STRE

Hertfordshire

First published in 1993 by

Philip's, a division of
Octopus Publishing Group Ltd
2-4 Heron Quays, London E14 4JP

Third colour edition 2004
First impression 2004

ISBN-10 0-540-08497-2 (pocket)
ISBN-13 978-0-540-08497-5 (pocket)

Printed and bound in Spain
by Cayfosa-Quebecor

Contents

III **Key to map symbols**

IV **Key to map pages**

VI **Route planning**

VIII **Administrative and Postcode boundaries**

1 **Street maps** at 2⅔ inches to 1 mile

177 **Index** of towns and villages

179 **Index** of streets, hospitals, industrial estates, railway stations, schools, shopping centres, universities and places of interest

Digital Data

The exceptionally high-quality mapping found in this atlas is available as digital data in TIFF format, which is easily convertible to other bitmapped (raster) image formats.

The index is also available in digital form as a standard database table. It contains all the details found in the printed index together with the National Grid reference for the map square in which each entry is named.

For further information and to discuss your requirements, please contact Philip's on 020 7644 6932 or james.mann@philips-maps.co.uk

PHILIP'S MAPS

the Gold Standard for serious driving

- Philip's street atlases cover every county in England, plus much of Wales and Scotland.
- All our atlases use the same style of mapping, with the same colours and symbols, so you can move with confidence from one atlas to the next
- Widely used by the emergency services, transport companies and local authorities.
- Created from the most up-to-date and detailed information available from Ordnance Survey
- Based on the National Grid

BEST BUY • BEST BUY • Auto EXPRESS • BEST BUY • BEST BUY

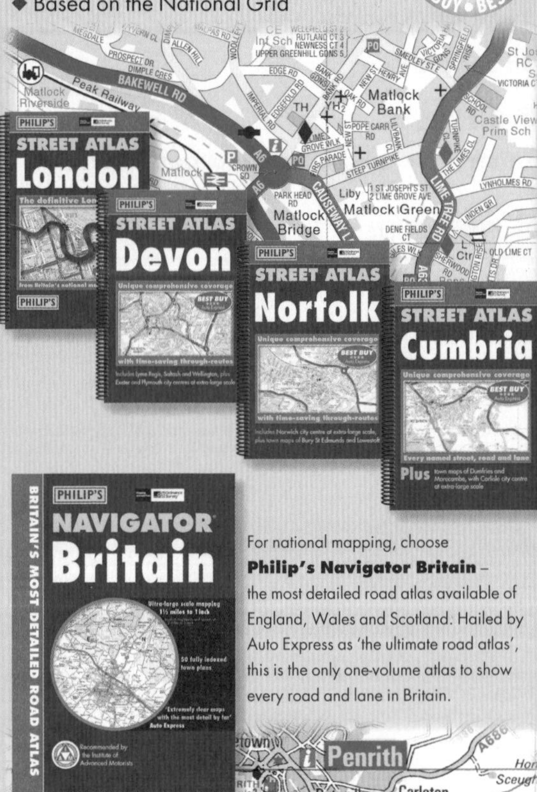

PHILIP'S NAVIGATOR Britain

BRITAIN'S MOST DETAILED ROAD ATLAS

For national mapping, choose **Philip's Navigator Britain** – the most detailed road atlas available of England, Wales and Scotland. Hailed by Auto Express as 'the ultimate road atlas', this is the only one-volume atlas to show every road and lane in Britain.

Penrith
Carleton
Pategill
Eamont Bridge
Belmount

All-England coverage

England

Bedfordshire
Berkshire
Birmingham and West Midlands
Bristol and Bath
Buckinghamshire
Cambridgeshire
Cheshire
Cornwall
Cumbria
Derbyshire
Devon
Dorset
County Durham and Teesside
Essex
North Essex
South Essex
Gloucestershire
North Hampshire
South Hampshire
Herefordshire Monmouthshire
Hertfordshire
Isle of Wight
East Kent
West Kent
Lancashire
Leicestershire and Rutland
Lincolnshire
London
Greater Manchester
Merseyside
Norfolk
Northamptonshire
Nottinghamshire
Oxfordshire
Shropshire
Somerset
Staffordshire
Suffolk
Surrey
East Sussex
West Sussex
Tyne and Wear Northumberland
Warwickshire
Birmingham and West Midlands
Wiltshire and Swindon
Worcestershire
East Yorkshire Northern Lincolnshire
North Yorkshire
South Yorkshire
West Yorkshire

Wales

Anglesey, Conwy and Gwynedd
Cardiff, Swansea and The Valleys
Denbighshire, Flintshire, Wrexham
Herefordshire Monmouthshire

Scotland

Aberdeenshire
Edinburgh and East Central Scotland
Fife and Tayside
Glasgow and West Central Scotland
Inverness and Moray

How to order

Philip's maps and atlases are available from bookshops, motorway services and petrol stations. You can order direct from the publisher by phoning **01903 828503** or online at **www.philips-maps.co.uk**
For bulk orders only, phone 020 7644 6940

Key to map symbols

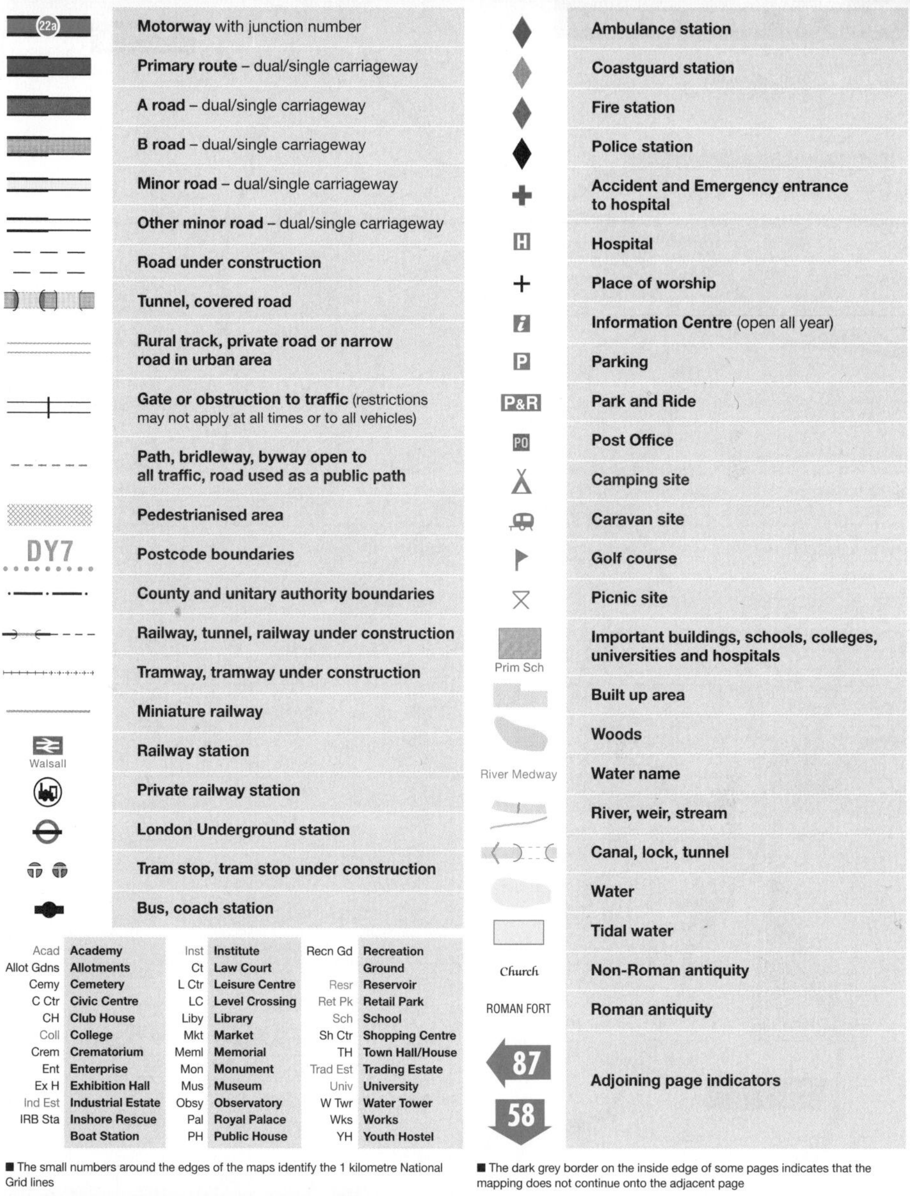

Acad	Academy	Inst	Institute	Recn Gd	Recreation Ground
Allot Gdns	Allotments	Ct	Law Court	Resr	Reservoir
Cemy	Cemetery	L Ctr	Leisure Centre	Ret Pk	Retail Park
C Ctr	Civic Centre	LC	Level Crossing	Sch	School
CH	Club House	Liby	Library	Sh Ctr	Shopping Centre
Coll	College	Mkt	Market	TH	Town Hall/House
Crem	Crematorium	Meml	Memorial	Trad Est	Trading Estate
Ent	Enterprise	Mon	Monument	Univ	University
Ex H	Exhibition Hall	Mus	Museum	W Twr	Water Tower
Ind Est	Industrial Estate	Obsy	Observatory	Wks	Works
IRB Sta	Inshore Rescue Boat Station	Pal	Royal Palace	YH	Youth Hostel
		PH	Public House		

■ The small numbers around the edges of the maps identify the 1 kilometre National Grid lines

■ The dark grey border on the inside edge of some pages indicates that the mapping does not continue onto the adjacent page

The scale of the maps on the pages numbered in blue is 4.2 cm to 1 km • 2⅔ inches to 1 mile • 1: 23810

0 ¼ ½ ¾ 1 mile

0 250 m 500 m 750 m 1 kilometre

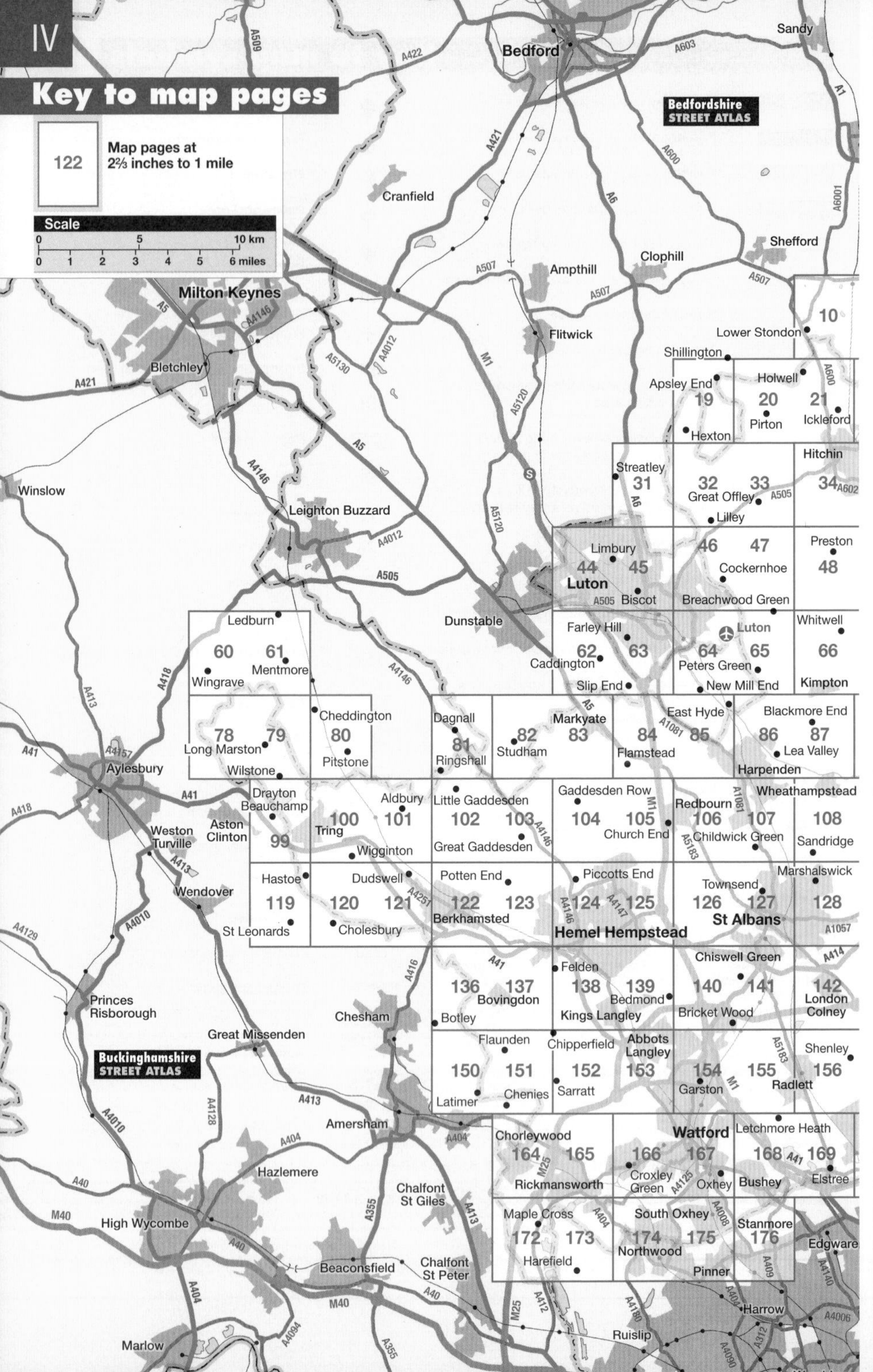
IV
Key to map pages
122
Map pages at 2⅔ inches to 1 mile
Scale
0
5
10 km
0
1
2
3
4
5
6 miles
Bedfordshire STREET ATLAS
Buckinghamshire STREET ATLAS
Bedford
Sandy
Cranfield
Ampthill
Clophill
Shefford
Milton Keynes
Flitwick
Bletchley
Lower Stondon
Shillington
Apsley End
Holwell
Pirton
Ickleford
Hexton
Winslow
Streatley
Great Offley
Lilley
Hitchin
Leighton Buzzard
Limbury
Luton
Biscot
Cockernhoe
Breachwood Green
Preston
Dunstable
Ledburn
Mentmore
Wingrave
Farley Hill
Caddington
Slip End
Peters Green
New Mill End
Whitwell
Kimpton
Cheddington
Pitstone
Long Marston
Wilstone
Dagnall
Ringshall
Studham
Markyate
Flamstead
East Hyde
Blackmore End
Lea Valley
Harpenden
Aylesbury
Drayton Beauchamp
Aston Clinton
Weston Turville
Tring
Aldbury
Wigginton
Little Gaddesden
Great Gaddesden
Gaddesden Row
Church End
Redbourn
Childwick Green
Wheathampstead
Sandridge
Hastoe
Wendover
St Leonards
Dudswell
Cholesbury
Potten End
Berkhamsted
Piccotts End
Hemel Hempstead
Townsend
St Albans
Marshalswick
Felden
Bovingdon
Botley
Kings Langley
Bedmond
Chiswell Green
Bricket Wood
London Colney
Princes Risborough
Chesham
Great Missenden
Flaunden
Chipperfield
Abbots Langley
Latimer
Chenies
Sarratt
Garston
Radlett
Shenley
Amersham
Chorleywood
Rickmansworth
Watford
Croxley Green
Oxhey
Letchmore Heath
Bushey
Elstree
Hazlemere
Chalfont St Giles
High Wycombe
Maple Cross
Harefield
South Oxhey
Northwood
Pinner
Stanmore
Edgware
Beaconsfield
Chalfont St Peter
Harrow
Ruislip
Marlow
Wembley
10
19
20
21
31
32
33
34
44
45
46
47
48
60
61
62
63
64
65
66
78
79
80
81
82
83
84
85
86
87
99
100
101
102
103
104
105
106
107
108
119
120
121
122
123
124
125
126
127
128
136
137
138
139
140
141
142
150
151
152
153
154
155
156
164
165
166
167
168
169
172
173
174
175
176

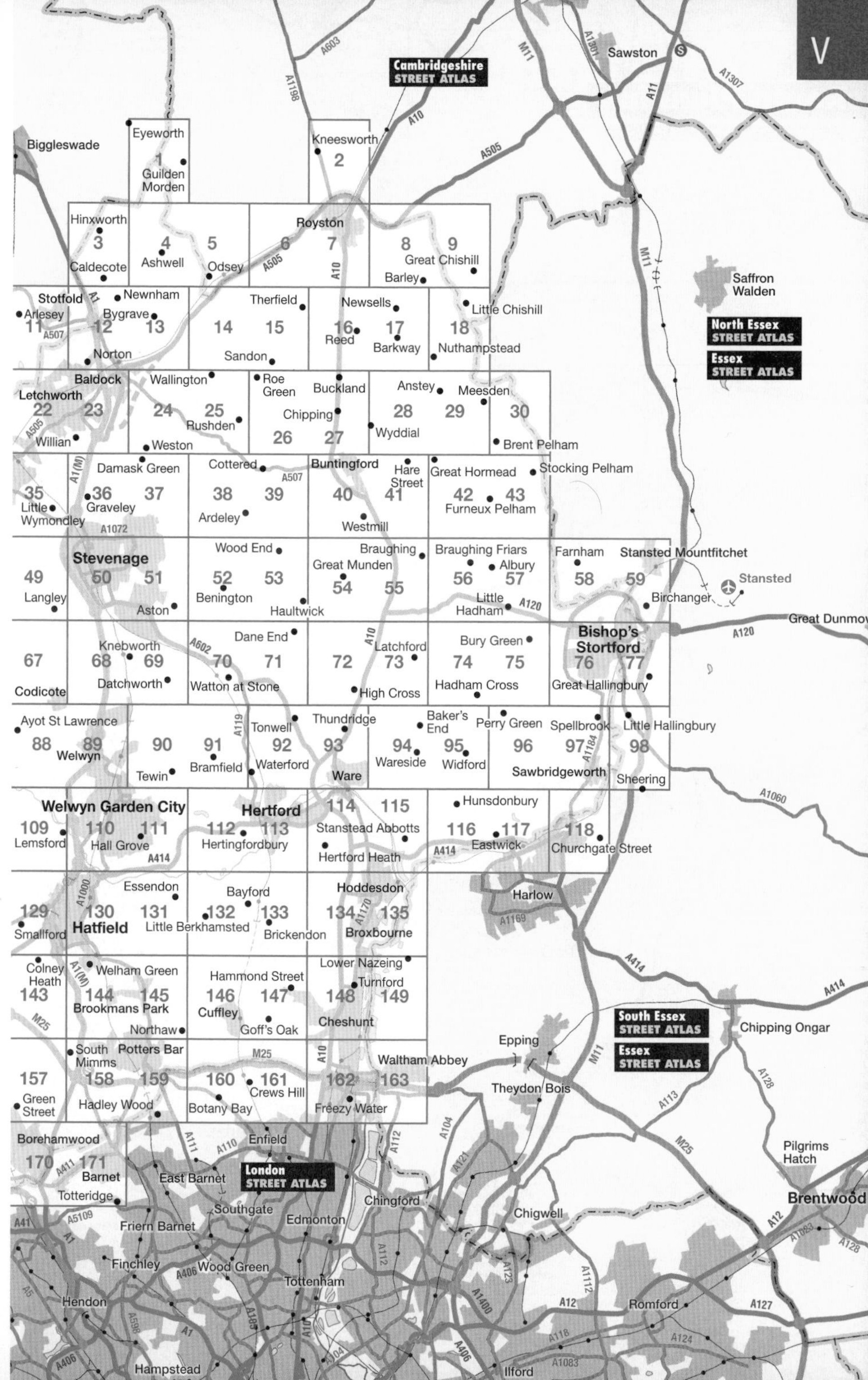

Cambridgeshire STREET ATLAS
North Essex STREET ATLAS
Essex STREET ATLAS
South Essex STREET ATLAS
Essex STREET ATLAS
London STREET ATLAS
Sawston
Biggleswade
Eyeworth
Guilden Morden
Kneesworth
Royston
Hinxworth
Caldecote
Ashwell
Odsey
Great Chishill
Barley
Saffron Walden
Stotfold
Newnham
Arlesey
Bygrave
Norton
Therfield
Sandon
Newsells
Reed
Barkway
Little Chishill
Nuthampstead
Baldock
Letchworth
Willian
Wallington
Rushden
Weston
Roe Green
Buckland
Chipping
Wyddial
Anstey
Meesden
Brent Pelham
Damask Green
Graveley
Little Wymondley
Cottered
Ardeley
Buntingford
Westmill
Hare Street
Great Hormead
Furneux Pelham
Stocking Pelham
Stevenage
Langley
Aston
Wood End
Benington
Haultwick
Braughing
Great Munden
Braughing Friars
Albury
Little Hadham
Farnham
Stansted Mountfitchet
Stansted
Birchanger
Great Dunmow
Bishop's Stortford
Knebworth
Datchworth
Codicote
Dane End
Watton at Stone
Latchford
High Cross
Bury Green
Hadham Cross
Great Hallingbury
Ayot St Lawrence
Welwyn
Tewin
Bramfield
Tonwell
Waterford
Thundridge
Ware
Baker's End
Wareside
Widford
Perry Green
Spellbrook
Sawbridgeworth
Little Hallingbury
Sheering
Welwyn Garden City
Lemsford
Hall Grove
Hertford
Hertingfordbury
Stanstead Abbotts
Hertford Heath
Hunsdonbury
Eastwick
Churchgate Street
Harlow
Essendon
Bayford
Hoddesdon
Smallford
Hatfield
Little Berkhamsted
Brickendon
Broxbourne
Colney Heath
Welham Green
Brookmans Park
Hammond Street
Cuffley
Goff's Oak
Lower Nazeing
Turnford
Cheshunt
Northaw
South Mimms
Potters Bar
Green Street
Hadley Wood
Botany Bay
Crews Hill
Freezy Water
Waltham Abbey
Epping
Theydon Bois
Chipping Ongar
Borehamwood
Barnet
Totteridge
East Barnet
Enfield
Southgate
Friern Barnet
Edmonton
Chingford
Chigwell
Pilgrims Hatch
Brentwood
Finchley
Wood Green
Tottenham
Hendon
Romford
Hampstead
Ilford
1 2 3 4 5 6 7 8 9 11 12 13 14 15 16 17 18 22 23 24 25 26 27 28 29 30
35 36 37 38 39 40 41 42 43 49 50 51 52 53 54 55 56 57 58 59
67 68 69 70 71 72 73 74 75 76 77 88 89 90 91 92 93 94 95 96 97 98
109 110 111 112 113 114 115 116 117 118 129 130 131 132 133 134 135
143 144 145 146 147 148 149 157 158 159 160 161 162 163 170 171
A603 A1198 A10 A505 A1301 M11 A11 A1307 A1 A507 A1(M) A1072 A602 A119 A120 A1184 A1060 A414 A1000 A1170 A1169 M25 A111 A110 A411 A5109 A41 A5 A406 A598 A1081 A112 A104 A121 A1400 A123 A1112 A12 A127 A118 A124 A1083 A113 A128 A1023

Route Planning

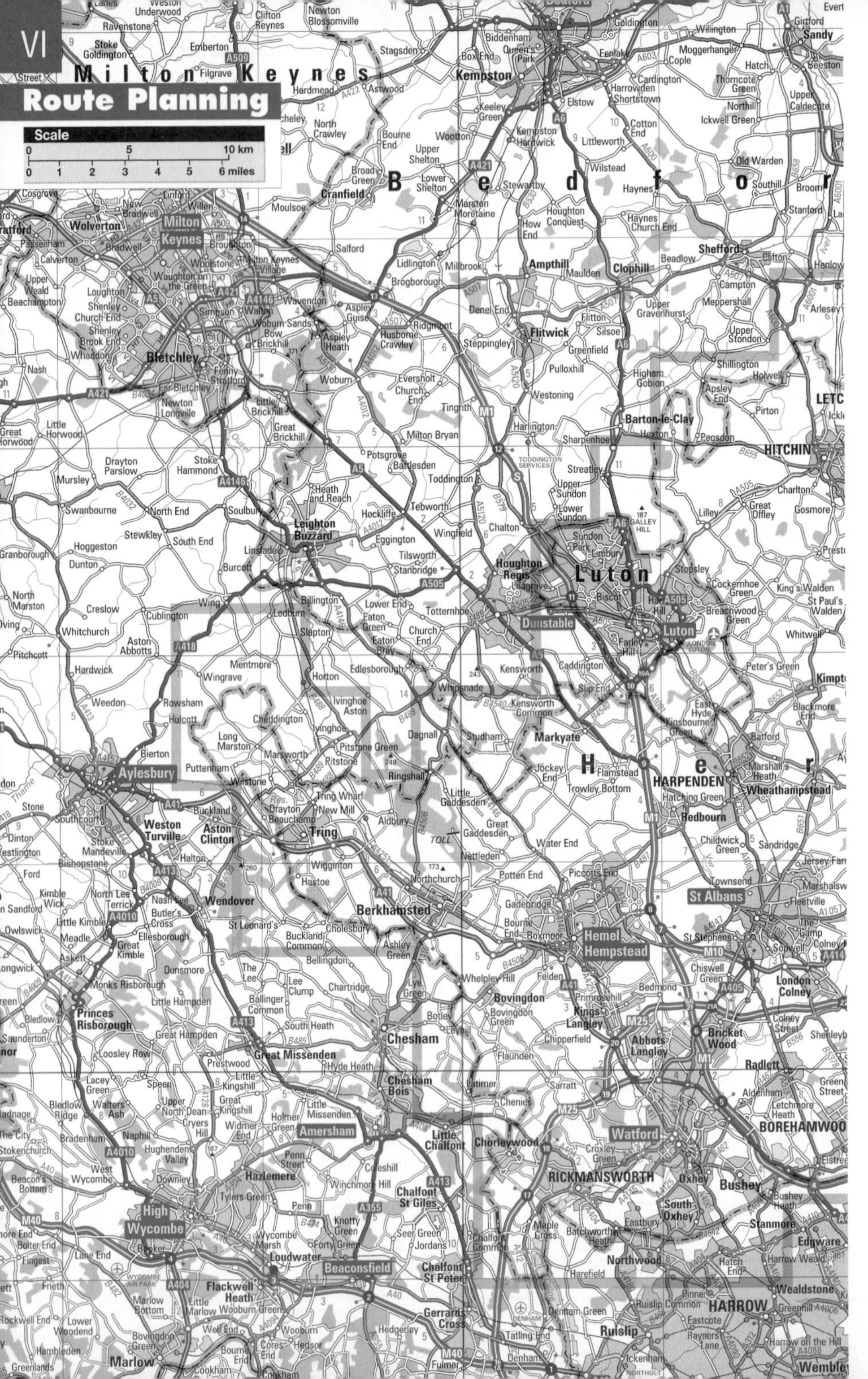

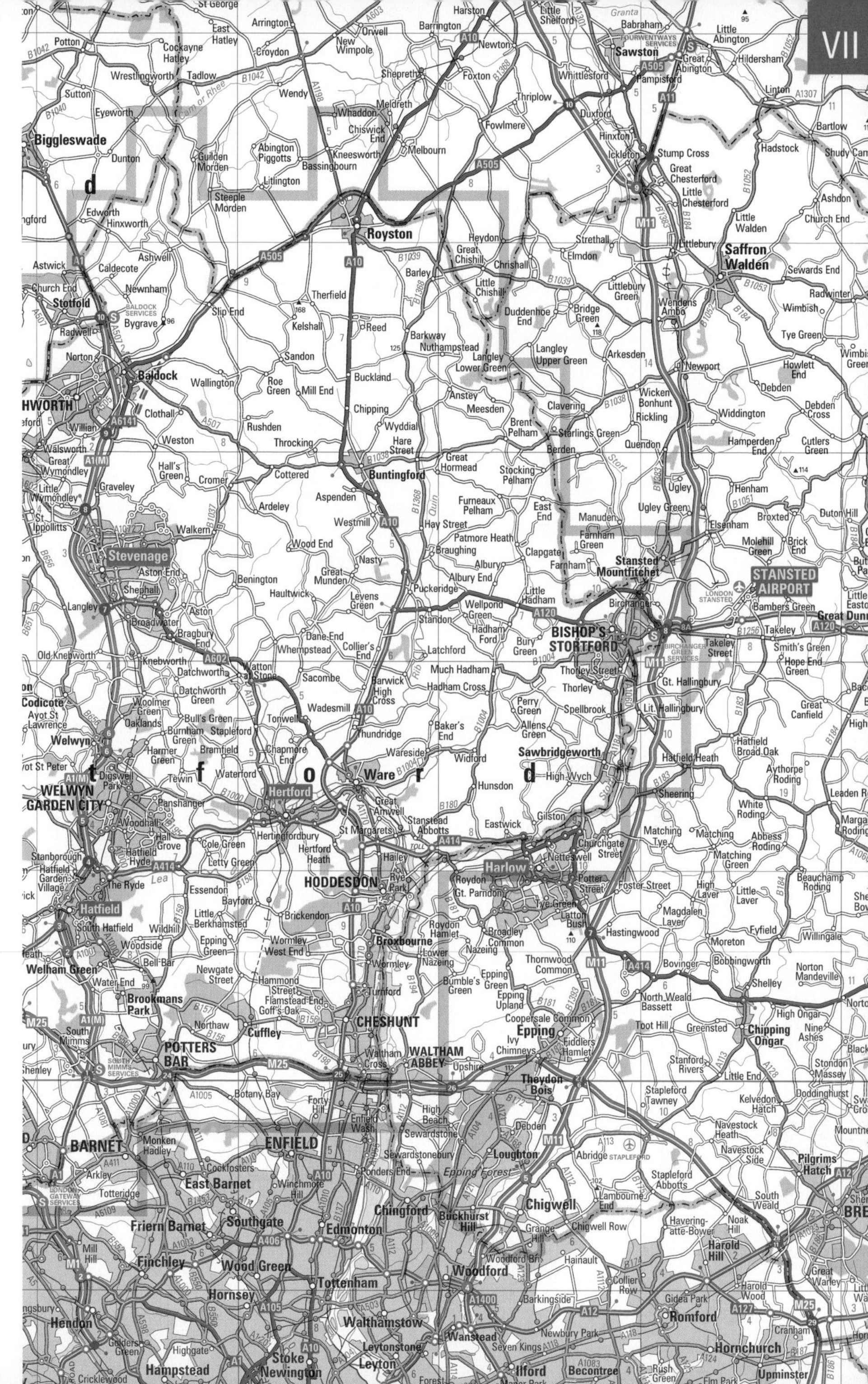

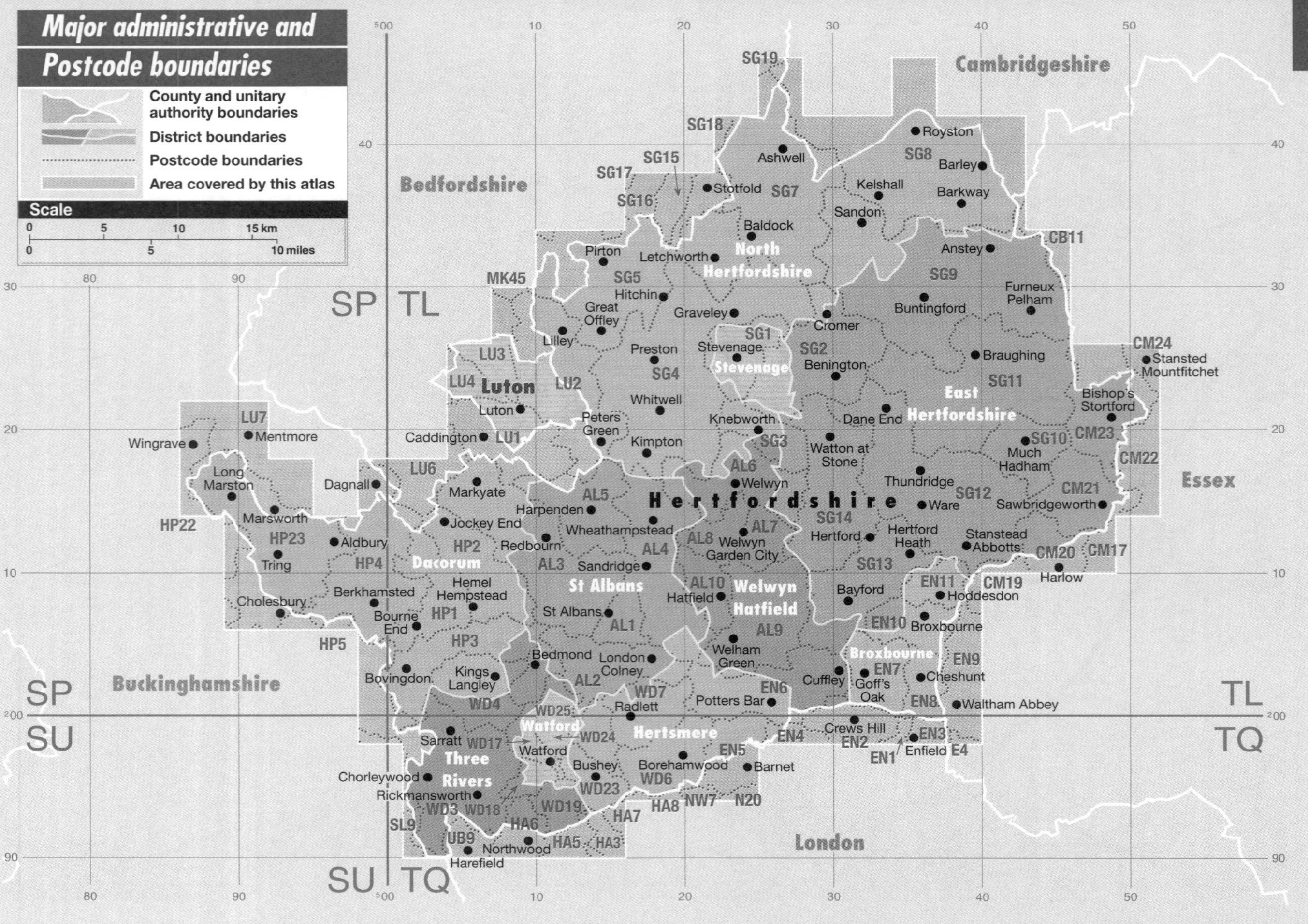
Major administrative and
Postcode boundaries
County and unitary authority boundaries
District boundaries
Postcode boundaries
Area covered by this atlas
Scale
0 5 10 15 km
0 5 10 miles
Cambridgeshire
Bedfordshire
Buckinghamshire
Essex
London
Hertfordshire
North Hertfordshire
East Hertfordshire
Stevenage
Luton
Dacorum
St Albans
Welwyn Hatfield
Broxbourne
Hertsmere
Watford
Three Rivers
SP
TL
SU
TQ
Royston
Ashwell
Barley
Kelshall
Barkway
Stotfold
Sandon
Baldock
Anstey
Pirton
Letchworth
Furneux Pelham
Hitchin
Buntingford
Great Offley
Graveley
Cromer
Lilley
Stevenage
Preston
Braughing
Stansted Mountfitchet
Benington
Bishop's Stortford
Whitwell
Luton
Peters Green
Knebworth
Dane End
Wingrave
Mentmore
Caddington
Watton at Stone
Much Hadham
Kimpton
Long Marston
Welwyn
Dagnall
Markyate
Thundridge
Harpenden
Ware
Sawbridgeworth
Marsworth
Jockey End
Wheathampstead
Aldbury
Welwyn Garden City
Hertford
Hertford Heath
Stanstead Abbotts
Tring
Redbourn
Sandridge
Harlow
Berkhamsted
Hemel Hempstead
Hatfield
Bayford
Hoddesdon
Cholesbury
Bourne End
St Albans
Broxbourne
Welham Green
Bedmond
London Colney
Cheshunt
Bovingdon
Kings Langley
Cuffley
Goff's Oak
Potters Bar
Waltham Abbey
Radlett
Sarratt
Crews Hill
Watford
Enfield
Chorleywood
Bushey
Borehamwood
Barnet
Rickmansworth
Northwood
Harefield
SG19
SG18
SG15
SG17
SG16
SG8
SG7
SG5
SG9
SG1
SG2
SG4
SG11
SG3
SG10
SG14
SG12
SG13
CB11
MK45
LU3
LU4
LU2
LU7
LU1
LU6
CM24
CM23
CM22
CM21
CM20
CM17
CM19
AL6
AL5
AL7
AL8
AL4
AL3
AL10
AL1
AL9
AL2
HP22
HP23
HP4
HP2
HP1
HP5
HP3
EN11
EN10
EN9
EN7
EN8
EN6
EN4
EN2
EN3
EN1
E4
EN5
WD4
WD7
WD25
WD17
WD24
WD23
WD6
WD3
WD18
WD19
SL9
UB9
HA6
HA5
HA3
HA7
HA8
NW7
N20
80
90
500
10
20
30
40
50
200

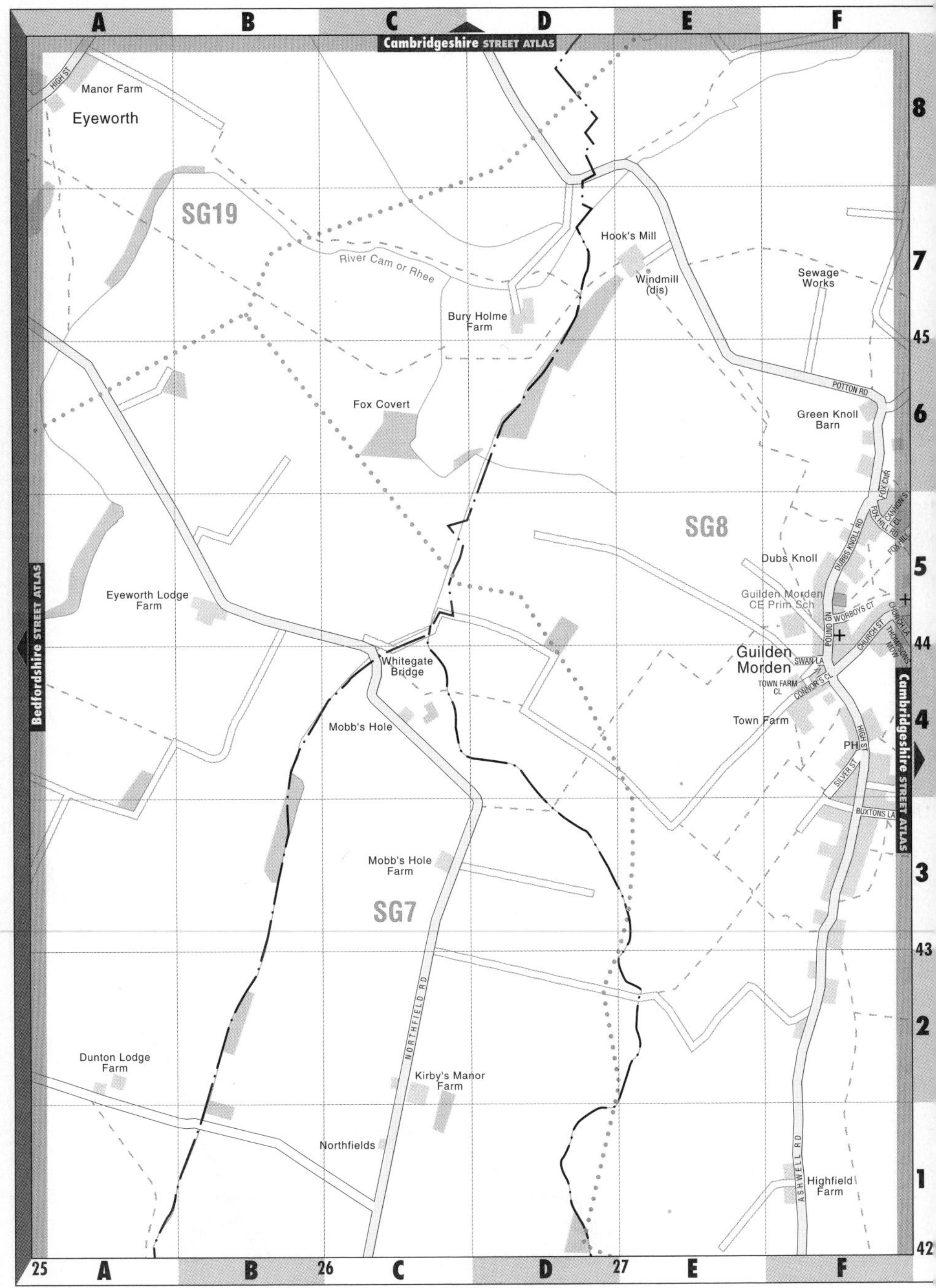
A
B
C
D
E
F
Cambridgeshire STREET ATLAS
Bedfordshire STREET ATLAS
Cambridgeshire STREET ATLAS
HIGH ST
Manor Farm
Eyeworth
SG19
River Cam or Rhee
Hook's Mill
Windmill (dis)
Bury Holme Farm
Sewage Works
POTTON RD
Green Knoll Barn
Fox Covert
SG8
FOX CNR
CANNONS CL
FOX HILL RD
DUBBS KNOLL RD
Dubs Knoll
Guilden Morden CE Prim Sch
WORBOYS CT
CHURCH LA
POUND GN
CHURCH ST
THOMPSONS MDW
Guilden Morden
SWAN LA
TOWN FARM CL
CONNOR'S CL
Town Farm
PH
HIGH ST
SILVER ST
BUXTONS LA
Eyeworth Lodge Farm
Whitegate Bridge
Mobb's Hole
Mobb's Hole Farm
SG7
NORTHFIELD RD
Dunton Lodge Farm
Kirby's Manor Farm
Northfields
ASHWELL RD
Highfield Farm
8
7
45
6
5
44
4
3
43
2
1
42
25
26
27

4

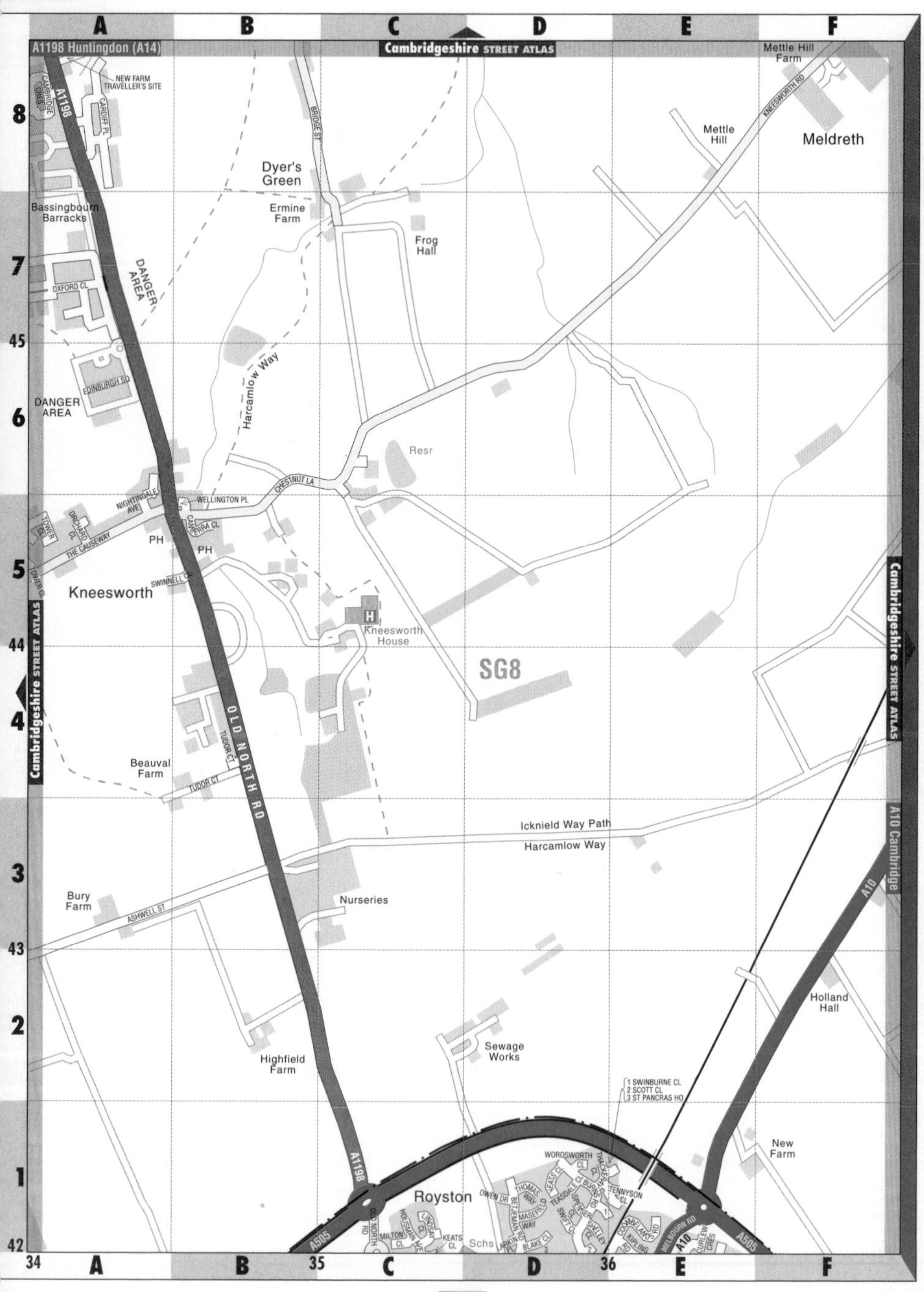
A1198 Huntingdon (A14)
Cambridgeshire STREET ATLAS
Meldreth
Mettle Hill Farm
Mettle Hill
Dyer's Green
Ermine Farm
Frog Hall
Bassingbourn Barracks
DANGER AREA
Harcamlow Way
Resr
Kneesworth
Kneesworth House
SG8
Beauval Farm
OLD NORTH RD
Icknield Way Path
Harcamlow Way
Bury Farm
Nurseries
Holland Hall
Highfield Farm
Sewage Works
1 SWINBURNE CL
2 SCOTT CL
3 ST PANCRAS HO
New Farm
Royston
Schs
A10 Cambridge
A505
A1198

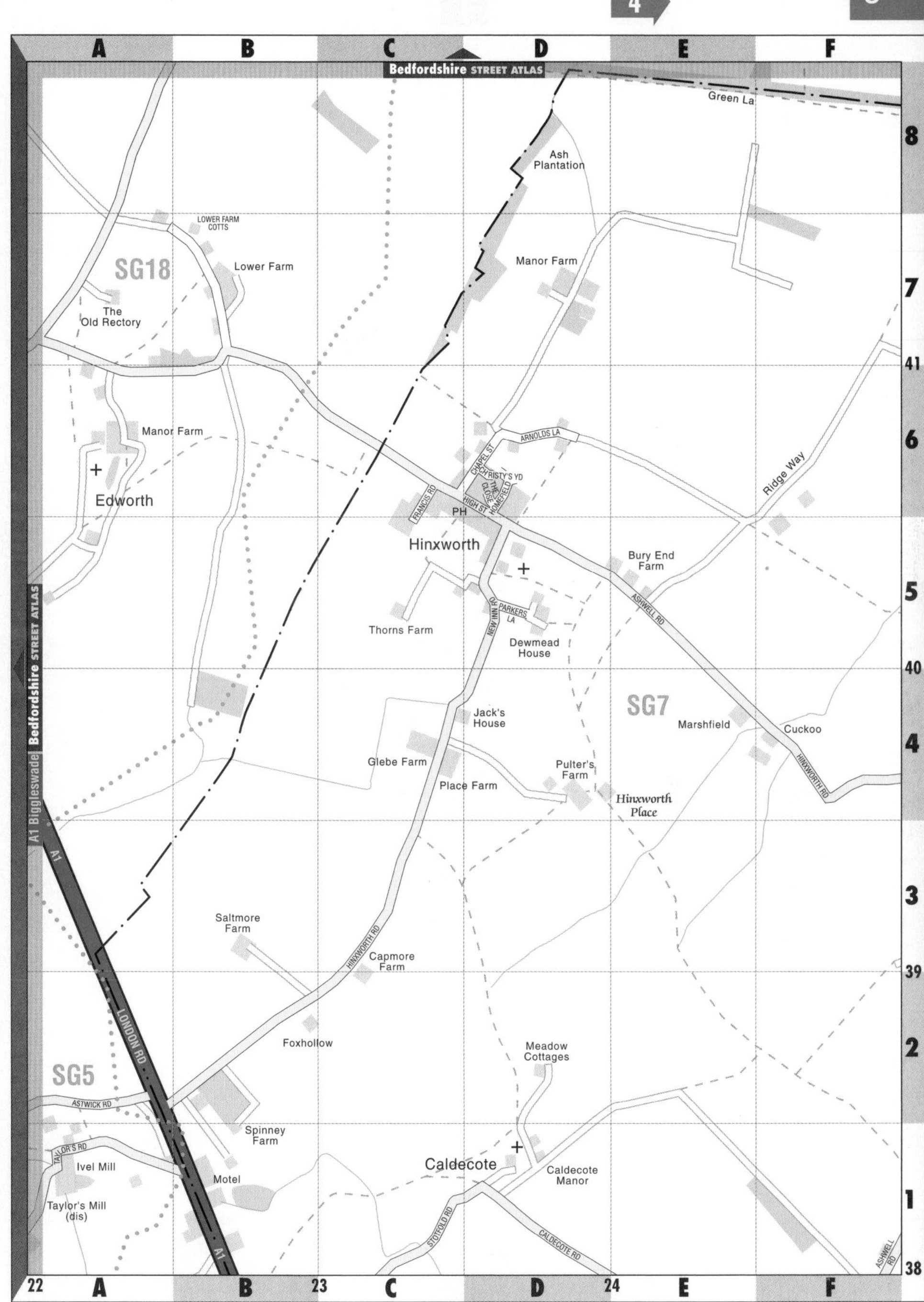

4
A
B
C
D
E
F
Bedfordshire STREET ATLAS
Green La
Ash Plantation
LOWER FARM COTTS
Lower Farm
SG18
Manor Farm
The Old Rectory
Manor Farm
Edworth
ARNOLDS LA
CHAPEL ST
CHRISTY'S YD
THE CLOSE
HOMEFIELD
FRANCIS RD
HIGH ST
PH
Hinxworth
Ridge Way
Bury End Farm
ASHWELL RD
OLD PARKERS LA
NEW INN RD
Thorns Farm
Dewmead House
Bedfordshire STREET ATLAS
A1 Biggleswade
SG7
Jack's House
Marshfield
Cuckoo
Glebe Farm
Pulter's Farm
Place Farm
HINXWORTH RD
Hinxworth Place
A1
Saltmore Farm
Capmore Farm
HINXWORTH RD
LONDON RD
Foxhollow
Meadow Cottages
SG5
ASTWICK RD
Spinney Farm
TAYLOR'S RD
Ivel Mill
Motel
Caldecote
Caldecote Manor
Taylor's Mill (dis)
STOTFOLD RD
CALDECOTE RD
ASHWELL RD
A1
8
7
41
6
5
40
4
3
39
2
1
38
22
23
24
12
4

3
1

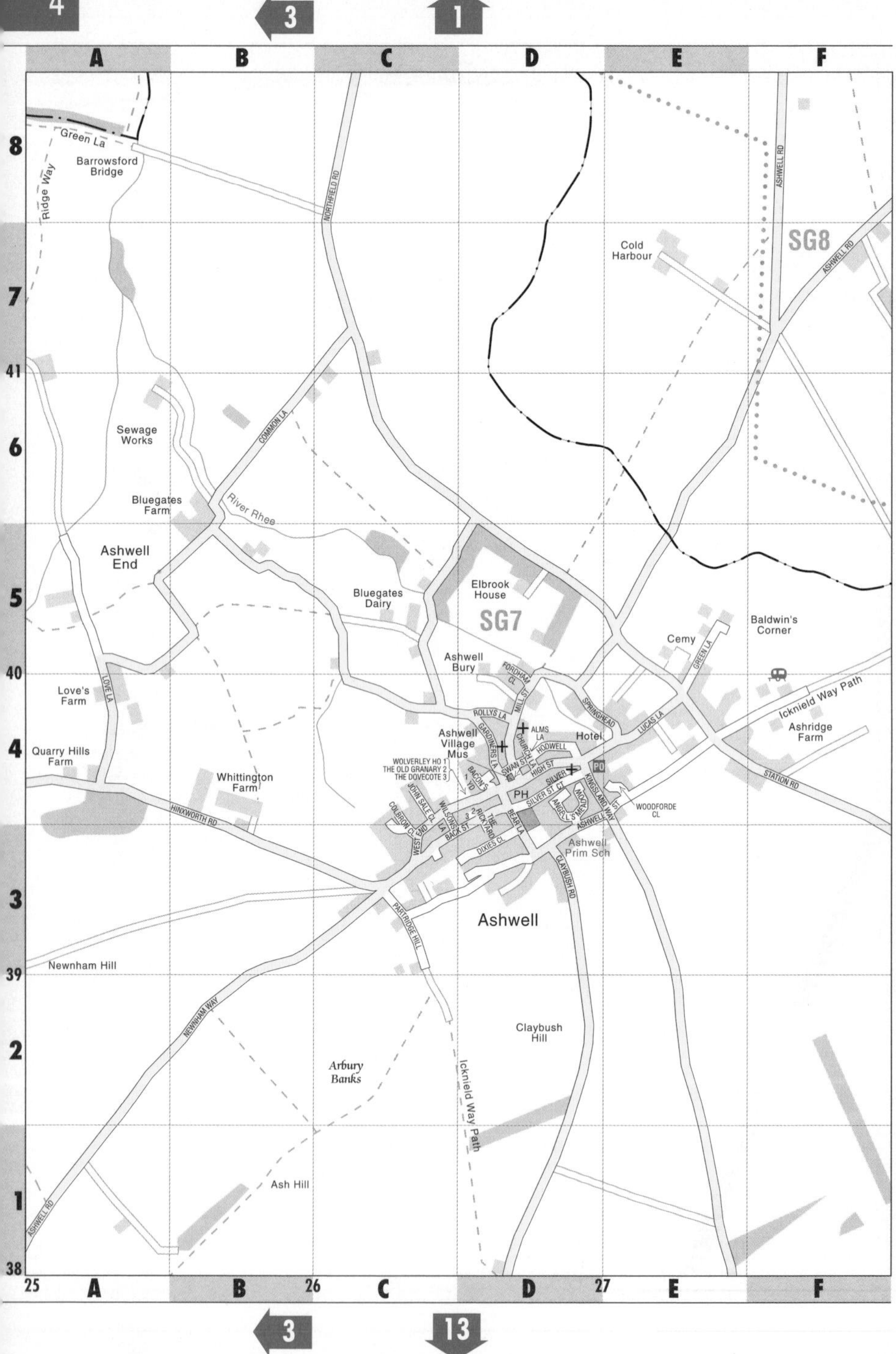
A
B
C
D
E
F
8
7
41
6
5
40
4
3
39
2
1
38
25
26
27
Green La
Barrowsford Bridge
Ridge Way
NORTHFIELD RD
ASHWELL RD
SG8
Cold Harbour
Sewage Works
COMMON LA
Bluegates Farm
River Rhee
Ashwell End
Bluegates Dairy
Elbrook House
SG7
Ashwell Bury
Cemy
GREEN LA
Baldwin's Corner
Love's Farm
LOVE LA
FORDHAM CL
MILL ST
ROLLYS LA
SPRINGHEAD
LUCAS LA
Icknield Way Path
Ashridge Farm
Ashwell Village Mus
ALMS LA
HODWELL
Hotel
Quarry Hills Farm
Whittington Farm
WOLVERLEY HO 1
THE OLD GRANARY 2
THE DOVECOTE 3
PH
PO
STATION RD
HINXWORTH RD
WOODFORDE CL
Ashwell Prim Sch
DIXIES CL
CLAYBUSH RD
PARTRIDGE HILL
Ashwell
Newnham Hill
NEWNHAM WAY
Claybush Hill
Arbury Banks
Icknield Way Path
Ash Hill
ASHWELL RD

3
13

A B C D E F

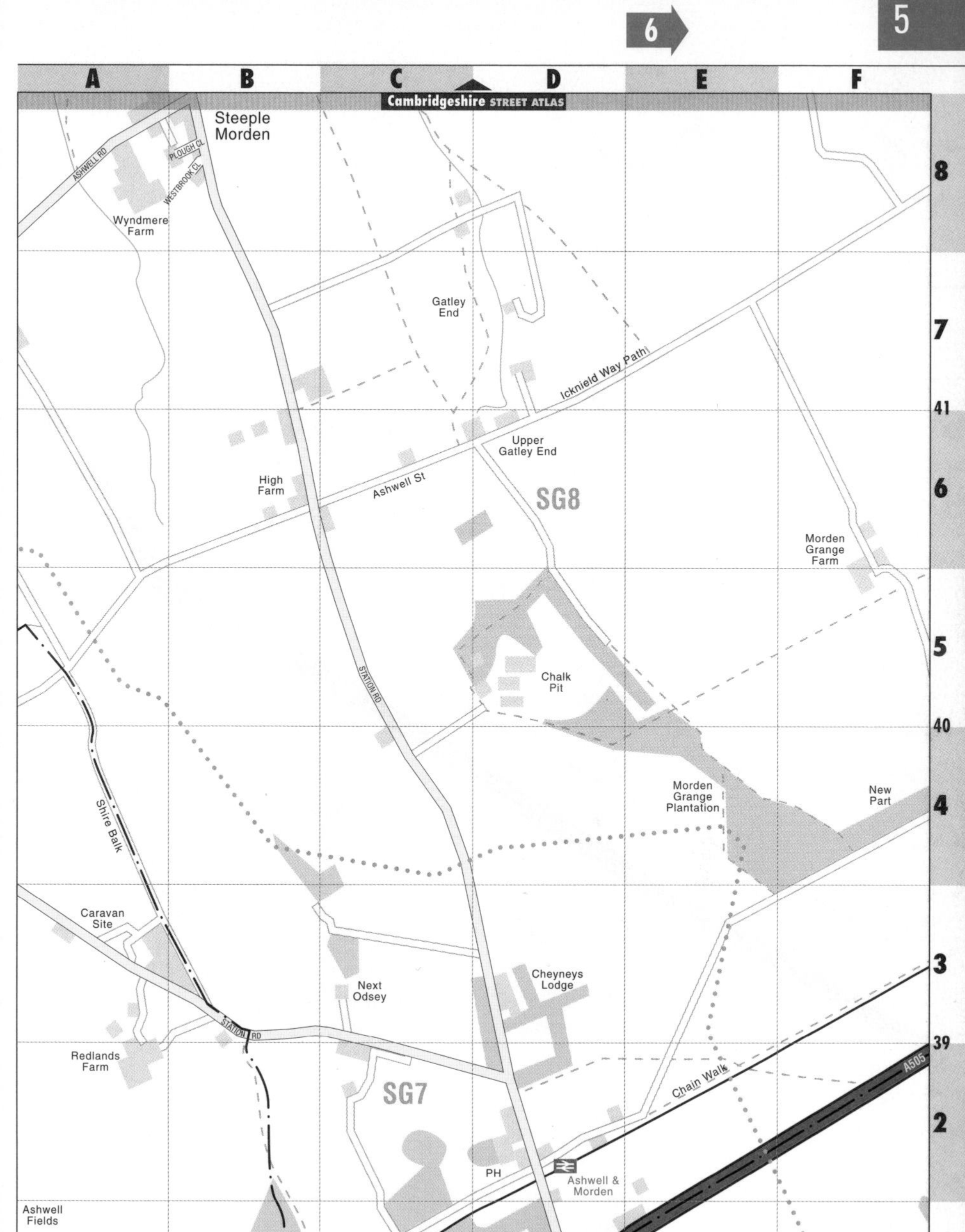

A B C D E F

5

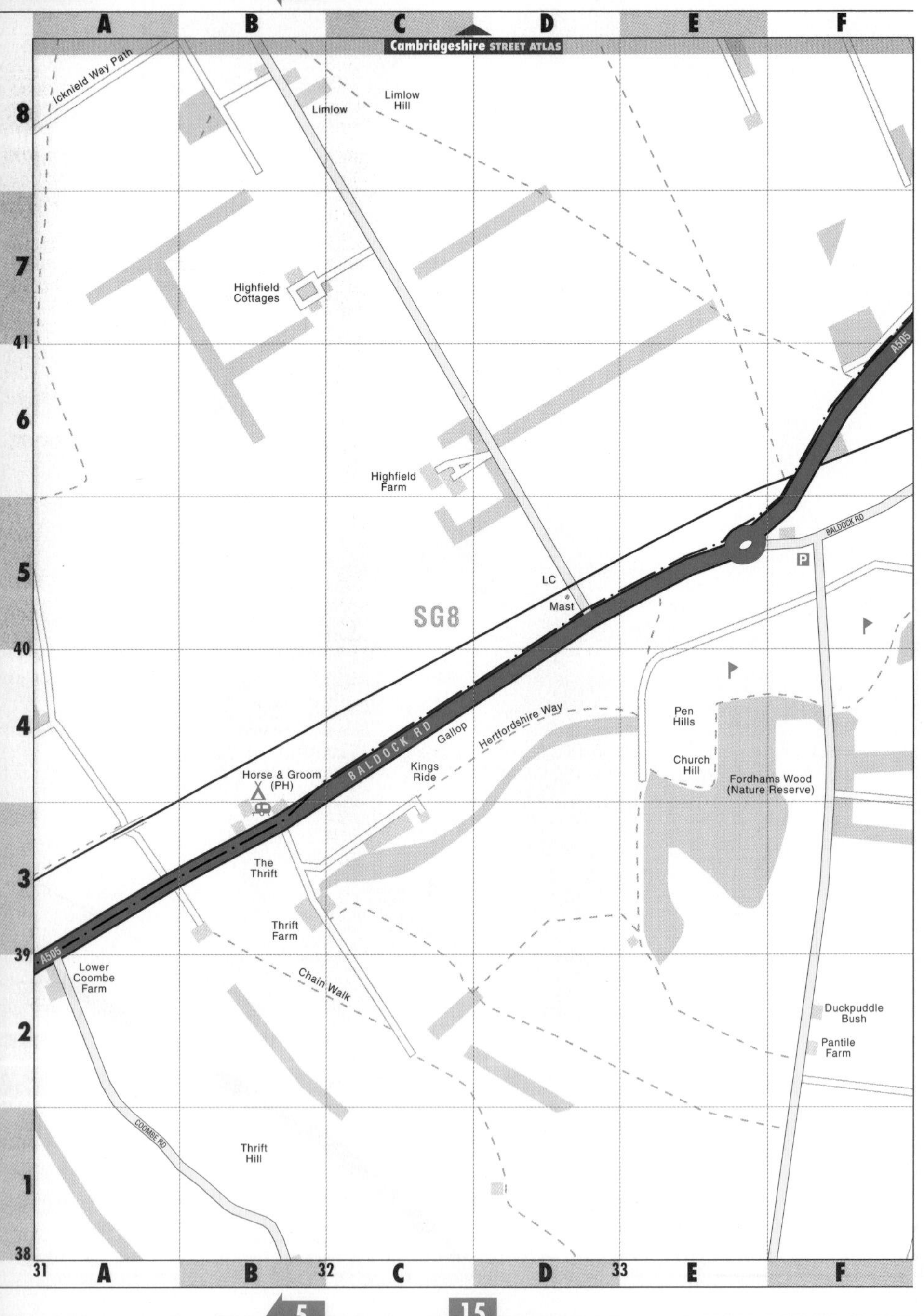
Cambridgeshire STREET ATLAS
Icknield Way Path
Limlow
Limlow Hill
Highfield Cottages
Highfield Farm
A505
BALDOCK RD
LC
Mast
SG8
Gallop
Hertfordshire Way
Kings Ride
Horse & Groom (PH)
The Thrift
Thrift Farm
Chain Walk
Lower Coombe Farm
COOMBE RD
Thrift Hill
Pen Hills
Church Hill
Fordhams Wood (Nature Reserve)
Duckpuddle Bush
Pantile Farm
A
B
C
D
E
F
8
7
41
6
5
40
4
3
39
2
1
38
31
32
33

5

15

2
8

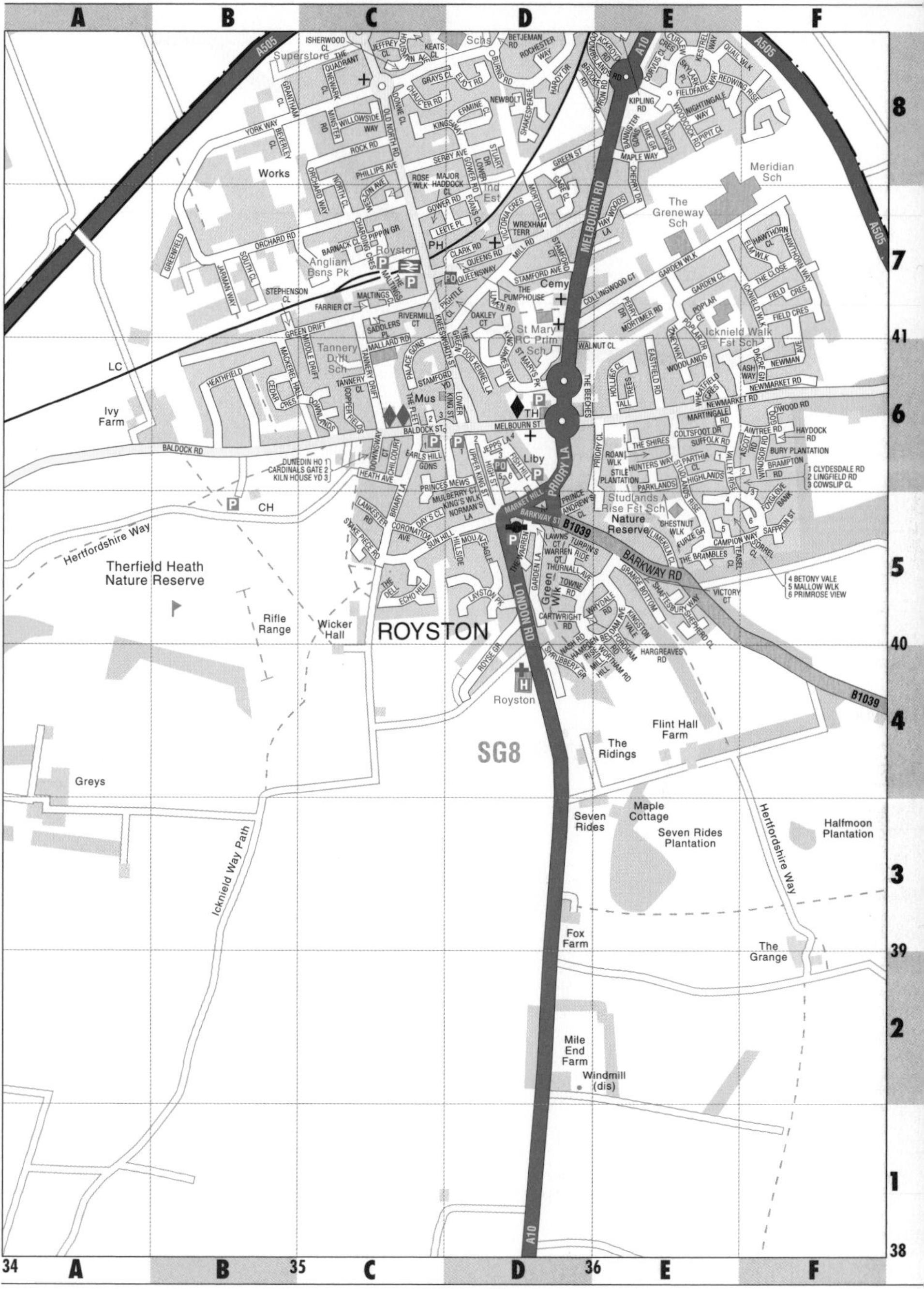

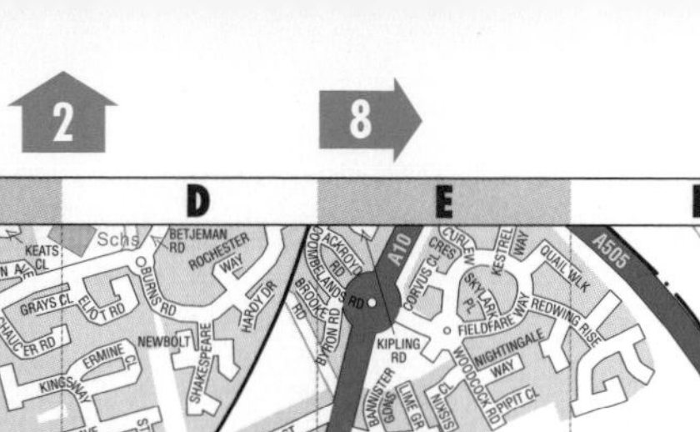

D6
1 ABBOTTS YD
2 KING ST
3 JOHN ST
4 CHURCH LA
5 GEORGE LA
6 MARKET HILL
7 ANGEL PAVEMENT

16
8

7

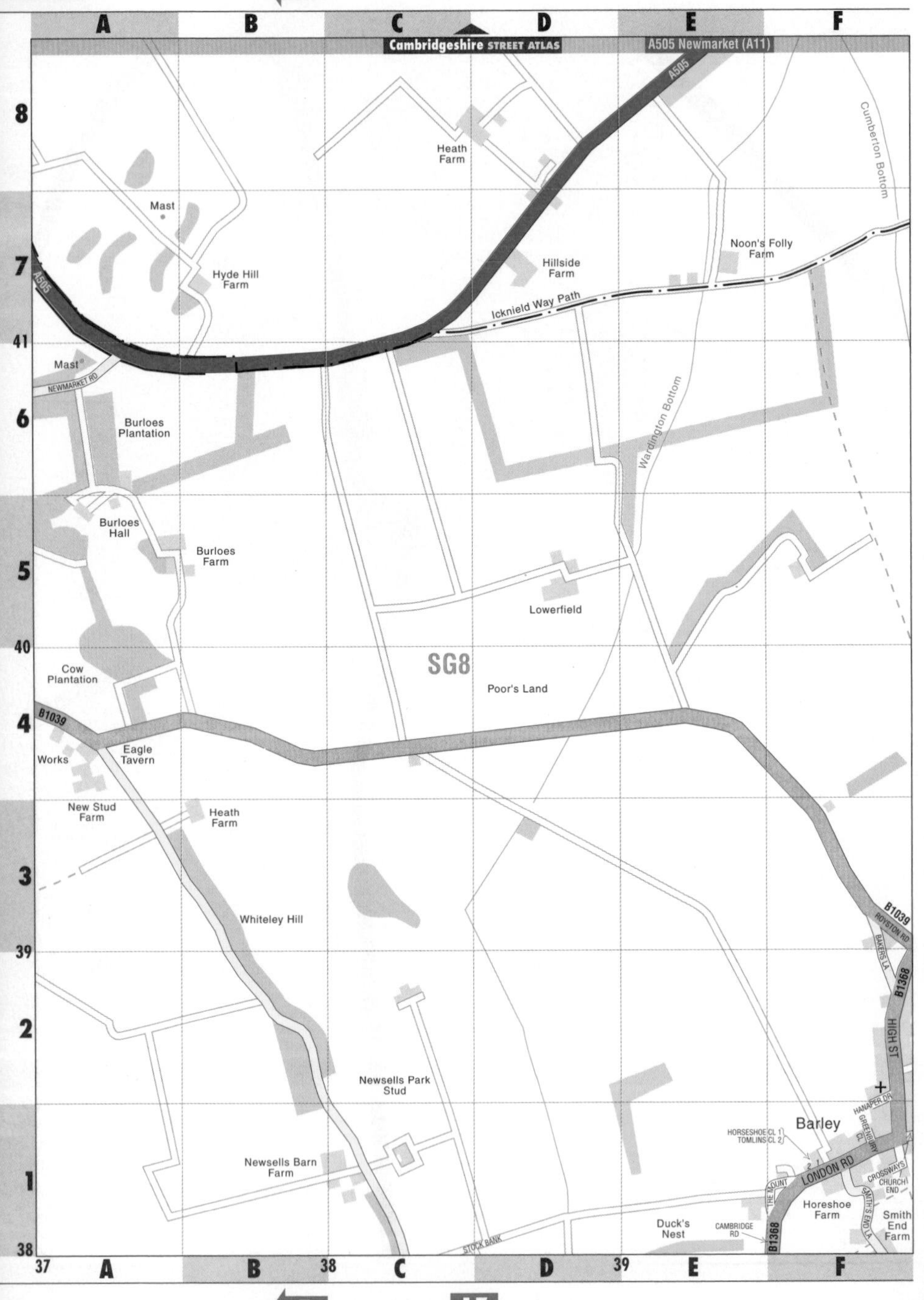
A
B
C
D
E
F
Cambridgeshire STREET ATLAS
A505 Newmarket (A11)
A505
Heath Farm
Cumberton Bottom
Mast
Noon's Folly Farm
Hillside Farm
Hyde Hill Farm
Icknield Way Path
Mast
NEWMARKET RD
Wardington Bottom
Burloes Plantation
Burloes Hall
Burloes Farm
Lowerfield
SG8
Cow Plantation
Poor's Land
B1039
Eagle Tavern
Works
New Stud Farm
Heath Farm
Whiteley Hill
B1039
ROYSTON RD
BAKERS LA
B1368
HIGH ST
Newsells Park Stud
HANAPER DR
Barley
GREENBURY CL
HORSESHOE CL 1
TOMLINS CL 2
Newsells Barn Farm
LONDON RD
CROSSWAYS
CHURCH END
THE MOUNT
SMITH'S END LA
Horeshoe Farm
Duck's Nest
CAMBRIDGE RD
Smith End Farm
B1368
STOCK BANK
8
7
41
6
5
40
4
3
39
2
1
38
37
38
39
A
B
C
D
E
F

7
17

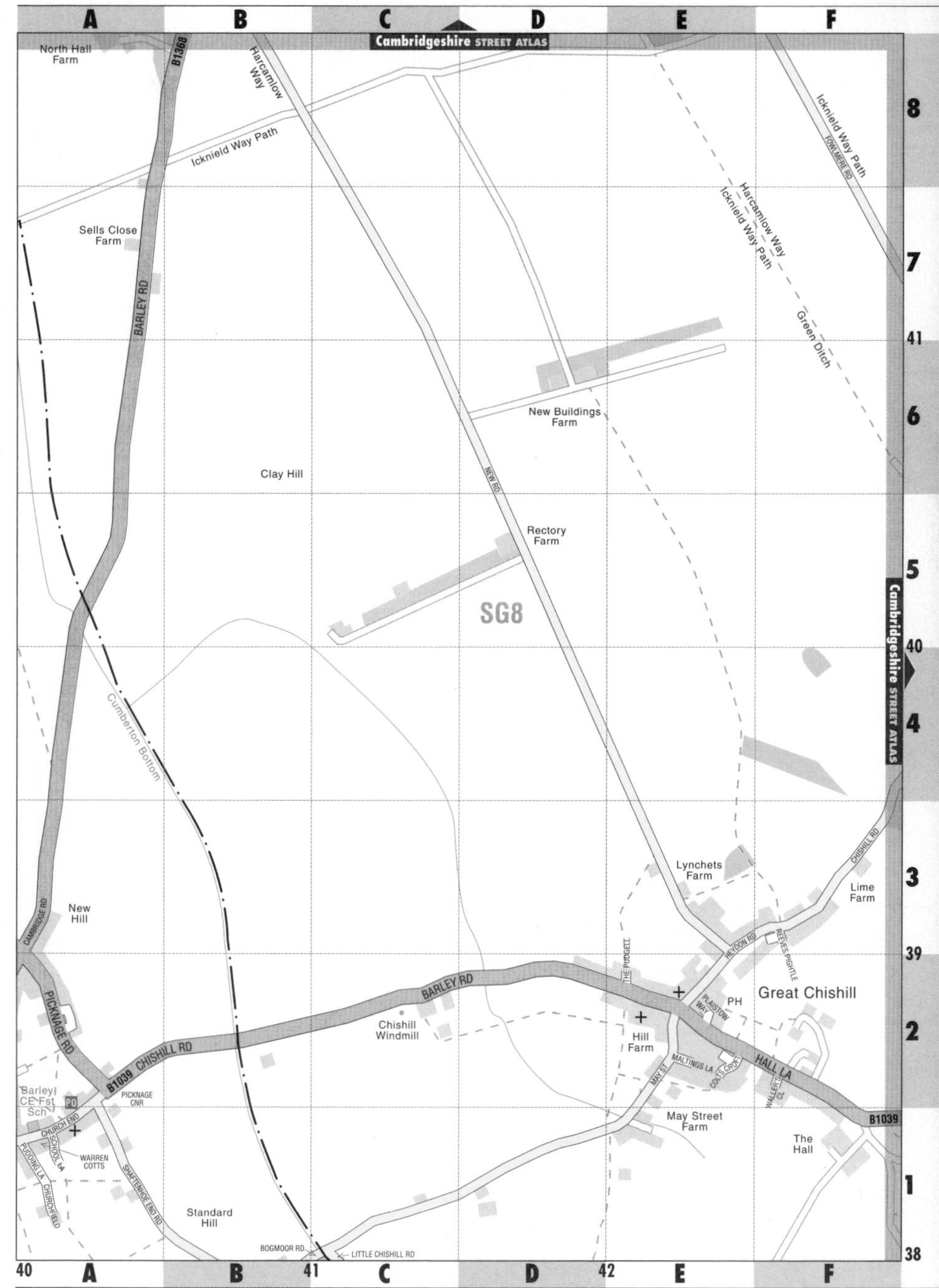
A
B
C
D
E
F
Cambridgeshire STREET ATLAS
North Hall Farm
B1368
Harcamlow Way
Icknield Way Path
Sells Close Farm
BARLEY RD
Harcamlow Way
Icknield Way Path
FOWLMERE RD
Green Ditch
New Buildings Farm
Clay Hill
NEW RD
Rectory Farm
SG8
Cumberton Bottom
Lynchets Farm
CHISHILL RD
Lime Farm
New Hill
CAMBRIDGE RD
PICKNAGE RD
BARLEY RD
THE PUDGELL
HEYDON RD
REEVES PIGHTLE
Great Chishill
PH
PLAISTOW WAY
Chishill Windmill
Hill Farm
B1039 CHISHILL RD
MALTINGS LA
COLTS CROFT
HALL LA
MAY ST
WALLER'S CL
B1039
Barley CE Fst Sch
PO
PICKNAGE CNR
CHURCH END
SCHOOL LA
WARREN COTTS
PUDDING LA
CHURCHFIELD
SHAFTENHOE END RD
May Street Farm
The Hall
Standard Hill
BOGMOOR RD
LITTLE CHISHILL RD
8
7
41
6
5
40
4
3
39
2
1
38
40
41
42

18

Bedfordshire STREET ATLAS
A6001 Biggleswade
A507 Flitwick
A507
ARLESEY RD
Henlow
PH
THE GARDENS
Arlesey Bridge
SG17
Old Manor Farm
Cityfield Farm
Westfield Farm
Middlefield Farm
Henlow Airfield
MIDDLEFIELD LA
HITCHIN RD
Middle Water
Sewage Works
SG16
Camp
A600 Bedford
Derwent Lower Sch
Playing Field
River Hiz
Laurels Grove
SG15
Susans Grove
Oldfield Farm
OLDFIELD FARM RD
Greyhound Stadium
STATION RD
PH
WILLOW TREES CVN SITE
Henlow Ind Est
Peckworth Ind Est
Lower Stondon
Playing Field
Lindas Grove
Works
MILL LA
STRAW PLAIT WAY
THREE STAR CVN PK
Cherry Tree Nurseries
BEDFORD RD
Old Ramerick
Holwellbury Farm
Holwell Bury House
Holwellbury
Ramerick Nursery
Ramerick Bottom
SG5
A600
LC

12

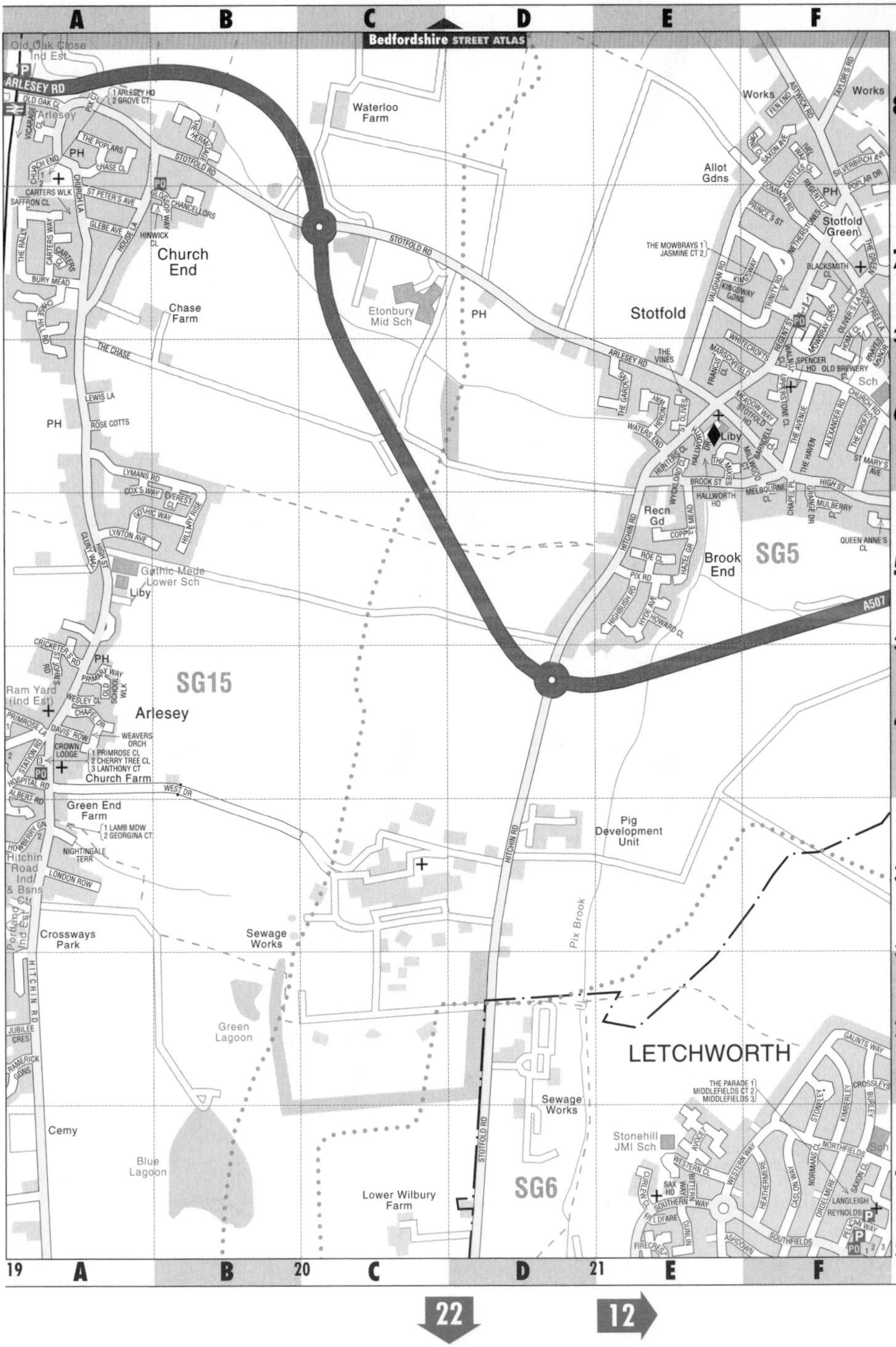
A
B
C
D
E
F
Bedfordshire STREET ATLAS
Old Oak Close Ind Est
ARLESEY RD
1 ARLESEY HO
2 GROVE CT
OLD OAK CL
Arlesey
VICARAGE CL
PIX CT
THE HERMITAGE
Waterloo Farm
THE POPLARS
PH
CHURCH END
CHASE CL
STOTFOLD RD
CARTERS WLK
SAFFRON CL
CHURCH LA
ST PETER'S AVE
GLOSSOP WAY
CHANCELLORS
GLEBE AVE
HOUSE LA
HINWICK CL
THE RALLY
CARTERS WAY
CARTERS CL
Church End
STOTFOLD RD
BURY MEAD
CHASE HILL RD
Chase Farm
Etonbury Mid Sch
PH
THE CHASE
LEWIS LA
ROSE COTTS
PH
LYMANS RD
COX'S WAY
EVEREST CL
GOTHIC WAY
HILLWAY RISE
LYNTON AVE
CLUNY WAY
HIGH ST
Gothic Mede Lower Sch
Liby
CRICKETERS RD
ST JOHN'S RD
PH
PRIMARY WAY
OLD SCHOOL WLK
SG15
Ram Yard (Ind Est)
WESLEY CL
CHAPEL DR
Arlesey
PRIMROSE LA
DAVIS' ROW
WEAVERS ORCH
CROWN LODGE
1 PRIMROSE CL
2 CHERRY TREE CL
3 LANTHONY CT
STATION RD
HOSPITAL RD
Church Farm
WEST DR
ALBERT RD
Green End Farm
1 LAMB MDW
2 GEORGINA CT
NIGHTINGALE TERR
Hitchin Road Ind/ & Bsns Ctr
LONDON ROW
Portland Ind Est
Crossways Park
Sewage Works
HITCHIN RD
JUBILEE CRES
RAMERICK GDNS
Green Lagoon
Cemy
Blue Lagoon
Lower Wilbury Farm
STOTFOLD RD
SG6
Sewage Works
Pix Brook
HITCHIN RD
Pig Development Unit
LETCHWORTH
Works
Works
FEN END
ASTWICK RD
TAYLOR'S RD
SAXON AVE
IVEL WAY
SILVERBIRCH AVE
POPLAR DR
Allot Gdns
CASTLES CL
COMMON RD
REGENT CT
PH
PRINCE'S ST
Stotfold Green
NETHERSTONES
THE GREEN
THE MOWBRAYS 1
JASMINE CT 2
KINGSWAY
KINGSWAY GDNS
TRINITY RD
VAUGHAN RD
BLACKSMITH CL
Stotfold
MOWBRAY CRES
OLIVER'S LA
ROCK TREE LA
HOME CL
BRAYES MANOR
PH
THE VINES
ARLESEY RD
WHITECROFTS
REGENT ST
WALNUT
SPENCER HO
OLD BREWERY CL
Sch
MARSCH FIELD
FRANCIS CL
UPPERSTONE CL
CHURCH RD
THE GARDENS
HERON WAY
ST OLIVES
MEADOW WAY
STOTFOLD HO
ALEXANDER RD
THE CROFTS
WATERS END
Liby
BARNDELL CL
THE AVENUE
THE HAVEN
ST MARY'S AVE
HUNTERS CL
HALLWORTH DR
MILLWOOD
THE MAXIES
BROOK ST
MELBOURNE CL
CHAPEL PL
GRANGE DR
HIGH ST
WYCKLOND CL
HALLWORTH HO
MULBERRY CL
Recn Gd
COPPICE MEAD
QUEEN ANNE'S CL
HITCHIN RD
SG5
ROE CL
HAZEL GR
Brook End
PIX RD
HIGHBUSH RD
HYDE AVE
HOWARD CL
A507
GAUNTS WAY
THE PARADE 1
MIDDLEFIELDS CT 2
MIDDLEFIELDS 3
CROSSLEYS
STONELEY
KIMBERLEY
BURLEY
Stonehill JMI Sch
AVOCET
NORTHFIELDS
Sch
WESTERN CL
WESTERN WAY
HEATHERMERE
CASLON WAY
NORMANS CL
ORDELMERE
SAXON CL
SAX HO
BITTERN WAY
SOUTHERN WAY
CURLEW CL
LANGLEIGH
REYNOLDS
FIELDFARE
DUNLIN
SOUTHFIELDS
ASHDOWN
FIRECREST
PELICAN WAY
1 2 3
8
7
37
6
5
36
4
3
35
2
1
34
19
20
21

22

12

11
3

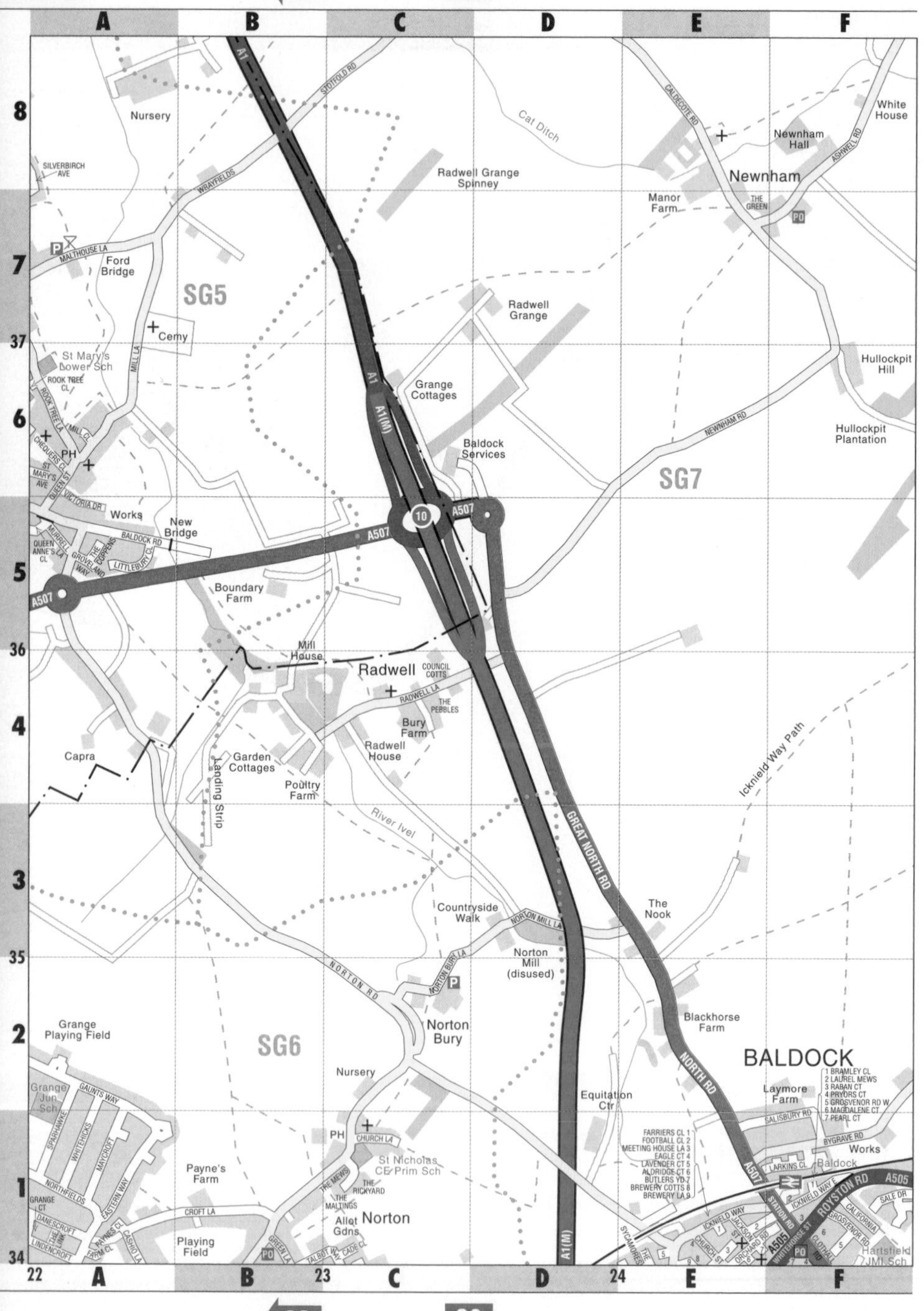
A
B
C
D
E
F
8
7
37
6
5
36
4
3
35
2
1
34
22
23
24
Nursery
SILVERBIRCH AVE
STOTFOLD RD
WRAYFIELDS
Cat Ditch
Radwell Grange Spinney
CALDECOTE RD
White House
Newnham Hall
ASHWELL RD
Newnham
Manor Farm
THE GREEN
PO
MALTHOUSE LA
Ford Bridge
SG5
Radwell Grange
Cemy
St Mary's Lower Sch
ROOK TREE CL
MILL LA
ROOK TREE LA
MILL CL
CHEQUERS CL
PH
ST MARY'S AVE
QUEEN ST
Grange Cottages
A1
A1(M)
Baldock Services
Hullockpit Hill
NEWNHAM RD
Hullockpit Plantation
SG7
VICTORIA DR
Works
New Bridge
BALDOCK RD
MURRELL LA
QUEEN ANNE'S CL
GROVELAND WAY
THE COPPINS
LITTLEBURY CL
A507
10
Boundary Farm
Mill House
Radwell
COUNCIL COTTS
RADWELL LA
THE PEBBLES
Bury Farm
Radwell House
Icknield Way Path
Capra
Garden Cottages
Landing Strip
Poultry Farm
River Ivel
GREAT NORTH RD
The Nook
Countryside Walk
NORTON MILL LA
Norton Mill (disused)
NORTON BURY LA
NORTON RD
P
Norton Bury
Blackhorse Farm
Grange Playing Field
SG6
NORTH RD
BALDOCK
Nursery
1 BRAMLEY CL
2 LAUREL MEWS
3 RABAN CT
4 PRYORS CT
5 GROSVENOR RD W
6 MAGDALENE CT
7 PEARL CT
Laymore Farm
SALISBURY RD
Grange Jun Sch
GAUNTS WAY
SPARHAWKE
WHITEHICKS
MAYCROFT
Equitation Ctr
PH
CHURCH LA
St Nicholas CE Prim Sch
FARRIERS CL 1
FOOTBALL CL 2
MEETING HOUSE LA 3
EAGLE CT 4
LAVENDER CT 5
ALDRIDGE CT 6
BUTLERS YD 7
BREWERY COTTS 8
BREWERY LA 9
BYGRAVE RD
Works
Baldock
LARKINS CL
Payne's Farm
NORTHFIELDS
EASTERN WAY
THE MEWS
THE RICKYARD
THE MALTINGS
GRANGE CT
DANESCROFT
LINDENCROFT
CROFT LA
Allot Gdns
Norton
ROYSTON RD
A505
SALE DR
CALIFORNIA
ICKNIELD WAY
GROSVENOR RD
STATION RD
WHITEHORSE ST
CLOTHALL RD
CHURCH ST
JACKSON ST
ORCHARD RD
SYCAMORES
FARM CL
PAYNES CL
CASHIO LA
Playing Field
GREEN LA
TALBOT WAY
CADE CL
PO
Hartsfield JMI Sch

11
23

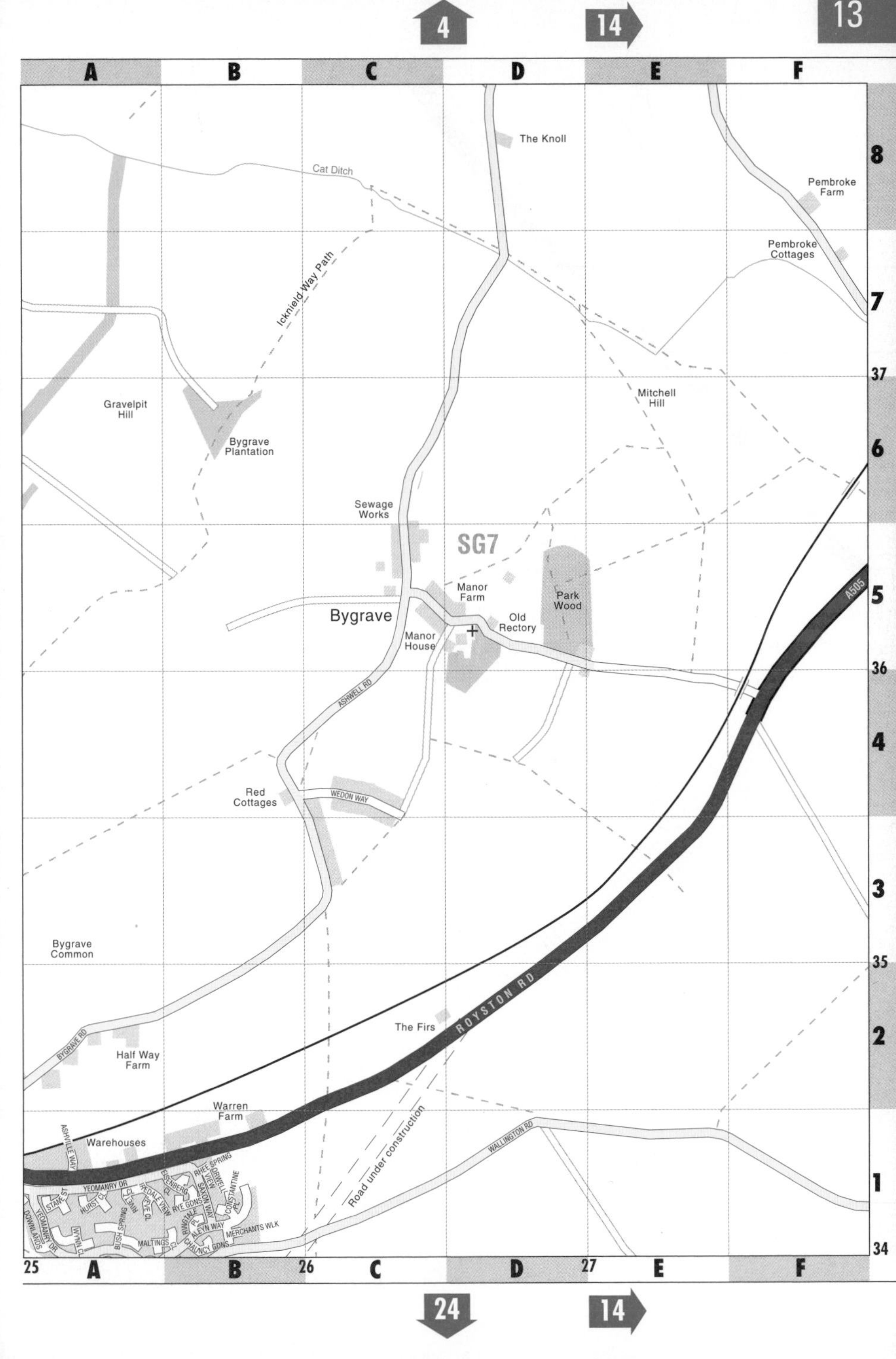
4
14
A
B
C
D
E
F
8
7
37
6
5
36
4
3
35
2
1
34
25
26
27
The Knoll
Cat Ditch
Pembroke
Farm
Pembroke
Cottages
Icknield Way Path
Mitchell
Hill
Gravelpit
Hill
Bygrave
Plantation
Sewage
Works
SG7
Manor
Farm
Park
Wood
Bygrave
Old
Rectory
Manor
House
A505
ASHWELL RD
Red
Cottages
WEDON WAY
Bygrave
Common
The Firs
ROYSTON RD
BYGRAVE RD
Half Way
Farm
Warren
Farm
Road under construction
WALLINGTON RD
Warehouses
ASHVILLE WAY
YEOMANRY DR
STANE ST
HURST CL
RIVETT CL
IREDALE VIEW
EVE CL
EISENBERG CL
RHEE SPRING
ORWELL VIEW
SAXON WAY
CONSTANTINE PL
RYE GDNS
RINGTALE PL
ALEYN WAY
MERCHANTS WLK
DOWNLANDS
YEOMANRY DR
WYNN CL
BUSH SPRING
MALTINGS CL
CHAUNCY GDNS
24
14

13
5

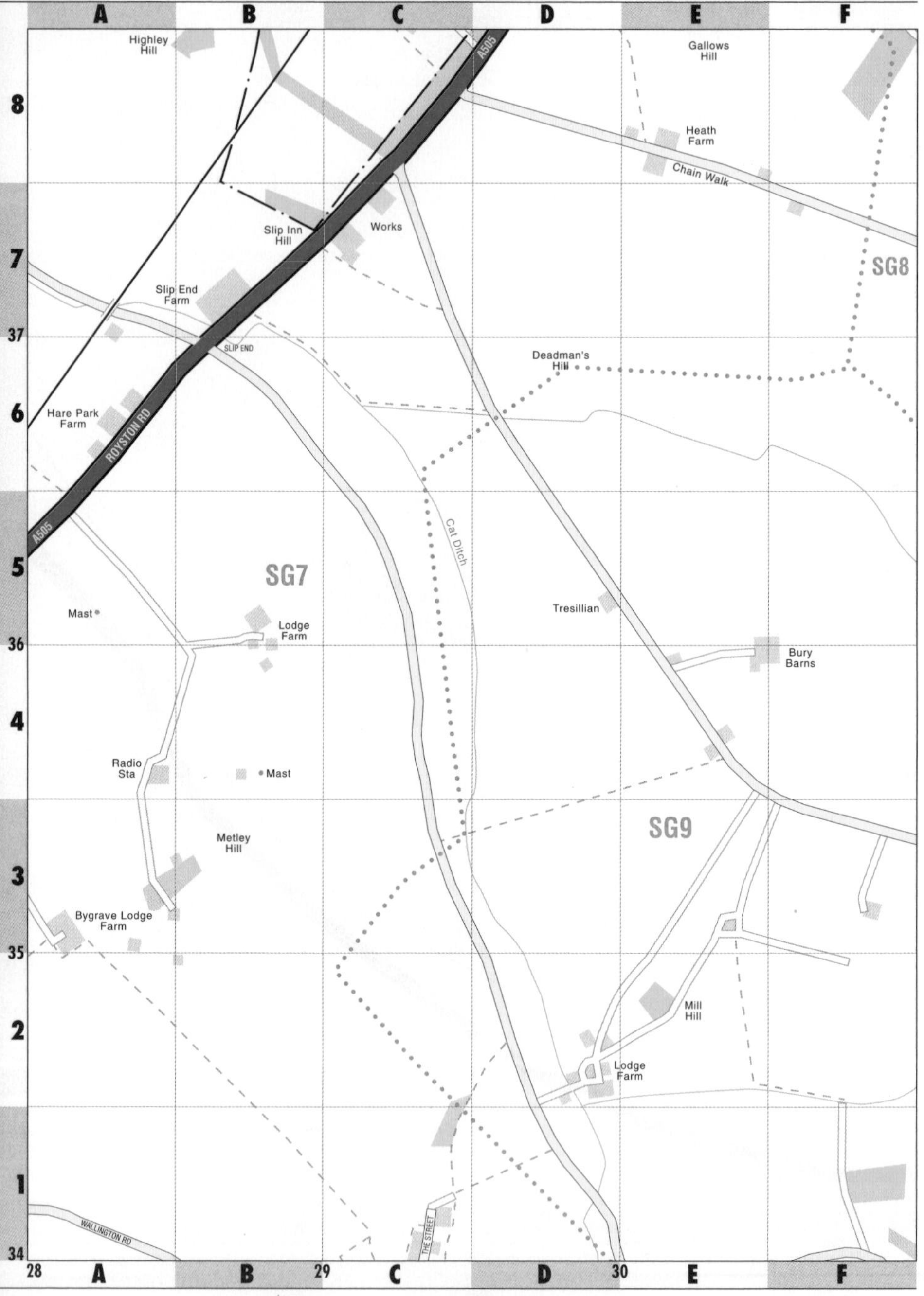
A
B
C
D
E
F
Highley Hill
Gallows Hill
A505
Heath Farm
Chain Walk
Slip Inn Hill
Works
SG8
Slip End Farm
SLIP END
Deadman's Hill
Hare Park Farm
ROYSTON RD
A505
Cat Ditch
SG7
Mast
Lodge Farm
Tresillian
Bury Barns
Radio Sta
Mast
Metley Hill
SG9
Bygrave Lodge Farm
Mill Hill
Lodge Farm
WALLINGTON RD
THE STREET
8
7
37
6
5
36
4
3
35
2
1
34
28
29
30

13
25

6
16

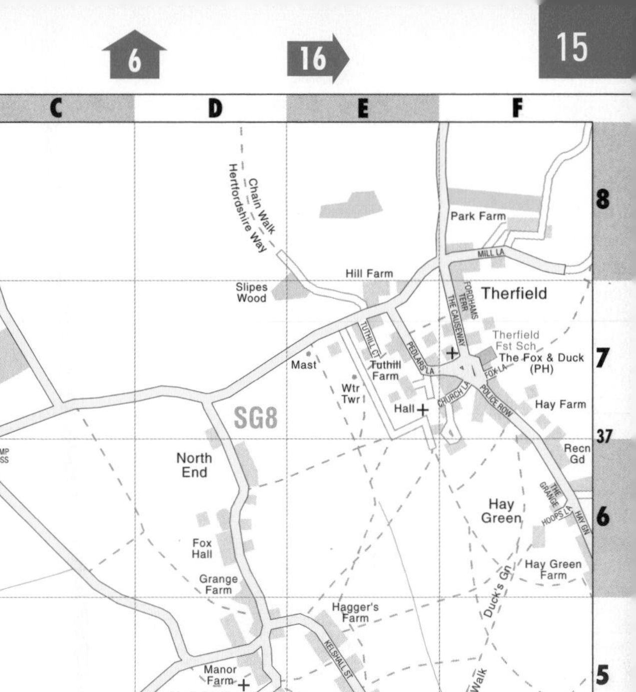
A
B
C
D
E
F
8
7
37
6
5
36
4
3
35
2
1
34
Coombe Farm
COOMBE RD
Chain Walk
Hertfordshire Way
Park Farm
MILL LA
Hill Farm
Slipes Wood
Therfield
FORDHAMS TERR
THE CAUSEWAY
TUTHILL CT
PEDLARS LA
Therfield Fst Sch
The Fox & Duck (PH)
FOX LA
CHURCH LA
POLICE ROW
Hay Farm
Horseshoe Wood Farm
Mast
Tuthill Farm
Wtr Twr
Hall
Crouch Hill
Chain Walk
STUMP CROSS
SG8
North End
Recn Gd
Mount Hill
THE GRANGE
HOOPS LA
HAY GN
Hay Green
Fox Hall
Grange Farm
Hay Green Farm
Duck's Gn
Hagger's Farm
KELSHALL ST
Manor Farm
Kelshall
Pott's Hill
Chain Walk
Rain Hill
Chain Walk
Hertfordshire Way
Kelshall La
Woodcotes
Wheat Hill
Gannock Farm
Lords Wood
SG9
Gannock Green
Little Sark
Philpott's Wood
Drift Way
Hertfordshire Way
Icknield Way Path
Hawkins Wood
Chestnut Hill
Partridge Hall Farm
Park Lane
The Mount
Notley La
Churchend Green
PAYNE END
Sandon Bury
Sandon
DARK LA
RUSHDEN RD
PO
Notley Green
Roe Wood
The Chequers (PH)
Sandon Jun Mix Inf Sch
Icknield Way Path
Cock's Lodge
31
32
33
A
B
C
D
E
F

26
16

15
7

A B C D E F
8
7
37
6
5
36
4
3
35
2
1
34
Icknield Way Path
Hatchpen
A10
Hertfordshire Way
Washingditch Green
MEADOW WAY
HAYWOOD LA
River Rib
Mardlebury
Mast
Reed End
SG8
THE JOINT
BRICKYARD LA
JACKSON'S LA
WILLOW CL
BLACKSMITH'S LA
HOBBS HAYES
CROW LA
Reed Fst Sch
Wisbridge Farm
Mast
Reed
Holborn Farm
ROOKS NEST LA
Southview
CHURCH LA
The Cabinet (PH)
HIGH ST
DRIFTWAY
Dane End
Queenbury
Mast
Rooksnest Farm
CHURCH CL
Reed Hall
DANE END
Gannock Grove
Kelshall La
Icknield Way Path
Gannock Green
Chapel Green
Reed Wood
River Rib
Hilly Wood
Sewage Works
Southfield Grove
Brandish Wood
SG9
Slate Hall Farm
34 A B 35 C D 36 E F

15
27

8
18

A
B
C
D
E
F
STOCK BANK
Ducks Nest
B1368
SMITH'S END LA
8
Newsells Park Stud
Cooper Green
Newsells
CAMBRIDGE RD
7
East Wood
37
Newsells Park
THE PENNS
BOGMOOR RD
6
Obelisk
BARKWAY HILL
Barkway Hill
THE JOINT
Mast
SG8
Mast
CAMBRIDGE RD
Sallow Wood
5
Walk Wood
ROYSTON RD
Periwinkle Hill
WINDMILL CL
PERIWINKLE CL
Cokenach
36
Bush Wood
Rokey Wood
WHITEHOUSE CT
Earl's Wood Cottage
4
CHURCH LA
Barkway
Manor Farm
Barkway CE Fst Sch
River Quin
BURRS LA
HIGH ST
Earl's Wood
3
Rushing Wells
Ashgrove
TOWNSEND CL
ASH MILL
Hertfordshire Way
Strawberry Grove
GAS LA
35
Sewage Works
Howlet's Farm
PH
2
NUTHAMPSTEAD RD
CH
LONDON RD
1
Barkway Equestrian Ctr
SG9
SG9
B1368
34
37
38
39

28
18

17 9

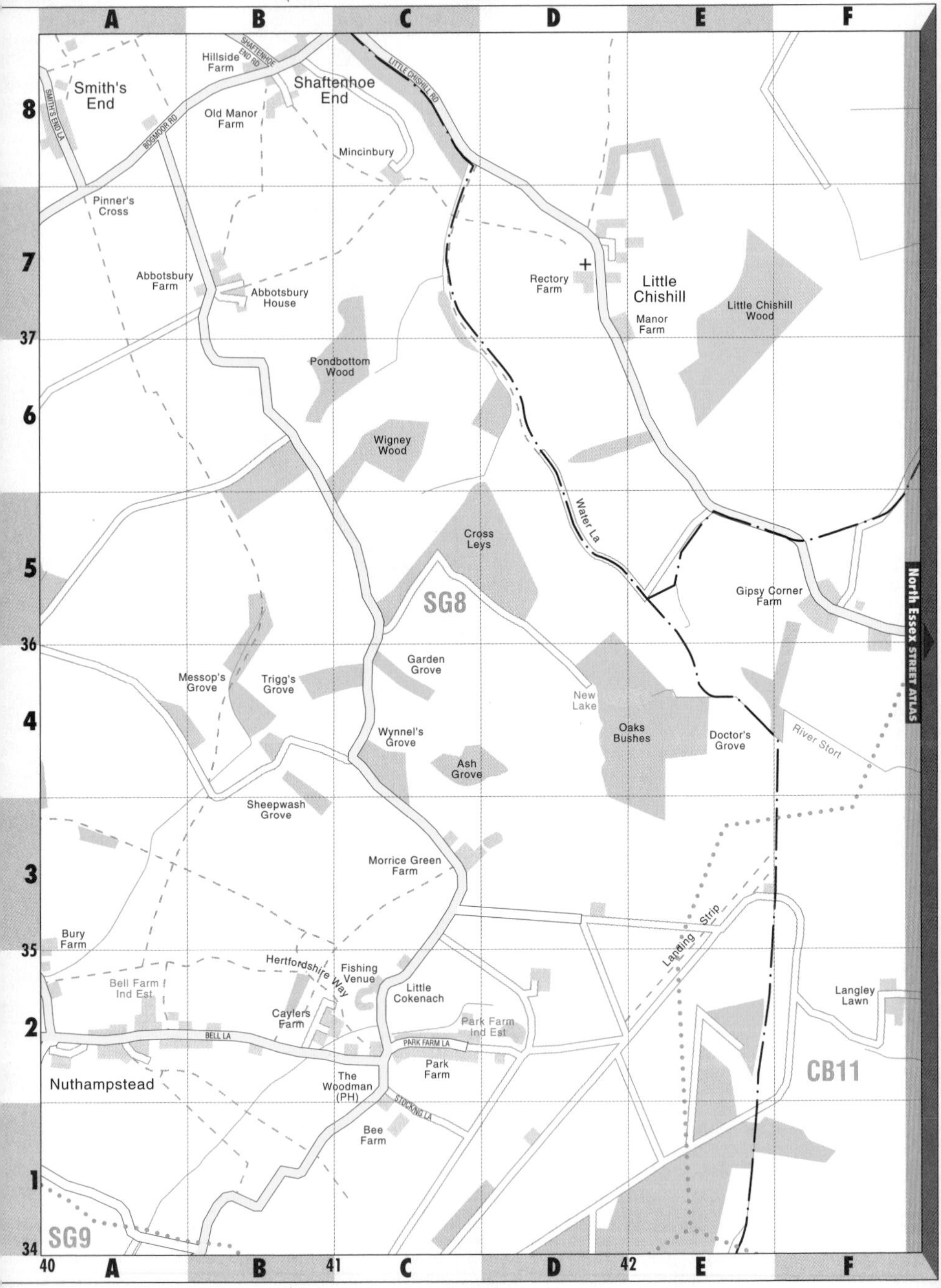

A B C D E F

8 7 37 6 5 36 4 3 35 2 1 34

Smith's End
SMITH'S END LA
Hillside Farm
SHAFTENHOE END RD
Shaftenhoe End
LITTLE CHISHILL RD
BOGMOOR RD
Old Manor Farm
Mincinbury
Pinner's Cross
Abbotsbury Farm
Abbotsbury House
Rectory Farm
Little Chishill
Manor Farm
Little Chishill Wood
Pondbottom Wood
Wigney Wood
Water La
Cross Leys
SG8
Gipsy Corner Farm
Garden Grove
Messop's Grove
Trigg's Grove
New Lake
Oaks Bushes
Doctor's Grove
River Stort
Wynnel's Grove
Ash Grove
Sheepwash Grove
Morrice Green Farm
Landing Strip
Bury Farm
Hertfordshire Way
Fishing Venue
Bell Farm Ind Est
Little Cokenach
Langley Lawn
Caylers Farm
Park Farm Ind Est
BELL LA
PARK FARM LA
Park Farm
CB11
Nuthampstead
The Woodman (PH)
STOCKING LA
Bee Farm
SG9

North Essex STREET ATLAS

40 A B 41 C D 42 E F

17 29

20

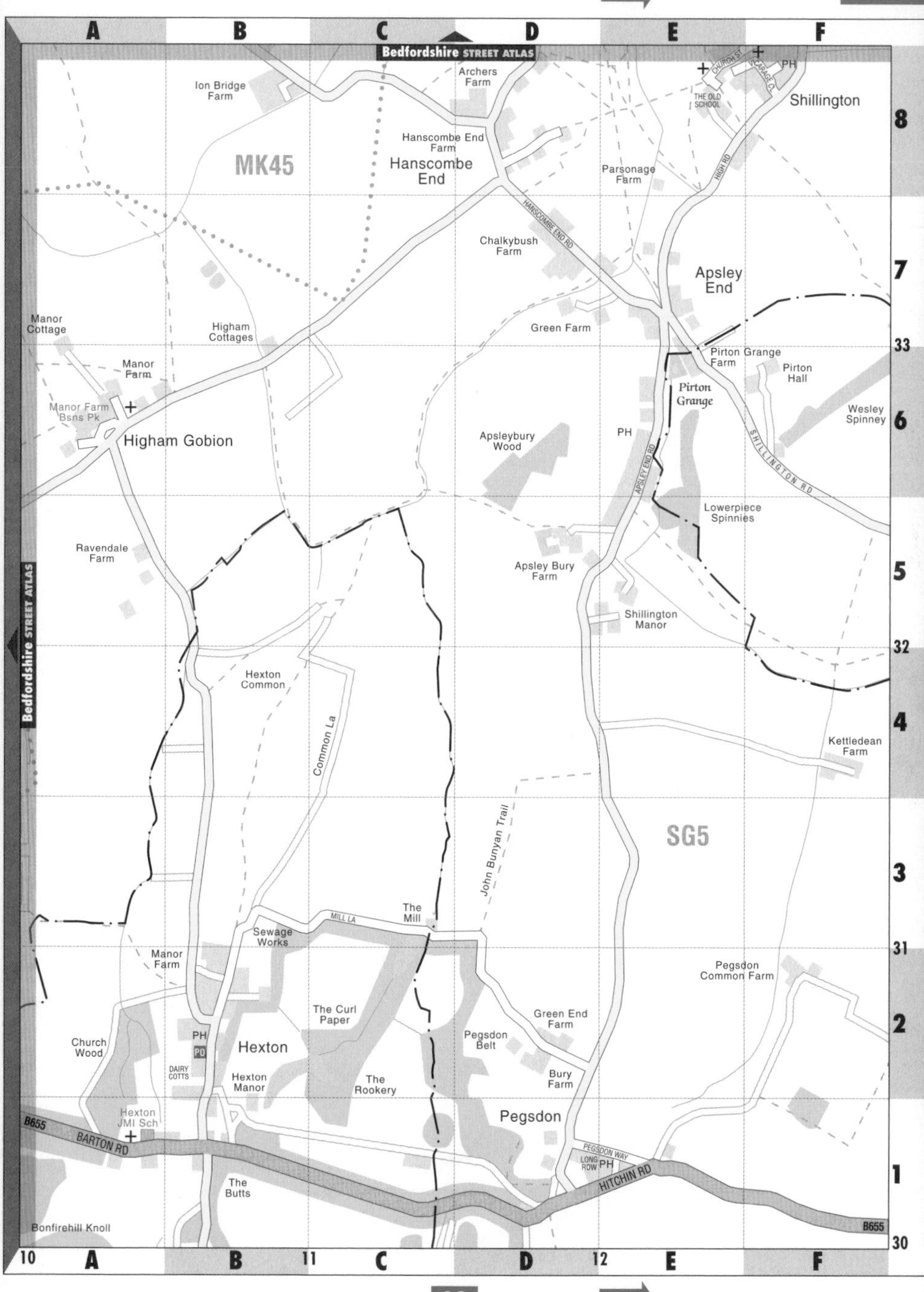
Bedfordshire STREET ATLAS
A
B
C
D
E
F
Ion Bridge Farm
Archers Farm
Shillington
THE OLD SCHOOL
CHURCH ST
VICARAGE CL
HIGH RD
PH
MK45
Hanscombe End Farm
Hanscombe End
Parsonage Farm
HANSCOMBE END RD
Chalkybush Farm
Apsley End
Manor Cottage
Higham Cottages
Green Farm
Pirton Grange Farm
Pirton Hall
Manor Farm
Pirton Grange
Manor Farm Bsns Pk
Higham Gobion
Apsleybury Wood
PH
Wesley Spinney
SHILLINGTON RD
APSLEY END RD
Lowerpiece Spinnies
Ravendale Farm
Apsley Bury Farm
Shillington Manor
Hexton Common
Common La
Kettledean Farm
SG5
John Bunyan Trail
MILL LA
The Mill
Sewage Works
Manor Farm
Pegsdon Common Farm
The Curl Paper
Green End Farm
Church Wood
PH
PD
Hexton
Pegsdon Belt
DAIRY COTTS
Hexton Manor
The Rookery
Bury Farm
Hexton JMI Sch
Pegsdon
B655
BARTON RD
PEGSDON WAY
LONG ROW
PH
HITCHIN RD
The Butts
Bonfirehill Knoll
B655
8
7
33
6
5
32
4
3
31
2
1
30
10
11
12

32
20

19

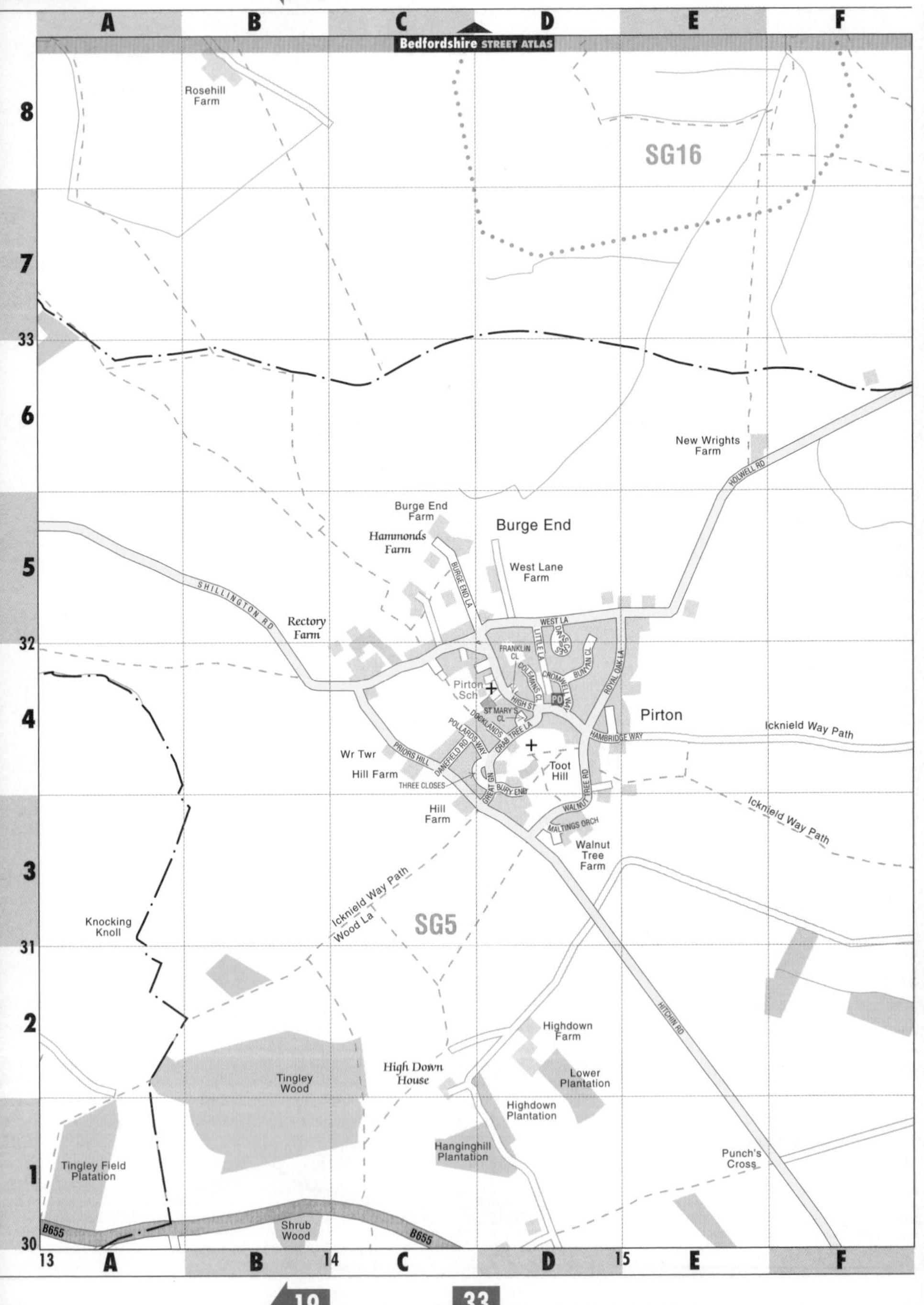

Bedfordshire STREET ATLAS
A
B
C
D
E
F
8
7
33
6
5
32
4
3
31
2
1
30
13
14
15
Rosehill Farm
SG16
New Wrights Farm
HOLWELL RD
Burge End Farm
Hammonds Farm
Burge End
West Lane Farm
BURGE END LA
SHILLINGTON RD
Rectory Farm
WEST LA
LITTLE LA
DANES CRES
FRANKLIN CL
BUNYAN CL
ROYAL OAK LA
COLEMANS CL
CROMWELL WAY
Pirton Sch
HIGH ST
PO
Pirton
ST MARY'S CL
DOCKLANDS
CRAB TREE LA
HAMBRIDGE WAY
Icknield Way Path
POLLARDS WAY
Wr Twr
PRIORS HILL
DANEFIELD RD
Toot Hill
Hill Farm
THREE CLOSES
GREAT GN
BURY END
WALNUT TREE RD
Hill Farm
WALNUT TREE RD
MALTINGS ORCH
Walnut Tree Farm
Icknield Way Path
Icknield Way Path
Wood La
SG5
Knocking Knoll
HITCHIN RD
Highdown Farm
High Down House
Tingley Wood
Lower Plantation
Highdown Plantation
Hanginghill Plantation
Tingley Field Platation
Punch's Cross
B655
Shrub Wood
B655

19
33

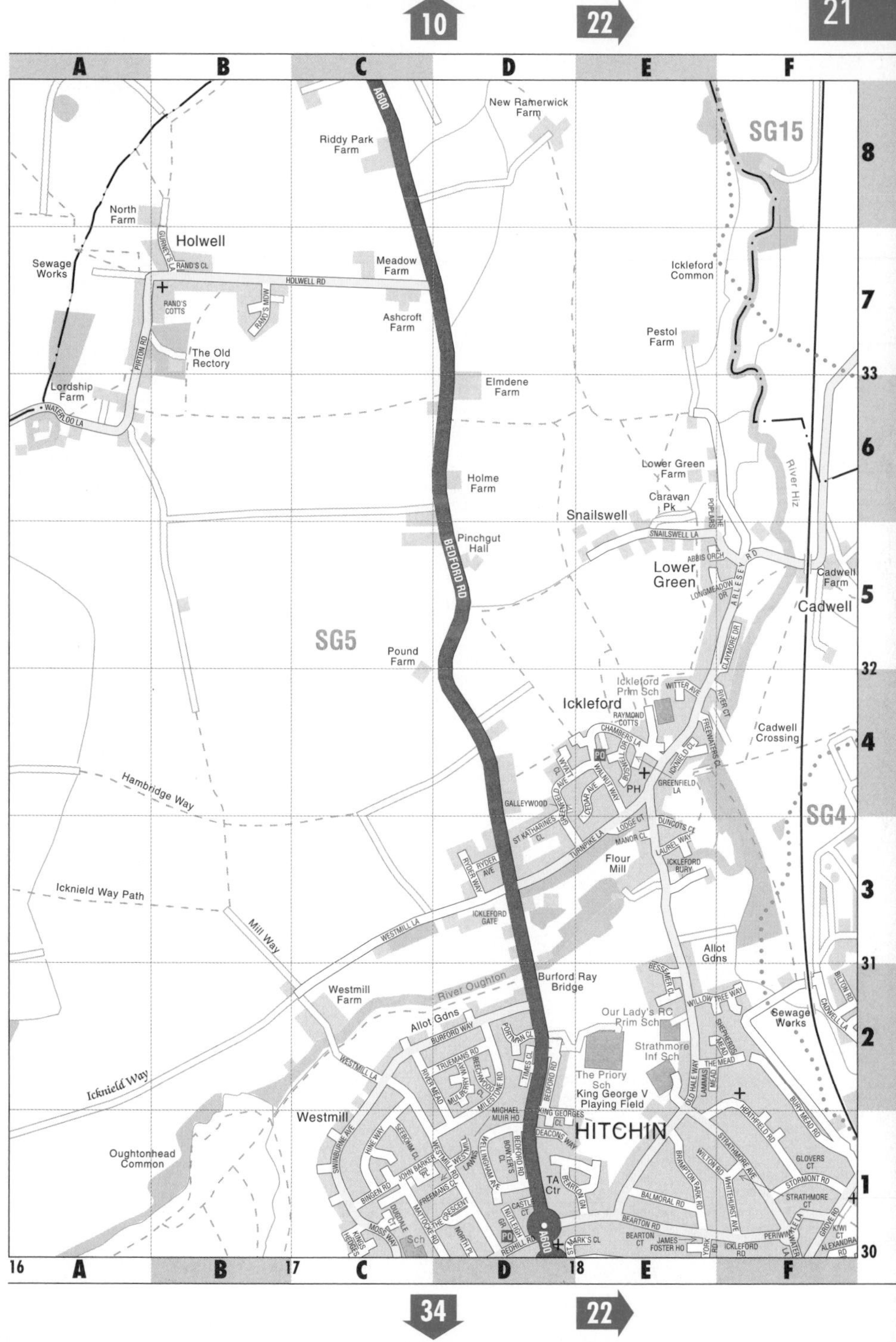
10
22
A
B
C
D
E
F
8
7
33
6
5
32
4
3
31
2
1
30
16
17
18
34
22
SG15
SG5
SG4
A600
New Ramerwick Farm
Riddy Park Farm
North Farm
Holwell
Sewage Works
GURNEY'S LA
RAND'S CL
HOLWELL RD
Meadow Farm
RAND'S COTTS
RAND'S MDW
Ashcroft Farm
Ickleford Common
Pestol Farm
PIRTON RD
The Old Rectory
Lordship Farm
WATERLOO LA
Elmdene Farm
Lower Green Farm
River Hiz
Holme Farm
Caravan Pk
Snailswell
THE POPLARS
Pinchgut Hall
SNAILSWELL LA
BEDFORD RD
ABBIS ORCH
ARLESEY RD
Lower Green
LONGMEADOW DR
Cadwell Farm
Cadwell
CLAYMORE DR
Pound Farm
Ickleford Prim Sch
WITTER AVE
RIVER CT
Ickleford
RAYMOND COTTS
CHAMBERS LA
FREEWATERS CL
Cadwell Crossing
ICKNIELD CL
WYATT CL
BOSWELL DR
WALNUT WAY
GREENFIELD AVE
CEDAR AVE
PO
PH
GREENFIELD LA
Hambridge Way
GALLEYWOOD
ST KATHARINES CL
LODGE CT
DUNCOTS CL
TURNPIKE LA
MANOR CL
LAUREL WAY
RYDER WAY
RYDER AVE
Flour Mill
ICKLEFORD BURY
Icknield Way Path
ICKLEFORD GATE
WESTMILL LA
Mill Way
Allot Gdns
Burford Ray Bridge
BESSEMER CL
Westmill Farm
River Oughton
WILLOW TREE WAY
Sewage Works
CADWELL LA
BILTON RD
Allot Gdns
Our Lady's RC Prim Sch
BURFORD WAY
PORTMAN CL
SHEPHERDS MEAD
Strathmore Inf Sch
TRUEMANS RD
TIMES CL
BEDFORD RD
THE MEAD
Icknield Way
RIVER MEAD
MULBERRY CL
BEECHWOOD CL
The Priory Sch
OLD HALE WAY
LAMMAS MEAD
MILESTONE RD
King George V Playing Field
BURY MEAD RD
HEATHFIELD RD
Westmill
MICHAEL MUIR HO
KING GEORGES CL
HITCHIN
DEACONS WAY
SWINBURNE AVE
HINE WAY
SEEBOHM CL
WESTMILL RD
WESTMILL LAWNS
WELLINGHAM AVE
BOWYER'S CL
STRATHMORE AVE
Oughtonhead Common
JOHN BARKER PL
TA Ctr
BEARTON GN
BRAMPTON PARK RD
WILTON RD
GLOVERS CT
STORMONT RD
WHITEHURST AVE
BINGEN RD
FREEMANS CL
BALMORAL RD
STRATHMORE CT
CASTLE CT
DURDALE CT
MATTOCK RD
THE CRESCENT
NUTLEIGH CT
NORTH PL
BEARTON RD
PERIWINKLE LA
WATER LA
GROVE RD
KIWI CT
MOSS WAY
KINGS HEDGES
Sch
GR
PO
REDHILL RD
ST MARK'S CL
BEARTON CT
JAMES FOSTER HO
YORK RD
ICKLEFORD RD
ALEXANDRA RD

21
11

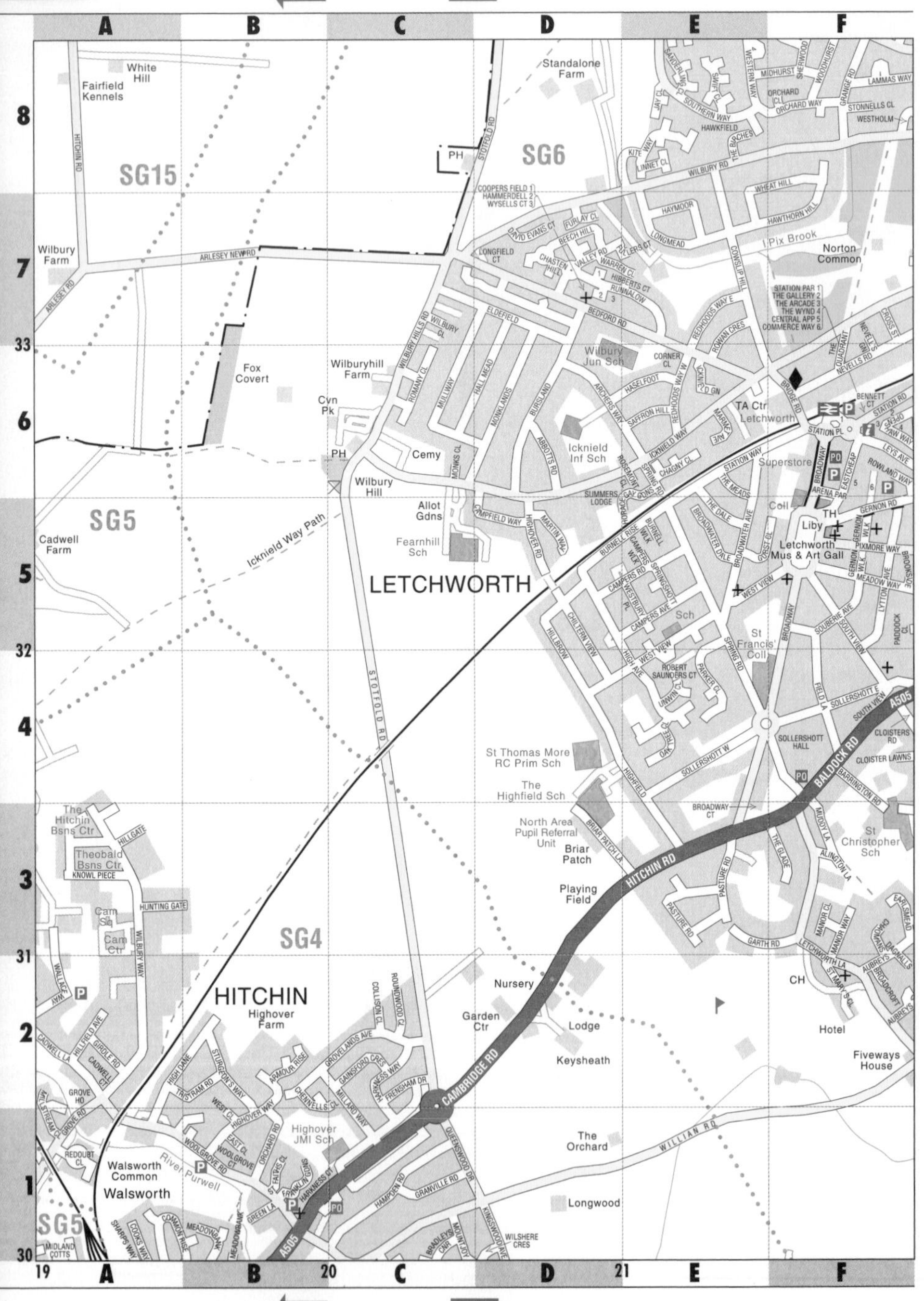
White Hill
Fairfield Kennels
Standalone Farm
SG15
SG6
SG5
SG4
Wilbury Farm
Fox Covert
Wilburyhill Farm
Cyn Pk
PH
Cemy
Wilbury Hill
Allot Gdns
Fearnhill Sch
Cadwell Farm
Icknield Way Path
LETCHWORTH
Wilbury Jun Sch
Icknield Inf Sch
TA Ctr Letchworth
Norton Common
Pix Brook
Superstore
Coll
Liby
TH
Letchworth Mus & Art Gall
St Francis' Coll
Sch
St Thomas More RC Prim Sch
The Highfield Sch
North Area Pupil Referral Unit
Briar Patch
Playing Field
St Christopher Sch
Nursery
Garden Ctr
Lodge
Keysheath
Hotel
Fiveways House
CH
The Orchard
Longwood
HITCHIN
Highover Farm
Highover JMI Sch
The Hitchin Bsns Ctr
Theobald Bsns Ctr
Cam Sq
Cam Ctr
Walsworth Common
Walsworth
River Purwell
HITCHIN RD
BALDOCK RD
CAMBRIDGE RD
A505
STOTFOLD RD
WILLIAN RD
ARLESEY NEW RD
ARLESEY RD
HITCHIN RD
BEDFORD RD
WILBURY RD
ICKNIELD WAY
STATION WAY
BROADWAY
SOLLERSHOTT W
SOLLERSHOTT E
GARTH RD
PASTURE RD
HIGHFIELD
HIGH AVE
SPRING RD
WEST VIEW
SOUTH VIEW
STATION PAR 1
THE GALLERY 2
THE ARCADE 3
THE WYND 4
CENTRAL APP 5
COMMERCE WAY 6
COOPERS FIELD 1
HAMMERDELL 2
WYSELLS CT 3
19
20
21
A B C D E F
8 7 6 5 4 3 2 1
33 32 31 30

21
35

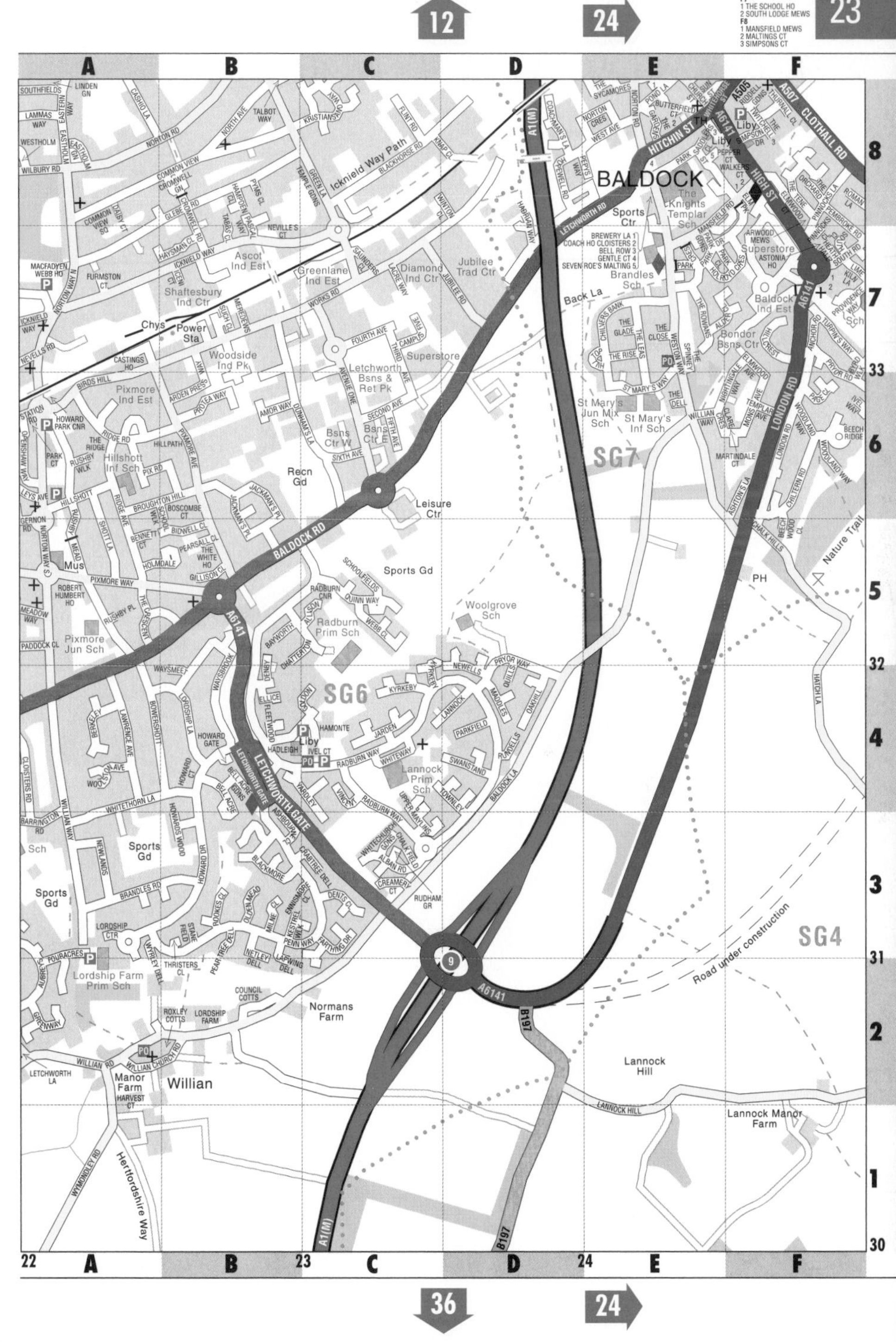
BALDOCK
Willian
SG6
SG7
SG4
Icknield Way Path
Hertfordshire Way
Road under construction
Nature Trail
Lannock Hill
Lannock Manor Farm
Normans Farm
Manor Farm
Ascot Ind Est
Greenlane Ind Est
Diamond Ind Ctr
Jubilee Trad Ctr
Shaftesbury Ind Ctr
Power Sta
Woodside Ind Pk
Pixmore Ind Est
Letchworth Bsns & Ret Pk
Superstore
Bsns Ctr W
Bsns Ctr E
Recn Gd
Leisure Ctr
Sports Gd
Hillshott Inf Sch
Mus
Pixmore Jun Sch
Radburn Prim Sch
Woolgrove Sch
Lannock Prim Sch
Lordship Farm Prim Sch
Sports Ctr
The Knights Templar Sch
Brandles Sch
Baldock Ind Est
Bondor Bsns Ctr
St Mary's Jun Mix Sch
St Mary's Inf Sch
BALDOCK RD
LETCHWORTH GATE
LONDON RD
HITCHIN ST
HIGH ST
CLOTHALL RD
LETCHWORTH RD
A1(M)
A6141
A505
A507
B197
Back La
LANNOCK HILL
NORTON RD
PIXMORE WAY
WORKS RD
RADBURN WAY
BALDOCK LA
WILLIAN RD
WYMONDLEY RD
HATCH LA
Sports Gd
PH

23
13

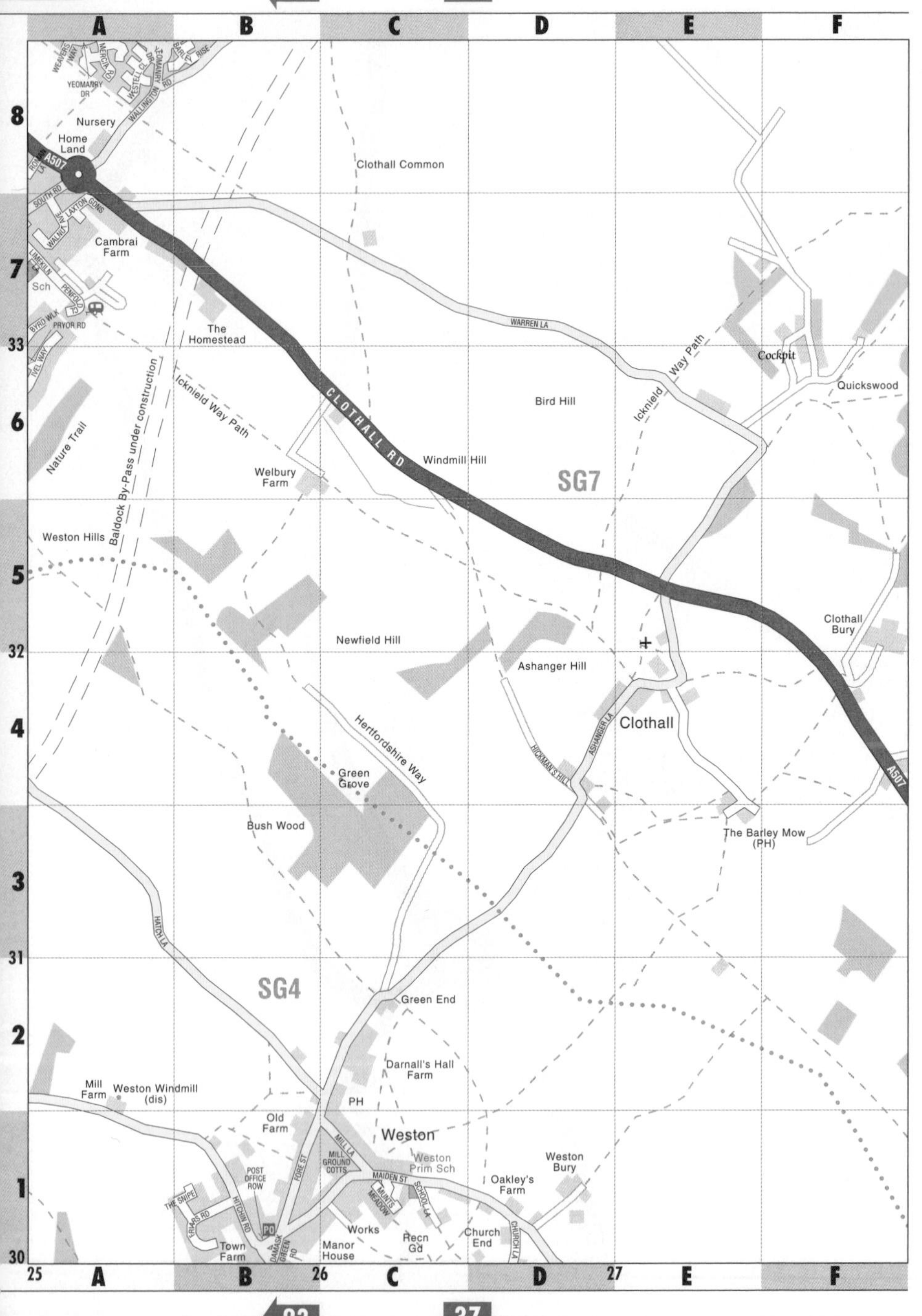
Clothall Common
Nursery
Home Land
A507
Cambrai Farm
Sch
The Homestead
Icknield Way Path
Baldock By-Pass under construction
Nature Trail
Welbury Farm
Weston Hills
CLOTHALL RD
Windmill Hill
WARREN LA
Bird Hill
SG7
Cockpit
Quickswood
Newfield Hill
Ashanger Hill
Clothall
Clothall Bury
Hertfordshire Way
Green Grove
Bush Wood
The Barley Mow (PH)
HATCH LA
SG4
Green End
Darnall's Hall Farm
Mill Farm
Weston Windmill (dis)
PH
Old Farm
Weston
Weston Prim Sch
Weston Bury
Oakley's Farm
Works
Recn Gd
Church End
Manor House
Town Farm
MAIDEN ST
SCHOOL LA
CHURCH LA
FORE ST
HITCHIN RD
POST OFFICE ROW
THE SNIPE
FRIARS RD
DAMASK GREEN RD
HICKMAN'S HILL
ASHANGER LA
A B C D E F
8 7 6 5 4 3 2 1
33 32 31 30
25 26 27

23
37

14
26

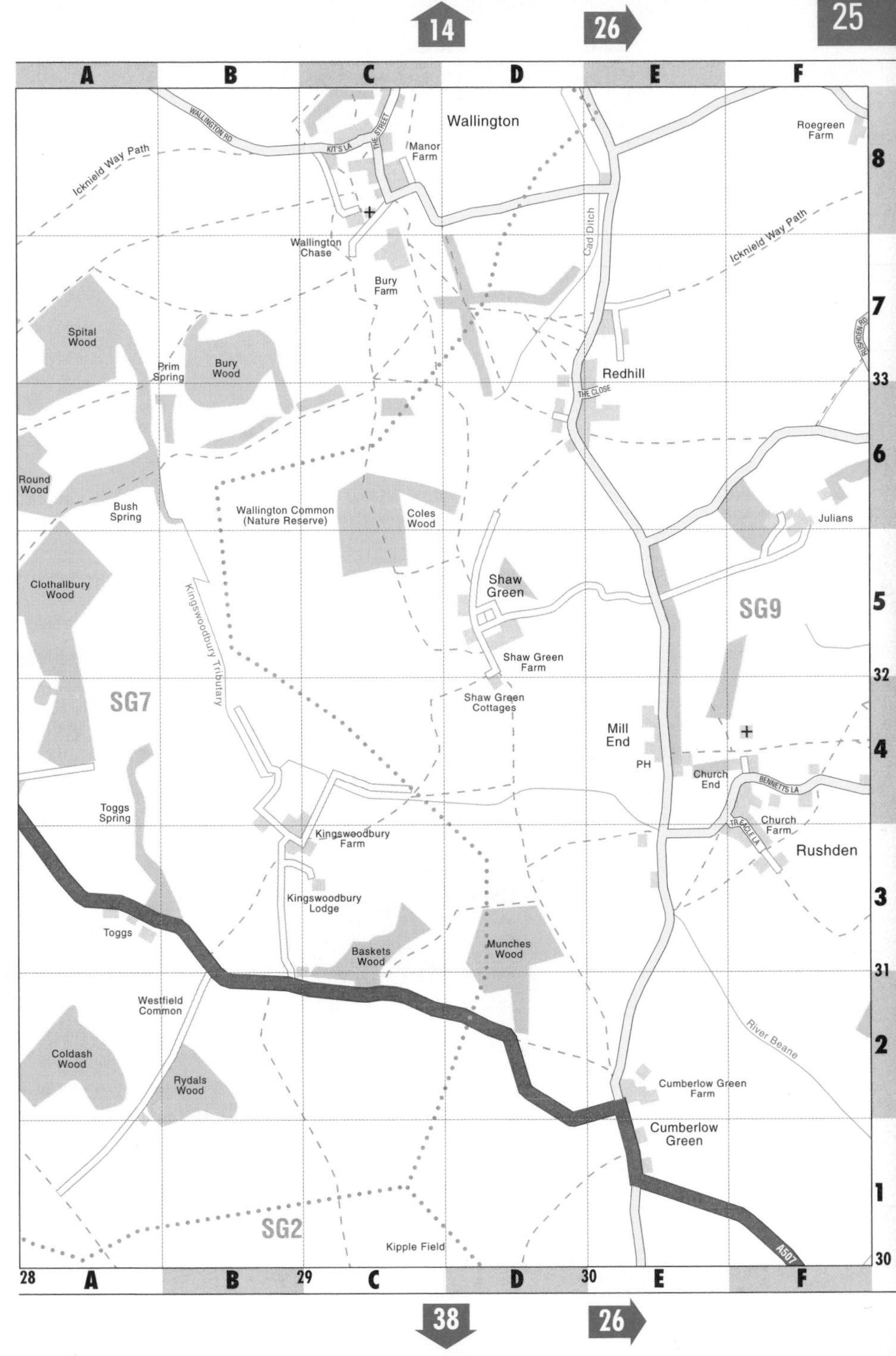
A
B
C
D
E
F
Wallington
WALLINGTON RD
KIT'S LA
THE STREET
Manor Farm
Icknield Way Path
Roegreen Farm
8
Cad Ditch
Icknield Way Path
Wallington Chase
Bury Farm
7
RUSHDEN RD
Spital Wood
Prim Spring
Bury Wood
Redhill
THE CLOSE
33
6
Round Wood
Bush Spring
Wallington Common (Nature Reserve)
Coles Wood
Julians
Clothallbury Wood
Kingswoodbury Tributary
Shaw Green
SG9
5
Shaw Green Farm
32
SG7
Shaw Green Cottages
Mill End
PH
4
Church End
BENNETTS LA
Toggs Spring
Church Farm
TREACLE LA
Kingswoodbury Farm
Rushden
Kingswoodbury Lodge
3
Toggs
Baskets Wood
Munches Wood
31
Westfield Common
River Beane
2
Coldash Wood
Rydals Wood
Cumberlow Green Farm
Cumberlow Green
1
SG2
Kipple Field
A507
30
28
29
30

38
26

25
15

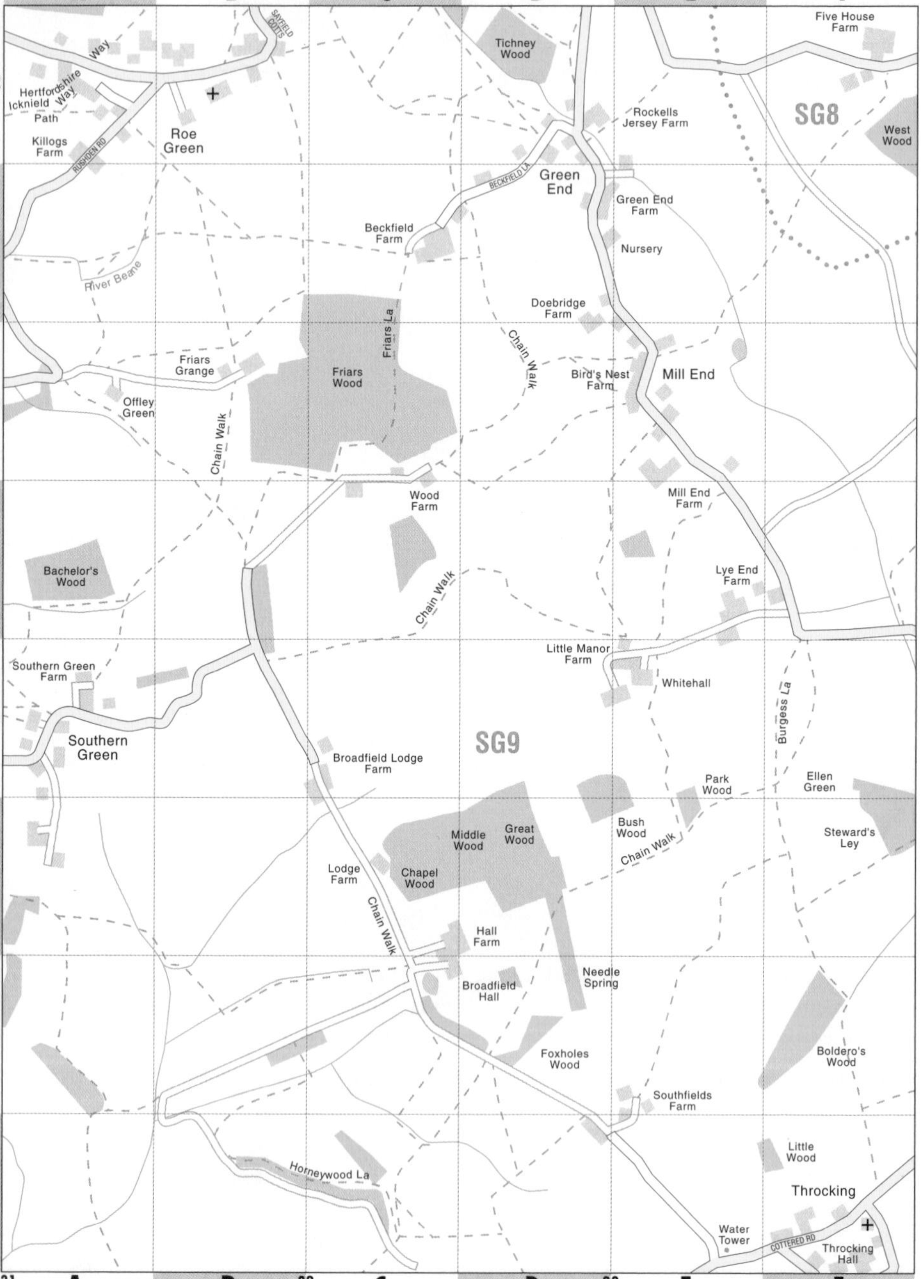

A
B
C
D
E
F
8
7
33
6
5
32
4
3
31
2
1
30
31
32
33
SAYFIELD COTTS
Tichney Wood
Five House Farm
Way
Hertfordshire Way
Icknield Path
Killogs Farm
RUSHDEN RD
Roe Green
Rockells Jersey Farm
SG8
West Wood
BECKFIELD LA
Green End
Green End Farm
Beckfield Farm
Nursery
River Beane
Doebridge Farm
Friars La
Chain Walk
Friars Grange
Friars Wood
Bird's Nest Farm
Mill End
Offley Green
Chain Walk
Wood Farm
Mill End Farm
Bachelor's Wood
Chain Walk
Lye End Farm
Little Manor Farm
Southern Green Farm
Whitehall
Burgess La
Southern Green
SG9
Broadfield Lodge Farm
Park Wood
Ellen Green
Middle Wood
Great Wood
Bush Wood
Steward's Ley
Chain Walk
Lodge Farm
Chapel Wood
Chain Walk
Hall Farm
Needle Spring
Broadfield Hall
Foxholes Wood
Boldero's Wood
Southfields Farm
Little Wood
Honeywood La
Throcking
Water Tower
COTTERED RD
Throcking Hall

25
39

16
28
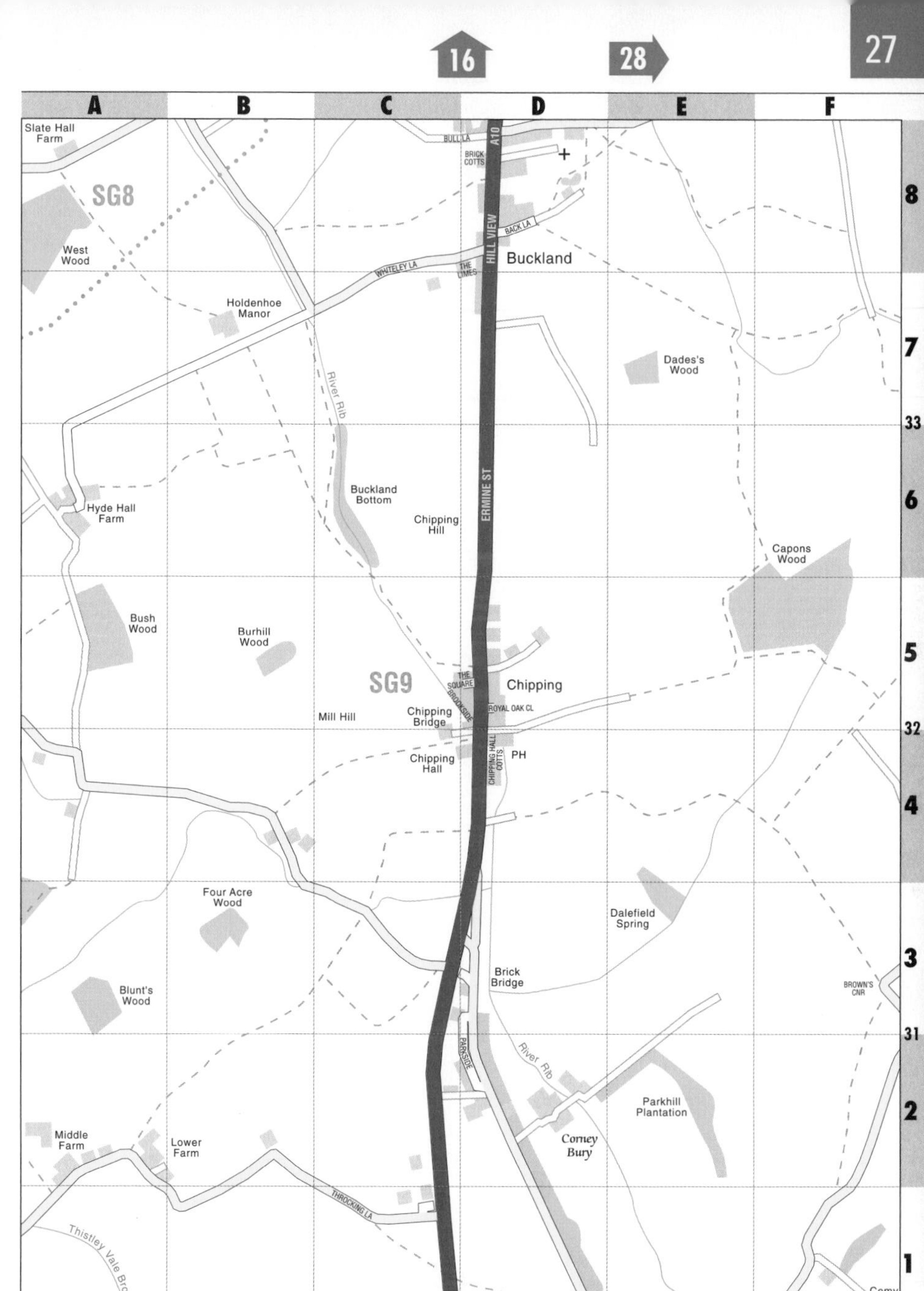
A
B
C
D
E
F
Slate Hall Farm
SG8
West Wood
BULL LA
A10
BRICK COTTS
BACK LA
HILL VIEW
Buckland
WHITELEY LA
THE LIMES
Holdenhoe Manor
Dades's Wood
River Rib
Buckland Bottom
Chipping Hill
ERMINE ST
Hyde Hall Farm
Capons Wood
Bush Wood
Burhill Wood
SG9
THE SQUARE
Chipping
BROOKSIDE
ROYAL OAK CL
Mill Hill
Chipping Bridge
Chipping Hall
CHIPPING HALL COTTS
PH
Four Acre Wood
Dalefield Spring
Brick Bridge
Blunt's Wood
BROWN'S CNR
PARKSIDE
River Rib
Parkhill Plantation
Middle Farm
Lower Farm
Corney Bury
THROCKING LA
Thistley Vale Brook
Freman Coll
Park Farm Ind Est
VICARAGE RD
Cemy
THE CAUSEWAY
A10
8
7
33
6
5
32
4
3
31
2
1
30
34
35
36
40
28

27 17

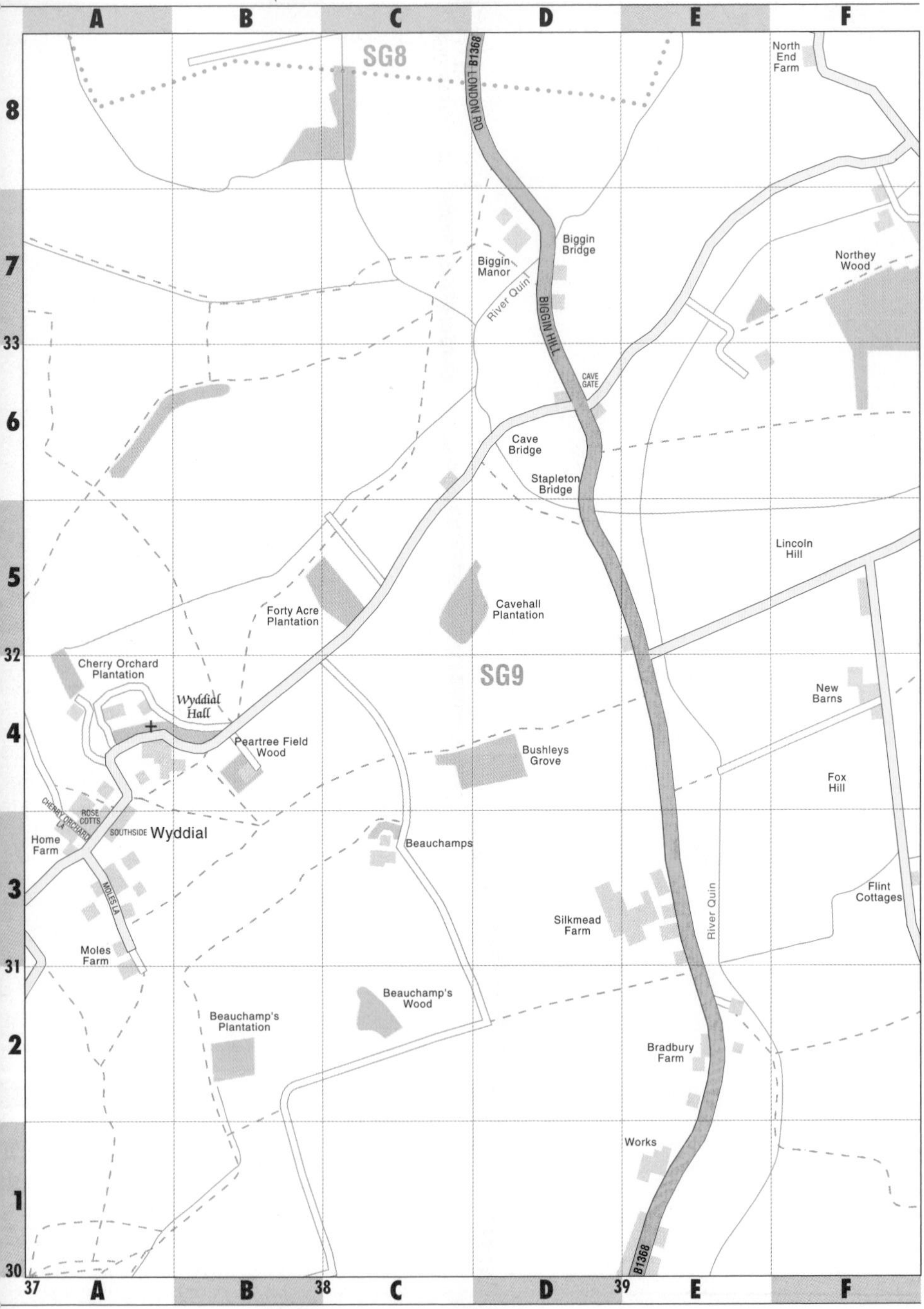

A B C D E F
8
7
33
6
5
32
4
3
31
2
1
30
37 38 39
SG8
B1368 LONDON RD
North End Farm
Biggin Bridge
Biggin Manor
River Quin
BIGGIN HILL
Northey Wood
CAVE GATE
Cave Bridge
Stapleton Bridge
Lincoln Hill
Forty Acre Plantation
Cavehall Plantation
Cherry Orchard Plantation
SG9
Wyddial Hall
New Barns
Peartree Field Wood
Bushleys Grove
Fox Hill
CHERRY ORCHARD LA
ROSE COTTS
SOUTHSIDE
Wyddial
Home Farm
Beauchamps
MOLES LA
Flint Cottages
Silkmead Farm
River Quin
Moles Farm
Beauchamp's Wood
Beauchamp's Plantation
Bradbury Farm
Works
B1368

27 41

18
30
A
B
C
D
E
F
CB11
SG8
Scales Park
8
Bandons
Pain's End
DIMSDALE COTTS
Northey Wood
Two Acres Farm
Cheapside
CASTLE COTTS
Anstey Castle
MOATSIDE
The Chequers (PH)
BURY FIELD
White Hill
7
33
ST GEORGES END
Anstey
The Hale
Lower Green
Anstey Fst Sch
ELM COTTS
Meesden
6
Snow End
The Fox (PH)
LINCOLN HILL
ROGER'S LA
Daw's End
Coltsfoot Farm
Manor Farm
SILVER ST
5
32
Anstey Bury
River Ash
Hertfordshire Way
4
Puttock's End
SG9
Cole Green
Mill Mound
3
Brick House Farm
31
2
B1038
ANDERSON'S LA
Borley Green Cottage
Hormead Hall
Black Ditch
Three Acre Wood
1
HALL LA
HALL COTTS
CONDUIT LA
B1038
Dane End House
30
40
41
42
42
30

29

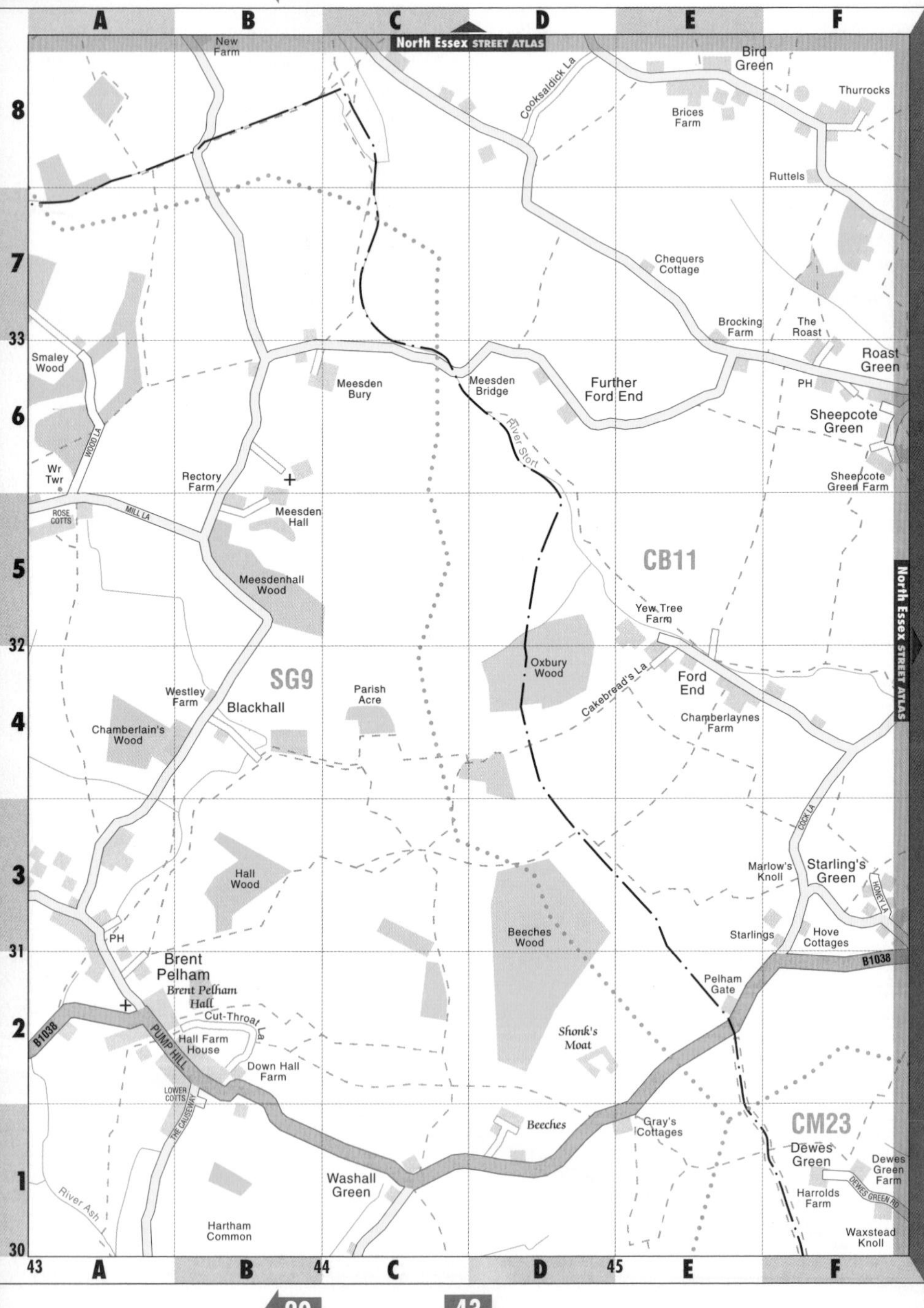
North Essex STREET ATLAS
New Farm
Bird Green
Thurrocks
Cooksaldick La
Brices Farm
Ruttels
Chequers Cottage
Smaley Wood
Brocking Farm
The Roast
Roast Green
Meesden Bury
Meesden Bridge
Further Ford End
PH
Sheepcote Green
River Stort
Wr Twr
WOOD LA
Rectory Farm
Sheepcote Green Farm
ROSE COTTS
MILL LA
Meesden Hall
CB11
Meesdenhall Wood
Yew Tree Farm
Oxbury Wood
SG9
Parish Acre
Westley Farm
Blackhall
Cakebread's La
Ford End
Chamberlain's Wood
Chamberlaynes Farm
COCK LA
Marlow's Knoll
Starling's Green
Hall Wood
HONEY LA
Beeches Wood
PH
Starlings
Hove Cottages
Brent Pelham
Brent Pelham Hall
Pelham Gate
B1038
Cut-Throat La
B1038
PUMP HILL
Hall Farm House
Shonk's Moat
Down Hall Farm
LOWER COTTS
THE CAUSEWAY
Beeches
Gray's Cottages
CM23
Dewes Green
Dewes Green Farm
Washall Green
Harrolds Farm
DEWES GREEN RD
River Ash
Hartham Common
Waxstead Knoll
A B C D E F
8 7 33 6 5 32 4 3 31 2 1 30
43 44 45

29
43

32
A
B
C
D
E
F
Bedfordshire STREET ATLAS
A6 Bedford
B655
A6
B655
East Hill
Barton Hills
Nature Reserve
SG5
Smithcombe Valley
MK45
Leet Wood
Ravensburgh Castle
Smithcombe Hill
Jeremiah's Tree
Watergutter Hole
Bartonhill Cutting
Stonley Wood
Cow Hole
Top Farm
LUTON RD
CHURCH RD
ST MARGARETS CL
PH
Barton Hill Farm
STANLEY RD
Streatley
SHARPENHOE RD
LU3
LU2
BURY LA
Streatley-Bury
Chiltern Way
SHARPENHOE RD
John Bunyan Trail
Swedish Cottages
Icknield Way Path
John Bunyan Trail
Maulden Firs
Bury Farm
New Farm
BARTON RD
George Wood
Galley Hill
Pasque Hospice
GREAT BRAMINGHAM LA
CH
HAYTON CL
SKELTON CL
DALTON CL
GATEHILL GDNS
TURNPIKE DR
LUTON
BURFORD CL
CATESBY GN
LAUNTON CL
QUANTOCK RISE
MILBURN CL
HOLFORD WAY
STATHAM CL
WOODMERE
WHITEHORSE VALE
HARLESTONE CL
ALBURY CL
CHARNDON CL
ELVINGTON GDNS
FARROW CL
DANVERS DR
ARBOUR CL
RYEFIELD
FERNHEATH
EDGCOTT CL
ALLENDALE
KIRBYS CL
AMES DR
ASHDALE GDNS
DEXTER CL 1
BALMORE WOOD 2
SPURCROFT 3
CHARD DR
SACOMBE GN
A6
Cardinal Newman RC Sec Sch
Warden Hill
8
7
29
6
5
28
4
3
27
2
1
26
07
08
09
45
32

31 19

A B C D E F
8
7
29
6
5
28
4
3
27
2
1
26
10 11 12
Butts Hill
Deacon Hill
Church Hole
Clark's Hill
Claypit Plantation
Lion Hill
Moor Hill
Cank Hill
The Meg
Devil's Ditch
Claypit Hole
Burwell Platation
Gravel Hill
Pegdons Spring
SG5
Wicks Spring
Hoo Bit
Fairy Hole
Icknield Way Path
Telegraph Hill
Nature Reserve
Muzzleford Wood
Wasgrove Wood
Staple Knoll
Lilley Hoo
Mortgrove Farm
John Bunyan Trail
Brogsdell Plantation
Newfield Wood
Brogsdell
Wasgrove Plantation
Walk Spring
Burnwell Spinneys
Lilley Manor
Kingshill Plantation
LU2
HEXTON RD
Kingshill La
Mazebeard Spring
Ward's Spring
Stockinghill Plantation
Pond Farm
Ward's Farm
Lilley Hoo Farm
RECTORY LA
Lilley
Ward's Wood
GREEN ACRES
John Bunyan Trail
Wardswood La
RUELEY DELL RD
LILLEYHOO LA
EAST ST
THE BAULK
A505
Lilleypark Plantation
Hollybush Hill
PH
Church Farm
George's Plantation
Lilley Park
WEST ST
HOLLYBUSH HILL
SG5
LILLEY BOTTOM
Mushroom Elders
Ralphs Farm
Lilleypark Wood
Allot Gdns
A505

31 46

20
34

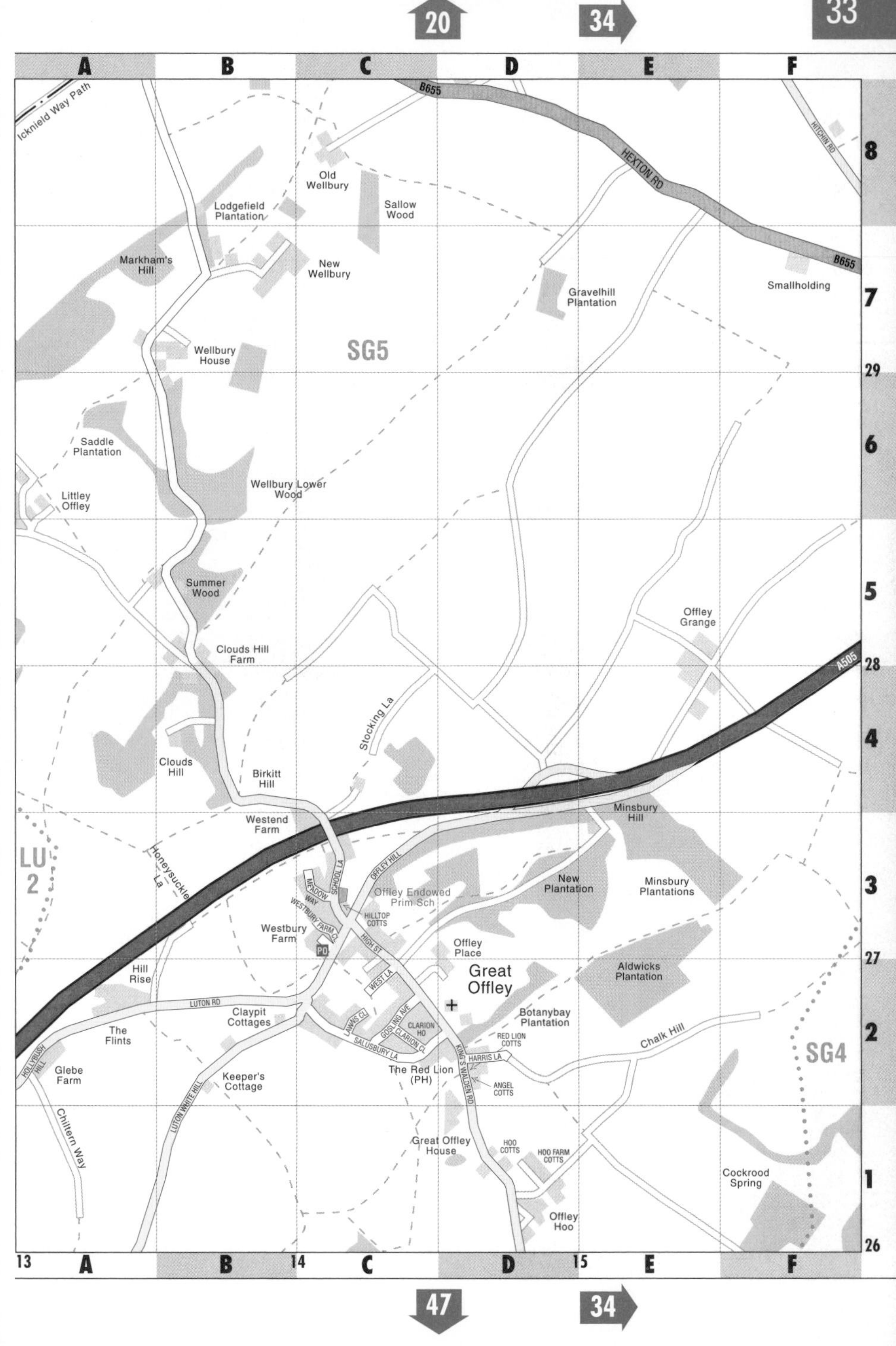
A
B
C
D
E
F
Icknield Way Path
B655
HEXTON RD
HITCHIN RD
Old Wellbury
Sallow Wood
Lodgefield Plantation
Markham's Hill
New Wellbury
Gravelhill Plantation
Smallholding
Wellbury House
SG5
Saddle Plantation
Wellbury Lower Wood
Littley Offley
Summer Wood
Offley Grange
Clouds Hill Farm
A505
Stocking La
Clouds Hill
Birkitt Hill
Westend Farm
Minsbury Hill
LU 2
Honeysuckle La
OFFLEY HILL
SCHOOL LA
MEADOW WAY
Offley Endowed Prim Sch
New Plantation
Minsbury Plantations
WESTBURY FARM CL
HILLTOP COTTS
Westbury Farm
HIGH ST
PO
Offley Place
Great Offley
Aldwicks Plantation
Hill Rise
WEST LA
LUTON RD
Claypit Cottages
LAWNS CL
GOSLING AVE
CLARION HO
Botanybay Plantation
The Flints
CLARION CL
SALUSBURY LA
RED LION COTTS
Chalk Hill
HOLLYBUSH HILL
Glebe Farm
KING'S WALDEN RD
HARRIS LA
SG4
The Red Lion (PH)
Keeper's Cottage
ANGEL COTTS
LUTON WHITE HILL
Chiltern Way
Great Offley House
HOO COTTS
HOO FARM COTTS
Cockrood Spring
Offley Hoo
8
7
29
6
5
28
4
3
27
2
1
26
13
14
15

47
34

33
21

D8
1 MATTOCKE RD
2 NORTH PL
3 BEAUMONT CL
4 CHESTNUT CT
5 SPELLBROOKE
6 BERKELEY CL
7 FOSMAN CL
8 CHALKDELL PATH

E7
1 MAPLES CT
2 BRAHAM CT
3 WEST ALLEY
4 ARCADE WLK
5 ARCADE
6 CHURCHYARD WLK
7 CHURCHGATE
F6
1 CANNON HO
2 ST ANDREW'S PL
3 KENDALE RD
4 WALTHAM RD
5 JEEVES YD
6 SAXON CT
F7
1 WOODCOTE HO
2 GARRISON CT
F8
1 ST AUGUSTINE CL
2 WATER LA
3 ANDERSON'S HO
4 REGAL CT
5 FORGE CL
6 GARDEN ROW
7 ST ANNE'S CT
8 OSIER CT

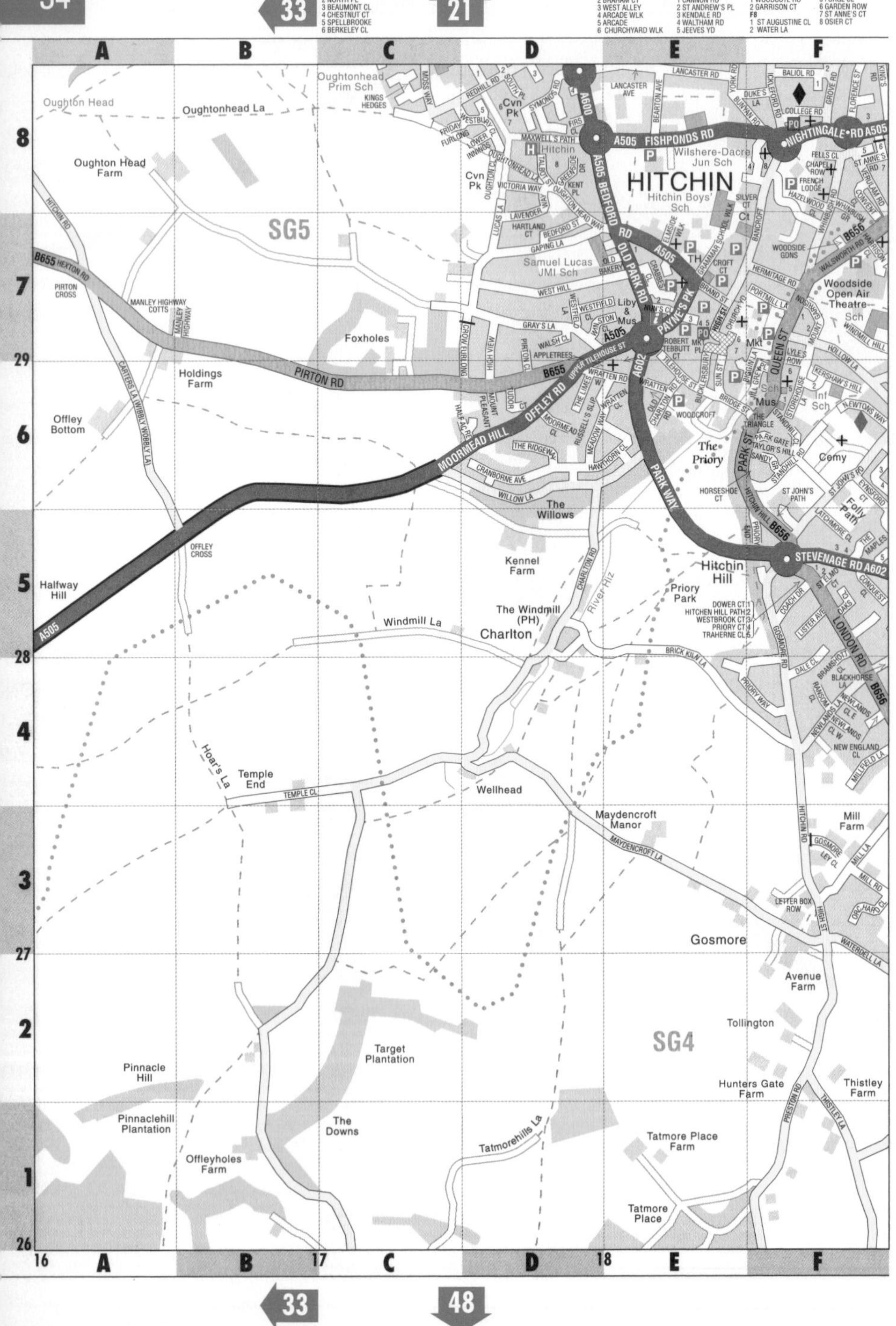

33
48

A B C D E F

8

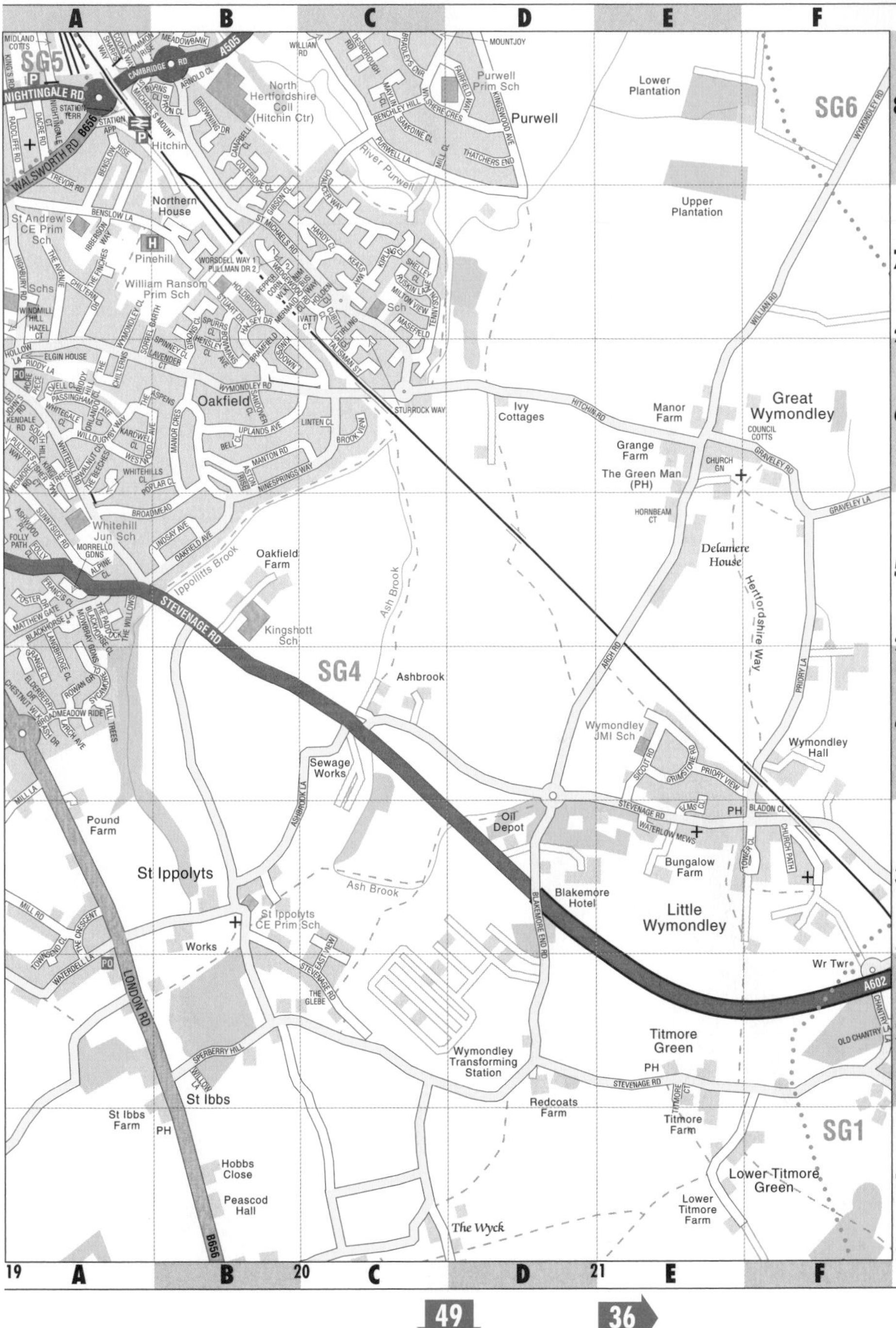

SG5
NIGHTINGALE RD
WALSWORTH RD
B656
CAMBRIDGE RD
A505
MEADOWBANK
MIDLAND COTTS
STATION TERR
STATION APP
Hitchin
North Hertfordshire Coll (Hitchin Ctr)
WILLIAN RD
DESBOROUGH RD
BRADLEYS CNR
FAIRFIELD WAY
MOUNTJOY
Purwell Prim Sch
Purwell
KINGSWOOD AVE
THATCHERS END
River Purwell
PURWELL LA
Lower Plantation
SG6
WYMONDLEY RD
Upper Plantation

7

Northern House
St Andrew's CE Prim Sch
BENSLOW LA
Pinehill
William Ransom Prim Sch
WORSDELL WAY 1
PULLMAN DR 2
ST MICHAELS RD
Schs
HIGHBURY RD
WINDMILL HILL
HAZEL CT
Sch
MILTON VIEW
MASEFIELD
TALISMAN ST
WILLIAN RD

29

HOLLOW LA
ELGIN HOUSE
RIDDY LA
WYMONDLEY RD
Oakfield
STURROCK WAY
Ivy Cottages
HITCHIN RD
Manor Farm
Great Wymondley
COUNCIL COTTS

6

UPLANDS AVE
LINTEN CL
BROOK VIEW
MANTON RD
NINESPRINGS WAY
Grange Farm
The Green Man (PH)
CHURCH GN
GRAVELEY RD
GRAVELEY LA
HORNBEAM CT
BROADMEAD
Whitehill Jun Sch
SUNNYSIDE RD
LINDSAY AVE
OAKFIELD AVE
Oakfield Farm
Delamere House

5

Ippollitts Brook
STEVENAGE RD
Kingshott Sch
Ash Brook
Hertfordshire Way
ARCH RD
PRIORY LA

28

SG4
Ashbrook
CHESTNUT WLK
MEADOW RIDE
TALL TREES

4

Wymondley JMI Sch
SIGCUT RD
GRIMSTONE RD
PRIORY VIEW
Wymondley Hall
Sewage Works
ASHBROOK LA
MILL LA
Pound Farm
Oil Depot
STEVENAGE RD
ELMS CL
PH
BLADON CL
WATERLOW MEWS
CHURCH PATH
TOWER CL

3

St Ippolyts
Ash Brook
Bungalow Farm
Blakemore Hotel
BLAKEMORE END RD
Little Wymondley
MILL RD
THE CRESCENT
TOWNSEND CL
WATERDELL LA
St Ippolyts CE Prim Sch
Works
EAST VIEW
STEVENAGE RD
THE GLEBE
LONDON RD

27

Wr Twr
A602
CHANTRY LA
OLD CHANTRY LA

2

SPERBERRY HILL
WILLOW LA
St Ibbs
Wymondley Transforming Station
Titmore Green
PH
STEVENAGE RD
TITMORE CT
Redcoats Farm
Titmore Farm
St Ibbs Farm
PH
SG1

1

Hobbs Close
Peascod Hall
Lower Titmore Green
Lower Titmore Farm
The Wyck
B656

26

19 A B 20 C D 21 E F

35
23

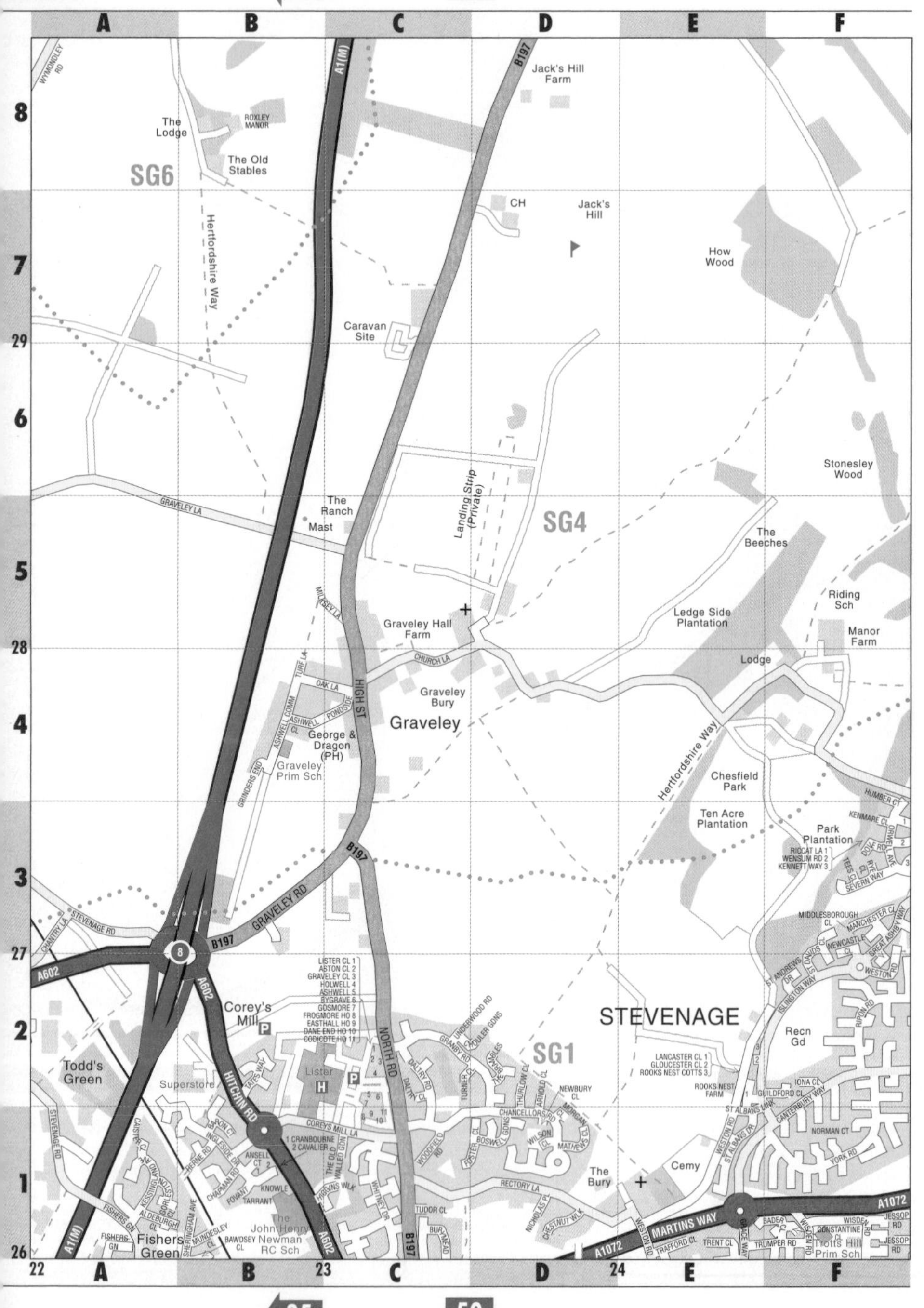
A
B
C
D
E
F
8
7
29
6
5
28
4
3
27
2
1
26
22
23
24
WYMONDLEY RD
A1(M)
B197
Jack's Hill Farm
The Lodge
ROXLEY MANOR
The Old Stables
SG6
Hertfordshire Way
CH
Jack's Hill
How Wood
Caravan Site
Stonesley Wood
The Ranch
Mast
GRAVELEY LA
Landing Strip (Private)
SG4
The Beeches
Riding Sch
Manor Farm
Ledge Side Plantation
Lodge
MILKSEY LA
Graveley Hall Farm
CHURCH LA
TURF LA
OAK LA
HIGH ST
Graveley Bury
ASHWELL COMM
ASHWELL CL
PONDSIDE
Graveley
George & Dragon (PH)
Graveley Prim Sch
GRINDERS END
Chesfield Park
Hertfordshire Way
Ten Acre Plantation
Park Plantation
HUMBER CT
KENMARE CL
RICCAT LA 1
WENSUM RD 2
KENNETT WAY 3
TEES CL
DOVE RD
ORWELL AVE
SEVERN WAY
GRAVELEY RD
CHANTRY LA
STEVENAGE RD
B197
A602
MIDDLESBOROUGH CL
MANCHESTER CL
NEWCASTLE CL
GREAT ASHBY WAY
ST DAVIDS CL
ST ANDREWS DR
WESTON
ISLINGTON WAY
LISTER CL 1
ASTON CL 2
GRAVELEY CL 3
HOLWELL 4
ASHWELL 5
BYGRAVE 6
GOSMORE 7
FROGMORE HO 8
EASTHALL HO 9
DANE END HO 10
CODICOTE HO 11
Corey's Mill
NORTH RD
UNDERWOOD RD
FOULER GDNS
GRANBY RD
BRAMBLES
STEVENAGE
RIPON RD
Recn Gd
Todd's Green
Lister
Superstore
YATES WAY
HITCHIN RD
DALTRY RD
DALTRY CL
TURNER CL
THURLOW CL
ARNOLD CL
SG1
NEWBURY CL
LANCASTER CL 1
GLOUCESTER CL 2
ROOKS NEST COTTS 3
ROOKS NEST FARM
IONA CL
GUILDFORD CL
CANTERBURY WAY
ST ALBANS LINK
ST ALBANS DR
WESTON RD
NORMAN CT
YORK RD
STEVENAGE RD
CAISTER CL
KESSINGLAND
REPHAM RD
INGLESIDE DR
COREYS MILL LA
1 CRANBOURNE
2 CAVALIER
ANSELL CT
CHAPMAN RD
FOVANT
KNOWLE
TARRANT
THE OLD WALLED GDN
WOODFIELD RD
FOSTER CL
BOSWELL GDNS
CHANCELLORS RD
MORGAN CL
WILSON CL
MATHEWS CL
The Bury
Cemy
RECTORY LA
PIPPINS WLK
WHITNEY DR
NICHOLAS PL
CHESTNUT WLK
TUDOR CL
BURYMEAD
GORLESTON
ALDEBURGH CL
FISHERS GN
SHERINGHAM AVE
MUNDESLEY CL
BAWDSEY CL
The John Henry Newman RC Sch
Fishers Green
A602
B197
A1072
MARTINS WAY
WESTON RD
TRAFFORD CL
TRENT CL
GRACE WAY
BADER CL
TRUMPER RD
WISDEN RD
CONSTANTINE CL
WISDEN
JESSOP RD
Trotts Hill Prim Sch
A1072

35
50

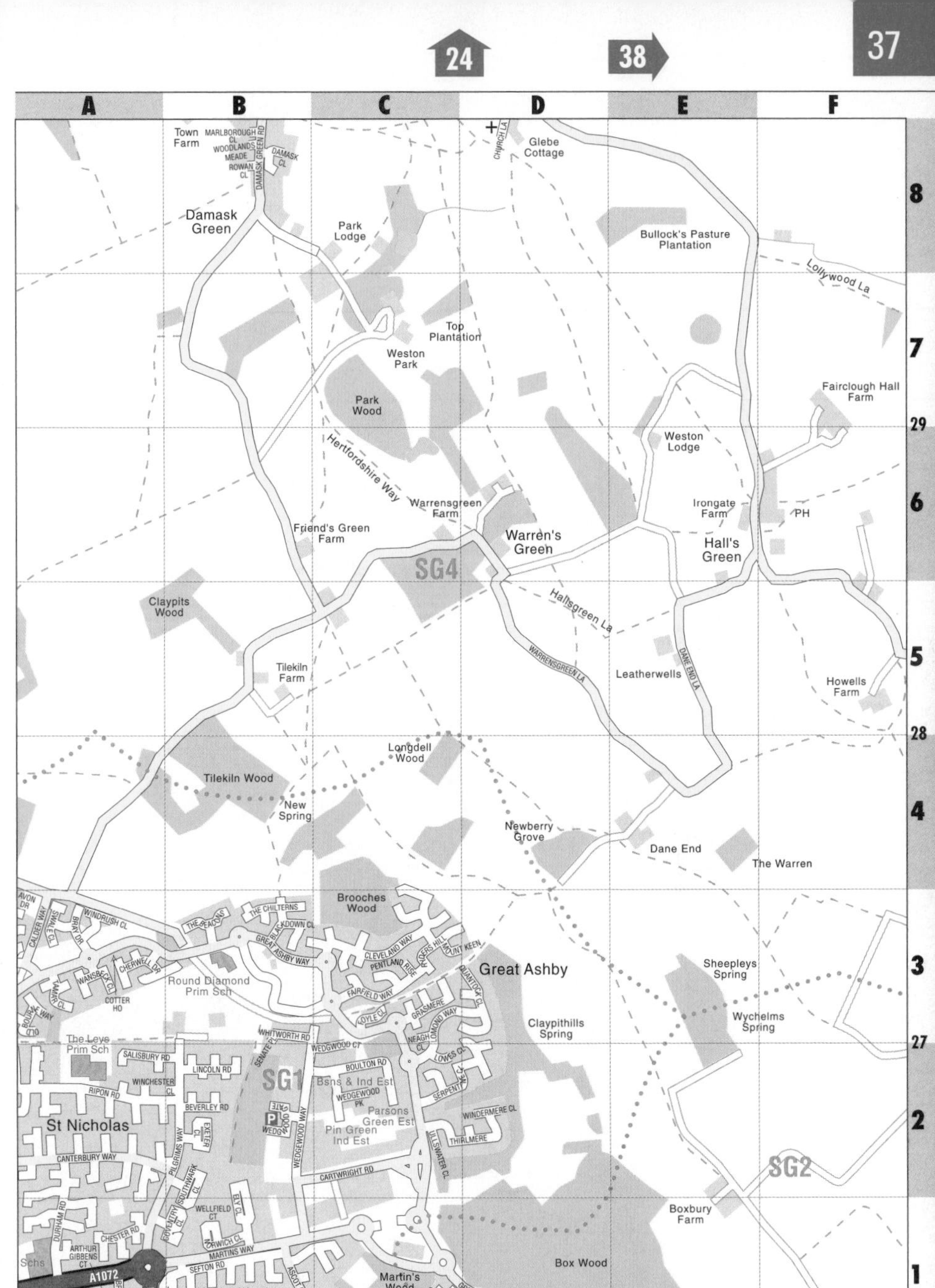
24
38
A
B
C
D
E
F
Town Farm
MARLBOROUGH CL
WOODLANDS
MEADE
ROWAN CL
DAMASK GREEN RD
DAMASK CL
CHURCH LA
Glebe Cottage
Damask Green
Park Lodge
Bullock's Pasture Plantation
Lollywood La
Top Plantation
Weston Park
Park Wood
Fairclough Hall Farm
Hertfordshire Way
Weston Lodge
Warrensgreen Farm
Irongate Farm
PH
Friend's Green Farm
Warren's Green
Hall's Green
SG4
Claypits Wood
Hallsgreen La
WARRENSGREEN LA
DANE END LA
Tilekiln Farm
Leatherwells
Howells Farm
Longdell Wood
Tilekiln Wood
New Spring
Newberry Grove
Dane End
The Warren
Brooches Wood
THE CHILTERNS
WINDRUSH CL
THE BEACONS
BLACKDOWN CL
GREAT ASHBY WAY
CLEVELAND WAY
PENTLAND RISE
MOUNT KEEN
QUANTOCK CL
Great Ashby
CHERWELL DR
Round Diamond Prim Sch
FAIRFIELD WAY
COTTER HO
Sheepleys Spring
Wychelms Spring
Claypithills Spring
GRASMERE
LOMOND WAY
WHITWORTH RD
WEDGWOOD CT
The Leys Prim Sch
SALISBURY RD
LINCOLN RD
SG1
Bsns & Ind Est
BOULTON RD
WINCHESTER CL
RIPON RD
WEDGEWOOD PK
SERPENTINE CL
Parsons Green Est
WINDERMERE CL
BEVERLEY RD
St Nicholas
Pin Green Ind Est
THIRLMERE
EXETER CL
PILGRIMS WAY
WEDGEWOOD WAY
ULLSWATER CL
CANTERBURY WAY
CARTWRIGHT RD
SG2
SOUTHWARK CL
WELLFIELD CT
ELY CL
DURHAM RD
COVENTRY CL
Boxbury Farm
CHESTER RD
NORWICH CL
ARTHUR GIBBENS CT
MARTINS WAY
Schs
SEFTON RD
Box Wood
A1072
VERITY WAY
A1155
Martin's Wood
Martins Wood Prim Sch
ASCOT CRES
GORDIAN WAY
GRESLEY WAY
JESSOP RD
THE OVAL
DERBY WAY
MILDMAY RD
LINGFIELD RD
VALERIAN WAY
TRAJAN GATE
NEPTUNE GATE
Boxwood Lodge
SANDOWN RD
JULIA GATE
PO
P
1
2
3
4
5
6
7
8
26
27
28
29
25
51
38

37
25

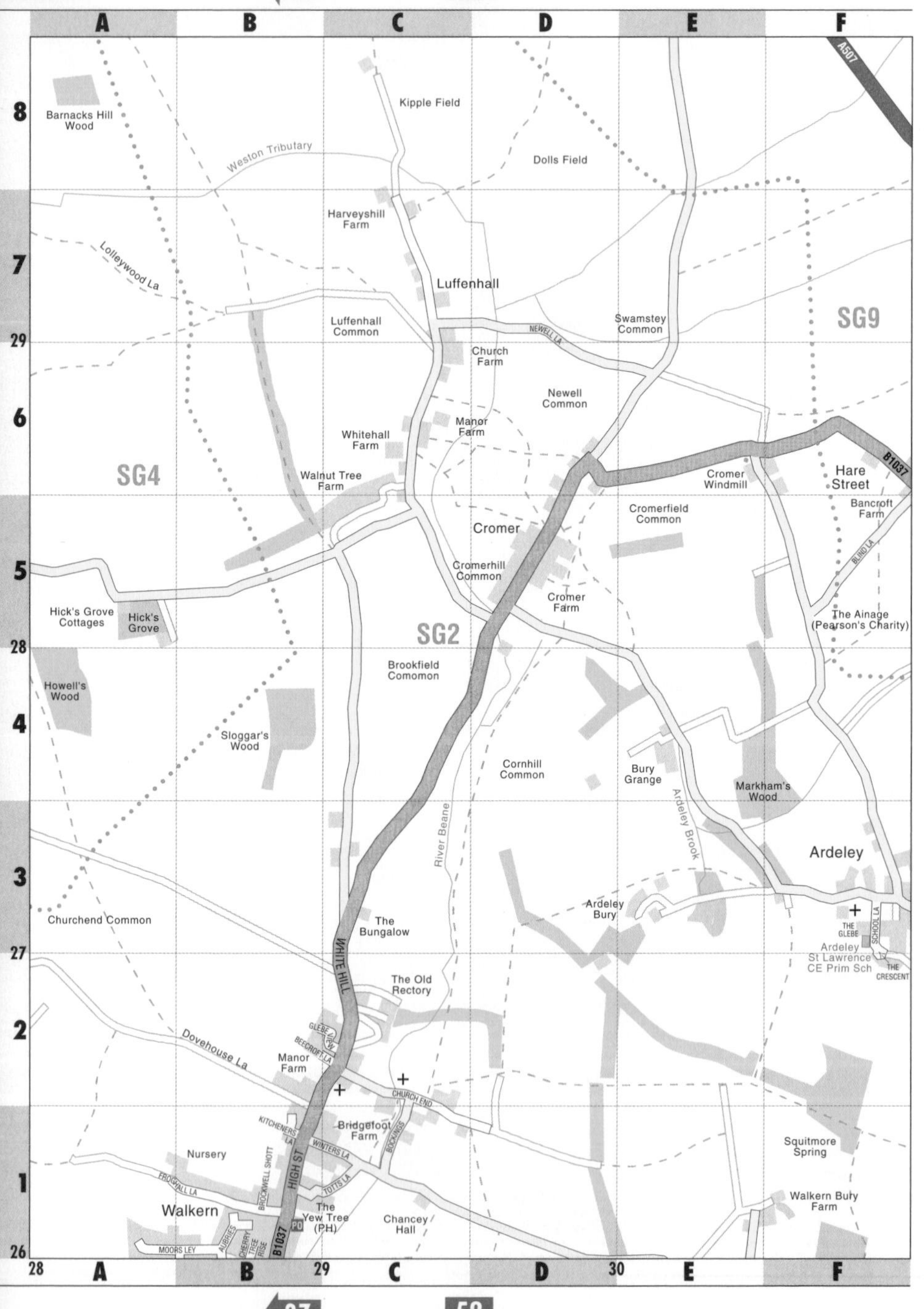
A
B
C
D
E
F
8
7
29
6
5
28
4
3
27
2
1
26
28
29
30
A507
Barnacks Hill Wood
Kipple Field
Weston Tributary
Dolls Field
Harveyshill Farm
Lolleywood La
Luffenhall
Luffenhall Common
Newell La
Swamstey Common
SG9
Church Farm
Newell Common
Manor Farm
Whitehall Farm
SG4
Walnut Tree Farm
B1037
Cromer Windmill
Hare Street
Cromerfield Common
Bancroft Farm
Cromer
Blind La
Cromerhill Common
Cromer Farm
Hick's Grove Cottages
Hick's Grove
The Ainage (Pearson's Charity)
SG2
Brookfield Comomon
Howell's Wood
Sloggar's Wood
Cornhill Common
Bury Grange
Markham's Wood
Ardeley Brook
River Beane
Ardeley
Churchend Common
The Bungalow
Ardeley Bury
The Glebe
School La
Ardeley St Lawrence CE Prim Sch
The Crescent
White Hill
The Old Rectory
Glebe View
Beecroft La
Dovehouse La
Manor Farm
Church End
Kitcheners La
Bridgefoot Farm
Bockings
Winters La
Nursery
Brockwell Shott
High St
Totts La
Squitmore Spring
Frogmall La
Walkern
The Yew Tree (PH)
PO
Chancey Hall
Walkern Bury Farm
Aubries
Cherry Tree Rise
Moors Ley

37
52

26
40

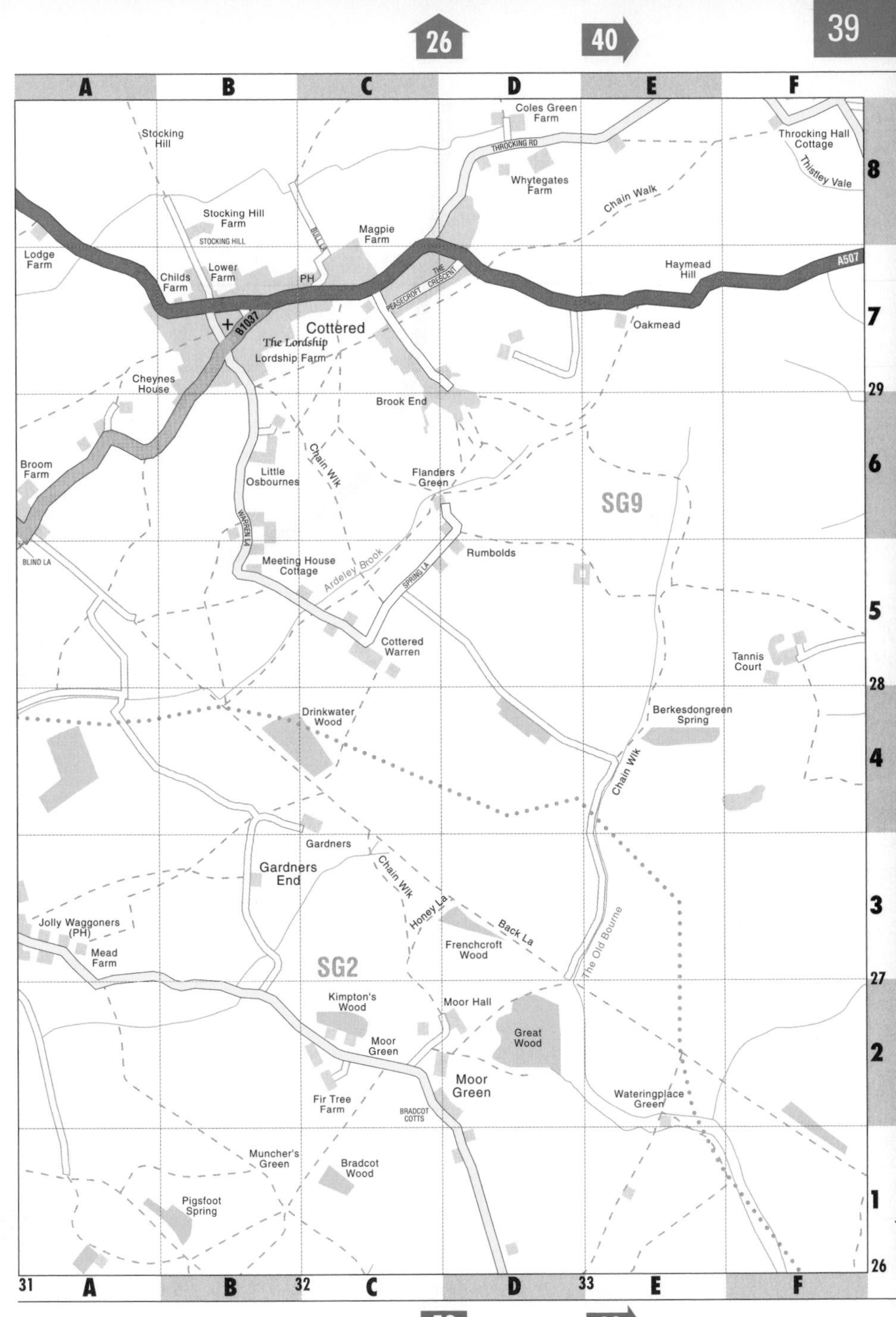
A
B
C
D
E
F
Coles Green Farm
Stocking Hill
Throcking Hall Cottage
THROCKING RD
Thistley Vale
Whytegates Farm
8
Chain Walk
Stocking Hill Farm
STOCKING HILL
BULL LA
Magpie Farm
Lodge Farm
Lower Farm
Childs Farm
PH
THE CRESCENT
PEASECROFT
Haymead Hill
A507
B1037
Cottered
The Lordship
Lordship Farm
Oakmead
7
Cheynes House
29
Brook End
Broom Farm
Chain Wlk
Little Osbournes
Flanders Green
6
SG9
WARREN LA
Meeting House Cottage
Rumbolds
BLIND LA
Ardeley Brook
SPRING LA
5
Cottered Warren
Tannis Court
28
Drinkwater Wood
Berkesdongreen Spring
Chain Wlk
4
Gardners
Gardners End
Chain Wlk
3
Jolly Waggoners (PH)
Honey La
Back La
Mead Farm
Frenchcroft Wood
The Old Bourne
SG2
27
Kimpton's Wood
Moor Hall
Great Wood
Moor Green
2
Moor Green
Fir Tree Farm
BRADCOT COTTS
Wateringplace Green
Muncher's Green
Bradcot Wood
Pigsfoot Spring
1
26
31
32
33

53
40

39
27

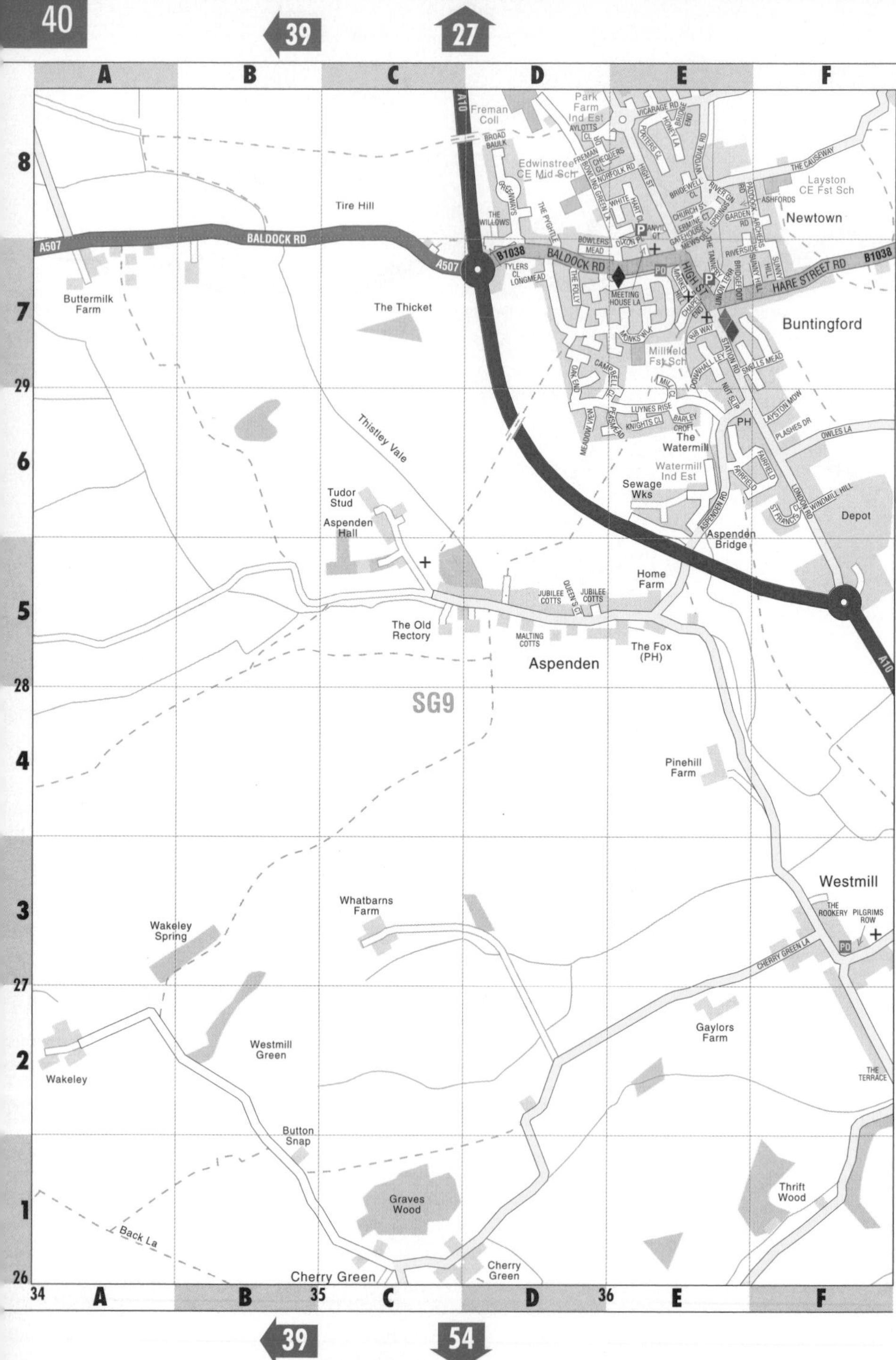
A B C D E F
8
7
29
6
5
28
4
3
27
2
1
26
34
35
36
A10
A507
BALDOCK RD
B1038
HARE STREET RD
Freman Coll
Park Farm Ind Est
Edwinstree CE Mid Sch
Layston CE Fst Sch
Newtown
Tire Hill
Buttermilk Farm
The Thicket
Buntingford
Millfield Fst Sch
Thistley Vale
The Watermill
Watermill Ind Est
Sewage Wks
Tudor Stud
Aspenden Hall
Aspenden Bridge
Depot
Home Farm
The Old Rectory
The Fox (PH)
Aspenden
SG9
Pinehill Farm
Westmill
Whatbarns Farm
Wakeley Spring
Gaylors Farm
Westmill Green
Wakeley
Button Snap
Graves Wood
Thrift Wood
Back La
Cherry Green
THE CAUSEWAY
OWLES LA
CHERRY GREEN LA
THE ROOKERY
PILGRIMS ROW
THE TERRACE
JUBILEE COTTS
QUEEN'S CT
MALTING COTTS
LONDON RD
WINDMILL HILL
ASPENDEN RD
HIGH ST
STATION RD
PLASHES DR
LAYSTON MDW
SNELLS MEAD
NUT SLIP
LUYNES RISE
KNIGHTS CL
BARLEY CROFT
MEADOW VIEW
PEASMEAD
OAK END
CAMPBELL CL
MILL CL
MONKS WLK
MEETING HOUSE LA
THE FOLLY
TYLERS CL
LONGMEAD
BOWLERS MEAD
THE PYGHTLE
THE WILLOWS
BROAD BAULK
GREENWAYS
VICARAGE RD
HONEY LA
BRIDGE END
WYDDIAL RD
PORTERS CL
HIGH ST
BRIDEWELL CL
CHURCH ST
ERMINE CT
GATEHOUSE
RIVER GN
PADDOCK RD
ASHFORDS
GARDEN RD
ARCHERS
RIVERSIDE
SUNNY HILL
BRIDGEFOOT
UNION TERR
THE TANNERY
MARKET HILL
CHAPEL END
RIB WAY
DOWNHALL LEY
FAIRFIELD
ST FRANCIS CL
NORFOLK RD
CHEQUERS
BOWLING GREEN LA
FREMAN CL
WHITE HART CL
AYLOTTS CL
DIXON PL
ANVIL CT
PH
PO
P

39
54

28
42

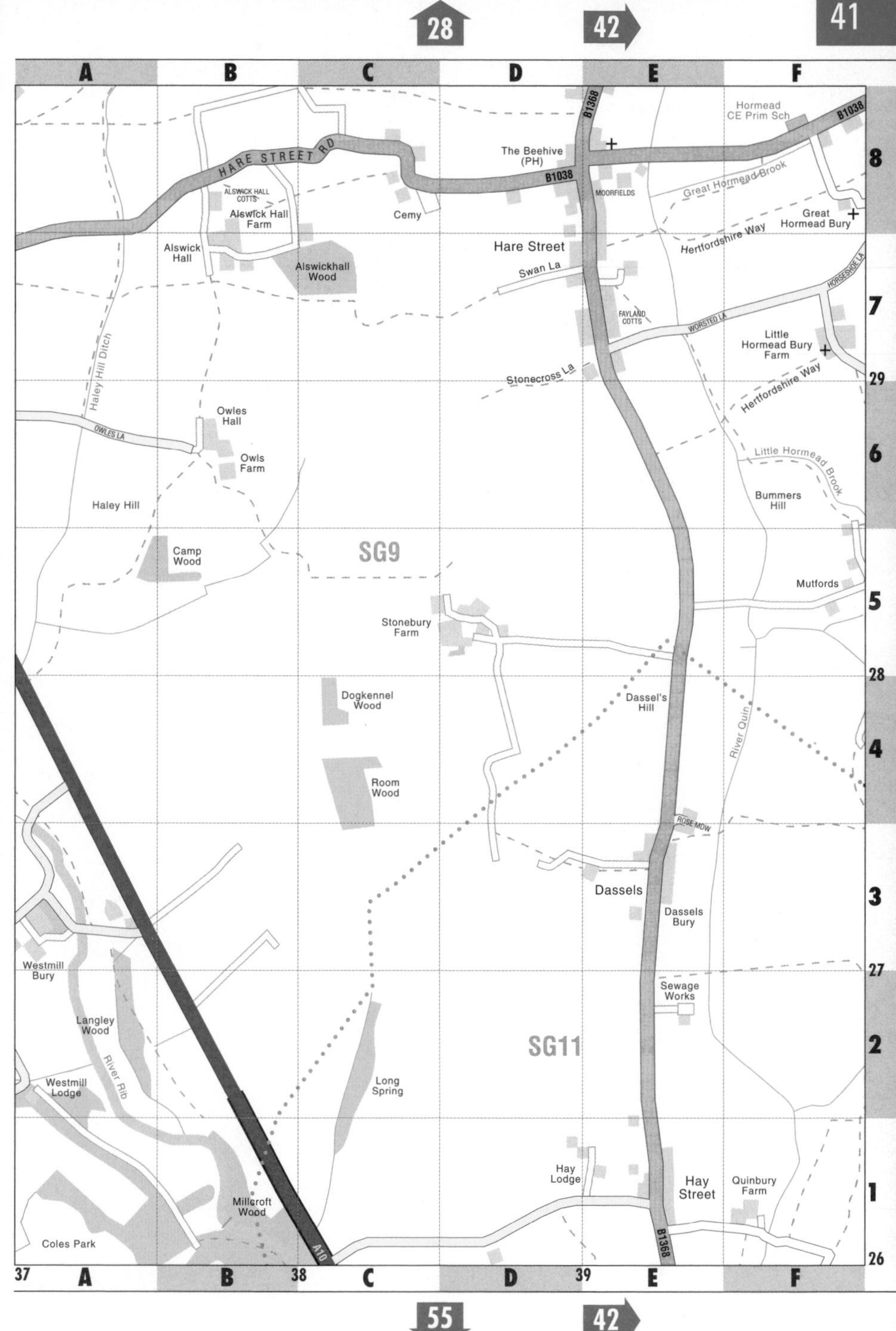
A
B
C
D
E
F
HARE STREET RD
B1368
B1038
Hormead CE Prim Sch
The Beehive (PH)
ALSWICK HALL COTTS
Alswick Hall Farm
Cemy
MOORFIELDS
Great Hormead Brook
Great Hormead Bury
Alswick Hall
Alswickhall Wood
Hare Street
Hertfordshire Way
Swan La
FAYLAND COTTS
WORSTED LA
HORSESHOE LA
Little Hormead Bury Farm
Haley Hill Ditch
Stonecross La
Hertfordshire Way
Owles Hall
OWLES LA
Owls Farm
Little Hormead Brook
Bummers Hill
Haley Hill
Camp Wood
SG9
Mutfords
Stonebury Farm
Dogkennel Wood
Dassel's Hill
River Quin
Room Wood
ROSE MDW
Dassels
Dassels Bury
Westmill Bury
Sewage Works
Langley Wood
River Rib
SG11
Westmill Lodge
Long Spring
Hay Lodge
Hay Street
Quinbury Farm
Millcroft Wood
Coles Park
A10
8
7
29
6
5
28
4
3
27
2
1
26
37
38
39

55
42

41
29

A
B
C
D
E
F
8
7
29
6
5
28
4
3
27
2
1
26
40
41
42
B1038
Three Tuns (PH)
Great Hormead
HORSESHOE HILL
JUBILEE COTTS
WILLOW CL
HORSESHOE LA
Church End Cottage
Sparksfield
The Thrift
Great Hormead Park
St Patrick's Wood
PARK VIEW
Glebe House
Little Hormead Brook
SG9
Balons Farm
Little Hormead
Bulls Farm
Fair Lady Wood
The Willows
Lady Wood
Mutfords
Mutton Hall
Duck Street Cottage
Hertfordshire Way
HALL BARNS
THE STREET
Shirley
Bradley Spring
High Wood
Hoare's La
Bozengreen Farm
Rotten Row
Patient End Farm
Patient End
Hertfordshire Way
Bozen Green
SG11
THE CAUSEWAY
Hole Farm Cott
Hole Farm

41
56

30

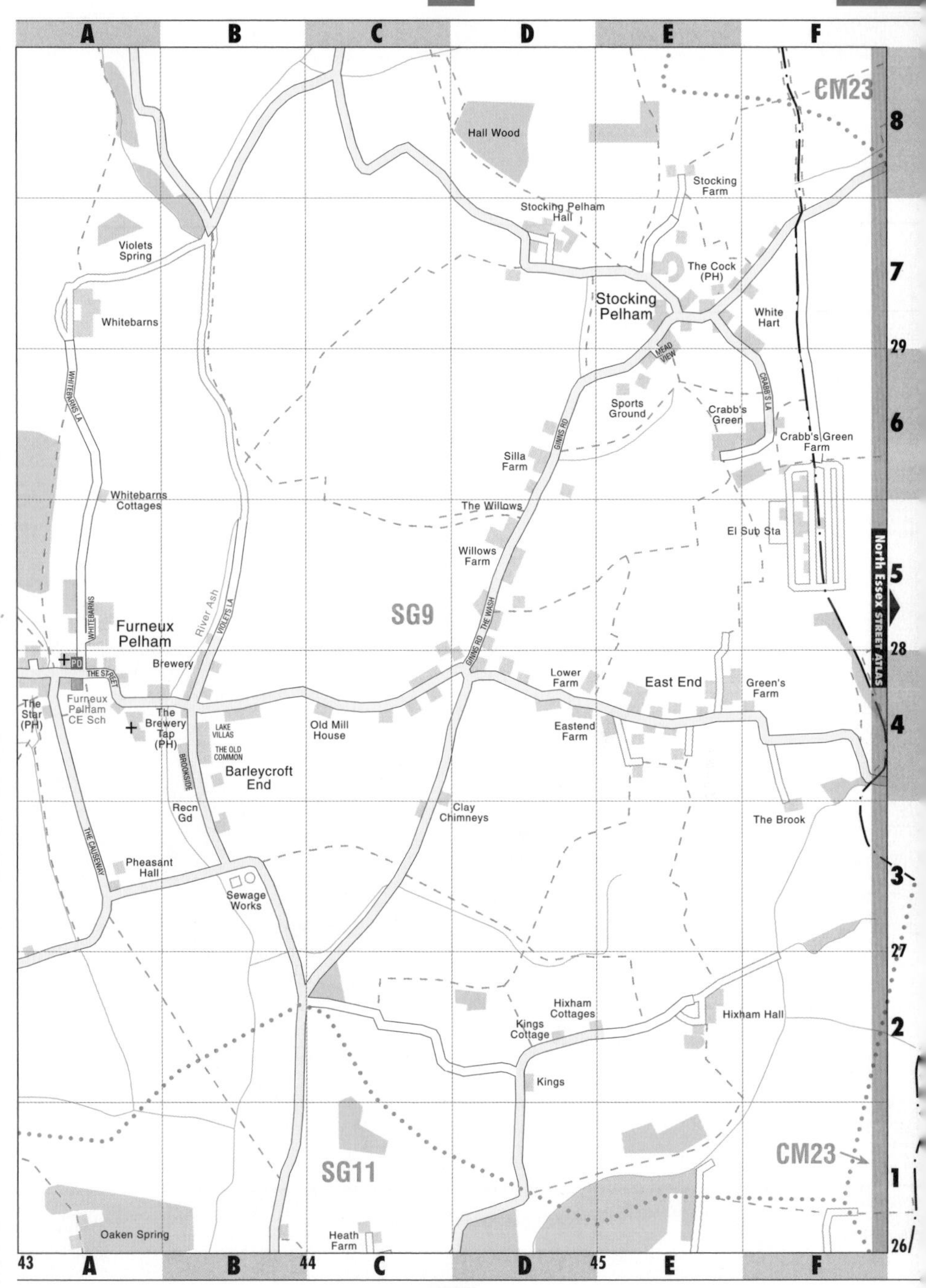

North Essex STREET ATLAS

57

C5
1 CHAWORTH GN
2 ACWORTH CT
3 MOSSDALE CT
4 WOLFSBURG CT
5 THORNTONDALE
6 GREEN CT
7 WHARFDALE

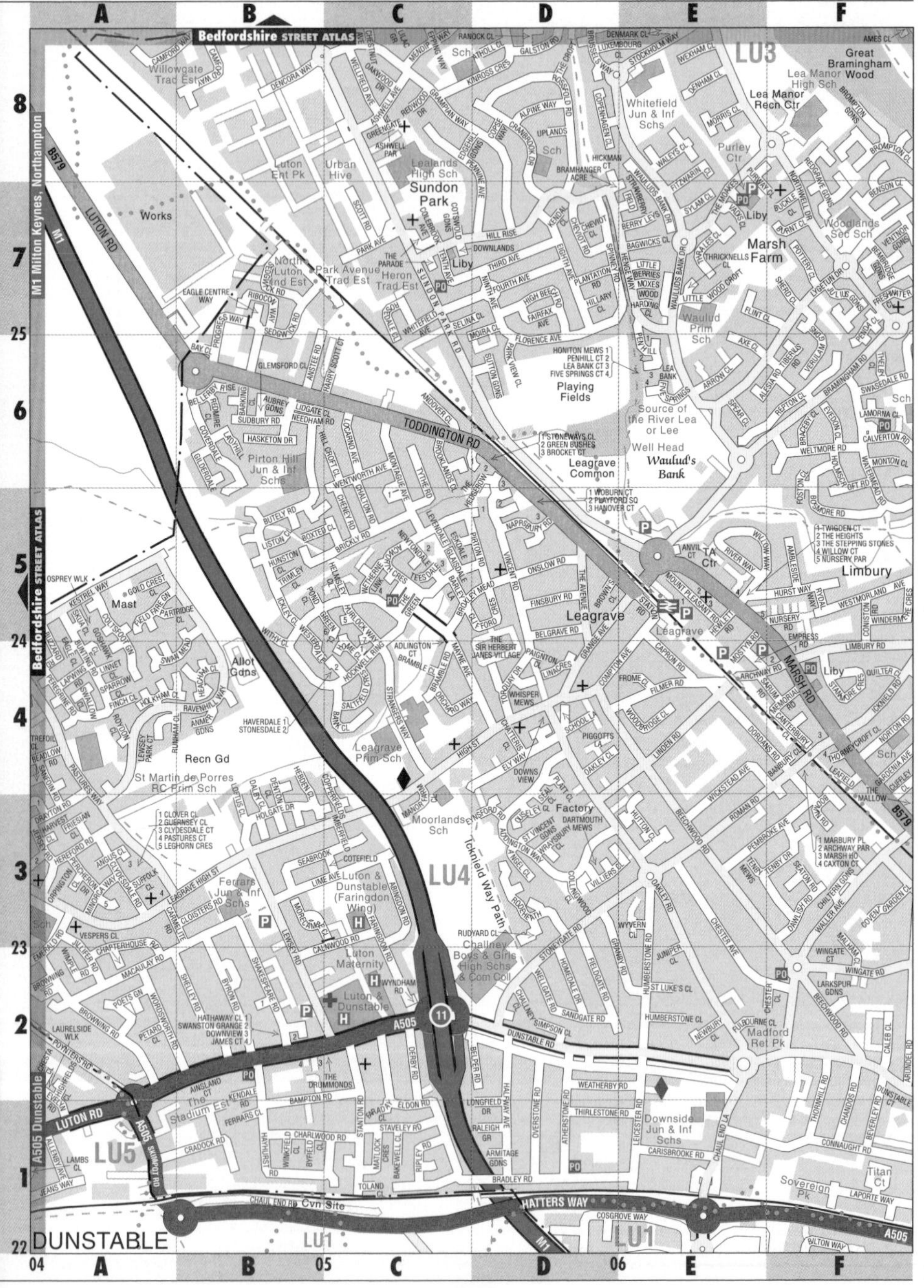

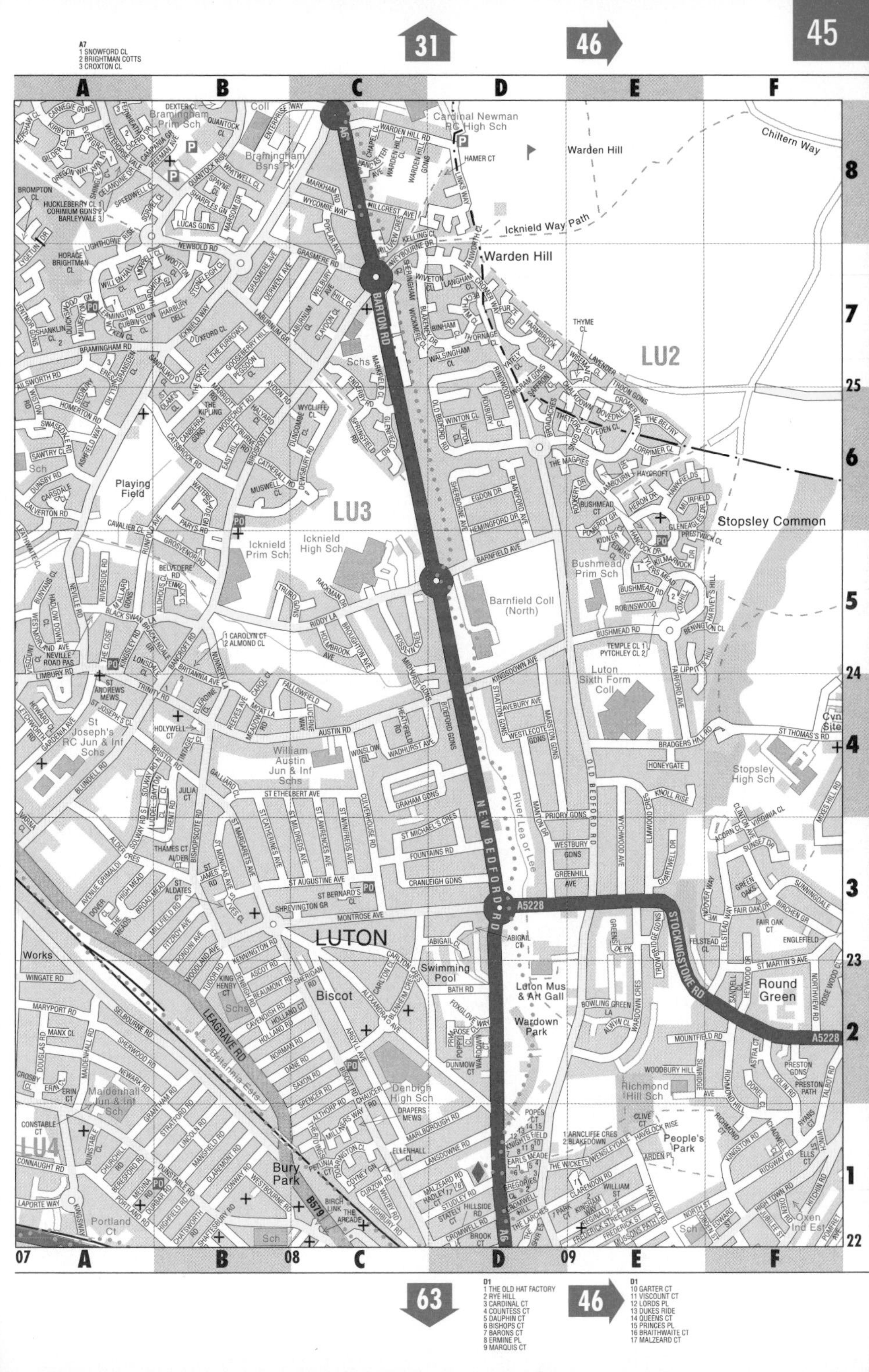

45
31
46
63
46
A7
1 SNOWFORD CL
2 BRIGHTMAN COTTS
3 CROXTON CL
A
B
C
D
E
F
8
7
25
6
5
24
4
3
23
2
1
22
07
08
09
Warden Hill
Chiltern Way
Icknield Way Path
Cardinal Newman RC High Sch
Bramingham Prim Sch
Bramingham Bsns Pk
LU2
LU3
LU4
Stopsley Common
Playing Field
Icknield Prim Sch
Icknield High Sch
Barnfield Coll (North)
Bushmead Prim Sch
Luton Sixth Form Coll
Stopsley High Sch
William Austin Jun & Inf Schs
St Joseph's RC Jun & Inf Schs
LUTON
Biscot
Swimming Pool
Luton Mus & Art Gall
Wardown Park
Round Green
Richmond Hill Sch
People's Park
Denbigh High Sch
Maidenhall Jun & Inf Sch
Bury Park
Portland Ct
Works
Oxen Ind Est
BARTON RD
NEW BEDFORD RD
OLD BEDFORD RD
STOCKINGSTONE RD
LEAGRAVE RD
A6
A5228
B579
River Lea or Lee
D1
1 THE OLD HAT FACTORY
2 RYE HILL
3 CARDINAL CT
4 COUNTESS CT
5 DAUPHIN CT
6 BISHOPS CT
7 BARONS CT
8 ERMINE PL
9 MARQUIS CT
D1
10 GARTER CT
11 VISCOUNT CT
12 LORDS PL
13 DUKES RIDE
14 QUEENS CT
15 PRINCES PL
16 BRAITHWAITE CT
17 MALZEARD CT

45
32

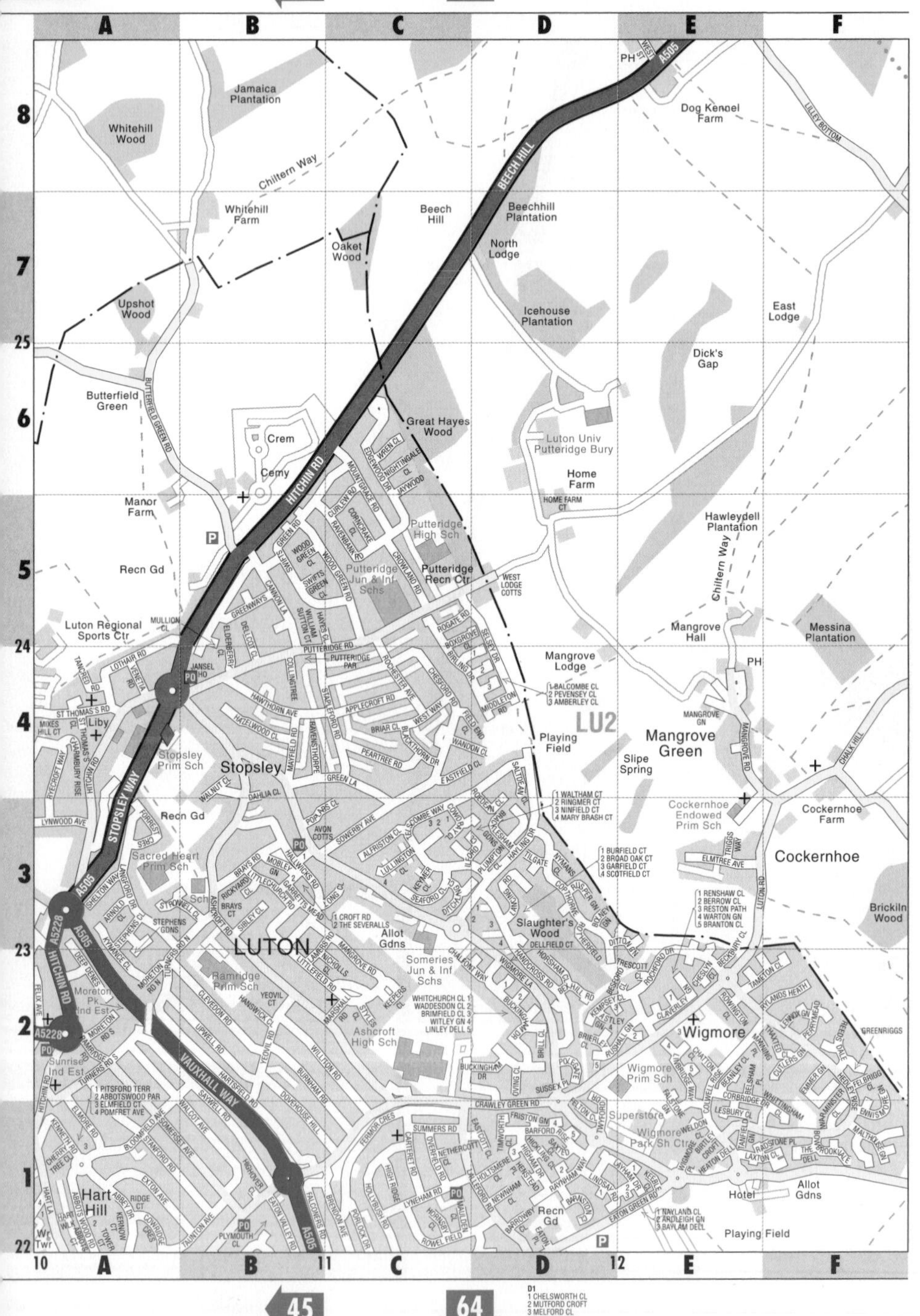

45
64

D1
1 CHELSWORTH CL
2 MUTFORD CROFT
3 MELFORD CL
4 PINFORD DELL
5 ALDERTON CL

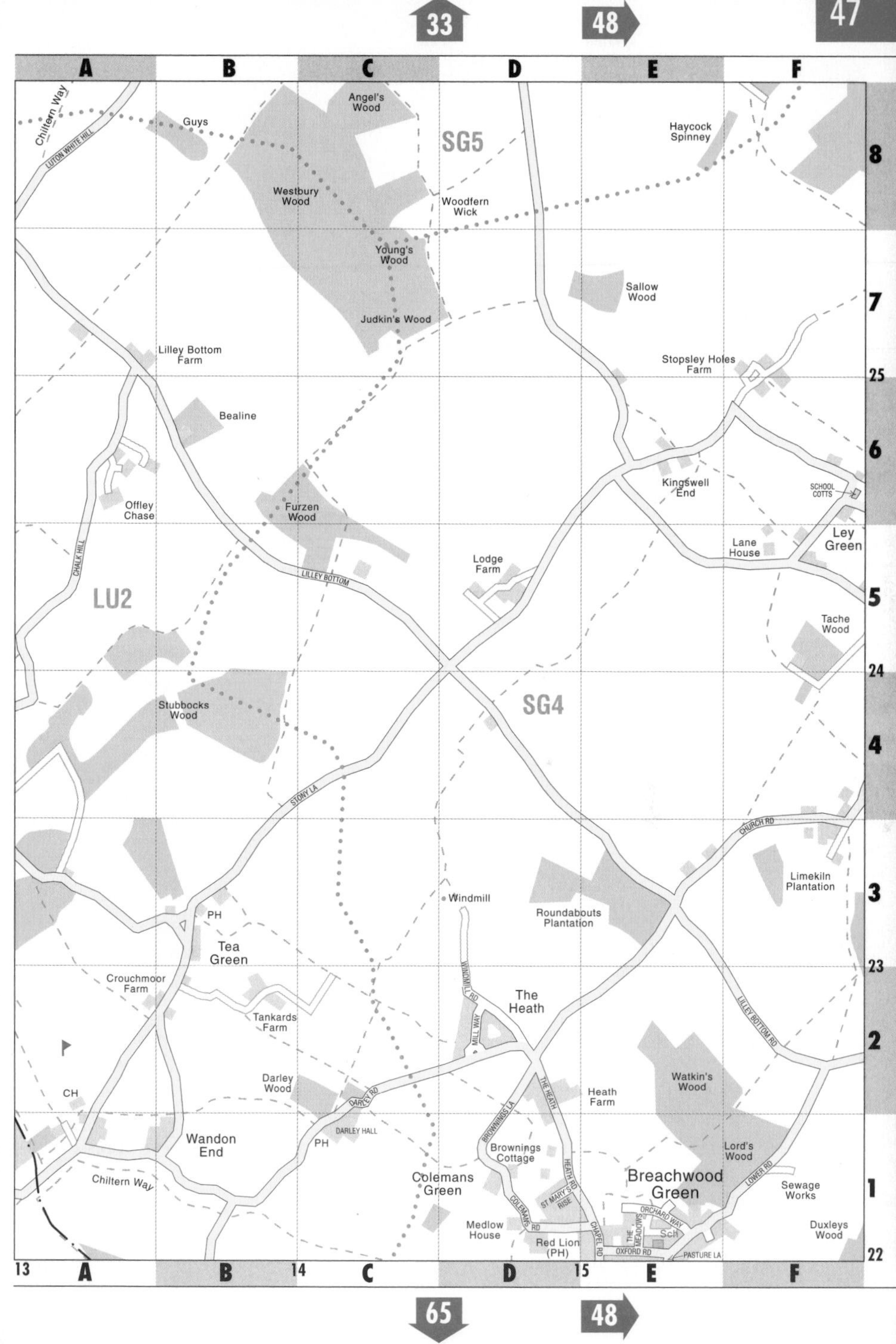
A
B
C
D
E
F
Chiltern Way
LUTON WHITE HILL
Guys
Angel's Wood
SG5
Haycock Spinney
8
Westbury Wood
Woodfern Wick
Young's Wood
Sallow Wood
7
Judkin's Wood
Lilley Bottom Farm
Stopsley Holes Farm
25
Bealine
6
Kingswell End
SCHOOL COTTS
Offley Chase
Furzen Wood
Ley Green
Lane House
CHALK HILL
Lodge Farm
LILLEY BOTTOM
LU2
5
Tache Wood
24
Stubbocks Wood
SG4
4
STONY LA
CHURCH RD
Limekiln Plantation
3
Windmill
PH
Roundabouts Plantation
Tea Green
23
Crouchmoor Farm
WINDMILL RD
The Heath
Tankards Farm
MILL WAY
LILLEY BOTTOM RD
2
Darley Wood
DARLEY RD
THE HEATH
Heath Farm
Watkin's Wood
CH
BROWNINGS LA
DARLEY HALL
Wandon End
PH
Brownings Cottage
Lord's Wood
HEATH RD
Chiltern Way
Colemans Green
Breachwood Green
LOWER RD
Sewage Works
1
COLEMANS RD
ST MARY'S RISE
ORCHARD WAY
THE MEADOWS
Sch
Medlow House
Duxleys Wood
Red Lion (PH)
CHAPEL RD
OXFORD RD
PASTURE LA
22
13
14
15

47
34

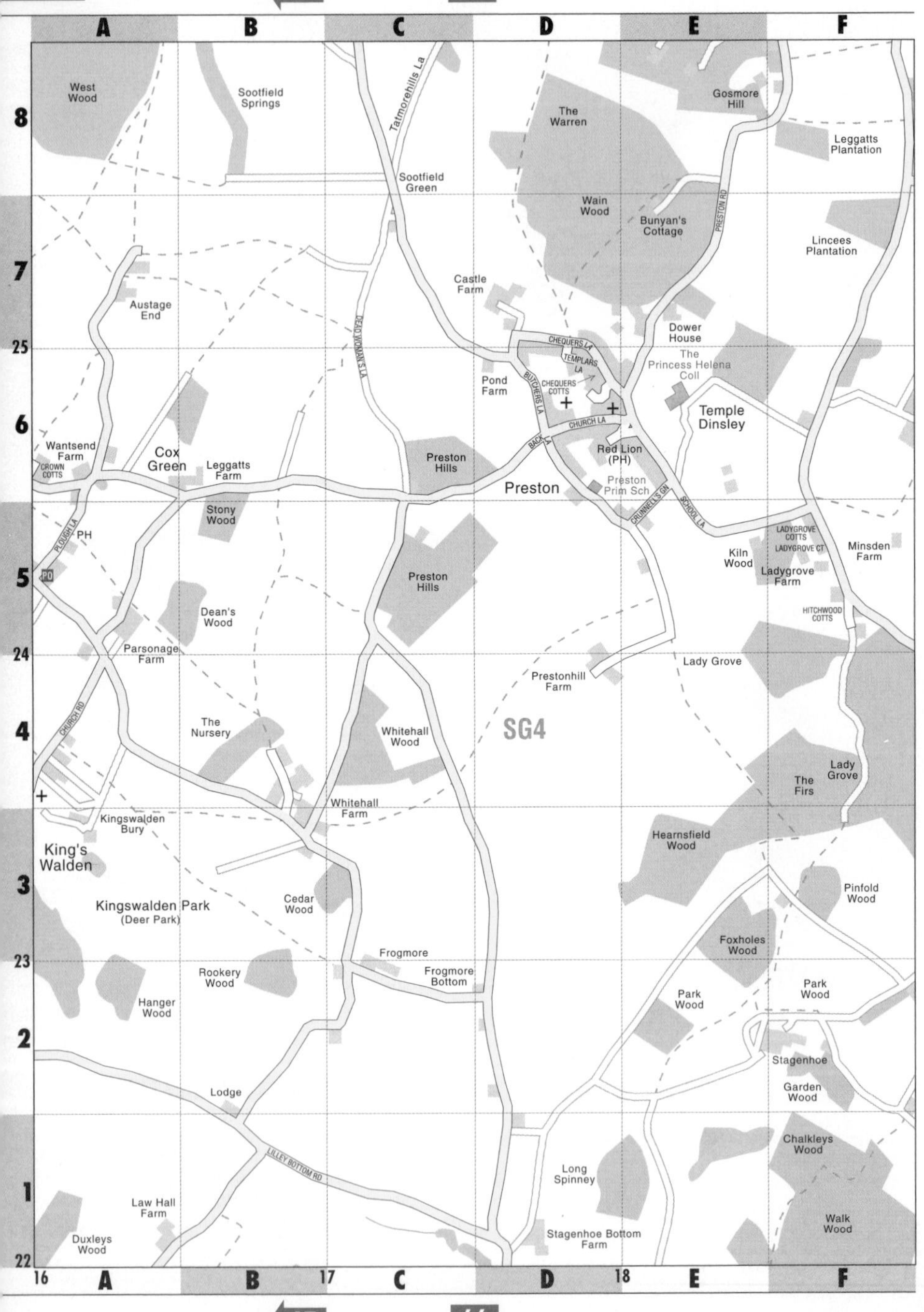

A
B
C
D
E
F
8
7
25
6
5
24
4
3
23
2
1
22
16
17
18
West Wood
Sootfield Springs
Tatmorehills La
The Warren
Gosmore Hill
Leggatts Plantation
Sootfield Green
Wain Wood
Bunyan's Cottage
PRESTON RD
Lincees Plantation
Castle Farm
Austage End
DEAD WOMAN'S LA
Dower House
CHEQUERS LA
TEMPLARS LA
CHEQUERS COTTS
The Princess Helena Coll
Pond Farm
BUTCHERS LA
CHURCH LA
Temple Dinsley
Wantsend Farm
CROWN COTTS
Cox Green
Leggatts Farm
Preston Hills
BACK LA
Red Lion (PH)
Preston
Preston Prim Sch
CRUNNELL'S GN
SCHOOL LA
Stony Wood
PLOUGH LA
PH
PO
LADYGROVE COTTS
LADYGROVE CT
Kiln Wood
Ladygrove Farm
Minsden Farm
Preston Hills
Dean's Wood
HITCHWOOD COTTS
Parsonage Farm
Lady Grove
Prestonhill Farm
CHURCH RD
The Nursery
Whitehall Wood
SG4
Lady Grove
The Firs
Whitehall Farm
Kingswalden Bury
King's Walden
Hearnsfield Wood
Pinfold Wood
Kingswalden Park
(Deer Park)
Cedar Wood
Foxholes Wood
Frogmore
Rookery Wood
Frogmore Bottom
Park Wood
Park Wood
Hanger Wood
Stagenhoe
Lodge
Garden Wood
LILLEY BOTTOM RD
Chalkleys Wood
Long Spinney
Law Hall Farm
Walk Wood
Duxleys Wood
Stagenhoe Bottom Farm

47
66

35
50

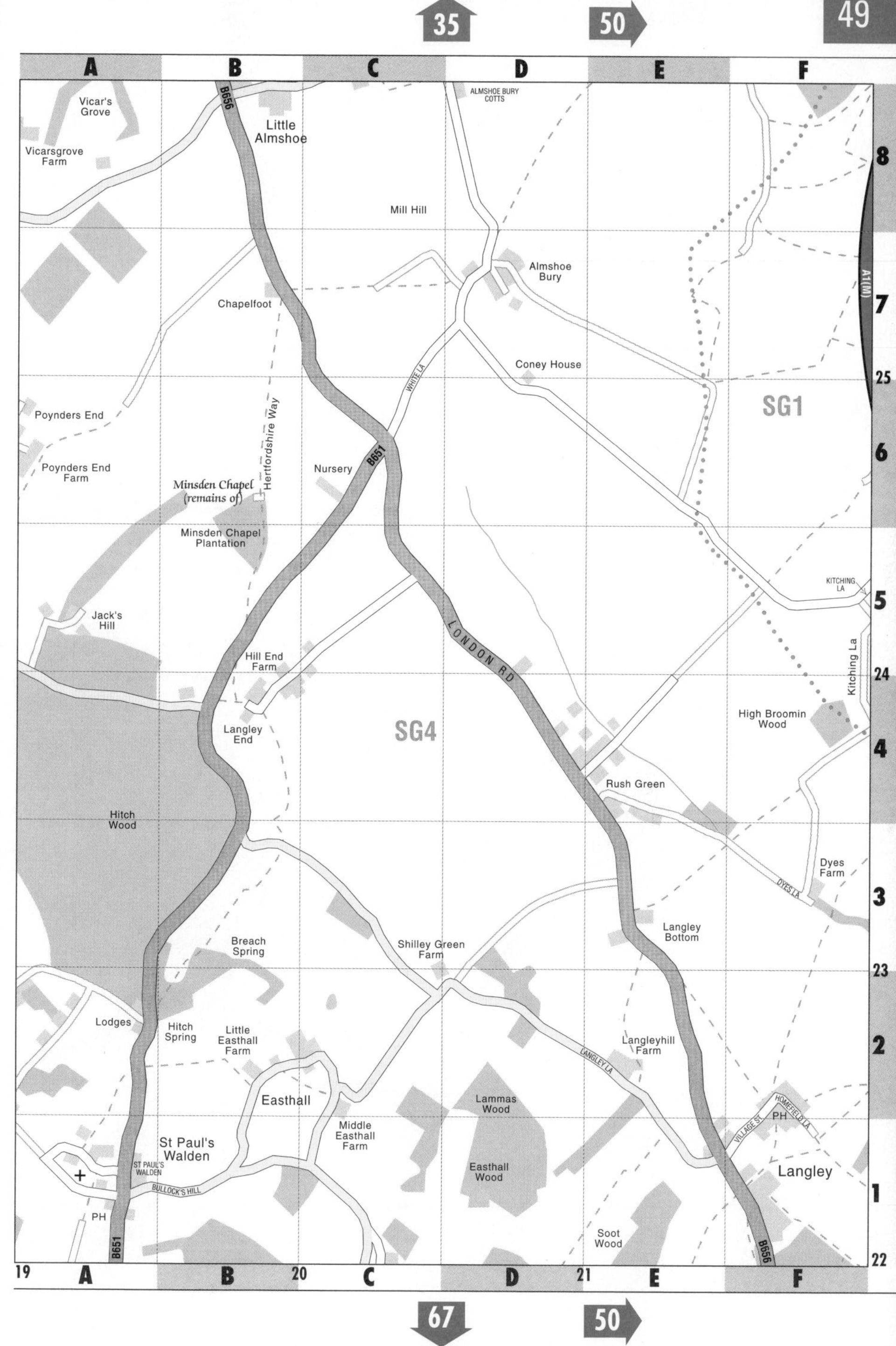
A
B
C
D
E
F
Vicar's Grove
Vicarsgrove Farm
B656
Little Almshoe
ALMSHOE BURY COTTS
Mill Hill
Almshoe Bury
Chapelfoot
Coney House
WHITE LA
Poynders End
Hertfordshire Way
Poynders End Farm
Minsden Chapel (remains of)
Nursery
B651
Minsden Chapel Plantation
SG1
A1(M)
KITCHING LA
Jack's Hill
LONDON RD
Hill End Farm
Kitching La
High Broomin Wood
Langley End
SG4
Rush Green
Hitch Wood
Dyes Farm
DYES LA
Langley Bottom
Breach Spring
Shilley Green Farm
Lodges
Hitch Spring
Little Easthall Farm
LANGLEY LA
Langleyhill Farm
Easthall
Lammas Wood
HOMEFIELD LA
PH
VILLAGE ST
Middle Easthall Farm
St Paul's Walden
ST PAUL'S WALDEN
BULLOCK'S HILL
Easthall Wood
Langley
PH
Soot Wood
B651
B656
8
7
25
6
5
24
4
3
23
2
1
22
19
20
21

67
50

B8
1 BAWDSEY CL
2 SHERINGHAM AVE
3 BOURNEMOUTH RD

49

C7
1 MIDDLE ROW
2 BAKER ST

36

E6
1 JOWITT HO
2 BATES HO
3 CHAUNCY HO
4 BERTRAM HO
5 EDWARDS HO
6 BLOOMFIELD HO

49

68

F1
1 ROEBUCK CT
2 HIGHCROFT
3 ST PAULS CT
4 PINEWOODS

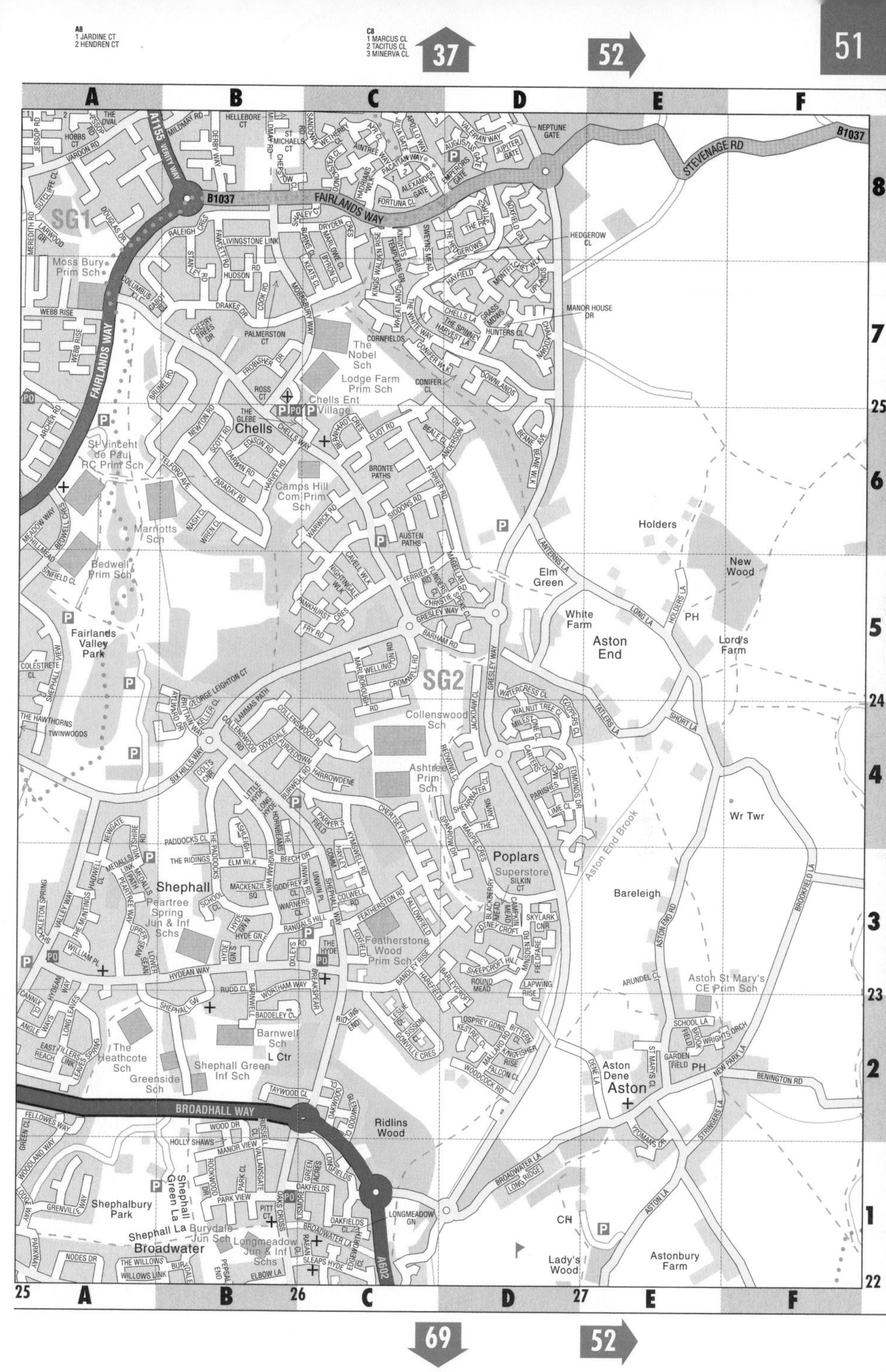
A8
1 JARDINE CT
2 HENDREN CT
C8
1 MARCUS CL
2 TACITUS CL
3 MINERVA CL
37
52
FAIRLANDS WAY
B1037
STEVENAGE RD
A1155
SG1
SG2
Moss Bury Prim Sch
The Nobel Sch
Lodge Farm Prim Sch
Chells Ent Village
Chells
St Vincent de Paul RC Prim Sch
Camps Hill Com Prim Sch
Marriotts Sch
Bedwell Prim Sch
Fairlands Valley Park
Holders
New Wood
Elm Green
White Farm
Aston End
Lord's Farm
Collenswood Sch
Ashtree Prim Sch
Wr Twr
Poplars
Superstore
Shephall
Peartree Spring Jun & Inf Schs
Bareleigh
Featherstone Wood Prim Sch
Aston St Mary's CE Prim Sch
The Heathcote Sch
Barnwell Sch
L Ctr
Shephall Green Inf Sch
Greenside Sch
Aston Dene
Aston
BROADHALL WAY
Ridlins Wood
Shephalbury Park
Shephall Green La
Shephall La
Burydale Jun Sch
Longmeadow Jun & Inf Schs
Broadwater
A602
Lady's Wood
Astonbury Farm
Aston End Brook
BENINGTON RD
BROOKFIELD LA
ASTON LA
69
52
25
26
27
22
23
24
A
B
C
D
E
F
1
2
3
4
5
6
7
8

51
38

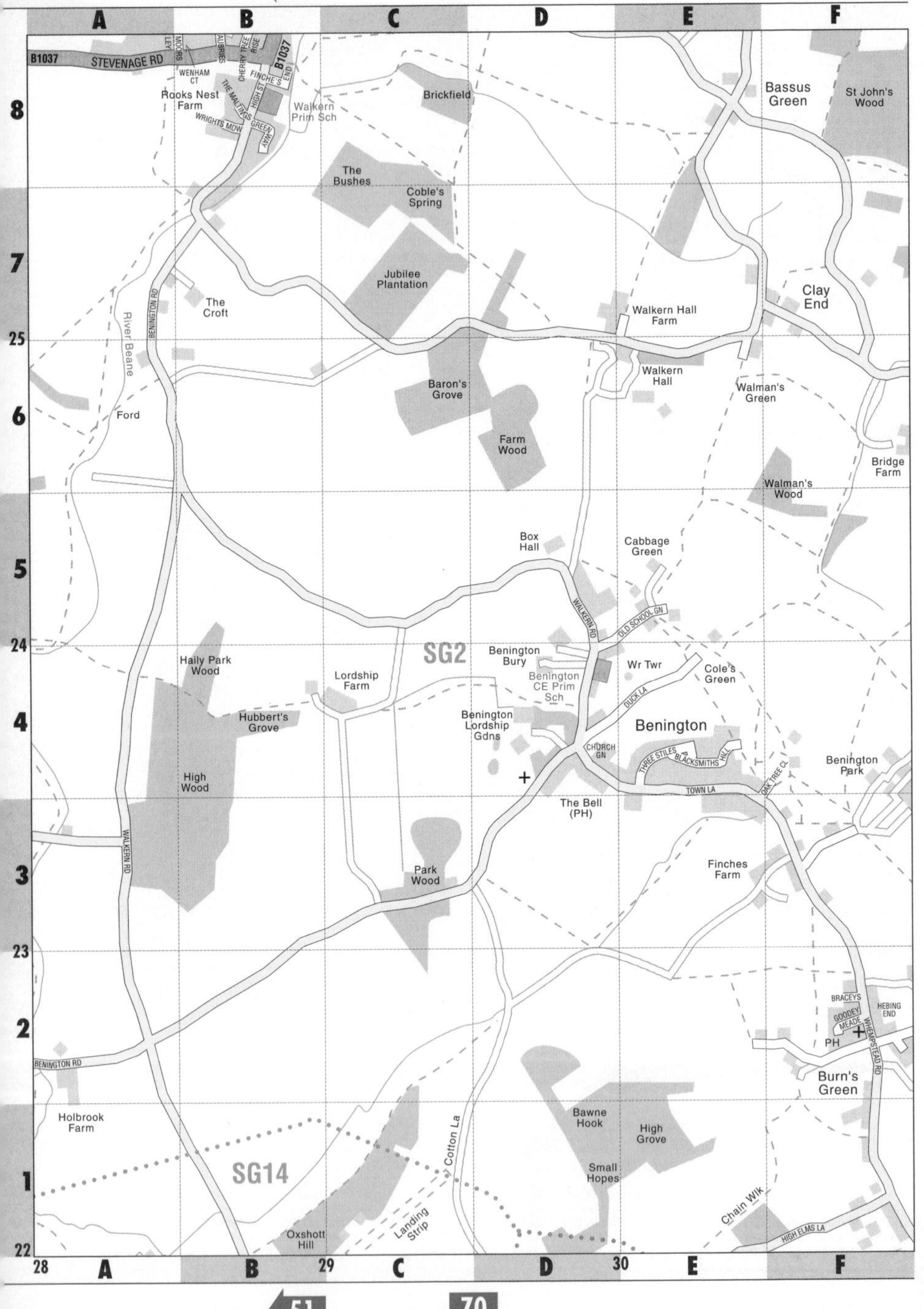
A
B
C
D
E
F
B1037
STEVENAGE RD
B1037
Rooks Nest Farm
Walkern Prim Sch
Brickfield
Bassus Green
St John's Wood
The Bushes
Coble's Spring
Jubilee Plantation
The Croft
River Beane
BENINGTON RD
Walkern Hall Farm
Clay End
Walkern Hall
Walman's Green
Baron's Grove
Ford
Farm Wood
Bridge Farm
Walman's Wood
Box Hall
Cabbage Green
WALKERN RD
OLD SCHOOL GN
SG2
Benington Bury
Wr Twr
Cole's Green
Haily Park Wood
Lordship Farm
Benington CE Prim Sch
DUCK LA
Benington
Hubbert's Grove
Benington Lordship Gdns
CHURCH GN
THREE STILES
BLACKSMITHS HILL
OAK TREE CL
Benington Park
High Wood
TOWN LA
The Bell (PH)
WALKERN RD
Park Wood
Finches Farm
BRACEYS
GOODEY MEADE
HEBING END
WHEMPSTEAD RD
PH
BENINGTON RD
Burn's Green
Holbrook Farm
Cotton La
Bawne Hook
High Grove
SG14
Small Hopes
Chain Wlk
Landing Strip
Oxshott Hill
HIGH ELMS LA
28
29
30
8
7
25
6
5
24
4
3
23
2
1
22

51
70

39
54

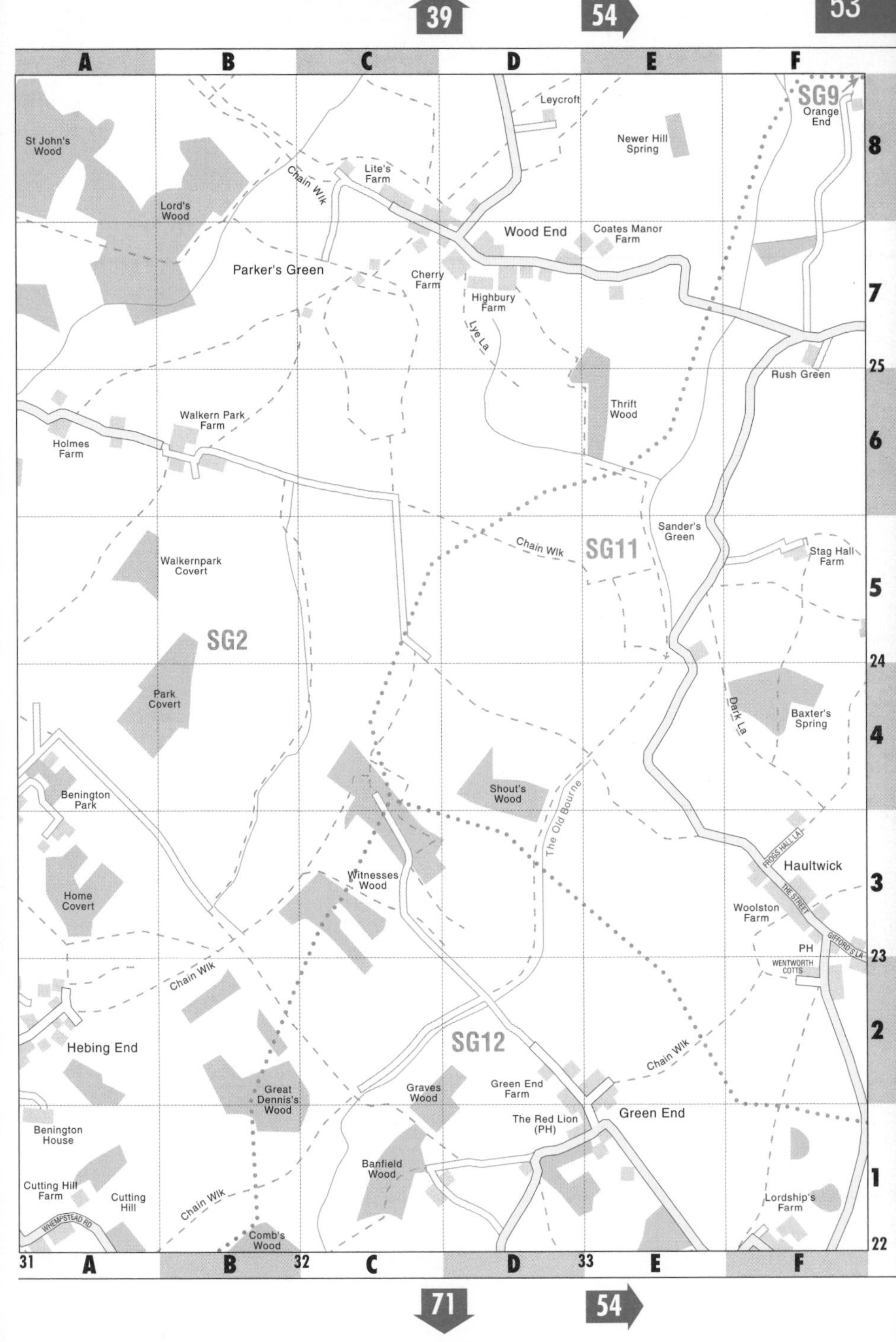
A
B
C
D
E
F
SG9
Orange End
Leycroft
Newer Hill Spring
St John's Wood
Lite's Farm
Chain Wlk
Lord's Wood
Wood End
Coates Manor Farm
Parker's Green
Cherry Farm
Highbury Farm
Lye La
Rush Green
Thrift Wood
Walkern Park Farm
Holmes Farm
Sander's Green
Chain Wlk
SG11
Stag Hall Farm
Walkernpark Covert
SG2
Park Covert
Dark La
Baxter's Spring
Benington Park
Shout's Wood
The Old Bourne
FROGS HALL LA
Haultwick
Witnesses Wood
THE STREET
Home Covert
Woolston Farm
GIFFORD'S LA
PH
WENTWORTH COTTS
Chain Wlk
Hebing End
SG12
Chain Wlk
Graves Wood
Green End Farm
Great Dennis's Wood
Green End
The Red Lion (PH)
Benington House
Banfield Wood
Cutting Hill Farm
Cutting Hill
Chain Wlk
Lordship's Farm
WHEMPSTEAD RD
Comb's Wood
8
7
25
6
5
24
4
3
23
2
1
22
31
32
33

71
54

53
40

A
B
C
D
E
F
8
7
25
6
5
24
4
3
23
2
1
22
34
35
36
Back La
Peasefield
Furtherfield
Spring
Tillers End
Farm
Coles
Park
The
Rectory
SG9
Cowley
Spring
Rush
Green
Cotts
Mill
Farm
The
Paddock
Bramble
Cottage
Nasty
Nobles
Farm
Munden
Bury
VALE
COTTS
Chain Wlk
Great Munden
SG11
HILLTOP
COTTS
MENTLEY LA
Bugby's
Farm
The Plough
(PH)
Great Munden
Farm
EDWARD
COTTS
Herringworth
Hall
Brockhold's
New Cover
Libury
Hall
Dane End Tributary
Stockalls
Great Munden
House
Foxdell
Wood
GIFFORD'S LA
Hornbeam
Common
Brockhold's
Farm
Overley
Common
King's
Hill
Camps
Farm
Levens
Green
Water
Twr
Bandy
Common
Fellowsfield
Common
The Horse
and Groom
(PH)
Levens Green
Farm
Old Hall
Green
PH
SG12
BEGGARMAN'S
LA

53
72

41
56

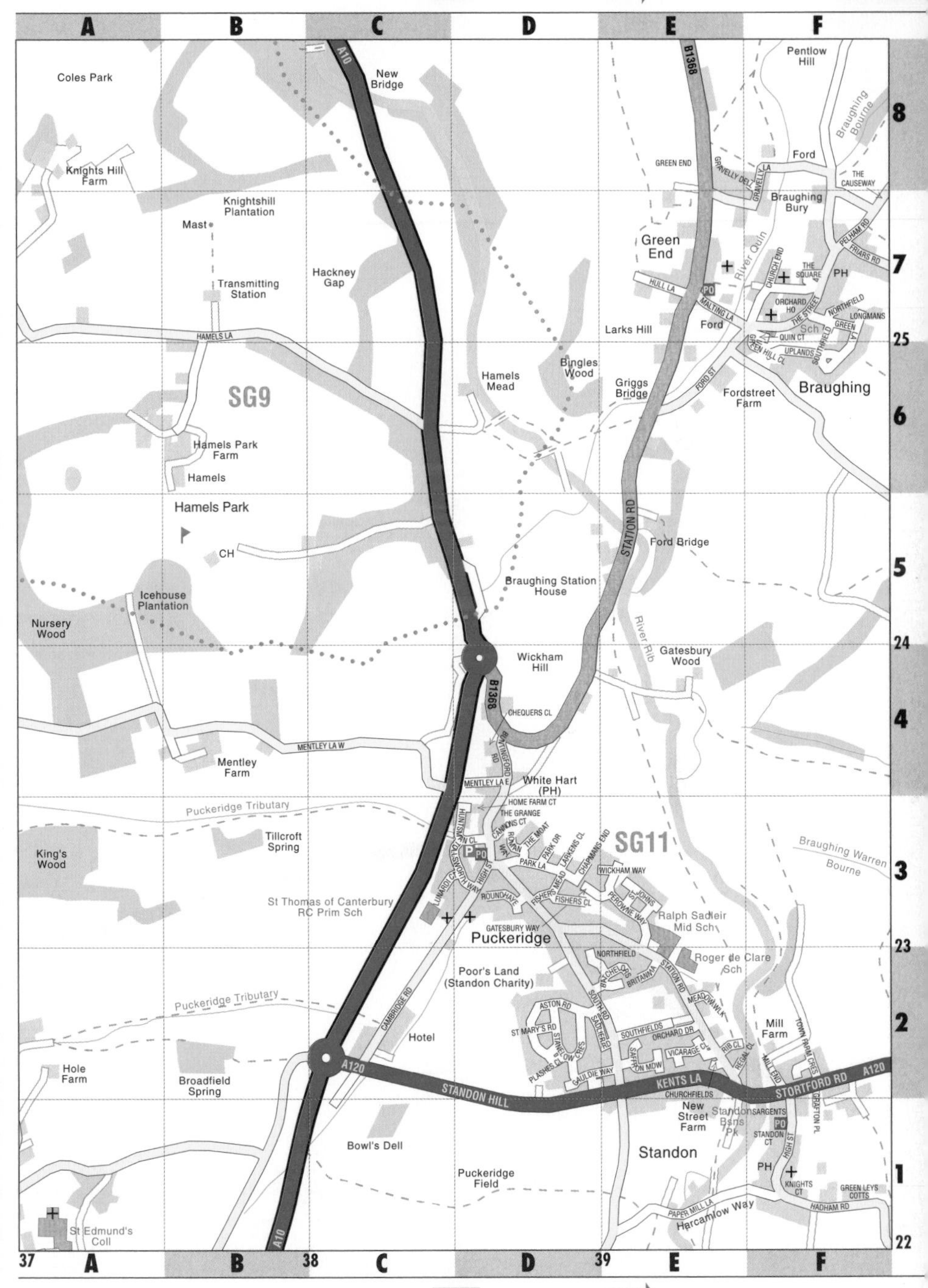
A
B
C
D
E
F
8
7
6
5
4
3
2
1
25
24
23
22
37
38
39
Coles Park
New Bridge
Pentlow Hill
Braughing Bourne
Knights Hill Farm
Knightshill Plantation
Mast
Transmitting Station
Hackney Gap
Green End
Ford
The Causeway
Braughing Bury
Green End
River Quin
Church End
The Square
PH
Pelham Rd
Friars Rd
Hull La
Malting La
Orchard Ho
The Street
Northfield
Longmans
Green La
Quin Ct
Uplands
Southfield
Green Hill Cl
Hamels La
Larks Hill
Ford St
Braughing
Fordstreet Farm
SG9
Hamels Mead
Bingles Wood
Griggs Bridge
Hamels Park Farm
Hamels
Hamels Park
Station Rd
Ford Bridge
CH
Braughing Station House
Icehouse Plantation
Nursery Wood
River Rib
Wickham Hill
Gatesbury Wood
B1368
A10
Chequers Cl
Mentley La W
Buntingford Rd
Mentley Farm
Mentley La E
White Hart (PH)
Home Farm Ct
The Grange
Cannons Ct
Puckeridge Tributary
Tillcroft Spring
King's Wood
SG11
Braughing Warren Bourne
Park La
The Moat
Park Dr
Larkens Cl
Chapmans End
Wickham Way
Roundhaye
Fishers Mead
Fishers Cl
Perowne Way
St Johns
St Thomas of Canterbury RC Prim Sch
Ralph Sadleir Mid Sch
Gatesbury Way
Puckeridge
Northfield
Roger de Clare Sch
Poor's Land (Standon Charity)
Batchelors
Britannia
Station Rd
Meadow Wlk
Puckeridge Tributary
Aston Rd
South Rd
St Mary's Rd
Southfields
Orchard Dr
Mill Farm
Town Farm Cres
Cambridge Rd
Hotel
Vicarage Cl
Rib Cl
Regal Cl
Mill End
Hole Farm
A120
Saffron Mdw
Plashes Cl
Kents La
Stortford Rd
Broadfield Spring
Standon Hill
Churchfields
New Street Farm
Standon Bsns Pk
Sargents
Grafton Pl
Standon Ct
Bowl's Dell
Standon
PH
High St
Puckeridge Field
Knights Ct
Green Leys Cotts
Paper Mill La
Hadham Rd
Harcamlow Way
St Edmund's Coll

73
56

55
42

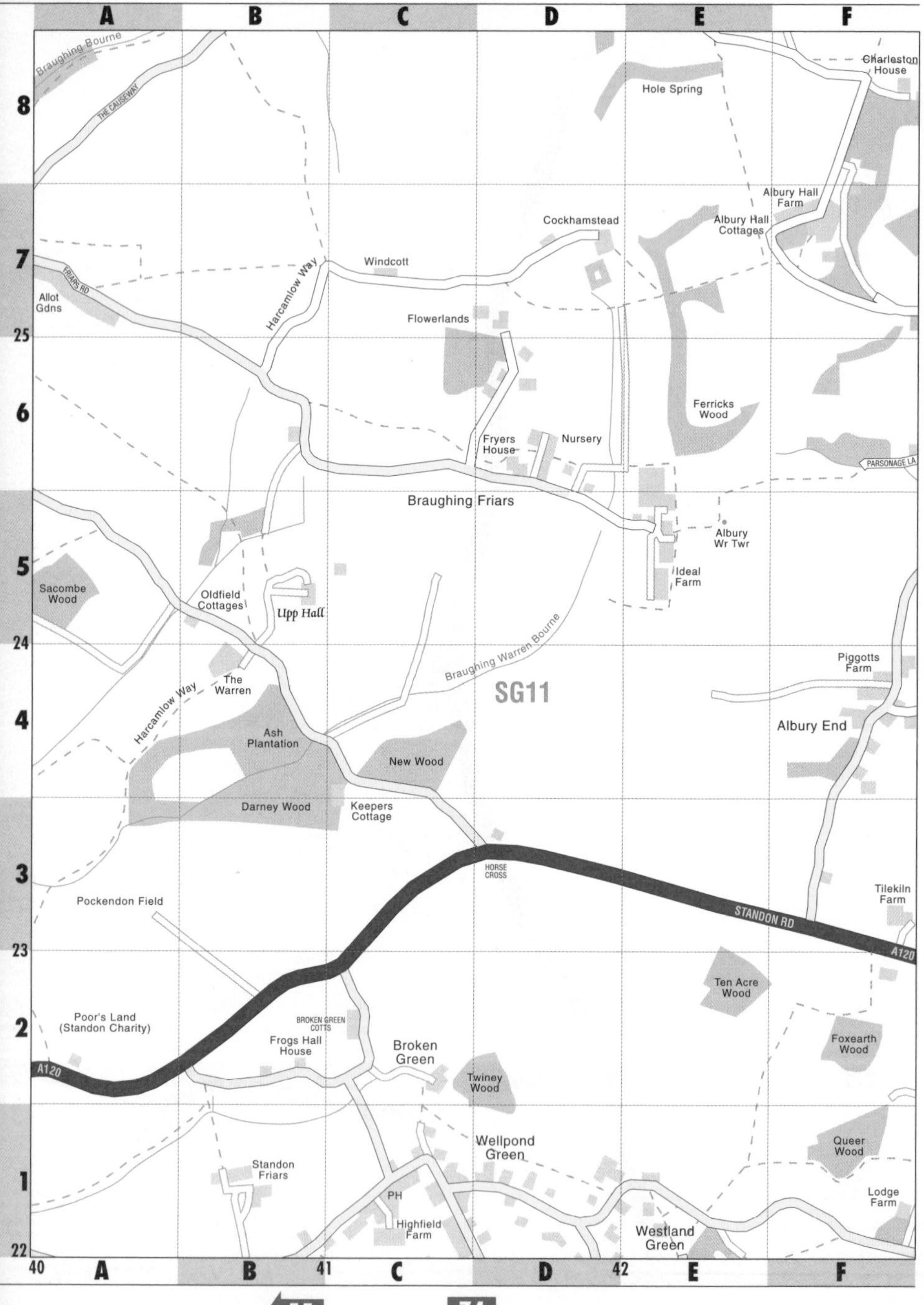
A
B
C
D
E
F
Braughing Bourne
THE CAUSEWAY
Charleston House
Hole Spring
Albury Hall Farm
Albury Hall Cottages
Cockhamstead
Windcott
Harcamlow Way
FRIARS RD
Allot Gdns
Flowerlands
Ferricks Wood
Fryers House
Nursery
PARSONAGE LA
Braughing Friars
Albury Wr Twr
Ideal Farm
Sacombe Wood
Oldfield Cottages
Upp Hall
Braughing Warren Bourne
Piggotts Farm
SG11
The Warren
Ash Plantation
New Wood
Albury End
Darney Wood
Keepers Cottage
HORSE CROSS
Pockendon Field
Tilekiln Farm
STANDON RD
A120
Ten Acre Wood
Poor's Land (Standon Charity)
BROKEN GREEN COTTS
Frogs Hall House
Broken Green
Twiney Wood
Foxearth Wood
Wellpond Green
Queer Wood
Standon Friars
PH
Highfield Farm
Westland Green
Lodge Farm
8
7
25
6
5
24
4
3
23
2
1
22
40
41
42

55
74

43
58

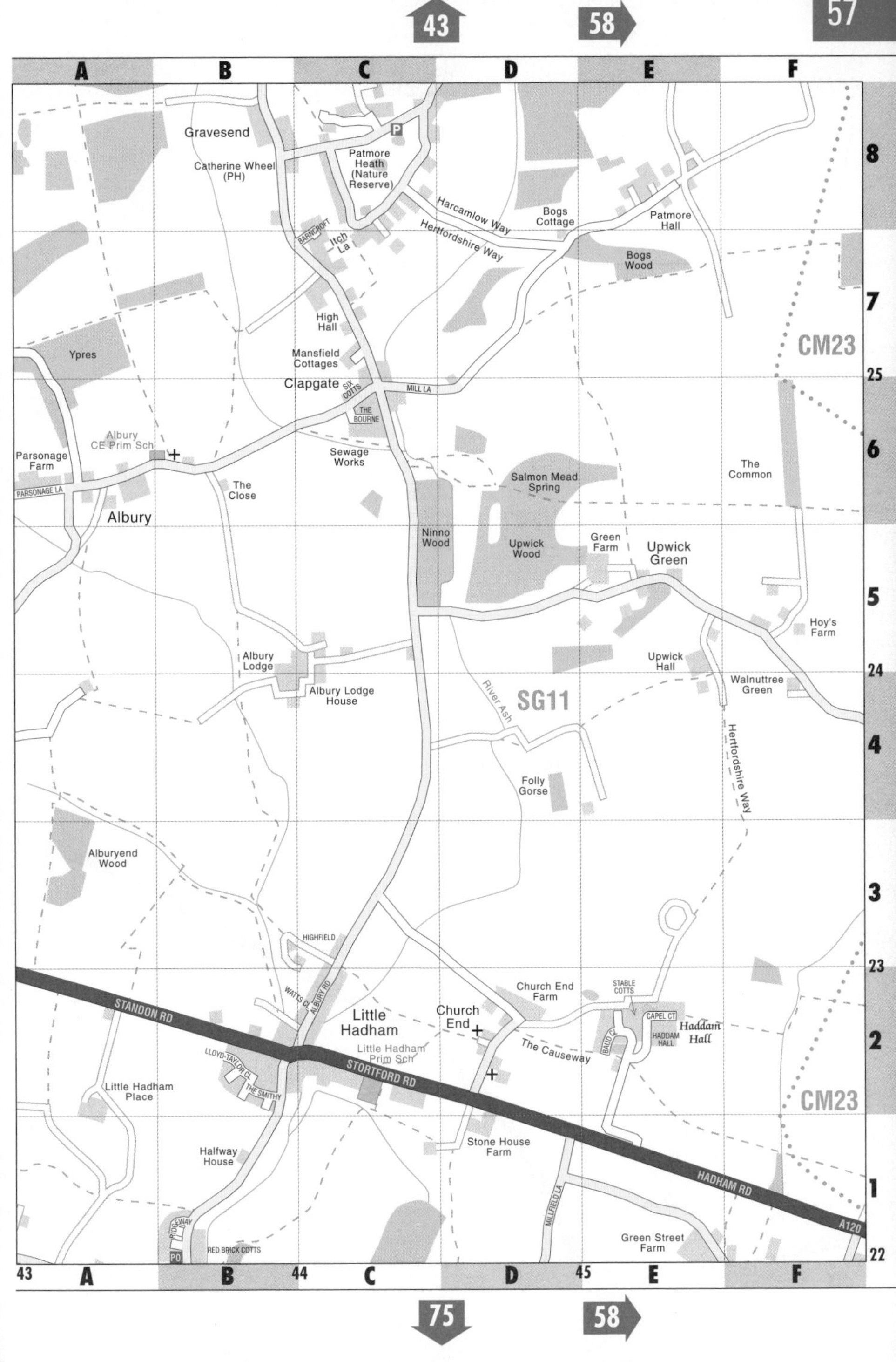
A
B
C
D
E
F
Gravesend
Catherine Wheel (PH)
Patmore Heath (Nature Reserve)
Harcamlow Way
Hertfordshire Way
Bogs Cottage
Patmore Hall
Bogs Wood
BARNCROFT
Itch La
High Hall
Mansfield Cottages
Clapgate
SIX COTTS
MILL LA
THE BOURNE
Ypres
CM23
Albury CE Prim Sch
Parsonage Farm
PARSONAGE LA
Sewage Works
The Close
Albury
Salmon Mead Spring
The Common
Ninno Wood
Upwick Wood
Green Farm
Upwick Green
Hoy's Farm
Albury Lodge
Albury Lodge House
Upwick Hall
Walnuttree Green
River Ash
SG11
Hertfordshire Way
Folly Gorse
Alburyend Wood
HIGHFIELD
WATTS CL
ALBURY RD
STANDON RD
Little Hadham
Church End
Church End Farm
STABLE COTTS
CAPEL CT
HADDAM HALL
BAUD CL
Haddam Hall
The Causeway
Little Hadham Prim Sch
STORTFORD RD
LLOYD-TAYLOR CL
THE SMITHY
Little Hadham Place
CM23
Halfway House
Stone House Farm
HADHAM RD
MILLFIELD LA
RIDGEWAY
PO
RED BRICK COTTS
Green Street Farm
A120
8
7
25
6
5
24
4
3
23
2
1
22
43
44
45

75
58

57

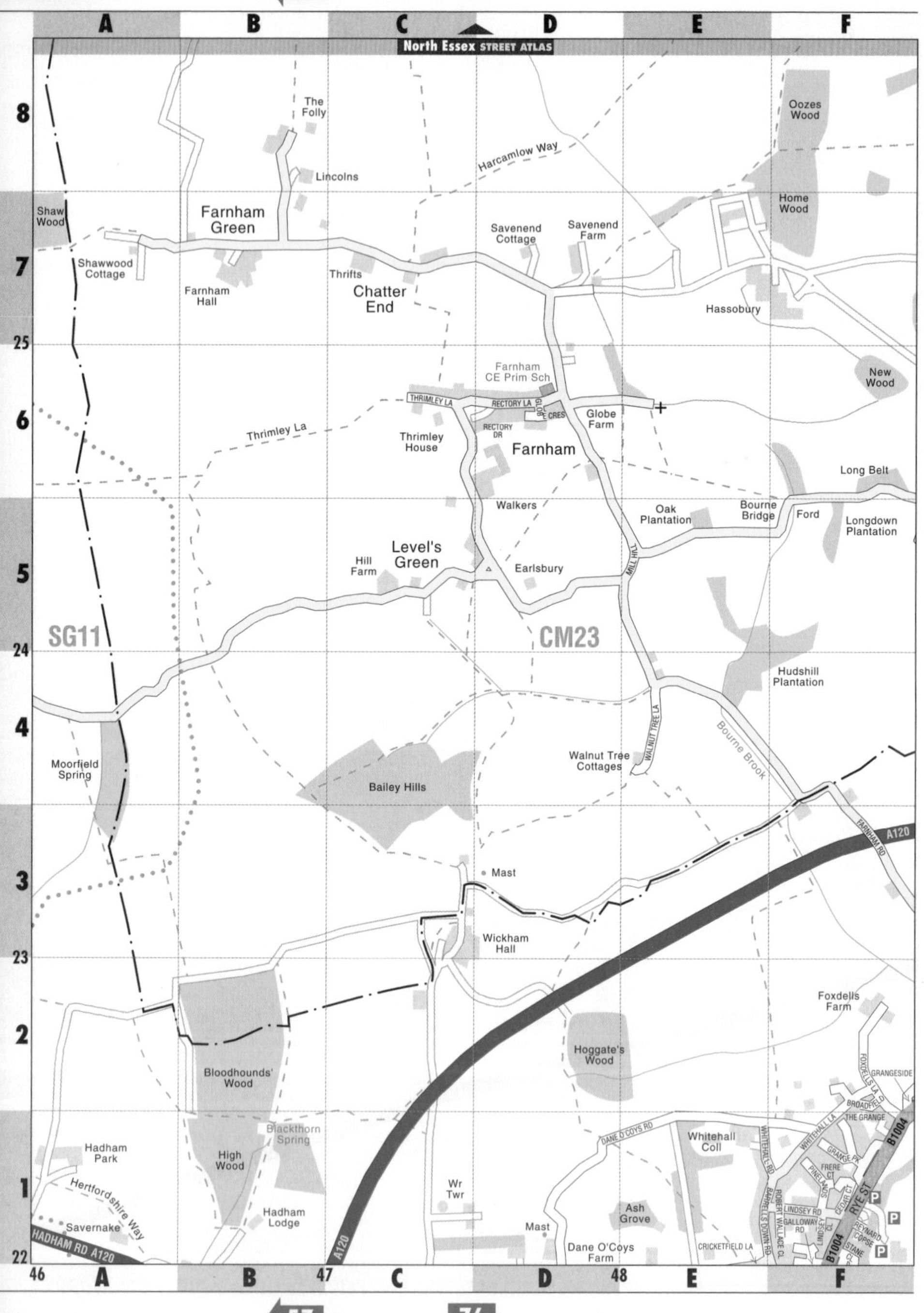

North Essex STREET ATLAS
A
B
C
D
E
F
8
7
6
5
4
3
2
1
25
24
23
22
46
47
48
The Folly
Lincolns
Harcamlow Way
Oozes Wood
Shaw Wood
Farnham Green
Home Wood
Savenend Cottage
Savenend Farm
Shawwood Cottage
Farnham Hall
Thrifts
Chatter End
Hassobury
New Wood
Farnham CE Prim Sch
THRIMLEY LA
RECTORY LA
GLOBE CRES
RECTORY DR
Globe Farm
Thrimley La
Thrimley House
Farnham
Long Belt
Walkers
Oak Plantation
Bourne Bridge
Ford
Longdown Plantation
MILL HILL
Hill Farm
Level's Green
Earlsbury
SG11
CM23
Hudshill Plantation
WALNUT TREE LA
Bourne Brook
Moorfield Spring
Walnut Tree Cottages
Bailey Hills
FARNHAM RD
A120
Mast
Wickham Hall
Foxdells Farm
Bloodhounds' Wood
Hoggate's Wood
FOXDELLS LA
GRANGESIDE
BROADFIELD
THE GRANGE
WHITEHALL LA
Blackthorn Spring
DANE O'COYS RD
Whitehall Coll
WHITEHALL RD
GRANGE PK
B1004
Hadham Park
High Wood
FRERE CT
PINELANDS
CEDAR CT
Hertfordshire Way
Wr Twr
ROBERT WALLACE CL
LINDSEY RD
GALLOWAY RD
LINDSEY CL
RYE ST
Ash Grove
P
Savernake
Hadham Lodge
Mast
REYNARD COPSE
HADHAM RD A120
Dane O'Coys Farm
CRICKETFIELD LA
BARRELLS DOWN RD
STANE CL

57
76

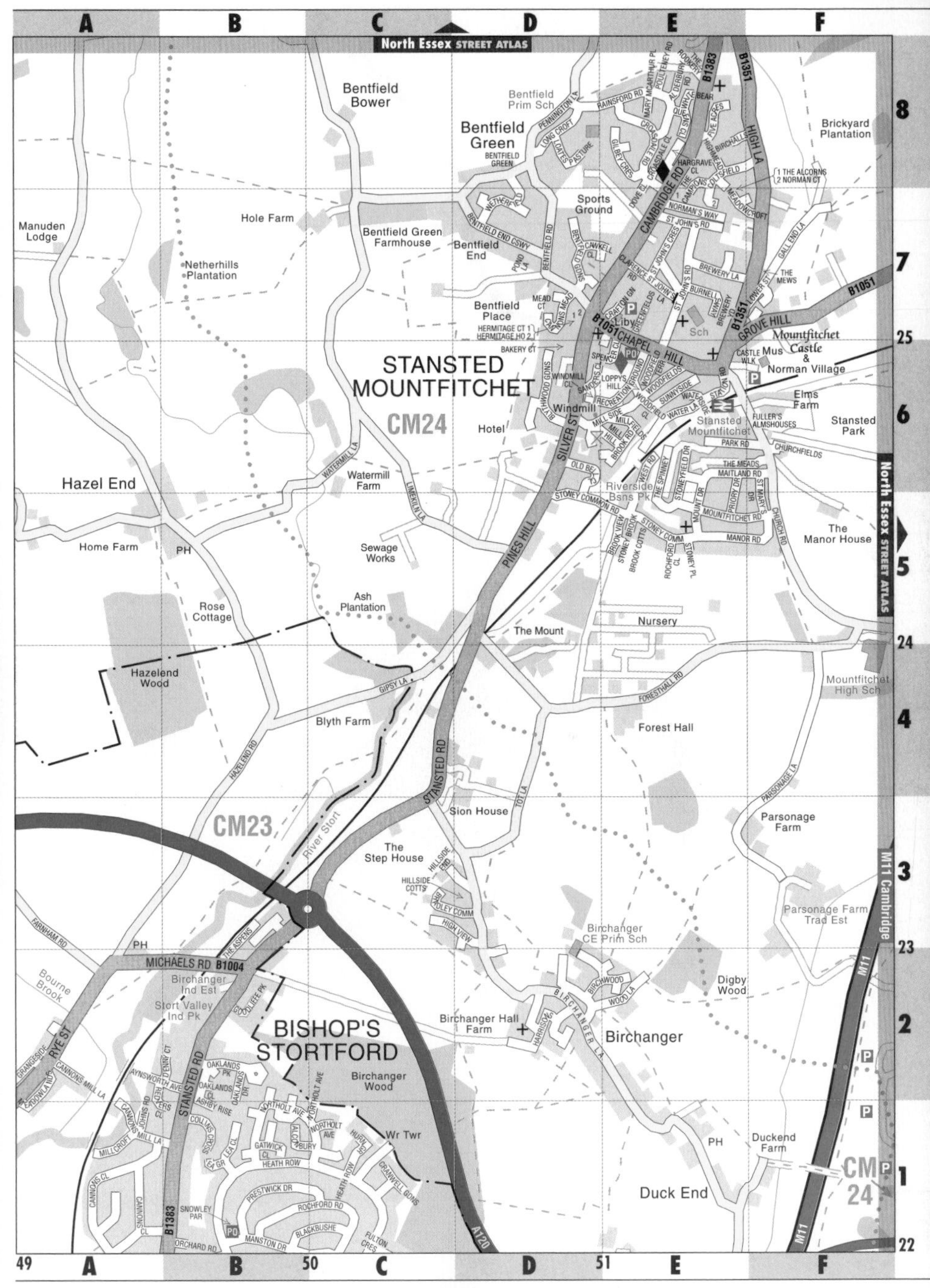
North Essex STREET ATLAS
Bentfield Bower
Bentfield Prim Sch
Bentfield Green
Brickyard Plantation
Manuden Lodge
Hole Farm
Sports Ground
Bentfield Green Farmhouse
Bentfield End
Netherhills Plantation
Bentfield Place
STANSTED MOUNTFITCHET
CM24
Hotel
Windmill
Mountfitchet Castle & Norman Village
Elms Farm
Stansted Park
Stansted Mountfitchet
Hazel End
Watermill Farm
Riverside Bsns Pk
Home Farm
Sewage Works
The Manor House
Rose Cottage
Ash Plantation
The Mount
Nursery
Hazelend Wood
Blyth Farm
Forest Hall
Mountfitchet High Sch
Sion House
Parsonage Farm
CM23
River Stort
The Step House
Parsonage Farm Trad Est
Birchanger CE Prim Sch
Birchanger Ind Est
Stort Valley Ind Pk
Digby Wood
BISHOP'S STORTFORD
Birchanger Hall Farm
Birchanger
Birchanger Wood
Wr Twr
Duckend Farm
Duck End
Bourne Brook
M11 Cambridge
B1383
B1351
B1051
B1004
A120
M11
CAMBRIDGE RD
HIGH LA
CHAPEL HILL
GROVE HILL
SILVER ST
PINES HILL
STANSTED RD
MICHAELS RD
RYE ST
FORESTHALL RD
GIPSY LA
HAZELEND RD
WATERMILL LA
LIMEKILN LA
TOT LA
BIRCHANGER LA
PARSONAGE LA
CHURCH RD
CHURCHFIELDS
PARK RD
MANOR RD
MOUNTFITCHET RD
STONEY COMMON RD
FARNHAM RD

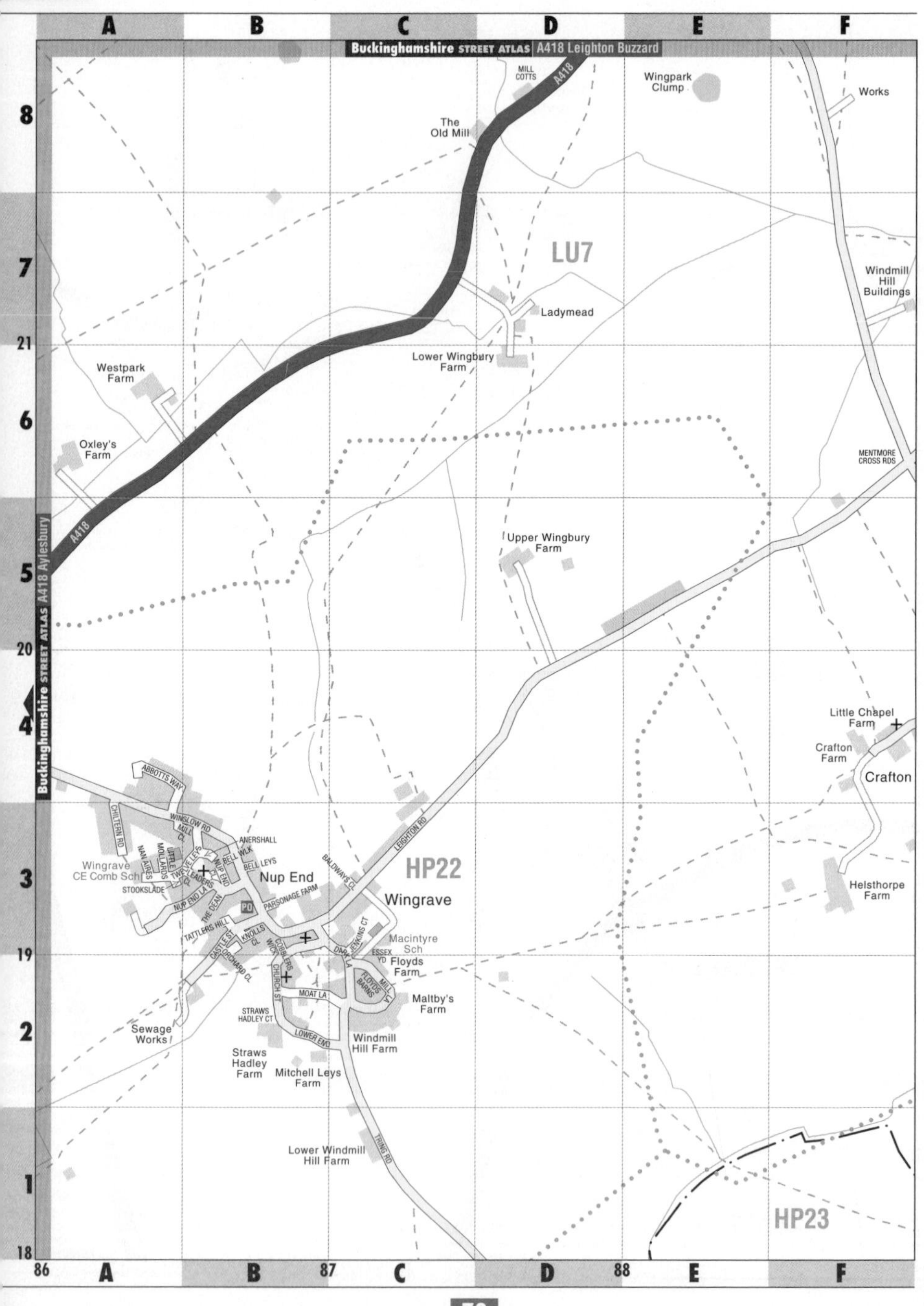

Buckinghamshire STREET ATLAS
A418 Leighton Buzzard
A418 Aylesbury
A418
MILL COTTS
The Old Mill
Wingpark Clump
Works
LU7
Windmill Hill Buildings
Ladymead
Lower Wingbury Farm
Westpark Farm
Oxley's Farm
MENTMORE CROSS RDS
Upper Wingbury Farm
Little Chapel Farm
Crafton Farm
Crafton
ABBOTTS WAY
CHILTERN RD
WINSLOW RD
MILL CL
ANERSHALL
BELL WLK
BELL LEYS
LEIGHTON RD
HP22
Wingrave CE Comb Sch
Nup End
BALDWAYS CL
PARSONAGE FARM
Wingrave
STOOKSLADE
NUP END LA
THE DEAN
TATTLERS HILL
KNOLLS CL
CASTLE ST
ORCHARD CL
COBBLERS WICK
CHURCH ST
JENKINS CT
DARK LA
ESSEX YD
Macintyre Sch
Floyds Farm
FLOYDS BARNS
MILL LA
MOAT LA
Maltby's Farm
Helsthorpe Farm
Sewage Works
STRAWS HADLEY CT
LOWER END
Windmill Hill Farm
Straws Hadley Farm
Mitchell Leys Farm
TRING RD
Lower Windmill Hill Farm
HP23
A B C D E F
8 7 21 6 5 20 4 3 19 2 1 18
86 87 88

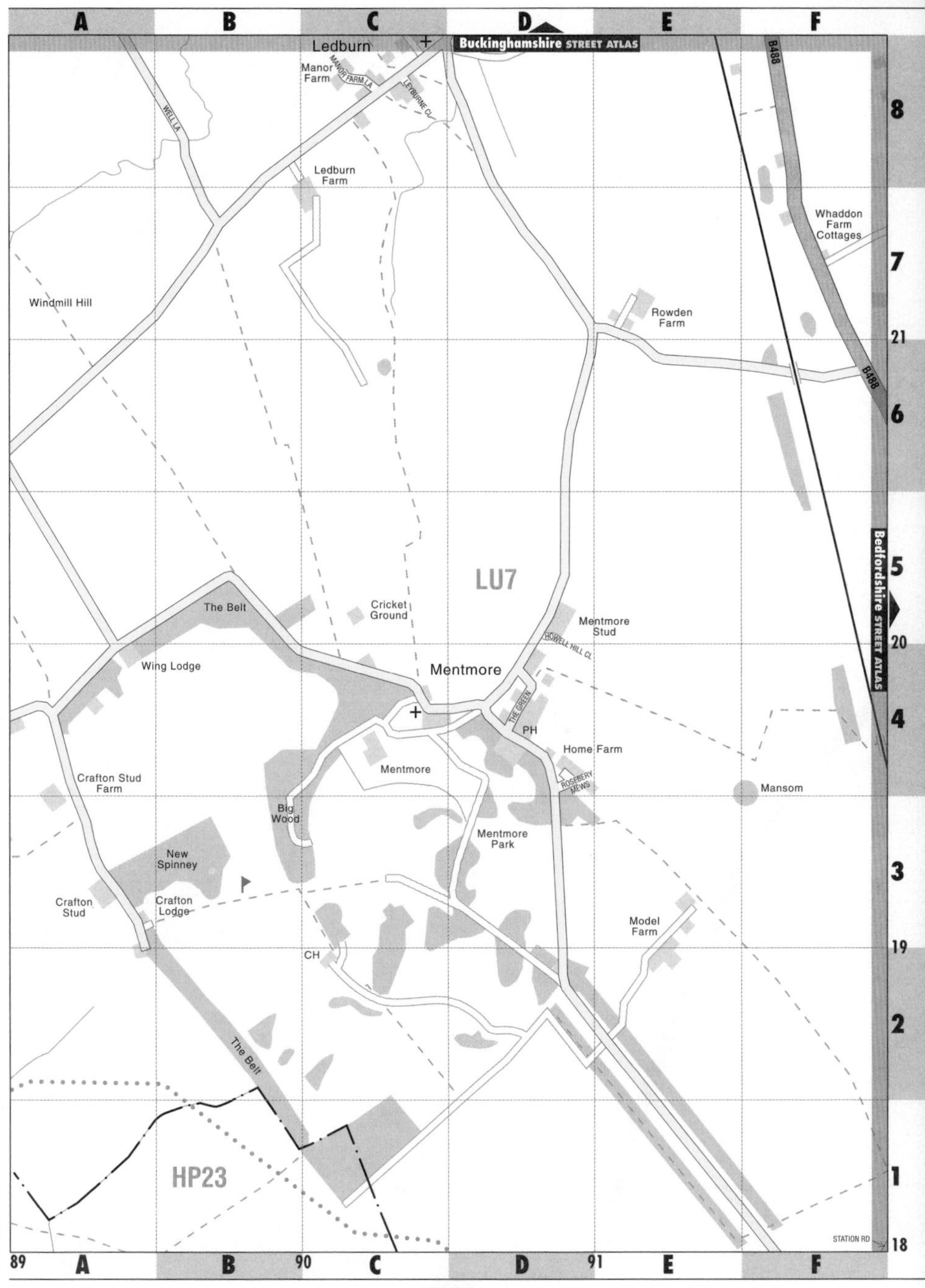
A
B
C
D
E
F
Ledburn
Buckinghamshire STREET ATLAS
B488
Manor Farm
MANOR FARM LA
LEYBURNE CL
WELL LA
8
Ledburn Farm
Whaddon Farm Cottages
7
Windmill Hill
Rowden Farm
21
B488
6
LU7
5
Bedfordshire STREET ATLAS
Cricket Ground
The Belt
Mentmore Stud
HOWELL HILL CL
20
Wing Lodge
Mentmore
THE GREEN
4
PH
Home Farm
Mentmore
ROSEBERY MEWS
Crafton Stud Farm
Mansom
Big Wood
Mentmore Park
New Spinney
3
Crafton Stud
Crafton Lodge
Model Farm
19
CH
2
The Belt
HP23
1
STATION RD
18
89
A
B
90
C
D
91
E
F

79

44

A
B
C
D
E
F
LU5
Skimpot Wood
LU4
Stanner's Wood
LU4
Mast
Cultivation Terraces
Foxdell Jun Sch
Ind Est
Works
COSGROVE WAY
COULSON CT
BILTON WAY
DALLOW RD
HAREFIELD CT
KENT RD
SUMMERFIELD RD
RUNLEY RD
WARREN RD
EASINGWOLD GDNS
HAREFIELD RD
M1
Chaul End Farm
Chaul End
Tunnels
Zouches Farm
Round Wood
Bush Wood
Badgerdell Wood
Mast
Twentynine Wood
CH
CHAUL END RD
BLUEBELL WOOD CL
Thirty Wood
Blossom Spring
Dame Ellen's Wood
Castlecroft Wood
Brickkiln Farm
LU1
Little John's Wood
Bedfordshire STREET ATLAS
Folly Wood
Cvn Pk
Manor Farm
A5 Dunstable, Milton Keynes
Turnpike Farm
Bury Farm
Cradle Spinney
FOLLY LA
COLLINGS WELLS CL
MANOR CT
LUTON RD
MEADOW CROFT
MEADOW WAY
HEATHFIELD CL
HYDE RD
PH
Lodge Farm
ORCHARD CL
DELFIELD GDNS
Heathfield Lower Sch
Willowfield Lower Sch
FIVE OAKS
MOSSMAN DR
HOLLY FARM CL
THE CRESCENT
Gatehouse
DUNSTABLE RD
HAWTHORN CRES
THE DELL
ELM AVE
Five Oaks Mid Sch
SUTTON GDNS
CULWORTH CL
ADSTONE RD
FAIRGREEN RD
Buncer's Wood
Garden Centre
EDGECOTE CL
THE GLEN
LEDWELL RD
Caddington
CROSSWAYS
ENSLOW CL
Jockey Farm
MILLFIELD WAY
MARDLE CL
LITTLEGREEN LA
WOODLANDS
MANOR RD
Tipplehill Farm
LU6
Kensworth House
PH
Herons Farm
Piper's Farm
MANCROFT RD
Cvn Pk
MILLFIELD LA
Cotswold Bsns Pk
Millfield Farm
Aley Green
Corner Farm
Nurseries
Cemy
Lynch Farm
PIPERS LA
Kensworth Lynch
AL3
Hill Farm
A5
8
7
21
6
5
20
4
3
19
2
1
18
04
05
06

83

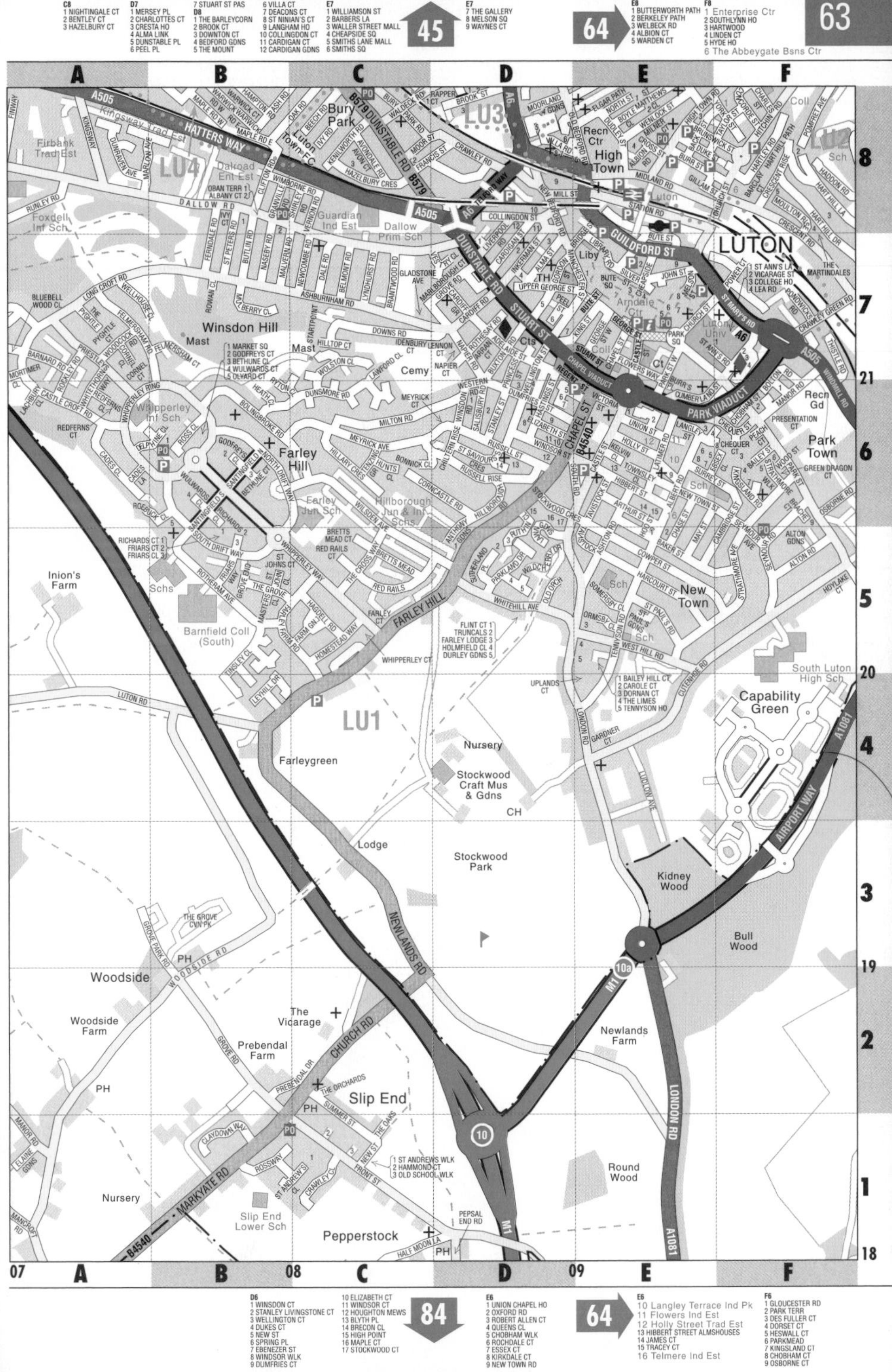
C8
1 NIGHTINGALE CT
2 BENTLEY CT
3 HAZELBURY CT
D7
1 MERSEY PL
2 CHARLOTTES CT
3 CRESTA HO
4 ALMA LINK
5 DUNSTABLE PL
6 PEEL PL
7 STUART ST PAS
D8
1 THE BARLEYCORN
2 BROOK CT
3 DOWNTON CT
4 BEDFORD GDNS
5 THE MOUNT
6 VILLA CT
7 DEACONS CT
8 ST NINIAN'S CT
9 LANGHAM HO
10 COLLINGDON CT
11 CARDIGAN CT
12 CARDIGAN GDNS
E7
1 WILLIAMSON ST
2 BARBERS LA
3 WALLER STREET MALL
4 CHEAPSIDE SQ
5 SMITHS LANE MALL
6 SMITHS SQ
45
E7
7 THE GALLERY
8 MELSON SQ
9 WAYNES CT
64
E8
1 BUTTERWORTH PATH
2 BERKELEY PATH
3 WELBECK RD
4 ALBION CT
5 WARDEN CT
F8
1 Enterprise Ctr
2 SOUTHLYNN HO
3 HARTWOOD
4 LINDEN CT
5 HYDE HO
6 The Abbeygate Bsns Ctr
A
B
C
D
E
F
8
7
21
6
5
20
4
3
19
2
1
18
07
08
09
LUTON
LU1
LU2
LU3
LU4
A505
HATTERS WAY
B579
DUNSTABLE RD
A6
GUILDFORD ST
STUART ST
PARK VIADUCT
CHAPEL VIADUCT
B4540
FARLEY HILL
NEWLANDS RD
CHURCH RD
MARKYATE RD
LONDON RD
A1081
AIRPORT WAY
M1
10
10a
Firbank Trad Est
Kingsway Trad Est
Dallow Ent Est
Foxdell Inf Sch
Bury Park
Luton Town FC
Guardian Ind Est
Dallow Prim Sch
Recn Ctr
High Town
Liby
TH
Arndale Ctr
Luton Univ
Cts
Coll
Ct
Winsdon Hill
Mast
Cemy
Whipperley Inf Sch
Farley Hill
Farley Jun Sch
Hillborough Jun & Inf Schs
Recn Gd
Park Town
Sch
New Town
Inion's Farm
Schs
Barnfield Coll (South)
South Luton High Sch
Capability Green
Farleygreen
Nursery
Stockwood Craft Mus & Gdns
CH
Lodge
Stockwood Park
Kidney Wood
Bull Wood
Woodside
PH
Woodside Farm
The Vicarage
Prebendal Farm
Newlands Farm
Slip End
Round Wood
Nursery
Slip End Lower Sch
Pepperstock
1 MARKET SQ
2 GODFREYS CT
3 BETHUNE CL
4 WULWARDS CT
5 OLYARD CT
1 ST ANN'S LA
2 VICARAGE ST
3 COLLEGE HO
4 LEA RD
RICHARDS CT 1
FRIARS CT 2
FRIARS CL 3
FLINT CT 1
TRUNCALS 2
FARLEY LODGE 3
HOLMFIELD CL 4
DURLEY GDNS 5
1 BAILEY HILL CT
2 CAROLE CT
3 DORNAN CT
4 THE LIMES
5 TENNYSON HO
1 ST ANDREWS WLK
2 HAMMOND CT
3 OLD SCHOOL WLK
A
B
C
D
E
F
D6
1 WINSDON CT
2 STANLEY LIVINGSTONE CT
3 WELLINGTON CT
4 DUKES CT
5 NEW ST
6 SPRING PL
7 EBENEZER ST
8 WINDSOR WLK
9 DUMFRIES CT
10 ELIZABETH CT
11 WINDSOR CT
12 HOUGHTON MEWS
13 BLYTH PL
14 BRECON CL
15 HIGH POINT
16 MAPLE CT
17 STOCKWOOD CT
84
E6
1 UNION CHAPEL HO
2 OXFORD RD
3 ROBERT ALLEN CT
4 QUEENS CL
5 CHOBHAM WLK
6 ROCHDALE CT
7 ESSEX CT
8 KIRKDALE CT
9 NEW TOWN RD
64
E6
10 Langley Terrace Ind Pk
11 Flowers Ind Est
12 Holly Street Trad Est
13 HIBBERT STREET ALMSHOUSES
14 JAMES CT
15 TRACEY CT
16 Telmere Ind Est
F6
1 GLOUCESTER RD
2 PARK TERR
3 DES FULLER CT
4 DORSET CT
5 HESWALL CT
6 PARKMEAD
7 KINGSLAND CT
8 CHOBHAM ST
9 OSBORNE CT

63
46

A
B
C
D
E
F
LUTON
LU1
LU2
London
Luton Airport
Terminal
Motor Vehicle
Works
Schs
Cemy
Luton
Ret Pk
PH
Hotel
Enterprise
Ctr
The
Bsns
Ctr
Luton
Airport
Parkway
Barratt
Ind Pk
Sports
Ctr
Masts
Hotel
Airport
Executive
Pk
VAUXHALL
WAY
A505
AIRPORT WAY
GIPSY LA
A1081
B653
LOWER HARPENDEN RD
Someries
Farm
Someries
Someries
Castle
Chiltern
Hall
Bush Pasture
COPT HALL
COTTAGES
Copt
Hall
Lower
Kidney Wood
George Wood
Stocking Wood
Horsley's
Wood
Hardingdell
Wood
Luton Hoo Park
Watbridge
Cottages
Fernell's
Wood
River Lea or Lee
Luton Hoo
Engine
Spring
The
Lodge
The Plain
Columnhill
Spring
The
Stable Yard
Birch
Wood
New Mill
End
THE LUTON DR
THE WARREN DR
TOWER RD
TOWER WAY
ABBOTS WOOD RD
ABBEY DR
COWRIDGE CRES
HART LA
DERWENT RD
BROOMS RD
WHITECROFT RD
CRAWLEY GREEN RD
LEYGREEN CL
BEACONSFIELD
BLAYDON RD
DURHAM RD
SILECROFT RD
NORFOLK RD
RUTLAND CRES
KETTON CL
KETTON CT
HART HILL DR
FARNLEY GR
CUCKOO'S NEST
RUTLAND CT 1
RUTLAND HALL 2
DEVON RD
BUCHANAN CT
BUCHANAN DR
GAYLAND AVE
EATON VALLEY RD
HARROWDEN RD
FALCONERS RD
BRENDON AVE
POLZEATH CL
MISTLETOE HILL
MISTLETOE CT
MOSSBANK AVE
CHERTSEY CL
EATON GREEN RD
GRESHAM CL
FRANK LESTER WAY
PRESIDENT WAY
PRINCE WAY
AIRPORT APPROACH RD
PROVOST WAY
1 HUNTING HALL
2 BRITANNIA HALL
3 MONARCH HALL
4 NAPIER HALL
5 EATON GREEN CT
6 HARROWDEN CT
PERCIVAL WAY
PROSPECT WAY
PROCTOR WAY
PRENTICE WAY
SPITTLESEA RD
AIRPORT WAY
KIMPTON RD
VAUXHALL RD
PARKWAY RD
OSBORNE RD
PARK ST
8
7
21
6
5
20
4
3
19
2
1
18
10
11
12

63
85

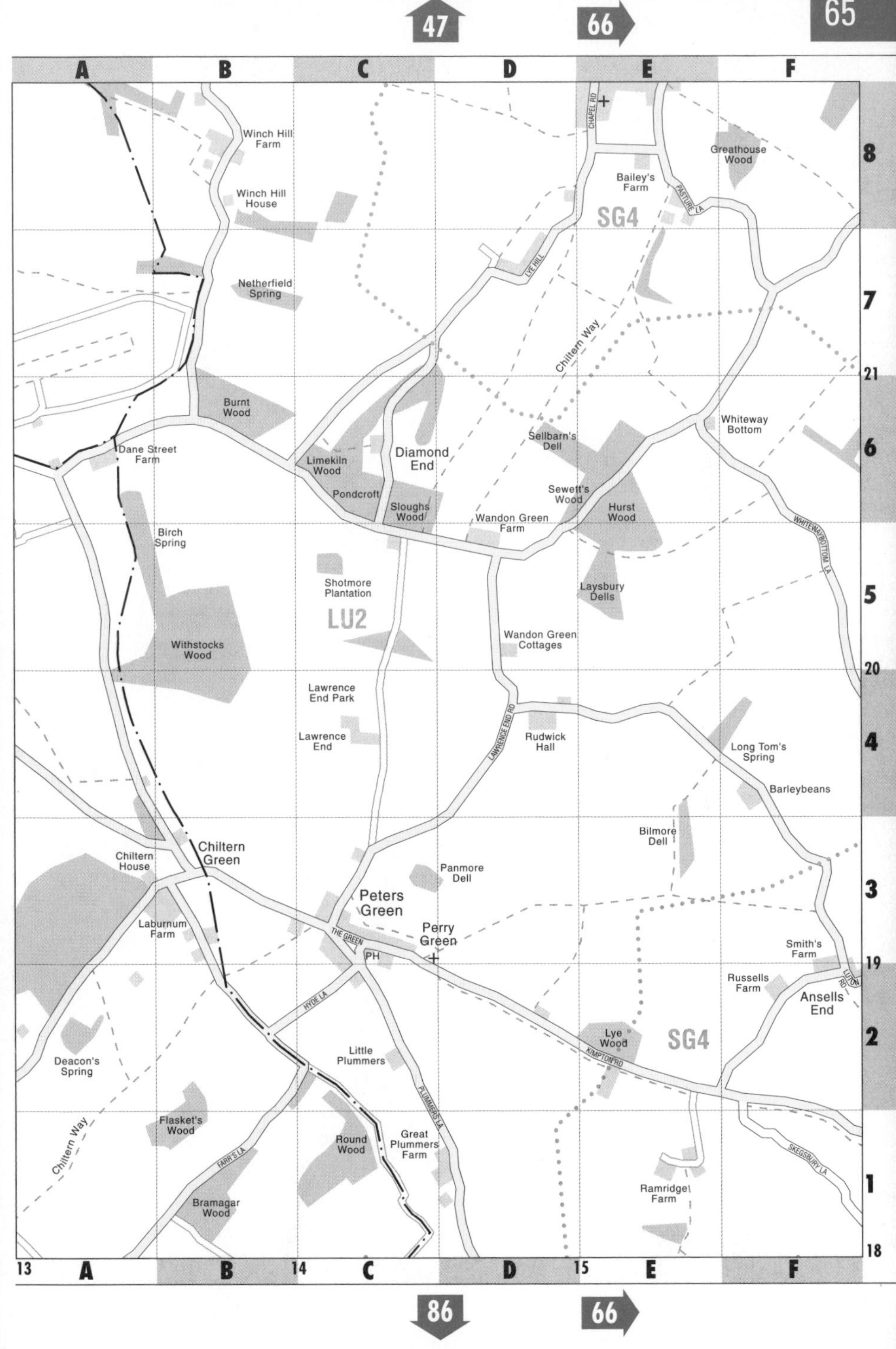
47
66
A
B
C
D
E
F
Winch Hill Farm
Winch Hill House
Chapel Rd
Greathouse Wood
Bailey's Farm
Pasture La
SG4
Lye Hill
Netherfield Spring
Chiltern Way
Burnt Wood
Whiteway Bottom
Dane Street Farm
Limekiln Wood
Diamond End
Sellbarn's Dell
Pondcroft
Sloughs Wood
Sewett's Wood
Hurst Wood
Wandon Green Farm
Whitewaybottom La
Birch Spring
Shotmore Plantation
Laysbury Dells
LU2
Withstocks Wood
Wandon Green Cottages
Lawrence End Park
Lawrence End Rd
Rudwick Hall
Lawrence End
Long Tom's Spring
Barleybeans
Bilmore Dell
Chiltern House
Chiltern Green
Panmore Dell
Peters Green
Laburnum Farm
The Green
Perry Green
PH
Smith's Farm
Russells Farm
Luton Rd
Ansells End
Hyde La
Lye Wood
SG4
Kimpton Rd
Deacon's Spring
Little Plummers
Plummers La
Flasket's Wood
Chiltern Way
Round Wood
Great Plummers Farm
Skegsbury La
Farr's La
Bramagar Wood
Ramridge Farm
8
7
21
6
5
20
4
3
19
2
1
18
13
14
15
86
66

65
48

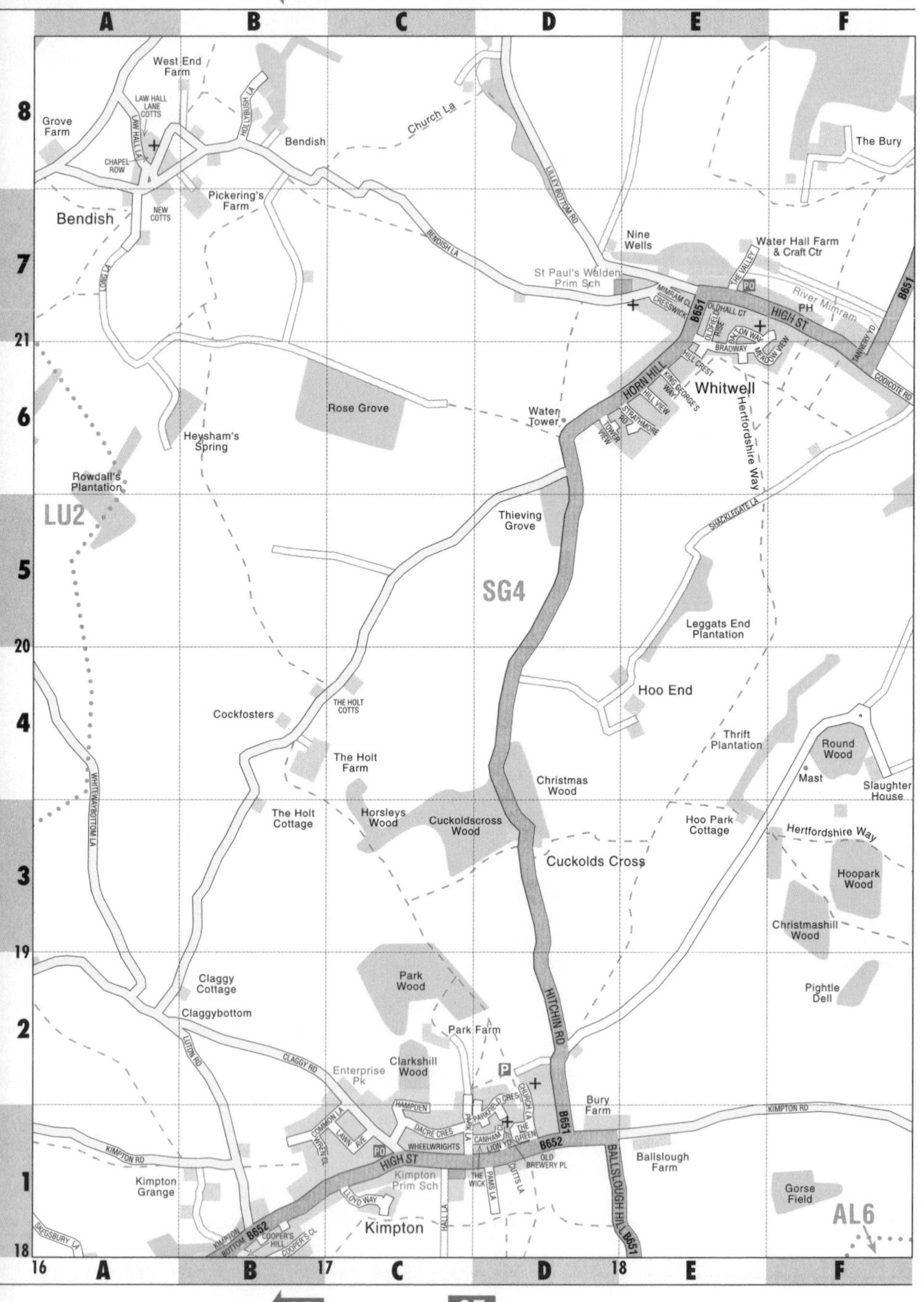
West End Farm
Grove Farm
Bendish
Pickering's Farm
Church La
Bendish La
Lilley Bottom Rd
The Bury
Nine Wells
Water Hall Farm & Craft Ctr
St Paul's Walden Prim Sch
River Mimram
High St
Whitwell
Horn Hill
Hertfordshire Way
Codicote Rd
Rose Grove
Water Tower
Heysham's Spring
Rowdall's Plantation
LU2
Thieving Grove
Shacklegate La
SG4
Leggats End Plantation
Hoo End
Cockfosters
The Holt Cotts
The Holt Farm
Thrift Plantation
Round Wood
Mast
Slaughter House
Christmas Wood
The Holt Cottage
Horsleys Wood
Cuckoldscross Wood
Hoo Park Cottage
Cuckolds Cross
Hoopark Wood
Christmashill Wood
Whitewaybottom La
Park Wood
Claggy Cottage
Claggybottom
Pightle Dell
Hitchin Rd
Park Farm
Clarkshill Wood
Enterprise Pk
Claggy Rd
Luton Rd
Bury Farm
Kimpton Rd
B651
B652
Ballsough Hill
Ballslough Farm
Kimpton Grange
Kimpton Prim Sch
Kimpton
Gorse Field
AL6

65
87

49
68

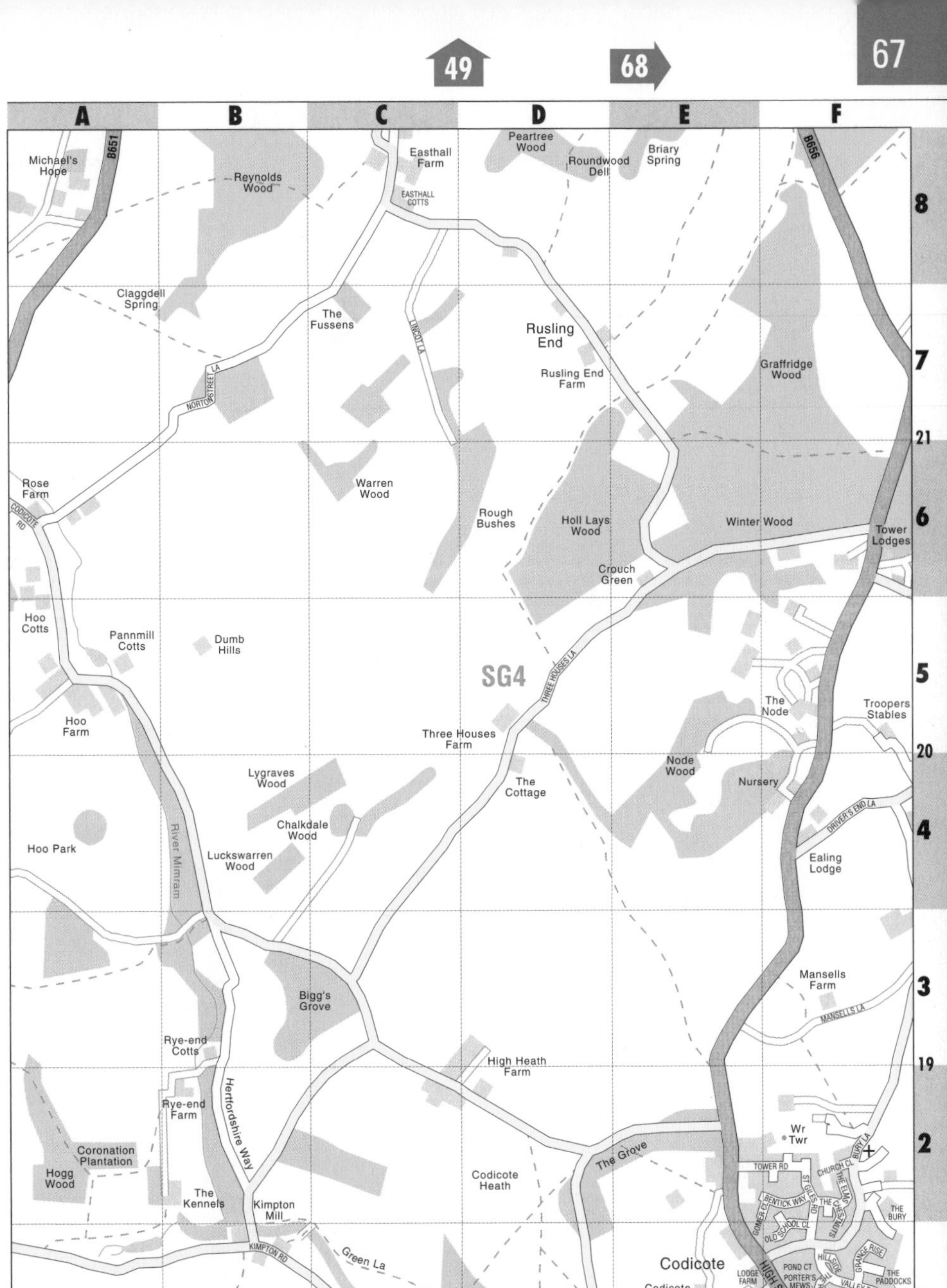
A
B
C
D
E
F
Michael's Hope
B651
Reynolds Wood
Easthall Farm
EASTHALL COTTS
Peartree Wood
Roundwood Dell
Briary Spring
B656
8
Claggdell Spring
The Fussens
LINCOT LA
Rusling End
Rusling End Farm
Graffridge Wood
7
NORTON STREET LA
21
Rose Farm
CODICOTE RD
Warren Wood
Rough Bushes
Holl Lays Wood
Winter Wood
Tower Lodges
6
Crouch Green
Hoo Cotts
Pannmill Cotts
Dumb Hills
SG4
THREE HOUSES LA
5
Hoo Farm
The Node
Troopers Stables
Three Houses Farm
20
Lygraves Wood
The Cottage
Node Wood
Nursery
Chalkdale Wood
DRIVER'S END LA
Hoo Park
River Mimram
Luckswarren Wood
Ealing Lodge
4
Bigg's Grove
Mansells Farm
3
MANSELLS LA
Rye-end Cotts
High Heath Farm
19
Rye-end Farm
Hertfordshire Way
Wr Twr
2
Coronation Plantation
The Grove
Hogg Wood
Codicote Heath
TOWER RD
CHURCH CL
BURY LA
ST GILES RD
THE ELMS
BENTICK WAY
THE CHESTNUTS
THE BURY
GOMER CL
OLD SCHOOL CL
The Kennels
Kimpton Mill
KIMPTON RD
Green La
Codicote
POND CT
HILLSIDE
GRANGE RISE
PORTER'S MEWS
THE PADDOCKS
LODGE FARM
HIGH ST
PH
VALLEY RD
RIDGEWAY
Codicote Lodge
THE CLOSE
1
HEATH HILL
HEATH LA
GLENBOURNE
PO
HILL RD
MEADOW WAY
THE GREEN
ST ALBANS RD
BAKER'S
FARRIERS
THE ORCHARD
TITHE CL
DOLLIMORE
POYNDERS MDW
NEW TOWN
MAYFLOWER CL
B656
TANYARD LA
AL6
Codicote CE Prim Sch
18
19
A
B
20
C
D
21
E
F

88
68

67
50

A
B
C
D
E
F
8
7
21
6
5
20
4
3
19
2
1
18
22
23
24
North Lodges
Burleigh Grove
Cowley's Corner Wood
Burleigh Farm
SG2
Hotel
LONDON RD
B197
STEVENAGE RD
Wintergreen Wood
B656
Knebworth Country Park
Mausoleum
OLD KNEBWORTH LA
Knebworth House
Miniature Rly
SG3
Manor Farm
Old Knebworth
Lodge Farm
CH
STOBARTS CL
PETERS WAY
NEW CL
WESTLAND RD
KEITHS WOOD
Knebworth
Mon
MANOR FARM STABLES
PARK LA
Martlets
Lytton Arms (PH)
ALMSHOUSES
MUIRHEAD WAY
BELLAMY CL
PH
STATION RD
Park Wood
DRIVER'S END LA
DRIVER'S END
SLIP LA
Nup End
STOCKENS DELL
HORNBEAM SPRING
GIBBONS WAY
GUN LA
Homewood
SG4
STOCKENS GN
GIPSY LA
CHERRY CL
GUN ROAD GDNS
MEADWAY
Hogsnorton
The Bothy
New Wood
CRAB TREE RD
WOODSTOCK
WADNAL WAY
BURY LA
Hornbeam Spring
Plummer's Farm
Thickney Wood
Robin Hood & Little John (PH)
SALLY DEARDS LA
Rableyheath
Wr Twr
Deard's Wood
SPINNEY LA
DARBY DR
WYCH ELM LA
The Iron House
Tagmore Green
Rableyheath Farm
AL6
NORMANS LA
NINNING'S LA
Ashley Grove
Arnold's Farm
Ninning's Wood
RABLEY HEATH RD
POTTERSHEATH RD
A1(M)
HEATH RD
Pottersheath
Heath Field
Little Wood
FALLOW END
Mardley Heath
Ridge Farm
1 THE BIRCHES
2 THE PADDOCKS
3 MAYFLOWER CL
CODICOTE HEIGHTS
Little Bury Farm
Arnold's Spring
DANESBURY PARK RD
CANONSFIELD RD
Welwyn Heath
MARDLEY WOOD
HEATHLANDS
MARDLEY HILL
MARDLEY DELL

67
89

51
70

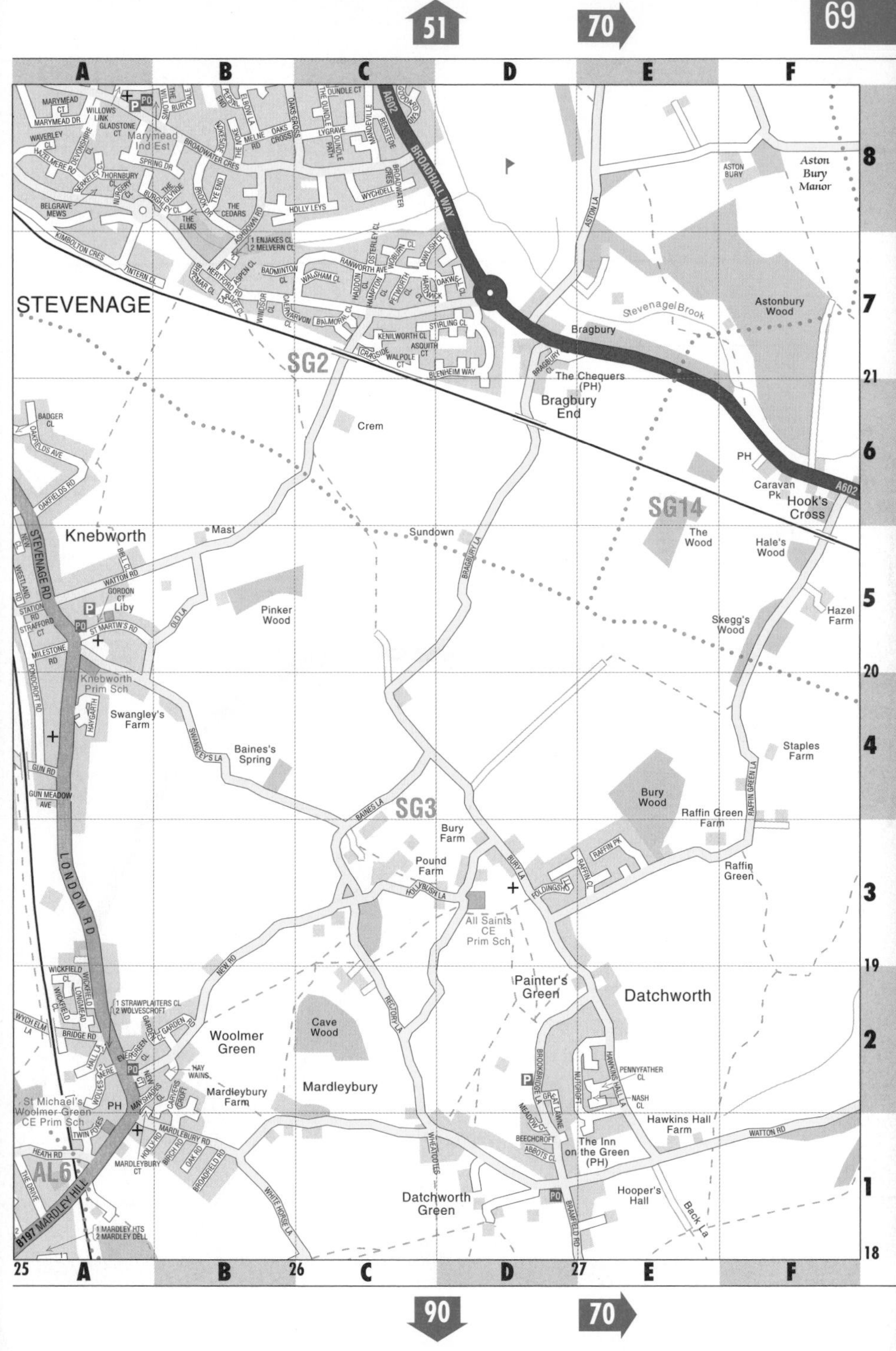
A
B
C
D
E
F
8
7
21
6
5
20
4
3
19
2
1
18
25
26
27
STEVENAGE
SG2
SG14
SG3
AL6
MARYMEAD CT
MARYMEAD DR
WILLOWS LINK
GLADSTONE CT
Marymead Ind Est
WAVERLEY CL
DEVONSHIRE CL
HAZELMERE RD
SPRING DR
BROADWATER CRES
THORNBURY CL
BERKELEY CL
NURSERY CL
BURGHLEY CL
THE GLYNDE
BELGRAVE MEWS
THE ELMS
THE CEDARS
TYE END
BROOK DR
ASHDOWN RD
KIMBOLTON CRES
TINTERN CL
1 ENJAKES CL
2 MELVERN CL
HERTFORD RD
ASPEN CL
BADMINTON CL
WALSHAM CL
RANWORTH AVE
HADDON CL
HAMPTON CL
OSTERLEY CL
WOBURN CL
PETWORTH CL
HARDWICK CL
DAWLISH CL
OAKWELL CL
WINDSOR CL
CAERNARVON CL
BALMORAL CL
STIRLING CL
KENILWORTH CL
ASQUITH CT
CRAGSIDE
WALPOLE CT
BLENHEIM WAY
HOLLY LEYS
WYCHDELL
BROADWATER CRES
THE MELNE RD
OAKS CROSS
LYGRAVE
OUNDLE PATH
THE OUNDLE
OUNDLE CT
MANDEVILLE
BENSTEDE
GODDARD END
ELBOW LA
PEPSAL END
YOKESIDE
THE WILLOWS
BURYDALE
A602
BROADHALL WAY
ASTON LA
ASTON BURY
Aston Bury Manor
Astonbury Wood
Stevenage Brook
Bragbury
BRAGBURY CL
The Chequers (PH)
Bragbury End
PH
Caravan Pk
Hook's Cross
The Wood
Hale's Wood
Hazel Farm
Skegg's Wood
Crem
Sundown
Mast
BRAGBURY LA
Knebworth
BADGER CL
OAKFIELDS AVE
OAKFIELDS RD
STEVENAGE RD
NEW RD
WESTLAND RD
STATION RD
STRAFFORD CT
MILESTONE RD
PONDCROFT RD
BELL CL
WATTON RD
GORDON CT
Liby
ST MARTIN'S RD
OLD LA
Pinker Wood
Knebworth Prim Sch
Swangley's Farm
HAYGARTH
SWANGLEY'S LA
Baines's Spring
GUN RD
GUN MEADOW AVE
LONDON RD
BAINES LA
Bury Farm
Pound Farm
HOLLYBUSH LA
All Saints CE Prim Sch
BURY LA
FOLDINGS
RAFFIN CL
RAFFIN PK
Bury Wood
Raffin Green Farm
RAFFIN GREEN LA
Raffin Green
Staples Farm
NEW RD
WICKFIELD CL
WICKFIELD
LONGMEAD
1 STRAWPLAITERS CL
2 WOLVESCROFT
GARDEN RD
WYCH ELM LA
BRIDGE RD
EVERSGREEN
HALL LA
WOLVES MERE
NEW CT
HAY WAINS
MAYSHADES CL
CARVERS CROFT
Woolmer Green
Cave Wood
RECTORY LA
Painter's Green
Datchworth
Mardleybury
Mardleybury Farm
St Michael's Woolmer Green CE Prim Sch
PH
TWIN FOXES
MARDLEBURY RD
HOLLY RD
BIRCH RD
OAK RD
BROADFIELD RD
MARDLEYBURY CT
HEATH RD
THE DRIVE
B197 MARDLEY HILL
1 MARDLEY HTS
2 MARDLEY DELL
WHITE HORSE LA
WHEATCOTES
Datchworth Green
BROOKBRIDGE LA
NUTCROFT
GREAT LAWNE
MEADOW CL
BEECHCROFT
ABBOTS CL
HAWKINS HALL LA
PENNYFATHER CL
NASH CL
Hawkins Hall Farm
WATTON RD
The Inn on the Green (PH)
BRAMFIELD RD
Hooper's Hall
Back La
P
PO

90
70

69
52
Sacombe Corner Wood
White Hall
Ford
Great Brookfield Wood
Cotton La
Stocking Spring
Leatherfield Common
HIGH ELMS LA
Idle Hill
Larkin's Wood
SG2
Leofield Grove
Gregory's Farm
SG12
FROGMORE HILL
Pallett's Wood
Lamsden Common
Harmer's Bushes
Frogmore
WALKERN RD
Frogmore Hall
Blue Hill Farm
Chain Walk
Arbury Wood
Oaks Cross Farm
A602
Gravel Pit
The Rookery
Blue Hill
Blackditch Wood
SG14
MILL LA
River Beane
BEANE RD
Stocking Grove
PH
LAMMAS RD
Watton at Stone
MOTTS CL
LONG MDW
AYLOTT CT
THE BEANSIDE
Toes Wood
Hopground Spring
Broom Hall Farm
GREAT INNINGS N
GREAT INNINGS S
NEWMANS CT
HIGH ST
WHITE HOUSE CL
RIVERSHILL
Depot
HAZELDELL
OLD SCHOOL ORCH
MOORYMEAD CL
STATION RD
RECTORY LA
HOCKERILL
SCHOOL LA
Watton at Stone
GLEBE CL
GLEBE CT
PO
WATTON HO
Well Wood
Watton at Stone Prim Sch
A602
WARE RD
Moorymead Spring
A119
Chapel Wood
WATTON RD
Watkin's Spring North
SG3
Brewers Wood
Watton Green
Hanginghill Wood
Chain Walk
Rivershill Green
Watkin's Hall Farm
PERRYWOOD LA
Chain Walk
Martin Spring
Perrywood Farm
69
91

53
72

A
B
C
D
E
F
Chain Walk
SG2
Comb's Wood
Apsley Common
Customs Wood
Little Munden CE Prim Sch
Short Whiteley Common
Easington Common
Dane End
CHURCH LA
GLADSTONE RD
WINDMILLS
Long Spring
The Old Bourne
KINGSFIELD RD
FOUNCELEY AVE
Chapel Farm
WHEMPSTEAD RD
KENNEDY
WHITELEY CL
PO
PAGET COTTS
MUNDEN RD
PH
Dane End House
Whempstead Green
PEARMAN DR
Whempstead
Home Farm
Cottonborough Common
Claypits Wood
MILL LA
Whempstead Farm
Hog's Wood
Whempstead Gate Farm
Wicks Wood
Lodge Farm
WHEMPSTEAD LA
Brookfield Common
Smart's Hill
Longcroft Wood
SG12
Bromley Common
Bushy Leys Spring
Willeycotes Wood
Dane End Tributary
Sacombe Hill Farm
Sacombe Hill
Bardolphspark Wood
SACOMBE GREEN RD
Sacombe
Bardolphs
SG14
WARE RD
SACOMBE POUND
Heath Mount Sch
Sacombebury Farm
The Springs
Sacombe House
Woodhall Park
Sacombe Park
The Clumps
Sacombe Lake
River Beane
Broad Water
Home Farm
The Cuts
Ware Lodge
King Edward's Gorse
A119
A602
8
7
21
6
5
20
4
3
19
2
1
18
31
32
33

71
54

A
B
C
D
E
F
High Trees Farm
Hatchett Farm
Beggarman's La
Beggarman's Wood
Hatchett Poultry Farm
Fullar's Common
Moorfield Common
Trenchern Hills
Hill Farm
Whitehill Farm
Langton's La
Shelly's Wood
Roughground Wood
CH
Cock's Wood
Rigery Farm
Potter's Green
Potter's Hall Farm
Labdens Farm
Rowney La
Rowney Priory
Black Grove
Willowtree Farm
Rowney Wood
Lowgate La
Standon Green End Farm
Knoll Farm
SG12
Standon Green End
SG11
Lowgate La
Sacombe Green
Mott's Wood
Barwick Tributary
Dane End Rd
Church Wood
Dilly Wood
The Bourne
Salmonsley Wood
A10
Low Wood
Home Wood
Home Farm
Marshall's La
Sutes
Cambridge Cotts
Pullar Memorial Prim Sch
High Cross
Gages Wood
Marshall's Farm
PH
Furzeground Wood
Marshall's
North Dr
Poplar Cl
Passfield Cotts
Hazelwood Farm
Rennesley Garden Wood
Mark's Wood
Highcross Hill
Gravelpit Wood
A10
SG12
8
7
21
6
5
20
4
3
19
2
1
18
34
35
36

71
93

55
74

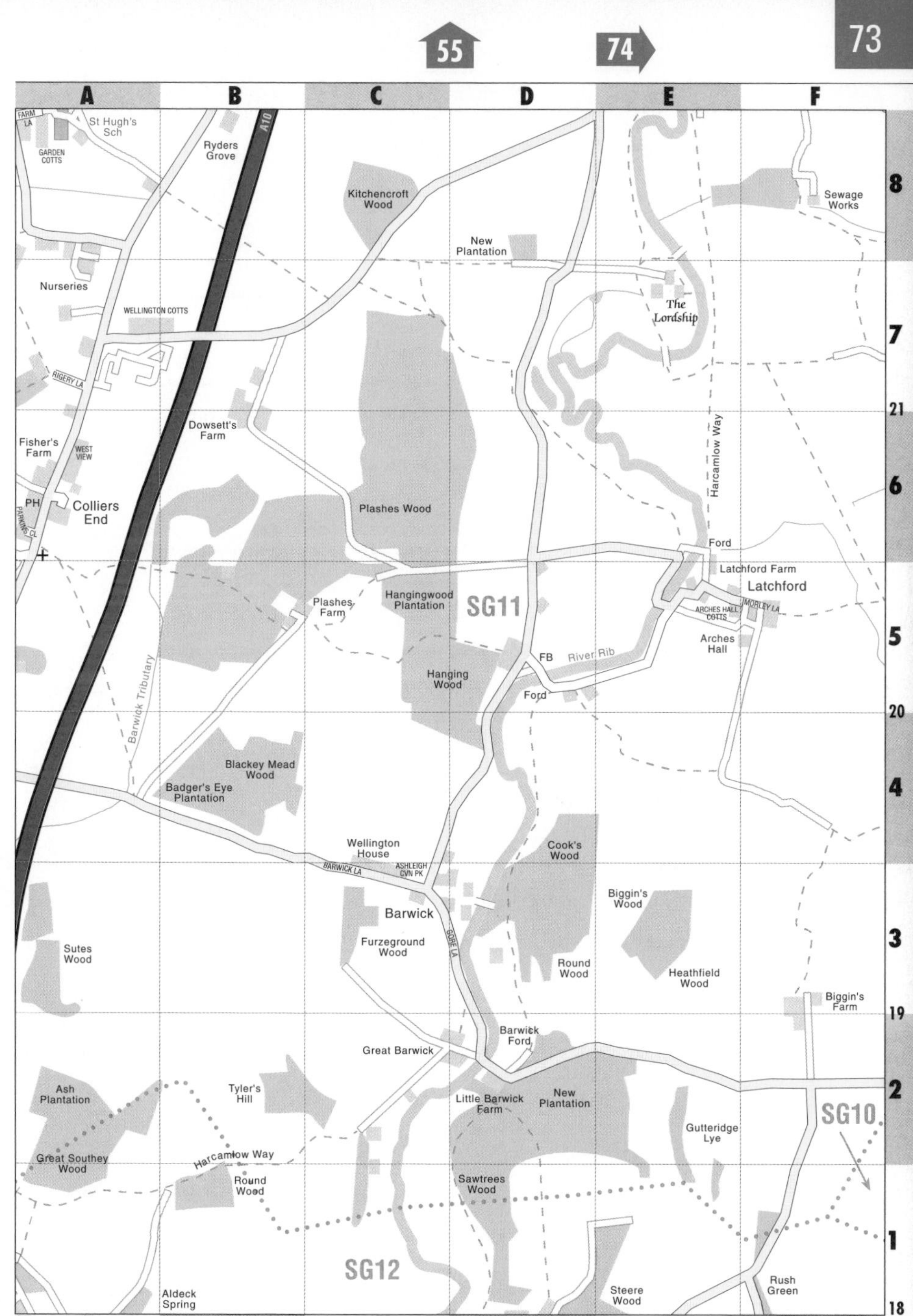
A
B
C
D
E
F
St Hugh's Sch
GARDEN COTTS
FARM LA
Ryders Grove
A10
Kitchencroft Wood
Sewage Works
New Plantation
Nurseries
WELLINGTON COTTS
The Lordship
RIGERY LA
Harcamlow Way
Dowsett's Farm
Fisher's Farm
WEST VIEW
PH
Colliers End
PARKINS CL
Plashes Wood
Ford
Latchford Farm
Latchford
Plashes Farm
Hangingwood Plantation
SG11
MORLEY LA
ARCHES HALL COTTS
Arches Hall
FB
River Rib
Hanging Wood
Ford
Barwick Tributary
Blackey Mead Wood
Badger's Eye Plantation
Wellington House
ASHLEIGH CVN PK
BARWICK LA
Cook's Wood
Biggin's Wood
Barwick
GORE LA
Furzeground Wood
Sutes Wood
Round Wood
Heathfield Wood
Biggin's Farm
Barwick Ford
Great Barwick
Ash Plantation
Tyler's Hill
Little Barwick Farm
New Plantation
SG10
Gutteridge Lye
Great Southey Wood
Harcamlow Way
Round Wood
Sawtrees Wood
SG12
Aldeck Spring
Steere Wood
Rush Green
8
7
21
6
5
20
4
3
19
2
1
18
37
38
39

94
74

73
56

A B C D E F
8
7
21
6
5
20
4
3
19
2
1
18
40 41 42
Alder Wood
Westfield Farm
Balsams
Bromley
Caley Wood
Little Balsams
Bowles Wood
Bromleyhall Farm
SG11
Damsel's Spring
Cambercroft Spring
The Wilderness
BROMLEY LA
CH
Standon Lodge Farm
Chaldean Farm
Rector's Springs
Vineyard Spring
Spindle Bridge
WINDING HILL
New Barns
NEW BARNS LA
Bartram's Wood
B1004
SG10
Much Hadham
THE SQUARE
HIGH ST
CHURCH LA
Cox La
The Bull Inn (PH)
PARK TERR
Brand's Farm
Moor Place
St Andrew's CE Prim Sch
Hertfordshire Way
TOWER HILL
OUDLE LA
Nimney Bourne
Blackcroft Farm
Hadham Cross
WALNUT CL
PO
ASH MDW
PH
MALTING LA
KETTLE GREEN RD
Old Hall Farm
CULVER CT
Nursery
BROADFIELD CL
BROADFIELD WAY
WIDFORD RD
Kettle Green Farm
WINDMILL WAY
LAURELDENE
MILLERS VIEW
STATION RD
Kettle Green
Moat Farm
SG12
B1004

73
95

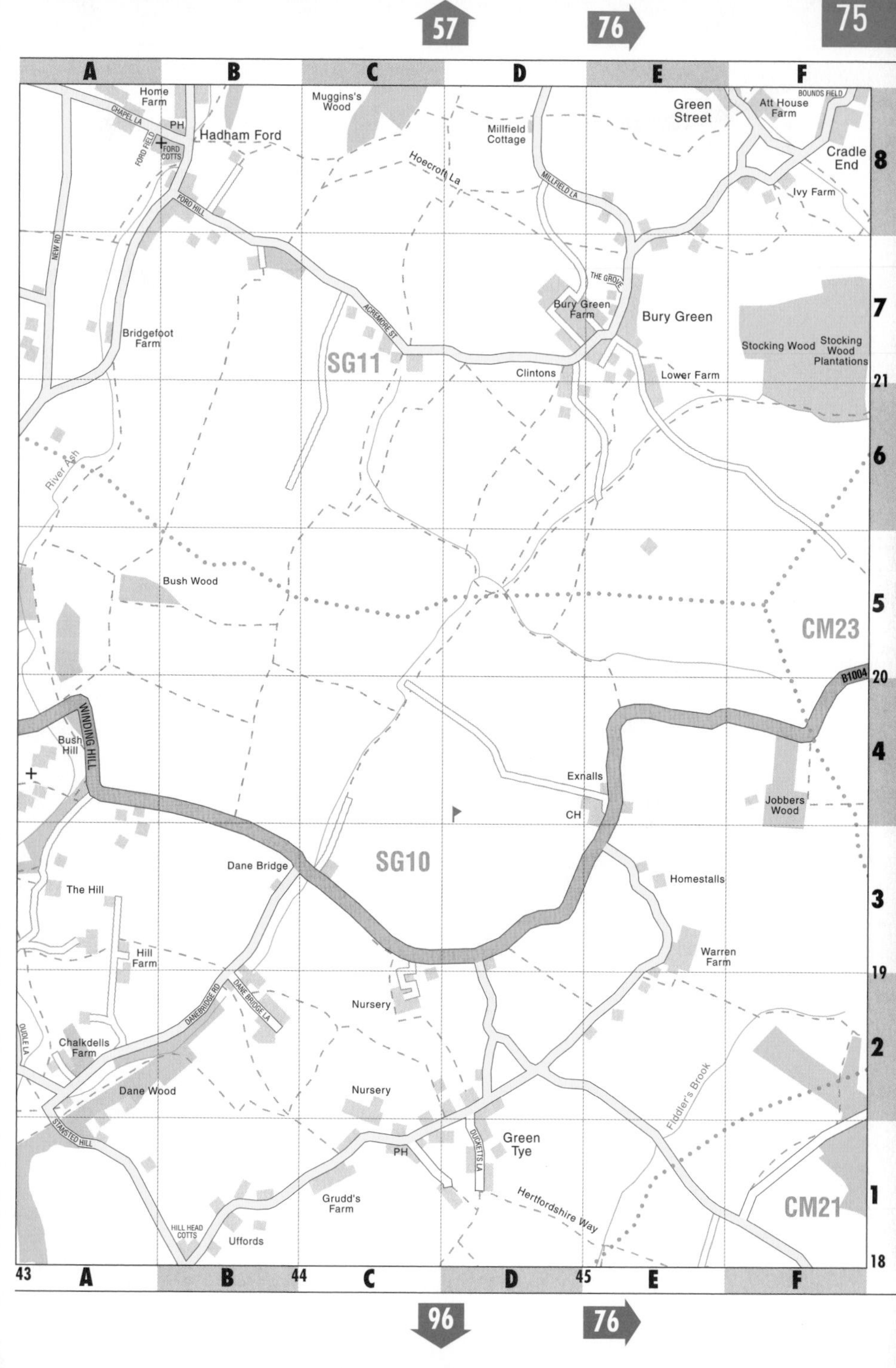
57
76
Home Farm
PH
Hadham Ford
Muggins's Wood
Millfield Cottage
Hoecroft La
Green Street
Att House Farm
BOUNDS FIELD
Cradle End
Ivy Farm
CHAPEL LA
FORD FIELD
FORD COTTS
FORD HILL
NEW RD
MILLFIELD LA
THE GROVE
ACREMORE ST
Bury Green Farm
Bury Green
Bridgefoot Farm
SG11
Clintons
Lower Farm
Stocking Wood
Stocking Wood Plantations
River Ash
Bush Wood
CM23
B1004
WINDING HILL
Bush Hill
Exnalls
CH
Jobbers Wood
Dane Bridge
SG10
Homestalls
The Hill
Hill Farm
Warren Farm
Nursery
DANEBRIDGE RD
DANE BRIDGE LA
OUDLE LA
Chalkdells Farm
Dane Wood
Nursery
Fiddler's Brook
STANSTED HILL
PH
DUCKETTS LA
Green Tye
Hertfordshire Way
Grudd's Farm
HILL HEAD COTTS
Uffords
CM21
A B C D E F
8 7 21 6 5 20 4 3 19 2 1 18
43 44 45
96
76

E5
1 BENHOOKS PL
2 MERRILL PL
3 BRITANNIA PL
4 MARGRAVE GDNS
5 OSBOURNE GDNS
6 SANDRINGHAM GDNS

F6
1 South St Commercial Ctr
2 SWAN CT
3 CHAPEL ROW
4 TUCKER'S ROW
5 MIDDLE ROW
6 ROYAL OAK GDNS

75

F6
7 APTON FIELDS
8 BARTHOLOMEW RD
9 STACEY CT
10 DUCKETTS WHARF
11 CYGNET CT
12 WHARF RD

58

F6
13 BRIDGEFORD HO
14 BOWLING CL
F7
1 KING STREET MEWS
2 BASBOW LA
3 SWORDERS YD
4 NORTH ST
5 BARRETT LA
6 MARKET SQ
7 MARKET ST
8 PALMERS LA
9 DEVOILS LA
10 JACKSON SQ
11 THE DELLS
12 MASTERMAN WHARF
13 DORSET HO
14 OAKTREE CL
15 NAILS LA
16 RIVERSIDE WLK
17 PORTLAND PL
18 VICARAGE CL
19 GROVE PL
20 SHERWOOD CT
21 CARELESS CT
F8
1 GALLOWAY CL
2 SQUIRRELS CL
3 BROOKHOUSE PL
4 ALPHA PL
5 NORTH TERR
6 THE CHANTRY
7 CONIFER CT
8 FLORENCE WLK

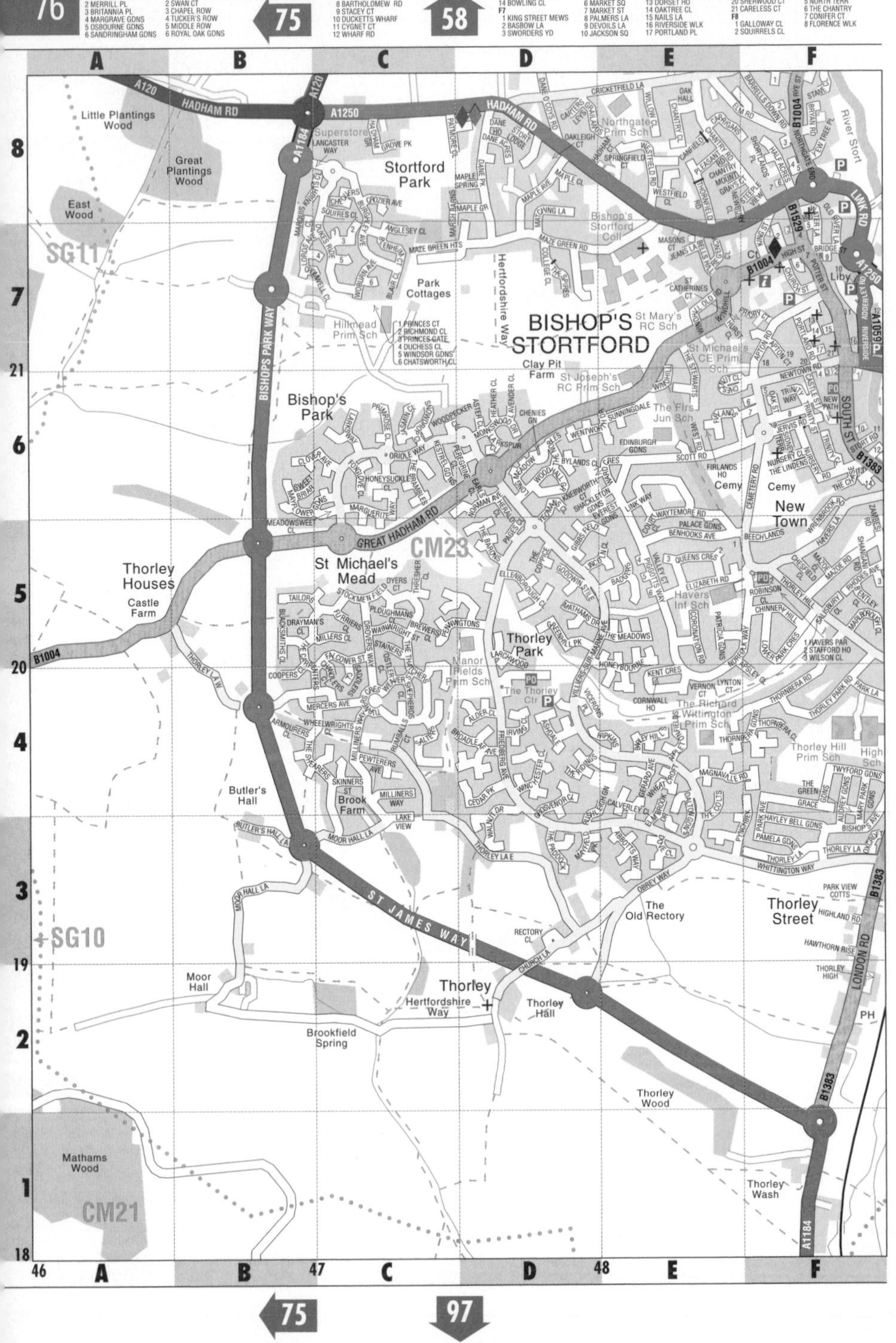

75
97

A7
1 THE CAUSEWAY
2 THE OLD MALTINGS
3 FULLER CT
4 LIMES CRES
5 RED LION CT
6 BAKERS CT
7 HOCKERILL CT
8 HARRINGTON CL
9 PRIORS
10 CLIFFORD CT
11 THOMAS HESKIN CT
12 THE PUMP HO

B8
1 BOYD CL
2 HEATH ROW
3 STORTFORD HALL RD
4 GROSVENOR HO
5 EATON HO
6 BELGRAVE HO

59

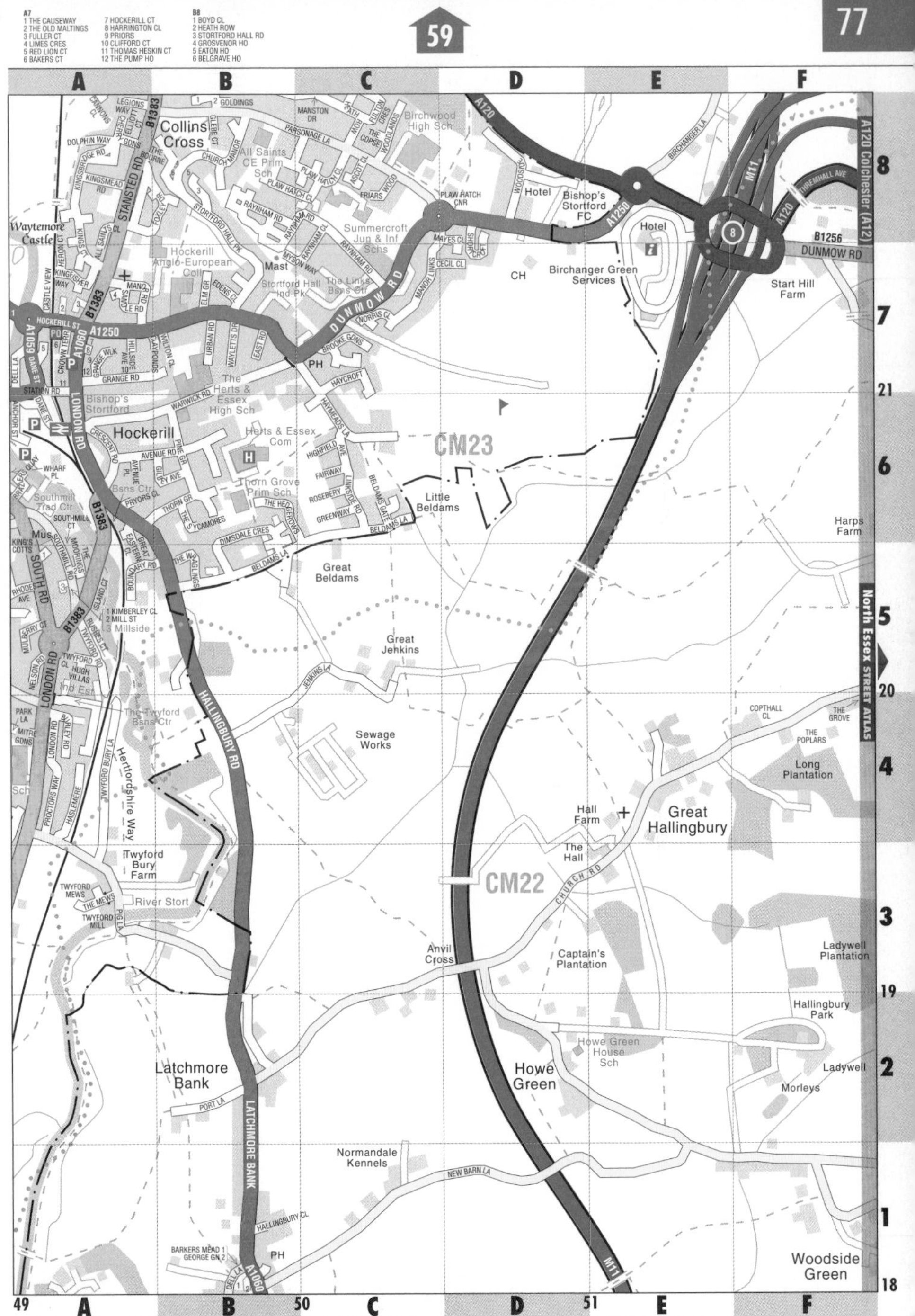

98

60

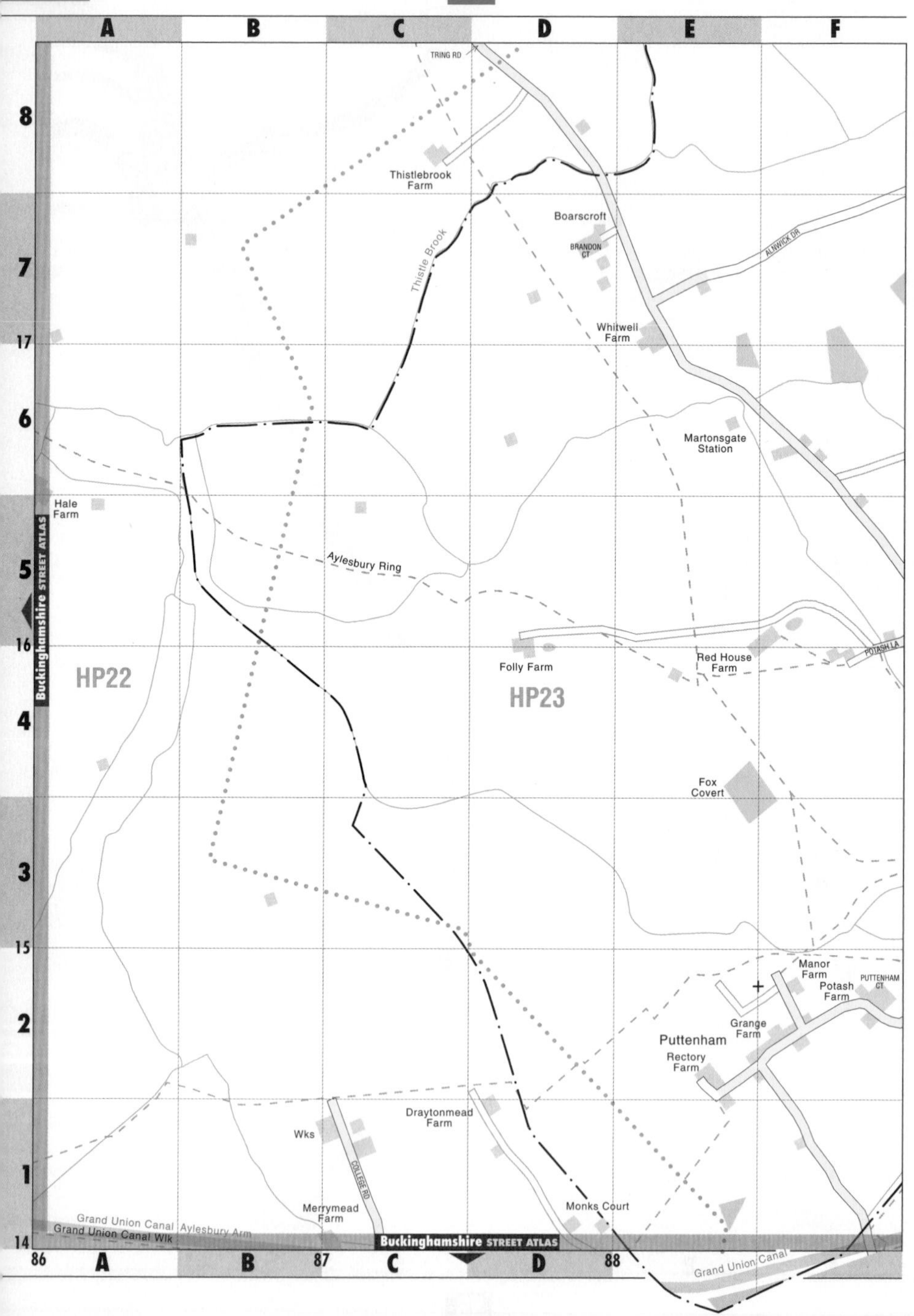

A
B
C
D
E
F
8
7
17
6
5
16
4
3
15
2
1
14
86
87
88
TRING RD
Thistlebrook Farm
Boarscroft
BRANDON CT
ALNWICK DR
Thistle Brook
Whitwell Farm
Martonsgate Station
Hale Farm
Aylesbury Ring
Buckinghamshire STREET ATLAS
HP22
Folly Farm
HP23
Red House Farm
POTASH LA
Fox Covert
Manor Farm
Potash Farm
PUTTENHAM CT
Grange Farm
Puttenham
Rectory Farm
Draytonmead Farm
Wks
COLLEGE RD
Merrymead Farm
Monks Court
Grand Union Canal Aylesbury Arm
Grand Union Canal Wlk
Grand Union Canal

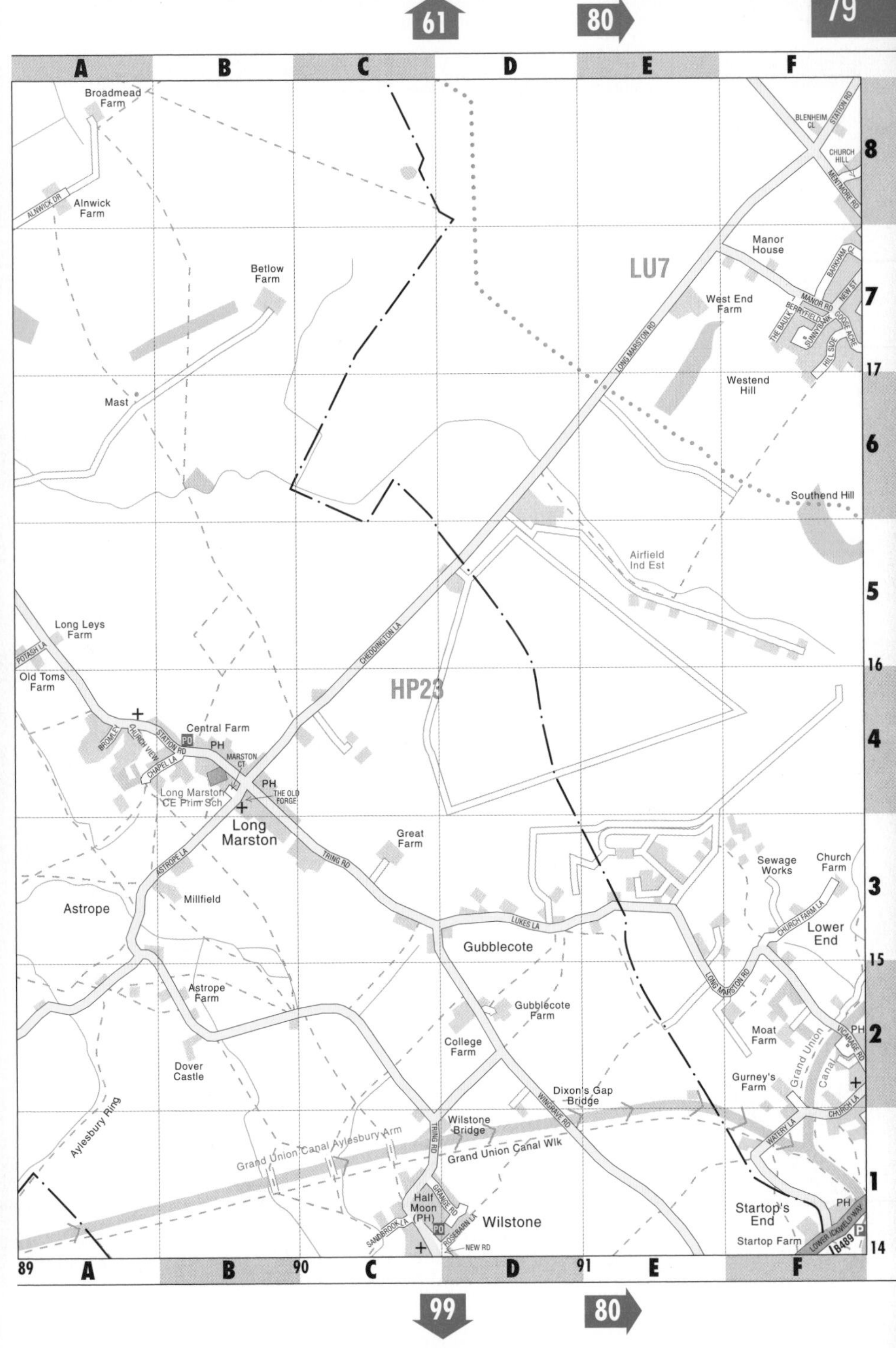
61
80
A
B
C
D
E
F
Broadmead Farm
Alnwick Farm
ALNWICK DR
Betlow Farm
Mast
LU7
BLENHEIM CL
STATION RD
CHURCH HILL
MENTMORE RD
Manor House
BARKHAM CL
West End Farm
MANOR RD
NEW ST
BERRYFIELD
THE BAULK
SUNNYBANK
GOOSE ACRE
HILL SIDE
LONG MARSTON RD
Westend Hill
Southend Hill
Airfield Ind Est
Long Leys Farm
POTASH LA
Old Toms Farm
CHEDDINGTON LA
HP23
Central Farm
PO
PH
BROMLEY
CHURCH VIEW
STATION RD
CHAPEL LA
MARSTON CT
THE OLD FORGE
Long Marston CE Prim Sch
Long Marston
ASTROPE LA
Great Farm
TRING RD
Astrope
Millfield
LUKES LA
Gubblecote
Sewage Works
Church Farm
CHURCH FARM LA
Lower End
LONG MARSTON RD
Astrope Farm
Gubblecote Farm
Moat Farm
Grand Union Canal
VICARAGE RD
Dover Castle
College Farm
Gurney's Farm
Dixon's Gap Bridge
WINGRAVE RD
CHURCH LA
Aylesbury Ring
Wilstone Bridge
TRING RD
Grand Union Canal Aylesbury Arm
Grand Union Canal Wlk
WATERY LA
Half Moon (PH)
GRANGE RD
SANDBROOK LA
ROSEBARN LA
NEW RD
Wilstone
Startop's End
Startop Farm
LOWER ICKNIELD WAY
B489
8
7
17
6
5
16
4
3
15
2
1
14
89
90
91
99
80

79

Buckinghamshire STREET ATLAS
Cheddington
Elsage House
Church Hill Farm
1 PAINES ORCH
2 ASHLEY CL
3 HORSESHOE CL
4 CHASESIDE CL
5 BARKHAM CL
6 LODGE CL
Cheddington Comb Sch
Vicarage Farm
Ivinghoe Bridge
Whistle Brook
Little Seabrook Farm
Seabrook Locks
The Old Swan (PH)
Falcon House
Great Seabrook Farm
Grand Union Canal Wlk
Grand Union Canal
Great Seabrook
Greatgap
Sewage Works
Ford End Farm
Yardley Farm
LU7
Brookmead Sch
Ivinghoe
STATION RD
HIGH ST
B489
B488
Liby
CH
TH
YH
PH
Brook End
Middle Path Farm
CHEDDINGTON RD
MARSWORTH RD
Pitstone
Pitstone Green Farm Mus
Pitstone Windmill
Pitstonegreen Farm
Church End
Moat Farm
VICARAGE RD
WHITEHILL LA
Manor Farm
HP23
Town Field Farm
Marsworth CE Inf Sch
College Farm
College Lake Wildlife Ctr
Chalk Pit
LOWER ICKNIELD WAY
UPPER ICKNIELD WAY
Marsworth
Manor House Farm
Folly Farm
Pitstone Hill
Ridgeway
92
93
94
A
B
C
D
E
F
8
7
17
6
5
16
4
3
15
2
1
14

79
100

82

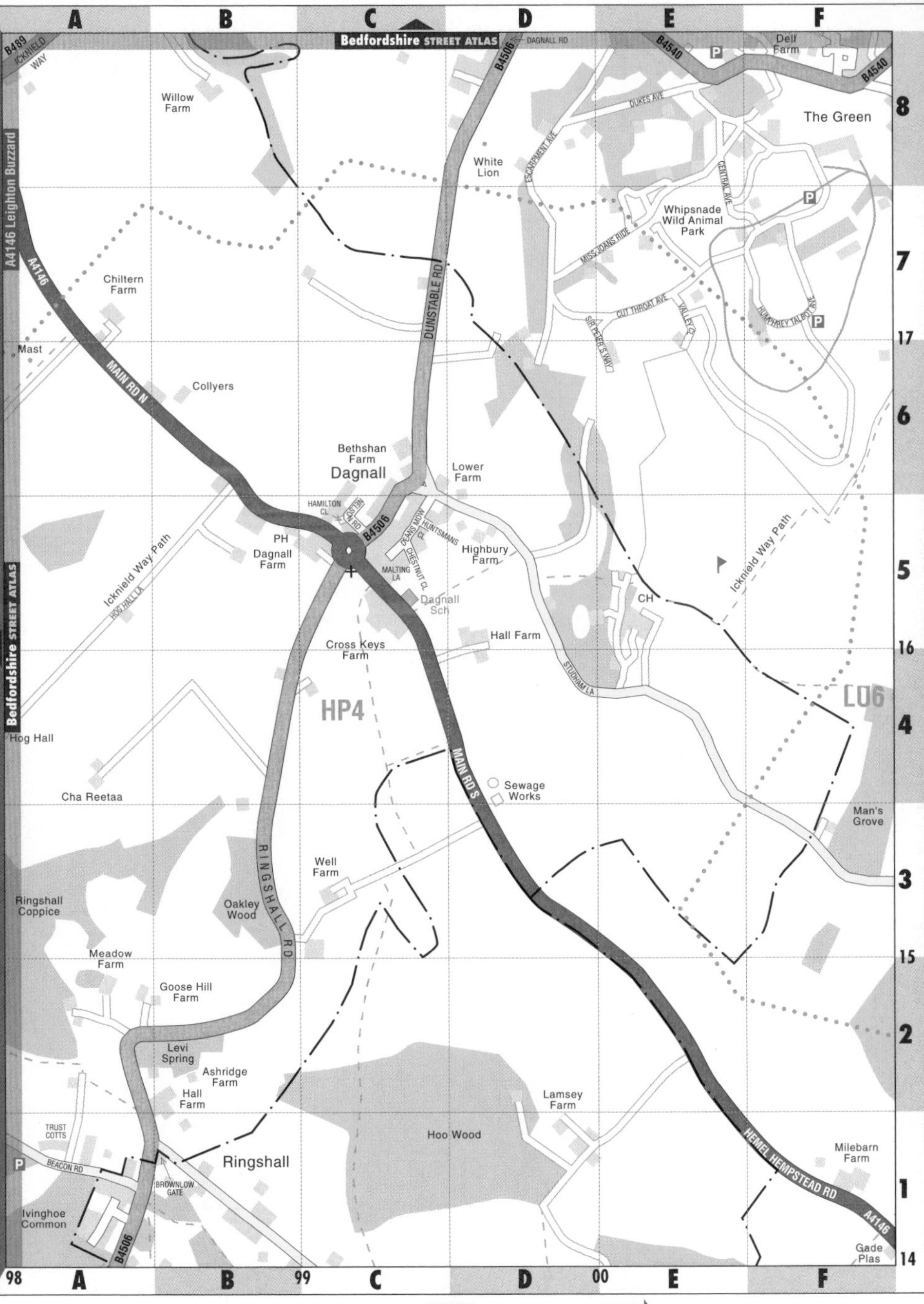

A
B
C
D
E
F
Bedfordshire STREET ATLAS
DAGNALL RD
B489
ICKNIELD WAY
B4506
B4540
Dell Farm
The Green
Willow Farm
DUKES AVE
ESCARPMENT AVE
CENTRAL AVE
White Lion
Whipsnade Wild Animal Park
MISS JOANS RIDE
A4146 Leighton Buzzard
A4146
Chiltern Farm
DUNSTABLE RD
CUT THROAT AVE
VALLEY CL
SIR PETER'S WAY
HUMPHREY TALBOT AVE
Mast
MAIN RD N
Collyers
Bethshan Farm
Dagnall
Lower Farm
HAMILTON CL
NELSON RD
DEANS MDW
HUNTSMANS CL
CHESTNUT CL
MALTING LA
PH
Dagnall Farm
Highbury Farm
Icknield Way Path
HOG HALL LA
Dagnall Sch
CH
Cross Keys Farm
Hall Farm
STUDHAM LA
HP4
LU6
Bedfordshire STREET ATLAS
Hog Hall
MAIN RD S
Sewage Works
Cha Reetaa
RINGSHALL RD
Man's Grove
Well Farm
Ringshall Coppice
Oakley Wood
Meadow Farm
Goose Hill Farm
Levi Spring
Ashridge Farm
Hall Farm
Lamsey Farm
TRUST COTTS
Hoo Wood
HEMEL HEMPSTEAD RD
Milebarn Farm
BEACON RD
Ringshall
BROWNLOW GATE
Ivinghoe Common
Gade Plas
8
7
17
6
5
16
4
3
15
2
1
14
98
99
00

102

82

81

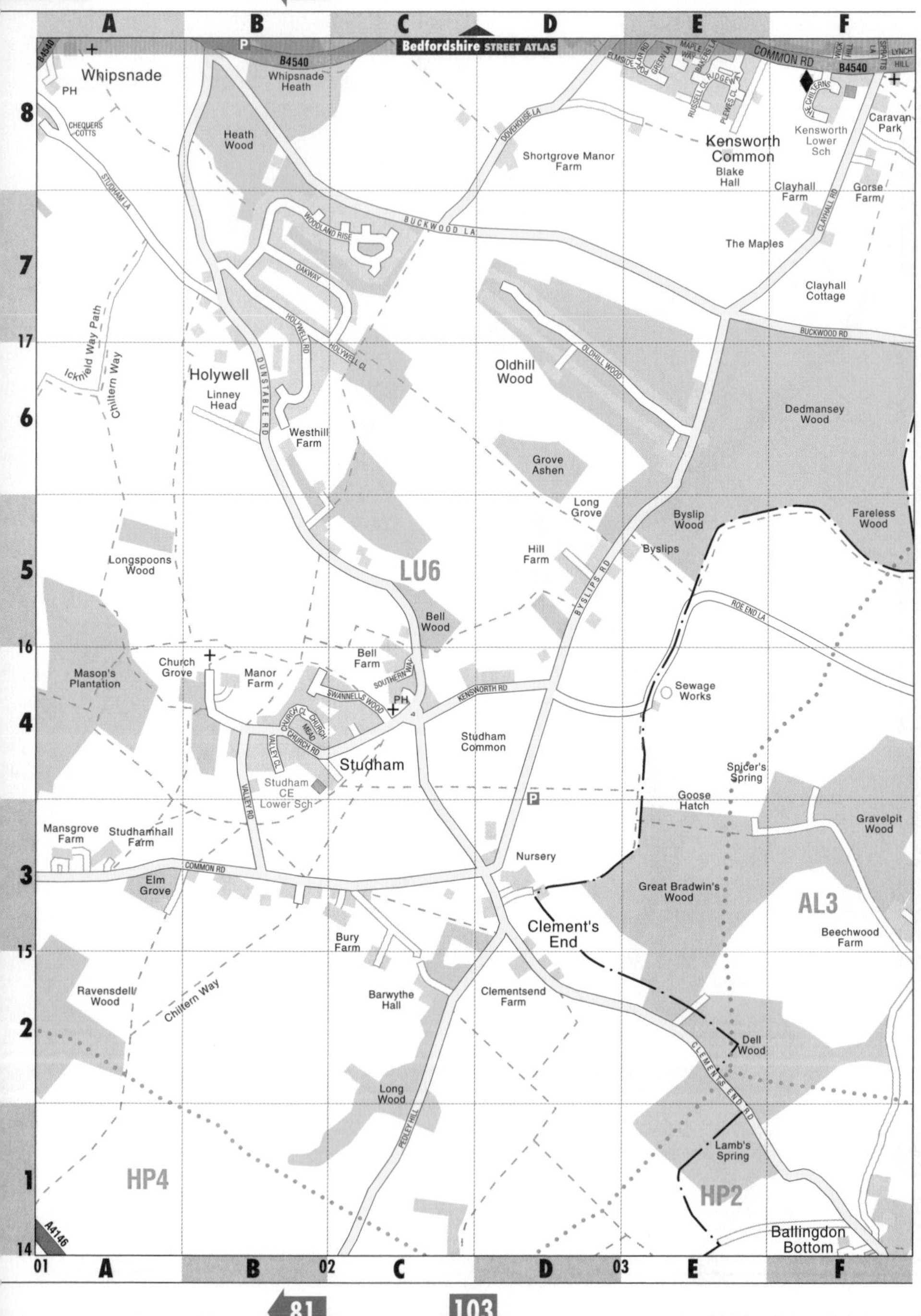
Bedfordshire STREET ATLAS
Whipsnade
PH
CHEQUERS COTTS
Whipsnade Heath
B4540
Heath Wood
STUDHAM LA
DOVEHOUSE LA
Shortgrove Manor Farm
Kensworth Common
Kensworth Lower Sch
Caravan Park
Blake Hall
Clayhall Farm
Gorse Farm
COMMON RD
B4540
THE CHILTERNS
ELMSIDE
POPLAR RD
GREEN LA
MAPLE WAY
BAKERS LA
RIDGEWAY
RUSSELL CL
PLEWES CL
WICK HILL
LA
SPRATTS
LYNCH HILL
CLAYHALL RD
The Maples
WOODLAND RISE
BUCKWOOD LA
OAKWAY
HOLYWELL RD
HOLYWELL CL
Clayhall Cottage
BUCKWOOD RD
Icknield Way Path
Chiltern Way
Holywell
Linney Head
DUNSTABLE RD
Westhill Farm
Oldhill Wood
OLDHILL WOOD
Dedmansey Wood
Grove Ashen
Long Grove
Byslip Wood
Fareless Wood
Byslips
Hill Farm
Longspoons Wood
LU6
BYSLIPS RD
ROE END LA
Bell Wood
Bell Farm
SOUTHERN WAY
Mason's Plantation
Church Grove
Manor Farm
SWANNELLS WOOD
PH
KENSWORTH RD
Sewage Works
CHURCH CL
CHURCH MEAD
CHURCH RD
VALLEY CL
Studham
Studham Common
Studham CE Lower Sch
Spicer's Spring
Goose Hatch
VALLEY RD
P
Mansgrove Farm
Studhamhall Farm
Gravelpit Wood
Nursery
COMMON RD
Elm Grove
Great Bradwin's Wood
AL3
Clement's End
Bury Farm
Beechwood Farm
Ravensdell Wood
Chiltern Way
Barwythe Hall
Clementsend Farm
Dell Wood
CLEMENTS END RD
Long Wood
PEDLEY HILL
Lamb's Spring
HP4
HP2
A4146
Ballingdon Bottom
A B C D E F
8 7 17 6 5 16 4 3 15 2 1 14
01 02 03

81

103

84

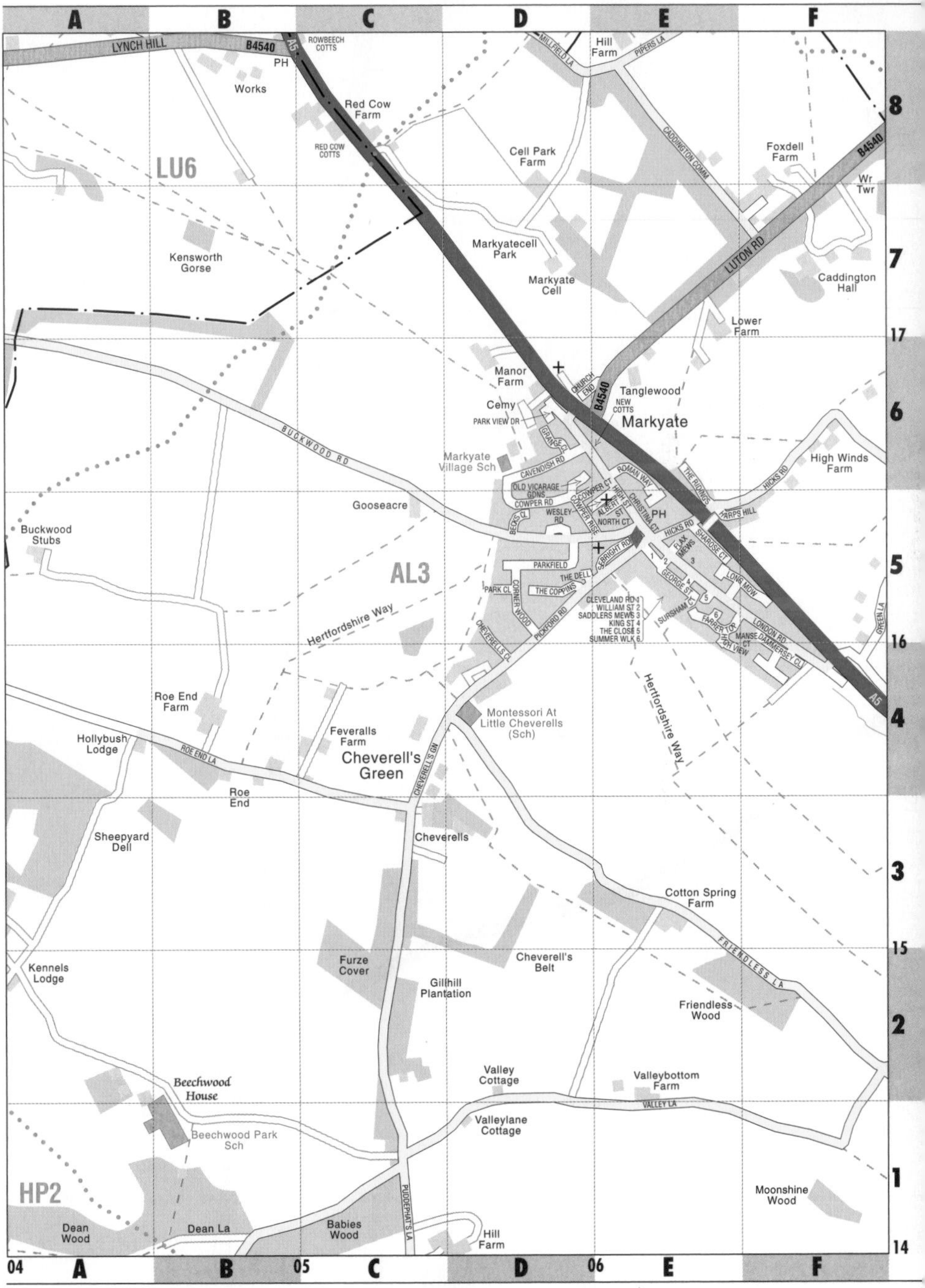

A B C D E F

Lynch Hill
B4540
A5
Rowbeech Cotts
PH
Works
Red Cow Farm
Red Cow Cotts
LU6
Millfield La
Hill Farm
Pipers La
Cell Park Farm
Caddington Comm
Foxdell Farm
B4540
Wr Twr
Kensworth Gorse
Markyatecell Park
Markyate Cell
Luton Rd
Caddington Hall
Lower Farm
Manor Farm
Church End
B4540
Tanglewood
New Cotts
Cemy
Park View Dr
Markyate
Buckwood Rd
Grange Cl
Markyate Village Sch
Cavendish Rd
Roman Way
The Ridings
Hicks Rd
High Winds Farm
Old Vicarage Gdns
Cowper Ct
Cowper Rd
Cowper Rise
Albert St
High St
Christina Ct
PH
Harps Hill
Gooseacre
Becks Cl
Wesley Rd
North Ct
Hicks Rd
Sharose Ct
Flax Mews
Buckwood Stubs
Parkfield
Sebright Rd
AL3
The Dell
George St
Long Mdw
Park Cl
Corner Wood
The Coppins
Cleveland Rd 1
William St 2
Saddlers Mews 3
King St 4
The Close 5
Summer Wlk 6
Sursham Ct
Farrer Top
Manse Ct
London Rd
Dammersey Cl
High View
Green La
Hertfordshire Way
Pickford Rd
Cheverells Cl
Hertfordshire Way
A5
Roe End Farm
Montessori At Little Cheverells (Sch)
Hollybush Lodge
Feveralls Farm
Roe End La
Cheverell's Green
Cheverell's Gn
Roe End
Sheepyard Dell
Cheverells
Cotton Spring Farm
Friendless La
Kennels Lodge
Furze Cover
Cheverell's Belt
Gillhill Plantation
Friendless Wood
Beechwood House
Valley Cottage
Valleybottom Farm
Valley La
Valleylane Cottage
Beechwood Park Sch
HP2
Moonshine Wood
Puddephat's La
Dean Wood
Dean La
Babies Wood
Hill Farm

8 7 17 6 5 16 4 3 15 2 1 14

04 A B 05 C D 06 E F

104

84

83
63

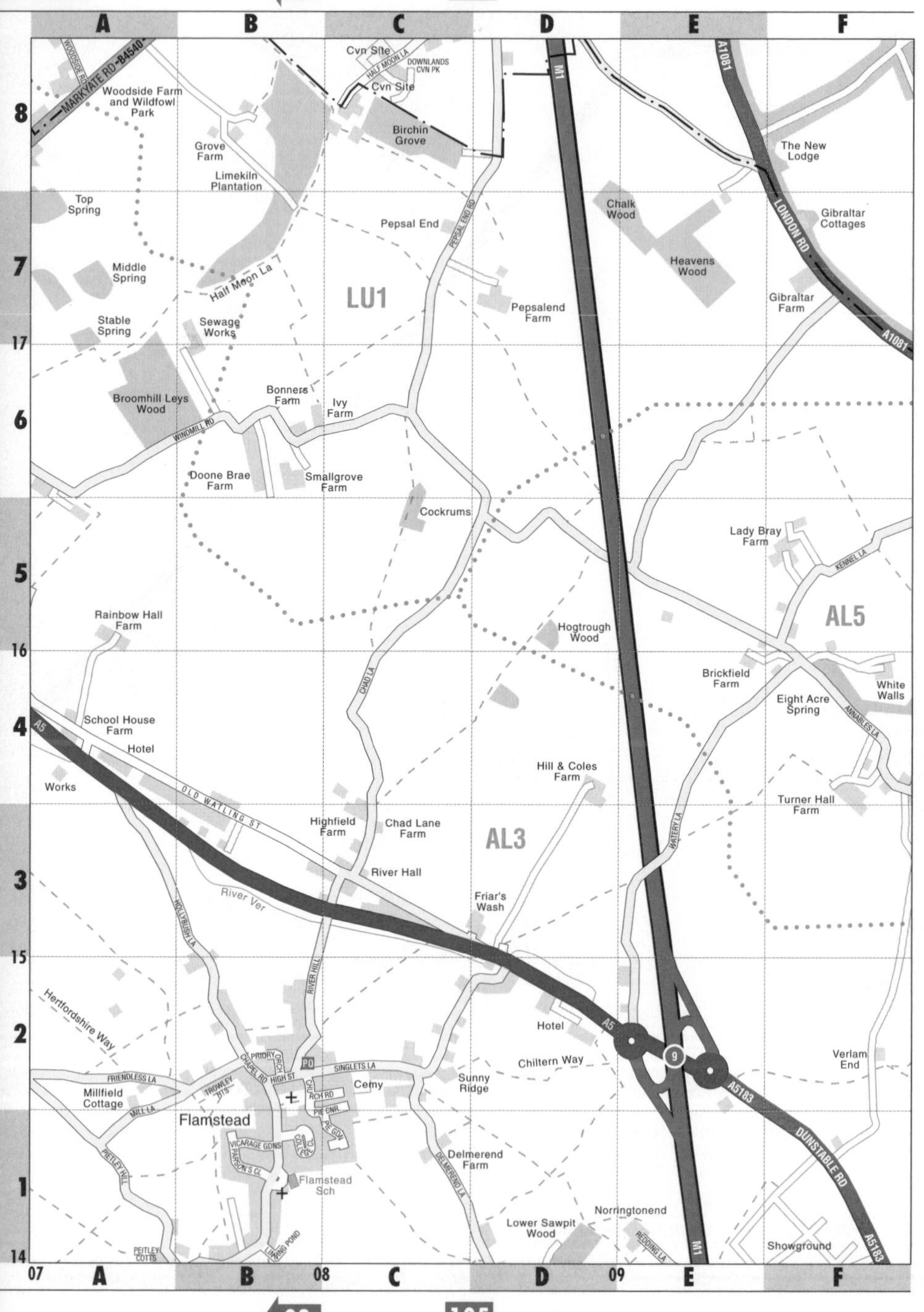
A
B
C
D
E
F
8
7
17
6
5
16
4
3
15
2
1
14
07
08
09
Woodside Farm and Wildfowl Park
MARKYATE RD-B4540
WOODSIDE RD
Cvn Site
HALF MOON LA
DOWNLANDS CVN PK
Cvn Site
Birchin Grove
Grove Farm
Limekiln Plantation
Top Spring
Pepsal End
PEPSAL END RD
M1
A1081
The New Lodge
Chalk Wood
LONDON RD
Gibraltar Cottages
Heavens Wood
Middle Spring
Half Moon La
LU1
Pepsalend Farm
Gibraltar Farm
Stable Spring
Sewage Works
Broomhill Leys Wood
Bonners Farm
Ivy Farm
WINDMILL RD
Doone Brae Farm
Smallgrove Farm
Cockrums
Lady Bray Farm
KENNEL LA
AL5
Rainbow Hall Farm
Hogtrough Wood
Brickfield Farm
Eight Acre Spring
White Walls
CHAD LA
ANNABLES LA
School House Farm
A5
Hotel
Works
Hill & Coles Farm
Turner Hall Farm
OLD WATLING ST
Highfield Farm
Chad Lane Farm
AL3
WATERY LA
River Hall
River Ver
Friar's Wash
HOLLYBUSH LA
RIVER HILL
Hertfordshire Way
Hotel
Chiltern Way
9
Verlam End
PRIORY
ORCH
CHAPEL RD
HIGH ST
PO
SINGLETS LA
FRIENDLESS LA
TROWLEY HILL
CHURCH RD
Cemy
Sunny Ridge
Millfield Cottage
MILL LA
PIE CNR
PIE GDN
A5183
Flamstead
VICARAGE GDNS
PARSON'S CL
COLLEGE CL
DUNSTABLE RD
PIETLEY HILL
Delmerend Farm
DELMEREND LA
Flamstead Sch
Norringtonend
Lower Sawpit Wood
REDDING LA
Showground
PEITLEY COTTS
LYBURY POND

83
105

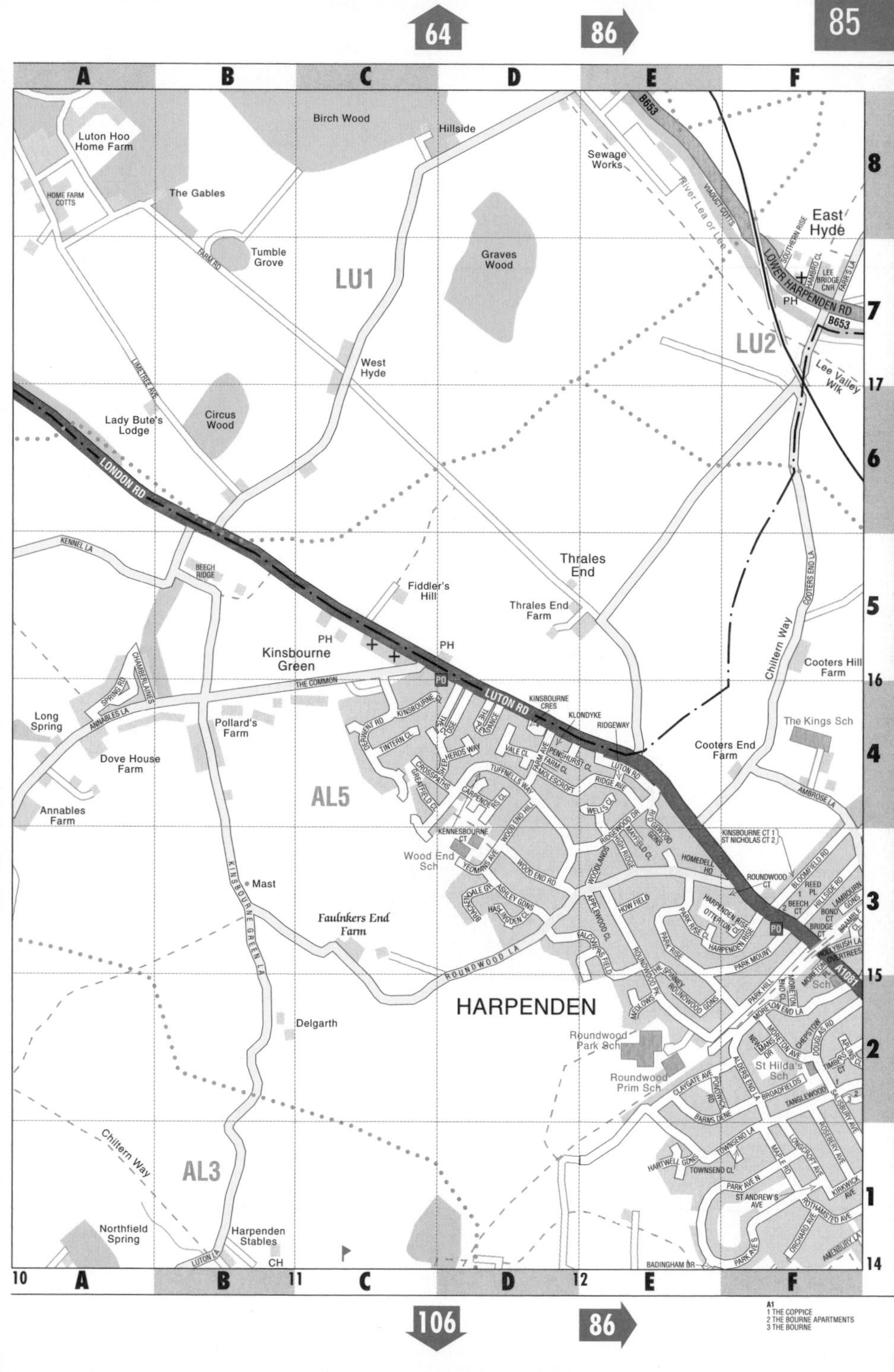

85
64
86
A
B
C
D
E
F
Birch Wood
Hillside
Luton Hoo
Home Farm
HOME FARM
COTTS
The Gables
Tumble
Grove
FARM RD
LU1
Graves
Wood
Sewage
Works
B653
River Lea or Lee
VIADUCT COTTS
East
Hyde
SOUTHERN RISE
HAMBRO CL
LEE
BRIDGE
CNR
FARR'S LA
LOWER HARPENDEN RD
PH
B653
LU2
Lee Valley
Wlk
West
Hyde
LIMETREE AVE
Lady Bute's
Lodge
Circus
Wood
LONDON RD
KENNEL LA
BEECH
RIDGE
Thrales
End
Fiddler's
Hill
Thrales End
Farm
PH
PH
Kinsbourne
Green
COOTERS END LA
Chiltern Way
Cooters Hill
Farm
CHAMBERLAINES
SPRING RD
THE COMMON
Long
Spring
ANNABLES LA
Pollard's
Farm
DERWENT RD
KINSBOURNE CL
TINTERN CL
THE CLOSE
THE PARADE
LUTON RD
KINSBOURNE
CRES
KLONDYKE
RIDGEWAY
The Kings Sch
Cooters End
Farm
Dove House
Farm
HERDS WAY
VALE CL
FARM AVE
PENSHURST CL
LUTON RD
CROSSPATHS
GREATFIELD CL
TUFFNELLS WAY
FARM CL
MOLESCROFT
RIDGE AVE
AMBROSE LA
AL5
CARPENDERS CL
WOOD END HILL
WELLS CL
Annables
Farm
KENNESBOURNE
CT
RIDGEWOOD DR
MAYFIELD CL
RIDGEWOOD
GDNS
KINSBOURNE CT 1
ST NICHOLAS CT 2
Wood End
Sch
YEOMANS AVE
WOOD END RD
WOODLANDS
HIGH RIDGE
HOMEDELL
HO
BLOOMFIELD RD
ROUNDWOOD
CT
REED
PL
HILLSIDE RD
KINSBOURNE GREEN LA
Mast
DALE GR
ASHLEY GDNS
HASLINGDEN CL
APPLEWOOD CL
HOW FIELD
HARPENDEN RISE
OTTERTON CL
PARK RISE CL
BEECH
CT
LAMBOURN
GDNS
BOND
CT
BRIDGE
CT
BRAMBLE
CL
Faulnkers End
Farm
PARK RISE
HARPENDEN RISE
PD
HOLLYBUSH LA
OVERTREES
ROUNDWOOD LA
FALCONERS FIELD
ROUNDWOOD PK
THE SPINNEY
ROUNDWOOD GDNS
PARK MOUNT
A1081
PARK HILL
MORETON END CL
MORETON
Sch
HARPENDEN
MEDLOWS
MORETON END LA
Delgarth
Roundwood
Park Sch
Roundwood
Prim Sch
NEWLANDS
MANS
DR
MORETON AVE
CHEPSTOW
DOUGLAS RD
St Hilda's
Sch
TIMBERS
CT
CLAYGATE AVE
POWDICH
RD
ALDERS END LA
BROADFIELDS
TANGLEWOOD
SALISBURY AVE
BARNS DENE
Chiltern Way
TOWNSEND LA
MAPLE RD
LONGCROFT AVE
ROSEBERY AVE
AL3
HARTWELL GDNS
TOWNSEND CL
PARK AVE N
KIRKWICK
AVE
ST ANDREW'S
AVE
ROTHAMSTED AVE
ORCHARD AVE
Northfield
Spring
Harpenden
Stables
LUTON LA
CH
BADINGHAM DR
PARK AVE S
AMENBURY LA
8
7
17
6
5
16
4
3
15
2
1
14
10
11
12
106
86
A1
1 THE COPPICE
2 THE BOURNE APARTMENTS
3 THE BOURNE

85
65

A B C D E F

Chiltern Way
Hyde Home Farm
Garden Wood
The Hyde
Home Wood
Little Cutts Farm
Hill Farm
Bishey Wood
Tallents Farm
SG4
B652
East Hyde Park
Dane Farm
LU2
B653
LOWER HARPENDEN RD
KIMPTON BOTTOM
Animal Welfare Centre
Dane Spring
Ladies Spring
Hyde Mill Farm
Broadlands
Wall Wood
Bower Heath Farm
Holly Farm
HOLLY LA
Old Raisins Farm
BOWER HEATH LA
Bower Heath
KINGS HEATH PK
THE SLYPE
SAUNCEY WOOD LA
River Lea or Lee
Lea Valley Wlk
COMMON LA
AL5
Turners Hall Farm
Cold Harbour
Westfield Wood
1 RIVERBANKS CL
2 BARLEY RISE
3 ST MARTINS CL
Sauncey Wood
The Lea Prim Sch
Cemy
Sauncey Wood Prim Sch
Mackerye End
Mackerye End Farm
Harpenden (private)
ST JAMES'S CT 1
CLARENDON CT 2
Riverside Est
Allied Bsns Ctr
LOWER LUTON RD
Manland Prim Sch
Sir John Lawes Sch
Batford
LEACROFT
MARTHAM CT
Lea Valley
St George's Sch
HARPENDEN
Ford
MANOR RD
LOWER LUTON RD
MARSHALLS WAY
A1081
LUTON RD
Harpenden Memorial
STATION RD
AL4
B653
Sewage Works
Lea Valley Wlk
Crabtree Inf Sch
1 DALEWOOD
2 FAIRFIELD CL
3 ENGLEHURST
HIGH ST
Liby
Coll
Piggottshill Wood
James Marshall Commercial Ctr
Harpenden
SOUTHDOWN RD
High Beeches Prim Sch
CH
ST ALBANS RD
LEASEY BRIDGE LA

13 A B 14 C D 15 E F

A2
1 LYDEKKER MEWS
2 GERARD CT
3 CORNELIA CT
4 HARDENWICK CT
5 SOUTHGATE CT
6 BERKELEY CT
7 FERNDALE
8 ANVIL HO

B1
1 CARLTON CT
2 CARLTON BANK
3 THE MEWS
4 CROFT CT
5 DEVONSHIRE RD
6 KINLOCH CT
7 VICTORIA RD
8 HARDING PAR
9 COLERIDGE CT

B1
10 BEAUMONT CT
11 COPPER BEECHES
12 MILTON CT
13 THE CEDARS
14 YARDLEY CT
15 KEATS HO
16 SHELLEY CT
17 AVON CT
18 FURZEDOWN CT
19 CHILTERN CT
20 HADDON CT

85
107

66
88

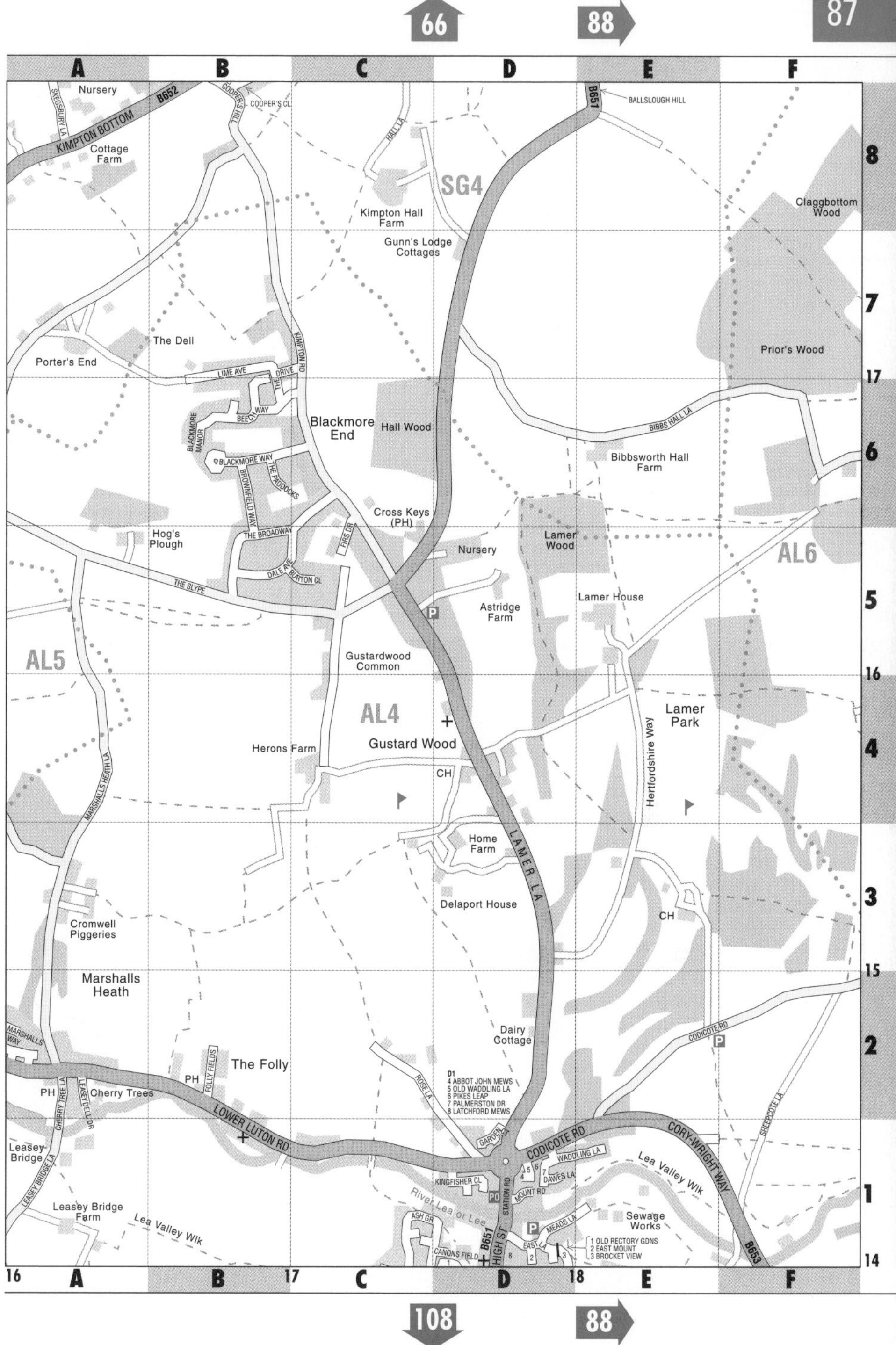
A
B
C
D
E
F
8
7
17
6
5
16
4
3
15
2
1
14
16
17
18
Nursery
SKEGSBURY LA
B652
KIMPTON BOTTOM
COOPER'S HILL
COOPER'S CL
B651
BALLSLOUGH HILL
HALL LA
Cottage Farm
SG4
Kimpton Hall Farm
Gunn's Lodge Cottages
Claggbottom Wood
Prior's Wood
The Dell
Porter's End
KIMPTON RD
LIME AVE
THE DRIVE
BEECH WAY
BLACKMORE MANOR
Blackmore End
Hall Wood
BIBBS HALL LA
BLACKMORE WAY
BROWNFIELD WAY
THE PADDOCKS
Bibbsworth Hall Farm
Cross Keys (PH)
Hog's Plough
FIRS DR
THE BROADWAY
Nursery
Lamer Wood
AL6
DALE AVE
BURTON CL
THE SLYPE
Astridge Farm
Lamer House
P
AL5
Gustardwood Common
AL4
Lamer Park
Herons Farm
Gustard Wood
Hertfordshire Way
CH
MARSHALLS HEATH LA
Home Farm
LAMER LA
Delaport House
CH
Cromwell Piggeries
Marshalls Heath
Dairy Cottage
CODICOTE RD
P
MARSHALLS WAY
The Folly
PH
FOLLY FIELDS
D1
4 ABBOT JOHN MEWS
5 OLD WADDLING LA
6 PIKES LEAP
7 PALMERSTON DR
8 LATCHFORD MEWS
ROSE LA
SHEEPCOTE LA
PH
CHERRY TREE LA
LEASEY DELL DR
Cherry Trees
LOWER LUTON RD
GARDEN CT
CODICOTE RD
CORY-WRIGHT WAY
WADDLING LA
Lea Valley Wlk
Leasey Bridge
DAWES LA
KINGFISHER CL
STATION RD
MOUNT RD
PO
River Lea or Lee
LEASEY BRIDGE LA
Leasey Bridge Farm
ASH GR
Sewage Works
MEADS LA
Lea Valley Wlk
B651
HIGH ST
EAST LA
CANONS FIELD
1 OLD RECTORY GDNS
2 EAST MOUNT
3 BROCKET VIEW
B653

108
88

87
67

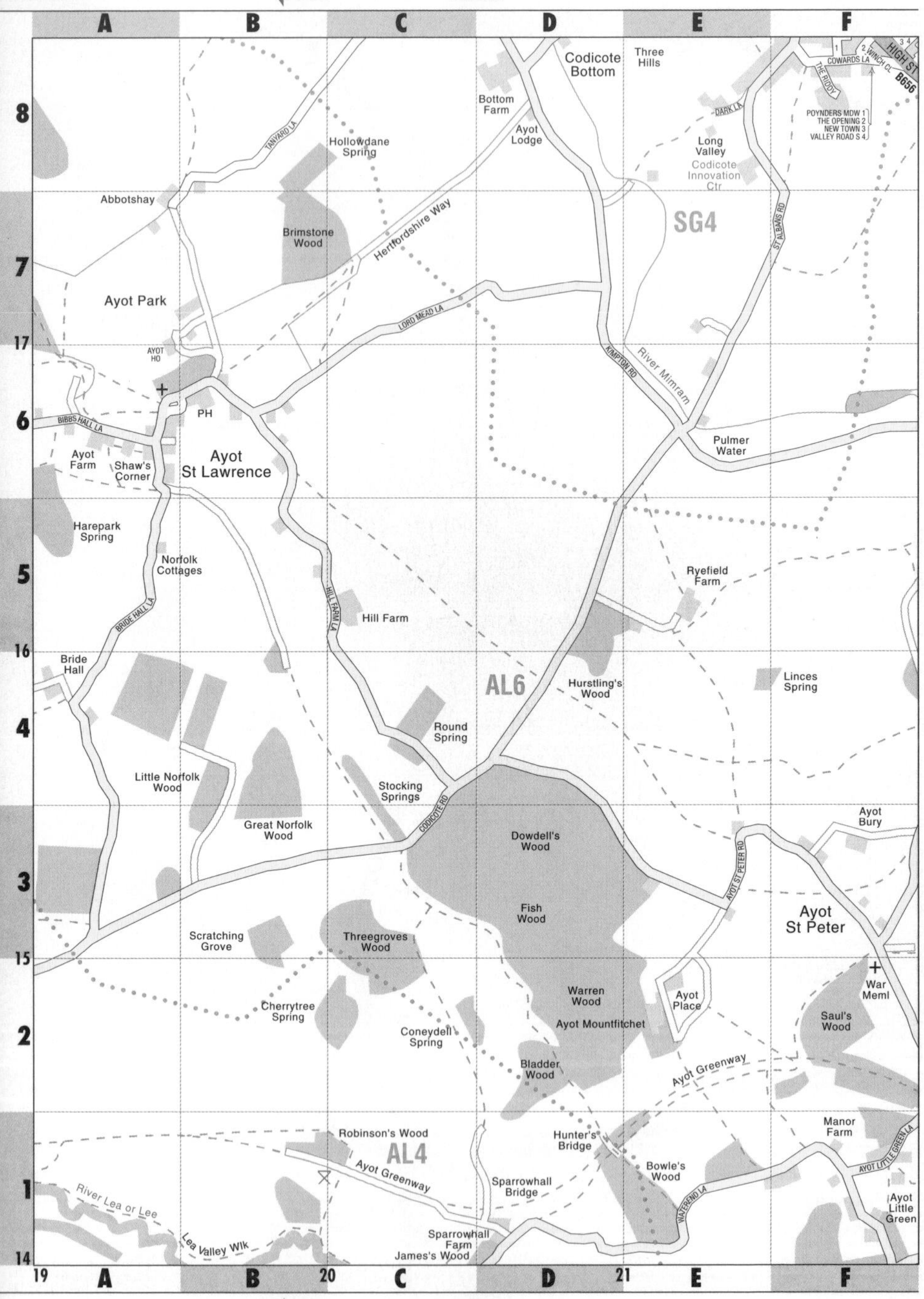
A
B
C
D
E
F
Codicote Bottom
Three Hills
COWARDS LA
WINCH CL
HIGH ST
THE RIDDY
B656
DARK LA
POYNDERS MDW 1
THE OPENING 2
NEW TOWN 3
VALLEY ROAD S 4
Bottom Farm
Ayot Lodge
TANYARD LA
Hollowdane Spring
Long Valley
Codicote Innovation Ctr
Abbotshay
Brimstone Wood
Hertfordshire Way
SG4
ST ALBANS RD
Ayot Park
LORD MEAD LA
AYOT HO
KIMPTON RD
River Mimram
PH
BIBBS HALL LA
Ayot Farm
Shaw's Corner
Ayot St Lawrence
Pulmer Water
Harepark Spring
Norfolk Cottages
Ryefield Farm
HILL FARM LA
Hill Farm
BRIDE HALL LA
Bride Hall
AL6
Hurstling's Wood
Linces Spring
Round Spring
Little Norfolk Wood
Stocking Springs
CODICOTE RD
Great Norfolk Wood
Dowdell's Wood
Ayot Bury
AYOT ST PETER RD
Fish Wood
Ayot St Peter
Scratching Grove
Threegroves Wood
War Meml
Warren Wood
Ayot Place
Cherrytree Spring
Ayot Mountfitchet
Saul's Wood
Coneydell Spring
Bladder Wood
Ayot Greenway
Robinson's Wood
Hunter's Bridge
Manor Farm
AL4
AYOT LITTLE GREEN LA
Ayot Greenway
Bowle's Wood
River Lea or Lee
Sparrowhall Bridge
WAFEREND LA
Ayot Little Green
Lea Valley Wlk
Sparrowhall Farm
James's Wood
8
7
17
6
5
16
4
3
15
2
1
14
19
20
21

87
109

68
90

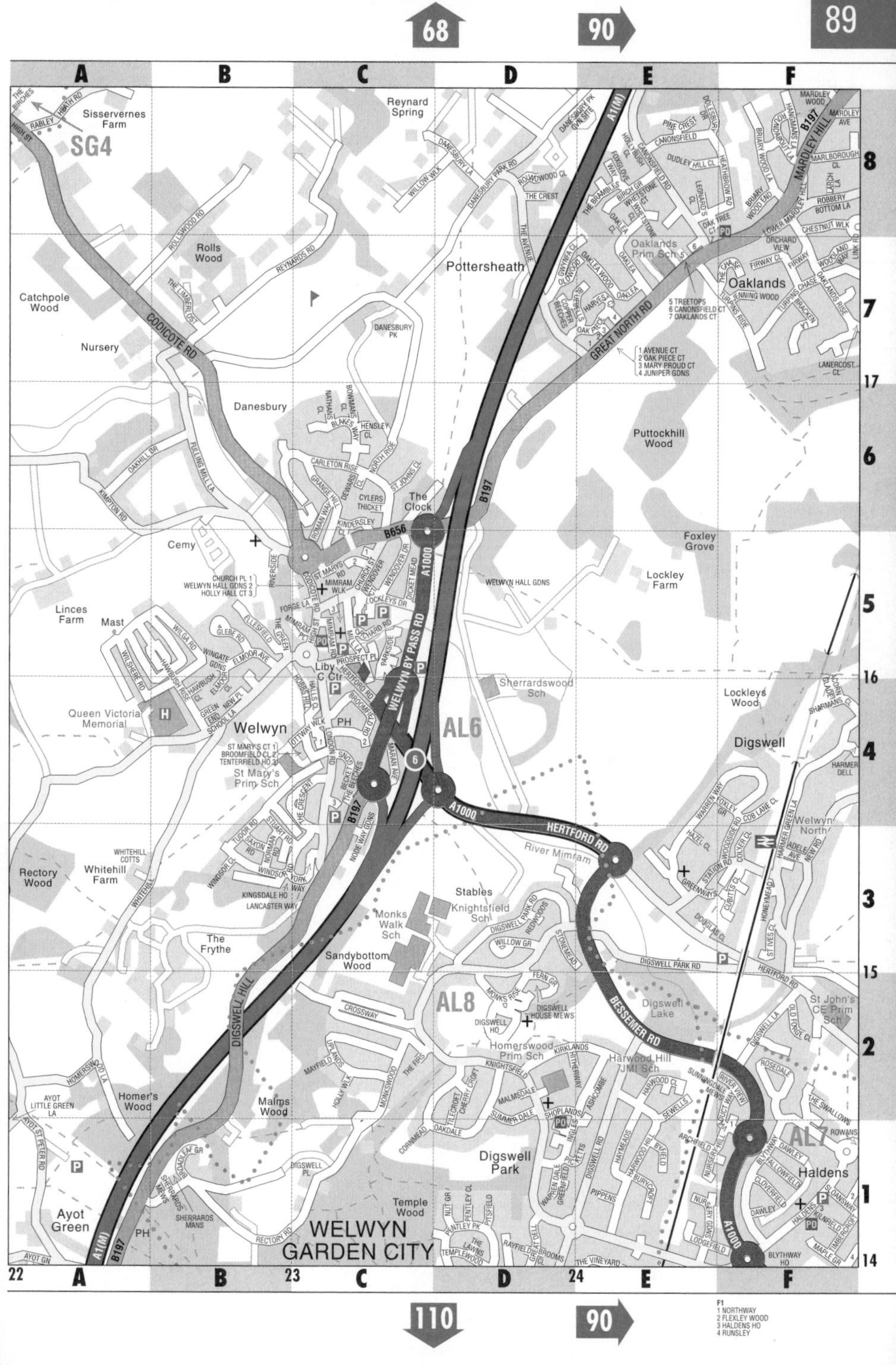

110
90

F1
1 NORTHWAY
2 FLEXLEY WOOD
3 HALDENS HO
4 RUNSLEY

89
69

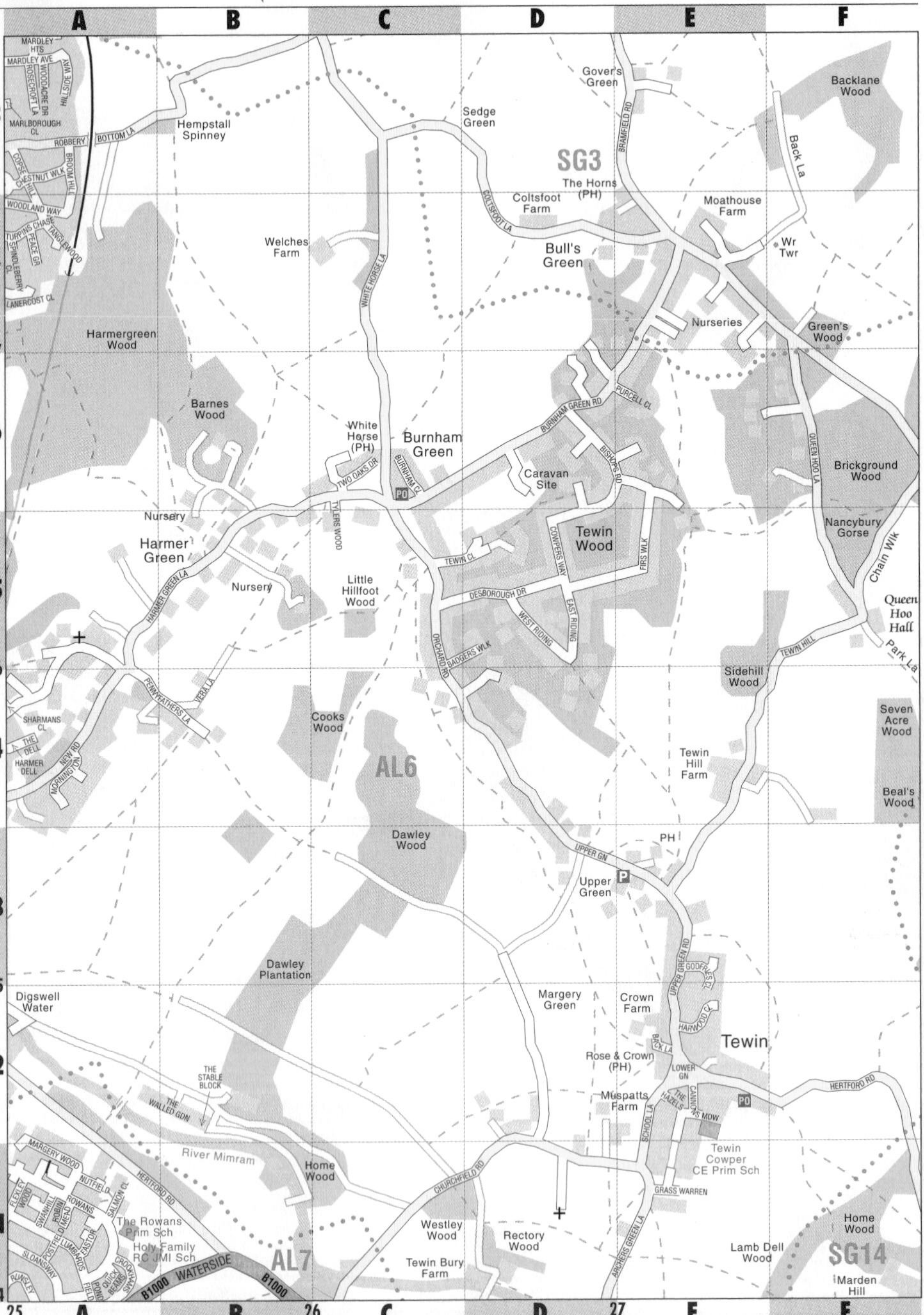

A B C D E F

8 7 17 6 5 16 4 3 15 2 1 14

MARDLEY HTS
MARDLEY AVE
ROSECROFT LA
WOODACRE DR
HILLSIDE WAY
MARLBOROUGH CL
ROBBERY
BOTTOM LA
BROOM HILL
COPSE HILL
CHESTNUT WLK
WOODLAND WAY
TURPINS CHASE
PEACE GR
TANGLEWOOD
SPINDLEBERRY CL
LANERCOST CL
Hempstall Spinney
Sedge Green
Gover's Green
Backlane Wood
Back La
SG3
BRAMFIELD RD
The Horns (PH)
Coltsfoot Farm
COLTSFOOT LA
Moathouse Farm
Welches Farm
WHITE HORSE LA
Bull's Green
Wr Twr
Nurseries
Green's Wood
Harmergreen Wood
Barnes Wood
White Horse (PH)
Burnham Green
BURNHAM GREEN RD
PURCELL CL
BISHOPS RD
QUEEN HOO LA
TWO OAKS DR
BURNHAM CL
PO
Caravan Site
Brickground Wood
Nursery
TYLERS WOOD
Tewin Wood
COWPERS WAY
FIRS WLK
Nancybury Gorse
Harmer Green
TEWIN CL
Chain Wlk
HARMER GREEN LA
Nursery
Little Hillfoot Wood
DESBOROUGH DR
EAST RIDING
WEST RIDING
Queen Hoo Hall
ORCHARD RD
BADGERS WLK
TEWIN HILL
Park La
Sidehill Wood
PENNYFATHERS LA
VERA LA
SHARMANS CL
THE DELL
HARMER DELL
NEW RD
MORNINGTON
Cooks Wood
AL6
Seven Acre Wood
Tewin Hill Farm
Beal's Wood
Dawley Wood
PH
UPPER GN
P
Upper Green
UPPER GREEN RD
GODFREYS CL
Dawley Plantation
Digswell Water
Margery Green
Crown Farm
HARWOOD CL
BACK LA
Tewin
Rose & Crown (PH)
LOWER GN
THE STABLE BLOCK
THE WALLED GDN
Muspatts Farm
THE HAZELS
CANNONS MDW
PO
HERTFORD RD
SCHOOL LA
River Mimram
Tewin Cowper CE Prim Sch
MARGERY WOOD
NUTFIELD
SALMON CL
HERTFORD RD
Home Wood
CHURCHFIELD RD
GRASS WARREN
FLEXLEY WOOD
SWANHILL
ROBIN MEAD
ROWANS
The Rowans Prim Sch
Westley Wood
Rectory Wood
ARCHERS GREEN LA
Home Wood
POSTFIELD
LUMBARDS
EASTOR
Holy Family RC JMI Sch
SG14
Lamb Dell Wood
SLOANSWAY
CROOKHAMS
FIELD
POND
QUICK BEAMS
RUNSLEY
B1000 WATERSIDE
B1000
AL7
Tewin Bury Farm
Marden Hill

25 A B 26 C D 27 E F

89
111

70
92

A
B
C
D
E
F
8
7
17
6
5
16
4
3
15
2
1
14
28
29
30
SG3
AL6
SG14
Perrywood Farm
Hazeldell Wood
Burgess Corner
Chain Wlk
Widow Bushes
Patchendon
Wrens Wood
Long Walk
PERRYWOOD LA
Lower Blackbuck Wood
Great Gobions Farm
Upper Blackbuck Wood
A119
Nicholson's Wood
Bramfield Woods
Back La
HIGH RD
Barber's Close
Bright's Hill
Valentine Spring
Warren Wood Ind Est
Open Bailey
Basil's Park
Greenhill
Winter Dell
Sally Rainbow's Dell
Symond's Wood
Row Wood
Greenhall Farm
Little Gobions
WINDING SHOTT
TURNERS CL
PH
Bramfield House
WELL GN
BURY LA
Priest Wood
Bramfield
MAIN RD
Bramfield Park Wood
HOLLY GROVE RD
Bramfield Place Farm
Bramfieldbury
Park La
Sewage Wks
BRAMFIELD LA
Well House
Westend Farm
TATTLE HILL
Bacon's Green
Westend
Tattle Hill
Gravel Pits
Bacon's Farm
Goldings
Oakfield Plantation
HERTFORD RD
BRAMFIELD RD

112
92

91
71

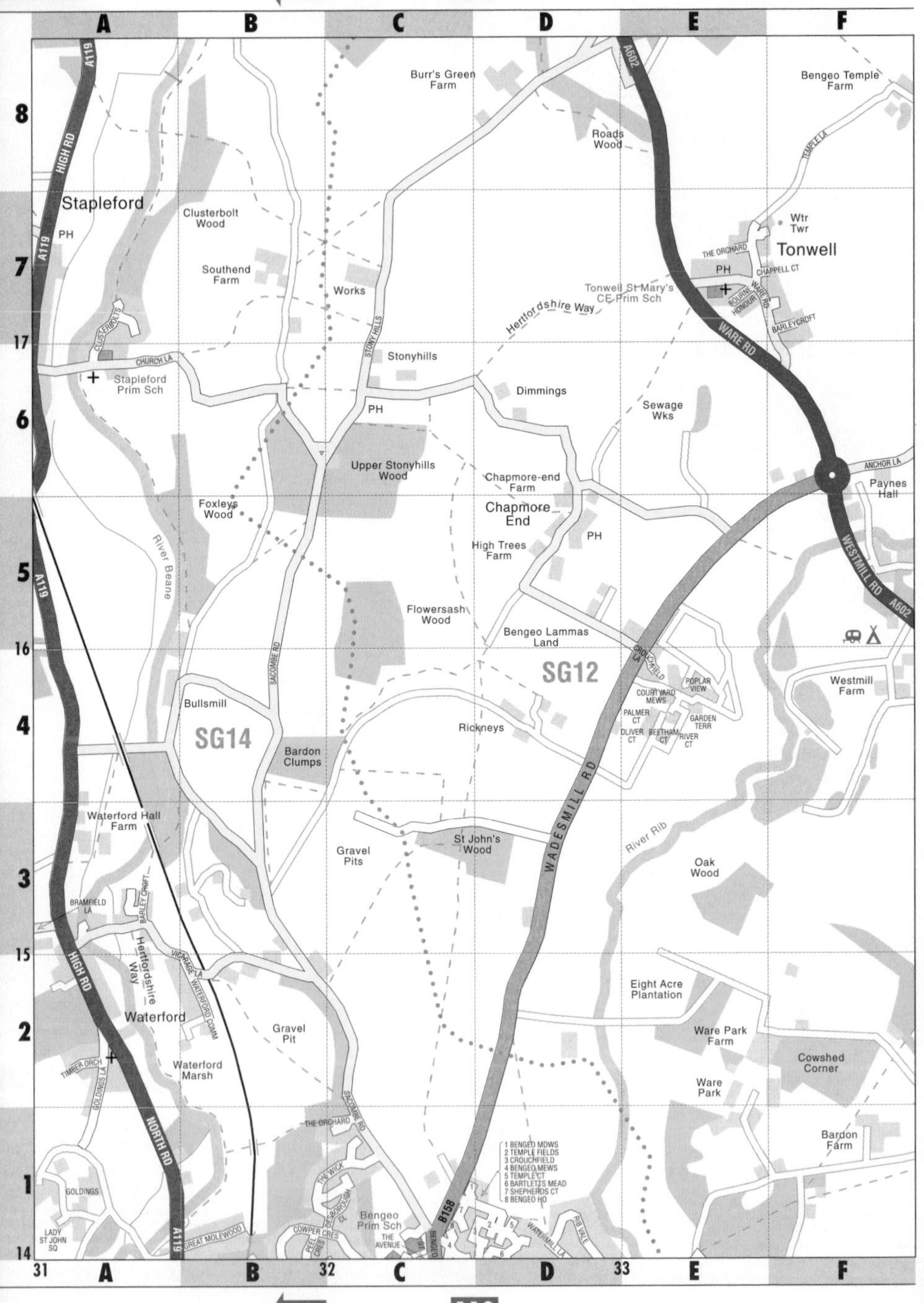
Stapleford
PH
Clusterbolt Wood
Southend Farm
Works
Burr's Green Farm
Roads Wood
Bengeo Temple Farm
Wtr Twr
Tonwell
THE ORCHARD
CHAPPELL CT
Tonwell St Mary's CE Prim Sch
Hertfordshire Way
BARLEYCROFT
WARE RD
CHURCH LA
Stapleford Prim Sch
Stonyhills
STONY HILLS
Dimmings
Sewage Wks
Upper Stonyhills Wood
Chapmore-end Farm
ANCHOR LA
Paynes Hall
Foxleys Wood
Chapmore End
High Trees Farm
River Beane
WESTMILL RD
A602
A119
HIGH RD
Flowersash Wood
Bengeo Lammas Land
SG12
Westmill Farm
SACOMBE RD
Bullsmill
SG14
Rickneys
Bardon Clumps
WADESMILL RD
Waterford Hall Farm
St John's Wood
Gravel Pits
River Rib
Oak Wood
BRAMFIELD LA
BARLEY CROFT
Hertfordshire Way
VICARAGE LA
WATERFORD COMM
Eight Acre Plantation
Waterford
Gravel Pit
Ware Park Farm
Cowshed Corner
Waterford Marsh
TIMBER ORCH
GOLDINGS LA
Ware Park
NORTH RD
THE ORCHARD
Bardon Farm
1 BENGEO MDWS
2 TEMPLE FIELDS
3 CROUCHFIELD
4 BENGEO MEWS
5 TEMPLE CT
6 BARTLETTS MEAD
7 SHEPHERDS CT
8 BENGEO HO
GOLDINGS
THE WICK
Bengeo Prim Sch
B158
LADY ST JOHN SQ
GREAT MOLEWOOD
COWPER CRES
PEEL CRES
THE AVENUE
WATERMILL LA
RIB VALE

91
113

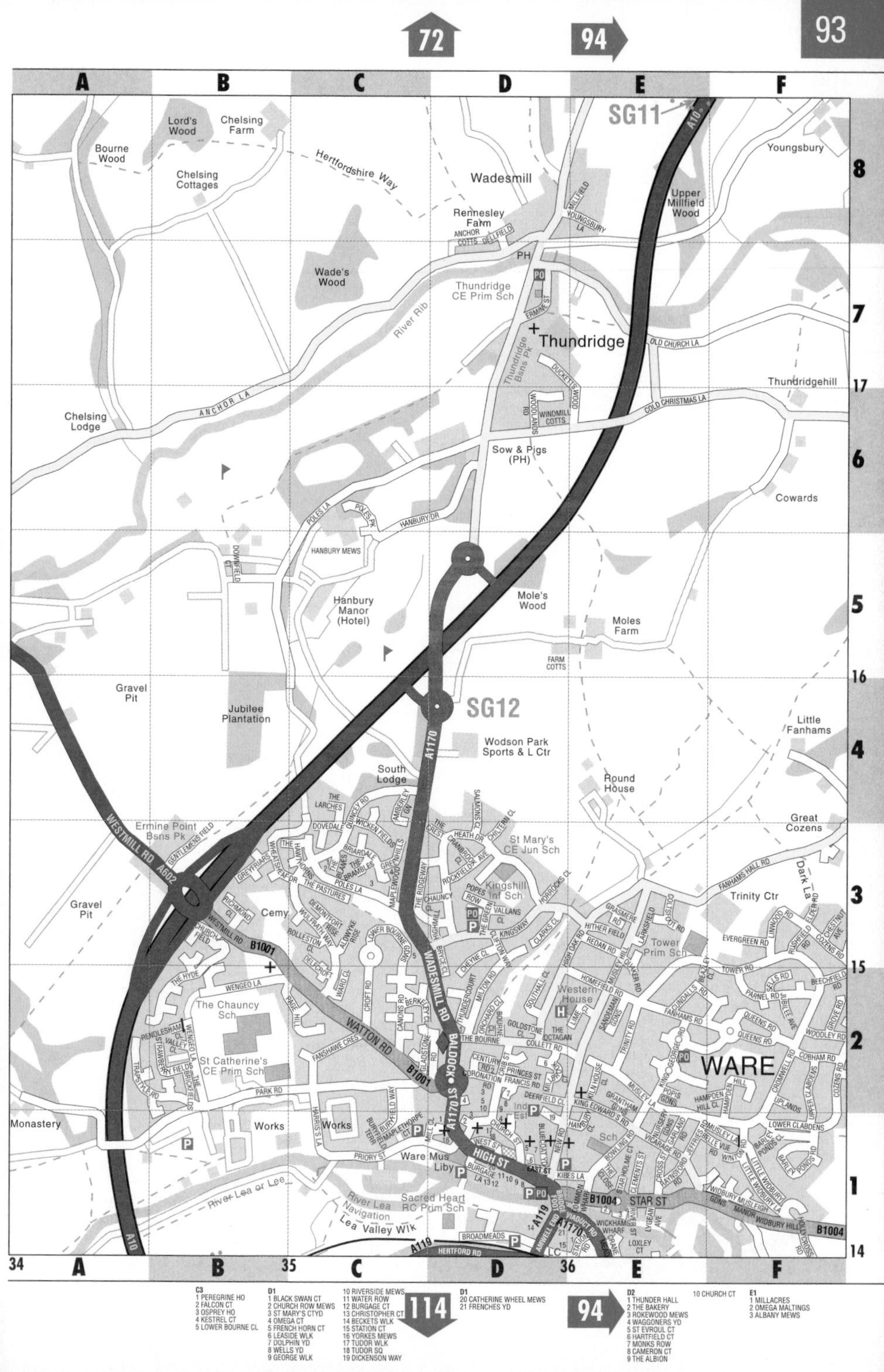

C3
1 PEREGRINE HO
2 FALCON CT
3 OSPREY HO
4 KESTREL CT
5 LOWER BOURNE CL

D1
1 BLACK SWAN CT
2 CHURCH ROW MEWS
3 ST MARY'S CTYD
4 OMEGA CT
5 FRENCH HORN CT
6 LEASIDE WLK
7 DOLPHIN YD
8 WELLS YD
9 GEORGE WLK
10 RIVERSIDE MEWS
11 WATER ROW
12 BURGAGE CT
13 CHRISTOPHER CT
14 BECKETS WLK
15 STATION CT
16 YORKES MEWS
17 TUDOR WLK
18 TUDOR SQ
19 DICKENSON WAY

D1
20 CATHERINE WHEEL MEWS
21 FRENCHES YD

D2
1 THUNDER HALL
2 THE BAKERY
3 ROKEWOOD MEWS
4 WAGGONERS YD
5 ST EVROUL CT
6 HARTFIELD CT
7 MONKS ROW
8 CAMERON CT
9 THE ALBION
10 CHURCH CT

E1
1 MILLACRES
2 OMEGA MALTINGS
3 ALBANY MEWS

93
73

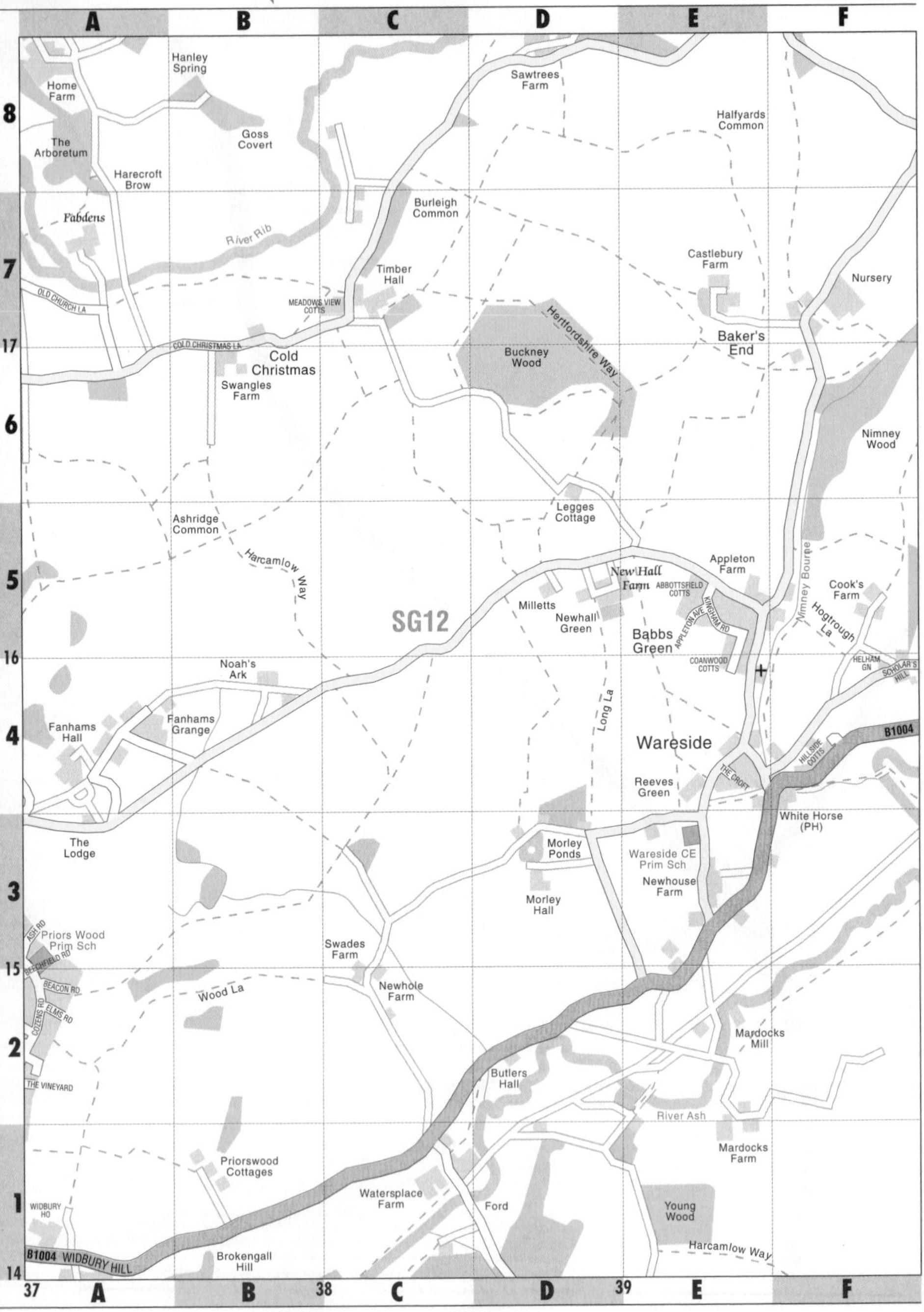

A B C D E F
8 7 17 6 5 16 4 3 15 2 1 14
Hanley Spring
Home Farm
The Arboretum
Goss Covert
Harecroft Brow
Fabdens
River Rib
Sawtrees Farm
Halfyards Common
Burleigh Common
Castlebury Farm
Timber Hall
Nursery
OLD CHURCH LA
MEADOWS VIEW COTTS
Hertfordshire Way
COLD CHRISTMAS LA
Cold Christmas
Swangles Farm
Buckney Wood
Baker's End
Nimney Wood
Ashridge Common
Legges Cottage
Harcamlow Way
Appleton Farm
New Hall Farm
ABBOTTSFIELD COTTS
Milletts
Newhall Green
Babbs Green
APPLETON AVE
KINGHAM RD
Cook's Farm
Hogtrough La
Nimney Bourne
SG12
COANWOOD COTTS
HELHAM GN
SCHOLAR'S HILL
Noah's Ark
Fanhams Hall
Fanhams Grange
Long La
Wareside
B1004
HILLSIDE COTTS
THE CROFT
Reeves Green
White Horse (PH)
The Lodge
Morley Ponds
Wareside CE Prim Sch
Newhouse Farm
Morley Hall
ASH RD
Priors Wood Prim Sch
BEECHFIELD RD
Swades Farm
BEACON RD
Wood La
Newhole Farm
COZENS RD
ELMS RD
Mardocks Mill
THE VINEYARD
Butlers Hall
River Ash
Mardocks Farm
Priorswood Cottages
Watersplace Farm
Ford
WIDBURY HO
Young Wood
Harcamlow Way
B1004 WIDBURY HILL
Brokengall Hill
37 38 39

93
115

74
96

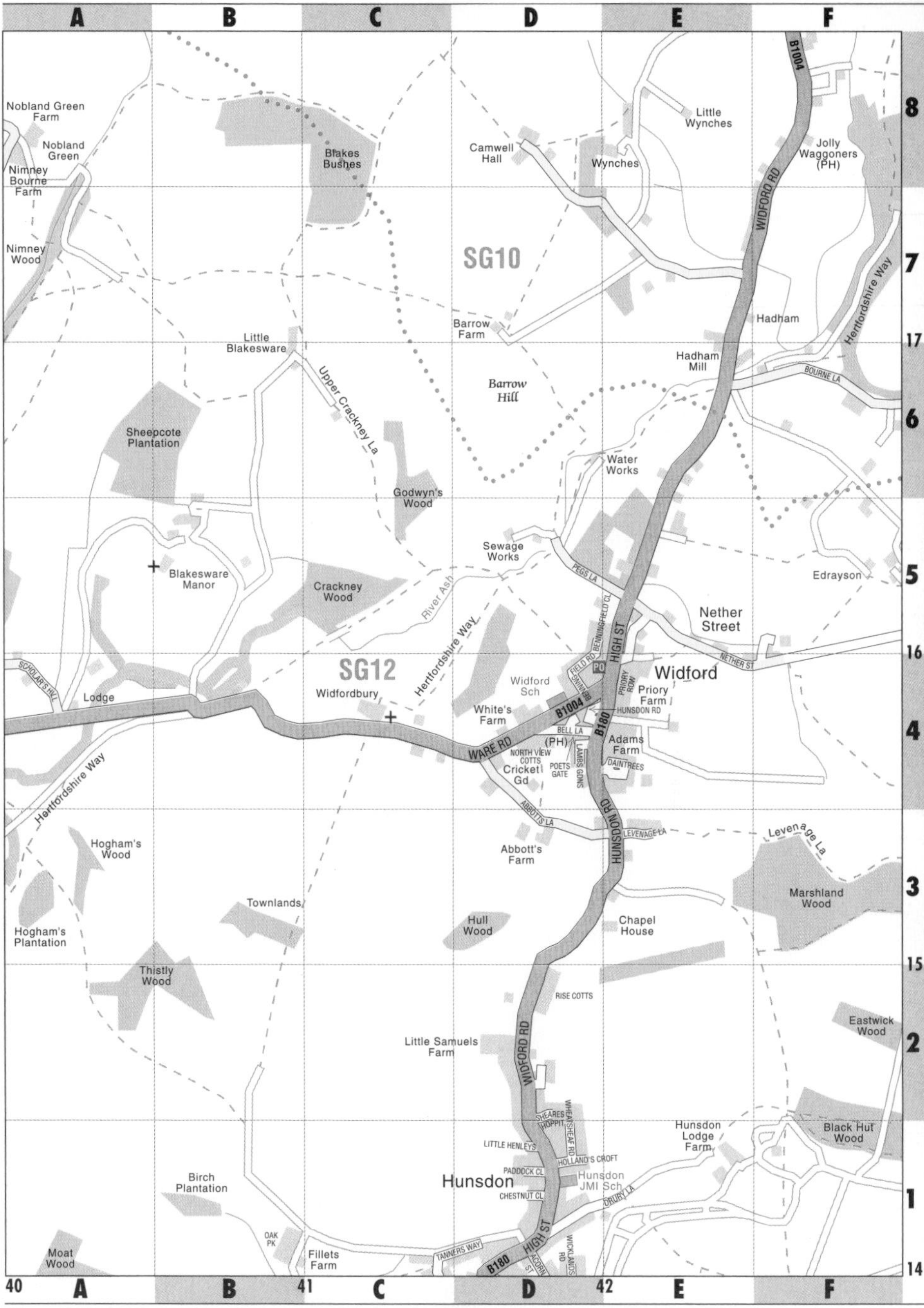

A B C D E F
8 7 17 6 5 16 4 3 15 2 1 14
40 41 42
Nobland Green Farm
Nobland Green
Nimney Bourne Farm
Nimney Wood
Blakes Bushes
Camwell Hall
Wynches
Little Wynches
Jolly Waggoners (PH)
B1004
WIDFORD RD
SG10
Hadham
Hertfordshire Way
Barrow Farm
Little Blakesware
Upper Crackney La
Barrow Hill
Hadham Mill
BOURNE LA
Sheepcote Plantation
Water Works
Godwyn's Wood
Sewage Works
Blakesware Manor
Crackney Wood
River Ash
PEGS LA
Edrayson
Nether Street
BENNINGFIELD CL
HIGH ST
NETHER ST
SCHOLAR'S HILL
SG12
FIELD RD
PO
Widford
Widford Sch
PRIORY ROW
Priory Farm
Lodge
Widfordbury
Hertfordshire Way
White's Farm
B1004
HUNSDON RD
B180
BELL LA
(PH)
Adams Farm
WARE RD
NORTH VIEW COTTS
POETS GATE
LAMBS GDNS
DAINTREES
Cricket Gd
Hertfordshire Way
ABBOTTS LA
LEVENAGE LA
HUNSDON RD
Levenage La
Hogham's Wood
Abbott's Farm
Marshland Wood
Townlands
Hull Wood
Chapel House
Hogham's Plantation
Thistly Wood
RISE COTTS
Eastwick Wood
Little Samuels Farm
WIDFORD RD
SHEARES HOPPIT
WHEATSHEAF RD
Hunsdon Lodge Farm
Black Hut Wood
LITTLE HENLEYS
HOLLAND'S CROFT
PADDOCK CL
Hunsdon JMI Sch
Birch Plantation
Hunsdon
CHESTNUT CL
DRURY LA
OAK PK
HIGH ST
WICKLANDS RD
Moat Wood
Fillets Farm
TANNERS WAY
B180
ACORN ST

116
96

95
75

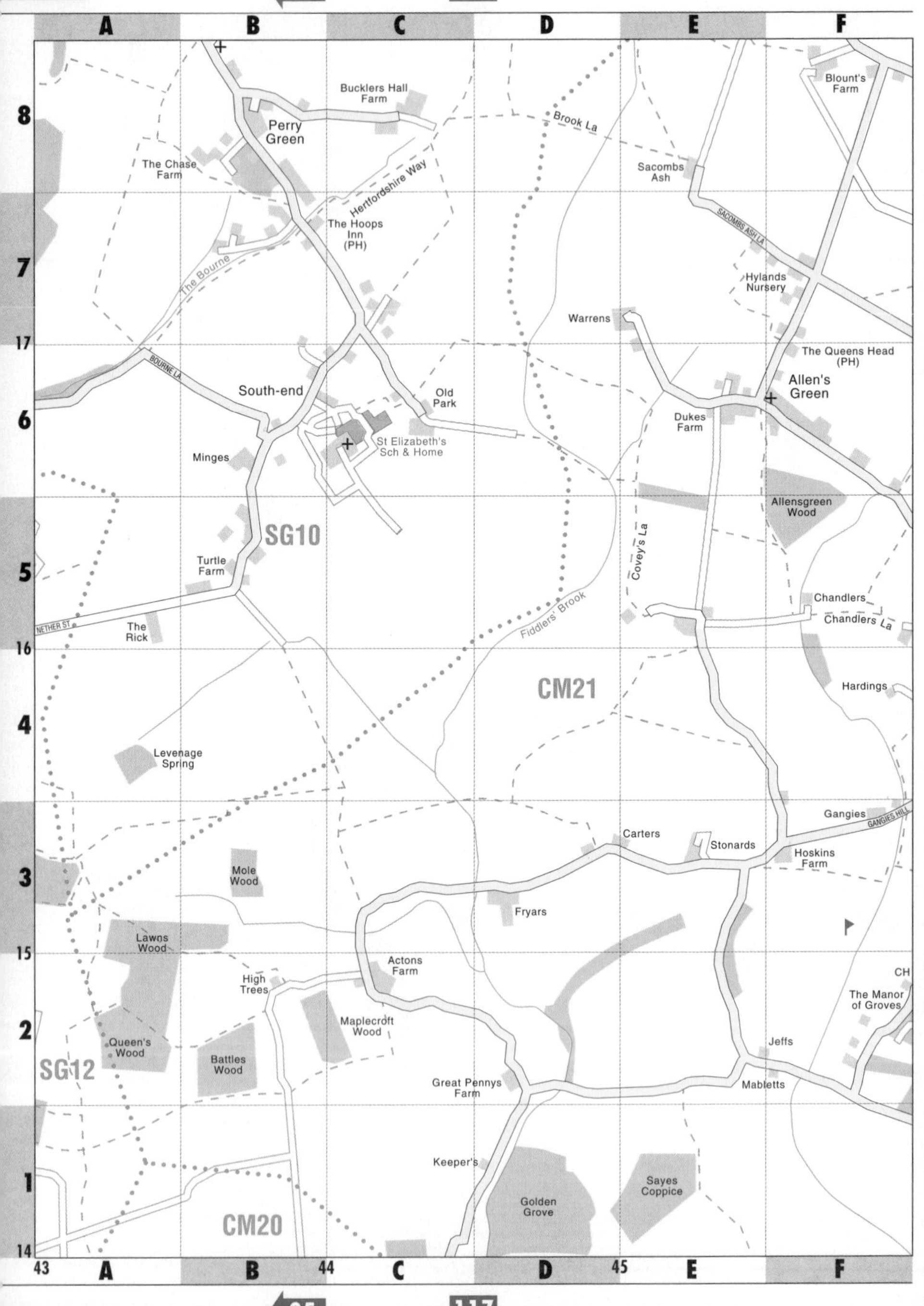
A
B
C
D
E
F
8
7
17
6
5
16
4
3
15
2
1
14
43
44
45
Bucklers Hall Farm
Perry Green
The Chase Farm
Brook La
Sacombs Ash
Blount's Farm
Hertfordshire Way
The Hoops Inn (PH)
SACOMBS ASH LA
Hylands Nursery
The Bourne
Warrens
The Queens Head (PH)
BOURNE LA
South-end
Old Park
Allen's Green
Dukes Farm
St Elizabeth's Sch & Home
Minges
Allensgreen Wood
SG10
Covey's La
Turtle Farm
Chandlers
Chandlers La
NETHER ST
The Rick
Fiddlers' Brook
CM21
Hardings
Levenage Spring
Gangies
GANGIES HILL
Carters
Stonards
Hoskins Farm
Mole Wood
Fryars
Lawns Wood
Actons Farm
CH
High Trees
The Manor of Groves
Maplecroft Wood
Queen's Wood
Battles Wood
Jeffs
SG12
Great Pennys Farm
Mabletts
Keeper's
Sayes Coppice
Golden Grove
CM20

95
117

76
98

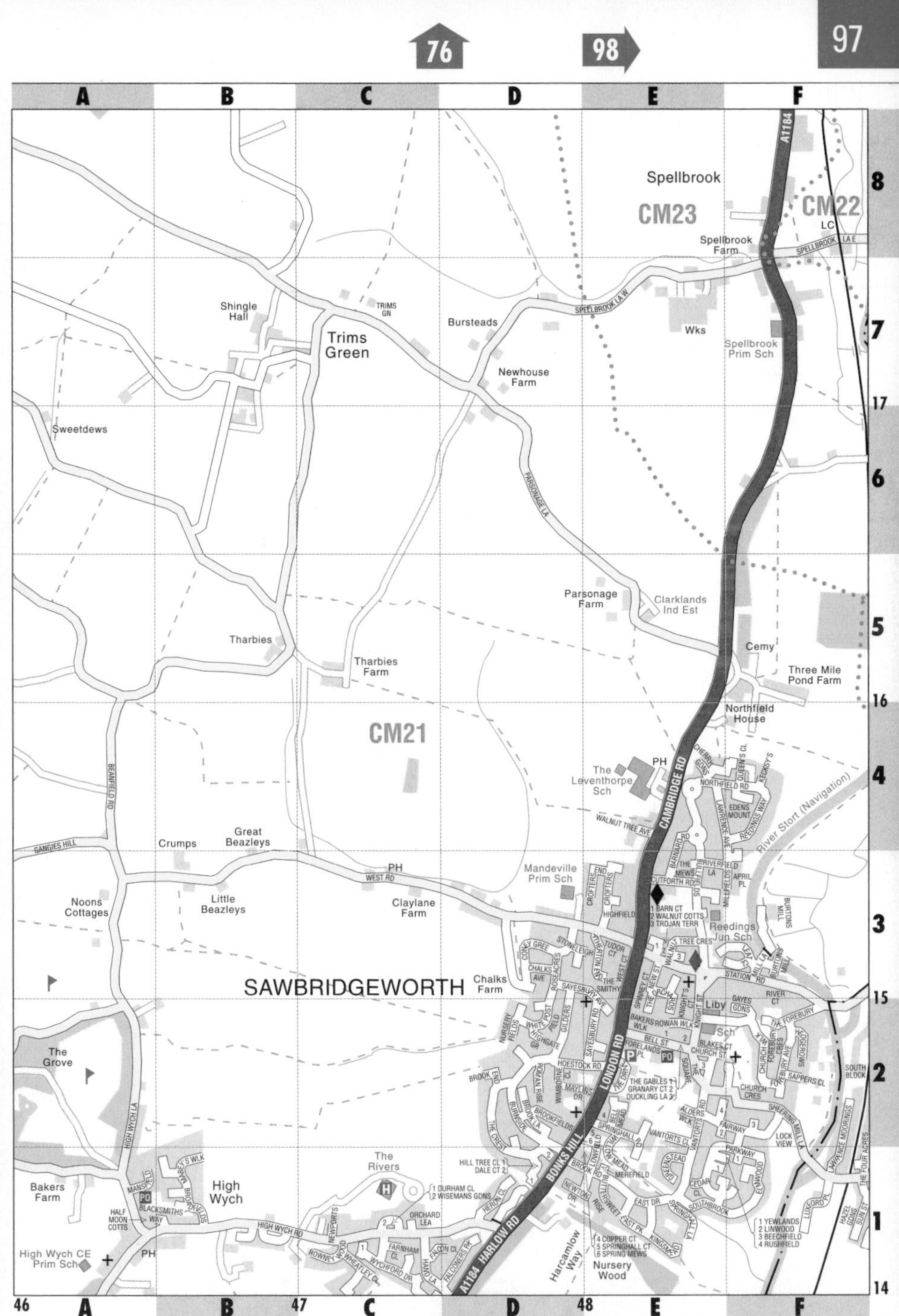
A
B
C
D
E
F
8
7
17
6
5
16
4
3
15
2
1
14
46
47
48
Spellbrook
CM23
CM22
LC
Spellbrook Farm
SPELLBROOK LA E
SPELLBROOK LA W
A1184
Shingle Hall
TRIMS GN
Trims Green
Bursteads
Wks
Spellbrook Prim Sch
Newhouse Farm
Sweetdews
PARSONAGE LA
Parsonage Farm
Clarklands Ind Est
Tharbies
Tharbies Farm
Cemy
Three Mile Pond Farm
Northfield House
CM21
BEANFIELD RD
PH
The Leventhorpe Sch
CAMBRIDGE RD
NORTHFIELD RD
EDENS MOUNT
REDINGS WAY
LAWRENCE AVE
River Stort (Navigation)
WALNUT TREE AVE
GANGIES HILL
Crumps
Great Beazleys
WEST RD
Mandeville Prim Sch
Noons Cottages
Little Beazleys
Claylane Farm
CROFTERS
CUTFORTH RD
1 BARN CT
2 WALNUT COTTS
3 TROJAN TERR
HIGHFIELD
Reedings Jun Sch
BURTONS MILL
STONELEIGH
TUDOR CT
STATION RD
SAWBRIDGEWORTH
Chalks Farm
SAYESBURY AVE
Liby
SAYES GDNS
RIVER CT
THE FOREBURY
Sch
BELL ST
BLAKES CT
CHURCH ST
FORELANDS PL
PO
HOESTOCK RD
LONDON RD
The Grove
THE GABLES 1
GRANARY CT 2
DUCKLING LA 3
SOUTH BLOCK
SAPPERS CL
CHURCH CRES
SHEERING MILL LA
BROOKFIELDS
VANTORTS CL
FAIRWAY
LOCK VIEW
PARKWAY
HIGH WYCH LA
HILL TREE CL 1
DALE CT 2
The Rivers
BONKS HILL
1 DURHAM CL
2 WISEMANS GDNS
High Wych
MANSFIELD
Bakers Farm
BLACKSMITHS WAY
HALF MOON COTTS
HIGH WYCH RD
ORCHARD LEA
HARLOW RD
EAST DR
SOUTHBROOK
1 YEWLANDS
2 LINWOOD
3 BEECHFIELD
4 RUSHFIELD
4 COPPER CT
5 SPRINGHALL CT
6 SPRING MEWS
Harcamlow Way
Nursery Wood
High Wych CE Prim Sch
FARNHAM CL
WYCHFORD DR
WHEATLEY CL
ROWNEY WOOD
FALCONERS PK

118
98

97
77

Wallbury
STADDLES
BARKERS MEAD 1
GEORGE GREEN VILLAS 2
REDBRICK ROW 3
A1060
Beadle Common
POST OFFICE COTTS
Little Hallingbury CE Prim Sch
Monksbury Farm
Little Hallingbury
M11
Sewage Works
Lock Farm
Nursery
GOOSE LA
SUTTON ACRES
LOWER RD
PO
Millhide Common
Gaston House
Gaston Common
Wright's Green
WRIGHTS GREEN LA
PYNCHON PADDOCKS
Gaston Green
BACK LA
OLD MILL LA
River Stort (Navigation)
Mill (dis)
Mott's Green
GRINSTEAD LA
Tednambury Farm
SAWBRIDGEWORTH RD
CM22
Little Bursteads
Little Hallingbury Park
Little Hallingbury Hall
South House Farm
Harcamlow Way
PH
Broadcroft
Spill Timbers Wood
Stone Hall
STORTFORD RD
Kecksy's Bridge
Camp Farm
HALLINGBURY RD
THE STABLES
THE GARDEN HOS
GREAT HYDE HALL
Round Spring
Oak Spring
Eighteenacre Spring
Little Hyde Hall
Wren's Spring
Hatfield Heath
A1060 Chelmsford
Sawbridgeworth
STATION RD
LC
Cowick
SAWBRIDGEWORTH RD
LITTLE HEATH 1
WAGON MEAD 2
FORGE COTTS 3
1 PRIORS CT
2 WATERSIDE PL
CM21
THE MEADOWS
ASH GROVES
THE FOUR ACRES
MEADOW WAY
SHEERING LOWER RD
Quickbury Farm
Stort Valley Way
B183
SHEERING MILL LA
Lower Sheering
Gladwyns
LADYWELL PROSPECT
MOORLANDS REACH
Sheering
THE STREET
PRIMLEY LA
CROWN CL
PLASHETS
HIGH PASTURES
Sheering CE Prim Sch
Shrubbs
BACK LA
PO
M11 Harlow
South Essex STREET ATLAS
A B C D E F
8 7 17 6 5 16 4 3 15 2 1 14
49 50 51

97

79
100

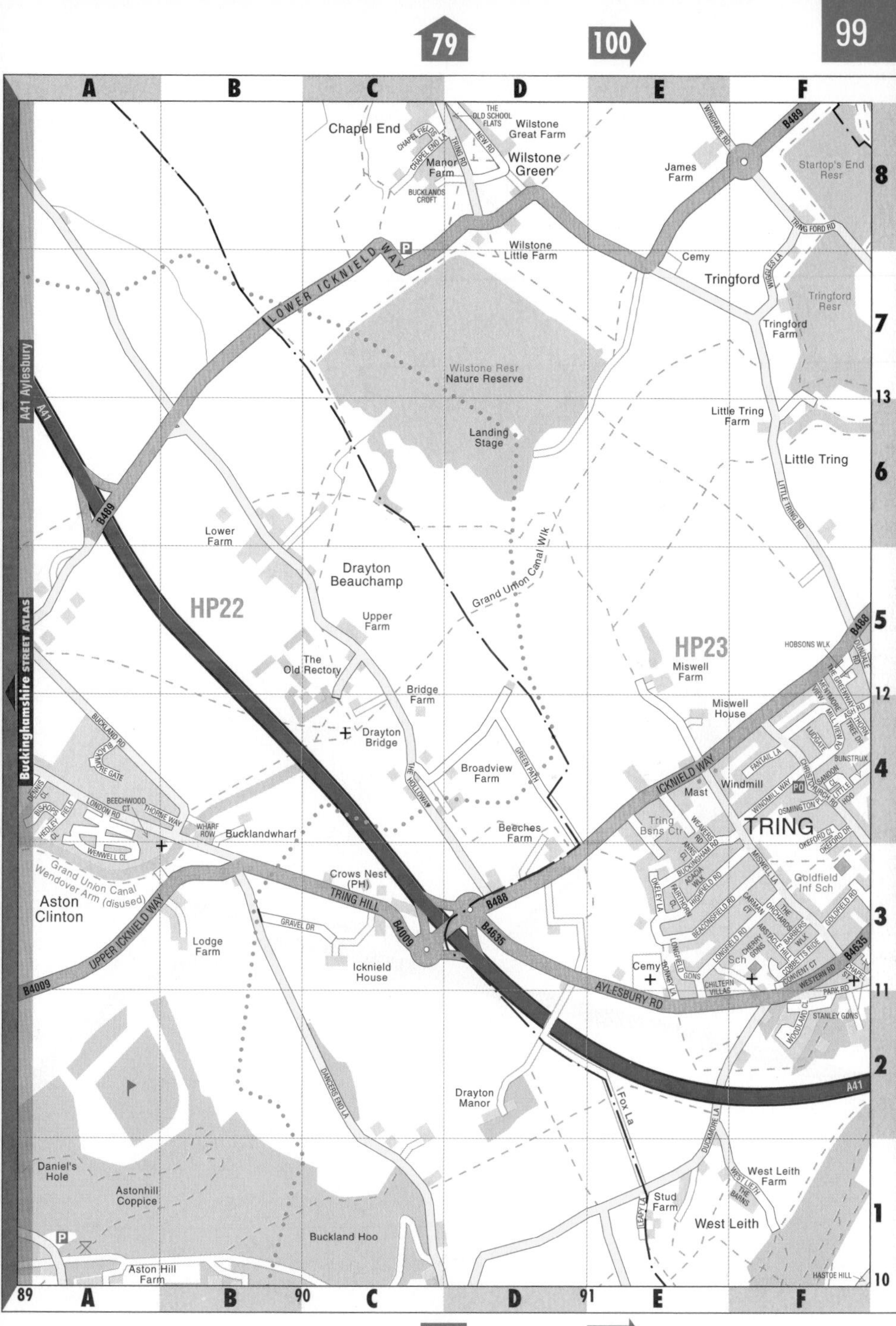

119
100

99
80

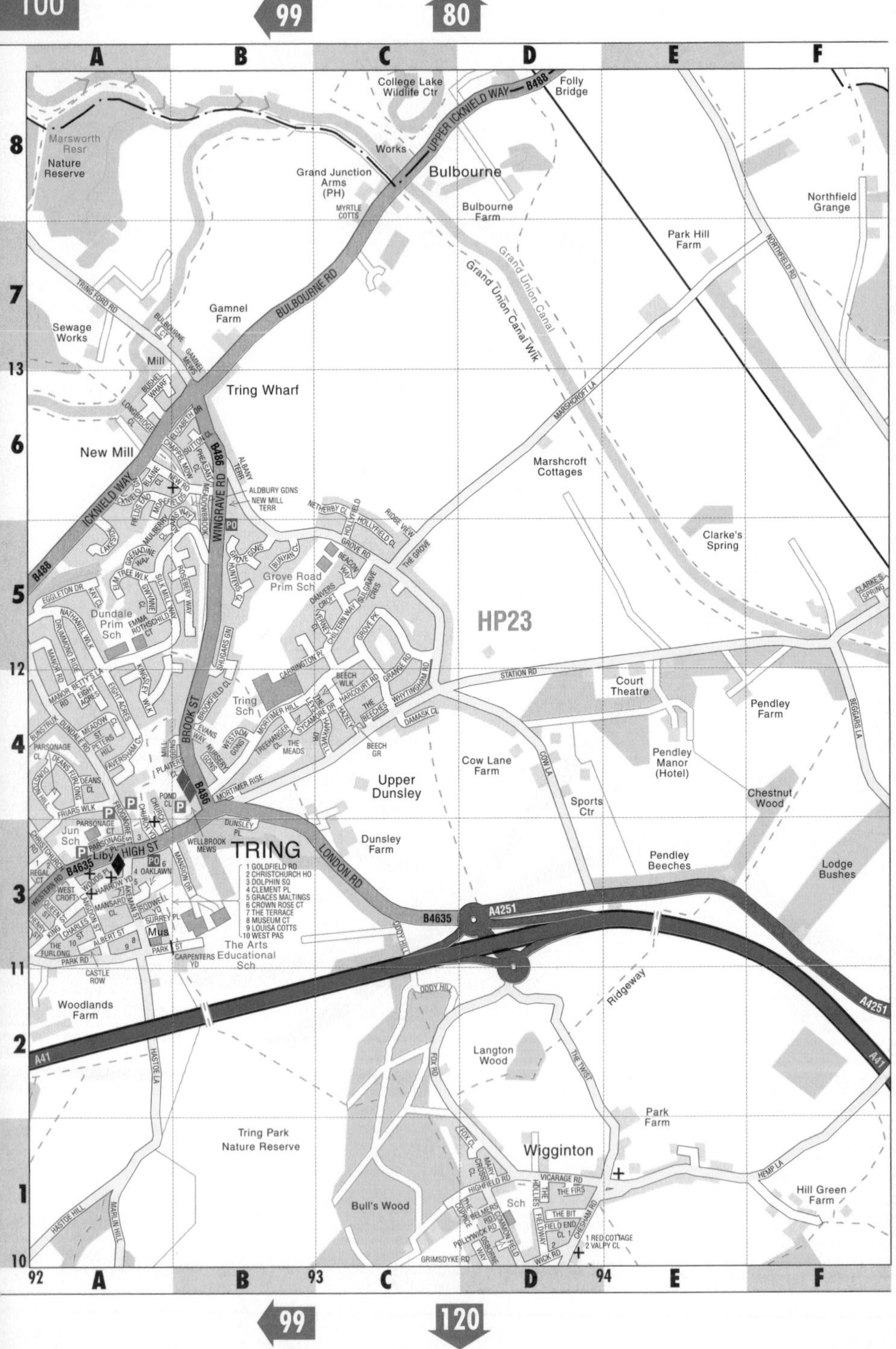
College Lake Wildlife Ctr
Folly Bridge
Marsworth Resr
Nature Reserve
Works
Grand Junction Arms (PH)
Bulbourne
Bulbourne Farm
Northfield Grange
Park Hill Farm
Gamnel Farm
Sewage Works
Mill
Tring Wharf
New Mill
Marshcroft Cottages
Clarke's Spring
Grove Road Prim Sch
Dundale Prim Sch
HP23
Court Theatre
Pendley Farm
Tring Sch
Cow Lane Farm
Pendley Manor (Hotel)
Upper Dunsley
Sports Ctr
Chestnut Wood
Jun Sch
Liby
TRING
Dunsley Farm
Pendley Beeches
Lodge Bushes
Mus
The Arts Educational Sch
Woodlands Farm
Ridgeway
Langton Wood
Park Farm
Tring Park Nature Reserve
Wigginton
Bull's Wood
Sch
Hill Green Farm
1 GOLDFIELD RD
2 CHRISTCHURCH HO
3 DOLPHIN SQ
4 CLEMENT PL
5 GRACES MALTINGS
6 CROWN ROSE CT
7 THE TERRACE
8 MUSEUM CT
9 LOUISA COTTS
10 WEST PAS
1 RED COTTAGE
2 VALPY CL
UPPER ICKNIELD WAY
B488
BULBOURNE RD
ICKNIELD WAY
WINGRAVE RD
B486
BROOK ST
HIGH ST
B4635
LONDON RD
A4251
A41
STATION RD
MARSHCROFT LA
NORTHFIELD RD
Grand Union Canal
Grand Union Canal Wlk
COW LA
BEGGARS LA
THE GROVE
GROVE RD
MORTIMER RISE
ODDY HILL
FOX RD
THE TWIST
HASTOE LA
HASTOE HILL
MARLIN HILL
HEMP LA
VICARAGE RD
CHESHAM RD
HIGHFIELD RD
GRIMSDYKE RD
WICK RD
A B C D E F
8 7 6 5 4 3 2 1
13 12 11 10
92 93 94

99
120

102

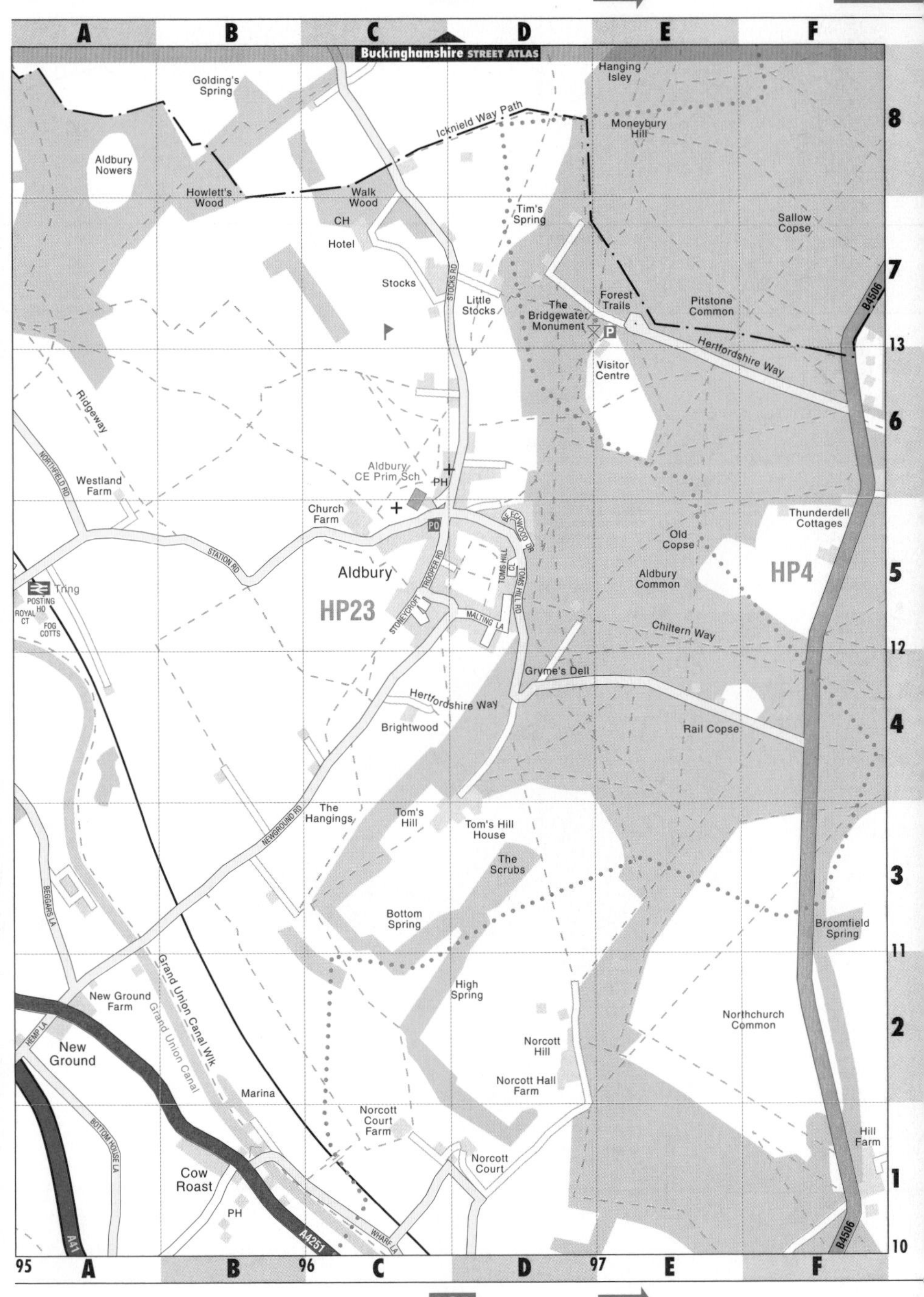

Buckinghamshire STREET ATLAS
A
B
C
D
E
F
8
7
6
5
4
3
2
1
13
12
11
10
95
96
97
Golding's Spring
Hanging Isley
Moneybury Hill
Icknield Way Path
Aldbury Nowers
Howlett's Wood
Walk Wood
CH
Hotel
Tim's Spring
Sallow Copse
Stocks
STOCKS RD
Little Stocks
The Bridgewater Monument
Forest Trails
Pitstone Common
B4506
Hertfordshire Way
Visitor Centre
Ridgeway
NORTHFIELD RD
Westland Farm
Aldbury CE Prim Sch
PH
Church Farm
PO
BEECHWOOD DR
Thunderdell Cottages
Old Copse
STATION RD
Aldbury
TROOPER RD
TOMS HILL CL
TOMS HILL RD
Aldbury Common
HP4
Tring
POSTING HO
ROYAL CT
FOG COTTS
HP23
STONEYCROFT
MALTING LA
Chiltern Way
Gryme's Dell
Hertfordshire Way
Brightwood
Rail Copse
NEWGROUND RD
The Hangings
Tom's Hill
Tom's Hill House
The Scrubs
BEGGARS LA
Bottom Spring
Broomfield Spring
Grand Union Canal Wlk
New Ground Farm
Grand Union Canal
High Spring
Northchurch Common
HEMP LA
New Ground
Norcott Hill
Norcott Hall Farm
Marina
BOTTOM HOUSE LA
Norcott Court Farm
Hill Farm
Cow Roast
Norcott Court
PH
A41
A4251
WHARF LA
B4506

121
102

101
81

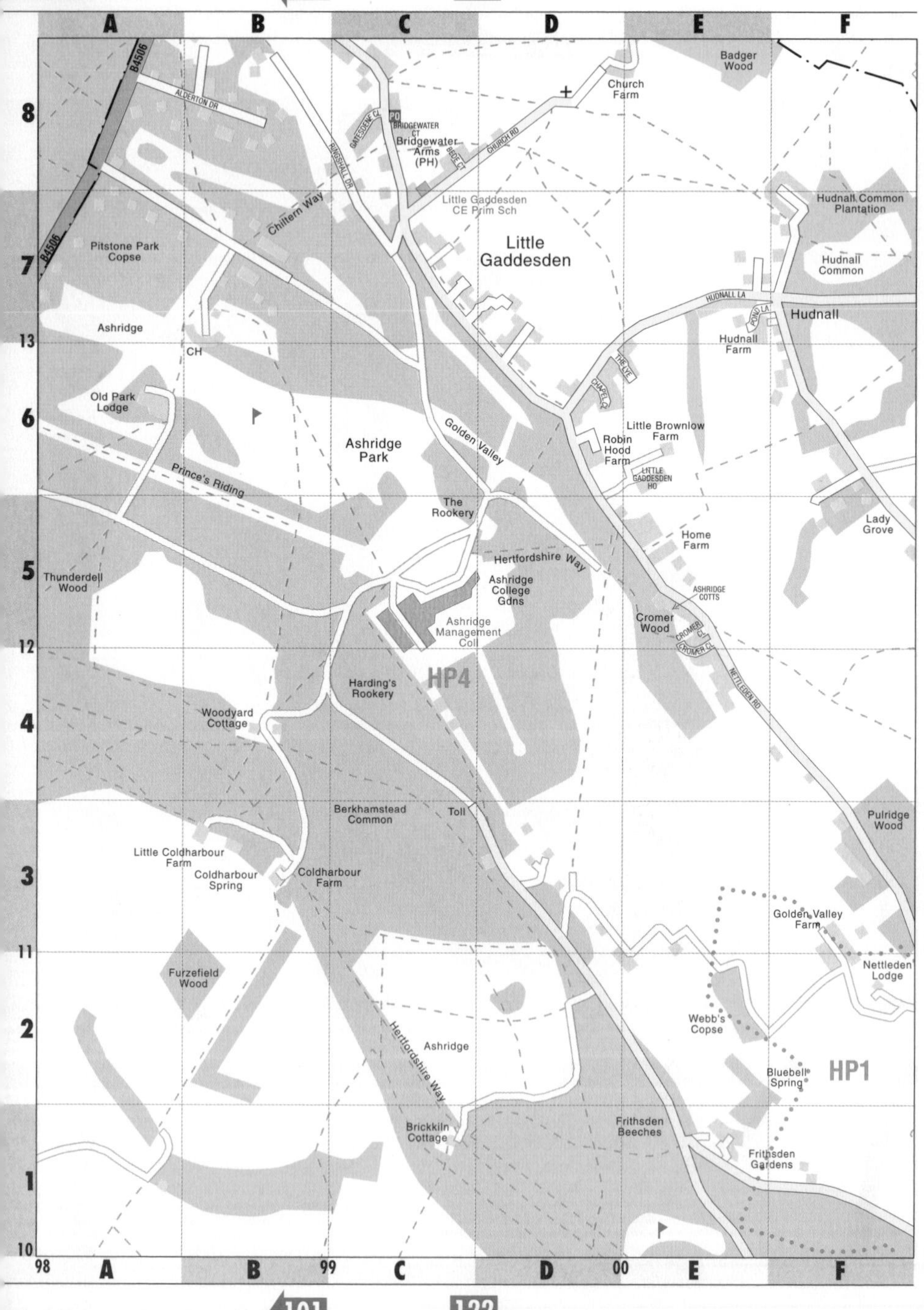

101
122

82
104

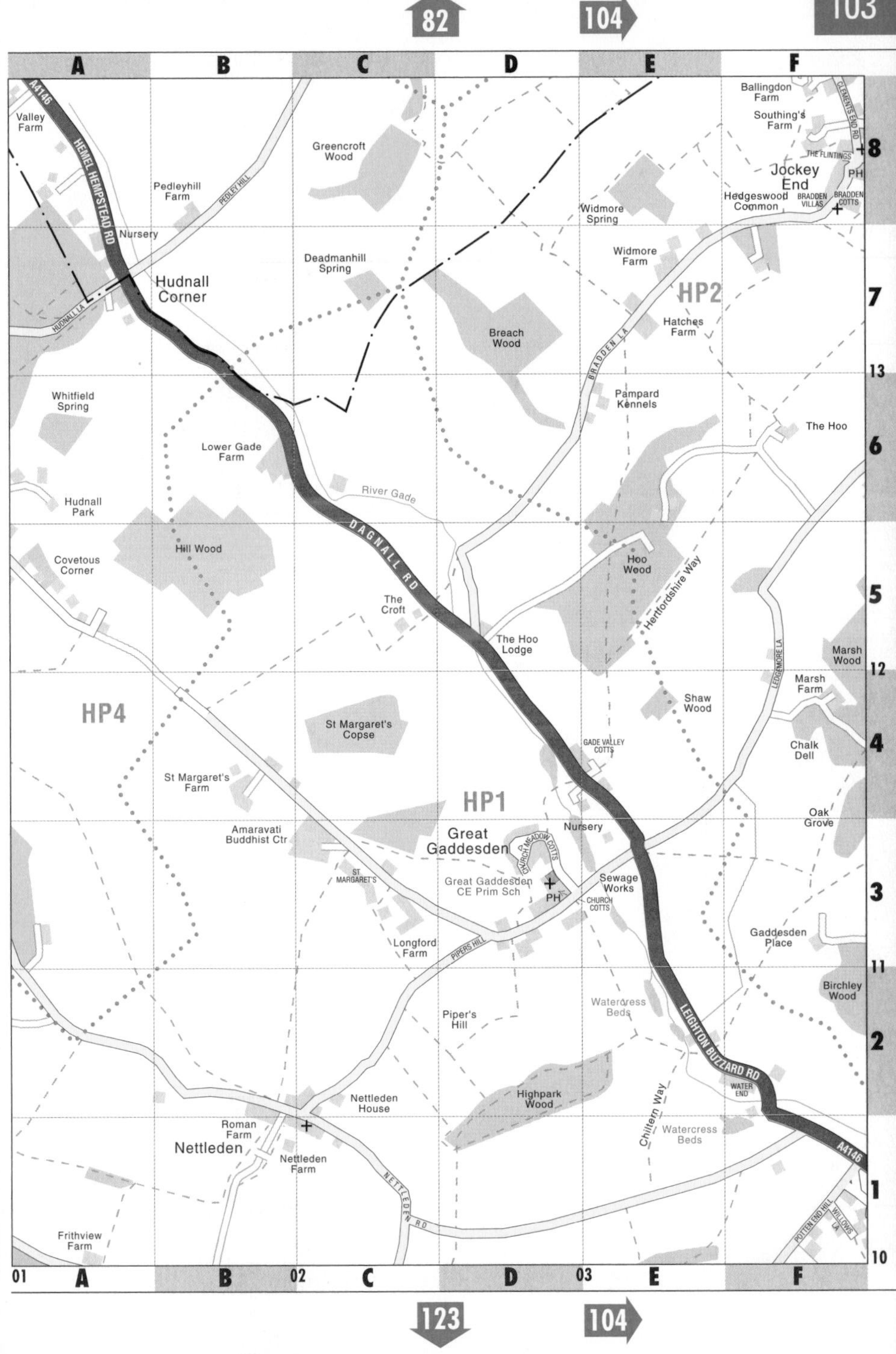

123
104

103
83

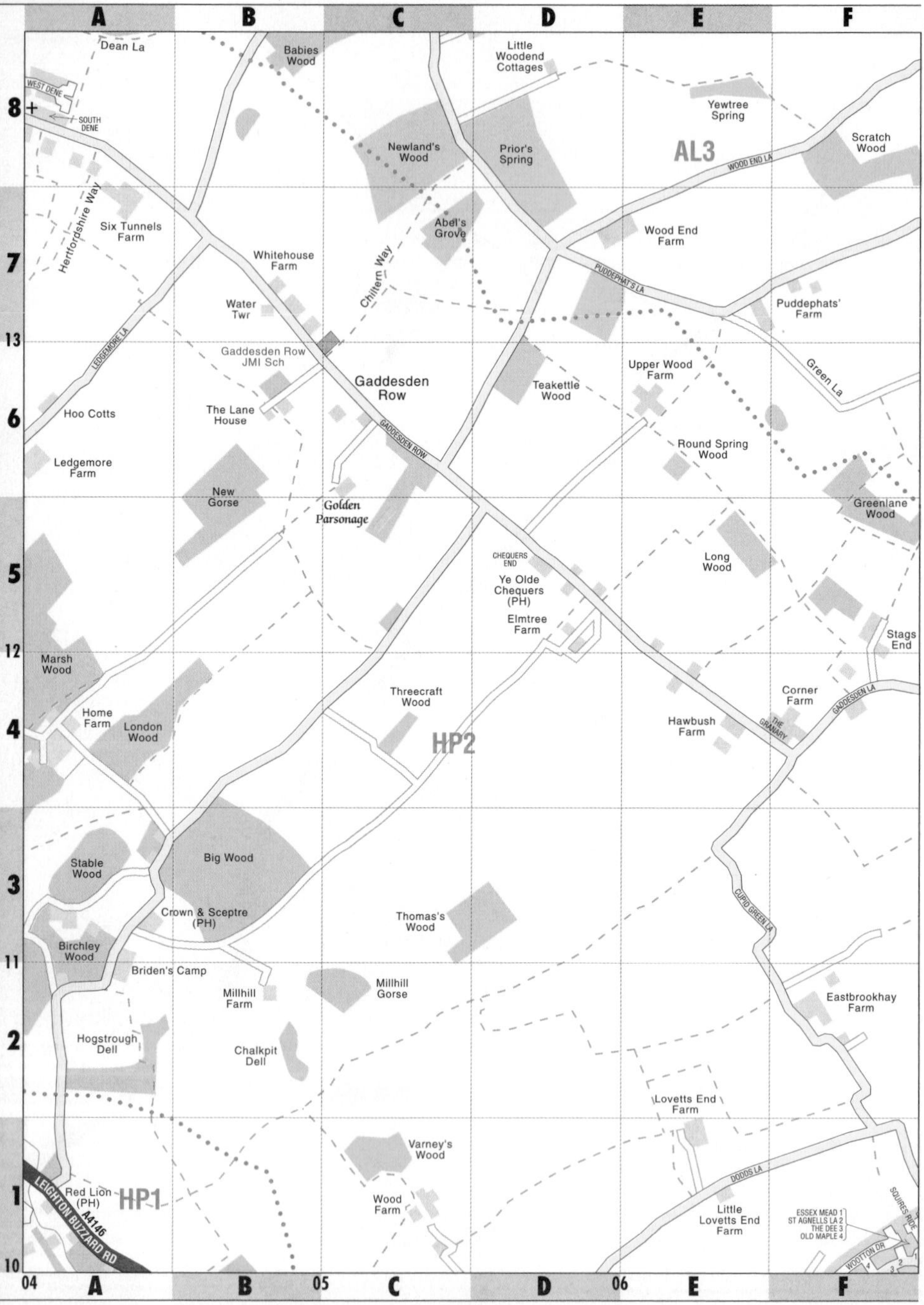

103
124

84
106
A
B
C
D
E
F
PH
Wood End La
Trowley Bottom
White Hill
Trowley Bottom
Trowley Bottom Farm
Delmerend La
St Agnells Farm
M1
Wr Twr
Redding Wood
Redding La
Dunstable Rd
A5183
8
Puddephat's La
Grove Farm
7
Lybury La
Nursery
Nicholls Farm
13
Green La
Hertfordshire Way
Nicholl's Great Wood
Rabbitfield Spring
Hilltop
Tassell Hall
The Square
Rains Bow Cl
Rose Acre
Nicholls Cl
6
Nirvana
Greenlane Farm
New Wood
Flamsteadbury Farm
Bury Cotts
Bury Wood
Down Edge
St Stephens Way
5
12
AL3
Mansdale Rd
Church End
4
Gaddesden La
Hay Wood
Saberton Cl
Hemel Hempstead Rd
B487
The Aubreys
3
Holtsmore End Farm
Holtsmore End
Woodside
Hotel
Great Revel End Farm
Pantake Wood
11
Aubrey La
HP2
Smallholding
The Beeches
2
Little Revel End
Hemel Hempstead Rd
1 Ashby Ct
2 Eversden Ct
3 Longstanton Ct
4 Sedgewick Ct
5 Haddenham Ct
6 Milton Ct
St Agnell's Farm Mews
High Wych Way
Aston View
Braemar
Turn
Blair Cl
Tattershall Dr
Valley Gn
Widford Terr
Elstree Rd
Bramfield Pl
Roydon Ct
Dunster Rd
Glamis Cl
Shenley Rd
Holtsmere End Lane
Brockswood Prim Sch
Nicky Way
1
Cupid Green La
Wareside
Sandridge Cl
Keats Cl
Darwin Cl
Coleridge Cres
Byron Pl
Essex Mead
Yeomans Ride
Horton Gdns
Perry Gn
Kipling Gr
Bronte Cres
Codicote Row
Dickens Ct
Burns Dr
Chaucer Wlk
Berkeley Sq
Nightingale Wlk
B487
M1
10
07
08
09
125
106

105
85

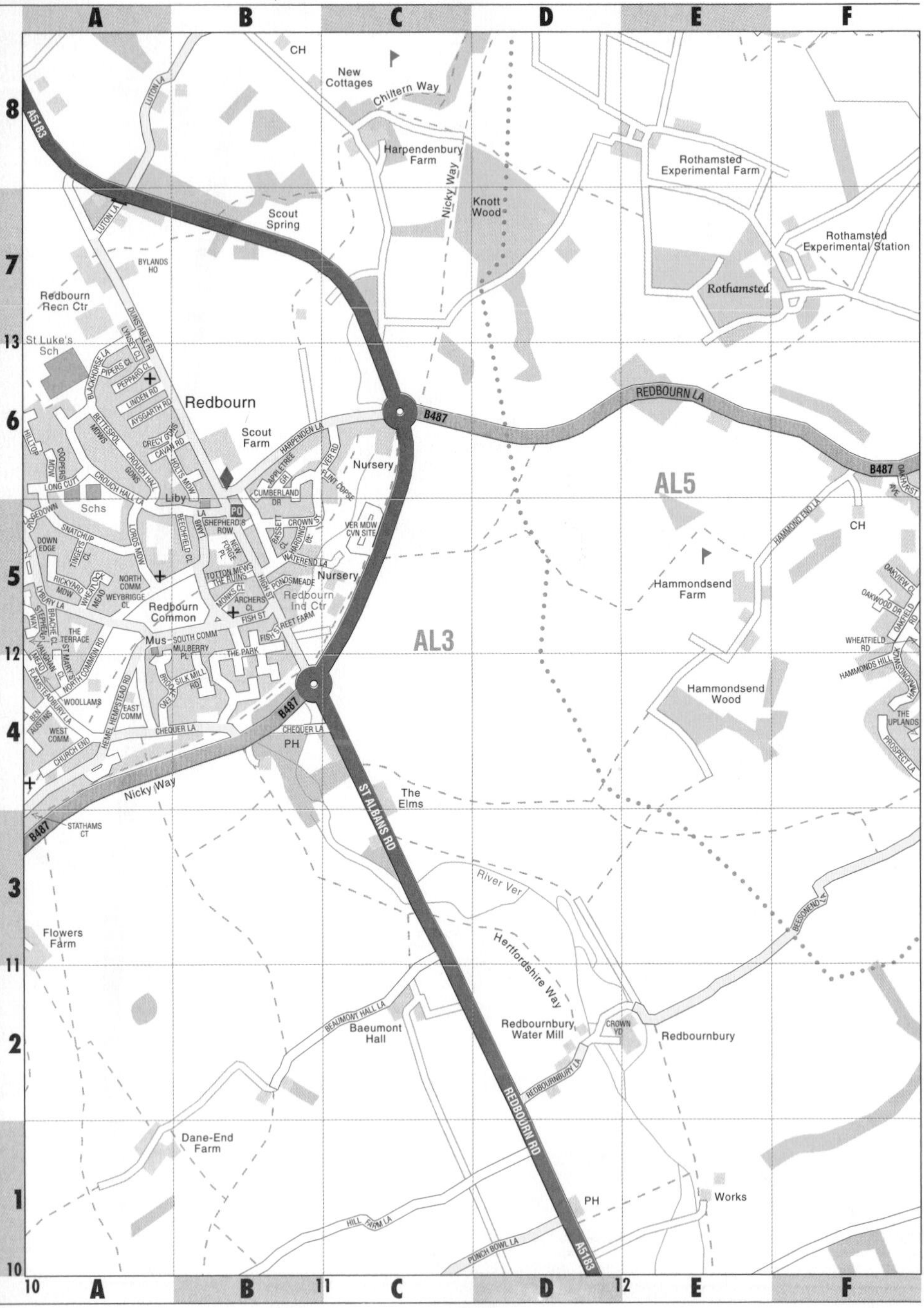
A
B
C
D
E
F
8
7
6
5
4
3
2
1
13
12
11
10
CH
New Cottages
Chiltern Way
Harpendenbury Farm
Rothamsted Experimental Farm
Knott Wood
Nicky Way
Scout Spring
Rothamsted Experimental Station
Rothamsted
A5183
LUTON LA
BYLANDS HO
Redbourn Recn Ctr
DUNSTABLE RD
St Luke's Sch
BLACKHORSE LA
PIPERS CL
PEPPARD CL
LINDEN RD
AYSGARTH RD
Redbourn
BETTESPOL MDWS
CRECY GDNS
CAVAN RD
HOLTS MDW
CROUCH HALL GDNS
Scout Farm
HARPENDEN LA
APPLETREE GR
VER RD
Nursery
B487
REDBOURN LA
HILLTOP
COOPERS MDW
LONG CUT
CROUCH HALL LA
Liby
CUMBERLAND DR
FLINT COPSE
AL5
B487
OAKHURST AVE
HAMMOND END LA
CH
RIDGEDOWN
Schs
LAMB LA
BEECHFIELD CL
PO
SHEPHERD'S ROW
NEW FORGE PL
BASSETT CL
CROWN ST
HARDING CL
VER MDW CVN SITE
WATEREND LA
DOWN EDGE
SNATCHUP
TINGEYS CL
LORDS MDW
Nursery
Hammondsend Farm
OAKVIEW CL
OAKWOOD DR
OAKFIELD RD
RICKYARD MDW
WHEATLOCK MEAD
NORTH COMM
WEYBRIGGE CL
TOTTON MEWS
THE RUINS
HIGH ST
PONDSMEADE
Redbourn Ind Ctr
LYBURY LA
Redbourn Common
MONKS CL
ARCHERS CL
FISH ST
FISH STREET FARM
AL3
WHEATFIELD RD
HAMMONDS HILL
STEPHENS WAY
BRACHE CL
THE TERRACE
ST MARY'S CL
VAUGHAN MEAD
NORTH COMMON RD
Mus
SOUTH COMM
MULBERRY PL
THE PARK
SILK MILL RD
BROOK END
FLAMSTEAD END
Hammondsend Wood
WOOLLAMS
HEMEL HEMPSTEAD RD
EAST COMM
BEN AUSTINS
REDBOURNBURY LA
WEST COMM
CHEQUER LA
B487
CHEQUER LA
THE UPLANDS
PROSPECT LA
PH
CHURCH END
Nicky Way
ST ALBANS RD
The Elms
B487
STATHAMS CT
River Ver
Flowers Farm
Hertfordshire Way
BEESONEND LA
BEAUMONT HALL LA
Baeumont Hall
Redbournbury Water Mill
CROWN YD
Redbournbury
REDBOURNBURY LA
REDBOURN RD
Dane-End Farm
PH
Works
HILL FARM LA
PUNCH BOWL LA
A5183
10
11
12

105
126

A B C D E F

8 7 6 5 4 3 2 1

13 12 11 10

Rothamsted Experimental Sta
Coach La
Hotel
St Dominic RC Prim Sch
Southdown Ind Est
Aldwickbury Farm
Aldwickbury Sch
Green La
The Grove Inf & Jun Schs
Grove Wood
Grove Farm
The Grove
Harpenden Common
Hatching Green
CH
Limbrick Hall
HARPENDEN
Cross Farm
Secret Spring
Clapper's Wood
Thames Wood
Mud La
Eight Acre Wood
Ayres End
AL4
AL5
Bamville Farm
Three Horseshoes (PH)
White House
Pudlen's Wood
Well Wood
Pismire Spring
Beesonend Farm
Childwick Stud
Childwick Hall
Hedge's Farm
Childwick Green
AL3
Green Wood
Cheapside Farm
The White House
Water Tower
Bush Wood
Greens Cottages
Childwick Bury Ho
A1081
ST ALBANS RD
HARPENDEN RD
B487
REDBOURN LA
AYRES END LA
BEESONEND LA
SANDRIDGEBURY LA
LEASEY BRIDGE LA
WHEATHAMPSTEAD RD
FERRERS LA
PIPERS LA
CROSS LA
LIMBRICK RD
WALKERS RD
EAST COMM
WEST COMM
MAPLE COTTS
1 HADLEIGH CT
2 TIVERTON CT
FURZEDOWN CT 1
HEATHVIEW 2

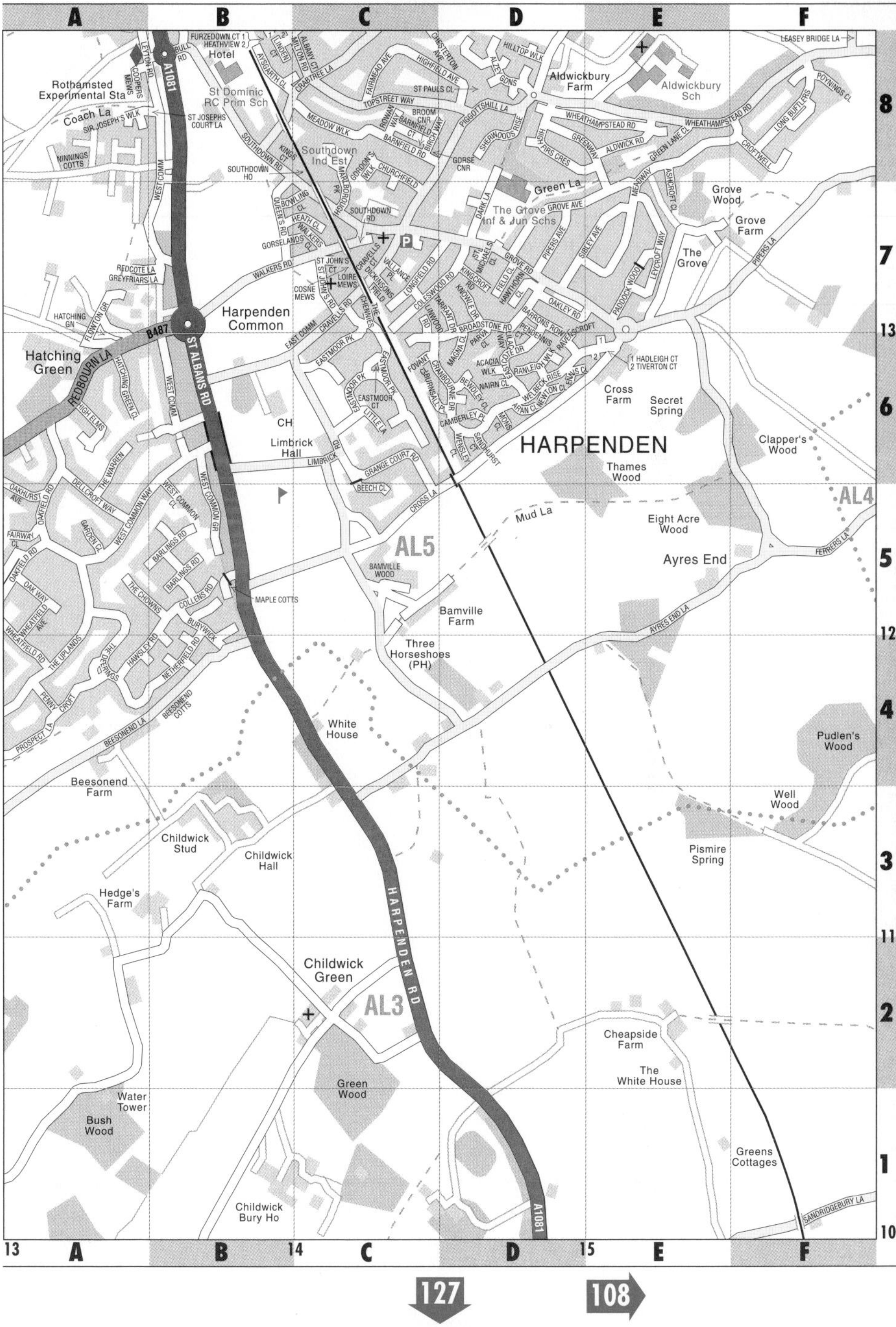

A B C D E F

13 14 15

107
87

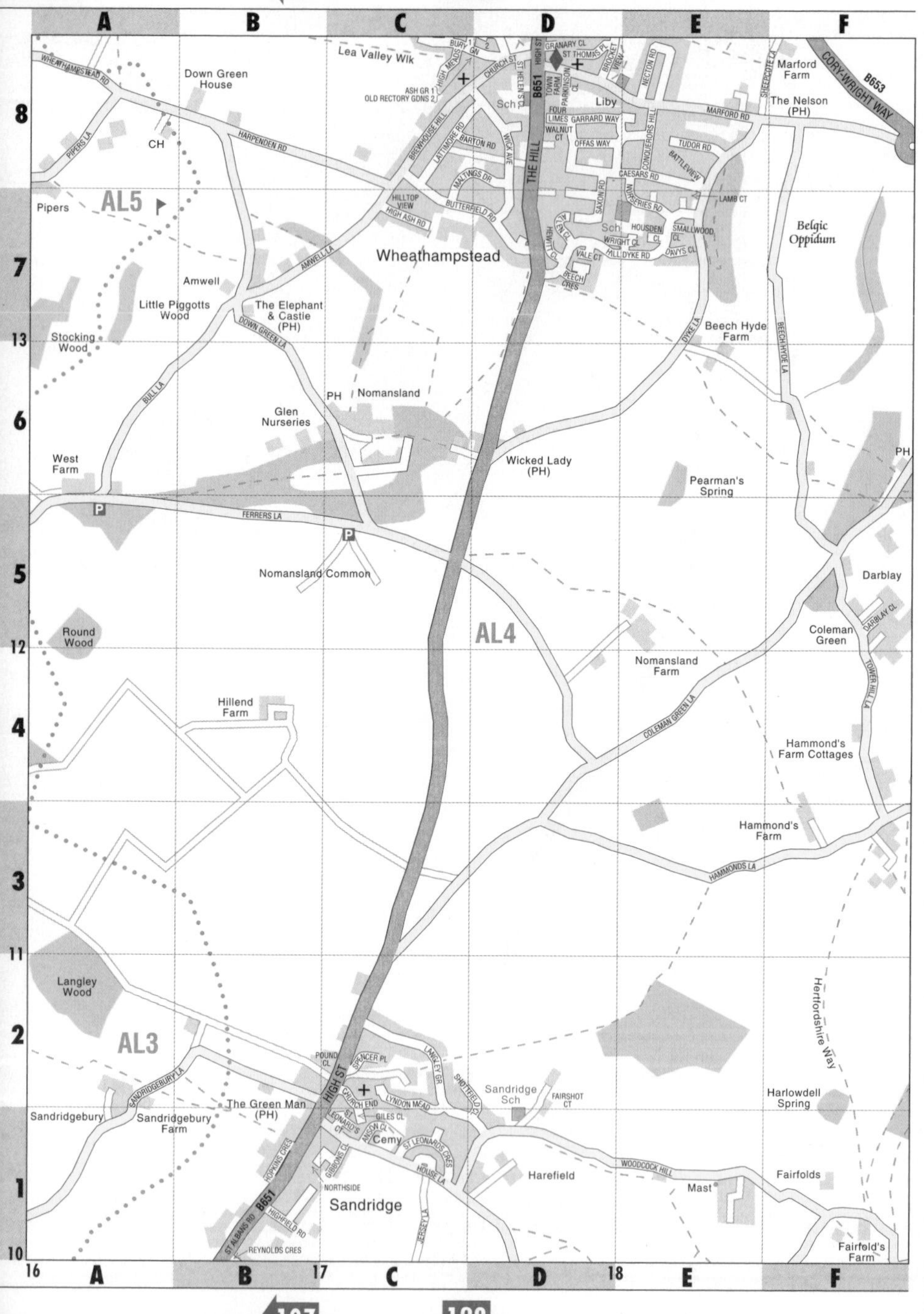

107
128

88
110

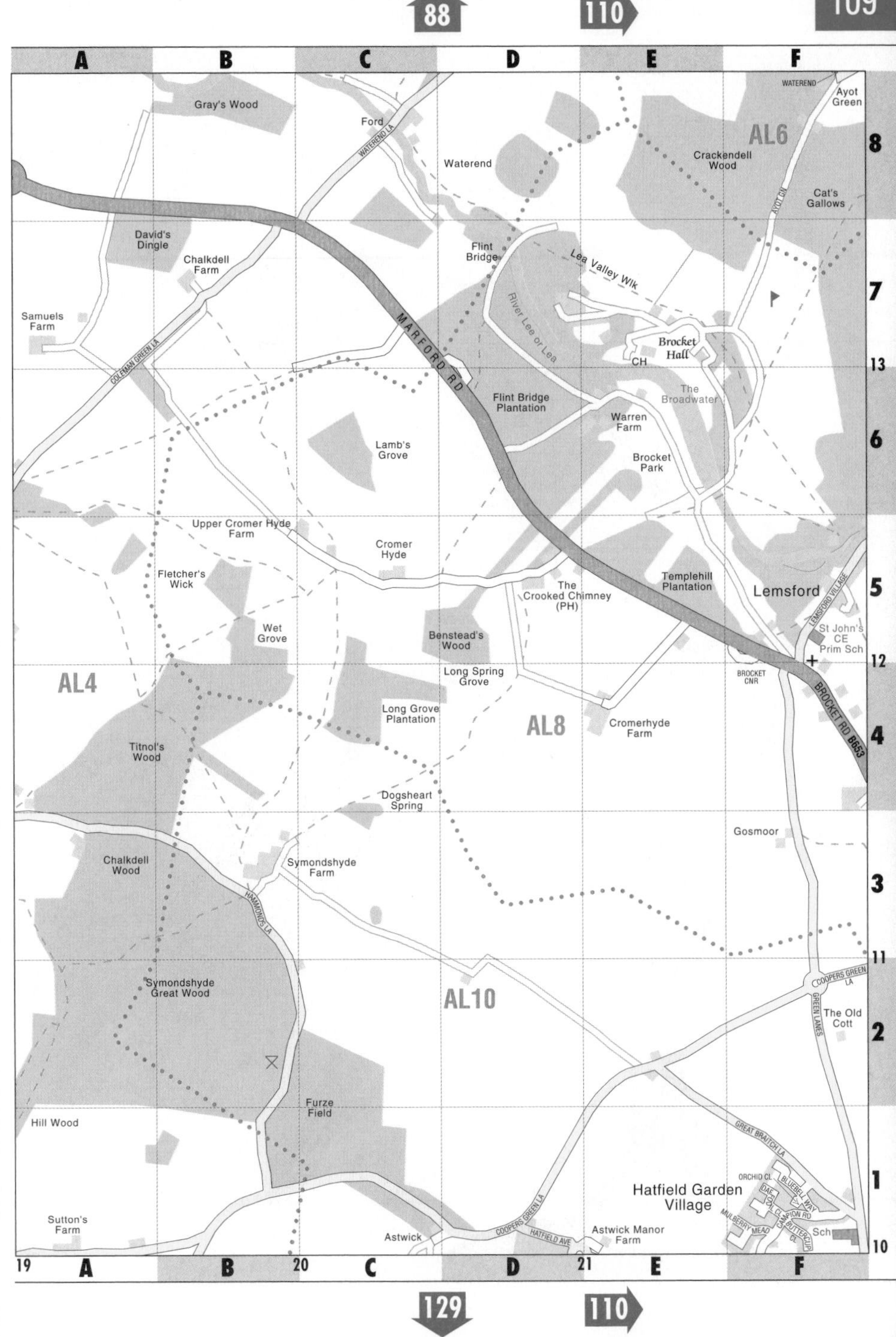

129
110

A B C D E F

8 7 13 6 5 12 4 3 11 2 1 10

AL6 Brock's Wood Six Ways Sherrardspark Wood Sherrardspark Templewood Prim Sch

DIGSWELL HILL AYOT GN PH BRICKWALL CL A1(M) B197 TEMPLEWOOD HAWTHORNS GREAT DELL LITTLE DELL THE VINEYARD VINE CL DIGSWELL CT KNIGHTSFIELD KESTREL WAY BLYTHWAY HO MAPLE GR Mundells Ct A1000 MUNDELLS THE BOULEVARD CENTRAL DR FALCON WAY LYLES LA DIGSWELL RISE CONEYDALE PENTLEY PK WOODLAND RISE ASHLEY CL MANDEVILLE RISE DIGSWELL RD BLAKEMERE RD THE ORCHARD GRESLEY CT WALDEN PL WALDEN RD PERRYWOOD THE GLADE SHERRARDSPARK RD DENSLEY CL SCHOLARS MEWS REDDINGS ROUNDWOOD DR

Oaklands Coll (Welwyn Campus) Liby JUNCTION COTTS WOODSIDE HOUSE THE CAMPUS COLLEGE WAY

WELWYN GARDEN CITY

BESSEMER RD MUNDELLS A1000 LITTLE MUNDELLS Haslemere Ind Est FAIR RD BLACK FAN RD

Nursery GREAT NORTH RD BROCKSWOOD LA BRIDGE RD THE QUADRANGLE HANDSIDE GN GUESSENS WLK YH ASQUITH HOUSE PARK HOUSE WIGMORES N STONEHILLS BRIDGE RD B195 Bridge Pk GARDEN CT BRIDGEFIELDS TEWIN RD SUTHERLAND CT Morrell Ct BROWNFIELDS BLENHEIM CT Martinfield Bsns Ctr MARTINFIELD SWIFTFIELDS SWALLOW END Bridgegate Bsns Ctr SWALLOWFIELDS SWALLOW CT BRIDGE RD E ALBANY PL

HIGH OAKS RD DOGNELL GN DELLCOTT CL THE VALLEY GN HIGH GR RUSSELLCROFT RD COLAYN GARTH PALMERSTON CT HOMERFIELD GUESSENS RD HOWARDSGATE The Howard Ctr OSBORN WAY HYDE WAY Welwyn Garden City

CH MANNICOTTS BROCKETT CL VALLEY RD LITTLE YOUNGS YOUNGS RISE GUESSENS CT GUESSENS GR LANEFIELD WLK CHURCH RD PARKWAY WIGMORES S FRETHERNE RD CHURCH RD CHURCHFIELD HOUSE PARKWAY CL

AL8 THE LINKS ELM GDNS HANDSIDE CL FARM CL APPLECROFT RD MEADOW GN HANDSIDE LA BARN CL BARNSIDE CT BARLEYCROFT GN THE CLOISTERS PARKFIELDS LYTTON GDNS BIRDCROFT RD Sch BARLEYCROFT RD PARKWAY GDNS LONGCROFT LA LONGCROFT GDNS OSBORN WAY

BROAD CT PEARTREE FARM RAVENFIELD RD HOME MEADOW LYNMOUTH RD HERONSWOOD RD WOODFIELD RD PEARTREE CL Peartree Prim Sch REGENT CL PEARTREE CT HOME LEY ESSENDON GDNS VERULAM RD KNELLA RD LONGMORE GDNS SHORTLANDS GN SHORTLANDS PL Peartree BROADWATER RD ATHELSTAN WLK N MOATWOOD GN

PH LEMSFORD VILLAGE MILL CL PH Lemsford LEMSFORD VILLAGE B197 B195 Applecroft Sch ATTIMORE RD ELMWOOD ATTIMORE CL THE OLD DR SCOTTS VIEW FEARNLEY RD TURMORE DALE HONEYCROFT Handside HOBBS WAY Sports Gd FORDWICH RD WILKINS GR ROOKS CL ROOKS HILL COLGROVE STANBOROUGH CL

Lemsford Springs (Nature Reserve) BROADFIELD PL NEWFIELDS MELBOURNE CT BROADWATER RD A6129 THE REEDS BY THE MOUNT BROADWATER CRES CHALKS MEAD GOBLINS GN EDGARS CT CRESWICK ATHELSTAN WLK S A1000 THE SPINNEY WELL GARTH BEDWELL CL POND CROFT BASSINGBURN WLK OAKTREE GARTH MILL GREEN RD DUNCAN CL ETHELRED CL LUDWICK WAY LUDWICK GN CRANBORNE GDNS ROSEMOOR CL SALISBURY GDNS ST AUDREYS GN SALISBURY RD GAINSWOOD EARTREE LA HOLWELL RD Holwell Prim Sch LONGLANDS RD WHEATLEY RD UPPERFIELD RD COWPER RD

Twentieth Mile Bridge LONGCROFT GN STANBOROUGH MEWS MARSDEN RD SPRINGFIELDS HO MARSDEN GN DOWNFIELDS LEMSFORD LA STACKLANDS SPRINGFIELDS HEATHER RD STANBOROUGH GN WOODHALL CT BEECHFIELD RD WOODHALL LA BARNFIELD RD PINEWOOD FURZEFIELD RD WOODHALL HO BURGUNDY CROFT LUDWICK CL COLE GREEN LA PH SANDPIT RD MOSS GN GOOSEACRE HYDE VALLEY Liby

Lakeside Sch Oaklands Coll (Lemsford Lane Campus) STANBOROUGH RD STANBOROUGH LA Gosling Sports Park Ski Ctr LITTLE BURROW BURROWFIELD SOUTHFIELD Our Lady RC Prim Sch Woodhall PH HANOVER HO MEADWAY RAYMONDS PLAIN HOLLYBUSH HO LEIGH COMM HOMESTEAD LA HOMESTEAD CT

Stanborough Sch WEST BURROWFIELD EAST BURROWFIELD HITHERBAULK TWELVE ACRES RAYMONDS CL GREAT LEY FOUR ACRES HUNTERS WAY TWO ACRES OAKEN GR HOLLYBUSH LA

B653 BROCKET RD NEW RD Stanborough Park Mast SIR JOHN NEWSOM WAY KENYON PL LAWRENCE HALL END SOUTH LEY AL7

Boating Lake Pol HQ CHEQUERS CHEQUERS FIELD CHAMBERS GR SOUTH LEY CT Cemy Hatfield Hyde Creswick JMI Sch LAYTON ST WALNUT CT WALNUT HOUSE WALNUT GR MOUNTWAY CL MOUNT WAY GREEN ACRES RYELANDS LITTLE WADE THE WADE

Stanborough The Bull (PH) B653 B197 A6129 BOUNDARY HO ROLLSWOOD ELLIOTT CL MIDDLEFIELD LINKFIELD HAREBELL LADY GR HOWLANDS THE CROFT

COOPERS GREEN LA Stanborough Bury THE HOLLIES GREAT NORTH RD River Lea or Lee DRYCROFT KATESCROFT PINNATE PL KENDALL CL CAMFIELD Amb HQ BOUNDARY LA BOUNDARY CT GOLDEN DELL KINGSLEY CT

Yachting Lake Cheswick Plantation HOLLYBUSH LA BENNETT CL WYNDHAMS END

Woodhall Farm Lea Valley Wlk ASCOTS LA

AL9 Lea Valley Walk GYPSY LA

AL10 A414 GREAT NORTH RD OLDINGS CNR COMET WAY A1001 A1(M) MILL GREEN LA A1000 HERTFORD RD A414

GREAT NORTH RD A414 MOUNT PLEASANT LA A414

10 22 A B 23 C D 24 E F

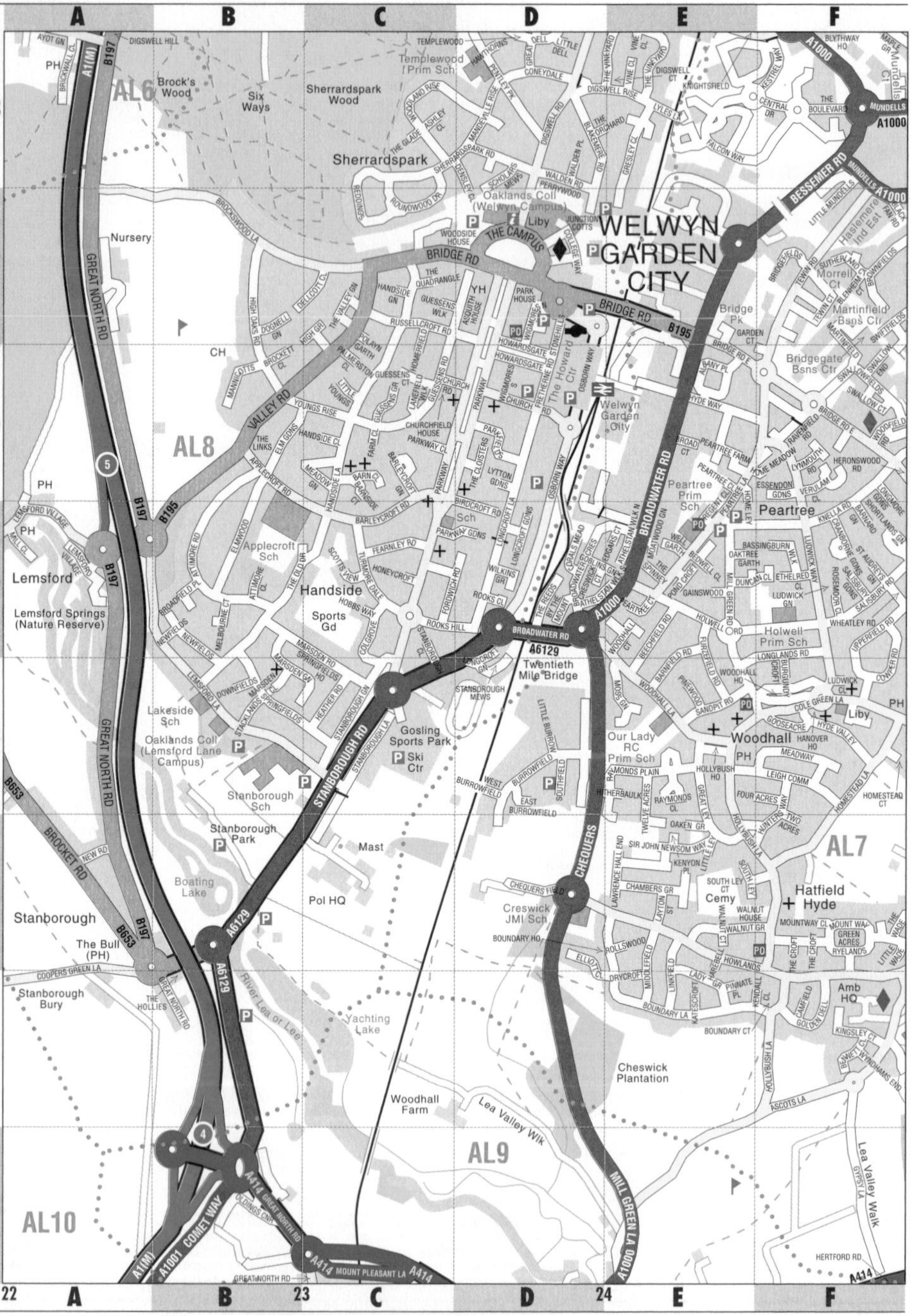

90
112

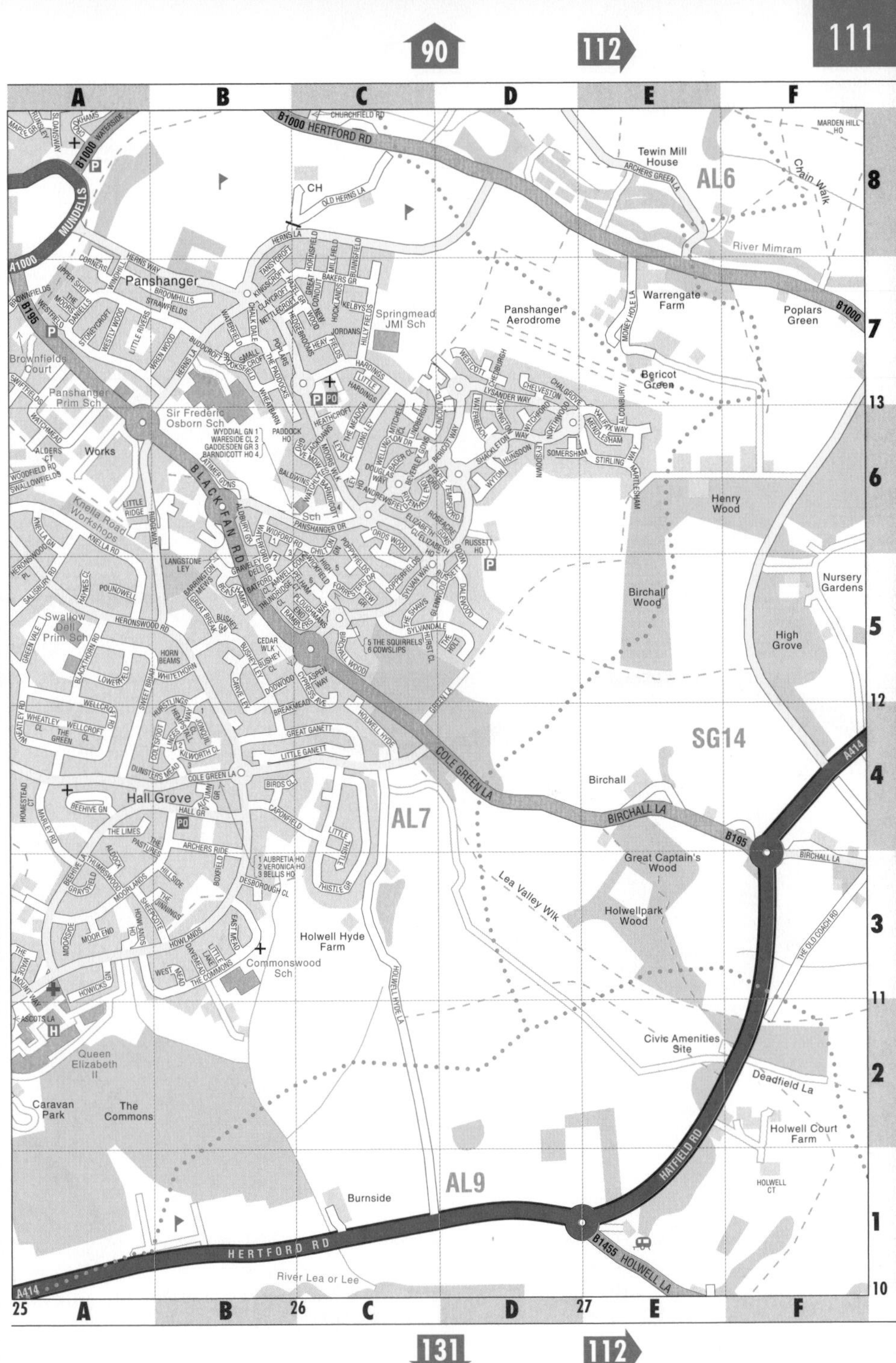

131
112

111 91

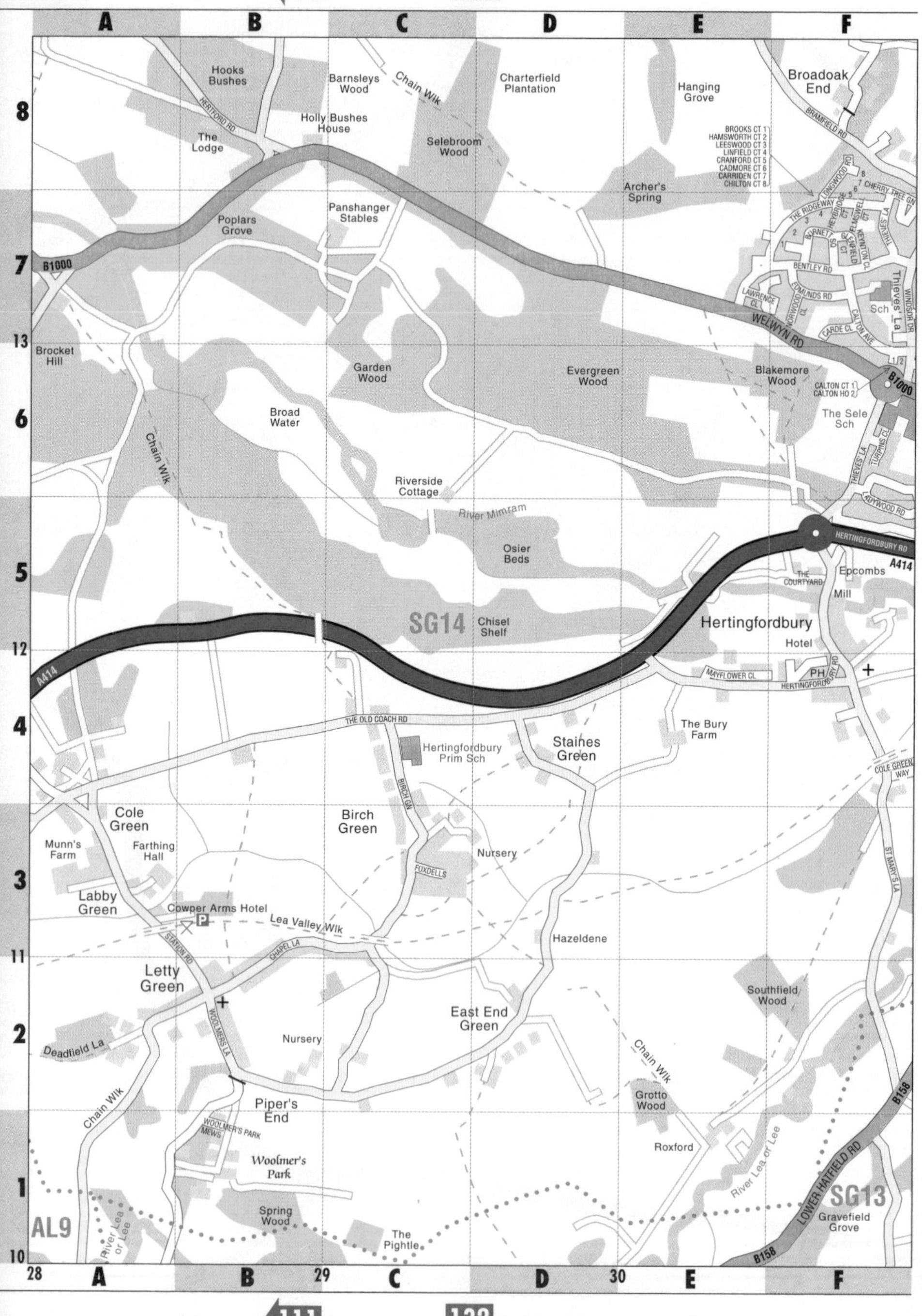

111 132

C6
1 ST ANDREW MEWS
2 MILLBRIDGE MEWS
3 TOWN MILL MEWS
D6
1 ADAM'S YD
2 DOLPHIN YD
3 MAIDENHEAD ST
4 EVRON PL
5 HONEY LA
6 MARKET PL
7 SALISBURY SQ
8 POST OFFICE WLK
9 The Bircherley Green Ctr
10 ODDFELLOWS CT
11 SHAFTESBURY QUAY
12 PRIORY WHARF
13 PRIORY CT
14 BIRCHERLEY CT
15 THE MALTHOUSE
16 WARREN PL
17 PROVIDENCE PL
18 BLUECOATS CT
19 CHAUNCY CT
20 MITRE CT
21 ST JOHN'S CT
92
114
HERTFORD
Bengeo
Hartham
SG14
SG12
SG13
Revel's Hall
Lea Valley Wlk
River Lee Navigation
Marshgate Trad Est
Mead Bsns Ctr
Duncombe Sch
L Ctr
Hertford North
Hertford East
Hollybush Prim Sch
St Joseph's RC Prim Sch
Cemy
Hertford County
River Beane
Superstore
TA Ctr
Liby
Castle
Mus
Simon Balle Sch
Balls Park
Richard Hale Sch
County Hall
University of Hertfordshire (Hertford Campus)
St Joseph's in the Park Sch
Chain Wlk
Nursery
Dunkirks Farm
Morgans JMI Sch
Terrace Wood
River Mimram
River Lea or Lee
Bayfordbury Park Farm
Bayford Brook
Hertfordshire Way
Swallow Grove Farm
Ducketts Cottages
Home Farm
Brickendonbury
Bayfordbury Coll (University of Hertfordshire)
Sailor's Grove
Thrift Cottages
Brickendon Brook
Home Farm
NORTH RD
WELWYN RD
HERTINGFORDBURY RD
GASCOYNE WAY
LONDON RD
WARE RD
HORNS MILL RD
LOWER HATFIELD RD
BULLOCK'S LA
PEG'S LA
HALE RD
PORT HILL
BENGEO ST
COWBRIDGE
Hagsdell La
MANGROVE RD
MORGAN'S WLK
BRICKENDON LA
A119
B158
B1000
A414
B1197
B1502
133
114

113 93

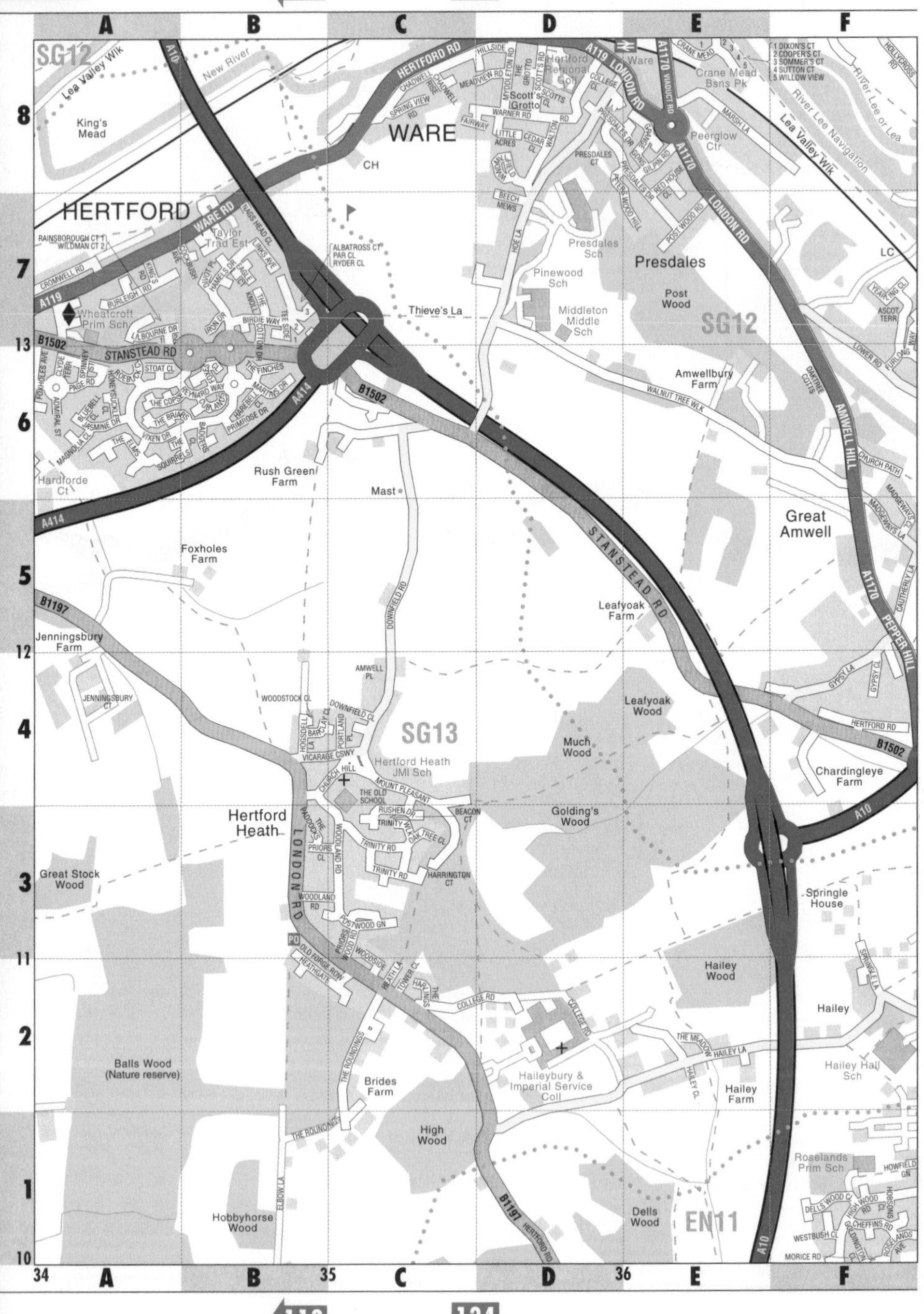

113 134

94
116

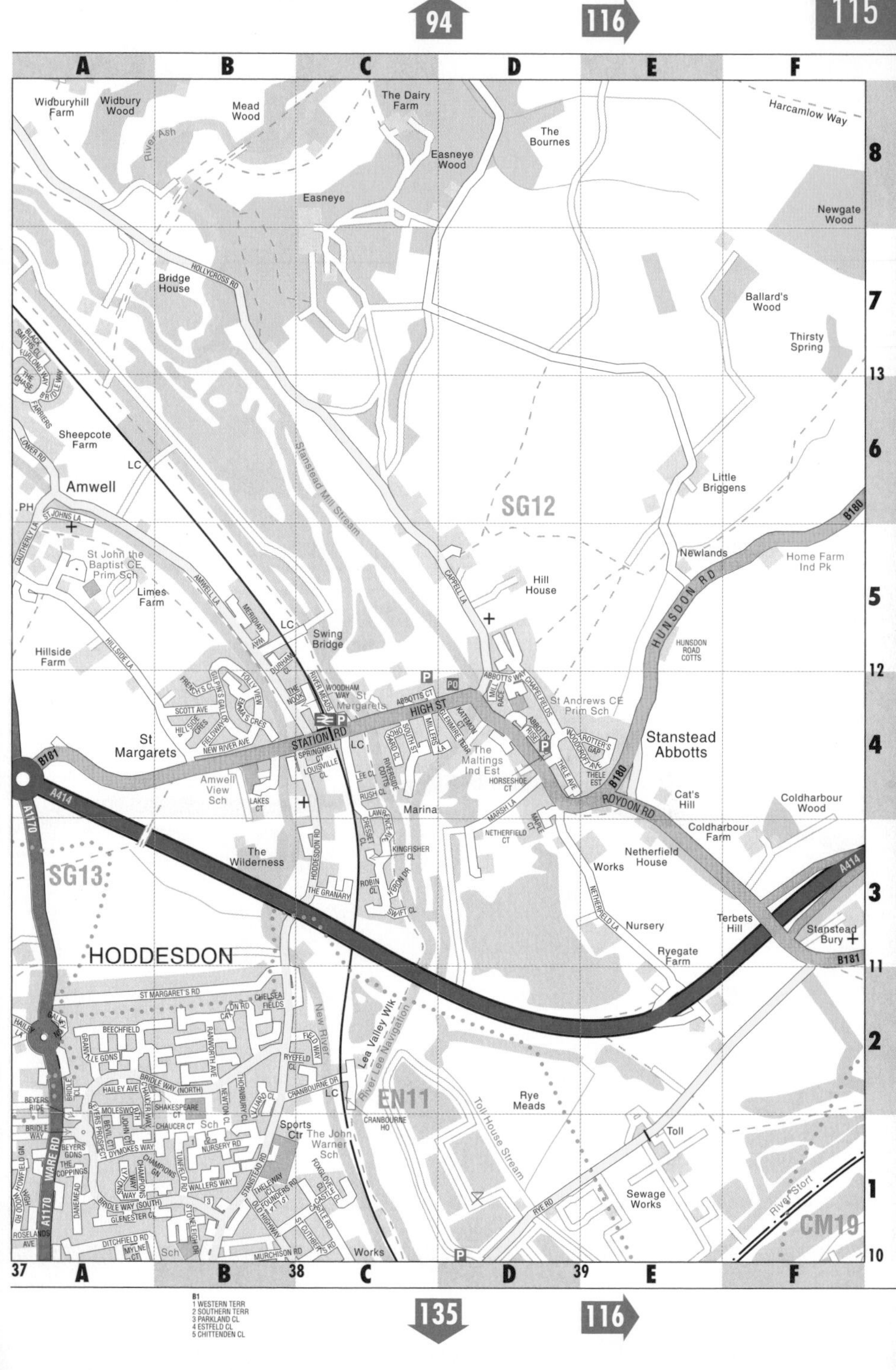

B1
1 WESTERN TERR
2 SOUTHERN TERR
3 PARKLAND CL
4 ESTFELD CL
5 CHITTENDEN CL

135
116

115 95

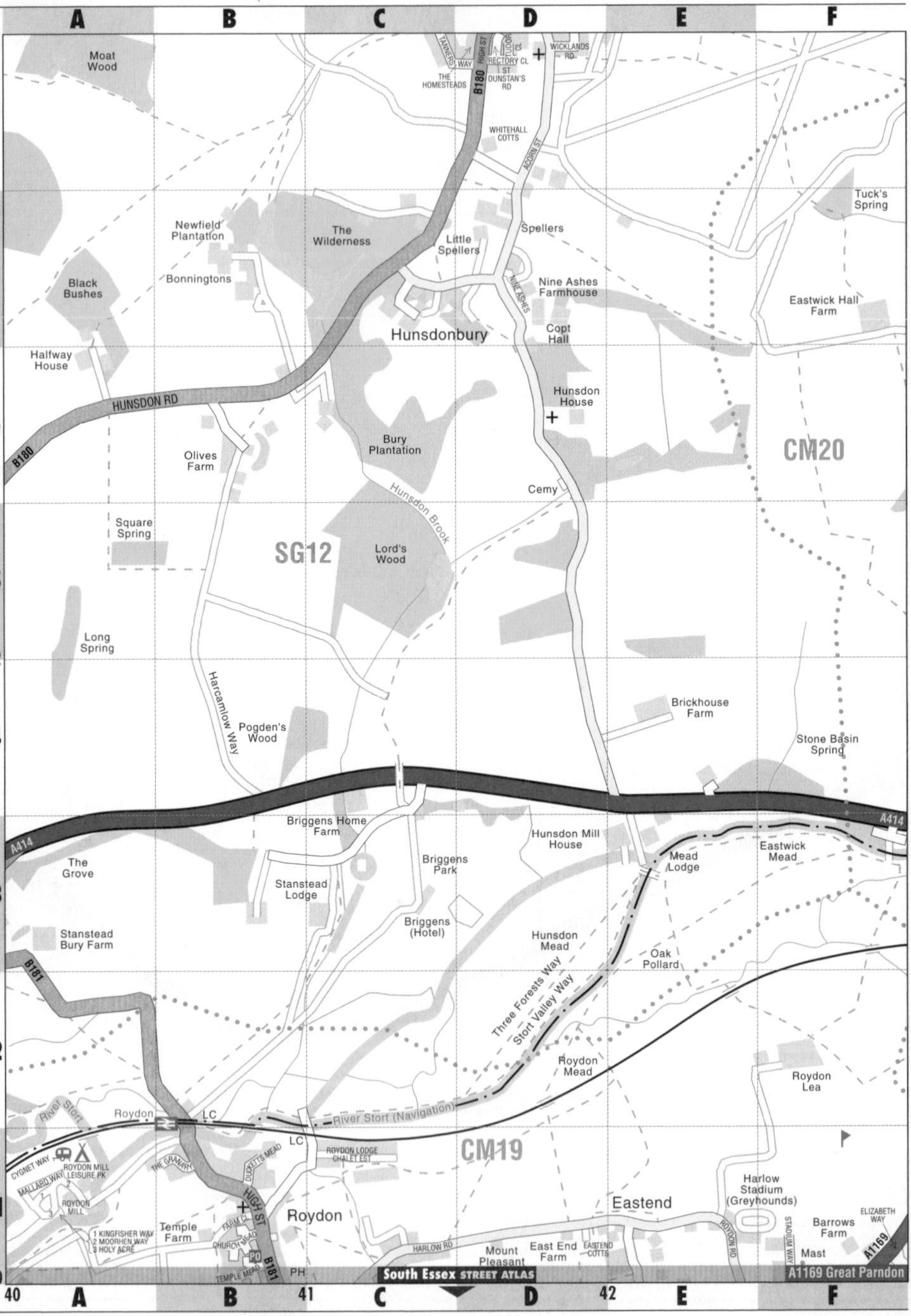

A B C D E F

8 7 13 6 5 12 4 3 11 2 1 10

Moat Wood
Newfield Plantation
The Wilderness
Little Spellers
Spellers
Nine Ashes Farmhouse
Tuck's Spring
Black Bushes
Bonningtons
Hunsdonbury
Copt Hall
Eastwick Hall Farm
Halfway House
HUNSDON RD
B180
Hunsdon House
Olives Farm
Bury Plantation
CM20
Cemy
Hunsdon Brook
Square Spring
SG12
Lord's Wood
Long Spring
Harcamlow Way
Pogden's Wood
Brickhouse Farm
Stone Basin Spring
A414
Briggens Home Farm
Hunsdon Mill House
Eastwick Mead
Mead Lodge
The Grove
Briggens Park
Stanstead Lodge
Briggens (Hotel)
Stanstead Bury Farm
Hunsdon Mead
Oak Pollard
B181
Three Forests Way
Stort Valley Way
Roydon Mead
Roydon Lea
River Stort
Roydon
LC
River Stort (Navigation)
ROYDON LODGE CHALET EST
CM19
CYGNET WAY
MALLARD WAY
ROYDON MILL LEISURE PK
ROYDON MILL
THE GRANARY
DUCKETTS MEAD
HIGH ST
Temple Farm
Roydon
Eastend
Harlow Stadium (Greyhounds)
ROYDON RD
STADIUM WAY
ELIZABETH WAY
Barrows Farm
1 KINGFISHER WAY
2 MOORHEN WAY
3 HOLY ACRE
FARM CL
CHURCH MEAD
PO
TEMPLE MEAD
PH
HARLOW RD
Mount Pleasant
East End Farm
EASTEND COTTS
Mast
A1169
TANNERS WAY
HIGH ST
THE HOMESTEADS
RECTORY CL
ST DUNSTAN'S RD
WICKLANDS RD
WHITEHALL COTTS
ACORN ST
NINE ASHES

South Essex STREET ATLAS

A1169 Great Parndon

40 A B 41 C D 42 E F

115

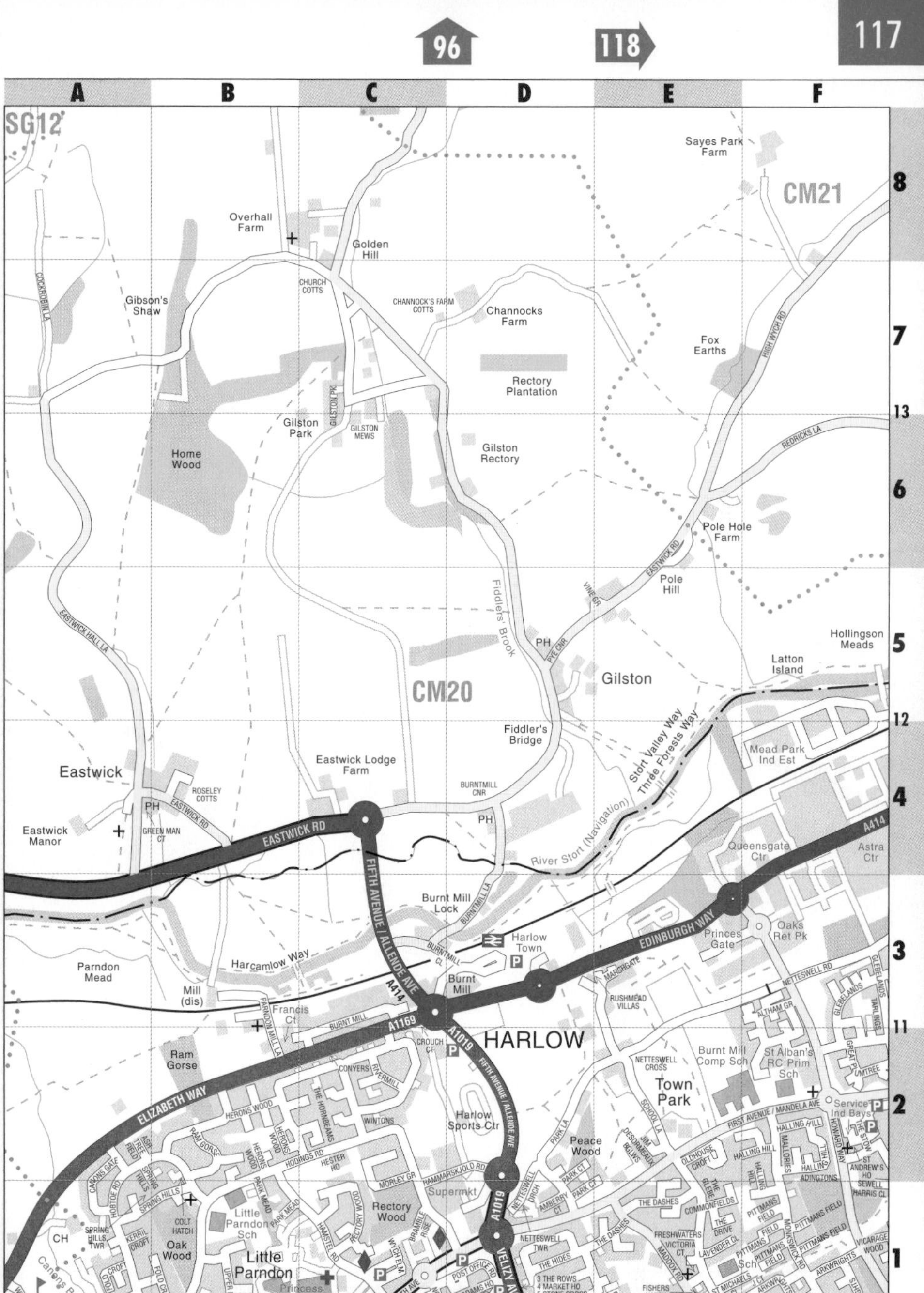
A
B
C
D
E
F
SG12
CM21
CM20
Sayes Park Farm
Overhall Farm
Golden Hill
Gibson's Shaw
CHURCH COTTS
CHANNOCK'S FARM COTTS
Channocks Farm
Fox Earths
Rectory Plantation
Gilston Park
GILSTON MEWS
Gilston Rectory
Home Wood
HIGH WYCH RD
REDRICKS LA
Pole Hole Farm
Pole Hill
EASTWICK RD
VINE GR
Fiddlers' Brook
EASTWICK HALL LA
PYE CNR
Gilston
Hollingson Meads
Latton Island
Fiddler's Bridge
Stort Valley Way
Three Forests Way
Mead Park Ind Est
Eastwick Lodge Farm
Eastwick
ROSELEY COTTS
BURNTMILL CNR
Eastwick Manor
GREEN MAN CT
River Stort (Navigation)
Queensgate Ctr
Astra Ctr
A414
FIFTH AVENUE / ALLENDE AVE
Burnt Mill Lock
BURNTMILL LA
Harlow Town
EDINBURGH WAY
Princes Gate
Oaks Ret Pk
Parndon Mead
Harcamlow Way
Burnt Mill
MARSHGATE
NETTESWELL RD
Mill (dis)
Francis Ct
RUSHMEAD VILLAS
ALTHAM GR
GLEBELANDS
HARLOW
A1169
A1019
CROUCH CT
Ram Gorse
NETTESWELL CROSS
Burnt Mill Comp Sch
St Alban's RC Prim Sch
ELIZABETH WAY
CONYERS
RIVERMILL
Town Park
THE HORNBEAMS
HERONS WOOD
SCHOOL LA
Harlow Sports Ctr
FIRST AVENUE / MANDELA AVE
Service Ind Bays
WINTONS
Peace Wood
HODINGS RD
HESTER HO
HAMMARSKJOLD RD
MORLEY GR
Supermkt
Rectory Wood
Little Parndon Sch
Oak Wood
COLT HATCH
SPRING HILLS TWR
Little Parndon
Princess Alexandra
Canons Brook
NETTESWELL TWR
THE HIDES
VELIZY AVE
3 THE ROWS
4 MARKET HO
5 STONE CROSS
Harlow Coll
STANFIELDS CT
FISHERS HATCH
VICTORIA CT
FRESHWATERS
THE DASHES
COMMONFIELDS
PITTMANS FIELD
ARKWRIGHTS
Netteswell
CORAL HO
STANTONS
WEST SQ 1
MITRE BLDGS 2
8
7
13
6
5
12
4
3
11
2
1
10
43
44
45

117
97

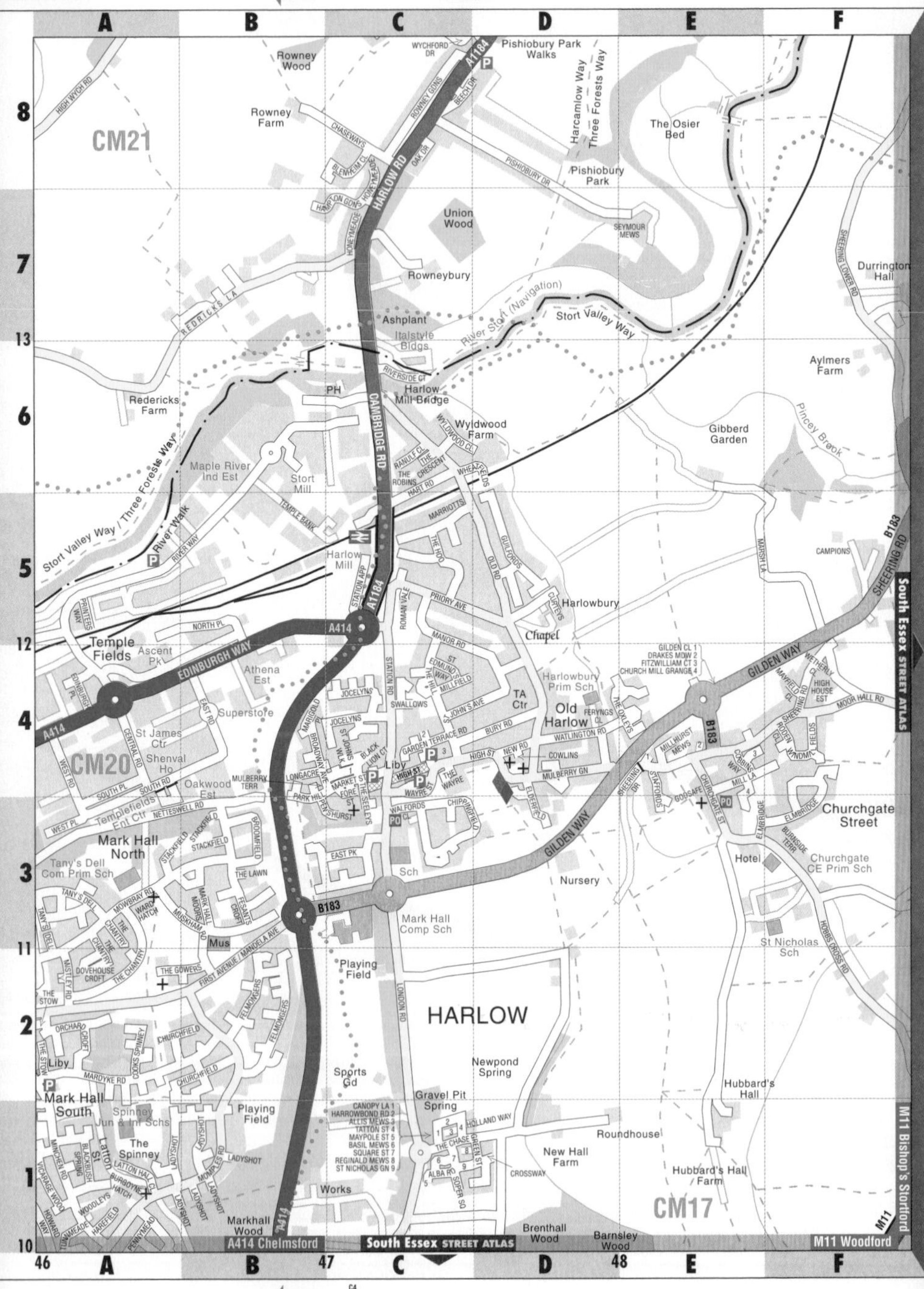

117

C4
1 DELLFIELD CT
2 CHERRY BLOSSOM CL
3 ROSEMARY CL

99
120

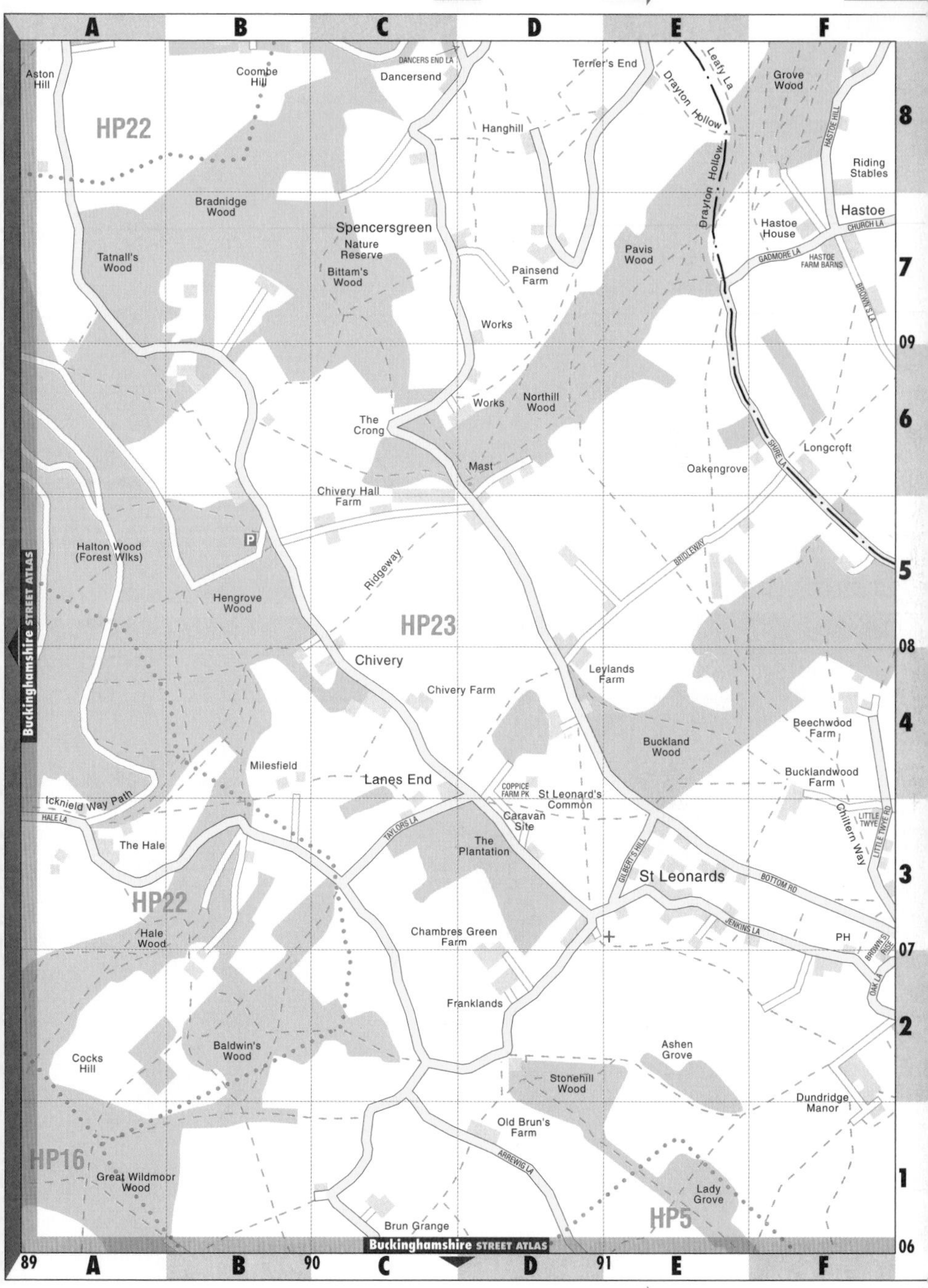
A
B
C
D
E
F
Aston Hill
Coombe Hill
DANCERS END LA
Dancersend
Terrier's End
Leafy La
Drayton Hollow
Grove Wood
HP22
Hanghill
HASTOE HILL
Riding Stables
Bradnidge Wood
Spencersgreen
Nature Reserve
Hastoe
Hastoe House
CHURCH LA
Tatnall's Wood
Bittam's Wood
Painsend Farm
Pavis Wood
GADMORE LA
HASTOE FARM BARNS
BROWN'S LA
Works
The Crong
Works
Northill Wood
SHIRE LA
Longcroft
Mast
Oakengrove
Chivery Hall Farm
Halton Wood (Forest Wlks)
P
Ridgeway
BRIDLEWAY
Hengrove Wood
HP23
Chivery
Leylands Farm
Chivery Farm
Beechwood Farm
Buckland Wood
Milesfield
Lanes End
Bucklandwood Farm
Icknield Way Path
COPPICE FARM PK
St Leonard's Common
HALE LA
Caravan Site
LITTLE TWYE
Chiltern Way
LITTLE TWYE RD
The Hale
TAYLORS LA
The Plantation
GILBERT'S HILL
St Leonards
BOTTOM RD
HP22
JENKINS LA
Chambres Green Farm
PH
Hale Wood
BROWN'S RISE
OAK LA
Franklands
Cocks Hill
Baldwin's Wood
Ashen Grove
Stonehill Wood
Dundridge Manor
Old Brun's Farm
HP16
ARREWIG LA
Great Wildmoor Wood
Lady Grove
HP5
Brun Grange
8
7
09
6
5
08
4
3
07
2
1
06
89
90
91
Buckinghamshire STREET ATLAS

120

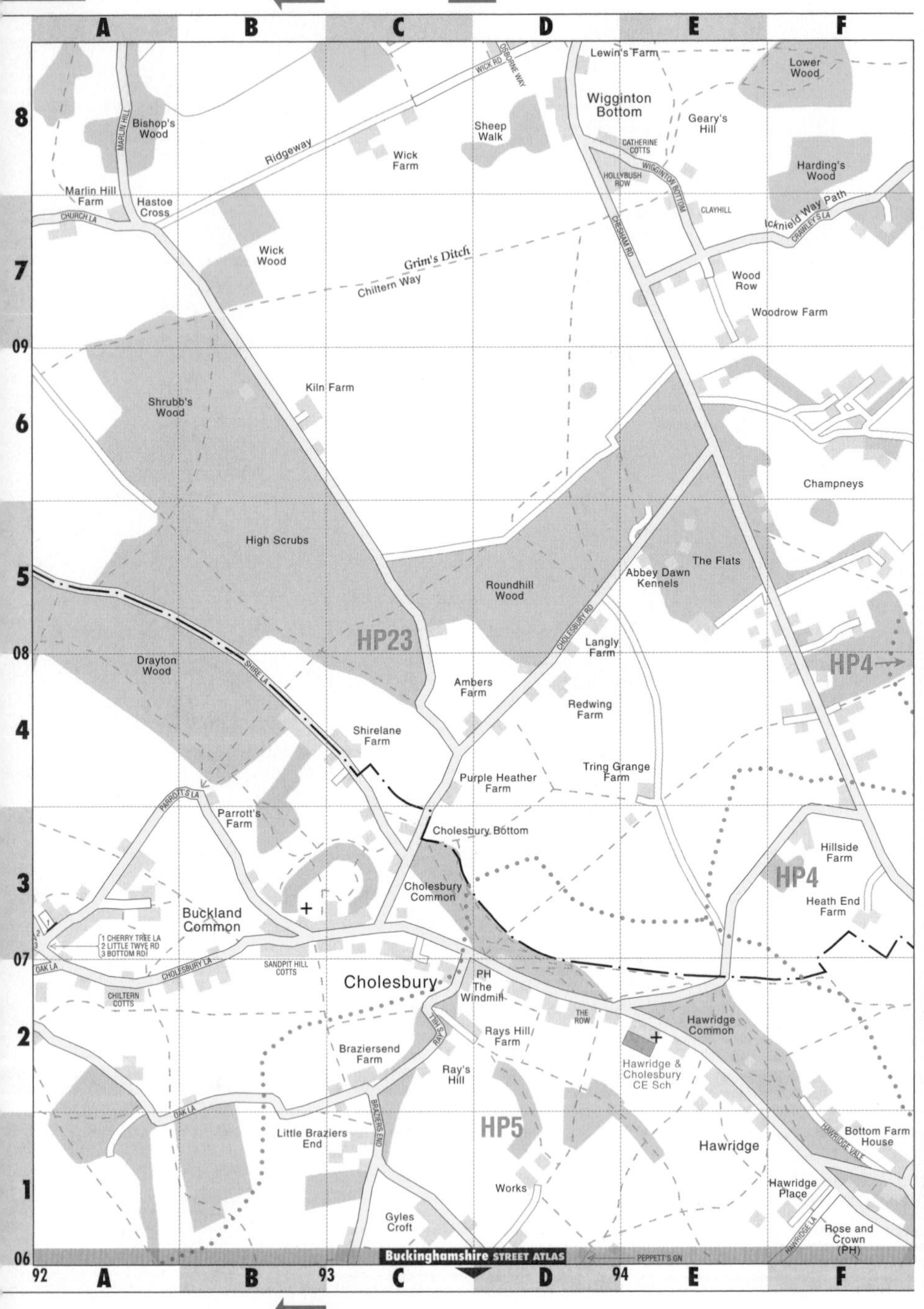
A B C D E F
8 7 09 6 5 08 4 3 07 2 1 06
92 93 94
Lewin's Farm
Lower Wood
Wigginton Bottom
Geary's Hill
Bishop's Wood
MARLIN HILL
WICK RD
OSBORNE WAY
Sheep Walk
Ridgeway
Wick Farm
CATHERINE COTTS
HOLLYBUSH ROW
WIGGINTON BOTTOM
Harding's Wood
Marlin Hill Farm
Hastoe Cross
CHURCH LA
CLAYHILL
Icknield Way Path
CRAWLEY'S LA
CHESHAM RD
Wick Wood
Grim's Ditch
Chiltern Way
Wood Row
Woodrow Farm
Kiln Farm
Shrubb's Wood
Champneys
High Scrubs
The Flats
Abbey Dawn Kennels
Roundhill Wood
HP23
Langly Farm
Drayton Wood
SHIRE LA
CHOLESBURY RD
HP4
Ambers Farm
Redwing Farm
Shirelane Farm
Tring Grange Farm
Purple Heather Farm
PARROTT'S LA
Parrott's Farm
Cholesbury Bottom
Hillside Farm
HP4
Cholesbury Common
Heath End Farm
Buckland Common
1 CHERRY TREE LA
2 LITTLE TWYE RD
3 BOTTOM RD
OAK LA
CHOLESBURY LA
SANDPIT HILL COTTS
Cholesbury
PH
The Windmill
CHILTERN COTTS
THE ROW
Hawridge Common
RAY'S HILL
Rays Hill Farm
Braziersend Farm
Ray's Hill
Hawridge & Cholesbury CE Sch
OAK LA
BRAZIERS END
HP5
Little Braziers End
Hawridge
HAWRIDGE VALE
Bottom Farm House
Works
Hawridge Place
HAWRIDGE LA
Gyles Croft
Rose and Crown (PH)
PEPPETT'S GN

101
122

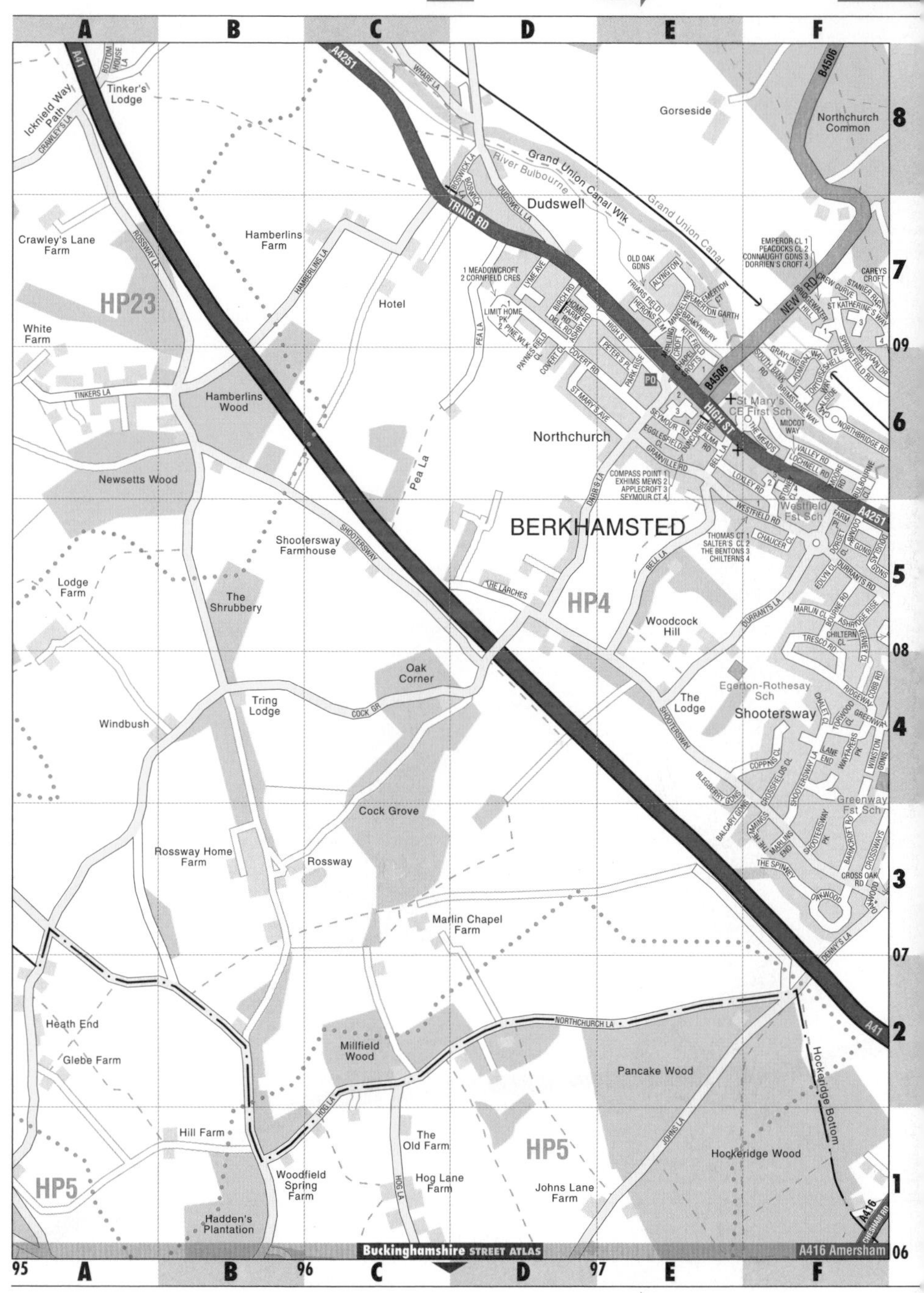
A
B
C
D
E
F
Tinker's Lodge
Icknield Way Path
Gorseside
Northchurch Common
Grand Union Canal Wlk
River Bulbourne
Grand Union Canal
Dudswell
TRING RD
Crawley's Lane Farm
Hamberlins Farm
HP23
Hotel
White Farm
Hamberlins Wood
Northchurch
Newsetts Wood
BERKHAMSTED
Shootersway Farmhouse
Lodge Farm
The Shrubbery
HP4
Woodcock Hill
Oak Corner
Tring Lodge
The Lodge
Egerton-Rothesay Sch
Shootersway
Windbush
Cock Grove
Greenway Fst Sch
Rossway Home Farm
Rossway
Marlin Chapel Farm
Heath End
Glebe Farm
Millfield Wood
Pancake Wood
Hockeridge Bottom
Hill Farm
The Old Farm
HP5
Hockeridge Wood
Woodfield Spring Farm
Hog Lane Farm
Johns Lane Farm
Hadden's Plantation
St Mary's CE First Sch
Westfield Fst Sch
HIGH ST
NEW RD
Pea La
NORTHCHURCH LA
HOG LA
JOHNS LA
SHOOTERSWAY
COCK GR
A41
A4251
B4506
A416
8
7
09
6
5
08
4
3
07
2
1
06
95
96
97
A416 Amersham

122

121
102

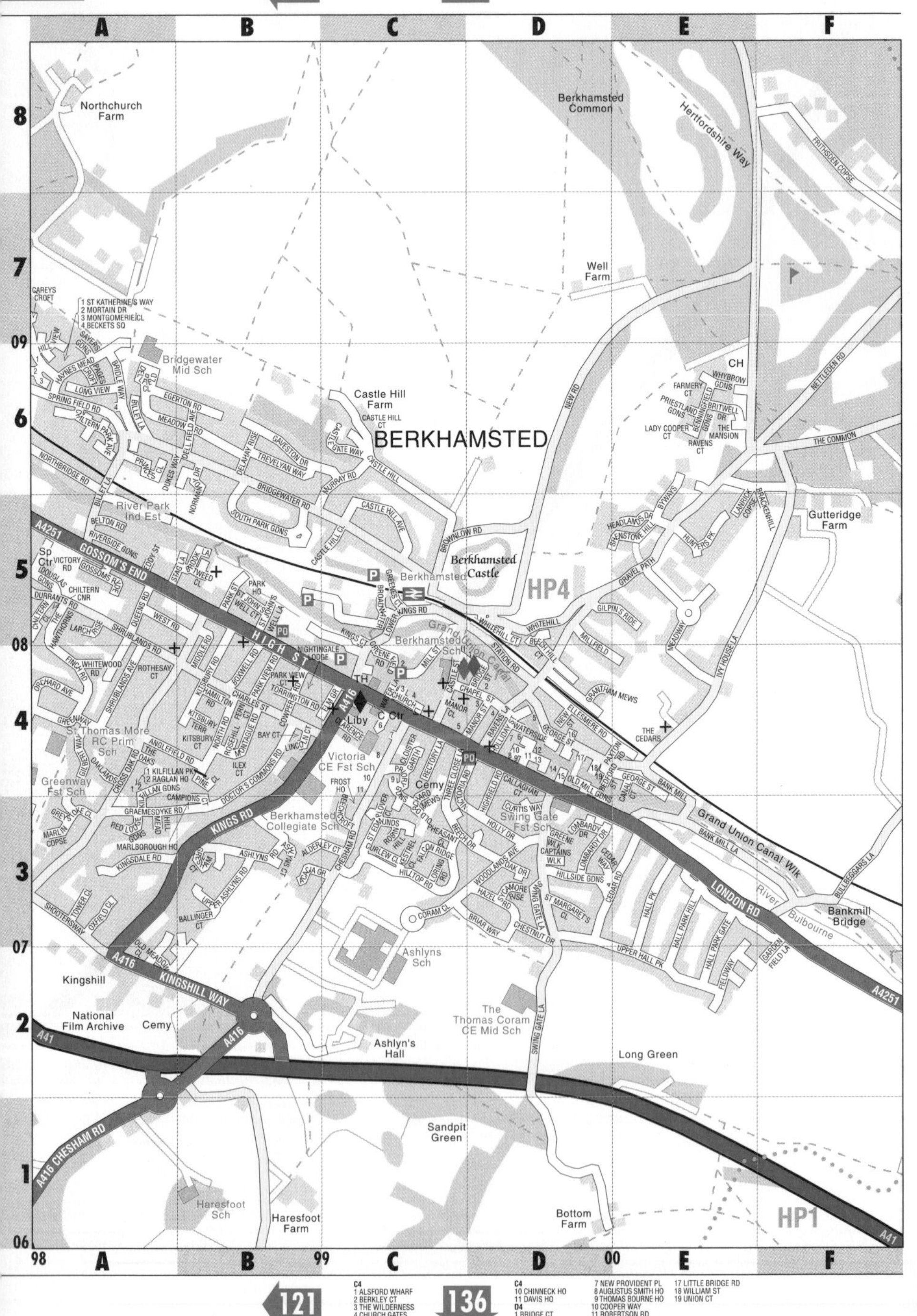

121
136

C4
1 ALSFORD WHARF
2 BERKLEY CT
3 THE WILDERNESS
4 CHURCH GATES
5 DOWER MEWS
6 PRINCE EDWARD ST
7 CAVALIER CT
8 DEANS LAWN
9 PRIORY CT

C4
10 CHINNECK HO
11 DAVIS HO

D4
1 BRIDGE CT
2 MASON'S YD
3 CASTLE MEWS
4 BARTRUM VILLAS
5 RAVENS WHARF
6 GLASSMILL HO
7 NEW PROVIDENT PL
8 AUGUSTUS SMITH HO
9 THOMAS BOURNE HO
10 COOPER WAY
11 ROBERTSON RD
12 COSTINS WLK
13 McDOUGALL RD
14 LONDRINA CT
15 LONDRINA TERR
16 CAMBRIDGE TERR
17 LITTLE BRIDGE RD
18 WILLIAM ST
19 UNION CT

103
124

A
B
C
D
E
F
Holly Bush Farm
Frithsden Vineyard
Frithsden
PH
Little Frithsden Copse
Crossways Farm
Heizdin's Wood
Strathgade Farm
Bingham's Park Childrens Farm
Spring Farm
Brown's Spring
Bingham's Park
Brown's Spring
Hollybush Wood
Rumblers Farm
Brown Springs Farm
Catstail Wood
Woodcroft Farm
Pottenend Farm
PH
Potten End CE Fst Sch
Potten End
Grim's Ditch
Boxted Farm
Amersfort
Little Heath
Little Heath Farm
Boxted House
Gutteridge Wood
HP4
Littleheath Great Farm
Lower Little Heath Farm
Fields End Farm
Fields End
Martindale Prim Sch
John F Kennedy RC Sch
Warners End
HP1
Hertfordshire Way
Bullbeggars Wood
HEMEL HEMPSTEAD
Shrub Hill Common
Sewage Works
Pouchen End
Pouchen End Hall
Pouchen End Farm
Chaulden
Chaulden Jun & Inf Schs
Pix Farm
Broadway Farm
Grand Union Canal
Grand Union Canal Wlk
Winkwell
Pixies Hill JMI Sch
Cress Farm
Hotel
River Bulbourne
Broadway Orchard
Bourne End Farm
Bourne End
Saw Mill
Moorend Farm
LONDON RD
A41
A4251
01
02
03
06
07
08
09
1
2
3
4
5
6
7
8

137
124

123
104

D5
1 SHARPCROFT
2 BROADCROFT
3 BOXHILL
4 PHYLLIS COURTNAGE HO
5 HELENA PL
6 BOWYERS

E6
1 WATLING CL
2 LANGDALE CT
3 ESKDALE CT
4 BORROWDALE CT
5 COTSWOLD
6 BARMOUTH ROW

F5
1 TANNSFIELD DR
2 TANNSMORE CL
3 WIDMORE DR

F6
1 MERCURY WLK

F7
1 SHERWOOD PL
2 PETERLEE CT

F8
1 TRESLIAN SQ
2 TORRIDGE WLK
3 THE DART
4 MARION WLK

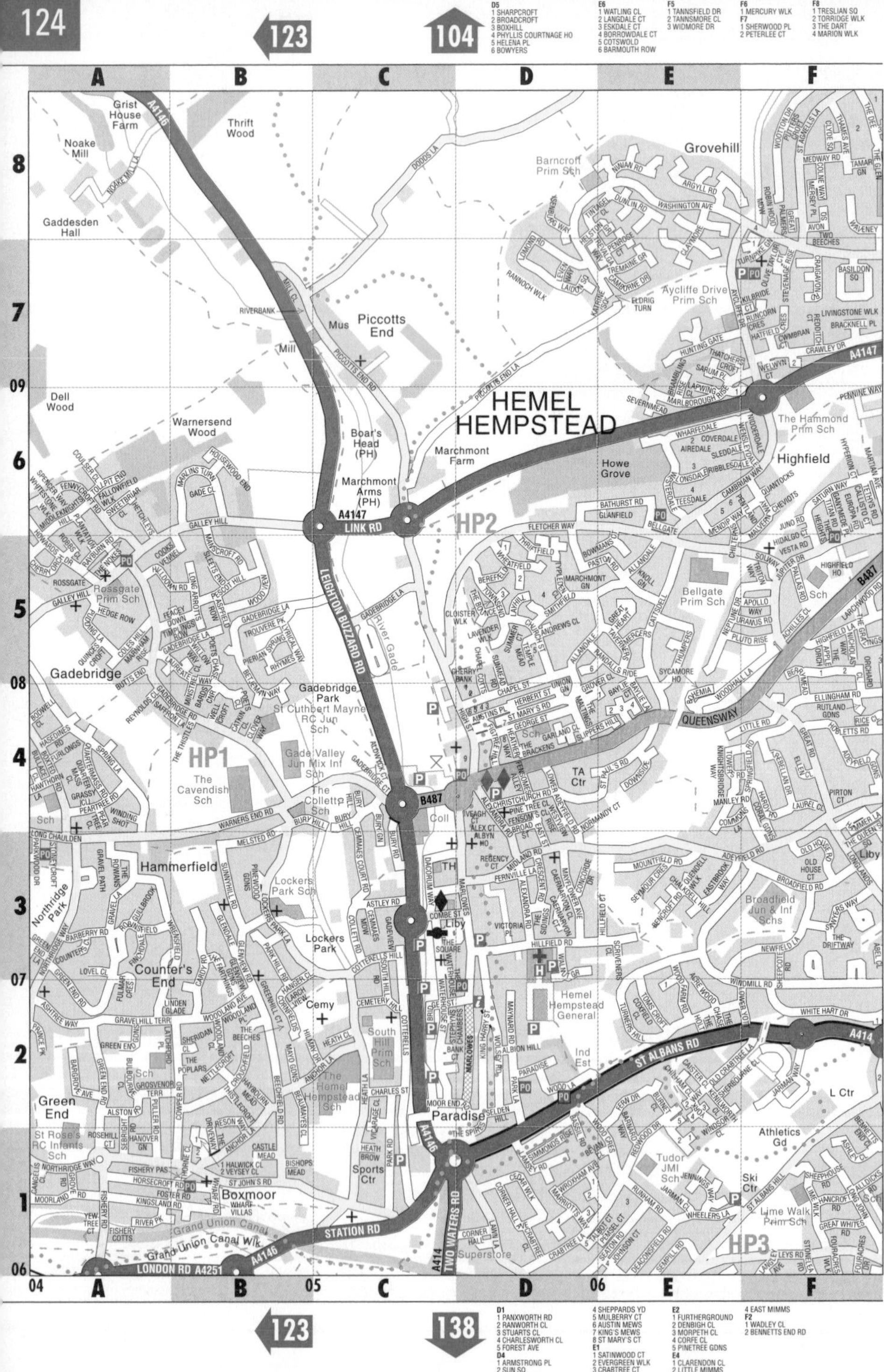

123
138

D1
1 PANXWORTH RD
2 RANWORTH CL
3 STUARTS CL
4 CHARLESWORTH CL
5 FOREST AVE

D4
1 ARMSTRONG PL
2 SUN SQ
3 THE GABLES
4 SHEPPARDS YD
5 MULBERRY CT
6 AUSTIN MEWS
7 KING'S MEWS
8 ST MARY'S CT

E1
1 SATINWOOD CT
2 EVERGREEN WLK
3 CRABTREE CT
4 WOODMAN RD

E2
1 FURTHERGROUND
2 DENBIGH CL
3 MORPETH CL
4 CORFE CL
5 PINETREE GDNS

E4
1 CLARENDON CL
2 LITTLE MIMMS
3 LONG MIMMS
4 EAST MIMMS

F2
1 WADLEY CL
2 BENNETTS END RD

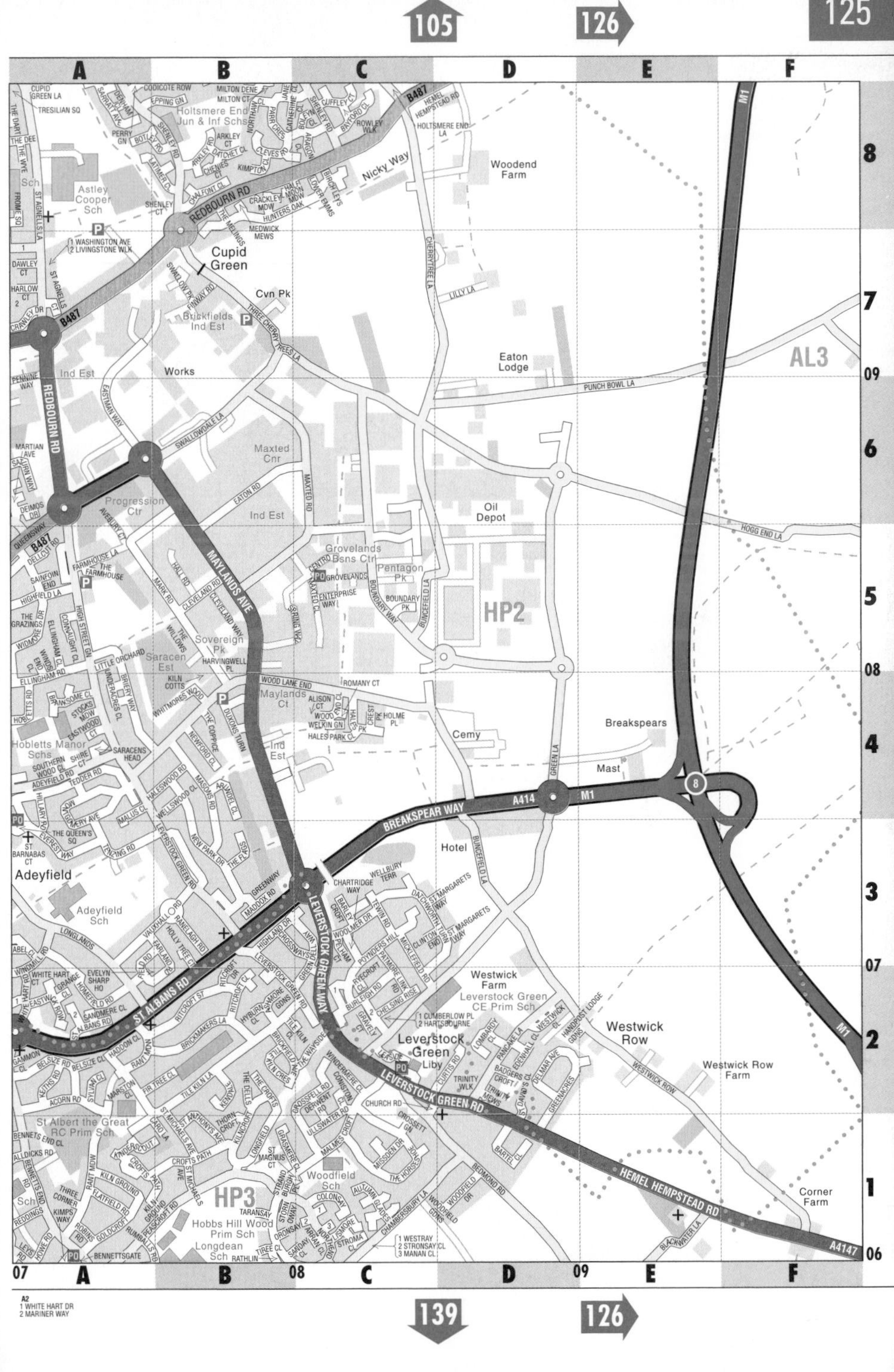

A2
1 WHITE HART DR
2 MARINER WAY

125
106

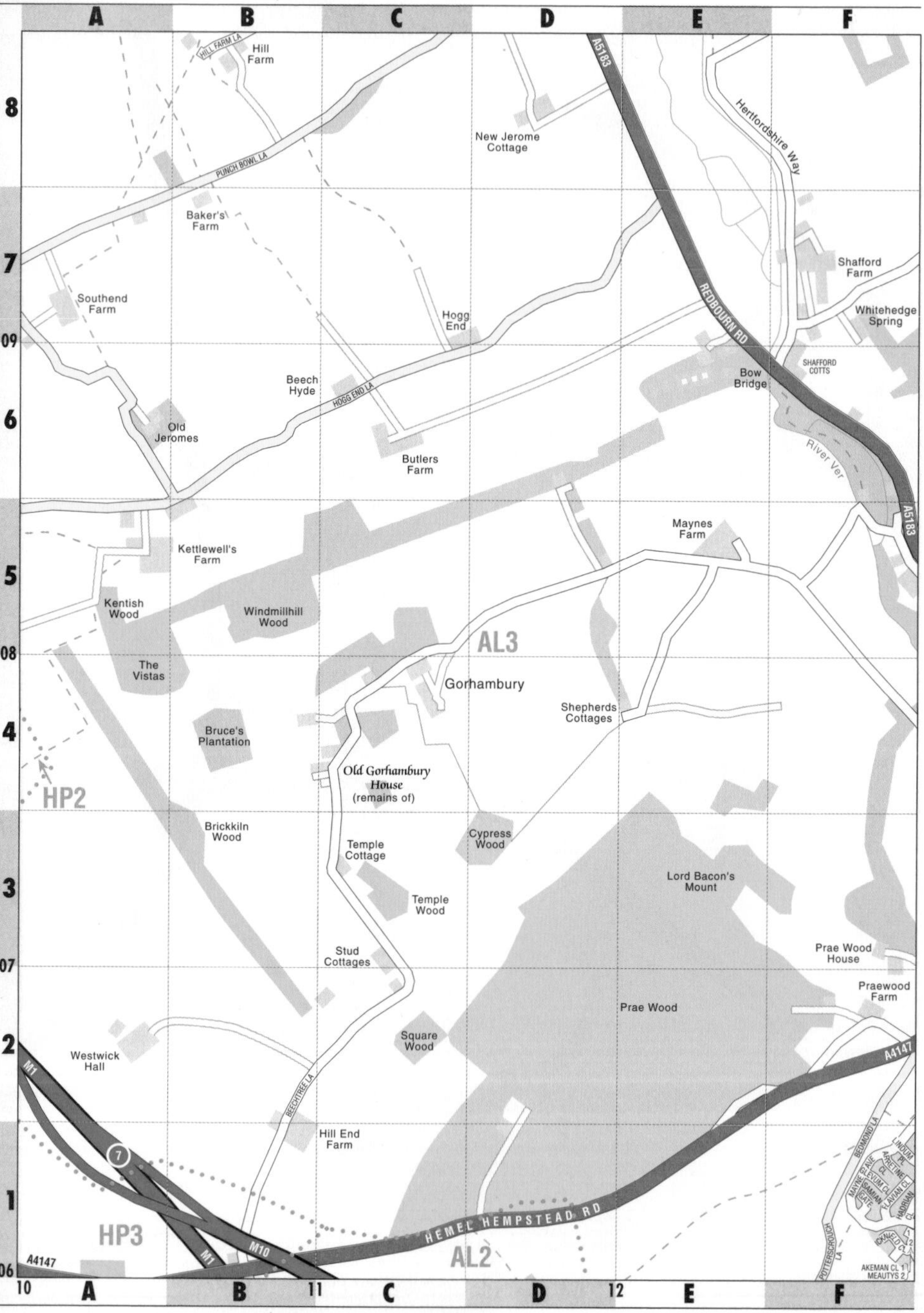

A B C D E F

8
7
09
6
5
08
4
3
07
2
1
06

HILL FARM LA
Hill Farm
PUNCH BOWL LA
Baker's Farm
New Jerome Cottage
A5183
Hertfordshire Way
Southend Farm
Hogg End
Shafford Farm
Whitehedge Spring
REDBOURN RD
SHAFFORD COTTS
Bow Bridge
Beech Hyde
HOGG END LA
Old Jeromes
Butlers Farm
River Ver
A5183
Maynes Farm
Kettlewell's Farm
Kentish Wood
Windmillhill Wood
AL3
The Vistas
Gorhambury
Shepherds Cottages
Bruce's Plantation
Old Gorhambury House
(remains of)
HP2
Brickkiln Wood
Cypress Wood
Temple Cottage
Lord Bacon's Mount
Temple Wood
Stud Cottages
Prae Wood House
Praewood Farm
Prae Wood
Square Wood
Westwick Hall
M1
A4147
BEECHTREE LA
Hill End Farm
BEDMOND LA
LINDUM PL
ARRETINE CL
MAYNE AVE
GLEVUM CL
SAMIAN GATE
FLAVIAN CL
HADRIAN CL
7
HEMEL HEMPSTEAD RD
POTTERSCROUCH LA
ICKNIELD CL
HP3
M1
M10
AL2
A4147
AKEMAN CL 1
MEAUTYS 2

10 A B 11 C D 12 E F

125
140

107
128

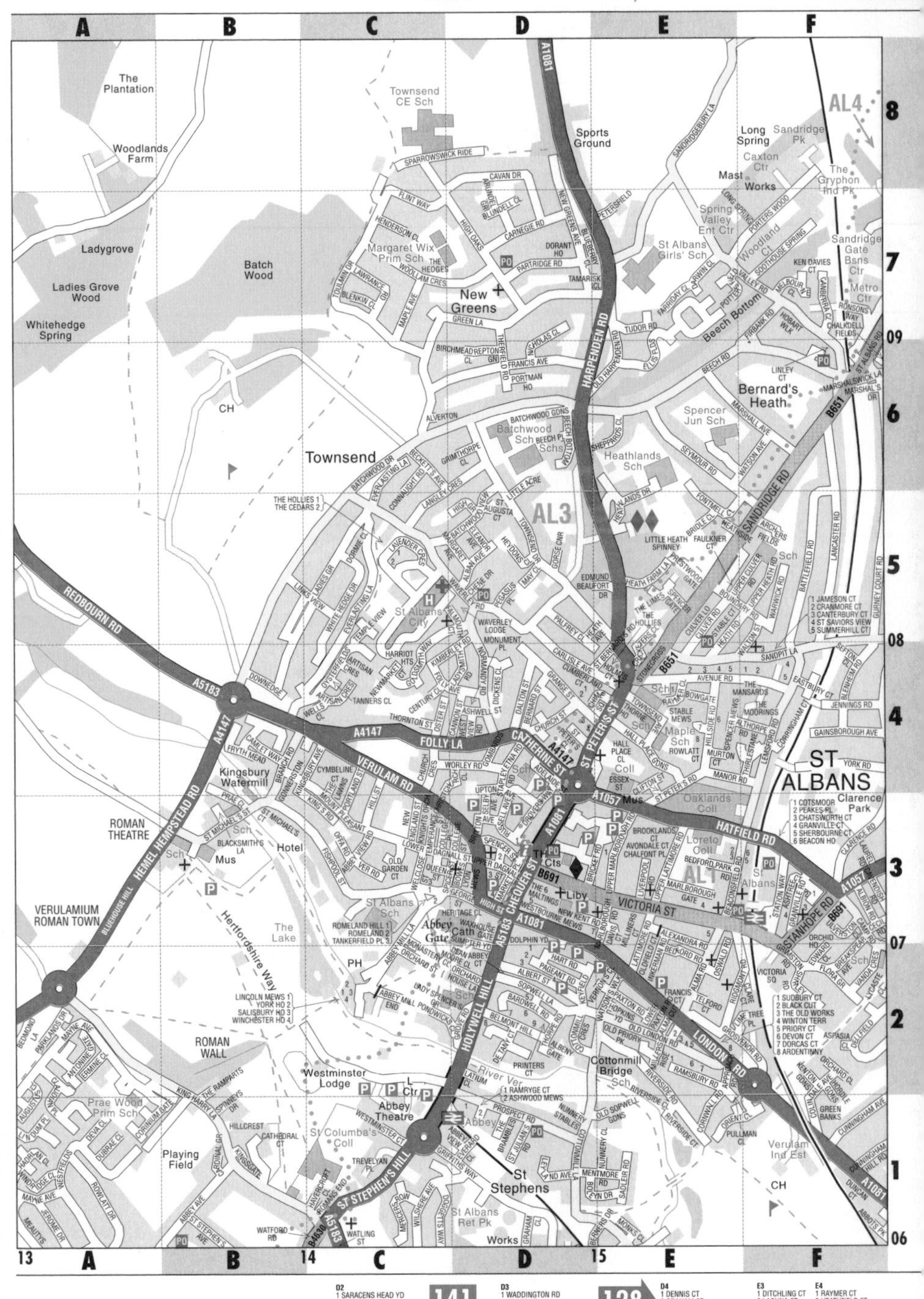

D2
1 SARACENS HEAD YD
2 SAMUEL SQ
3 RYDER SEED MEWS
4 PEARCES WLK
5 MALTHOUSE CT
6 BARDWELL CT
7 BELMONT CT
8 THE SYCAMORES
9 PAT LARNER HO

141

D3
1 WADDINGTON RD
2 CROSS ST
3 CHRISTOPHER PL
4 FRENCH ROW
5 HALF MOON MEWS
6 ART SCHOOL YD
7 WESLEY HO

128

D4
1 DENNIS CT
2 GRAHAM CT
3 GRANGE CT
4 PEMBERTON ALMSHOUSES

E3
1 DITCHLING CT
2 LAGUNA CT
3 YARRA HO
4 GARLAND CT
5 MIDLAND HO

E4
1 RAYMER CT
2 HEATHFIELD CT
3 WEYVER CT
4 HIGHCLERE CT
5 ST RAPHAELS CT
6 HILLSIDE GATE
7 RAMSEY LODGE CT
8 HILLSIDE CT

127
108

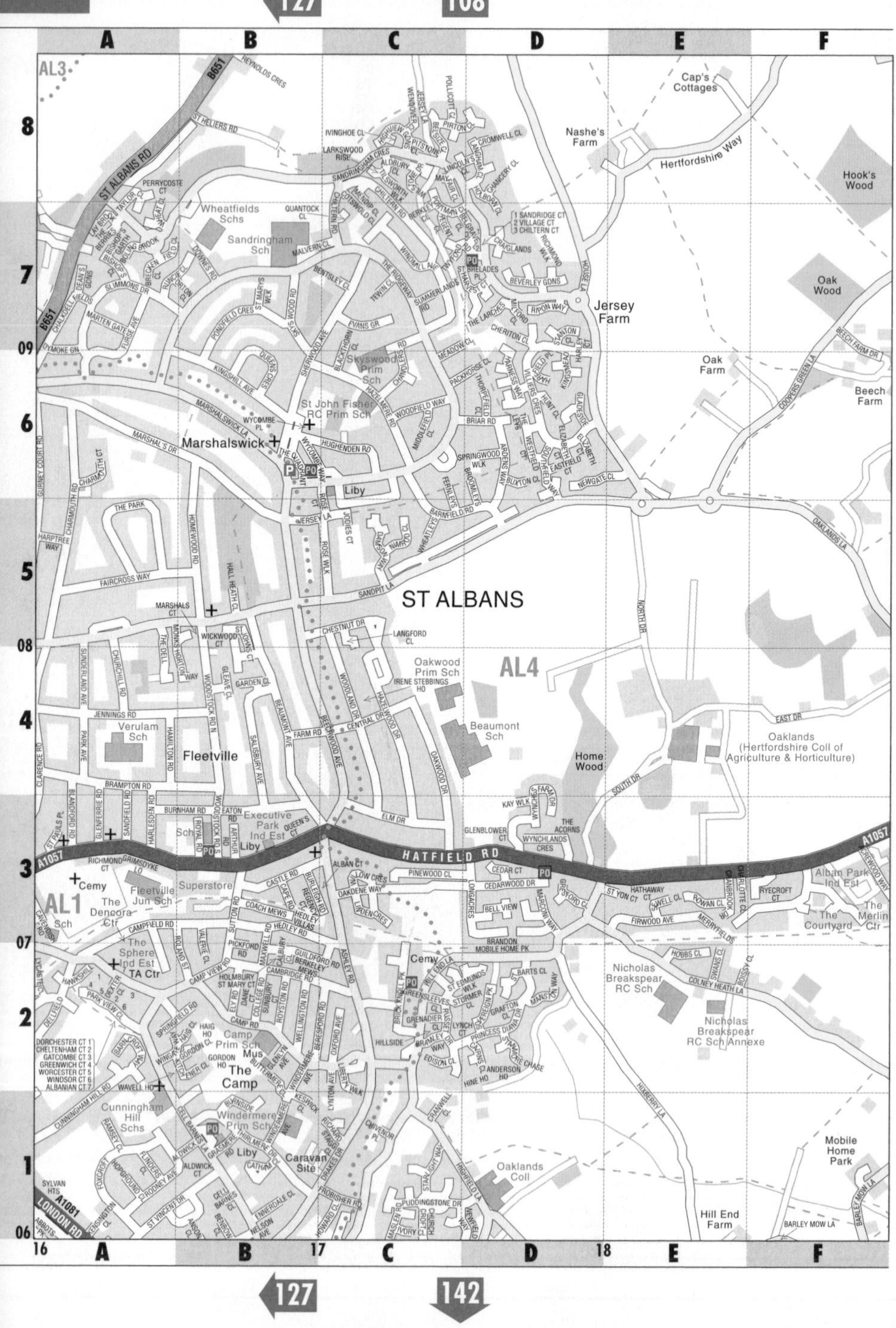

127
142

109
130

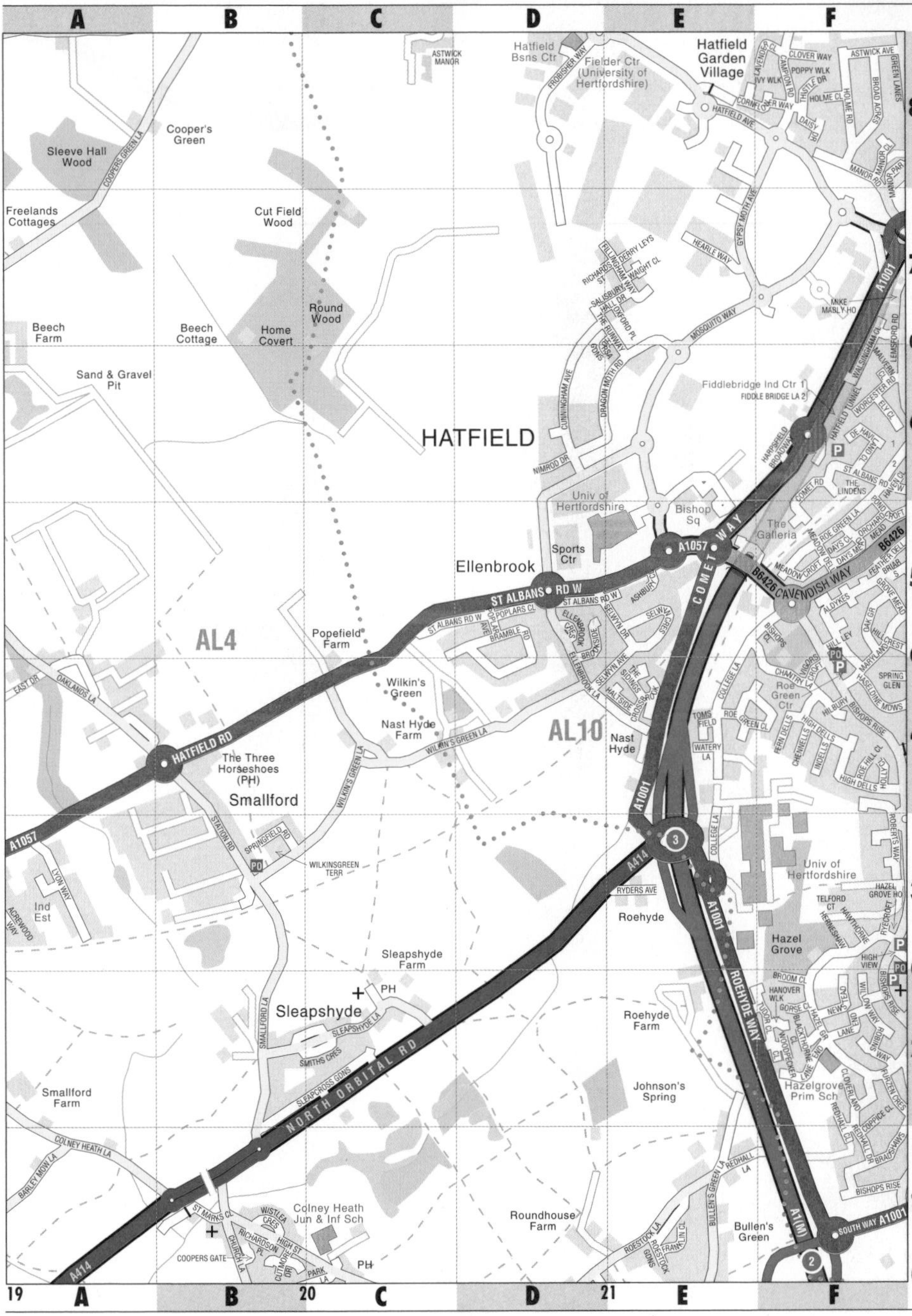

A B C D E F

Hatfield Bsns Ctr
ASTWICK MANOR
Fielder Ctr (University of Hertfordshire)
Hatfield Garden Village
FROBISHER WAY
LAVENDER CL
CLOVER WAY
ASTWICK AVE
GREEN LANES
CAMPION RD
POPPY WLK
IVY WLK
THISTLE DR
CORNFLOWER WAY
HOLME CL
HOLME RD
BROAD ACRES
DAISY DR
HATFIELD AVE
MANOR CL
MANOR RD
Cooper's Green
Sleeve Hall Wood
COOPERS GREEN LA
Freelands Cottages
Cut Field Wood
HEARLE WAY
GYPSY MOTH AVE
FILLINGHAM WAY
DERRY LEYS
RICHARDS ST
WAIGHT CL
SALISBURY HALL DR
OXFORD PL
THE RUNWAY
TIRSA GDNS
MOSQUITO WAY
MIKE MABLY HO
A1001
LEMSFORD RD
WALSINGHAM CL
MALVERN CL
Beech Farm
Beech Cottage
Round Wood
Home Covert
Sand & Gravel Pit
CUNNINGHAM AVE
DRAGON MOTH RD
Fiddlebridge Ind Ctr 1
FIDDLE BRIDGE LA 2
WORCESTER RD
ELY CL
HATFIELD TUNNEL
HATFIELD
HARPSFIELD BROADWAY
NIMROD DR
COMET RD
ST ALBANS RD
THE LINDENS
Univ of Hertfordshire
Bishop Sq
The Galleria
ROE GREEN LA
DAYS CL
ORCHARD
Sports Ctr
A1057
COMET WAY
MEADOW DELL
DAYS MEAD
B6426
CAVENDISH WAY
FEATHER DELL
Ellenbrook
ST ALBANS RD W
POPLARS CL
ASHBURY CL
SELWYN CRES
ALDYKES
GROVE MEAD
AL4
Popefield Farm
BRAMBLE RD
ELLENBROOK CRES
BROOKSIDE
SELWYN DR
BISHOPS CL
OAK GR
HILLCREST
HILL LEY
MARYLANDS
SELWYN AVE
THE SIDINGS
CHANTRY LA
VIGORS CROFT
Roe Green Ctr
HASELDINE MDWS
SPRING GLEN
EAST DR
OAKLANDS LA
Wilkin's Green
ELLENBROOK LA
HALTSIDE
CROSSBROOK
COLLEGE LA
HILBURY
BISHOPS RISE
TOMS FIELD
ROE GREEN CL
HIGH DELLS
Nast Hyde Farm
AL10
FERN DELLS
CHENNELLS
INGELLS
ROE HILL CL
HATFIELD RD
WILKIN'S GREEN LA
Nast Hyde
WATERY LA
HIGH DELLS
CLAYTON
The Three Horseshoes (PH)
Smallford
ROBERTS WAY
A1001
STATION RD
SPRINGFIELD RD
WILKINSGREEN TERR
A414
Univ of Hertfordshire
LYON WAY
RYDERS AVE
HAZEL GROVE HO
TELFORD CT
HAWTHORNE
Ind Est
ACREWOOD WAY
Roehyde
A1001
HERNESHAW
RYECROFT
Hazel Grove
Sleapshyde Farm
HIGH VIEW
BROOM CL
HANOVER WLK
PH
GORSE CL
Sleapshyde
SMALLFORD LA
SLEAPSHYDE LA
Roehyde Farm
ROEHYDE WAY
TUDOR CL
HAZEL GR
NEWSTEAD
WILLOW WAY
ROBINS WAY
BISHOPS RISE
SMITHS CRES
NORTH ORBITAL RD
BLACKTHORN CL
WOODPECKER CL
LANE END
BIRCH LANE
CLOVERLAND
Smallford Farm
SLEAPCROSS GDNS
Johnson's Spring
Hazelgrove Prim Sch
FURZEN CRES
REDHALL CL
COPPICE CL
REDHALL DR
BRADSHAWS
COLNEY HEATH LA
BARLEY MOW LA
BULLEN'S GREEN LA
REDHALL LA
BISHOPS RISE
ST MARKS CL
WISTLEA CRES
Colney Heath Jun & Inf Sch
Roundhouse Farm
Bullen's Green
SOUTH WAY
A1001
A1(M)
RICHARDSON PL
HIGH ST
COOPERS GATE
CHURCH LA
GUTMORE DR
PARK LA
PH
ROESTOCK LA
ROESTOCK GDNS
FRANKLIN CL
A414

8
7
09
6
5
08
4
3
07
2
1
06

19 A B 20 C D 21 E F

143
130

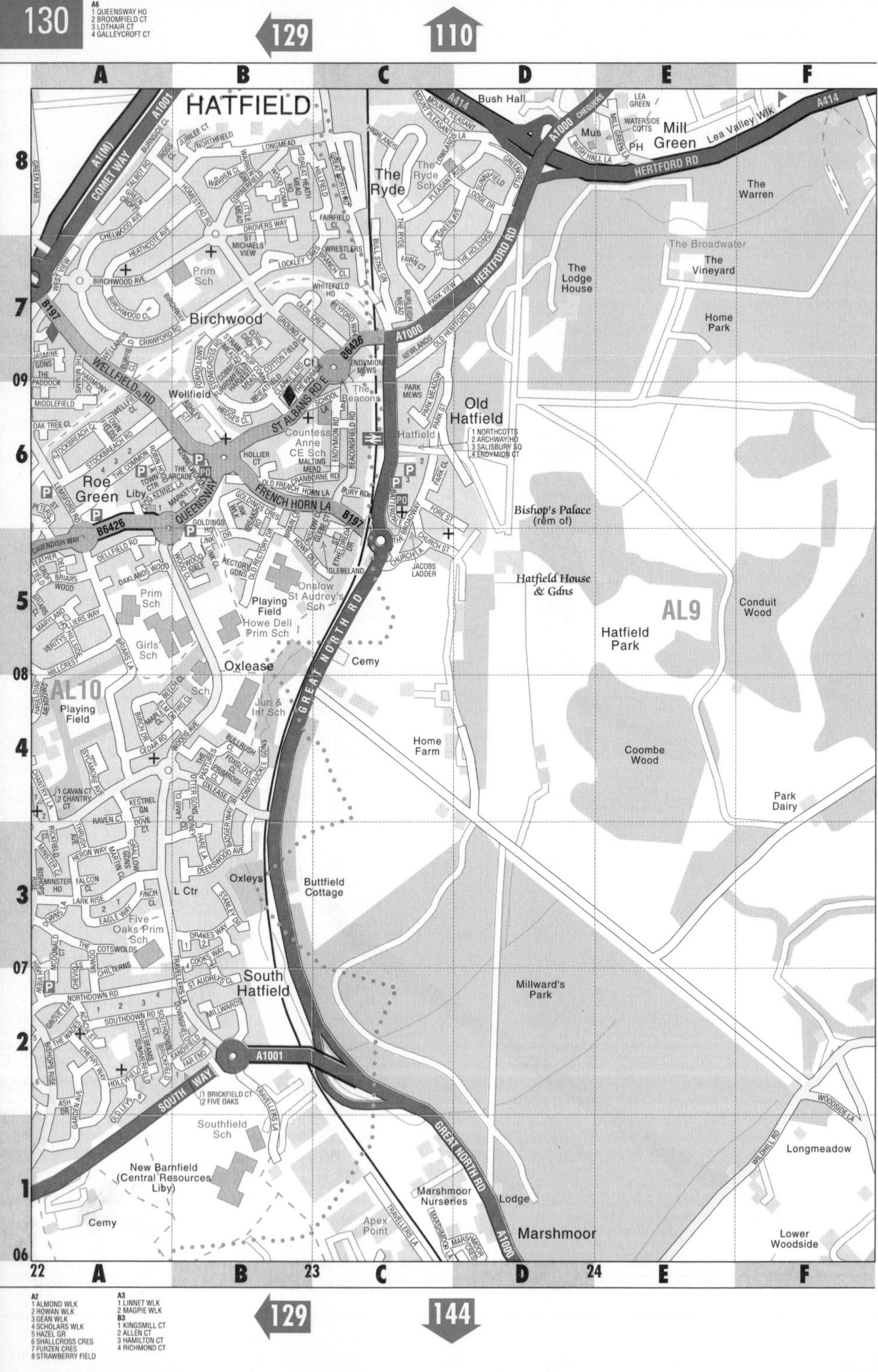
A6
1 QUEENSWAY HO
2 BROOMFIELD CT
3 LOTHAIR CT
4 GALLEYCROFT CT
129
110
HATFIELD
The Ryde
The Ryde Sch
Bush Hall
Mill Green
Mus
PH
Lea Valley Wlk
HERTFORD RD
HERTFORD RD
The Warren
The Broadwater
The Vineyard
The Lodge House
Home Park
Birchwood
Prim Sch
Wellfield
Old Hatfield
1 NORTHCOTTS
2 ARCHWAY HO
3 SALISBURY SQ
4 ENDYMION CT
The Beacons
Countess Anne CE Sch
Hatfield
Roe Green
Liby
Bishop's Palace (rem of)
Hatfield House & Gdns
AL9
Conduit Wood
Hatfield Park
Onslow St Audrey's Sch
Playing Field
Howe Dell Prim Sch
Prim Sch
Girls Sch
Oxlease
Cemy
AL10
Playing Field
Sch
Jun & Inf Sch
GREAT NORTH RD
Home Farm
Coombe Wood
Park Dairy
Oxleys
L Ctr
Buttfield Cottage
Five Oaks Prim Sch
South Hatfield
Millward's Park
A1001
SOUTH WAY
1 BRICKFIELD CT
2 FIVE OAKS
Southfield Sch
New Barnfield (Central Resources Liby)
Cemy
Marshmoor Nurseries
Lodge
Apex Point
Marshmoor
Longmeadow
Lower Woodside
WOODSIDE LA
WILDHILL RD
A1(M)
COMET WAY
A1001
A414
A1000
B197
B6426
WELLFIELD RD
ST ALBANS RD E
QUEENSWAY
FRENCH HORN LA
CAVENDISH WAY
A2
1 ALMOND WLK
2 ROWAN WLK
3 GEAN WLK
4 SCHOLARS WLK
5 HAZEL GR
6 SHALLCROSS CRES
7 FURZEN CRES
8 STRAWBERRY FIELD
A3
1 LINNET WLK
2 MAGPIE WLK
B3
1 KINGSMILL CT
2 ALLEN CT
3 HAMILTON CT
4 RICHMOND CT
129
144

111
132

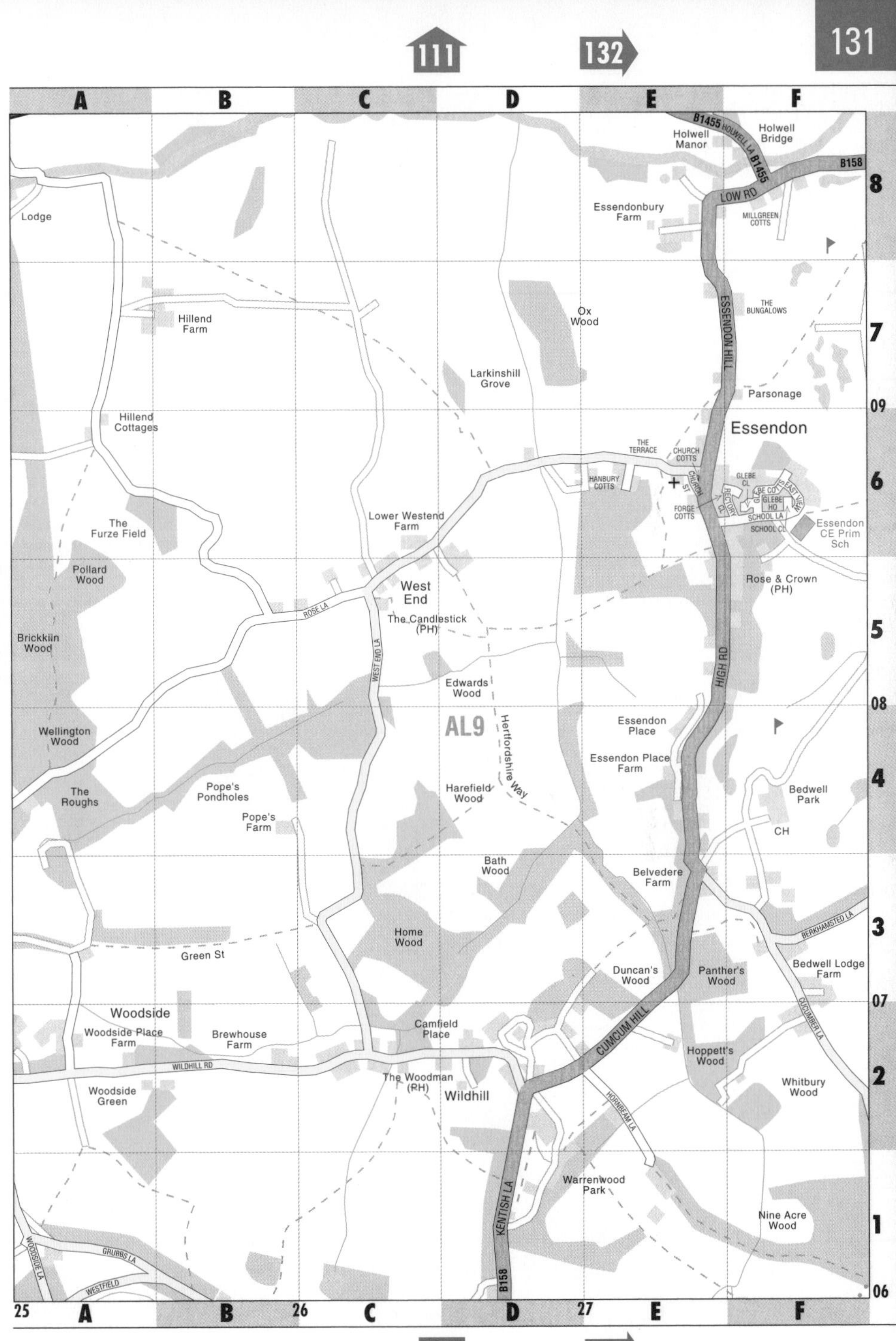

145
132

131
112

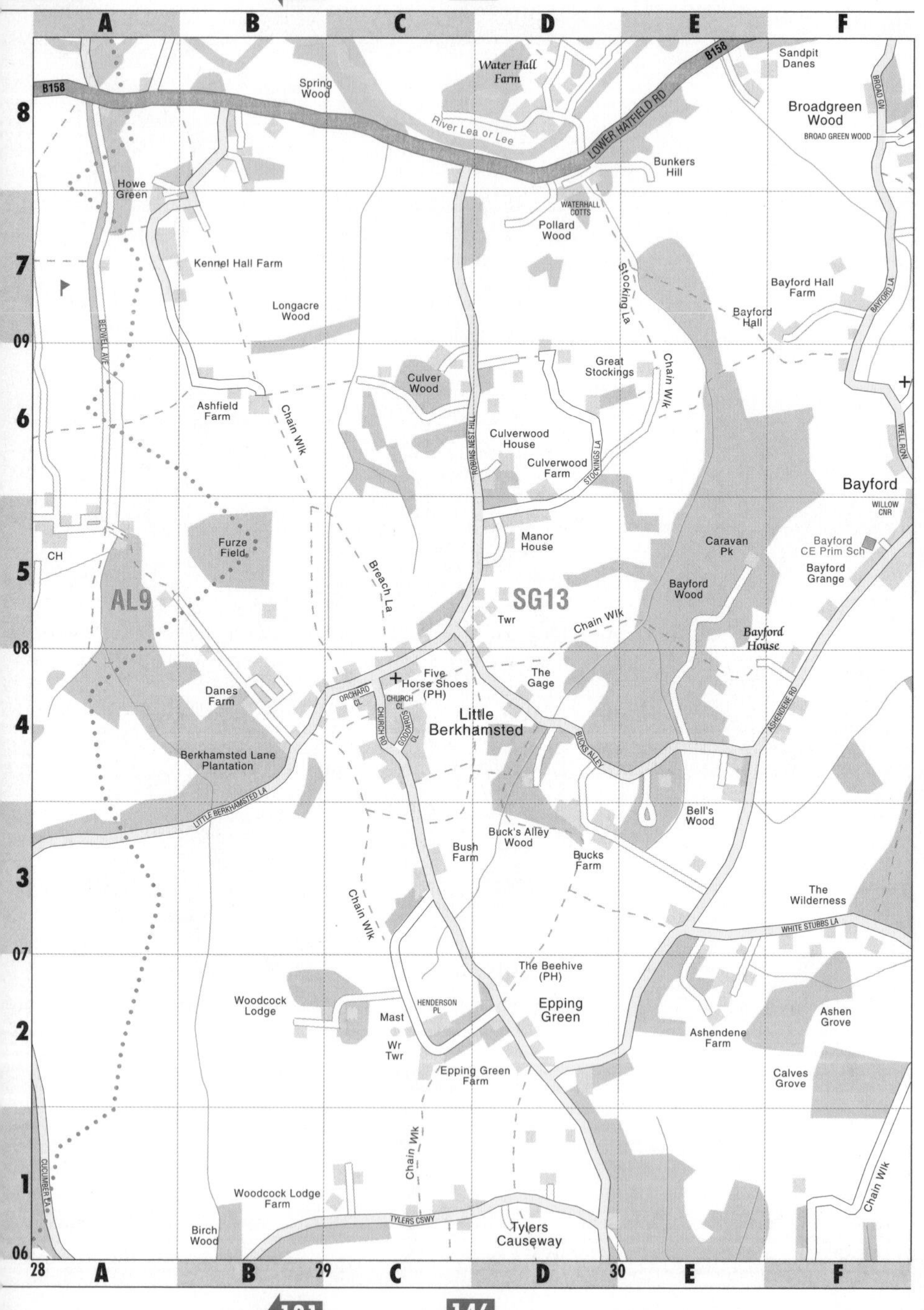

131
146

A B C D E F

8
Hook's Grove
Clements Farm
CLEMENTSBURY
Blackfields Farm
The Grove
BROAD GREEN WOOD
Broadgreen Wood

7
Weepings Wood
Hertfordshire Way
Owls Hatch Cottages
Back La
Edwards Green Farm
MANGROVE LA
Monk's Wood

09

6
Warren House
Bayford Brook
Harmond's Wood
BRICKENDON LA
Sewards Farm
BAYFORD GN
Monks Green
Jepp's Wood
WELL-ROW
Manor House
Great Groves
SG13
FOURWAYS
PH
Mast
Bayford
Sewage Wks

5
ASHENDENE RD
Bourne Orchard
Bramble's Wood
Fanshaws
FANSHAWS LA
Stocking La
Chain Wlk
Bourne Wood
Fanshaws Farm

08
The Farmer's Boy (PH)
Brickendon

4
Brickendon Grange
Cowheath Wood
Morley Grove
CH
Broad Riding Wood
Nature Trails
Blackfan Wood
Claypits Wood

3
Broxbourne Wood
Hedgerows Wood
Hedgegrove Farm
Devil's La
Nature Reserve

07
PEMBRIDGE LA
WOOD HOUSE LA
Old Claypits Farm
Calais Wood
Pembridge Lane Farm
Paradise Wildlife Park

2
Ettridge Farm
Stocking Wood
Ponsbourne Tunnel
EN10
WHITE STUBBS LA
Mortals Wood
Old Grove
Emanuel Pollards
Bencroft Wood

1
Chain Wlk
Nature Trail
Wormley Wood
Westlea
Manor Farm
WEST END RD

06

31 A B 32 C D 33 E F

133
114

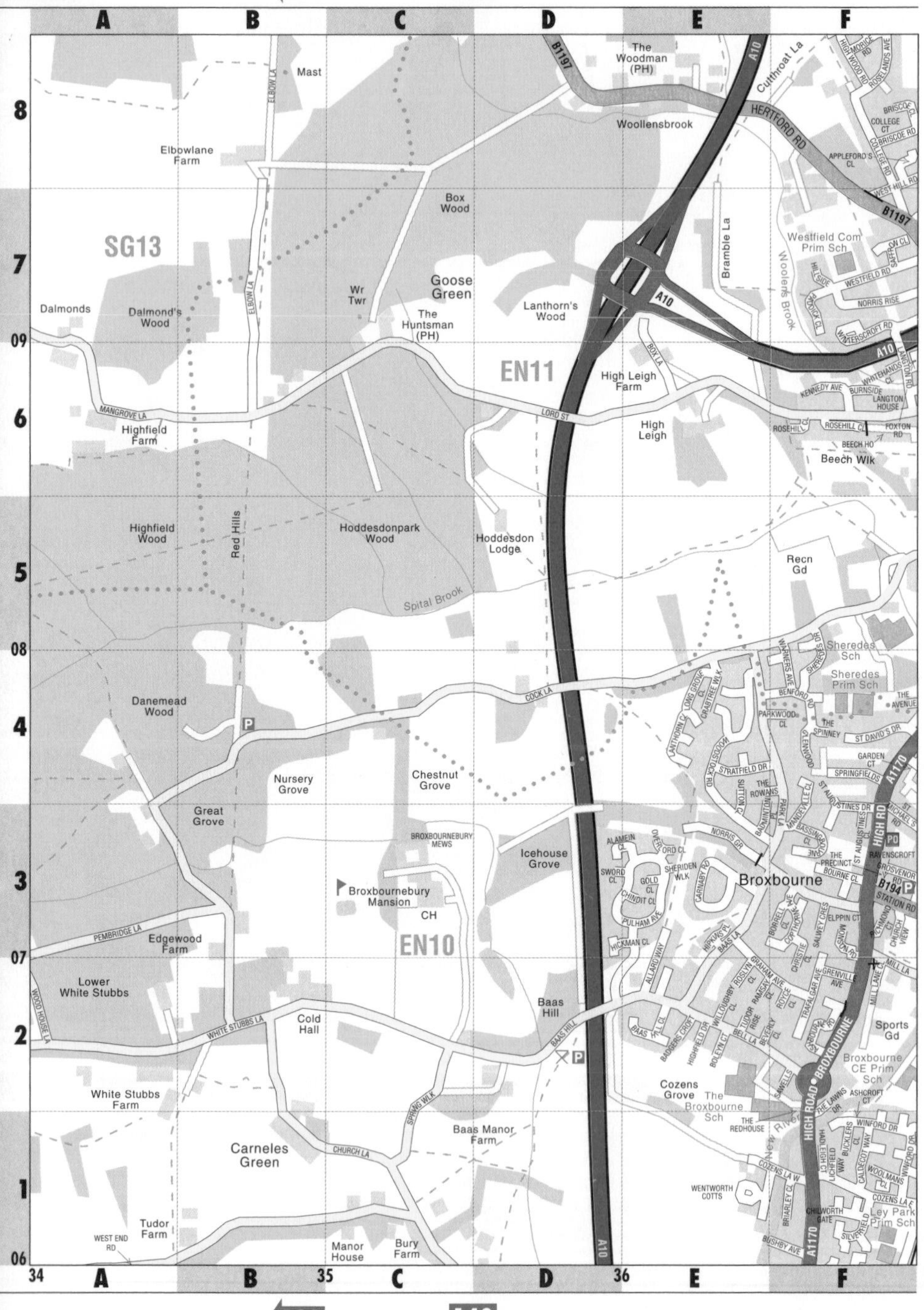

133
148

A7
1 FOURWAYS CT
2 CUMBERLAND CT
3 WESTFIELD RD
4 NORRIS RISE
5 WINTERSCROFT RD
6 BELCHER RD
7 ROMAN MEWS
8 ROMAN ST
9 BURFORD MEWS
10 BURFORD PL

115

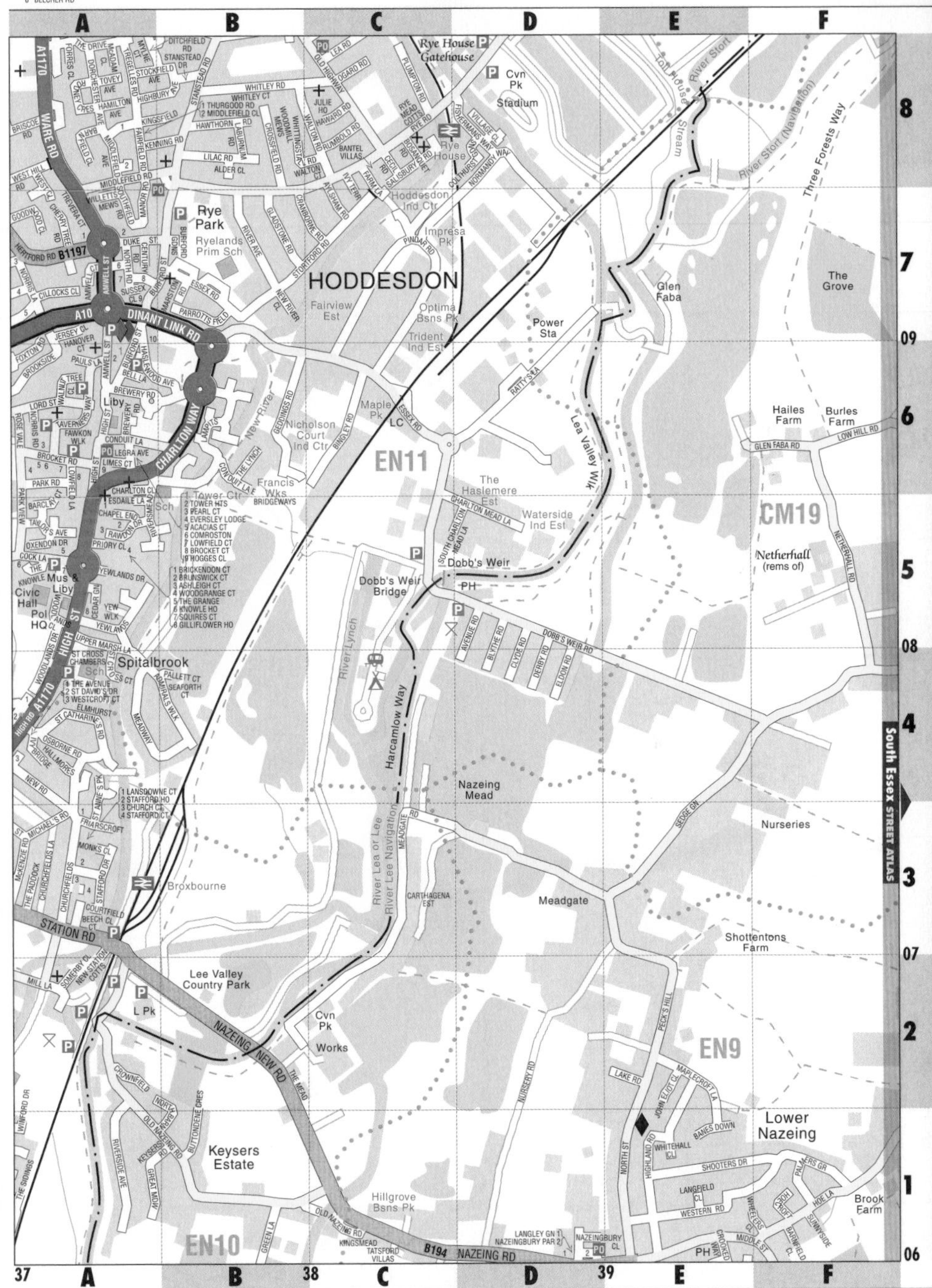

149

122

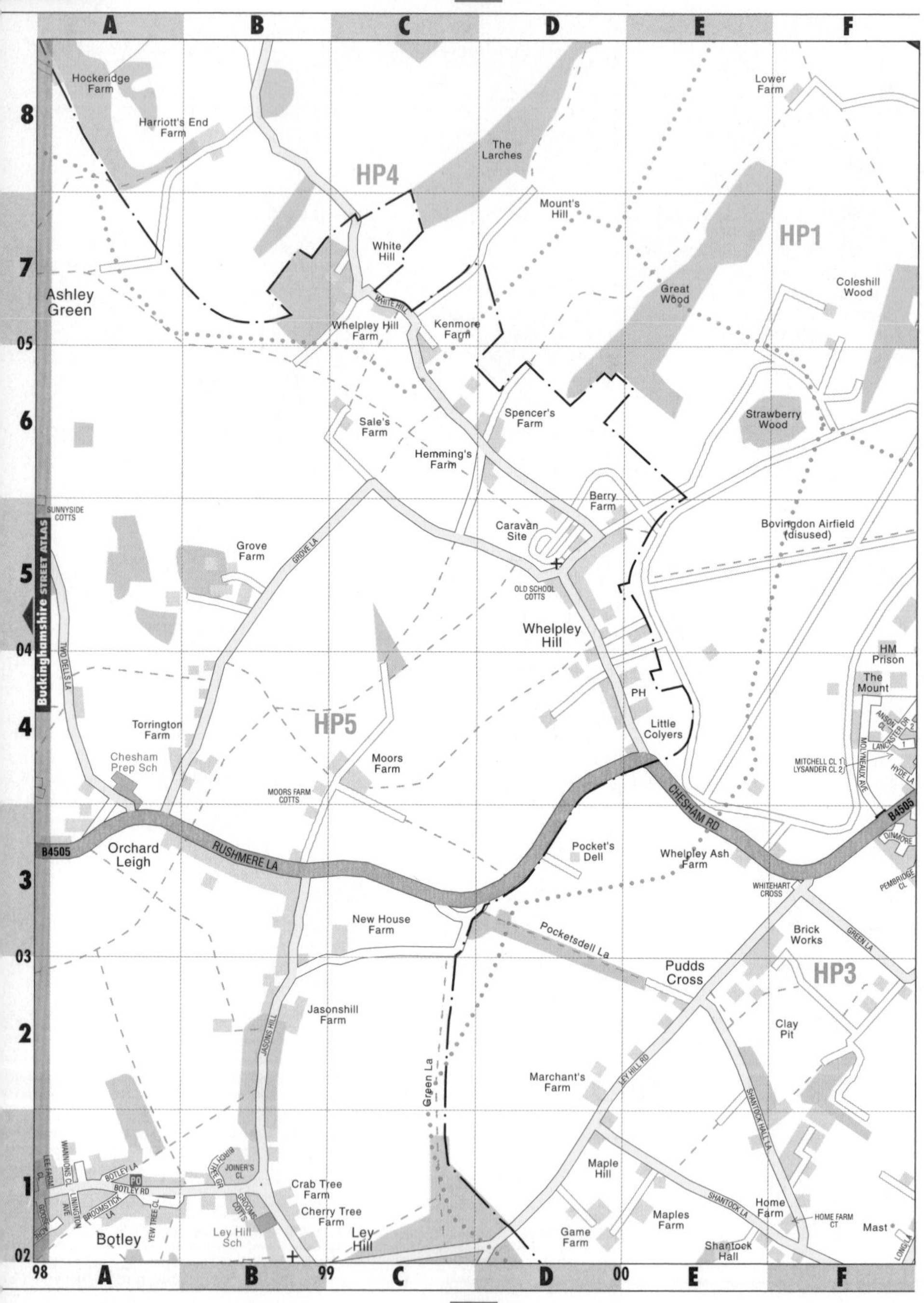

A
B
C
D
E
F
8
7
05
6
5
04
4
3
03
2
1
02
98
99
00
Hockeridge Farm
Harriott's End Farm
HP4
The Larches
Mount's Hill
White Hill
HP1
Lower Farm
Coleshill Wood
Ashley Green
Great Wood
WHITE HILL
Whelpley Hill Farm
Kenmore Farm
Spencer's Farm
Strawberry Wood
Sale's Farm
Hemming's Farm
Berry Farm
SUNNYSIDE COTTS
Caravan Site
Bovingdon Airfield (disused)
Grove Farm
GROVE LA
Buckinghamshire STREET ATLAS
OLD SCHOOL COTTS
Whelpley Hill
HM Prison
TWO DELLS LA
The Mount
PH
Torrington Farm
HP5
Little Colyers
ANSON CL
LANCASTER DR
MOLYNEAUX AVE
Chesham Prep Sch
Moors Farm
MITCHELL CL
LYSANDER CL
HYDE LA
MOORS FARM COTTS
CHESHAM RD
B4505
B4505
Orchard Leigh
RUSHMERE LA
Pocket's Dell
Whelpley Ash Farm
DINMORE
PEMBRIDGE CL
WHITEHART CROSS
New House Farm
Pocketsdell La
Brick Works
GREEN LA
Pudds Cross
HP3
Jasonshill Farm
JASONS HILL
Clay Pit
Marchant's Farm
LEY HILL RD
Green La
SHANTOCK HALL LA
WANNIONS CL
LEE FARM CL
BOTLEY LA
BOTLEY RD
LININGTON AVE
BROOMSTICK LA
GOOSE ACRE
YEW TREE CL
BIRCH TREE GR
JOINER'S CL
GROOMS COTTS
PO
Maple Hill
Crab Tree Farm
Cherry Tree Farm
SHANTOCK LA
Maples Farm
Home Farm
HOME FARM CT
Mast
LONG LA
Botley
Ley Hill Sch
Ley Hill
Game Farm
Shantock Hall

150

123
138

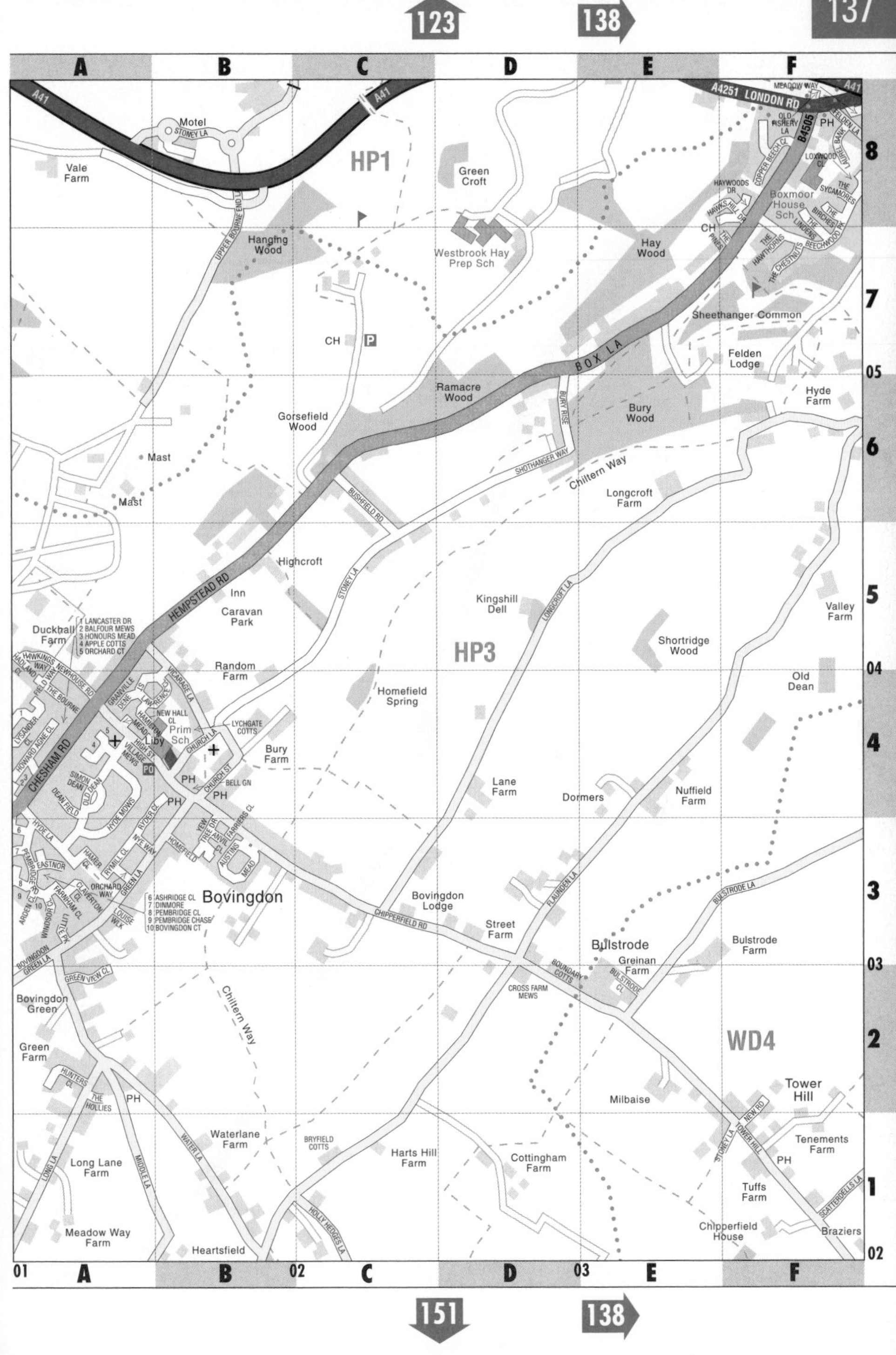

151
138

137
124

137
152

140

A B C D E F

8 7 05 6 5 04 4 3 03 2 1 02

HEMEL HEMPSTEAD

HP3

WD4

WD5

Bennetts End
Longdean Sch
Chambersbury Prim Sch
Nash Mills
Abbot's Hill Sch
St Nicholas House Prep Sch
Shaffond Knoll Farm
New Plantation
Pimlico House
White House Farm
Hyde Farm
Hyde Meadow Farm
Mast
Bunker's Farm
BUNKER'S FARM COTTS
Well Farm
Highwood Hall Farm
High Herts Farm
Pimlico
The Swan (PH)
Blackwater Wood
Homefield Farm
NEWLANDS CVN SITE
Verulam Farm
Hart Hall Farm
Bedmond
Bedmond Green
Bedmond Village Prim Sch
Hilltop Farm
Leewood Farm
Langley Wharf
River Gade
Grand Union Canal
Grand Union Canal Wlk
Happy Valley Ind Pk
Kings Park Ind Est
Sunderland Est
Benmore Farm
Hertfordshire Way
NUMBERS FARM
Ovaltine Dairy Farm
Mansion House Farm
Parsonage Farm
Long Wood
Round Wood
Ovaltine Egg Farm
Abbots Langley
Kings Langley
Home Park Ind Est
Wayside Farm
Broadfield Farm
Liby
Sch
PH
PO
M25
A4251

HEMPSTEAD RD
HIGH ST
WATFORD RD
LOWER RD
RED LION LA
BUNKERS LA
HIGHWOODHALL LA
HYDE LA
HARTHALL LA
TOMS LA
SHEPPEY'S LA
BEDMOND RD
CUMBERLAND CL
HYDE TERR
ROSE ACRE
BLACKWATER LA
CHURCH HILL
ST ALBANS LA
SERGEHILL LA
MILLHOUSE LA
WOODLAND WAY
CHAPEL WAY
BLUEBELL DR
HIGH ST
BELL CL
BELL LA
EAST LA
MEADOW WAY
HENDERSON PL
HILLTOP RD
SEABROOK RD
WOODLANDS
SHAFTESBURY WAY
GROSVENOR AVE
BELGRAVE DR
RAILWAY TERR
WOODLANDS RD
PRIMROSE HILL
STATION RD
EGG FARM LA
ROMAN GDNS
HOMEPARK COTTS
STATION APP
HOME PARK MILL LINK RD
STATION FOOTPATH
JUBILEE WLK
CATSDELL BOTTOM
HANDA CL
RATHLYN
BARRA CL
NORTHEND
MILLFIELD
PEASCROFT RD
WINCHDELLS
SIX ACRES
CHILDWICK CT
RUMBALLS CL
CANDLEFIELD RD
CANDLEFIELD CL
CANDLEFIELD WLK
GREAT ELMS RD
HORSELERS
BARNACRES RD
HILL COMM
MARKET OAK LA
CHAMBERSBURY LA
HIGHCLERE DR
SILVERTHORN DR
LONGDEAN PK
LINSEY CL
THE LEAS
GEORGEWOOD RD
MEADOW RD
POND RD
HIGHBARNS
EAST GN
MILL CL
SANDERS RD
SANDERS CL
OAK ST
CHAFFINCHES GN
SHAFFORD COTTS
CONISTON RD
BELHAM RD
HAVELOCK RD
WHITLARS DR
KINGS MDW
GADE AV
RECTORY LA
REGENT CL
CHANTRY CL
MILL LA
TOOVEYS MILL CL
COMMON LA
THE GLEBE
VICARAGE LA
THE NAP
SADDLERS WLK
FISHER CL
LITTLE HAYES
WILLOW EDGE
BLACKWELL RD
WATERSIDE
WATERSIDE CT
KINGFISHER LURE
WATER LA
PETERSLEA
RIVERSIDE CL
LANGLEY HILL
LANGLEY HILL CL
EDMUND MEWS
THE ORCHARD
CHURCH LA
CLOISTERS
ALEXANDRA RD
MEADOWBANK
WINDSOR CT
YORK CL
PALACE CL
FRIARS WAY
GREAT PK
MEADOW WAY
BEECHFIELD RD
LANGLEY CRES
AVENUE APP
RADCLIFFE AVE
ANTOINETTE CT
DAIRY WAY
TITHE BARN CT
LOVE LA
PARNELL CL
HANOVER GDNS
BREAKSPEAR CT
TIBBS HILL RD
SUMMERHOUSE WAY
SHEPHERD CL
THE CRESCENT
PARSONAGE CL
ST LAWRENCE CL
ABBOTS RD
DELLMEADOW
STANDFIELD

07 A B 08 C D 09 E F

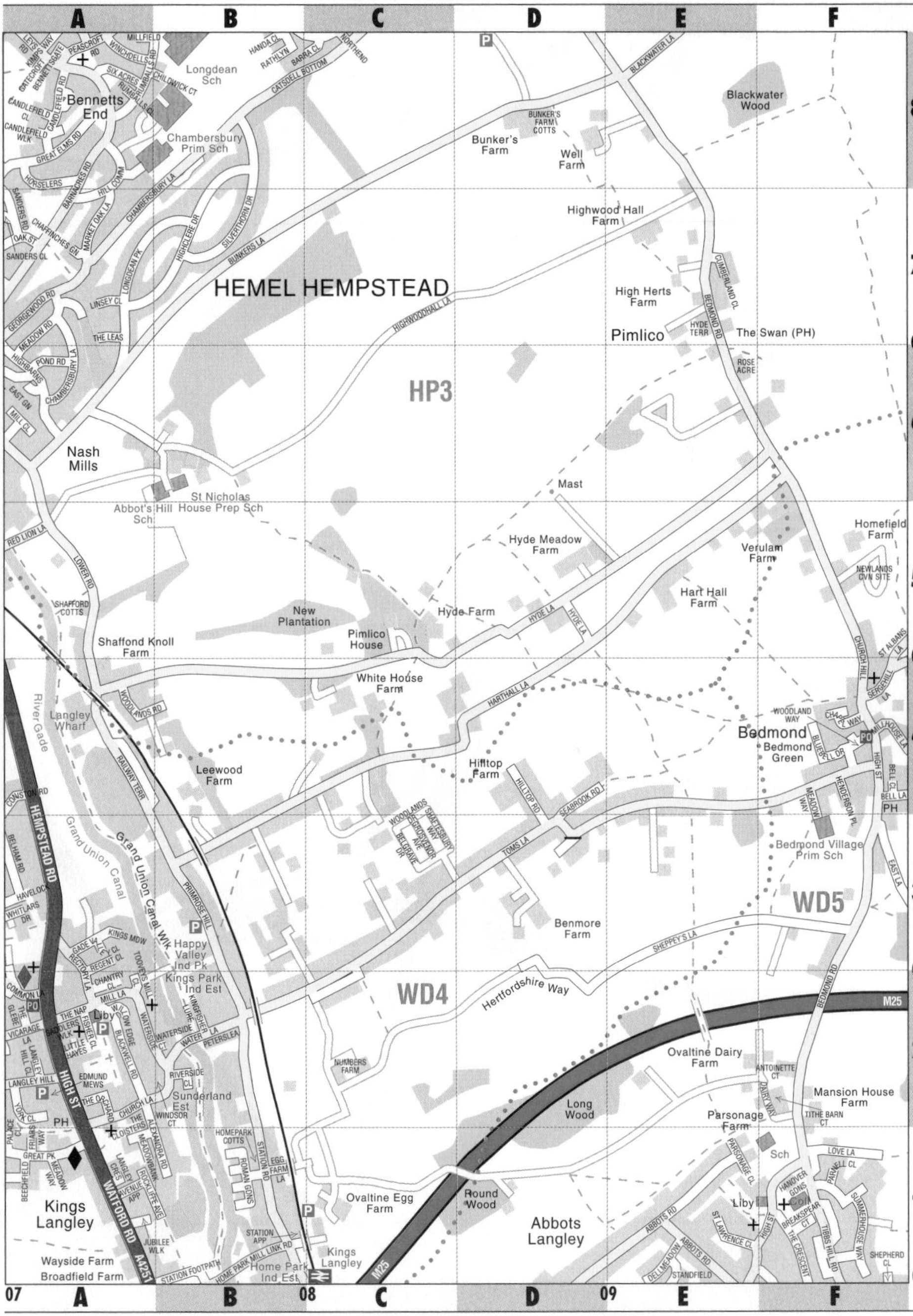

153

140

139 126

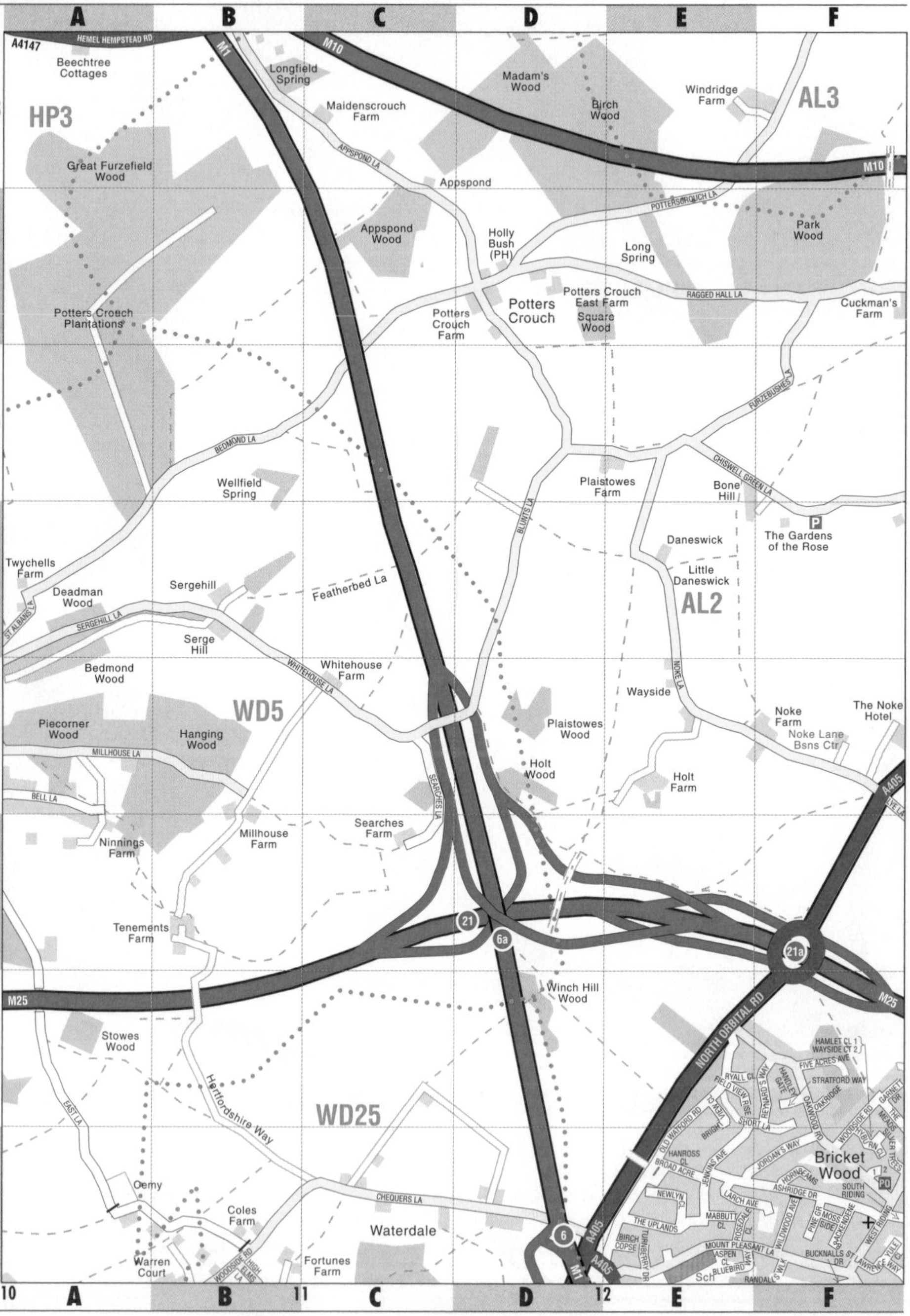
A4147
HEMEL HEMPSTEAD RD
M1
M10
HP3
AL3
AL2
WD5
WD25
Beechtree Cottages
Longfield Spring
Maidenscrouch Farm
Madam's Wood
Birch Wood
Windridge Farm
Great Furzefield Wood
APPSPOND LA
Appspond
Appspond Wood
Holly Bush (PH)
POTTERSCROUCH LA
Park Wood
Long Spring
Potters Crouch East Farm
RAGGED HALL LA
Cuckman's Farm
Potters Crouch Plantations
Potters Crouch Farm
Potters Crouch
Square Wood
FURZEBUSHES LA
BEDMOND LA
Wellfield Spring
BLUNTS LA
Plaistowes Farm
CHISWELL GREEN LA
Bone Hill
The Gardens of the Rose
Daneswick
Little Daneswick
Twychells Farm
Deadman Wood
Sergehill
Featherbed La
ST ALBANS LA
SERGEHILL LA
Serge Hill
Bedmond Wood
WHITEHOUSE LA
Whitehouse Farm
NOKE LA
Wayside
Noke Farm
The Noke Hotel
Noke Lane Bsns Ctr
Piecorner Wood
Hanging Wood
Plaistowes Wood
MILLHOUSE LA
SEARCHES LA
Holt Wood
Holt Farm
BELL LA
A405
LYE LA
Ninnings Farm
Millhouse Farm
Searches Farm
Tenements Farm
21
6a
21a
M25
Winch Hill Wood
NORTH ORBITAL RD
Stowes Wood
Hertfordshire Way
EAST LA
HAMLET CL 1
WAYSIDE CT 2
FIVE ACRES AVE
RYALL CL
HANDLEY GATE
STRATFORD WAY
FIELD VIEW RISE
REYNARD'S WAY
OAKRIDGE
OAKWOOD RD
GARNETT DR
THE MEADS
SILVER TREES
LILAC CL
OLD WATFORD RD
BRIGHT
SHORT LA
WOODSIDE RD
HAZEL CL
HANROSS CL
JENKINS AVE
JORDAN'S WAY
HORNBEAMS
Bricket Wood
BROAD ACRE
ASHRIDGE DR
SOUTH RIDING
PO
NEWLYN CL
LARCH AVE
Oemy
Coles Farm
CHEQUERS LA
Waterdale
THE UPLANDS
MABBUTT CL
ROSEDALE CL
WILDWOOD AVE
PINE GR
MOSS SIDE
BRACKENDENE
WEST RIDING
6
BIRCH COPSE
MOUNT PLEASANT LA
ASPEN CL
BLUEBIRD WAY
BUCKNALLS DR
ST LAWRENCE WAY
YULE CL
Warren Court
WOODSIDE RD
HIGH ELMS LA
Fortunes Farm
TURNBERRY DR
Sch
RANDALLS WLK
8
7
05
6
5
04
4
3
03
2
1
02
10
11
12
A B C D E F

127
142

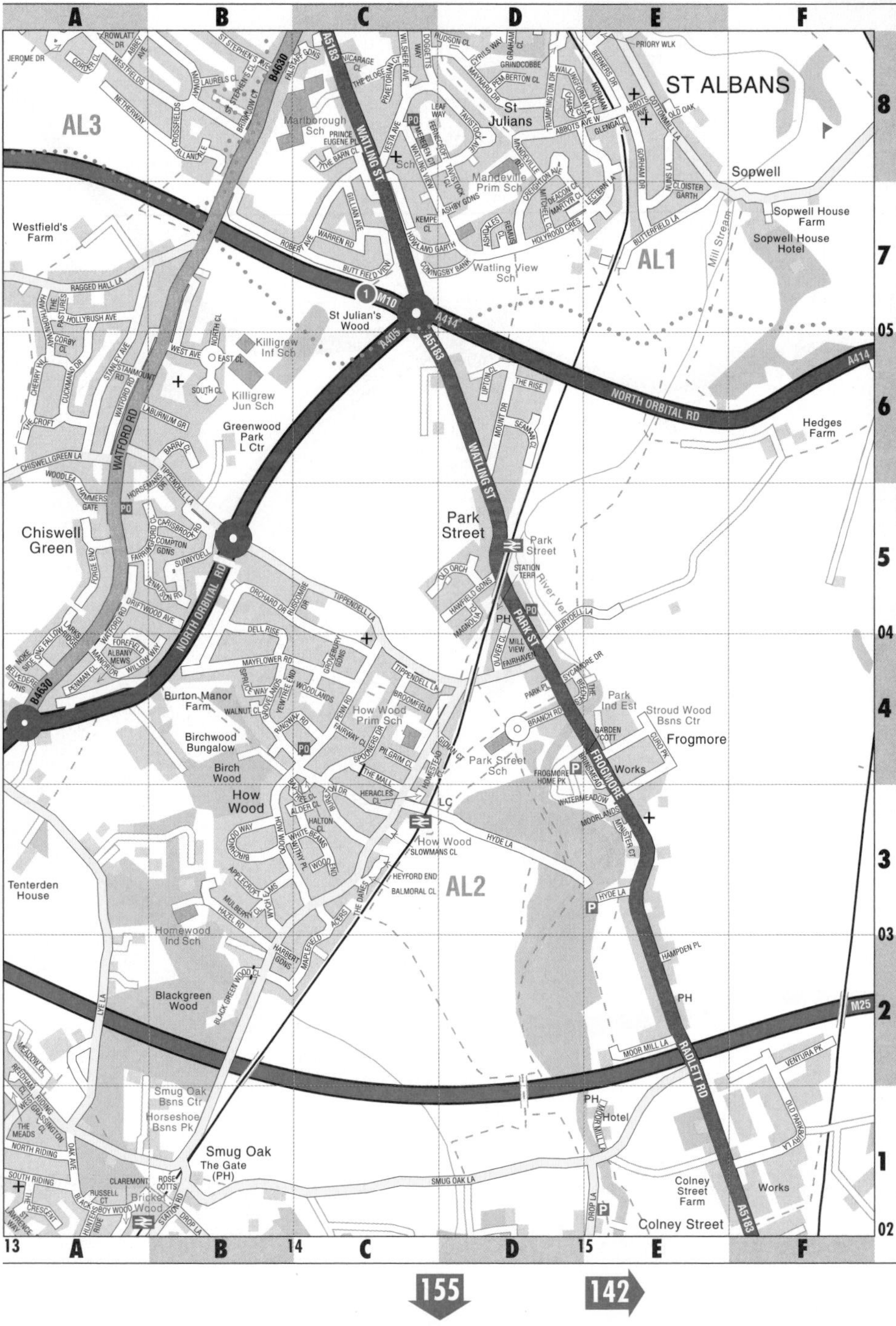
A
B
C
D
E
F
ST ALBANS
AL3
AL1
AL2
St Julians
Sopwell
Marlborough Sch
Mandeville Prim Sch
Watling View Sch
Sopwell House Farm
Sopwell House Hotel
Westfield's Farm
St Julian's Wood
Killigrew Inf Sch
Killigrew Jun Sch
Greenwood Park L Ctr
Hedges Farm
Chiswell Green
Park Street
Park Ind Est
Stroud Wood Bsns Ctr
Frogmore
Works
Burton Manor Farm
Birchwood Bungalow
Birch Wood
How Wood
How Wood Prim Sch
Park Street Sch
Tenterden House
Homewood Ind Sch
Blackgreen Wood
Smug Oak Bsns Ctr
Horseshoe Bsns Pk
Smug Oak
The Gate (PH)
Bricket Wood
Colney Street Farm
Colney Street
Hotel
WATLING ST
PARK ST
FROGMORE
RADLETT RD
NORTH ORBITAL RD
WATFORD RD
TIPPENDELL LA
HYDE LA
SMUG OAK LA
MOOR MILL LA
CHISWELLGREEN LA
RAGGED HALL LA
HOLLYBUSH AVE
A5183
A414
A405
B4630
M10
M25
8
7
6
5
4
3
2
1
05
04
03
02
13
14
15

155
142

141 128

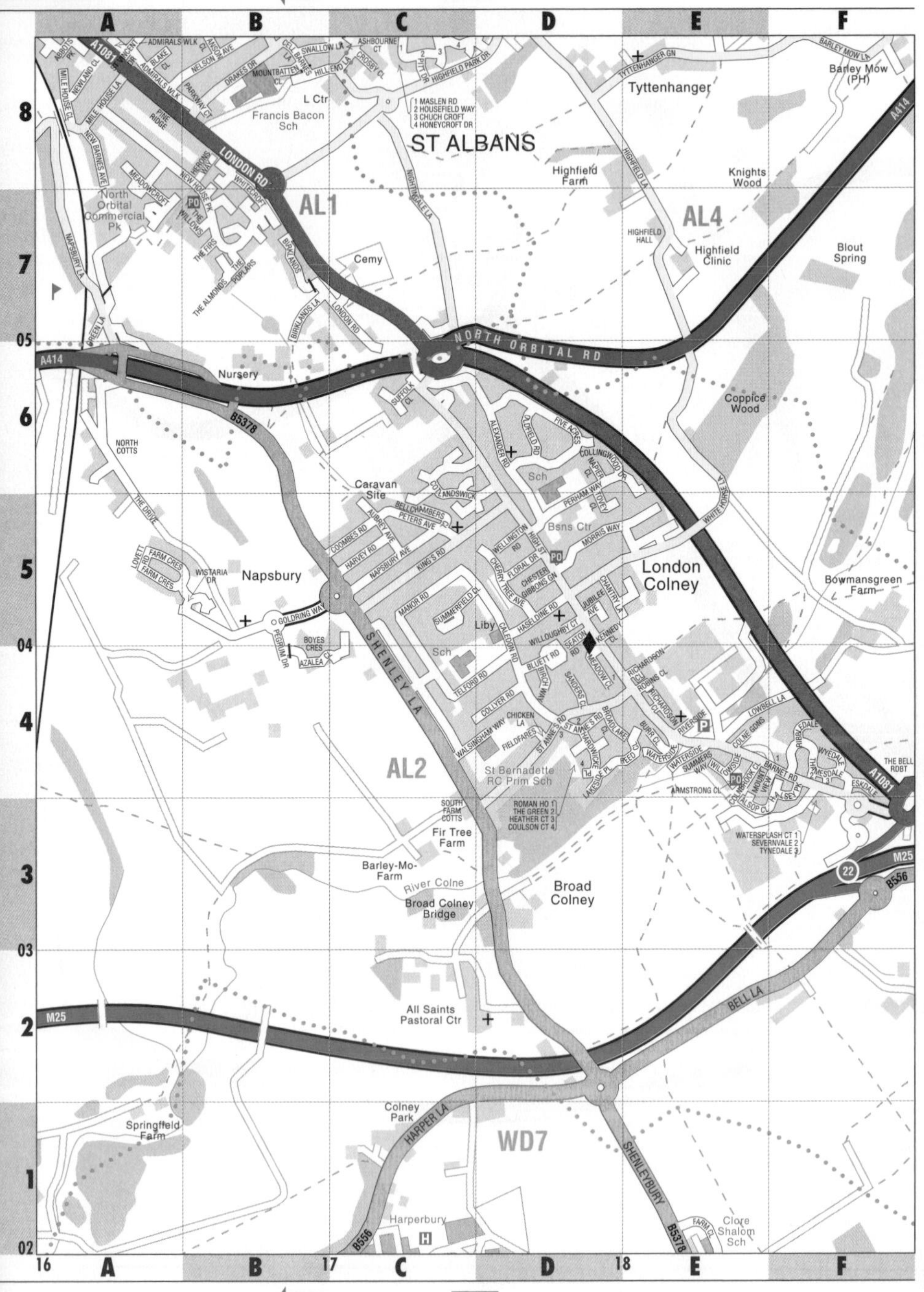

141 156

129
144

157
144

143
130

143
158

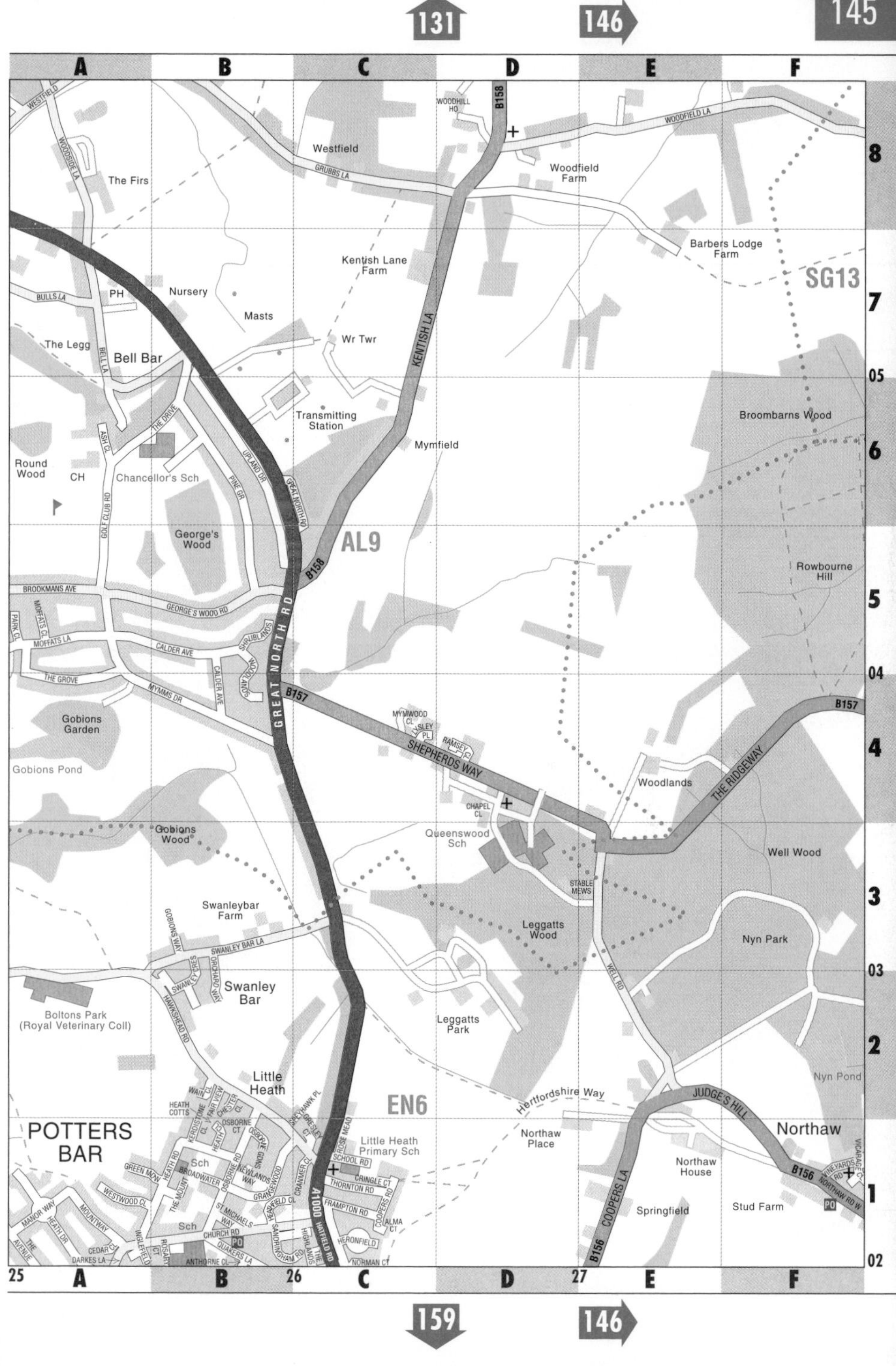
131
146
A
B
C
D
E
F
8
7
05
6
5
04
4
3
03
2
1
02
25
26
27
Westfield
Woodhill Ho
B158
Woodfield La
Woodside La
The Firs
Grubbs La
Woodfield Farm
Barbers Lodge Farm
SG13
Kentish Lane Farm
Bulls La
PH
Nursery
Masts
Wr Twr
Kentish La
The Legg
Bell La
Bell Bar
Transmitting Station
Broombarns Wood
The Drive
Ash Cl
Upland Dr
Mymfield
Round Wood
CH
Chancellor's Sch
Pine Gr
Great North Rd
Golf Club Rd
George's Wood
AL9
Rowbourne Hill
Brookmans Ave
George's Wood Rd
Moffats Cl
Park Cl
Moffats La
Calder Ave
Shrublands
Woodlands
The Grove
Mymms Dr
B157
Mymwood Cl
Linsley Pl
Ramsey Cl
Shepherds Way
Gobions Garden
Gobions Pond
Woodlands
The Ridgeway
Chapel Cl
Queenswood Sch
Gobions Wood
Well Wood
Stable Mews
Swanleybar Farm
Gobions Way
Leggatts Wood
Nyn Park
Swanley Bar La
Swanley Cres
Orchard Way
Swanley Bar
Well Rd
Boltons Park (Royal Veterinary Coll)
Hawkshead Rd
Leggatts Park
Little Heath
Nyn Pond
Hertfordshire Way
Judge's Hill
Wain Cl
Fair View
Chester Rd
Heath Cotts
Keroistone Cl
Osborne Ct
Sparrowhawk Pl
Gresley Ct
EN6
Northaw Place
Northaw
Vicarage Cl
POTTERS BAR
Sch
Rose Mead
Little Heath Primary Sch
School Rd
Cringle Ct
Northaw House
Vineyards Rd
B156
Northaw Rd W
Green Mdw
Heath Rd
The Mount
Broadwater
Osborne Rd
Newlands Way
Grangewood
Cranmer Cl
Thornton Rd
Coopers Rd
Coopers La
Westwood Cl
Manor Way
Mountway
Heath Dr
St Michaels Way
Hatfield Rd
Frampton Rd
Alma Ct
Springfield
Stud Farm
PO
The Avenue
Sch
Church Rd
Sandringham Rd
The Highlands
Heronfield
Darkes La
Cedar Ct
Inglefield
Rosary Ct
Anthorne Cl
Quakers La
Norman Ct
A1000
159
146

145
132

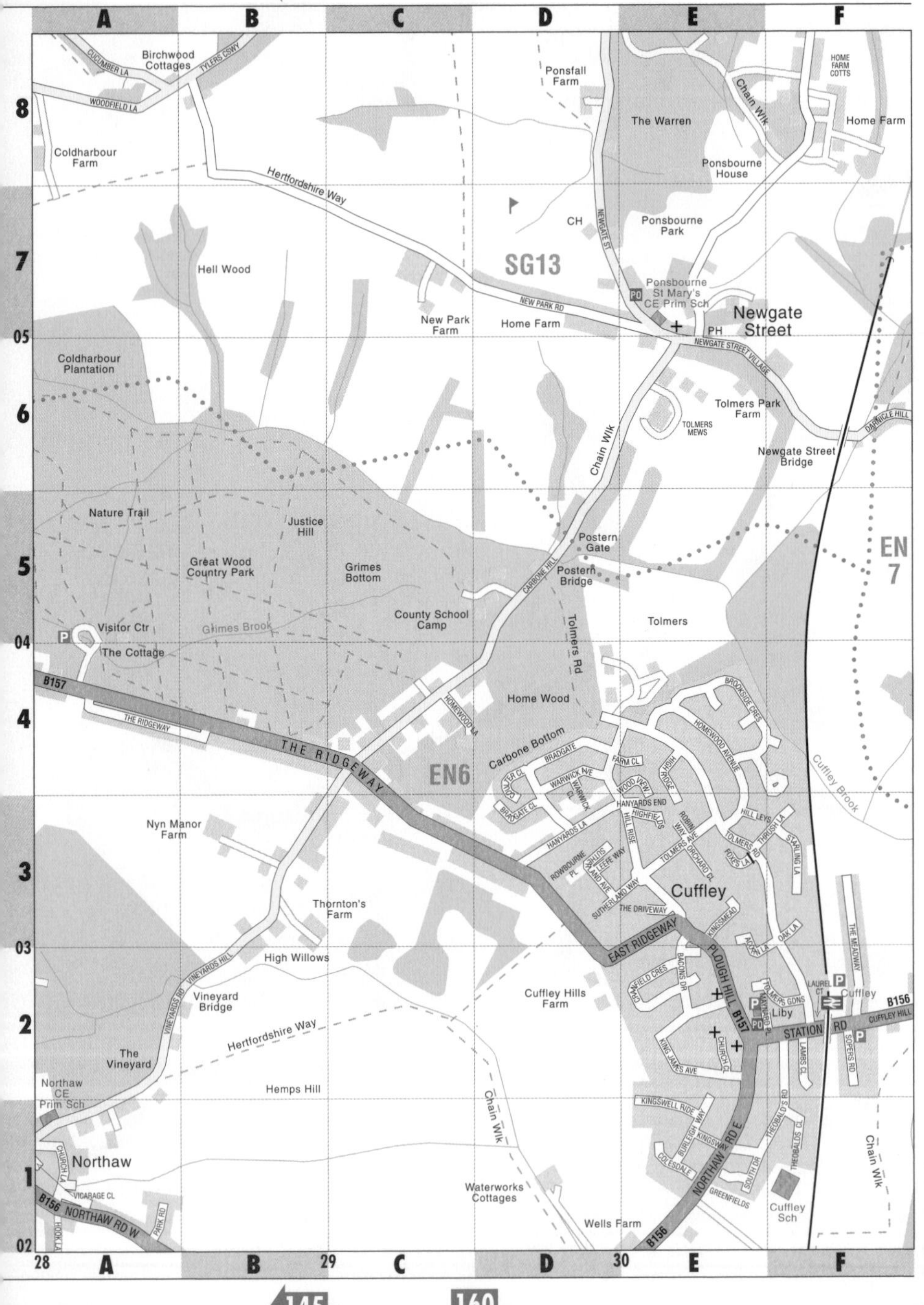

145
160

133
148

161
148

E5
1 SOUTHVIEW CL
2 THE POPLARS
3 HAZEL CL
4 WHITEBEAM CL
5 NUTWOOD GDNS
6 FRIERN CL
7 CONY CL

147
134

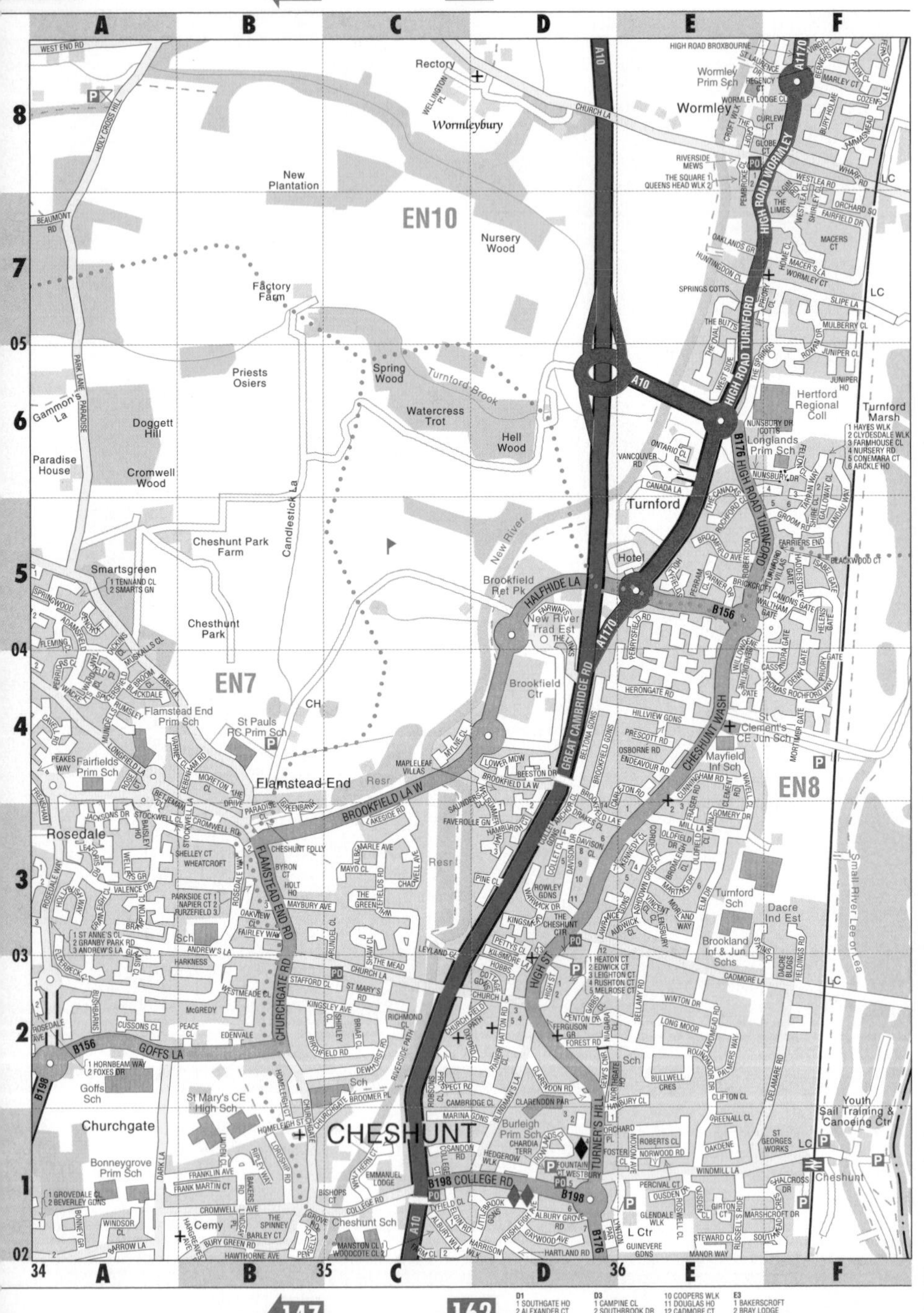

D1	D3		E3
1 SOUTHGATE HO	1 CAMPINE CL	10 COOPERS WLK	1 BAKERSCROFT
2 ALEXANDER CT	2 SOUTHBROOK DR	11 DOUGLAS HO	2 BRAY LODGE
3 ROWLANDS CT	3 THE SPUR	12 CADMORE CT	3 CUNNINGHAM CT
4 ANCIENT ALMHOS	4 CRAIGS WLK	13 SYMONDS CT	4 GOODWIN CT
5 NEWNHAM PAR	5 BREEZE TERR	14 BROOKFIELD CT	5 BEECHOLM MEWS
6 MANORCROFT PAR	6 THE WHITE HO		6 FAIRFIELD WLK
7 CLAYTON PAR	7 THE COLONNADE		
	8 CEDAR LODGE		
	9 BLAXLAND TERR		

147
162

135

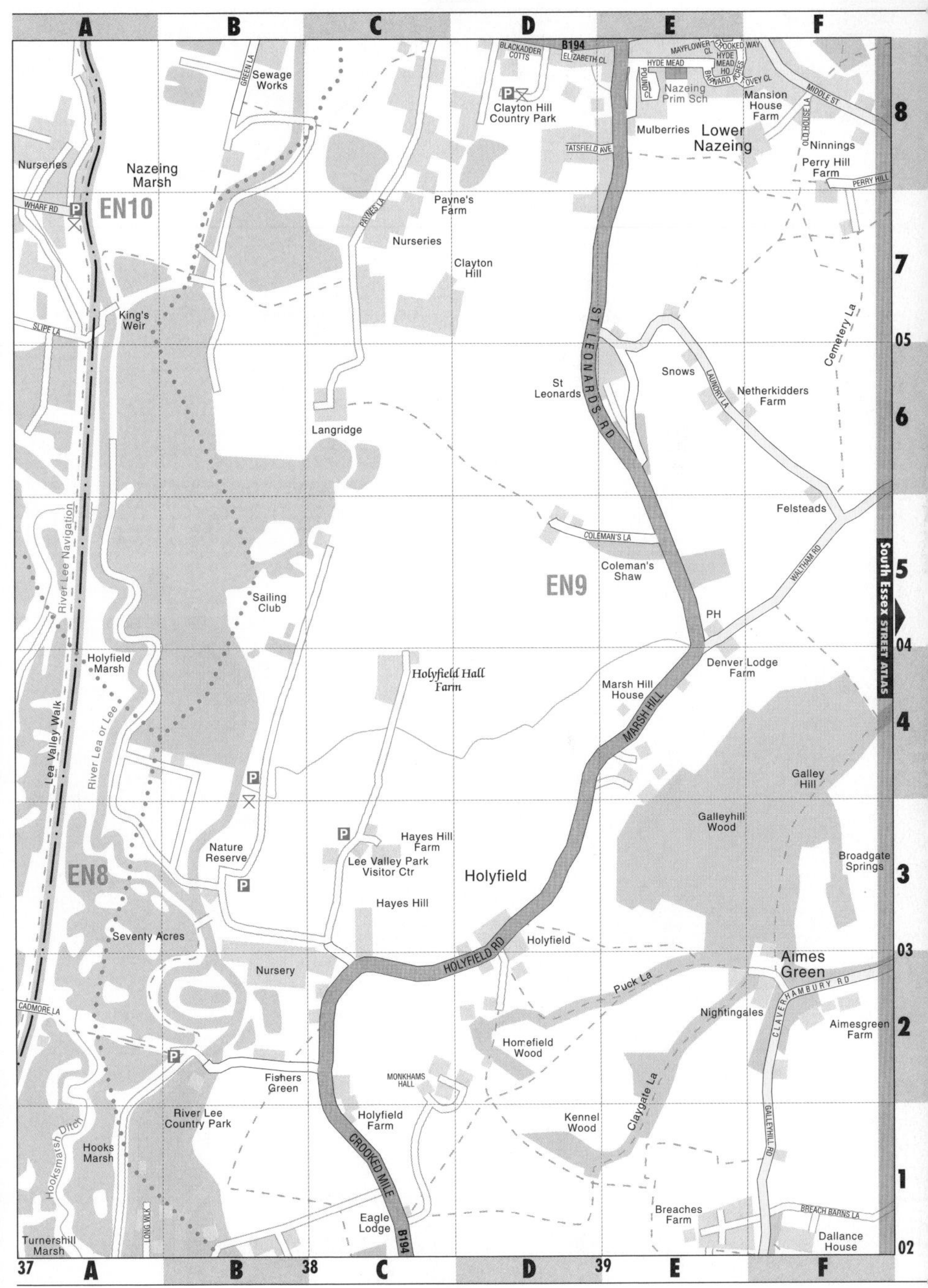
A
B
C
D
E
F
8
7
05
6
5
04
4
3
03
2
1
02
37
38
39
Sewage Works
GREEN LA
BLACKADDER COTTS
B194
ELIZABETH CL
MAYFLOWER CL
CROOKED WAY
HYDE MEAD
HYDE MEAD HO
POUND CL
BARNARD ACRES
TOVEY CL
Nazeing Prim Sch
Clayton Hill Country Park
Mansion House Farm
MIDDLE ST
OLD HOUSE LA
Mulberries
Lower Nazeing
Ninnings
Perry Hill Farm
PERRY HILL
TATSFIELD AVE
Nurseries
Nazeing Marsh
WHARF RD
EN10
Payne's Farm
PAYNES LA
Nurseries
Clayton Hill
King's Weir
SLIPE LA
ST LEONARDS RD
Cemetery La
Snows
LAUNDRY LA
Netherkidders Farm
St Leonards
Langridge
Felsteads
COLEMAN'S LA
WALTHAM RD
Coleman's Shaw
EN9
River Lee Navigation
Sailing Club
PH
Holyfield Marsh
Holyfield Hall Farm
Denver Lodge Farm
Marsh Hill House
MARSH HILL
Lea Valley Walk
River Lea or Lee
Galley Hill
Galleyhill Wood
Hayes Hill Farm
Nature Reserve
Lee Valley Park Visitor Ctr
Broadgate Springs
EN8
Holyfield
Hayes Hill
Seventy Acres
Holyfield
HOLYFIELD RD
Aimes Green
Nursery
Puck La
CLAVERHAMBURY RD
CADMORE LA
Nightingales
Aimesgreen Farm
Homefield Wood
Fishers Green
MONKHAMS HALL
Claygate La
Holyfield Farm
Kennel Wood
River Lee Country Park
GALLEYHILL RD
Hooksmarsh Ditch
Hooks Marsh
CROOKED MILE
Breaches Farm
BREACH BARNS LA
Eagle Lodge
LONG WLK
B194
Turnershill Marsh
Dallance House
South Essex STREET ATLAS

163

136

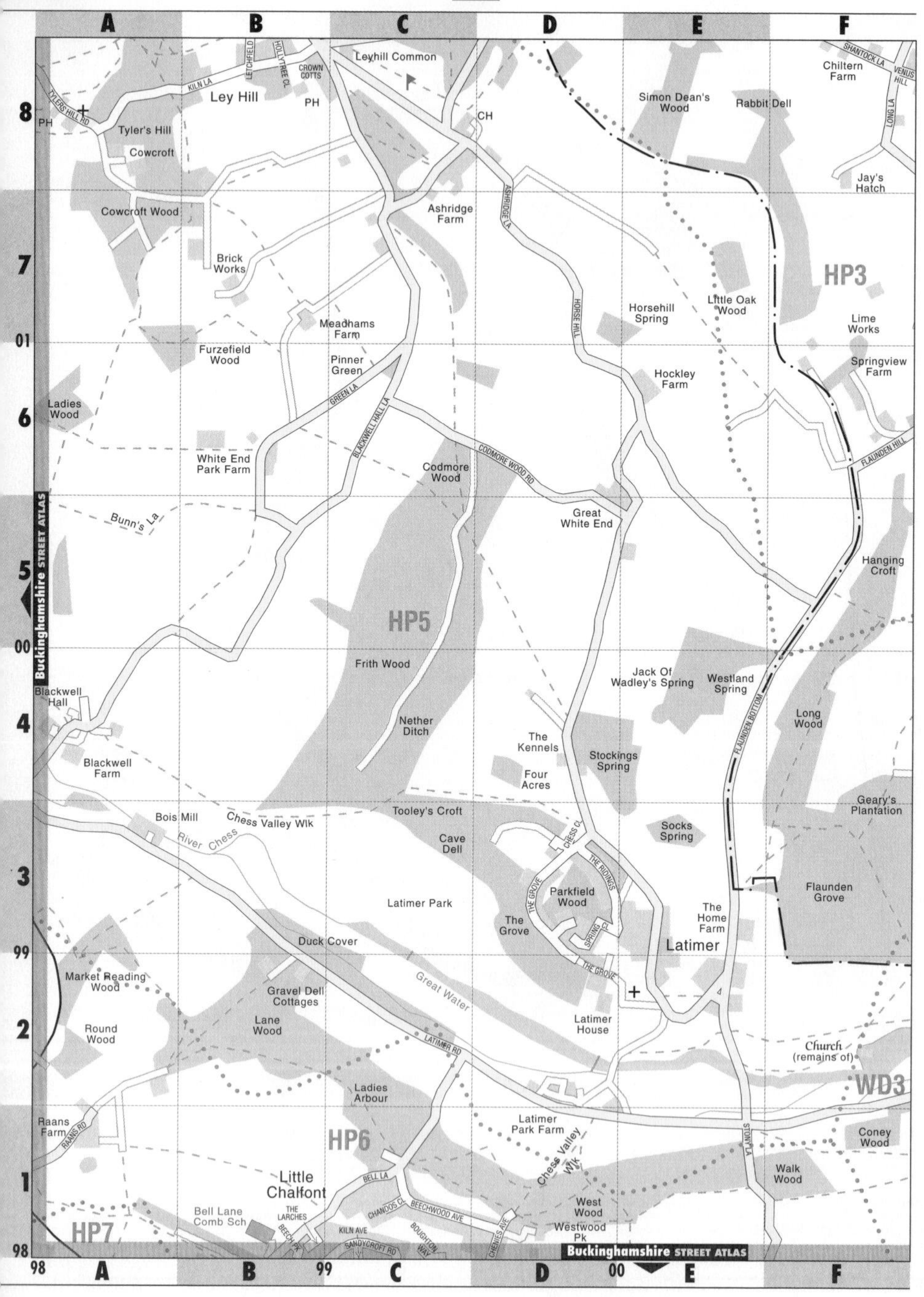
A
B
C
D
E
F
Leyhill Common
Ley Hill
PH
CROWN COTTS
LETCHFIELD
HOLLYTREE CL
KILN LA
TYLERS HILL RD
PH
Tyler's Hill
Cowcroft
Cowcroft Wood
CH
ASHRIDGE LA
Ashridge Farm
Brick Works
Simon Dean's Wood
Rabbit Dell
SHANTOCK LA
VENUS HILL
Chiltern Farm
LONG LA
Jay's Hatch
HP3
Horsehill Spring
HORSE HILL
Little Oak Wood
Lime Works
Meadhams Farm
Furzefield Wood
Pinner Green
GREEN LA
BLACKWELL HALL LA
Hockley Farm
Springview Farm
Ladies Wood
FLAUNDEN HILL
CODMORE WOOD RD
White End Park Farm
Codmore Wood
Great White End
Bunn's La
Hanging Croft
HP5
Frith Wood
Jack Of Wadley's Spring
Westland Spring
FLAUNDEN BOTTOM
Blackwell Hall
Nether Ditch
The Kennels
Stockings Spring
Long Wood
Blackwell Farm
Four Acres
Bois Mill
Chess Valley Wlk
Tooley's Croft
Geary's Plantation
River Chess
Cave Dell
CHESS CL
Socks Spring
THE RIDINGS
Latimer Park
THE GROVE
Parkfield Wood
The Grove
SPRING CL
The Home Farm
Flaunden Grove
Duck Cover
Latimer
Market Reading Wood
Gravel Dell Cottages
Great Water
Lane Wood
Round Wood
Latimer House
LATIMER RD
Church (remains of)
Ladies Arbour
WD3
Raans Farm
RAANS RD
HP6
Latimer Park Farm
Chess Valley Wlk
STONY LA
Coney Wood
Walk Wood
Little Chalfont
BELL LA
West Wood
Bell Lane Comb Sch
THE LARCHES
CHANDOS CL
BEECHWOOD AVE
BOUGHTON WAY
CHENIES AVE
Westwood Pk
HP7
BEECH PK
KILN AVE
SANDYCROFT RD
Buckinghamshire STREET ATLAS
8
7
01
6
5
00
4
3
99
2
1
98
98
99
00

137
152

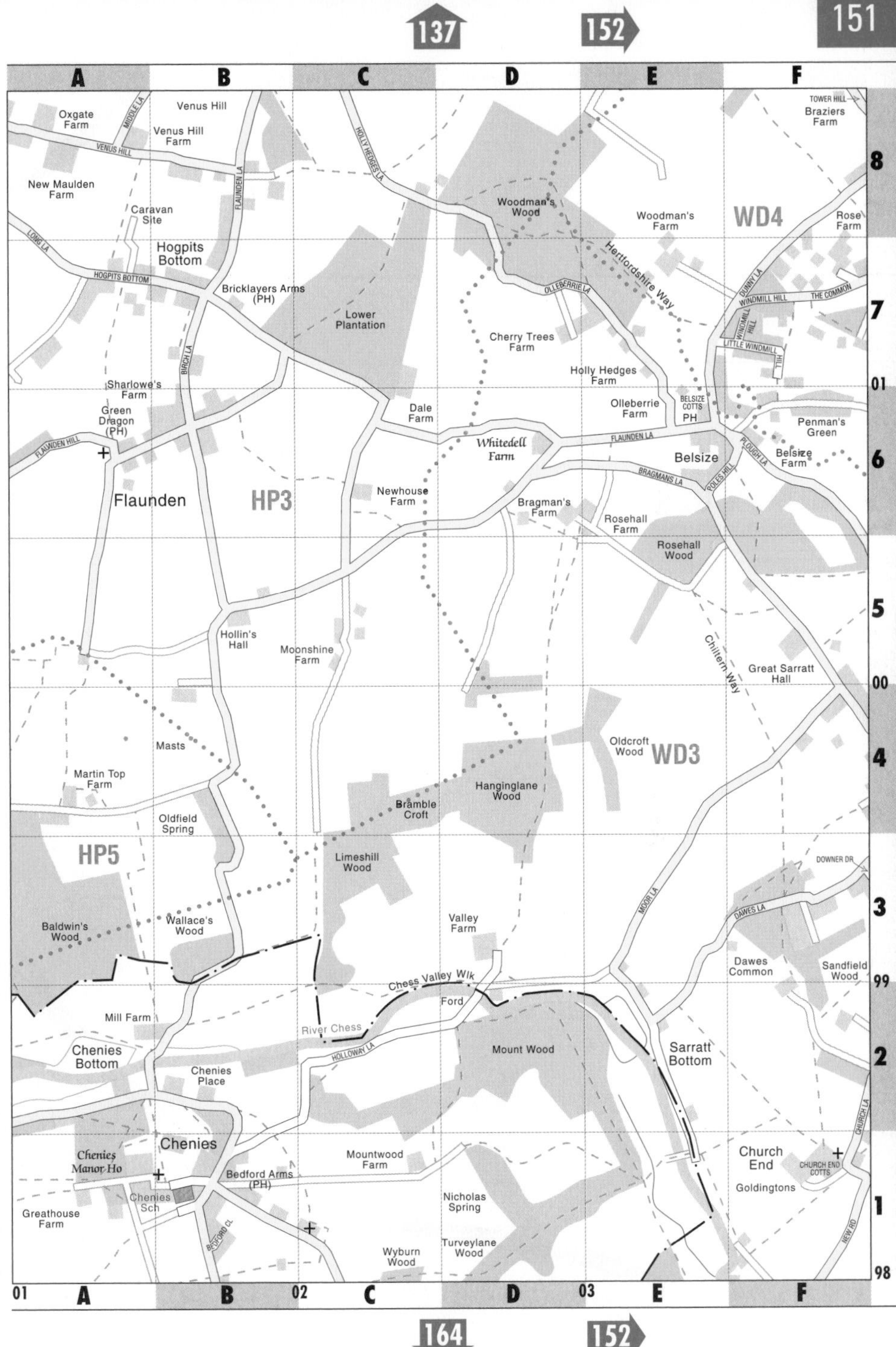

164
152

151
138

A B C D E F

8 7 01 6 5 00 4 3 99 2 1 98

Chipperfield
St Paul's CE Prim Sch
PH
Manor House
Rookery Wood
Hertfordshire Way
Berrybush Farm
Mast
Middle Farm
Langley Lodge Farm
Langley Lodge
Chipperfield Common
Topcommon
Hunterswood
Callipers Hall
Penmans
Jeffery's Farm
Berrybushes Wood
Hillmeads Farm
Cart & Horses (PH)
WD4
Baytree Farm
Commonwood
Bucks Hill
Model Farm
Commonwood Common
Bucks Hill Farm
Little Westwood Farm
Red Lion Farm
Bucks Hill House
Great Westwood Farm
Briar Cottage
The Boot (PH)
Sarratt
High Spring
Juniper Hill
WD3
Buckshill Bottom
Templepan Wood
Newhall Farm
Sarratt CE Prim Sch
White House
Yew Court Farm
Green End Bsns Ctr
Potten Farm
Micklefield Green
Great Wood
Chandler's Farm
Micklefield Green Farm
Clarendon Arms (PH)
Scrubbs Farm
Great Wood Cottages
Chandler's Cross
Cottage Farm
Scrubbs Wood
Coltspring School of Riding

CROFT LA, CHAPEL CROFT, TOWER HILL, DUNNY LA, THE STREET, FORGE CL, LANGLEY RD, KING'S LA, NUNFIELD, KINGS CL, HAVENSFIELD, THE COMMON, QUEEN ST, LANGLEY LODGE LA, QUICKMOOR LA, PLOUGH LA, BUCKS HILL, RED LION LA, BOTTOM LA, OLD HOUSE LA, THE GREEN, DAWES LA, ALEXANDRA RD, DOWNER DR, MYRTLE COTTS, CLUTTERBUCKS, GEORGE V WAY, CAROON DR, DIMMOCKS LA, DEADMAN'S ASH LA, TOM'S HILL, TEMPLEPAN LA, CHURCH LA, CHANDLER'S LA, LONG PIGHTLE MOBILE HOME PK, WHITE SHACK LA, SARRATT RD, FIR TREE HILL, REDHALL LA, ROUSEBARN LA, SARRATT RD 1, SARRATT LA 2, A41, M25

04 A B 05 C D 06 E F

151
165

139
154

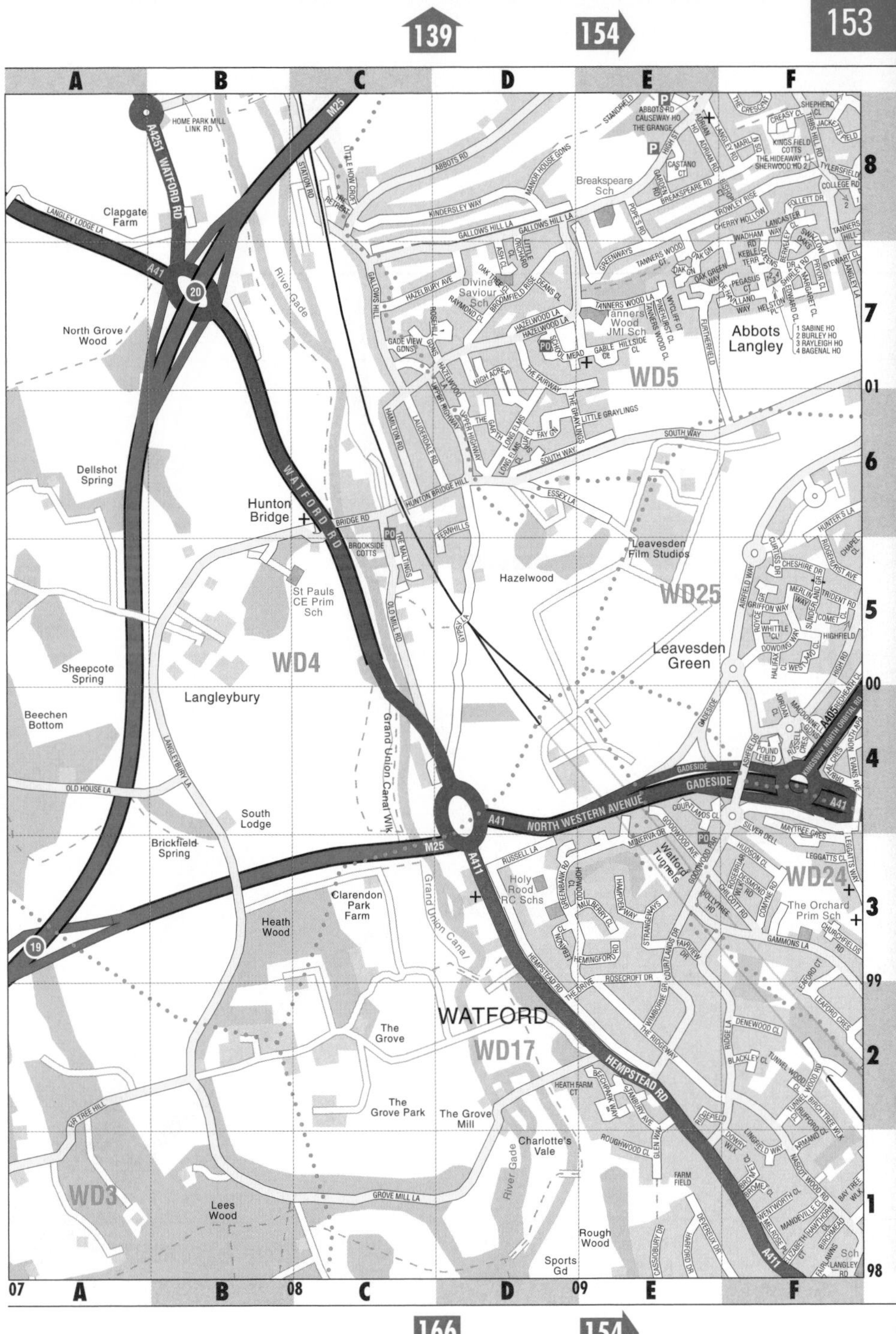
A
B
C
D
E
F
8
7
01
6
5
00
4
3
99
2
1
98
07
08
09
M25
A4251 WATFORD RD
HOME PARK MILL LINK RD
LANGLEY LODGE LA
Clapgate Farm
A41
20
North Grove Wood
River Gade
STATION RD
LITTLE HOW CROFT
THE RETREAT
ABBOTS RD
MANOR HOUSE GDNS
KINDERSLEY WAY
GALLOWS HILL LA
GALLOWS HILL
HAZELBURY AVE
ASH CL
LITTLE ORCHARD CL
OAK TREE CL
Divine Saviour Sch
BROOMFIELD RISE
DEANS CL
RAYMOND CL
ROSEHILL GDNS
GADE VIEW GDNS
HAZELWOOD LA
SCHOOL MEAD
GABLE CL
HILLSIDE CL
Tanners Wood JMI Sch
TANNERS WOOD LA
PINEHURST CL
WYCLIF CT
FURTHERFIELD
GREENWAYS
TANNERS WOOD CT
POPE'S RD
Breakspeare Sch
STANDFIELD
ABBOTS RD
CAUSEWAY HO
THE GRANGE
HIGH ST
CASTANO CT
GARDEN RD
BREAKSPEARE RD
ADRIAN RD
LANGLEY RD
THE CRESCENT
CREASY CL
MARLIN SQ
SHEPHERD CL
JACKETTS FIELD
KINGS FIELD COTTS
THE HIDEAWAY 1
SHERWOOD HO 2
TIBBS HILL RD
TYLERSFIELD
COLLEGE RD
FOLLETT DR
TROWLEY RISE
CHERRY HOLLOW
LANCASTER WAY
WADHAM
KEBLE TERR
QUEENS
BERKELEY CL
SWALLOW OAKS
PRYOR CL
TANNERS HILL
STEWART CL
LANGLEY LA
OAK GREEN WAY
PEGASUS CT
DE HAVILLAND WAY
HELSTON PL
EDWARD CL
SHIRLEY RD
MARGARET CL
Abbots Langley
1 SABINE HO
2 BURLEY HO
3 RAYLEIGH HO
4 BAGENAL HO
WD5
HIGH ACRE
THE FAIRWAY
THE GRAYLINGS
LITTLE GRAYLINGS
THE GARTH
LONG ELMS
FAY GN
SOUTH WAY
HAMILTON RD
LAUDERDALE RD
UPPER HIGHWAY
HAZELWOOD LA
HUNTON BRIDGE HILL
ESSEX LA
Dellshot Spring
Hunton Bridge
BRIDGE RD
WATFORD RD
BROOKSIDE COTTS
THE MALTINGS
FERNHILLS
St Pauls CE Prim Sch
OLD MILL RD
GYPSY LA
Hazelwood
Leavesden Film Studios
WD25
HUNTER'S LA
CURTISS DR
CHESHIRE DR
RIDGEHURST AVE
CHAPEL CL
AIRFIELD WAY
MERLIN WAY
TRIDENT RD
ROYCE GR
GRIFFON WAY
SUNDERLAND GR
COMET CL
WHITTLE CL
DOWDING WAY
HIGHFIELD
HALIFAX CL
WESTLAND CL
HIGH RD
Leavesden Green
Sheepcote Spring
WD4
Langleybury
Beechen Bottom
LANGLEYBURY LA
Grand Union Canal Wlk
GADESIDE
JORDAN CL
MACDONNELL GDNS
A405
REDHEATH CL
NORTH ORBITAL RD
KINGSWAY NORTH ORBITAL RD
ASHFIELDS
POUND FIELD
RUSSELL CRES
EVANS AVE
OLD HOUSE LA
South Lodge
A41 NORTH WESTERN AVENUE
COURTLANDS CL
SILVER DELL
MAYTREE CRES
LEGGATTS WAY
LEGGATTS CL
Brickfield Spring
M25
A411
RUSSELL LA
MINERVA DR
GOODWOOD AVE
GOODWOOD PDE
Watford Tuggels
HUDSON CL
ROSEBRIAR WLK
DESMOND RD
CHILCOTT RD
COMYNE RD
WD24
Holy Rood RC Schs
GREENBANK RD
HOPWOOD CL
MULBERRY CL
HAMPDEN WAY
STRANGEWAYS
HOLLYTREE HO
The Orchard Prim Sch
GAMMONS LA
CHURCHFIELDS
Clarendon Park Farm
Heath Wood
Grand Union Canal
19
HEMINGFORD RD
HEMPSTEAD RD
ROSECROFT DR
COURTLANDS DR
FAIRVIEW DR
LEAFORD CT
LEAFORD CRES
THE DRIVE
WIMBORNE GR
THE RIDGEWAY
RIDGE LA
DENEWOOD CL
BLACKLEY CL
TUNNEL WOOD CL
TUNNEL WOOD RD
WATFORD
WD17
The Grove
HEMPSTEAD RD
HEATH FARM CT
BEECHPARK WAY
STANBURY AVE
RIDGEFIELD
FIR TREE HILL
The Grove Park
The Grove Mill
Charlotte's Vale
ROUGHWOOD CL
GLEN WAY
DOWRY WLK
LINGFIELD WAY
BIRCH TREE WLK
ARMAND CL
NASCOT WOOD RD
FARM FIELD
River Gade
BROMET CL
BAY TREE WLK
WD3
Lees Wood
GROVE MILL LA
Rough Wood
CASSIOBURY DR
DEVEREUX DR
HARFORD DR
WENTWORTH CL
MANDEVILLE CL
MELROSE PL
ELIZABETH CT
HAWTHORN CL
BIRCHMEAD
FAIRLAWNS
A411
Sports Gd
Sch
LANGLEY RD

153
140

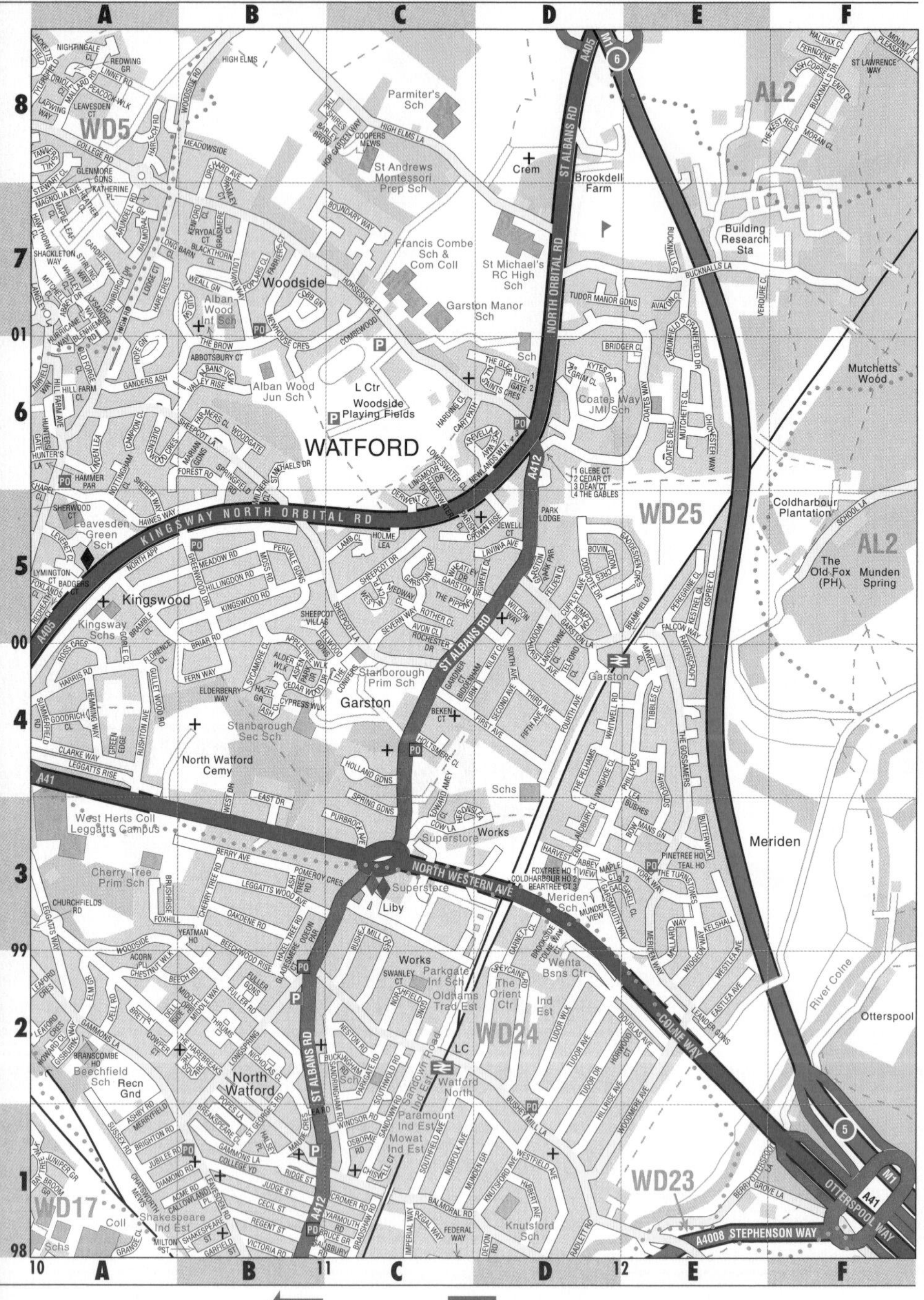

153
167

A B C D E F

8

Hamilton Cl
Rowan Cl
Juniper Ave
Claremont
Hunters Ride
Mount Pleasant La
Station Rd
St Lawrence Way
Nottlers Wood
Nottlers House
L Ctr
Bricket Wood Training & Con Ctr
Lower Stud
Waterside Farm
Colneystreet Bridge
Bridgefoot Cotts
Works
A5183 Radlett Rd
Drop La
River Ver

7

WD25
Bricket Wood Common
New Plantation
School La
River Colne
Netherwylde Farm
Oakridge La
B556
Harper La

01

AL2
Little Munden Farm
Commonmeadow La
Hill Farm
A5183
Watling Knoll
Brook Dr
The Close

6

Kitswell Way
Meadow Mead
Oakridge Ave
Four Acre Plantation
Peartree Wood
Crab Wood
Links Dr
Goodyers Ave
Oakridge La

5

Ford
Munden House
Sewage Works
Penne Cl
Newlands Ave
Hertfordshire Way
Blackbirds La
WD7

00

WD25
Crab La
The Folly
1 Darnhills
2 High Firs
Abbey View
B462
Blackbirds Farm

4

RADLETT
Hawtrees
Scotscraig
Delfield Cl
Watford Rd
The Chase
Highfields
Oaks Cl
Hambleden Pl
Gills Hill
Folly Pathway
Gills Hollow
Wall Hall (Univ Campus)
Kemprow
Folly Cl
St Johns CE Inf Sch
Willow Way
Kemprow Farm
Fairfield Jun Sch
Gills Hill La
Elm Wlk

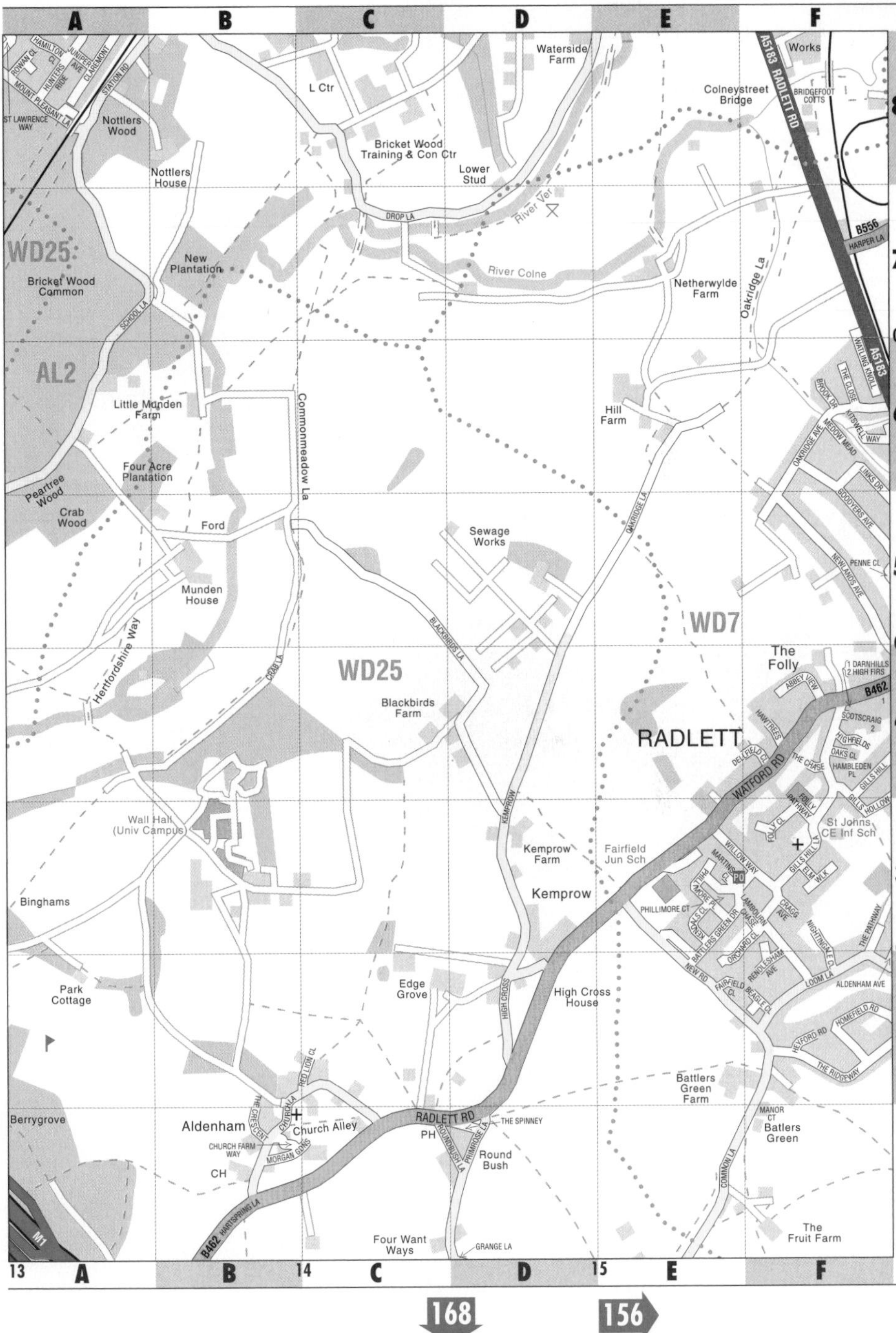

3

Martins Cl
Phillimore Pl
PO
Binghams
Kemprow
Phillimore Ct
Kendals Cl
Battlers Green Dr
Lamboum Chase
Cragg Ave
Nightingale Cl
The Pathway
Orchard Cl
Rendlesham Ave

99

New Rd
Fairfield Cl
Beagle Cl
Loom La
Aldenham Ave
Park Cottage
Edge Grove
High Cross
High Cross House
Homefield Rd
Heyford Rd

2

The Ridgeway
Battlers Green Farm
Manor Ct
Batlers Green
Berrygrove
Aldenham
The Crescent
Church La
Red Lion Cl
Church Alley
Radlett Rd
PH
Roundbush La
Primrose La
The Spinney
Round Bush
Church Farm Way
Morgan Gdns
CH
Common La

1

M1
B462 Hartspring La
Four Want Ways
Grange La
The Fruit Farm

98

13 A B 14 C D 15 E F

155
142

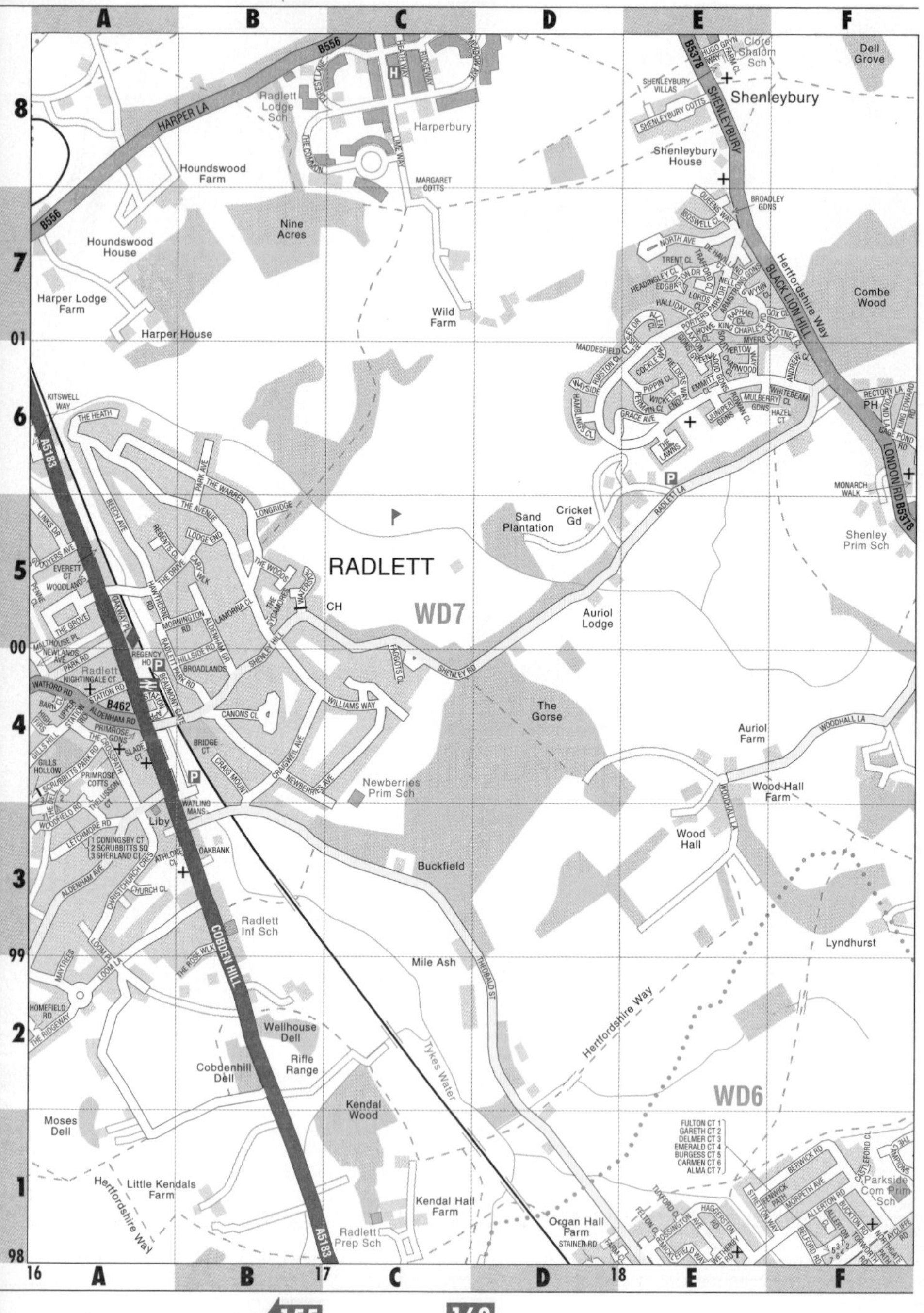

155
169

143
158

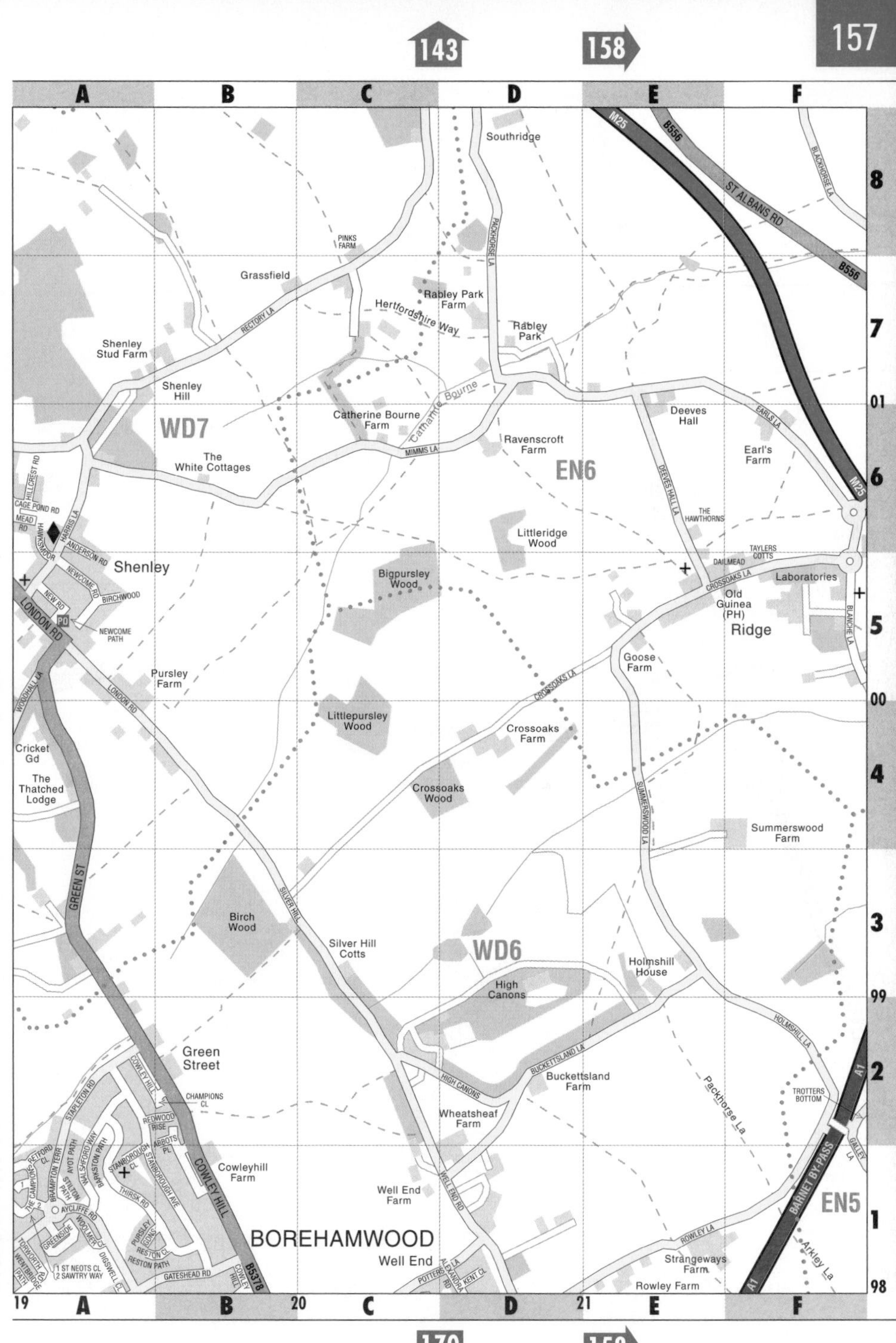

170
158

157
144

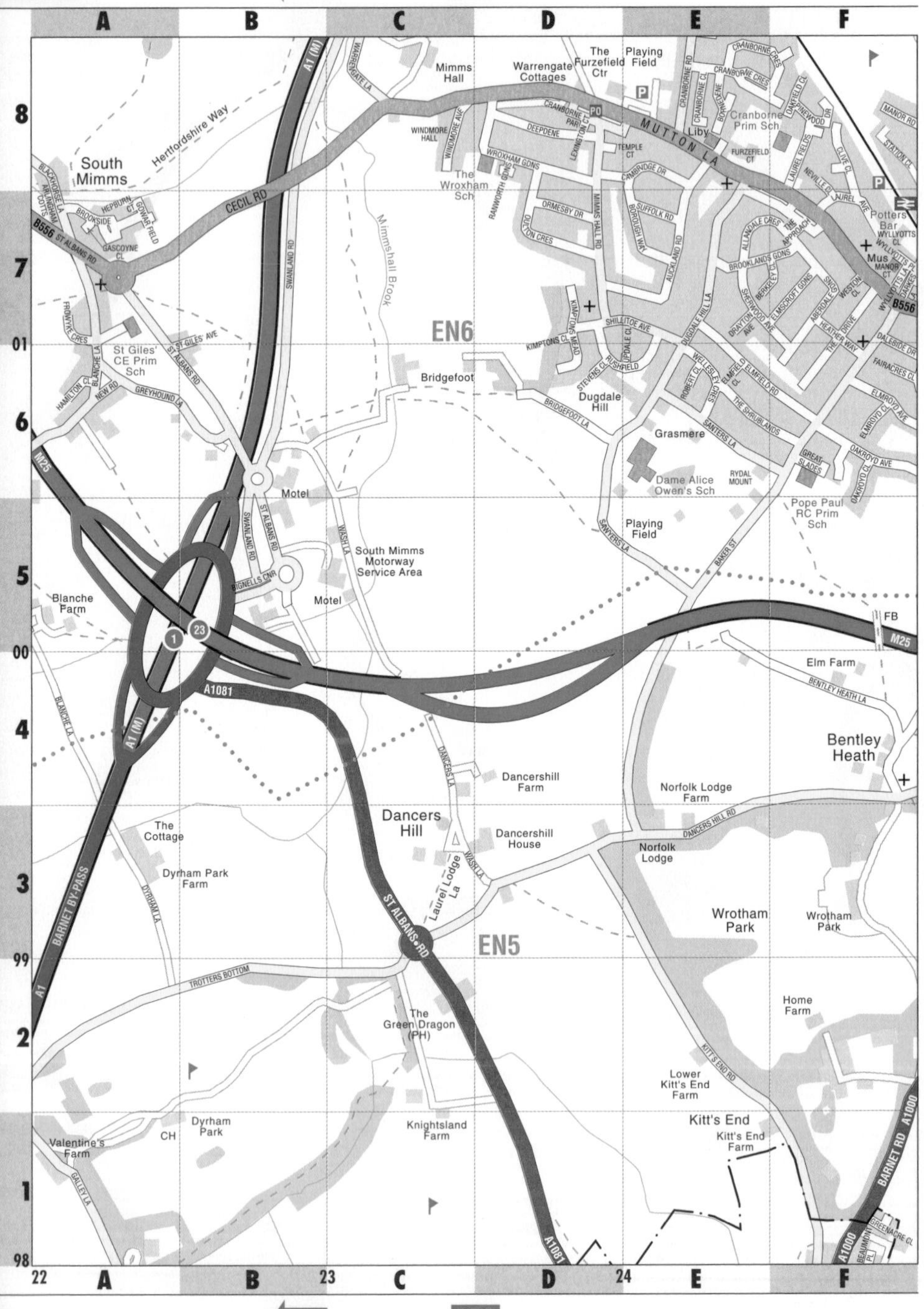

157
171

145

160

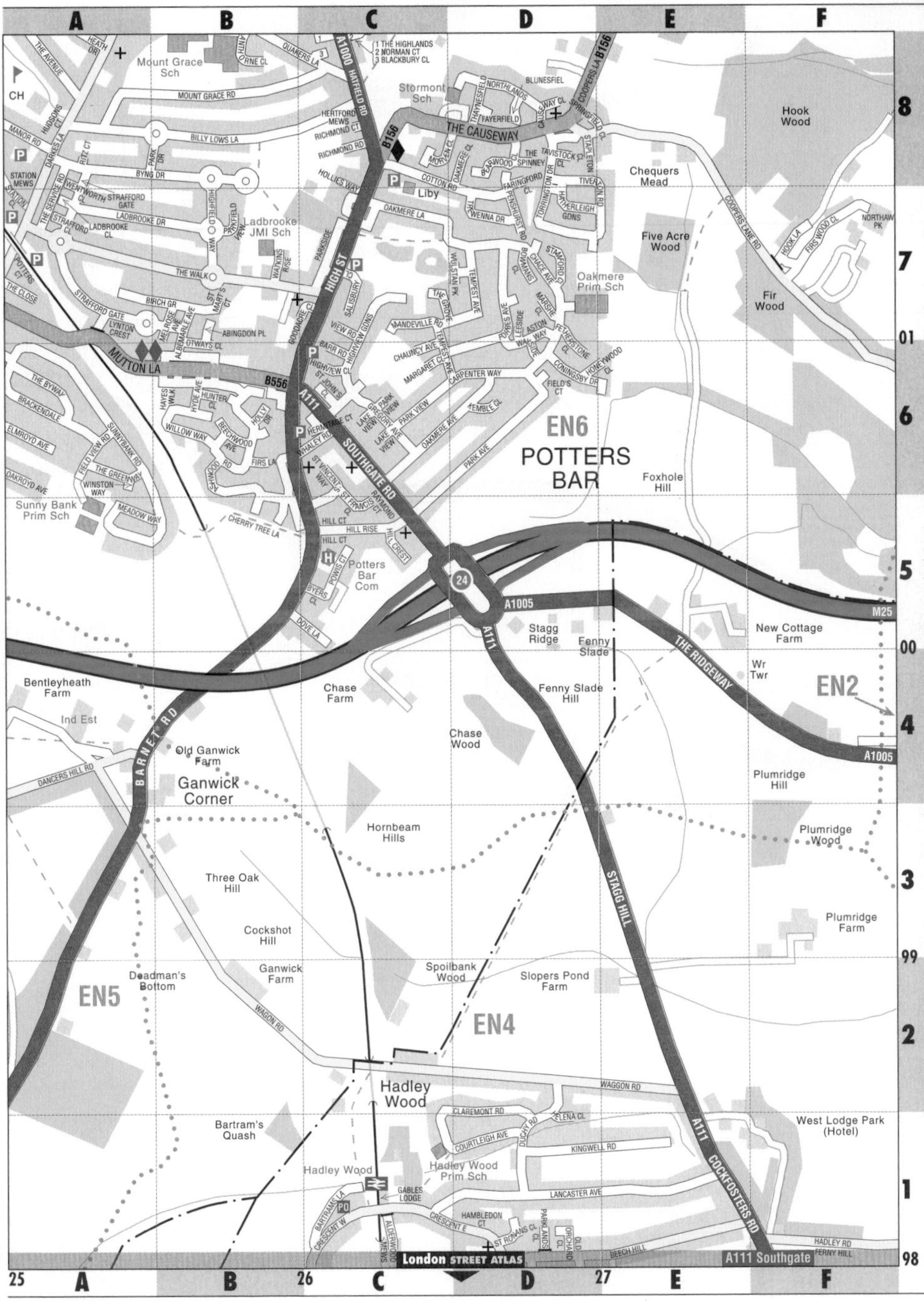

A
B
C
D
E
F
8
7
01
6
5
00
4
3
99
2
1
98
25
26
27
Mount Grace Sch
Stormont Sch
Hook Wood
Chequers Mead
Five Acre Wood
Fir Wood
Oakmere Prim Sch
Ladbrooke JMI Sch
Liby
EN6
POTTERS BAR
Foxhole Hill
Sunny Bank Prim Sch
Potters Bar Com
Stagg Ridge
Fenny Slade
New Cottage Farm
Wr Twr
EN2
Bentleyheath Farm
Ind Est
Chase Farm
Fenny Slade Hill
Chase Wood
Old Ganwick Farm
Ganwick Corner
Plumridge Hill
Hornbeam Hills
Plumridge Wood
Three Oak Hill
Cockshot Hill
Plumridge Farm
Deadman's Bottom
Ganwick Farm
Spoilbank Wood
Slopers Pond Farm
EN5
EN4
Hadley Wood
Bartram's Quash
Hadley Wood Prim Sch
West Lodge Park (Hotel)
THE CAUSEWAY
MUTTON LA
HATFIELD RD
HIGH ST
SOUTHGATE RD
BARNET RD
STAGG HILL
COCKFOSTERS RD
THE RIDGEWAY
A1000
A111
A1005
B156
B556
M25
WAGGON RD
WAGON RD
DANCERS HILL RD
COOPERS LANE RD
CHERRY TREE LA
MOUNT GRACE RD
BILLY LOWS LA
BYNG DR
LADBROOKE DR
THE WALK
STRAFFORD GATE
DARKES LA
THE SERVICE RD
THE BYWAY
BRACKENDALE
ELMROYD AVE
OAKROYD AVE
MEADOW WAY
CLAREMONT RD
COURTLEIGH AVE
KINGWELL RD
LANCASTER AVE
CRESCENT E
CRESCENT W
BEECH HILL
HADLEY RD
FERNY HILL
1 THE HIGHLANDS
2 NORMAN CT
3 BLACKBURY CL
London STREET ATLAS
A111 Southgate

160

159
146

A
B
C
D
E
F
8
7
01
6
5
00
4
3
99
2
1
98
28
29
30
Park Farm
B156
NORTHAW RD W
Coles Hill
Colesdale Farm
NORTHAW RD E B156
Northaw Brook
Chain Wlk
CATTLEGATE COTTS
EN7
Nursery Plantation
Northaw Brook
CATTLEGATE HILL
EN6
Barvin Park
OAKWELL DR
Cattlegate Wood
Cattlegate Farm
Abbotswood
WOODGATE AVE
COOPERS LANE RD
Barvin Hill
Woodhurst Farm Cottages
CATTLEGATE RD
M25
Hooke Hill
Woodhurst Farm
Owls Hall
Turkey Brook
M25
Holly Hill Farm
South Hill
Crews Hill
CH
CREWS HILL
Crews Hill
North Lodge Farm
St Nicholas House
EN2
Chain Wlk
South Barvin Farm
A1005
Holyhill Brook
EAST LODGE LA
Vault Hill
Botany Bay
Parting Hill
THE RIDGEWAY
East Lodge
Little Beechhill Wood
LITTLE BEECHHILL
Vault Hill Wood
Robin Hood (PH)
Bay Farm
Roundhedge Hill
London Loop
Rectory Farm
Duncan's Wood
Salmon's Brook
EN4
Cuckolds Hill
WILLIAM COVELL CL 1
HIGH OAKS 2
KINGFISHER CT 3
HIGHRIDGE PL 4
London Loop
Ash Wood
ROUNDHEDGE WAY
ARAGON CL
Park Farm
Parkside Farm
Hotel
A1005
FERNY HILL
Obelisk
Moat Wood
Ride Wood
HADLEY RD
OAK AVE
MOUNT VIEW
Ferny Hill Farm
London STREET ATLAS
A1005 Enfield

159

147
162

A B C D E F
8
7
01
6
5
00
4
3
99
2
1
98
31 32 33
Woodgreen Farm
Broadfield Farm
BARROW LA
B198
LIEUTENANT ELLIS WAY
Burnt Farm
Chain Wlk
Theobalds
Burnt Farm Cottage
Cattlins
Dysons Osiers
OLDPARK RIDE
Home Wood
Chain Wlk
EN7
Hanging Plantation
BURNTFARM RIDE
Home Plantation
Spring Farm
Theobalds Manor
Tilekiln Osiers
Gunsite Stud
The Paddocks
Chain Wlk
South Osiers
Crews Hill Piggeries
Nurseries
Glasgow Stud
Whitewebbs Farm
Cemy
Sloemans Farm
M25
CATTLEGATE RD
SANDER'S CNR
Crews Hill
WHITEWEBBS RD
Whitewebbs Mus of Transport
WHITEWEBBS LA
King & Tinker (PH)
BEECH AVE
ROSEWOOD DR
ASH RIDE
WROXHAM GDNS
GOLF RIDE
CYPRESS AVE
Nurseries
Whitewebbs Wood
Whitewebbs Park
Water Garden Ctr
Chain Wlk
White Webbs
Nurseries
THEOBALDS PARK RD
New River (Old Course)
EN2
Turkey Brook
Chain Wlk
St John's CE Prim Sch
FLASH LA
Cuffley Brook
London Loop
King's Oak Plain
ROSSENDALE CL
STRAYFIELD RD
Brayside Farm
CH
London Loop
The Red House
Queenswood Farm
PH
Forty Hall Farm
Clay Hill
CLAY HILL
BRAMLEY HOUSE CT
ST JOHN'S TERR
STRATTON AVE
Turkey Brook
ACACIA RD 1
LAVENDER RD 2
VIOLET AVE 3
ENFIELD
Forty Hall
THE CLOCK HO
PARK NOOK GDNS
Allot Gdns
TUDOR CRES 1
YORK TERR 2
RIPLEY RD 3
WETHERBY RD 4
Hilly Fields Park
ELM GDNS
1 WADDESTON CT
2 KENSINGTON CT
3 HOWARD CT
CARTERHATCH LA 1
BRIDGENHALL RD 2
LAYARD RD 3
CHINNERY CL 4
DOWLAND HO 5
The Kings Oak Private
COOK'S HOLE RD
HILLSIDE CRES
BROWNING RD
LINTON DR
WOODBINE GR
FORTY HILL
FORTY HILL HO
Worcesters Primary Sch
PHIPPS HATCH LA
CONWAY GDNS
HENRY CL
PORTLAND DR
KENILWORTH CRES
LIME TREE WALK
Cemy
CEDAR
PARK RD
ST LUKE'S AVE
MORLEY HILL
BIRKBECK RD
MYRTLE GR
BURNHAM CL
PH
ST GEORGE'S RD
GOAT LA
SPRING COURT RD
Chase Farm
RENDLESHAM RD
GLOUCESTER RD
BRIGADIER AVE
BRODIE RD
WOODLANDS RD
Lavender Prim Sch
Enfield Cty Lwr Sch
BAKER ST
MAYDELTON AVE
ADELAIDE CL
HALSIDE RD
OLD FORGE RD
RUSSELL RD
THE RIDGEWAY
CEDAR RD
BLOSSOM LA
CHANTRY CL
BRIGADIER HILL
GLENVILLE AVE
MERTON RD
STERLING RD
HAWTHORN GR
RIDLER RD
EN1
GARNAULT RD
LAVENDER GDNS
BEDALE RD

162

161
148

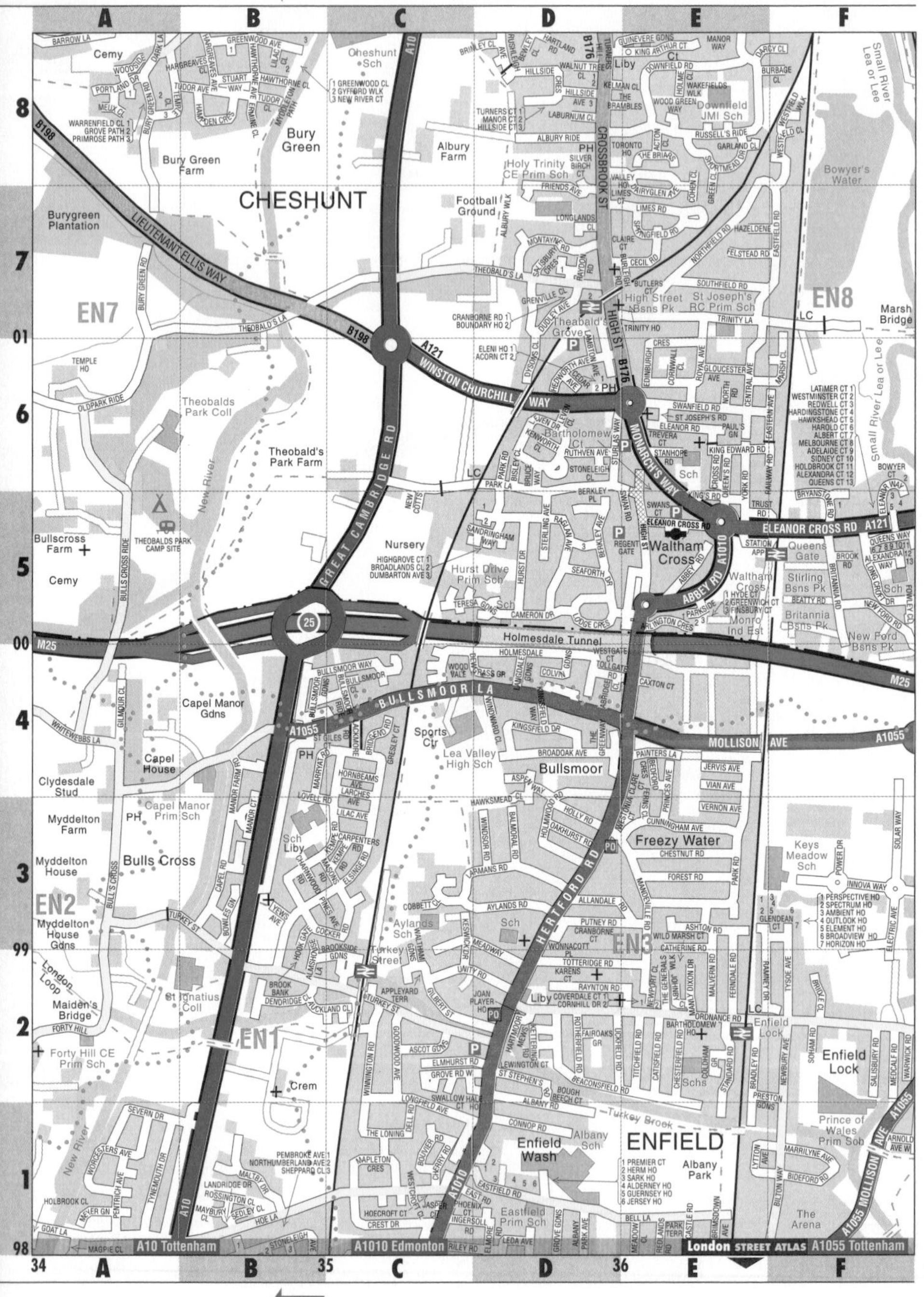
A
B
C
D
E
F
8
7
01
6
5
00
4
3
99
2
1
98
34
35
36
CHESHUNT
ENFIELD
EN7
EN8
EN2
EN1
EN3
Cemy
Oheshunt Sch
Bury Green
Bury Green Farm
Albury Farm
Holy Trinity CE Prim Sch
Downfield JMI Sch
Bowyer's Water
Small River Lea or Lee
Burygreen Plantation
Football Ground
LIEUTENANT ELLIS WAY
THEOBALD'S LA
High Street Bsns Pk
St Joseph's RC Prim Sch
Marsh Bridge
Theobald's Grove
WINSTON CHURCHILL WAY
GREAT CAMBRIDGE RD
CROSSBROOK ST
HIGH ST
MONARCH'S WAY
Theobalds Park Coll
Theobald's Park Farm
New River
THEOBALDS PARK CAMP SITE
Bullscross Farm
Nursery
Hurst Drive Prim Sch
Waltham Cross
ELEANOR CROSS RD
Queens Gate
Stirling Bsns Pk
Britannia Bsns Pk
Monro Ind Est
New Ford Bsns Pk
Holmesdale Tunnel
M25
Capel Manor Gdns
BULLSMOOR LA
Sports Ctr
Lea Valley High Sch
Bullsmoor
MOLLISON AVE
A1055
Capel House
Clydesdale Stud
Capel Manor Prim Sch
Myddelton Farm
Myddelton House
Bulls Cross
Freezy Water
Keys Meadow Sch
Myddelton House Gdns
Aylands Sch
Turkey Street
HERTFORD RD
London Loop
Maiden's Bridge
St Ignatius Coll
Forty Hill CE Prim Sch
Crem
Enfield Lock
Enfield Wash
Albany Sch
Albany Park
Prince of Wales Prim Sch
The Arena
Eastfield Prim Sch
Turkey Brook
A10 Tottenham
A1010 Edmonton
A1055 Tottenham
London STREET ATLAS

161

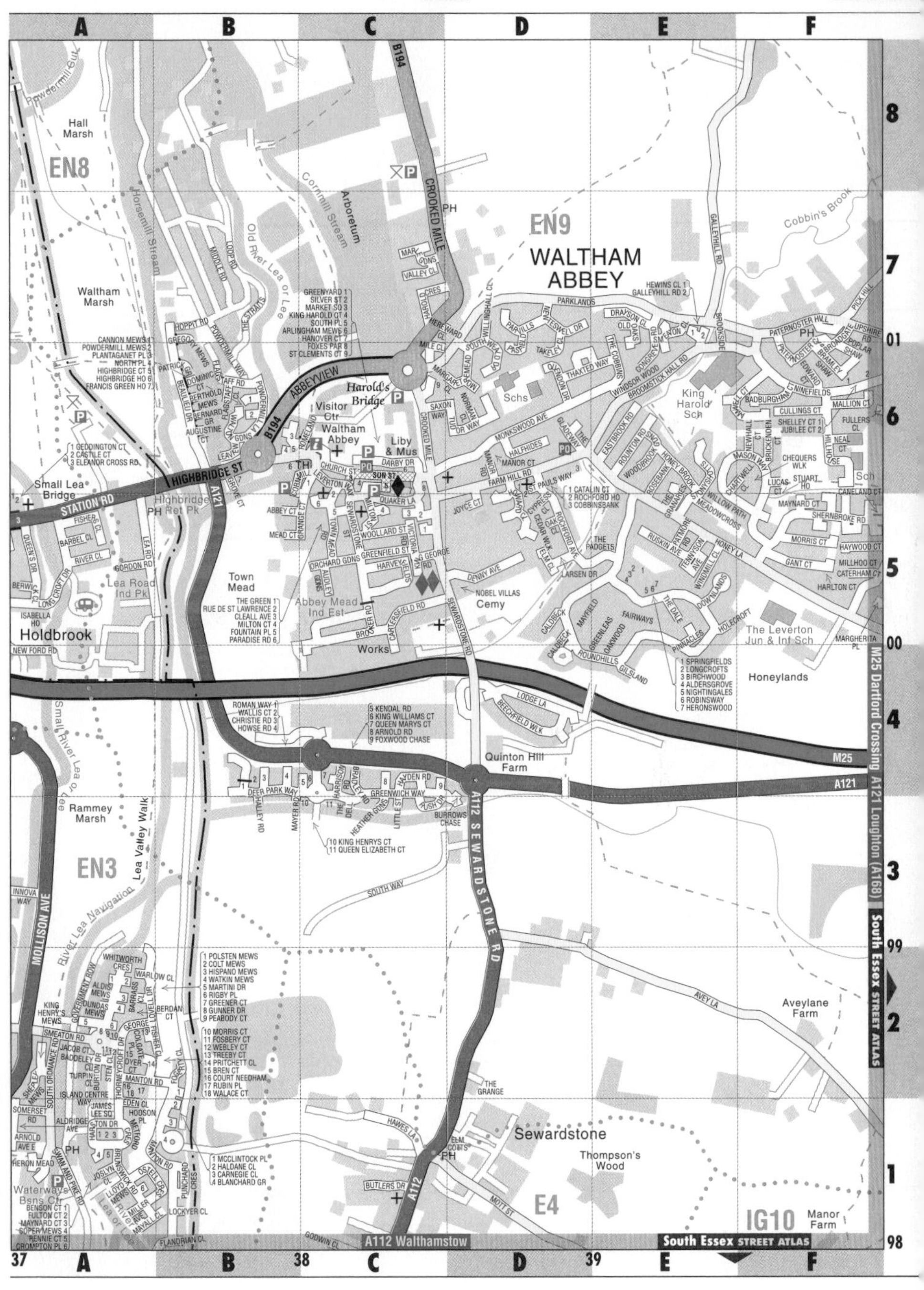
A
B
C
D
E
F
8
7
01
6
5
00
4
3
99
2
1
98
37
38
39
Powdermill Cut
Hall Marsh
EN8
Horsemill Stream
Old River Lea or Lee
Cornmill Stream
Arboretum
B194
CROOKED MILE
PH
EN9
WALTHAM ABBEY
Cobbin's Brook
GALLEYHILL RD
Waltham Marsh
MIDDLE RD
LOOP RD
THE STRAITS
GREENYARD 1
SILVER ST 2
MARKET SQ 3
KING HAROLD CT 4
SOUTH PL 5
ARLINGHAM MEWS 6
HANOVER CT 7
FOXES PAR 8
ST CLEMENTS CT 9
MARY GDNS
VALLEY CL
HAROLD CRES
HEREWARD CL
MILE CL
HEWINS CL 1
GALLEYHILL RD 2
PARKLANDS
DRAYSON CL
OLD OAKS
BROOKSIDE
PATERNOSTER HILL
UPSHIRE RD
PICK HILL
CANNON MEWS 1
POWDERMILL MEWS 2
PLANTAGANET PL 3
NORTH PL 4
HIGHBRIDGE CT 5
HIGHBRIDGE HO 6
FRANCIS GREEN HO 7
HOPPIT RD
GREGORY MEWS
POWDERMILL WAY
PATRICK GR
DOMINIC CT
BEAULIEU DR
BERTHOLD MEWS
BERNARD GR
AUGUSTINE CT
FLAGSTAFF RD
LEAVEN GDNS
ABBEYVIEW
Harold's Bridge
Visitor Ctr
Waltham Abbey
Liby & Mus
TH
PO
Schs
MARGARET AVE
NORMAN CL
SAXON WAY
TUDOR WAY
MONKSWOOD AVE
WINDSOR WOOD
BROOMSTICK HALL RD
THAXTED WAY
THE COBBINS
TAKELEY CL
NEWTESWELL DR
King Harold Sch
PH
BADBURGHAM CT
NINEFIELDS
MALLION CT
CULLINGS CT
SHELLEY CT 1
JUBILEE CT 2
FULLERS CL
NEAL CT
HILLHOUSE
CHEQUERS WLK
LUCAS CT
STUART HO
Sch
CANELAND CT
MAYNARD CT
SHERNBROKE RD
MORRIS CT
HAYWOOD CT
GANT CT
MILLHOO CT
CATERHAM CT
HARLTON CT
1 GEDDINGTON CT
2 CASTLE CT
3 ELEANOR CROSS RD
Small Lea Bridge
HIGHBRIDGE ST
STATION RD
A121
Highbridge Ret Pk
PH
CHURCH ST
SUN ST
DARBY DR
QUAKER LA
HALFHIDES
MANOR CT
FARM HILL RD
ST PAULS WAY
1 CATALIN CT
2 ROCHFORD HO
3 COBBINSBANK
EASTBROOK RD
ROUNTON RD
WOODBROOK
HONEY BROOK
WILLOW PATH
MEADOWCROSS
HONEY LA
JOYCE CT
CYPRESS PATH
CEDAR WLK
ELM CL
ROCHFORD AVE
THE PADGETS
RUSKIN AVE
PATMORE RD
TENNYSON AVE
WINDMILL CL
ABBEY CT
MEAD CT
GRANGE CT
SEWARDSTONE ST
WOOLLARD ST
GREENFIELD ST
VICTORIA RD
KING GEORGE RD
HARVEY FIELDS
ORCHARD GDNS
AUDLEY GDNS
FISHER CL
BARBEL CL
RIVER CL
GORDON RD
LEA RD
QUEEN'S DR
BERWICK CL
LONGCROFT DR
Lea Road Ind Pk
Town Mead
THE GREEN 1
RUE DE ST LAWRENCE 2
CLEALL AVE 3
MILTON CT 4
FOUNTAIN PL 5
PARADISE RD 6
Abbey Mead Ind Est
DENNY AVE
NOBEL VILLAS
Cemy
LARSEN DR
CALDBECK
MAYFIELD
GREENLEAS
OAKWOOD
FAIRWAYS
THE DALE
DOWNLANDS
HOLECROFT
PINNACLES
ROUNDHILLS
GILSLAND
The Leverton Jun & Inf Sch
MARGHERITA PL
ISABELLA HO
Holdbrook
NEW FORD RD
BROOKER RD
CARTERSFIELD RD
Works
SEWARDSTONE RD
1 SPRINGFIELDS
2 LONGCROFTS
3 BIRCHWOOD
4 ALDERSGROVE
5 NIGHTINGALES
6 ROBINSWAY
7 HERONSWOOD
Honeylands
M25 Dartford Crossing
A121 Loughton (A168)
ROMAN WAY 1
WALLIS CT 2
CHRISTIE RD 3
HOWSE RD 4
5 KENDAL RD
6 KING WILLIAMS CT
7 QUEEN MARYS CT
8 ARNOLD RD
9 FOXWOOD CHASE
LODGE LA
BEECHFIELD WLK
Small River Lea or Lee
Quinton Hill Farm
M25
A121
DEER PARK WAY
HARRISON DR
BRADLEY RD
HAYDEN RD
GREENWICH WAY
HALLEY RD
MAYER RD
THE DELL
HEATHER GDNS
LITTLE ST
RUSH DR
BURROWS CHASE
Rammey Marsh
Lea Valley Walk
10 KING HENRYS CT
11 QUEEN ELIZABETH CT
A112 SEWARDSTONE RD
EN3
SOUTH WAY
River Lea Navigation
INNOVA WAY
MOLLISON AVE
South Essex STREET ATLAS
WHITWORTH CRES
WARLOW CL
1 POLSTEN MEWS
2 COLT MEWS
3 HISPANO MEWS
4 WATKIN MEWS
5 MARTINI DR
6 RIGBY PL
7 GREENER CT
8 GUNNER DR
9 PEABODY CT
ALDIS MEWS
DUNDAS MEWS
BARRASS CL
LOVELL DR
BERDAN CT
GOVERNMENT ROW
KING HENRY'S MEWS
SMEATON RD
JACOB CT
BADDELEY CL
TURPIN
BURTON DR
COLGATE PL
DYER CT
MANTON RD
10 MORRIS CT
11 FOSBERY CT
12 WEBLEY CT
13 TREEBY CT
14 PRITCHETT CL
15 BREN CT
16 COURT NEEDHAM
17 RUBIN PL
18 WALACE CT
AVEY LA
Aveylane Farm
THE GRANGE
ISLAND CENTRE WAY
SOUTH ORDNANCE RD
HORNEYCROFT DR
STEN CL
EDEN CL
HODSON PL
JAMES LEE SQ
SOMERSET RD
ALDRIDGE AVE
HARSTON DR
ARNOLD AVE E
PH
HERON MEAD
SWAN AND PIKE RD
BRUNSWICK RD
METFORD CRES
OSTELL CRES
JOSLYN CL
LLOYD MEWS
MILLER AVE
MAVALL CL
Waterways Bsns Ctr
BENSON CT 1
FULTON CT 2
MAYNARD CT 3
COPER MEWS 4
RENNIE CT 5
CROMPTON PL 6
PUNCHARD CRES
1 MCCLINTOCK PL
2 HALDANE CL
3 CARNEGIE CL
4 BLANCHARD GR
LOCKYER CL
FLANDRIAN CL
HAWES LA
ELM COTTS
PH
Sewardstone
Thompson's Wood
BUTLERS DR
A112
MOTT ST
E4
IG10
Manor Farm
GODWIN CL
A112 Walthamstow
South Essex STREET ATLAS

151

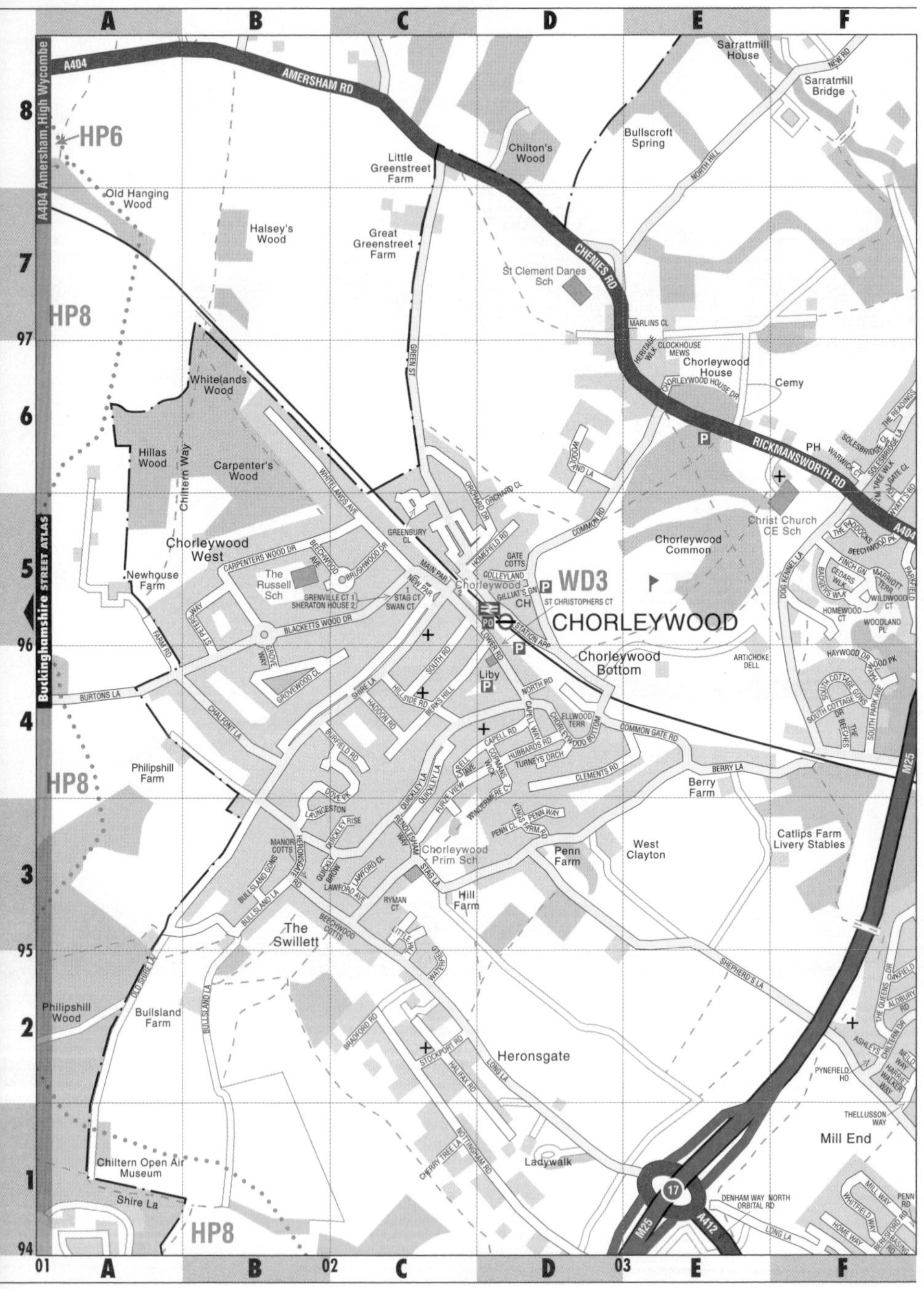

A404
AMERSHAM RD
HP6
A404 Amersham, High Wycombe
Old Hanging Wood
Halsey's Wood
Little Greenstreet Farm
Great Greenstreet Farm
Chilton's Wood
Bullscroft Spring
Sarrattmill House
Sarrattmill Bridge
NEW RD
NORTH HILL
CHENIES RD
St Clement Danes Sch
HP8
MARLINS CL
HERITAGE WLK
CLOCKHOUSE MEWS
Chorleywood House
CHORLEYWOOD HOUSE DR
Cemy
GREEN ST
Whitelands Wood
Hillas Wood
Chiltern Way
Carpenter's Wood
WHITELANDS AVE
ORCHARD DR
ORCHARD CL
WOODLAND LA
COMMON RD
RICKMANSWORTH RD
PH
Christ Church CE Sch
Chorleywood Common
A404
Chorleywood West
Newhouse Farm
CARPENTERS WOOD DR
BEECHWOOD AVE
BRUSHWOOD DR
The Russell Sch
GREENBURY CL
HOMEFIELD RD
GATE COTTS
COLLEYLAND
MAIN PAR
NEW PAR
Chorleywood
GILLIAT'S GN
CH
WD3
ST CHRISTOPHERS CT
GRENVILLE CT 1
SHERATON HOUSE 2
1 STAG CT
SWAN CT
BLACKETTS WOOD DR
ST PETERS WAY
CHORLEYWOOD
STATION APP
LOWER RD
Chorleywood Bottom
ARTICHOKE DELL
FARM RD
GROVE WAY
GROVEWOOD CL
Liby
BURTONS LA
SHIRE LA
SOUTH RD
HILLSIDE RD
BERKS HILL
NORTH RD
CHALFONT LA
HADDON RD
CAPELL WAY
CHORLEYWOOD BOTTOM
ELLWOOD TERR
COMMON GATE RD
BURFIELD RD
CAPELL RD
HUBBARDS RD
TURNEYS ORCH
CLEMENTS RD
BERRY LA
Berry Farm
Philipshill Farm
HP8
DOVER CL
LAUNCESTON
QUICKLEY LA
QUICKLEY RISE
FURZE VIEW
CAPELL AVE
COPMANS WICK
WINDERMERE CL
KINGS FARM RD
PENN WAY
PENN CL
MANOR COTTS
HERONSGATE RD
QUICKLEY BROW
REDNDLESHAM WAY
Chorleywood Prim Sch
Penn Farm
West Clayton
Catlips Farm Livery Stables
BULLSLAND GDNS
BULLSLAND LA
LAWFORD CL
LAWFORD AVE
STAG LA
RYMAN CT
Hill Farm
The Swillett
BEECHWOOD COTTS
WATERFIELD
SHEPHERD'S LA
M25
THE READINGS
SOLESBRIDGE CL
SOLESBRIDGE LA
WARWICK CT
ELM TREE WLK
LYCH GATE CL
HYATT'S RD
THE PADDOCKS
BEECHWOOD PK
PARKFIELD
DOG KENNEL LA
FINCH GN
CEDARS WLK
MARRIOTT TERR
BADGERS WLK
WILDWOOD CT
HOMEWOOD CT
WOODLAND PL
HAYWOOD DR
HAYWOOD PK
SOUTH COTTAGE GDNS
SOUTH COTTAGE DR
THE BEECHES
SOUTH PARK AVE
Philipshill Wood
OLD SHIRE LA
Bullsland Farm
BULLSLAND LA
BRADFORD RD
STOCKPORT RD
HALIFAX RD
Heronsgate
LONG LA
THE QUEENS DR
OAKFIELD
ALDBURY RD
CHILTERN DR
ASHLEYS
NELL GWYNNE
HARRIER
WALKER
PYNEFIELD HO
THELLUSSON WAY
Mill End
Chiltern Open Air Museum
Shire La
CHERRY TREE LA
NOTTINGHAM RD
Ladywalk
17
M25
A412
DENHAM WAY NORTH ORBITAL RD
LONG LA
MILL WAY
WHITFIELD WAY
PENN RD
HOME WAY
BERESFORD RD
BASING
HP8
Buckinghamshire STREET ATLAS
A B C D E F
8 7 97 6 5 96 4 3 95 2 1 94
01 02 03

172

152
166

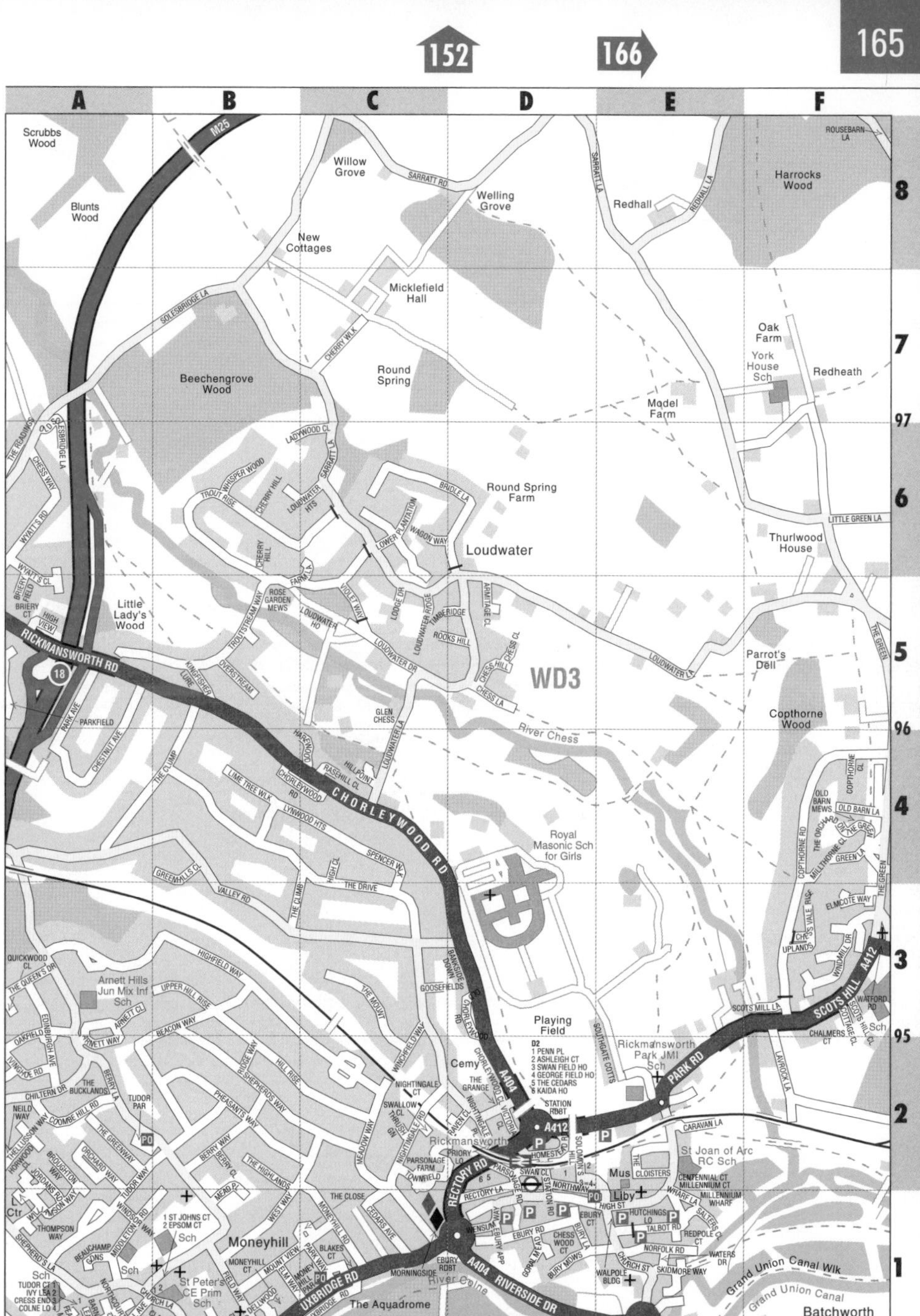

173
166

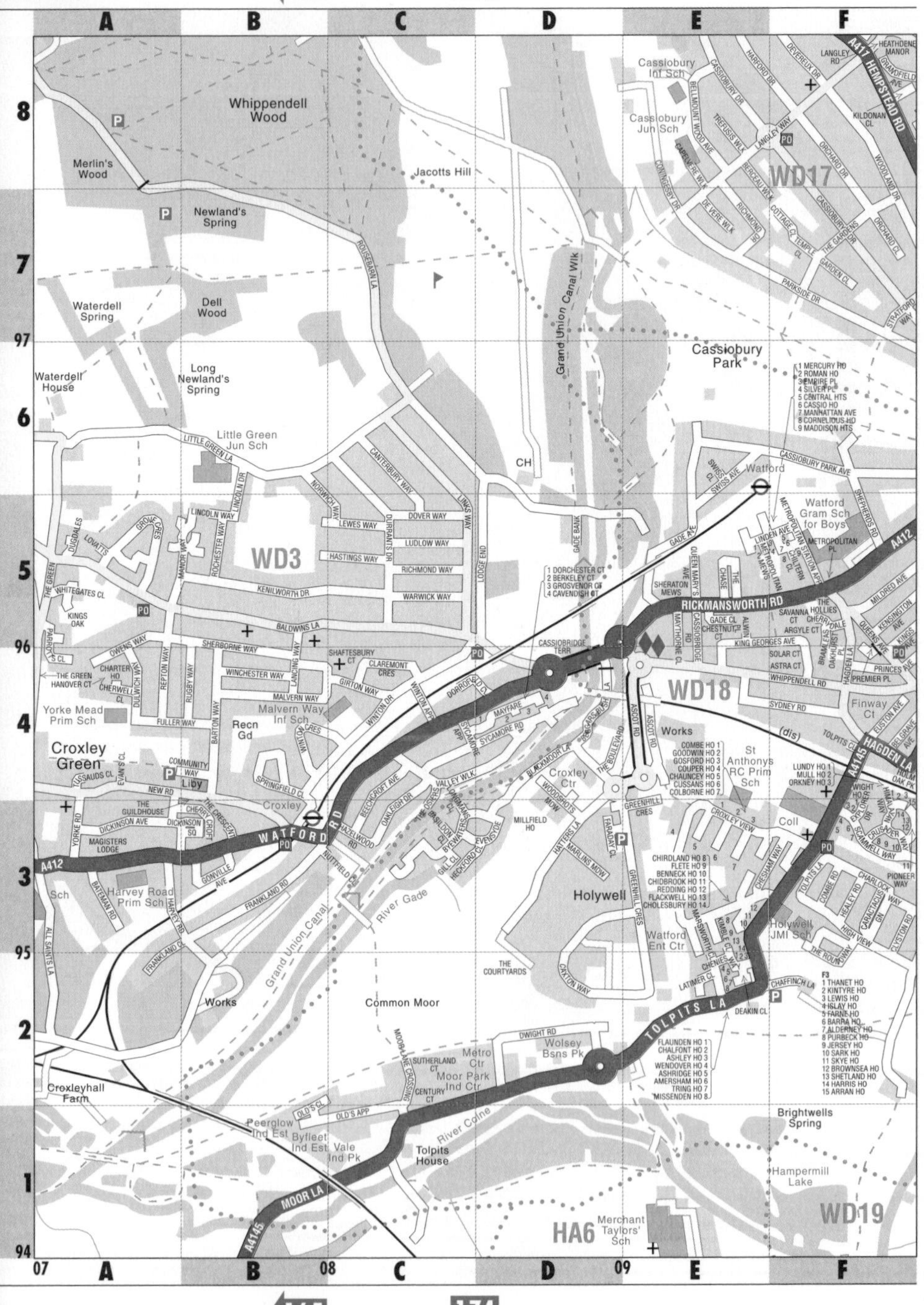
Whippendell Wood
Merlin's Wood
Newland's Spring
Jacotts Hill
Cassiobury Inf Sch
Cassiobury Jun Sch
WD17
Waterdell Spring
Dell Wood
Grand Union Canal Wlk
Cassiobury Park
Waterdell House
Long Newland's Spring
Little Green Jun Sch
Watford
Watford Gram Sch for Boys
WD3
RICKMANSWORTH RD
WD18
Yorke Mead Prim Sch
Malvern Way Inf Sch
Recn Gd
Croxley Green
Croxley
Croxley Ctr
Works
St Anthonys RC Prim Sch
Harvey Road Prim Sch
Holywell
Watford Ent Ctr
Holywell JMI Sch
Common Moor
Wolsey Bsns Pk
Metro Ctr
Moor Park Ind Ctr
Croxleyhall Farm
Peerglow Ind Est
Byfleet Ind Est
Vale Ind Pk
Tolpits House
Brightwells Spring
Hampermill Lake
HA6
Merchant Taylors' Sch
WD19
TOLPITS LA
MOOR LA
WATFORD RD
HAGDEN LA
HEMPSTEAD RD

154
168

A8
1 CURZON GATE CT
2 BLOCK 14
3 BLOCK 12
4 BLOCK 10
5 BEECHFIELD CT
6 LANGWOOD

B6
1 BALLINGER CT
2 THE BEECHES
3 BURVALE CT
4 CRAKERS MEAD
5 BRIDGEFORD HO
6 FAIRCROSS HO

C7
1 WELLINGTON HO
2 CHELTENHAM HO
3 ROEDEAN HO
4 CANTERBURY HO
5 LANCING HO
6 WESTMINSTER HO
7 ELIZABETH HO
8 BADMINTON HO
9 ETON HO
10 ANDREW REED CT
11 ALEXANDRA CT
12 REEDS CHAPEL

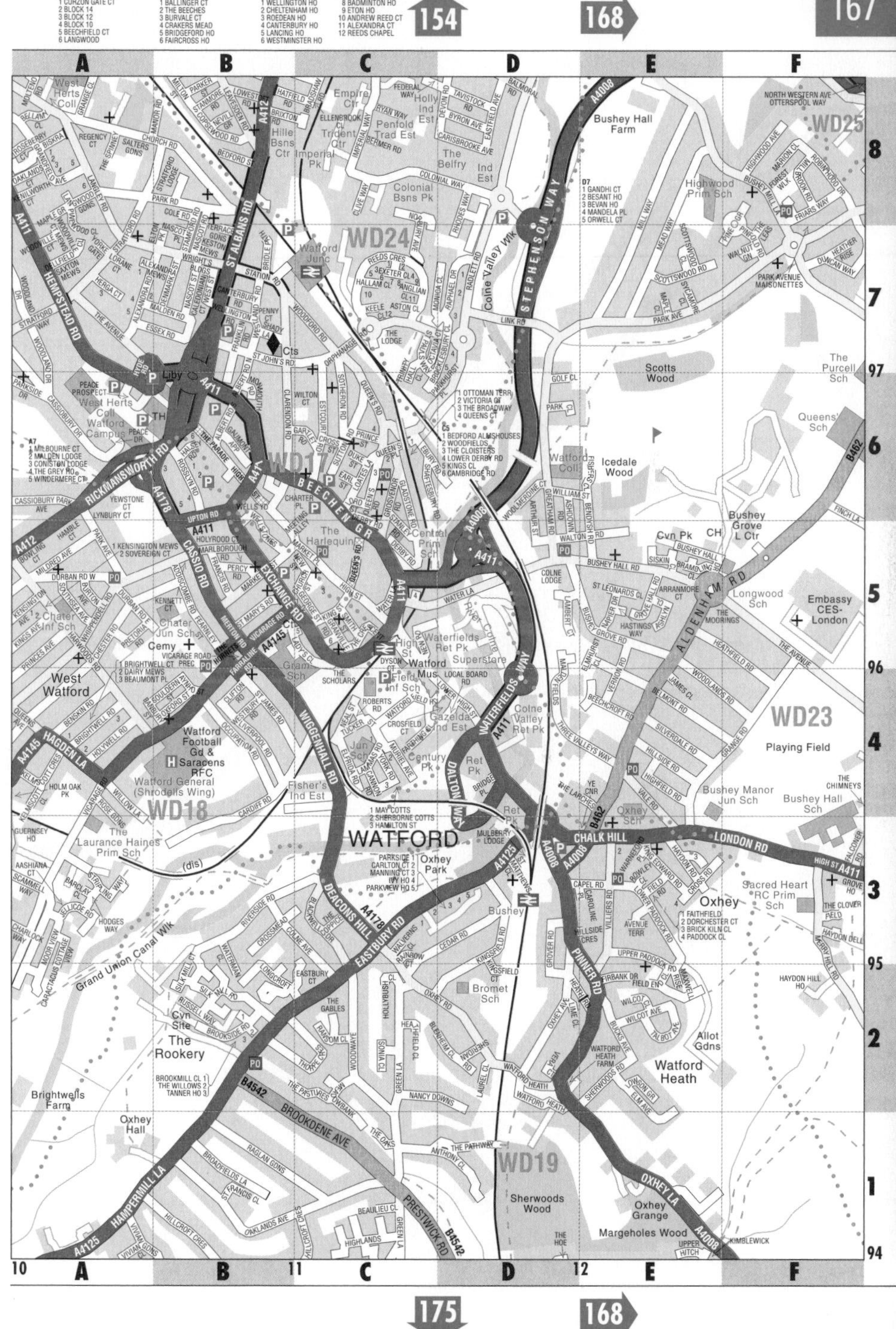

175
168

167 155

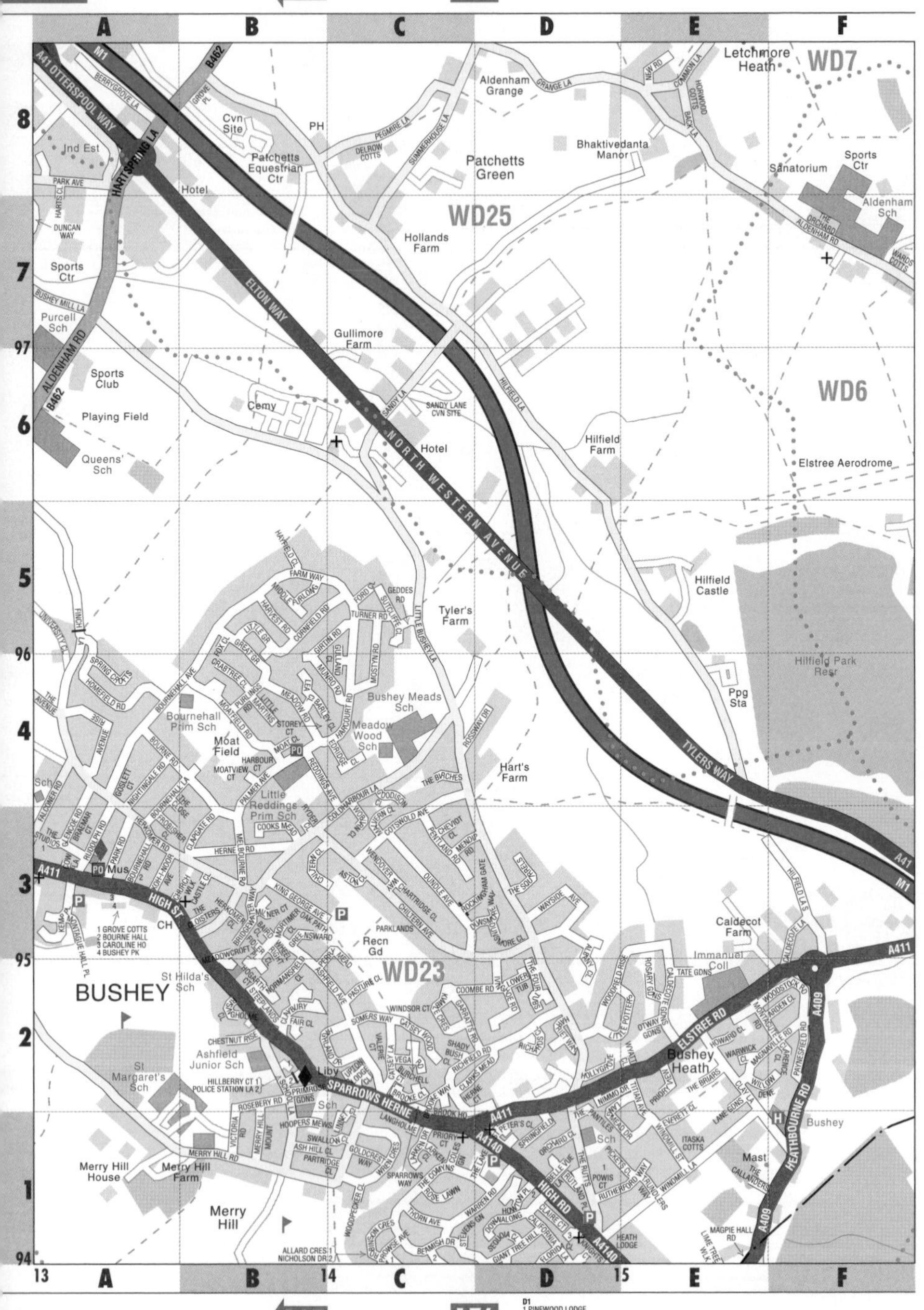

167 176

D1
1 PINEWOOD LODGE
2 CALIFORNIA CT
3 UPLANDS CT

A
B
C
D
E
F
Little Kendals Wood
WD7
Medburn House
Tykeswater La
Wards La
Medburn Lodge
North Medburn Farm
Slades Farm
Butterfly La
Letchmore Lodge
PH
The Haberdashers' Aske's Sch for Boys
Medburn Bridge
South Medburn Farm
CH
Ham Farm
Aldenham Park
Flying Club
Hogg La
Haberdashers' Aske's Sch for Girls
WD6
Page's Farm
Aldenham Rd
Home Farm
Lister Cotts
Aldenham Country Park
London Loop
Laboratory
Dagger La
Cemy
Elstree Hill N
B5378
Aldenham Resr
St Nicholas Elstree CE Prim Sch
Elstree
Watford Rd
High St
Tylers Way
Elstree Rd
PH
Abbotsbury
Barnet La
A411
Lismirrane Ind Pk
North Western Ave
Edgwarebury House Farm
The Leys
Penniwells Farm
Centennial Pk
Centennial Ave
Elstree Hill S
Watford By-Pass
Centennial Ct
WD23
A5183
Edgwarebury Country Club
M1
Brockleyhill Farm
Brockley Hill
Edgware Way
A41
HA7
Brockley Grange
Royal National Orthopaedic
Brockley Hill HO
HA8
A5
Meryfield Prim Sch
Borehamwood Ent Ctr
Brickfield Cotts
Orchard Cl
Boreham Holt
Allum La
Woodside
Hollywood Ct
London Loop
Hartfield Ave
The Rise
Lowther Cl
Watling Ct 1
Stuart Ct 2
West View Ct 3
Potters Mews 4
The Bartons
Lands End
Schubert Rd
Sullivan Way
Beethoven Rd
Elgar Cl
Coates Rd
West View Gdns
May Gdns
Fortune La
Georges Mead
Northgate Path 1
Torworth Rd 2
Milby Ct 3
1 Chiltern Cl
2 Badgers Cl
Tilehouse Cl 1
Red Lodge 2
8
7
97
6
5
96
4
3
95
2
1
94
16
17
18

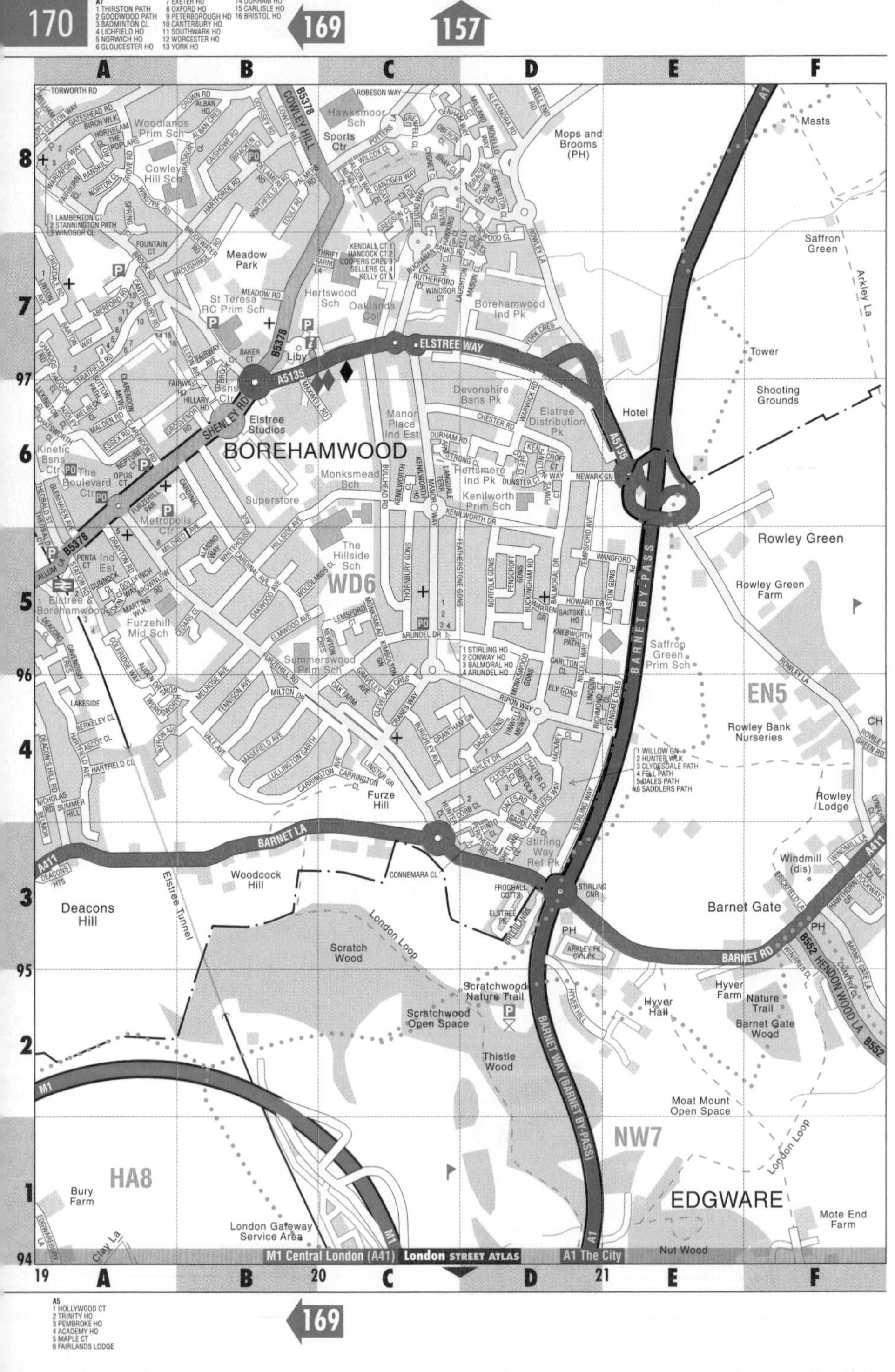

170
A7
1 THIRSTON PATH
2 GOODWOOD PATH
3 BADMINTON CL
4 LICHFIELD HO
5 NORWICH HO
6 GLOUCESTER HO
7 EXETER HO
8 OXFORD HO
9 PETERBOROUGH HO
10 CANTERBURY HO
11 SOUTHWARK HO
12 WORCESTER HO
13 YORK HO
14 DURHAM HO
15 CARLISLE HO
16 BRISTOL HO
169
157
A
B
C
D
E
F
8
7
97
6
5
96
4
3
95
2
1
94
19
20
21
BOREHAMWOOD
WD6
EN5
NW7
HA8
EDGWARE
Woodlands Prim Sch
Cowley Hill Sch
Hawksmoor Sch
Sports Ctr
Mops and Brooms (PH)
Masts
Saffron Green
Arkley La
Meadow Park
St Teresa RC Prim Sch
Hertswood Sch
Oaklands Coll
Borehamwood Ind Pk
Tower
Shooting Grounds
ELSTREE WAY
A5135
B5378
COWLEY HILL
SHENLEY RD
Liby
Bsns Ctr
Elstree Studios
Devonshire Bsns Pk
Manor Place Ind Est
Elstree Distribution Pk
Hotel
Kinetic Bsns Ctr
The Boulevard Ctr
Monksmead Sch
Hertsmere Ind Pk
Kenilworth Prim Sch
Superstore
Metropolis Ctr
The Hillside Sch
Rowley Green
Rowley Green Farm
Elstree & Borehamwood
Ind Est
Furzehill Mid Sch
Saffron Green Prim Sch
Summerswood Prim Sch
BARNET BY-PASS
1 STIRLING HO
2 CONWAY HO
3 BALMORAL HO
4 ARUNDEL HO
Rowley Bank Nurseries
1 WILLOW GN
2 HUNTER WLK
3 CLYDESDALE PATH
4 FELL PATH
5 DALES PATH
6 SADDLERS PATH
Furze Hill
Rowley Lodge
BARNET LA
A411
Stirling Way Ret Pk
Windmill (dis)
Woodcock Hill
CONNEMARA CL
STIRLING CNR
Deacons Hill
Elstree Tunnel
London Loop
Barnet Gate
Scratch Wood
PH
BARNET RD
B552
HENDON WOOD LA
Scratchwood Nature Trail
Scratchwood Open Space
Hyver Hall
Hyver Farm
Nature Trail
Barnet Gate Wood
Thistle Wood
BARNET WAY (BARNET BY-PASS)
M1
Moat Mount Open Space
Bury Farm
London Gateway Service Area
Clay La
Mote End Farm
Nut Wood
A1
M1 Central London (A41)
London STREET ATLAS
A1 The City
A5
1 HOLLYWOOD CT
2 TRINITY HO
3 PEMBROKE HO
4 ACADEMY HO
5 MAPLE CT
6 FAIRLANDS LODGE
169

158

E5
1 HERTSWOOD CT
2 SUNBURY CT
3 MERIDEN HO
4 NORFOLK CT
5 MORRISON CT
6 KINGSHILL CT
7 BARONSMERE CT
8 CHARTWELL CT

E6
1 RICHARD CT
2 ALSTON CT
3 RIDGELEIGH CT
4 BARLETTS COTTS
5 NURSERY ROW
6 HADLEY PAR
7 EXCHANGE BLDGS
8 CHIPPING CL
9 BRUCE RD
10 HART LODGE
11 HOLKHAM HO
12 LEATHERSELLERS CL
13 BRADDON CT

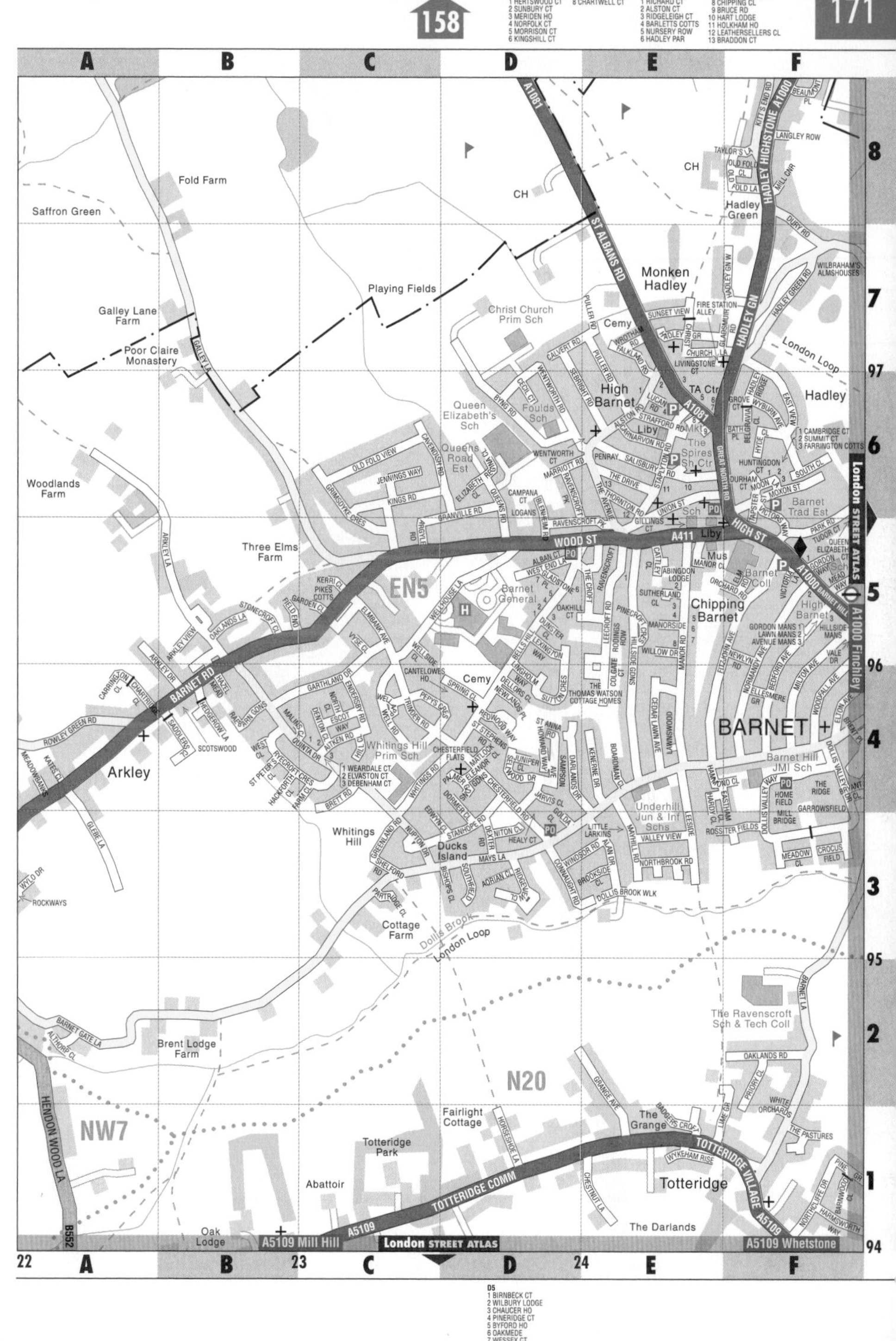

D5
1 BIRNBECK CT
2 WILBURY LODGE
3 CHAUCER HO
4 PINERIDGE CT
5 BYFORD HO
6 OAKMEDE
7 WESSEX CT

164

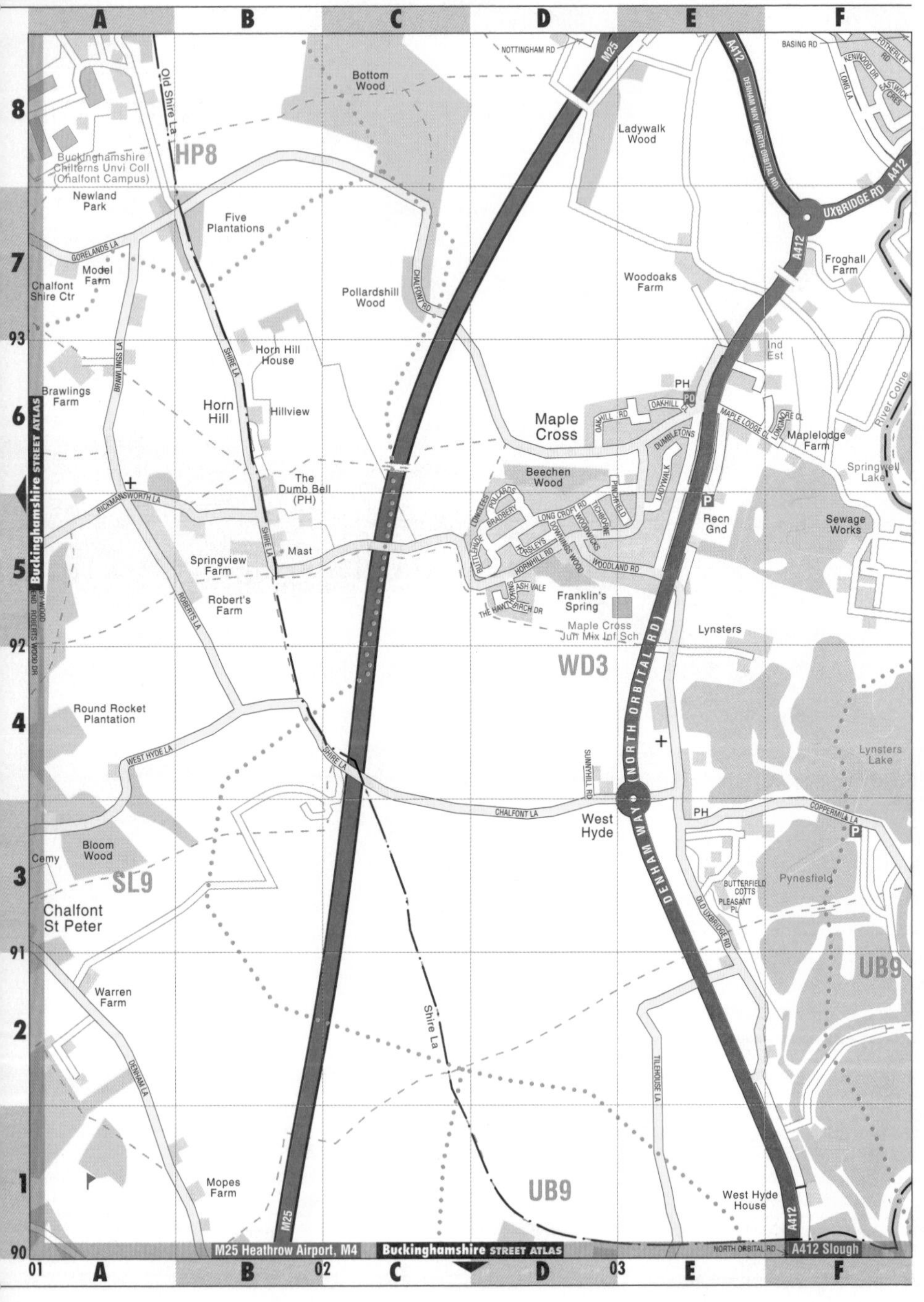

A
B
C
D
E
F
8
7
93
6
5
92
4
3
91
2
1
90
01
02
03
Old Shire La
Bottom Wood
NOTTINGHAM RD
M25
A412
BASING RD
FOTHERLEY RD
KENWOOD DR
LONG LA
EASTWICK CRES
DENHAM WAY (NORTH ORBITAL RD)
Ladywalk Wood
HP8
Buckinghamshire Chilterns Unvi Coll (Chalfont Campus)
Newland Park
Five Plantations
UXBRIDGE RD
GORELANDS LA
Model Farm
Chalfont Shire Ctr
Pollardshill Wood
CHALFONT RD
Woodoaks Farm
Froghall Farm
SHIRE LA
Horn Hill House
BRAWLINGS LA
Brawlings Farm
Ind Est
PH
PO
OAKHILL RD
OAKHILL CL
MAPLE LODGE CL
Horn Hill
Hillview
Maple Cross
DUMBLETONS
Maplelodge Farm
River Colne
Springwell Lake
Beechen Wood
The Dumb Bell (PH)
RICKMANSWORTH LA
LONGCROFT RD
TICHBORNE
PINCHFIELD
LADYWALK
Recn Gnd
Sewage Works
Mast
Springview Farm
Robert's Farm
ROBERTS LA
HORNHILL RD
WOODLAND RD
ASH VALE
BIRCH DR
THE HAWTHORNS
Franklin's Spring
Maple Cross Jun Mix Inf Sch
Lynsters
WD3
ROBERTS WOOD DR
Round Rocket Plantation
WEST HYDE LA
SUNNYHILL RD
Lynsters Lake
CHALFONT LA
West Hyde
PH
COPPERMILL LA
Bloom Wood
Cemy
SL9
Chalfont St Peter
BUTTERFIELD COTTS
PLEASANT PL
OLD UXBRIDGE RD
Pynesfield
UB9
Warren Farm
DENHAM LA
Shire La
TILEHOUSE LA
Mopes Farm
UB9
West Hyde House
NORTH ORBITAL RD
M25 Heathrow Airport, M4
A412 Slough
Buckinghamshire STREET ATLAS

165
174

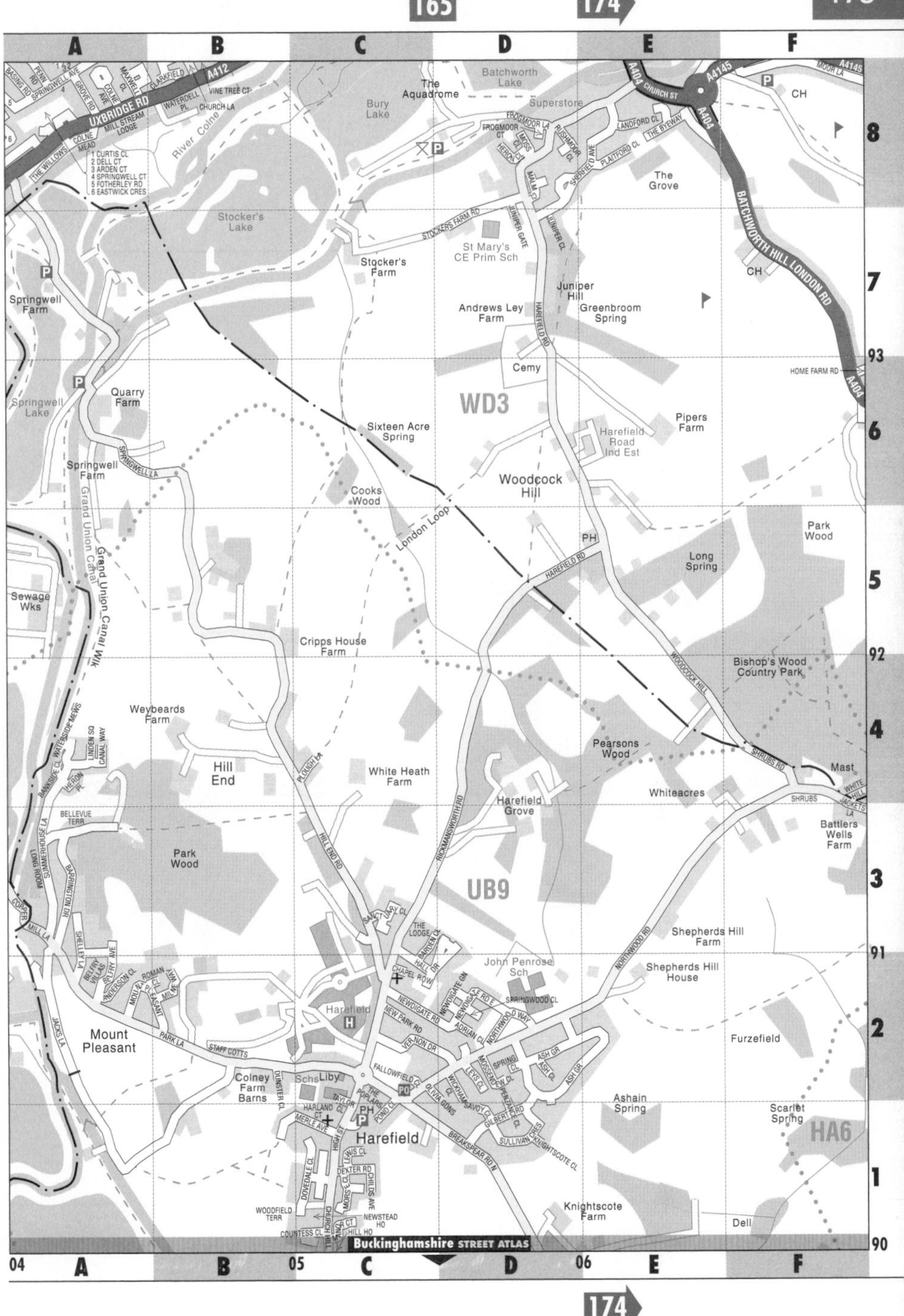
A
B
C
D
E
F
8
7
93
6
5
92
4
3
91
2
1
90
04
05
06
UXBRIDGE RD
A412
The Aquadrome
Batchworth Lake
Bury Lake
Superstore
River Colne
Stocker's Lake
Stocker's Farm
St Mary's CE Prim Sch
Springwell Farm
Springwell Lake
Quarry Farm
Andrews Ley Farm
Juniper Hill
Greenbroom Spring
The Grove
Cemy
WD3
Sixteen Acre Spring
Harefield Road Ind Est
Pipers Farm
Woodcock Hill
Cooks Wood
London Loop
Grand Union Canal
Grand Union Canal Wlk
Sewage Wks
Park Wood
Long Spring
Cripps House Farm
Bishop's Wood Country Park
Weybeards Farm
Pearsons Wood
Hill End
White Heath Farm
Whiteacres
Mast
Harefield Grove
Battlers Wells Farm
Park Wood
UB9
Shepherds Hill Farm
John Penrose Sch
Shepherds Hill House
Mount Pleasant
Harefield
Furzefield
Colney Farm Barns
Schs
Liby
Ashain Spring
Scarlet Spring
HA6
Harefield
Knightscote Farm
Dell
BATCHWORTH HILL LONDON RD
A404
A4145
CHURCH ST
MOOR LA
CH
HOME FARM RD
STOCKERS FARM RD
HAREFIELD RD
JUNIPER CL
JUNIPER GATE
WOODCOCK HILL
SHRUBS RD
RICKMANSWORTH RD
NORTHWOOD RD
HILL END RD
PLOUGH LA
SPRINGWELL LA
PARK LA
STAFF COTTS
BREAKSPEAR RD N
HIGH ST
CHURCH HILL
JACKS LA
COPPER MILL LA
LONG ROOM
SUMMERHOUSE LA
BARRINGTON DR
BELLEVUE TERR
1 CURTIS CL
2 DELL CT
3 ARDEN CT
4 SPRINGWELL CT
5 FOTHERLEY RD
6 EASTWICK CRES
PH
PO
H
Buckinghamshire STREET ATLAS

174

173
166

E5
1 ABBOTSFORD LODGE
2 THE LIMES
F5
1 WILLOWTREE LODGE
2 THE MANOR HO
3 MAPLEWOOD CT
4 HIGH OAKS
5 MARKAB RD
6 ADMIRALS CT
7 CLARENDON CT

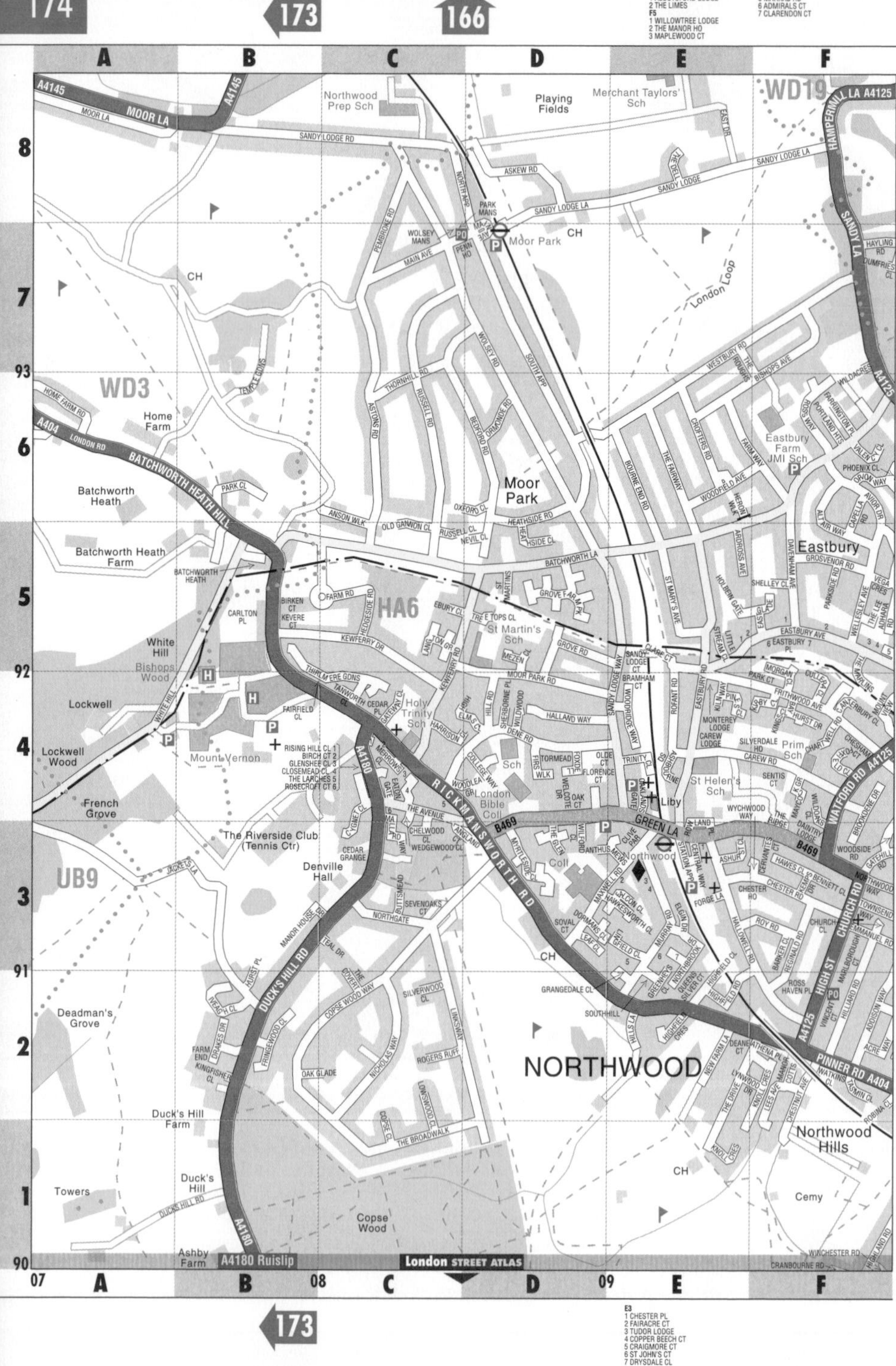

173

E3
1 CHESTER PL
2 FAIRACRE CT
3 TUDOR LODGE
4 COPPER BEECH CT
5 CRAIGMORE CT
6 ST JOHN'S CT
7 DRYSDALE CL

C7
1 KIRKCALDY GN
2 HARROGATE RD
3 SWANSTON PATH
4 LALSHAM HO
5 GOSFORTH LA
6 ALDERWOOD HO
7 FORFAR HO
8 ENVILLE HO
9 DUNFERMLINE HO
10 DENTON HO
11 LINDRICK HO
12 PADGATE HO
13 OFFERTON HO
14 PENN HO
15 MALDEN HO

D7
1 LUFFENHAM HO
2 ST ANDREWS RD
3 PENNARD HO
4 LAWRENCE CT
5 ERSKINE HO
6 FILTON HO
7 HARTCRAN HO
8 MANSCOTT HO

167

176

E8
1 CHOLESBURY
2 PRESTWOOD
3 CHAMPNEYS

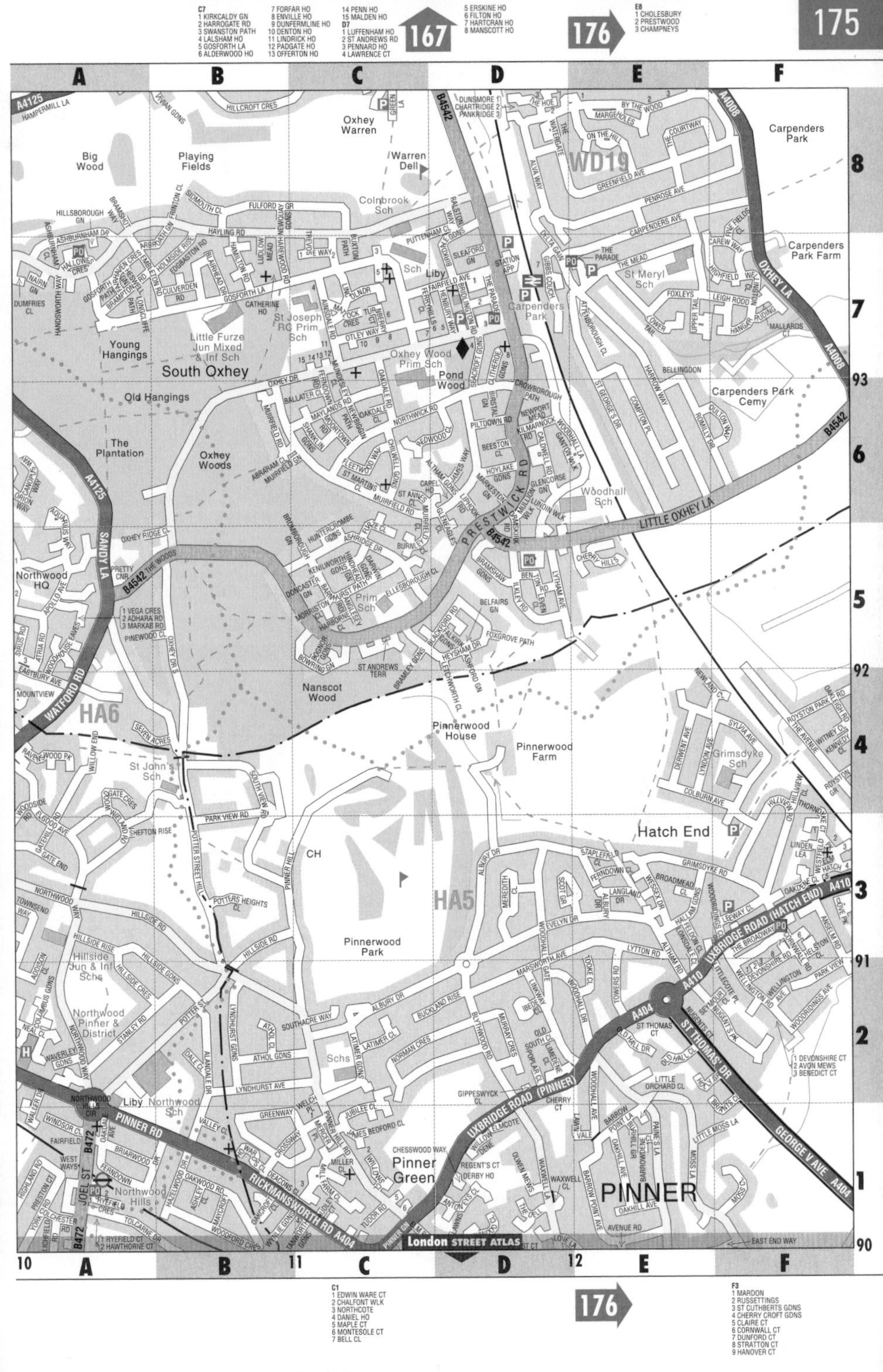

C1
1 EDWIN WARE CT
2 CHALFONT WLK
3 NORTHCOTE
4 DANIEL HO
5 MAPLE CT
6 MONTESOLE CT
7 BELL CL

176

F3
1 MARDON
2 RUSSETTINGS
3 ST CUTHBERTS GDNS
4 CHERRY CROFT GDNS
5 CLAIRE CT
6 CORNWALL CT
7 DUNFORD CT
8 STRATTON CT
9 HANOVER CT

175

168

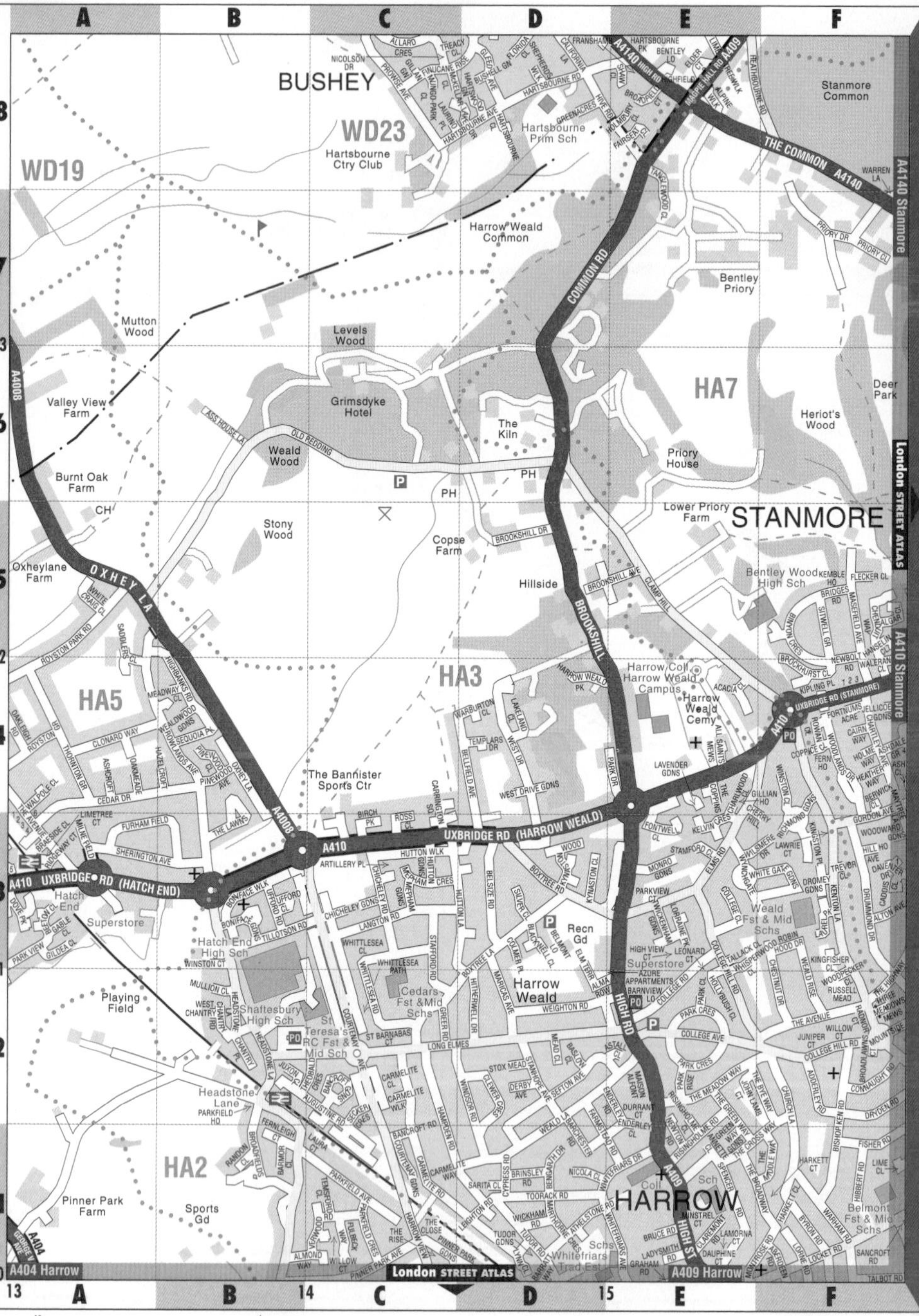
A B C D E F
8
7
93
6
5
92
4
3
91
2
1
90
13 14 15
BUSHEY
WD23
WD19
Hartsbourne Ctry Club
Hartsbourne Prim Sch
Stanmore Common
THE COMMON A4140
A4140 Stanmore
Harrow Weald Common
COMMON RD
Bentley Priory
Mutton Wood
Levels Wood
Grimsdyke Hotel
HA7
Deer Park
Heriot's Wood
Valley View Farm
OLD REDDING
Weald Wood
The Kiln
Priory House
Burnt Oak Farm
PH
CH
Stony Wood
Lower Priory Farm
STANMORE
Copse Farm
Oxheylane Farm
OXHEY LA
Hillside
BROOKSHILL
Bentley Wood High Sch
A410 Stanmore
HA5
HA3
Harrow Coll Harrow Weald Campus
Harrow Weald Cemy
UXBRIDGE RD (STANMORE)
The Bannister Sports Ctr
A4008
A410
UXBRIDGE RD (HARROW WEALD)
A410 UXBRIDGE RD (HATCH END)
Hatch End
Superstore
Hatch End High Sch
Recn Gd
Weald Fst & Mid Schs
Playing Field
Cedars Fst & Mid Schs
Harrow Weald
Shaftesbury High Sch
St Teresa's RC Fst & Mid Sch
HIGH RD
Headstone Lane
HA2
Pinner Park Farm
Sports Gd
HARROW
A409
HIGH ST
Belmont Fst & Mid Schs
Whitefriars Trad Est
A404 Harrow
London STREET ATLAS
A409 Harrow

A3
1 ASHWOOD HO
2 ROSEMARY CT
3 RANDOLPH CT
4 AVON CT
5 CHERRY CROFT GDNS
6 ALDEN MEAD

175

F3
1 CASTELLANE CL
F4
1 CYGNET HO
2 CORONET HO
3 AMBERDENE
4 KENNETH GDNS

Index

Church Rd **6** Beckenham BR2.......... **53** C6

Place name	Location number	Locality, town or village	Postcode district	Page and grid square
May be abbreviated on the map	Present when a number indicates the place's position in a crowded area of mapping	Shown when more than one place has the same name	District for the indexed place	Page number and grid reference for the standard mapping

Public and commercial buildings are highlighted in magenta **Places of interest** are highlighted in blue with a star★

Abbreviations used in the index

Acad	**Academy**	Comm	**Common**	Gd	**Ground**	L	**Leisure**	Prom	**Promenade**
App	**Approach**	Cott	**Cottage**	Gdn	**Garden**	La	**Lane**	Rd	**Road**
Arc	**Arcade**	Cres	**Crescent**	Gn	**Green**	Liby	**Library**	Recn	**Recreation**
Ave	**Avenue**	Cswy	**Causeway**	Gr	**Grove**	Mdw	**Meadow**	Ret	**Retail**
Bglw	**Bungalow**	Ct	**Court**	H	**Hall**	Meml	**Memorial**	Sh	**Shopping**
Bldg	**Building**	Ctr	**Centre**	Ho	**House**	Mkt	**Market**	Sq	**Square**
Bsns, Bus	**Business**	Ctry	**Country**	Hospl	**Hospital**	Mus	**Museum**	St	**Street**
Bvd	**Boulevard**	Cty	**County**	HQ	**Headquarters**	Orch	**Orchard**	Sta	**Station**
Cath	**Cathedral**	Dr	**Drive**	Hts	**Heights**	Pal	**Palace**	Terr	**Terrace**
Cir	**Circus**	Dro	**Drove**	Ind	**Industrial**	Par	**Parade**	TH	**Town Hall**
Cl	**Close**	Ed	**Education**	Inst	**Institute**	Pas	**Passage**	Univ	**University**
Cnr	**Corner**	Emb	**Embankment**	Int	**International**	Pk	**Park**	Wk, Wlk	**Walk**
Coll	**College**	Est	**Estate**	Intc	**Interchange**	Pl	**Place**	Wr	**Water**
Com	**Community**	Ex	**Exhibition**	Junc	**Junction**	Prec	**Precinct**	Yd	**Yard**

Index of localities, towns and villages

A

Abbots Langley 153 F7
Adeyfield 125 A3
Aimes Green 149 F2
Albury 57 A6
Albury End 56 F4
Aldbury 101 C5
Aldenham 155 B3
Aley Green 62 E1
Allen's Green 96 F6
Amwell 115 A6
Ansells End 65 F2
Anstey 29 B6
Apsley End 19 E7
Ardeley 38 F3
Arkley 171 A4
Arlesey 11 A4
Ashley Green 136 A7
Ashwell 4 D3
Ashwell End 4 A5
Aspenden 40 D5
Aston 51 E2
Aston Clinton 99 A3
Aston End 51 E5
Astrope 79 A3
Ayot Green 89 A1
Ayot St Lawrence 88 B6
Ayot St Peter 88 F3
Ayres End 107 E5

B

Babbs Green 94 E5
Baker's End 94 E7
Baldock 23 E8
Ballingdon Bottom 82 F1
Barkway 17 D4
Barley 8 F1
Barleycroft End 43 B4
Barnet 171 F4
Barnet Gate 170 F3
Barwick 73 C3
Bassus Green 52 F8
Batchworth 165 F1
Batford 86 D3
Bayford 132 F6
Bedmond 139 F4
Bedwell 50 E5
Bell Bar 145 A7
Belsize 151 E6
Bendish 66 A7
Bengeo 113 C8
Benington 52 E4
Bennetts End 139 A8
Bentfield Green 59 D8
Bentley Heath 158 F4
Berkhamsted 122 C6
Bernard's Heath 127 F6
Birchanger 59 E2
Birch Green 112 C3
Birchwood 130 B7
Biscot 45 C2
Bishop's Park 76 B6
Bishop's Stortford 76 D7
Blackmore End 87 C6
Blue Hill 70 D5
Borehamwood 170 B6
Botany Bay 160 D3
Botley 136 A1
Bourne End 123 E2
Bovingdon 137 B3
Boxmoor 124 B1
Bragbury End 69 D6
Bramfield 91 C4
Braughing 55 F6
Braughing Friars 56 C5
Breachwood Green 47 E1
Brent Pelham 30 A2
Brickendon 133 C4
Bricket Wood 140 F1
Broad Colney 142 D3
Broadgreen Wood 132 F8
Broadoak End 112 F8
Broadwater 51 A1
Broken Green 56 C2
Brookmans Park 144 F5
Broxbourne 134 F3
Buckland 27 D8
Buckland Common 120 B3
Bulbourne 100 C8
Bulls Cross 162 A3
Bull's Green 90 D7
Bullsmoor 162 D4
Bullstrode 137 E3
Buntingford 40 F7
Burge End 20 D5
Burnham Green 90 C6
Burns Green 52 F2
Bury Green
Bishop's Stortford 75 E7
Bury Green Cheshunt 162 B8
Bury Park 45 B1
Bushey 168 A2
Bushey Heath 168 E2
Bygrave 13 C5

C

Caddington 62 D3
Cadwell 21 F5
Caldecote 3 C1
Capability Green 63 F4
Chalfont St Peter 172 A3
Chandler's Cross 152 F1
Chapel End 99 C8
Chapmore End 92 D5
Charlton 34 D5
Chatter End 58 C7
Chaulden 123 E2
Chaul End 62 C7
Cheapside 29 B7
Cheddington 80 A8
Chells 51 B6
Chenies 151 B1
Cherry Green 40 C1
Cheshunt 148 C1
Cheverell's Green 83 C4
Childwick Green 107 C2
Chiltern Green 65 B3
Chipperfield 152 B8
Chipping 27 D5
Chipping Barnet 171 F5
Chiswellgreen 141 A5
Cholesbury 120 C2
Chorleywood 164 E5
Chorleywood West 164 B5
Church End Arlesey 11 B7
Church End Little Hadham ..57 D2
Church End Pitstone 80 D3
Church End Redbourn 105 F4
Church End Sarratt 151 F1
Churchgate 148 A1
Churchgate Street 118 F3
Clapgate 57 C6
Clay End 52 F7
Clement's End 82 D3
Clothall 24 E4
Cockernhoe 46 F3
Codicote 67 E1
Codicote Bottom 88 D8
Cold Christmas 94 B6
Cole Green 112 A3
Colliers End 73 A6
Collins Cross 77 B8
Colney Heath 143 D8
Colney Street 141 E1
Commonwood 152 B5
Corey's Mill 36 B2
Cottered 39 C7
Counter's End 124 A3
Cow Roast 101 B1
Cradle End 75 F8
Crafton 60 F4
Crews Hill 161 B4
Cromer 38 D5
Croxley Green 166 A4
Cuckolds Cross 66 D3
Cuffley 146 E3
Cumberlow Green 25 E1
Cupid Green 125 B7

D

Dagnall 81 C6
Damask Green 37 B8
Dancers Hill 158 C3
Dane End 71 F8
Datchworth 69 E2
Datchworth Green 69 C1
Deacons Hill 170 A3
Dewes Green 30 F1
Digswell 89 F4
Digswell Park 89 D1
Drayton Beauchamp 99 C5
Duck End 59 E1

Dudswell 121 D7
Dunstable 44 A1
Dyer's Green 2 B8

E

Eastbury 174 F5
Eastend 116 E1
East End 43 E4
East End Green 112 D2
Easthall 49 B2
East Hyde 85 F8
Eastwick 117 A4
Edgware 170 E1
Edworth 3 A6
Ellenbrook 129 D5
Elstree 169 E3
Enfield 162 E1
Enfield Lock 162 F2
Enfield Wash 162 D1
Epping Green 132 D2
Essendon 131 F6
Eyeworth 1 A8

F

Farley Hill 63 B6
Farnham 58 D6
Farnham Green 58 B7
Felden 138 A8
Fields End 123 D4
Fishers Green 50 A8
Flamstead 84 B1
Flamstead End 148 B4
Flaunden 151 A6
Fleetville 128 B4
Ford End 30 E4
Freezy Water 162 E3
Frithsden 123 B8
Frogmore 141 E4
Frogmore End 138 E7
Furneux Pelham 43 A5
Further Ford End 30 D6

G

Gaddesden Row 104 C6
Gadebridge 124 A5
Ganwick Corner 159 B4
Garston 154 C4
Gaston Green 98 B7
Gilston 117 E5
Goff's Oak 147 C3
Gorhambury 126 C4
Graveley 36 C4
Gravesend 57 B8
Great Amwell 114 F5
Great Ashby 37 D3
Great Chishill 9 F2
Great Gaddesden 103 D3
Great Hallingbury 77 E4
Great Hormead 42 A8
Great Munden 54 C5
Great Offley 33 D2
Great Wymondley 35 F6
Green End Braughing 55 E7
Green End Buntingford 26 D7
Green End Dane End 53 E1
Green End Hemel Hempstead 124 A2
Green Street Bishop's Stortford 75 E8
Green Street Borehamwood 157 B2
Green Tye 75 D1
Grovehill 124 E8
Gubblecote 79 D3
Guilden Morden 1 F4
Gustard Wood 87 D4

H

Hadham Cross 74 E2
Hadham Ford 75 B8
Hadley 171 F6
Hadley Wood 159 C2
Haldens 89 F1
Hall Grove 111 B4
Hammerfield 124 A3
Hammond Street 147 D5
Handside 110 C5
Hanscombe End 19 C8
Harefield 173 C1
Hare Street Buntingford 41 D7
Hare Street Cottered 38 F6
Harlow 117 D2
Harmer Green 90 B5
Harpenden 86 B2
Harpenden Common 107 B7
Harrow 176 E1
Harrow Weald 176 D2
Hart Hill 46 A1
Hastoe 119 F7
Hatch End 175 E3
Hatching Green 107 A6
Hatfield 130 B8
Hatfield Garden Village 129 E8
Hatfield Heath 98 E3
Hatfield Hyde 110 F3
Haultwick 53 F3
Hawridge 120 E1
Hay Green 15 F6
Hazel End 59 A6
Hebing End 53 A2
Hemel Hempstead 124 D6
Henlow 10 D8
Heronsgate 164 D2
Hertford 113 C5
Hertford Heath 114 B3
Hertingfordbury 112 E5
Hexton 19 B2
Higham Gobion 19 A6
High Barnet 171 E6
High Cross 72 F2
Highfield 124 F6
High Town 63 E8
High Wych 97 B1
Hill End 173 B4
Hinxworth 3 C5
Hitchen Hill 34 E5
Hitchin 34 E8
Hockerill 77 A6
Hoddesdon 135 C7
Hogpits Bottom 151 B7
Holdbrook 163 A5
Holwell 21 B7
Holwellbury 10 B1
Holyfield 149 D3
Holywell Watford 166 D3
Holywell Whipsnade 82 B6
Hoo End 66 E4
Hook's Cross 69 F6
Horn Hill 172 B6
Howe Green 77 D2
How Wood 141 B3
Hudnall 102 F7
Hudnall Corner 103 B7
Hunsdon 95 D1
Hunsdonbury 116 D7
Hunton Bridge 153 C6

I

Ickleford 21 E4
Ivinghoe 80 F5

J

Jockey End 103 F8

K

Kelshall 15 D5
Kemprow 155 D3
Kensworth Common 82 E8
Kensworth Lynch 62 A1
Kettle Green 74 C1
Keysers Estate 135 B1
Kimpton 66 C1
Kings Langley 139 A1
King's Walden 48 A3
Kinsbourne Green 85 C5
Kitt's End 158 E1
Knebworth 69 A5
Kneesworth 2 A5

L

Lanes End 119 C4
Langley 49 F1
Langleybury 153 B4
Latchford 73 F5
Latchmore Bank 77 B2
Latimer 150 E3
Leagrave 44 D5
Lea Valley 86 F2
Leavesden Green 153 E5
Ledburn 61 C8
Lemsford 110 A5
Letchmore Heath 168 E8
Letchworth 22 C5
Letty Green 112 B2
Level's End 58 C5
Levens Green 54 C1
Leverstock Green 125 C2
Ley Green 47 F5
Ley Hill 150 B8
Lilley 32 D2
Limbury 44 F5
Little Berkhamsted 132 C4
Little Chalfont 150 B1
Little Chishill 18 E7
Little Gaddesden 102 D7
Little Hadham 57 C2
Little Hallingbury 98 D8
Little Heath Hemel Hempstead 123 B5
Little Heath Potters Bar 145 B2
Little Hormead 42 A6
Little Parndon 117 B1
Little Tring 99 F6
Little Wymondley 35 E3
London Colney 142 E5
Long Marston 79 B3
Loudwater 165 D6
Lower End 79 F3
Lower Green Ickleford 21 E5
Lower Green Meesden 29 E6
Lower Nazeing 149 E8
Lower Sheering 98 A1
Lower Stondon 10 A3
Lower Titmore Green 35 F1
Luffenhall 38 C7
Luton 45 C3

M

Mackerye End 86 F4
Mangrove Green 46 E4
Maple Cross 172 D6
Mardleybury 69 C2
Mark Hall North 118 A3
Mark Hall South 118 A1
Markyate 83 E6
Marshalls Heath 87 A2
Marshalswick 128 B6
Marsh Farm 44 E7
Marsworth 80 A1
Meesden 29 F6
Meldreth 2 F8
Mentmore 61 D4
Meriden 154 E3
Merry Hill 168 B1
Micklefield Green 152 B1
Mill End Buntingford 26 E6
Mill End Rickmansworth 164 F1
Mill Green 130 E8
Moneyhill 165 B1
Monken Hadley 171 E7
Moor Green 39 D2
Moor Park 174 D6
Mount Pleasant 173 A2
Much Hadham 74 F3

N

Napsbury 142 B5
Nash Mills 139 A6
Nasty 54 D6
Nazeing Marsh 149 A8
Nether Street 95 E5
Nettleden 103 B1
Newgate Street 146 F7
New Greens 127 D7
New Ground 101 A2
New Mill 100 A6
Newmill End 64 D1
Newnham 12 E8
Newsells 17 D7
Newtown 40 F8
New Town Bishop's Stortford 76 F6
New Town Luton 63 E5
Northaw 146 A1
North End 15 D6
North Mymms 144 A5
North Watford 154 B2
Northwood 174 E2
Northwood Hills 174 F1
Norton 12 C1
Norton Bury 12 C2
Norton Green 50 B3
Nup End 60 B3
Nuthampstead 18 A2

O

Oakfield 35 B6
Oaklands 89 F7
Odsey 5 C1
Old Hall Green 54 F1
Old Harlow 118 D4
Old Hatfield 130 D6
Old Knebworth 68 C6
Old Town 50 C8
Orchard Leigh 136 A3
Oxhey 167 E3
Oxlease 130 B5

P

Painter's Green 69 D2
Panshanger 111 B7
Park Street 141 D5
Patchetts Green 168 D8
Peartree 110 F5
Pegsdon 19 D1
Pepperstock 63 C1
Perry Green 96 B8
Peters Green 65 C3
Piccotts End 124 C7
Pimlico 139 E7
Pin Green 50 F8
Pinner 175 E1
Pinner Green 175 C1
Pirton 20 E4
Pitstone 80 D4
Poplars 51 D3
Potten End 123 C7
Potters Bar 159 D6
Potters Crouch 140 D7
Pottersheath 89 D7
Pouchen End 123 D2
Presdales 114 E7
Preston 48 D6
Puckeridge 55 D3
Pudds Cross 136 E2
Purwell 35 D8
Puttenham 78 E2

R

Rableyheath 68 D3
Radlett 156 C5
Radwell 12 C4
Redbourn 106 B6
Reed 16 F5
Reed End 16 B5
Rickmansworth 165 C1
Ridge 157 F5
Ringshall 81 B1
Roast Green 30 F6
Roe Green Hatfield 130 A6
Roe Green Sandon 26 B8
Roestock 143 E8
Rosedale 148 A3
Round Green 45 F2
Rowley Green 170 F5
Roydon 116 C1
Royston 7 C5
Rucklers Lane 138 E5
Rushden 25 F3
Rusling End 67 D7
Rye Park 135 B7

S

Sacombe 71 E3
Sacombe Green 72 A4
St Albans 127 F4
St Ibbs 35 B2
St Ippolyts 35 B3
St Julians 141 D8
St Leonards 119 E3
St Margarets 115 B4
St Michael's Mead 76 C5
St Nicholas 37 A2
St Paul's Walden 49 B1
St Stephens 127 D1
Sandon 15 B1
Sandridge 108 C1
Sarratt 152 A4
Sarrett Bottom 151 E2
Sawbridgeworth 97 C3
Sewardstone 163 D1
Shaftenhoe End 18 B8
Shaw Green 25 D5
Sheepcote Green 30 F6
Sheering 98 C1
Shenley 157 A5
Shenleybury 156 E8
Shephall 51 B3
Sherrardspark 110 C8
Shillington 19 F8
Shootersway 121 F4
Sleapshyde 129 C2
Slip End 63 C2
Smallford 129 B4
Smith's End 18 A8
Smug Oak 141 B1
Snailswell 21 E6
Sopwell 141 F8
South-end 96 B6
Southern Green 26 A4
South Hatfield 130 B2
South Mimms 158 A8
South Oxhey 175 B7
Spellbrook 97 E8
Spencerswood 119 C7
Spitalbrook 135 A4
Staines Green 112 D4
Stanborough 110 A3
Standon 55 E1
Standon Green End 72 E4
Stanmore 176 F5
Stanstead Abbotts 115 E4
Stansted Mountfitchet 59 C6
Stapleford 92 A7
Starling's Green 30 F3
Startop's End 79 F1
Steeple Morden 5 B8
Stevenage 50 D8
Stocking Pelham 43 E7
Stopsley 46 B4
Stortford Park 76 C8
Stotfold 11 E7
Streatley 31 A5
Studham 82 C4
Sundon Park 44 E7
Swanley Bar 145 B2
Symonds Green 50 A7

T

Temple Fields 118 A4
Tewin 90 E2
Tewin Wood 90 D5
The Camp 128 B2
The Green 81 F8
Therfield 15 F7
The Rookery 167 B2
The Ryde 130 C8
The Swillett 164 B3
Thorley 76 C3
Thorley Park 76 D5
Thorley Street 76 F3
Throcking 26 F1
Thundridge 93 E7
Titmore Green 35 E2
Todd's Green 36 A2
Tonwell 92 F7
Totteridge 171 E1
Tower Hill 137 F2
Town Park 117 E2
Townsend 127 C6
Trims Green 97 C7
Tring 100 B3
Tringford 99 F7
Tring Wharf 100 B6
Trowley Bottom 105 B8
Turnford 148 E5
Two Waters 138 C8
Tylers Causeway 132 D1
Tyttenhanger 142 E8

U

Upper Dunsley 100 C4

W

Wadesmill 93 D8
Walkern 38 A1
Wallington 25 D8
Walsworth 22 A1
Waltham Abbey 163 D7
Waltham Cross 162 E5
Warden Hill 45 D7
Ware 93 F2
Wareside 94 E4
Warners End 123 F4
Warren's Green 37 D6
Washall Green 30 C1
Waterdale 140 C1
Waterford 92 A2
Watford 167 C3
Watford Heath 167 E2
Watton at Stone 70 D4
Welham Green 144 C7
Well End 157 C1
Wellpond Green 56 D1
Welwyn 89 B4
Welwyn Garden City 110 E7
West End 131 C5
Westland Green 56 E1
West Leith 99 F1
Westmill Buntingford 40 F3
Westmill Hitchin 21 C1
Weston 24 C1
West Watford 167 A4
Westwick Row 125 E2
Wheathampstead 108 C7
Whelpley Hill 136 D5
Whempstead 71 B7
Whippendell Bottom 138 C1
Whipsnade 82 A8
Whitwell 66 E6
Widford 95 E4
Wigginton 100 D1
Wigginton Bottom 120 D8
Wigmore 46 E2
Wildhill 131 D2
Willian 23 B2
Wilstone 79 D1
Wilstone Green 99 D8
Wingrave 60 C3
Winsdon Hill 63 B7
Woodcock Hill 173 D6
Wood End 53 D7
Woodhall 110 E4
Woodside Luton 63 A2
Woodside Watford 154 B7
Woodside 131 A2
Woodside Green 77 F1
Woolmer Green 69 B2
Wormley 148 E8
Wormley West End 147 F8
Wyddial 28 A3

A

Aashiana Ct WD18 ... 167 A3
Abbey Ave AL3 ... 127 B1
Abbey CE Prim Sch The AL1 ... 127 D2
Abbey Ct St Albans AL1 ... 127 D2
Waltham Abbey EN9 ... 163 B5
Abbey Dr
Abbots Langley WD5 ... 154 A7
Luton LU2 ... 46 A1
Abbey Mead Ind Est EN9 ... 163 C5
Abbey Mill End AL3 ... 127 C2
Abbey Mill La AL3 ... 127 C2
Abbey Rd EN8 ... 162 E5
Abbey Sta AL1 ... 127 D1
Abbey Theatre AL1 ... 127 C1
Abbey View Radlett WD7 ... 155 F4
St Albans AL1 ... 127 D1
Watford WD25 ... 154 D3
Abbey View Rd AL3 ... 127 C3
Abbeygate Bsns Ctr The 6 LU2 ... 63 F8
Abbeyview EN9 ... 163 C6
Abbis Orch SG5 ... 21 E5
Abbot John Mews 4 AL4 ... 87 D1
Abbots Ave AL1 ... 141 E8
Abbots Ave W AL1 ... 141 D8
Abbots Cl SG3 ... 69 D1
Abbots Ct LU2 ... 46 A1
Abbots Gr SG1 ... 50 F5
Abbots Langley Sch WD5 ... 139 F1
Abbots Pk AL1 ... 128 A1
Abbots Pl WD6 ... 157 B2
Abbots Rd WD5 ... 139 E1
Abbots Rise WD4 ... 138 F5
Abbots View WD4 ... 138 F4
Abbots Wood Rd LU2 ... 64 A8
Abbotsbury Ct WD25 ... 154 B7
Abbotsford Lodge 1 HA6 ... 174 E5
Abbotswood Par LU2 ... 46 A1
Abbotts Ct SG12 ... 115 C4
Abbotts La SG12 ... 95 D3
Abbotts Rd SG6 ... 22 D6
Abbotts Rise SG12 ... 115 D4
Abbotts Way
Bishop's Stortford CM23 ... 76 E3
Stanstead Abbotts SG12 ... 115 D4
Wingrave HP22 ... 60 A4
Abbotts Yd 1 SG8 ... 7 D6
Abbottsfield Cotts SG12 ... 94 E5
Abdale La AL9 ... 144 C4
Abel Cl HP2 ... 125 A3
Abel Smith Sch SG13 ... 113 D6
Aberdale Gdns EN6 ... 158 F7
Aberdeen Rd HA3 ... 176 F1
Aberford Rd WD6 ... 170 A7
Abigail Cl LU3 ... 45 D3
Abigail Ct LU3 ... 45 D3
Abingdon Lodge EN5 ... 171 E5
Abingdon Pl EN6 ... 159 B7
Abingdon Rd LU4 ... 44 C3
Abinger Cl SG1 ... 50 E3
Aboyne Lodge Jun Mix Inf Sch AL3 ... 127 D4
Abraham Cl WD19 ... 175 B6
Abridge Cl EN8 ... 162 D4
Abstacle Hill HP23 ... 99 F3
Acacia Cl
Hammond Street EN7 ... 147 E4
Stanmore HA7 ... 176 E4
Acacia Gr HP4 ... 122 B3
Acacia Rd EN2 ... 161 D1
Acacia St AL10 ... 130 A2
Acacia Wlk
Harpenden AL5 ... 107 D6
Tring HP23 ... 99 E3
Acacias Ct EN11 ... 135 A6
Academy Ho 4 WD6 ... 170 A5
Acers AL2 ... 141 C3
Achilles Cl HP2 ... 124 F5
Ackroyd Rd SG8 ... 7 E8
Acme Rd WD24 ... 154 B1
Acorn Cl LU2 ... 45 F3
Acorn Ct EN8 ... 162 D6
Acorn Glade AL6 ... 89 F4
Acorn La EN6 ... 146 E2
Acorn Pl WD24 ... 154 A2
Acorn Rd HP3 ... 125 A2
Acorns The AL4 ... 128 D3
Acre Piece SG4 ... 35 A6
Acre Way HA6 ... 174 F2
Acre Wood HP2 ... 124 E2
Acremore St SG11 ... 75 C7
Acrewood Way AL4 ... 128 F3
Acton Cl EN8 ... 162 E8
Acworth Cres LU4 ... 44 C5
Acworth Ct 2 LU4 ... 44 C5
Adam's Yd 1 SG14 ... 113 D6
Adams Ho CM20 ... 117 D1
Adams Way HP23 ... 100 B6
Adamsfield EN7 ... 148 A5
Adderley Rd
Bishop's Stortford CM23 ... 76 F7
Harrow HA3 ... 176 F2
Addington Way LU4 ... 44 D3
Addiscombe Rd WD18 ... 167 B5
Addison Cl HA6 ... 175 A2
Addison Way HA6 ... 174 F2
Adelaide Cl EN1 ... 161 F1
Adelaide Ct EN8 ... 162 F5
Adelaide St Luton LU1 ... 63 D7
St Albans AL3 ... 127 D4
Adele Ave AL6 ... 89 F3
Adeyfield Gdns HP2 ... 124 F4
Adeyfield Rd HP2 ... 124 F3
Adeyfield Sch HP2 ... 125 A3
Adhara Rd HA6 ... 175 A5
Adingtons CM20 ... 117 F2
Adlington Ct LU4 ... 44 C4
Admiral St SG13 ... 114 A6
Admiral Way HP4 ... 121 F6
Admirals Cl AL4 ... 143 E8
Admirals Ct 6 HA6 ... 174 F5
Admirals Wlk
Hoddesdon EN11 ... 135 B4
St Albans AL1 ... 142 A8
Adrian Cl Barnet EN5 ... 171 D3
Harefield UB9 ... 173 D2
Adrian Ho WD5 ... 153 E8
Adrian Rd WD5 ... 153 E8
Adstone Rd LU1 ... 62 F3
Ailsworth Rd LU3 ... 45 A7
Ainsdale Rd WD19 ... 175 C7
Ainsland Ct LU4 ... 44 B2
Aintree Rd SG8 ... 7 F6
Aintree Way SG1 ... 51 C8
Airedale HP2 ... 124 E6
Airfield Ind Est HP23 ... 79 E5
Airfield Way WD25 ... 153 F5
Airport Approach Rd
Luton LU2 ... 64 D7
Luton LU2 ... 64 D8
Airport Executive Pk LU2 ... 64 D8
Airport Way LU1,LU2 ... 64 A5
Aitken Rd EN5 ... 171 C4
Akeman Cl AL3 ... 126 F1
Akeman St HP23 ... 100 A3
Akrill Ho AL5 ... 86 A3
Alamein Cl EN10 ... 134 E3
Alan Dr EN5 ... 171 E3
Alandale Dr HA5 ... 175 B2
Alba Rd CM17 ... 118 C1
Alban Ave AL3 ... 127 D5
Alban Cres WD6 ... 170 B8
Alban Ct Barnet EN5 ... 171 D5
St Albans AL1 ... 128 C3
Alban Ho WD6 ... 170 B8
Alban Pk Ind Est AL4 ... 128 F3
Alban Rd SG6 ... 23 C3
Alban Wood Inf Sch WD25 ... 154 B7
Alban Wood Jun Sch WD25 ... 154 B6
Albanian Ct AL1 ... 128 A2
Albans View WD25 ... 154 B6
Albany Cl WD23 ... 168 D3
Albany Ct Harpenden AL5 ... 107 C8
Luton LU1 ... 63 B8
Albany Mews
Chiswell Green AL2 ... 141 A4
3 Ware SG12 ... 93 E1
Albany Park Ave EN3 ... 162 D1
Albany Pl AL7 ... 110 E6
Albany Rd EN3 ... 162 D1
Albany Sch EN3 ... 162 D1
Albany Terr HP23 ... 100 B6
Albatross Ct SG13 ... 114 B7
Albemarle Ave
Cheshunt EN8 ... 148 C3
Potters Bar EN6 ... 159 B7
Albeny Gate AL1 ... 127 D2
Albert Ct EN8 ... 162 F5
Albert Rd Arlesey SG15 ... 11 A4
Luton LU1 ... 63 E6
Albert Rd N WD17 ... 167 B6
Albert Rd S WD17 ... 167 B6
Albert St Markyate AL3 ... 83 E5
St Albans AL1 ... 127 D2
Stevenage SG1 ... 50 D7
Tring HP23 ... 100 A3
Albion Cl SG13 ... 113 E7
Albion Ct 4 LU2 ... 63 E8
Albion Hill HP2 ... 124 D2
Albion Rd Luton LU2 ... 63 E8
Pitstone LU7 ... 80 D5
St Albans AL1 ... 127 F3
Albion The 9 SG12 ... 93 D2
Albury CE Prim Sch SG11 ... 57 A6
Albury Cl LU3 ... 31 A1
Albury Dr Pinner HA5 ... 175 D3
Pinner HA5 ... 175 E3
Albury Grove Rd EN8 ... 148 D1
Albury Rd SG11 ... 57 C2
Albury Ride EN8 ... 162 D8
Albury Wlk EN8 ... 148 C1
Albyn Ho HP2 ... 124 D3
Alconbury
Bishop's Stortford CM23 ... 59 B1
Welwyn Garden City AL7 ... 111 E6
Alcorns The CM24 ... 59 E7
Aldbury CE Prim Sch HP23 ... 101 C6
Aldbury Cl St Albans AL4 ... 128 C8
Watford WD25 ... 154 D3
Aldbury Gdns HP23 ... 100 B6
Aldbury Gr AL7 ... 111 B6
Aldbury Rd WD3 ... 164 F2
Aldeburgh Cl SG1 ... 36 A1
Alden Mead 6 HA5 ... 176 A3
Aldenham Ave WD7 ... 156 A3
Aldenham Ctry Pk* WD6 ... 169 B4
Aldenham Gr WD7 ... 156 B5
Aldenham Rd
Bushey WD23 ... 168 A6
Elstree WD6,WD25 ... 169 B5
Radlett WD7 ... 156 A4
Watford WD23 ... 167 E5
Aldenham Sch WD6 ... 168 F7
Alder Cl Baldock SG7 ... 23 F7
Bishop's Stortford CM23 ... 76 D4
Chiswell Green AL2 ... 141 C3
Hoddesdon EN11 ... 135 B8
Alder Cres LU3 ... 45 A3
Alder Ct LU3 ... 45 B3
Alder Wlk WD25 ... 154 B4
Alderbury Rd CM24 ... 59 E8
Alderley Ct HP4 ... 122 C3
Alderman Cl AL9 ... 144 C7
Alderney Ho Enfield EN3 ... 162 D1
7 Watford WD18 ... 166 F3
Alders Ct AL7 ... 111 A6
Alders End La AL5 ... 85 F2
Alders Wlk CM21 ... 97 E2
Aldersgrove EN9 ... 163 E5
Alderton Cl 5 LU2 ... 46 D1
Alderton Dr HP4 ... 102 B8
Alderwood Ho 6 WD19 ... 175 C7
Alderwood Mews EN4 ... 159 C1
Aldhous Cl LU3 ... 45 B5
Aldis Mews EN3 ... 163 A2
Aldock AL7 ... 111 A3
Aldock Rd SG1 ... 50 E7
Aldridge Ave EN3 ... 163 A1
Aldridge Ct SG7 ... 12 E1
Aldwick AL1 ... 128 B1
Aldwick Ct AL1 ... 128 B1
Aldwick Rd AL5 ... 107 E8
Aldwickbury Cres AL5 ... 86 D1
Aldwickbury Sch AL5 ... 107 E8
Aldwyck Ct HP1 ... 124 C4
Aldwyke Rise SG12 ... 93 C3
Aldykes AL10 ... 129 F5
Alesia Rd LU3 ... 44 F6
Alex Ct HP2 ... 124 D4
Alexander Ct 2 EN8 ... 148 D1
Alexander Gate SG1 ... 51 C8
Alexander Rd
Hertford SG14 ... 113 A6
London Colney AL2 ... 142 D6
Stotfold SG5 ... 11 F6
Alexandra Ave LU3 ... 45 C2
Alexandra Ct
Cheshunt EN8 ... 162 F5
11 Watford WD24 ... 167 C7
Alexandra Mews WD17 ... 167 A7
Alexandra Rd
Borehamwood WD6 ... 170 D8
Chipperfield WD4 ... 138 A1
Hemel Hempstead HP2 ... 124 D4
Hitchin SG5 ... 21 F1
Sarratt WD3 ... 152 A3
St Albans AL1 ... 127 E3
Watford WD17 ... 167 A7
Kings Langley WD4 ... 139 B1
Alexandra Way EN8 ... 162 F5
Aleyn Way SG7 ... 13 B1
Alfriston Cl LU2 ... 46 C3
Algar Cl HA7 ... 176 F5
Alington La SG6 ... 22 F3
Alison Ct HP2 ... 125 C4
All Saints CE Prim Sch
Bishop's Stortford CM23 ... 77 B8
Datchworth SG3 ... 69 D3
All Saints Cl CM23 ... 77 A8
All Saints Cres WD25 ... 154 D6
All Saints La WD3 ... 166 A3
All Saints Mews HA3 ... 176 E4
Allandale
Hemel Hempstead HP2 ... 124 D5
St Albans AL3 ... 141 B8
Allandale Cres EN6 ... 158 E7
Allandale Rd EN3 ... 162 D3
Allard Cl EN7 ... 147 F4
Allard Cres WD23 ... 168 C1
Allard Way EN10 ... 134 E2
Alldicks Rd HP3 ... 124 F1
Allen Cl Shenley WD7 ... 156 E7
Wheathampstead AL4 ... 108 D7
Allen Ct 2 AL10 ... 130 B3
Allenby Ave LU5 ... 44 A1
Allendale LU3 ... 31 A1
Allerton Cl WD6 ... 156 F1
Allerton Rd WD6 ... 156 F1
Alleyns Rd SG1 ... 50 D7
Allied Bsns Ctr AL5 ... 86 C3
Allis Mews CM17 ... 118 C1
Allison SG6 ... 23 C5
Allton Rd SG16 ... 10 A4
Allum La WD6 ... 169 E5
Allwood Rd EN7 ... 147 F4
Alma Ct
Borehamwood WD6 ... 156 F1
Potters Bar EN6 ... 145 C1
Alma Cut AL1 ... 127 E2
Alma Link 4 LU1 ... 63 D7
Alma Rd
Berkhamsted HP4 ... 121 E6
St Albans AL1 ... 127 E2
Alma Row HA3 ... 176 D2
Alma St LU1 ... 63 D7
Almond Cl LU3 ... 45 B4
Almond Hill Jun Sch SG1 ... 50 E8
Almond Way
Borehamwood WD6 ... 170 B5
Harrow HA2 ... 176 C1
Almond Wlk 1 AL10 ... 130 A2
Almonds La SG1 ... 50 E8
Almonds The AL1 ... 142 B7
Alms La SG7 ... 4 D4
Almshoe Bury Cotts SG4 ... 49 D8
Almshouse La EN1 ... 162 B2
Almshouses SG3 ... 68 B5
Alnwick Dr HP23 ... 78 F7
Alpha Bsns Pk AL9 ... 144 C8
Alpha Pl 4 CM23 ... 76 F8
Alpine Cl SG4 ... 35 A5
Alpine Way LU3 ... 44 D8
Alpine Wlk HA7 ... 176 E8
Alsford Wharf 1 HP4 ... 122 C4
Alsop Cl AL2 ... 142 E3
Alston Ct 2 EN5 ... 171 E6
Alston Rd Barnet EN5 ... 171 E6
Hemel Hempstead HP1 ... 124 A2
Alswick Hall Cotts SG9 ... 41 B8
Altair Way HA6 ... 174 F5
Altham Gdns WD19 ... 175 D6
Altham Gr CM20 ... 117 F3
Altham Rd HA5 ... 175 E3
Althorp Cl EN5 ... 171 A2
Althorp Rd LU3 ... 45 C1
Althorpe Rd AL1 ... 127 F4
Alton Ave HA7 ... 176 F3
Alton Gdns LU1 ... 63 F5
Alton Rd LU1 ... 63 F5
Altwood AL5 ... 86 D1
Alva Way WD19 ... 175 D8
Alverton AL3 ... 127 C6
Alwin Pl WD18 ... 166 E5
Alwyn Cl
Borehamwood WD6 ... 169 F3
Luton LU2 ... 45 E2
Alyngton HP4 ... 121 E7
Alzey Gdns AL5 ... 107 D8
Amberdene 3 HA7 ... 176 F4
Amberley Cl
Harpenden AL5 ... 86 B2
Luton LU2 ... 46 D4
Amberley Gn SG12 ... 93 C4
Amberry Ct CM20 ... 117 D1
Ambient Ho EN3 ... 162 F3
Ambleside Harpenden AL5 ... 86 D2
Luton LU3 ... 44 F5
Ambrose La AL5 ... 85 F4
Amenbury Ct AL5 ... 86 A1
Amenbury La AL5 ... 86 A1
Amersham Ho WD18 ... 166 E2
Amersham Rd WD3 ... 164 B8
Ames Cl Luton LU3 ... 31 A1
Luton LU3 ... 44 F8
Amor Way SG6 ... 23 B6
Amwell Cl WD25 ... 154 E4
Amwell Comm AL7 ... 111 C5
Amwell Ct
Hoddesdon EN11 ... 135 A7
Waltham Abbey EN9 ... 163 E6
Amwell End SG12 ... 93 D1
Amwell Hill SG12 ... 114 F6
Amwell La
Stanstead Abbotts SG12 ... 115 B5
Wheathampstead AL4 ... 108 B7
Amwell Pl SG13 ... 114 C4
Amwell St EN11 ... 135 A7
Amwell View Sch SG12 ... 115 B4
Anchor Cl EN8 ... 148 D3
Anchor Cotts SG12 ... 93 D7
Anchor La
Hemel Hempstead HP1 ... 124 B1
Hemel Hempstead HP1 ... 124 C2
Tonwell SG12 ... 93 B6
Anchor Rd SG7 ... 23 F7
Anchor St CM23 ... 77 A6
Ancient Almhos 4 EN8 ... 148 D1
Anderson Cl UB9 ... 173 A2
Anderson Ho AL4 ... 128 D2
Anderson Rd
Shenley WD7 ... 157 A6
Stevenage SG2 ... 51 D6
Anderson's Ho 3 SG5 ... 34 F8
Anderson's La SG9 ... 29 A1
Andover Cl LU4 ... 44 C6
Andrew Cl WD7 ... 156 F6
Andrew Reed Ct 10 WD24 ... 167 C7
Andrew's La
Cheshunt EN7 ... 148 B3
Goff's Oak EN7 ... 147 F3
Andrews Cl HP2 ... 124 D5
Andrews Lane Prim Sch EN7 ... 148 B3
Andrewsfield AL7 ... 111 C6
Anelle Rise HP3 ... 138 F7
Anershall HP22 ... 60 B3
Angel Cl LU4 ... 44 D3
Angel Cotts SG5 ... 33 D2
Angel Pavement 7 SG8 ... 7 D6
Angell's Mdw SG7 ... 4 D4
Angle Ways SG2 ... 51 B1
Anglefield Rd HP4 ... 122 A4
Anglesey Cl CM23 ... 76 C7
Anglesey Rd WD19 ... 175 C5
Anglian Bsns Pk SG8 ... 7 C7
Anglian Cl WD24 ... 167 C7
Angotts Mead SG1 ... 50 B6
Angus Cl LU4 ... 44 A3
Anmer Gdns LU4 ... 44 B4
Annables La AL5 ... 85 A4
Annette Cl HA3 ... 176 E1
Anns Cl HP23 ... 99 E3
Ansell Ct SG1 ... 36 B1
Anselm Rd HA5 ... 175 F3
Anson Cl Bovingdon HP3 ... 136 F4
Sandridge AL4 ... 108 C1
St Albans AL1 ... 128 B1
Anson Wlk HA6 ... 174 C6
Anstee Rd LU4 ... 44 B6
Anstey Fst Sch SG9 ... 29 A6
Anthony Cl WD19 ... 167 D1
Anthony Gdns LU1 ... 63 D6
Anthony Rd WD6 ... 169 F7
Anthorne Cl EN6 ... 159 B8
Anthus Mews HA6 ... 174 E3
Antoinette Ct WD5 ... 139 F2
Antoneys Cl HA5 ... 175 D1
Antonine Gate AL3 ... 127 A2
Anvil Cl HP3 ... 137 B3
Anvil Ct Buntingford SG9 ... 40 E8
Luton LU3 ... 44 E5
Anvil Ho 8 AL5 ... 86 A2
Apex Point AL9 ... 130 C1
Aplins Cl AL5 ... 86 A2
Apollo Ave HA6 ... 175 A5
Apollo Way
Hemel Hempstead HP2 ... 124 F5
Stevenage SG2 ... 51 C8
Apple Cotts HP3 ... 137 A4
Apple Orch The HP2 ... 124 F5
Appleby St EN7 ... 147 E5
Applecroft
Berkhamsted HP4 ... 121 E6
Chiswell Green AL2 ... 141 B3
Lower Stondon SG16 ... 10 B3
Applecroft Rd Luton LU2 ... 46 C4
Welwyn Garden City AL8 ... 110 B6
Applecroft Sch AL8 ... 110 B5
Appleford's Cl EN11 ... 134 F8
Appleton Ave SG12 ... 94 E5
Appleton Fields CM23 ... 76 E4
Appletree Gr AL3 ... 106 B6
Appletree Wlk WD25 ... 154 B4
Appletrees SG5 ... 34 D6
Applewood Cl AL5 ... 85 E3
Appleyard Terr EN3 ... 162 C2
Approach Rd AL1 ... 127 E2
Approach The EN6 ... 158 F7
Appspond La AL2 ... 140 C8
April Pl CM21 ... 97 F3
Apsley Cl CM23 ... 76 F4
Apsley End Rd SG5 ... 19 E6
Apsley Grange HP3 ... 138 E6
Apsley Ind Est HP3 ... 138 D7
Apsley Manor Farm Barns HP3 ... 138 D5
Apsley Mills Ret Pk HP3 ... 138 E7
Apsley Sta HP3 ... 138 E6
Apton Ct CM23 ... 76 F7
Apton Fields 7 CM23 ... 76 F6
Apton Rd CM23 ... 76 F7
Aquarius Way HA6 ... 175 A6
Aragon Cl Enfield EN2 ... 160 F1
Hemel Hempstead HP2 ... 125 C8
Aran Cl AL5 ... 107 D6
Arbour Cl LU3 ... 31 A1
Arbour The SG13 ... 113 D4
Arbroath Gn WD19 ... 175 B7
Arcade 5 SG5 ... 34 E7
Arcade The Hatfield AL10 ... 130 B6
Letchworth SG6 ... 22 F6
Luton LU4 ... 45 C1
Arcade Wlk 4 SG5 ... 34 E7
Arcadian Ct AL5 ... 86 A2
Arch Rd SG4 ... 35 E4
Archer Cl WD4 ... 138 F2
Archer Rd SG1 ... 51 A6
Archers SG9 ... 40 F8
Archers Cl Hertford SG14 ... 113 C7
Redbourn AL3 ... 106 B5
Archers Fields AL1 ... 127 F5
Archers Green La AL6 ... 111 E8
Archers Ride AL7 ... 111 B4
Archers Way SG6 ... 22 D6
Arches Hall Cotts SG11 ... 73 E5
Archfield AL7 ... 89 E1
Archway Ho AL9 ... 130 C6
Archway Par LU3 ... 44 F4
Archway Rd LU3 ... 44 E4
Arckle Ho EN10 ... 148 F5
Ardeley St Lawrence CE Prim Sch SG2 ... 38 F3
Arden Cl Bovingdon HP3 ... 137 A3
Bushey WD23 ... 168 F2
Arden Ct WD3 ... 173 A8
Arden Gr AL5 ... 86 B1
Arden Pl LU2 ... 45 E1
Arden Press Way SG6 ... 23 B6
Ardens Way AL4 ... 128 D6
Ardentinny AL1 ... 127 E2
Ardleigh Gn LU2 ... 46 E1
Ardross Ave HA6 ... 174 E5
Arena Par SG6 ... 22 F6
Arena The EN3 ... 162 F1
Argent Way EN7 ... 147 D5
Argyle Ct WD18 ... 166 F5
Argyle Rd EN5 ... 171 C5
Argyle Way SG1 ... 50 C5
Argyll Ave LU3 ... 45 C2
Argyll Rd HP2 ... 124 E8
Arkley Ct HP2 ... 125 B8
Arkley Dr EN5 ... 171 B4
Arkley La EN5 ... 171 B5
Arkley Pk Cvn Pk EN5 ... 170 D3
Arkley Rd HP2 ... 125 B8
Arkley View EN5 ... 171 B5
Arkwrights CM20 ... 117 F1
Arlesey Ho SG15 ... 11 A8
Arlesey New Rd SG15,SG6 ... 22 B7
Arlesey Rd Henlow SG16 ... 10 D8
Henlow SG16 ... 10 E8
Ickleford SG5 ... 21 F5
Stotfold SG5 ... 11 E6
Arlesey Sta SG15 ... 11 A8
Arlingham Cotts EN6 ... 158 A7
Arlingham Mews EN9 ... 163 C6
Arlington Cres EN8 ... 162 E5
Armand Cl WD17 ... 153 F1
Armitage Cl WD3 ... 165 D5
Armitage Gdns LU4 ... 44 D1
Armour Rise SG4 ... 22 B2
Armourers Cl CM23 ... 76 B4

Armstrong Cl
Borehamwood WD6 ...170 C6
London Colney AL2 ...142 E4
Armstrong Gdns WD7 ...156 E7
Armstrong Pl 1 HP1 ...124 D4
Arncliffe Cres LU2 ...45 E1
Arndale Ctr LU1 ...63 E7
Arnett Cl WD3 ...165 A3
Arnett Hills Jun Mix Inf Sch WD3 ...165 A3
Arnett Way WD3 ...165 A2
Arnold Ave E EN3 ...163 A1
Arnold Ave W EN3 ...162 F1
Arnold Cl Hitchin SG4 ...35 B8
Luton LU2 ...46 A3
Stevenage SG1 ...36 D2
Arnold Rd EN9 ...163 C4
Arnolds La SG7 ...3 D6
Arran Cl HP3 ...125 C1
Arran Ct LU1 ...63 D7
Arran Ho 15 WD18 ...166 F3
Arranmore Ct WD23 ...167 E5
Arretine Cl AL3 ...126 F1
Arrewig La HP5,HP23 ...119 D1
Arrow Cl LU3 ...44 E6
Art School Yd 6 AL1 ...127 D3
Arthur Gibbens Ct SG1 ...37 A1
Arthur Rd AL1 ...128 B3
Arthur St Luton LU1 ...63 E6
Watford WD23 ...167 D5
Artichoke Dell WD3 ...164 E4
Artillery Pl HA3 ...176 C3
Artisan Cres AL3 ...127 C4
Arts Educational Sch The HP23 ...100 B3
Arundel Cl Aston SG2 ...51 E3
Cheshunt EN8 ...148 C3
Hemel Hempstead HP2 ...125 B4
Arundel Dr WD6 ...170 C5
Arundel Gr AL3 ...127 D7
Arundel Ho WD6 ...170 C5
Arundel Rd LU4 ...44 F2
Arundell Rd WD5 ...154 A7
Arwood Mews SG7 ...23 F7
Ascent Pk CM20 ...118 A4
Ascot Cl
Bishop's Stortford CM23 ...77 C8
Borehamwood WD6 ...170 A4
Ascot Cres SG1 ...37 B1
Ascot Gdns EN3 ...162 C2
Ascot Ind Est SG6 ...23 B7
Ascot Rd Luton LU3 ...45 B2
Royston SG8 ...7 F6
Watford WD18 ...166 E4
Ascot Terr SG12 ...114 F7
Ascots La AL7 ...110 F2
Ash Cl
Abbots Langley WD5 ...153 D7
Brookmans Park AL9 ...145 A6
Harefield UB9 ...173 D2
Harrow HA7 ...176 F4
Watford WD25 ...154 B4
Ash Copse AL2 ...154 F8
Ash Dr Hatfield AL10 ...130 A2
Hitchin SG4 ...35 A4
Ash Gr Harefield UB9 ...173 D2
Hemel Hempstead HP3 ...138 F7
Wheathampstead AL4 ...87 C1
Ash Groves CM21 ...98 A2
Ash Hill Cl WD23 ...168 B1
Ash Mdw SG10 ...74 F2
Ash Mill SG8 ...17 C3
Ash Rd Luton LU4 ...63 B8
Tring HP23 ...99 F4
Ware SG12 ...94 A3
Ash Ride EN2 ...161 A4
Ash Tree Field CM20 ...117 A2
Ash Tree Rd WD24 ...154 B3
Ash Vale WD3 ...172 D5
Ash Way SG8 ...7 F6
Ashanger La SG7 ...24 D4
Ashbourne Cl SG6 ...23 B3
Ashbourne Ct AL4 ...142 C8
Ashbourne Rd EN10 ...134 F2
Ashbourne Sq HA6 ...174 E4
Ashbrook La SG4 ...35 C3
Ashburnam Wlk SG2 ...50 F1
Ashburnham Cl WD19 ...175 A7
Ashburnham Dr WD19 ...175 A7
Ashburnham Rd LU1 ...63 C7
Ashbury Cl AL10 ...129 E5
Ashby Ct HP2 ...105 B1
Ashby Gdns AL1 ...141 D7
Ashby Rd
Berkhamsted HP4 ...121 D7
Watford WD24 ...154 A1
Ashby Rise CM23 ...59 B1
Ashcombe AL8 ...89 E2
Ashcroft HA5 ...176 A4
Ashcroft Cl AL5 ...107 E8
Ashcroft Ct EN10 ...134 F1
Ashcroft High Sch LU2 ...46 C2
Ashcroft Rd LU2 ...46 B3
Ashdale CM23 ...76 D4
Ashdale Gdns LU3 ...31 A1
Ashdale Gr HA7 ...176 F4
Ashdales AL1 ...141 D7
Ashdown SG6 ...11 F1
Ashdown Cres EN8 ...148 E3
Ashdown Dr WD6 ...169 F7
Ashdown Rd
Stevenage SG2 ...69 B8
Watford WD23 ...167 D6
Ashendene Rd SG13 ...132 F4
Ashfield Ave WD23 ...168 C2
Ashfield Jun Sch WD23 ...168 B2
Ashfield Way LU3 ...45 A6
Ashfields WD24,WD25 ...153 F4
Ashford Gn WD19 ...175 D5
Ashfords SG9 ...40 E8
Ashleigh SG2 ...51 B4
Ashleigh Ct
Hoddesdon EN11 ...135 A5
2 Rickmansworth WD3 ...165 D2
Ashleigh Cvn Pk SG11 ...73 C3
Ashley Cl Cheddington LU7 ...80 A8
Hemel Hempstead HP3 ...124 F1
Pinner HA5 ...175 B1
Welwyn Garden City AL8 ...110 C8
Ashley Ct AL10 ...130 B6
Ashley Dr WD6 ...170 D4
Ashley Gdns AL5 ...85 D3
Ashley Ho WD18 ...166 E2
Ashley Rd Hertford SG14 ...113 B5
St Albans AL1 ...128 C2
Ashleys WD3 ...164 F2
Ashlyn Cl WD23 ...167 E5
Ashlyns Ct HP4 ...122 B3
Ashlyns Rd HP4 ...122 B3
Ashlyns Sch HP4 ...122 C2
Ashmore Gdns HP3 ...125 B2
Ashridge Cl HP3 ...137 A3
Ashridge College Gdns* HP4 ...102 D5
Ashridge Cotts HP4 ...102 E5
Ashridge Dr
Bricket Wood AL2 ...140 F1
South Oxhey WD19 ...175 C5
Ashridge Estate Visitor Ctr* HP4 ...101 E6
Ashridge Ho WD18 ...166 E2
Ashridge La HP5 ...150 D7
Ashridge Management Coll HP4 ...102 C5
Ashridge Rise HP4 ...121 F5
Ashton Rd Enfield EN3 ...162 E3
Luton LU1 ...63 E5
Ashton's La SG7 ...23 F6
Ashtree Ct AL1 ...127 F3
Ashtree Prim Sch SG2 ...51 C4
Ashtree Way HP1 ...124 A2
Ashurst Cl HA6 ...174 E3
Ashville Way SG7 ...13 A1
Ashwell SG1 ...36 C2
Ashwell & Morden Sta SG7 ...5 D2
Ashwell Ave LU3 ...44 C8
Ashwell Cl SG4 ...36 B4
Ashwell Comm SG4 ...36 B4
Ashwell Par LU3 ...44 C8
Ashwell Pk AL5 ...86 D1
Ashwell Prim Sch SG7 ...4 D4
Ashwell Rd Bygrave SG7 ...13 C4
Guilden Morden SG8 ...1 F1
Hinxworth SG7 ...3 E5
Newnham SG7 ...12 F8
Ashwell St Ashwell SG7 ...4 D4
Kneesworth SG8 ...2 A3
St Albans AL3 ...127 D4
Ashwell Village Mus* SG7 ...4 D4
Ashwood Ho 1 HA5 ...176 A3
Ashwood Mews AL1 ...127 D1
Ashwood Pl SG4 ...35 A5
Ashwood Rd EN6 ...159 B6
Askew Rd HA6 ...174 D8
Aspasia Cl AL1 ...127 F2
Aspen Cl
Bricket Wood AL2 ...140 E1
Stevenage SG2 ...69 B7
Aspen Park Dr WD25 ...154 B4
Aspen Way Enfield EN3 ...162 D4
Welwyn Garden City AL7 ...111 C5
Aspenden Rd SG9 ...40 E6
Aspens The
Bishop's Stortford CM23 ...59 B3
Hitchin SG4 ...35 A6
Aspfield Row HP1 ...124 B5
Asquith Ct SG2 ...69 C7
Asquith Ho AL8 ...110 D7
Ass House La HA3 ...176 B6
Astall Cl HA3 ...176 E2
Aster Cl CM23 ...76 D6
Asters The EN7 ...147 D3
Astley Cooper Sch HP2 ...125 A8
Astley Gn LU2 ...46 D2
Astley Rd HP1 ...124 C3
Aston Bury SG2 ...69 F8
Aston Cl Bushey WD23 ...168 C3
Stevenage SG1 ...36 C2
Watford WD24 ...167 C7
Aston End Rd SG2 ...51 E3
Aston Grange SG14 ...113 D8
Aston La SG2 ...69 E8
Aston Rd SG11 ...55 D2
Aston Rise SG4 ...35 B6
Aston St Mary's CE Prim Sch SG2 ...51 E2
Aston View HP2 ...105 A1
Aston Way EN6 ...159 D7
Astonia Ho SG7 ...23 F7
Astons Rd HA6 ...174 C6
Astra Ct Luton LU2 ...45 F2
Watford WD18 ...166 F4
Astra Ctr CM20 ...117 F4
Astral Cl SG16 ...10 B3
Astrope La HP23 ...79 B3
Astwick Ave AL10 ...129 F8
Astwick Manor AL10 ...129 C8
Astwick Rd Stotfold SG5 ...11 F8
Stotfold SG5 ...3 A2
Athelstan Rd HP3 ...138 F8
Athelstan Wlk N AL7 ...110 E5
Athelstan Wlk S AL7 ...110 D5
Athelstone Rd HA3 ...176 D1
Athena Est CM20 ...118 B4
Athena Pl HA6 ...174 F2
Athenia Cl EN7 ...147 B2
Atherstone Rd LU4 ...44 D1
Atherton End CM21 ...97 E3
Athlone Cl WD7 ...156 B3
Athol Cl HA5 ...175 B2
Athol Gdns HA5 ...175 B2
Atholl Cl LU3 ...44 D8
Atria Rd HA6 ...175 A5
Attenborough Cl WD19 ...175 E7
Attimore Cl AL8 ...110 B5
Attimore Rd AL8 ...110 B5
Aubretia Ho AL7 ...111 B4
Aubrey Ave AL2 ...142 C5
Aubrey Gdns LU4 ...44 B6
Aubrey La AL3 ...105 E2
Aubreys SG6 ...23 A2
Aubreys Rd HP1 ...123 E3
Aubries SG2 ...38 B1
Auckland Cl EN1 ...162 B2
Auckland Rd EN6 ...158 E7
Auden Dr WD6 ...170 A4
Audley Cl WD6 ...170 A6
Audley Ct HA5 ...175 C1
Audley Gdns EN9 ...163 C5
Audrey Gdns CM23 ...76 F4
Audwick Cl EN8 ...148 E3
Augustine Ct EN9 ...163 B6
Augustine Rd HA3 ...176 C2
Augustus Cl AL3 ...127 A1
Augustus Gate SG2 ...51 D8
Augustus Smith Ho 8 HP4 ...122 D4
Austen Paths SG2 ...51 C6
Austin Mews 6 HP1 ...124 D4
Austin Rd LU3 ...45 C4
Austins Mead HP3 ...137 B3
Austins Pl HP2 ...124 D4
Autumn Glades HP3 ...125 C1
Autumn Gr AL7 ...111 B4
Avalon Cl WD25 ...154 E7
Avebury Ave LU2 ...45 D4
Avebury Ct HP2 ...125 A5
Avenue App WD4 ...139 A1
Avenue Ct AL6 ...89 E7
Avenue Grimaldi LU3 ...45 A3
Avenue Mans EN5 ...171 F5
Avenue One SG6 ...23 C6
Avenue Pl CM23 ...77 A6
Avenue Rd
Bishop's Stortford CM23 ...77 B6
Hoddesdon EN11 ...135 D5
Pinner HA5 ...175 E1
St Albans AL1 ...127 E4
Avenue Rise WD23 ...168 A4
Avenue St Nicholas AL5 ...86 A1
Avenue Terr WD19 ...167 E3
Avenue The Barnet EN5 ...171 E6
Bushey WD23 ...167 F5
Harrow HA3 ...176 F2
Hemel Hempstead HP1 ...123 E4
Hertford SG14 ...113 B8
Hitchin SG4 ...35 A7
Luton LU4 ...44 D5
Northwood HA6 ...174 C4
Oaklands AL6 ...89 D7
Pinner HA5 ...175 F4
Potters Bar EN6 ...145 A1
Radlett WD7 ...156 B5
Stevenage SG1 ...50 D8
Stotfold SG5 ...11 F6
Watford WD17 ...167 A7
Avey La EN9 ...163 E2
Avia Cl HP3 ...138 D7
Avior Dr HA6 ...174 F6
Avocet SG6 ...11 E1
Avon Chase SG16 ...10 C4
Avon Cl WD25 ...154 C5
Avon Cotts LU2 ...46 B3
Avon Ct 17 Harpenden AL5 ...86 B1
Luton LU1 ...63 C8
4 Pinner HA5 ...176 A3
Avon Dr SG1 ...37 A3
Avon Mews HA5 ...175 F2
Avon Rd SG16 ...10 B4
Avon Sq HP2 ...124 F8
Avondale Ct AL1 ...127 E3
Avondale Rd LU1 ...63 C8
Axe Cl LU3 ...44 E6
Aycliffe Dr HP2 ...124 E7
Aycliffe Drive Prim Sch HP2 ...124 E7
Aycliffe Rd WD6 ...156 F1
Aydon Rd LU3 ...45 B6
Aylands Rd EN3 ...162 D3
Aylands Sch EN3 ...162 C3
Aylesbury Rd HP23 ...99 E3
Aylott Ct SG14 ...70 D4
Aylotts Cl SG9 ...40 D8
Aylsham Rd EN11 ...135 C8
Aylward Dr SG2 ...51 B4
Aynho St WD18 ...167 B4
Aynsworth Ave CM23 ...59 B2
Ayot Gn Ayot St Peter AL6 ...89 A1
Hatfield AL6 ...109 F8
Ayot Ho AL6 ...88 A6
Ayot Little Green La AL6 ...88 F1
Ayot Path WD6 ...157 A1
Ayot St Peter Rd AL6 ...88 E3
Ayr Cl SG1 ...51 C8
Ayres End La AL3,AL5 ...107 E5
Aysgarth Cl AL5 ...107 B8
Aysgarth Rd AL3 ...106 A6
Azalea Cl AL2 ...142 B4
Azure Appartments HA3 ...176 E2

B

Baas Hill EN10 ...134 D2
Baas Hill Cl EN10 ...134 E2
Baas La EN10 ...134 E3
Babbage Rd SG1 ...50 B5
Back La Buckland SG9 ...27 D8
Little Hallingbury CM22 ...98 B7
Preston SG4 ...48 D6
Radlett WD25 ...168 E8
Sheering CM22 ...98 B1
Tewin AL6 ...90 E2
Back St Ashwell SG7 ...4 C3
Luton LU2 ...63 E8
Back The HP4 ...123 B7
Bacon's Yd SG7 ...4 D4
Bacons Dr EN6 ...146 E2
Badburgham Ct EN9 ...163 F6
Baddeley Cl
Holdbrook EN3 ...163 A2
Stevenage SG2 ...51 B2
Bader Cl Stevenage SG1 ...36 F1
Welwyn Garden City AL7 ...111 C6
Badger Cl SG3 ...69 A6
Badger Way AL10 ...130 B3
Badgers CM23 ...76 E5
Badgers Cl
Borehamwood WD6 ...169 F7
Hertford SG13 ...114 B6
Stevenage SG1 ...50 E4
Badgers Croft
Barnet HP2 ...171 E1
Hemel Hempstead HP2 ...125 D2
Hoddesdon EN10 ...134 E2
Badgers Ct WD25 ...154 A5
Badgers Wlk
Chorleywood WD3 ...164 F5
Tewin AL6 ...90 C5
Badingham Dr AL5 ...85 E1
Badminton Cl
3 Borehamwood WD6 ...170 A7
Stevenage SG2 ...69 B7
Badminton Ho 8 WD24 ...167 C7
Badminton Pl EN10 ...134 E3
Bagenal Ho WD5 ...153 F7
Bagwicks Cl LU3 ...44 E7
Bailey Hill Ct LU1 ...63 E5
Bailey St LU1 ...63 F6
Baines La SG3 ...69 C4
Baird Cl WD23 ...168 B3
Bairstow Cl WD6 ...169 E8
Baisley Ho EN7 ...148 A3
Baker Ct WD6 ...170 B7
Baker St Enfield EN1 ...161 E1
Hertford SG13 ...113 E6
Luton LU1 ...63 E5
Potters Bar EN6 ...158 E5
2 Stevenage SG1 ...50 C7
Baker's La SG4 ...67 F1
Bakers Ct 6 CM23 ...77 A7
Bakers Gr AL7 ...111 C7
Bakers La Barley SG8 ...8 F2
Kensworth Common LU6 ...82 E8
Bakers Rd EN7 ...148 B1
Bakers Wlk CM21 ...97 E2
Bakerscroft 1 EN8 ...148 E3
Bakery Ct CM24 ...59 D6
Bakery The 2 SG12 ...93 D2
Bakewell Cl LU4 ...44 C1
Balcary Gdns HP4 ...121 F4
Balcombe Cl LU2 ...46 D4
Balcon Way WD6 ...170 C8
Baldock Ind Est SG7 ...23 F7
Baldock La SG6 ...23 D4
Baldock Rd Aspenden SG9 ...40 B8
Letchworth SG6 ...23 B5
Royston SG8 ...6 C4
Stotfold SG5 ...12 A5
Baldock St Royston SG8 ...7 C6
Ware SG12 ...93 D2
Baldock Sta SG7 ...12 F1
Baldock Way WD6 ...169 F8
Baldways Cl HP22 ...60 C3
Baldwins AL7 ...111 C6
Baldwins La WD3 ...166 B5
Balfour Ct AL5 ...86 C3
Balfour Mews HP3 ...137 A4
Balfour St SG14 ...113 C7
Baliol Rd SG5 ...34 F8
Ballater Cl WD19 ...175 C6
Ballinger Ct
Berkhamsted HP4 ...122 B3
1 Watford WD18 ...167 B6
Balloon Cnr AL9 ...144 B8
Ballslough Hill SG4 ...66 D1
Balmoral Cl
Chiswell Green AL2 ...141 C3
Stevenage SG2 ...69 C7
Balmoral Dr WD6 ...170 D5
Balmoral Ho WD6 ...170 C5
Balmoral Rd
Abbots Langley WD5 ...154 A7
Enfield EN3 ...162 D3
Hitchin SG5 ...21 E1
Watford WD24 ...154 C1
Balmore Wood LU3 ...31 B1
Balsams Cl SG13 ...113 D4
Bampton Rd LU4 ...44 B2
Bamville Wood AL5 ...107 C5
Banbury Cl LU4 ...44 F4
Banbury St WD18 ...167 B4
Bancroft SG5 ...34 F7
Bancroft Gdns HA3 ...176 C2
Bancroft Rd Harrow HA3 ...176 C1
Bancroft Rd *continued*
Luton LU3 ...45 B5
Bandley Rise SG2 ...51 C3
Banes Down EN9 ...135 E1
Bank Cl LU4 ...44 C4
Bank Ct HP1 ...124 C2
Bank Mill HP4 ...122 E4
Bank Mill La HP4 ...122 E3
Banks Rd WD6 ...170 C7
Bankside Cl UB9 ...173 A4
Bankside Down WD3 ...165 D3
Bannister Gdns SG8 ...7 E8
Bantel Villas EN11 ...135 C8
Barbel Cl EN8 ...163 A5
Barberry Rd HP1 ...124 A3
Barbers La 2 LU1 ...63 E7
Barbers Wlk HP23 ...99 F3
Barchester Rd HA3 ...176 D1
Barclay Cl
Hertford Heath SG13 ...114 B4
Watford WD18 ...167 A3
Barclay Cres SG1 ...50 E7
Barclay Ct
Hoddesdon EN11 ...135 A5
Luton LU2 ...63 F8
Barclay Sch SG1 ...50 D8
Barden Cl UB9 ...173 C3
Bards Cnr HP1 ...124 B4
Bardwell Ct 6 AL1 ...127 D2
Bardwell Rd AL1 ...127 D2
Barfolds AL9 ...144 C8
Barford Rise LU2 ...46 D1
Barge Ho HP3 ...138 E7
Bargrove Ave HP1 ...124 A2
Barham Ave WD6 ...169 F5
Barham Rd SG2 ...51 C5
Barker Cl HA6 ...174 F3
Barkers Mead
Bishop's Stortford CM22 ...77 B1
Little Hallingbury CM22 ...98 B8
Barkham Cl LU7 ...79 F7
Barking Cl LU4 ...44 B6
Barkston Path WD6 ...157 A1
Barkway CE Fst Sch SG8 ...17 C4
Barkway Hill SG8 ...17 E6
Barkway Rd SG8 ...7 E5
Barkway St SG8 ...7 D5
Barley Brow WD25 ...154 C8
Barley CE Fst Sch SG8 ...9 A1
Barley Cl WD23 ...168 B4
Barley Croft
Hemel Hempstead HP2 ...125 C3
Hertford SG14 ...113 D8
Stapleford SG14 ...92 A3
Barley Ct EN7 ...148 B1
Barley Hills CM23 ...76 E4
Barley La LU4 ...44 C5
Barley Mow La AL4 ...142 F8
Barley Ponds Cl SG12 ...93 F1
Barley Ponds Rd SG12 ...93 F1
Barley Rd Barley SG8 ...9 A7
Great Chishill SG8 ...9 C2
Barley Rise Baldock SG7 ...24 B8
Harpenden AL5 ...86 C4
Barleycorn The 1 LU3 ...63 D8
Barleycroft
Buntingford SG9 ...40 E6
Stevenage SG2 ...51 D3
Tonwell SG12 ...92 F7
Barleycroft Gn AL8 ...110 C6
Barleycroft Rd AL8 ...110 C5
Barleyvale LU3 ...45 A8
Barlings Rd AL5 ...107 B5
Barmor Cl HA2 ...176 B1
Barmouth Row 6 HP2 ...124 E6
Barn Cl
Hemel Hempstead HP3 ...138 F8
Radlett WD7 ...156 A4
Welwyn Garden City AL8 ...110 C6
Barn Ct CM21 ...97 E3
Barn Lea WD3 ...165 A1
Barnack Cl SG8 ...7 C7
Barnacres Rd HP3 ...139 A8
Barnard Acres EN9 ...149 E8
Barnard Gn AL7 ...110 F5
Barnard Rd Luton LU1 ...63 A7
Sawbridgeworth CM21 ...97 E4
Barnard Way HP3 ...124 E1
Barncroft SG11 ...57 C7
Barncroft Prim Sch HP2 ...124 D8
Barncroft Rd HP4 ...121 F3
Barncroft Way AL1 ...128 A2
Barndell Cl SG5 ...11 F6
Barndicott AL7 ...111 C6
Barndicott Ho AL7 ...111 C6
Barnes La WD4 ...138 D3
Barnes Rise WD4 ...138 F4
Barnet By-Pass
Borehamwood WD6 ...170 E5
Dancers Hill EN5 ...158 A3
Barnet Coll EN5 ...171 F5
Barnet Gate La EN5 ...170 F3
Barnet General Hospl EN5 ...171 D5
Barnet Hill EN5 ...171 F5
Barnet Hill Jun Mix Inf Sch EN5 ...171 F4
Barnet La
Borehamwood WD6 ...170 B3
Totteridge EN5,N20 ...171 F2
Barnet Mus* EN5 ...171 E5
Barnet Rd Barnet EN5 ...170 E3
Ganwick Corner EN6,EN5 ...159 A4
London Colney AL2 ...142 F4
Barnet Stall Market EN5 ...171 E6
Barnet Trad Est EN5 ...171 F6

Barnet Way (Barnet By-Pass)
NW7 170 D2
Barnfield HP3 138 F8
Barnfield Ave LU2 45 D5
Barnfield Cl
Hoddesdon EN11 135 A8
Lower Nazeing EN9 135 F1
Barnfield Coll LU3 45 B8
Barnfield Coll (North)
Luton LU2 63 F8
Luton, Stopsley Common
LU2 45 D5
Barnfield Coll (South)
LU1 63 B5
Barnfield Ct AL5 107 C8
Barnfield Rd
Harpenden AL5 107 C8
St Albans AL4 128 C5
Welwyn Garden City AL7 110 E4
Barnhurst Path WD19 175 C5
Barns Dene AL5 85 E2
Barns The HP23 99 F1
Barnsdale Cl WD6 169 F8
Barnside Ct AL8 110 C6
Barnston Cl LU2 46 D1
Barnsway WD4 138 E3
Barnview Lo HA3 176 E2
Barnwell SG2 51 B2
Barnwell Sch SG2 51 B2
Barnwood Cl N20 171 F1
Baron Ct SG1 36 B1
Barons Ct 7 LU2 45 D1
Barons The CM23 76 D5
Baronsmere Ct 7 EN5 171 E5
Barr Rd EN6 159 C6
Barra Cl HP3 139 C8
Barra Ho 6 WD18 166 F3
Barrass Cl EN3 163 A2
Barratt Ind Pk LU2 64 C6
Barratt Way HA3 176 D1
Barrells Down Rd CM23 58 E1
Barrett La 5 CM23 76 F7
Barrington Dr UB9 173 A3
Barrington Mews AL7 111 B5
Barrington Rd SG6 22 F4
Barrons Row AL5 107 D7
Barrow La EN7 147 F1
Barrow Point Ave HA5 175 E1
Barrow Point La HA5 175 E1
Barrowby Cl LU2 46 D1
Barrowdene Cl HA5 175 E1
Barry Cl AL2 141 B6
Barry Ct SG1 50 B8
Bartel Cl HP3 125 D1
Bartholomew Court Sh
Pavilion EN8 162 E6
Bartholomew Ho EN3 162 E2
Bartholomew Rd 8
CM23 76 F6
Bartletts Cotts 4 EN5 171 E6
Bartletts Mead SG14 92 D1
Barton Cl AL5 86 C3
Barton Rd Hexton SG5 19 A1
Luton LU3 45 C7
Wheathampstead AL4 108 C8
Barton Way
Borehamwood WD6 170 A7
Croxley Green WD3 166 B4
Bartons The WD6 169 D3
Bartrams La EN4 159 C1
Bartrop Cl EN7 147 D3
Bartrum Villas 4 HP4 122 D4
Barwick La SG11 73 C3
Basbow La 2 CM23 76 F7
Basil Mews CM17 118 C1
Basildon Cl WD18 166 C3
Basildon Sq HP2 124 F7
Basils Rd SG1 50 D7
Baslow Cl HA3 176 D2
Bassett Cl AL3 106 B5
Bassil Rd HP2 124 D2
Bassingbourne Cl EN10 134 F3
Bassingburn Wlk AL7 110 F5
Bassus Gn SG2 52 F8
Batchelors SG11 55 E2
Batchwood Dr AL3 127 C6
Batchwood Gdns AL3 127 D6
Batchwood Sch AL3 127 D6
Batchwood View AL3 127 D5
Batchworth Heath WD3 174 B5
Batchworth Heath Hill
WD3 174 A6
Batchworth Hill London Rd
WD3 173 F7
Batchworth La HA6 174 D5
Bateman Rd WD3 166 A3
Bates Ho 2 SG1 50 E6
Batford Cl AL7 111 B5
Batford Rd AL5 86 D3
Bath Pl EN5 171 F6
Bath Rd LU3 45 D2
Bathurst Rd HP2 124 E6
Batterdale AL9 130 C6
Battlefield Rd AL1 127 F5
Battlers Green Dr WD7 155 E3
Battleview AL4 108 E8
Baud Cl SG11 57 E2
Baulk The
Cheddington LU7 79 F7
Lilley LU2 32 D2
Pitstone LU7 80 F5
Bay Cl LU4 44 B6
Bay Ct HP4 122 B4
Bay Tree Cl
Chiswell Green AL2 141 C3
Hammond Street EN7 147 F4
Bay Tree Wlk WD17 154 A1
Bayford CE Prim Sch
SG13 132 F5
Bayford Cl
Hemel Hempstead HP2 125 C8
Hertford SG13 113 C4
Bayford Gn SG13 133 A6
Bayford La SG13 132 F7
Bayford Sta SG13 133 B5
Bayfordbury Coll (Univ of
Hertfordshire) SG13 113 B1
Bayhurst Dr HA6 174 F4
Baylam Dell LU2 46 E1
Bayley Hall Mews SG14 113 D5
Baylie Ct HP2 124 E4
Baylie La HP2 124 E4
Bayworth SG6 23 B5
Beacon Ct SG13 114 C3
Beacon Ho AL1 127 F3
Beacon Rd Ringshall HP4 81 A1
Ware SG12 94 A2
Beacon Way
Rickmansworth WD3 165 B3
Tring HP23 100 C5
Beacons The
Hatfield AL10 130 C6
Stevenage SG1 37 B3
Beaconsfield LU2 64 B8
Beaconsfield Rd
Enfield EN3 162 D2
Hatfield AL10 130 C6
St Albans AL1 127 E3
Tring HP23 99 E3
Beadles The CM22 98 B8
Beadlow Rd LU4 44 A4
Beagle Cl WD7 155 F2
Beale Cl SG2 51 C6
Beamish Dr WD23 168 C1
Beane Ave SG2 51 D6
Beane Rd Hertford SG14 113 B7
Watton at S SG14 70 D4
Beane River View SG14 113 C6
Beane Wlk SG2 51 D6
Beaneside The SG14 70 D4
Beanfield Rd CM21 97 A4
Beanley Cl LU2 46 E2
Bear La SG7 4 D4
Bearton Ave SG5 34 E8
Bearton Ct SG5 21 E1
Bearton Gn SG5 21 D1
Bearton Rd SG5 21 E1
Bearwood Cl EN6 159 D8
Beatty Rd EN8 162 F5
Beauchamp Gdns WD3 165 A1
Beauchamps AL7 111 B5
Beaulieu Cl WD19 167 C1
Beaulieu Dr EN9 163 B6
Beaumayes Cl HP1 124 B2
Beaumont Ave AL1 128 B4
Beaumont Cl 3 SG5 34 D8
Beaumont Ct 10 AL5 86 B1
Beaumont Gate WD7 156 A4
Beaumont Hall La AL3 106 C2
Beaumont Pl Barnet EN5 171 F8
Watford WD18 167 A4
Beaumont Rd
Hammond Street EN7 147 F7
Luton LU3 45 B2
Beaumont Sch AL4 128 C4
Beaumont View EN7 147 D5
Beazley Cl SG12 93 E2
Beckbury Cl LU2 46 E2
Becket Gdns AL6 89 C4
Beckets Sq HP4 122 A6
Beckets Wlk 14 SG12 93 D1
Beckett's Ave AL3 127 C6
Becketts SG14 113 A5
Beckfield La SG9 26 D7
Beckham Cl LU2 45 D7
Becks Cl AL3 83 D5
Bedale Rd EN2 161 C1
Bede Cl HA5 175 D2
Bede Ct HP4 102 C8
Bedford Almshouses 1
WD18 167 C5
Bedford Ave EN5 171 F4
Bedford Cl WD3 151 B1
Bedford Cres EN3 162 E4
Bedford Gdns 4 LU2 63 D8
Bedford Park Rd AL1 127 E3
Bedford Rd Hitchin SG5 34 E7
Ickleford SG5 21 D5
Letchworth SG6 22 D7
Lower Stondon SG16 10 B3
Moor Park HA6 174 D6
St Albans AL1 127 E2
Bedford St
Berkhamsted HP4 122 D4
Hitchin SG5 34 D7
Watford WD24 167 B8
Bedmond La
Bricket Wood AL3,WD5 140 B6
St Albans AL3 126 F1
Bedmond Rd
Abbots Langley WD5 139 F2
Hemel Hempstead HP3 125 D1
Pimlico HP3 139 E7
Bedmond Village Prim Sch
WD5 139 F3
Bedwell Ave AL9,SG13 132 A7
Bedwell Cl AL7 110 E5
Bedwell Cres SG1 50 F5
Bedwell Prim Sch SG1 51 A5
Bedwell Rise SG1 50 E5
Beech Ave
Crews Hill EN2 161 A4
Radlett WD7 156 A5
Beech Bottom AL3 127 D6
Beech Cl Harpenden AL5 107 C5
Beech Cl *continued*
Hatfield AL10 130 A4
Beech Cres AL4 108 D7
Beech Ct Harpenden AL5 85 F3
Hoddesdon EN10 135 A3
Beech Dr
Berkhamsted HP4 122 C3
Borehamwood WD6 169 F7
Sawbridgeworth CM21 118 C8
Stevenage SG2 51 B3
Beech Farm Dr AL4 128 F7
Beech Gr HP23 100 C4
Beech Hill
Hadley Wood EN4 159 E1
Letchworth SG6 22 D7
Luton LU2 46 D8
Beech Hill Com Prim Sch
LU4 45 B1
Beech Hill Ct HP4 122 D4
Beech Ho EN11 134 F6
Beech Hyde La AL4 108 F6
Beech Hyde Prim Sch
AL4 108 D7
Beech Mews SG12 114 D7
Beech Pk HP6 150 B1
Beech Pl AL3 127 D6
Beech Rd Luton LU1 63 C8
St Albans AL3 127 E6
Watford WD24 154 B2
Beech Ridge Baldock SG7 23 F6
Harpenden AL5 85 B5
Beech Way AL4 87 B6
Beech Wlk HP23 100 C4
Beechcroft
Berkhamsted HP4 122 C3
Datchworth SG3 69 D1
Beechcroft Ave WD3 166 C4
Beechcroft Rd WD23 167 E4
Beechen Gr WD17 167 C6
Beeches The
Chorleywood WD3 164 F4
Hemel Hempstead HP1 124 B2
Hitchin SG4 35 A6
Park Street AL2 141 D4
Royston SG8 7 D6
Tring HP23 100 C4
2 Watford WD18 167 B6
Welwyn AL6 89 C4
Beechfield
Hoddesdon EN11 115 A2
Kings Langley WD4 138 F1
Sawbridgeworth CM21 97 F2
Beechfield Cl
Borehamwood WD6 169 E7
Redbourn AL3 106 B5
Beechfield Ct 5 WD17 167 A8
Beechfield Rd
Hemel Hempstead HP1 124 B2
Ware SG12 93 F2
Welwyn Garden City AL7 110 E5
Beechfield Sch WD24 154 A2
Beechfield Wlk EN9 163 D4
Beeching Cl AL5 86 B4
Beechlands CM23 76 F5
Beecholm Mews 5 EN8 148 E3
Beechpark Way WD17 153 E2
Beechtree La AL3 126 B2
Beechwood Ave
Chorleywood WD3 164 B5
Little Chalfont HP6 150 C1
Potters Bar EN6 159 B6
St Albans AL1 128 C4
Beechwood Cl
Baldock SG7 23 F5
Hammond Street EN7 147 E5
Hertford SG13 113 F6
Hitchin SG5 21 D2
Beechwood Cotts WD3 164 C3
Beechwood Ct HP22 99 A4
Beechwood Dr HP23 101 D5
Beechwood Park Sch
AL3 83 B1
Beechwood Pk
Chorleywood WD3 164 F5
Hemel Hempstead HP3 137 F7
Beechwood Rd LU4 44 E3
Beechwood Rise WD24 154 B2
Beecroft La SG2 38 C2
Beehive Cl WD6 169 D3
Beehive Gn AL7 111 A4
Beehive La AL7 111 A3
Beehive Rd EN7 147 B3
Beesonend Cotts AL5 107 B4
Beesonend La AL3,AL5 106 E3
Beeston Cl WD19 175 D6
Beeston Dr EN8 148 D4
Beetham Ct SG12 92 E4
Beethoven Rd WD6 169 D3
Beeton Cl HA5 176 A3
Beggarman's La SG11 72 D8
Beggars Bush La WD18,
WD3 166 D4
Beggars La HP23 101 A3
Beken Ct WD25 154 C4
Belcher Rd 6 EN11 135 A7
Beldam Ave SG8 7 E5
Beldams Gate CM23 77 B5
Beldams La CM23 77 B5
Belfairs WD19 175 D5
Belford Rd WD6 156 F1
Belfry Ave UB9 173 A2
Belfry The Luton LU2 45 E6
Watford WD24 167 D8
Belfry Villas UB9 173 A2
Belgrave Ave WD18 166 F4
Belgrave Cl AL4 128 C7
Belgrave Dr WD4 139 C3
Belgrave Ho 6 CM23 77 B8
Belgrave Mews SG2 69 A8
Belgrave Rd LU4 44 D5
Belgravia Cl EN5 171 F6
Belham Rd WD4 139 A3
Bell Acre SG6 23 B4
Bell Acre Gdns SG6 23 B4
Bell Cl Bedmond WD5 139 F4
Hitchin SG4 35 B6
Knebworth SG3 69 A5
7 Pinner HA5 175 C1
Bell Farm Ind Est SG8 18 A2
Bell Gn HP3 137 B4
Bell La
Abbots Langley WD5 140 A4
Berkhamsted HP4 121 E5
Brookmans Park AL9 145 A7
Enfield EN3 162 E1
Hertford SG14 113 D6
Hoddesdon EN11 135 A6
Hoddesdon, Broxbourne
EN11 134 E2
Little Chalfont HP6 150 C1
Nuthampstead SG8 18 B2
Shenley AL2 142 E2
Stevenage SG1 50 C7
Widford SG12 95 D4
Bell Lane Comb Sch
HP6 150 B1
Bell Leys HP22 60 B3
Bell Mead CM21 97 E2
Bell Rdbt The AL2 142 F4
Bell Row SG7 23 E7
Bell St CM21 97 E2
Bell View AL4 128 D3
Bell Wlk HP22 60 B3
Bellamy Cl Knebworth SG3 68 F5
Watford WD17 167 A8
Bellamy Rd EN8 148 E2
Bellchambers Cl AL2 142 C5
Belle Vue La WD23 168 D1
Belle Vue Rd SG12 93 F1
Bellerby Rise LU4 44 B6
Bellevue Terr UB9 173 A3
Bellfield Ave HA3 176 D4
Bellgate HP2 124 E6
Bellgate Prim Sch HP2 124 E5
Bellingdon WD19 175 E7
Bellis Ho AL7 111 B4
Bellmount Wood Ave
WD17 166 E8
Bells Hill Barnet EN5 171 D5
Bishop's Stortford CM23 76 E7
Belmers Rd HP23 100 D1
Belmont Ct 7 AL1 127 D2
Belmont Fst Sch HA3 176 F1
Belmont Hill AL1 127 D2
Belmont Lodge HA3 176 D3
Belmont Mid Sch HA3 176 F1
Belmont Rd
Hemel Hempstead HP3 138 E8
Luton LU1 63 C7
Watford WD23 167 E4
Belmor WD6 170 A3
Belper Rd LU4 44 D2
Belsham Pl LU2 46 E2
Belsize Cl
Hemel Hempstead HP3 125 A2
St Albans AL4 128 C8
Belsize Cotts WD3 151 E6
Belsize Rd Harrow HA3 176 D3
Hemel Hempstead HP3 125 A2
Belswains Gn HP3 138 E8
Belswains La HP3 138 F7
Belswains Prim Sch
HP3 138 F7
Belton Rd HP4 122 A5
Beltona Gdns EN8 148 D4
Belvedere Gdns AL2 141 A4
Belvedere Rd LU3 45 B5
Bembridge Gdns LU3 44 F7
Ben Austins AL3 106 A4
Benbow Cl AL1 128 B1
Benchley Hill SG4 35 C8
Benchleys Rd HP1 123 F2
Bencroft EN7 148 A5
Bencroft Rd HP2 124 E3
Bencroft Wood* EN10 133 D1
Bendish La SG4 66 C7
Bendysh Rd WD23 167 E5
Benedict Ct HA5 175 F2
Benedictine Gate EN8 148 E4
Benford Rd EN11 134 F4
Bengarth Dr HA3 176 D1
Bengeo Ho SG14 92 C1
Bengeo Mdws SG14 92 C1
Bengeo Mews SG14 92 C1
Bengeo Prim Sch SG14 92 C1
Bengeo St SG14 113 C8
Benhooks Ave CM23 76 E5
Benhooks Pl 1 CM23 76 E5
Benington CE Prim Sch
SG2 52 D4
Benington Cl LU2 45 F5
Benington Lordship Gdns*
SG2 52 D4
Benington Rd Aston SG2 51 F2
Benington SG2 52 A7
Benneck Ho WD18 166 E3
Bennett Cl
Northwood HA6 174 F3
Welwyn Garden City AL7 110 F2
Bennett Ct Letchworth SG6 22 F6
Letchworth SG6 23 A5
Bennetts Cl AL4 143 D8
Bennetts End Cl HP3 124 F1
Bennetts End Rd HP3 125 A1
Bennetts La SG9 25 F4
Bennettsgate HP3 139 A8
Benningfield Cl SG12 95 D5
Benningfield Gdns HP4 122 E6
Benningfield Rd SG12 95 D4
Benskin Rd WD18 167 A4
Benslow La SG4 35 A7
Benslow Rise SG4 35 A8
Benson Cl LU3 44 F7
Benson Ct EN3 163 A1
Benstede SG2 69 C8
Bentfield Bower CM24 59 C8
Bentfield End Cswy
CM24 59 D7
Bentfield Gdns CM24 59 D7
Bentfield Gn CM24 59 D8
Bentfield Prim Sch CM24 59 D8
Bentfield Rd CM24 59 D7
Bentick Way SG4 67 F2
Bentley Cl CM23 76 F5
Bentley Ct 2 LU1 63 C8
Bentley Heath La EN5 158 F4
Bentley Lodge WD23 176 E8
Bentley Rd SG14 112 F7
Bentley Wood High Sch
HA7 176 F5
Benton Rd WD19 175 D5
Bentons The HP4 121 F6
Bentsley Cl AL4 128 C7
Berceau Wlk WD17 166 E8
Berdan Ct EN3 163 A2
Berefeld HP2 124 D5
Beresford Rd Luton LU4 45 A1
Rickmansworth WD3 164 F1
St Albans AL1 128 C2
Bericot Way AL7 111 D6
Berkeley SG6 23 A4
Berkeley Cl
Abbots Langley WD5 153 F8
Borehamwood WD6 170 A4
6 Hitchin SG5 34 D8
Potters Bar EN6 158 F7
Stevenage SG2 69 A8
Ware SG12 93 C2
Berkeley Ct
Croxley Green WD3 166 D4
6 Harpenden AL5 86 A2
Berkeley Mews AL1 128 B2
Berkeley Path 2 LU2 63 E8
Berkeley Sq HP2 105 C1
Berkhamsted Castle*
HP4 122 D5
Berkhamsted Collegiate Sch
Berkhamsted HP4 122 B4
Berkhamsted HP4 122 C4
Berkhamsted Rd HP1 123 E5
Berkhamsted Sta HP4 122 C5
Berkley Ave EN8 162 D5
Berkley Cl Pitstone LU7 80 D3
St Albans AL4 128 C7
Berkley Ct 2 HP4 122 C4
Berkley Pl EN8 162 D5
Berks Hill WD3 164 C4
Bermer Rd WD24 167 C8
Bernard Gr EN9 163 B6
Bernard St AL3 127 D4
Bernard's Heath Inf Sch
AL1 127 F5
Berners Dr AL1 141 E8
Berners Way EN10 148 F8
Bernhardt Cres SG2 51 C6
Berries The AL4 128 A7
Berrow Cl LU2 46 E2
Berry Ave WD24 154 B3
Berry Cl WD3 165 B2
Berry Grove La WD24,
WD25 154 E1
Berry La WD3 165 A2
Berry Leys LU3 44 E7
Berry Way WD3 165 B2
Berryfield LU7 79 F7
Berrygrove La WD25 168 A8
Berrymead HP2 124 F5
Berthold Mews EN9 163 B6
Bertram Ho 4 SG1 50 E6
Berwick Cl Harrow HA7 176 F4
Holdbrook EN8 163 A5
Stevenage SG1 50 A8
Berwick Rd WD6 156 F1
Besant Ho 2 WD24 167 D7
Besford Cl LU2 46 E2
Bessemer Cl SG5 21 E2
Bessemer Dr SG1 50 B4
Bessemer Rd AL7,AL8 89 E2
Bethune Cl LU1 63 B6
Bethune Ct LU1 63 B6
Betjeman Cl
Cheshunt EN7 148 A3
Harpenden AL5 86 C1
Betjeman Rd SG8 2 D1
Betjeman Way HP1 124 B4
Betony Vale SG8 7 E5
Bettespol Mdws AL3 106 A6
Betty's La HP23 100 A4
Bevan Cl HP3 124 E1
Bevan Ho 3 WD24 167 D7
Beverley Cl SG8 7 B8
Beverley Gdns
Cheshunt EN7 148 A1
St Albans AL4 128 D7
Welwyn Garden City AL7 111 C6
Beverley Rd Luton LU4 44 F1
Stevenage SG1 37 B2
Beverly Cl EN10 134 E2
Bevil Ct EN11 115 A1
Bewdley Cl AL5 107 D6
Bewley Cl EN8 162 D8

Bexhill Rd LU2 ....46 D2
Beyers Gdns EN11 ....115 A1
Beyers Prospect EN11 ....115 A1
Beyers Ride EN11 ....115 A1
Bibbs Hall La SG4,AL6 ....87 E6
Biddenham Turn WD25 ....154 C4
Bideford Gdns LU3 ....45 D4
Bideford Rd EN3 ....162 F1
Bidwell Cl SG6 ....23 B5
Biggin Hill SG9 ....28 D7
Biggin La SG5 ....34 F7
Biggs Grove Rd EN7 ....147 E4
Bignells Cnr EN6 ....158 B5
Billet La HP4 ....122 A6
Billy Lows La EN6 ....159 B8
Bilton Rd SG4 ....21 F2
Bilton Way Enfield EN3 ....162 F1
Luton LU1 ....44 F1
Bingen Rd SG5 ....21 C1
Bingham Cl HP1 ....123 F5
Bingham's Park Childrens Farm* HP1 ....123 E8
Bingley Rd EN11 ....135 C6
Binham Cl LU2 ....45 D7
Binyon Cres HA7 ....176 F5
Birch Copse AL2 ....140 E1
Birch Ct HA6 ....174 C4
Birch Dr Hatfield AL10 ....130 A4
Maple Cross WD3 ....172 D5
Birch Gn
Hemel Hempstead HP1 ....123 F5
Hertingfordbury SG14 ....112 C4
Birch Gr Oaklands AL6 ....89 E8
Potters Bar EN6 ....159 B7
Birch La HP3 ....151 B7
Birch Leys HP2 ....125 C8
Birch Link LU4 ....45 C1
Birch Pk HA3 ....176 C3
Birch Rd
Berkhamsted HP4 ....121 D7
Woolmer Green SG3 ....69 B1
Birch Tree Gr HP5 ....136 B1
Birch Tree Wlk WD17 ....153 F2
Birch Way
Harpenden AL5 ....107 C8
London Colney AL2 ....142 D4
Birch Wlk WD6 ....170 A8
Birchall La SG14 ....111 E4
Birchall Wood AL7 ....111 C5
Birchalls CM24 ....59 E8
Birchanger CE Prim Sch CM23 ....59 D2
Birchanger Ind Est CM23 ....59 B2
Birchanger La CM23 ....59 D2
Birchen Gr LU2 ....45 F3
Bircherley Ct 14 SG14 ....113 D6
Bircherley Green Ctr The 9 SG14 ....113 D6
Bircherley St SG14 ....113 D6
Birches The
Bushey WD23 ....168 C4
Codicote SG4 ....89 A8
Hemel Hempstead HP3 ....137 F8
Letchworth SG6 ....22 E8
Birchfield Rd EN8 ....148 C2
Birchmead WD17 ....153 F1
Birchmead Cl AL3 ....127 D6
Birchway AL10 ....130 B7
Birchwood
Birchanger CM23 ....59 D2
Shenley WD7 ....157 A5
Waltham Abbey EN9 ....163 E5
Birchwood Ave AL10 ....130 A7
Birchwood Avenue Prim Sch AL10 ....130 B7
Birchwood Cl AL10 ....130 A7
Birchwood High Sch CM23 ....77 C8
Birchwood Way AL2 ....141 B3
Birdcroft Rd AL8 ....110 D5
Birdie Way SG13 ....114 B7
Birds Cl AL7 ....111 B4
Birds Hill SG6 ....23 A6
Birdsfoot La LU3 ....45 B6
Birkbeck Rd EN2 ....161 D1
Birkdale Gdns WD19 ....175 D7
Birken Ct HA6 ....174 B5
Birklands AL1 ....142 B7
Birklands La AL1 ....142 B7
Birling Dr LU2 ....46 C4
Birnbeck Ct 1 EN5 ....171 D5
Birstal Gn WD19 ....175 D6
Birtley Croft LU2 ....46 E1
Biscot Rd LU3 ....45 C2
Bishop Ct WD5 ....153 F8
Bishop Ken Rd HA3 ....176 F2
Bishop Sq AL10 ....129 E5
Bishop Wood CE Jun Sch HP23 ....100 A3
Bishop's Ave CM23 ....76 F3
Bishop's Cl AL4 ....128 A7
Bishop's Garth AL4 ....128 A7
Bishop's Hatfield Girls' Sch AL10 ....130 A5
Bishop's Palace (rem of)* AL9 ....130 D6
Bishop's Stortford Bsns Ctr CM23 ....77 A6
Bishop's Stortford Coll CM23 ....76 E7
Bishop's Stortford High Sch The CM23 ....76 F4
Bishop's Stortford Sta CM23 ....77 A6
Bishop's Wood Ctry Pk* WD3 ....173 F4
Bishops Ave
Borehamwood WD6 ....169 F4
Moor Park HA6 ....174 F7
Bishops Cl Barnet EN5 ....171 D3
Hatfield AL10 ....129 F5
Bishops Ct Cheshunt EN8 ....148 B1
6 Luton LU3 ....45 D1
Bishops Field HP22 ....99 A4
Bishops Mead HP1 ....124 B1
Bishops Park Way CM23 ....76 B7
Bishops Rd AL6 ....90 E6
Bishops Rise AL10 ....129 F2
Bishops Wood Hospl HA6 ....174 B4
Bishopscote Rd LU3 ....45 B3
Biskra WD17 ....167 A8
Bisley Cl EN8 ....162 D6
Bit The HP23 ....100 D1
Bittern Cl
Hammond Street EN7 ....147 C6
Hemel Hempstead HP3 ....138 F6
Stevenage SG2 ....51 D2
Bittern Way SG6 ....11 E1
Black Boy Wood AL2 ....141 A1
Black Cut AL1 ....127 E2
Black Fan Rd
Welwyn Garden City AL7 ....110 F7
Welwyn Garden City AL7 ....111 B6
Black Green Wood Cl AL2 ....141 B2
Black Lion Ct CM17 ....118 C4
Black Lion Hill WD7 ....156 F7
Black Smiths Cl SG12 ....115 A7
Black Swan Ct 1 SG12 ....93 D1
Black Swan La LU3 ....45 A5
Blackadder Cotts EN9 ....149 D8
Blackberry Mead SG2 ....51 D3
Blackbirds La WD25 ....155 C5
Blackbury Cl EN6 ....159 C8
Blackbush Spring CM20 ....118 A1
Blackbushe CM23 ....59 C1
Blackdale EN7 ....148 A4
Blackdown Cl SG1 ....37 B3
Blacketts Wood Dr WD3 ....164 B5
Blackford Rd WD19 ....175 D5
Blackhorse Cl SG4 ....35 A5
Blackhorse La Hitchin SG4 ....35 A5
Redbourn AL3 ....106 A6
Ridge EN6 ....157 F8
Blackhorse Rd SG6 ....23 C8
Blackley Cl WD17 ....153 F2
Blackmoor La WD18 ....166 D4
Blackmore SG6 ....23 B3
Blackmore Gate HP22 ....99 A4
Blackmore Manor AL4 ....87 B6
Blackmore Way AL4 ....87 B6
Blacksmith Cl SG5 ....11 F7
Blacksmith's La
Reed SG8 ....16 D5
St Albans AL3 ....127 B3
Blacksmiths Cl CM23 ....76 B5
Blacksmiths Hill SG2 ....52 E4
Blacksmiths Way CM21 ....97 B1
Blackthorn Cl
St Albans AL4 ....128 C6
Watford WD25 ....154 B7
Blackthorn Dr LU2 ....46 C4
Blackthorn Rd AL7 ....111 A5
Blackthorne Cl AL10 ....129 F2
Blackwater La HP3 ....125 E1
Blackwell Cl HA3 ....176 D3
Blackwell Dr WD19 ....167 C3
Blackwell Hall La HP5 ....150 C6
Blackwell Rd WD4 ....139 A2
Blackwood Ct EN7 ....148 F5
Bladon Cl SG4 ....35 F3
Blaine Cl HP23 ....100 A6
Blair Cl
Bishop's Stortford CM23 ....76 C7
Hemel Hempstead HP2 ....105 B1
Stevenage SG2 ....50 F1
Blairhead Dr WD19 ....175 B7
Blake Cl Royston SG8 ....2 D1
St Albans AL1 ....142 A8
Blakedown LU2 ....45 E1
Blakemere Rd AL8 ....110 D8
Blakemore End Rd SG4 ....35 D3
Blakeney Dr LU2 ....45 C7
Blakeney Ho SG1 ....50 A7
Blakeney Rd SG1 ....50 A7
Blakes Ct
Rickmansworth WD3 ....165 C1
Sawbridgeworth CM21 ....97 E2
Blakes Way AL6 ....89 C6
Blanchard Gr EN3 ....163 B1
Blanche La EN6 ....157 F5
Blandford Ave LU2 ....45 D6
Blandford Rd AL1 ....128 A3
Blanes The SG12 ....93 C3
Blattner Cl WD6 ....169 E5
Blaxland Terr 9 EN8 ....148 D3
Blaydon Rd LU2 ....64 A8
Blegberry Gdns HP4 ....121 E4
Blenheim Cl
Cheddington LU7 ....79 F8
Sawbridgeworth CM21 ....118 C8
Watford WD19 ....167 D2
Blenheim Cres LU3 ....45 C2
Blenheim Ct
Bishop's Stortford CM23 ....76 C7
Welwyn Garden City AL7 ....110 F7
Blenheim Rd Barnet EN5 ....171 D5
St Albans AL1 ....127 F4
Blenheim Way SG2 ....69 D7
Blenhiem Rd WD5 ....154 A7
Blenkin Cl AL3 ....127 C7
Blind La SG2,SG9 ....38 F5
Blindman's La EN8 ....148 D2
Block 10 4 WD17 ....167 A8
Block 12 3 WD17 ....167 A8
Block 14 2 WD17 ....167 A8
Bloomfield Ave LU2 ....46 A1
Bloomfield Ho 6 SG1 ....50 E6
Bloomfield Rd
Hammond Street EN7 ....147 C6
Harpenden AL5 ....85 F3
Blossom La EN2 ....161 C1
Blue Bridge Rd AL9 ....144 E4
Bluebell Cl
Hemel Hempstead HP1 ....123 E2
Hertford SG13 ....114 A6
Bluebell Dr
Bedmond WD5 ....139 F4
Goff's Oak EN7 ....147 D3
Bluebell Way AL10 ....109 F1
Bluebell Wood Cl LU1 ....63 A7
Bluebells AL6 ....89 D7
Blueberry Cl AL3 ....127 D7
Bluebird Way AL2 ....140 E1
Bluebridge Ave AL9 ....144 F4
Bluecoat Yd SG12 ....93 D1
Bluecoats Ave SG14 ....113 D6
Bluecoats Ct 18 SG14 ....113 D6
Bluehouse Hill AL3 ....127 A3
Bluett Rd AL2 ....142 D4
Blundell Cl AL3 ....127 D7
Blundell Rd LU3 ....45 A4
Blunesfield EN6 ....159 D8
Blunts La AL2 ....140 D5
Blyth Cl
Borehamwood WD6 ....170 A8
Stevenage SG1 ....50 A7
Blyth Pl 13 LU1 ....63 D6
Blythe Rd EN11 ....135 D5
Blythway AL7 ....89 F1
Blythway Ho AL7 ....89 F1
Blythwood Gdns CM24 ....59 D6
Blythwood Rd HA5 ....175 D2
Boardman Cl EN5 ....171 E4
Bockings SG2 ....38 C1
Bodmin Rd LU4 ....44 F3
Bodwell Cl HP1 ....124 A4
Bogmoor Rd SG8 ....18 A8
Bognor Gdns WD19 ....175 C5
Bohemia HP2 ....124 E4
Boissy Cl AL4 ....128 E2
Boleyn Cl HP2 ....125 C8
Boleyn Ct EN10 ....134 E2
Boleyn Dr AL1 ....127 D1
Boling Brook AL4 ....128 A7
Bolingbroke Rd LU1 ....63 B6
Bolney Gn LU2 ....46 D3
Bolton Rd LU1 ....63 F7
Boltons Park (Royal Veterinary Coll) EN6 ....145 A2
Bond Ct AL5 ....85 F3
Bondor Bsns Ctr SG7 ....23 F7
Boniface Gdns HA3 ....176 B3
Boniface Wlk HA3 ....176 B3
Bonks Hill CM21 ....97 D1
Bonney Gr EN7 ....148 A1
Bonneygrove Prim Sch EN7 ....148 A1
Bonnick Cl LU1 ....63 C6
Booths Cl AL9 ....144 D7
Boreham Holt WD6 ....169 F5
Borehamwood Ent Ctr WD6 ....169 F6
Borehamwood Ind Pk WD6 ....170 D7
Bornedene EN6 ....158 E8
Borodale AL5 ....86 A1
Borough Way EN6 ....158 E7
Borrell Cl EN10 ....134 F3
Borrowdale Ct 4 HP2 ....124 E6
Borton Ave SG16 ....10 B4
Bosanquet Rd EN11 ....135 C8
Boscombe Ct SG6 ....23 B6
Bosmore Rd LU3 ....44 F5
Boswell Cl WD7 ....156 E7
Boswell Dr SG5 ....21 E4
Boswell Gdns SG1 ....36 D1
Boswick La HP4 ....121 D8
Botley La HP5 ....136 A1
Botley Rd Botley HP5 ....136 A1
Hemel Hempstead HP2 ....125 B8
Bottom House La HP23 ....101 A1
Bottom La WD3,WD4 ....152 C4
Bottom Rd HP23 ....119 F3
Bough Beech Ct EN3 ....162 D2
Boughton Way HP6 ....150 C1
Boulevard Ctr The WD6 ....170 A6
Boulevard The
Watford WD18 ....166 D4
Welwyn Garden City AL7 ....110 F8
Boulton Rd SG1 ....37 C2
Bounce The HP2 ....124 D5
Boundary Cl EN5 ....171 F8
Boundary Cotts HP3 ....137 D2
Boundary Ct AL7 ....110 F2
Boundary Dr SG14 ....113 D8
Boundary Ho
Cheshunt EN8 ....162 D7
Welwyn Garden City AL7 ....110 D3
Boundary La AL7 ....110 E2
Boundary Pk HP2 ....125 C5
Boundary Rd
Bishop's Stortford CM23 ....77 A5
St Albans AL1 ....127 E5
Boundary Way
Hemel Hempstead HP2 ....125 C5
Watford WD25 ....154 C7
Bounds Field SG11 ....75 F8
Bourne Apartments The 2 AL5 ....85 F2
Bourne Cl
Hoddesdon EN10 ....134 F3
Ware SG12 ....93 D2
Bourne End Cotts HP1 ....123 C1
Bourne End Rd HA6 ....174 E6
Bourne Hall WD23 ....168 A3
Bourne Honour SG12 ....92 E7
Bourne La SG10 ....96 A6
Bourne Rd
Berkhamsted HP4 ....121 F5
Bushey WD23 ....168 A4
Bourne The
Bishop's Stortford CM23 ....77 A8
Bovingdon HP3 ....137 A4
Clapgate SG11 ....57 C6
3 Harpenden AL5 ....85 F2
Ware SG12 ....93 D2
Bournehall Ave WD23 ....168 A4
Bournehall La WD23 ....168 A4
Bournehall Prim Sch WD23 ....168 B4
Bournehall Rd WD23 ....168 A3
Bournemouth Rd 3 SG1 ....50 B8
Bouvier Rd EN3 ....162 C1
Bovingdon Cres WD25 ....154 D5
Bovingdon Ct HP3 ....137 A3
Bovingdon Prim Sch HP3 ....137 B4
Bowbrookvale LU2 ....46 F1
Bowcock Wlk SG1 ....50 E3
Bower Heath La AL5 ....86 C6
Bower's Par AL5 ....86 A1
Bowers Way AL5 ....86 A1
Bowershott SG6 ....23 A4
Bowes Lyon Mews AL3 ....127 D3
Bowgate AL1 ....127 E4
Bowlers Mead SG9 ....40 D7
Bowles Gn EN1 ....162 B3
Bowling Cl
14 Bishop's Stortford CM23 ....76 F6
Harpenden AL5 ....107 C7
Bowling Ct WD18 ....167 A5
Bowling Gn SG1 ....50 C8
Bowling Green La
Buntingford SG9 ....40 D8
Luton LU2 ....45 E2
Bowling Rd SG12 ....93 E1
Bowman Trad Est SG1 ....50 B5
Bowmans Ave SG4 ....35 B6
Bowmans Cl
Potters Bar EN6 ....159 D7
Welwyn AL6 ....89 C6
Bowmans Ct HP2 ....124 E5
Bowmans Gn WD25 ....154 E3
Bowmansgreen Prim Sch AL2 ....142 C4
Bowring Gn WD19 ....175 C5
Bowyer Ct EN8 ....162 F6
Bowyer's Cl SG5 ....21 D1
Bowyers 6 HP2 ....124 D5
Box La
Hemel Hempstead HP3 ....137 E7
Hoddesdon EN11 ....134 E6
Boxberry Cl SG1 ....50 E6
Boxfield AL7 ....111 B3
Boxfield Gn SG2 ....51 D8
Boxgrove Cl LU2 ....46 C5
Boxhill 3 HP2 ....124 D5
Boxmoor House Sch HP3 ....137 F8
Boxmoor Prim Sch HP1 ....124 A2
Boxted Cl LU4 ....44 C5
Boxted Rd HP1 ....123 F5
Boxtree La HA3 ....176 D3
Boxtree Rd HA3 ....176 D3
Boxwell Rd HP4 ....122 B4
Boyce Cl WD6 ....169 E8
Boyd Cl 1 CM23 ....77 B8
Boyes Cres AL2 ....142 B5
Boyle Cl LU2 ....63 E8
Brace Cl EN7 ....147 B6
Braceby Cl LU3 ....44 F6
Braceys SG2 ....52 F2
Brache Cl AL3 ....106 A5
Brache Ct LU1 ....63 F6
Bracken Cl WD6 ....170 B8
Bracken La AL6 ....89 F7
Brackendale EN6 ....159 A6
Brackendale Gr
Harpenden AL5 ....85 D3
Luton LU3 ....45 B5
Brackendene AL2 ....140 F1
Brackenhill HP4 ....122 F5
Brackens The HP2 ....124 D4
Bracklesham Gdns LU2 ....46 D3
Bracknell Pl HP2 ....124 F7
Bradbery WD3 ....172 D5
Bradbury Cl WD6 ....170 B8
Bradcot Cotts SG2 ....39 C2
Bradden Cotts HP2 ....103 F8
Bradden La HP1,HP2 ....103 E7
Bradden Villas HP2 ....103 F8
Braddon Ct 18 EN5 ....171 E6
Bradford Rd WD3 ....164 C2
Bradgate EN6 ....146 D4
Bradgate Cl EN6 ....146 D3
Bradgers Hill Rd LU2 ....45 E4
Bradley Comm CM23 ....59 C3
Bradley Rd Enfield EN3 ....162 E2
Luton LU4 ....44 D1
Waltham Abbey EN9 ....163 C4
Bradleys Cnr SG4 ....35 C8
Bradman Way SG1 ....37 A1
Bradmore Gn AL9 ....144 E5
Bradmore La AL9 ....144 C5
Bradmore Way AL9 ....144 E5
Bradshaw Rd WD24 ....154 C1
Bradshaws AL10 ....129 F1
Bradway SG4 ....66 E6
Braemar Cl SG2 ....69 B7
Braemar Ct WD23 ....168 A3
Braemar Turn HP2 ....105 B1
Braeside Cl HA5 ....176 A3
Bragbury Cl SG2 ....69 D7
Bragbury La SG2,SG3 ....69 D5
Bragmans La WD3 ....151 E6
Braham Ct 2 SG5 ....34 E7
Brain Cl AL10 ....130 B6
Braithwaite Ct 16 LU3 ....45 D1
Brakynbery HP4 ....121 E7
Bramble Cl Harpenden AL5 ....85 F3
Luton LU4 ....44 C4
Watford WD25 ....154 A5
Bramble Rd
Hatfield AL10 ....129 D5
Luton LU4 ....44 C4
Bramble Rise CM20 ....117 C1
Brambles The
Bishop's Stortford CM23 ....76 C6
Cheshunt EN8 ....162 D8
Oaklands AL6 ....89 E8
Royston SG8 ....7 E5
St Albans AL1 ....127 D1
Stevenage SG1 ....36 D2
Ware SG12 ....93 C3
Brambling Cl WD23 ....167 E5
Brambling Rise HP2 ....124 E6
Bramfield Hitchin SG4 ....35 B6
Watford WD25 ....154 E5
Bramfield Ct SG14 ....113 A7
Bramfield La SG14 ....91 F3
Bramfield Pl HP2 ....105 A1
Bramfield Rd
Datchworth SG3 ....90 E8
Hertford SG14 ....112 F8
Bramham Ct HA6 ....174 E4
Bramhanger Acre LU3 ....44 D7
Bramingham Bsns Pk LU3 ....45 B8
Bramingham Prim Sch LU3 ....45 B8
Bramingham Rd LU3 ....44 F6
Bramleas WD18 ....166 F5
Bramley Cl SG7 ....12 F1
Bramley Ct WD25 ....154 B8
Bramley Gdns WD19 ....175 C5
Bramley House Ct EN2 ....161 D2
Bramley Shaw EN9 ....163 F6
Bramley Way AL4 ....128 C2
Brampton Cl
Cheshunt EN7 ....148 A3
Harpenden AL5 ....86 D1
Brampton Park Rd SG5 ....21 E1
Brampton Rd Royston SG8 ....7 F6
South Oxhey WD19 ....175 A7
St Albans AL1 ....128 A4
Brampton Terr WD6 ....157 A1
Bramshaw Gdns WD19 ....175 D5
Bramshot Way WD19 ....175 A8
Bramshott Cl SG4 ....34 F5
Branch Cl AL10 ....130 C7
Branch Rd
Park Street AL2 ....141 D4
St Albans AL3 ....127 B4
Brand St SG5 ....34 E7
Brandles Rd SG6 ....23 A3
Brandles Sch SG7 ....23 E7
Brandon Cl EN7 ....147 F5
Brandon Ct HP23 ....78 D7
Brandon Mobile Home Pk AL4 ....128 D2
Branksome Cl HP2 ....125 A4
Branscombe Ho WD24 ....154 A2
Branton Cl LU2 ....46 E2
Brantwood Rd LU1 ....63 C7
Brawlings La SL9 ....172 A6
Bray Cl WD6 ....170 C8
Bray Dr SG1 ....37 A3
Bray Lodge 2 EN8 ....148 E3
Brayes Manor SG5 ....11 F6
Brays Ct LU2 ....46 B3
Brays Rd LU2 ....46 B3
Braziers End HP5 ....120 C1
Braziers Field SG13 ....113 F6
Braziers Quay CM23 ....77 A6
Breach Barns La EN9 ....149 F1
Breachwood Green Jun Mix Inf Sch SG4 ....47 E1
Bread & Cheese La EN7 ....147 D6
Breadcroft La AL5 ....86 B1
Breakmead AL7 ....111 B4
Breaks Rd AL10 ....130 B6
Breakspear SG2 ....51 C3
Breakspear Ave AL1 ....127 F2
Breakspear Coll WD5 ....139 F1
Breakspear Ct WD5 ....139 F1
Breakspear Rd N UB9 ....173 D1
Breakspear Way HP2 ....125 C4
Breakspeare Cl WD24 ....154 B1
Breakspeare Rd WD5 ....153 E8
Breakspeare Sch WD5 ....153 E8
Brecken Cl AL4 ....128 A7
Brecon Cl 14 LU1 ....63 D6
Breeze Terr 5 EN8 ....148 D3
Bren Ct EN3 ....163 A2
Brendon Ave LU2 ....46 C1
Brent Ct SG1 ....50 E5
Brent Pl EN5 ....171 F4
Brett Pl WD24 ....154 A2
Brett Rd EN5 ....171 C4
Bretts Mead LU1 ....63 C5
Bretts Mead Ct LU1 ....63 C5
Brewers Cl CM23 ....76 C5
Brewery Cotts SG7 ....12 E1

Brewery La Baldock SG7 ...23 E8
Stansted Mountfitchet
CM24 ...59 E7
Brewery Rd EN11 ...135 A6
Brewery Yd CM24 ...59 F7
Brewhouse Hill AL4 ...108 C8
Brewhouse La SG14 ...113 C6
Briants Cl HA5 ...175 F1
Briar Cl Cheshunt EN8 ...148 C2
Luton LU2 ...46 C4
Potten End HP4 ...123 A7
Briar Patch La SG6 ...22 D3
Briar Rd St Albans AL4 ...128 D6
Watford WD25 ...154 B4
Briar Way HP4 ...122 D3
Briarcliff HP1 ...123 E4
Briardale Stevenage SG1 ...50 E4
Ware SG12 ...93 C3
Briarley Cl EN10 ...134 F1
Briars Cl AL10 ...130 A5
Briars La AL10 ...130 A5
Briars The Bushey WD23 ...168 E2
Cheshunt EN8 ...162 E8
Hertford SG13 ...114 A6
Sarratt WD3 ...152 A3
Briars Wood AL10 ...130 A5
Briarswood EN7 ...147 E3
Briarwood Dr HA6 ...175 A1
Briary La SG8 ...7 C5
Briary Wood End AL6 ...89 F8
Briary Wood La AL6 ...89 F8
Brick Cotts SG9 ...27 D8
Brick Kiln Cl WD19 ...167 E3
Brick Kiln La SG4 ...34 E5
Brick Kiln Rd SG1 ...50 C6
Brick Knoll Pk AL1 ...128 C2
Brickcroft EN10 ...148 E5
Brickenden Ct EN9 ...163 F6
Brickendon Ct EN11 ...135 A5
Brickendon La SG13 ...133 D6
Bricket Rd AL1 ...127 D3
Bricket Wood Sta AL2 ...141 A1
Brickfield AL10 ...130 A2
Brickfield Ave HP3 ...125 B2
Brickfield Cotts WD6 ...169 F6
Brickfield Ct AL10 ...130 B2
Brickfield La EN5 ...170 F3
Brickfields Ind Est HP2 ...125 B7
Brickfields The SG12 ...93 B2
Brickly Rd LU4 ...44 C5
Brickmakers La HP3 ...125 B2
Brickwall Cl AL6 ...110 A8
Brickyard La SG8 ...16 E5
Bride Hall La AL6 ...88 A5
Bridewell Cl SG9 ...40 E8
Bridge Ct
1 Berkhamsted HP4 ...122 D4
Harpenden AL5 ...85 F3
Radlett WD7 ...156 B4
Bridge End SG9 ...40 E8
Bridge Foot SG12 ...93 D1
Bridge Pk AL7 ...110 E7
Bridge Pl WD17 ...167 D4
Bridge Rd
Abbots Langley WD4 ...153 C6
Letchworth SG6 ...22 F6
Stevenage SG1 ...50 C7
Welwyn Garden City AL8 ...110 C7
Woolmer Green SG3 ...69 A2
Bridge Rd E AL7 ...110 F6
Bridge Rd W SG1 ...50 B7
Bridge St
Berkhamsted HP4 ...122 D4
Bishop's Stortford CM23 ...76 F7
Hemel Hempstead HP1 ...124 C2
Hitchin SG5 ...34 E6
Kneesworth SG8 ...2 B8
Luton LU1 ...63 E8
Bridgefields AL7 ...110 F7
Bridgefoot SG9 ...40 E7
Bridgefoot Cotts AL2 ...155 F8
Bridgefoot La EN6 ...158 D6
Bridgeford Ho
13 Bishop's Stortford CM23 ...76 F6
5 Watford WD18 ...167 B6
Bridgegate Bsns Ctr
AL7 ...110 F7
Bridgend Rd EN1 ...162 C4
Bridgenhall Rd EN1 ...161 F1
Bridger Cl WD25 ...154 E6
Bridges Ct SG14 ...113 C6
Bridges Rd HA7 ...176 F5
Bridgewater Ct HP4 ...102 C8
Bridgewater Hill HP4 ...121 F7
Bridgewater Mid Sch
HP4 ...122 A6
Bridgewater Monument
The* HP4 ...101 E7
Bridgewater Rd HP4 ...122 B5
Bridgewater Way WD23 ...168 B3
Bridgeways EN11 ...135 B5
Bridle Cl Enfield EN3 ...162 F2
Hoddesdon EN11 ...115 A2
St Albans AL3 ...127 E5
Bridle La WD3 ...165 D6
Bridle Path WD17 ...167 B7
Bridle Way
Berkhamsted HP4 ...122 A6
Great Amwell SG12 ...115 A6
Hoddesdon EN11 ...115 A1
Bridle Way (N) EN11 ...115 B2
Bridle Way (S) EN11 ...115 A1
Bridleway HP23 ...119 E5
Bridlington Rd WD19 ...175 D7
Brierley Cl LU2 ...46 D2
Briery Ct WD3 ...165 A5
Briery Field WD3 ...165 A5
Briery Way HP2 ...125 A4
Brigadier Ave EN2 ...161 C1
Brigadier Hill EN2 ...161 C1
Brightman Cotts 2 LU3 ...45 A7
Brighton Rd WD24 ...154 A1
Brighton Way SG1 ...50 A8
Brightview Cl AL2 ...140 E2
Brightwell Ct WD18 ...167 A4
Brightwell Rd WD18 ...167 A4
Brill Cl LU2 ...46 D2
Brimfield Cl LU2 ...46 D2
Brimsdown Ave EN3 ...162 E1
Brimstone Way HP4 ...121 F6
Brindley Way HP3 ...138 F6
Brinklow Ct AL3 ...141 B8
Brinley Cl EN8 ...162 D8
Brinsley Rd HA3 ...176 D1
Brinsmead AL2 ...141 E4
Briscoe Cl EN11 ...134 F8
Briscoe Rd EN11 ...134 F8
Bristol Ho 16 WD6 ...170 A7
Bristol Rd LU3 ...45 B4
Britannia SG11 ...55 E2
Britannia Ave LU3 ...45 B4
Britannia Bsns Pk EN8 ...162 F5
Britannia Ests LU3,LU4 ...45 B2
Britannia Hall LU2 ...64 C8
Britannia Pl 3 CM23 ...76 E5
Britannia Rd EN8 ...162 F5
Brittain Way SG2 ...51 B4
Britten Cl WD6 ...169 D3
Britton Ave AL3 ...127 D3
Britwell Dr HP4 ...122 E6
Brixham Cl SG1 ...50 B7
Brixton Rd WD24 ...167 B8
Broad Acre AL2 ...140 E1
Broad Acres AL10 ...129 F8
Broad Baulk SG9 ...40 D8
Broad Ct AL7 ...110 E6
Broad Gn SG13 ...132 F8
Broad Green Wood
SG13 ...133 A8
Broad Mead LU3 ...45 A3
Broad Oak Ct LU2 ...46 D3
Broad Oak Way SG2 ...50 F1
Broad St HP2 ...124 D4
Broad Wlk CM20 ...117 D1
Broadacres LU2 ...45 D6
Broadcroft
2 Hemel Hempstead HP2 ...124 D5
Letchworth SG6 ...22 F2
Broadfield
Bishop's Stortford CM23 ...58 F2
Harlow CM20 ...117 E1
Broadfield Cl SG10 ...74 E1
Broadfield Ct WD23 ...176 E8
Broadfield Inf Sch HP2 ...124 F3
Broadfield Jun Sch HP2 ...124 F3
Broadfield Pl AL8 ...110 B5
Broadfield Rd
Hemel Hempstead HP2 ...124 F3
Woolmer Green SG3 ...69 B1
Broadfield Way SG10 ...74 F1
Broadfields
Goff's Oak EN7 ...147 B2
Harpenden AL5 ...85 F2
Harrow HA2 ...176 B1
High Wych CM21 ...97 B1
Broadfields La WD19 ...167 B1
Broadfields Prim Sch
CM20 ...117 E1
Broadgate EN9 ...163 F7
Broadgreen Rd EN7 ...147 D5
Broadhall Way SG2 ...51 B2
Broadlake Cl AL2 ...142 D4
Broadlands WD7 ...156 B4
Broadlands Cl EN8 ...162 D5
Broadlawns Ct HA3 ...176 F2
Broadleaf Ave CM23 ...76 D4
Broadleaf Gr AL8 ...89 B1
Broadley Gdns WD7 ...156 E7
Broadmead SG4 ...35 B5
Broadmead Cl HA5 ...175 E3
Broadmead Ind Sch LU1 ...63 E5
Broadmeadow Ride SG4 ...35 A4
Broadmeads SG12 ...93 D1
Broadoak Ave EN3 ...162 D4
Broadstone Rd AL5 ...107 D7
Broadview SG1 ...50 E6
Broadview Ho EN3 ...162 F3
Broadwalk The HA6 ...174 C1
Broadwater
Berkhamsted HP4 ...122 C5
Potters Bar EN6 ...145 B1
Broadwater Ave SG6 ...22 E5
Broadwater Cres
Stevenage SG2 ...69 C8
Welwyn Garden City AL7 ...110 D5
Broadwater Dale SG6 ...22 E5
Broadwater La SG2 ...51 D1
Broadwater Rd AL7 ...110 E6
Broadway SG6 ...22 F5
Broadway Ave CM17 ...118 B4
Broadway Ct SG6 ...22 E3
Broadway The
Harrow HA3 ...176 F1
Hatfield AL9 ...130 C6
Kimpton AL4 ...87 B5
Pinner HA5 ...175 F3
Watford WD17 ...167 C6
Brocket Cnr AL8 ...109 F4
Brocket Ct
Hoddesdon EN11 ...135 A6
Luton LU4 ...44 D5
Brocket Rd Hatfield AL8 ...110 A3
Hoddesdon EN11 ...135 A6
Brocket View AL4 ...108 D8
Brockett Cl AL8 ...110 B6
Brockhurst Cl HA7 ...176 F4
Brocklesbury Cl WD24 ...167 D7
Brockley Hill HA7 ...169 C1
Brockley Hill Ho HA7 ...169 C1
Brockswood La AL8 ...110 B7
Brockswood Prim Sch
HP2 ...105 C1
Brockwell Shott SG2 ...38 B1
Brodewater Rd WD6 ...170 B7
Brodie Rd EN2 ...161 C1
Broken Green Cotts
SG11 ...56 C2
Bromborough Gn WD19 ...175 C5
Bromet Cl WD17 ...153 F1
Bromet Sch WD19 ...167 D2
Bromleigh Cl EN8 ...148 E3
Bromley HP23 ...79 A4
Bromley La SG10,SG11 ...74 D6
Brompton Cl LU3 ...44 F8
Brompton Gdns LU3 ...44 F8
Bronte Cres HP2 ...105 B1
Bronte Paths SG2 ...51 C6
Brook Bank EN1 ...162 B2
Brook Cl WD6 ...170 B7
Brook Cotts CM24 ...59 E5
Brook Ct LU3 ...45 D1
Brook Dr Radlett WD7 ...155 F6
Stevenage SG2 ...69 B8
Brook End CM21 ...97 D2
Brook Field SG2 ...51 E2
Brook Ho WD23 ...168 C1
Brook La
Berkhamsted HP4 ...122 B5
Sawbridgeworth CM21 ...97 D2
Brook Rd
Borehamwood WD6 ...170 A7
Cheshunt EN8 ...162 F5
Sawbridgeworth CM21 ...97 E1
Stansted Mountfitchet
CM24 ...59 E6
Brook St Luton LU3 ...63 D8
Stotfold SG5 ...11 E6
Tring HP23 ...100 B4
Brook View Hitchin SG4 ...35 C6
Stansted Mountfitchet
CM24 ...59 E5
Brookbridge La SG3 ...69 D2
Brookdene Ave WD19 ...167 C1
Brookdene Dr HA6 ...174 F4
Brooke Cl WD23 ...168 C2
Brooke End AL3 ...106 A4
Brooke Gdns CM23 ...77 C7
Brooke Rd SG8 ...7 D8
Brooke Way WD23 ...168 C2
Brooker Rd EN9 ...163 C5
Brookfield Cl HP23 ...100 B4
Brookfield Ct 14 EN8 ...148 D3
Brookfield Ctr EN8 ...148 D4
Brookfield Gdns EN8 ...148 D4
Brookfield La SG2 ...51 F3
Brookfield La E EN8 ...148 D3
Brookfield La W EN8 ...148 C4
Brookfield Ret Pk EN8 ...148 D5
Brookfields CM21 ...97 D2
Brookhill SG2 ...68 F8
Brookhouse Pl 3 CM23 ...76 F8
Brookland Inf Sch EN8 ...148 E3
Brookland Jun Sch EN8 ...148 E3
Brooklands Cl LU4 ...44 C6
Brooklands Ct AL1 ...127 E3
Brooklands Gdns EN6 ...158 E7
Brookmans Ave AL9 ...144 F5
Brookmans Park Prim Sch
AL9 ...144 E5
Brookmans Park Sta
AL9 ...144 E5
Brookmead Sch LU7 ...80 E5
Brookmill Cl WD19 ...167 B2
Brooks Ct SG14 ...112 F7
Brooksfield AL7 ...111 B7
Brookshill HA3 ...176 D5
Brookshill Ave HA3 ...176 E5
Brookshill Dr HA3 ...176 D5
Brookside Buckland SG9 ...27 D5
Furneux Pelham SG9 ...43 B4
Hatfield AL10 ...129 D5
Hertford SG13 ...113 E5
Hoddesdon EN11 ...135 A6
Letchworth SG6 ...22 F5
South Mimms EN6 ...158 A7
Waltham Abbey EN9 ...163 E7
Watford WD24 ...154 D3
Brookside Cl EN5 ...171 E3
Brookside Cotts WD4 ...153 C5
Brookside Cres EN6 ...146 E4
Brookside Gdns EN1 ...162 C2
Brookside Rd WD19 ...167 B2
Broom Barns Jun Mix Inf Sch
SG1 ...50 E5
Broom Cl
Hammond Street EN7 ...148 A4
Hatfield AL10 ...129 F2
Broom Cnr AL5 ...107 C8
Broom Gr Knebworth SG3 ...68 F5
Watford WD17 ...154 A1
Broom Hill
Hemel Hempstead HP1 ...123 E2
Welwyn AL6 ...90 A8
Broom Wlk SG1 ...50 E5
Broomer Pl EN8 ...148 C2
Broomfield
Chiswell Green AL2 ...141 C4
Harlow CM20 ...118 B3
Broomfield Ave EN10 ...148 E5
Broomfield Cl AL6 ...89 C4
Broomfield Ct 2 AL10 ...130 A6
Broomfield Rd AL6 ...89 C4
Broomfield Rise WD5 ...153 D7
Broomhills AL7 ...111 B7
Broomleys AL4 ...128 D6
Brooms Cl AL8 ...89 D1
Brooms Rd LU2 ...64 A8
Broomstick Hall Rd
EN9 ...163 E6
Broomstick La HP5 ...136 A1
Broughinge Rd WD6 ...170 B7
Broughton Ave LU3 ...45 C5
Broughton Hill SG6 ...23 B6
Broughton Way WD3 ...165 A2
Brow The WD25 ...154 B6
Brown's Cl LU4 ...44 D5
Brown's Cnr SG9 ...27 F3
Brown's La HP23 ...119 F7
Brown's Rise HP23 ...119 F3
Brownfield Way AL4 ...87 B6
Brownfields AL7 ...110 F7
Brownfields Ct AL7 ...111 A7
Browning Dr SG4 ...35 B8
Browning Rd Enfield EN2 ...161 D1
Harpenden AL5 ...86 C2
Luton LU4 ...44 A2
Brownings La SG4 ...47 D1
Brownlow Gate HP4 ...81 B1
Brownlow La LU7 ...80 A7
Brownlow Rd
Berkhamsted HP4 ...122 C5
Borehamwood WD6 ...170 A5
Browns Hedge LU7 ...80 C3
Browns Spring HP4 ...123 C7
Brownsea Ho 12 WD18 ...166 F3
Brox Dell SG1 ...50 E6
Broxbourne CE Prim Sch
EN10 ...134 F2
Broxbourne Sch The
EN10 ...134 E1
Broxbourne Sta EN10 ...135 A3
Broxbournebury Mews
EN10 ...134 C3
Broxley Mead LU4 ...44 D5
Bruce Gr WD24 ...154 C1
Bruce Rd 9 Barnet EN5 ...171 E6
Harrow HA3 ...176 E1
Bruce Way EN8 ...162 D6
Brunel Rd SG2 ...51 B7
Brunswick Ct EN11 ...135 A5
Brunswick Rd EN3 ...163 A1
Brunswick St LU2 ...63 F8
Brushrise WD24 ...154 A3
Brushwood Dr WD3 ...164 C5
Brussels Way LU3 ...44 D8
Bryan Rd CM23 ...76 F8
Bryanstone Rd EN8 ...162 F5
Bryant Cl EN5 ...171 F4
Bryant Ct AL5 ...86 A3
Bryce Cl SG12 ...93 D3
Bryfield Cotts HP3 ...137 C1
Bsns Ctr E SG6 ...23 C6
Bsns Ctr The LU2 ...64 B6
Bsns Ctr W SG6 ...23 C6
Buchanan Ct
Borehamwood WD6 ...170 C7
Luton LU2 ...64 B8
Buchanan Dr LU2 ...64 B8
Buckettsland La WD6 ...157 D2
Buckingham Dr LU2 ...46 D2
Buckingham Rd
Borehamwood WD6 ...170 D5
Tring HP23 ...99 E3
Watford WD24 ...154 C2
Buckinghamshire Chilterns
Unvi Coll (Chalfont Campus)
HP8 ...172 A8
Buckland Rd HP22 ...99 A4
Buckland Rise HA5 ...175 D2
Bucklands Croft HP23 ...99 C8
Bucklands The WD3 ...165 A2
Buckle Cl LU3 ...44 F7
Bucklers Cl EN10 ...134 F1
Bucklersbury SG5 ...34 E6
Bucknalls Cl WD25 ...154 E7
Bucknalls Dr AL2 ...154 F8
Bucknalls La WD25 ...154 E7
Bucks Alley SG13 ...132 D4
Bucks Ave WD19 ...167 E2
Bucks Hill WD4 ...152 C5
Buckthorn Ave SG1 ...50 E4
Buckton Rd WD6 ...156 F1
Buckwood La LU6 ...82 C7
Buckwood Rd AL3 ...83 C6
Buddcroft AL7 ...111 B7
Bude Cres SG1 ...50 A7
Bulbourne Cl
Berkhamsted HP4 ...121 F6
Hemel Hempstead HP1 ...124 A2
Bulbourne Ct HP23 ...100 A7
Bulbourne Rd HP23 ...100 B7
Bull La Buckland SG9 ...27 C8
Cottered SG9 ...39 C8
Wheathampstead AL4 ...108 A6
Bull Plain SG14 ...113 D6
Bull Rd AL5 ...107 B8
Bull Stag Gn AL9 ...130 C7
Bull's Cross EN2 ...162 A3
Bullace Cl HP1 ...124 A4
Bullbeggars La HP4 ...123 A4
Bullen's Green La AL4 ...143 E8
Bullfields CM21 ...97 E3
Bullhead Rd WD6 ...170 C6
Bullock's Hill SG4 ...49 B1
Bullock's La SG13 ...113 C4
Bullrush Cl AL10 ...130 B4
Bulls Cross Ride EN7 ...162 A5
Bulls La AL9 ...144 E7
Bullsland Gdns WD3 ...164 B3
Bullsland La WD3 ...164 B2
Bullsmoor Cl EN8 ...162 C4
Bullsmoor Gdns EN8 ...162 B4
Bullsmoor La EN1,EN3 ...162 C4
Bullsmoor Ride EN8 ...162 C4
Bullsmoor Way EN8 ...162 C4
Bullwell Cres EN8 ...148 E2
Bulstrode Cl WD4 ...137 E2
Bulstrode La
Chipperfield WD4 ...137 F3
Hemel Hempstead HP3 ...138 A5
Bulwer Link SG1 ...50 E3
Buncefield La HP2 ...125 C5
Bungalows The
Essendon AL9 ...131 F7
Harpenden AL5 ...86 C3
Bunker's Farm Cotts
HP3 ...139 D8
Bunkers La HP3 ...139 B7
Bunnsfield AL7 ...111 C7
Bunstrux HP23 ...100 A4
Bunting Rd LU4 ...44 A4
Buntingford Rd SG11 ...55 D4
Bunyan Cl Pirton SG5 ...20 D4
Tring HP23 ...100 B5
Bunyan Rd SG5 ...34 F8
Bunyans Cl LU3 ...45 A5
BUPA Bushey Hospl
WD23 ...168 F1
Burbage Cl EN8 ...162 F8
Burchell Ct WD23 ...168 C2
Burfield Cl AL10 ...130 A7
Burfield Ct LU2 ...46 D3
Burfield Rd WD3 ...164 C4
Burford Cl LU3 ...31 A1
Burford Gdns EN11 ...135 B7
Burford Mews 9 EN11 ...135 A7
Burford Pl 10 EN11 ...135 A7
Burford St EN11 ...135 A7
Burford Way SG5 ...21 D2
Burgage Ct 12 SG12 ...93 D1
Burgage La SG12 ...93 D1
Burge End La SG5 ...20 C5
Burgess Cl EN7 ...147 C6
Burgess Ct WD6 ...156 F1
Burghley Ave
Bishop's Stortford CM23 ...76 C7
Borehamwood WD6 ...170 C4
Burghley Cl SG2 ...69 B8
Burgoyne Hatch CM20 ...118 A1
Burgundy Croft AL7 ...110 F4
Burhill Gr HA5 ...175 E1
Burleigh Mead AL9 ...130 C7
Burleigh Prim Sch EN8 ...148 D1
Burleigh Rd
Cheshunt EN8 ...162 E7
Hemel Hempstead HP2 ...125 C2
Hertford SG13 ...114 A7
St Albans AL1 ...128 B3
Burleigh Way EN6 ...146 E1
Burley SG6 ...11 F2
Burley Ho WD5 ...153 F7
Burley Rd CM23 ...77 A4
Burn's Gn SG2 ...52 F2
Burnell Rise SG6 ...22 D5
Burnell Wlk SG6 ...22 E5
Burnells Way CM24 ...59 E7
Burnet Cl HP3 ...124 E2
Burnett Ave SG16 ...10 B4
Burnett Sq SG14 ...112 F7
Burnham Cl
Datchworth AL6 ...90 C6
Enfield EN1 ...161 E1
Burnham Green Rd AL6,
SG3 ...90 D6
Burnham Rd Luton LU2 ...46 B2
St Albans AL1 ...128 B3
Burnley Cl WD19 ...175 C5
Burns Cl Hitchin SG4 ...35 B8
Stevenage SG2 ...51 C8
Burns Dr HP2 ...105 B1
Burns Rd SG8 ...7 D8
Burnsall Pl AL5 ...107 C6
Burnside Hertford SG14 ...113 A5
Hoddesdon EN11 ...134 F6
Sawbridgeworth CM21 ...97 D2
St Albans AL1 ...128 B1
Burnside Cl AL10 ...130 A8
Burnside Terr CM17 ...118 F3
Burnt Cl LU3 ...44 F7
Burnt Mill CM20 ...117 C3
Burnt Mill Comp Sch
CM20 ...117 F2
Burntfarm Ride EN2,EN7 ...161 B7
Burntmill Cl CM20 ...117 C3
Burntmill Cnr CM20 ...117 D4
Burntmill La CM20 ...117 D3
Burr Cl AL2 ...142 E4
Burr St LU2 ...63 E8
Burr's Pl LU1 ...63 E6
Burrowfield AL7 ...110 D4
Burrows Chase EN9 ...163 D3
Burrs La SG8 ...17 C3
Bursland SG6 ...22 D6
Burston Dr AL2 ...141 C3
Burton Ave WD18 ...167 A5
Burton Cl AL4 ...87 C5
Burton Dr EN3 ...163 A2
Burton Grange EN7 ...147 E4
Burton La EN7 ...147 E3
Burtons La WD3 ...164 A4
Burtons Mill CM21 ...97 F3
Burvale Ct 3 WD18 ...167 B6
Burwell Rd SG2 ...51 B4
Bury Cotts AL3 ...105 E5
Bury End SG5 ...20 D4
Bury Field SG9 ...29 B7

Bury Gn
Hemel Hempstead HP1 124 C4
Wheathampstead AL4 108 C8
Bury Green Rd
Cheshunt EN7 162 A7
Cheshunt EN7 162 A8
Bury Hill HP1 124 C4
Bury Hill Cl HP1 124 C4
Bury Holme EN10 148 F8
Bury La Bramfield SG14 91 B4
Codicote SG4 67 F2
Datchworth SG3 69 D3
Rickmansworth WD3 165 D1
Streatley LU3 31 A5
Bury Mdws WD3 165 D1
Bury Mead SG15 11 A7
Bury Mead Rd SG5 21 F1
Bury Park Rd LU1 63 C8
Bury Plantation SG8 7 F6
Bury Rd Harlow CM17 118 D4
Hatfield AL10 130 C6
Hemel Hempstead HP1 124 C3
Bury Rise HP3 137 D6
Bury The SG4 67 F2
Burycroft AL8 89 E1
Burydale SG2 69 B8
Burydale Jun Sch SG2 51 B1
Burydell La AL2 141 D5
Buryfield Terr SG12 93 C1
Buryfield Way SG12 93 C1
Burymead SG1 36 C1
Burywick AL5 107 B5
Bush Hall La AL9 130 D8
Bush Spring SG7 13 A1
Bushbarns EN7 148 A2
Bushby Ave EN10 134 F1
Bushel Wharf HP23 100 A6
Bushell Gn WD23 176 D8
Bushey Cl AL7 111 B5
Bushey Gn AL7 111 B5
Bushey Grove Rd WD23 167 E5
Bushey Hall Dr WD23 167 E5
Bushey Hall Rd WD23 167 E5
Bushey Hall Sch WD23 167 F4
Bushey Heath Prim Sch WD23 168 D1
Bushey Ley AL7 111 B5
Bushey Manor Jun Sch WD23 167 E4
Bushey Meads Sch WD23 168 C4
Bushey Mill Cres WD24 154 C3
Bushey Mill La
Watford WD23 167 E8
Watford,North Watford WD24 154 D1
Bushey Mus* WD23 168 A3
Bushey Pk WD23 168 A3
Bushey Sta WD19 167 D3
Bushfield Rd HP3 137 C6
Bushmead Ct LU2 45 E6
Bushmead Prim Sch LU2 45 E5
Bushmead Rd LU2 45 E5
Bushwood Cl AL9 144 B8
Butchers La SG4 48 D6
Bute Sq LU1 63 E7
Bute St LU1 63 E7
Butely Rd LU4 44 B5
Butler's Hall La CM23 76 B3
Butlers Ct EN8 162 E7
Butlers Dr E4 163 C1
Butlers Yd SG7 12 E1
Butlin Rd LU1 63 B7
Butt Field View AL1 141 C7
Buttercup Cl AL10 109 F1
Butterfield Cotts WD3 172 E3
Butterfield Ct SG7 23 E8
Butterfield Green Rd LU2 46 A6
Butterfield La AL1 141 E7
Butterfield Rd AL4 108 C7
Butterfly La WD6 169 B7
Buttermere Cl AL1 128 B2
Buttersweet Rise CM21 97 E1
Butterwick WD25 154 E3
Butterworth Path 1 LU2 63 E8
Buttlehide WD3 172 D5
Butts End HP1 124 A5
Butts The EN10 148 E7
Buttsmead HA6 174 C3
Buxton Cl AL4 128 D6
Buxton Path WD19 175 C7
Buxton Rd LU1 63 D7
Buxtons La SG8 1 F3
Buzzard Rd LU4 44 A4
By The Mount AL7 110 D5
By The Wood WD19 175 E8
By-Wood End SL9 172 A5
Byde St SG14 113 C7
Bye Way The HA3 176 F2
Byers Cl EN6 159 C5
Byewaters WD18 166 C3
Byeway The WD3 173 E8
Byfield AL8 89 E1
Byfield Cl LU4 44 B1
Byfleet Ind Est WD18 166 B1
Byford Ho 5 EN5 171 D5
Bygrave SG1 36 C2
Bygrave Rd SG7 12 F1
Bylands Cl CM23 76 D6
Bylands Ho AL3 106 A7
Byng Dr EN6 159 A8
Byng Rd EN5 171 D6
Byrd Wlk SG7 23 F7
Byron Ave
Borehamwood WD6 170 A4
Watford WD24 167 D8
Byron Cl
Hammond Street EN7 147 F4
Hitchin SG4 35 B8
Stevenage SG2 51 C7
Byron Ct EN8 148 B3
Byron Pl HP2 105 B1
Byron Rd Harpenden AL5 86 A2
Harrow HA3 176 F1
Luton LU4 44 B2
Royston SG8 7 E8
Byslips Rd LU6 82 D5
Byway The EN6 159 A6
Byways HP4 122 E5

C

Cabot Cl SG2 51 A7
Caddington Comm AL3 83 E8
Caddis Cl HA7 176 F3
Cade Cl SG6 12 C1
Cades Cl LU1 63 A6
Cades La LU1 63 A6
Cadia Cl LU1 62 E4
Cadmore Ct
12 Cheshunt EN8 148 D3
Hertford SG14 112 F7
Cadmore La EN8 148 E2
Cadwell Ct SG4 22 A2
Cadwell La SG4 22 A2
Caernarvon Cl
Hemel Hempstead HP2 124 D3
Stevenage SG2 69 B7
Caernarvon Ct HP2 124 D3
Caesars Rd AL4 108 E8
Cage Pond Rd WD7 156 F6
Cairn Way HA7 176 F4
Cairns Cl AL4 128 D2
Caishowe Rd WD6 170 B8
Caister Cl
Hemel Hempstead HP2 124 E2
Stevenage SG1 36 A1
Calais Cl EN7 147 D5
Calbury Cl AL1 128 B2
Caldbeck EN9 163 D5
Caldecot Ave EN7 147 F2
Caldecot Way EN10 134 F1
Caldecote Gdns WD23 168 E2
Caldecote La WD23 168 F3
Caldecote Rd SG7 12 E8
Calder Ave AL9 145 B5
Calder Way SG1 37 A3
Caldwell Rd WD19 175 D6
Caleb Cl LU4 44 F2
Caledon Rd AL2 142 D5
Caledonian Ct WD17 167 B7
California SG7 12 F1
California Ct 2 WD23 168 D1
California La WD23 168 D1
Callaghan Ct HP4 122 D4
Callanders The WD23 168 E1
Callisto Ct HP2 124 F6
Callowland Pl WD24 154 B1
Calnwood Rd LU4 44 C3
Calton Ave SG14 112 F7
Calton Ct SG14 112 F6
Calton Ho SG14 112 F6
Calverley Cl CM23 76 E4
Calvert Rd EN5 171 D7
Calverton Rd LU3 45 A6
Cam Ctr SG4 22 A3
Cam Sq SG4 22 A3
Camberley Pl AL5 107 D6
Camborne Dr HP2 124 E7
Cambrian Way HP2 124 F6
Cambridge Cl EN8 148 C2
Cambridge Cotts SG11 72 E2
Cambridge Cres SG8 2 A8
Cambridge Ct EN5 171 F6
Cambridge Dr EN6 158 E8
Cambridge Rd
Barkway SG8 17 D5
Barley SG8 9 A3
Harlow CM20 118 C6
Hitchin SG4 22 C2
Sawbridgeworth CM21 97 E4
St Albans AL1 128 B2
Standon SG11 55 C2
Stansted Mountfitchet CM24 59 E8
6 Watford WD18 167 C5
Cambridge St LU1 63 F6
Cambridge Terr 16 HP4 122 D4
Cameron Ct 8 SG12 93 D2
Cameron Dr EN8 162 D5
Camfield AL7 110 F2
Camford Way LU3 44 A8
Camlet Way AL3 127 B4
Camp Prim Sch AL1 128 B2
Camp Rd AL1 128 B2
Camp View Rd AL1 128 B2
Campana Ct EN5 171 D6
Campania Gr LU3 45 A8
Campbell Cl
Buntingford SG9 40 E7
Hitchin SG4 35 B8
Campers Ave SG6 22 E5
Campers Rd SG6 22 E5
Campers Wlk SG6 22 E5
Campfield Rd
Hertford SG14 113 B5
St Albans AL1 128 A3
Campfield Way SG6 22 D5
Campine Cl 1 EN8 148 D3
Campion Cl WD25 154 A6
Campion Ct SG1 50 C8
Campion Rd
Hatfield AL10 129 F8
Hemel Hempstead HP1 123 E2
Campion Way SG8 7 E5
Campions CM17 118 F5
Campions Ct HP4 122 B3
Campions The
Borehamwood WD6 157 A1
Stansted Mountfitchet CM24 59 E8
Campkin Mead SG2 51 D3
Camps Hill Com Prim Sch SG2 51 C6
Campus Five SG6 23 C7
Campus The AL8 110 D7
Canada La EN10 148 E6
Canadas The EN10 148 E6
Canal Ct HP4 122 E4
Canal Way UB9 173 A4
Canalside HP4 121 F6
Canberra Cl
Kneesworth SG8 2 B5
St Albans AL3 127 F7
Canberra Gdns LU3 45 B6
Candlefield Cl HP3 139 A8
Candlefield Rd HP3 139 A8
Candlefield Wlk HP3 139 A8
Caneland Ct EN9 163 F5
Canfield CM23 76 E8
Cangelis Cl HP1 124 A1
Canham Cl SG4 66 D1
Cannix Cl SG2 51 A2
Cannon Ho 1 SG4 34 F6
Cannon La LU2 46 B5
Cannon Mews EN9 163 B6
Cannon Rd WD18 167 C4
Cannon St AL3 127 D4
Cannon's Cl SG8 1 F5
Cannons Cl CM23 59 A1
Cannons Ct SG11 55 D3
Cannons Mdw AL6 90 E2
Cannons Mead CM24 59 D7
Cannons Mill La CM23 59 A1
Canons Cl WD7 156 B4
Canons Field AL6 87 D1
Canons Gate
Cheshunt EN8 148 F5
Harlow CM20 117 A2
Canons Rd SG12 93 C2
Canonsfield AL6 89 E8
Canonsfield Ct AL6 89 E7
Canonsfield Rd AL6 89 E8
Canopus Way HA6 175 A6
Canopy La CM17 118 C1
Cantelowes Ho EN5 171 D4
Canterbury Cl Luton LU3 44 F4
Northwood HA6 174 F4
Canterbury Ct AL1 127 F4
Canterbury Ho
10 Borehamwood WD6 170 A7
4 Watford WD24 167 C7
Canterbury Rd
Borehamwood WD6 170 A7
Watford WD17 167 B7
Canterbury Way
Croxley Green WD3 166 C6
Stevenage SG1 36 F2
Cape Rd AL1 128 B3
Capel Ct SG11 57 E2
Capel Ho WD19 175 D6
Capel Manor Gdns* EN1,EN7 162 B4
Capel Manor Prim Sch EN1 162 B4
Capel Rd Enfield EN1 162 B3
Watford WD19 167 E3
Capell Ave WD3 164 C4
Capell Rd WD3 164 D4
Capell Way WD3 164 D4
Capella Rd HA6 174 F6
Capelvere Wlk WD17 166 E8
Caponfield AL7 111 B4
Capron Rd LU4 44 E4
Captains Wlk HP4 122 D3
Caractacus Cottage View WD18 167 A3
Caractacus Gn WD18 166 F3
Caravan La WD3 165 E2
Carbone Hill EN6,SG13 146 D5
Carde Cl SG14 112 F7
Cardiff Cl SG2 69 B7
Cardiff Gr LU1 63 D7
Cardiff Pl SG8 2 A8
Cardiff Rd Luton LU1 63 D7
Watford WD18 167 B4
Cardiff Way WD5 154 A7
Cardigan Ct 11 LU1 63 D8
Cardigan Gdns 12 LU1 63 D8
Cardigan St LU1 63 D7
Cardinal Ave WD6 170 B5
Cardinal Cl EN7 147 F5
Cardinal Ct
Borehamwood WD6 170 B6
3 Luton LU2 45 D1
Cardinal Gr AL3 127 B1
Cardinal Newman RC Sec Sch LU2 31 C1
Cardinals Gate SG8 7 C6
Cardy Rd HP1 124 B3
Careless Ct 21 CM23 76 F7
Carew Lodge HA6 174 E4
Carew Rd HA6 174 F4
Carew Way WD19 175 F7
Careys Croft HP4 122 A7
Carisbrook Rd AL2 141 B5
Carisbrooke Ave WD24 167 D8
Carisbrooke Rd
Harpenden AL5 86 C2
Luton LU4 44 E1
Carleton Rd EN8 148 E4
Carleton Rise AL6 89 C6
Carlisle Ave AL3 127 D4
Carlisle Ho 15 WD6 170 A7
Carlton Bank 2 AL5 86 B1
Carlton Cl
Borehamwood WD6 170 D5
Luton LU3 45 C2
Carlton Cres LU3 45 C2
Carlton Ct
1 Harpenden AL5 86 B1
Watford WD19 167 C3
Carlton Pl HA6 174 B5
Carlton Rd AL5 86 B2
Carman Ct HP23 99 F3
Carmelite Cl HA3 176 C2
Carmelite Rd
Harrow HA3 176 C1
Luton LU4 44 A3
Carmelite Way HA3 176 C1
Carmelite Wlk HA3 176 C2
Carmen Ct WD6 156 F1
Carnaby Rd EN10 134 E3
Carnarvon Rd EN5 171 E6
Carnegie Cl EN3 163 B1
Carnegie Gdns LU3 45 A8
Carnegie Rd AL3 127 D7
Caro La HP3 125 B1
Carol Cl LU3 45 B4
Carole Ct LU1 63 E5
Caroline Ho WD23 168 A3
Caroline Pl WD19 167 E3
Carolyn Ct LU3 45 B4
Caroon Dr WD3 152 B3
Carpenders Ave WD19 175 E8
Carpenders Cl AL5 85 D4
Carpenders Park Sta WD19 175 D7
Carpenter Way EN6 159 D6
Carpenters Rd EN1 162 C3
Carpenters The CM23 76 B5
Carpenters Wood Dr WD3 164 B5
Carpenters Yd HP23 100 A3
Carriden Ct SG14 112 F8
Carrigans CM23 76 E8
Carrington Ave WD6 170 C4
Carrington Cl
Arkley EN5 171 A4
Borehamwood WD6 170 C4
Carrington Pl HP23 100 C5
Carrington Sq HA3 176 C3
Carsdale Cl LU3 45 A6
Cart Path WD25 154 C6
Cart Tk The HP3 138 F6
Carteret Rd LU2 46 C1
Carterhatch La EN1 161 F1
Carters Cl Arlesey SG15 11 A7
Aston SG2 51 D4
Carters La (Wibbly Wobbly La) SG5 34 A6
Carters Leys CM23 76 D8
Carters Way SG15 11 A7
Carters Wlk SG15 11 A7
Cartersfield Rd EN9 163 C5
Carthagena Est EN9 135 C3
Cartwright Rd Royston SG8 7 D5
Stevenage SG1 37 C2
Carve Ley AL7 111 B5
Carvers Croft SG3 69 B2
Cary Wlk WD7 156 B5
Cashio La SG6 23 A8
Caslon Way SG6 11 F1
Cassandra Gate EN8 148 F4
Cassio Ho WD18 166 F5
Cassio Rd WD18 167 B5
Cassiobridge Rd WD18 166 E5
Cassiobridge Terr WD3 166 D4
Cassiobury Dr WD17 166 F7
Cassiobury Inf Sch WD17 166 E8
Cassiobury Jun Sch WD17 166 E8
Cassiobury Park Ave WD18 166 F6
Castano Ct WD5 153 E8
Castellane Cl 1 HA7 176 F3
Castile Ct EN8 163 A5
Castile Gdns WD4 138 F2
Castings Ho SG6 23 A7
Castle Cl Bushey WD23 168 B3
Hoddesdon EN11 115 C1
Pitstone LU7 80 D3
Castle Cotts SG9 29 B7
Castle Croft Rd LU1 63 A6
Castle Ct SG5 21 D1
Castle Gate SG14 113 C5
Castle Gate Way HP4 122 C6
Castle Hill HP4 122 C6
Castle Hill Ave HP4 122 C5
Castle Hill Cl HP4 122 C5
Castle Hill Ct HP4 122 C6
Castle Mead HP1 124 B1
Castle Mead Gdns SG14 113 C6
Castle Mews 8 HP4 122 D4
Castle Rd Enfield EN3 162 E1
Hoddesdon EN11 115 C1
St Albans AL1 128 B3
Castle Rise AL4 86 F2
Castle Row HP23 100 A3
Castle St
Berkhamsted HP4 122 C4
Bishop's Stortford CM23 76 F6
Hertford SG14 113 D5
Luton,High Town LU1 63 E7
Castle St *continued*
Luton,New Town LU1 63 E6
Wingrave HP22 60 B3
Castle View CM23 77 A7
Castle Wlk CM24 59 E6
Castleford Cl WD6 156 F1
Castles Cl SG5 11 F8
Catalin Ct EN9 163 D6
Caterham Ct EN9 163 F5
Catesby Gn LU3 31 A1
Catham Cl AL1 128 B1
Cathedral & Abbey Church of St Alban* AL3 127 D3
Cathedral Ct AL3 127 B1
Catherall Rd LU3 45 B6
Catherine Cl HP2 125 B8
Catherine Cotts HP23 120 E8
Catherine Ho WD19 175 B7
Catherine Rd EN3 162 E3
Catherine St AL3 127 D4
Catherine Wheel Mews 20 SG12 93 D1
Catisfield Rd EN3 162 E2
Catkin Cl HP1 124 B4
Catlin St HP3 138 B8
Catsbrook Rd LU3 45 B6
Catsdell Bottom HP3 139 B8
Catsey La WD23 168 C2
Catsey Wood WD23 168 C2
Catterick Way WD6 169 F8
Cattlegate Cotts EN6 160 D8
Cattlegate Hill EN6 160 D7
Cattlegate Rd
Crews Hill EN2 161 A5
Northaw EN6 160 D6
Cattley Cl EN5 171 E5
Cattlins Cl EN7 147 F2
Cattsdell HP2 124 E5
Causeway Cl EN6 159 D8
Causeway Ho WD5 153 E8
Causeway The
1 Bishop's Stortford CM23 77 A7
Braughing SG9,SG11 42 D1
Brent Pelham SG9 30 B1
Buntingford SG9 40 F8
Furneux Pelham SG9 43 A3
Kneesworth SG8 2 A5
Potters Bar EN6 159 D8
Therfield SG8 15 F7
Cautherly La SG12 115 A5
Cavalier SG1 36 B1
Cavalier Cl LU3 45 A5
Cavalier Ct 7 HP4 122 C4
Cavan Ct AL10 130 A4
Cavan Dr AL3 127 D8
Cavan Rd AL3 106 A6
Cave Gate SG9 28 D6
Cavell Rd EN7 148 A4
Cavell Wlk SG2 51 C5
Cavendish Cres WD6 170 A5
Cavendish Ct
Croxley Green WD3 166 D4
Hemel Hempstead HP3 138 E6
Cavendish Rd
Barnet EN5 171 C6
Luton LU3 45 B2
Markyate AL3 83 D6
St Albans AL1 127 F3
Stevenage SG1 50 B5
Cavendish Sch The HP1 124 B4
Cavendish Way AL10 129 F5
Cawkell Cl CM24 59 D7
Caxton Ct Enfield EN3 162 E4
Luton LU3 44 F4
Caxton Ctr AL3 127 F8
Caxton Hill SG13 113 F6
Caxton Rd EN11 115 B2
Caxton Way
Stevenage SG1 50 B4
Watford WD18 166 D2
Cecil Cl CM23 77 D7
Cecil Cres AL10 130 B7
Cecil Ct EN5 171 D6
Cecil Rd Brickendon SG13 113 C3
Cheshunt EN8 162 E7
Hoddesdon EN11 135 C8
South Mimms EN6 158 B7
St Albans AL1 127 F3
Cecil St WD24 154 B1
Cedar Ave Cheshunt EN8 162 D6
Ickleford SG5 21 E4
Cedar Cl Hertford SG14 113 B6
Potters Bar EN6 145 A1
Sawbridgeworth CM21 97 E1
Ware SG12 114 D8
Cedar Cres SG8 7 B6
Cedar Ct
Bishop's Stortford CM23 58 F1
St Albans AL4 128 D3
Watford WD25 154 D6
Cedar Dr HA5 176 A4
Cedar Gn EN11 135 A5
Cedar Grange HA6 174 C3
Cedar Lawn Ave EN5 171 E4
Cedar Lodge 8 EN8 148 D3
Cedar Park Rd EN2 161 C1
Cedar Pk CM23 76 D4
Cedar Pl HA6 174 C4
Cedar Rd
Berkhamsted HP4 122 E3
Enfield EN2 161 C1
Hatfield AL10 130 A4
Watford WD19 167 D3
Cedar Way HP4 122 D3
Cedar Wlk
Hemel Hempstead HP3 124 D1
Waltham Abbey EN9 163 D5
Welwyn Garden City AL7 111 B5

Cedar Wood Dr WD25 ....154 B4
Cedars Ave WD3 ....165 C1
Cedars Cl WD6 ....170 B5
Cedars Fst Sch HA3 ....176 C2
Cedars Mid Sch HA3 ....176 C2
Cedars The
Berkhamsted HP4 ....122 E4
18 Harpenden AL5 ....86 B1
5 Rickmansworth WD3 ....165 D2
St Albans AL3 ....127 C5
Stevenage SG2 ....69 B8
Cedars Wlk WD3 ....164 F5
Cedarwood Dr AL4 ....128 D3
Celandine Dr LU3 ....45 A8
Cell Barnes Cl AL1 ....128 B1
Cell Barnes La AL1 ....128 B1
Cemetery Hill HP1 ....124 C2
Cemetery Rd CM23 ....76 F6
Cemmaes Court Rd
HP1 ....124 C3
Cemmaes Mdw HP1 ....124 C3
Centennial Ave WD6 ....169 C2
Centennial Ct
Rickmansworth WD3 ....165 E2
Stanmore WD6 ....169 C2
Centennial Pk WD6 ....169 C2
Central App SG6 ....22 F6
Central Ave
Cheshunt EN8 ....162 E6
Lower Stondon SG16 ....10 B3
Whipsnade LU6 ....81 E8
Central Dr St Albans AL4 .128 C4
Welwyn Garden City AL7 ....110 F8
Central Hts WD18 ....166 F5
Central Prim Sch WD18 .167 C5
Central Rd CM20 ....118 A4
Central Way HA6 ....174 E3
Centro HP2 ....125 C5
Century Cl AL3 ....127 C4
Century Ct WD18 ....166 C2
Century Pk WD17 ....167 C4
Century Rd
Hoddesdon EN11 ....135 A7
Ware SG12 ....93 D2
Cervantes Ct HA6 ....174 F3
Chace Ave EN6 ....159 D7
Chace The SG2 ....50 F1
Chad La AL3 ....84 C4
Chadwell SG12 ....114 C8
Chadwell Ave EN8 ....148 C3
Chadwell Cl LU2 ....45 F1
Chadwell Rd SG1 ....50 B3
Chadwell Rise SG12 ....114 C8
Chaffinch La WD18 ....166 F2
Chaffinches Gn HP3 ....139 A7
Chagny Cl SG6 ....22 E6
Chalet Cl HP4 ....121 F4
Chalfont Cl HP2 ....125 B8
Chalfont Ho WD18 ....166 E2
Chalfont La
Chorleywood WD3 ....164 B4
Maple Cross WD3 ....172 D3
Chalfont Pl AL1 ....127 E3
Chalfont Rd WD3,SL9,
HP8 ....172 C7
Chalfont Shire Ctr*
HP8 ....172 A7
Chalfont Way LU2 ....46 D2
Chalfont Wlk 2 HA5 ....175 C1
Chalgrove AL7 ....111 D7
Chalk Dale AL7 ....111 B7
Chalk Field SG6 ....23 C3
Chalk Hill Great Offley LU2 .47 A5
Watford WD19 ....167 E3
Chalk Hills SG7 ....23 F5
Chalkdell Fields AL4 ....128 A7
Chalkdell Hill HP2 ....124 E3
Chalkdell Path 8 SG5 ....34 D8
Chalkdown Luton LU2 ....45 E6
Stevenage SG2 ....51 D7
Chalks Ave CM21 ....97 D3
Challney Boys High Sch &
Com Coll LU4 ....44 D2
Challney Cl LU4 ....44 D2
Challney Girls High Sch
LU4 ....44 D2
Chalmers Ct WD3 ....165 F3
Chalton Rd LU4 ....44 C5
Chamberlaines AL5 ....85 A5
Chambers Gate SG1 ....50 D7
Chambers Gr AL7 ....110 E3
Chambers La SG5 ....21 E4
Chambers' St SG14 ....113 C6
Chambersbury La HP3 ..139 A7
Chambersbury Prim Sch
HP3 ....139 B8
Champions Cl WD6 ....157 B2
Champions Gn EN11 ....115 A1
Champions Way EN11 ....115 A1
Champneys 3 WD19 ....175 E8
Chancellor's Sch AL9 ....145 A6
Chancellors SG15 ....11 B7
Chancellors Rd SG1 ....36 D1
Chancery Cl AL4 ....128 D8
Chandler's La WD3 ....152 E2
Chandlers Cl CM23 ....76 C4
Chandlers Rd AL4 ....128 C6
Chandlers Way SG14 ....113 A6
Chandos Cl HP6 ....150 C1
Chandos Rd
Borehamwood WD6 ....170 A7
Luton LU4 ....44 F1
Channock's Farm Cotts
CM20 ....117 C7
Chantry Cl
Bishop's Stortford CM23 ....76 E8
Edgware NW7 ....170 F2
Enfield EN2 ....161 C1

Chantry Cl *continued*
Kings Langley WD4 ....139 A2
Chantry Ct AL10 ....130 A4
Chantry La Hatfield AL10 .129 F4
Hatfield AL10 ....130 A4
Little Wymondley SG4 ....35 F2
London Colney AL2 ....142 D5
Chantry Mount CM23 ....76 E8
Chantry Pl HA3 ....176 B2
Chantry Rd
Bishop's Stortford CM23 ....76 E8
Harrow HA3 ....176 B2
Chantry The
6 Bishop's Stortford CM23 .76 F8
Harlow CM20 ....118 A2
Chaomans SG6 ....22 F3
Chapel Cl
Brookmans Park AL9 ....145 D4
Little Gaddesden HP4 ....102 D6
Luton LU2 ....45 C8
St Albans AL1 ....141 D8
Chapel Cotts HP2 ....124 D4
Chapel Croft WD4 ....152 A8
Chapel Crofts HP4 ....121 E6
Chapel Dr SG15 ....11 A4
Chapel End
Buntingford SG9 ....40 E7
Hoddesdon EN11 ....135 A5
Chapel End La HP23 ....99 C8
Chapel Fields HP23 ....99 C8
Chapel Hill CM24 ....59 E6
Chapel La
Letty Green SG14 ....112 B3
Little Hadham SG11 ....75 A8
Long Marston HP23 ....79 B4
Chapel Pl SG5 ....11 F6
Chapel Rd
Breachwood Green SG4 ....65 E8
Flamstead AL3 ....84 B2
Chapel Row
3 Bishop's Stortford CM23 .76 F6
Harefield UB9 ....173 C2
Hitchin SG5 ....34 F8
Whitwell SG4 ....66 A8
Chapel St
Berkhamsted HP4 ....122 D4
Hemel Hempstead HP2 ....124 D4
Hinxworth SG7 ....3 D6
Luton,High Town LU1 ....63 E7
Luton,New Town LU1 ....63 E6
Tring HP23 ....99 F3
Chapel Viaduct LU1 ....63 E7
Chapel Way WD5 ....139 F4
Chapelfields SG12 ....115 D4
Chapman Rd SG1 ....36 B1
Chapmans End SG11 ....55 D3
Chappel Mdw HP23 ....100 B6
Chappell Ct SG12 ....92 E7
Chapterhouse Rd LU4 ....44 A3
Chard Dr LU3 ....31 B1
Chardia Terr EN8 ....148 D1
Charding Cres SG8 ....7 C7
Chardins Cl HP1 ....123 F4
Charkham Mews AL9 ....144 C7
Charles St
Berkhamsted HP4 ....122 B4
Hemel Hempstead HP1 ....124 C2
Luton LU2 ....63 F8
Tring HP23 ....100 A3
Charlesworth Cl 4 HP3 .124 D1
Charlock Way WD18 ....166 F3
Charlotte Cl AL4 ....128 E3
Charlottes Ct 2 LU1 ....63 D7
Charlton Cl EN11 ....135 A6
Charlton Mead La EN11 .135 D5
Charlton Rd SG5 ....34 D5
Charlton Way EN11 ....135 B6
Charlwood Cl HA3 ....176 E4
Charlwood Rd LU4 ....44 B1
Charmbury Rise LU2 ....46 A4
Charmouth Ct AL1 ....128 A6
Charmouth Rd AL1 ....128 A5
Charndon Cl LU3 ....31 B1
Charnwood Rd EN1 ....162 B3
Charter Ho WD3 ....166 A4
Charter Pl WD17 ....167 C6
Chartley Ave HA7 ....176 F4
Chartridge WD19 ....175 D8
Chartridge Cl Arkley EN5 .171 A4
Bushey WD23 ....168 C3
Chartridge Way HP2 ....125 C3
Chartwell Cl EN9 ....163 E6
Chartwell Ct 8 EN5 ....171 E5
Chartwell Dr LU2 ....45 E3
Chartwell Rd HA6 ....174 F4
Charwood Cl WD7 ....156 E6
Chasden Rd HP1 ....123 F5
Chase Cl SG15 ....11 A8
Chase Farm Hospl EN2 ..161 A1
Chase Hill Rd SG15 ....11 A7
Chase St LU1 ....63 E6
Chase The Arlesey SG15 ....11 A6
Bishop's Stortford CM23 ....76 F6
Goff's Oak EN7 ....147 B3
Great Amwell SG12 ....115 A6
Harlow CM17 ....118 C1
Hemel Hempstead HP2 ....124 E2
Hertford SG13 ....113 F6
Oaklands AL6 ....89 F7
Radlett WD7 ....155 F4
Watford WD18 ....166 E5
Chaseside Cl LU7 ....80 A7
Chaseways CM21 ....118 C8
Chasten Hill SG6 ....22 D7
Chater Inf Sch WD18 ....167 A5
Chater Jun Sch WD18 ....167 B5
Chatsworth Cl
Bishop's Stortford CM23 ....76 C7

Chatsworth Cl *continued*
Borehamwood WD6 ....170 A6
Chatsworth Ct
St Albans AL1 ....127 F3
Stevenage SG2 ....50 F1
Chatsworth Mews
WD24 ....154 A1
Chatsworth Rd LU4 ....45 B1
Chatter End CM23 ....58 C7
Chatteris Cl LU4 ....44 D4
Chatterton SG6 ....23 C5
Chatton Cl LU2 ....46 E2
Chaucer Cl HP4 ....121 F5
Chaucer Ct EN11 ....115 A1
Chaucer Ho 3 EN5 ....171 D5
Chaucer Rd Luton LU3 ....45 C2
Royston SG8 ....7 C8
Chaucer Way Hitchin SG4 ..35 C7
Hoddesdon EN11 ....115 A2
Chaucer Wlk HP2 ....105 B1
Chaul End La LU4 ....44 E1
Chaul End Rd
Caddington LU1 ....62 D6
Luton LU4 ....44 B1
Chaulden House Gdns
HP1 ....123 F1
Chaulden Jun & Inf Schs
HP1 ....123 F2
Chaulden La HP1 ....123 E1
Chaulden Terr HP1 ....123 F2
Chauncey Ho WD18 ....166 E3
Chauncy Ave EN6 ....159 C6
Chauncy Cl SG12 ....93 D3
Chauncy Ct 19 SG14 ....113 D6
Chauncy Gdns SG7 ....13 B1
Chauncy Ho 3 SG1 ....50 E6
Chauncy Rd SG1 ....50 E6
Chauncy Sch The SG12 ....93 B2
Chaworth Gn 1 LU4 ....44 C5
Cheapside LU1 ....63 E7
Cheapside Sq 4 LU1 ....63 E7
Chedburgh AL7 ....111 D7
Cheddington Comb Sch
LU7 ....80 A7
Cheddington La HP23 ....79 C5
Cheddington Rd LU7 ....80 C4
Cheffins Rd EN11 ....114 F1
Chells Ent Village SG2 ....51 C6
Chells La SG2 ....51 D7
Chells Way SG2 ....51 B6
Chelmsford Rd SG14 ....113 B5
Chelsea Fields EN11 ....115 B2
Chelsing Rise HP2 ....125 C2
Chelsworth Cl 1 LU2 ....46 D1
Cheltenham Ct AL1 ....128 A2
Cheltenham Ho 2
WD24 ....167 C7
Chelveston AL7 ....111 D7
Chelwood Ave AL10 ....130 A8
Chelwood Cl HA6 ....174 C3
Chenduit Way HA7 ....176 F5
Chene Dr AL3 ....127 D5
Cheney Rd LU4 ....44 C5
Chenies Ave HP6 ....150 D1
Chenies Ct HP2 ....125 B8
Chenies Gn CM23 ....76 D6
Chenies Manor Ho*
WD3 ....151 A1
Chenies Rd WD3 ....164 D7
Chenies Sch WD3 ....151 B1
Chenies Way WD18 ....166 E2
Chennells AL10 ....129 F4
Chennells Cl SG4 ....22 B2
Chennies The AL5 ....107 C7
Chepstow AL5 ....85 F2
Chepstow Cl SG1 ....51 B8
Chequer Ct LU1 ....63 F6
Chequer La AL3 ....106 B4
Chequer St Luton LU1 ....63 F6
St Albans AL1 ....127 D3
Chequers
Bishop's Stortford CM23 ....76 C8
Hatfield AL9 ....130 D8
Welwyn Garden City AL7 ....110 D3
Chequers Bridge Rd SG1 .50 C6
Chequers Cl
Buntingford SG9 ....40 D8
Pitstone LU7 ....80 C4
Standon SG11 ....55 D4
Stotfold SG5 ....12 A6
Chequers Cotts
Preston SG4 ....48 D6
Whipsnade LU6 ....82 A8
Chequers End HP2 ....104 D5
Chequers Field AL7 ....110 D3
Chequers La
Abbots Langley WD2 ....140 C1
Pitstone LU7 ....80 C5
Preston SG4 ....48 D7
Chequers Wlk EN9 ....163 F6
Cheriton Cl AL4 ....128 D7
Cherry Bank HP2 ....124 D5
Cherry Blossom Cl 2
CM17 ....118 C4
Cherry Cl SG3 ....68 F4
Cherry Croft
Croxley Green WD3 ....166 B3
Welwyn Garden City AL8 ....89 D2
Cherry Croft Gdns 4
HA5 ....175 F3
Cherry Ct HA5 ....175 D2
Cherry Dr SG8 ....7 E7
Cherry Gdns
Bishop's Stortford CM23 ....77 A8
Sawbridgeworth CM21 ....97 E4
Tring HP23 ....99 F3
Cherry Green La SG9 ....40 F3

Cherry Hill
Chiswell Green AL2 ....141 A6
Harrow HA3 ....176 E4
Rickmansworth WD3 ....165 B6
Cherry Hills WD19 ....175 E5
Cherry Hollow WD5 ....153 F8
Cherry Orch HP1 ....124 A5
Cherry Orchard La SG9 ..28 A3
Cherry Rd EN3 ....162 C1
Cherry Tree Ave AL2 ....142 D5
Cherry Tree Cl
Arlesey SG15 ....11 A4
Luton LU2 ....46 A1
Cherry Tree Gn SG14 ....112 F7
Cherry Tree La
Cholesbury HP23 ....120 A3
Chorleywood WD3 ....164 C1
Potters Bar EN6 ....159 B5
Wheathampstead AL4 ....87 A2
Cherry Tree Prim Sch
WD24 ....154 A3
Cherry Tree Rd
Hoddesdon EN11 ....135 A7
Watford WD24 ....154 B3
Cherry Tree Rise SG2 ....38 B1
Cherry Trees SG16 ....10 B3
Cherry Trees Dr SG2 ....51 B7
Cherry Way AL10 ....130 A2
Cherry Wlk WD3 ....165 C7
Cherrydale WD18 ....166 F5
Cherrytree La HP2 ....125 C7
Chertsey Cl LU2 ....64 D8
Chertsey Rise SG2 ....51 C4
Cherwell Cl WD3 ....166 A4
Cherwell Dr SG1 ....37 A3
Chesfield Cl CM23 ....76 F5
Chesford Rd LU2 ....46 C4
Chesham Ct HA6 ....174 F4
Chesham Prep Sch HP5 .136 A4
Chesham Rd
Berkhamsted HP4 ....122 C3
Bovingdon HP3,HP3 ....136 E3
Wigginton HP23 ....120 E7
Chesham Way WD18 ....166 F3
Cheshire Dr WD25 ....153 F5
Cheshunt Centre The
EN8 ....148 D3
Cheshunt Folly EN8 ....148 B3
Cheshunt Sch EN8 ....148 C1
Cheshunt Sta EN8 ....148 F1
Cheshunt Wash EN8 ....148 E4
Cheslyn Cl LU2 ....46 E2
Chess Cl Latimer HP5 ....150 D3
Rickmansworth WD3 ....165 D5
Chess Hill WD3 ....165 D5
Chess La WD3 ....165 D5
Chess Vale Rise WD3 ....165 F3
Chess Way WD3 ....165 A6
Chesswood Ct WD3 ....165 D1
Chesswood Way HA5 ....175 D1
Chester Ave LU4 ....44 E3
Chester Cl Luton LU4 ....44 F2
Potters Bar EN6 ....145 B2
Chester Gibbons Gn
AL2 ....142 D5
Chester Ho HA6 ....174 F3
Chester Pl 1 HA6 ....174 E3
Chester Rd
Borehamwood WD6 ....170 D6
Northwood HA6 ....174 F3
Stevenage SG1 ....37 A1
Watford WD18 ....167 A5
Chesterfield Flats EN5 ....171 D4
Chesterfield Inf & Jun Schs
EN3 ....162 E2
Chesterfield Rd
Barnet EN5 ....171 D4
Enfield EN3 ....162 E2
Chesterton Ave AL5 ....86 D1
Chestnut Ave
Lower Stondon SG16 ....10 C3
Luton LU3 ....44 C8
Northwood HA6 ....174 F2
Rickmansworth WD3 ....165 A4
Ware SG12 ....93 F3
Chestnut Cl
Bishop's Stortford CM23 ....76 E6
Dagnall HP4 ....81 C5
Hunsdon SG12 ....95 D1
Potten End HP4 ....123 B6
Chestnut Ct
4 Hitchin SG5 ....34 D8
Watford WD18 ....166 E5
Chestnut Dr
Berkhamsted HP4 ....122 D3
Harrow HA3 ....176 F2
Hatfield Heath CM22 ....98 F3
St Albans AL4 ....128 C5
Chestnut La
Kneesworth SG8 ....2 B6
Totteridge N20 ....171 E1
Chestnut Rd EN3 ....162 E3
Chestnut Rise WD23 ....168 B2
Chestnut Wlk Hitchin SG4 .35 A4
Royston SG8 ....7 E5
Stevenage SG1 ....36 D1
Watford WD24 ....154 A2
Chestnuts The
Codicote SG4 ....67 F2
Hemel Hempstead HP3 ....137 F7
Hertford SG13 ....113 D5
Cheverell's Gn AL3 ....83 C4
Cheverells Cl AL3 ....83 D4
Cheviot Cl Bushey WD23 .168 C3
Luton LU3 ....44 D7
Cheviot Rd LU3 ....44 D7
Cheviots Hatfield AL10 ....130 A3
Hemel Hempstead HP2 ....124 F6

Cheyne Cl Pitstone LU7 ....80 D4
Ware SG12 ....93 D3
Cheynes Inf Sch LU3 ....44 D8
Chicheley Gdns HA3 ....176 C3
Chicheley Rd HA3 ....176 C3
Chichester Way WD25 ....154 E6
Chicken La AL2 ....142 D4
Chidbrook Ho WD18 ....166 E3
Chigwell Hurst Ct HA5 ..175 D1
Chilcott Rd WD24 ....153 F3
Chilcourt SG8 ....7 C6
Childs Ave UB9 ....173 C1
Childwick Ct HP3 ....139 B8
Childwick Gn AL3 ....107 C2
Chilham Cl HP2 ....124 E2
Chiltern Ave WD23 ....168 C3
Chiltern Cl
Borehamwood WD6 ....169 F7
Bushey WD23 ....168 B3
Goff's Oak EN7 ....147 B4
Ware SG12 ....93 D3
Watford WD18 ....166 F5
Berkhamsted HP4 ....121 F5
Chiltern Cnr HP4 ....122 A5
Chiltern Cotts HP23 ....120 A2
Chiltern Ct
19 Harpenden AL5 ....86 B1
St Albans AL4 ....128 D7
Chiltern Dr WD3 ....165 A2
Chiltern Gdns LU4 ....44 F3
Chiltern Open Air Mus*
HP8 ....164 A1
Chiltern Park Ave HP4 ..122 A6
Chiltern Rd Baldock SG7 ..23 F6
Hitchin SG4 ....35 A7
St Albans AL4 ....128 C7
Wingrave HP22 ....60 A3
Chiltern Rise LU1 ....63 D6
Chiltern View SG6 ....22 D5
Chiltern Villas HP23 ....99 E3
Chiltern Way HP23 ....100 C5
Chilterns
Berkhamsted HP4 ....121 F6
Hatfield AL10 ....130 A2
Hemel Hempstead HP2 ....124 E5
Chilterns The Hitchin SG4 ..35 A6
Kensworth Common LU6 ....82 F8
Stevenage SG1 ....37 B3
Chilton Ct SG14 ....112 F8
Chilton Gn AL7 ....111 C6
Chilvers Bank SG7 ....23 E7
Chilwell Gdns WD19 ....175 C6
Chilworth Gate EN10 ....134 F1
Chime Sq AL3 ....127 E4
Chimneys The WD23 ....167 F4
Chindit Cl EN10 ....134 E3
Chinneck Ho 10 HP4 ....122 C4
Chinnery Cl EN1 ....161 F1
Chinnery Hill CM23 ....76 F5
Chipperfield Rd
Bovingdon HP3 ....137 C3
Hemel Hempstead HP3 ....138 C7
Kings Langley WD4 ....138 D2
Chipping Cl 8 EN5 ....171 E6
Chipping Hall Cotts SG9 .27 D4
Chippingfield CM17 ....118 C3
Chirdland Ho WD18 ....166 E3
Chishill Rd Barley SG8 ....9 A2
Great Chishill SG8 ....9 F3
Chishill Windmill* SG8 ....9 C2
Chiswell Ct WD24 ....154 C1
Chiswell Green La AL2 ..140 E6
Chittenden Cl 5 EN9 ....115 B1
Chivenor Pl AL4 ....128 C1
Chobham Ct 8 LU1 ....63 F6
Chobham St LU1 ....63 F6
Chobham Wlk 5 LU1 ....63 E6
Cholesbury 1 WD19 ....175 E8
Cholesbury Ho WD18 ....166 E3
Cholesbury La HP23 ....120 B2
Cholesbury Rd HP23 ....120 D5
Chorleywood Bottom
WD3 ....164 D4
Chorleywood Cl WD3 ....165 D2
Chorleywood House Dr
WD3 ....164 E6
Chorleywood Prim Sch
WD3 ....164 C3
Chorleywood Rd WD3 ....165 C4
Chorleywood Sta WD3 ....164 D5
Chouler Gdns SG1 ....36 C2
Chowns The AL5 ....107 A5
Christ Church CE Prim Sch
SG12 ....93 E1
Christ Church CE Sch
WD3 ....164 F5
Christ Church La EN5 ....171 E7
Christ Church Prim Sch
EN5 ....171 D7
Christchurch Cl AL3 ....127 D4
Christchurch Cres WD7 .156 A3
Christchurch Ho HP23 ....100 A3
Christchurch Pl SG14 ....113 C6
Christchurch Rd
Hemel Hempstead HP2 ....124 D4
Tring HP23 ....99 F4
Christie Cl EN10 ....134 F3
Christie Rd Stevenage SG2 .51 D5
Waltham Abbey EN9 ....163 B4
Christina Ct AL3 ....83 E5
Christopher Ct
Hemel Hempstead HP3 ....138 D8
13 Ware SG12 ....93 D1
Christopher Pl 3 AL3 ....127 D3
Christy's Yd SG7 ....3 D6

Church Cl Codicote SG4 ....67 F2
Cuffley EN6 ....146 E2
Little Berkhamsted SG13 ..132 C4
Northwood HA6 ....174 F3
Radlett WD7 ....156 A3
Reed SG8 ....16 E4
Studham LU6 ....82 B4
Church Cotts
Essendon AL9 ....131 E6
Gilston CM20 ....117 C7
Great Gaddesden HP1 ....103 D3
Church Cres
Sawbridgeworth CM21 .....97 F2
St Albans AL3 ....127 C4
Church Ct
Hoddesdon EN10 ....135 A3
[10] Ware SG12 ....93 D2
Church End Arlesey SG15 ..11 A8
Barley SG8 ....9 A1
Braughing SG11 ....55 F7
Markyate AL3 ....83 D6
Redbourn AL3 ....106 A4
Sandridge AL4 ....108 C2
Walkern SG2 ....38 C2
Church End Cotts WD3 ..151 F1
Church Farm La HP23 ....79 F3
Church Farm Way
WD25 ....155 B1
Church Field SG12 ....93 B3
Church Field Path EN8 ..148 C2
Church Gates [4] HP4 ....122 C4
Church Gn Benington SG2 ..52 D4
Great Wymondley SG4 ......35 E6
Harpenden AL5 ....86 A1
Church Green Row AL5 ..86 A1
Church Hill
Bedmond WD5 ....139 F4
Cheddington LU7 ....80 A8
Harefield UB9 ....173 C1
Hertford Heath SG13 ....114 C4
Church La Arlesey SG15 ...11 A7
Ashwell SG7 ....4 D4
Barkway SG8 ....17 C4
Berkhamsted HP4 ....122 C4
Bishop's Stortford CM23 ....76 D3
Bovingdon HP3 ....137 B4
Cheddington LU7 ....80 A8
Cheshunt EN8 ....148 C2
Colney Heath AL4 ....143 B8
Dane End SG12 ....71 F8
Graveley SG4 ....36 C4
Guilden Morden SG8 ....1 F5
Harrow HA3 ....176 F2
Hatfield AL9 ....130 C5
Hoddesdon EN10 ....134 C1
Kimpton SG4 ....66 D1
Kings Langley WD4 ....139 A2
Letchworth SG6 ....12 C1
Marsworth HP23 ....79 F1
Much Hadham SG10 ....74 F3
Northaw EN6 ....146 A1
Preston SG4 ....48 D6
Radlett WD25 ....155 B1
Reed SG8 ....16 E5
Rickmansworth WD3 ......165 B1
[4] Royston SG8 ....7 D6
Sarratt WD3 ....152 A2
Stapleford SG14 ....92 A6
Stevenage SG1 ....50 C7
Therfield SG8 ....15 F7
Tring HP23 ....120 A7
Weston SG4 ....24 D1
Church Manor CM23 .....77 B8
Church Mead
Roydon CM19 ....116 B1
Studham LU6 ....82 B4
Church Meadow Cotts
HP1 ....103 D3
Church Mill Grange
CM17 ....118 E4
Church Path
Great Amwell SG12 ......114 F6
Little Wymondley SG4 .....35 F3
Church Pl AL6 ....89 C5
Church Rd Flamstead AL3 ..84 B2
Great Hallingbury CM22 ....77 D3
Hemel Hempstead HP3 ...125 C2
Hertford SG14 ....113 C7
King's Walden SG4 ....47 F3
Little Berkhamsted SG13 ..132 C4
Little Gaddesden HP4 .....102 D8
Northwood HA6 ....174 F3
Pitstone, Church End LU7 ...80 E3
Pitstone, Ivinghoe LU7 .....80 F5
Potten End HP4 ....123 B6
Potters Bar EN6 ....145 B1
Slip End LU1 ....63 C2
Stansted Mountfitchet CM24 .59 F5
Stotfold SG5 ....11 F6
Streatley LU3 ....31 A6
Studham LU6 ....82 B4
Watford WD17 ....167 B8
Welwyn Garden City AL8 ..110 D6
Church Row Mews [2]
SG12 ....93 D1
Church St Baldock SG7 ....12 E1
Bishop's Stortford CM23 ....76 F7
Bovingdon HP3 ....137 B4
Buntingford SG9 ....40 E8
Essendon AL9 ....131 E6
Guilden Morden SG8 ....1 F5
Hatfield AL9 ....130 C5
Hemel Hempstead HP2 ...124 D5
Hertford SG14 ....113 D6
Luton LU2 ....63 E7
Church St *continued*
Luton,High Town LU2 ....63 F8
Rickmansworth WD3 .....165 E1
Sawbridgeworth CM21 .....97 E2
Shillington SG5 ....19 E8
St Albans AL3 ....127 D4
Waltham Abbey EN9 ......163 C6
Ware SG12 ....93 D1
Watford WD18 ....167 C5
Welwyn AL6 ....89 C5
Wheathampstead AL4 .....108 D8
Wingrave HP22 ....60 B2
Church Street Ind Est
SG12 ....93 D1
Church View
Hoddesdon EN10 ....134 F3
Long Marston HP23 ....79 A4
Church Wlk
Bushey WD23 ....168 A3
Sawbridgeworth CM21 .....97 F2
Church Yd Hitchin SG5 .....34 E7
Tring HP23 ....100 A3
Churchfield Barley SG8 .....9 A1
Harlow CM20 ....118 B2
Harpenden AL5 ....107 C8
Churchfield Ho AL8 .....110 C6
Churchfield Rd AL6 ......90 C1
Churchfields
Hertford SG13 ....113 D5
Hoddesdon EN10 ....135 A3
Standon SG11 ....55 E2
Stansted Mountfitchet CM24 .59 F6
Churchfields La EN10 ...135 A3
Churchfields Rd WD24 ..153 F3
Churchgate
Cheshunt EN8 ....148 B1
[7] Hitchin SG5 ....34 E7
Churchgate CE Prim Sch
CM17 ....118 F3
Churchgate Rd EN8 .....148 B2
Churchgate St CM17 ....118 E4
Churchill Cres AL9 ......144 C8
Churchill Rd Luton LU4 ....45 A1
St Albans AL1 ....128 A4
Churchyard Wlk [6] SG5 ..34 E7
Cicero Dr LU3 ....45 A8
Cillocks Cl EN11 ....135 A7
Claggy Rd SG4 ....66 B2
Claire Ct Bushey WD23 ...168 D1
Cheshunt EN8 ....162 D7
[5] Pinner HA5 ....175 F3
Clamp Hill HA7 ....176 E5
Clapgate Rd WD23 ......168 B3
Clare Cl WD6 ....169 F3
Clare Cres SG7 ....23 E6
Clare Ct Enfield EN3 .....162 E4
Northwood HA6 ....174 E5
St Albans AL1 ....127 F2
Claremont
Bricket Wood AL2 ....155 A8
Goff's Oak EN7 ....147 F2
Claremont Cres WD3 ....166 C4
Claremont Rd
Hadley Wood EN4 ....159 D2
Harrow HA3 ....176 E1
Luton LU4 ....45 B1
Clarence Cl WD23 ....168 F2
Clarence Rd
Berkhamsted HP4 ....122 C4
Harpenden AL5 ....86 A3
St Albans AL1 ....128 A4
Stansted Mountfitchet
CM24 ....59 E7
Clarendon Cl [1] HP2 ....124 E4
Clarendon Ct
Harpenden AL5 ....86 B3
[7] Northwood HA6 ....174 F5
Clarendon Mews WD6 ..170 A6
Clarendon Par EN8 .....148 D2
Clarendon Rd
Borehamwood WD6 ......170 A6
Cheshunt EN8 ....148 D2
Harpenden AL5 ....86 B3
Luton LU2 ....45 E1
Watford WD17 ....167 B6
Clarion Cl SG5 ....33 C2
Clarion Ho SG5 ....33 C2
Clark Rd SG8 ....7 D7
Clarke Way WD25 ....154 A4
Clarke's Rd AL10 ....130 B7
Clarke's Spring HP23 ....100 F5
Clarkfield WD3 ....165 B1
Clarklands Ind Est*
CM21 ....97 E5
Clarks Cl SG12 ....93 D3
Clarks Mead WD23 ......168 D2
Claudian Pl AL3 ....127 A1
Claverhambury Rd EN9 ..149 F2
Claverley Gn LU2 ....46 E2
Claverton Cl HP3 ....137 A3
Clay End SG2 ....52 F7
Clay Hill EN2 ....161 D2
Clay La WD23 ....168 E2
Claybury WD23 ....168 B2
Claybush Rd SG7 ....4 D3
Claycroft AL7 ....111 B7
Claydon Cl LU3 ....45 C7
Claydown Way LU1 ....63 B1
Claygate Ave AL5 ....85 E2
Clayhall Rd LU6 ....82 F7
Clayhill HP23 ....120 E7
Claymore HP2 ....124 E7
Claymore Dr SG5 ....21 F5
Claymores SG1 ....50 E6
Clayponds CM23 ....77 B7
Clayton Hill Ctry Pk*
EN9 ....149 D8
Clayton Par [7] EN8 .....148 D1
Cleall Ave EN9 ....163 C5
Cleave The AL5 ....86 D1
Clement Pl HP23 ....100 A3
Clement Rd EN8 ....148 E4
Clements End Rd LU6,
HP2 ....82 E2
Clements Rd WD3 ....164 D4
Clements St SG12 ....93 E1
Clementsbury SG13 .....133 C8
Clevedon Rd LU2 ....46 B2
Cleveland Cres WD6 ....170 C4
Cleveland Rd
Hemel Hempstead HP2 ....125 B5
Markyate AL3 ....83 E5
Cleveland Way
Hemel Hempstead HP2 ....125 B5
Stevenage SG1 ....37 C3
Cleves Rd HP2 ....125 B8
Cleviscroft SG1 ....50 E4
Clewer Cres HA3 ....176 D2
Clifford Cres LU4 ....44 D5
Clifford Ct [10] CM23 .....77 A7
Clifton Cl EN8 ....148 E2
Clifton Rd Luton LU1 ......63 B8
Watford WD18 ....167 B4
Clifton St AL1 ....127 E4
Clifton Way
Borehamwood WD6 ......170 A8
Ware SG12 ....93 D3
Climb The WD3 ....165 B3
Clinton Ave LU2 ....45 F3
Clinton End HP2 ....125 C3
Clitheroe Gdns WD19 ...175 D7
Clive Cl EN6 ....158 F8
Clive Ct LU2 ....45 E1
Clive Par HA6 ....174 E3
Clive Way WD24 ....167 C8
Clock Ho The EN2 ....161 F2
Clockhouse Mews WD3 ..164 E6
Cloister Garth
Berkhamsted HP4 ....122 C4
St Albans AL1 ....141 E7
Cloister Lawns SG6 ....22 F4
Cloister Wlk HP2 ....124 D5
Cloisters Rd
Letchworth SG6 ....23 A4
Luton LU4 ....44 B3
Cloisters The
Bushey WD23 ....168 B3
Kings Langley WD4 ......139 A2
Rickmansworth WD3 .....165 E2
[3] Watford WD17 ....167 C5
Welwyn Garden City AL8 ..110 D6
Clonard Way HA5 ....176 A4
Clore Shalom Sch
London Colney WD7 ......142 E1
Shenleybury WD7 ....156 E8
Close The Baldock SG7 ....23 E7
Brookmans Park AL9 .....144 E5
Bushey WD23 ....168 A4
Codicote SG4 ....67 F1
Harpenden AL5 ....85 D4
Harrow HA2 ....176 C1
Hinxworth SG7 ....3 D6
Luton LU3 ....45 A5
Markyate AL3 ....83 E5
Potters Bar EN6 ....159 A7
Radlett WD7 ....155 F6
Rickmansworth WD3 .....165 B1
Royston SG8 ....7 F7
St Albans AL1 ....141 C8
Wallington SG9 ....25 E6
Ware SG12 ....93 E1
Closemead Cl HA6 ......174 C4
Clothall Rd Baldock SG7 ...23 F8
Clothall SG7 ....24 C6
Clovelly Way SG1 ....50 A7
Clover Ave CM23 ....76 B6
Clover Cl LU4 ....44 A3
Clover Field The WD23 ..167 F3
Clover Way Hatfield AL10 .129 F8
Hemel Hempstead HP1 ...124 B4
Cloverfield AL7 ....89 F1
Cloverland AL10 ....129 F2
Clump The WD3 ....165 B4
Cluny Way SG15 ....11 A5
Clusterbolts SG14 ....92 A7
Clutterbucks WD3 ......152 A3
Clyde Rd EN11 ....135 D5
Clyde Sq HP2 ....124 F8
Clyde Terr SG13 ....114 A6
Clydesdale Cl WD6 .....170 D4
Clydesdale Ct LU4 ....44 A3
Clydesdale Path WD6 ...170 D4
Clydesdale Rd Luton LU4 ..44 A3
Royston SG8 ....7 E6
Clydesdale Wlk EN10 ....148 F6
Clyfton Cl EN10 ....148 F8
Clyston Rd WD18 ....166 F3
Coach Dr SG4 ....34 F5
Coach House Cloisters
SG7 ....23 E7
Coach Mews AL1 ....128 B3
Coachman's La SG7 ......23 D8
Coanwood Cotts SG12 ....94 E4
Coates Dell WD25 ....154 E6
Coates Rd WD6 ....169 D2
Coates Way WD25 ....154 E6
Coates Way Jun Mix Inf Sch
WD25 ....154 E6
Cob Lane Cl AL6 ....89 F4
Cobb Cl WD6 ....170 C4
Cobb Gn WD25 ....154 B7
Cobb Rd HP4 ....121 F4
Cobbett Cl EN3 ....162 C3
Cobbetts Ride HP23 ......99 F3
Cobbins The EN9 ....163 E6
Cobbins Way CM17 .....118 E4
Cobbinsbank EN9 ....163 D6
Cobblers Wick HP22 ......60 B3
Cobden Hill WD7 ....156 B2
Cobden St LU2 ....45 F1
Cobham Rd SG12 ....93 F2
Cobmead AL10 ....130 B7
Cock Gr HP23 ....121 C4
Cock La Brent Pelham CB11 ..30 F3
Hoddesdon EN11 ....134 D4
Cockbush Ave SG13 .....114 B7
Cocker Rd EN1 ....162 C3
Cockernhoe Endowed Prim
Sch LU2 ....46 E3
Cockfosters Rd EN4 .....159 E1
Cockle Way WD7 ....156 E6
Cockrobin La CM20 ......117 A7
Codicote CE Prim Sch
SG4 ....67 E1
Codicote Dr WD25 ....154 D5
Codicote Ho SG1 ....36 C1
Codicote Hts SG4 ....68 B1
Codicote Innovation Ctr
SG4 ....88 E8
Codicote Rd
Ayot St Lawrence AL4,AL6,
SG4 ....88 C3
Welwyn AL6 ....89 B7
Wheathampstead AL4 ......87 D1
Whitwell SG4 ....66 F6
Codicote Row HP2 ......105 B1
Codmore Wood Rd HP5 .150 D6
Cohen Cl EN8 ....162 E8
Colborne Ho WD18 ......166 E3
Colbron Cl SG7 ....4 C4
Colburn Ave HA5 ....175 E4
Colchester Rd HA6 ......175 A1
Cold Christmas La SG12 ..93 E6
Coldham Gr EN3 ....162 E2
Coldharbour La
Bushey WD23 ....168 C4
Harpenden AL5 ....86 C4
Cole Green La AL7 ......111 B4
Cole Green Way SG14 ...113 A4
Cole Rd WD17 ....167 B8
Colebrook Ave LU3 ....44 C7
Coleman Green La
Sandridge AL4 ....108 E4
Wheathampstead AL4 .....109 A7
Coleman's La EN9 ....149 E5
Colemans Cl SG5 ....20 D4
Colemans Rd SG4 ....47 D1
Coleridge Cl
Hammond Street EN7 .....147 F4
Hitchin SG4 ....35 B8
Coleridge Cres HP2 .....105 B1
Coleridge Ct [9] AL5 .....86 B1
Coleridge Way WD6 .....170 A5
Coles Gn WD23 ....168 C1
Coles Hill HP1 ....124 A5
Colesdale EN6 ....146 E1
Colestrete SG1 ....50 F5
Colestrete Cl SG1 ....51 A5
Coleswood Rd AL5 ......107 C7
Colgate Ct EN5 ....171 E4
Colgate Pl EN3 ....163 A2
Colgrove AL8 ....110 C5
Colin Rd LU2 ....45 F2
Colindale Ave AL1 ....127 F1
College Ave HA3 ....176 E2
College Cl
Bishop's Stortford CM23 ....76 D7
Flamstead AL3 ....84 B1
Harrow HA3 ....176 E3
Ware SG12 ....114 D8
College Ct Cheshunt EN8 .148 C1
Hoddesdon EN11 ....134 F8
College Hill Rd HA3 .....176 E3
College Ho LU1 ....63 F7
College La AL10 ....129 E4
College Lake Wildlife Ctr*
HP23 ....100 C8
College Pl AL3 ....127 C3
College Rd
Abbots Langley WD5 .....154 A8
Aston Clinton HP22 ....78 C1
Cheshunt EN8 ....148 D1
Harrow HA3 ....176 E2
Hertford Heath SG13 ....114 D2
Hitchin SG5 ....34 F8
Hoddesdon EN11 ....134 F8
St Albans AL1 ....128 B2
College St AL3 ....127 D3
College Way
Northwood HA6 ....174 D4
Welwyn Garden City AL8 ..110 D7
College Yd WD24 ....154 B1
Collens Rd AL5 ....107 B5
Collenswood Rd SG2 .....51 B4
Collenswood Sch SG2 ......51 C4
Collet Cl EN8 ....148 D3
Collet Gdns EN8 ....148 D3
Collett Rd
Hemel Hempstead HP1 ...124 C3
Ware SG12 ....93 D2
Collett Sch The HP1 .....124 B4
Colleyland WD3 ....164 D5
Collingdon Ct [10] LU1 .....63 D8
Collingdon St LU1 ....63 D8
Collings Wells Cl LU1 .....62 E4
Collingtree LU2 ....46 B4
Collingwood Cl LU4 ....44 D3
Collingwood Ct SG8 ....7 D7
Collingwood Dr AL2 .....142 D6
Collins Cross CM23 ....59 B1
Collison Cl SG4 ....22 C2
Collyer Rd AL2 ....142 D4
Colmer Pl HA3 ....176 D3
Colnbrook Cl AL2 ....142 E4
Colnbrook Sch WD19 ....175 C7
Colne Ave
Rickmansworth WD3 .....173 A8
Watford WD19 ....167 C3
Colne Bridge Ret Pk
WD17 ....167 D4
Colne Gdns AL2 ....142 E4
Colne Lo WD3 ....165 A1
Colne Lodge WD23 ......167 D5
Colne Mead WD3 ....173 A8
Colne Valley Ret Pk
WD17 ....167 D4
Colne Way
Hemel Hempstead HP2 ....124 F8
Watford WD24,WD25 .....154 E2
Colne Way Ct WD24 .....154 D3
Colney Heath Jun & Inf Sch
AL4 ....129 C1
Colney Heath La AL4 ....128 E2
Colonial Bsns Pk WD24 ..167 C8
Colonial Way WD24 .....167 D8
Colonnade The [7] EN8 ...148 D3
Colonsay HP3 ....125 C1
Colston Cres EN7 ....147 B4
Colt Hatch CM20 ....117 B1
Colt Mews EN3 ....163 A2
Colthurst Gdns EN11 ....135 D8
Colts Cnr SG2 ....51 B4
Colts Croft SG8 ....9 E2
Colts The CM23 ....76 E4
Coltsfield CM24 ....59 E8
Coltsfoot AL7 ....111 B4
Coltsfoot Dr SG8 ....7 E6
Coltsfoot Gn LU4 ....44 A5
Coltsfoot La SG3 ....90 D7
Coltsfoot Rd SG12 ....93 E3
Coltsfoot The HP1 ....123 E2
Columbus Cl SG2 ....51 A7
Columbus Gdns HA6 ....175 A2
Colvin Gdns EN8 ....162 D4
Colwell Rd SG2 ....51 C3
Colwell Rise LU2 ....46 E2
Colwyn Cl SG1 ....50 B7
Colyer Cl AL6 ....89 F3
Combe Ho WD18 ....166 E3
Combe Rd WD18 ....166 F3
Combe St HP1 ....124 C3
Combewood WD25 ......154 C7
Comet Cl WD25 ....153 F5
Comet Rd AL10 ....129 F6
Comet Way AL10 ....129 E5
Commerce Way SG6 ......22 F6
Common Field HP23 .....100 D1
Common Gate Rd WD3 ..164 E4
Common Gdns HP4 ......123 B6
Common La Ashwell SG7 ....4 B6
Harpenden AL5 ....86 D5
Kimpton SG4 ....66 B1
Kings Langley WD4 ......138 F3
Radlett WD7,WD25 ....155 E1
Common Rd
Chorleywood WD3 ....164 D5
Kensworth Common LU6 ....82 F8
Stanmore HA7 ....176 D7
Stotfold SG5 ....11 F7
Studham LU6 ....82 B3
Common Rise SG4 ....22 A1
Common The
Chipperfield WD4 ....152 B8
Harpenden AL5 ....85 C4
Hatfield AL10 ....130 A6
London Colney WD7 ......156 B8
Potten End HP4 ....123 A6
Stanmore HA7 ....176 F8
Common View SG6 ....23 B8
Common View Sq SG6 ....23 A8
Common Wharf SG12 .....93 E1
Commonfields CM20 ....117 E1
Commons La HP2 ....124 E4
Commons The AL7 ....111 B3
Commonswood Sch
AL7 ....111 B3
Community Way WD3 ...166 B4
Compass Point HP4 .....121 E6
Compton Ave LU4 ....44 D4
Compton Gdns AL2 ......141 B5
Compton Pl WD19 ....175 E6
Comroston EN11 ....135 A6
Comyne Rd WD24 ....153 F3
Comyns The WD23 ......168 C1
Concorde Dr HP2 ....124 D3
Concorde St LU2 ....63 F8
Conduit La
Great Hormead SG9 ....29 B1
Hoddesdon EN11 ....135 A6
Conduit La E EN11 ....135 B6
Conemara Ct EN10 ....148 F5
Coney Cl AL10 ....130 B3
Coney Gree CM21 ....97 D3
Coneydale AL8 ....110 D8
Congreve Rd EN9 ....163 E6
Conifer Cl
Goff's Oak EN7 ....147 F2
Stevenage SG2 ....51 D7
Conifer Ct [7] CM23 ....76 F8
Conifer Wlk SG2 ....51 C7
Conifers The WD25 ......154 C4
Coningesby Dr WD17 ....166 E7
Coningsby Bank AL1 .....141 D7
Coningsby Cl AL9 ....144 D7
Coningsby Ct WD7 ......156 A3
Coningsby Dr EN6 ......159 D6
Coniston Cl HP3 ....125 C2
Coniston Lodge [3]
WD17 ....167 A7
Coniston Rd
Kings Langley WD4 ....138 F3
Luton LU3 ....44 F5

Connaught Cl HP2 125 A5
Connaught Gdns HP4 121 F7
Connaught Rd
Barnet EN5 171 D3
Harpenden AL5 86 B2
Harrow HA3 176 F2
Luton LU4 44 F1
St Albans AL3 127 C6
Connemara Cl WD6 170 D3
Connop Rd EN3 162 D1
Connor's Cl SG8 1 F4
Conquerors Hill AL4 108 E8
Conquest Cl SG4 34 F5
Constable Ct LU4 45 A1
Constantine Cl SG1 36 F1
Constantine Pl SG7 13 B1
Convent Cl SG5 34 F8
Convent Ct HP23 99 F3
Conway Gdns EN2 161 E1
Conway Ho WD6 170 C5
Conway Rd LU4 45 B1
Cony Cl 7 EN7 147 E5
Conyers CM20 117 C2
Cook Rd SG2 51 B7
Cook's Hole Rd EN2 161 C1
Cooks Mead WD23 168 B3
Cooks Spinney CM20 118 A2
Cooks Vennel HP1 124 B5
Cooks Way Hatfield AL10 130 B3
Hitchin SG4 22 A1
Coombe Gdns HP4 121 F5
Coombe Hill Rd WD3 165 A2
Coombe Rd
Bushey WD23 168 D2
Kelshall SG8 6 A1
Coombelands Rd SG8 2 E1
Coombes Rd AL2 142 C5
Cooper Way 10 HP4 122 D4
Cooper's Cl SG4 66 B1
Cooper's Ct SG12 114 E8
Cooper's Hill SG4 87 B8
Coopers Cl Aston SG2 51 D4
Bishop's Stortford CM23 76 B4
Coopers Cres WD6 170 C8
Coopers Ct SG14 113 D6
Coopers Field SG6 22 D7
Coopers Gate AL4 129 B1
Coopers Green La AL4, AL10 109 D1
Coopers La EN6 145 E1
Coopers Lane Rd EN6 160 B6
Coopers Mdw AL3 106 A6
Coopers Mews
Harpenden AL5 107 A8
Watford WD25 154 C8
Coopers Rd EN6 145 C1
Coopers Wlk 10 EN8 148 D3
Cooters End La AL5 85 F5
Copenhagen Cl LU3 44 D8
Copmans Wick WD3 164 D4
Coppens The SG5 12 A5
Copper Beech Cl HP3 137 F8
Copper Beech Ct 4 HA6 174 E3
Copper Beeches
11 Harpenden AL5 86 B1
Oaklands AL6 89 D7
Copper Ct CM21 97 E2
Copperfields Luton LU4 44 C3
Royston SG8 7 C6
Welwyn Garden City AL7 111 C5
Coppermill La WD3,UB9 172 F3
Copperwood SG13 113 F6
Coppice Cl Harrow HA7 176 F4
Hatfield AL10 129 F1
Coppice Farm Pk HP23 119 D4
Coppice Mead SG5 11 E5
Coppice The
Bishop's Stortford CM23 76 D5
1 Harpenden AL5 85 F2
Hemel Hempstead HP2 125 B4
Watford WD19 167 C3
Wigginton HP23 100 C1
Coppings The EN11 115 A1
Coppins Cl HP4 121 F4
Coppins The
Harrow HA3 176 E4
Markyate AL3 83 D5
Copse Cl HA6 174 C1
Copse Hill AL6 90 A8
Copse The
Bishop's Stortford CM23 77 C8
Hemel Hempstead HP1 123 E5
Hertford SG13 114 A6
Copse Way LU3 44 D8
Copse Wood Way HA6 174 C2
Copsewood Rd WD24 167 B8
Copt Hall Cotts LU2 64 E4
Copthall Cl CM22 77 F4
Copthorne LU2 46 D3
Copthorne Ave EN10 134 F3
Copthorne Cl WD3 165 F4
Copthorne Rd WD3 165 F4
Coral Gdns HP2 124 F3
Coral Ho CM20 117 A1
Corals Mead AL7 110 D5
Coram Cl HP4 122 C3
Corbridge Dr LU2 46 E1
Corby Cl AL2 141 A6
Cordell Cl EN8 148 E3
Corder Cl AL3 141 A8
Coreys Mill La SG1 36 C1
Corfe Cl
Borehamwood WD6 170 D6
4 Hemel Hempstead HP2 124 E2
Corinium Gate AL3 127 A1
Corinium Gdns LU3 45 A8
Corncastle Rd LU1 63 D6
Corncrake Cl LU2 46 C5
Corncroft AL10 130 B7
Cornel Cl LU1 63 A7
Cornel Ct LU1 63 A7
Cornelia Ct 3 AL5 86 A2
Cornelious Ho WD18 166 F5
Corner Cl SG6 22 E6
Corner Hall HP3 124 D1
Corner Hall Ave HP3 124 D1
Corner View AL9 144 C7
Corner Wood AL3 83 D5
Cornerfield AL10 130 B8
Corners AL7 111 A7
Cornfield Cres HP4 121 D7
Cornfield Rd WD23 168 B5
Cornfields
Hemel Hempstead HP1 124 B2
Stevenage SG2 51 C4
Cornflower Way AL10 129 E8
Cornhill Dr EN3 162 E2
Cornmead AL8 89 C1
Cornmill EN9 163 C6
Cornwall Cl EN8 162 E6
Cornwall Ct 6 HA6 175 F3
Cornwall Ho CM23 76 E4
Cornwall Rd
Harpenden AL5 86 B2
Pinner HA5 175 F3
St Albans AL1 127 E1
Coronation Ave SG8 7 C5
Coronation Rd
Bishop's Stortford CM23 76 E5
Ware SG12 93 D2
Coronet Ho 2 HA7 176 F4
Corringham Ct AL1 127 F4
Corton Cl SG1 50 B8
Corvus Cl SG8 7 E8
Cory-Wright Way AL4 87 E1
Cosgrove Way LU1 44 D1
Cosne Mews AL5 107 C7
Costins Wlk 12 HP4 122 D4
Cotefield LU4 44 C3
Cotesmore Rd HP1 123 E2
Cotlandswick AL2 142 C5
Cotney Croft SG2 51 D3
Cotsmoor AL1 127 F3
Cotswold HP2 124 E6
Cotswold Ave WD23 168 C3
Cotswold Bsns Pk LU1 62 D2
Cotswold Cl AL4 128 C8
Cotswold Gdns LU3 44 C7
Cotswolds AL10 130 A3
Cottage Cl
Croxley Green WD3 165 F3
Watford WD17 166 F7
Cottage Gdns EN8 148 D2
Cotter Ho SG1 37 A3
Cottered Rd SG9 26 F1
Cotterells HP1 124 C2
Cotterells Hill HP1 124 C3
Cotton Dr SG13 114 B7
Cotton Field AL10 130 B7
Cotton Rd EN6 159 C8
Cottonmill Cres AL1 127 D2
Cottonmill La AL1 127 D1
Coulser Cl HP1 124 A6
Coulson Ct
London Colney AL2 142 D4
Luton LU1 62 F8
Coulter Cl EN6 146 D4
Council Cotts
Great Wymondley SG4 35 F6
Letchworth SG6 23 B2
Radwell SG7 12 C4
Counters Cl HP1 124 A3
Countess Anne CE Prim Sch AL9 130 C6
Countess Cl UB9 173 C1
Countess Ct 4 LU2 45 D1
Couper Ho WD18 166 E3
Coursers Farm Cotts AL4 143 C6
Coursers Rd AL2,AL4 143 C6
Court Cl CM23 76 E5
Court Needham EN3 163 A2
Courtaulds WD4 138 B1
Courtenay Ave HA3 176 C2
Courtenay Gdns HA3 176 C1
Courtfield Cl EN10 135 A3
Courtfields AL5 86 D1
Courtlands Cl WD24 153 E4
Courtlands Dr WD17 153 E3
Courtleigh Ave EN4 159 D1
Courtway The WD19 175 E8
Courtyard Mews SG12 92 E4
Courtyard The
Hemel Hempstead HP3 138 D5
Hertingfordbury SG14 112 F5
St Albans AL4 128 F3
Courtyards The WD18 166 D2
Covent Garden Cl LU4 44 F3
Coventry Cl SG1 37 B1
Coverdale
Hemel Hempstead HP2 124 E6
Luton LU4 44 B6
Coverdale Ct EN3 162 E2
Covert Cl HP4 121 D6
Covert Rd HP4 121 D6
Covert The HA6 174 C2
Cow La Bushey WD23 168 A3
Tring HP23 100 D4
Watford WD25 154 C3
Cowards La SG4 88 F8
Cowbridge SG14 113 C6
Cowdray Cl LU2 46 C3
Cowles EN7 147 F4
Cowley Hill WD6 157 B1
Cowley Hill Sch WD6 170 A8
Cowlins CM17 118 D4
Cowper Cres SG14 92 B1
Cowper Ct Markyate AL3 83 D5
Watford WD24 154 A2
Cowper Rd
Berkhamsted HP4 122 B4
Harpenden AL5 86 C1
Hemel Hempstead HP1 124 B2
Markyate AL3 83 D5
Welwyn Garden City AL7 110 F4
Cowper Rise AL3 83 D5
Cowper St LU1 63 E5
Cowpers Way AL6 90 D5
Cowridge Cres LU2 64 A8
Cowslip Cl SG8 7 F5
Cowslip Hill SG6 22 E7
Cowslips AL7 111 C5
Cox Cl WD7 156 F7
Cox's Way SG15 11 A6
Coxfield Cl HP2 124 E2
Coyney Gn LU3 45 C1
Cozens La E EN10 134 F1
Cozens La W EN10 134 F1
Cozens Rd SG12 94 A2
Crab La WD25 155 B4
Crab Tree La SG5 20 D4
Crab Tree Rd SG3 68 F4
Crabb's La SG9 43 F6
Crabbes Cl SG5 34 E7
Crabtree Cl
Bushey WD23 168 B4
Hemel Hempstead HP3 124 D1
Crabtree Ct 3 HP3 124 E1
Crabtree Dell SG6 23 B3
Crabtree Inf Sch AL5 86 C1
Crabtree La
Harpenden AL5 86 C1
Hemel Hempstead HP3 124 D1
Crabtree Wlk EN10 134 E4
Crackley Mdw HP2 125 B8
Cradock Rd LU4 44 B1
Crafton Gn CM24 59 E7
Cragg Ave WD7 155 F3
Cragside SG2 69 C7
Craig Mount WD7 156 B4
Craigavon Rd HP2 124 F7
Craiglands AL4 128 D7
Craigmore Ct 5 HA6 174 E3
Craigs Wlk 4 EN8 148 D3
Craigweil Ave WD7 156 B4
Crakers Mead 4 WD18 167 B6
Cranborne Ave
Hitchin SG5 34 D6
Potters Bar EN6 144 E1
Cranborne Cl
Brickendon SG13 113 C3
Potters Bar EN6 158 E8
Cranborne Cres EN6 158 E8
Cranborne Ct EN3 162 D3
Cranborne Gdns AL7 110 F5
Cranborne Ind Est EN6 144 E1
Cranborne Par EN6 158 D8
Cranborne Prim Sch EN6 158 F8
Cranborne Rd
Cheshunt EN8 162 D7
Hatfield AL10 130 B6
Hoddesdon EN11 135 C7
Potters Bar EN6 144 E1
Cranbourne SG1 36 B1
Cranbourne Dr
Harpenden AL5 107 D6
Hoddesdon EN11 115 C2
Cranbourne Ho EN11 115 C2
Cranbourne Prim Sch The EN11 115 B2
Cranbourne Rd HA6 174 F1
Cranbrook Cl SG12 93 D3
Cranbrook Dr Luton LU3 44 D8
St Albans AL4 128 E3
Crane Mead SG12 114 E8
Crane Mead Bsns Pk SG12 114 E8
Cranefield Dr WD25 154 E6
Cranes Way WD6 170 C4
Cranfield Cres EN6 146 E2
Cranford Ct
Harpenden AL5 86 C1
Hertford SG14 112 F7
Cranleigh Cl EN7 148 A3
Cranleigh Gdns LU3 45 D3
Cranmer Cl EN6 145 C1
Cranmore Ct AL1 127 F4
Cranwell Cl AL4 128 C1
Cranwell Gdns CM23 59 C1
Cravells Ct AL5 107 C7
Cravells Rd AL5 107 C7
Crawford Rd AL10 130 A7
Crawley Cl LU1 63 C1
Crawley Dr HP2 124 F7
Crawley Green Inf Sch LU2 64 B8
Crawley Green Rd
Luton, Hart Hill LU2 64 A8
Luton, Wigmore LU2 46 D1
Crawley Rd LU1 63 D8
Crawley's La HP23 120 F7
Creamery Ct SG6 23 C3
Creasy Cl WD5 153 F8
Crecy Gdns AL3 106 A6
Creighton Ave AL1 141 D8
Crescent E EN4 159 C1
Crescent Rd
Bishop's Stortford CM23 77 A6
Hemel Hempstead HP2 124 D3
Luton LU2 63 F8
Crescent Rise LU2 63 F8
Crescent The
Abbots Langley WD5 139 F1
Ardeley SG2 38 F2
Bricket Wood AL2 141 A1
Caddington LU1 62 E3
Cottered SG9 39 D7
Croxley Green WD3 166 B3
Harlow CM17 118 C6
Hitchin SG5 21 D1
Letchworth SG6 23 A5
Lower Stondon SG16 10 C4
Marsworth HP23 80 A1
Pitstone LU7 80 C4
Radlett WD25 155 B1
St Ippolyts SG4 35 A3
Watford WD18 167 C5
Welwyn AL6 89 C4
Crescent W EN4 159 C1
Cress End WD3 165 A1
Cresset Cl SG12 115 C3
Cresswick SG4 66 E7
Crest Dr EN3 162 C1
Crest Pk HP2 125 C4
Crest The
Goff's Oak EN7 147 B4
Luton LU3 45 B7
Oaklands AL6 89 D8
Sawbridgeworth CM21 97 D2
Ware SG12 93 D3
Cresta Cl LU5 44 A2
Cresta Ho 3 LU1 63 D7
Creswick Ct AL7 110 D5
Creswick Jun Mix Inf Sch AL7 110 D3
Crew Curve HP4 121 F7
Crews Hill EN2 160 F5
Crews Hill Sta EN2 160 F5
Crib St SG12 93 D2
Cricketer's Rd SG15 11 A4
Cricketers Cl AL3 127 E4
Cricketfield La CM23 76 E8
Cringle Ct EN6 145 C1
Crispin Field LU7 80 C4
Croasdaile Rd CM24 59 E8
Croasdale Cl CM24 59 E8
Crocus Field EN5 171 F3
Croft Cl WD4 138 A1
Croft Ct
Borehamwood WD6 170 D6
4 Harpenden AL5 86 B1
Hitchin SG5 34 E7
Croft End Rd WD4 138 A1
Croft Field
Chipperfield WD4 138 A1
Hatfield AL10 130 A5
Croft La
Chipperfield WD4 138 A1
Letchworth SG6 12 B1
Croft Mdw WD4 138 A1
Croft Mdws LU7 80 A7
Croft Rd Luton LU2 46 B3
Ware SG12 93 C2
Croft The Barnet EN5 171 E5
Chiswell Green AL2 141 A6
Hoddesdon EN10 148 E8
Luton LU3 44 D8
Wareside SG12 94 E4
Welwyn Garden City AL7 110 F3
Croft Wlk EN10 148 E8
Crofters CM21 97 E3
Crofters End CM21 97 E3
Crofters Rd HA6 174 E6
Crofts Path HP3 125 B1
Crofts The
Hemel Hempstead HP3 125 B2
Stotfold SG5 11 F6
Croftwell AL5 107 F8
Cromer Cl HP4 102 E5
Cromer Rd WD24 154 C1
Cromer Way
Luton, Stopsley Common LU2 45 E6
Luton, Warden Hill LU2 45 D7
Cromer Windmill* SG2 38 E6
Crompton Pl EN3 163 A1
Crompton Rd SG1 50 A6
Cromwell Ave EN7 148 B1
Cromwell Cl
Bishop's Stortford CM23 76 B7
St Albans AL4 128 D8
Cromwell Gn SG6 23 B8
Cromwell Hill LU2 45 D1
Cromwell Rd
Borehamwood WD6 169 E8
Cheshunt EN7 148 B3
Hertford SG13 114 A7
Letchworth SG6 23 B8
Luton LU3 45 D1
Stevenage SG2 51 C5
Ware SG12 93 F2
Cromwell Way SG5 20 D4
Crooked Mile
Waltham Abbey EN9 163 C6
Waltham Abbey EN9 163 C7
Crooked Way EN9 135 E1
Crookhams AL7 90 A1
Crop Comm AL10 130 B7
Crosby Cl Luton LU4 45 A2
St Albans AL4 142 C8
Crosfield Ct WD17 167 D4
Cross Farm Mews HP3 137 D2
Cross La Harpenden AL5 107 C5
Hertford SG14 113 B6
Cross Oak Rd HP4 122 A4
Cross Rd Cheshunt EN8 162 E6
Hertford SG14 113 C7
Watford WD19 167 E3
Cross St Letchworth SG6 22 F7
Cross St *continued*
Luton LU2 63 E8
2 St Albans AL3 127 D3
Ware SG12 93 E1
Watford WD17 167 C6
Cross Way AL5 86 C3
Cross Way The
Harrow HA3 176 E1
Luton LU1 63 C5
Crossbrook AL10 129 E4
Crossbrook St EN8 162 D8
Crossett Gn HP3 125 C1
Crossfell Rd HP3 125 C2
Crossfield Rd EN11 135 B8
Crossfields AL3 141 B8
Crossfields Cl HP4 121 F4
Crossgates SG1 50 E5
Crosslands LU1 62 E3
Crossleys SG6 11 F2
Crossmead WD19 167 B3
Crossoaks La EN6 157 F5
Crosspath The WD7 156 A4
Crosspaths AL5 85 C4
Crossway Harlow CM17 118 D1
Pinner HA5 175 B1
Welwyn Garden City AL8 89 C2
Crossways Barley SG8 8 F1
Berkhamsted HP4 121 F3
Hemel Hempstead HP3 125 B3
Crouch Ct CM20 117 C3
Crouch Hall Gdns AL3 106 A6
Crouch Hall La AL3 106 A6
Crouch La EN7 147 C4
Crouchfield
Hemel Hempstead HP1 124 B2
Hertford SG14 92 C1
Crouchfield La SG12 92 E4
Crow Furlong SG5 34 D7
Crow La SG8 16 F5
Crowborough Path WD19 175 D6
Crowland Rd LU2 46 C5
Crown Cl CM22 98 C1
Crown Cotts Botley HP5 150 B8
King's Walden SG4 48 A6
Crown Lodge SG15 11 A4
Crown Rd WD6 170 B8
Crown Rise WD25 154 D5
Crown Rose Ct HP23 100 A3
Crown St AL3 106 B5
Crown Terr CM23 77 A7
Crown Wlk HP3 138 E7
Crown Yd AL3 106 D2
Crownfield EN10 135 A2
Croxdale Rd WD6 170 A7
Croxley Ctr WD18 166 D4
Croxley Sta WD3 166 B3
Croxley View WD18 166 E3
Croxton Cl 3 LU3 45 A7
Crozier Ave CM23 76 C8
Crunnell's Gn SG4 48 E5
Crusader Way WD18 166 F3
Cubbington Cl LU3 45 A7
Cubitt Cl SG4 35 C7
Cubitts Cl AL6 89 F3
Cublands SG13 114 B6
Cuckmans Dr AL2 141 A6
Cuckoo's Nest LU2 64 A7
Cucumber La AL9,SG13 132 A1
Cuffley Ave WD25 154 D5
Cuffley Cl LU3 44 F4
Cuffley Ct HP2 125 C8
Cuffley Hill EN7 147 B2
Cuffley Sch EN6 146 F1
Cuffley Sta EN6 146 F2
Cullera Cl HA6 174 F4
Cullings Ct EN9 163 F6
Culver Ct SG10 74 F1
Culver Lo AL1 127 E5
Culver Rd AL1 127 E5
Culverden Rd WD19 175 B7
Culverhouse Rd LU3 45 C3
Culworth Cl LU1 62 E3
Cumberland Cl
Hertford SG14 113 C8
Pimlico HP3 139 E7
Cumberland Ct
2 Hoddesdon EN11 135 A7
St Albans AL3 127 E4
Cumberland Dr AL3 106 B6
Cumberland St LU1 63 E6
Cumberlow Pl HP2 125 C2
Cumcum Hill AL9 131 E2
Cundalls Rd SG12 93 E2
Cunningham Ave
Enfield EN3 162 E3
Hatfield AL10 129 D6
St Albans AL1 127 F1
Cunningham Ct 3 EN8 148 E3
Cunningham Hill Inf Sch AL1 128 A1
Cunningham Hill Jun Sch AL1 128 A1
Cunningham Hill Rd AL1 128 A1
Cunningham Rd EN8 148 E4
Cupid Green La
Flamstead HP2 104 E3
Hemel Hempstead HP2 105 A1
Curlew Cl
Berkhamsted HP4 122 C3
Letchworth SG6 11 E1
Curlew Cres SG8 7 E8
Curlew Ct EN10 148 F8
Curlew Rd LU2 46 C5

Curo Pk AL2 ....141 E4
Currie St SG13 ....113 E6
Curteys CM17 ....118 D5
Curtis Cl WD3 ....165 A1
Curtis Rd HP3 ....125 D2
Curtis Way HP4 ....122 D3
Curtiss Dr WD25 ....153 F5
Curzon Gate Ct 1
WD17 ....167 A8
Curzon Rd LU3 ....45 C1
Cussans Ho WD18 ....166 E3
Cussons Cl EN7 ....148 A2
Cut Throat Ave HP4,LU6 ....81 E7
Cutenhoe Rd LU1 ....63 E4
Cutforth Rd CM21 ....97 E3
Cuthbert Cl EN7 ....147 F2
Cutlers Gn LU2 ....46 F2
Cutmore Dr AL4 ....129 B1
Cutts La SG4 ....66 D1
Cuttsfield Terr HP1 ....123 F2
Cuttys La SG1 ....50 E5
Cwmbran Ct HP2 ....124 F7
Cygnet Cl
Borehamwood WD6 ....170 C8
Northwood HA6 ....174 C4
Cygnet Ct 11 CM23 ....76 F6
Cygnet Ho
Hemel Hempstead HP3 ....138 F6
1 Stanmore HA7 ....176 F4
Cygnet Way CM19 ....116 A1
Cylers Thicket AL6 ....89 C6
Cymbeline Ct AL3 ....127 C4
Cypress Ave
Crews Hill EN2 ....161 A4
Welwyn Garden City AL7 ....111 C5
Cypress Cl EN9 ....163 D5
Cypress Rd HA3 ....176 D1
Cypress Wlk WD25 ....154 B4
Cyrils Way AL1 ....141 D8

D

Dacorum Way HP1 ....124 C3
Dacre Bldgs EN8 ....148 F2
Dacre Cres SG4 ....66 C1
Dacre Gdns WD6 ....170 D4
Dacre Gn SG8 ....7 F6
Dacre Ind Est EN8 ....148 F3
Dacre Rd SG5 ....35 A8
Daffodil Cl AL10 ....109 F1
Dagger La WD6 ....169 B4
Daggs Dell Rd HP1 ....123 E5
Dagnall Rd
Great Gaddesden HP1 ....103 C5
Whipsnade HP4,LU6 ....81 D8
Dagnall Sch HP4 ....81 C5
Dagnalls SG6 ....22 F2
Dahlia Cl
Hammond Street EN7 ....147 C6
Luton LU2 ....46 B4
Dailmead EN6 ....157 F5
Daintrees SG12 ....95 E4
Daintry Lodge HA6 ....174 F3
Dairy Cotts SG5 ....19 B2
Dairy Mews WD18 ....167 A4
Dairy Way WD5 ....139 F2
Dairyglen Ave EN8 ....162 E7
Daisy Ct SG6 ....23 A8
Daisy Dr AL10 ....129 F8
Dalby Cl LU4 ....44 B3
Dale Ave AL4 ....87 B5
Dale Cl Hitchin SG4 ....34 F4
Pinner HA5 ....175 B2
Dale Ct CM21 ....97 D1
Dale Rd LU1 ....63 C7
Dale The Letchworth SG6 ....22 E5
Waltham Abbey EN9 ....163 E5
Dales Path WD6 ....170 D4
Dales Rd WD6 ....170 D4
Daleside Dr EN6 ....158 F6
Dalewood Harpenden AL5 ....86 D1
Welwyn Garden City AL7 ....111 D5
Dalkeith Rd AL5 ....86 C1
Dallow Prim Sch LU1 ....63 C8
Dallow Rd LU1 ....63 B8
Dalroad Ent Est LU1 ....63 B8
Dalton Cl LU3 ....31 B1
Dalton Gdns CM23 ....76 E4
Dalton St AL3 ....127 D4
Dalton Way
Watford WD17 ....167 D4
Whitwell SG4 ....66 E7
Daltry Cl SG1 ....36 C2
Daltry Rd SG1 ....36 C2
Damask Cl Tring HP23 ....100 C4
Weston SG4 ....37 B8
Damask Gn HP1 ....123 E2
Damask Green Rd SG4 ....37 B8
Dame Alice Owen's Sch
EN6 ....158 E6
Dammersey Cl AL3 ....83 F4
Damson Way AL4 ....128 C5
Dancers End La HP23 ....99 C2
Dancers Hill Rd EN5 ....158 E3
Dancers La EN5 ....158 C4
Dancote SG3 ....68 F5
Dane Acres CM23 ....76 D8
Dane Bridge La SG10 ....75 B2
Dane Cl
Harpenden AL5 ....86 C4
Stotfold SG5 ....11 F8
Dane Ct AL1 ....128 B2
Dane End SG8 ....16 B4
Dane End Ho SG1 ....36 C1
Dane End La SG4 ....37 E5
Dane End Rd SG11 ....72 E3
Dane Ho CM23 ....76 D8
Dane O'Coys Rd CM23 ....58 E1
Dane Pk CM23 ....76 D8
Dane Rd LU3 ....45 C2
Dane St CM23 ....77 A7
Danebridge Rd SG10 ....75 B2
Danefield Rd SG5 ....20 C4
Danemead EN11 ....115 A1
Danes The AL2 ....141 C3
Danesbury La AL6 ....89 D8
Danesbury Park Rd AL6 ....89 D8
Danesbury Pk
Hertford SG14 ....113 D7
Welwyn AL6 ....89 C7
Danesbury Pk Cvn Site
AL6 ....89 D8
Danescroft SG6 ....12 A1
Danesgate SG1 ....50 D4
Danestrete SG1 ....50 D5
Daniel Ho 4 HA5 ....175 C1
Daniells AL7 ....111 A7
Danvers Croft HP23 ....100 C5
Danvers Dr LU3 ....31 C1
Danziger Way WD6 ....170 C8
Darblay Cl AL4 ....108 F5
Darby Dr
Waltham Abbey EN9 ....163 C6
Welwyn AL6 ....68 E3
Darcy Cl EN8 ....162 E8
Dark La
Cheshunt EN7 ....148 A1
Codicote SG4 ....88 E8
Harpenden AL5 ....107 D7
Sandon SG9 ....15 B1
Wingrave HP22 ....60 C3
Darkes La EN6 ....159 A8
Darlands Dr EN5 ....171 D4
Darley Hall LU2 ....47 C1
Darley Rd LU2,SG4 ....47 C2
Darnhills WD7 ....155 F4
Darnicle Hill EN7 ....147 A6
Darr's La HP4 ....121 D6
Darrington Rd WD6 ....169 E8
Dart The HP2 ....125 A8
Dartmouth Mews LU4 ....44 D3
Darwin Cl
Hemel Hempstead HP2 ....105 B1
St Albans AL3 ....127 E7
Darwin Gdns WD19 ....175 C5
Darwin Rd SG2 ....51 B6
Dashes The CM20 ....117 E1
Datchet Cl HP2 ....125 B8
Datchworth Turn HP2 ....125 C3
Dauphin Ct 5 LU2 ....45 D1
Dauphine Ct HA3 ....176 E1
Davenham Ave HA6 ....174 F5
Daventer Dr HA7 ....176 F3
David Evans Ct SG6 ....22 D7
Davies St SG13 ....113 E6
Davis Cres SG5 ....20 D4
Davis Ct AL1 ....127 E3
Davis Ho 11 HP4 ....122 C4
Davis' Row SG15 ....11 A4
Davison Cl EN8 ....148 D3
Davison Dr EN8 ....148 D3
Davys Cl AL4 ....108 E7
Dawes La Sarratt WD3 ....151 F3
Wheathampstead AL4 ....87 D1
Dawley AL7 ....89 F1
Dawley Ct HP2 ....125 A7
Dawlish Cl SG2 ....69 C7
Dawlish Rd LU4 ....44 F3
Dawson Cl SG16 ....10 C5
Day's Cl SG8 ....7 C5
Dayemead AL7 ....111 B3
Days Cl AL10 ....129 F5
Days Mead AL10 ....129 F5
De Haviland Cl AL10 ....129 F6
De Havilland Aircraft
Heritage Mus The*
AL2 ....143 B2
De Havilland Ct WD7 ....156 E7
De Havilland Way WD5 ....153 F7
De Tany Ct AL1 ....127 D2
De Vere Wlk WD17 ....166 E7
Deacon Cl AL1 ....141 D7
Deacon's Hill Rd WD6 ....170 A4
Deacons Cl
Borehamwood WD6 ....170 A5
Pinner HA5 ....175 B1
Deacons Ct 7 LU2 ....63 D8
Deacons Hill WD19 ....167 C3
Deacons Hts WD6 ....170 A3
Deacons Way SG5 ....21 D1
Deaconsfield Rd HP3 ....138 E8
Dead Woman's La SG4 ....48 C7
Deadman's Ash La
WD3 ....152 B3
Deakin Cl WD18 ....166 E2
Dean Ct WD25 ....154 D6
Dean Field HP3 ....137 A4
Dean Moore Cl AL1 ....127 D2
Dean The HP22 ....60 B3
Dean's Gdns AL4 ....128 A7
Deane Ct HA6 ....174 E2
Deans Cl
Abbots Langley WD5 ....153 D7
Tring HP23 ....100 A4
Deans Furlong HP23 ....100 A4
Deans Lawn 8 HP4 ....122 C4
Deans Mdw HP4 ....81 C5
Deanscroft SG3 ....68 F5
Deansway HP3 ....138 F8
Deard's End La SG3 ....68 F6
Deards Wood SG3 ....68 F5
Debenham Ct EN5 ....171 C4
Debenham Rd EN7 ....148 B4
Dee The HP2 ....124 F8
Deep Denes LU2 ....46 A2
Deepdene EN6 ....158 D8
Deeping Cl SG3 ....68 F4
Deer Cl SG13 ....113 F6
Deer Park Way EN9 ....163 B4
Deerfield Cl SG12 ....93 D2
Deerings The AL5 ....107 A4
Deerswood Ave AL10 ....130 B3
Deeves Hall La EN6 ....157 E6
Deimos Dr HP2 ....125 A6
Delahay Rise HP4 ....122 B6
Delamare Rd EN8 ....148 F2
Delamere Rd WD6 ....170 B8
Delfcroft SG12 ....93 C2
Delfield Gdns LU1 ....62 E4
Delius Cl WD6 ....169 C3
Dell Cl AL5 ....86 B3
Dell Ct WD3 ....173 A8
Dell Field Ave HP4 ....122 B6
Dell La
Bishop's Stortford, Hockerill
CM23 ....77 A7
Bishop's Stortford,
Latchmore Bank CM22 ....77 B1
Spellbrook CM22 ....98 A8
Dell Mdw HP3 ....138 E7
Dell Rd
Berkhamsted HP4 ....121 D7
Enfield EN3 ....162 C1
Watford WD24 ....154 A2
Dell Rise AL2 ....141 B5
Dell Side WD24 ....154 A2
Dell Springs SG9 ....40 E8
Dell The Baldock SG7 ....23 E6
Brickendon SG13 ....113 C3
Caddington LU1 ....62 E3
Luton LU2 ....46 F1
Markyate AL3 ....83 D5
Moor Park HA6 ....174 E8
Pinner HA5 ....175 D1
Radlett WD7 ....156 A4
Royston SG8 ....7 C5
St Albans AL1 ....128 A4
Stevenage SG1 ....50 E5
Waltham Abbey EN9 ....163 C3
Welwyn AL6 ....90 A4
Dellcot Cl LU2 ....46 B4
Dellcott Cl AL8 ....110 C7
Dellcroft Way AL5 ....107 A5
Dellcut Rd HP2 ....125 A5
Dellfield
St Albans AL1 ....127 F2
Thundridge SG12 ....93 D8
Dellfield Cl
Berkhamsted HP4 ....122 A6
Radlett WD7 ....155 F4
Watford WD17 ....167 A7
Dellfield Ct
1 Harlow CM17 ....118 C4
Luton LU2 ....46 D2
Dellfield Rd AL10 ....130 A5
Dellmeadow WD5 ....139 E1
Dellors Cl EN5 ....171 D4
Dells The
11 Bishop's Stortford CM23 ....76 F7
Hemel Hempstead HP3 ....125 B2
Dells Wood Cl EN11 ....114 F1
Dellsome La
Colney Heath AL4 ....143 E8
Welham Green AL9 ....144 B8
Dellswood Cl SG13 ....113 E5
Dellwood WD3 ....165 B1
Delmar Ave HP2 ....125 D2
Delmer Ct WD6 ....156 F1
Delmerend La AL3 ....84 C1
Delphine Cl LU1 ....63 B6
Delrow Cotts WD25 ....168 C8
Delta Gain WD19 ....175 D7
Demontfort Rise SG12 ....93 C3
Denbigh Cl 2 HP2 ....124 E2
Denbigh High Sch LU3 ....45 C2
Denbigh Inf Sch LU3 ....45 B2
Denbigh Jun Sch LU3 ....45 B2
Denbigh Rd LU3 ....45 B2
Denby SG6 ....23 B4
Dencora Ctr The AL1 ....128 A3
Dencora Way LU3 ....44 B8
Dendridge Cl EN1 ....162 B2
Dene La SG2 ....51 E2
Dene Rd HA6 ....174 D4
Denes The HP3 ....138 F7
Denewood Cl WD17 ....153 F2
Denham Cl
Hemel Hempstead HP2 ....125 A8
Luton LU3 ....44 E8
Denham La SL9 ....172 A2
Denham Way WD6 ....170 C8
Denham Way (North Orbital
Rd) WD3 ....172 E4
Denmark Cl LU3 ....44 E8
Denmark St WD17 ....167 B7
Dennis Cl HP22 ....99 A4
Dennis Ct 1 AL3 ....127 D4
Denny Ave EN9 ....163 D5
Denny Ct CM23 ....59 B2
Denny Gate EN8 ....148 F4
Denny's La HP4 ....121 F3
Densley Cl AL8 ....110 D8
Denton Cl
Barnet EN5 ....171 C4
Luton LU4 ....44 B3
Denton Ho 10 WD19 ....175 C7
Denton Rd SG1 ....50 E4
Dents Cl SG6 ....23 C3
Derby Ave HA3 ....176 D2
Derby Ho HA5 ....175 D1
Derby Rd
Hoddesdon EN11 ....135 D5
Luton LU4 ....44 C2
Watford WD18 ....167 C5
Derby Way SG1 ....51 B8
Derry Leys AL10 ....129 E7
Derwent Ave Luton LU3 ....45 B7
Pinner HA5 ....175 E4
Derwent Cl WD25 ....154 C5
Derwent Lower Sch
SG16 ....10 B5
Derwent Rd
Harpenden AL5 ....85 C4
Hemel Hempstead HP3 ....125 C2
Lower Stondon SG16 ....10 B4
Luton LU2 ....64 A8
Des Fuller Ct 3 LU1 ....63 F6
Desborough Cl
Hertford SG14 ....92 C1
Welwyn Garden City AL7 ....111 B3
Desborough Dr AL6 ....90 D5
Desborough Rd SG4 ....35 C8
Desmond Rd WD24 ....153 F3
Deva Cl AL3 ....127 A1
Devereux Dr WD17 ....153 E1
Devoils La 9 CM23 ....76 F7
Devon Ct AL1 ....127 E2
Devon Rd Luton LU2 ....64 B8
Watford WD24 ....167 D8
Devonshire Bsns Pk
WD6 ....170 D6
Devonshire Cl SG2 ....69 A8
Devonshire Ct HA5 ....175 F2
Devonshire Rd
5 Harpenden AL5 ....86 B1
Pinner HA5 ....175 F2
Dewars Cl AL6 ....89 C6
Dewes Green Rd
CM23 ....30 F1
Dewgrass Gr EN8 ....162 D4
Dewhurst Rd EN8 ....148 C2
Dewhurst St Mary CE Prim
Sch EN8 ....148 C2
Dewpond Cl SG1 ....50 C8
Dewsbury Rd LU3 ....45 C6
Dexter Cl Luton LU3 ....31 B1
St Albans AL1 ....128 A2
Dexter Rd
Barnet EN5 ....171 D3
Harefield UB9 ....173 C1
Diamond Ind Ctr SG6 ....23 C7
Diamond Rd WD24 ....154 A1
Dickens Cl AL3 ....127 D4
Dickens Ct HP2 ....105 B1
Dickenson Way 19 SG12 ....93 D1
Dicker Mill SG13 ....113 D7
Dicket Mead AL6 ....89 C5
Dickins Cl EN7 ....148 A5
Dickinson Ave WD3 ....166 A3
Dickinson Quay HP3 ....138 F7
Dickinson Sq WD3 ....166 A3
Dickinsons Field AL5 ....107 C7
Dickson EN7 ....147 F4
Dig Dag Hill EN7 ....147 F4
Digswell Cl WD6 ....157 A1
Digswell Ct AL8 ....110 E8
Digswell Hill AL6 ....89 B2
Digswell Ho AL8 ....89 D2
Digswell House Mews
AL8 ....89 D2
Digswell La AL7 ....89 F2
Digswell Park Rd
Welwyn Garden City AL8 ....89 D3
Welwyn Garden City AL8 ....89 E3
Digswell Pl AL8 ....89 C1
Digswell Rd AL8 ....89 E1
Digswell Rise AL8 ....110 E8
Dimmocks La WD3 ....152 B3
Dimsdale Cotts SG9 ....29 B7
Dimsdale Cres CM23 ....77 B6
Dimsdale St SG14 ....113 C6
Dinant Link Rd EN11 ....135 B7
Dingle Cl EN5 ....170 F3
Dinmore HP3 ....136 F3
Ditchfield Rd EN11 ....115 A1
Ditchling Cl LU2 ....46 C3
Ditchling Ct 1 AL1 ....127 E3
Ditchmore La SG1 ....50 D6
Ditton Gn LU2 ....46 E3
Divine Saviour RC Prim Sch
WD5 ....153 D7
Divot Pl SG13 ....114 B7
Dixies Cl SG7 ....4 D3
Dixon Pl SG9 ....40 E7
Dixon's Ct SG12 ....114 E8
Dixons Hill Cl AL9 ....144 B6
Dixons Hill Rd AL9 ....144 C7
Dobb's Weir Rd EN11,
CM19 ....135 D5
Docklands SG5 ....20 D4
Doctor's Commons Rd
HP4 ....122 B4
Dodds La HP2 ....104 E1
Dodwood AL7 ....111 B5
Dog Kennel La
Chorleywood WD3 ....164 F5
Hatfield AL10 ....130 A6
Royston SG8 ....7 D6
Doggetts Way AL1 ....127 C1
Dognell Gn AL8 ....110 B7
Dolesbury Dr AL6 ....89 E8
Dollimore Cl SG4 ....67 F1
Dollis Brook Wlk EN5 ....171 E3
Dollis Valley Dr EN5 ....171 F4
Dollis Valley Way
EN5 ....171 F3
Dolphin Sq HP23 ....100 A3
Dolphin Way CM23 ....77 A8
Dolphin Yd
2 Hertford SG14 ....113 D6
St Albans AL1 ....127 D3
7 Ware SG12 ....93 D1
Dominic Ct EN9 ....163 B6
Doncaster Cl SG1 ....51 C8
Doncaster Gn WD19 ....175 C5
Donkey La HP23 ....99 E2
Donne Cl SG8 ....7 C8
Dorant Ho AL3 ....127 D7
Dorcas Ct AL1 ....127 E2
Dorchester Ave EN11 ....135 A8
Dorchester Ct
Croxley Green WD3 ....166 D4
St Albans AL1 ....128 A2
Watford WD19 ....167 E3
Dordans Rd LU4 ....44 F4
Dorel Cl LU2 ....45 F2
Dormans Cl HA6 ....174 D3
Dormer Cl EN5 ....171 D4
Dormie Cl AL3 ....127 C5
Dornan Ct LU1 ....63 E5
Dorrien's Croft HP4 ....121 F7
Dorrington Cl LU3 ....45 C1
Dorrofield Cl WD3 ....166 D4
Dorset Cl HP4 ....121 F5
Dorset Ct 4 LU1 ....63 F6
Dorset Ho 13 CM23 ....76 F7
Douglas Ave WD24 ....154 E2
Douglas Cl AL6 ....89 E3
Douglas Dr SG1 ....51 A8
Douglas Ho 11 EN8 ....148 D3
Douglas Rd
Harpenden AL5 ....85 F2
Luton LU4 ....45 A2
Douglas Way AL7 ....111 C6
Dove Cl
Bishop's Stortford CM23 ....76 E3
Stansted Mountfitchet
CM24 ....59 E8
Dove Ct AL10 ....130 A3
Dove La EN6 ....159 C5
Dove Pk
Chorleywood WD3 ....164 C4
Pinner HA5 ....176 A3
Dove Rd SG1 ....36 F3
Dovecote The SG7 ....4 D4
Dovedale Luton LU2 ....45 E6
Stevenage SG2 ....51 B4
Ware SG12 ....93 C3
Dovedale Cl UB9 ....173 C1
Dovehouse Croft CM20 ....118 A2
Dovehouse Hill LU2 ....46 B1
Dovehouse La LU6 ....82 D8
Dover Cl Luton LU3 ....45 A3
Pitstone LU7 ....80 D2
Dover Way WD3 ....166 C5
Doverfield EN7 ....147 C2
Dowding Way WD25 ....153 F5
Dower Ct SG4 ....34 F5
Dower Mews 5 HP4 ....122 C4
Dowland Ho EN1 ....161 F1
Dowling Ct HP3 ....138 D8
Down Edge AL3 ....105 F5
Down Green La AL4 ....108 B7
Downalong WD23 ....168 D1
Downedge AL3 ....127 B4
Downer Dr WD3 ....152 A3
Downes Rd AL4 ....128 B7
Downfield Cl SG13 ....114 C4
Downfield Ct SG12 ....93 B5
Downfield Jun Mix Inf Sch
EN8 ....162 E8
Downfield Rd
Cheshunt EN8 ....162 E8
Hertford Heath SG13 ....114 C5
Downfields AL8 ....110 B4
Downhall Ley SG9 ....40 E7
Downings Wood WD3 ....172 D5
Downlands Baldock SG7 ....13 A1
Luton LU3 ....44 C7
Royston SG8 ....7 C6
Stevenage SG2 ....51 D7
Waltham Abbey EN9 ....163 E5
Downlands Cvn Pk LU1 ....84 C8
Downs La AL10 ....130 A3
Downs Rd LU1 ....63 C7
Downs The AL10 ....130 A3
Downs View LU4 ....44 D4
Downsfield AL10 ....130 B2
Downside HP2 ....124 E4
Downside Inf Sch LU4 ....44 E1
Downside Jun Sch LU4 ....44 E1
Downsway Ct SG8 ....7 C6
Downton Ct 3 LU3 ....63 D8
Downview LU4 ....44 B2
Dowry Wlk WD17 ....153 F1
Dragon Moth Rd AL10 ....129 D6
Drakes Cl EN8 ....148 D3
Drakes Dr
Northwood HA6 ....174 B2
St Albans AL1 ....128 C1
Stevenage SG2 ....51 B7
Drakes Mdw CM17 ....118 E4
Drakes Way AL10 ....130 B3
Drapers Mews LU3 ....45 C1
Drapers Way SG1 ....50 C7
Drayman's Cl CM23 ....76 B5
Drayson Cl EN9 ....163 E7
Drayton Ave EN6 ....158 E7
Drayton Rd
Borehamwood WD6 ....170 A5
Luton LU4 ....44 A3
Driftway SG8 ....16 E4
Driftway The HP2 ....124 F3
Driftwood Ave AL2 ....141 B5
Drive The Barnet EN5 ....171 E6
Brookmans Park AL9 ....145 B6

Drive The *continued*
Cheshunt EN7 .... 148 B3
Goff's Oak EN7 .... 147 B3
Harlow CM20 .... 117 E1
Harpenden AL5 .... 86 A1
Hertford SG14 .... 113 C8
Hoddesdon EN11 .... 135 A8
Kimpton AL4 .... 87 B7
London Colney AL2 .... 142 A5
Northwood HA6 .... 174 E2
Oaklands AL6 .... 69 A1
Potters Bar EN6 .... 158 F7
Radlett WD7 .... 156 A5
Rickmansworth WD3 .... 165 C3
Sawbridgeworth CM21 .... 97 E2
Watford WD17 .... 153 E2
Driver's End SG4 .... 68 A4
Driver's End La SG4,SG3 .... 68 A4
Driveway The
Cuffley EN6 .... 146 E3
Hemel Hempstead HP1 .... 124 B1
Dromey Gdns HA3 .... 176 F3
Drop La AL2 .... 155 C7
Drovers Way
Bishop's Stortford CM23 .... 76 C5
Hatfield AL10 .... 130 B8
St Albans AL1 .... 127 D3
Drummond Dr HA7 .... 176 F3
Drummond Ride HP23 .... 100 A5
Drummonds The LU4 .... 44 C2
Drury La SG12 .... 95 E1
Drycroft AL7 .... 110 E2
Dryden Cres SG2 .... 51 C8
Dryden Rd HA3 .... 176 F2
Drysdale Cl 7 HA6 .... 174 E3
Dubbs Knoll Rd SG8 .... 1 F5
Dubrae Cl AL3 .... 127 A1
Duchess Cl CM23 .... 76 C7
Duchy Rd EN4 .... 159 D1
Duck End CM23 .... 59 E1
Duck La SG2 .... 52 E4
Duck's Hill Rd HA6 .... 174 B1
Ducketts La SG10 .... 75 D1
Ducketts Mead CM19 .... 116 B1
Ducketts Wharf 10 CM23 .... 76 F6
Ducketts Wood SG12 .... 93 E6
Duckling La CM21 .... 97 E2
Duckmore La HP23 .... 99 E2
Dudley Ave EN8 .... 162 D7
Dudley Hill Cl AL6 .... 89 E8
Dudley St LU2 .... 63 E8
Dudswell La HP4 .... 121 D7
Dugdale Ct SG5 .... 21 C1
Dugdale Hill La EN6 .... 158 E7
Dugdales WD3 .... 166 A5
Duke St Hoddesdon EN11 .... 135 A7
Luton LU2 .... 63 E8
Watford WD17 .... 167 C6
Duke's La SG5 .... 34 F8
Dukes Ave LU6 .... 81 E8
Dukes Ct 4 LU1 .... 63 D6
Dukes Ride
Bishop's Stortford CM23 .... 76 C7
13 Luton LU2 .... 45 D1
Dukes Way HP4 .... 122 A6
Dulwich Way WD3 .... 166 A4
Dumbarton Ave EN8 .... 162 D5
Dumbletons WD3 .... 172 E6
Dumfries Cl WD19 .... 175 A7
Dumfries Ct 9 LU1 .... 63 D6
Dumfries St LU1 .... 63 D6
Duncan Cl AL7 .... 110 E5
Duncan Ct AL1 .... 127 F1
Duncan Way WD23 .... 167 F7
Duncombe Cl
Hertford SG14 .... 113 C8
Luton LU3 .... 45 C6
Duncombe Rd
Berkhamsted HP4 .... 121 E6
Hertford SG14 .... 113 C8
Duncombe Sch SG14 .... 113 C7
Duncots Cl SG5 .... 21 E3
Dundale Prim Sch
HP23 .... 100 A5
Dundale Rd HP23 .... 100 A4
Dundas Mews EN3 .... 163 A2
Dunedin Ho SG8 .... 7 C6
Dunfermline Ho 9
WD19 .... 175 C7
Dunford Ct 7 HA5 .... 175 F3
Dunham's La SG6 .... 23 C6
Dunkirks Mews SG13 .... 113 D4
Dunlin SG6 .... 11 E1
Dunlin Rd HP2 .... 124 E8
Dunmow Ct LU3 .... 45 D2
Dunmow Rd CM23 .... 77 C7
Dunn Cl SG1 .... 50 E3
Dunnock Cl WD6 .... 170 A5
Dunny La WD4 .... 151 F7
Dunraven Ave LU1 .... 63 A8
Dunsby Rd LU3 .... 45 A6
Dunsley Pl HP23 .... 100 B3
Dunsmore WD19 .... 175 D8
Dunsmore Cl WD23 .... 168 D3
Dunsmore Rd LU1 .... 63 C6
Dunsmore Way WD23 .... 168 D3
Dunstable Cl LU4 .... 45 A1
Dunstable Ct LU4 .... 44 F2
Dunstable Pl 5 LU1 .... 63 D7
Dunstable Rd
Caddington LU1,LU6 .... 62 C3
Dagnall HP4,LU6 .... 81 C7
Luton LU4 .... 44 D2
Luton,Bury Park LU1,LU4 .... 45 B1
Redbourn AL3 .... 106 A7
Studham LU6 .... 82 B6
Dunster Cl Barnet EN5 .... 171 D5
Harefield UB9 .... 173 B2
Dunster Ct WD6 .... 170 D6
Dunster Rd HP2 .... 105 B1
Dunsters Mead AL7 .... 111 B4
Dunston Hill HP23 .... 100 A4
Durban Rd E WD18 .... 167 A5
Durban Rd W WD18 .... 167 A5
Durbar Rd LU4 .... 45 B1
Durham Cl
Sawbridgeworth CM21 .... 97 C1
Stanstead Abbotts SG12 .... 115 B5
Durham Ct EN5 .... 171 F6
Durham Ho 14 WD6 .... 170 A7
Durham Rd
Borehamwood WD6 .... 170 C6
Luton LU2 .... 64 A7
Stevenage SG1 .... 37 A1
Durley Gdns LU1 .... 63 D5
Durrant Ct HA3 .... 176 E2
Durrants Dr WD3 .... 166 C5
Durrants Hill Rd HP3 .... 138 D8
Durrants La HP4 .... 121 F5
Durrants Rd HP4 .... 121 F5
Dury Rd EN5 .... 171 F7
Duxford Cl LU3 .... 45 B7
Duxons Turn HP2 .... 125 B4
Dwight Rd WD18 .... 166 D2
Dyer Ct EN3 .... 163 A2
Dyers Ct CM23 .... 76 C5
Dyes La SG4 .... 49 F3
Dyke La AL4 .... 108 E7
Dylan Cl WD6 .... 169 D2
Dymoke Gn AL4 .... 128 A7
Dymokes Way EN11 .... 115 A1
Dyrham La EN5 .... 158 A3
Dyson Ct WD17 .... 167 C5
Dysons Cl EN8 .... 162 D6

E

Eagle Centre Way LU4 .... 44 B7
Eagle Cl LU4 .... 44 A4
Eagle Ct Baldock SG7 .... 12 E1
Hertford SG13 .... 114 B7
Eagle Way AL10 .... 130 A3
Ealing Cl WD6 .... 170 D8
Earl St WD17 .... 167 C6
Earls Cl CM23 .... 76 D6
Earls Hill Gdns SG8 .... 7 C6
Earls La EN6 .... 157 F6
Earls Meade LU2 .... 45 D1
Earlsmead SG6 .... 22 F3
Easington Rd SG12 .... 71 E7
Easingwold Gdns LU1 .... 62 F8
East Burrowfield AL7 .... 110 D4
East Cl
Chiswell Green AL2 .... 141 B6
Hitchin SG4 .... 22 B1
Stevenage SG1 .... 50 F5
East Comm
Harpenden AL5 .... 107 C7
Redbourn AL3 .... 106 A4
East Dr Moor Park WD1 .... 174 E8
Sawbridgeworth CM21 .... 97 E1
St Albans AL4 .... 128 F4
Watford WD25 .... 154 B3
East End Way HA5 .... 175 F1
East Flint HP1 .... 123 F4
East Gate CM20 .... 117 D1
East Gn HP3 .... 139 A6
East Hertfordshire Sec Ctr
(PRU) EN8 .... 162 D5
East Hill LU3 .... 45 B6
East La
Abbots Langley WD5 .... 140 A2
Wheathampstead AL4 .... 87 D1
East Lodge La EN2 .... 160 E4
East Mead AL7 .... 111 B3
East Mimms 4 HP2 .... 124 E4
East Mount AL4 .... 87 D1
East Pk Harlow CM17 .... 118 C3
Sawbridgeworth CM21 .... 97 E1
East Rd
Bishop's Stortford CM23 .... 77 B7
Enfield EN3 .... 162 C1
Harlow CM20 .... 118 B4
East Reach SG2 .... 51 A2
East Ridgeway EN6 .... 146 E3
East Riding AL6 .... 90 D5
East St
Hemel Hempstead HP2 .... 124 D3
Lilley LU2 .... 32 D2
Ware SG12 .... 93 D1
East View Barnet EN5 .... 171 F6
Essendon AL9 .... 131 F6
St Ippolyts SG4 .... 35 C2
East Wlk CM20 .... 117 D1
Eastbourne Ave SG1 .... 50 A6
Eastbrook Prim Sch
HP2 .... 125 A8
Eastbrook Rd EN9 .... 163 E6
Eastbrook Way HP2 .... 124 E3
Eastbury Ave HA6 .... 174 F5
Eastbury Ct
St Albans AL1 .... 127 F4
Watford WD19 .... 167 C2
Eastbury Farm Jun Mix Inf
Sch HA6 .... 174 F6
Eastbury Pl HA6 .... 174 F5
Eastbury Rd
Northwood HA6 .... 174 E4
Watford WD19 .... 167 C3
Eastcheap SG6 .... 22 F6
Eastcote Dr AL5 .... 107 D6
Eastcott Cl LU2 .... 46 D1
Eastend Cotts CM19 .... 116 D1
Eastern Ave
Cheshunt EN8 .... 162 F6
Eastern Ave *continued*
Lower Stondon SG16 .... 10 C3
Eastern Way SG6 .... 12 A1
Eastfield Ave WD24 .... 167 D8
Eastfield Cl LU2 .... 46 C4
Eastfield Ct AL4 .... 128 D6
Eastfield Prim Sch EN3 .... 162 D1
Eastfield Rd
Cheshunt EN8 .... 162 F7
Enfield EN3 .... 162 D1
Royston SG8 .... 7 E6
Eastgate SG1 .... 50 D5
Eastglade HA6 .... 174 F5
Easthall Cotts SG4 .... 67 C8
Easthall Ho SG1 .... 36 C1
Eastham Cl EN5 .... 171 F4
Eastholm SG6 .... 23 A8
Eastholm Gn SG6 .... 23 A8
Eastlea Ave WD25 .... 154 E2
Eastman Way HP2 .... 125 A6
Eastmoor Ct AL5 .... 107 C6
Eastmoor Pk AL5 .... 107 C6
Eastnor HP3 .... 137 A3
Easton Gdns WD6 .... 170 E5
Eastor AL7 .... 90 A1
Eastwick Cres WD3 .... 172 F8
Eastwick Hall La CM20 .... 117 A5
Eastwick Rd
Eastwick CM20 .... 117 B4
Gilston CM20 .... 117 E6
Eastwick Row HP2 .... 125 A2
Eastwood Ct HP2 .... 125 A4
Eaton Gate HA6 .... 174 C4
Eaton Green Ct LU2 .... 64 C8
Eaton Green Rd LU2 .... 64 C8
Eaton Ho 5 CM23 .... 77 B8
Eaton Pl LU2 .... 46 D1
Eaton Rd
Hemel Hempstead HP2 .... 125 B6
St Albans AL1 .... 128 B3
Eaton Valley Rd LU2 .... 64 B8
Ebberns Rd HP3 .... 138 E8
Ebenezer St 7 LU1 .... 63 D6
Ebury App WD3 .... 165 D1
Ebury Cl HA6 .... 174 C5
Ebury Ct WD3 .... 165 D1
Ebury Rd
Rickmansworth WD3 .... 165 D1
Watford WD17 .... 167 C6
Ebury Rdbt WD3 .... 165 D1
Echo Hill SG8 .... 7 C5
Eddy St HP4 .... 122 A5
Eden Cl EN3 .... 163 A1
Edenhall Cl HP2 .... 125 D2
Edens Cl CM23 .... 77 B7
Edens Mount CM21 .... 97 F4
Edenvale EN7 .... 148 B2
Edgars Ct AL7 .... 110 E5
Edgbaston Dr WD7 .... 156 E7
Edgbaston Rd WD19 .... 175 B7
Edgcott Cl LU3 .... 31 B1
Edgecote Cl LU1 .... 62 E3
Edgehill Gdns LU3 .... 44 C8
Edgewood Dr LU2 .... 46 C6
Edgeworth Cl SG2 .... 51 C1
Edgware Way HA8 .... 169 D1
Edgwarebury La WD6,
HA8 .... 169 F1
Edinburgh Ave WD3 .... 165 A2
Edinburgh Cres EN8 .... 162 E6
Edinburgh Dr WD5 .... 154 A7
Edinburgh Gdns CM23 .... 76 E6
Edinburgh Pl CM20 .... 118 A4
Edinburgh Sq SG8 .... 2 A6
Edinburgh Way CM20 .... 117 E3
Edison Cl AL4 .... 128 C2
Edison Rd SG2 .... 51 B6
Edkins Cl LU2 .... 45 E5
Edlyn Cl HP4 .... 121 F5
Edmonds Dr SG2 .... 51 D4
Edmund Beaufort Dr
AL3 .... 127 E5
Edmund Mews WD4 .... 139 A2
Edmunds Rd SG14 .... 112 F7
Edridge Cl WD23 .... 168 C4
Edulf Rd WD6 .... 170 B8
Edward Amey Cl WD25 .... 154 C3
Edward Cl
Abbots Langley WD5 .... 153 F7
St Albans AL1 .... 127 F2
Edward Cotts SG11 .... 54 C3
Edward Ct
Hemel Hempstead HP3 .... 138 D7
Waltham Abbey EN9 .... 163 F6
Edward St LU2 .... 45 F1
Edwards Ho 5 SG1 .... 50 E6
Edwick Ct EN8 .... 148 D2
Edwin Ware Ct 1 HA5 .... 175 C1
Edwinstree CE Mid Sch
SG9 .... 40 D8
Edwyn Cl EN5 .... 171 D3
Egdon Dr LU2 .... 45 D6
Egerton Rd HP4 .... 122 B6
Egerton-Rothesay Sch
HP4 .... 121 E4
Egg Farm La WD4 .... 139 B1
Egglesfield Cl HP4 .... 121 E6
Eggleton Dr HP23 .... 100 A5
Eight Acres HP23 .... 100 A4
Eighth Ave LU3 .... 44 D7
Eisenberg Cl SG7 .... 13 B1
Elaine Gdns LU1 .... 63 A1
Elbow La
Hertford Heath SG13 .... 134 B7
Stevenage SG2 .... 51 B1
Eldefield SG6 .... 22 D7
Elder Ct WD23 .... 176 E8
Elder Rd SG12 .... 93 F3
Elder Way SG1 .... 50 E3
Elderbeck Cl EN7 .... 148 A2
Elderberry Cl LU2 .... 46 B4
Elderberry Dr SG4 .... 35 A4
Elderberry Way WD25 .... 154 B4
Elderfield CM17 .... 118 D4
Eldon Ave WD6 .... 170 B7
Eldon Rd
Hoddesdon EN11 .... 135 D4
Luton LU4 .... 44 C1
Eldrig Turn HP2 .... 124 E7
Eleanor Ave AL3 .... 127 D5
Eleanor Cross Rd EN8 .... 162 F5
Eleanor Gdns EN5 .... 171 D4
Eleanor Rd Cheshunt EN8 .... 162 E6
Hertford SG14 .... 113 C7
Eleanor Way EN8 .... 162 F5
Electric Ave EN3 .... 162 F3
Element Ho EN3 .... 162 F3
Eleni Ho EN8 .... 162 D6
Elfrida Rd WD18 .... 167 C4
Elgar Cl WD6 .... 169 D2
Elgar Path LU2 .... 63 E8
Elgin Dr HA6 .... 174 E3
Elgin Ho SG4 .... 35 A6
Elgin Rd Cheshunt EN8 .... 148 C1
Hoddesdon EN10 .... 148 F8
Elgood Ave HA6 .... 175 A3
Eliot Rd Royston SG8 .... 7 D8
Stevenage SG2 .... 51 C6
Elizabeth Cl Barnet EN5 .... 171 D6
Lower Nazeing EN9 .... 149 D8
Welwyn Garden City AL7 .... 111 C6
Elizabeth Ct 10 Luton LU1 .... 63 D6
St Albans AL4 .... 128 D6
Watford WD17 .... 153 F1
Elizabeth Dr HP23 .... 100 B6
Elizabeth Ho
7 Watford WD24 .... 167 C7
Welwyn Garden City AL7 .... 111 C6
Elizabeth Rd CM23 .... 76 E5
Elizabeth St LU1 .... 63 D6
Elizabeth Way CM20 .... 117 B2
Ellen Cl HP2 .... 124 F4
Ellenborough Cl CM23 .... 76 D5
Ellenbrook Cl WD24 .... 167 C8
Ellenbrook Cres AL10 .... 129 D5
Ellenbrook La AL10 .... 129 D4
Ellenhall Cl LU3 .... 45 C1
Ellerdine Cl LU3 .... 45 B4
Ellesborough Cl WD19 .... 175 C5
Ellesfield AL6 .... 89 B5
Ellesmere Gr EN5 .... 171 F4
Ellesmere Rd HP4 .... 122 D4
Ellice SG6 .... 23 B4
Ellingham Cl HP2 .... 125 A5
Ellingham Rd HP2 .... 124 F4
Elliott Cl AL7 .... 110 D3
Elliott Ct CM23 .... 77 A8
Ellis Ave SG1 .... 50 E8
Ellis Fields AL3 .... 127 E6
Elliswick Rd AL5 .... 86 B2
Ells Ct LU2 .... 45 F1
Ellwood Gdns WD25 .... 154 C5
Ellwood Terr WD3 .... 164 D4
Elm Ave Caddington LU1 .... 62 E3
Watford WD19 .... 167 E2
Elm Cl EN9 .... 163 D5
Elm Cotts Holdbrook EN9 .... 163 D1
Meesden SG9 .... 29 F6
Elm Dr Cheshunt EN8 .... 148 E3
Hatfield AL10 .... 130 A4
St Albans AL4 .... 128 C3
Elm Gdns Enfield EN2 .... 161 D1
Welwyn Garden City AL8 .... 110 B6
Elm Gn HP1 .... 123 E5
Elm Gr Berkhamsted HP4 .... 122 C4
Bishop's Stortford CM23 .... 77 B7
Watford WD24 .... 154 A2
Elm Hatch HA5 .... 175 F3
Elm Park Rd HA5 .... 175 D1
Elm Pk SG7 .... 23 F8
Elm Rd Barnet EN5 .... 171 F5
Bishop's Stortford CM23 .... 76 F8
Elm Terr HA3 .... 176 D2
Elm Tree Wlk
Chorleywood WD3 .... 164 F5
Tring HP23 .... 100 A5
Elm Way WD3 .... 165 B1
Elm Wlk Radlett WD7 .... 155 F3
Royston SG8 .... 7 F7
Stevenage SG2 .... 51 B3
Elmbank Ave EN5 .... 171 C5
Elmbridge CM17 .... 118 F3
Elmbrook Dr CM23 .... 76 E3
Elmcote HA5 .... 175 D1
Elmcote Way WD3 .... 165 F3
Elmfield Cl EN6 .... 158 E6
Elmfield Ct LU2 .... 46 A1
Elmfield Rd EN6 .... 158 E6
Elmhurst EN10 .... 135 A4
Elmhurst Cl WD23 .... 167 E5
Elmhurst Rd EN3 .... 162 C2
Elmoor Ave AL6 .... 89 B5
Elmoor Cl AL6 .... 89 B4
Elmore Rd Enfield EN3 .... 162 D1
Luton LU2 .... 46 A1
Elmroyd Ave EN6 .... 158 F6
Elmroyd Cl EN6 .... 158 F6
Elms Cl SG4 .... 35 E3
Elms Rd Harrow HA3 .... 176 E3
Ware SG12 .... 94 A2
Elms The Codicote SG4 .... 67 F2
Hertford SG13 .... 114 A6
Stevenage SG2 .... 69 B8
Elmscroft Gdns EN6 .... 158 F7
Elmside LU6 .... 82 E8
Elmside Wlk SG5 .... 34 E7
Elmswell Ct SG14 .... 112 F7
Elmtree Ave LU2 .... 46 E3
Elmwood
Sawbridgeworth CM21 .... 97 F1
Welwyn Garden City AL8 .... 110 B5
Elmwood Ave Baldock SG7 .... 23 F7
Borehamwood WD6 .... 170 B5
Elmwood Cres LU2 .... 45 E3
Elmwood Ct SG7 .... 23 F8
Elppin Ct EN10 .... 134 F3
Elsinge Rd EN1 .... 162 C3
Elstree & Borehamwood Sta
WD6 .... 170 A5
Elstree Distribution Pk
WD6 .... 170 D6
Elstree Hill N WD6 .... 169 D4
Elstree Hill S WD6 .... 169 D2
Elstree Pk WD6 .... 170 D3
Elstree Rd Bushey WD23 .... 168 E2
Elstree WD6 .... 169 A3
Hemel Hempstead HP2 .... 105 A1
Elstree Way WD6 .... 170 C7
Elton Ave EN5 .... 171 F4
Elton Ct SG14 .... 113 C7
Elton Pk WD17 .... 167 B7
Elton Rd SG14 .... 113 C7
Elton Way WD25 .... 168 B7
Elvaston Ct EN5 .... 171 C4
Elveden Cl LU2 .... 45 E6
Elvington Gdns LU3 .... 31 B1
Ely Cl Hatfield AL10 .... 129 F6
Stevenage SG1 .... 37 B1
Ely Gdns WD6 .... 170 D4
Ely Rd AL1 .... 128 B2
Ely Way LU4 .... 44 D4
Embleton Rd WD19 .... 175 A7
Emerald Ct WD6 .... 156 F1
Emerald Rd LU4 .... 44 A3
Emerton Ct HP4 .... 121 E7
Emerton Garth HP4 .... 121 E7
Emma Rothschild Ct
HP23 .... 100 A5
Emma's Cres SG12 .... 115 B4
Emmanuel Lodge EN8 .... 148 C1
Emmanuel Rd HA6 .... 174 F3
Emmer Gn LU2 .... 46 F2
Emmitt Cl WD7 .... 156 E6
Emperor Cl HP4 .... 121 F7
Emperors Gate SG2 .... 51 D8
Empire Ctr WD24 .... 167 C8
Empire Pl WD18 .... 166 F5
Empress Rd LU3 .... 44 E4
Endeavour Rd EN8 .... 148 E4
Enderby Rd LU3 .... 45 C6
Enderley Cl HA3 .... 176 E2
Enderley Rd HA3 .... 176 E2
Endersby Rd EN5 .... 171 C4
Endymion Ct AL10 .... 130 C6
Endymion Mews AL10 .... 130 C6
Endymion Rd AL10 .... 130 C6
Enfield Cty Lower Sch
EN2 .... 161 E1
Enfield Lock Sta EN3 .... 162 E2
Englefield LU2 .... 45 F3
Englehurst AL5 .... 86 D1
Enid Cl AL2 .... 154 F8
Enjakes Cl SG2 .... 69 B7
Ennerdale Cl AL1 .... 128 B1
Ennis Cl AL5 .... 107 D6
Ennismore Cl SG6 .... 23 C3
Ennismore Gn LU2 .... 46 F1
Enslow Cl LU1 .... 62 E3
Enterprise Ctr Luton LU2 .... 64 B6
1 Luton,High Town LU2 .... 63 F8
Enterprise Ctr The
Potters Bar EN6 .... 144 E1
Stevenage SG1 .... 50 B7
Enterprise Pk SG4 .... 66 C2
Enterprise Way
Hemel Hempstead HP2 .... 125 C5
Luton LU3 .... 45 B8
Enville Ho 8 WD19 .... 175 C7
Epping Forest District Mus*
EN9 .... 163 C6
Epping Gn HP2 .... 125 B8
Epping Way LU3 .... 44 C8
Epsom Ct WD3 .... 165 B1
Ereswell Rd LU3 .... 45 A7
Erin Cl LU4 .... 45 A2
Erin Ct LU4 .... 45 A2
Ermine Cl Cheshunt EN7 .... 162 B8
Royston SG8 .... 7 D8
St Albans AL3 .... 127 A2
Ermine Ct SG9 .... 40 E8
Ermine Pl 8 LU2 .... 45 D1
Ermine Point Bsns Pk
SG12 .... 93 B3
Ermine St Buckland SG9 .... 27 D6
Thundridge SG12 .... 93 D7
Erskine Ho 5 WD19 .... 175 D7
Escarpment Ave HP4,LU6 .... 81 D8
Escot Way EN5 .... 171 C4
Esdaile La EN11 .... 135 A5
Eskdale
London Colney AL2 .... 142 F4
Luton LU4 .... 44 C5
Eskdale Ct 3 HP2 .... 124 E6
Essendon CE Prim Sch
AL9 .... 131 F6
Essendon Gdns AL7 .... 110 F6
Essendon Hill AL9 .... 131 F7
Essex Cl LU1 .... 63 F6
Essex Ct 7 LU1 .... 63 E6
Essex La WD4 .... 153 D6
Essex Mead HP2 .... 105 A1

Essex Rd
Borehamwood WD6 170 A6
Hoddesdon EN11 135 C6
Stevenage SG1 50 B8
Watford WD17 167 B7
Essex St AL1 127 E4
Essex Yd HP22 60 C3
Estcourt Rd WD17 167 C6
Estfeld Cl 4 EN11 115 B1
Ethelred Cl AL7 110 F5
Etna Rd AL3 127 D4
Eton Ho 9 WD24 167 C7
Etonbury Mid Sch SG15 11 C7
Europa Rd HP2 124 F6
Euston Ave WD18 166 F4
Evan's Cl WD3 166 A4
Evans Ave WD25 153 F4
Evans Cl SG8 7 D7
Evans Gr AL4 128 C7
Evans Way HP23 100 B4
Evans Wharf HP3 138 E7
Evedon Cl LU3 44 F6
Evelyn Dr HA5 175 D3
Evelyn Rd LU5 44 A1
Evelyn Sharp Ho HP2 125 A2
Evensyde WD18 166 D3
Everard Cl AL1 127 D1
Everest Cl SG15 11 B5
Everest Gdns CM23 76 E6
Everest Way HP2 125 A3
Everett Cl Bushey WD23 168 E1
Hammond Street EN7 147 C6
Everett Ct WD7 156 A5
Evergreen Cl SG3 69 A2
Evergreen Rd SG12 93 F3
Evergreen Way LU3 45 A8
Evergreen Wlk 2 HP3 124 E1
Everlasting La AL3 127 C5
Eversden Ct HP2 105 B1
Eversley Lodge EN11 135 A6
Evron Pl 4 SG14 113 D6
Exchange Bldgs 7 EN5 171 E6
Exchange Rd
Stevenage SG1 50 F5
Watford WD18 167 B5
Executive Pk Ind Est
AL1 128 B3
Exeter Cl Stevenage SG1 37 B2
Watford WD24 167 C7
Exeter Ho 7 WD6 170 A7
Exhims Mews HP4 121 E6
Explorer Dr WD18 166 F3
Extension Rd SG13 113 F6
Exton Ave LU2 46 A1
Eynsford Ct SG4 34 F6
Eynsford Rd LU4 44 D3

F

Faggots Cl WD7 156 C4
Faints Cl EN7 147 F2
Fair Cl WD23 168 B2
Fair Oak Ct LU2 45 F3
Fair Oak Dr LU2 45 F3
Fair View EN6 145 B2
Fairacre HP3 138 F7
Fairacre Ct 2 HA6 174 E3
Fairacres Cl EN6 158 F6
Fairburn Cl WD6 170 A8
Faircross Ho 6 WD17 167 B6
Faircross Way AL1 128 A5
Fairfax Ave LU3 44 D7
Fairfax Rd SG13 113 F7
Fairfield Buntingford SG9 40 F6
Northwood HA6 175 A1
Pinner HA6 175 A1
Fairfield Ave WD19 175 D7
Fairfield Cl
Harpenden AL5 86 D1
Hatfield AL10 130 C8
Northwood HA6 174 B4
Radlett WD7 155 E2
Fairfield Dr EN10 148 F7
Fairfield Jun Sch WD7 155 E3
Fairfield Rd EN11 135 A8
Fairfield Way Hitchin SG4 35 D8
Stevenage SG1 37 C3
Fairfield Wlk 6 EN8 148 E3
Fairfields Prim Sch
EN7 148 A4
Fairfolds WD25 154 E4
Fairford Ave LU2 45 E4
Fairgreen Rd LU1 62 F3
Fairhaven AL2 141 D4
Fairhaven Cres WD19 175 A7
Fairhill HP3 138 F7
Fairlands Lo WD6 170 A5
Fairlands Lodge 6
WD6 170 A5
Fairlands Prim Sch SG1 50 D6
Fairlands Way SG1 51 A7
Fairlawns Pinner HA5 175 D1
Watford WD17 153 F1
Fairley Way EN7 148 B3
Fairmead Ave AL5 107 C8
Fairoaks Gr EN3 162 D2
Fairseat Cl WD23 176 E8
Fairshot Ct AL4 108 D2
Fairthorn Cl HP23 99 E3
Fairview Dr WD17 153 E3
Fairview Est EN11 135 C7
Fairview Rd SG1 50 B7
Fairway
Bishop's Stortford CM23 77 C6
Fairway *continued*
Hemel Hempstead HP3 138 F7
Sawbridgeworth CM21 97 F2
Ware SG12 114 C8
Fairway Ave WD6 170 B7
Fairway Cl
Chiswell Green AL2 141 C4
Harpenden AL5 107 A5
Fairway Ct HP3 138 F7
Fairway Ho WD6 170 B6
Fairway The
Abbots Langley WD5 153 D7
Moor Park HA6 174 E6
Fairways Cheshunt EN8 148 D5
Waltham Abbey EN9 163 E5
Faithfield WD19 167 E3
Falcon Cl Hatfield AL10 130 A3
Northwood HA6 174 E3
Sawbridgeworth CM21 97 C1
Stevenage SG2 51 D2
Falcon Ct 2 SG12 93 C3
Falcon Ridge HP4 122 C3
Falcon Way
Watford WD25 154 E5
Welwyn Garden City AL7 110 E8
Falconer Rd WD23 168 A3
Falconer Sch WD23 168 A4
Falconer St CM23 76 C5
Falconers Field AL5 85 E3
Falconers Pk CM21 97 D1
Falconers Rd LU2 46 B1
Falkirk Gdns WD19 175 D5
Falkland Rd EN5 171 E7
Fallow End AL6 68 D1
Fallow Rise SG13 113 F6
Fallowfield Luton LU3 45 C4
Stevenage SG2 51 C3
Welwyn Garden City AL7 89 F1
Fallowfield Cl UB9 173 C2
Fallowfield Wlk HP1 124 A6
Fallows Gn AL5 86 B3
Falmouth Ct AL3 127 D5
Falstaff Gdns AL1 141 C8
Falstone Gn LU2 46 E1
Fanhams Hall Rd SG12 93 F3
Fanhams Rd SG12 93 E2
Fanshaw Ct SG14 113 C7
Fanshawe Cres SG12 93 C2
Fanshawe St SG14 113 B7
Fanshaws La SG13 133 C5
Fantail La HP23 99 F4
Far End AL10 130 B2
Faraday Cl Luton LU4 44 C1
Watford WD18 166 D3
Faraday Rd SG2 51 B6
Faringdon Rd LU4 44 C3
Faringford Cl EN6 159 D8
Farland Rd HP2 125 B3
Farley Ct LU1 63 C5
Farley Farm Rd LU1 63 B5
Farley Hill LU1 63 C5
Farley Jun Sch LU1 63 C6
Farley Lodge LU1 63 D5
Farm Ave AL5 85 D4
Farm Cl Barnet EN5 171 C4
Borehamwood WD6 156 E1
Cheshunt EN8 148 C1
Cuffley EN6 146 E4
Harpenden AL5 85 D4
Hertford SG14 113 A6
Letchworth SG6 12 A1
London Colney WD7 142 E1
Roydon CM19 116 B1
Shenleybury WD7 156 E8
Stevenage SG1 50 E4
Welwyn Garden City AL8 110 C6
Farm Cotts SG12 93 D5
Farm Cres AL2 142 A5
Farm End HA6 174 B2
Farm Field WD17 153 E1
Farm Gn LU1 63 C5
Farm Hill Rd EN9 163 D6
Farm La Hoddesdon EN11 135 C8
Rickmansworth WD3 165 C6
Standon SG11 73 A8
Farm Pl HP4 121 F5
Farm Rd
Little Chalfont WD3 164 A5
Northwood HA6 174 C5
Slip End LU1 85 B7
St Albans AL1 128 B4
Farm Way Bushey WD23 168 B5
Moor Park HA6 174 F6
Farmbrook LU2 45 D7
Farmers Cl WD25 154 B6
Farmery Ct HP4 122 E6
Farmhouse Cl EN10 148 F6
Farmhouse La HP2 125 A5
Farmhouse The HP2 125 A5
Farmstead Rd HA3 176 D1
Farne Ho 5 WD18 166 F3
Farnham CE Prim Sch
CM23 58 D6
Farnham Cl
Bovingdon HP3 137 A3
Sawbridgeworth CM21 97 C1
Farnham Gn CM23 58 B7
Farnley Gr LU2 64 A7
Farquhar St SG14 113 C7
Farr's La LU2 65 B1
Farraline Rd WD18 167 B5
Farrant Way WD6 169 E8
Farrer Top AL3 83 E5
Farriday Cl AL3 127 E7
Farrier Ct SG8 7 C7
Farriers SG12 115 A6
Farriers Cl Baldock SG7 12 E1
Bovingdon HP3 137 B3
Farriers Cl *continued*
Codicote SG4 67 F1
Farriers Ct WD25 154 B7
Farriers End EN10 148 F5
Farriers Way WD6 170 D4
Farringford Cl AL2 141 B5
Farrington Cotts EN5 171 F6
Farrington Pl HA6 174 F6
Farrow Cl LU3 31 C1
Farthing Cl WD18 167 C4
Farthing Dr SG6 23 C3
Farthings The HP1 124 B3
Faulkner Ct AL1 127 E5
Faverolle Gn EN8 148 D3
Faversham Cl HP23 100 A4
Fawbert & Barnard Inf Sch
CM21 97 E2
Fawbert & Barnard Sch
CM17 118 C3
Fawcett Rd SG2 51 B8
Fawkon Wlk EN11 135 A6
Fawn Ct AL9 130 C7
Fay Gn WD5 153 D6
Fayerfield EN6 159 D8
Fayland Cotts SG9 41 E7
Feacey Down HP1 124 B5
Fearney Mead WD3 165 A1
Fearnhill Sch SG6 22 C5
Fearnley Rd AL8 110 C5
Fearnley St WD18 167 B5
Feather Dell AL10 130 A5
Featherbed La HP3 138 B7
Featherston Rd SG2 51 C3
Featherstone Gdns
WD6 170 C5
Featherstone Wood Prim Sch
SG2 51 C3
Federal Way WD24 167 C8
Felbrigg Cl LU2 46 F2
Felden Cl Pinner HA5 175 E3
Watford WD25 154 D5
Felden Dr HP3 138 A7
Felden La HP3 138 A7
Felden Lawns HP3 138 A7
Felix Ave LU2 46 A2
Fell Path WD6 170 D4
Fellowes La AL4 143 E8
Fellowes Way SG2 51 A2
Fells Cl SG5 34 F8
Felmersham Ct LU1 63 B7
Felmersham Rd LU1 63 A7
Felmongers CM20 118 B2
Felstead Cl LU2 45 F3
Felstead Rd EN8 162 E7
Felstead Way LU2 45 F3
Felton Cl
Borehamwood WD6 156 E1
Cheshunt EN10 148 F6
Luton LU2 46 D1
Fen End SG5 11 F8
Fennycroft Rd HP1 124 A6
Fensom's Cl HP2 124 D4
Fensomes Alley HP2 124 D4
Fenwick Cl LU3 45 B5
Fenwick Path WD6 156 F1
Ferguson Gr EN8 148 D2
Fermor Cres LU2 46 C1
Fern Cl EN10 148 F8
Fern Ct HP4 122 B4
Fern Dells AL10 129 F4
Fern Dr HP3 124 E2
Fern Gr AL8 89 D2
Fern Ho HA7 176 F4
Fern Way WD25 154 B4
Ferndale
7 Harpenden AL5 86 A2
Much Hadham SG10 74 F2
Ferndale Rd Enfield EN3 162 E2
Luton LU1 63 B7
Ferndene AL2 154 F8
Ferndown HA6 175 A1
Ferndown Cl HA5 175 E3
Ferndown Rd WD19 175 C6
Fernecroft AL1 141 D8
Ferney Rd EN7 147 D5
Fernheath LU3 31 A1
Fernhills WD4 153 D6
Fernleigh Ct HA2 176 B1
Fernleys AL4 128 C5
Ferns Cl EN3 162 E3
Fernville La HP2 124 D3
Ferny Hill EN4 159 F1
Ferrars Cl LU4 44 B1
Ferrars Inf Sch LU4 44 B3
Ferrars Jun Sch LU4 44 B3
Ferrers La AL4 108 B5
Ferrier Rd SG2 51 C6
Ferryhills Cl WD19 175 C7
Feryngs Cl CM17 118 D4
Fesants Croft CM20 118 B3
Fetherstone Cl EN6 159 D7
Fiddle Bridge La AL10 129 F6
Fiddlebridge Ind Ctr
AL10 129 F6
Fidler Pl WD23 168 B3
Field Cl Harpenden AL5 107 D7
St Albans AL4 128 A7
Field Cres SG8 7 F7
Field End EN5 171 B5
Field End Cl Luton LU2 46 C4
Watford WD19 167 E2
Wigginton HP23 100 D1
Field Fare Gn LU4 44 A5
Field Inf Sch WD18 167 C4
Field Jun Sch WD18 167 C4
Field La SG6 22 F4
Field Rd
Hemel Hempstead HP2 125 A3
Field Rd *continued*
Watford WD19 167 E3
Field View Rd EN6 159 A6
Field View Rise AL2 140 E2
Field Way Bovingdon HP3 137 A4
Hoddesdon EN11 115 C2
Rickmansworth WD3 165 B1
Field's Ct EN6 159 D6
Fielder Ctr (Univ of Herts)
AL10 129 D8
Fielders Way WD7 156 E6
Fieldfare Letchworth SG6 11 E1
Stevenage SG2 51 D3
Fieldfare Way SG8 7 E8
Fieldfares AL2 142 D4
Fieldgate Ho SG1 50 F5
Fieldgate Rd LU4 44 D2
Fieldings Rd EN8 148 F2
Fields End HP23 100 A6
Fields End La HP1 123 E5
Fieldway
Berkhamsted HP4 122 E2
Stanstead Abbotts SG12 115 B4
Wigginton HP23 100 D1
Fifth Ave Letchworth SG6 23 C6
Watford WD25 154 D4
Fifth Avenue / Allende Ave
CM20 117 C3
Figtree Hill HP2 124 D4
Filey Cl SG1 50 A7
Fillingham Way AL10 129 E7
Filmer Rd LU4 44 E4
Filton Ho 6 WD19 175 D7
Finch Cl Hatfield AL10 130 A3
Luton LU4 44 A4
Finch Gn WD3 164 F5
Finch La WD23 168 A5
Finch Rd HP4 122 A4
Finchdale HP1 124 A3
Finche's End SG2 52 B8
Finches The
Hertford SG13 114 B6
Hitchin SG4 35 A7
Finley Rd AL5 86 D3
Finsbury Ct EN8 162 E5
Finsbury Rd LU4 44 D5
Finucane Rise WD23 176 C8
Finway LU1 63 A8
Finway Ct WD18 166 F4
Finway Rd HP2 125 B7
Fir Cl SG2 50 F1
Fir Tree Cl HP3 125 B2
Fir Tree Ct WD6 169 F5
Fir Tree Hill WD3 153 A2
Firbank Dr WD19 167 E2
Firbank Rd AL3 127 F7
Firbank Trad Est LU1 63 A8
Fire Station Alley EN5 171 E7
Firecrest SG6 11 E1
Firlands CM23 76 E6
Firlands Ho CM23 76 E6
Firs Cl Hatfield AL10 130 B4
Hitchin SG5 34 D8
Firs Dr AL4 87 C5
Firs Jun Sch The CM23 76 E6
Firs La EN6 159 B6
Firs The
Hammond Street EN7 147 E4
Harpenden AL5 86 D2
St Albans AL1 142 B7
Welwyn Garden City AL8 89 C2
Wigginton HP23 100 D1
Firs Wlk Northwood HA6 174 D4
Tewin AL6 90 E5
Firs Wood Cl EN6 159 F7
First Ave WD25 154 D4
First Avenue / Mandela Ave
CM20 117 F2
First Garden City Heritage
Mus* SG6 23 A5
Firthesden Vinyard*
HP4 123 B8
Firway AL6 89 F7
Firway Cl AL6 89 F7
Firwood Ave AL4 128 E3
Fish Hill SG8 7 D6
Fish St AL3 106 B5
Fish Street Farm AL3 106 B5
Fisher Cl Holdbrook EN3 163 A2
Kings Langley WD4 139 A2
Fisher Rd HA3 176 F1
Fisher's Green Rd SG1 50 B8
Fisher's Ind Est WD18 167 C4
Fishermans Way EN11 135 D8
Fishers Cl Holdbrook EN8 163 A5
Standon SG11 55 D3
Watford WD23 167 E6
Fishers Gn SG1 36 A1
Fishers Hatch CM20 117 E1
Fishers Mead SG11 55 D3
Fishery Cotts HP1 124 A1
Fishery Pas HP1 124 B1
Fishery Rd HP1 124 A1
Fishponds Rd SG5 34 E8
Fishpool St AL3 127 C3
Fitzjohn Ave EN5 171 F5
Fitzroy Ave LU3 45 B3
Fitzwarin Cl LU3 44 E8
Fitzwilliam Ct CM17 118 E4
Five Acres
Kings Langley WD4 138 F2
London Colney AL2 142 D6
Stansted Mountfitchet
CM24 59 E8
Five Acres Ave AL2 140 F2
Five Fields Cl WD19 175 F7
Five Oaks Caddington LU1 62 F4
Hatfield AL10 130 B2
Five Oaks Mid Sch LU1 62 F3
Five Oaks Prim Sch
AL10 130 A3
Five Springs LU3 44 E6
Five Springs Ct LU3 44 E6
Flackwell Ho WD18 166 E3
Flags The HP2 125 B3
Flagstaff Cl EN9 163 B6
Flagstaff Rd EN9 163 B6
Flamstead End Prim Sch
EN7 148 A4
Flamstead End Rd EN8 148 B3
Flamstead Sch AL3 84 B1
Flamsteadbury La AL3 106 A4
Flandrian Cl EN3 163 B1
Flash La EN2 161 C3
Flatfield Rd HP3 125 A1
Flaunden Bottom HP3,
HP5 150 E4
Flaunden Hill HP3 151 A6
Flaunden Ho WD18 166 E2
Flaunden La
Bovingdon HP3 137 D3
Sarratt WD3 151 E6
Flavian Cl AL3 126 F1
Flax Mews AL3 83 E5
Flecker Cl HA7 176 F5
Fleet The SG8 7 C6
Fleetville Inf Sch AL1 128 B3
Fleetville Jun Sch AL1 128 A3
Fleetwood SG6 23 B4
Fleetwood Cres SG1 50 B7
Fleetwood Way WD19 175 C6
Fleming Cl EN7 148 A5
Fleming Cres SG14 113 A6
Fletcher Way HP2 124 D6
Flete Ho WD18 166 E3
Flexley Wood AL7 90 A1
Flight Path SG16 10 B3
Flinders Cl St Albans AL1 128 A1
Stevenage SG2 51 D5
Flint Cl LU3 44 E7
Flint Copse AL3 106 C6
Flint Ct LU1 63 D5
Flint Rd SG6 23 C8
Flint Way AL3 127 C7
Flintings The HP2 103 F8
Flora Gr AL1 127 F2
Floral Dr AL2 142 D5
Florence Ave LU3 44 D6
Florence Cl WD25 154 A4
Florence Ct HA6 174 E4
Florence St SG5 34 F8
Florence Wlk 8 CM23 76 F8
Florida Cl WD23 176 D8
Flowers Ind Est 11 LU1 63 E6
Flowers Way LU1 63 E7
Flowton Gr AL5 107 A7
Floyds Barns HP22 60 C2
Fog Cotts HP23 101 A5
Fogerty Cl EN3 163 B2
Fold Croft CM20 117 A1
Foldingshott SG3 69 D3
Follett Dr WD5 153 F8
Folly Ave AL3 127 C4
Folly Cl Hitchin SG4 35 A5
Radlett WD7 155 F3
Folly Fields AL4 87 B2
Folly La Caddington LU1 62 E4
St Albans AL3 127 C4
Folly Path SG4 35 A5
Folly Pathway WD7 155 F3
Folly The Buntingford SG9 40 D7
Hertford SG14 113 D6
Folly View SG12 115 B4
Fontmell Cl AL3 127 E5
Fontwell Cl HA3 176 E3
Football Cl SG7 12 E1
Forbes Ave EN6 159 D7
Ford Cl WD23 168 C5
Ford Cotts SG11 75 B8
Ford Field SG11 75 A8
Ford Hill SG11 75 B8
Ford St SG11 55 E6
Fordham Cl SG7 4 D4
Fordham Rd SG8 7 E5
Fordhams Terr SG8 15 F7
Fordhams Wood (Nature
Reserve)* SG8 6 E4
Fordwich Cl SG14 113 A6
Fordwich Hill SG14 113 A6
Fordwich Rd AL8 110 C5
Fordwich Rise SG14 113 A6
Fore St Harlow CM17 118 C4
Hatfield AL9 130 C6
Hertford SG14 113 D6
Weston SG4 24 B1
Forebury Ave CM21 97 F2
Forebury Cres CM21 97 F2
Forebury The CM21 97 F2
Forefield AL2 141 A4
Forelands Pl CM21 97 E2
Forest Ave 5 HP3 124 D1
Forest La WD7 156 B8
Forest Rd Cheshunt EN8 148 D2
Enfield EN3 162 E3
Watford WD25 154 B6
Forest Row SG2 50 F1
Forest Wlk WD23 167 F8
Foresters Cl EN7 147 E4
Foresthall Rd CM24 59 E4
Forfar Ho 7 WD19 175 C7
Forge Cl
Chipperfield WD4 152 A8
5 Hitchin SG5 34 F8
Forge Cotts
Essendon AL9 131 E6
Hatfield Heath CM22 98 F3

Forge End AL2 ... 141 A5
Forge La Northwood HA6 ... 174 E3
Welwyn AL6 ... 89 C5
Forres Cl EN11 ... 135 A8
Forres Prim Sch EN11 ... 115 B1
Forrest Cres LU2 ... 46 A3
Forresters Dr AL7 ... 111 C5
Fortnums Acre HA7 ... 176 F4
Fortuna Cl SG1 ... 51 C8
Fortune La WD6 ... 169 D3
Forty Hall* EN2 ... 161 F2
Forty Hill EN2 ... 161 F1
Forty Hill CE Prim Sch EN2 ... 162 A2
Forty Hill Ho EN2 ... 161 F1
Forum The SG1 ... 50 D5
Fosbery Ct EN3 ... 163 A2
Fosman Cl 7 SG5 ... 34 D8
Foster Cl Cheshunt EN8 ... 148 E1
Stevenage SG1 ... 36 D1
Foster Dr SG4 ... 35 A5
Foster Rd HP1 ... 124 B1
Foston Cl LU3 ... 44 F6
Fotherley Rd WD3 ... 172 F8
Foulds Sch EN5 ... 171 D6
Founceley Ave SG12 ... 71 F8
Founders Rd EN11 ... 115 B1
Fountain Ct
Borehamwood WD6 ... 170 A7
Cheshunt EN8 ... 148 D1
Fountain Dr SG13 ... 113 F7
Fountain Pl EN9 ... 163 C5
Fountains Rd LU3 ... 45 D3
Four Acres Stevenage SG1 ... 50 D7
Welwyn Garden City AL7 ... 110 F4
Four Acres The CM21 ... 98 A2
Four Limes AL4 ... 108 D8
Four Swannes Prim Sch EN8 ... 162 E6
Four Tubs The WD23 ... 168 D2
Fouracres SG6 ... 23 A3
Fouracres Dr HP3 ... 124 F1
Fouracres Wlk HP3 ... 124 F1
Fourdrinier Way HP3 ... 138 D8
Fourth Ave Harlow CM20 ... 117 C1
Letchworth SG6 ... 23 C7
Luton LU3 ... 44 D7
Watford WD25 ... 154 D4
Fourways SG13 ... 133 A5
Fourways Ct 1 EN11 ... 135 A7
Fourways Market AL9 ... 144 C7
Fovant SG1 ... 36 B1
Fovant Cl AL5 ... 107 C6
Fowley Cl EN8 ... 162 F5
Fowlmere Rd SG8 ... 9 F8
Fox Cl Bushey WD23 ... 168 B5
Elstree WD6 ... 169 D3
Wigginton HP23 ... 100 D1
Fox Cnr SG8 ... 1 F5
Fox Hill SG8 ... 1 F5
Fox Hill Rd SG8 ... 1 F5
Fox La SG8 ... 15 F7
Fox Rd Stevenage SG1 ... 50 E4
Wigginton HP23 ... 100 C2
Fox's La AL9 ... 144 F7
Foxbury Cl LU2 ... 45 D6
Foxcroft AL1 ... 128 A1
Foxdell HA6 ... 174 D4
Foxdell Inf Sch LU1 ... 63 A8
Foxdell Jun Sch LU1 ... 62 E8
Foxdells SG14 ... 112 C3
Foxdells La CM23 ... 58 F2
Foxes Cl SG13 ... 114 B6
Foxes Dr EN7 ... 148 A2
Foxes La EN6 ... 146 E3
Foxes Par EN9 ... 163 C6
Foxfield SG2 ... 51 C3
Foxfield Cl HA6 ... 174 F4
Foxglove Bank SG8 ... 7 F5
Foxglove Cl
Bishop's Stortford CM23 ... 76 C6
Hatfield AL10 ... 130 B4
Hoddesdon EN11 ... 115 C1
Foxglove Way Luton LU3 ... 45 D2
Oaklands AL6 ... 89 E8
Foxgloves The HP1 ... 123 E2
Foxgrove Path WD19 ... 175 D5
Foxhill Luton LU2 ... 45 E5
Watford WD24 ... 154 A3
Foxholes Ave SG13 ... 113 F6
Foxhollows AL10 ... 130 B7
Foxlands Cl WD25 ... 154 A5
Foxley Dr CM23 ... 77 B8
Foxley Gr AL6 ... 89 F4
Foxleys WD19 ... 175 E7
Foxton Rd EN11 ... 135 A6
Foxtree Ho WD25 ... 154 E3
Foxwood Chase EN9 ... 163 C4
Foyle Cl SG1 ... 37 C3
Frampton Rd EN6 ... 145 C1
Frampton St SG14 ... 113 D6
Francis Ave AL3 ... 127 D6
Francis Bacon Sch AL1 ... 142 B8
Francis Cl Hitchin SG4 ... 35 A5
Stotfold SG5 ... 11 E6
Francis Combe Sch & Com Coll WD25 ... 154 C7
Francis Ct Harlow CM20 ... 117 B2
St Albans AL1 ... 127 E2
Francis Green Ho EN9 ... 163 B6
Francis House Prep Sch HP23 ... 99 F3
Francis Rd Hinxworth SG7 ... 3 C6
Ware SG12 ... 93 D2
Watford WD18 ... 167 B5
Francis St LU1 ... 63 D8
Francis Wks EN11 ... 135 B6
Frank Lester Way LU2 ... 64 D8
Frank Martin Ct EN7 ... 148 B1
Frankland Cl WD3 ... 166 A2
Frankland Rd WD3 ... 166 B3
Franklin Ave EN7 ... 148 B1
Franklin Cl
Colney Heath AL4 ... 129 E1
Hemel Hempstead HP3 ... 138 E8
Pirton SG5 ... 20 D4
Franklin Gdns SG4 ... 22 B1
Franklin Rd WD17 ... 167 B7
Franklin's Rd SG1 ... 50 C8
Franks Cl SG16 ... 10 B5
Franshams WD23 ... 176 D8
Fraser Rd EN8 ... 148 E3
Fred Millard Ct SG1 ... 50 E5
Frederick St LU2 ... 45 E1
Frederick Street Pas LU2 ... 45 E1
Freeman Ave LU3 ... 45 B8
Freemans Cl SG5 ... 21 D1
Freewaters Cl SG5 ... 21 E4
Freezywater St George's Prim Sch EN3 ... 162 D3
Freman Coll SG9 ... 40 D8
Freman Dr SG9 ... 40 D8
French Horn Ct 5 SG12 ... 93 D1
French Horn La AL10 ... 130 B6
French Lodge SG5 ... 34 F8
French Row 4 AL3 ... 127 D3
French's Cl SG12 ... 115 B4
Frenches Yd 21 SG12 ... 93 D1
Frensham EN7 ... 148 A4
Frensham Dr SG4 ... 22 C2
Frere Ct CM23 ... 58 F1
Freshwater Cl LU3 ... 44 F7
Freshwaters CM20 ... 117 E1
Fretherne Rd AL8 ... 110 D6
Friars Cl LU1 ... 63 B5
Friars Ct LU1 ... 63 B5
Friars Field HP4 ... 121 E7
Friars Rd Braughing SG11 ... 56 A7
Weston SG4 ... 24 B1
Friars Way
Kings Langley WD4 ... 139 A1
Luton LU1 ... 63 B5
Watford WD23 ... 167 F8
Friars Wlk HP23 ... 100 A4
Friars Wood CM23 ... 77 C8
Friarscroft EN10 ... 135 A3
Friday Furlong SG5 ... 34 C8
Friedberg Ave CM23 ... 76 D4
Friendless La AL3 ... 83 F2
Friends Ave EN8 ... 162 D7
Friern Cl 6 EN7 ... 147 E5
Friesian Cl LU4 ... 44 A3
Frimley Rd HP1 ... 123 E4
Fringewood Cl HA6 ... 174 B2
Frinton Cl WD19 ... 175 B8
Friston Gn LU2 ... 46 D1
Frithsden Copse HP4 ... 122 F8
Frithwood Ave HA6 ... 174 F4
Frithwood Prim Sch HA6 ... 174 F4
Frobisher Cl WD23 ... 168 A3
Frobisher Dr SG2 ... 51 B7
Frobisher Rd AL1 ... 128 C1
Frobisher Way AL10 ... 129 D8
Froghall Cotts WD6 ... 170 D3
Froghall La SG2 ... 38 B1
Frogmoor Ct WD3 ... 173 D8
Frogmoor La WD3 ... 173 D8
Frogmore AL2 ... 141 E4
Frogmore Hill SG14 ... 70 B7
Frogmore Ho SG1 ... 36 C1
Frogmore Home Pk AL2 ... 141 D4
Frogmore Rd HP3 ... 138 D8
Frogmore Road Ind Est HP3 ... 138 D8
Frogmore St HP23 ... 100 A3
Frogs Hall La SG11 ... 53 F3
Frome Cl LU4 ... 44 E4
Frome Sq HP2 ... 125 A8
Front St LU1 ... 63 C1
Front The HP4 ... 123 B7
Frost Ho HP4 ... 122 C3
Frowick Cl AL9 ... 144 B8
Frowyke Cres EN6 ... 158 A7
Fry Rd SG2 ... 51 C5
Fryth Mead AL3 ... 127 B4
Fulbeck Way HA2 ... 176 C1
Fulbourne Cl LU4 ... 44 E2
Fulford Gr WD19 ... 175 B8
Fuller Ct 3 CM23 ... 77 A7
Fuller Gdns WD24 ... 154 B2
Fuller Rd WD24 ... 154 B2
Fuller Way WD3 ... 166 A4
Fuller's Almshouses CM24 ... 59 F6
Fullers Cl EN9 ... 163 F6
Fullers Ct SG6 ... 22 E7
Fulling Mill La AL6 ... 89 B6
Fulmar Cres HP1 ... 124 A3
Fulmore Cl AL5 ... 86 D4
Fulton Cl SG1 ... 50 C5
Fulton Cres CM23 ... 77 C8
Fulton Ct
Borehamwood WD6 ... 156 F1
Holdbrook EN3 ... 163 A1
Furham Field HA5 ... 176 A3
Furlay Cl SG6 ... 22 D7
Furlong The HP23 ... 100 A3
Furlong Way SG12 ... 115 A7
Furlongs HP1 ... 124 A4
Furmston Ct SG6 ... 23 A7
Furneux Pelham CE Sch SG9 ... 43 A4
Furriers Cl CM23 ... 76 C5
Furrowfield AL10 ... 130 B7
Furrows The LU3 ... 45 B7
Furse Ave AL4 ... 128 A7
Furtherfield WD5 ... 153 E7
Furtherground 1 HP2 ... 124 E2
Furze Cl Luton LU2 ... 45 D7
South Oxhey WD19 ... 175 C5
Furze Gr SG8 ... 7 E5
Furze Rd HP1 ... 123 E2
Furze View WD3 ... 164 C4
Furzebushes La AL2 ... 140 F6
Furzedown SG2 ... 51 B4
Furzedown Ct 18 AL5 ... 86 B1
Furzefield EN8 ... 148 B3
Furzefield Ct EN6 ... 158 E8
Furzefield Ctr The EN6 ... 158 D8
Furzefield Rd AL7 ... 110 E4
Furzehill Mid Sch WD6 ... 170 A5
Furzehill Par WD6 ... 170 A6
Furzehill Rd WD6 ... 170 B5
Furzen Cres AL10 ... 129 F2

G

Gable Cl
Abbots Langley WD5 ... 153 E7
Pinner HA5 ... 176 A3
Gables Ave WD6 ... 169 F6
Gables Lodge EN4 ... 159 C1
Gables The
3 Hemel Hempstead HP1 ... 124 D4
Sawbridgeworth CM21 ... 97 E2
Watford WD19 ... 167 C2
Watford,Woodside WD25 ... 154 D6
Gaddesden Cres WD25 ... 154 E5
Gaddesden Gr AL7 ... 111 B6
Gaddesden La AL3 ... 105 C4
Gaddesden Row HP2 ... 104 C6
Gaddesden Row Jun Mix Inf Sch HP2 ... 104 B6
Gade Ave WD18 ... 166 E5
Gade Bank WD1 ... 166 D5
Gade Cl
Hemel Hempstead HP1 ... 124 B6
Watford WD18 ... 166 E5
Gade Twr HP3 ... 138 F6
Gade Valley Cl WD4 ... 139 A3
Gade Valley Cotts HP1 ... 103 E4
Gade Valley Jun Mix Inf Sch HP1 ... 124 B4
Gade View Gdns WD4 ... 153 C7
Gadebridge Ct HP1 ... 124 C4
Gadebridge La
Hemel Hempstead HP1 ... 124 B5
Hemel Hempstead HP1 ... 124 C5
Gadebridge Rd HP1 ... 124 B4
Gadeside WD24,WD25 ... 153 E4
Gadeview HP1 ... 124 C3
Gadeview Rd HP3 ... 138 D7
Gadmore La HP23 ... 119 F7
Gadswell Cl WD25 ... 154 E3
Gage Cl SG8 ... 7 D7
Gainsborough Ave AL1 ... 127 F4
Gainsford Cres SG4 ... 22 C2
Gainswood AL7 ... 110 E5
Gaitskell Ho WD6 ... 170 D5
Gall End La CM24 ... 59 F7
Galleria The AL10 ... 129 F5
Gallery The
Letchworth SG6 ... 22 F6
7 Luton LU1 ... 63 E7
Galley Gn SG13 ... 115 A2
Galley Hill HP1 ... 124 B6
Galley La EN5 ... 171 B7
Galleycroft Ct 4 AL10 ... 130 A6
Galleyhill Rd EN9 ... 163 E7
Galleywood SG5 ... 21 D4
Galliard Cl LU3 ... 45 B4
Galloway Cl
1 Bishop's Stortford CM23 ... 76 F8
Cheshunt EN10 ... 148 F5
Galloway Rd CM23 ... 58 F1
Gallows Hill WD4 ... 153 C7
Gallows Hill La WD5 ... 153 D8
Galston Rd LU3 ... 44 D8
Gammon Cl HP3 ... 125 A2
Gammons La WD17, WD24 ... 154 A2
Gamnel Mews HP23 ... 100 B7
Ganders Ash WD25 ... 154 A6
Gandhi Ct 1 WD24 ... 167 D7
Gangies Hill CM21 ... 97 A4
Gant Ct EN9 ... 163 F5
Ganton Wlk WD19 ... 175 E6
Ganymede Pl HP2 ... 124 F6
Gaping La SG5 ... 34 D7
Garden Ave AL10 ... 130 A2
Garden Cl Barnet EN5 ... 171 C5
Harpenden AL5 ... 107 A5
Royston SG8 ... 7 E7
St Albans AL1 ... 128 B4
Watford WD17 ... 166 F7
Woolmer Green SG3 ... 69 B2
Garden Cott AL2 ... 141 E4
Garden Cotts SG11 ... 73 A8
Garden Ct
Hoddesdon EN10 ... 134 F4
Welwyn Garden City AL7 ... 110 E7
Wheathampstead AL4 ... 87 D1
Garden Field SG2 ... 51 E2
Garden Field La HP4 ... 122 F2
Garden Fields Jun Mix Inf Sch AL3 ... 127 D6
Garden Ho SG13 ... 113 C5
Garden Hos The CM21 ... 98 B3
Garden La SG8 ... 7 D5
Garden Rd
Abbots Langley WD5 ... 153 E8
Garden Rd *continued*
Buntingford SG9 ... 40 E8
Woolmer Green SG3 ... 69 B2
Garden Row 6 SG5 ... 34 F8
Garden Terr SG12 ... 92 E4
Garden Terrace Rd CM17 ... 118 C4
Garden Wlk Royston SG8 ... 7 E7
Stevenage SG1 ... 50 E5
Gardenia Ave LU3 ... 45 A4
Gardens of the Rose The* AL2 ... 140 F5
Gardens The Baldock SG7 ... 23 E8
Brookmans Park AL9 ... 144 E4
Henlow SG16 ... 10 D8
Stotfold SG5 ... 11 E6
Watford WD17 ... 166 F7
Gardiners La SG7 ... 4 D4
Gardner Ct Luton LU1 ... 63 E4
Watford WD25 ... 154 C4
Gareth Ct WD6 ... 156 F1
Garfield Ct LU2 ... 46 D3
Garfield St WD24 ... 154 B1
Garland Cl Cheshunt EN8 ... 162 E8
Hemel Hempstead HP2 ... 124 D4
Garland Ct 4 AL1 ... 127 E3
Garland Rd SG12 ... 93 E1
Garnault Rd EN1 ... 161 F1
Garner Dr EN10 ... 148 E5
Garnett Cl WD24 ... 154 D3
Garnett Dr AL2 ... 140 F2
Garrard Way AL4 ... 108 D8
Garratts Rd WD23 ... 168 C2
Garretts Cl SG14 ... 113 C6
Garretts Mead LU2 ... 46 B3
Garrison Ct 2 SG4 ... 34 F7
Garrowsfield EN5 ... 171 F4
Garsmouth Way WD25 ... 154 D3
Garston Cres WD25 ... 154 C5
Garston Dr WD25 ... 154 C5
Garston Inf Sch WD25 ... 154 D4
Garston La WD25 ... 154 D5
Garston Manor Sch WD25 ... 154 C7
Garston Park Par WD25 ... 154 D5
Garston Sta WD25 ... 154 D4
Garter Ct 10 LU2 ... 45 D1
Garth Rd SG6 ... 22 E3
Garth The WD5 ... 153 D6
Garthland Dr EN5 ... 171 C4
Gartlet Rd WD17 ... 167 C6
Gas La SG8 ... 17 C3
Gascoyne Cl EN6 ... 158 A7
Gascoyne Way SG13, SG14 ... 113 D5
Gatcombe Ct AL1 ... 128 A2
Gate Cl WD6 ... 170 C8
Gate Cotts WD3 ... 164 D5
Gate End HA6 ... 175 A3
Gatecroft HP3 ... 139 A8
Gatehill Gdns LU3 ... 31 B1
Gatehill Rd HA6 ... 175 A3
Gatehouse Mews SG9 ... 40 E8
Gates Way SG1 ... 50 C6
Gatesbury Way SG11 ... 55 D3
Gatesdene Cl HP4 ... 102 C8
Gateshead Rd WD6 ... 170 A8
Gateway Cl HA6 ... 174 C4
Gateways The EN7 ... 147 E3
Gatwick Cl CM23 ... 59 B1
Gauldie Way SG11 ... 55 D2
Gaumont App WD17 ... 167 B6
Gaunts Way SG6 ... 12 A2
Gaveston Dr HP4 ... 122 B6
Gayland Ave LU2 ... 64 B8
Gayton Cl LU3 ... 45 B4
Gaywood Ave EN8 ... 148 D1
Gazelda Ind Est WD17 ... 167 D4
Gean Wlk 3 AL10 ... 130 A2
Geddes Rd WD23 ... 168 C5
Geddings Rd EN11 ... 135 B6
Geddington Ct EN8 ... 163 A5
Generals Wlk The EN3 ... 162 E2
Gentle Ct SG7 ... 23 E8
Gentlemens Field SG12 ... 93 B3
George Field Ho 4 WD3 ... 165 D2
George Gn CM22 ... 77 B1
George Green Villas CM22 ... 98 B8
George La 5 SG8 ... 7 D6
George Leighton Ct SG2 ... 51 B4
George Lovell Dr EN3 ... 163 A2
George St
Berkhamsted HP4 ... 122 D4
Hemel Hempstead HP2 ... 124 D4
Hertford SG14 ... 113 C6
Luton LU1 ... 63 E7
Markyate AL3 ... 83 E5
St Albans AL3 ... 127 D3
Watford WD18 ... 167 C5
George St W LU1 ... 63 E7
George Street Prim Sch HP2 ... 124 D4
George V Ave HA5 ... 175 F1
George V Way WD3 ... 152 B3
George Wlk 9 SG12 ... 93 D1
George's Wood Rd AL9 ... 145 B5
Georges Mead WD6 ... 169 E3
Georgewood Rd HP3 ... 139 A7
Georgina Ct SG15 ... 11 A3
Gerard Ave CM23 ... 76 E4
Gerard Ct 2 AL5 ... 86 A2
Gernon Rd SG6 ... 22 F5
Gernon Wlk SG6 ... 22 F5
Gew's Cnr EN8 ... 148 D2
Giant Tree Hill WD23 ... 168 D1
Gibbons Cl
Borehamwood WD6 ... 169 E8
Sandridge AL4 ... 108 C1
Gibbons Way SG3 ... 68 F5
Gibbs Cl EN8 ... 148 D2
Gibbs Couch WD19 ... 175 D7
Gibbs Field CM23 ... 76 D5
Gibraltar Lodge AL5 ... 86 D3
Gibson Cl SG4 ... 35 B7
Gidian Ct AL2 ... 141 D4
Gifford's La SG11 ... 54 A2
Gilbert Ct AL5 ... 86 B4
Gilbert Rd UB9 ... 173 D1
Gilbert St EN3 ... 162 C2
Gilbert Way HP4 ... 122 A4
Gilbert's Hill HP23 ... 119 E3
Gilbey Ave CM23 ... 77 B6
Gilbey Cres CM24 ... 59 E8
Gildea Cl HA5 ... 176 A3
Gilden Cl CM17 ... 118 E4
Gilden Way CM17 ... 118 D3
Gilder Cl LU3 ... 45 A8
Gilderdale LU4 ... 44 B6
Gilders CM21 ... 97 D2
Giles Cl AL4 ... 108 C1
Giles Inf Sch The SG1 ... 37 A1
Giles Jun Sch SG1 ... 37 A1
Gill Cl WD18 ... 166 C3
Gillam St LU2 ... 63 E8
Gillan Gn WD23 ... 176 C8
Gillian Ave AL1 ... 141 C7
Gillian Ho HA3 ... 176 E4
Gilliat's Gn WD3 ... 164 D5
Gilliflower Ho EN11 ... 135 A5
Gillings Ct EN5 ... 171 E5
Gillison Cl SG6 ... 23 B5
Gills Hill WD7 ... 155 F4
Gills Hill La WD7 ... 155 F3
Gills Hollow WD7 ... 155 F3
Gilmour Cl EN2 ... 162 A4
Gilpin Gn AL5 ... 86 C1
Gilpin Rd SG12 ... 114 E8
Gilpin's Gallop SG12 ... 115 B4
Gilpin's Ride HP4 ... 122 E5
Gilsland EN9 ... 163 E4
Gilston Mews CM20 ... 117 C6
Gilston Pk CM20 ... 117 C7
Ginns Rd SG9 ... 43 D6
Gippeswyck Cl HA5 ... 175 D2
Gipsy La
Bishop's Stortford CM23, CM24 ... 59 C4
Knebworth AL6,SG3 ... 68 E4
Luton LU1 ... 64 A6
Girdle Rd SG4 ... 22 A2
Girons Cl SG4 ... 35 B7
Girtin Rd WD23 ... 168 C5
Girton Ct EN8 ... 148 E1
Girton Way WD3 ... 166 C4
Gisburne Way WD24 ... 154 A2
Gladding Rd EN7 ... 147 B6
Glade The Baldock SG7 ... 23 E7
Letchworth SG6 ... 22 F3
Welwyn Garden City AL8 ... 110 C8
Glades The HP1 ... 123 E4
Gladeside AL4 ... 128 D6
Gladesmere Ct WD24 ... 154 B2
Gladeway The EN9 ... 163 D6
Gladsmuir Rd EN5 ... 171 E7
Gladstone Ave LU1 ... 63 C7
Gladstone Ct SG2 ... 69 A8
Gladstone Pl EN5 ... 171 D5
Gladstone Rd
Dane End SG12 ... 71 F8
Hoddesdon EN11 ... 135 B7
Ware SG12 ... 93 C2
Watford WD17 ... 167 C6
Glaisdale LU4 ... 44 C5
Glamis Cl Cheshunt EN7 ... 148 A2
Hemel Hempstead HP2 ... 105 B1
Glanfield HP2 ... 124 E6
Glassmill Ho 6 HP4 ... 122 D4
Gleave Cl AL1 ... 128 B4
Glebe Ave SG15 ... 11 A7
Glebe Cl Essendon AL9 ... 131 F6
Hemel Hempstead HP3 ... 138 E7
Hertford SG14 ... 113 D8
Pitstone LU7 ... 80 D5
Watton at S SG14 ... 70 D3
Glebe Cotts AL9 ... 131 F6
Glebe Ct
Bishop's Stortford CM23 ... 77 B8
Hatfield AL10 ... 130 C6
Watford WD25 ... 154 D6
Watton at S SG14 ... 70 E3
Glebe Ho AL9 ... 131 F6
Glebe La EN5 ... 171 A3
Glebe Rd Hertford SG14 ... 113 D8
Letchworth SG6 ... 23 B8
Welwyn AL6 ... 89 B5
Glebe The Ardeley SG2 ... 38 F3
Harlow CM20 ... 117 E1
Kings Langley WD4 ... 139 A2
St Ippolyts SG4 ... 35 C2
Stevenage SG2 ... 51 B6
Watford WD25 ... 154 D6
Glebe View SG2 ... 38 C2
Glebeland AL10 ... 130 C5
Glebelands CM20 ... 117 F3
Gleed Ave WD23 ... 176 D8
Glemsford Cl LU4 ... 44 B6
Glemsford Dr AL5 ... 86 D2
Glen Chess WD3 ... 165 C5
Glen Faba Rd CM19 ... 135 F6
Glen The Caddington LU1 ... 62 E3

Glen The *continued*
Hemel Hempstead HP2 ....124 F8
Northwood HA6 ....174 D3
Glen Way WD17 ....153 E1
Glenblower Ct AL4 ....128 D3
Glenbourne SG4 ....67 F1
Glencoe Rd WD23 ....168 A3
Glencorse Gn WD19 ....175 D6
Glendale HP1 ....124 B3
Glendale Wlk EN8 ....148 E1
Glendean Ct EN3 ....162 F3
Gleneagles Cl WD19 ....175 D6
Gleneagles Dr LU2 ....45 E6
Glenester Cl EN11 ....115 A1
Glenferrie Rd AL1 ....128 A3
Glenfield Ct SG14 ....112 F7
Glenfield Rd LU3 ....45 C6
Glengall Pl AL1 ....141 E8
Glenhaven Ave WD6 ....170 A6
Glenlyn Ave AL1 ....128 B2
Glenmire Terr SG12 ....115 D4
Glenmore Gdns WD5 ....154 A7
Glenshee Cl HA6 ....174 C4
Glenview Gdns HP1 ....124 B3
Glenview Rd HP1 ....124 B3
Glenville Ave EN2 ....161 D1
Glenwood
Hoddesdon EN10 ....134 F4
Welwyn Garden City AL7 ....111 D5
Glenwood Cl SG2 ....51 C2
Glevum Cl AL3 ....126 F1
Globe Cl AL5 ....86 B1
Globe Cres CM23 ....58 D6
Globe Ct Hertford SG14 ....113 C8
Hoddesdon EN10 ....148 F8
Glossop Way SG15 ....11 B7
Gloucester Ave EN8 ....162 E6
Gloucester Cl SG1 ....36 E2
Gloucester Ho 6 WD6 ....170 A7
Gloucester Rd
Enfield EN2 ....161 C1
1 Luton LU1 ....63 F6
Glover Cl EN7 ....147 F4
Glovers Cl SG13 ....113 C4
Glovers Ct SG5 ....21 F1
Glynde The SG2 ....69 B8
Goat La EN1 ....161 F1
Gobions Way EN6 ....145 B3
Goblins Gn AL7 ....110 D5
Goddard End SG2 ....69 C8
Goddards Cl SG13 ....132 C4
Godfrey Cl SG2 ....51 B3
Godfreys Cl LU1 ....63 B6
Godfreys Ct LU1 ....63 B6
Godfries Cl AL6 ....90 E3
Godsafe CM17 ....118 E4
Godwin Cl E4 ....163 C1
Goff's La EN7 ....147 E2
Goff's Oak Ave EN7 ....147 C3
Goffs Cres EN7 ....147 C2
Goffs La EN7 ....148 A2
Goffs Oak Jun Mix Inf Sch EN7 ....147 B3
Goffs Sch EN7 ....148 A2
Gold Cl EN10 ....134 E3
Gold Crest Cl LU4 ....44 A5
Golda Cl EN5 ....171 D3
Goldcrest Way WD23 ....168 C1
Goldcroft HP3 ....125 A1
Golden Dell AL7 ....110 F2
Goldfield Inf Sch HP23 ....99 F3
Goldfield Rd HP23 ....99 F3
Goldfinch Way WD6 ....170 A5
Goldings
Bishop's Stortford CM23 ....77 B8
Hertford SG14 ....92 A1
Goldings Cres AL10 ....130 B6
Goldings Ho AL10 ....130 B6
Goldings La SG14 ....92 A2
Goldington Cl EN11 ....114 F1
Goldon SG6 ....23 C4
Goldring Way AL2 ....142 B5
Goldsmith Way AL3 ....127 C4
Goldstone Cl SG12 ....93 D2
Golf Cl WD23 ....167 D6
Golf Club Rd AL9 ....145 A6
Golf Ride EN2 ....161 A4
Gombards AL3 ....127 D4
Gomer Cl SG4 ....67 E2
Gonnerston AL3 ....127 B4
Gonville Ave WD3 ....166 B3
Gonville Cres SG2 ....51 C2
Goodacre Cl EN6 ....159 C7
Goodey Meade SG2 ....52 F2
Goodison Cl WD23 ....168 C4
Goodliffe Pk CM23 ....59 B2
Goodrich Cl WD25 ....154 A4
Goodwin Ct 4 EN8 ....148 E3
Goodwin Ho WD18 ....166 E3
Goodwin Stile CM23 ....76 D5
Goodwins Mead LU7 ....80 A7
Goodwood Ave
Enfield EN3 ....162 C2
Watford WD24 ....153 E3
Goodwood Cl EN11 ....135 A7
Goodwood Par WD24 ....153 E3
Goodwood Path 2 WD6 ....170 A7
Goodwood Rd SG8 ....7 F6
Goodyers Ave WD7 ....155 F5
Goose Acre Botley HP5 ....136 A1
Cheddington LU7 ....80 A7
Goose La CM22 ....98 E7
Gooseacre AL7 ....110 F4
Gooseberry Hill LU3 ....45 B7
Goosecroft HP1 ....123 F4
Goosefields WD3 ....165 C3
Goral Mead WD3 ....165 D1
Gordian Way SG2 ....37 C1
Gordon Ave HA7 ....176 F4
Gordon Cl AL1 ....128 B2
Gordon Ct SG3 ....69 A5
Gordon Ho AL1 ....128 B2
Gordon Mans EN5 ....171 F5
Gordon Rd EN9 ....163 A5
Gordon St LU1 ....63 D7
Gordon Way EN5 ....171 F5
Gordon's Wlk AL5 ....107 C8
Gore La SG11 ....73 D3
Gorelands La HP8 ....172 A7
Gorham Dr AL1 ....141 E8
Gorhambury* AL3 ....126 C4
Gorle Cl WD25 ....154 A4
Gorleston Cl SG1 ....36 A1
Gorse Cl AL10 ....129 F2
Gorse Cnr
Harpenden AL5 ....107 C8
St Albans AL3 ....127 D5
Gorselands AL5 ....107 B7
Gorst Cl SG6 ....22 E5
Gosford Ho WD18 ....166 E3
Gosforth La
South Oxhey WD19 ....175 B7
5 South Oxhey WD19 ....175 C7
Gosforth Path WD19 ....175 A7
Goshawk Cl LU4 ....44 A4
Goslett Ct WD23 ....168 A4
Gosling Ave SG5 ....33 C2
Gosling Ski Ctr* AL8 ....110 C4
Gosmore SG1 ....36 C2
Gosmore Ley Cl SG4 ....34 F3
Gosmore Rd SG4 ....34 F5
Gossamers The WD25 ....154 E4
Gosselin Ho SG14 ....113 D8
Gosselin Rd SG14 ....113 C8
Gossom's End HP4 ....122 A5
Gossoms Ryde HP4 ....122 A5
Gothic Mede Lower Sch SG15 ....11 A5
Gothic Way SG15 ....11 B5
Gould Cl AL9 ....144 B7
Government Row EN3 ....163 A2
Gowar Field EN6 ....158 A7
Gower Rd SG8 ....7 C7
Gowers The CM20 ....118 B2
Grace Ave WD7 ....156 E6
Grace Cl WD6 ....170 D8
Grace Gdns CM23 ....76 F4
Grace Way SG1 ....50 E7
Graces Maltings HP23 ....100 A3
Graemesdyke Rd HP4 ....122 A3
Grafton Cl AL4 ....128 D2
Grafton Pl SG11 ....55 F1
Graham Ave EN10 ....134 E2
Graham Cl AL1 ....127 D1
Graham Ct 2 AL3 ....127 D4
Graham Gdns LU3 ....45 C4
Graham Rd HA3 ....176 E1
Grailands CM23 ....76 D8
Grammar School Wlk SG5 ....34 E7
Grampian Way LU3 ....44 C8
Granaries The EN9 ....163 E5
Granary Cl AL4 ....108 D8
Granary Ct CM21 ....97 E2
Granary La AL5 ....86 C1
Granary The
Flamstead HP2 ....104 F4
Roydon CM19 ....116 B1
Stanstead Abbotts SG12 ....115 C3
Granby Ave AL5 ....86 D2
Granby Ct AL5 ....86 D2
Granby Rd Luton LU4 ....44 E2
Stevenage SG1 ....36 C2
Grandfield Ave WD17 ....167 A8
Grange Ave Luton LU4 ....44 D4
Totteridge N20 ....171 E2
Grange Bottom SG8 ....7 E5
Grange Cl
Hemel Hempstead HP2 ....125 A2
Hertford SG14 ....113 B6
Hitchin SG4 ....35 A4
Markyate AL3 ....83 D6
Watford WD17 ....167 A8
Grange Court Rd AL5 ....107 C6
Grange Ct Hertford SG14 ....113 C7
Letchworth SG6 ....12 A1
3 St Albans AL3 ....127 D4
Waltham Abbey EN9 ....163 C5
Grange Dr SG5 ....11 F5
Grange Gdns SG12 ....114 E8
Grange Hill AL6 ....89 C6
Grange Jun Sch SG6 ....12 A2
Grange La WD25 ....168 D8
Grange Pk CM23 ....58 F1
Grange Rd
Bishop's Stortford CM23 ....77 A7
Borehamwood WD6 ....169 F4
Letchworth SG6 ....22 F8
Pitstone LU7 ....80 D5
Tring HP23 ....100 C5
Watford WD23 ....167 F4
Wilstone HP23 ....79 D1
Grange Rise SG4 ....67 F1
Grange St AL3 ....127 D4
Grange The
Abbots Langley WD5 ....153 E8
Bishop's Stortford CM23 ....58 F1
Hoddesdon EN11 ....135 A5
Rickmansworth WD3 ....165 D2
Sewardstone EN9 ....163 D2
Standon SG11 ....55 D3
Therfield SG8 ....15 F6
Grange Wlk CM23 ....77 A7
Grangedale Cl HA6 ....174 E2
Grangeside CM23 ....59 A2
Grangewood EN6 ....145 B1
Gransden Cl LU3 ....45 A7
Grant Gdns AL5 ....86 B2
Grantham Cl SG8 ....7 B8
Grantham Gdns SG12 ....93 E2
Grantham Gn WD6 ....170 C4
Grantham Mews HP4 ....122 D4
Grantham Rd LU4 ....45 B1
Granville Ct AL1 ....127 F3
Granville Dene HP3 ....137 A4
Granville Gdns EN11 ....115 A2
Granville Rd Barnet EN5 ....171 D6
Hitchin SG4 ....22 C1
Luton LU1 ....63 B8
St Albans AL1 ....127 F3
Watford WD18 ....167 C5
Berkhamsted HP4 ....121 E6
Grasmere SG1 ....37 C3
Grasmere Ave
Harpenden AL5 ....86 C1
Luton LU3 ....45 B7
Grasmere Cl
Hemel Hempstead HP3 ....125 B1
Watford WD25 ....154 B7
Grasmere Rd Luton LU3 ....45 C7
St Albans AL1 ....128 B1
Ware SG12 ....93 E3
Grass Mdws SG2 ....51 D7
Grass Warren AL6 ....90 E1
Grassington Cl AL2 ....141 A1
Grassy Cl HP1 ....124 A4
Gravel Dr HP23 ....99 B3
Gravel La HP1 ....124 A3
Gravel Path
Berkhamsted HP4 ....122 E5
Hemel Hempstead HP1 ....124 A3
Graveley Ave WD6 ....170 C4
Graveley Cl SG1 ....36 C2
Graveley Dell AL7 ....111 B5
Graveley La SG4 ....36 B5
Graveley Prim Sch SG4 ....36 B4
Graveley Rd Graveley SG1 ....36 B3
Great Wymondley SG4 ....35 F6
Gravelhill Terr HP1 ....124 A2
Gravelly Dell SG11 ....55 F8
Gravelly La SG11 ....55 F8
Gravely Ct HP2 ....125 C2
Gray's La SG5 ....34 D7
Grayling Ct HP4 ....121 F6
Graylings The WD5 ....153 D6
Grays Cl SG8 ....7 C8
Grays Ct CM23 ....76 E8
Graysfield AL7 ....111 A3
Grazings The HP2 ....124 F5
Great Ashby Way SG1 ....37 B3
Great Braitch La AL10 ....109 F1
Great Bramingham La LU3 ....31 B2
Great Break AL7 ....111 B5
Great Cambridge Rd
Cheshunt EN8 ....148 D4
Enfield EN1 ....162 C6
Great Conduit AL7 ....111 C7
Great Dell AL8 ....89 D1
Great Eastern Cl CM23 ....77 A6
Great Elms Rd HP3 ....138 F7
Great Gaddesden CE Prim Sch HP1 ....103 D3
Great Ganett AL7 ....111 C4
Great Gn SG5 ....20 D4
Great Gr WD23 ....168 B5
Great Groves EN7 ....147 E3
Great Hadham Rd CM23 ....76 C5
Great Heart HP2 ....124 E5
Great Heath AL10 ....130 B8
Great Hyde Hall CM21 ....98 B3
Great Innings N SG14 ....70 D4
Great Innings S SG14 ....70 D3
Great Lawne SG3 ....69 D2
Great Ley AL7 ....110 E4
Great Mdw EN10 ....135 A1
Great Molewood SG14 ....92 B1
Great North Rd
Barnet EN5 ....171 E6
Brookmans Park AL9,EN6 ....145 B5
Hatfield AL9 ....130 C5
Oaklands AL6 ....89 E7
Radwell SG7 ....12 D3
Welwyn Garden City AL8 ....110 A7
Great Palmers HP2 ....124 F8
Great Pk WD4 ....139 A1
Great Plumtree CM20 ....117 F2
Great Rd HP2 ....124 F4
Great Slades EN6 ....158 F6
Great Stockwood Rd EN7 ....147 D5
Great Sturgess Rd HP1 ....123 F3
Great Whites Rd HP3 ....124 F1
Great Wood Ctry Pk* EN6 ....146 B5
Greatfield Cl AL5 ....85 C4
Greatham Rd WD23 ....167 D6
Green Acres Lilley LU2 ....32 D2
Stevenage SG2 ....51 C1
Welwyn Garden City AL7 ....110 F3
Green Banks AL1 ....127 F1
Green Bushes LU4 ....44 D6
Green Cl
Brookmans Park AL9 ....144 E5
Cheshunt EN8 ....162 E8
Luton LU4 ....44 C5
Stevenage SG2 ....50 F2
Green Croft AL10 ....130 A8
Green Ct 6 LU4 ....44 C5
Green Dell Way HP3 ....125 C3
Green Dragon Ct LU1 ....63 F6
Green Drift SG8 ....7 C7
Green Edge WD25 ....154 A4
Green End Braughing SG11 ....55 E8
Welwyn AL6 ....89 B4
Green End Bsns Ctr WD3 ....152 A2
Green End Gdns HP1 ....124 A2
Green End La HP1 ....123 F3
Green End Rd HP1 ....124 A2
Green Hill Cl SG11 ....55 F7
Green La Ashwell SG7 ....4 E5
Bovingdon HP3 ....137 A3
Bovingdon,Pudds Cross HP3 ....136 F3
Braughing SG11 ....55 F7
Croxley Green WD3 ....165 F4
Hemel Hempstead HP2 ....125 D4
Hitchin SG4 ....22 B1
Hoddesdon EN10 ....149 B8
Kensworth Common LU6 ....82 E8
Latimer HP5 ....150 C6
Letchworth SG6 ....23 C8
Luton LU2 ....46 C4
Markyate AL3 ....83 F5
Northwood HA6 ....174 E3
Pitstone LU7 ....80 E5
St Albans, New Greens AL3 ....127 D7
St Albans, Sopwell AL1 ....142 A7
Watford WD19 ....167 C2
Welwyn Garden City AL7 ....111 D5
Green Lane Cl AL5 ....107 E8
Green Lanes AL10 ....109 F2
Green Lanes Prim Sch AL10 ....109 F1
Green Leys Cotts SG11 ....55 F1
Green Man Ct CM20 ....117 A4
Green Mdw EN6 ....145 A1
Green Milverton LU3 ....45 A7
Green Oaks LU2 ....45 F3
Green Path HP22,HP23 ....99 D4
Green St
Chorleywood WD3 ....164 C6
Harlow CM17 ....118 D1
Royston SG8 ....7 D8
Shenley WD6,WD7 ....157 A3
Stevenage SG1 ....50 C7
Green The
Bishop's Stortford CM23 ....76 F4
Cheddington LU7 ....80 A7
Cheshunt EN8 ....148 C3
Codicote SG4 ....67 F1
Kimpton SG4 ....66 D1
Knebworth SG3 ....68 C5
London Colney AL2 ....142 D4
Luton LU4 ....44 C5
Mentmore LU7 ....61 D4
Newnham SG7 ....12 E7
Peters Green LU2 ....65 C3
Pitstone LU7 ....80 D4
Potten End HP4 ....123 B6
Royston SG8 ....7 D6
Sarratt WD3 ....152 A3
Stotfold SG5 ....11 F7
Waltham Abbey EN9 ....163 C5
Ware SG12 ....93 D3
Welwyn AL6 ....89 B5
Welwyn Garden City AL7 ....111 A4
Green Vale AL7 ....111 A5
Green View Cl HP3 ....137 A2
Green Way Gdns HA3 ....176 E1
Green Way The HA3 ....176 E2
Greenacre Cl EN5 ....158 F1
Greenacres
Bushey WD23 ....176 D8
Hemel Hempstead HP2 ....125 D2
Pitstone LU7 ....80 C4
Greenall Cl EN8 ....148 E1
Greenbank EN8 ....148 B3
Greenbank Rd WD17 ....153 D3
Greenbury Cl Barley SG8 ....8 F1
Chorleywood WD3 ....164 C5
Greencoates SG13 ....113 E5
Greene Field Rd HP4 ....122 C4
Greene Wlk HP4 ....122 D3
Greener Ct EN3 ....163 A2
Greenes Ct HP4 ....122 C5
Greenfield Hatfield AL9 ....130 D8
Royston SG8 ....7 B7
Welwyn Garden City AL8 ....89 D1
Greenfield Ave
Ickleford SG5 ....21 D4
South Oxhey WD19 ....175 E8
Greenfield La SG5 ....21 E4
Greenfield Rd SG1 ....50 E7
Greenfield St EN9 ....163 C5
Greenfields Cuffley EN6 ....146 E1
Stansted Mountfitchet CM24 ....59 E7
Greenfields Prim Sch WD19 ....175 C5
Greengate LU3 ....44 C8
Greenheys Cl HA6 ....174 E2
Greenhill Ave LU2 ....45 E3
Greenhill Cres WD18 ....166 E3
Greenhill Ct HP1 ....124 B2
Greenhill Pk CM23 ....76 D5
Greenhills SG12 ....93 C3
Greenhills Cl WD3 ....165 B4
Greenland Rd EN5 ....171 C3
Greenlands WD6 ....170 D3
Greenlane Ind Est SG6 ....23 C7
Greenleas EN9 ....163 E5
Greenriggs LU2 ....46 F2
Greenside WD6 ....157 A1
Greenside Dr SG5 ....34 D8
Greenside Pk LU2 ....45 E3
Greenside Sch SG2 ....51 B2
Greensleeves Cl AL4 ....128 C2
Greenstead CM21 ....97 E1
Greensward WD23 ....168 B3
Greenway
Berkhamsted HP4 ....122 A4
Bishop's Stortford CM23 ....77 C6
Harpenden AL5 ....107 E8
Hemel Hempstead HP2 ....125 B3
Letchworth SG6 ....23 A2
Pinner HA5 ....175 B1
Walkern SG2 ....52 B8
Greenway Fst Sch HP4 ....121 F4
Greenway The
Enfield EN3 ....162 D4
Potters Bar EN6 ....159 A6
Rickmansworth WD3 ....165 A2
Tring HP23 ....99 F5
Greenways
Abbots Langley WD5 ....153 E7
Buntingford SG9 ....40 D8
Goff's Oak EN7 ....147 B2
Hertford SG14 ....113 B6
Luton LU2 ....46 B5
Stevenage SG1 ....50 E6
Welwyn AL6 ....89 E3
Greenwich Ct
Cheshunt EN8 ....162 E5
St Albans AL1 ....128 A2
Greenwich Way EN9 ....163 C4
Greenwood Ave EN7 ....162 B8
Greenwood Cl EN7 ....162 B8
Greenwood Dr WD25 ....154 B5
Greenwood Gdns WD7 ....156 E6
Greenyard EN9 ....163 C6
Greer Rd HA3 ....176 C2
Gregories Cl LU3 ....45 D1
Gregory Ave EN6 ....159 C6
Gregory Mews EN9 ....163 B7
Gregson Cl WD6 ....170 C8
Grenadier Cl AL4 ....128 C2
Grenadine Cl EN7 ....147 F4
Grenadine Way HP23 ....100 A5
Greneway Sch The SG8 ....7 E7
Grenfell Cl WD6 ....170 C8
Grenville Ave EN10 ....134 F2
Grenville Cl EN8 ....162 D7
Grenville Ct WD3 ....164 C5
Grenville Way SG2 ....51 A1
Gresford Cl AL4 ....128 D3
Gresham Cl LU2 ....64 D8
Gresham Ct HP4 ....122 B3
Gresley Cl AL8 ....110 E8
Gresley Ct Enfield EN1 ....162 C4
Potters Bar EN6 ....145 C1
Gresley Way SG2 ....51 D5
Greville Cl AL9 ....144 C7
Grey House The 4 WD17 ....167 A7
Greycaine Rd WD24 ....154 D2
Greydells Rd SG1 ....50 E6
Greyfriars SG12 ....93 B3
Greyfriars La AL5 ....107 A7
Greyhound La EN6 ....158 A6
Greystoke Cl HP4 ....122 A3
Griffiths Way AL1 ....127 C1
Griffon Way WD25 ....153 F5
Grimsdyke Cres EN5 ....171 C6
Grimsdyke Fst & Mid Sch HA5 ....175 F4
Grimsdyke Lo AL1 ....128 A3
Grimsdyke Rd
Pinner HA5 ....175 E3
Wigginton HP23 ....100 D1
Grimston Rd AL1 ....127 F2
Grimstone Rd SG4 ....35 E4
Grimthorpe Cl AL3 ....127 D6
Grindcobbe AL1 ....141 D8
Grinders End SG4 ....36 B4
Grinstead La CM22 ....98 C6
Groom Rd EN10 ....148 F5
Grooms Cotts HP5 ....136 B1
Groomsby Dr LU7 ....80 E5
Grosvenor Ave WD4 ....139 C3
Grosvenor Cl CM23 ....76 D4
Grosvenor Ct
Croxley Green WD3 ....166 D4
Stevenage SG1 ....50 A7
Grosvenor Ho 4 CM23 ....77 B8
Grosvenor Rd Baldock SG7 ....12 F1
Borehamwood WD6 ....170 B6
Hoddesdon EN10 ....134 F3
Luton LU3 ....45 B5
Moor Park HA6 ....174 F5
St Albans AL1 ....127 E2
Watford WD17 ....167 C6
Grosvenor Rd W SG7 ....12 F1
Grosvenor Terr HP1 ....124 A2
Grotto The SG12 ....114 D8
Ground La AL10 ....130 B7
Grove Ave AL5 ....107 D7
Grove Cotts WD23 ....168 A3
Grove Cres WD3 ....166 A5
Grove Ct Arlesey SG15 ....11 A8
Barnet EN5 ....171 F6
Waltham Abbey EN9 ....163 B6
Grove Cvn Pk The LU1 ....63 B3
Grove End LU1 ....63 B5
Grove Farm Pk HA6 ....174 D5
Grove Gdns Enfield EN3 ....162 D1
Tring HP23 ....100 B5
Grove Hall Rd WD23 ....167 E5
Grove Hill CM24 ....59 E7
Grove Ho Bushey WD23 ....167 F3
Cheshunt EN8 ....148 B1
Hitchin SG4 ....22 A2
Grove Inf Sch The AL5 ....107 D7
Grove Jun Sch The AL5 ....107 D7

Grove La HP5 136 B5
Grove Lea AL10 130 A2
Grove Mdw AL7 111 C6
Grove Mead AL10 129 F5
Grove Mill La WD3, WD17 153 C1
Grove Park Rd LU1 63 B3
Grove Path EN7 162 A8
Grove Pk
Bishop's Stortford CM23 76 C8
Tring HP23 100 C5
Grove Pl
19 Bishop's Stortford CM23 76 F7
Bushey WD25 168 B8
Welham Green AL9 144 C7
Grove Rd
Borehamwood WD6 170 A8
Harpenden AL5 107 D7
Hemel Hempstead HP1 124 A1
Hitchin SG4 21 F1
Luton LU1 63 D7
Northwood HA6 174 D5
Rickmansworth WD3 173 A8
Slip End LU1 63 B2
St Albans AL1 127 D2
Stevenage SG1 50 D7
Tring HP23 100 C5
Ware SG12 93 F2
Grove Rd W EN3 162 C2
Grove Road Prim Sch HP23 100 C5
Grove The
Brookmans Park AL9 145 A4
Chipperfield WD4 138 C1
Great Hallingbury CM22 77 F4
Latimer HP5 150 D3
Little Hadham SG11 75 E7
Luton LU1 63 B5
Potters Bar EN6 159 C7
Radlett WD7 156 A5
Tring HP23 100 C5
Grove Way WD3 164 B4
Grove Wlk SG14 113 C8
Grovebury Gdns AL2 141 C4
Grovedale Cl EN7 147 F1
Groveland Way SG5 12 A5
Grovelands
Chiswell Green AL2 141 B4
Hemel Hempstead HP2 125 C5
Grovelands Ave SG4 22 C2
Grovelands Bsns Ctr HP2 125 C5
Grover Cl HP2 124 D4
Grover Rd WD19 167 D3
Grovewood Cl WD3 164 B4
Grubbs La AL9 145 C8
Gryphon Ind Pk The AL3 127 F8
Guardian Ind Est LU1 63 C8
Guernsey Cl LU4 44 A3
Guernsey Ho Enfield EN3 162 D1
Watford WD18 167 A3
Guessens Ct AL8 110 C6
Guessens Gr AL8 110 C6
Guessens Rd AL8 110 C6
Guessens Wlk AL8 110 C7
Guilden Morden CE Prim Sch SG8 1 F5
Guildford Cl SG1 36 F2
Guildford Rd AL1 128 B2
Guildford St LU1 63 E7
Guildhouse The WD3 166 B3
Guilfords CM17 118 D5
Guinevere Gdns EN8 162 E8
Gulland Cl WD23 168 C4
Gullbrook HP1 124 A3
Gullet Wood Rd WD25 154 A4
Gullicot Way LU7 80 D4
Gulphs The SG13 113 D5
Gun La SG3 68 F4
Gun Meadow Ave SG3 69 A4
Gun Rd SG3 69 A4
Gun Road Gdns SG3 68 F4
Gunnels Wood Ind Est SG1 50 D3
Gunnels Wood Rd SG1 50 B5
Gunner Dr EN3 163 A2
Gurney Court Rd AL1 127 F5
Gurney's La SG5 21 B7
Gwent Cl WD25 154 D5
Gwynfa Cl AL6 89 D7
Gwynne Cl HP23 100 A5
Gwynns Wlk SG13 113 E6
Gyfford Wlk EN7 162 B8
Gypsy Cl SG12 114 F4
Gypsy La
Abbots Langley WD4 153 D5
Great Amwell SG12 114 F4
Welwyn Garden City AL7 110 F1
Gypsy Moth Ave AL10 129 E7

H

Haberdashers' Aske's Sch for Boys WD6 169 B6
Haberdashers' Aske's Sch for Girls WD6 169 B5
Hackforth Cl EN5 171 B4
Hackney Cl WD6 170 D4
Haddam Hall SG11 57 E2
Haddenham Ct HP2 105 B1
Haddestoke Gate EN8 148 F5
Haddon Cl
Borehamwood WD6 170 A6
Hemel Hempstead HP3 125 A2
Stevenage SG2 69 C7
Haddon Ct 20 AL5 86 B1
Haddon Rd
Chorleywood WD3 164 C4
Luton LU2 63 F8
Hadham Ct CM23 76 E8
Hadham Gr CM23 76 C8
Hadham Ho CM23 76 D8
Hadham Rd
Bishop's Stortford CM23 76 D8
Little Hadham SG11 57 F1
Standon SG11 55 F1
Hadland Cl HP3 137 A5
Hadleigh SG6 23 B4
Hadleigh Ct
Hoddesdon EN10 134 F1
Wheathampstead AL5 107 E6
Hadley Cl WD6 169 F3
Hadley Ct LU3 45 D1
Hadley Gn EN5 171 F7
Hadley Gn W EN5 171 F7
Hadley Gr EN5 171 E7
Hadley Green Rd EN5 171 F7
Hadley Highstone EN5 171 F8
Hadley Par 6 EN5 171 E6
Hadley Rd EN2,EN4 160 C1
Hadley Ridge EN5 171 F6
Hadley Wood Prim Sch EN4 159 C1
Hadley Wood Sta EN4 159 C1
Hadlow Down Cl LU3 45 A5
Hadrian Cl AL3 127 A1
Hadrian Way SG7 23 D7
Hadrians Wlk SG1 51 C8
Hadwell Cl SG2 51 A3
Hagdell Rd LU1 63 C5
Hagden La WD18 167 A4
Haggerston Rd WD6 156 E1
Hagsdell Rd SG13 113 D5
Haig Cl AL1 128 B2
Haig Ho AL1 128 B2
Hailey Ave EN11 115 A2
Hailey Cl SG13 114 E2
Hailey Hall Sch SG13 114 F2
Hailey La SG13 114 E2
Haileybury & Imperial Service Coll SG13 114 D2
Haines Way WD25 154 A5
Haldane Cl EN3 163 B1
Haldens AL7 89 F1
Haldens Ho 3 AL7 89 F1
Hale Ct SG13 113 D5
Hale Ho EN3 162 D2
Hale La HP22 119 A3
Hale Rd SG13 113 D5
Hales Mdw AL5 86 A2
Hales Park Cl HP2 125 C4
Hales Pk HP2 125 C4
Haleswood Rd HP2 125 B4
Half Acre SG5 34 D6
Half Acres CM23 76 F8
Half Moon Cotts CM21 97 B1
Half Moon La LU1 84 C8
Half Moon Mdw HP2 125 C8
Half Moon Mews 5 AL1 127 D3
Halfhide La EN8 148 D5
Halfhides EN9 163 D6
Halfway Ave LU4 44 D1
Halifax Cl
Bricket Wood AL2 154 F8
Watford WD25 153 F5
Halifax Rd WD3 164 C2
Halifax Way AL7 111 E6
Hall Barns SG9 42 F4
Hall Cl WD3 165 A1
Hall Cotts SG9 29 A1
Hall Dr UB9 173 C2
Hall Gdns AL4 143 D8
Hall Gr AL7 111 B4
Hall Heath Cl AL1 128 B5
Hall La Great Chishill SG8 9 F2
Great Hormead SG9 29 A1
Kimpton SG4 87 C8
Woolmer Green SG3 69 A2
Hall Mead SG6 22 D6
Hall Park Gate HP4 122 E3
Hall Park Hill HP4 122 E3
Hall Pk HP4 122 E3
Hall Place Cl AL1 127 E4
Hall Place Gdns AL1 127 E4
Hall Rd HP2 125 B5
Hallam Cl WD24 167 C7
Hallam Gdns HA5 175 E3
Halland Way HA6 174 D4
Halley Rd EN9 163 B3
Halleys Ridge SG14 113 A5
Halliday Cl WD7 156 E7
Halling Hill CM20 117 F2
Hallingbury Cl CM22 77 B1
Hallingbury Rd
Bishop's Stortford CM22 77 B4
Sawbridgeworth CM21 98 A4
Hallmores EN10 135 A4
Hallowell Rd HA6 174 E3
Hallowes Cres WD19 175 A7
Halls Cl AL6 89 C4
Hallside Rd EN1 161 F1
Hallwicks Rd LU2 46 B3
Hallworth Dr SG5 11 E6
Hallworth Ho SG5 11 E6
Halsey Dr
Hemel Hempstead HP1 123 F5
Hitchin SG4 35 B7
Halsey Pk AL2 142 F4
Halsey Pl WD24 154 B1
Halsey Rd WD18 167 B6
Halstead Hill EN7 147 E1
Halter Cl WD6 170 D4
Halton Cl AL2 141 C3
Halton Wood (Forest Wlks)* HP23 119 A5
Haltside AL10 129 E4
Halwick Cl HP1 124 B1
Halyard Cl LU3 45 B6
Halyard High Sch LU4 44 A3
Hamberlins La HP4 121 C7
Hamble Ct WD18 167 A5
Hambleden Pl WD7 155 F4
Hambledon Ct EN4 159 D1
Hamblings Cl WD7 156 D6
Hambridge Way SG5 20 D4
Hambro Cl LU2 85 F7
Hamburgh Ct EN8 148 D3
Hamels Dr SG13 114 B7
Hamels La SG9 55 B7
Hamer Cl HP3 137 A3
Hamer Ct LU2 45 D8
Hamilton Ave EN11 135 A8
Hamilton Cl
Bricket Wood AL2 155 A8
Dagnall HP4 81 C5
South Mimms EN6 158 A6
Hamilton Ct 3 AL10 130 B3
Hamilton Mead HP3 137 A4
Hamilton Rd
Abbots Langley WD4 153 C6
Berkhamsted HP4 122 B4
South Oxhey WD19 175 B7
St Albans AL1 128 A4
Hamilton St WD18 167 C4
Hamlet Cl AL2 140 F1
Hamlet The HP4 123 A7
Hammarskjold Rd CM20 117 D2
Hammer La HP2 124 F4
Hammer Par WD25 154 A6
Hammerdell SG6 22 D7
Hammers Gate AL2 141 A5
Hammond Cl Barnet EN5 171 E4
Hammond Street EN7 147 F5
Stevenage SG1 50 D6
Hammond Ct LU1 63 C1
Hammond End La AL5 106 F5
Hammond Prim Sch The HP2 124 F6
Hammonds Hill AL5 106 F4
Hammonds La AL10 109 B3
Hammondstreet Rd EN7 147 D5
Hammondswick AL5 106 F4
Hamonte SG6 23 C4
Hampden SG4 66 C1
Hampden Cl SG6 23 B8
Hampden Cres EN7 162 B8
Hampden Hill SG12 93 F2
Hampden Hill Cl SG12 93 F2
Hampden Pl AL2 141 E2
Hampden Rd
Harrow HA3 176 C1
Hitchin SG4 22 C1
Hampden Rise SG8 7 D4
Hampden Way WD17 153 E3
Hampermill La WD19 167 A1
Hampton Cl SG2 69 C7
Hampton Gdns CM21 118 C7
Hampton Rd LU4 63 B8
Hamstel Rd CM20 117 C1
Hamsworth Ct SG14 112 F7
Hanaper Dr SG8 8 F2
Hanbury Cl Cheshunt EN8 148 E2
Ware SG12 93 E1
Hanbury Cotts AL9 131 E6
Hanbury Dr SG12 93 C6
Hanbury Mews SG12 93 C5
Hancock Ct WD6 170 C8
Hancock Dr LU2 45 E5
Hancroft Rd HP3 124 F1
Hand La CM21 97 C1
Handa Cl HP3 139 B8
Handcross Rd LU2 46 D2
Handley Gate AL2 140 F2
Handpost Lodge Gdns HP2 125 D2
Handside Cl AL8 110 C6
Handside Gn AL8 110 C7
Handside La AL8 110 C6
Handsworth Way WD19 175 A7
Hangar Ruding WD19 175 F7
Hanger Cl HP1 124 B2
Hangmans La AL6 89 F8
Hanover Cl SG2 50 F1
Hanover Ct
Croxley Green WD3 166 A4
Hoddesdon EN11 135 A7
Luton LU4 44 D5
9 Pinner HA5 175 F3
Waltham Abbey EN9 163 C6
Hanover Gdns WD5 139 F1
Hanover Gn HP1 124 A1
Hanover Ho AL7 110 F4
Hanover Wlk AL10 129 F2
Hanross Cl AL2 140 E1
Hanscombe End Rd SG5 19 D7
Hanselin Cl HA7 176 F5
Hanswick Cl LU2 46 B2
Hanworth Cl LU2 45 D7
Hanyards End EN6 146 E3
Hanyards La EN6 146 D3
Happy Valley Ind Pk WD4 139 B3
Harbert Gdns AL2 141 C2
Harborne Cl WD19 175 C5
Harbour Ct WD23 168 B4
Harbury Dell LU3 45 B7
Harcourt Rd
Bushey WD23 168 C4
Tring HP23 100 C4
Harcourt St LU1 63 E5
Hardenwick Ct 4 AL5 86 A2
Harding Cl Luton LU3 44 E7
Redbourn AL3 106 B5
Watford WD25 154 C6
Harding Ct AL5 86 B4
Harding Par 8 AL5 86 B1
Hardings AL7 111 C7
Hardingstone Ct EN8 162 F5
Hardwick Cl SG2 69 C7
Hardwick Gn LU3 45 B7
Hardwicke Pl AL2 142 D4
Hardy Cl Barnet EN5 171 E4
Hitchin SG4 35 C7
Hardy Dr SG8 7 D8
Hardy Rd HP2 124 F4
Hare Cres WD25 154 A7
Hare La AL10 130 B3
Hare Street Rd SG9 41 B8
Harebell AL7 110 E3
Harebell Cl SG13 114 B6
Harebreaks The WD24 154 B2
Harefield Harlow CM20 118 A1
Stevenage SG2 51 C3
Harefield Ct LU1 62 F8
Harefield Hospl UB9 173 C2
Harefield Inf Sch UB9 173 C2
Harefield Jun Sch UB9 173 C2
Harefield Pl AL4 128 D6
Harefield Rd Luton LU1 62 F8
Rickmansworth WD3 173 D7
Harefield Road Ind Est WD3 173 E6
Harepark Cl HP1 123 F4
Haresfoot Sch HP4 122 B1
Harewood WD3 165 C4
Harewood Ct HA3 176 E2
Harewood Rd WD19 175 B7
Harford Dr WD17 166 E8
Harforde Ct SG13 114 A6
Hargrave Cl CM24 59 E8
Hargreaves Ave EN7 162 B8
Hargreaves Cl EN7 162 B8
Hargreaves Rd SG8 7 D5
Harkett Cl HA3 176 F1
Harkett Ct HA3 176 F1
Harkness EN7 148 B2
Harkness Ct SG4 22 B1
Harkness Ind Est WD6 170 A5
Harkness Way SG4 22 C2
Harland Ct UB9 173 C1
Harlech Rd WD5 154 A8
Harlequin The WD17 167 C5
Harlesden Rd AL1 128 A3
Harlestone Cl LU3 31 A1
Harley Ct AL4 128 D7
Harlings The SG13 114 C2
Harlow Coll CM20 117 D1
Harlow Ct HP2 125 A7
Harlow Mill Sta CM20 118 C5
Harlow Rd Roydon CM19 116 C1
Sawbridgeworth CM21 118 C8
Harlow Sports Ctr CM20 117 D2
Harlow Stad (Greyhounds) CM19 116 E1
Harlow Town Sta CM20 117 D3
Harlowbury Prim Sch CM17 118 D4
Harlton Ct EN9 163 F5
Harmer Dell AL6 89 F4
Harmer Green La AL6 90 B5
Harmony Cl AL10 130 A7
Harmsworth Way N20 171 F1
Harness Way AL4 128 D6
Harold Cres EN9 163 C7
Harold Ct EN8 162 F5
Harpenden Hospl (private) AL5 86 A4
Harpenden La AL3 106 B6
Harpenden Meml Hospl AL5 86 B2
Harpenden Prep Sch AL5 85 F2
Harpenden Rd
Wheathampstead AL5,AL4 108 B8
St Albans AL3 127 E6
Harpenden Rise AL5 85 F3
Harpenden Sta AL5 86 B1
Harper Ct SG1 50 F5
Harper La WD7 156 B8
Harperbury Hospl WD7 156 C8
Harps Hill AL3 83 E5
Harpsfield Broadway AL10 129 F6
Harptree Way AL1 128 A5
Harriet Walker Way WD3 164 F2
Harriet Way WD23 168 D2
Harrington Cl 8 CM23 77 A7
Harrington Ct SG13 114 C3
Harriot Hts AL3 127 C4
Harris Ho 14 WD18 166 F3
Harris La Great Offley SG5 33 D2
Shenley WD7 157 A6
Harris Rd WD25 154 A4
Harris's La SG12 93 C1
Harrison Cl Hitchin SG4 34 F7
Northwood HA6 174 C4
Harrison Rd EN9 163 C4
Harrison Wlk EN8 148 D1
Harrisons CM23 59 D2
Harrogate Rd 2 WD19 175 C7
Harrow Coll, Harrow Weald Campus HA3 176 E4
Harrow Ct SG1 50 E5
Harrow View HA2 176 C1
Harrow Way WD19 175 E6
Harrow Weald Pk HA3 176 D4
Harrow Yd HP23 100 A3
Harrowbond Rd CM17 118 C1
Harrowden Ct LU2 64 C8
Harrowden Rd LU2 64 B8
Harrowdene SG2 51 C4
Harry Scott Ct LU4 44 C6
Harston Dr EN3 163 A1
Hart Hill Dr LU2 63 F8
Hart Hill La LU2 63 F8
Hart Hill Path LU2 63 F8
Hart Hill Prim Sch LU2 63 F8
Hart La LU2 64 A8
Hart Lodge 10 EN5 171 E6
Hart Rd Harlow CM17 118 C6
St Albans AL1 127 D2
Hart Wlk LU2 46 A1
Hartcran Ho 7 WD19 175 D7
Hartfield Ave WD6 170 A4
Hartfield Cl WD6 170 A4
Hartfield Ct 6 SG12 93 D2
Hartforde Rd WD6 170 B8
Harthall La WD4,HP3 139 D4
Hartham La SG14 113 D6
Hartham Villas SG14 113 C7
Hartland Ct SG5 34 D7
Hartland Rd EN8 148 D1
Hartley Rd LU2 63 F8
Hartmoor Mews EN3 162 D2
Harts Cl WD23 168 A8
Hartsbourne Ave WD23 176 D8
Hartsbourne Cl WD23 176 D8
Hartsbourne Pk WD23 176 E8
Hartsbourne Prim Sch WD23 176 D8
Hartsbourne Rd WD23 176 D8
Hartsbourne Way HP2 125 C2
Hartsfield Jun Mix Inf Sch SG7 12 F1
Hartsfield Rd LU2 46 B2
Hartspring La WD23, WD25 168 A8
Hartswood Gn WD23 176 D8
Hartwell Gdns AL5 85 E1
Hartwood 3 LU2 63 F8
Harvest Cl LU4 44 A3
Harvest Ct Letchworth SG6 23 A2
Oaklands AL6 89 E7
St Albans AL4 128 D7
Harvest End WD25 154 D3
Harvest La SG2 51 D7
Harvest Mead AL10 130 B7
Harvest Rd WD23 168 B5
Harvey Rd
Croxley Green WD3 166 A3
London Colney AL2 142 C5
Stevenage SG2 51 B6
Harvey Road Prim Sch WD3 166 A3
Harvey's Hill LU2 45 F5
Harveyfields EN9 163 C5
Harvingwell Pl HP2 125 B5
Harwood Cl Tewin AL6 90 E2
Welwyn Garden City AL8 89 E2
Harwood Hill AL8 89 E1
Harwood Hill Jun Mix Inf Sch AL8 89 E2
Harwoods Rd WD18 167 A5
Hasedines Rd HP1 124 A4
Haseldine Mdws AL10 129 F4
Haseldine Rd AL2 142 D5
Haselfoot SG6 22 E6
Hasketon Dr LU4 44 B6
Haslemere CM23 77 A4
Haslemere Est The EN11 135 D6
Haslemere Ind Est AL7 110 F7
Haslewood Ave EN11 135 A6
Haslingden Cl AL5 85 D3
Hastings Cl SG1 50 A8
Hastings St LU1 63 D6
Hastings Way
Croxley Green WD3 166 C5
Watford WD23 167 E5
Hastoe Farm Barns HP23 119 F7
Hastoe La HP23 100 A2
Hatch End High Sch HA3 176 B2
Hatch End Sta HA5 176 A3
Hatch Gn CM22 98 B8
Hatch La SG4 24 A3
Hatching Gn AL5 107 A6
Hatching Green Cl AL5 107 A6
Hatfield Ave AL10 129 E8
Hatfield Bsns Ctr AL10 129 D8
Hatfield Cres HP2 124 F7
Hatfield House & Gdns* AL9 130 D5
Hatfield Rd
Essendon AL9 111 E1
Potters Bar EN6 159 C8
St Albans AL1,AL4 128 C3
Watford WD24 167 B8
Hatfield Sta AL9 130 C6
Hatfield Tunnel AL10 129 F6
Hathaway Cl LU4 44 B2
Hathaway Ct AL4 128 E3
Hatherleigh Gdns EN6 159 D7
Hatters La WD18 166 D3
Hatters Way LU1,LU4 44 D1
Hatton Rd EN8 148 D2
Havelock Rd
Kings Langley WD4 138 F3
Luton LU2 45 E1
Havelock Rise LU2 45 E1

Haven Cl AL10 129 F6
Haven The SG5 11 F6
Havensfield WD4 152 B8
Havercroft Cl AL3 127 C1
Haverdale LU4 44 C4
Havers Inf Sch CM23 76 E5
Havers La CM23 76 F5
Havers Par CM23 76 F5
Haward Rd EN11 135 C8
Hawbush Cl AL6 89 B4
Hawbush Rise AL6 89 B5
Hawes Cl HA6 174 F3
Hawes La E4 163 C1
Haweswater Dr WD25 154 C6
Hawfield Gdns AL2 141 D5
Hawkesworth Cl HA6 174 E3
Hawkfield SG6 22 E8
Hawkfields LU2 45 E6
Hawkings Way HP3 137 A5
Hawkins Cl WD6 170 C7
Hawkins Hall La SG3 69 E2
Hawkshead Ct EN8 162 F5
Hawkshead La AL9 144 D3
Hawkshead Rd EN6 145 B2
Hawkshill AL1 128 A2
Hawkshill Dr HP3 137 F8
Hawksmead Cl EN3 162 D3
Hawksmoor WD7 157 A6
Hawksmoor Sch WD6 170 C8
Hawkwell Dr HP23 100 C4
Hawridge & Cholesbury CE Sch HP5 120 E2
Hawridge La HP5 120 F1
Hawridge Vale HP5 120 F1
Hawsley Rd AL5 107 A4
Hawthorn Ave LU2 46 B4
Hawthorn Cl
Abbots Langley WD5 154 A7
Harpenden AL5 107 D7
Hertford SG14 113 A7
Hitchin SG5 34 E6
Royston SG8 7 F7
Watford WD17 153 F1
Hawthorn Cres LU1 62 E3
Hawthorn Gr Barnet EN5 170 F3
Enfield EN2 161 D1
Hawthorn Hill SG6 22 F7
Hawthorn La HP1 123 F4
Hawthorn Rd EN11 135 B8
Hawthorn Rise CM23 76 F3
Hawthorn Way
Chiswell Green AL2 141 A7
Royston SG8 7 F7
Hawthorne Ave EN7 162 B8
Hawthorne Cl EN7 162 B8
Hawthorne Ct HA6 175 A1
Hawthorne Rd WD7 156 A5
Hawthornes AL10 129 F3
Hawthorns AL8 110 D8
Hawthorns The
Berkhamsted HP4 122 A5
Hemel Hempstead HP3 137 F7
Maple Cross WD3 172 D5
Ridge EN6 157 E6
Stevenage SG1 51 A4
Ware SG12 93 C3
Hawtrees WD7 155 F4
Hay Cl WD6 170 C7
Hay Gn SG8 15 F6
Hay La AL5 86 A1
Hay Wains SG3 69 B2
Haybourn Mead HP1 124 B2
Haycroft
Bishop's Stortford CM23 77 C7
Luton LU2 45 E6
Haycroft Rd SG1 50 E7
Hayden Rd EN9 163 C4
Haydock Rd SG8 7 F6
Haydon Dell WD23 167 F3
Haydon Hill Ho WD23 167 F2
Haydon Rd WD19 167 E3
Hayes Cl LU2 46 C5
Hayes Hill Farm* EN9 149 C3
Hayes Wlk
Cheshunt EN10 148 F6
Potters Bar EN6 159 B6
Hayfield SG2 51 D7
Hayfield Cl WD23 168 B5
Haygarth SG3 69 A4
Hayhurst Rd LU4 44 B1
Hayley Bell Gdns CM23 76 F3
Hayley Comm SG2 51 C3
Hayling Dr LU2 46 D3
Hayling Rd WD19 175 B8
Haymeads AL8 89 E1
Haymeads La CM23 77 C6
Haymoor SG6 22 E7
Haynes Cl AL7 111 A5
Haynes Mead HP4 122 A6
Haysman Cl SG6 23 B7
Hayton Cl LU3 31 B2
Haywood Cl HA5 175 D1
Haywood Ct EN9 163 F5
Haywood Dr WD3 164 F4
Haywood La SG8 16 A6
Haywood Pk WD3 164 F4
Haywoods Dr HP3 137 F8
Haywoods La SG8 7 E7
Hazel Cl
3 Hammond Street EN7 147 E5
Welwyn AL6 89 E3
Hazel Ct Hitchin SG4 35 A7
Shenley WD7 156 F6
Hazel End CM23 59 A5
Hazel Gdns CM21 97 F1
Hazel Gr Hatfield AL10 129 F2
Stotfold SG5 11 E5
Watford WD25 154 B4
Welwyn Garden City AL7 111 C7
Hazel Grove Ho AL10 129 F3
Hazel Mead EN5 171 B4
Hazel Rd
Berkhamsted HP4 122 D3
Chiswell Green AL2 141 B3
Hazel Tree Rd WD24 154 B3
Hazelbury Ave WD5 153 C7
Hazelbury Cres LU1 63 C8
Hazelbury Ct 3 LU1 63 C8
Hazelcroft HA5 176 B4
Hazeldell SG14 70 D3
Hazeldell Link HP1 123 E2
Hazeldell Rd HP1 123 F2
Hazeldene EN8 162 E7
Hazelend Rd CM23 59 B4
Hazelgrove Prim Sch AL10 129 F2
Hazelmere Rd
St Albans AL4 128 C6
Stevenage SG2 69 A8
Hazels The AL6 90 E2
Hazelwood Cl Hitchin SG5 34 F8
Luton LU2 46 B4
Hazelwood Dr
Pinner HA5 175 B1
St Albans AL4 128 C4
Hazelwood La WD5 153 D7
Hazelwood Rd WD3 166 C3
Hazely HP23 100 C4
Heacham Cl LU4 44 B4
Headingley Cl
Hammond Street EN7 147 F5
Shenley WD7 156 E7
Stevenage SG1 50 E8
Headlands Dr HP4 122 E5
Headstone La HA3 176 B2
Headstone Lane Sta HA3 176 B2
Healey Rd WD18 166 F3
Healy Ct EN5 171 D3
Hearle Way AL10 129 E7
Heath Ave Royston SG8 7 C6
St Albans AL3 127 D5
Heath Brow HP1 124 C1
Heath Cl Harpenden AL5 107 C7
Hemel Hempstead HP1 124 C2
Luton LU1 63 B6
Potters Bar EN6 145 B1
Heath Cotts EN6 145 B1
Heath Dr Potters Bar EN6 145 A1
Ware SG12 93 D3
Heath Farm Ct WD17 153 D2
Heath Farm La AL1,AL3 127 E5
Heath Hall SG7 23 F7
Heath Hill SG4 67 D1
Heath La Codicote SG4 67 E1
Hemel Hempstead HP1 124 C2
Hertford Heath SG13 114 C2
Heath Lodge WD23 168 D1
Heath Mount Sch SG14 71 B2
Heath Rd
Breachwood Green SG4 47 D1
Oaklands AL6 68 F1
Potters Bar EN6 145 B1
St Albans AL1 127 E5
Watford WD19 167 E2
Heath Row CM23 59 B1
Heath The
Breachwood Green SG4 47 D2
Radlett WD7 156 A6
Heath Way WD7 156 C8
Heathbourne Rd WD23 168 F1
Heathbrow Rd AL6 89 F8
Heathcote Ave AL10 130 A7
Heathcote Sch The SG2 51 A2
Heathcroft AL7 111 C6
Heathdene Manor WD17 166 F8
Heather Cl
Abbots Langley WD5 154 A7
Bishop's Stortford CM23 76 D6
Heather Ct AL2 142 D4
Heather Gdns EN9 163 C3
Heather Rd AL8 110 C4
Heather Rise WD23 167 F7
Heather Way
Harrow HA7 176 F4
Hemel Hempstead HP2 124 D4
Potters Bar EN6 158 F7
Heathermere SG6 11 F1
Heathfield SG8 7 B6
Heathfield Cl
Caddington LU1 62 F4
Potters Bar EN6 145 B1
Watford WD19 167 C2
Heathfield Ct 2 AL1 127 E4
Heathfield Lower Sch LU1 62 E4
Heathfield Rd Hitchin SG5 21 F1
Luton LU3 45 C4
Watford WD23 167 F5
Heathgate SG13 114 B2
Heathlands AL6 68 F1
Heathlands Dr AL3 127 E5
Heathlands Sch AL3 127 E6
Heathside
Colney Heath AL4 143 B8
St Albans AL1 127 E5
Heathside Cl HA6 174 D5
Heathside Rd HA6 174 D6
Heathview AL5 107 B8
Heaton Ct EN8 148 D2
Heaton Dell LU2 46 E1
Heay Fields AL7 111 C7
Hebden Cl LU4 44 B4
Hebing End SG2 52 F2
Heckford Cl WD18 166 C3
Hedge Row HP1 124 A5
Hedgebrooms AL7 111 C7
Hedgerow Cl SG2 51 D8
Hedgerow La EN5 171 B4
Hedgerow The LU4 44 D6
Hedgerow Wlk EN8 148 D1
Hedgerows CM21 97 F2
Hedgerows The
Bishop's Stortford CM23 77 B6
Stevenage SG2 51 D8
Hedges Cl AL10 130 B6
Hedges The AL3 127 C7
Hedgeside HP4 123 A7
Hedgeside Rd HA6 174 C5
Hedley Cl HP22 99 A4
Hedley Rd AL1 128 B3
Hedley Rise LU2 46 F2
Hedley Villas AL1 128 B3
Hedworth Ave EN8 162 D6
Heights The
Hemel Hempstead HP2 124 F6
Luton LU3 44 E5
Helena Cl EN4 159 D1
Helena Pl 5 HP2 124 D5
Helens Gate EN8 148 F5
Helham Gn SG12 94 F4
Hellards Rd SG1 50 D7
Hellebore Ct SG1 51 B8
Helmsley Cl LU4 44 C5
Helston Cl HA5 175 F3
Helston Gr HP2 124 D8
Helston Pl WD5 153 F7
Hemel Hempstead General Hospl HP2 124 D3
Hemel Hempstead Rd
Great Gaddesden HP4 81 F1
Hemel Hempstead HP2, HP3 125 E1
Redbourn AL3,HP2 105 E2
St Albans HP3,AL2,AL3 126 D1
Hemel Hempstead Sch The HP1 124 C2
Hemel Hempstead Sta HP3 138 A8
Hemingford Dr LU2 45 D6
Hemingford Rd WD17 153 E3
Hemming Way WD25 154 A4
Hemmings The HP4 121 F3
Hemp La HP23 100 F1
Hempstall AL7 111 B4
Hempstead La HP4 123 C6
Hempstead Rd
Bovingdon HP3 137 B5
Kings Langley WD4 139 A3
Watford WD17 153 E2
Henbury Way WD19 175 D7
Henderson Cl AL3 127 C7
Henderson Pl
Bedmond WD5 139 F4
Little Berkhamsted SG13 132 C2
Hendon Wood La NW7 171 A1
Hendren Ct SG1 51 A8
Henge Way LU3 44 E7
Henlow Ind Est SG16 10 B4
Henry Cl EN2 161 E1
Henry St
Hemel Hempstead HP3 138 D7
Tring HP23 100 A3
Hensley Cl Hitchin SG4 35 B6
Welwyn AL6 89 C6
Henstead Pl LU2 46 D1
Hepburn Ct EN6 158 A7
Heracles Cl AL2 141 C3
Herald Cl CM23 76 D6
Herbert St HP2 124 D4
Hereford Rd LU4 44 A3
Hereward Cl EN9 163 C7
Herga Ct WD17 167 A7
Heritage Cl AL3 127 D3
Heritage Wlk WD3 164 E6
Herkomer Cl WD23 168 B3
Herkomer Rd WD23 168 A3
Herm Ho EN3 162 D1
Hermitage Ct
Potters Bar EN6 159 C6
Stansted Mountfitchet CM24 59 D7
Hermitage Ho CM24 59 D7
Hermitage Rd SG5 34 F7
Hermitage The SG15 11 B8
Herne Ct WD23 168 C2
Herne Rd Bushey WD23 168 B3
Stevenage SG1 36 B1
Herneshaw AL10 129 F3
Herns La AL7 111 B8
Herns Way AL7 111 A7
Heron Cl
Hemel Hempstead HP3 138 F6
Rickmansworth WD3 173 D8
Sawbridgeworth CM21 97 D1
Heron Ct CM23 77 A7
Heron Dr Luton LU2 45 E6
Stanstead Abbotts SG12 115 C3
Heron Mead EN3 163 A1
Heron Pl UB9 173 A4
Heron Trad Est LU3 44 C7
Heron Way Hatfield AL10 130 A3
Stotfold SG5 11 E6
Heron Wlk HA6 174 E6
Heronfield EN6 145 C1
Herongate Rd EN8 148 E4
Herons Elm HP4 121 E7
Herons Way AL1 142 B8
Herons Wood CM20 117 B2
Heronsgate Rd WD3 164 B3
Heronslea WD25 154 C3
Heronswood EN9 163 E5
Heronswood Pl AL7 111 A5
Heronswood Rd AL7 111 A5
Hertford Castle* SG14 113 C5
Hertford County Hospl SG14 113 B6
Hertford East Sta SG13 113 E6
Hertford Heath Jun Mix Inf Sch SG13 114 C4
Hertford Mews EN6 159 C8
Hertford Mus* SG14 113 D6
Hertford North Sta SG14 113 B6
Hertford Rd Enfield EN3 162 D3
Great Amwell SG12 114 F4
Hatfield AL9 111 B1
Hoddesdon EN11 134 E8
Stevenage SG2 69 B7
Tewin AL6 90 F2
Welwyn AL6 89 D3
Hertford Regional Coll
Cheshunt EN10 148 F6
Ware SG12 114 D8
Hertford St Andrew CE Prim Sch SG14 112 F7
Hertfordshire & Essex High Sch The CM23 77 B7
Hertfordshire Bsns Ctr AL2 142 D5
Hertfordshire Theatre Sch SG4 34 F6
Hertingfordbury Prim Sch SG14 112 C4
Hertingfordbury Rd
Hertford SG14 113 B5
Hertingfordbury SG14 112 F4
Herts & Essex Com Hospl CM23 77 B6
Hertsmere Ind Pk WD6 170 D6
Hertswood Ct 1 EN5 171 E5
Hertswood Sch WD6 170 C7
Hester Ho CM20 117 C2
Heswall Ct 5 LU1 63 F6
Heswall Gn WD19 175 A7
Hetchleys HP1 124 A6
Hever Cl LU7 80 D2
Hewins Cl EN9 163 E7
Hewitt Cl AL4 108 D7
Hewlett Rd LU3 44 E5
Hexton Jun Mix Inf Sch SG5 19 A1
Hexton Rd
Great Offley SG5 33 E8
Lilley LU2 32 C4
Heybridge Ct SG14 112 F7
Heydon Rd SG8 9 E3
Heydons Cl AL3 127 D5
Heyford End AL2 141 C3
Heyford Rd WD7 155 F2
Heyford Way AL10 130 C7
Heysham Dr WD19 175 D5
Heywood Dr LU2 45 F2
Hibbert Ave WD24 154 D1
Hibbert Rd HA3 176 F1
Hibbert St LU1 63 E6
Hibbert Street Almshouses 13 LU1 63 E6
Hibberts Ct SG6 22 E7
Hickling Cl LU2 46 D1
Hickling Way AL5 86 C3
Hickman Cl EN10 134 D3
Hickman Ct LU3 44 D8
Hickman's Hill SG7 24 D4
Hicks Rd AL3 83 F6
Hidalgo Ct HP2 124 F6
Hideaway The WD5 153 F8
Hides The CM20 117 D1
Higgins Rd EN7 147 D4
Higgins Wlk SG1 36 C1
High Acres WD5 153 D7
High Ash Rd AL4 108 C7
High Ave SG6 22 E4
High Barnet Sta EN5 171 F5
High Beech Rd LU3 44 D7
High Beeches Prim Sch AL5 86 D1
High Canons WD6 157 D2
High Cl WD3 165 C4
High Cross WD25 155 D2
High Dane SG4 22 A2
High Dells AL10 129 F4
High Elms
Harpenden AL5 107 A6
Watford WD25 154 B8
High Elms Cl HA6 174 D4
High Elms La
Abbots Langley WD25, WD5 154 C8
Benington SG2 52 F1
High Firs Radlett WD7 155 F4
Radlett WD7 156 A4
High Firs Cres AL5 107 D8
High Gr St Albans AL3 127 D5
Welwyn Garden City AL8 110 C7
High House Est CM17 118 F4
High La CM24 59 F8
High Mead LU3 45 A3
High Meads AL4 108 C8
High Oak Rd SG12 93 E3
High Oaks Enfield EN2 160 F1
4 Northwood HA6 174 F5
St Albans AL3 127 D7
High Oaks Rd AL8 110 B7
High Pastures CM22 98 D1
High Plash SG1 50 E5
High Point 15 LU1 63 D6
High Rd Bushey WD23 168 D1
High Rd *continued*
Essendon AL9 131 E5
Harrow HA3 176 E3
Hoddesdon EN10 134 F4
Shillington SG5 19 E8
Stapleford SG14 92 A2
Watford WD25 154 A7
High Ridge Cuffley EN6 146 E4
Harpenden AL5 85 E3
Luton LU2 46 C1
High Ridge Cl HP3 138 D6
High Ridge Rd HP3 138 D7
High Road Broxbourne EN10 134 F1
High Road Turnford EN10 148 E6
High Road Wormley EN10 148 F8
High St
Abbots Langley WD5 139 F1
Arlesey SG15 11 A5
Ashwell SG7 4 D4
Baldock SG7 23 F8
Barkway SG8 17 C3
Barley SG8 8 F2
Barnet EN5 171 F5
Bedmond WD5 139 F4
Berkhamsted HP4 122 B4
Berkhamsted, Northchurch HP4 121 E6
Bishop's Stortford CM23 76 F7
Bovingdon HP3 137 A4
Buntingford SG9 40 E8
Bushey WD23 168 A3
Cheddington LU7 80 A7
Cheshunt EN8 148 D2
Cheshunt, Theabald's Grove Sta EN8 162 D7
Cheshunt, Waltham Cross EN8 162 E5
Codicote SG4 67 F1
Colney Heath AL4 129 B1
Elstree WD6 169 D3
Eyeworth SG19 1 A8
Flamstead AL3 84 B2
Graveley SG4 36 C4
Great Offley SG5 33 C3
Guilden Morden SG8 1 F4
Harefield UB9 173 C1
Harlow CM17 118 D4
Harpenden AL5 86 A1
Harrow HA3 176 E1
Hemel Hempstead HP1, HP3 124 D4
Hinxworth SG7 3 D6
Hitchin SG5 34 E7
Hitchin, Gosmore SG4 34 F3
Hoddesdon EN11 135 A5
Hunsdon SG12 95 D1
Kimpton SG4 66 C1
Kings Langley WD4 139 A2
London Colney AL2 142 D5
Luton LU4 44 C4
Markyate AL3 83 E5
Much Hadham SG10 74 F3
Northwood HA6 174 F2
Pirton SG5 20 D4
Pitstone LU7 80 E5
Potters Bar EN6 159 C7
Redbourn AL3 106 B5
Reed SG8 16 E5
Rickmansworth WD3 165 E1
Roydon CM19 116 B1
Royston SG8 7 D6
Sandridge AL4 108 C2
St Albans AL3 127 D3
Standon SG11 55 F1
Standon, Puckeridge SG11 55 D3
Stanstead Abbotts SG12 115 C4
Stevenage SG1 50 C7
Stotfold SG5 11 F6
Tring HP23 100 A3
Walkern SG2 38 B1
Ware SG12 93 D1
Watford WD17 167 B6
Watford WD17 167 C5
Watton at S SG14 70 E3
Welwyn AL6 89 C5
Wheathampstead AL4 87 D1
Whitwell SG4 66 F7
Widford SG12 95 E5
High Street Bsns Pk EN8 162 E7
High Street Gn HP2 125 A5
High Town Rd LU2 45 F1
High Tree Cl CM21 97 D1
High View
Birchanger CM23 59 D3
Chorleywood WD3 165 A5
Hatfield AL10 130 A2
Hitchin SG5 34 D7
Markyate AL3 83 E5
Watford WD18 166 F3
High View Ct HA3 176 E3
High Wickfield AL7 111 C5
High Wood Cl LU1 62 F7
High Wood Rd EN11 114 F1
High Wych CE Prim Sch CM21 97 A1
High Wych La CM21 97 A2
High Wych Rd
Gilston CM21 117 F7
High Wych CM21 97 B1
High Wych Way HP2 105 A1
Higham Dr LU2 46 D1
Highbanks Rd HA5 176 B4
Highbarns HP3 139 A6
Highbridge Ct EN9 163 B6

Highbridge Ho EN9 163 B6
Highbridge Ret Pk EN9 163 B5
Highbridge St EN9 163 B6
Highbury Ho (North Herts Music Sch) SG4 35 A7
Highbury Inf Sch SG4 34 F6
Highbury Rd Hitchin SG4 35 A7
Luton LU3 45 C1
Highbush Rd SG5 11 E5
Highclere Ct 4 AL1 127 E4
Highclere Dr HP3 139 B7
Highcroft 2 SG2 50 F1
Highcroft Rd HP3 138 B6
Highfield Bushey WD23 176 E8
Kings Langley WD4 138 E3
Letchworth SG6 22 E4
Little Hadham SG11 57 C3
Sawbridgeworth CM21 97 E3
South Oxhey WD19 175 F7
Watford WD25 153 F5
Highfield Ave
Bishop's Stortford CM23 77 C6
Harpenden AL5 107 C8
Highfield Cl HA6 174 E2
Highfield Cres HA6 174 E2
Highfield Ct
Hertford SG13 113 D4
Stevenage SG1 50 F7
Highfield Dr EN10 134 E2
Highfield Hall AL4 142 E7
Highfield Ho HP2 124 F5
Highfield La
Colney Heath AL4 142 E8
Hemel Hempstead HP2 124 F5
Highfield Oval AL5 86 A4
Highfield Park Dr AL4 142 C8
Highfield Rd
Berkhamsted HP4 122 D4
Hammond Street EN7 147 E5
Hertford SG13 113 D4
Luton LU4 45 B1
Northwood HA6 174 E2
Sandridge AL4 108 B1
Tring HP23 99 E3
Watford WD23 167 E4
Wigginton HP23 100 D1
Highfield Sch The SG6 22 D4
Highfield Way WD3 165 B3
Highfields Cuffley EN6 146 E3
Radlett WD7 155 F4
Highfields Cl LU5 44 A2
Highfiled Way EN6 159 B7
Highgate Gr CM21 97 D2
Highgrove Ct EN8 162 D5
Highland Dr
Bushey WD23 168 C2
Hemel Hempstead HP3 125 B3
Highland Rd
Bishop's Stortford CM23 76 F3
Lower Nazeing EN9 135 E1
Northwood HA6 175 A1
Highlands Hatfield AL9 130 C8
Royston SG8 7 E6
Watford WD19 167 C1
Highlands The
Potters Bar EN6 145 C1
Rickmansworth WD3 165 B2
Highmead CM24 59 E8
Highmill SG12 93 D3
Highmoor AL5 86 A4
Highover Cl LU2 46 B1
Highover Jun Mix Inf Sch SG4 22 C1
Highover Rd SG6 22 D5
Highover Way SG4 22 B1
Highridge Pl EN2 160 F1
Highview Cl EN6 159 C6
Highview Gdns
Potters Bar EN6 159 C6
St Albans AL4 128 C8
Highway The HA7 176 F2
Highwood Ave WD23 167 F8
Highwood Prim Sch WD23 167 E8
Highwoodhall La HP3 139 C7
Hilbury AL10 129 F4
Hilfield La WD25 168 D6
Hilfield La S WD23 168 F3
Hill Cl Barnet EN5 171 C4
Harpenden AL5 86 C4
Luton LU3 45 C7
Hill Comm HP3 139 A8
Hill Crest
Potters Bar EN6 159 C5
Whitwell SG4 66 E6
Hill Crest Lodge WD6 169 F5
Hill Croft Cl LU4 44 C6
Hill Ct EN6 159 C5
Hill Dyke Rd AL4 108 E7
Hill End La AL4 128 C2
Hill End Rd UB9 173 C3
Hill Farm Ave WD25 154 A6
Hill Farm Cl WD25 154 A6
Hill Farm La
Ayot St Lawrence AL6 88 C5
Redbourn AL3 106 C1
Hill Head Cotts SG10 75 B1
Hill Ho Harefield UB9 173 C1
Hertford SG13 113 C5
Hill House Ave HA7 176 F3
Hill Ley AL10 129 F5
Hill Leys EN6 146 E3
Hill Mead HP4 122 A3
Hill Milford AL5 86 D3
Hill Pickford AL5 86 D4
Hill Rd Codicote SG4 67 E1
Northwood HA6 174 D4
Hill Rise Cuffley EN6 146 E3
Hill Rise *continued*
Luton LU3 44 D7
Potters Bar EN6 159 C5
Rickmansworth WD3 165 B2
Hill Side LU7 79 F7
Hill St AL3 127 C3
Hill The Harlow CM17 118 C4
Wheathampstead AL4 108 D8
Hill Top SG7 23 E7
Hill View
Berkhamsted HP4 122 A6
Buckland SG9 27 D8
Whitwell SG4 66 E6
Hillary Cl LU3 44 D7
Hillary Cres LU1 63 C6
Hillary Ho WD6 170 B6
Hillary Rd HP2 125 A4
Hillary Rise SG15 11 B5
Hillberry Ct WD23 168 B2
Hillborough Inf Sch LU1 63 C6
Hillborough Jun Sch LU1 63 C6
Hillborough Rd LU1 63 D6
Hillbrow SG6 22 D5
Hillcrest Baldock SG7 23 F7
Hatfield AL10 130 A5
St Albans AL3 127 B1
Stevenage SG1 50 F5
Hillcrest Ave LU2 45 C8
Hillcrest Cl EN7 147 C2
Hillcrest Rd WD7 157 A6
Hillcroft Cres WD19 175 B8
Hilldown Rd HP1 124 A5
Hille Bsns Ctr WD24 167 B8
Hillfield AL10 130 C8
Hillfield Ave SG4 22 A2
Hillfield Ct HP2 124 E3
Hillfield Rd HP2 124 D3
Hillgate SG4 22 A3
Hillgrove Bsns Pk EN9 135 C1
Hillhouse EN9 163 F6
Hillhouse CE Prim Sch EN9 163 F6
Hilliard Rd HA6 174 F2
Hillingdon Rd WD25 154 B5
Hillmead SG1 51 A6
Hillmead Prim Sch CM23 76 C7
Hillpath SG6 23 B6
Hillpoint WD3 165 C4
Hillrise Ave WD24 154 D2
Hills La HA6 174 E2
Hillsborough Gn WD19 175 A7
Hillshott SG6 23 A6
Hillshott Inf Sch SG6 23 A6
Hillside Codicote SG4 67 F1
Hatfield AL10 130 A5
Hoddesdon EN11 134 F7
Royston SG8 7 D5
St Albans AL4 128 C2
Stevenage SG1 50 F5
Ware SG12 114 D8
Welwyn Garden City AL7 111 B3
Hillside Ave
Bishop's Stortford CM23 77 A7
Borehamwood WD6 170 B5
Cheshunt EN8 162 D8
Hillside Cl WD5 153 E7
Hillside Cotts
Birchanger CM23 59 C3
Wareside SG12 94 F4
Hillside Cres Enfield EN2 161 D1
Northwood HA6 175 A2
Stanstead Abbotts SG12 115 B4
Watford WD19 167 D3
Hillside Ct Cheshunt EN8 162 D8
8 St Albans AL1 127 E4
Hillside End CM23 59 C3
Hillside Gate 6 AL1 127 E4
Hillside Gdns
Barnet EN5 171 E5
Berkhamsted HP4 122 D3
Pinner HA6 175 B2
Hillside Ho SG1 50 F5
Hillside Jun & Inf Schs HA6 175 A3
Hillside La SG12 115 A5
Hillside Mans EN5 171 F5
Hillside Rd
Chorleywood WD3 164 C4
Harpenden AL5 85 F3
Luton LU3 45 D1
Pinner HA5 175 B3
Radlett WD7 156 B4
St Albans AL1 127 E4
Watford WD23 167 E4
Hillside Rise HA6 175 A3
Hillside Sch The WD6 170 C5
Hillside Terr SG13 113 C4
Hillside Way AL6 90 A8
Hilltop AL3 105 F6
Hilltop Cl EN7 147 F5
Hilltop Cotts
Great Munden SG11 54 D4
Great Offley SG5 33 C3
Hilltop Ct LU1 63 C7
Hilltop Rd Bedmond WD4 139 D4
Berkhamsted HP4 122 C3
Hilltop View AL4 108 C7
Hilltop Wlk AL5 107 D8
Hillview Cl HA5 175 F4
Hillview Cres LU2 45 C8
Hillview Gdns EN8 148 E4
Hillview Rd HA5 175 F4
Hilly Fields AL7 111 C7
Hilmay Dr HP1 124 C2
Hilton Cl SG1 50 B7
Himalayan Way WD18 166 F3
Hindhead Gn WD19 175 C5
Hine Ho AL4 128 D2
Hine Way SG5 21 C1
Hinwick Cl SG15 11 B7
Hinxworth Rd Ashwell SG7 4 B4
Hinxworth SG7 3 C3
Hipkins CM23 76 E4
Hipkins Pl EN10 134 E3
Hispano Mews EN3 163 A2
Hitchen Hill Path SG4 34 F5
Hitchens Cl HP1 123 F4
Hitchin Boys' Sch SG5 34 E8
Hitchin British Schools Mus* SG5 34 F6
Hitchin Bsns Ctr The SG4 22 A3
Hitchin Girls' Sch SG4 34 F7
Hitchin Hill SG4 34 F5
Hitchin Hospl SG5 34 D8
Hitchin Mus* SG5 34 E7
Hitchin Rd Arlesey SG15 11 A2
Great Wymondley SG4 35 D6
Hexton SG5 19 E1
Hitchin SG4 34 F3
Kimpton SG4 66 D2
Letchworth SG6 22 E3
Lower Stondon SG16 10 C6
Luton LU2 46 A4
Pirton SG5 20 E2
Stevenage SG1 36 B1
Stotfold SG5 11 E5
Weston SG4 24 B1
Hitchin Road Ind & Bsns Ctr SG15 11 A3
Hitchin St SG7 23 E8
Hitchin Sta SG4 35 A8
Hitchwood Cotts SG4 48 F5
Hither Field SG12 93 E3
Hitherbaulk AL7 110 E4
Hitherfield La AL5 86 A2
Hitherway AL8 89 D2
Hitherwell Dr HA3 176 D2
Hive Cl WD23 176 D8
Hive Rd WD23 176 E8
Hixberry La AL4 128 E1
Hobart Wlk AL3 127 F7
Hobbs Cl Cheshunt EN8 148 D2
St Albans AL4 128 E2
Hobbs Cross Rd CM17 118 F3
Hobbs Ct SG1 51 A8
Hobbs Hayes SG8 16 E5
Hobbs Hill AL6 89 C4
Hobbs Hill Rd HP3 138 F8
Hobbs Hill Wood Prim Sch HP3 125 B1
Hobbs Way AL8 110 C5
Hobby Horse Cl EN7 147 D5
Hobletts Manor Inf Sch HP2 125 A4
Hobletts Manor Jun Sch HP2 125 A4
Hobletts Rd HP2 124 F4
Hobsons Cl EN11 114 F1
Hobsons Wlk HP23 99 F5
Hobtoe Rd CM20 117 A1
Hockerill SG14 70 E3
Hockerill Anglo-European Coll CM23 77 B7
Hockerill Ct 7 CM23 77 A7
Hockerill St CM23 77 A7
Hocklands AL7 111 C7
Hockwell Ring LU4 44 C4
Hoddesdon Ind Ctr EN11 135 C7
Hoddesdon Rd SG12 115 C3
Hodges Way WD18 167 A3
Hodings Rd CM20 117 C2
Hodson Pl EN3 163 A1
Hodwell SG7 4 D4
Hoe La Enfield EN1,EN3 162 B1
Lower Nazeing EN9 135 F1
Ware SG12 114 D7
Hoe The WD19 175 D8
Hoecroft EN9 135 F1
Hoecroft Ct EN3 162 C1
Hoestock Rd CM21 97 D2
Hog Hall La HP4 81 A5
Hog La HP5 121 C1
Hogarth Ct WD23 168 B2
Hogg End La AL3 126 C6
Hogg La WD6 169 A5
Hogges Cl EN11 135 A6
Hogpits Bottom HP3 151 A7
Hogsdell La SG13 114 B4
Holbeck La EN7 147 F5
Holbein Gate HA6 174 E5
Holborn Cl AL4 128 D8
Holbrook Cl EN1 162 A1
Holcroft Rd AL5 86 D3
Holdbrook SG4 35 B7
Holdbrook Ct EN8 162 F5
Holdbrook Prim Sch EN8 162 F5
Holden Cl Hertford SG13 113 E7
Hitchin SG4 35 C7
Holders La SG2 51 E5
Holdings The AL9 130 D7
Holecroft EN9 163 E5
Holford Way LU3 31 B1
Holgate Dr LU4 44 B3
Holkham Cl LU4 44 A4
Holkham Ho 11 EN5 171 E6
Holland Ct LU3 45 C2
Holland Gdns WD25 154 C4
Holland Rd LU3 45 B2
Holland Way CM17 118 C1
Holland's Croft SG12 95 D1
Holliday St HP4 122 D4
Hollier Ct AL10 130 B6
Holliers Way AL10 130 A5
Hollies Cl SG8 7 E6
Hollies The
Bovingdon HP3 137 A2
St Albans AL3 127 E4
St Albans, Townsend AL3 127 C5
Watford WD18 166 F5
Welwyn Garden City AL8 110 B2
Wigginton HP23 100 D1
Hollies Way EN6 159 C8
Hollow La SG4 34 F7
Holloway La WD3 151 C2
Holloway The HP23,HP22 99 C4
Holloways La AL9 144 D7
Holly Cl AL10 129 F4
Holly Copse SG1 50 F4
Holly Croft SG14 113 A7
Holly Dell SG13 113 C4
Holly Dr
Berkhamsted HP4 122 D3
Potters Bar EN6 159 B6
Holly Farm Cl LU1 62 E3
Holly Gr HA5 175 E2
Holly Grove Rd SG14 91 C3
Holly Hall Ct AL6 89 C5
Holly Hedges La HP3 151 C8
Holly Ind Est WD24 167 C8
Holly La AL5 86 E6
Holly Leys SG2 69 C8
Holly Rd Enfield EN3 162 D3
Woolmer Green SG3 69 B1
Holly Shaws SG2 51 B1
Holly St LU1 63 E6
Holly Street Trad Est 12 LU1 63 E6
Holly Tree Ct HP2 125 B3
Holly Wlk Harpenden AL5 86 D1
Welwyn Garden City AL8 89 C2
Hollybush Ave AL2 141 A7
Hollybush Cl
Harrow HA3 176 E2
Oaklands AL6 89 E8
Potten End HP4 123 D7
Watford WD19 167 C2
Hollybush Hill LU2,SG5 32 F1
Hollybush Ho AL7 110 E4
Hollybush La
Datchworth SG3 69 C3
Flamstead AL3 84 B3
Harpenden AL5 86 A3
Hemel Hempstead HP1 123 F4
Welwyn Garden City AL7 110 E3
Whitwell SG4 66 B8
Hollybush Prim Sch SG14 113 A6
Hollybush Rd LU2 46 C1
Hollybush Row HP23 120 D8
Hollybush Way EN7 148 A3
Hollycross Rd SG12 115 B7
Hollyfield Hatfield AL10 130 A2
Tring HP23 100 C5
Hollyfield Cl HP23 100 C5
Hollyfields EN10 148 E5
Hollygrove WD23 168 D2
Hollyhock Cl HP1 123 E4
Hollytree Cl HP5 150 B8
Hollytree Ho WD24 153 E3
Hollywood Ct WD6 169 F5
Holm Oak Pk WD18 167 A4
Holmbrook Ave LU3 45 C5
Holmbury Cl WD23 176 E8
Holmbury St Mary Ct AL1 128 B2
Holmdale SG6 23 B5
Holmdale Cl WD6 169 F7
Holme Cl Cheshunt EN8 162 E8
Hatfield AL10 129 F8
Holme Lea WD25 154 C5
Holme Pk WD6 169 F7
Holme Pl HP2 125 C4
Holme Rd AL10 129 F8
Holme Way HA7 176 F4
Holmes Ct AL3 127 E4
Holmesdale EN8 162 D4
Holmfield Cl LU1 63 D5
Holmscroft Rd LU3 44 F6
Holmshill La EN5,WD6 157 F2
Holmside Rise WD19 175 B7
Holmwood Rd EN3 162 D3
Holroyd Cres SG7 23 F7
Holt Cl WD6 169 F5
Holt Cotts The SG4 66 C4
Holt Ho EN8 148 B3
Holt The
Hemel Hempstead HP2 124 E2
Welwyn Garden City AL7 111 D5
Holts Mdw AL3 106 B6
Holtsmere Cl Luton LU2 46 D1
Watford WD25 154 C4
Holtsmere End Inf Sch HP2 125 B8
Holtsmere End Jun Sch HP2 125 B8
Holtsmere End La HP2 105 C1
Holwell SG1 36 C2
Holwell Ct AL9 111 F1
Holwell Hyde AL7 111 C4
Holwell Hyde La AL7 111 C3
Holwell La AL9 131 F8
Holwell Prim Sch AL7 110 F5
Holwell Rd Holwell SG5 21 C7
Pirton SG5 20 E6
Welwyn Garden City AL7 110 E5
Holy Acre CM19 116 A1
Holy Cross Hill EN10 148 A8
Holy Family RC Jun Mix Inf Sch AL7 90 A1
Holy Rood RC Inf Sch WD17 153 D3
Holy Rood RC Jun Sch WD17 153 D3
Holy Trinity CE Prim Sch
Cheshunt EN8 162 D7
Northwood HA6 174 C4
Holyfield Hall Farm* EN9 149 C4
Holyfield Rd EN9 149 D2
Holyrood Cres AL1 141 D7
Holyrood Ct WD18 167 B5
Holywell Cl LU6 82 C6
Holywell Ct LU3 45 B4
Holywell Hill AL1 127 D2
Holywell Jun Mix Inf Sch WD18 166 F3
Holywell Rd Studham LU6 82 B6
Watford WD18 167 A4
Home Cl Cheshunt EN10 148 F7
Luton LU4 44 C4
Stotfold SG5 11 F7
Home Farm Cotts
Newgate Street SG13 146 F8
Slip End LU1 85 A8
Home Farm Ct
Bovingdon HP3 136 F1
Cockernhoe LU2 46 D5
Standon SG11 55 D3
Home Farm Ind Pk SG12 115 F5
Home Farm Rd
Berkhamsted HP4 121 D7
Rickmansworth WD3 174 A6
Home Field EN5 171 F4
Home Ley AL7 110 E6
Home Mdw AL7 110 F6
Home Park Ind Est WD4 139 B1
Home Park Mill Link Rd WD4 139 B1
Home Way WD3 164 F1
Homedale Dr LU4 44 D2
Homedell Ho AL5 85 E3
Homefield
Bovingdon HP3 137 B3
Hinxworth SG7 3 D6
Potten End HP4 123 B7
Homefield La SG4 49 F2
Homefield Rd
Bushey WD23 168 A4
Chorleywood WD3 164 D5
Hemel Hempstead HP2 125 A2
Radlett WD7 155 F2
Ware SG12 93 E2
Homeleigh Ct EN8 148 B1
Homeleigh St EN8 148 B1
Homepark Cotts WD4 139 B1
Homerfield AL8 110 C7
Homerswood La AL6 89 A2
Homerswood Prim Sch AL8 89 D2
Homerton Rd LU3 45 A6
Homestead Cl AL2 141 C4
Homestead Ct AL7 110 F4
Homestead La AL7 110 F4
Homestead Moat SG1 50 E4
Homestead Rd
Hatfield AL10 130 B8
Rickmansworth WD3 165 D2
Homestead Way LU1 63 C5
Homesteads The SG12 116 D8
Homewood Ave EN6 146 E4
Homewood Ct WD3 164 F5
Homewood Ind Sch AL2 141 B3
Homewood La EN6 146 C4
Homewood Rd AL1 128 B5
Honey Brook EN9 163 E6
Honey La
Brent Pelham CB11 30 F3
Buntingford SG9 40 E8
5 Hertford SG14 113 D6
Waltham Abbey EN9 163 E5
Honeybourne CM23 76 E4
Honeycroft AL8 110 C5
Honeycroft Dr AL4 142 C8
Honeycross Rd HP1 123 E2
Honeygate LU2 45 E4
Honeymead AL6 89 F3
Honeymeade CM21 118 C7
Honeysuckle Cl
Bishop's Stortford CM23 76 C6
Hertford SG13 114 A6
Honeysuckle Gdns AL10 130 B4
Honeyway SG8 7 E6
Honeywood Cl EN6 159 D6
Honilands Prim Sch EN1 162 B3
Honiton Mews LU3 44 E6
Honours Mead HP3 137 A4
Hoo Cotts SG5 33 D1
Hoo Farm Cotts SG5 33 D1
Hoo St LU1 63 E5
Hoo The CM17 118 C5
Hook Gate EN1 162 B3
Hook La Northaw EN6 159 F7
Northaw EN6 160 A8
Hook's Cross SG14 69 F6
Hoopers Mews WD23 168 B1
Hoops La SG8 15 F6
Hop Garden Way WD25 154 C8
Hope Gn WD25 154 A6
Hopewell Rd SG7 23 D8
Hopground Cl AL1 128 A1
Hopkins Cres AL4 108 B1
Hopkins Yd AL1 127 E2
Hoppit Rd EN9 163 B7

Hopton Rd SG1 50 A8
Hopwood Cl WD17 153 E3
Horace Brightman Cl
LU3 45 A7
Horace Gay Gdns SG6 22 E6
Horbeam Cl WD6 170 A8
Hordle Gdns AL1 127 F2
Horizon Ho EN3 162 F3
Hormead CE Prim Sch
SG9 41 F8
Horn Hill SG4 66 E6
Hornbeam Cl SG14 113 B7
Hornbeam Ct SG4 35 E5
Hornbeam La AL9 131 E2
Hornbeam Spring SG3 68 F4
Hornbeam Way EN7 147 F2
Hornbeams
Bricket Wood AL2 140 F1
Welwyn Garden City AL7 111 B5
Hornbeams Ave EN1 162 C4
Hornbeams The
Harlow CM20 117 C2
Stevenage SG2 51 B4
Hornets The WD18 167 B5
Hornhill Rd WD3 172 D5
Horns Cl SG13 113 C4
Horns Mill Rd SG13 113 C3
Horns Rd SG13 113 C5
Hornsby Cl LU2 46 C1
Hornsfield AL7 111 C7
Horrocks Cl SG12 93 D3
Horsa Gdns AL10 129 E7
Horse Cross SG11 56 D3
Horse Hill HP5 150 D7
Horsecroft Rd HP1 124 A1
Horselers HP3 139 A8
Horsemans Dr AL2 141 B6
Horseshoe Bsns Pk AL2 141 B1
Horseshoe Cl Barley SG8 8 F1
Cheddington LU7 80 A7
Horseshoe Ct Hitchin SG4 34 E6
Stanstead Abbotts SG12 115 D4
Horseshoe Hill SG9 42 A8
Horseshoe La
Great Hormead SG9 42 A8
Totteridge N20 171 D1
Watford WD25 154 C7
Horseshoe The HP3 125 C1
Horsham Cl LU2 46 D2
Horsleys WD3 172 D5
Horton Gdns HP2 105 A1
Horwood Cl WD3 165 A2
Horwood Cotts WD25 168 E8
Horwood Ct WD24 154 E2
Hospital Rd SG15 11 A4
Houghton Mews 12 LU1 63 D6
Housden Cl AL4 108 E7
House La Arlesey SG15 11 A7
Sandridge AL4 108 C1
St Albans AL4 128 D7
House On The Hill Toy Mus*
CM24 59 F6
Housefield Way AL4 142 C8
Housewood End HP1 124 B6
Housman Ave SG8 2 C1
How Field AL5 85 E3
How Wood AL2 141 B3
How Wood Prim Sch
AL2 141 C4
How Wood Sta AL2 141 C3
Howard Agne Cl HP3 137 A4
Howard Cl Bushey WD23 168 E2
Luton LU3 45 A4
St Albans AL1 128 C1
Stotfold SG5 11 E5
Waltham Abbey EN9 163 D5
Watford WD24 154 A2
Howard Ct Enfield EN1 161 E1
Letchworth SG6 23 B4
Howard Ctr The AL8 110 D6
Howard Dr
Borehamwood WD6 170 D5
Letchworth SG6 23 B3
Howard Gate SG6 23 B4
Howard Park Cnr SG6 23 A6
Howard Way Barnet EN5 171 D4
Harlow CM20 117 F2
Howards Cl HA5 175 B1
Howards Dr HP1 124 A5
Howards Wood SG6 23 B3
Howardsgate AL8 110 D6
Howberry Gn SG15 11 A3
Howe Cl WD7 156 E7
Howe Dell AL10 130 B5
Howe Dell Prim Sch
AL10 130 B5
Howe Green House Sch
CM22 77 D2
Howe Rd HP3 125 A1
Howell Hill Cl LU7 61 D5
Howfield Gn EN11 115 A1
Howicks Gn AL7 111 A3
Howland Garth AL1 141 C7
Howlands AL7 111 B3
Howlands Ho AL7 111 A3
Howse Rd EN9 163 B4
Howton Pl WD23 168 D1
Hoylake Ct LU1 63 F5
Hoylake Gdns WD19 175 D6
Hubbards Rd WD3 164 D4
Huckleberry Cl LU3 45 A8
Hudnall La HP4 102 E7
Hudson Cl St Albans AL1 141 D8
Watford WD24 153 F3
Hudson Rd SG2 51 B7
Hudsons Ct EN6 159 A8
Huggins La AL9 144 C8
Hugh Villas CM23 77 A5
Hughenden Rd AL4 128 C6
Hugo Gryn Way WD7 156 E8
Hull Cl EN7 147 D5
Hull La SG11 55 E7
Humber Ct SG1 36 F3
Humberstone Cl LU4 44 E2
Humberstone Rd LU4 44 E2
Humphrey Talbot Ave
LU6 81 F7
Hunsdon AL7 111 D6
Hunsdon Jun Mix Inf Sch
SG12 95 D1
Hunsdon Rd
Stanstead Abbotts SG12 115 E5
Widford SG12 95 E3
Hunsdon Road Cotts
SG12 115 E5
Hunston Cl LU4 44 B5
Hunt Cl AL4 128 D6
Hunter Cl
Borehamwood WD6 170 C4
Potters Bar EN6 159 B6
Hunter Wlk WD6 170 D4
Hunter's La WD25 153 F6
Huntercrombe Gdns
WD19 175 C5
Hunters Cl
Bovingdon HP3 137 A2
Stevenage SG2 51 D7
Stotfold SG5 11 E6
Tring HP23 100 B5
Hunters Gate WD25 154 A6
Hunters Oak HP2 125 B8
Hunters Pk HP4 122 E5
Hunters Reach EN7 147 F2
Hunters Ride AL2 155 A8
Hunters Way Royston SG8 7 E5
Welwyn Garden City AL7 110 F3
Hunting Gate
Hemel Hempstead HP2 124 E7
Hitchin SG4 22 A3
Hunting Hall LU2 64 C8
Huntingdon Cl EN10 148 E7
Huntingdon Ct EN5 171 F6
Huntingdon Rd SG1 50 B8
Hunton Bridge Hill
WD4 153 C6
Hunts Cl LU1 63 C6
Huntsman Cl SG11 55 D3
Huntsmans Cl HP4 81 C5
Huntsmill Rd HP1 123 E2
Hurlock Way LU4 44 C5
Hurn Gr CM23 59 C1
Hurricane Way WD5 154 A7
Hurst Cl Baldock SG7 13 A1
Bishop's Stortford CM23 76 E7
Welwyn Garden City AL7 111 C5
Hurst Dr EN8 162 D5
Hurst Drive Prim Sch
EN8 162 D5
Hurst Pl HA6 174 B2
Hurst Way LU3 44 F5
Hurstlings AL7 111 B5
Hutchings Lo WD3 165 E1
Hutton Cl Hertford SG14 113 A6
Luton LU4 44 E3
Hutton Gdns HA3 176 C3
Hutton La HA3 176 D3
Hutton Wlk HA3 176 C3
Hyatt Ind Est SG1 50 A5
Hyburn Cl
Bricket Wood AL2 140 F1
Hemel Hempstead HP3 125 B2
Hyde Ave
Potters Bar EN6 159 B6
Stotfold SG5 11 E5
Hyde Cl Barnet EN5 171 F6
Harpenden AL5 86 B4
Hyde Ct EN8 162 E5
Hyde Gn E SG2 51 B3
Hyde Gn N SG2 51 B3
Hyde Gn S SG2 51 B3
Hyde Ho 5 LU2 63 F8
Hyde La Bedmond HP3 139 D5
Bovingdon HP3 137 A3
Park Street AL2 141 D3
Peters Green LU2 65 C2
Hyde Mdws HP3 137 A4
Hyde Mead EN9 149 E8
Hyde Mead Ho EN9 149 E8
Hyde Rd Caddington LU1 62 F4
Watford WD17 167 A7
Hyde Terr HP3 139 E7
Hyde The Stevenage SG2 51 C3
Ware SG12 93 B2
Hyde Valley AL7 110 F4
Hyde View Rd AL5 86 B4
Hyde Way AL7 110 E6
Hydean Way SG2 51 B3
Hyperion Ct HP2 124 F6
Hyver Hill NW7 170 D2

I

Ibberson Way SG4 35 A7
Iceni Ct SG6 23 B7
Ickleford Bury SG5 21 E3
Ickleford Gate SG5 21 E3
Ickleford Prim Sch SG5 21 E4
Ickleford Rd SG5 34 F8
Ickley Cl LU4 44 B5
Icknield Cl Ickleford SG5 21 E4
St Albans AL3 126 F1
Icknield Gn
Letchworth SG6 22 E6
Tring HP23 100 A6
Icknield High Sch LU3 45 C5
Icknield Inf Sch SG6 22 D6
Icknield Prim Sch LU3 45 B5
Icknield Rd LU3 44 F4
Icknield Walk Fst Sch SG8 7 E7
Icknield Way Baldock SG7 12 E1
Dagnall LU6 81 A8
Letchworth SG6 22 E6
Luton LU3 45 B7
Tring HP23 99 E4
Icknield Way E SG7 12 F1
Icknield Wlk SG8 7 F7
Idenbury Ct LU1 63 C7
Ilex Ct HP4 122 B4
Ilford Cl LU2 46 D3
Ilkley Rd WD19 175 D5
Imberfield LU4 44 C3
Immanuel Coll WD23 168 E2
Imperial Pk WD24 167 C8
Imperial Way
Hemel Hempstead HP3 138 E7
Watford WD24 167 C8
Impresa Pk EN11 135 C7
Indells AL10 129 F4
Ingelheim Ct SG1 50 D7
Ingersoll Rd EN3 162 C1
Inglefield EN6 145 A1
Ingles AL8 89 E2
Ingleside Dr SG1 36 B1
Ingram Gdns LU2 45 D7
Inkerman Rd AL1 127 E2
Inkerman St LU1 63 D7
Inn's Cl SG1 50 D6
Innes Ct HP3 138 D8
Innova Way Enfield EN3 162 F3
Holdbrook EN3 163 A3
Inskip Cres SG1 50 E5
Iona Cl SG1 36 F2
Iredale View SG7 13 A1
Irene Stebbings Ho AL4 128 C4
Iron Dr SG13 114 B7
Irving Cl CM23 76 D4
Irving Cres LU7 80 A8
Isabel Gate EN8 148 F5
Isabella Ho EN8 163 A5
Isabelle Cl EN7 147 C2
Isenburg Way HP2 124 D8
Isherwood Cl SG8 7 C8
Island Centre Way EN3 163 A2
Island Ct CM23 77 A5
Islay Ho 4 WD18 166 F3
Islington Way SG1 36 F2
Italstyle Bldgs CM20 118 C6
Itaska Cotts WD23 168 E1
Ivatt Ct SG4 35 C7
Iveagh Cl HA6 174 B2
Iveagh Ct HP2 124 D4
Ivel Ct SG6 23 C4
Ivel Rd SG1 50 C7
Ivel Way Baldock SG7 24 A6
Stotfold SG5 11 F8
Ives Rd SG14 113 B7
Ivinghoe Cl
St Albans AL4 128 C8
Watford WD25 154 D4
Ivinghoe Rd
Bushey WD23 168 D2
Rickmansworth WD3 165 A2
Ivory Cl AL4 128 C1
Ivory Ct HP3 138 E8
Ivy Ct LU1 63 B8
Ivy Ho WD19 167 D3
Ivy House La HP4 122 E4
Ivy Lea WD3 165 A1
Ivy Rd LU1 63 C8
Ivy Terr EN11 135 C8
Ivy Wlk AL10 129 F8
Ivybridge EN10 135 A4

J

J Ct CM20 117 F1
Jackdaw Cl SG2 51 D4
Jackdaws AL7 111 C6
Jackets La HA6 174 B3
Jacketts Field WD5 153 F8
Jackman's Pl SG6 23 B5
Jacks La UB9 173 A2
Jackson Sq 10 CM23 76 F7
Jackson St SG7 12 E1
Jackson's La SG8 16 E5
Jacksons Dr EN7 148 A3
Jacob Ct EN3 163 A2
Jacobs Ladder AL9 130 C5
James Bedford Cl HA5 175 C1
James Cl WD23 167 E4
James Ct Luton LU4 44 B2
14 Luton,New Town LU1 63 E6
James Foster Ho SG5 21 E1
James Lee Sq EN3 163 A1
James Marshall Commercial
Ctr AL5 86 A1
James Way
South Oxhey WD19 175 D6
Stevenage SG1 50 C7
Jameson Ct AL1 127 F4
Jameson Rd AL5 86 B3
Jane Cl HP2 125 B8
Jansel Ho LU2 46 B4
Jarden SG6 23 C4
Jardine Ct SG1 51 A8
Jarman Cl HP3 124 E1
Jarman Way
Hemel Hempstead HP2 124 F2
Jarman Way *continued*
Royston SG8 7 B7
Jarvis Cl EN5 171 D4
Jarvis Cleys EN7 147 F5
Jasmin Cl
Bishop's Stortford CM23 76 C6
Northwood HA6 174 F2
Jasmin Way HP1 123 E4
Jasmine Ct SG5 11 F7
Jasmine Dr SG13 114 A6
Jasmine Gdns AL10 130 A7
Jasons Hill HP5 136 B2
Jasper Cl EN3 162 C1
Jay Cl SG6 22 E8
Jaywood LU2 46 C6
Jeans La CM23 76 E7
Jeans Way LU5 44 A1
Jeeves Yd 5 SG4 34 F6
Jeffrey Cl SG8 7 C8
Jeffries Rd SG12 93 E1
Jellicoe Gdns HA7 176 F4
Jellicoe Rd WD18 167 A3
Jenkins Ave AL2 140 E1
Jenkins Ct HP22 60 C3
Jenkins La
Bishop's Stortford CM22 77 C5
St Leonards HP23 119 E3
Jenning Wood AL6 89 F7
Jennings Cl SG1 50 E3
Jennings Rd AL1 128 A4
Jennings Way
Barnet EN5 171 C6
Hemel Hempstead HP3 124 E1
Jenningsbury Ct SG13 114 A4
Jenyns Sch SG11 55 F7
Jepps Cl EN7 147 E4
Jepps La SG8 7 D6
Jerome Dr AL3 127 A1
Jersey Cl EN11 135 A7
Jersey Ho Enfield EN3 162 D1
9 Watford WD18 166 F3
Jersey La
St Albans, Marshalswick
AL4 128 B5
St Albans, Sandridge AL4 128 C8
Jersey Rd LU4 44 A3
Jervis Ave EN3 162 E4
Jervis Rd CM23 76 F6
Jessop Rd SG1 37 A1
Jeve Cl SG7 13 A1
Jewell Ct WD25 154 D5
Jill Grey Pl SG4 34 F6
Jillifer Rd LU4 44 A2
Jim Desormeaux Bglws
CM20 117 E2
Jinnings The AL7 111 B3
Jocelyns CM17 118 C4
Jocketts Hill HP1 123 F3
Jocketts Rd HP1 123 F2
Jodies Ct AL4 128 C5
Joel St HA6 175 A1
John Barker Pl SG5 21 C1
John Ct EN11 115 A1
John Eliot Cl EN9 135 E2
John F Kennedy RC Sch
HP1 123 F4
John Henry Newman RC Sch
The SG1 36 B1
John Lamb Ct HA3 176 E2
John Penrose Sch UB9 173 D2
John Sale Cl SG7 4 C4
John St Luton LU1 63 E7
3 Royston SG8 7 D6
John Tate Rd SG13 113 F6
John Warner Sch The
EN11 115 B1
Johnby Cl EN3 162 E2
Johns La HP5 121 E1
Johns Rd CM23 59 A1
Johnson Ct HP3 124 E1
Joiner's Cl HP5 136 B1
Joint The SG8 16 E6
Jones Rd EN7 147 B1
Jonquil Cl AL7 111 B4
Jordan Cl WD25 153 F4
Jordan's Way AL2 140 F1
Jordans AL7 111 C7
Jordans Rd WD3 165 A1
Joslyn Cl EN3 163 A1
Jowitt Ho 1 SG1 50 E6
Joyce Ct EN9 163 D5
Jubilee Ave
London Colney AL2 142 D5
Ware SG12 93 F2
Jubilee Cl
Lower Stondon SG16 10 B3
Pinner HA5 175 C1
Jubilee Cotts
Aspenden SG9 40 D5
Great Hormead SG9 42 A8
Jubilee Cres SG15 11 A2
Jubilee Ct Harpenden AL5 86 C3
Hatfield AL10 130 B8
Waltham Abbey EN9 163 F6
Jubilee Meml Ave SG1 50 D8
Jubilee Rd
Letchworth SG6 23 D7
Stevenage SG1 50 B8
Watford WD24 154 A1
Jubilee St LU2 45 F1
Jubilee Trad Ctr SG6 23 D7
Jubilee Wlk WD4 139 A1
Judge St WD24 154 B1
Judge's Hill EN6 145 F2
Julia Ct LU3 45 B4
Julia Gate SG2 51 C8
Julian's Ct SG1 50 C8
Julian's Rd SG1 50 B8
Julie Ho EN11 135 C8
Julius Gdns LU3 44 F7
Junction Cotts AL8 110 D7
Juniper Ave AL2 155 A8
Juniper Cl Barnet EN5 171 D4
Cheshunt EN10 148 F6
Luton LU4 44 E2
Rickmansworth WD3 173 D7
Juniper Ct HA3 176 F2
Juniper Gate WD3 173 D8
Juniper Gdns
Oaklands AL6 89 E7
Shenley WD7 156 E6
Juniper Gn HP1 123 E3
Juniper Gr WD17 154 A1
Juniper Ho EN10 148 F6
Juno Rd HP2 124 F6
Jupiter Dr HP2 124 F5
Jupiter Drive Jun Mix & Inf
Sch HP2 124 F5
Jupiter Gate SG2 51 D8
Juxon Cl HA3 176 B2

K

Kaida Ho 6 WD3 165 D2
Kardwell Cl SG4 35 A6
Karen Ho SG16 10 A4
Karens Ct EN3 162 D2
Katemon Ct SG12 115 D4
Kates Cl EN5 171 A4
Katescroft AL7 110 E2
Katherine Cl HP3 138 E8
Katherine Pl WD5 154 A7
Katrine Sq HP2 124 E7
Kay Cl HP23 100 A5
Kay Wlk AL4 128 D3
Keats Cl
Hemel Hempstead HP2 105 B1
Royston SG8 7 C8
Stevenage SG2 51 C7
Keats Ho 15 AL5 86 B1
Keats Way SG4 35 C7
Keble Terr WD5 153 F7
Kecksy's CM21 97 F4
Keeble Cl LU2 46 E1
Keele Cl WD24 167 C7
Keepers Cl
Cheddington LU7 80 A7
Luton LU2 46 C2
Keiths Rd HP3 125 A2
Keiths Wood SG3 68 F5
Kelbys AL7 111 C7
Keller Cl SG2 51 B4
Kelling Cl LU2 45 C8
Kelly Cl WD6 170 D7
Kelly Ct WD6 170 C7
Kelman Cl EN8 162 D8
Kelmscott Cl WD18 167 A4
Kelmscott Cres WD18 167 A4
Kelshall WD25 154 E3
Kelshall St SG8 15 E5
Kelvin Cl LU1 63 E6
Kelvin Cres HA3 176 E3
Kemble Cl EN6 159 D6
Kemble Ho HA7 176 F5
Kemp Pl WD23 168 A3
Kempe Cl AL1 141 C7
Kempe Rd EN1 162 C3
Kemprow WD25 155 D3
Kemps Dr HA6 174 F3
Kempsey Cl LU2 46 D2
Ken Davies Ct AL3 127 F7
Kendal Cl LU3 44 D7
Kendal Rd EN9 163 C4
Kendale HP3 125 B2
Kendale Rd 3 Hitchin SG4 34 F6
Luton LU4 44 B2
Kendall Cl AL7 110 F2
Kendall Ct WD6 170 C8
Kendals Cl WD7 155 E3
Kenerne Dr EN5 171 E4
Kenford Cl WD25 154 B7
Kenilworth Cl
Borehamwood WD6 170 C6
Hemel Hempstead HP2 124 E2
Stevenage SG2 69 C7
Kenilworth Cres EN1 161 E1
Kenilworth Ct WD17 167 A8
Kenilworth Dr
Borehamwood WD6 170 D6
Croxley Green WD3 166 B5
Kenilworth Gdns WD19 175 C5
Kenilworth Ho WD6 170 C6
Kenilworth Prim Sch
WD6 170 D6
Kenilworth Rd LU1 63 C8
Kenmare Cl SG1 36 F3
Kennedy Ave EN11 134 F6
Kennedy Cl
Cheshunt EN8 148 E3
London Colney AL2 142 D5
Pinner HA5 175 F4
Kennedy Rd SG12 71 E7
Kennel La AL5 85 A5
Kennelwood La AL10 130 B6
Kennesbourne Ct AL5 85 D4
Kenneth Gdns 4 HA7 176 F4
Kenneth Rd LU2 46 A1
Kennett Way SG1 36 F3
Kenning Rd EN11 135 B8
Kennington Rd LU3 45 B3
Kensington Ave WD18 166 F5
Kensington Cl AL1 128 A1
Kensington Ct EN1 161 E1
Kensington Mews
WD18 167 A5

Kensington Way WD6 .170 D6
Kensworth Lower Sch LU6 .82 F8
Kensworth Rd LU6 .82 D4
Kent Cl WD6 .157 D1
Kent Cres CM23 .76 E4
Kent Pl SG5 .34 D8
Kent Rd LU1 .62 F8
Kentish La AL9 .145 C7
Kenton Gdns AL1 .127 F2
Kenton La HA3 .176 F3
Kents Ave HP3 .138 D7
Kents La SG11 .55 E2
Kenwood Dr WD3 .172 F8
Kenworth Cl EN8 .162 D6
Kenyon Pl AL7 .110 E3
Kerdistone Cl EN6 .145 B1
Kernow Ct LU2 .46 A1
Kerr Cl SG3 .68 F5
Kerri Cl EN5 .171 C5
Kerril Croft CM20 .117 A1
Kershaw Cl LU3 .45 A8
Kershaw's Hill SG4 .34 F6
Kessingland Ave SG1 .36 A1
Keston Mews WD17 .167 B7
Kestrel Cl
Berkhamsted HP4 .122 C3
Stevenage SG2 .51 D2
Watford WD25 .154 E5
Kestrel Ct 4 SG12 .93 C3
Kestrel Gdns CM23 .76 C6
Kestrel Gn AL10 .130 A4
Kestrel Way Luton LU4 .44 A5
Royston SG8 .7 E8
Welwyn Garden City AL7 .110 F8
Kestrel Wlk SG6 .23 B3
Kestrels The AL2 .154 F8
Keswick Cl AL1 .128 B1
Keswick Dr EN3 .162 C3
Kettering Rd EN3 .162 D2
Kettle Green Rd SG10 .74 E2
Ketton Cl LU2 .64 A7
Ketton Ct LU2 .64 A7
Kevere Ct HA6 .174 B5
Kewferry Dr HA6 .174 C5
Kewferry Rd HA6 .174 C5
Keyfield AL1 .127 D2
Keymer Cl LU2 .46 C3
Keynton Cl SG14 .112 F7
Keysers Rd EN10 .135 B1
Kibes La SG12 .93 E1
Kidner Cl LU2 .45 E5
Kilbride Ct HP2 .124 F7
Kilby Cl WD25 .154 D4
Kildonan Cl WD17 .166 F8
Kilfillan Gdns HP4 .122 A4
Kilfillan Pk HP4 .122 A4
Killigrew Inf Sch AL2 .141 B6
Killigrew Jun Sch AL2 .141 B6
Kilmarnock Dr LU2 .45 E5
Kilmarnock Rd WD19 .175 D6
Kiln Ave HP6 .150 C1
Kiln Cl HP4 .123 B6
Kiln Cotts HP2 .125 B4
Kiln Ground HP3 .125 A1
Kiln House Cl SG12 .93 E2
Kiln House Yd SG8 .7 C6
Kiln La HP5 .150 B8
Kiln Way HA6 .174 E4
Kilncroft HP3 .125 B1
Kilnfield AL7 .89 F1
Kilsmore La EN8 .148 D2
Kilvinton Dr EN2 .161 D1
Kilworth Cl AL7 .111 B4
Kimberley SG6 .11 F2
Kimberley Cl CM23 .77 A5
Kimberley Rd AL3 .127 D4
Kimble Cl WD18 .166 E2
Kimble Cres WD23 .168 C2
Kimblewick WD19 .167 E1
Kimbolton Cres SG2 .69 A7
Kimbolton Gn WD6 .170 C5
Kimps Way HP3 .139 A8
Kimpton Bottom AL5,SG4 .86 E7
Kimpton Cl HP2 .125 B8
Kimpton Pl WD25 .154 D5
Kimpton Prim Sch SG4 .66 C1
Kimpton Rd
Ayot St Peter AL6 .89 A6
Codicote SG4 .67 B1
Kimpton SG4,AL4 .87 C7
Luton LU1,LU2 .64 A6
Peters Green LU2,SG4 .65 E2
Kimptons Cl EN6 .158 D7
Kimptons Mead EN6 .158 D7
Kinderscout HP3 .125 A1
Kindersley Cl AL6 .89 C6
Kindersley Way WD5 .153 D8
Kinetic Bsns Ctr WD6 .170 A6
King Arthur Ct EN8 .162 E8
King Charles Rd WD7 .156 E7
King Edward Rd
Cheshunt EN8 .162 E6
Shenley WD7 .156 F6
Watford WD19 .167 E3
King Edward St HP3 .138 D7
King Edward's Rd SG12 .93 E2
King George Ave WD23 .168 B3
King George Cl SG1 .50 E6
King George Rd
Waltham Abbey EN9 .163 C5
Ware SG12 .93 E2
King George's Way SG4 .66 E6
King Georges Ave WD18 .166 E5
King Georges Cl SG5 .21 D1
King Harold Ct EN9 .163 C6
King Harold Sch EN9 .163 E6
King Harry La AL3 .127 B1
King Harry St HP2 .124 D2
King Henry Ct LU3 .45 B2
King Henry's Mews EN3 .163 A2
King Henrys Ct EN9 .163 C3
King James Ave EN6 .146 E2
King James Way SG8 .7 D6
King St
Bishop's Stortford CM23 .76 F7
Luton LU1 .63 E7
Markyate AL3 .83 E5
2 Royston SG8 .7 D6
Tring HP23 .100 A3
Watford WD18 .167 C5
King Street Mews 1 CM23 .76 F7
King Williams Ct EN9 .163 C4
King's Cotts CM23 .77 A6
King's La WD4 .152 B8
King's Mews 7 HP2 .124 D4
King's Rd Cheshunt EN8 .162 E5
Hertford SG13 .114 A7
Hitchin SG5 .34 F8
London Colney AL2 .142 C5
St Albans AL3 .127 C3
King's Walden Rd SG5 .33 D2
King's Wlk SG8 .7 D5
Kingcroft Rd AL5 .107 D7
Kingfisher Cl
Harrow HA3 .176 F3
Northwood HA6 .174 B2
Stanstead Abbotts SG12 .115 C3
Wheathampstead AL4 .87 D1
Kingfisher Ct Enfield EN2 .160 F1
Hitchin SG4 .35 A6
Kingfisher Dr HP3 .138 F6
Kingfisher Lure
Kings Langley WD4 .139 B2
Rickmansworth WD3 .165 B5
Kingfisher Rise SG2 .51 D2
Kingfisher Way
Bishop's Stortford CM23 .77 A7
Roydon CM19 .116 A1
Kingham Rd SG12 .94 E5
Kinghamway LU2 .45 E1
Kings Ave
Hemel Hempstead HP3 .138 F7
Watford WD18 .167 A5
Kings Cl
Chipperfield WD4 .152 B8
Northwood HA6 .174 F4
5 Watford WD18 .167 C5
Kings Ct
Berkhamsted HP4 .122 C5
Bishop's Stortford CM23 .77 A8
Harpenden AL5 .107 B8
Kings Farm Rd WD3 .164 D3
Kings Field Cotts WD5 .153 F8
Kings Heath Pk AL5 .86 C6
Kings Hedges SG5 .34 C8
Kings Langley Prim Sch WD4 .138 F3
Kings Langley Sch WD4 .138 E3
Kings Langley Sta WD4 .139 C1
Kings Mdw WD4 .139 A3
Kings Oak WD3 .166 A5
Kings Oak Private Hospl The EN2 .161 A1
Kings Park Ind Est WD4 .139 B2
Kings Rd Barnet EN5 .171 C6
Berkhamsted HP4 .122 B3
Stevenage SG1 .50 D4
Kings Sch The AL5 .85 F4
Kings Walden Rise SG2 .51 C8
Kingsbridge Rd CM23 .77 A8
Kingsbury Ave AL3 .127 C4
Kingsbury Watermill* AL3 .127 B4
Kingscroft AL7 .111 B7
Kingsdale Ho AL6 .89 B3
Kingsdale Rd HP4 .122 A3
Kingsdown SG4 .35 B6
Kingsdown Ave LU2 .45 D5
Kingsfield EN11 .135 A8
Kingsfield Ct WD19 .167 D2
Kingsfield Dr EN3 .162 D4
Kingsfield Rd
Dane End SG12 .71 E8
Watford WD19 .167 D3
Kingsfield Way EN3 .162 D4
Kingsgate AL3 .127 B1
Kingshill Ave AL4 .128 B6
Kingshill Ct 6 EN5 .171 E5
Kingshill Inf Sch SG12 .93 D3
Kingshill Way HP4 .122 B2
Kingshott Sch SG4 .35 B5
Kingsland Ct 7 LU1 .63 F6
Kingsland Rd
Hemel Hempstead HP1 .124 A1
Luton LU1 .63 F6
Kingsland Way SG7 .4 D4
Kingsley Ave
Borehamwood WD6 .169 F7
Cheshunt EN8 .148 C2
Kingsley Ct AL7 .110 F2
Kingsley Rd LU3 .45 A5
Kingsley Wlk HP23 .100 A4
Kingsmead
Cheshunt EN8 .148 D3
Cuffley EN6 .146 E3
Lower Nazeing EN9 .135 C1
Sawbridgeworth CM21 .97 E1
St Albans AL4 .128 D6
Kingsmead Rd CM23 .77 A8
Kingsmill Ct 1 AL10 .130 B3
Kingston Pl HA3 .176 F3
Kingston Rd LU2 .45 F1
Kingston Vale SG8 .7 E5
Kingsway Cuffley EN6 .146 E1
Luton LU4 .45 A1
Royston SG8 .7 C8
Stotfold SG5 .11 F7
Ware SG12 .93 D3
Kingsway Gdns SG5 .11 F7
Kingsway Ind Est LU1 .63 A8
Kingsway Inf Sch WD25 .154 A5
Kingsway Jun Sch WD25 .154 A5
Kingsway North Orbital Rd WD25 .154 B5
Kingswell Ride EN6 .146 E1
Kingswood Ave SG4 .35 D8
Kingswood Rd WD25 .154 B5
Kingwell Rd EN4 .159 D1
Kinloch Ct 6 AL5 .86 B1
Kinross Cres LU3 .44 D8
Kinsbourne Cl AL5 .85 C4
Kinsbourne Cres AL5 .85 D4
Kinsbourne Ct AL5 .85 F3
Kinsbourne Green La AL5 .85 B3
Kintyre Ho 2 WD18 .166 F3
Kipling Cl SG4 .35 C7
Kipling Gr HP2 .105 B1
Kipling Pl HA7 .176 F4
Kipling Rd SG8 .2 E1
Kipling The LU3 .45 B6
Kipling Way AL5 .86 B1
Kirby Cl HA6 .174 F4
Kirby Dr LU3 .45 A8
Kirkcaldy Gn 1 WD19 .175 C7
Kirkdale Ct 8 LU1 .63 E6
Kirkdale Rd AL5 .86 A2
Kirklands AL8 .89 D2
Kirkwick Ave AL5 .86 A1
Kit's La SG7 .25 C8
Kitchener Cl AL1 .128 B2
Kitcheners La SG2 .38 B1
Kitching La
St Ippolyts SG4 .49 F5
Stevenage SG1 .50 A5
Kite Field HP4 .121 E7
Kite Way SG6 .22 E8
Kitsbury Ct HP4 .122 B4
Kitsbury Rd HP4 .122 B4
Kitsbury Terr HP4 .122 B4
Kitson Way CM20 .117 C1
Kitswell Rd WD7 .156 A6
Kitswell Way WD7 .155 F6
Kitt's End Rd EN5 .158 E2
Kiwi Ct SG5 .21 F1
Klondyke AL5 .85 D4
Knap Cl SG6 .23 D8
Knebworth Ct CM23 .76 D6
Knebworth Ctry Pk* SG3 .68 C7
Knebworth Ho* SG3 .68 B6
Knebworth Path WD6 .170 D5
Knebworth Prim Sch SG3 .69 A5
Knebworth Sta SG3 .68 F5
Kneesworth House Hospl SG8 .2 C5
Kneesworth Rd SG8 .2 F8
Kneesworth St SG8 .7 C6
Knella Gn AL7 .111 A6
Knella Rd AL7 .111 A6
Knella Road Workshops AL7 .111 A6
Knight St CM21 .97 E2
Knight's Ct CM21 .97 E2
Knights Cl
Bishop's Stortford CM23 .76 C8
Buntingford SG9 .40 E6
Knights Ct Bushey WD23 .168 D1
Standon SG11 .55 F1
Knights Field LU2 .45 D1
Knights Orch
Hemel Hempstead HP1 .123 F5
St Albans AL3 .127 C3
Knights Templar Sch The SG7 .23 E8
Knights Templars Gn SG2 .51 C8
Knightsbridge Way HP2 .124 E4
Knightscote Cl UB9 .173 D1
Knightsfield AL8 .89 D2
Knightsfield Sch AL8 .89 D3
Knoll Cres HA6 .174 F2
Knoll Gn HP2 .124 E5
Knoll Rise LU2 .45 E4
Knoll The SG13 .114 B7
Knolles Cres AL9 .144 B7
Knolls Cl HP22 .60 B3
Knowl Piece SG4 .22 A3
Knowl Pk WD6 .169 E4
Knowl Way WD6 .169 F4
Knowle SG1 .36 B1
Knowle Dr AL5 .107 D7
Knowle Ho EN11 .135 A5
Knowle The EN11 .135 A5
Knutsford Ave WD24 .154 D1
Knutsford Sch WD24 .154 D1
Koh-I-Noor Ave WD23 .168 A3
Kristiansand Way SG6 .23 C8
Kymswell Rd SG2 .51 C3
Kynance Cl LU2 .46 A2
Kynaston Cl HA3 .176 D3
Kynaston Wood HA3 .176 D3
Kyrkeby SG6 .23 C4
Kytes Dr WD25 .154 D6

L

Laburnum Cl
Cheshunt EN8 .162 D8
Luton LU3 .45 C7
Laburnum Gr
Chiswell Green AL2 .141 B6
Luton LU3 .45 B7
Laburnum Rd EN11 .135 B8
Lachbury Cl LU1 .63 A6
Lackmore Rd EN1 .162 C4
Lacre Way SG6 .23 C7
Ladbrooke Cl EN6 .159 A7
Ladbrooke Dr EN6 .159 A7
Ladbrooke JMI Sch EN6 .159 B7
Ladies Gr AL3 .127 C5
Lady Cooper Ct HP4 .122 E6
Lady Gr AL7 .110 E2
Lady Spencer's Gr AL1 .127 C2
Lady St John Sq SG14 .92 A1
Lady Zia Wernher Sch LU2 .46 B3
Lady's Cl WD18 .167 C5
Ladygrove Cotts SG4 .48 F5
Ladygrove Ct SG4 .48 F5
Ladyhill LU4 .44 B6
Ladymeadow HP3 .138 D4
Ladyshot CM20 .118 B1
Ladysmith Rd
Harrow HA3 .176 E1
Pitstone LU7 .80 E5
St Albans AL3 .127 D4
Ladywalk WD3 .172 E6
Ladywell Prospect CM21 .98 A1
Ladywood Cl WD3 .165 C6
Ladywood Rd SG14 .112 F6
Laguna Ct 2 AL1 .127 E3
Laidon Sq HP2 .124 D7
Lake Dr WD23 .176 D8
Lake Rd EN9 .135 E2
Lake The WD23 .168 D1
Lake View
Bishop's Stortford CM23 .76 B3
Potters Bar EN6 .159 C6
Lake Villas SG9 .43 B4
Lakeland Cl HA3 .176 D4
Lakes Ct SG12 .115 B4
Lakeside
Borehamwood WD6 .170 A4
Tring HP23 .100 A5
Lakeside Pl AL2 .142 D4
Lakeside Rd EN8 .148 C3
Lakeside Sch AL8 .110 B4
Lalleford Rd LU2 .46 D1
Lalsham Ho 4 WD19 .175 C7
Lamb Cl Hatfield AL10 .130 B4
Watford WD25 .154 C5
Lamb Ct AL4 .108 E7
Lamb La AL3 .106 B5
Lamb Mdw SG15 .11 A3
Lambert Ct WD23 .167 D5
Lamberton Ct WD6 .170 A8
Lambourn Chase WD7 .155 F3
Lambourn Dr LU2 .45 E6
Lambourn Gdns AL5 .85 F3
Lambs Cl Cuffley EN6 .146 F2
Dunstable LU5 .44 A1
Lambs Gdns SG12 .95 D4
Lambton Ave EN8 .162 D6
Lamer La AL4 .87 D3
Lamers Rd LU2 .46 B2
Lammas Mead SG5 .21 E2
Lammas Path SG2 .51 B4
Lammas Rd
Cheddington LU7 .80 A7
Watford WD18 .167 C4
Watton at S SG14 .70 D4
Lammas Way SG6 .22 F8
Lammasmead EN10 .148 F8
Lamorna Cl Luton LU3 .44 F6
Radlett WD7 .156 B5
Lamorna Ct HA3 .176 E1
Lampits EN11 .135 B6
Lamsey Rd HP3 .124 D1
Lancaster Ave
Hadley Wood EN4 .159 D1
Hitchin SG5 .34 E8
Luton LU2 .45 C8
Lancaster Cl SG1 .36 E2
Lancaster Dr HP3 .136 F4
Lancaster Rd Hitchin SG5 .34 E8
St Albans AL1 .127 F5
Lancaster Way
Abbots Langley WD5 .153 F8
Bishop's Stortford CM23 .76 C8
Welwyn AL6 .89 C3
Lancing Ho 5 WD24 .167 C7
Lancing Rd LU2 .46 D3
Lancing Way WD3 .166 B4
Landau Way EN10 .148 F5
Landford Cl WD3 .173 E8
Landmead Rd EN8 .148 E2
Landridge Dr EN1 .162 B1
Lands' End WD6 .169 D3
Lane End
Berkhamsted HP4 .121 F4
Hatfield AL10 .129 F2
Lane Gdns WD23 .168 E2
Lanefield Wlk AL8 .110 C6
Lanercost Cl AL6 .90 A7
Langbridge Cl SG4 .35 A4
Langdale Ave AL5 .86 D2
Langdale Ct 2 HP2 .124 E6
Langdale Gdns EN3 .162 D4
Langdale Terr WD6 .170 C6
Langdon St HP23 .100 A3
Langfield Cl EN9 .135 E1
Langford Cl AL4 .128 C5
Langford Dr LU2 .46 A3
Langham Cl Luton LU2 .45 D7
St Albans AL4 .128 D8
Langham Ho 9 LU1 .63 D8
Langholme WD23 .168 C1
Langland Ct HA6 .174 D3
Langland Dr HA5 .175 E3
Langleigh SG6 .11 F1
Langley Ave HP3 .138 F8
Langley Cres
Kings Langley WD4 .139 A1
St Albans AL3 .127 C5
Langley Ct EN7 .147 C3
Langley Gn EN9 .135 D1
Langley Gr AL4 .108 C2
Langley Hill WD4 .138 F2
Langley Hill Cl WD4 .139 A2
Langley La
Abbots Langley WD5 .153 F7
Langley SG4 .49 E2
Langley Lodge La WD4 .153 A8
Langley Rd
Abbots Langley WD5 .153 F8
Chipperfield WD4 .138 B1
Watford WD17 .167 A8
Langley Row EN5 .171 F8
Langley St LU1 .63 E6
Langley Terrace Ind Pk 10 LU1 .63 E6
Langley Way WD17 .166 F8
Langley Wharf WD4 .139 A4
Langleybury La WD4 .153 B4
Langmead Dr WD23 .168 D1
Langstone Ley AL7 .111 B5
Langthorne Ave SG1 .50 E6
Langton Gr HA6 .174 C5
Langton Ho EN11 .134 F6
Langton Rd Harrow HA3 .176 C3
Hoddesdon EN11 .134 F6
Langwood 6 WD17 .167 A8
Langwood Gdns WD17 .167 A8
Langworthy HA5 .176 A4
Lankester Rd SG8 .7 C5
Lannock SG6 .23 D4
Lannock Hill SG4 .23 E1
Lannock Prim Sch SG6 .23 C4
Lanrick Copse HP4 .122 E5
Lansdowne Cl WD25 .154 D4
Lansdowne Ct EN10 .135 A3
Lansdowne Rd LU3 .45 D1
Lanterns La SG2 .51 D5
Lanthony Ct SG15 .11 A4
Lanthorn Cl EN10 .134 E4
Laporte Way LU4 .44 F1
Lapwing Cl HP2 .124 E6
Lapwing Dell SG6 .23 B3
Lapwing Rd LU4 .44 A4
Lapwing Rise SG2 .51 D3
Lapwing Way WD5 .154 A8
Larch Ave
Bricket Wood AL2 .140 E1
Hitchin SG4 .35 A4
Larch Cl EN7 .147 E4
Larch La AL6 .89 F8
Larch Rise HP4 .122 A5
Larch View HP1 .124 B2
Larches Ave EN1 .162 C4
Larches The
Berkhamsted HP4 .121 D5
Little Chalfont HP6 .150 B1
Luton LU2 .45 D1
Northwood HA6 .174 C4
St Albans AL4 .128 D7
Ware SG12 .93 C4
Watford WD23 .167 E4
Larchwood CM23 .76 D5
Lark Rise AL10 .130 A3
Larken Cl WD23 .168 C1
Larken Dr WD23 .168 C1
Larkens Cl SG11 .55 D3
Larkin Pl SG8 .2 D1
Larkins Cl SG7 .12 F1
Larkinson SG1 .50 C7
Larks Ridge AL2 .141 A4
Larksfield SG12 .93 E3
Larkspur Cl
Bishop's Stortford CM23 .76 D6
Hemel Hempstead HP1 .123 E4
Larkspur Gdns LU4 .44 F2
Larksway CM23 .76 C6
Larkswood Rise AL4 .128 C8
Larmans Rd EN3 .162 D3
Larsen Dr EN9 .163 D5
Larwood Gr SG1 .51 A8
Larwood Sch SG1 .50 F7
Latchford Mews 8 AL4 .87 D1
Latchford Pl HP1 .124 A2
Latchmore Bank CM22 .77 B2
Latchmore Cl SG4 .34 F5
Latimer Cl
Hemel Hempstead HP2 .125 B8
Pinner HA5 .175 C2
Watford WD18 .166 E2
Latimer Ct EN8 .162 F5
Latimer Gdns
Pinner HA5 .175 C2
Welwyn Garden City AL7 .111 B6
Latimer Rd
Little Chalfont HP6,HP5 .150 C2
Luton LU1 .63 E6
Latium Cl AL1 .127 D2
Lattimore Rd
St Albans AL1 .127 E3
Wheathampstead AL4 .108 C8

Latton Hall Cl CM20 118 A1
Lauderdale Rd WD4 153 C6
Laughton Ct WD6 170 D7
Launceston WD3 164 B3
Laundry La EN9 149 E6
Launton Cl LU3 31 B1
Laura Ct HA2 176 C1
Laural Ct EN6 146 E2
Laurance Haines Prim Sch The WD18 167 A3
Laureate Way HP1 124 B5
Laurel Ave EN6 158 F7
Laurel Bank HP3 137 F8
Laurel Cl
Hemel Hempstead HP2 124 F4
Watford WD19 167 D2
Laurel Ct EN6 146 F1
Laurel Fields EN6 158 F8
Laurel Mews SG7 12 F1
Laurel Pk HA3 176 F3
Laurel Rd AL1 127 F3
Laurel Way SG5 21 E3
Laureldene SG10 74 F1
Laurels Cl AL3 141 B8
Laurels The
Bushey WD23 176 E8
Hammond Street EN7 147 E5
Potten End HP4 123 C6
Laurelside Wlk LU5 44 A2
Lauries Cl HP1 123 C1
Laurino Pl WD23 176 C8
Lavender Cl
Bishop's Stortford CM23 76 D6
Hammond Street EN7 147 F4
Harlow CM20 117 E1
Hatfield AL10 129 F8
Luton LU2 45 E7
Lavender Cres AL3 127 C5
Lavender Ct Baldock SG7 12 E1
Hitchin SG4 35 B6
Lavender Gdns
Enfield EN2 161 B1
Harrow HA3 176 E4
Lavender Prim Sch EN2 161 E1
Lavender Rd EN2 161 D1
Lavender Way SG5 34 D7
Lavender Wlk HP2 124 D5
Lavinia Ave WD25 154 D5
Lavrock La WD3 165 F2
Law Hall La SG4 66 A8
Law Hall Lane Cotts SG4 66 A8
Lawford Ave WD3 164 C3
Lawford Cl
Chorleywood WD3 164 C3
Luton LU1 63 C7
Lawn Ave SG4 66 C1
Lawn Gdns LU1 63 D5
Lawn La HP3 138 D8
Lawn Mans EN5 171 F5
Lawn The CM20 118 B3
Lawn Vale HA5 175 E1
Lawns Cl SG5 33 C2
Lawns Ct SG8 7 D5
Lawns Dr The EN10 134 F2
Lawns The Harrow HA5 176 B3
Hemel Hempstead HP1 123 E4
Shenley WD7 156 E6
St Albans AL3 127 C4
Stevenage SG2 51 D4
Welwyn Garden City AL8 89 D1
Lawnswood EN5 171 E4
Lawrance Gdns EN8 148 D3
Lawrance Rd AL3 127 C7
Lawrence Ave
Letchworth SG6 23 A4
Sawbridgeworth CM21 97 E4
Stanstead Abbotts SG12 115 C3
Stevenage SG1 50 E7
Lawrence Cl SG14 112 E7
Lawrence Ct 4 WD19 175 D7
Lawrence End Rd LU2 65 D4
Lawrence Hall End AL7 110 E3
Lawrence Moorings CM21 97 F2
Lawrie Ct HA3 176 F3
Laxton Cl LU2 46 E1
Laxton Gdns Baldock SG7 24 A7
Shenley WD7 156 E7
Lay Brook AL4 128 A7
Layard Rd EN1 161 F1
Layham Dr LU2 46 E1
Layhill HP2 124 D5
Layston CE Fst Sch SG9 40 F8
Layston Mdw SG9 40 F6
Layston Pk SG8 7 D5
Layton St AL7 110 E3
Le Corte Cl WD4 138 F2
Lea Bank LU3 44 E6
Lea Bank Ct LU3 44 E6
Lea Bushes WD25 154 E4
Lea Cl
Bishop's Stortford CM23 59 B1
Bushey WD23 168 B4
Lea Ct AL5 86 A3
Lea Farm Jun Sch WD25 154 D4
Lea Gn AL9 130 E8
Lea Gr CM23 59 B1
Lea Manor High Sch LU3 44 F8
Lea Manor Recn Ctr LU3 44 F8
Lea Mount EN7 147 E3
Lea Prim Sch The AL5 86 B4
Lea Rd Harpenden AL5 86 B3
Hoddesdon EN11 135 C8
Holdbrook EN9 163 A5
Lea Rd *continued*
Luton LU1 63 F7
Watford WD24 154 B1
Lea Road Ind Pk EN9 163 A5
Lea Valley High Sch EN3 162 C4
Lea Valley Park Visitor Ctr* EN9 163 C6
Lea Wlk AL5 86 C4
Leacroft AL5 86 D3
Leaders Cl HP22 60 B3
Leaf Cl HA6 174 D3
Leaf Way AL1 141 D8
Leafield LU3 44 F4
Leaford Cres WD24 153 F2
Leaford Ct WD24 153 F3
Leaforis Rd EN7 148 A3
Leafy La HP23 99 E1
Leagrave High St LU4 44 B3
Leagrave Prim Sch LU4 44 C4
Leagrave Rd LU4 45 B2
Leagrave Sta LU4 44 E5
Leahoe Gdns SG13 113 C5
Lealands High Sch LU3 44 C8
Leamington Rd LU3 45 A7
Leander Gdns WD25 154 E2
Leas The Baldock SG7 23 E7
Hemel Hempstead HP3 139 A7
Watford WD23 167 F7
Leasey Bridge La AL4 87 A1
Leasey Dell Dr AL4 87 A2
Leaside HP2 125 C2
Leaside Ct AL5 86 C3
Leaside Wlk 6 SG12 93 D1
Leat Cl CM21 97 F3
Leathersellers Cl 12 EN5 171 E6
Leathwaite Cl LU3 45 A6
Leaves Spring SG2 51 A2
Leavesden Ct WD5 154 A8
Leavesden Film Studios WD4 153 E5
Leavesden Green Jun Mix Inf Sch WD25 154 A5
Leavesden Rd WD24 154 B1
Leaview EN9 163 B6
Lebanon Cl WD17 153 D3
Lectern La AL1 141 E7
Leda Ave EN3 162 D1
Ledgemore La HP1,HP2 103 F5
Ledwell Rd LU1 62 F3
Lee Bridge Cnr LU2 85 F7
Lee Cl Hertford SG13 113 C4
Stanstead Abbotts SG12 115 C4
Lee Farm Cl HP5 136 A1
Lee The HA6 174 F5
Lee Valley Ctry Pk* EN10 135 B2
Leeches Way LU7 80 A7
Leecroft Rd EN5 171 E5
Leefe Way EN6 146 D3
Leeming Rd WD6 169 F8
Lees Ave HA6 174 F2
Leeside Barnet EN5 171 E3
Potters Bar EN6 159 D7
Leeswood Ct SG14 112 F7
Leete Pl SG8 7 D7
Leeway Cl HA5 175 F3
Leggatts Cl WD24 153 F3
Leggatts Rise WD25 154 A4
Leggatts Way WD24 154 A3
Leggatts Wood Ave WD24 154 B3
Leggett Gr SG1 50 E8
Leggfield Terr HP1 123 F3
Leghorn Cres LU4 44 A3
Legions Way CM23 77 A8
Legra Ave EN11 135 A6
Leicester Rd LU4 44 E1
Leigh Comm AL7 110 F4
Leigh Ct WD6 170 D7
Leigh Rodd WD19 175 F7
Leighton Buzzard Rd
Great Gaddesden HP1 103 E2
Hemel Hempstead HP1 124 C5
Leighton Ct EN8 148 D2
Leighton Rd Harrow HA3 176 D1
Wingrave HP22 60 C3
Lemonfield Dr WD25 154 E6
Lemsford Ct WD6 170 C5
Lemsford La AL8 110 B4
Lemsford Rd
Hatfield AL10 130 A6
St Albans AL1 127 F4
Lemsford Springs (Nature Reserve)* AL8 110 A5
Lemsford Village AL8 109 F5
Lennon Ct LU1 63 D7
Lennox Gn LU2 46 F2
Lensbury Cl EN8 148 E3
Leonard Ct HA3 176 E3
Leonard's Cl AL6 89 E8
Lesbury Cl LU2 46 E1
Leslie Cl SG2 51 C2
Letchfield HP5 150 B8
Letchmore Cl SG1 50 D6
Letchmore Inf Sch SG1 50 D7
Letchmore Rd
Radlett WD7 156 A3
Stevenage SG1 50 D7
Letchworth Bsns & Ret Pk SG6 23 C6
Letchworth Cl WD19 175 D5
Letchworth Gate SG6 23 B4
Letchworth La SG6 22 F3
Letchworth Mus & Art Gall* SG6 22 F5
Letchworth Rd
Baldock SG7 23 D7
Luton LU3 45 A4
Letchworth Sta SG6 22 F6
Letter Box Row SG4 34 F3
Level's Gn CM23 58 C5
Leven Cl Cheshunt EN8 162 D6
South Oxhey WD19 175 D5
Leven Dr EN8 162 D6
Leven Way HP2 124 D7
Levenage La SG12 95 E3
Levendale LU4 44 C5
Leventhorpe Sch The CM21 97 E4
Leveret Cl WD25 154 A5
Leverstock Green CE Prim Sch HP2 125 D2
Leverstock Green Rd
Hemel Hempstead HP2 125 B3
Hemel Hempstead HP2, HP3 125 C2
Leverstock Green Way HP2,HP3 125 C3
Leverton Jun & Inf Sch The EN9 163 F5
Leverton Way EN9 163 C6
Lewes Way WD3 166 C5
Lewington Ct EN3 162 D2
Lewis Cl UB9 173 C1
Lewis Ho 3 WD18 166 F3
Lewis La SG15 11 A6
Lewsey Park Ct LU4 44 A4
Lewsey Rd LU4 44 B2
Lexington Cl WD6 169 F6
Lexington Ct EN6 158 D8
Lexington Way EN5 171 D5
Ley Hill Rd HP3 136 E2
Ley Hill Sch HP5 136 B1
Ley Ho AL7 111 C6
Ley Park Prim Sch EN10 134 F1
Ley Wlk AL7 111 C6
Leyburne Cl LU7 61 C8
Leyburne Rd LU3 45 B6
Leycroft Way AL5 107 E7
Leyden Rd SG1 50 D2
Leygreen Cl LU2 64 A8
Leyhill Dr LU1 63 B4
Leyland Ave AL1 127 D1
Leyland Cl EN8 148 C2
Leys Ave SG6 22 F6
Leys Cl UB9 173 D2
Leys Prim Sch The SG1 37 A2
Leys Rd HP3 124 F1
Leys The St Albans AL4 128 D6
Tring HP23 100 B4
Leysdown AL7 111 D6
Leyton Gn AL5 86 A1
Leyton Rd AL5 86 A1
Liberty Cl SG13 113 C3
Liberty Wlk AL1 128 C2
Library Rd LU1 63 E7
Lichfield Ho 4 WD6 170 A7
Lichfield Rd HA6 175 A1
Lichfield Way EN10 134 F1
Liddel Cl LU3 45 B3
Lidgate Cl LU4 44 B6
Lieutenant Ellis Way EN7,EN8 162 A7
Lighthorne Rise LU3 45 A7
Lightswood Cl EN7 147 D4
Lilac Ave EN1 162 C3
Lilac Cl EN7 162 B8
Lilac Gr LU3 44 C8
Lilac Rd EN11 135 B8
Lilac Way AL5 107 D6
Lilbourne Dr SG13 114 A7
Lilley Bottom LU2,SG4 47 C5
Lilley Bottom Rd SG4 48 B1
Lilleyhoo La LU2,SG5 32 F2
Lilliard Cl EN11 115 B2
Lilly La HP2 125 D7
Limberlost The AL6 89 B7
Limbrick Rd AL5 107 C6
Limbury Rd LU3 44 F4
Lime Ave Kimpton AL4 87 B7
Luton LU4 44 C3
Lime Cl Aston SG2 51 D4
Harrow HA3 176 F1
Ware SG12 93 E2
Watford WD19 167 D2
Lime Gr Royston SG8 7 E8
Totteridge N20 171 F1
Lime Tree Pl AL1 127 E2
Lime Tree Wlk
Bushey WD23 176 E8
Enfield EN2 161 C1
Rickmansworth WD3 165 B4
Lime Walk Prim Sch HP2 124 F1
Lime Way WD7 156 C8
Lime Wlk HP3 124 F1
Limedene Cl HA5 175 D2
Limekiln Cl SG8 7 E5
Limekiln La Baldock SG7 23 F7
Stansted Mountfitchet CM24 59 C5
Limes Cres 4 CM23 77 A7
Limes Ct Cheshunt EN8 162 D7
Hoddesdon EN11 135 A6
Limes Rd EN8 162 E7
Limes The Buckland SG9 27 D8
Cheshunt EN10 148 F7
Hertford SG14 113 C6
Hitchin SG5 34 D6
Luton LU1 63 E5
2 Northwood HA6 174 E5
St Albans AL1 127 E5
Limes The *continued*
Welwyn Garden City AL7 111 A4
Limetree Ave LU1 85 A7
Limetree Ct HA5 176 A3
Limit Home Pk HP4 121 D7
Linacres LU4 44 D4
Linbridge Way LU2 46 E2
Linces Way AL7 111 B4
Lincoln Cl
Bishop's Stortford CM23 76 D5
Welwyn Garden City AL7 111 D6
Lincoln Ct
Berkhamsted HP4 122 B4
Borehamwood WD6 170 D4
Lincoln Dr
Croxley Green WD3 166 B6
South Oxhey WD19 175 C7
Lincoln Hill SG9 29 A5
Lincoln Mews AL3 127 C2
Lincoln Rd Luton LU4 45 B1
Stevenage SG1 37 B2
Lincoln Way WD3 166 B5
Lincoln's Cl AL4 128 D8
Lincot La SG4 67 C7
Lindbergh AL7 111 C6
Linden Ave WD18 166 F5
Linden Cl EN7 148 B1
Linden Cres AL1 128 C3
Linden Ct Harpenden AL5 107 B8
4 Luton LU2 63 F8
Linden Glade HP1 124 A2
Linden Gn SG6 23 A8
Linden Lea WD25 154 A6
Linden Rd Luton LU4 44 E4
Redbourn AL3 106 A6
Linden Sq UB9 173 A4
Lindencroft SG6 12 A1
Lindens The
Bishop's Stortford CM23 76 F6
Hatfield AL10 129 F6
Hemel Hempstead HP3 137 F8
Stevenage SG1 50 E4
Lindley Cl AL5 86 A4
Lindlings HP1 123 E2
Lindrick Ho 11 WD19 175 C7
Lindsay Ave SG4 35 B5
Lindsay Cl SG8 2 C1
Lindsay Pl EN7 148 B1
Lindsay Rd LU2 46 D1
Lindsey Cl CM23 58 F1
Lindsey Rd CM23 58 F1
Lindum Pl AL3 127 A1
Linfield Ct SG14 112 F7
Lingfield Cl HA6 174 E3
Lingfield Rd Royston SG8 7 F6
Stevenage SG1 37 C1
Lingfield Way WD17 153 F1
Lingholm Way EN5 171 D4
Lingmoor Dr WD25 154 C6
Linington Ave HP5 136 A1
Link Cl AL10 130 B5
Link Dr AL10 130 B5
Link Rd
Bishop's Stortford CM23 76 F8
Hemel Hempstead HP1 124 C6
Oaklands AL6 89 F8
Watford WD24 167 D7
Link The SG6 12 A1
Link Way CM23 76 E6
Link Wlk AL10 130 B6
Linkfield AL7 110 E2
Links Ave SG13 114 B7
Links Bsns Ctr The CM23 77 C7
Links Dr
Borehamwood WD6 169 F5
Radlett WD7 155 F6
Links The Cheshunt EN8 148 D5
Welwyn Garden City AL8 110 B6
Links View AL3 127 C5
Links Way
Croxley Green WD3 166 C5
Luton LU2 45 D8
Linkside Rd CM23 77 C6
Linksway HA6 174 C2
Linkway HA5 175 D2
Linkways E SG1 50 F5
Linkways W SG1 50 F5
Linley Ct AL3 127 F6
Linley Dell LU2 46 D2
Linnet Cl Bushey WD23 168 C1
Letchworth SG6 22 E8
Luton LU4 44 A4
Linnet Rd WD5 154 A8
Linnet Wlk 1 AL10 130 A3
Linning Pond AL3 84 B1
Linsey Cl HP3 139 A7
Linster Gr WD6 170 C4
Linten Cl SG4 35 C6
Linton Ave WD6 169 F7
Lintott Cl SG1 50 D6
Linwood CM21 97 E2
Linwood Rd
Harpenden AL5 107 C7
Ware SG12 93 F3
Lion Ct WD6 170 C8
Lion Yd SG4 66 D1
Liphook Rd WD19 175 D6
Lippitts Hill LU2 45 E5
Lismirrane Ind Pk WD6 169 B3
Lismore
Hemel Hempstead HP3 125 C1
Stevenage SG2 51 C1
Lister Ave SG4 34 F5
Lister Cl SG1 36 C2
Lister Cotts WD6 169 A4
Lister Hospl SG1 36 B2
Liston Cl LU4 44 B5
Little Acre AL3 127 D6
Little Acres SG12 114 D8
Little Beechill EN2 160 D3
Little Berkhamsted La AL9,SG13 132 B3
Little Berries LU3 44 E7
Little Bridge Rd 17 HP4 122 D4
Little Burrow AL7 110 D4
Little Bushey La WD23 168 C5
Little Catherells HP1 123 F5
Little Chishill Rd SG8 18 C8
Little Dell AL8 110 D8
Little Furze Jun Mix & Inf Sch WD19 175 B7
Little Gaddesden CE Prim Sch HP4 102 C8
Little Gaddesden Ho HP4 102 E6
Little Ganett AL7 111 C4
Little Gr WD23 168 B5
Little Graylings WD5 153 E6
Little Green Jun Sch WD3 166 B6
Little Green La WD3 166 B6
Little Grove Ave EN7 147 E4
Little Hadham Prim Sch SG11 57 C2
Little Hallingbury CE Prim Sch CM22 98 C7
Little Hardings AL7 111 C7
Little Hayes WD4 139 A2
Little Heath CM22 98 F3
Little Heath La HP4 123 B4
Little Heath Prim Sch EN6 145 C1
Little Heath Spinney AL3 127 E5
Little Henleys SG12 95 D1
Little Hill WD3 164 C3
Little Hoo HP23 99 F4
Little How Croft WD5 153 C8
Little Hyde SG2 51 B4
Little La Harpenden AL5 107 C6
Pirton SG5 20 D5
Little Lake AL7 111 B3
Little Larkins EN5 171 E3
Little Ley AL7 110 E3
Little Martins WD23 168 B4
Little Mead AL10 130 B8
Little Mimms 2 HP2 124 E4
Little Mollards HP22 60 A3
Little Moss La HA5 175 E1
Little Mundells AL7 110 F8
Little Munden CE Prim Sch SG12 71 E8
Little Orch HP2 125 A5
Little Orchard Cl
Abbots Langley WD5 153 D7
Pinner HA5 175 E1
Little Oxhey La WD19 175 E6
Little Parndon Sch CM20 117 B1
Little Piper's Cl EN7 147 B2
Little Pk HP3 137 A3
Little Potters WD23 168 E2
Little Rd HP2 124 F4
Little Reddings Prim Sch WD23 168 B4
Little Ridge AL7 111 A6
Little Rivers AL7 111 A7
Little St EN9 163 C3
Little Stock Rd EN7 147 D5
Little Stream Cl HA6 174 E5
Little Thistle AL7 111 C4
Little Tring Rd HP23 99 F6
Little Twye HP23 119 F3
Little Twye Rd HP23 119 F3
Little Wade AL7 110 F3
Little Widbury SG12 93 F1
Little Widbury La SG12 93 F1
Little Windmill Hill WD4 151 F7
Little Wood Croft LU3 44 E7
Little Youngs AL8 110 C6
Littlebrook Gdns EN8 148 D1
Littlebury Cl SG5 12 A5
Littlechurch Rd LU2 46 B3
Littlecote Pl HA5 175 E2
Littlefield Rd LU2 46 B2
Littlegreen La LU1 62 E3
Liverpool Rd Luton LU1 63 D7
St Albans AL1 127 E3
Watford WD18 167 B4
Livingstone Ct EN5 171 E7
Livingstone Link SG2 51 B8
Livingstone Wlk HP2 124 F7
Lloyd Mews EN3 163 A1
Lloyd Way SG4 66 C1
Lloyd-Taylor Cl SG11 57 B2
Loates La WD17 167 C6
Loates Pasture CM24 59 D8
Local Board Rd WD17 167 D4
Locarno Ave LU4 44 C6
Lochinver House Sch EN6 145 B1
Lochnell Rd HP4 121 F6
Lock Ho HP3 138 E7
Lock View CM21 97 F2
Lockers Park La HP1 124 B3
Lockers Park Sch HP1 124 B3
Locket Rd HA3 176 F1
Lockley Cres AL10 130 B7
Lockleys Dr AL6 89 C5
Lockyer Cl EN3 163 B1
Lodge Ave WD6 169 F4
Lodge Cl Cheddington LU7 80 A7
Hertford SG14 113 C8
Lodge Cres EN8 162 D5

Lodge Ct
Abbots Langley WD25 .....154 A7
Ickleford SG5 .....21 E3
Lodge Dr Hatfield AL9 .....130 D8
Rickmansworth WD3 .....165 C5
Lodge End
Croxley Green WD3 .....166 D5
Radlett WD7 .....156 B5
Lodge Farm SG4 .....67 E1
Lodge Farm Prim Sch SG2 .....51 C7
Lodge Gdns AL5 .....86 A2
Lodge La EN9 .....163 D4
Lodge The Harefield UB9 .173 C3
Watford WD24 .....167 C7
Lodge Way SG2 .....51 A1
Lodgefield AL7 .....89 E1
Loftus Cl LU4 .....44 B3
Logans EN5 .....171 D6
Loire Mews AL5 .....107 C7
Lombardy Cl HP2 .....125 D2
Lombardy Dr HP4 .....122 D3
Lombardy Way WD6 .....169 E7
Lomond Rd HP2 .....124 D7
Lomond Way SG1 .....37 C3
London Bible Coll HA6 ..174 D4
London Coll of Professional Studies LU1 .....63 E7
London Colney Jun Mix Inf Sch AL2 .....142 D6
London Luton Airport LU2 .....64 D7
London Rd
Aston Clinton HP22 .....99 A4
Baldock SG7 .....23 F6
Barkway SG8 .....17 D1
Barley SG8 .....8 F1
Berkhamsted HP4 .....122 E3
Bishop's Stortford CM23 .....77 A5
Buntingford SG9 .....40 F6
Bushey WD23 .....167 F3
Harlow CM17 .....118 C2
Hemel Hempstead HP1, HP3 .....124 A1
Hertford SG13 .....113 E5
Hertford Heath SG13 .....114 B3
Hitchin SG4 .....34 F5
Knebworth SG3 .....69 A3
Langley SG4 .....49 D5
Luton LU1 .....84 F7
Luton,New Town LU1 .....63 E4
Markyate AL3 .....83 F5
Rickmansworth WD3 .....173 E8
Royston SG8 .....7 D5
Sawbridgeworth CM21 .....97 E2
Shenley WD7 .....157 A5
St Albans AL1 .....142 C7
Stevenage SG1,SG2 .....50 D3
Stotfold SG5 .....3 A2
Tring HP23 .....100 C3
Ware SG12 .....114 E7
Welwyn AL6 .....89 C4
London Row SG15 .....11 A3
Londrina Ct 14 HP4 .....122 D4
Londrina Terr 15 HP4 .....122 D4
Long Arrotts HP1 .....124 B5
Long Barn Cl WD25 .....154 A7
Long Buftlers AL5 .....107 F8
Long Chaulden HP1 .....123 E3
Long Cl LU2 .....46 C3
Long Croft CM24 .....59 D8
Long Croft Dr EN8 .....163 A5
Long Croft Rd Luton LU1 ..63 A7
Maple Cross WD3 .....172 D5
Long Cutt AL3 .....106 A6
Long Elmes HA3 .....176 C2
Long Elms WD5 .....153 D6
Long Elms Cl WD5 .....153 D6
Long Fallow AL2 .....141 A4
Long Grove Cl EN10 .....134 E4
Long Hale LU7 .....80 C3
Long Hedge LU7 .....80 C4
Long Hyde SG2 .....51 B4
Long John HP3 .....124 F1
Long La Aston SG2 .....51 E5
Bovingdon HP3 .....150 F8
Chorleywood WD3 .....164 D2
Rickmansworth WD3 .....172 F8
Whitwell SG4 .....66 A7
Long Leaves SG2 .....51 A2
Long Ley Cheddington LU7 .80 A7
Harlow CM20 .....117 F1
Welwyn Garden City AL7 ..111 C6
Long Marston CE Prim Sch HP23 .....79 B4
Long Marston Rd
Cheddington HP23,LU7 .....79 E7
Marsworth HP23 .....79 F2
Long Mdw
Bishop's Stortford CM23 .....76 D6
Markyate AL3 .....83 F5
Watton at S SG14 .....70 D4
Long Mimms 8 HP2 .....124 E4
Long Moor EN8 .....148 E2
Long Pightle Mobile Home Pk WD3 .....152 F2
Long Ridge SG2 .....51 D1
Long Room UB9 .....173 A3
Long Row SG5 .....19 D1
Long Spring AL3 .....127 F7
Long View HP4 .....122 A6
Longacre CM17 .....118 B4
Longacres AL4 .....128 D3
Longbridge Cl HP23 .....100 A6
Longcliffe Path WD19 .....175 A7
Longcroft WD19 .....167 B2
Longcroft Ave AL5 .....85 F1
Longcroft Gdns AL8 .....110 D5
Longcroft Gn AL8 .....110 D5
Longcroft La
Bovingdon HP3 .....137 D5
Welwyn Garden City AL8 ..110 D5
Longcroft Rd SG1 .....50 E7
Longcrofts EN9 .....163 E5
Longdean Pk HP3 .....139 A7
Longdean Sch HP3 .....139 B8
Longfield HP3 .....125 B1
Longfield Ave EN3 .....162 C1
Longfield Ct SG6 .....22 D7
Longfield Dr LU4 .....44 D1
Longfield Gdns HP23 .....99 E3
Longfield La EN7 .....148 A4
Longfield Rd
Harpenden AL5 .....107 C7
Tring HP23 .....99 F3
Longfields SG2 .....51 C1
Longlands HP2 .....125 A3
Longlands Cl EN8 .....162 D7
Longlands Prim Sch EN10 .....148 F6
Longlands Rd AL7 .....110 F5
Longlees WD3 .....172 D5
Longman Ct HP3 .....138 E6
Longmans SG11 .....55 F7
Longmans Cl WD18 .....166 C3
Longmead
Buntingford SG9 .....40 D7
Hatfield AL10 .....130 B8
Letchworth SG6 .....22 E7
Woolmer Green SG3 .....69 A2
Longmeadow Dr SG5 .....21 F5
Longmeadow Gn SG2 .....51 C1
Longmeadow Jun & Inf Schs SG2 .....51 B1
Longmore Cl WD3 .....172 F6
Longmore Gdns AL7 .....110 F6
Longridge WD7 .....156 B5
Longspring WD24 .....154 B2
Longstanton Ct HP2 .....105 B1
Longwood Rd SG14 .....112 F8
Longwood Sch WD23 .....167 F5
Loning The EN3 .....162 C1
Lonsdale HP2 .....124 E6
Lonsdale Cl Luton LU3 .....45 B5
Pinner HA5 .....175 E2
Lonsdale Ct SG1 .....50 F7
Lonsdale Rd SG1 .....50 F7
Lonsdale Sch SG1 .....50 F7
Loom La WD7 .....156 A2
Loom Pl WD7 .....156 A3
Loop Rd EN9 .....163 B7
Loppys Hill CM24 .....59 E6
Lorane Ct WD17 .....167 A7
Lord Mead La AL6,SG4 .....88 C7
Lord St Hoddesdon EN11 ..134 D6
Watford WD17 .....167 C6
Lords Ave CM23 .....76 B7
Lords Cl WD7 .....156 E7
Lords Mdw AL3 .....106 A5
Lords Pl 12 LU2 .....45 D1
Lords Wood AL7 .....111 C6
Lordship Ctr SG6 .....23 A3
Lordship Farm SG6 .....23 B2
Lordship Farm Prim Sch SG6 .....23 A3
Lordship La SG6 .....23 B4
Lordship Rd EN7 .....148 B1
Loreto Coll AL1 .....127 E3
Loring Rd HP4 .....122 C3
Lorne Rd HA3 .....176 F1
Lorraine Pk HA3 .....176 E3
Lorrimer Cl LU2 .....45 E6
Lothair Ct 3 AL10 .....130 A6
Lothair Rd LU2 .....46 A4
Loudwater Dr WD3 .....165 C5
Loudwater Ho WD3 .....165 C5
Loudwater Hts WD3 .....165 C6
Loudwater La WD3 .....165 E5
Loudwater Ridge WD3 ..165 C5
Louisa Cotts HP23 .....100 A3
Louise Wlk HP3 .....137 A3
Louisville Cl SG12 .....115 C4
Louvain Way WD25 .....154 B7
Lovatts WD3 .....166 A5
Love La
Abbots Langley WD5 .....139 F1
Ashwell SG7 .....4 A4
Kings Langley WD4 .....138 E3
Pinner HA5 .....175 E1
Lovel Cl HP1 .....124 A3
Lovell Cl SG4 .....35 A6
Lovell Rd EN1 .....162 B3
Lovering Rd EN7 .....147 C6
Lovett Rd AL2 .....142 A5
Low Hill Rd CM19 .....135 F6
Low Rd AL9 .....131 F8
Lowbell La AL2 .....142 E4
Lower Adeyfield Rd HP2 .....124 D4
Lower Barn HP3 .....138 F8
Lower Bourne Cl 5 SG12 .....93 C3
Lower Bourne Gdns SG12 .....93 C3
Lower Clabdens SG12 .....93 F1
Lower Cotts SG9 .....30 B2
Lower Dagnall St AL3 ..127 C3
Lower Derby Rd 4 WD17 .....167 C5
Lower Emms HP2 .....125 C8
Lower End HP22 .....60 B2
Lower Farm Cotts SG7 .....3 B7
Lower Gn AL6 .....90 E2
Lower Gower Rd SG8 .....7 D8
Lower Harpenden Rd LU1,LU2 .....64 C3
Lower Hatfield Rd SG13 .112 F1
Lower High St WD17 .....167 D4
Lower Icknield Way
Marsworth HP23 .....80 A1
Wilstone HP22,HP23 .....99 C7
Lower Innings SG5 .....34 D8
Lower King St SG8 .....7 D6
Lower Kings Rd HP4 .....122 C5
Lower Luton Rd AL4,AL5 ..86 C3
Lower Mardley Hill AL6 ..89 F8
Lower Mdw EN8 .....148 D4
Lower Paddock Rd WD19 .....167 E3
Lower Park Cres CM23 .....76 F5
Lower Paxton Rd AL1 .....127 E2
Lower Plantation WD3 ..165 C6
Lower Rd
Breachwood Green SG4 .....47 F1
Chorleywood WD3 .....164 D5
Great Amwell SG12 .....114 F6
Hemel Hempstead HP3 .....139 A5
Little Hallingbury CM22 .....98 C7
Lower Sales HP1 .....123 F2
Lower Sean SG2 .....51 A3
Lower Shott EN7 .....147 F5
Lower St CM24 .....59 F7
Lower Tail WD19 .....175 E7
Lower Tub WD23 .....168 D2
Lower Yott HP2 .....124 F2
Lowerfield AL7 .....111 A5
Lowes Cl SG1 .....37 C2
Lowestoft Rd WD24 .....167 B8
Loweswater Cl WD25 .....154 C6
Lowfield CM21 .....97 E1
Lowfield Ct EN11 .....135 A6
Lowfield La EN11 .....135 A6
Lowgate La
Dane End SG12 .....72 A4
Thundridge SG12 .....72 C5
Lowlands AL9 .....130 C8
Lowson Gr WD19 .....167 E2
Lowswood Cl HA6 .....174 C2
Lowther Cl WD6 .....169 F4
Loxley Ct SG12 .....93 E1
Loxley Rd HP4 .....121 F6
Loxwood Cl HP3 .....137 F8
Lucan Rd EN5 .....171 E6
Lucas Ct EN9 .....163 F6
Lucas Gdns LU3 .....45 B8
Lucas La Ashwell SG7 .....4 E4
Hitchin SG5 .....34 D7
Lucern Cl EN7 .....147 E4
Lucerne Way LU3 .....45 C4
Lucks Hill HP1 .....123 E3
Ludgate HP23 .....99 F4
Ludlow Ave LU1 .....63 E4
Ludlow Mead WD19 .....175 B7
Ludlow Way WD3 .....166 C5
Ludwick Cl AL7 .....110 F4
Ludwick Gn AL7 .....110 F5
Ludwick Way AL7 .....110 F5
Luffenham Ho 1 WD19 .175 D7
Lukes La HP23 .....79 D3
Lukes Lea HP23 .....80 A1
Lullington Cl LU2 .....46 C3
Lullington Garth WD6 ...170 B4
Lulworth Ave EN7 .....147 B2
Lumbards AL7 .....90 A1
Lumen Rd SG8 .....7 D7
Lunardi Ct SG11 .....55 C3
Lundin Wlk WD19 .....175 D6
Lundy Ho WD18 .....166 F4
Luton & Dunstable Hospl LU4 .....44 C2
Luton & Dunstable Hospl (Faringdon Wing) LU4 ..44 C3
Luton Airport Parkway Sta LU1 .....64 B5
Luton Dr The LU1 .....64 B3
Luton Ent Pk LU3 .....44 B8
Luton La Harpenden AL3 ..85 B1
Redbourn AL3 .....106 A8
Luton Maternity Hospl LU4 .....44 C2
Luton Mus & Art Gall* LU3 .....45 D2
Luton Rd Caddington LU1 ..63 A4
Cockernhoe LU2 .....46 E3
Dunstable LU5 .....44 A1
Great Offley SG5 .....33 B2
Harpenden AL5 .....85 D4
Kimpton SG4 .....66 B2
Luton LU4 .....44 A7
Markyate AL3 .....83 F7
Streatley LU3 .....31 A6
Luton Regional Sports Ctr LU2 .....46 A5
Luton Ret Pk LU1 .....64 A6
Luton Sixth Form Coll LU2 .....45 E4
Luton Sta LU2 .....63 E8
Luton Town FC LU1 .....63 C8
Luton Univ LU1 .....63 F7
Luton Univ, Putteridge Bury LU2 .....46 D6
Luton White Hill
Great Offley SG5 .....33 B2
Lilley LU2 .....46 F8
Luxembourg Cl LU3 .....44 D8
Luxford Pl CM21 .....97 F1
Luynes Rise SG9 .....40 E6
Lybury La AL3 .....105 F7
Lycaste Cl AL1 .....128 A2
Lych Gate WD25 .....154 D6
Lychgate Cotts HP3 .....137 B4
Lydekker Mews 1 AL5 .....86 A2
Lydia Ct AL9 .....144 C7
Lydia Mews AL9 .....144 C7
Lye Hill SG4 .....65 D7
Lye La AL2 .....141 A2
Lye The HP4 .....102 D6
Lygean Ave SG12 .....93 E1
Lygetun Dr LU3 .....44 F7
Lygrave SG2 .....69 C8
Lyle's Row SG4 .....34 F6
Lyles La AL8 .....110 E8
Lymans Rd SG15 .....11 A6
Lyme Ave HP4 .....121 D7
Lymington Ct WD25 .....154 A5
Lymington Rd SG1 .....50 B8
Lynbury Ct WD18 .....167 A6
Lynch Ct AL4 .....128 D2
Lynch Hill LU6 .....83 A8
Lynch The EN11 .....135 B6
Lyndale SG1 .....50 E4
Lyndhurst Ave HA5 .....175 B2
Lyndhurst Cl AL5 .....86 C2
Lyndhurst Dr AL5 .....86 C2
Lyndhurst Gdns HA5 .....175 B2
Lyndhurst Rd LU1 .....63 C7
Lyndon Ave HA5 .....175 E4
Lyndon Mead AL4 .....108 C2
Lyne Way HP1 .....123 F5
Lyneham Rd LU2 .....46 C1
Lynford Cl EN5 .....170 F4
Lynmouth Rd AL7 .....110 F6
Lynn Cl HA3 .....176 D1
Lynsey Cl AL3 .....106 A6
Lynton Ave Arlesey SG15 ..11 A5
St Albans AL1 .....128 C2
Lynton Crest EN6 .....159 A7
Lynton Ct CM23 .....76 E4
Lynton Par EN8 .....148 D1
Lynwood Ave LU2 .....46 A3
Lynwood Dr HA6 .....174 F2
Lynwood Hts WD3 .....165 C4
Lyon Way AL4 .....129 A3
Lyrical Way HP1 .....124 B5
Lys Hill Gdns SG14 .....113 B8
Lysander Cl HP3 .....137 A4
Lysander Way
Abbots Langley WD5 .....154 A7
Welwyn Garden City AL7 ..111 D7
Lysley Pl AL9 .....145 C4
Lytham Ave WD19 .....175 D5
Lytton Ave Enfield EN3 ...162 E1
Letchworth SG6 .....22 F5
Lytton Fields SG3 .....68 F5
Lytton Gdns AL8 .....110 D6
Lytton Rd HA5 .....175 E3
Lytton Way SG1 .....50 C6
Lyttons Way EN11 .....115 A1

M

Mabbutt Cl AL2 .....140 E1
Mabey's Wlk CM21 .....97 B1
Macaulay Rd LU4 .....44 A2
Macdonnell Gdns WD25 .153 F4
Macer's La EN10 .....148 F7
Macers Ct EN10 .....148 F7
Macfadyen Webb Ho SG6 .....23 A7
Macintosh Cl EN7 .....147 D5
Macintyre Sch HP22 .....60 C3
Mackenzie Sq SG2 .....51 B3
Mackerel Hall SG8 .....7 B6
Maddesfield Ct WD7 .....156 E6
Maddison Hts WD18 .....166 F5
Maddles SG6 .....23 D4
Maddox Rd Harlow CM20 .117 E1
Hemel Hempstead HP2 .....125 B3
Made Feld SG1 .....50 F5
Madford Ret Pk LU4 .....44 F2
Madgeways Cl SG12 .....114 F5
Madgeways La SG12 .....114 F5
Magdalene Ct SG7 .....12 F1
Magellan Cl SG2 .....51 D5
Magisters Lodge WD3 ..166 A3
Magna Cl AL5 .....107 D6
Magnaville Rd
Bishop's Stortford CM23 .....76 E4
Bushey WD23 .....168 F2
Magnolia Ave WD5 .....154 A7
Magnolia Cl
Hertford SG13 .....114 A6
Park Street AL2 .....141 D5
Magpie Cl EN1 .....162 A1
Magpie Cres SG2 .....51 D4
Magpie Hall Rd WD23 .....176 E8
Magpie Wlk 2 AL10 .....130 A3
Magpies The LU2 .....45 E6
Maiden St SG4 .....24 C1
Maidenhall Inf Sch LU4 ..45 A2
Maidenhall Jun Sch LU4 .45 A2
Maidenhall Rd LU4 .....45 A2
Maidenhead St 3 SG14 .113 D6
Maidenhead Yd SG14 ..113 D6
Main Ave HA6 .....174 C7
Main Par WD3 .....164 C5
Main Rd SG14 .....91 D3
Main Rd N HP4 .....81 A6
Main Rd S HP4 .....81 D4
Maison Alfont HA3 .....176 E2
Maitland Rd CM24 .....59 E6
Major Haddock Cl SG8 .....7 C7
Malden Fields WD23 .....167 D4
Malden Ho 15 WD19 .....175 C7
Malden Lodge 2 WD17 .167 A7
Malden Rd
Borehamwood WD6 .....170 A6
Watford WD17 .....167 B7
Maldon Ct AL5 .....86 B2
Malham Cl LU4 .....44 F2
Malins Cl EN5 .....171 C4
Mall The AL2 .....141 C4
Mallard Gdns LU3 .....45 A5
Mallard Rd Royston SG8 .....7 C6
Stevenage SG2 .....51 D2
Watford WD5 .....154 A8
Mallard Way
Northwood HA6 .....174 C3
Roydon CM19 .....116 A1
Watford WD25 .....154 E3
Mallards Ct WD19 .....175 F7
Mallards The HP3 .....138 F6
Mallion Ct EN9 .....163 F6
Mallories CM20 .....117 F2
Mallow The LU3 .....44 F3
Mallow Wlk
Goff's Oak EN7 .....147 D3
Royston SG8 .....7 E5
Malm Cl WD3 .....173 D8
Malmes Croft HP3 .....125 C1
Malmsdale AL8 .....89 D2
Maltby Dr EN1 .....162 B1
Malthouse Ct 5 AL1 .....127 D2
Malthouse Gn LU2 .....46 F1
Malthouse La SG5 .....12 A7
Malthouse Pl WD7 .....156 A5
Malthouse The 15 SG14 .113 D6
Malting Cotts SG9 .....40 D5
Malting La Aldbury HP23 .101 D5
Braughing SG11 .....55 E7
Dagnall HP4 .....81 C5
Much Hadham SG10 .....74 F2
Malting Mead AL10 .....130 C6
Maltings Cl Baldock SG7 ...13 B1
Royston SG8 .....7 C7
Maltings Ct 2 SG7 .....23 F8
Maltings Dr AL4 .....108 C8
Maltings Ind Est The SG12 .....115 D4
Maltings La SG8 .....9 E2
Maltings Mews SG13 .....113 C5
Maltings Orch SG5 .....20 D3
Maltings The
Abbots Langley WD4 .....153 C5
Hemel Hempstead HP2 ...124 D4
Letchworth SG6 .....12 C1
Royston SG8 .....7 C7
St Albans AL1 .....127 D3
Walkern SG2 .....52 B8
Malus Cl HP2 .....125 A4
Malvern Cl Bushey WD23 .168 C3
Hatfield AL10 .....129 F6
St Albans AL4 .....128 C7
Malvern Rd Enfield EN3 ..162 E2
Luton LU1 .....63 B7
Malvern Way
Croxley Green WD3 .....166 B4
Hemel Hempstead HP2 .....124 F6
Malvern Way Inf Sch WD3 .....166 C4
Malzeard Ct 17 LU3 .....45 D1
Malzeard Rd LU3 .....45 D1
Manan Cl HP3 .....125 C1
Manchester Cl SG1 .....36 F3
Manchester St LU1 .....63 E7
Mancroft Rd LU1 .....62 E2
Mandela Pl 4 WD24 .....167 D7
Mandelyns HP4 .....121 E7
Mandeville SG2 .....69 C8
Mandeville Cl
Hertford SG13 .....113 C3
Hoddesdon EN10 .....134 F3
Watford WD17 .....153 F1
Mandeville Dr AL1 .....141 D8
Mandeville Prim Sch
Sawbridgeworth CM21 .....97 D3
St Albans AL1 .....141 D8
Mandeville Rd
Enfield EN3 .....162 E3
Hertford SG13 .....113 C3
Potters Bar EN6 .....159 C7
Mandeville Rise AL8 .....110 D8
Mangrove Dr SG13 .....113 E4
Mangrove Gn LU2 .....46 E4
Mangrove La SG13 .....113 E2
Mangrove Rd
Cockernhoe LU2 .....46 E4
Hertford SG13 .....113 E5
Luton LU2 .....46 C2
Manhattan Ave WD18 .....166 F5
Manland Ave AL5 .....86 C2
Manland Prim Sch AL5 ...86 B3
Manland Way AL5 .....86 C3
Manley Highway SG5 .....34 B7
Manley Highway Cotts SG5 .....34 A7
Manley Rd HP2 .....124 E4
Manly Dixon Dr EN3 .....162 E2
Mannicotts AL8 .....110 B6
Manning Ct WD19 .....167 D3
Manning Pl LU2 .....46 E2
Manor Ave HP3 .....138 D8
Manor Cl Barnet EN5 .....171 E5
Berkhamsted HP4 .....122 C4
Hatfield AL10 .....129 F8
Hertford SG14 .....113 D8
Ickleford SG5 .....21 E3
Letchworth SG6 .....22 F3
Manor Cotts
Chorleywood WD3 .....164 B3
Northwood HA6 .....174 F2
Manor Cres SG4 .....35 B6
Manor Ct Caddington LU1 ..62 F4
Cheshunt EN8 .....162 D8
Enfield EN1 .....162 B3
Harefield UB9 .....173 C1

Manor Ct *continued*
Potters Bar EN6 158 F7
Radlett WD7 155 F1
Waltham Abbey EN9 163 D6
Manor Dr AL2 141 A4
Manor Farm Bsns Pk SG5 19 A6
Manor Farm Cl LU4 44 C3
Manor Farm La LU7 61 C8
Manor Farm Rd EN1 162 B4
Manor Farm Stables SG3 68 C5
Manor Fields Prim Sch CM23 76 D5
Manor Ho The [2] HA6 174 F5
Manor House Dr
Northwood HA6 174 B3
Stevenage SG2 51 D7
Manor House Gdns WD5 153 D8
Manor Links CM23 77 C7
Manor Lodge Sch WD7 143 C1
Manor Par AL10 129 F8
Manor Place Ind Est WD6 170 C6
Manor Pound Rd LU7 80 A7
Manor Rd Barnet EN5 171 E5
Bishop's Stortford CM23 77 A7
Caddington LU1 62 F2
Cheddington LU7 79 F7
Harlow CM17 118 C5
Hatfield AL10 129 F8
Hoddesdon EN11 135 A7
Lea Valley AL4 86 F2
London Colney AL2 142 C5
Luton LU1 63 F6
Potters Bar EN6 159 A8
St Albans AL1 127 E4
Stansted Mountfitchet CM24 59 E5
Tring HP23 100 A4
Waltham Abbey EN9 163 D6
Watford WD17 167 B8
Manor St HP4 122 D4
Manor View SG2 51 B1
Manor Way
Borehamwood WD6 170 C6
Cheshunt EN8 148 E1
Croxley Green WD3 166 B5
Letchworth SG6 22 F3
Potters Bar EN6 145 A1
Manorcroft Par [6] EN8 148 D1
Manorside EN5 171 E5
Manorville Rd HP3 138 C7
Mansard Cl HP23 100 A3
Mansards The AL1 127 F4
Manscott Ho [8] WD19 175 D7
Manscroft Rd HP1 124 B5
Mansdale Rd AL3 105 F4
Manse Ct AL3 83 F5
Mansells La SG4 67 F3
Mansfield CM21 97 A1
Mansfield Ct SG14 113 C8
Mansfield Gdns SG14 113 C8
Mansfield Mews [1] SG7 23 F8
Mansfield Rd Baldock SG7 23 E8
Luton LU4 45 B1
Mansion Dr HP23 100 B3
Mansion The HP4 122 E6
Manston Cl EN8 148 C1
Manston Dr CM23 59 B1
Manston Way AL4 128 D2
Manton Dr LU2 45 D3
Manton Rd Hitchin SG4 35 B6
Holdbrook EN3 163 A1
Manx Cl LU4 45 A2
Maple Ave
Bishop's Stortford CM23 76 D8
St Albans AL3 127 C7
Maple Cl
Bishop's Stortford CM23 76 D8
Hatfield AL10 130 A4
Watford WD23 167 E7
Maple Cotts AL5 107 B5
Maple Cross Jun Mix Inf Sch WD3 172 E5
Maple Ct
[5] Borehamwood WD6 170 A5
[16] Luton LU1 63 D6
[5] Pinner HA5 175 C1
Stanstead Abbotts SG12 115 D3
Watford WD25 154 D3
Maple Flats AL5 86 A3
Maple Gn HP1 123 E5
Maple Gr
Bishop's Stortford CM23 76 D8
Watford WD17 167 A8
Welwyn Garden City AL7 89 F1
Maple Leaf Cl WD5 154 A7
Maple Lodge SG14 113 C5
Maple Lodge Cl WD3 172 E6
Maple Pk EN11 135 C6
Maple Rd AL5 85 F1
Maple Rd E LU4 63 B8
Maple Rd W LU4 63 B8
Maple River Ind Est CM20 118 B6
Maple Sch AL1 127 E4
Maple Spring CM23 76 D8
Maple Way
Kensworth Common LU6 82 E8
Royston SG8 7 E8
Maplecroft La EN9 135 E2
Maplefield AL2 141 C2
Mapleleaf Villas EN8 148 D4
Maples Ct [1] SG5 34 E7
Maples The
Goff's Oak EN7 147 E3
Hitchin SG4 34 F5
Maplethorpe Ct SG12 93 C1
Mapleton Cres EN3 162 C1
Maplewood SG12 93 C3
Maplewood Ct [3] HA6 174 F5
Maran Ave AL6 89 C4
Marbury Pl LU3 44 F4
Marchmont Gn HP2 124 D5
Marconi Way AL4 128 D3
Marcus Cl [1] SG1 51 C8
Marden Hill Ho AL6 111 F8
Mardle Cl LU1 62 E2
Mardlebury Rd SG3 69 B1
Mardley Ave AL6 90 A8
Mardley Dell AL6 68 F1
Mardley Hill AL6 69 A1
Mardley Hts AL6 69 A1
Mardley Wood AL6 68 F1
Mardleybury Ct SG3 69 A1
Mardon [1] HA5 175 F3
Mardyke Rd CM20 118 A2
Marford Rd
Hatfield AL4,AL6 109 C7
Wheathampstead AL4 108 E8
Margaret Ave AL3 127 D5
Margaret Cl
Abbots Langley WD5 153 F7
Potters Bar EN6 159 C6
Waltham Abbey EN9 163 D6
Margaret Cotts WD7 156 C8
Margaret Wix Prim Sch AL3 127 C7
Margeholes WD19 175 E8
Margery Wood AL7 90 A1
Margherita Pl EN9 163 F5
Margrave Gdns [4] CM23 76 E5
Marguerite Way CM23 76 C6
Marian Gdns WD25 154 B6
Maricas Ave HA3 176 D2
Marigold Pl CM17 118 B4
Marina Gdns EN8 148 C1
Mariner Way [2] HP2 125 A2
Marion Cl WD23 167 F8
Marion Wlk [4] HP2 124 F8
Mark Hall Comp Sch CM17 118 C3
Mark Hall Cycle Mus & Gdns* CM20 118 B3
Mark Hall Moors CM20 118 B3
Mark Rd HP2 125 B5
Markab Rd HA6 175 A5
Markeston Gn WD19 175 D6
Market Hill
Buntingford SG9 40 E7
[6] Royston SG8 7 D6
Royston SG8 7 D5
Market Ho CM20 117 D1
Market Oak La HP3 139 A7
Market Pl Hatfield AL10 130 B6
[6] Hertford SG14 113 D6
Hitchin SG5 34 E7
St Albans AL3 127 D3
Stevenage SG1 50 D5
Watford WD17 167 C5
Market Sq
[6] Bishop's Stortford CM23 76 F7
Luton LU1 63 B6
Stevenage SG1 50 D5
Waltham Abbey EN9 163 C6
Market St
[7] Bishop's Stortford CM23 76 F7
Harlow CM17 118 C4
Hertford SG14 113 D6
Watford WD18 167 B5
Markfield Cl LU3 45 C7
Markham Cl WD6 169 F6
Markham Rd
Hammond Street EN7 147 C6
Luton LU3 45 C8
Markyate Rd LU1 63 B1
Markyate Village Sch AL3 83 D6
Marlborough Cl
Bishop's Stortford CM23 76 F5
Oaklands AL6 89 F8
Weston SG4 37 B8
Marlborough Ct
Luton LU1 63 D7
Northwood HA6 174 F3
Marlborough Gate AL1 127 E3
Marlborough Ho HP4 122 B3
Marlborough Pk AL5 107 C7
Marlborough Rd
Luton LU3 45 D1
St Albans AL1 127 E3
Stevenage SG2 51 C5
Watford WD18 167 B5
Marlborough Rise HP2 124 E6
Marlborough Sch AL1 141 C8
Marle Gdns EN9 163 C7
Marley Ct EN10 148 F8
Marley Rd AL7 111 A4
Marlin Cl HP4 121 F5
Marlin Copse HP4 122 A3
Marlin Hill HP23 120 A8
Marlin Sq WD5 153 F8
Marlins Cl WD3 164 E7
Marlins End HP4 121 F3
Marlins Mdw WD18 166 D3
Marlins The HA6 174 F5
Marlins Turn HP1 124 B6
Marlow Ave LU1 63 A8
Marlowe Cl SG2 51 C8
Marlowes HP1 124 D3
Marmet Ave SG6 22 E6
Marnham Rise HP1 124 A5
Marquis Cl
Bishop's Stortford CM23 76 B7
Harpenden AL5 86 D2
Marquis Ct [9] LU2 45 D1
Marquis La AL5 86 D2
Marrilyne Ave EN3 162 F1
Marriott Rd Barnet EN5 171 D6
Luton LU3 45 B6
Marriott Terr WD3 164 F5
Marriotts CM17 118 C5
Marriotts Sch SG2 51 A6
Marriotts Way HP3 124 D1
Marryat Rd EN1 162 B4
Marschefield SG5 11 E6
Marsden Cl AL8 110 B4
Marsden Gn AL8 110 B4
Marsden Rd AL8 110 C5
Marsh Cl EN8 162 F6
Marsh Hill EN9 149 E4
Marsh Ho LU3 44 F4
Marsh La Harlow CM17 118 E5
Stanstead Abbotts SG12 115 D4
Ware SG12 114 E8
Marsh Rd LU3 44 F4
Marshal's Dr AL1 128 A6
Marshall Ave AL3 127 F6
Marshall Rd LU2 46 C2
Marshall's La SG12,SG11 72 C2
Marshalls Heath La AL4, AL5 87 A4
Marshalls Way AL4 86 F2
Marshals Ct AL1 128 B5
Marshalswick La AL1 128 B6
Marshbarns CM23 76 C8
Marshcroft Dr EN8 148 F1
Marshcroft La HP23 100 D6
Marshe Cl EN6 159 D7
Marshgate Harlow CM20 117 E3
Stevenage SG1 50 D5
Marshgate Dr SG13 113 E7
Marshgate Trad Est SG13 113 E7
Marshmoor Cres AL9 130 D1
Marshmoor La AL9 144 D8
Marsom Gr LU3 45 B8
Marston Cl HP3 125 A2
Marston Ct HP23 79 B4
Marston Gdns LU2 45 D4
Marston Rd EN11 135 B7
Marsworth Ave HA5 175 D2
Marsworth CE Inf Sch HP23 80 A2
Marsworth Cl WD18 166 E2
Marsworth Rd LU7 80 D4
Marsworth Resr Nature Reserve* HP23 100 A8
Marten Gate AL4 128 A7
Martham Ct AL5 86 C3
Marthorne Cres HA3 176 D1
Martian Ave HP2 124 F6
Martin Cl AL10 130 A3
Martin Way SG6 22 D5
Martindale Ct SG7 23 F6
Martindale Prim Sch HP1 123 F4
Martindale Rd HP1 123 F4
Martindales The LU2 63 F7
Martinfield AL7 110 F7
Martinfield Bsns Ctr AL7 110 F7
Martingale Rd SG8 7 E6
Martini Dr EN3 163 A2
Martins Cl WD7 155 E3
Martins Dr Cheshunt EN8 148 E3
Hertford SG13 114 B6
Martins Way SG1 36 E1
Martins Wlk WD6 170 A5
Martins Wood Prim Sch SG1 37 B1
Martlesham AL7 111 E6
Martyr Cl AL1 141 D7
Marwood Cl WD4 138 F2
Mary Brash Ct LU2 46 C3
Mary Cross Cl HP23 100 D1
Mary Exton Jun Mix Inf Sch SG4 35 C7
Mary McArthur Pl CM24 59 E8
Mary Park Gdns CM23 76 F4
Mary Proud Ct AL6 89 E7
Maryland AL10 129 F5
Marymead Ct SG2 69 A8
Marymead Dr SG2 69 A8
Marymead Ind Est SG2 69 B8
Maryport Rd LU4 45 A2
Masefield SG4 35 C7
Masefield Ave
Borehamwood WD6 170 B4
Stanmore HA7 176 F5
Masefield Ct AL5 86 B4
Masefield Rd AL5 86 B4
Masefield Way SG8 2 D1
Maslen Rd AL4 128 C1
Mason Cl WD6 170 D7
Mason Way EN9 163 F6
Mason's Yd [2] HP4 122 D4
Masons Ct CM23 76 E7
Masons Rd Enfield EN1 162 C3
Hemel Hempstead HP2 125 B4
Masterman Wharf [12] CM23 76 F7
Masters Cl LU1 63 B5
Matching La CM23 76 D8
Mathams Dr CM23 76 D5
Mathews Cl SG1 36 D1
Matlock Cl EN5 171 D4
Matlock Cres Luton LU4 44 C1
South Oxhey WD19 175 C7
Matthew Gate SG4 35 A5
Mattocke Rd SG5 21 C1
Maud Jane's Cl LU7 80 E5
Maude Cres WD24 154 B1
Maulden Cl LU2 46 C1
Maxted Cl HP2 125 C5
Maxted Cnr HP2 125 B6
Maxted Rd HP2 125 C6
Maxwell Cl WD3 173 A8
Maxwell Rd
Borehamwood WD6 170 B6
Northwood HA6 174 E3
St Albans AL1 128 B2
Stevenage SG1 50 B5
Maxwell Rise WD19 167 E2
Maxwell's Path SG5 34 D8
May Cl AL3 127 D5
May Cotts WD18 167 C4
May Gdns WD6 169 D3
May St Great Chishill SG8 9 E2
Luton LU1 63 E5
Mayall Cl EN3 163 A1
Maybury Ave EN8 148 B3
Maybury Cl EN1 162 B1
Maycock Gr HA6 174 F4
Maycroft Letchworth SG6 12 A1
Pinner HA5 175 B1
Maycroft Rd EN7 147 E5
Maydencroft La SG4 34 E3
Maydwell Lodge WD6 169 F7
Mayer Rd EN9 163 B3
Mayes Cl CM23 77 D8
Mayfair Cl AL4 128 C8
Mayfare WD3 166 D4
Mayfield
Waltham Abbey EN9 163 D5
Welwyn Garden City AL8 89 C2
Mayfield Cl Harlow CM17 118 F4
Harpenden AL5 85 E3
Mayfield Inf Sch EN8 148 E4
Mayfield Pk CM23 76 D3
Mayfield Rd LU2 46 B4
Mayflower Ave HP2 124 D3
Mayflower Cl
Codicote SG4 67 F1
Hertingfordbury SG14 112 E4
Lower Nazeing EN9 149 E8
Mayflower Gdns CM23 76 B6
Mayflower Rd AL2 141 B4
Mayhill Rd EN5 171 E3
Maylands Ave HP2 125 B5
Maylands Ct HP2 125 B4
Maylands Rd WD19 175 C6
Mayles Cl SG1 50 B7
Maylin Cl SG4 35 C8
Maylins Dr CM21 97 D2
Maynard Ct
Holdbrook EN3 163 A1
Waltham Abbey EN9 163 F5
Maynard Dr AL1 141 D8
Maynard Pl EN6 146 E2
Maynard Rd HP2 124 D2
Mayne Ave Luton LU4 44 C4
St Albans AL3 127 A2
Mayo Cl EN8 148 C3
Mayo Gdns HP1 124 B2
Maypole St CM17 118 C1
Mays La EN5 171 D3
Mayshades Cl SG3 69 A2
Maythorne Cl WD18 166 E5
Maytree Cres WD24 153 F4
Maytree La HA7 176 F3
Maytrees Hitchin SG4 35 A6
Radlett WD7 156 A2
Maze Green Hts CM23 76 C7
Maze Green Rd CM23 76 D7
Mazoe Cl CM23 76 F5
Mazoe Rd CM23 76 F5
McAdam Cl EN11 135 A8
Mcclintock Pl EN3 163 B2
McDonald Ct AL10 130 A3
McDougall Rd [13] HP4 122 D4
McGredy EN7 148 B2
McKellar Cl WD23 176 C8
McKenzie Rd EN10 135 A3
Mead Bsns Ctr SG13 113 E7
Mead Cl Harrow HA3 176 D2
Stevenage SG1 50 F6
Mead Ct
Stansted Mountfitchet CM24 59 D7
Waltham Abbey EN9 163 B5
Mead Ho AL10 130 B8
Mead La SG13 113 E7
Mead Park Ind Est CM20 117 F4
Mead Pl WD3 165 B1
Mead Rd WD7 157 A6
Mead The Cheshunt EN8 148 C2
Hitchin SG5 21 F2
Hoddesdon EN10 135 B2
South Oxhey WD19 175 E7
Mead View SG9 43 E6
Mead Way WD23 167 E7
Meadgate Rd EN9 135 C3
Meadow Ave WD7 156 C8
Meadow Cl Barnet EN5 171 F3
Bricket Wood AL2 141 A2
Datchworth SG3 69 D1
Enfield EN3 162 E1
Hertford SG13 113 F7
London Colney AL2 142 D4
St Albans AL4 128 C6
Tring HP23 100 A4
Welham Green AL9 144 D7
Meadow Croft
Caddington LU1 62 F4
Hatfield AL10 129 F5
Meadow Dell AL10 129 F5
Meadow Gn AL8 110 C6
Meadow La LU7 80 E3
Meadow Rd
Berkhamsted HP4 122 B6
Borehamwood WD6 170 B7
Bushey WD23 168 B4
Hemel Hempstead HP3 139 A7
Luton LU3 45 B4
Watford WD25 154 B5
Meadow The
Hertford Heath SG13 114 E2
Welwyn Garden City AL7 111 C6
Meadow View
Buntingford SG9 40 D6
Whitwell SG4 66 E6
Meadow Way
Bedmond WD5 139 F4
Caddington LU1 62 E4
Codicote SG4 67 E1
Great Offley SG5 33 C3
Hitchin SG5 34 D6
Kings Langley WD4 139 A1
Letchworth SG6 22 F5
Potters Bar EN6 159 A5
Rickmansworth WD3 165 C2
Sawbridgeworth CM21 98 A1
Stevenage SG1 50 F5
Stotfold SG5 11 F6
Therfield SG8 16 A6
Meadow Way The HA3 176 E2
Meadow Wlk
Harpenden AL5 107 C8
Standon SG11 55 E2
Meadow Wood Sch WD23 168 C4
Meadowbank Hitchin SG4 22 B1
Kings Langley WD4 139 A1
Watford WD19 167 C2
Meadowbanks EN5 171 A4
Meadowbrook HP23 100 B6
Meadowcroft
Berkhamsted HP4 121 D7
Bushey WD23 168 B3
St Albans AL1 142 A8
Stansted Mountfitchet CM24 59 E7
Meadowcross EN9 163 E5
Meadowlands CM23 59 A2
Meadows The
Bishop's Stortford CM23 76 E5
Breachwood Green SG4 47 E1
Hemel Hempstead HP1 123 E4
Sawbridgeworth CM21 98 A2
Meadows View Cotts SG12 94 C7
Meadowside WD25 154 B8
Meadowsweet Cl CM23 76 C6
Meads La AL4 87 D1
Meads Prim Sch The LU3 45 A6
Meads The
Berkhamsted HP4 121 F6
Bricket Wood AL2 140 F2
Letchworth SG6 22 E6
Luton LU3 45 A3
Stansted Mountfitchet CM24 59 F6
Tring HP23 100 B4
Meadview Rd SG12 114 D8
Meadway Barnet EN5 171 F5
Berkhamsted HP4 122 E5
Colney Heath AL4 143 D8
Enfield EN3 162 D3
Harpenden AL5 107 E8
Hoddesdon EN11 135 A4
Knebworth SG3 68 F4
Stevenage SG1 50 A6
Welwyn Garden City AL7 110 F4
Stevenage SG1 50 B7
Meadway Cl HA5 176 B4
Meadway The EN6 146 F2
Meautys AL3 127 A1
Medalls Link SG2 51 A3
Medalls Path SG2 51 A3
Medcalf Rd EN3 162 F2
Medina Rd LU4 45 A1
Medlows AL5 85 E2
Medow Mead WD7 155 F6
Medway Cl WD25 154 C5
Medway Rd HP2 124 F8
Medwick Mews HP2 125 B8
Mees Cl LU3 31 A1
Meeting Alley WD17 167 C5
Meeting House La
Baldock SG7 12 E1
Buntingford SG9 40 E7
Megg La WD4 138 B1
Melbourn Rd SG8 7 D7
Melbourn St SG8 7 D6
Melbourne Cl
St Albans AL3 127 F7
Stotfold SG5 11 F6
Melbourne Ct
Cheshunt EN8 162 F5
Welwyn Garden City AL8 110 B5
Melbourne Rd WD23 168 B3
Melford Cl [3] LU2 46 D1
Melings The HP2 125 B8
Melne Rd SG2 69 B8
Melrose Ave
Borehamwood WD6 170 B4
Potters Bar EN6 159 B7
Melrose Ct EN8 148 D2
Melrose Pl WD17 153 F1
Melson Sq [8] LU1 63 E7
Melson St LU1 63 E7
Melsted Rd HP1 124 B3
Melvern Cl SG2 69 B7
Melvyn Cl EN7 147 B3

Memorial Rd LU3 ....44 F4
Mendip Cl AL4 ....128 C8
Mendip Rd WD23 ....168 C3
Mendip Way
Hemel Hempstead HP2 ....124 E6
Luton LU3 ....44 C8
Mendlesham AL7 ....111 E6
Mentley La SG11 ....54 E4
Mentley La E SG11 ....55 D4
Mentley La W SG11 ....55 C4
Mentmore* LU7 ....61 C4
Mentmore Cross Rds
LU7 ....60 F6
Mentmore Rd
Cheddington LU7 ....79 F8
St Albans AL1 ....127 E1
Mentmore View HP23 ....99 F5
Mepham Cres HA3 ....176 C3
Mepham Gdns HA3 ....176 C3
Mercer Pl HA5 ....175 C1
Mercers HP2 ....124 E5
Mercers Ave CM23 ....76 B4
Mercers Row AL1 ....127 C1
Merchant Dr SG13 ....113 F7
Merchant Taylors' Sch
HA6 ....166 E1
Merchants Wlk SG7 ....13 B1
Mercia Rd SG7 ....24 A8
Mercury Ho WD18 ....166 E5
Mercury Wlk 1 HP2 ....124 F6
Mereden Ct AL1 ....141 C8
Meredews SG6 ....23 B7
Meredith Cl HA5 ....175 D3
Meredith Rd SG1 ....51 A8
Merefield CM21 ....97 E1
Meriden Ho 3 EN5 ....171 E5
Meriden Prim Sch
WD25 ....154 D3
Meriden Way WD25 ....154 E2
Meridian Sch SG8 ....7 E7
Meridian Way SG12 ....115 B5
Merle Ave UB9 ....173 C1
Merlin Ctr The AL4 ....128 F3
Merlin Way WD25 ....153 F5
Merling Croft HP4 ....121 E7
Mermaid Cl SG4 ....35 B7
Merrill Pl 2 CM23 ....76 E5
Merritt Wlk AL9 ....144 B8
Merrow Dr HP1 ....123 E4
Merrows Cl HA6 ....174 C4
Merry Hill Inf Sch
WD23 ....168 B2
Merry Hill Mount WD23 ....168 B1
Merry Hill Rd WD23 ....168 B1
Merryfield WD17 ....154 A1
Merryfields AL4 ....128 E3
Mersey Pl
Hemel Hempstead HP2 ....124 F8
1 Luton LU1 ....63 D7
Merton Rd Enfield EN2 ....161 D1
Watford WD18 ....167 B5
Meryfield Cl WD6 ....169 F7
Meryfield Prim Sch
WD6 ....169 F8
Metford Cres EN3 ....163 A1
Metro Ctr St Albans AL4 ....127 F7
Watford WD18 ....166 D2
Metropolis Ctr WD6 ....170 A6
Metropolitan Mews
WD18 ....166 E5
Metropolitan Pl WD18 ....166 F5
Metropolitan Station App
WD18 ....166 F5
Meux Cl EN7 ....162 A8
Mews The
Bishop's Stortford CM22 ....77 A3
3 Harpenden AL5 ....86 B1
Letchworth SG6 ....12 C1
Sawbridgeworth CM21 ....97 E3
Stansted Mountfitchet CM24 ....59 F7
Meyer Gn EN1 ....162 A1
Meyrick Ave LU1 ....63 C6
Meyrick Ct LU1 ....63 D6
Mezen Cl HA6 ....174 D5
Michael Muir Ho SG5 ....21 D1
Michaels Rd CM23 ....59 A2
Micklefield Rd HP2 ....125 C3
Micklefield Way WD6 ....156 E1
Micklem Dr HP1 ....123 F4
Micklem Prim Sch HP1 ....124 A4
Midcot Way HP4 ....121 F6
Middle Drift SG8 ....7 C6
Middle Furlong WD23 ....168 B5
Middle Hill HP1 ....123 E3
Middle La HP3 ....137 A1
Middle Ope WD24 ....154 B2
Middle Rd
Berkhamsted HP4 ....122 B4
Waltham Abbey EN9 ....163 B7
Middle Row
5 Bishop's Stortford CM23 ....76 F6
1 Stevenage SG1 ....50 C7
Middle St EN9 ....149 F8
Middle Way WD24 ....154 B2
Middle Way The HA3 ....176 F1
Middlefield
Hatfield AL10 ....130 A6
Welwyn Garden City AL7 ....110 E3
Middlefield Ave EN11 ....135 A8
Middlefield Cl
Hoddesdon EN11 ....135 A8
St Albans AL4 ....128 C6
Middlefield La SG16 ....10 C7
Middlefield Rd EN11 ....135 A8
Middlefields SG6 ....11 F1
Middlefields Ct SG6 ....11 F1
Middleknights Hill HP1 ....124 A6
Middlesborough Cl SG1 ....36 F2
Middleton Mid Sch
SG12 ....114 D7
Middleton Rd Luton LU2 ....46 D4
Rickmansworth WD3 ....165 A1
Midhurst SG6 ....22 F8
Midhurst Gdns LU3 ....45 C4
Midland Cotts SG5 ....22 A1
Midland Ho 5 AL1 ....127 E3
Midland Rd
Hemel Hempstead HP2 ....124 D3
Luton LU2 ....63 E8
Midland Way SG16 ....10 B3
Midway AL3 ....141 B8
Mike Mably Ho AL10 ....129 F7
Milbourne Ct 1 WD17 ....167 A7
Milburn Cl LU3 ....31 B1
Milby Ct WD6 ....169 F8
Mildmay Rd SG1 ....37 B1
Mildred Ave
Borehamwood WD6 ....170 B5
Watford WD18 ....167 A5
Mile Cl EN9 ....163 C6
Mile House Cl AL1 ....142 A8
Mile House La AL1 ....142 A8
Milestone Cl SG2 ....51 D4
Milestone Rd Hitchin SG5 ....21 D2
Knebworth SG3 ....69 A5
Milford Cl AL4 ....128 D7
Milford Hill AL5 ....86 D4
Milksey La SG4 ....36 C5
Mill Bridge Barnet EN5 ....171 F3
Hertford SG14 ....113 C6
Mill Cl Buntingford SG9 ....40 E7
Hatfield AL8 ....110 A5
Hemel Hempstead, Nash Mills
HP3 ....139 A6
Hemel Hempstead, Piccotts End
HP1 ....124 B7
Hitchin SG4 ....35 C8
Stotfold SG5 ....12 A6
Ware SG12 ....93 D1
Wingrave HP22 ....60 A3
Mill Cnr EN5 ....171 F8
Mill Cotts LU7 ....60 D8
Mill End SG11 ....55 F2
Mill Farm Cl HA5 ....175 C1
Mill Gdns HP23 ....100 A4
Mill Green La AL9 ....110 E1
Mill Green Mus & Mill*
AL9 ....130 E8
Mill Green Rd AL7 ....110 E5
Mill Ground Cotts SG4 ....24 C1
Mill Hill Farnham CM23 ....58 E5
Royston SG8 ....7 E4
Stansted Mountfitchet
CM24 ....59 E6
Mill La Albury SG11 ....57 C6
Arlesey SG15 ....10 F4
Cheshunt EN8 ....148 E3
Flamstead AL3 ....84 A1
Harlow CM17 ....118 E4
Hatfield Heath CM22 ....98 F3
Hexton SG5 ....19 C3
Hitchin SG4 ....34 F3
Hoddesdon EN10 ....135 A2
Kings Langley WD4 ....139 A2
Meesden SG9 ....30 A5
Sawbridgeworth CM21 ....97 F3
Stotfold SG5 ....12 A6
Therfield SG8 ....15 F8
Watton at S SG12 ....71 A6
Welwyn AL6 ....89 C5
Weston SG4 ....24 C1
Wingrave HP22 ....60 C2
Mill Lane Cl EN10 ....134 F2
Mill Mead Prim Sch
SG14 ....113 C6
Mill Race SG12 ....115 D4
Mill Rd Hertford SG14 ....113 D6
Royston SG8 ....7 D7
St Ippolyts SG4 ....35 A3
Mill Side CM24 ....59 E6
Mill St Ashwell SG7 ....4 D4
Berkhamsted HP4 ....122 C4
Bishop's Stortford CM23 ....77 A5
Hemel Hempstead HP3 ....138 D8
Luton LU1 ....63 D8
Mill Stream Lodge WD3 ....173 A8
Mill View AL2 ....141 D4
Mill View Rd HP23 ....99 F4
Mill Way
Breachwood Green SG4 ....47 D2
Rickmansworth WD3 ....164 F1
Watford WD23 ....167 E8
Millacres 1 SG12 ....93 E1
Milland Ct WD6 ....170 D8
Millard Way SG4 ....22 C1
Millbank HP3 ....138 D7
Millbridge Mews 2
SG14 ....113 C6
Millbrook Ct SG12 ....93 D2
Millbrook Rd WD23 ....167 F8
Millbrook Sch EN8 ....148 E2
Millcrest Rd EN7 ....147 B3
Millcroft CM23 ....59 A1
Millennium Ct WD3 ....165 E2
Millennium Wharf WD3 ....165 E1
Miller Ave EN3 ....163 A1
Miller Cl HA5 ....175 C1
Millers Cl CM23 ....76 C5
Millers Ct SG14 ....113 D5
Millers La SG12 ....115 C4
Millers Rise AL1 ....127 E2
Millers View SG10 ....74 E1
Millfield
Berkhamsted HP4 ....122 D5
Harlow CM17 ....118 C4
Thundridge SG12 ....93 E8
Millfield *continued*
Welwyn Garden City AL7 ....111 C7
Millfield Fst Sch SG9 ....40 E7
Millfield Ho WD18 ....166 D3
Millfield La
Caddington LU1 ....62 D2
Hitchin SG4 ....34 F4
Little Hadham SG11 ....75 D8
Millfield Rd LU3 ....45 B3
Millfield Way LU1 ....62 D3
Millfield Wlk HP3 ....139 A8
Millfields
Sawbridgeworth CM21 ....97 F3
Stansted Mountfitchet
CM24 ....59 E6
Millgreen Cotts AL9 ....131 F8
Millhoo Ct EN9 ....163 F5
Millhouse La WD5 ....140 A4
Millhurst Mews CM17 ....118 E4
Milliners Ct AL1 ....127 E3
Milliners Way
Bishop's Stortford CM23 ....76 C4
Luton LU3 ....45 C1
Millmead Way SG14 ....113 B6
Millside CM23 ....77 A5
Millstream Cl
Hertford SG14 ....113 B6
Hitchin SG4 ....22 A1
Millthorne Cl WD3 ....165 F4
Millwards AL10 ....130 B2
Millwood Ct SG5 ....11 F6
Millwright Wlk HP3 ....138 F6
Milne Cl SG6 ....23 B3
Milne Field HA5 ....176 A3
Milner Cl WD25 ....154 B6
Milner Ct Bushey WD23 ....168 B3
Luton LU2 ....63 E8
Milneway UB9 ....173 B2
Milton Ave EN5 ....171 F4
Milton Cl SG8 ....2 C1
Milton Ct
Hammond Street EN7 ....147 F5
12 Harpenden AL5 ....86 B1
Hemel Hempstead HP2 ....105 B1
Waltham Abbey EN9 ....163 C5
Milton Dene HP2 ....125 B8
Milton Dr WD6 ....170 B4
Milton Rd Harpenden AL5 ....86 B1
Luton LU1 ....63 C6
Ware SG12 ....93 D2
Milton St
Waltham Abbey EN9 ....163 C5
Watford WD24 ....167 B8
Milton View SG4 ....35 C7
Milverton Gn LU3 ....45 A7
Mimms Hall Rd EN6 ....158 D7
Mimms La EN6,WD7 ....157 C6
Mimram Cl SG4 ....66 E7
Mimram Pl AL6 ....89 C5
Mimram Rd
Hertford SG14 ....113 B5
Welwyn AL6 ....89 C5
Mimram Wlk AL6 ....89 C5
Minchen Rd CM20 ....118 A1
Minderhall Ct SG1 ....50 C7
Minehead Way SG1 ....50 A7
Minerva Cl 3 SG1 ....51 C8
Minerva Dr WD24 ....153 E3
Minims The AL10 ....130 A7
Minister Ct AL2 ....141 E3
Minoan Dr HP3 ....138 E7
Minorca Way LU4 ....44 A3
Minsden Rd SG2 ....51 D3
Minster Cl AL10 ....130 A3
Minster Ho AL10 ....130 A3
Minster Rd SG8 ....7 C8
Minstrel Cl HP1 ....124 B4
Minstrel Ct HA3 ....176 E1
Miss Joans Ride HP4,LU6 ....81 E7
Missden Dr HP3 ....125 C1
Missenden Ho WD18 ....166 E2
Mistletoe Ct LU2 ....64 C8
Mistletoe Hill LU2 ....64 C8
Mistley Rd CM20 ....118 A2
Miswell La HP23 ....99 F3
Mitchell Cl
Abbots Langley WD5 ....154 A7
Bovingdon HP3 ....136 F4
St Albans AL1 ....141 D7
Welwyn Garden City AL7 ....111 C6
Mitre Bldgs CM20 ....117 C1
Mitre Ct 20 SG14 ....113 D6
Mitre Gdns CM23 ....77 A4
Mixes Hill Ct LU2 ....46 A4
Mixes Hill Rd LU2 ....45 F4
Mixies The SG5 ....11 E6
Moakes The LU3 ....44 E7
Moat Cl WD23 ....168 B4
Moat La Luton LU3 ....45 B4
Wingrave HP22 ....60 B2
Moat The SG11 ....55 D3
Moatfield Rd WD23 ....168 B4
Moatside SG9 ....29 B7
Moatview Ct WD23 ....168 B4
Moatwood Gn AL7 ....110 E5
Mobbsbury Way SG2 ....51 C7
Mobley Gn LU2 ....46 B3
Moffats Cl AL9 ....145 A5
Moffats La AL9 ....144 F5
Moira Cl LU3 ....44 D7
Moles La SG9 ....28 A3
Molescroft AL5 ....85 D4
Molesworth EN11 ....115 A2
Molewood Rd SG14 ....113 B7
Mollison Ave EN3 ....163 A3
Molteno Rd WD17 ....167 A8
Molyneaux Ave HP3 ....136 F4
Momples Rd CM20 ....118 B1
Monarch Hall LU2 ....64 C8
Monarch Wlk WD7 ....156 F6
Monarch's Way EN8 ....162 E6
Monastery Cl AL3 ....127 C3
Money Hole La AL6 ....111 E7
Moneyhill Ct WD3 ....165 B1
Moneyhill Par WD3 ....165 C1
Moneyhill Rd WD3 ....165 C1
Monica Cl WD24 ....167 D7
Monkhams Hall EN9 ....149 C2
Monklands SG6 ....22 D6
Monks Cl
Hoddesdon EN10 ....135 A3
Letchworth SG6 ....22 C6
Redbourn AL3 ....106 B5
St Albans AL1 ....127 E1
Monks Horton Way AL1 ....128 A4
Monks Rise AL8 ....89 D2
Monks Row 7 SG12 ....93 D2
Monks View SG2 ....50 F2
Monks Walk Sch AL8 ....89 C3
Monks Wlk SG9 ....40 E7
Monksmead WD6 ....170 C5
Monksmead Sch WD6 ....170 C6
Monkswick Rd CM20 ....117 F1
Monkswood AL8 ....89 C2
Monkswood Ave EN9 ....163 D6
Monkswood Dr CM23 ....76 D6
Monkswood Gdns WD6 ....170 D5
Monkswood Ret Pk SG1 ....50 E3
Monkswood Way SG1 ....50 E3
Monmouth Rd WD17 ....167 B6
Monro Gdns HA3 ....176 E3
Monro Ind Est EN8 ....162 E5
Mons Ave SG7 ....23 F6
Mons Cl AL5 ....107 D6
Monson Rd EN10 ....134 F3
Montacute Rd WD23 ....168 E2
Montague Ave LU4 ....44 C6
Montague Hall Pl WD23 ....168 A3
Montague Rd HP4 ....122 B4
Montayne Rd EN8 ....162 D7
Monterey Lodge HA6 ....174 E4
Montesole Ct 6 HA5 ....175 C1
Montessori At Little
Cheverells (Sch) AL3 ....83 D4
Montfitchet Wlk SG2 ....51 D7
Montgomerie Cl HP4 ....122 A6
Montgomery Ave HP2 ....125 A4
Montgomery Dr EN8 ....148 E3
Monton Cl LU3 ....44 F6
Montrose Ave LU3 ....45 C3
Montrose Rd HA3 ....176 F1
Monument Pl AL3 ....127 D4
Moon La EN5 ....171 F6
Moor End Rd HP1 ....124 C2
Moor Hall La CM23 ....76 B3
Moor Hall Rd CM17 ....118 F4
Moor La Moor Park WD3 ....174 A8
Sarratt WD3 ....151 E3
Moor Lane Crossing
WD18 ....166 C2
Moor Mill La AL2 ....141 E2
Moor Park Rd HA6 ....174 D4
Moor Park Sta HA6 ....174 D7
Moor Pk Ind Ctr WD18 ....166 C2
Moor St LU1 ....63 C8
Moor View WD18 ....167 A3
Moore Rd HP4 ....121 F6
Moorend AL7 ....111 A3
Moorfields SG9 ....41 E8
Moorhen Way CM19 ....116 A1
Moorhurst Ave EN7 ....147 B2
Moorings The
Bishop's Stortford CM23 ....77 A5
St Albans AL1 ....127 F4
Watford WD23 ....167 E5
Moorland Gdns LU2 ....63 D8
Moorland Rd
Harpenden AL5 ....86 B4
Hemel Hempstead HP1 ....124 A1
Moorlands
Park Street AL2 ....141 E3
Welwyn Garden City AL7 ....111 A3
Moorlands Reach CM21 ....98 A1
Moorlands Sch LU4 ....44 C3
Moormead Cl SG5 ....34 D6
Moormead Hill SG5 ....34 D6
Moors Farm Cotts HP5 ....136 B4
Moors Ley SG2 ....38 B1
Moors The AL7 ....111 A7
Moors Wlk AL7 ....111 C6
Moorside
Hemel Hempstead HP3 ....138 B8
Welwyn Garden City AL7 ....111 A3
Moortown Rd WD19 ....175 C6
Moorymead Cl SG14 ....70 D3
Moran Cl AL2 ....154 F8
Morecambe Cl Luton LU4 ....44 B3
Stevenage SG1 ....50 B7
Morefields HP23 ....100 A6
Moremead EN9 ....163 D6
Moreton Ave AL5 ....85 F2
Moreton Cl EN7 ....148 B4
Moreton End Cl AL5 ....85 F2
Moreton End La AL5 ....85 F2
Moreton Pk Ind Est LU2 ....46 A2
Moreton Pl AL5 ....85 F3
Moreton Rd N LU2 ....46 A2
Moreton Rd S LU2 ....46 A2
Morgan Cl
Northwood HA6 ....174 F4
Stevenage SG1 ....36 D1
Morgan Gdns WD25 ....155 B2
Morgan's Rd SG13 ....113 D4
Morgan's Wlk SG13 ....113 D3
Morgans Cl SG13 ....113 D4
Morgans Jun Mix Inf Sch
SG13 ....113 D4
Morice Rd EN11 ....134 F8
Morland Way EN8 ....148 E3
Morley Gr CM20 ....117 C2
Morley Hill EN2 ....161 D1
Morley La SG11 ....73 F5
Morningside WD3 ....165 C1
Mornington AL6 ....90 A4
Mornington Rd WD7 ....156 B5
Morpeth Ave WD6 ....156 F1
Morpeth Cl 3 HP2 ....124 E2
Morrell Cl LU3 ....45 A7
Morrell Ct AL7 ....110 F7
Morrello Gdns SG4 ....35 A5
Morris Cl
Lower Stondon SG16 ....10 C5
Luton LU3 ....44 E8
Morris Ct Holdbrook EN3 ....163 A2
Waltham Abbey EN9 ....163 F5
Morris Way AL2 ....142 D5
Morrison Ct 5 EN5 ....171 E5
Morriston Cl WD19 ....175 C5
Morse Cl UB9 ....173 C1
Mortain Dr HP4 ....121 F6
Mortimer Cl
Bushey WD23 ....168 B3
Luton LU1 ....63 A7
Mortimer Gate EN8 ....148 F4
Mortimer Hill HP23 ....100 B4
Mortimer Rd SG8 ....7 E7
Mortimer Rise HP23 ....100 B4
Morton Cl LU7 ....80 C4
Morton St SG8 ....7 D7
Morven Cl EN6 ....159 C8
Mosquito Way AL10 ....129 E7
Moss Bury Prim Sch SG1 ....51 A7
Moss Cl Pinner HA5 ....175 F1
Rickmansworth WD3 ....173 D8
Moss Gn AL7 ....110 E4
Moss La HA5 ....175 E1
Moss Rd WD25 ....154 B5
Moss Side AL2 ....140 F1
Moss Way SG5 ....21 C1
Mossbank Ave LU2 ....64 C8
Mossdale Ct 3 LU4 ....44 C5
Mossendew Cl UB9 ....173 D2
Mossman Dr LU1 ....62 E4
Mostyn Rd Bushey WD23 ....168 C4
Luton LU3 ....44 E4
Mott St E4 ....163 D1
Motts Cl SG14 ....70 D4
Moulton Rise LU2 ....63 F8
Mount Cl HP1 ....123 F3
Mount Dr
Park Street AL2 ....141 D6
Stansted Mountfitchet
CM24 ....59 E5
Mount Garrison SG4 ....34 F7
Mount Grace Rd EN6 ....159 B8
Mount Grace Sch EN6 ....159 B8
Mount Keen SG1 ....37 C3
Mount Pleasant
Harefield UB9 ....173 A2
Hertford Heath SG13 ....114 C4
Hitchin SG5 ....34 D6
St Albans AL3 ....127 C3
Mount Pleasant Cl AL9 ....130 D8
Mount Pleasant Flats
SG1 ....50 E8
Mount Pleasant La
Bricket Wood AL2 ....140 E1
Hatfield AL9 ....130 C8
Mount Pleasant Lane Jun Mix
& Inf Sch AL2 ....140 E1
Mount Pleasant Rd LU3 ....44 E5
Mount Rd Hertford SG14 ....113 A5
Wheathampstead AL4 ....87 D1
Mount The Barley SG8 ....8 F1
Hammond Street EN7 ....147 D5
5 Luton LU3 ....63 D8
Potters Bar EN6 ....145 B1
Rickmansworth WD3 ....165 C3
Mount Vernon Hospl
HA6 ....174 B4
Mount View Enfield EN2 ....160 F1
London Colney AL2 ....142 F4
Rickmansworth WD3 ....165 B1
Mount Way AL7 ....110 F3
Mountbatten Cl AL1 ....142 B8
Mounteagle SG8 ....7 D5
Mountfield Rd
Hemel Hempstead HP2 ....124 E3
Luton LU2 ....45 E2
Mountfitchet Castle &
Norman Village* CM24 ....59 F6
Mountfitchet High Sch
CM24 ....59 F4
Mountfitchet Rd CM24 ....59 E5
Mountgrace Rd LU2 ....46 C6
Mountjoy SG4 ....22 C1
Mountside HA7 ....176 F2
Mountsorrel SG13 ....113 F6
Mountview HA6 ....174 F4
Mountview Rd EN7 ....147 E5
Mountway EN6 ....145 A1
Mountway Cl AL7 ....110 F3
Mowat Ind Est WD24 ....154 C1
Mowbray Cres SG5 ....11 F7
Mowbray Gdns SG4 ....35 A5
Mowbray Rd CM20 ....118 A3
Mowbrays The SG5 ....11 F7
Moxes Wood LU3 ....44 E7
Moxom Ave EN8 ....148 E1
Moxon St EN5 ....171 F6

Mozart Ct SG1 .....50 C5
Muddy La SG6 .....22 F3
Muirfield LU2 .....45 E6
Muirfield Cl WD19 .....175 C6
Muirfield Gn WD19 .....175 C6
Muirfield Rd WD19 .....175 B6
Muirhead Way SG3 .....68 F5
Mulberry Cl
Cheshunt EN10 .....148 F7
Chiswell Green AL2 .....141 B3
Luton LU1 .....63 B7
Stotfold SG5 .....11 F5
Tring HP23 .....100 A5
Watford WD17 .....153 E3
Mulberry Ct
Bishop's Stortford CM23 .....77 A5
5 Hemel Hempstead HP1 .124 D4
Royston SG8 .....7 D5
Mulberry Gdns WD7 .....156 E6
Mulberry Gn CM17 .....118 D4
Mulberry Lodge WD19 ..167 D3
Mulberry Mead AL10 .....109 F1
Mulberry Pl AL3 .....106 B4
Mulberry Terr CM17 .....118 B4
Mulberry Way SG5 .....21 D2
Mull Ho WD18 .....166 F4
Mullion Cl Harrow HA3 ..176 B2
Luton LU2 .....46 B5
Mullion Wlk WD19 .....175 D6
Mullway SG6 .....22 C6
Mulready Wlk HP3 .....138 E7
Mundells
Hammond Street EN7 .....148 A4
Welwyn Garden City AL7 ..111 A8
Mundells Ct AL7 .....110 F8
Munden Gr WD24 .....154 D1
Munden Rd SG12 .....71 E7
Munden View WD25 .....154 D3
Mundesley Cl
South Oxhey WD19 .....175 C6
Stevenage SG1 .....36 B1
Mungo-Park Cl WD23 ...176 C8
Munro Rd WD23 .....168 C4
Muntings The SG2 .....51 A3
Munts Mdw SG4 .....24 C1
Murchison Rd EN11 .....115 B1
Muriel Ave WD18 .....167 C4
Murray Cres HA5 .....175 D2
Murray Rd
Berkhamsted HP4 .....122 C6
Northwood HA6 .....174 E3
Murrell La SG5 .....12 A5
Murton Ct AL1 .....127 E4
Museum Ct HP23 .....100 A3
Museum of St Albans*
AL1 .....127 E3
Musgrave Cl EN7 .....147 F4
Musk Hill HP1 .....123 E2
Muskalls Cl EN7 .....148 A4
Muskham Rd CM20 .....118 B3
Musleigh Manor SG12 ....93 F1
Musley Hill SG12 .....93 E2
Musley Inf Sch SG12 .....93 E2
Musley La SG12 .....93 E2
Mussons Path LU2 .....45 E1
Muswell Cl LU3 .....45 B6
Mutchetts Cl WD25 .....154 E6
Mutford Croft 2 LU2 .....46 D1
Mutton La EN6 .....158 E8
Myddelton Ave EN1 .....161 E1
Myddelton House Gdns*
EN2 .....162 A3
Myddleton Path EN7 .....162 B8
Myddleton Rd SG12 .....114 D8
Myers Cl WD7 .....156 E7
Myles Ct EN7 .....147 C2
Mylne Cl EN8 .....148 C4
Mylne Ct EN11 .....115 A1
Mymms Dr AL9 .....145 B4
Mymwood Cl AL9 .....145 C4
Myrtle Cotts
Sarratt WD3 .....152 A3
Tring HP23 .....100 C8
Myrtle Gn HP1 .....123 E4
Myrtle Gr EN2 .....161 D1
Myrtleside Cl HA6 .....174 D3
Myson Way CM23 .....77 B7

N

Nags Head Cl SG13 .....114 B7
Nails La 15 CM23 .....76 F7
Nairn Cl AL5 .....107 D6
Nairn Gn WD19 .....175 A7
Nan Aires HP22 .....60 A3
Nancy Downs WD19 .....167 C2
Nap The WD4 .....139 A2
Napier Cl AL2 .....142 D6
Napier Ct Cheshunt EN8 ..148 B3
Luton LU1 .....63 D7
Napier Dr WD23 .....167 E5
Napier Hall LU2 .....64 C8
Napier Rd LU1 .....63 D7
Nappsbury Rd LU4 .....44 D5
Napsbury Ave AL2 .....142 C5
Napsbury La AL1 .....142 A7
Nascot Pl WD17 .....167 B7
Nascot Rd WD17 .....167 B7
Nascot St WD17 .....167 B7
Nascot Wood Inf Sch
WD17 .....154 A1
Nascot Wood Jun Sch
WD17 .....154 A1
Nascot Wood Rd WD17 ..153 F1
Naseby Rd LU1 .....63 B7
Nash Cl
Borehamwood WD6 .....169 F5
Datchworth SG3 .....69 E2
Stevenage SG2 .....51 B6
Welham Green AL9 .....144 D8
Nash Gn HP3 .....138 F6
Nash Mills CE Prim Sch
HP3 .....138 F6
Nash Mills La HP3 .....138 F5
Nash Rd SG8 .....7 D5
Nathaniel Wlk HP23 .....100 A5
Nathans Cl AL6 .....89 C6
Nayland Cl LU2 .....46 E1
Nazeing New Rd EN10 ..135 B2
Nazeing Prim Sch EN9 ..149 E8
Nazeing Rd EN9 .....135 D1
Nazeingbury Cl EN9 .....135 D1
Nazeingbury Par EN9 ...135 D1
Neagh Cl SG1 .....37 C3
Neagle Cl WD6 .....170 C8
Neal Cl HA6 .....175 A2
Neal Ct Hertford SG14 .....113 C6
Waltham Abbey EN9 .....163 F6
Neal St WD18 .....167 C4
Necton Rd AL4 .....108 E8
Needham Rd LU4 .....44 B6
Neild Way WD3 .....164 F2
Nell Gwynn Cl WD7 .....156 E7
Nelson Ave AL1 .....142 B8
Nelson Rd
Bishop's Stortford CM23 .....77 A5
Dagnall HP4 .....81 C5
Nelson St SG14 .....113 B7
Nene Rd SG16 .....10 B4
Neptune Ct WD6 .....170 A6
Neptune Dr HP2 .....124 E5
Neptune Gate SG2 .....51 D8
Neston Rd WD24 .....154 C2
Nether St SG12 .....95 E4
Netherby Cl HP23 .....100 C6
Nethercott Cl LU2 .....46 C1
Netherfield Ct SG12 .....115 D3
Netherfield La SG12 .....115 E3
Netherfield Rd AL5 .....107 B4
Netherhall Rd CM19 .....135 F5
Netherstones SG5 .....11 F7
Netherway AL3 .....141 A8
Netley Dell SG6 .....23 B3
Netteswell Cross CM20 ..117 E2
Netteswell Orch CM20 ...117 D1
Netteswell Rd CM20 .....117 F3
Netteswell Twr CM20 ....117 D1
Nettlecroft
Hemel Hempstead HP1 ....124 B2
Welwyn Garden City AL7 ..111 B7
Nettleden Rd
Little Gaddesden HP4 .....102 E4
Nettleden HP1 .....103 C1
Potten End HP4 .....123 B8
Nevell's Gn SG6 .....22 F6
Nevells Rd SG6 .....22 F6
Nevil Cl HA6 .....174 D5
Nevill Gr WD24 .....167 B8
Neville Cl EN6 .....158 F8
Neville Rd LU3 .....45 A5
Neville Road Pas LU3 ....45 A5
Neville's Ct SG6 .....23 B7
New Barn La CM22 .....77 D1
New Barnes Ave AL1 ....142 A8
New Barns La SG10 .....74 E4
New Bedford Rd
Luton LU3 .....45 D3
Luton,High Town LU1 .....63 D8
New Briars Prim Sch
AL10 .....130 A5
New Cl SG3 .....68 F6
New Cotts
Brookmans Park AL9 .....144 D3
Cheshunt EN8 .....162 C5
Markyate AL3 .....83 E6
Whitwell SG4 .....66 A7
New Ct SG3 .....69 A2
New England Cl SG4 .....34 F4
New England St AL3 .....127 C3
New Farm La HA6 .....174 E2
New Farm Traveller's Site
SG8 .....2 A8
New Ford Bsns Pk EN8 ..162 F5
New Ford Rd EN8 .....162 F5
New Forge Pl AL3 .....106 B5
New Greens Ave AL3 ....127 D7
New Hall Cl HP3 .....137 A4
New House Pk AL1 .....142 B7
New Inn Rd SG7 .....3 D5
New Kent Rd AL1 .....127 D3
New Mill Terr HP23 .....100 B6
New Par WD3 .....164 C5
New Park Dr HP2 .....125 B3
New Park La SG2 .....51 F2
New Park Rd
Harefield UB9 .....173 C2
Newgate Street SG13 .....146 D7
New Path CM23 .....76 F6
New Pl AL6 .....89 B4
New Provident Pl 7
HP4 .....122 D4
New Rd
Berkhamsted HP4 .....122 D6
Berkhamsted, Northchurch
HP4 .....121 F7
Chipperfield WD4 .....137 F1
Croxley Green WD3 .....166 A4
Elstree WD6 .....169 D3
Great Chishill SG8 .....9 D6
Harlow CM17 .....118 D4
Hatfield AL8 .....110 A3
Hertford SG14 .....113 D8
New Rd *continued*
Hoddesdon EN10 .....135 A4
Little Hadham SG11 .....75 A7
Lower Stondon SG17 .....10 A8
Radlett WD7 .....155 E2
Radlett, Letchmore Heath
WD25 .....168 E8
Sarratt WD3 .....151 F1
Shenley WD7 .....157 A5
South Mimms EN6 .....158 A6
Tring HP23 .....100 B6
Ware SG12 .....93 D1
Watford WD17 .....167 C5
Welwyn AL6 .....89 F3
Woolmer Green SG3 .....69 B3
New River Ave SG12 .....115 B4
New River Cl EN11 .....135 B7
New River Ct EN7 .....162 B8
New River Trad Est
EN8 .....148 D5
New St Berkhamsted HP4 .122 D4
Cheddington LU7 .....79 F7
5 Luton LU1 .....63 D6
Sawbridgeworth CM21 .....97 E3
Slip End LU1 .....63 C1
Watford WD18 .....167 C5
New Station Cotts EN10 .135 A3
New Town SG4 .....67 F1
New Town Rd 9 LU1 .....63 E6
New Town St LU1 .....63 E6
New Wood AL7 .....111 C7
Newark Cl SG8 .....7 C8
Newark Gn WD6 .....170 D6
Newark Rd LU4 .....45 A2
Newberries Ave WD7 ...156 B4
Newberries Prim Sch
WD7 .....156 C4
Newbiggin Path WD19 ..175 C6
Newbold Rd LU3 .....45 B7
Newbolt SG8 .....7 D8
Newbolt Rd HA7 .....176 F5
Newbury Ave EN3 .....162 F2
Newbury Cl
Bishop's Stortford CM23 ....76 E8
Luton LU4 .....44 E2
Stevenage SG1 .....36 D1
Newcastle Cl SG1 .....36 F2
Newcombe Rd LU1 .....63 C7
Newcome Path WD7 .....157 A5
Newcome Rd WD7 .....157 A5
Newdigate Gn UB9 .....173 D2
Newdigate Rd UB9 .....173 C2
Newdigate Rd E UB9 .....173 D2
Newell La SG2 .....38 D7
Newell Rd HP3 .....138 E8
Newell Rise HP3 .....138 E8
Newells SG6 .....23 D4
Newells Hedge LU7 .....80 D5
Newfield La HP2 .....124 F3
Newfield Way AL4 .....128 D1
Newfields AL8 .....110 B5
Newford Cl HP2 .....125 B4
Newgate SG2 .....51 A4
Newgate Cl AL4 .....128 D6
Newgate St SG13 .....146 D7
Newgate Street Village
SG13 .....146 E6
Newgatestreet Rd EN7 ..147 B4
Newground Rd HP23 .....101 B3
Newhall Ct EN9 .....163 F6
Newhouse Cres WD25 ...154 B6
Newhouse Rd HP3 .....137 A4
Newland Cl Pinner HA5 ...175 F4
St Albans AL1 .....142 A8
Newland Gdns SG13 .....113 E6
Newlands Hatfield AL9 ...130 C7
Letchworth SG6 .....23 A3
Newlands Ave WD7 .....155 F5
Newlands Cl E SG4 .....34 F4
Newlands Cl W SG4 .....34 F4
Newlands Cvn Site WD5 .139 F5
Newlands La SG4 .....34 F4
Newlands Pl EN5 .....171 D4
Newlands Rd
Hemel Hempstead HP1 ....123 E3
Luton LU1 .....63 C3
Newlands Way EN6 .....145 B1
Newlands Wlk WD25 .....154 D6
Newlyn Cl
Bricket Wood AL2 .....140 E1
Stevenage SG1 .....50 A6
Newlyn Rd EN5 .....171 F5
Newman Ave SG8 .....7 F6
Newmans Ct SG14 .....70 D3
Newmans Dr AL5 .....85 F2
Newmarket Ct AL3 .....127 C4
Newmarket Rd
Royston SG8 .....7 E6
Royston SG8 .....7 F6
Newnham Cl LU2 .....46 D1
Newnham Par 5 EN8 ...148 D1
Newnham Rd SG7 .....12 E6
Newnham Way SG7 .....4 B2
Newport Cl EN3 .....162 E2
Newport Mead WD19 ...175 D6
Newports CM21 .....97 C1
Newquay Gdns WD19 ...175 B8
Newstead AL10 .....129 F2
Newstead Ho UB9 .....173 C1
Newteswell Dr EN9 .....163 D7
Newton Cl
Harpenden AL5 .....107 D6
Hoddesdon EN11 .....115 B2
Newton Cres WD6 .....170 C5
Newton Dr CM21 .....97 D1
Newton Rd Harrow HA3 ..176 E1
Stevenage SG2 .....51 B6
Newtondale LU4 .....44 C5
Newtons Way SG4 .....34 F6
Newtown Rd CM23 .....76 F6
Niagara Cl EN8 .....148 D2
Nicholas Breakspear RC Sch
AL4 .....128 E2
Nicholas Cl
St Albans AL3 .....127 D6
Watford WD24 .....154 B2
Nicholas La SG14 .....113 D6
Nicholas Pl SG1 .....36 D1
Nicholas Rd WD6 .....169 F4
Nicholas Way
Hemel Hempstead HP2 ....124 F5
Northwood HA6 .....174 C2
Nicholls Cl Luton LU2 .....46 C2
Redbourn AL3 .....105 F5
Nicholson Court Ind Ctr
EN11 .....135 B6
Nicola Cl HA3 .....176 D1
Nicoll Way WD6 .....170 D5
Nicolson Dr WD23 .....176 C8
Nidderdale HP2 .....124 F6
Nightingale Ave SG8 .....2 A5
Nightingale Cl Luton LU2 ..46 C6
Radlett WD7 .....155 F3
Watford WD5 .....154 A8
Nightingale Ct
Hertford SG14 .....113 C6
Hitchin SG5 .....35 A8
1 Luton LU3 .....63 C8
Radlett WD7 .....156 A4
Rickmansworth WD3 .....165 C2
Nightingale La AL1,AL4 ..142 C7
Nightingale Lodge HP4 .122 B4
Nightingale Pl WD3 .....165 D2
Nightingale Rd
Bushey WD23 .....168 A4
Hammond Street EN7 .....147 C6
Hitchin SG5 .....34 F8
Rickmansworth WD3 .....165 C2
Nightingale Terr SG15 .....11 A3
Nightingale Way
Baldock SG7 .....23 F6
Royston SG8 .....7 E8
Nightingale Wlk
Hemel Hempstead HP2 ...105 C1
Stevenage SG2 .....51 C5
Nightingales EN9 .....163 E5
Nimbus Way SG4 .....35 C7
Nimmo Dr WD23 .....168 D2
Nimrod Cl AL4 .....128 C5
Nimrod Dr AL10 .....129 D6
Nine Ashes SG12 .....116 D7
Ninefields EN9 .....163 F6
Ninesprings Way SG4 ....35 B6
Ninfield Ct LU2 .....46 C3
Ninian Rd HP2 .....124 E8
Ninning's La AL6 .....68 D2
Ninnings Cotts AL5 .....107 A8
Ninth Ave LU3 .....44 D7
Niton Cl EN5 .....171 D3
Niven Cl WD6 .....170 C8
Noake Mill La HP1 .....124 A8
Nobel Sch The SG2 .....51 C7
Nobel Villas EN9 .....163 D5
Nobles The CM23 .....76 D6
Node Way Gdns AL6 .....89 C3
Nodes Dr SG2 .....51 A1
Noke La AL2 .....140 E4
Noke Lane Bsns Ctr AL2 .140 F4
Noke Shot AL5 .....86 C4
Noke Side AL2 .....141 A4
Noke The SG2 .....69 B8
Nokes The HP1 .....124 A5
Nokeside SG2 .....69 B8
Nook The SG12 .....115 B4
Norbury Ave WD24 .....167 C7
Norfolk Ave WD24 .....154 C1
Norfolk Ct 4 EN5 .....171 E5
Norfolk Gdns WD6 .....170 D5
Norfolk Rd
Buntingford SG9 .....40 E8
Luton LU2 .....64 A7
Rickmansworth WD3 .....165 E1
Norfolk Way CM23 .....76 F5
Norman Ave CM23 .....76 D6
Norman Cl St Albans AL1 .141 E8
Waltham Abbey EN9 .....163 D6
Norman Cres HA5 .....175 C2
Norman Ct
Potters Bar EN6 .....145 C1
Stansted Mountfitchet
CM24 .....59 E7
Stevenage SG1 .....36 F1
Norman Rd Luton LU3 .....45 B2
Welwyn AL6 .....89 B3
Norman's La SG8 .....7 D5
Norman's Way CM24 .....59 E7
Normandy Ave EN5 .....171 F5
Normandy Ct HP1 .....124 D4
Normandy Dr HP4 .....122 B6
Normandy Rd AL3 .....127 D4
Normandy Way EN11 ....135 D8
Normans Cl SG6 .....11 F1
Normans La AL6 .....68 E2
Normansfield Cl WD23 ..168 B2
Norris Cl CM23 .....77 C7
Norris Gr EN10 .....134 E3
Norris La EN11 .....135 A7
Norris Rd EN11 .....135 A6
Norris Rise EN11 .....134 F7
North App
Moor Park HA6 .....174 C8
Watford WD25 .....154 A5
North Area Pupil Referral
Unit SG6 .....22 D3
North Ave Letchworth SG6 .23 B8
Shenley WD7 .....156 E7
North Barn EN10 .....135 B1
North Cl Barnet EN5 .....171 C4
Chiswell Green AL2 .....141 B6
Royston SG8 .....7 C7
North Comm AL3 .....106 A5
North Common Rd AL3 .106 A4
North Cotts AL2 .....142 A6
North Ct AL3 .....83 E5
North Dr St Albans AL4 ...128 E5
Thundridge SG11 .....72 E1
North Drift Way LU1 .....63 B6
North End SG8 .....15 D6
North Gate CM20 .....117 C1
North Hertfordshire Coll
Letchworth SG6 .....22 F5
Stevenage SG1 .....50 D4
North Hertfordshire Coll
(Hitchin Ctr) SG4 .....35 B8
North Hill WD3 .....164 E8
North Luton Ind Est LU4 ..44 B7
North Orbital Commercial Pk
AL1 .....142 A7
North Orbital Rd
Bricket Wood AL2 .....140 E2
Chiswell Green AL2 .....141 B5
Colney Heath AL4 .....129 C2
London Colney AL1,AL2,
AL4 .....142 D6
Park Street AL2 .....141 E6
Watford WD25 .....154 D7
North Pl Harlow CM20 ....118 B5
Hitchin SG5 .....21 D1
Waltham Abbey EN9 .....163 B6
North Rd Baldock SG7 .....12 E2
Berkhamsted HP4 .....122 B4
Cheshunt EN8 .....162 E6
Chorleywood WD3 .....164 D4
Hertford SG14 .....113 A7
Hertford SG14 .....113 C6
Hoddesdon EN11 .....135 A7
Stevenage SG1 .....36 C2
North Ride AL6 .....89 C6
North Riding AL2 .....141 A1
North Road Ave SG14 ...113 A7
North Road Gdns SG14 ..113 B6
North St
4 Bishop's Stortford CM23 .76 F7
Lower Nazeing EN9 .....135 E1
Luton, Hart Hill LU2 .....45 E1
Luton,High Town LU2 .....63 E8
North Terr 5 CM23 .....76 F8
North View Cotts SG12 ....95 D4
North Western Ave
Stanmore WD6 .....169 A2
Watford,Garston WD24 ..154 C3
Watford,Leavesden Green
WD2 .....153 D4
Bushey WD23,W25 .....168 C6
Northaw CE Prim Sch
EN6 .....146 A1
Northaw Cl HP2 .....125 B8
Northaw Pk EN6 .....159 F7
Northaw Rd E EN6 .....146 E1
Northaw Rd W EN6 .....160 C8
Northbridge Rd HP4 ....122 A6
Northbrook Dr HA6 .....174 E3
Northbrook Rd EN5 .....171 E3
Northchurch La HP4,
HP5 .....121 D2
Northchurch St Mary's CE
Fst Sch HP4 .....121 E6
Northcliffe Dr N20 .....171 F1
Northcote 3 HA5 .....175 C1
Northcotts AL9 .....130 C6
Northcourt WD3 .....165 A1
Northdown Rd AL10 .....130 A2
Northend HP3 .....125 C1
Northern Ave SG16 .....10 C3
Northern Ho SG4 .....35 B7
Northfield Braughing SG11 .55 F7
Hatfield AL10 .....130 B8
Standon SG11 .....55 E2
Northfield Gdns WD24 ..154 C2
Northfield Rd
Aldbury HP23 .....100 F7
Borehamwood WD6 .....170 B8
Cheshunt EN8 .....162 E7
Guilden Morden SG7 .....1 C2
Harpenden AL5 .....86 C4
Sawbridgeworth CM21 .....97 E4
Northfields SG6 .....11 F1
Northfields Inf Sch SG6 ..11 F1
Northgate HA6 .....174 C3
Northgate End CM23 .....76 F8
Northgate Ho EN8 .....148 D2
Northgate Path WD6 .....169 F8
Northgate Prim Sch
CM23 .....76 E8
Northlands EN6 .....159 D8
Northolt Ave CM23 .....59 B1
Northridge Way HP1 .....124 A3
Northside AL4 .....108 B1
Northumberland Ave
EN1 .....162 B1
Northview Rd LU2 .....45 F2
Northway
Rickmansworth WD3 .....165 D2
1 Welwyn Garden City AL7 .89 F1
Northwell Dr LU3 .....44 F7
Northwick Rd WD19 .....175 C6
Northwood AL7 .....111 D6
Northwood & Pinner District
Hospl HA6 .....175 A2
Northwood Cl EN7 .....147 F4
Northwood Coll HA6 .....174 D3
Northwood Hills Cir
HA6 .....175 A2

Northwood Hills Sta HA6 ....175 A1
Northwood Prep Sch WD3 ....174 C8
Northwood Rd UB9 ....173 E3
Northwood Sch HA6 ....175 B2
Northwood Sta HA6 ....174 E3
Northwood Way
Harefield UB9 ....173 D2
Northwood HA6 ....175 A3
Norton Bury La SG6 ....12 C2
Norton Cl WD6 ....170 A8
Norton Cres SG7 ....23 E8
Norton Gn SG1 ....50 B3
Norton Green Rd SG1 ....50 C4
Norton Mill La SG6 ....12 D3
Norton Rd
Letchworth SG5,SG6,SG7 ...12 C2
Luton LU3 ....44 F4
Stevenage SG1 ....50 D4
Norton Road Prim Sch LU3 ....44 F4
Norton Way N SG6 ....23 A7
Norton Way S SG6 ....23 A5
Nortonstreet La SG4 ....67 B7
Norvic Rd HP23 ....80 A1
Norwich Cl SG1 ....37 B1
Norwich Ho 5 WD6 ....170 A7
Norwich Way WD3 ....166 B5
Norwood Cl SG14 ....112 F7
Norwood Rd EN8 ....148 E1
Nottingham Cl WD25 ...154 A6
Nottingham Rd WD3 ....164 C1
Novello Way WD6 ....170 D8
Nugent's Pk HA5 ....175 F2
Nugents Ct HA5 ....175 E2
Numbers Farm WD4 ....139 C2
Nun's Cl SG5 ....34 E7
Nunfield WD4 ....152 B8
Nunnery Cl AL1 ....127 E1
Nunnery La LU3 ....45 B5
Nunnery Stables AL1 ...127 D1
Nuns La AL1 ....141 E8
Nunsbury Dr EN10 ....148 E6
Nunsbury Drive Cotts EN10 ....148 E6
Nup End Cl HP22 ....60 B3
Nup End La HP22 ....60 B3
Nupton Dr EN5 ....171 C3
Nurseries Rd AL4 ....108 E7
Nursery Cl
Bishop's Stortford CM23 ....76 F6
Stevenage SG2 ....69 A8
Nursery Cotts SG1 ....50 A6
Nursery Fields CM21 ....97 D2
Nursery Gdns
Goff's Oak EN7 ....147 D3
Tring HP23 ....100 B4
Ware SG12 ....93 E1
Welwyn Garden City AL7 ....89 E1
Nursery Hill AL7 ....89 E1
Nursery Par LU3 ....44 E5
Nursery Rd
Bishop's Stortford CM23 ....76 F6
Cheshunt EN10 ....148 F6
Hoddesdon EN11 ....115 B1
Lower Nazeing EN9 ....135 D2
Luton LU3 ....44 F5
Nursery Row 5 EN5 ....171 E6
Nursery Terr HP4 ....123 B7
Nut Gr AL8 ....89 D1
Nut Slip SG9 ....40 E6
Nutcroft SG3 ....69 D2
Nutfield AL7 ....90 A1
Nuthampstead Rd SG8 ...17 E2
Nutleigh Gr SG5 ....21 D1
Nuttfield Cl WD3 ....166 B3
Nutwood Gdns 5 EN7 ....147 E5
Nye Way HP3 ....137 A3
Nymans Cl LU2 ....46 D3

O

Oak Ave
Bricket Wood AL2 ....141 A1
Enfield EN2 ....160 F1
Oak Cl
Hemel Hempstead HP3 ....138 F7
Waltham Abbey EN9 ....163 D5
Oak Ct HA6 ....174 D4
Oak Dr Berkhamsted HP4 .122 D3
Sawbridgeworth CM21 ....118 C8
Oak End SG9 ....40 D7
Oak Farm WD6 ....170 C4
Oak Glade HA6 ....174 B2
Oak Gn WD5 ....153 E7
Oak Gr Hatfield AL10 ....129 F5
Hertford SG13 ....113 E4
Oak Green Way WD5 ....153 E7
Oak Hall CM23 ....76 E8
Oak La Cholesbury HP23 ..120 B2
Cuffley EN6 ....146 F3
Graveley SG4 ....36 C4
Oak Path WD23 ....168 B3
Oak Piece AL6 ....89 E7
Oak Piece Ct AL6 ....89 E7
Oak Pk SG12 ....95 B1
Oak Rd Luton LU4 ....63 C8
Woolmer Green SG3 ....69 B1
Oak St
Bishop's Stortford CM23 ....76 F6
Hemel Hempstead HP3 ....138 F7
Oak Tree Cl
Abbots Langley WD5 ....153 D7
Benington SG2 ....52 F4
Hatfield AL10 ....130 A6
Hertford Heath SG13 ....114 C3
Oak Tree Cl *continued*
Letchworth SG6 ....22 E4
Oak Tree Ct Elstree WD6 .169 D3
Oaklands AL6 ....89 E8
Oak Way AL5 ....107 A5
Oakbank WD7 ....156 B3
Oakcroft Cl HA5 ....175 B1
Oakdale AL8 ....89 D1
Oakdale Ave HA6 ....175 A1
Oakdale Cl WD19 ....175 C6
Oakdale Rd WD19 ....175 C6
Oakdene EN8 ....148 E1
Oakdene Cl HA5 ....175 F3
Oakdene Rd
Hemel Hempstead HP3 ....138 F7
Watford WD24 ....154 B3
Oakdene Way AL1 ....128 C3
Oaken Gr AL7 ....110 E3
Oakfield WD3 ....165 A2
Oakfield Ave SG4 ....35 B5
Oakfield Cl EN6 ....158 F8
Oakfield Rd AL5 ....107 A5
Oakfields SG2 ....51 C1
Oakfields Ave SG3 ....69 A6
Oakfields Cl SG2 ....51 C1
Oakfields Rd SG3 ....69 A6
Oakhill SG6 ....23 D4
Oakhill Ave HA5 ....175 E1
Oakhill Cl WD3 ....172 E6
Oakhill Ct EN5 ....171 D5
Oakhill Dr AL6 ....89 A6
Oakhill Rd WD3 ....172 D6
Oakhurst Ave AL5 ....107 A5
Oakhurst Pl WD18 ....166 F5
Oakhurst Rd EN3 ....162 D3
Oakington AL7 ....111 D6
Oaklands HP4 ....122 A4
Oaklands (Herts Coll of Agriculture & Hort) AL4 ....128 E4
Oaklands Ave
Brookmans Park AL9 ....144 E4
Watford WD19 ....167 B1
Oaklands Cl CM23 ....59 B2
Oaklands Coll
St Albans AL1 ....127 E3
St Albans,The Camp AL4 ..128 D1
Oaklands Coll (Boreham Wood Campus) WD6 ...170 C7
Oaklands Coll (Harpenden Campus) AL5 ....86 B1
Oaklands Coll (Lemsford Lane Campus) AL8 ....110 B4
Oaklands Coll (Welwyn Garden City Campus) AL8 ....110 D7
Oaklands Ct Oaklands AL6 .89 E7
Watford WD17 ....167 A8
Oaklands Dr CM23 ....59 B2
Oaklands Gate HA6 ....174 E4
Oaklands Gr EN10 ....148 E7
Oaklands La Arkley EN5 ..171 B5
St Albans AL4 ....128 F5
Oaklands Pk CM23 ....59 B2
Oaklands Prim Sch AL6 ..89 E7
Oaklands Rd
Hammond Street EN7 ....147 E5
Totteridge N20 ....171 F2
Oaklands Rise AL6 ....89 F7
Oaklands Wood AL10 ...130 A5
Oaklawn HP23 ....100 A3
Oaklea AL6 ....89 E7
Oaklea Cl AL6 ....89 E8
Oaklea Wood AL6 ....89 E7
Oakleigh Ct CM23 ....76 D8
Oakleigh Dr WD3 ....166 C3
Oakleigh Rd HA5 ....175 F4
Oakley Cl LU4 ....44 D4
Oakley Ct SG8 ....7 D7
Oakley Rd
Harpenden AL5 ....107 D7
Luton LU4 ....44 E3
Oakmeade HA5 ....176 A4
Oakmede 6 EN5 ....171 D5
Oakmere Ave EN6 ....159 C6
Oakmere Cl EN6 ....159 D8
Oakmere La EN6 ....159 C7
Oakmere Prim Sch EN6 .159 D7
Oakridge AL2 ....140 F2
Oakridge Ave WD7 ....155 F6
Oakridge La WD7 ....155 E5
Oakroyd Ave EN6 ....158 F6
Oakroyd Cl EN6 ....158 F6
Oaks Cl Hitchin SG4 ....34 F5
Radlett WD7 ....155 F4
Oaks Cross SG2 ....51 B1
Oaks Ret Pk CM20 ....117 F3
Oaks The
Berkhamsted HP4 ....122 A4
Slip End LU1 ....63 C1
Watford WD19 ....167 C1
Oaktree Cl
14 Bishop's Stortford CM23 .76 F7
Goff's Oak EN7 ....147 B3
Oaktree Cotts SG12 ....114 F6
Oaktree Garth AL7 ....110 E5
Oakview Cl Cheshunt EN7 .148 B3
Harpenden AL5 ....106 F5
Oakway LU6 ....82 B7
Oakway Pl WD7 ....156 A5
Oakwell Cl SG2 ....69 D7
Oakwell Dr EN6 ....160 B7
Oakwood
Berkhamsted HP4 ....121 F3
Waltham Abbey EN9 ....163 E5
Oakwood Ave WD6 ....170 B5
Oakwood Cl SG2 ....51 C2
Oakwood Dr
Harpenden AL5 ....106 F5
Luton LU3 ....44 C8
St Albans AL4 ....128 C4
Oakwood Est CM20 ....118 B4
Oakwood Prim Sch AL4 .128 C4
Oakwood Rd
Bricket Wood AL2 ....140 F2
Pinner HA5 ....175 B1
Oban Terr LU1 ....63 B8
Oberon Cl WD6 ....170 C8
Obrey Way CM23 ....76 E3
Occupation Rd WD18 ...167 B4
Octagan The SG12 ....93 D2
Octavia Ct WD24 ....167 C7
Oddfellows Ct 10 SG14 ..113 D6
Oddy Hill Tring HP23 ....100 C3
Wigginton HP23 ....100 C2
Odeon Par WD24 ....154 B3
Odyssey Rd WD6 ....170 B8
Offa Rd AL3 ....127 C3
Offas Way AL4 ....108 D8
Offerton Ho 13 WD19 ....175 C7
Offley Cross SG5 ....34 B5
Offley Endowed Prim Sch SG5 ....33 C3
Offley Hill SG5 ....33 C3
Offley Rd SG5 ....34 D6
Ogard Rd EN11 ....135 C8
Okeford Cl HP23 ....99 F4
Okeford Dr HP23 ....99 F4
Okeley La HP23 ....99 E3
Old Bakery SG5 ....34 E7
Old Barn La WD3 ....165 F4
Old Barn Mews WD3 ....165 F4
Old Bedford Rd Luton LU2 .45 E4
Luton, Warden Hill LU2 ....45 D6
Old Bell Cl CM24 ....59 D6
Old Bourne Way SG1 ....37 A3
Old Brewery Cl SG5 ....11 F7
Old Brewery Pl SG4 ....66 D1
Old Chantry La SG4 ....35 F2
Old Charlton Rd SG5 ....34 E6
Old Chorleywood Rd WD3 ....165 D3
Old Church La SG12 ....93 E7
Old Coach Rd The SG14 .112 C4
Old Common The SG9 ....43 B4
Old Crabtree La HP2 ....124 E2
Old Cross SG14 ....113 C6
Old Dean HP3 ....137 A4
Old Dr The AL8 ....110 B5
Old Farm LU7 ....80 D4
Old Fishery La
Hemel Hempstead HP1 ....123 F1
Hemel Hempstead HP1 ....137 F8
Old Fold Cl EN5 ....171 F8
Old Fold La EN5 ....171 F8
Old Fold View EN5 ....171 C6
Old Forge Cl
Abbots Langley WD25 ....154 A6
Welwyn Garden City AL7 ....89 F2
Old Forge Rd EN1 ....161 F1
Old Forge Row SG13 ....114 B3
Old Forge The HP23 ....79 B4
Old French Horn La AL10 ....130 B6
Old Gannon Cl HA6 ....174 C5
Old Garden Ct AL3 ....127 C3
Old Gorhanbury Ho* AL3 ....126 C4
Old Granary The SG7 ....4 D4
Old Grove Cl EN7 ....147 D5
Old Hale Way SG5 ....21 E2
Old Hall Cl HA5 ....175 E2
Old Hall Dr HA5 ....175 E2
Old Harpenden Rd AL3 ..127 E6
Old Hat Factory The 1 LU2 ....45 D1
Old Herns La AL7 ....111 C8
Old Hertford Rd AL9 ....130 C7
Old Highway EN11 ....135 C8
Old House Ct HP2 ....124 F3
Old House La
Lower Nazeing EN9 ....149 F8
Sarratt WD4 ....152 F4
Old House Rd HP2 ....124 F3
Old Knebworth La SG3, SG2 ....68 D8
Old La SG3 ....69 B5
Old Leys AL10 ....130 A2
Old London Rd
Hertford SG13 ....113 E6
St Albans AL1 ....127 E2
Old Maltings The 2 CM23 ....77 A7
Old Maple HP2 ....104 F1
Old Meadow Cl HP4 ....122 A2
Old Mill Gdns HP4 ....122 D4
Old Mill La CM22 ....98 B6
Old Mill Rd WD4 ....153 C5
Old Nazeing Rd EN9, EN10 ....135 C1
Old North Rd
Kneesworth SG8 ....2 B4
Royston SG8 ....7 C8
Old Oak AL1 ....141 E8
Old Oak Cl SG15 ....11 A8
Old Oak Close Ind Est SG15 ....11 A8
Old Oak Gdns HP4 ....121 E7
Old Oaks EN9 ....163 E7
Old Orch Luton LU1 ....63 D5
Park Street AL2 ....141 D5
Old Orchard Cl EN4 ....159 D1
Old Orchard Mews HP4 .122 C3
Old Park Rd SG5 ....34 E7
Old Parkbury La AL2 ....141 F1
Old Parkway Sch AL8 ...110 C5
Old Priory Pk AL1 ....127 E2
Old Rd CM17 ....118 D5
Old Rectory Cl AL5 ....86 A2
Old Rectory Dr AL10 ....130 B5
Old Rectory Gdns AL4 ..108 D8
Old Redding HA3 ....176 C6
Old River La CM23 ....76 F7
Old School Cl SG4 ....67 F1
Old School Cotts HP5 ...136 D5
Old School Flats The HP23 ....99 D8
Old School Gn SG2 ....52 E5
Old School Orch SG14 ....70 E3
Old School The
Hertford Heath SG13 ....114 C4
Shillington SG5 ....19 E8
Old School Wlk
Arlesey SG15 ....11 A4
Slip End LU1 ....63 C1
Old Shire La WD3 ....164 A2
Old Solesbridge La WD3 ....165 A6
Old Sopwell Gdns AL1 ..127 E1
Old South Cl HA5 ....175 D2
Old Uxbridge Rd WD3 ...172 E3
Old Vicarage Gdns AL3 ...83 D6
Old Waddling La 5 AL4 ..87 D1
Old Walled Gdn The SG1 .36 C1
Old Watford Rd AL2 ....140 E2
Old Watling St AL3 ....84 B3
Old Works The AL1 ....127 E2
Old's App WD18 ....166 C1
Old's Cl WD18 ....166 B1
Olde Ct HA6 ....174 E4
Olde Swann Ct SG1 ....50 C8
Olden Mead SG6 ....23 B3
Oldfield Cl EN8 ....148 E3
Oldfield Ct AL1 ....127 E3
Oldfield Dr EN8 ....148 E3
Oldfield Farm Rd
Lower Stondon SG16 ....10 B4
Lower Stondon SG16 ....10 C4
Oldfield Rd
Hemel Hempstead HP1 ....123 E2
London Colney AL2 ....142 D6
Oldfield Rise SG4 ....66 E7
Oldhall Ct SG4 ....66 E7
Oldhall St SG14 ....113 D6
Oldhams Trad Est WD24 ....154 C2
Oldhill Wood LU6 ....82 D6
Oldhouse Croft CM20 ...117 E2
Oldings Cnr AL9 ....110 B1
Oldpark Ride EN7 ....161 D7
Oldwood AL6 ....89 D7
Olive Taylor Ct HP2 ....124 F7
Oliver Cl
Hemel Hempstead HP3 ....138 E7
Park Street AL2 ....141 D4
Oliver Ct SG12 ....92 E4
Oliver Rd HP3 ....138 F7
Oliver Rise HP3 ....138 E7
Oliver's La SG5 ....11 F7
Olivers Cl HP4 ....123 C7
Olivia Gdns UB9 ....173 C2
Olleberrie La HP3,WD3 ...151 D7
Olwen Mews HA5 ....175 D1
Olyard Ct LU1 ....63 B6
Olympus Rd SG16 ....10 B4
Omega Ct 4 SG12 ....93 D1
Omega Maltings 2 SG12 .93 E1
On The Hill WD19 ....175 E8
Onslow Cl AL10 ....130 B5
Onslow Rd LU4 ....44 D5
Onslow St Audrey's Sch AL10 ....130 B5
Ontario Cl EN10 ....148 E6
Opening The SG4 ....88 F8
Openshaw Way SG6 ....23 A6
Optima Bsns Pk EN11 ...135 C7
Opus Ct WD6 ....170 A6
Oram Pl HP3 ....138 D8
Orbital Cres WD25 ....153 F4
Orchard Ave
Berkhamsted HP4 ....122 A4
Harpenden AL5 ....85 F1
Watford WD25 ....154 B8
Orchard Cl
Borehamwood WD6 ....169 F6
Bushey WD23 ....168 D1
Caddington LU1 ....62 E4
Chorleywood WD3 ....164 D5
Cuffley EN6 ....146 E3
Hemel Hempstead HP2 ....124 F5
Kneesworth SG8 ....2 A5
Letchworth SG6 ....22 F8
Little Berkhamsted SG13 ..132 C4
Radlett WD7 ....155 E3
St Albans AL1 ....127 F2
St Ippolyts SG4 ....34 F3
Stanstead Abbotts SG12 ..115 C4
Ware SG12 ....93 D2
Watford WD17 ....166 F7
Wingrave HP22 ....60 B3
Orchard Cres SG1 ....50 C7
Orchard Croft CM20 ....118 A2
Orchard Ct HP9 ....137 A4
Orchard Dr
Chiswell Green AL2 ....141 B5
Chorleywood WD3 ....164 D5
Standon SG11 ....55 E2
Watford WD17 ....166 F8
Orchard Gdns EN9 ....163 C5
Orchard Ho SG11 ....55 F7
Orchard House La AL1 ..127 D2
Orchard Lea CM21 ....97 C1
Orchard Mead AL10 ....129 F5
Orchard On The Green The WD3 ....165 F4
Orchard Pl EN8 ....148 D1
Orchard Prim Sch The WD24 ....153 F3
Orchard Rd Baldock SG7 ...12 E1
Barnet EN5 ....171 F5
Bishop's Stortford CM23 ....59 B1
Hitchin SG4 ....22 B1
Royston SG8 ....7 B7
Stevenage SG1 ....50 C7
Tewin AL6 ....90 C5
Welwyn AL6 ....89 C5
Orchard Sq EN10 ....148 F7
Orchard St
Hemel Hempstead HP3 ...138 D8
St Albans AL3 ....127 C2
Orchard The Baldock SG7 ..23 F8
Codicote SG4 ....67 F1
Hertford SG14 ....92 C1
Kings Langley WD4 ....139 A2
Radlett WD6 ....168 F7
Tonwell SG12 ....92 E7
Welwyn Garden City AL8 ..110 D8
Orchard View AL6 ....89 F7
Orchard Way
Bovingdon HP3 ....137 A3
Breachwood Green SG4 ....47 E1
Goff's Oak EN7 ....147 B3
Knebworth SG3 ....68 E5
Letchworth SG6 ....22 F8
Lower Stondon SG16 ....10 B3
Luton LU4 ....44 C4
Pitstone LU7 ....80 E5
Potters Bar EN6 ....145 B2
Rickmansworth WD3 ....165 A2
Royston SG8 ....7 C8
Orchards The
Sawbridgeworth CM21 ....97 E3
Slip End LU1 ....63 C2
Tring HP23 ....99 F3
Orchid Cl
Goff's Oak EN7 ....147 C1
Hatfield AL10 ....109 F1
Orchid Ho AL1 ....127 F3
Ordelmere SG6 ....11 F1
Ordnance Rd EN3 ....162 E2
Oregon Way LU3 ....45 A8
Organ Hall Rd WD6 ....169 E8
Orient Cl AL1 ....127 E1
Orient Ctr The WD24 ....154 D2
Oriole Cl WD5 ....154 A8
Oriole Way CM23 ....76 C6
Orion Gate SG1 ....50 F5
Orion Way HA6 ....175 A6
Orkney Ho WD18 ....166 F4
Orlando Cl SG4 ....35 A6
Ormesby Dr EN6 ....158 D7
Ormonde Rd HA6 ....174 D6
Ormsby Cl LU1 ....63 E5
Ormskirk Rd WD19 ....175 D5
Oronsay HP3 ....125 B1
Orphanage Rd WD17, WD24 ....167 C7
Orpington Cl LU4 ....44 A3
Orton Cl AL4 ....128 A7
Orwell Ave SG1 ....36 F3
Orwell Ct 5 WD24 ....167 D7
Orwell View SG7 ....13 B1
Osborn Way AL8 ....110 D6
Osborne Ct 9 Luton LU1 ..63 F6
Potters Bar EN6 ....145 B1
Osborne Gdns EN6 ....145 B1
Osborne Rd
Cheshunt EN8 ....148 E4
Hoddesdon EN10 ....135 A4
Luton LU1 ....63 F6
Potters Bar EN6 ....145 B1
Watford WD24 ....154 C1
Osborne Way HP23 ....100 D1
Osbourne Ave WD4 ....138 F3
Osbourne Gdns 5 CM23 ..76 E5
Osier Ct 8 SG5 ....34 F8
Osiers The WD3 ....166 C4
Osmington Pl HP23 ....99 F4
Osprey Cl WD25 ....154 E5
Osprey Gdns SG2 ....51 D2
Osprey Ho 3 SG12 ....93 C3
Osprey Wlk LU4 ....44 A5
Ostell Cres EN3 ....163 A1
Oster St AL3 ....127 C4
Osterley Cl SG2 ....69 C7
Ostler Cl CM23 ....76 C4
Oswald Rd AL1 ....127 E2
Otley Way WD19 ....175 C7
Otter Gdns AL10 ....130 B4
Otterspool La WD25 ....154 E1
Otterspool Way WD25 ...154 F1
Otterton Cl AL5 ....85 F3
Ottoman Terr WD17 ....167 C6
Ottway Wlk AL6 ....89 C4
Otway Gdns WD23 ....168 E2
Otways Cl EN6 ....159 B6
Oudle La SG10 ....74 F2
Oughton Cl SG5 ....34 C8
Oughton Head Way SG5 ..34 D8
Oughton Prim Sch SG5 ...21 C1
Oughtonhead La SG5 ....34 C8
Oughtonhead Prim Sch SG5 ....34 C8
Oulton Cres EN6 ....158 D7
Oulton Rise AL5 ....86 C3
Oulton Way WD19 ....175 F6
Oundle Ave WD23 ....168 C3
Oundle Ct SG2 ....69 C8

Oundle Path SG2 69 C8
Oundle The SG2 69 C8
Our Lady RC Prim Sch AL7 110 E4
Our Lady's RC Prim Sch SG5 21 E2
Ousden Cl EN8 148 E1
Ousden Dr EN8 148 E1
Ouseley Cl LU4 44 D3
Outlook Ho EN3 162 F3
Oval The Cheshunt EN10 148 E7
Lower Stondon SG16 10 C3
Stevenage SG1 37 A1
Overfield Rd LU2 46 C1
Overlord Cl EN10 134 E3
Overstone Rd
Harpenden AL5 86 C1
Luton LU4 44 D1
Overstream WD3 165 B5
Overtrees AL5 85 F3
Oving Cl LU2 46 D2
Owen Dr SG8 2 D1
Owen Jones Cl SG16 10 C5
Owens Way WD3 166 A5
Owles La SG9 41 A6
Ox La AL5 86 B3
Oxcroft CM23 76 F3
Oxen Ind Est LU2 45 F1
Oxen Rd LU2 45 F1
Oxendon Dr EN11 135 A5
Oxfield Cl HP4 122 A3
Oxford Ave AL1 128 C2
Oxford Cl Cheshunt EN8 148 D2
Kneesworth SG8 2 A7
Moor Park HA6 174 D6
Oxford Ho 8 WD6 170 A7
Oxford Pl AL10 129 E7
Oxford Rd
Breachwood Green SG4 47 E1
2 Luton LU1 63 E6
Oxford St WD18 167 B4
Oxhey Ave WD19 167 D2
Oxhey Dr S WD19 175 B7
Oxhey Inf Sch WD23 167 E4
Oxhey La Pinner HA5 176 A5
South Oxhey WD19 175 F7
Watford WD19 167 D2
Oxhey Rd WD19 167 D2
Oxhey Ridge Cl HA6 175 B5
Oxhey Wood Prim Sch WD19 175 C7
Oxlease Dr AL10 130 B4
Oxleys Rd SG2 51 B3
Oxleys The CM17 118 E4
Oysterfields AL3 127 C4

P

Pacatian Way SG1 51 C8
Packhorse Cl AL4 128 C6
Packhorse La EN6 157 D8
Paddick Cl EN11 134 F7
Paddock Cl Hunsdon SG12 95 D1
Letchworth SG6 23 A5
Watford WD19 167 E3
Paddock Ho AL7 111 B6
Paddock Rd SG9 40 E8
Paddock The
Bishop's Stortford CM23 76 D3
Hatfield AL10 130 A6
Hitchin SG4 35 A5
Hoddesdon EN10 135 A3
Paddock Way HP1 123 E3
Paddock Wood AL5 107 E7
Paddocks Cl SG2 51 B4
Paddocks The
Chorleywood WD3 164 F5
Codicote SG4 68 A1
Hertford Heath SG13 114 B3
Kimpton AL4 87 B6
Stevenage SG2 51 B3
Welwyn Garden City AL7 111 B7
Padgate Ho 12 WD19 175 C7
Padgets The EN9 163 E5
Page Cl SG7 23 F6
Page Hill SG12 93 C2
Page Rd SG13 114 A6
Pageant Rd AL1 127 D2
Pages Cl CM23 76 D5
Pages Croft HP4 122 A6
Paget Cotts SG12 71 F7
Paignton Cl LU4 44 D4
Paine's La HA5 175 E1
Paines Orch LU7 80 A8
Painters La EN3 162 E4
Palace Cl WD4 139 A1
Palace Gdns
Bishop's Stortford CM23 76 E5
Royston SG8 7 C6
Palfrey Cl AL3 127 D5
Pallas Rd HP2 124 F5
Pallett Ct EN11 135 B4
Palmer Ave WD23 168 B4
Palmer Cl SG14 113 C8
Palmer Ct SG12 92 E4
Palmer Gdns EN5 171 D4
Palmer Rd SG14 113 D8
Palmers Gr EN9 135 F1
Palmers La 8 CM23 76 F7
Palmers Rd WD6 170 B8
Palmers Way EN8 148 E2
Palmerston Cl AL8 110 C6
Palmerston Ct SG2 51 B7
Palmerston Dr 7 AL4 87 D1
Pamela Ave HP3 138 F8
Pamela Gdns CM23 76 F3
Pams La SG4 66 D1
Pancake La HP2 125 D2
Pankhurst Cres SG2 51 C5
Pankhurst Pl WD24 167 C6
Pankridge WD19 175 D8
Panshanger Aerodrome AL6,AL7 111 D7
Panshanger Dr AL7 111 C6
Panshanger Prim Sch AL7 111 A7
Pantiles The WD23 168 D1
Panxworth Rd 1 HP3 124 D1
Paper Mill La SG11 55 E1
Par Cl SG13 114 B7
Parade The
Hatfield AL10 130 C7
Letchworth SG6 11 F1
Luton LU3 44 C7
South Oxhey WD19 175 D7
South Oxhey WD19 175 E7
Watford WD17 167 B6
Paradise HP2 124 D2
Paradise Cl EN7 148 B3
Paradise Rd EN9 163 C5
Paradise Wildlife Pk* EN10 133 F2
Paramount Ind Est WD24 154 C1
Parish Cl WD25 154 C5
Parishes Mead SG2 51 D4
Park Ave
Bishop's Stortford CM23 76 F3
Luton LU3 44 C7
Potters Bar EN6 159 D6
Radlett WD7 156 B6
Rickmansworth WD3 165 A5
St Albans AL1 128 A4
Watford WD23 167 E7
Watford,West Watford WD18 167 A5
Park Ave N AL5 85 F1
Park Ave S AL5 85 F1
Park Avenue Maisonettes WD23 167 F7
Park Avenue Trad Est LU3 44 C7
Park Cl Baldock SG7 23 F7
Brookmans Park AL9 145 A5
Harrow HA3 176 E2
Hatfield AL9 130 C6
Markyate AL3 83 D5
Rickmansworth WD3 174 B6
Stevenage SG2 51 B1
Watford WD23 167 D6
Park Cnr AL4 143 B8
Park Cres Baldock SG7 23 E7
Borehamwood WD6 169 F6
Harrow HA3 176 E2
Park Ct Harlow CM20 117 D2
Letchworth SG6 23 A6
Luton LU2 45 D1
Northwood HA6 174 F4
Park Dr Baldock SG7 23 E7
Potters Bar EN6 159 B8
Standon SG11 55 D3
Stanmore HA3 176 E4
Park Farm Cl SG16 10 D8
Park Farm Ind Est SG9 40 D8
Park Farm Ind Pk SG8 18 F2
Park Farm La SG8 18 C2
Park Gate SG4 34 F6
Park Gdns SG7 23 E7
Park Hill Harlow CM17 118 B4
Harpenden AL5 85 F2
Park Hill Rd HP1 124 B3
Park Ho
Berkhamsted HP4 122 B5
Welwyn Garden City AL8 110 D7
Park Ind Est AL2 141 E4
Park La
Bishop's Stortford CM23 76 F4
Cheshunt EN7 162 D6
Colney Heath AL4 129 C1
Hammond Street EN7 148 A4
Harefield UB9 173 B2
Harlow CM20 117 D2
Hemel Hempstead HP2 124 D2
Hoddesdon EN10 134 F3
Kimpton SG4 66 C1
Knebworth SG3 68 D5
Standon SG11 55 D3
Park Lane Paradise EN7 148 A6
Park Lodge WD25 154 D5
Park Mans HA6 174 C7
Park Mdw AL9 130 C6
Park Mead CM20 117 B1
Park Mews AL9 130 C6
Park Mount AL5 85 F3
Park Nook Gdns EN2 161 D2
Park Pl Park Street AL2 141 D4
Stevenage SG1 50 D5
Park Place Chambers SG1 50 D5
Park Rd Barnet EN5 171 F5
Bushey WD23 168 A3
Cheshunt EN8 162 D6
Enfield EN3 162 E3
Hemel Hempstead HP1 124 C1
Hertford SG13 113 E6
Hoddesdon EN11 135 A6
Northaw EN6 146 A1
Radlett WD7 156 A4
Rickmansworth WD3 165 E2
Stansted Mountfitchet CM24 59 E6
Park Rd *continued*
Tring HP23 100 A3
Ware SG12 93 B2
Watford WD17 167 B8
Park Rise
Berkhamsted HP4 121 E6
Harpenden AL5 85 E3
Harrow HA3 176 E2
Park Rise Cl AL5 85 E3
Park Sq LU1 63 E7
Park St Baldock SG7 23 E8
Berkhamsted HP4 122 B5
Hatfield AL9 130 C6
Hitchin SG4 34 E6
Luton LU1 63 F6
Park Street AL2 141 D5
Tring HP23 100 A3
Park St W LU1 63 E7
Park Street CE Sch AL2 141 D4
Park Street La AL2 141 C3
Park Street Sta AL2 141 D5
Park Terr Enfield EN3 162 E1
2 Luton LU1 63 F6
Much Hadham SG10 74 F3
Park The Redbourn AL3 106 B5
St Albans AL1 128 A5
Park Viaduct LU1 63 F6
Park View
Great Hormead SG9 42 A7
Hatfield AL9 130 C7
Hoddesdon EN11 135 A5
Pinner HA5 175 F2
Potters Bar EN6 159 C6
Stevenage SG2 51 B1
Park View Cl Luton LU3 44 D6
St Albans AL1 128 A2
Park View Cotts CM23 76 F3
Park View Ct HP4 122 B4
Park View Dr AL3 83 D6
Park View Rd
Berkhamsted HP4 122 B4
Pinner HA5 175 B3
Park Way Hitchin SG5 34 E6
Rickmansworth WD3 165 C1
Parker Ave SG14 113 D8
Parker Cl SG6 22 E4
Parker St WD24 167 B8
Parker's Field SG2 51 C4
Parkers La SG7 3 D5
Parkfield
Chorleywood WD3 164 F5
Letchworth SG6 23 D4
Markyate AL3 83 D5
Parkfield Ave HA2 176 C1
Parkfield Cres
Harrow HA2 176 C1
Kimpton SG4 66 D1
Parkfield Ho HA2 176 B2
Parkfield View EN6 159 B7
Parkfields AL8 110 D6
Parkgate Inf Sch WD24 154 C2
Parkgate Jun Sch WD24 154 C2
Parkgate Rd WD24 154 C2
Parkhurst Rd SG14 113 C7
Parkins Cl SG11 73 A6
Parkinson Cl AL4 108 D8
Parkland Cl 3 EN11 115 B1
Parkland Dr LU1 63 D5
Parklands Bushey WD23 168 C3
Hemel Hempstead HP1 123 F5
Royston SG8 7 E6
Waltham Abbey EN9 163 D7
Parklands Cl EN4 159 D1
Parklands Dr AL3 127 A2
Parkmead 6 LU1 63 F6
Parkside Cheshunt EN8 162 E5
Potters Bar EN6 159 C7
Watford WD19 167 C3
Welwyn AL6 89 C5
Wyddial SG9 27 D2
Parkside Com Prim Sch WD6 156 F1
Parkside Ct EN7 148 B3
Parkside Dr WD17 166 F7
Parkside Rd HA6 174 F5
Parkview Ct HA3 176 E3
Parkview Ho WD19 167 D3
Parkway
Sawbridgeworth CM21 97 F1
Stevenage SG2 51 A1
Welwyn Garden City AL8 110 C6
Parkway Cl AL8 110 C6
Parkway Ct AL1 142 B8
Parkway Gdns AL8 110 D5
Parkway Rd LU1 64 B5
Parkwood Cl EN10 134 F4
Parkwood Dr HP1 123 F3
Parliament Sq SG14 113 D6
Parmiter's Sch WD25 154 C8
Parndon Mill La CM20 117 B3
Parnel Rd SG12 93 F2
Parnell Cl WD5 139 F1
Parr Cres HP2 125 B8
Parrott's La HP23 120 A4
Parrotts Cl WD3 166 A4
Parrotts Field EN11 135 B7
Parson's Cl AL3 84 B1
Parsonage Cl
Abbots Langley WD5 139 E1
Tring HP23 100 A4
Parsonage Ct HP23 100 A3
Parsonage Farm
Rickmansworth WD3 165 C2
Wingrave HP22 60 B3
Parsonage Farm Trad Est CM24 59 F3
Parsonage La Albury SG11 57 A6
Parsonage La *continued*
Bishop's Stortford CM23 77 C8
Spellbrook CM21 97 D6
Stansted Mountfitchet CM24 59 F4
Welham Green AL9 144 B8
Parsonage Pl HP23 100 A3
Parsonage Rd
Rickmansworth WD3 165 D2
Welham Green AL9 144 B8
Parsons Green Est SG1 37 C2
Parthia Cl SG8 7 E6
Partridge Cl Barnet EN5 171 C3
Bushey WD23 168 C1
Luton LU4 44 A5
Partridge Hill SG7 4 C3
Partridge Rd AL3 127 D7
Parva Cl AL5 107 D6
Parvills EN9 163 D7
Parys Rd LU3 45 B6
Pascal Way SG6 23 B8
Pasfield EN9 163 D6
Passfield Cotts SG11 72 F1
Passingham Ave SG4 35 A6
Paston Rd HP2 124 E5
Pasture Cl WD23 168 C2
Pasture La SG4 65 E8
Pasture Rd SG6 22 E3
Pastures Ct LU4 44 A3
Pastures The
Chiswell Green AL2 141 A7
Hatfield AL10 130 B4
Hemel Hempstead HP1 123 E4
Stevenage SG2 51 D8
Totteridge N20 171 F1
Ware SG12 93 C3
Watford WD19 167 C2
Welwyn Garden City AL7 111 B4
Pastures Way LU4 44 A4
Pat Larner Ho 9 AL1 127 D2
Paternoster Cl EN9 163 F6
Paternoster Hill EN9 163 F7
Pathway The
Radlett WD7 155 F3
Watford WD19 167 D1
Patmore Cl CM23 76 C8
Patmore Heath (Nature Reserve)* SG11 57 D8
Patmore Link Rd HP2 125 C2
Patmore Rd EN9 163 E5
Patricia Gdns CM23 76 E5
Patrick Gr EN9 163 B6
Paul's Gn EN8 162 E6
Pauls La EN11 135 A6
Paxton Rd
Berkhamsted HP4 122 D4
St Albans AL1 127 E2
Payne End SG9 15 B1
Payne's Pk SG5 34 E7
Paynes Cl SG6 12 A1
Paynes Field Cl HP4 121 D7
Paynes La EN9 149 C7
Paynesfield Rd WD23 168 F2
Pea La HP4 121 D7
Peabody Ct EN3 163 A2
Peace Cl EN7 148 B2
Peace Dr WD17 167 A6
Peace Gr AL6 90 A7
Peace Prospect WD17 167 A6
Peach Ct LU1 63 F6
Peacock Wlk WD5 154 A8
Peacocks Cl HP4 121 F6
Peakes La EN7 147 F4
Peakes Pl AL1 127 F3
Peakes Way EN7 147 F4
Pear Tree Cl SG16 10 B3
Pear Tree Dell SG6 23 B3
Pear Tree Wlk EN7 147 E5
Pearces Wlk 4 AL1 127 D2
Pearl Ct Baldock SG7 12 F1
Hoddesdon EN11 135 A6
Pearman Dr SG12 71 E7
Pearsall Cl SG6 23 B5
Pearson Ave SG13 113 C4
Pearsons Cl SG13 113 C4
Peartree Cl
Hemel Hempstead HP1 124 A4
Welwyn Garden City AL7 110 E6
Peartree Ct
Watford WD24 154 D3
Welwyn Garden City AL7 110 E5
Peartree Farm AL7 110 E6
Peartree La AL7 110 E6
Peartree Prim Sch AL7 110 E5
Peartree Rd
Hemel Hempstead HP1 124 A4
Luton LU2 46 C4
Peartree Spring Inf Sch SG2 51 B3
Peartree Spring Jun Sch SG2 51 B3
Peartree Way SG2 51 A3
Peascroft Rd HP3 125 B1
Peasecroft SG9 39 C7
Peasmead SG9 40 E6
Pebbles The SG7 12 C4
Peck's Hill EN9 135 E2
Peckworth Ind Est SG16 10 A4
Pedlars La SG8 15 E7
Pedley Hill HP4,LU6 82 C1
Peel Cres SG14 113 C8
Peel Pl 6 LU1 63 D7
Peel St LU1 63 D7
Peerglow Ctr SG12 114 E8
Peerglow Ind Est WD18 166 B1
Peg's La SG13 113 D5
Pegasus Ct WD5 153 F7
Pegasus Pl AL3 127 D5
Pegmire La WD25 168 C8
Pegrum Dr AL2 142 B5
Pegs La SG12 95 D5
Pegsdon Cl LU3 45 B7
Pegsdon Way SG5 19 E1
Peitley Cotts AL3 84 A1
Pelham Ct
Hemel Hempstead HP2 125 C3
Welwyn Garden City AL7 111 C5
Pelham Rd SG11 55 F7
Pelhams The WD25 154 D4
Pelican Way SG6 11 F1
Pemberton Almshouses 4 AL3 127 D4
Pemberton Cl AL1 141 D8
Pembridge Chase HP3 137 A3
Pembridge La EN10 133 E2
Pembridge Rd HP3 137 A3
Pembroke Ave
Enfield EN1 162 B1
Luton LU4 44 F3
Pembroke Cl EN10 148 E8
Pembroke Dr EN7 147 B2
Pembroke Ho 3 WD6 170 A5
Pembroke Rd Baldock SG7 23 F8
Moor Park HA6 174 C7
Pemsel Ct HP3 124 E1
Penda Cl LU3 44 F7
Pendennis Ct AL5 107 D7
Penfold Cl SG7 24 A7
Penfold Trad Est WD24 167 C8
Pengelly Cl EN7 148 B1
Penhill LU3 44 E6
Penhill Ct LU3 44 E6
Penman Cl AL2 141 A4
Penn Cl WD3 164 D3
Penn Ho Moor Park HA6 174 C7
14 South Oxhey WD19 175 C7
Penn Pl 1 WD3 165 D2
Penn Rd
Chiswell Green AL2 141 C4
Rickmansworth WD3 165 A1
Stevenage SG1 50 E4
Penn Way
Chorleywood WD3 164 D3
Letchworth SG6 23 B3
Pennard Ho 3 WD19 175 D7
Penne Cl WD7 156 A5
Pennine Ave LU3 44 D8
Pennine Way HP2 125 A7
Pennington La CM24 59 D8
Penningtons CM23 76 C5
Penns The SG8 17 E6
Penny Croft AL5 107 A4
Penny Ct WD17 167 B7
Pennyfather Cl SG3 69 E2
Pennyfathers La AL6 90 B4
Pennymead CM20 118 A1
Penray EN5 171 E6
Penrose Ave WD19 175 E8
Penrose Ct HP2 124 E7
Penscroft Gdns WD6 170 D5
Penshurst CM17 118 C3
Penshurst Cl AL5 85 D4
Penshurst Rd EN6 159 D7
Penta Ct WD6 170 A5
Pentagon Pk HP2 125 C5
Pentland HP2 124 F6
Pentland Rd WD23 168 C3
Pentland Rise SG1 37 C3
Pentley Cl AL8 89 D1
Pentley Pk AL8 89 D1
Penton Dr EN8 148 D2
Pentrich Ave EN1 162 A1
Penzance Cl UB9 173 D1
Peplins Cl AL9 144 E5
Peplins Way AL9 144 E5
Peppard Cl AL3 106 A6
Pepper Ct SG7 23 F8
Pepper Hill SG12 114 F4
Peppercorn Wlk SG4 35 B7
Peppett's Gn HP5 120 D1
Pepsal End SG2 69 B8
Pepsal End Rd LU1 84 C7
Pepys Cres EN5 171 C4
Pepys Way SG7 23 E8
Percheron Dr LU4 44 A3
Percheron Rd WD6 170 D3
Percival Ct EN8 148 E1
Percival Way LU2 64 C7
Percy Rd WD18 167 B5
Peregrine Cl
Bishop's Stortford CM23 76 D6
Watford WD25 154 E5
Peregrine Ho 1 SG12 93 C3
Peregrine Rd LU4 44 A4
Perham Way AL2 142 D6
Perivale Gdns WD25 154 B5
Periwinkle Cl SG8 17 C5
Periwinkle La SG5 21 F1
Permain Cl WD7 156 E6
Perowne Way SG11 55 E3
Perram Cl EN10 148 E5
Perriors Cl EN7 148 A4
Perry Dr SG8 7 E7
Perry Gn HP2 105 A1
Perry Hill EN9 149 F8
Perry Mead WD23 168 C3
Perrycoste Ct AL4 128 A8
Perrymead LU2 46 F2
Perrysfield Rd EN8 148 E5
Perrywood AL8 110 D8
Perrywood La SG14 91 B7
Perspective Ho EN3 162 E3
Pescot Hill HP1 124 B5
Petard Cl LU4 44 A2
Peter's Pl HP4 121 E6
Peterborough Ho 9 WD6 170 A7

Peterlee Ct 2 HP2 ... 124 F7
Peters Ave AL2 ... 142 C5
Peters Way SG3 ... 68 F6
Peters Wood Hill SG12 ... 114 E7
Petersfield AL3 ... 127 E7
Peterslea WD4 ... 139 B2
Pettys Cl EN8 ... 148 D3
Petunia Ct LU3 ... 45 C1
Petworth Cl SG2 ... 69 C7
Pevensey Cl LU2 ... 46 D4
Pewterers Ave CM23 ... 76 C4
Pheasant Cl
Berkhamsted HP4 ... 122 C3
Tring HP23 ... 100 B6
Pheasants Way WD3 ... 165 B2
Phillimore Ct WD7 ... 155 E3
Phillimore Pl WD7 ... 155 E3
Phillipers WD25 ... 154 E4
Phillips Ave SG8 ... 7 C8
Phipps Hatch La EN2 ... 161 C1
Phoenix Cl HA6 ... 174 F6
Phoenix Ct EN3 ... 162 C1
Phyllis Courtnage Ho 4 HP2 ... 124 D5
Piccotts End La HP2 ... 124 D7
Piccotts End Rd HP1 ... 124 C7
Pick Hill EN9 ... 163 F7
Pickets Cl WD23 ... 168 E1
Picketts AL8 ... 89 D1
Pickford Hill AL5 ... 86 C3
Pickford Rd Markyate AL3 ... 83 D5
St Albans AL1 ... 128 B2
Picknage Cnr SG8 ... 9 A2
Picknage Rd SG8 ... 9 A2
Pie Cnr AL3 ... 84 C1
Pie Gdn AL3 ... 84 C1
Pierian Spring HP1 ... 124 B5
Pietley Hill AL3 ... 84 A1
Pig La CM22 ... 77 A3
Pigeonwick AL5 ... 86 B3
Piggotts La LU4 ... 44 D4
Piggotts Way CM23 ... 76 E5
Piggottshill La AL5 ... 107 D8
Pightle Cl SG8 ... 7 D7
Pightle The LU7 ... 80 D3
Pike End SG1 ... 50 D6
Pikes Cotts EN5 ... 171 C5
Pikes Leap 6 AL4 ... 87 D1
Pilgrim Cl
Chiswell Green AL2 ... 141 C4
Watford WD25 ... 154 D6
Pilgrims Row SG9 ... 40 F3
Pilgrims Way SG1 ... 37 B2
Piltdown Rd WD19 ... 175 D6
Pin Green Ind Est SG1 ... 37 C2
Pin Green Prim Sch SG1 ... 50 F6
Pinchfield WD3 ... 172 D5
Pindar Rd EN11 ... 135 C7
Pine Cl Berkhamsted HP4 ... 122 B4
Cheshunt EN8 ... 148 D3
Pine Crest AL6 ... 89 E8
Pine Gr
Bishop's Stortford CM23 ... 77 B6
Bricket Wood AL2 ... 140 F1
Brookmans Park AL9 ... 145 B6
Totteridge N20 ... 171 F1
Watford WD23 ... 167 F8
Pine Ridge AL1 ... 142 A8
Pine Tree Cl HP2 ... 124 D4
Pine Wlk HP4 ... 121 D7
Pinecroft HP3 ... 138 F7
Pinecroft Cres EN5 ... 171 E5
Pinecroft Ct HP3 ... 138 F7
Pinehill Hospl SG4 ... 35 A7
Pinehurst Cl WD5 ... 153 E7
Pinelands CM23 ... 58 F1
Pineridge Ct 4 EN5 ... 171 D5
Pines Ave EN1 ... 162 B3
Pines Cl HA6 ... 174 E4
Pines Hill CM24 ... 59 D5
Pines The
Borehamwood WD6 ... 169 F7
Hemel Hempstead HP3 ... 137 F7
Pinetree Gdns 5 HP2 ... 124 E2
Pinetree Ho WD25 ... 154 E3
Pinewood AL7 ... 110 E4
Pinewood Ave HA5 ... 176 B4
Pinewood Cl
Borehamwood WD6 ... 170 D7
Pinner HA5 ... 176 B4
South Oxhey WD19 ... 175 B5
St Albans AL4 ... 128 C3
Watford WD17 ... 167 A8
Pinewood Dr EN6 ... 158 F8
Pinewood Gdns HP1 ... 124 B3
Pinewood Lodge 1 WD23 ... 168 D1
Pinewood Sch SG12 ... 114 D7
Pinewoods 4 SG2 ... 50 F1
Pinfold Rd WD23 ... 167 F7
Pinford Dell 4 LU2 ... 46 D1
Pinks Farm WD7 ... 157 C8
Pinnacles EN9 ... 163 E5
Pinnate Pl AL7 ... 110 E2
Pinner Gn HA5 ... 175 C1
Pinner Hill HA5 ... 175 B3
Pinner Hill Rd HA5 ... 175 C1
Pinner Park Ave HA2 ... 176 C1
Pinner Park Gdns HA2 ... 176 C1
Pinner Rd
Northwood HA6 ... 175 A1
Watford WD19 ... 167 E2
Pinner Wood Fst & Mid Schs HA5 ... 175 C2
Pinnocks Cl SG7 ... 23 F7
Pinnocks La SG7 ... 23 F8
Pinto Cl WD6 ... 170 D3
Pioneer Way WD18 ... 166 F3
Pipers Ave AL5 ... 107 D7
Pipers Cl AL3 ... 106 A6
Pipers Hill HP1 ... 103 D3
Pipers La
Caddington AL3,LU1 ... 62 F1
Wheathampstead AL5 ... 107 F7
Pipit Cl SG8 ... 7 E8
Pippens AL8 ... 89 E1
Pippin Cl WD7 ... 156 E6
Pippin Gr SG8 ... 7 C7
Pippins The WD25 ... 154 C5
Pirton Cl Hitchin SG5 ... 34 D6
St Albans AL4 ... 128 C8
Pirton Cross SG5 ... 34 A7
Pirton Ct HP2 ... 124 F4
Pirton Hill Inf Sch LU4 ... 44 B6
Pirton Hill Jun Sch LU4 ... 44 B6
Pirton Rd Hitchin SG5 ... 34 C6
Holwell SG5 ... 21 A7
Luton LU4 ... 44 D5
Pirton Sch SG5 ... 20 D4
Pishiobury Dr CM21 ... 118 D8
Pitsfield AL8 ... 89 D1
Pitsford Terr LU2 ... 46 A1
Pitstone Cl AL4 ... 128 C8
Pitstone Common Forest Trails* HP4 ... 101 E7
Pitstone Green Farm Mus* LU7 ... 80 D4
Pitstone Windmill* LU7 ... 80 F4
Pitt Ct SG2 ... 51 B1
Pitt Dr AL4 ... 142 C8
Pitteway Wlk SG14 ... 113 C6
Pittmans Field CM20 ... 117 F1
Pix Ct SG15 ... 11 A8
Pix Farm La HP1 ... 123 C2
Pix Rd Letchworth SG6 ... 23 A6
Stotfold SG5 ... 11 E5
Pixies Hill Cres HP1 ... 123 F2
Pixies Hill Jun Mix Inf Sch HP1 ... 123 F2
Pixies Hill Rd HP1 ... 123 F2
Pixmore Ave SG6 ... 23 B6
Pixmore Ind Est SG6 ... 23 A6
Pixmore Jun Sch SG6 ... 23 A5
Pixmore Way SG6 ... 23 A5
Plaistow Way SG8 ... 9 E2
Plaiters Cl HP23 ... 100 B4
Plaitford Cl WD3 ... 173 E8
Plantaganet Pl EN9 ... 163 B6
Plantation Rd LU3 ... 44 D7
Plantation Wlk HP1 ... 124 A6
Plash Dr SG1 ... 50 E5
Plashes Cl SG11 ... 55 D2
Plashes Dr SG9 ... 40 F6
Plashets CM22 ... 98 D1
Platt Cl LU4 ... 44 D4
Plaw Hatch Cl CM23 ... 77 B8
Plaw Hatch Cnr CM23 ... 77 D8
Playford Sq LU4 ... 44 D5
Pleasance The AL5 ... 85 D4
Pleasant Pl WD3 ... 172 E3
Pleasant Rd CM23 ... 76 E8
Pleasant Rise AL9 ... 130 C8
Plewes Cl LU6 ... 82 E8
Plough Cl SG8 ... 5 B8
Plough Hill EN6 ... 146 E2
Plough La Harefield UB9 ... 173 C4
King's Walden SG4 ... 48 A5
Potten End HP4 ... 123 B7
Sarratt WD3 ... 151 F6
Ploughmans Cl CM23 ... 76 C5
Ploughmans End AL7 ... 111 C5
Plover Cl HP4 ... 122 C3
Plum Tree Rd SG16 ... 10 B2
Plummers La LU2 ... 65 C2
Plumpton Cl LU2 ... 46 D3
Plumpton Rd EN11 ... 135 C8
Pluto Rise HP2 ... 124 F5
Plymouth Cl LU2 ... 46 B1
Poets Chase HP1 ... 124 B5
Poets Cl HP1 ... 124 B4
Poets Ct AL5 ... 86 B1
Poets Gate
Goff's Oak EN7 ... 147 E3
Widford SG12 ... 95 D4
Poets Gn LU4 ... 44 A2
Polayn Garth AL8 ... 110 C7
Polegate LU2 ... 46 D2
Polehanger La HP1 ... 123 E5
Poles Hill WD3 ... 151 E6
Poles La Thundridge SG12 ... 93 C6
Ware SG12 ... 93 C3
Poles Pk SG12 ... 93 C6
Police Row SG8 ... 15 F7
Police Station La WD23 ... 168 B2
Pollard Gdns SG1 ... 50 F8
Pollards WD3 ... 172 D5
Pollards Cl EN7 ... 147 C2
Pollards Way SG5 ... 20 D4
Pollicott Cl AL4 ... 128 C8
Pollywick Rd HP23 ... 100 D1
Polsten Mews EN3 ... 163 A2
Polzeath Cl LU2 ... 64 C8
Pomeroy Cres WD24 ... 154 B3
Pomeroy Gr LU2 ... 45 E6
Pomfret Ave LU2 ... 45 F1
Pond Cl Harefield UB9 ... 173 C1
Luton LU4 ... 44 B5
Stevenage SG1 ... 50 C7
Tring HP23 ... 100 A4
Pond Croft Hatfield AL10 ... 129 F5
Welwyn Garden City AL7 ... 110 E5
Pond Ct SG4 ... 67 F1
Pond Field AL7 ... 90 A1
Pond La Baldock SG7 ... 23 E8
Little Gaddesden HP4 ... 102 E7
Pond La *continued*
Stansted Mountfitchet CM24 ... 59 D7
Pond Rd HP3 ... 139 A6
Pondcroft Rd SG3 ... 69 A4
Pondfield Cres AL4 ... 128 B7
Pondside SG4 ... 36 C4
Pondsmeade AL3 ... 106 B5
Pondwick Rd AL5 ... 85 E2
Pondwicks Cl AL1 ... 127 C2
Pondwicks Rd LU1 ... 63 F7
Ponsbourne St Mary's CE Prim Sch SG13 ... 146 E7
Pooleys La AL9 ... 144 C8
Pope Paul RC Prim Sch EN6 ... 158 F6
Pope's Rd WD5 ... 153 E8
Popes Ct LU2 ... 45 D1
Popes La WD24 ... 154 B1
Popes Row SG12 ... 93 D3
Popis Gdns SG12 ... 93 E2
Poplar Ave Hatfield AL10 ... 129 D5
Luton LU3 ... 45 C8
Poplar Cl Hitchin SG4 ... 35 B6
Pinner HA5 ... 175 D2
Royston SG8 ... 7 E7
Thundridge SG11 ... 72 F2
Poplar Dr Royston SG8 ... 7 E7
Stotfold SG5 ... 11 F8
Poplar Rd LU6 ... 82 E8
Poplar Shaw EN9 ... 163 F6
Poplar View SG12 ... 92 E4
Poplars AL7 ... 111 B7
Poplars Cl Hatfield AL10 ... 129 D5
Luton LU2 ... 46 B3
Watford WD25 ... 154 B7
Poplars The Arlesey SG15 ... 11 A8
Borehamwood WD6 ... 170 A8
Great Hallingbury CM22 ... 77 F4
2 Hammond Street EN7 ... 147 E5
Harefield UB9 ... 173 C2
Hemel Hempstead HP1 ... 124 B2
Ickleford SG5 ... 21 F5
St Albans AL1 ... 142 B7
Popple Way SG1 ... 50 E6
Poppy Cl
Hemel Hempstead HP1 ... 123 E4
Luton LU3 ... 45 D2
Poppy Mead SG1 ... 50 F4
Poppy Wlk
Goff's Oak EN7 ... 147 D3
Hatfield AL10 ... 129 F8
Poppyfields AL7 ... 111 C5
Porlock Dr LU2 ... 46 C1
Port Hill SG14 ... 113 C7
Port La CM22 ... 77 B2
Port Vale SG14 ... 113 C6
Porter's Mews SG4 ... 67 F1
Porters Cl SG9 ... 40 E8
Porters Hill AL5 ... 86 C4
Porters Park Dr WD7 ... 156 E7
Porters Wood AL3 ... 127 F7
Portland Ct LU4 ... 45 A1
Portland Dr
Cheshunt EN7 ... 162 A8
Enfield EN2 ... 161 E1
Portland Hts HA6 ... 174 F6
Portland Ind Est SG15 ... 11 A3
Portland Pl
17 Bishop's Stortford CM23 ... 76 F7
Hertford Heath SG13 ... 114 C4
Portland Rd
Bishop's Stortford CM23 ... 76 F7
Luton LU4 ... 45 A1
Portland St AL3 ... 127 C4
Portman Cl Hitchin SG5 ... 21 D2
St Albans AL4 ... 128 C7
Portman Ho AL3 ... 127 D6
Portmill La SG5 ... 34 F7
Post Office Cotts CM22 ... 98 C8
Post Office Rd CM20 ... 117 D1
Post Office Row SG4 ... 24 B1
Post Office Wlk 8 SG14 ... 113 D6
Post Wood Rd SG12 ... 114 E7
Postfield AL7 ... 90 A1
Posting Ho HP23 ... 101 A5
Postwood Gn SG13 ... 114 C3
Potash La HP23 ... 79 A5
Potten End CE Fst Sch HP4 ... 123 B6
Potten End Hill HP1 ... 123 E8
Potter St
Bishop's Stortford CM23 ... 76 F7
Pinner HA5 ... 175 B2
Potter Street Hill HA5 ... 175 B3
Potters Bar Com Hospl EN6 ... 159 C5
Potters Bar Mus* EN6 ... 158 F7
Potters Bar Sta EN6 ... 158 F7
Potters Ct EN6 ... 159 A7
Potters Field AL3 ... 127 E7
Potters Heights Cl HA5 ... 175 B3
Potters La
Borehamwood WD6 ... 170 C8
Stevenage SG1 ... 50 B4
Potters Mews WD6 ... 169 D3
Potterscrouch La AL2, AL3 ... 140 E7
Pottersheath Rd AL6 ... 68 D1
Pottery Cl LU3 ... 44 F7
Potton Rd SG8 ... 1 F6
Pouchen End La HP1 ... 123 D3
Poulteney Rd CM24 ... 59 E8
Poultney Cl WD7 ... 156 F7
Pound Ave SG1 ... 50 D6
Pound Cl
Lower Nazeing EN9 ... 149 E8
Pound Cl *continued*
Sandridge AL4 ... 108 C2
Pound Gn SG8 ... 1 F5
Pound La WD7 ... 156 F6
Poundfield WD25 ... 153 F4
Poundwell AL7 ... 111 A5
Powdermill La EN9 ... 163 B6
Powdermill Mews EN9 ... 163 B6
Powdermill Way EN9 ... 163 B6
Power Ct LU1 ... 63 F7
Power Dr EN3 ... 162 F3
Powis Ct Bushey WD23 ... 168 D1
Potters Bar EN6 ... 159 C5
Powys Ct WD6 ... 170 D6
Poynders Hill HP2 ... 125 C3
Poynders Mdw SG4 ... 88 F8
Poynings Cl AL5 ... 107 F8
Poynters Rd LU5 ... 44 A2
Prae Cl AL3 ... 127 B3
Prae Wood Prim Sch AL3 ... 127 A1
Praetorian Ct AL1 ... 141 C8
Prebendal Dr LU1 ... 63 B2
Precinct The EN10 ... 134 F3
Premier Ct EN3 ... 162 D1
Premier Pl WD18 ... 166 F4
Prentice Way LU2 ... 64 D7
Prescott Rd EN8 ... 148 E4
Presdales Ct SG12 ... 114 D8
Presdales Dr SG12 ... 114 E8
Presdales Sch SG12 ... 114 D7
Presentation Ct LU1 ... 63 F6
President Way LU2 ... 64 D8
Prestatyn Cl SG1 ... 50 B8
Preston Ct HA6 ... 175 A1
Preston Gdns
Enfield EN3 ... 162 E2
Luton LU2 ... 45 F2
Preston Path LU2 ... 45 F2
Preston Prim Sch SG4 ... 48 D6
Preston Rd Preston SG4 ... 48 E7
St Ippolyts SG4 ... 34 F1
Prestwick Cl LU2 ... 45 E5
Prestwick Dr CM23 ... 59 B1
Prestwick Rd WD19 ... 175 D6
Prestwood 2 WD19 ... 175 E8
Prestwood Gate AL1 ... 127 E5
Pretoria Rd WD18 ... 167 A5
Pretty Cnr HA6 ... 175 A5
Priestland Gdns HP4 ... 122 E6
Priestleys LU1 ... 63 A7
Primary Way SG15 ... 11 A4
Primett Rd SG1 ... 50 C7
Primley La CM22 ... 98 C1
Primrose Cl Arlesey SG15 ... 11 A4
Bishop's Stortford CM23 ... 76 C6
Hatfield AL10 ... 130 B4
Hemel Hempstead HP1 ... 123 E2
Luton LU3 ... 45 D2
Primrose Cotts WD7 ... 156 A4
Primrose Ct SG1 ... 50 D7
Primrose Dr SG13 ... 114 B6
Primrose Gdns
Bushey WD23 ... 168 B2
Radlett WD7 ... 156 A4
Primrose Hill WD4 ... 139 B3
Primrose Hill Rd SG1 ... 50 D7
Primrose La Arlesey SG15 ... 11 A4
Radlett WD25 ... 155 D1
Primrose Path EN7 ... 162 A8
Primrose View SG8 ... 7 F5
Prince Andrew's Cl SG8 ... 7 D5
Prince Edward St 6 HP4 ... 122 C4
Prince Eugene Pl AL1 ... 141 C8
Prince of Wales Prim Sch EN3 ... 162 F2
Prince Pk HP1 ... 124 A2
Prince St WD17 ... 167 C6
Prince Way LU2 ... 64 D8
Prince's St SG5 ... 11 F7
Princes Ave Enfield EN3 ... 162 E4
Watford WD18 ... 167 A5
Princes Cl HP4 ... 122 A6
Princes Ct
Bishop's Stortford CM23 ... 76 C7
Hemel Hempstead HP3 ... 138 B8
Princes Gate
Bishop's Stortford CM23 ... 76 C7
Harlow CM20 ... 117 E3
Princes Mews SG8 ... 7 C6
Princes Pl 15 LU2 ... 45 D1
Princes St SG12 ... 93 D2
Princess Alexandra Hospl CM20 ... 117 C1
Princess Diana Dr AL4 ... 128 D2
Princess Helena Coll The SG4 ... 48 E6
Princess St LU1 ... 63 D7
Printers Ct AL1 ... 127 D2
Printers Way CM20 ... 118 A5
Priors 9 CM23 ... 77 A7
Priors Cl SG13 ... 114 B3
Priors Ct CM22 ... 98 A2
Priors Hill SG5 ... 20 C4
Priors Wood Prim Sch SG12 ... 94 A3
Priors Wood Rd SG13 ... 114 C3
Priory Ave CM17 ... 118 C5
Priory Cl Cheshunt EN10 ... 148 E7
Hoddesdon EN11 ... 135 A5
Royston SG8 ... 7 E6
Stanmore HA7 ... 176 F7
Totteridge N20 ... 171 F2
Priory Ct
9 Berkhamsted HP4 ... 122 C4
Bishop's Stortford CM23 ... 76 F7
Bushey WD23 ... 168 C1
Priory Ct *continued*
13 Hertford SG14 ... 113 D6
Hitchin SG4 ... 34 F5
St Albans AL1 ... 127 E2
Priory Dell SG1 ... 50 F5
Priory Dr Stanmore HA7 ... 176 F7
Stansted Mountfitchet CM24 ... 59 E5
Priory End SG4 ... 34 F5
Priory Gate EN8 ... 148 F4
Priory Gdns
Berkhamsted HP4 ... 122 C4
Luton LU2 ... 45 D4
Priory La
Great Wymondley SG4 ... 35 F4
Royston SG8 ... 7 D6
Priory Lo WD3 ... 165 D2
Priory Orch AL3 ... 84 B2
Priory Row SG12 ... 95 E4
Priory Sch The SG5 ... 21 E2
Priory St Hertford SG14 ... 113 D6
Ware SG12 ... 93 C1
Priory View
Bushey WD23 ... 168 E2
Little Wymondley SG4 ... 35 E4
Priory Way SG4 ... 34 F4
Priory Wharf 12 SG14 ... 113 D6
Priory Wlk AL1 ... 141 E8
Pritchett Cl EN3 ... 163 A2
Proctor Way LU2 ... 64 C7
Proctors Way CM23 ... 77 A4
Progress Way LU4 ... 44 B7
Progression Ctr HP2 ... 125 A6
Prospect La AL5 ... 107 A4
Prospect Pl AL6 ... 89 C5
Prospect Rd
Cheshunt EN8 ... 148 C2
St Albans AL1 ... 127 D1
Prospect Way LU2 ... 64 C7
Protea Way SG6 ... 23 B6
Providence Gr SG1 ... 50 E8
Providence Pl 17 SG14 ... 113 D6
Providence Way SG7 ... 23 F7
Provost Way LU2 ... 64 C8
Prowse Ave WD23 ... 176 C8
Pryor Cl WD5 ... 153 F7
Pryor Rd SG7 ... 23 F6
Pryor Way SG6 ... 23 D5
Pryors Cl CM23 ... 77 A6
Pryors Ct SG7 ... 12 F1
Puddephat's La AL3 ... 104 D7
Pudding La Barley SG8 ... 9 A1
Hemel Hempstead HP1 ... 124 A5
Puddingstone Dr AL4 ... 128 C1
Pudgell The SG8 ... 9 E2
Pulham Ave EN10 ... 134 E3
Pullar Meml Prim Sch SG11 ... 72 E2
Puller Rd Barnet EN5 ... 171 E7
Hemel Hempstead HP1 ... 124 A2
Pulleys Cl HP1 ... 123 F4
Pulleys La HP1 ... 123 F4
Pullman Cl AL1 ... 127 E1
Pullman Dr SG4 ... 35 B7
Pulter's Way SG4 ... 35 A6
Pump Hill SG9 ... 30 A2
Pump Ho The 12 CM23 ... 77 A7
Pumphouse The SG8 ... 7 D7
Punch Bowl La AL3 ... 126 B8
Punchard Cres EN3 ... 163 B1
Purbeck Ho 8 WD18 ... 166 F3
Purbrock Ave WD25 ... 154 C3
Purcell Cl Datchworth AL6 ... 90 E6
Radlett WD6 ... 169 D8
Purcell Ct SG1 ... 50 C8
Purcell Sch WD23 ... 168 A7
Purkiss Rd SG13 ... 113 C3
Purley Ctr LU3 ... 44 E7
Purlings Rd WD23 ... 168 B4
Pursley Gdns WD6 ... 157 A1
Purway Cl LU3 ... 44 E7
Purwell La SG4 ... 35 C8
Purwell Prim Sch SG4 ... 35 D8
Putney Rd EN3 ... 162 D3
Puttenham Cl WD19 ... 175 D8
Puttenham Ct HP23 ... 78 F2
Putteridge High Sch LU2 ... 46 C5
Putteridge Inf Sch LU2 ... 46 C5
Putteridge Jun Sch LU2 ... 46 C5
Putteridge Par LU2 ... 46 B4
Putteridge Rd LU2 ... 46 C4
Putteridge Recn Ctr LU2 ... 46 C5
Putterills The AL5 ... 86 A1
Putters Croft HP2 ... 124 F8
Puttocks Cl AL9 ... 144 C8
Puttocks Dr AL9 ... 144 C8
Pye Cnr CM20 ... 117 D5
Pyghtle Ct LU1 ... 63 A7
Pyghtle The
Buntingford SG9 ... 40 D7
Luton LU1 ... 63 A7
Pyms Cl SG6 ... 23 B8
Pynchbek CM23 ... 76 E3
Pynchon Paddocks CM22 ... 98 D7
Pynefield Ho WD3 ... 164 F2
Pytchley Cl LU2 ... 45 E5

Q

Quadrangle The AL8 ... 110 C7
Quadrant The
Letchworth SG6 ... 22 F6
Royston SG8 ... 7 C8
St Albans AL4 ... 128 B6

Quadrant The *continued*
Stevenage SG1 . . . . .50 D4
Quail Wlk SG8 . . . . .7 E8
Quaker La EN9 . . . . .163 C5
Quaker Rd SG12 . . . . .93 E3
Quakers La EN6 . . . . .159 B8
Quantock Cl Luton LU3 . . . .45 B8
St Albans AL4 . . . . .128 C7
Stevenage SG1 . . . . .37 D3
Quantock Rise LU3 . . . . . . .31 B1
Quantocks HP2 . . . . .124 F6
Quartermass Cl HP1 . . . .124 A4
Quartermass Rd HP1 . . .124 A4
Queen Anne's Cl SG5 . . . . .11 F5
Queen Elizabeth Ct
Barnet EN5 . . . . .171 F5
Waltham Abbey EN9 . . . . . .163 C3
Queen Elizabeth II Hospl
AL7 .111 A2
Queen Elizabeth's Girls Sch
EN5 . . . . .171 F5
Queen Elizabeth's Sch
EN5 . . . . .171 D6
Queen Hoo La AL6 . . . . . . .90 F6
Queen Mary's Ave
WD18 . . . . .166 E5
Queen Marys Ct EN9 . . . .163 C4
Queen St
Chipperfield WD4 . . . . .152 A7
Hitchin SG4,SG5 . . . . .34 F7
Pitstone LU7 . . . . .80 D4
St Albans AL3 . . . . .127 C3
Stotfold SG5 . . . . .12 A6
Tring HP23 . . . . .100 A3
Queen Victoria Meml Hospl
AL6 .89 B4
Queen's Cl CM21 . . . . .97 F4
Queen's Ct
Aspenden SG9 . . . . .40 D5
Hertford SG13 . . . . .113 D5
St Albans AL1 . . . . .128 B3
Queen's Dr EN8 . . . . .163 A5
Queen's Dr The WD3 . . . .165 A3
Queen's Pl WD17 . . . . . . .167 C6
Queen's Rd
Cheshunt EN8 . . . . .162 E6
Harpenden AL5 . . . . .107 B7
Hertford SG13 . . . . .113 D5
Watford WD17 . . . . .167 C6
Queen's Sq The HP2 . . . .124 F4
Queens Ave WD18 . . . . . .166 F5
Queens Cl 4 Luton LU1 . . .63 E6
Stansted Mountfitchet
CM24 . . . . .59 E8
Queens Cres
Bishop's Stortford CM23 . . . .76 E5
St Albans AL4 . . . . .128 B6
Queens Ct Cheshunt EN8 .162 F5
14 Luton LU2 . . . . .45 D1
Watford WD17 . . . . .167 C6
Queens Dr WD5 . . . . .153 F7
Queens Head Wlk EN10 . .148 E8
Queens Rd Barnet EN5 . . .171 D6
Berkhamsted HP4 . . . . .122 A5
Royston SG8 . . . . .7 D7
Ware SG12 . . . . .93 F2
Queens Road Est EN5 . . .171 D6
Queens Silver Ct HA6 . . .174 E2
Queens Way
Cheshunt EN8 . . . . .162 F5
Shenley WD7 . . . . .156 E7
Queens' Sch WD23 . . . . . .168 A6
Queensgate EN8 . . . . . . .162 F5
Queensgate Ctr CM20 . . .117 F4
Queensway
Hemel Hempstead HP1,
HP2 . . . . .124 E4
Royston SG8 . . . . .7 D7
Stevenage SG1 . . . . .50 D5
Queensway Ho 1 AL10 . .130 A6
Queenswood Cres
WD25 . . . . .154 A6
Queenswood Dr SG4 . . . . .22 C1
Queenswood Sch AL9 . . .145 D3
Quendell Wlk HP2 . . . . . .124 E3
Quendon Dr EN9 . . . . . . .163 D6
Quickbeams AL7 . . . . .90 A1
Quickbury Farm CM21 . . . .98 B2
Quickley La WD3 . . . . . . .164 C4
Quickley Rise WD3 . . . . .164 C3
Quickly Brow WD3 . . . . . .164 B3
Quickmoor La WD4 . . . . .152 C6
Quickswood LU3 . . . . .45 A7
Quickwood Cl WD3 . . . . .165 A3
Quills SG6 . . . . .23 D4
Quilter Cl LU3 . . . . .44 F4
Quin Ct SG11 . . . . .55 F7
Quinces Croft HP1 . . . . . .124 A5
Quincey Rd SG12 . . . . .93 C4
Quinn Way SG6 . . . . .23 C5
Quinta Dr EN5 . . . . .171 C4

R

Raans Rd HP6 . . . . .150 A1
Raban Cl SG2 . . . . .51 C1
Raban Ct SG7 . . . . .12 F1
Rabley Heath Rd AL6 . . . . .68 B2
Rackman Dr LU3 . . . . .45 C5
Radburn Cnr SG6 . . . . .23 C5
Radburn Prim Sch SG6 . . .23 C5
Radburn Way SG6 . . . . .23 C4
Radcliffe Rd SG5 . . . . .35 A8
Radlett Inf Sch WD7 . . . .156 B3
Radlett La WD7 . . . . .156 E6
Radlett Lodge Sch WD7 .156 B8
Radlett Park Rd WD7 . . .156 A4
Radlett Prep Sch WD7 . .156 C1
Radlett Rd
London Colney AL2 . . . . . . .141 E2
Watford WD24 . . . . .167 D7
Radlett Sta WD7 . . . . . . .156 A4
Radnor Ct HA3 . . . . .176 F2
Radstone Pl LU2 . . . . .46 E1
Radwell La SG7 . . . . .12 C4
Raebarn Gdns EN5 . . . . . .171 B4
Raffin Cl SG3 . . . . .69 E3
Raffin Green La SG3 . . . . . .69 F4
Raffin Pk SG3 . . . . .69 E3
Ragged Hall La AL2 . . . . .140 E7
Raglan Ave EN8 . . . . .162 D5
Raglan Gdns WD19 . . . . .167 B1
Raglan Ho HP4 . . . . .122 A4
Rags La EN7 . . . . .147 E4
Railway Pl SG13 . . . . .113 E6
Railway Rd EN8 . . . . .162 F6
Railway St SG13,SG14 . . .113 D6
Railway Terr WD4 . . . . . .139 A4
Rainbow Cl AL3 . . . . .105 F6
Rainbow Ct WD19 . . . . . .167 C3
Rainer Cl EN8 . . . . .148 D2
Rainsborough Ct SG13 . .114 A7
Rainsford Rd CM24 . . . . . . .59 E8
Raleigh Cres SG2 . . . . .51 B8
Raleigh Gr LU4 . . . . .44 D1
Rally The SG15 . . . . .11 A7
Ralph Sadleir Mid Sch
SG11 . . . . .55 E3
Ralston Way WD19 . . . . .175 D8
Ram Gorse CM20 . . . . . . .117 B2
Ram Yard (Ind Est) SG15 . .11 A4
Ramblers Way AL7 . . . . . .111 C5
Rambling Way HP4 . . . . .123 C6
Ramerick Gdns SG15 . . . . .11 A2
Ramney Dr EN3 . . . . .162 E2
Ramparts The AL3 . . . . . .127 B2
Ramridge Prim Sch LU2 . .46 B2
Ramridge Rd LU2 . . . . .46 A2
Ramryge Ct AL1 . . . . .127 D1
Ramsay Cl EN10 . . . . .134 E2
Ramsbury Rd AL1 . . . . . .127 E2
Ramsdell SG1 . . . . .50 F5
Ramsey Cl
Brookmans Park AL9 . . . . .145 D4
St Albans AL1 . . . . .128 A1
Ramsey Lodge Ct 7
AL1 . . . . .127 E4
Ramson Rise HP1 . . . . . . .123 E2
Rand's Cl SG5 . . . . .21 B7
Rand's Cotts SG5 . . . . .21 B7
Rand's Mdw SG5 . . . . .21 B7
Randalls Ride HP2 . . . . . .124 E5
Randalls Wlk AL2 . . . . . . .140 F1
Randals Hill SG2 . . . . .51 C3
Randolph Ct 3 HA5 . . . . .176 A3
Randon Cl HA2 . . . . .176 B1
Ranelagh Rd HP2 . . . . . . .125 B3
Ranleigh Wlk AL5 . . . . . .107 D6
Rannoch Wlk HP2 . . . . . .124 D7
Ranock Cl LU3 . . . . .44 D8
Ranskill Rd WD6 . . . . . . .170 A8
Ransom Cl Hitchin SG4 . . . .34 F4
Watford WD19 . . . . .167 C2
Rant Mdw
Hemel Hempstead HP3 . . . .125 A1
Hemel Hempstead HP3 . . . .125 A2
Ranulf Cl CM17 . . . . .118 C6
Ranworth Ave
Hoddesdon EN11 . . . . .115 B2
Stevenage SG2 . . . . .69 C7
Ranworth Cl 2 HP3 . . . .124 D1
Ranworth Gdns EN6 . . . .158 D8
Raphael Cl WD7 . . . . .156 E7
Raphael Dr WD24 . . . . . . .167 D7
Rapper Ct LU3 . . . . .63 D8
Rasehill Cl WD3 . . . . .165 C4
Rathlyn HP3 . . . . .139 B8
Ratty's La EN11,CM19 . . .135 D6
Raven Cl WD3 . . . . .165 D2
Raven Ct AL10 . . . . .130 A4
Ravenbank Rd LU2 . . . . . . .46 C5
Ravenfield Rd AL7 . . . . . .110 F6
Ravenhill Way LU4 . . . . . . .44 B4
Ravens Ct HP4 . . . . .122 E6
Ravens La HP4 . . . . .122 D4
Ravens Wharf 5 HP4 . . .122 D4
Ravenscroft Barnet EN5 . .171 E5
Harpenden AL5 . . . . .107 D6
Hoddesdon EN10 . . . . .134 F3
Watford WD25 . . . . .154 E4
Ravenscroft Pk EN5 . . . . .171 D5
Ravenscroft Sch & Tech Coll
The N20 . . . . .171 F2
Ravensdell HP1 . . . . .123 F4
Ravensthorpe LU2 . . . . . . .46 B4
Ravenswood Pk HA6 . . . .175 A4
Rawdon Dr EN11 . . . . . . .135 A5
Ray's Hill HP5 . . . . .120 C2
Rayburn Rd HP1 . . . . .124 A5
Raydon Rd EN8 . . . . .162 D7
Rayfield AL8 . . . . .89 D1
Rayleigh Ho WD5 . . . . . . .153 F7
Raymer Cl AL1 . . . . .127 E4
Raymer Ct 1 AL1 . . . . . . .127 E4
Raymond Cl WD5 . . . . . . .153 D7
Raymond Cotts SG5 . . . . . .21 E4
Raymond Ct EN6 . . . . . . .159 C5
Raymonds Cl AL7 . . . . . . .110 E4
Raymonds Plain AL7 . . . .110 E4
Raynham Cl CM23 . . . . . . .77 C8
Raynham Rd CM23 . . . . . . .77 B8
Raynham St SG13 . . . . . . .113 E6
Raynham Way LU2 . . . . . . .46 D1
Raynsford Rd SG12 . . . . . . .93 E1
Raynton Rd EN3 . . . . .162 D2
Readings The WD3 . . . . . .164 F6
Recreation Ground CM24 . .59 E6
Rectory Cl
Bishop's Stortford CM23 . . . .76 D3
Essendon AL9 . . . . .131 F6
Hunsdon SG12 . . . . .116 D8
Rectory Dr CM23 . . . . .58 D6
Rectory Gdns AL10 . . . . . .130 B5
Rectory La
Berkhamsted HP4 . . . . .122 C4
Datchworth SG3 . . . . .69 C2
Farnham CM23 . . . . .58 D6
Kings Langley WD4 . . . . . . .139 A3
Lilley LU2 . . . . .32 D2
Rickmansworth WD3 . . . . . .165 D1
Shenley WD7 . . . . .157 B7
Stevenage SG1 . . . . .36 D1
Watton at S SG14 . . . . .70 D3
Rectory Rd
Rickmansworth WD3 . . . . . .165 D2
Welwyn Garden City AL8 . . . .89 B1
Rectory Wood CM20 . . . . .117 C1
Red Brick Cotts SG11 . . . .57 B1
Red Cottage HP23 . . . . . .100 D1
Red Cow Cotts LU6 . . . . . .83 C8
Red House Cl SG12 . . . . .114 E8
Red Lion Cl WD25 . . . . . .155 C2
Red Lion Cotts SG5 . . . . . .33 D2
Red Lion Ct 5 CM23 . . . . .77 A7
Red Lion La
Hemel Hempstead HP3 . . .139 A5
Sarratt WD3 . . . . .152 A4
Red Lodge WD6 . . . . .169 F6
Red Lodge Gdns HP4 . . . .122 A3
Red Rails LU1 . . . . .63 C5
Red Rails Ct LU1 . . . . .63 C5
Red Rd WD6 . . . . .169 F6
Redan Rd SG12 . . . . .93 E3
Redbourn Ind Ctr AL3 . . .106 B5
Redbourn Inf Sch AL3 . . .106 A6
Redbourn Jun Sch AL3 . . .106 A6
Redbourn La AL3,AL5 . . . .106 E6
Redbourn Rd
Hemel Hempstead HP2 . . . .125 B8
St Albans AL3 . . . . .126 E7
Redbourn Village Mus*
AL3 . . . . .106 A5
Redbournbury La AL3 . . .106 D2
Redbournbury Water Mill*
AL3 . . . . .106 D2
Redbrick Row CM22 . . . . . .98 B8
Redcar Dr SG1 . . . . .50 A6
Redcote La AL5 . . . . .107 A7
Redding Ho WD18 . . . . . .166 E3
Redding La AL3 . . . . .105 F8
Reddings
Hemel Hempstead HP3 . . .125 A1
Welwyn Garden City AL8 . .110 C7
Reddings Ave WD23 . . . . .168 B4
Reddings Prim Sch The
HP3 . . . . .125 A1
Reddings The WD6 . . . . . .169 F6
Redditch Ct HP2 . . . . .124 F7
Redferns Cl LU1 . . . . .63 A6
Redferns Ct LU1 . . . . .63 A6
Redgrave Gdns LU3 . . . . . .44 F7
Redhall Cl AL10 . . . . .129 F1
Redhall Dr AL10 . . . . .129 F1
Redhall La
Colney Heath AL4 . . . . .129 E1
Sarratt WD3 . . . . .165 E8
Redheath Cl WD25 . . . . . .153 F4
Redhill Rd SG5 . . . . .34 D8
Redhoods Way E SG6 . . . .22 E7
Redhoods Way W SG6 . . . .22 E6
Redhouse The EN10 . . . . .134 F1
Redlands Rd EN3 . . . . . . .162 E1
Redmire Cl LU4 . . . . .44 B6
Redoubt Cl SG4 . . . . .22 A1
Redpole Ct WD3 . . . . .165 E1
Redricks La CM21 . . . . . . .118 A6
Redvers Cl CM23 . . . . .59 A2
Redwell Ct EN8 . . . . .162 F5
Redwing Cl SG2 . . . . .51 D4
Redwing Gr WD5 . . . . . . .154 A8
Redwing Rise SG8 . . . . .7 E8
Redwood Cl WD19 . . . . . .175 D6
Redwood Dr
Hemel Hempstead HP3 . . . .124 E1
Luton LU3 . . . . .44 C8
Redwood Rise WD6 . . . . .157 B2
Redwood Way EN5 . . . . . .171 D4
Redwoods Hertford SG14 .113 C7
Welwyn Garden City AL8 . . .89 D3
Reed Cl AL2 . . . . .142 E4
Reed Fst Sch SG8 . . . . . . .16 E5
Reed Pl AL5 . . . . .85 F3
Reedham Cl AL2 . . . . .141 A2
Reedings Jun Sch CM21 . . .97 E3
Reedings Way CM21 . . . . . .97 F4
Reeds Chapel 12 WD24 . .167 C7
Reeds Cres WD24 . . . . . . .167 C7
Reeds Dale LU2 . . . . .46 F2
Reeds The AL7 . . . . .110 D5
Reeves Ave LU3 . . . . .45 B4
Reeves Pightle SG8 . . . . . . .9 F3
Regal Cl SG11 . . . . .55 E2
Regal Ct 4 Hitchin SG5 . . . .34 F8
Tring HP23 . . . . .100 A3
Regal Way WD24 . . . . . . .154 C1
Regency Cl CM23 . . . . .76 E7
Regency Ct
Hemel Hempstead HP2 . . .124 D3
Hoddesdon EN10 . . . . .148 F8
St Albans AL1 . . . . .128 B3
Regency Ct *continued*
Watford WD17 . . . . .167 A8
Regency Ho WD7 . . . . . . .156 A4
Regent Cl
Kings Langley WD4 . . . . . . .139 A3
St Albans AL4 . . . . .128 C7
Welwyn Garden City AL7 . .110 E5
Regent Ct SG5 . . . . .11 F7
Regent Gate EN8 . . . . . . .162 E5
Regent St Luton LU1 . . . . . .63 E7
Stotfold SG5 . . . . .11 F7
Watford WD24 . . . . .154 B1
Regent's Ct HA5 . . . . .175 D1
Regents Ct WD7 . . . . .156 A5
Regina Cl EN5 . . . . .171 D6
Reginald Mews CM17 . . .118 C1
Reginald Rd HA6 . . . . . . .174 F3
Reginald St LU2 . . . . .45 E1
Remus Cl AL1 . . . . .141 D7
Rendlesham Ave WD7 . . .155 F2
Rendlesham Cl SG12 . . . . .93 B2
Rendlesham Rd EN2 . . . .161 B1
Rendlesham Way WD3 . .164 C3
Rennie Ct EN3 . . . . .163 A1
Rennison Cl EN7 . . . . . . .147 F4
Renshaw Cl LU2 . . . . .46 E2
Repton Cl LU3 . . . . .44 F6
Repton Gn AL3 . . . . .127 D6
Repton Way WD3 . . . . . . .166 A4
Reson Way HP1 . . . . .124 B2
Reston Cl WD6 . . . . .157 B1
Reston Path
Borehamwood WD6 . . . . . .157 A1
Luton LU2 . . . . .46 E2
Retford Cl WD6 . . . . .157 A1
Retreat The WD5 . . . . . . .153 C8
Revels Cl SG14 . . . . .113 D8
Revels Rd SG14 . . . . .113 D8
Reynard Copse CM23 . . . . .58 F1
Reynard Way SG13 . . . . . .114 B6
Reynard's Way AL2 . . . . .140 F2
Reynards Rd AL6 . . . . .89 C7
Reynolds SG6 . . . . .11 F1
Reynolds Cl HP1 . . . . . . .124 A4
Reynolds Cres AL4 . . . . . .128 B8
Rhee Spring SG7 . . . . .13 B1
Rhodes Ave CM23 . . . . . . .76 F5
Rhodes Meml Mus &
Commonwealth Ctr*
CM23 . . . . .77 A6
Rhodes Way WD24 . . . . . .167 D8
Rhymes HP1 . . . . .124 B5
Rib Cl SG11 . . . . .55 E2
Rib Vale SG14 . . . . .92 D1
Rib Way SG9 . . . . .40 E7
Ribbledale AL2 . . . . .142 F4
Ribblesdale HP2 . . . . .124 E6
Ribocon Way LU4 . . . . . . .44 B7
Ribston Cl WD7 . . . . .156 D6
Riccat La SG1 . . . . .36 F3
Rice Cl HP2 . . . . .124 F4
Richard Ct 1 EN5 . . . . . . .171 E6
Richard Hale Sch SG13 . .113 D5
Richard Stagg Cl AL1 . . .128 C1
Richard Wittington Prim Sch
The CM23 . . . . .76 E4
Richards Cl
Bushey WD23 . . . . .168 D2
Luton LU1 . . . . .63 B6
Richards Ct LU1 . . . . .63 B5
Richards St AL10 . . . . . . .129 E7
Richardson Cl AL2 . . . . . .142 E4
Richardson Cres EN7 . . .147 B6
Richardson Pl AL4 . . . . . .129 B1
Richfield Rd WD23 . . . . . .168 C2
Richmond Cl
Bishop's Stortford CM23 . . . .76 C7
Borehamwood WD6 . . . . . .170 D4
Cheshunt EN8 . . . . .148 C2
Ware SG12 . . . . .93 B3
Richmond Ct
4 Hatfield AL10 . . . . .130 B3
Hoddesdon EN10 . . . . .134 F3
Luton LU2 . . . . .45 F1
Potters Bar EN6 . . . . .159 C8
St Albans AL1 . . . . .128 A3
Richmond Dr WD17 . . . . .166 E7
Richmond Gdns HA3 . . . .176 F3
Richmond Hill LU2 . . . . . . .45 F2
Richmond Hill Sch LU2 . . .45 E2
Richmond Rd EN6 . . . . . .159 C8
Richmond Way WD3 . . . .166 C5
Richmond Wlk AL4 . . . . .128 D7
Rickfield Cl AL10 . . . . . . .130 A3
Rickmansworth La SL9 . .172 A5
Rickmansworth Park Jun Mix
Inf Sch WD3 . . . . .165 E2
Rickmansworth Rd
Chorleywood WD3 . . . . . . .164 F6
Harefield UB9 . . . . .173 D3
Northwood HA6 . . . . .174 D3
Pinner HA5 . . . . .175 C1
Watford WD18 . . . . .166 E5
Rickmansworth Sch
WD3 . . . . .165 F3
Rickmansworth Sta
WD3 . . . . .165 D2
Rickyard Cl LU2 . . . . .46 B3
Rickyard Mdw AL3 . . . . . .106 A5
Rickyard The Ashwell SG7 . .4 D3
Letchworth SG6 . . . . .12 C1
Riddell Gdns SG7 . . . . .23 F8
Riddy Hill Cl SG4 . . . . .35 A6
Riddy La Hitchin SG4 . . . . .35 A6
Luton LU3 . . . . .45 C5
Riddy The SG4 . . . . .88 F8
Ridge Ave Harpenden AL5 . .85 E4
Letchworth SG6 . . . . .23 A6
Ridge Ct LU2 . . . . .46 A1
Ridge La WD17 . . . . .153 F2
Ridge Lea HP1 . . . . .123 F2
Ridge Rd SG6 . . . . .23 A6
Ridge St WD24 . . . . .154 B1
Ridge The Barnet EN5 . . . .171 F4
Letchworth SG6 . . . . .23 A6
Northwood HA6 . . . . .174 F3
Ridge View HP23 . . . . . . .100 C5
Ridge Way WD3 . . . . .165 B2
Ridgedown AL3 . . . . .106 A5
Ridgefield WD17 . . . . .153 E2
Ridgehurst Ave WD25 . . .153 F5
Ridgeleigh Ct 3 EN5 . . . .171 E6
Ridgeview Cl EN5 . . . . . .171 D3
Ridgeway
Berkhamsted HP4 . . . . .121 F4
Harpenden AL5 . . . . .85 E4
Kensworth Common LU6 . . . .82 E8
Little Hadham SG11 . . . . .57 B1
London Colney WD7 . . . . . .156 C8
Stevenage SG1 . . . . .50 F5
Welwyn Garden City AL7 . .111 B6
Ridgeway Cl HP3 . . . . . . .138 F5
Ridgeway Ct HA5 . . . . . . .176 A3
Ridgeway The
Codicote SG4 . . . . .67 F1
Cuffley EN6 . . . . .146 A4
Hadley Wood EN2,EN4 . . . .160 D3
Hertford SG14 . . . . .112 F7
Hitchin SG5 . . . . .34 D6
Radlett WD7 . . . . .155 F2
St Albans AL4 . . . . .128 C7
Ware SG12 . . . . .93 C3
Watford WD17 . . . . .153 E2
Ridgewood Dr AL5 . . . . . . .85 E4
Ridgewood Gdns AL5 . . . .85 E4
Ridgmont Rd AL1 . . . . . . .127 E2
Ridgway Rd LU2 . . . . .45 F1
Ridings The
Bishop's Stortford CM23 . . . .76 D4
Hertford SG14 . . . . .113 A5
Latimer HP5 . . . . .150 D3
Luton LU3 . . . . .45 C1
Markyate AL3 . . . . .83 E6
Stevenage SG2 . . . . .51 B3
Ridler Rd EN1 . . . . .161 E1
Ridlins End SG2 . . . . .51 C2
Rigby Pl EN3 . . . . .163 A2
Rigery La SG11 . . . . .73 A7
Riley Rd EN3 . . . . .162 C1
Ringmer Ct LU2 . . . . .46 C3
Ringshall Dr HP4 . . . . . . .102 C8
Ringshall Rd HP4 . . . . .81 B3
Ringtale Pl SG7 . . . . .13 B1
Ringway Rd AL2 . . . . .141 C4
Ringwood Rd LU2 . . . . .45 D7
Ripley Rd Enfield EN2 . . .161 C1
Luton LU4 . . . . .44 C1
Ripley Way Cheshunt EN7 .148 B1
Hemel Hempstead HP1 . . . .123 E4
Ripon Rd SG1 . . . . .37 A2
Ripon Way
Borehamwood WD6 . . . . . .170 D4
St Albans AL4 . . . . .128 D7
Rise Cotts SG12 . . . . .95 D2
Rise The Baldock SG7 . . . . .23 E7
Borehamwood WD6 . . . . . .169 F4
Harrow HA3 . . . . .176 C1
Park Street AL2 . . . . .141 D6
Risedale Cl HP3 . . . . .138 E8
Risedale Hill HP3 . . . . . . .138 E8
Risedale Rd HP3 . . . . .138 E8
Rising Hill Cl HA6 . . . . . .174 C4
Risingholme Cl
Bushey WD23 . . . . .168 B2
Harrow HA3 . . . . .176 E2
Risingholme Rd HA3 . . . .176 E1
Ritcroft Cl HP3 . . . . .125 B2
Ritcroft Dr HP3 . . . . .125 B2
Ritcroft St HP3 . . . . .125 B2
Ritz Ct EN6 . . . . .159 A8
Rivenhall End AL7 . . . . . .111 C6
River Ave EN11 . . . . .135 B7
River Cl EN8 . . . . .163 A5
River Ct Ickleford SG5 . . . . .21 F4
Sacombe SG12 . . . . .92 E4
Sawbridgeworth CM21 . . . . .97 F3
River Gn SG9 . . . . .40 E8
River Hill AL3 . . . . .84 B2
River Lee Ctry Pk* EN9 .149 B1
River Mead SG5 . . . . .21 C2
River Meads SG12 . . . . . . .115 C4
River Park Ind Est HP4 . .122 A5
River Pk HP1 . . . . .124 A1
River St SG12 . . . . .93 E1
River View AL7 . . . . .89 F2
River Way Harlow CM20 . .118 B5
Luton LU3 . . . . .44 E5
Riverbank HP1 . . . . .124 B7
Riverbanks Cl AL5 . . . . . . .86 C4
Riverfield La CM21 . . . . . . .97 E3
Riverford Cl AL5 . . . . .86 B4
Rivermill CM20 . . . . .117 C2
Rivermill Ct SG8 . . . . .7 C7
Rivers Hospl The CM21 . . .97 C1
Riversend Rd HP3 . . . . . .138 C8
Rivershill SG14 . . . . .70 E3
Riverside
Bishop's Stortford CM23 . . . .76 F7
Buntingford SG9 . . . . .40 E7
Hemel Hempstead HP3 . . . .138 F6
Hertford SG14 . . . . .113 D6
London Colney AL2 . . . . . . .142 E4
Welwyn AL6 . . . . .89 B5
Riverside Ave EN10 . . . . .135 A1
Riverside Bsns Pk CM24 . .59 E6

Riverside Cl
Kings Langley WD4 ... 139 B2
St Albans AL1 ... 127 E1
Riverside Club (Tennis Ctr)
The HA6 ... 174 B3
Riverside Cotts SG12 ... 115 C4
Riverside Ct
Harlow CM20 ... 118 C6
St Albans AL1 ... 127 E1
Riverside Dr WD3 ... 165 D1
Riverside Est AL5 ... 86 C4
Riverside Gdns HP4 ... 122 A5
Riverside Mews
Hoddesdon EN10 ... 148 E8
10 Ware SG12 ... 93 D1
Riverside Path EN8 ... 148 C2
Riverside Rd Luton LU3 ... 45 A5
St Albans AL1 ... 127 E2
Watford WD19 ... 167 B3
Riverside Wlk 16 CM23 ... 76 F7
Riversmead EN11 ... 135 A5
Riversmeet SG14 ... 113 B5
Rivett Cl SG7 ... 13 A1
Roan Wlk SG8 ... 7 E6
Roaring Meg Ret Pk SG1 ... 50 E3
Robbery Bottom La AL6 ... 90 A8
Robbs Cl HP1 ... 124 A5
Robe End HP1 ... 123 F5
Robert Allen Ct 3 LU1 ... 63 E6
Robert Ave AL1 ... 141 C7
Robert Cl EN6 ... 158 E6
Robert Humbert Ho SG6 ... 23 A5
Robert Saunders Ct SG6 ... 22 E4
Robert Tebbutt Ct SG5 ... 34 E6
Robert Wallace Cl CM23 ... 58 F1
Roberts Cl EN8 ... 148 E1
Roberts La SL9 ... 172 B5
Roberts Rd WD18 ... 167 C4
Roberts Way AL10 ... 129 F3
Roberts Wood Dr SL9 ... 172 A5
Robertson Cl EN10 ... 148 E5
Robertson Rd 11 HP4 ... 122 D4
Robeson Way WD6 ... 170 C8
Robin Cl SG12 ... 115 C3
Robin Ct AL5 ... 86 B4
Robin Hill HP4 ... 122 C3
Robin Hood Dr
Harrow HA3 ... 176 F3
Watford WD23 ... 167 F8
Robin Hood La AL10 ... 130 A6
Robin Hood Mdw HP2 ... 124 F8
Robin Mead AL7 ... 90 A1
Robin Way EN6 ... 146 E3
Robina Cl HA6 ... 174 F2
Robins Cl AL2 ... 142 E4
Robins Nest Hill SG13 ... 132 C6
Robins Rd HP3 ... 125 A1
Robins The CM17 ... 118 C6
Robins Way AL10 ... 129 F2
Robinsfield HP1 ... 124 A3
Robinson Ave EN7 ... 147 B3
Robinson Cl CM23 ... 76 F5
Robinson Cres WD23 ... 168 C1
Robinsway EN9 ... 163 E5
Robinswood LU2 ... 45 E5
Robsons Cl EN8 ... 148 C2
Rochdale Ct 6 LU1 ... 63 E6
Rochester Ave LU2 ... 46 C4
Rochester Dr WD25 ... 154 C4
Rochester Way
Croxley Green WD3 ... 166 B5
Royston SG8 ... 7 D8
Rochford Ave EN9 ... 163 D5
Rochford Cl
Cheshunt EN10 ... 148 E5
Stansted Mountfitchet
CM24 ... 59 E5
Rochford Dr LU2 ... 46 E2
Rochford Ho EN9 ... 163 D6
Rochford Rd CM23 ... 59 C1
Rock Rd SG8 ... 7 C8
Rockfield Ave SG12 ... 93 D3
Rockingham Gate
WD23 ... 168 C3
Rockingham Way SG1 ... 50 E4
Rockleigh SG14 ... 113 C6
Rockley Rd LU1 ... 63 A7
Rockliffe Ave WD4 ... 139 A1
Rockways EN5 ... 170 F3
Rodeheath LU4 ... 44 D3
Roden Cl CM17 ... 118 F4
Rodgers Cl WD6 ... 169 D3
Rodings Row EN5 ... 171 E5
Rodney Ave AL1 ... 128 A1
Rodney Cres EN11 ... 135 A8
Rodwell Yd HP23 ... 100 A3
Roe Cl SG5 ... 11 E5
Roe End La AL3 ... 83 B4
Roe Green Cl AL10 ... 129 F4
Roe Green Ctr AL10 ... 129 F4
Roe Green La AL10 ... 129 F5
Roe Hill Cl AL10 ... 129 F4
Roebuck Cl
Hertford SG13 ... 114 A6
Luton LU1 ... 63 B6
Roebuck Ct 1 SG2 ... 50 F1
Roebuck Gate SG2 ... 50 F1
Roebuck Prim Sch SG2 ... 50 F2
Roebuck Ret Pk SG1 ... 50 E2
Roecroft Lower Sch SG5 ... 11 F6
Roedean Ave EN3 ... 162 C1
Roedean Cl LU2 ... 46 D3
Roedean Ho 3 WD24 ... 167 C7
Roefields Cl HP3 ... 138 A7
Roehyde Way AL10 ... 129 E2
Roestock Gdns AL4 ... 129 E1
Roestock La AL4 ... 129 E1
Rofant Rd HA6 ... 174 E4
Rogate Rd LU2 ... 46 C5
Roger de Clare Sch SG11 ... 55 E2
Roger's La SG9 ... 29 A5
Rogers Cl EN7 ... 147 D4
Rogers Ruff HA6 ... 174 C2
Rokewood Mews 3
SG12 ... 93 D2
Roland St AL1 ... 128 B2
Rolleston Cl SG12 ... 93 C3
Rollswood AL7 ... 110 E3
Rollswood Rd AL6 ... 89 B8
Rollys La SG7 ... 4 D4
Roman Cl UB9 ... 173 B2
Roman Gdns WD4 ... 139 B1
Roman Ho
London Colney AL2 ... 142 D4
Watford WD18 ... 166 E5
Roman La SG7 ... 24 A8
Roman Mews 7 EN11 ... 135 A7
Roman Rd LU4 ... 44 E3
Roman Rise CM21 ... 97 D2
Roman St 8 EN11 ... 135 A7
Roman Vale CM17 ... 118 C5
Roman Way Markyate AL3 ... 83 E6
Standon SG11 ... 55 D3
Waltham Abbey EN9 ... 163 B4
Welwyn AL6 ... 89 C6
Roman Way Fst Sch SG8 ... 7 C8
Romans End AL3 ... 127 C1
Romany Cl SG6 ... 22 C6
Romany Ct HP2 ... 125 C4
Romeland Elstree WD6 ... 169 D3
St Albans AL3 ... 127 C3
Waltham Abbey EN9 ... 163 C6
Romeland Hill AL3 ... 127 C3
Romilly Dr WD19 ... 175 F6
Rondini Ave LU3 ... 45 B3
Ronsons Way AL4 ... 127 F7
Rook Tree Cl SG5 ... 12 A6
Rook Tree La SG5 ... 12 A6
Rookery Dr LU2 ... 45 E6
Rookery The
Hatfield AL9 ... 144 D8
Stansted Mountfitchet
CM24 ... 59 E8
Westmill SG9 ... 40 F3
Rookery Yd SG1 ... 50 C7
Rookes Cl SG6 ... 23 B3
Rooks Cl AL8 ... 110 D5
Rooks Hill
Rickmansworth WD3 ... 165 D5
Welwyn Garden City AL8 ... 110 C5
Rooks Nest Cotts SG1 ... 36 E2
Rooks Nest Farm SG1 ... 36 E2
Rooks Nest La SG8 ... 16 A5
Rookwood Dr SG2 ... 51 B1
Rosary Ct EN6 ... 145 B1
Rosary Gdns WD23 ... 168 E2
Rose Acre Pimlico HP3 ... 139 E6
Redbourn AL3 ... 105 F6
Rose Cotts Arlesey SG15 ... 11 A6
Bricket Wood AL2 ... 141 B1
Meesden SG9 ... 30 A5
Wyddial SG9 ... 28 A3
Rose Ct
Hammond Street EN7 ... 148 A4
St Albans AL4 ... 128 C5
Rose Garden Mews
WD3 ... 165 B5
Rose Gdns WD18 ... 167 A4
Rose La Essendon AL9 ... 131 C5
Wheathampstead AL4 ... 87 C2
Rose Lawn WD23 ... 168 C1
Rose Mdw SG11 ... 41 E4
Rose Mead EN6 ... 145 C1
Rose Vale EN11 ... 135 A6
Rose Wlk Royston SG8 ... 7 C7
St Albans AL4 ... 128 C5
Rose Wlk The WD7 ... 156 B3
Rose Wood Cl LU2 ... 45 F3
Roseacre Gdns AL7 ... 111 D6
Roseacres CM21 ... 97 D3
Rosebank EN9 ... 163 E6
Rosebarn La HP23 ... 79 D1
Roseberry Ct WD17 ... 167 A8
Rosebery CM23 ... 77 C6
Rosebery Ave AL5 ... 85 F1
Rosebery Mews LU7 ... 61 D4
Rosebery Rd WD23 ... 168 B2
Rosebery Way HP23 ... 100 B5
Rosebriar Wlk WD24 ... 153 F3
Rosecroft Ct HA6 ... 174 C4
Rosecroft Dr WD17 ... 153 E3
Rosecroft La AL6 ... 90 A8
Rosedale AL7 ... 89 F2
Rosedale Ave EN7 ... 147 F2
Rosedale Cl
Bricket Wood AL2 ... 140 E1
Luton LU3 ... 44 C7
Rosedale Way EN7 ... 148 A3
Roseheath HP1 ... 123 E4
Rosehill HP4 ... 122 B4
Rosehill Cl EN11 ... 134 F6
Rosehill Ct HP1 ... 124 A1
Rosehill Gdns WD5 ... 153 C7
Roselands Ave EN11 ... 114 F1
Roselands Prim Sch
EN11 ... 114 F1
Roseley Cotts CM20 ... 117 B4
Rosemary Cl 3 CM17 ... 118 C4
Rosemary Ct 2 HA5 ... 176 A3
Rosemont Cl SG6 ... 22 E6
Rosemoor Cl AL7 ... 110 F5
Rosewood Ct HP1 ... 123 E4
Rosewood Dr EN2 ... 161 A4
Roslyn Cl EN10 ... 134 E2
Ross Cl Hatfield AL10 ... 130 A8
Luton LU1 ... 63 B6
Ross Cl *continued*
Stanmore HA3 ... 176 C3
Ross Cres WD25 ... 154 A4
Ross Ct SG2 ... 51 B7
Ross Haven Pl HA6 ... 174 F2
Ross Way HA6 ... 174 F6
Rossendale Cl EN2 ... 161 B3
Rossfold Rd LU3 ... 44 D8
Rossgate HP1 ... 124 A5
Rossgate Prim Sch HP1 ... 124 A5
Rossington Ave WD6 ... 156 E1
Rossington Cl EN1 ... 162 B1
Rossiter Fields EN5 ... 171 F3
Rosslyn Cres LU3 ... 45 C5
Rosslyn Rd WD18 ... 167 B6
Rossway LU1 ... 63 B1
Rossway Dr WD23 ... 168 D4
Rossway La HP4 ... 121 A7
Roswell Cl EN8 ... 148 E1
Rothamsted Ave AL5 ... 86 A1
Rothamsted Ct AL5 ... 86 A1
Rothamsted Experimental Sta
AL5 ... 107 A8
Rother Cl WD25 ... 154 C5
Rotheram Ave LU1 ... 63 B5
Rotherfield LU2 ... 46 D3
Rotherfield Rd EN3 ... 162 D2
Rothesay Ct HP4 ... 122 A4
Rothesay Rd LU1 ... 63 D7
Roughdown Ave HP3 ... 138 A8
Roughdown Rd HP3 ... 138 B8
Roughdown Villas HP3 ... 138 A8
Roughdown Villas Rd
HP3 ... 138 A8
Roughs The HA6 ... 174 E7
Roughwood Cl WD17 ... 153 E1
Round Diamond Prim Sch
SG1 ... 37 B3
Round Mead SG2 ... 51 D3
Roundabout Ho HA6 ... 175 A2
Roundabout La AL6 ... 89 F8
Roundbush La WD25 ... 155 C1
Roundcroft EN7 ... 147 F5
Roundfield Ave AL5 ... 86 D3
Roundhaye SG11 ... 55 D3
Roundhedge Way EN2 ... 160 F1
Roundhills EN9 ... 163 E4
Roundings The SG13 ... 114 C2
Roundmoor Dr EN8 ... 148 E2
Roundway The WD18 ... 166 F2
Roundwood HP3 ... 138 E4
Roundwood Cl
Hitchin SG4 ... 22 C2
Oaklands AL6 ... 89 D8
Roundwood Ct AL5 ... 85 F3
Roundwood Dr AL8 ... 110 C7
Roundwood Gdns AL5 ... 85 E2
Roundwood La AL5 ... 85 D3
Roundwood Park Sch
AL5 ... 85 E2
Roundwood Pk AL5 ... 85 E3
Roundwood Prim Sch
AL5 ... 85 E2
Rounton Rd EN9 ... 163 E6
Rousebarn La WD3 ... 166 C7
Row The HP5 ... 120 D2
Rowan Cl
Bricket Wood AL2 ... 155 A8
Harrow HA7 ... 176 F4
Luton LU1 ... 63 B7
Shenley WD7 ... 156 E6
St Albans AL4 ... 128 E3
Weston SG4 ... 37 B8
Rowan Cres
Letchworth SG6 ... 22 E7
Stevenage SG1 ... 50 E7
Rowan Dr EN10 ... 148 F6
Rowan Gr SG4 ... 35 A4
Rowan Way AL5 ... 107 C8
Rowan Wlk
2 Hatfield AL10 ... 130 A2
Sawbridgeworth CM21 ... 97 E2
Rowans AL7 ... 90 A1
Rowans Prim Sch The
AL7 ... 90 A1
Rowans The Baldock SG7 ... 23 E7
Hemel Hempstead HP1 ... 124 A3
Hoddesdon EN10 ... 134 F4
Rowbeech Cotts LU6 ... 83 C8
Rowbourne Pl EN6 ... 146 D3
Rowcroft HP1 ... 123 E2
Rowel Field LU2 ... 46 C1
Rowington Cl LU2 ... 46 E2
Rowland Pl HA6 ... 174 E3
Rowland Rd SG1 ... 50 F4
Rowland Way SG6 ... 22 F6
Rowlands Ave HA5 ... 176 B4
Rowlands Cl EN8 ... 148 D1
Rowlands Ct 3 EN8 ... 148 D1
Rowlatt Ct AL1 ... 127 E4
Rowlatt Dr AL3 ... 127 A1
Rowley Cl WD19 ... 167 E3
Rowley Gdns EN8 ... 148 D3
Rowley Green Rd EN5 ... 171 A4
Rowley La Barnet EN5 ... 170 F5
Borehamwood WD6 ... 170 D7
Rowley Wlk HP2 ... 125 C8
Rowley's Rd SG13 ... 113 F7
Rowney Gdns CM21 ... 118 C8
Rowney La SG12 ... 72 B5
Rowney Wood CM21 ... 97 C1
Rows The CM20 ... 117 D1
Roxley Cotts SG6 ... 23 B2
Roxley Manor SG6 ... 36 B8
Roy Rd HA6 ... 174 F3
Royal Ave EN8 ... 162 E6
Royal Ct Aldbury HP23 ... 101 A5
Hemel Hempstead HP3 ... 138 E8
Royal Masonic Sch for Girls
WD3 ... 165 D4
Royal National Orthopaedic
Hospl HA7 ... 169 B1
Royal Oak Cl SG9 ... 27 D5
Royal Oak Gdns 6 CM23 ... 76 F6
Royal Oak La SG5 ... 20 D4
Royal Rd AL1 ... 128 B3
Royal Veterinary Coll
AL9 ... 144 D3
Royce Cl EN10 ... 134 F2
Royce Gr WD25 ... 153 F5
Roydon Cl LU4 ... 44 A4
Roydon Ct HP2 ... 105 A1
Roydon Lodge Chalet Est
CM19 ... 116 C1
Roydon Mill CM19 ... 116 A1
Roydon Mill Leisure Pk
CM19 ... 116 A1
Roydon Rd Harlow CM19 ... 116 E1
Stanstead Abbotts SG12 ... 115 E4
Roydon Sta CM19 ... 116 B2
Royse Gr SG8 ... 7 D4
Roysia Mid Sch SG8 ... 7 D8
Royston & District Mus*
SG8 ... 7 C6
Royston Cl SG14 ... 113 B6
Royston Gr HA5 ... 176 A4
Royston Hospl SG8 ... 7 D4
Royston Park Rd HA5 ... 176 A5
Royston Rd Baldock SG7 ... 13 D2
Barkway SG8 ... 17 C5
Barley SG8 ... 8 F3
St Albans AL1 ... 128 B2
Royston Sta SG8 ... 7 C7
Rubin Pl EN3 ... 163 A2
Rucklers La WD4 ... 138 C4
Ruckles Cl SG1 ... 50 E5
Rudd Cl SG2 ... 51 B3
Rudham Gr SG6 ... 23 C3
Rudolf Steiner Sch
WD4 ... 138 E2
Rudolph Rd WD23 ... 168 A3
Rudyard Cl LU4 ... 44 D3
Rue de St Lawrence
EN9 ... 163 C5
Rueley Dell Rd LU2 ... 32 D2
Rufford Cl WD17 ... 153 F2
Rugby Way WD3 ... 166 B4
Ruins The AL3 ... 106 B5
Rumballs Cl HP3 ... 139 A8
Rumballs Ct CM23 ... 76 C4
Rumballs Rd HP3 ... 139 A8
Rumbold Rd EN11 ... 135 C8
Rumsley EN7 ... 148 A4
Runcie Cl AL4 ... 128 A7
Runcorn Cres HP2 ... 124 F7
Rundells SG6 ... 23 D4
Runfold Ave LU3 ... 45 A5
Runham Cl LU4 ... 44 A4
Runham Rd HP3 ... 124 E1
Runley Rd LU1 ... 62 F7
Runnalow SG6 ... 22 E7
Runsley AL7 ... 90 A1
Runswick Ct SG1 ... 50 A7
Runway The AL10 ... 129 E7
Ruscombe Dr AL2 ... 141 C5
Rush Cl SG12 ... 115 C4
Rush Dr EN9 ... 163 C3
Rushall Gn LU2 ... 46 E2
Rushby Mead SG6 ... 23 A5
Rushby Pl SG6 ... 23 A5
Rushby Wlk SG6 ... 23 A6
Rushden Rd SG9 ... 26 A8
Rushen Dr SG13 ... 114 C3
Rushendon Furlong LU7 ... 80 E5
Rushes Ct CM23 ... 77 A5
Rushfield
Potters Bar EN6 ... 158 E6
Sawbridgeworth CM21 ... 97 E2
Rushfield Rd SG12 ... 93 F3
Rushleigh Ave EN8 ... 148 D1
Rushleigh Gn CM23 ... 76 D4
Rushmead Villas CM20 ... 117 E3
Rushmere Ct HP3 ... 138 E7
Rushmere La HP5 ... 136 B3
Rushmoor Cl WD3 ... 173 D8
Rushmore Cl LU1 ... 62 E4
Rushton Ave WD25 ... 154 A4
Rushton Ct EN8 ... 148 D2
Ruskin Ave EN9 ... 163 E5
Ruskin Cl EN7 ... 147 E5
Ruskin La SG4 ... 35 C7
Rusper Gn LU2 ... 46 D3
Russell Ave AL3 ... 127 D3
Russell Cl
Kensworth Common LU6 ... 82 E8
Moor Park HA6 ... 174 C5
Stevenage SG2 ... 51 B2
Russell Cres WD25 ... 153 F4
Russell Ct AL2 ... 141 A1
Russell La WD17 ... 153 D3
Russell Mead HA3 ... 176 F2
Russell Pl HP3 ... 138 B8
Russell Rd Enfield EN1 ... 161 F1
Moor Park HA6 ... 174 C6
Russell Rise LU1 ... 63 D6
Russell Sch The WD3 ... 164 B5
Russell St Hertford SG14 ... 113 C6
Luton LU1 ... 63 D6
Russell Way WD19 ... 167 B2
Russell's Ride EN8 ... 162 E8
Russell's Slip SG5 ... 34 D6
Russellcroft Rd AL8 ... 110 C7
Russet Cl EN7 ... 147 E5
Russet Dr Shenley WD7 ... 156 E7
St Albans AL4 ... 128 C2
Russett Ho AL7 ... 111 D6
Russett Wood AL7 ... 111 D5
Russettings 2 HA5 ... 175 F3
Rutherford Cl
Borehamwood WD6 ... 170 C7
Stevenage SG1 ... 50 A6
Rutherford Way WD23 ... 168 E1
Ruthin Cl LU1 ... 63 D5
Ruthven Ave EN8 ... 162 D6
Rutland Cres LU2 ... 64 A7
Rutland Ct LU2 ... 64 A7
Rutland Gdns HP2 ... 124 F4
Rutland Hall LU2 ... 64 A7
Rutland Pl WD23 ... 168 D1
Rutts The WD23 ... 168 D1
Ryall Cl AL2 ... 140 E2
Ryan Way WD24 ... 167 C8
Ryans Ct LU2 ... 45 F1
Rydal Ct WD25 ... 154 B7
Rydal Mount EN6 ... 158 E6
Rydal Way LU3 ... 44 F5
Ryde Sch The AL9 ... 130 C8
Ryde The AL9 ... 130 C8
Ryder Ave SG5 ... 21 D3
Ryder Cl Bovingdon HP3 ... 137 A4
Bushey WD23 ... 168 B3
Hertford SG13 ... 114 B7
Ryder Seed Mews 3
AL1 ... 127 D2
Ryder Way SG5 ... 21 D3
Ryders Ave AL4 ... 129 E3
Ryders Hill SG1 ... 37 C3
Rye Cl Harpenden AL5 ... 86 B4
Stevenage SG1 ... 36 F3
Rye Gdns SG7 ... 13 B1
Rye Hill Harpenden AL5 ... 86 B4
2 Luton LU2 ... 45 D1
Rye House Gatehouse*
EN11 ... 135 D8
Rye House Sta EN11 ... 135 C8
Rye Mead Cotts EN11 ... 135 C8
Rye Rd EN11 ... 135 C8
Rye St CM23 ... 58 F1
Ryecroft Hatfield AL10 ... 129 F3
Stevenage SG1 ... 50 E7
Ryecroft Cl HP2 ... 125 C2
Ryecroft Cres EN5 ... 171 B4
Ryecroft Ct AL4 ... 128 F3
Ryecroft Way LU2 ... 46 A4
Ryefeld Cl EN11 ... 115 B2
Ryefield LU3 ... 31 A1
Ryefield Cres HA6 ... 175 A1
Ryelands AL7 ... 110 F3
Ryelands Prim Sch
EN11 ... 135 B7
Rylands Heath LU2 ... 46 F2
Ryley Cl SG16 ... 10 B5
Ryman Ct WD3 ... 164 C3
Rymill Cl HP3 ... 137 A3
Ryton Cl LU1 ... 63 B6

S

Saberton Cl AL3 ... 105 F4
Sabine Ho WD5 ... 153 F7
Sacombe Gn LU3 ... 31 B1
Sacombe Green Rd SG12 ... 71 E4
Sacombe Pound SG12 ... 71 E3
Sacombe Rd
Hemel Hempstead HP1 ... 123 F5
Hertford SG14 ... 92 C1
Stapleford SG14 ... 92 B4
Sacombs Ash La CM21 ... 96 E7
Sacred Heart Language Coll
The HA3 ... 176 E1
Sacred Heart Prim Sch
LU2 ... 46 A3
Sacred Heart RC Prim Sch
Bushey WD23 ... 167 F3
Ware SG12 ... 93 D1
Saddlers Cl Arkley EN5 ... 171 B4
Baldock SG7 ... 23 E8
Bishop's Stortford CM23 ... 76 C4
Borehamwood WD6 ... 170 D3
Pinner HA5 ... 176 A4
Saddlers Mews AL3 ... 83 E5
Saddlers Path WD6 ... 170 D4
Saddlers Pl SG8 ... 7 C7
Saddlers Wlk WD4 ... 139 A2
Sadleir Rd AL1 ... 127 E1
Sadler Cl EN7 ... 147 C6
Sadlers Way SG14 ... 113 A6
Sadlier Rd SG11 ... 55 E2
Saffron Cl Arlesey SG15 ... 11 A7
Hoddesdon EN11 ... 134 F7
Luton LU2 ... 45 D7
Saffron Green Prim Sch
WD6 ... 170 E5
Saffron Hill SG6 ... 22 E6
Saffron La HP1 ... 124 B4
Saffron Mdw SG11 ... 55 E2
Saffron St SG8 ... 7 F5
Sainfoin End HP2 ... 125 A5
St Adrian's RC Prim Sch
AL1 ... 141 C8
St Agnell's Farm Mews
HP2 ... 105 A1
St Agnells Ct HP2 ... 125 A7
St Agnells La HP2 ... 125 A8
St Alban & St Stephen RC Inf
Sch AL1 ... 127 F2
St Alban & St Stephen RC
Jun Sch AL1 ... 128 A3
St Alban's RC Prim Sch
CM20 ... 117 F2

St Albans City Hospl AL3 127 C5
St Albans Dr SG1 36 E1
St Albans Girls' Sch AL3 127 E7
St Albans High Sch for Girls AL1 127 E4
St Albans Hill HP3 124 F1
St Albans La WD5 140 A5
St Albans Link SG1 36 E1
St Albans Music Sch AL3 127 D6
St Albans Rd Barnet EN5 171 E7
Codicote SG4 88 F7
Dancers Hill EN5 158 C3
Harpenden AL5 107 B6
Hemel Hempstead HP2, HP3 124 E2
Redbourn AL3 106 C3
Ridge EN6 157 F8
Sandridge AL4 108 B1
St Albans AL4 128 A8
St Albans Rd E AL10 130 B6
St Albans Rd W AL10 129 D5
St Albans Ret Pk AL1 127 D1
St Albans Roman Theatre* AL3 127 A3
St Albans Sch AL3 127 C3
St Albans Sta AL1 127 F3
St Albert the Great RC Prim Sch HP3 125 A2
St Aldates Ct LU3 45 B3
St Andrew Mews 1 SG14 113 C6
St Andrew St SG14 113 C6
St Andrew's Ave AL5 85 F1
St Andrew's CE Prim Sch SG4 35 A7
St Andrew's CE Prim Sch SG10 74 F2
St Andrew's Cl LU1 63 B1
St Andrew's Ho CM20 117 F2
St Andrew's Pl 2 SG4 34 F6
St Andrew's Rd HP3 138 D7
St Andrews CE Prim Sch SG12 115 D4
St Andrews Dr SG1 36 F2
St Andrews Mews LU3 45 A4
St Andrews Montessori Prep Sch WD25 154 C8
St Andrews Rd 2 WD19 175 D7
St Andrews Terr WD19 175 C5
St Andrews Wlk LU1 63 C1
St Ann's La LU1 63 F7
St Ann's Rd LU1 63 F7
St Anna Rd EN5 171 D4
St Anne's Cl EN7 148 A3
St Anne's Ct 7 SG5 34 F8
St Anne's Pk EN10 135 A4
St Anne's Rd Hitchin SG5 34 F8
London Colney AL2 142 D4
St Annes Cl WD19 175 C6
St Anthonys Ave HP3 125 B1
St Anthonys RC Prim Sch WD18 166 E4
St Audreys Cl AL10 130 B2
St Audreys Gn AL7 110 F5
St Augusta Ct AL3 127 D5
St Augustine Ave LU3 45 C3
St Augustine Cl 1 SG5 34 F8
St Augustine RC Prim Sch EN11 135 B6
St Augustines Cl EN10 134 F3
St Augustines Dr EN10 134 F3
St Barnabas Ct Harrow HA3 176 C2
Hemel Hempstead HP2 125 A3
St Bartholomew's CE Prim Sch HP23 100 D1
St Barts Cl AL4 128 D2
St Bernadette RC Prim Sch AL2 142 D4
St Bernard's Cl LU3 45 C3
St Bernard's Rd AL3 127 E4
St Brelades Pl AL4 128 D7
St Catharine's Rd EN10 135 A4
St Catherine of Siena RC Prim Sch WD25 154 D6
St Catherine's CE Prim Sch SG12 93 B2
St Catherines Ave LU3 45 B3
St Catherines Ct CM23 76 E7
St Christopher Sch SG6 22 F3
St Christophers Ct WD3 164 D5
St Clement Danes Sch WD3 164 D7
St Clement's CE Jun Sch EN8 148 E4
St Clements Ct EN9 163 C6
St Columba's Coll AL3 127 C1
St Cross Chambers EN11 135 A4
St Cross Ct EN11 135 A4
St Cross RC Prim Sch EN11 135 A4
St Cuthbert Mayne RC Jun Sch HP1 124 B4
St Cuthberts Gdns 3 HA5 175 F3
St Cuthberts Rd EN11 115 C1
St David's Cl HP2 125 D2
St David's Dr EN10 134 F4
St Davids Cl SG1 36 F2
St Dominic RC Prim Sch AL5 107 B8
St Dunstan's Rd SG12 116 D8
St Edmund's Coll SG11 55 A1
St Edmund's Way CM17 118 C4
St Edmunds HP4 122 C3
St Edmunds Wlk AL4 128 D2
St Elizabeth's Sch & Home SG10 96 C6
St Elmo Ct SG4 34 F5
St Ethelbert Ave LU3 45 C4
St Etheldreda's Dr AL10 130 C5
St Evroul Ct 5 SG12 93 D2
St Faiths Cl SG4 22 B1
St Francis Cl Buntingford SG9 40 F6
Potters Bar EN6 159 C5
Watford WD19 167 B1
St Francis' Coll SG6 22 E4
St George's Dr WD19 175 E6
St George's Rd Enfield EN1 161 F1
Hemel Hempstead HP3 138 C7
Watford WD24 154 B1
St George's Sch AL5 86 B2
St George's Way SG1 50 D5
St Georges End SG9 29 A6
St Georges Works EN8 148 F1
St Giles Ct EN8 162 C4
St Giles Rd SG4 67 F2
St Giles' Ave EN6 158 B7
St Giles' CE Prim Sch EN6 158 A7
St Helen's CE Prim Sch AL4 108 D8
St Helen's Cl AL4 108 D8
St Helen's Sch HA6 174 E4
St Heliers Rd AL4 128 B8
St Hilda's Sch Bushey WD23 168 B2
Harpenden AL5 85 F2
St Hugh's Sch SG11 73 A8
St Ignatius Coll EN1 162 B2
St Ippolyts CE Prim Sch SG4 35 B3
St Ives Cl Luton LU3 45 B3
Welwyn AL6 89 F3
St James Ctr CM20 118 A4
St James Rd Harpenden AL5 86 B4
Watford WD18 167 B4
St James Way CM23 76 C3
St James' Rd LU3 45 B3
St James's Ct AL5 86 B3
St James's Rd EN7 147 D3
St Joan of Arc RC Sch WD3 165 E2
St John Cl LU1 63 B5
St John Fisher RC Prim Sch AL4 128 C6
St John RC Prim Sch SG7 23 F7
St John The Baptist CE Prim Sch SG12 115 A5
St John's Ave CM17 118 D4
St John's CE Prim Sch Crews Hill EN2 161 B2
Hatfield AL8 109 F5
Welwyn Garden City AL6 89 F2
St John's Cl EN6 159 C6
St John's Cres CM24 59 E7
St John's Ct Harpenden AL5 107 C7
21 Hertford SG13 113 D6
6 Northwood HA6 174 E3
St John's La CM24 59 E7
St John's Path SG4 34 F5
St John's RC Prim Sch WD3 165 B1
St John's Rd Arlesey SG15 11 A4
Harpenden AL5 107 C7
Hemel Hempstead HP1 124 B1
Hitchin SG4 34 F6
Stansted Mountfitchet CM24 59 E7
Watford WD17 167 B7
St John's Sch HA6 175 B4
St John's St SG13 113 D6
St John's Terr EN2 161 D2
St John's Well Ct HP4 122 B5
St John's Well La HP4 122 B5
St Johns SG11 55 E3
St Johns CE Inf Sch WD7 155 F4
St Johns Cl AL6 89 C6
St Johns Ct Luton LU1 63 B5
Rickmansworth WD3 165 B1
St Albans AL1 128 B5
St Johns La SG12 115 A6
St Johns Wlk CM17 118 C4
St Joseph RC Prim Sch WD19 175 C7
St Joseph's Cl LU3 45 A4
St Joseph's in the Park Sch SG14 113 A4
St Joseph's RC Inf Sch LU3 45 A4
St Joseph's RC Jun Sch LU3 45 A4
St Joseph's RC Prim Sch Bishop's Stortford CM23 76 E6
Cheshunt EN8 162 E7
Hertford SG14 113 A7
St Joseph's Rd EN8 162 E6
St Josephs Court La AL5 107 B8
St Julian's Rd AL1 127 D1
St Katharines Cl SG5 21 D3
St Katherine's Way HP4 121 F7
St Laurence Dr EN10 148 F8
St Lawrence Cl Abbots Langley HP3 139 E1
Bovingdon HP3 137 A4
St Lawrence Way AL2 140 F1
St Lawrences Ave LU3 45 C3
St Leonard's Ct AL4 108 C1
St Leonard's Rd SG14 113 D8
St Leonards Cl Hertford SG14 113 E8
Watford WD23 167 E5
St Leonards Cres AL4 108 C1
St Leonards Rd EN9 149 D6
St Luke's Ave EN2 161 D1
St Luke's Cl LU4 44 E2
St Luke's Sch AL3 106 A6
St Magnus Ct HP3 125 C1
St Margaret Clitheroe RC Prim Sch SG2 50 F2
St Margaret of Scotland Jun Sch LU1 63 B5
St Margaret of Scotland RC Inf Sch LU1 63 B5
St Margaret's Cl HP4 122 D3
St Margaret's Rd SG12 115 B2
St Margaret's Sch WD23 168 A2
St Margarets SG2 50 F2
St Margarets Ave LU3 45 B3
St Margarets Cl LU3 31 A6
St Margarets Sta SG12 115 C4
St Margarets Way HP2 125 D3
St Mark's Cl SG5 21 D1
St Marks Cl AL4 129 B1
St Martha's Convent Jun Sch EN5 171 E5
St Martin de Porres RC Prim Sch LU4 44 A4
St Martin's Ave LU2 45 F2
St Martin's Rd SG3 69 A5
St Martin's Sch HA6 174 D5
St Martins HA6 174 D5
St Martins Cl Harpenden AL5 86 C4
South Oxhey WD19 175 C6
St Mary RC Prim Sch SG8 7 D7
St Mary's Ave Berkhamsted UB2 121 D6
Moor Park HA6 174 E5
Stotfold SG5 11 F6
St Mary's CE High Sch EN8 148 B1
St Mary's CE Jun Sch SG12 93 D3
St Mary's CE Prim Sch WD3 173 D7
St Mary's CE Prim Sch Stansted Mountfitchet CM24 59 E7
Welham Green AL9 144 B8
St Mary's Cl Letchworth SG6 22 F2
Pirton SG5 20 D4
Redbourn AL3 106 A4
St Mary's Ct 8 Hemel Hempstead HP2 124 D4
Potters Bar EN6 159 B7
Welwyn AL6 89 C4
St Mary's Ctyd 3 SG12 93 D1
St Mary's Dr CM24 59 F5
St Mary's Inf Sch SG7 23 E6
St Mary's Jun Mix Sch SG7 23 E6
St Mary's La SG14 112 F3
St Mary's Lower Sch SG5 12 A6
St Mary's Prim Sch AL6 89 B4
St Mary's RC Sch CM23 76 E7
St Mary's Rd Cheshunt EN8 148 C2
Hemel Hempstead HP2 124 D4
Luton LU1 63 F7
Standon SG11 55 D2
Watford WD18 167 B5
St Mary's Rise SG4 47 D1
St Mary's Way SG7 23 E6
St Marys Ct SG2 51 E2
St Marys Pk SG8 7 D6
St Marys Rd AL6 89 C5
St Marys Wlk AL4 128 B7
St Matthew's Inf Sch LU2 45 E1
St Matthews Cl Luton LU2 63 E8
Watford WD19 167 D3
St Meryl Sch WD19 175 E7
St Michael's CE Prim Sch Bishop's Stortford CM23 76 F7
St Albans AL3 127 B3
St Michael's Cres LU3 45 D3
St Michael's Ct AL3 127 B3
St Michael's Mount SG4 35 A8
St Michael's RC High Sch WD25 154 D7
St Michael's Rd EN10 135 A3
St Michael's St AL3 127 B3
St Michael's Woolmer Green CE Prim Sch Woolmer Green CE Prim Sch Woolmer Green CE Prim Sch SG3 69 A1
St Michaels Ave HP3 125 B1
St Michaels Cl Harlow CM20 117 E1
Harpenden AL5 107 D7
St Michaels Ct SG1 51 B8
St Michaels Dr WD25 154 B6
St Michaels Rd SG4 35 B7
St Michaels View AL10 130 B7
St Michaels Way EN6 145 B1
St Mildreds Ave LU3 45 C3
St Monicas Ave LU3 45 B3
St Neots Cl WD6 157 A1
St Nicholas CE Prim Sch Harpenden AL5 86 A1
Letchworth SG6 12 C1
Stevenage SG2 50 F4
St Nicholas Cl WD6 169 D3
St Nicholas Ct AL5 85 F3
St Nicholas Elstree CE Prim Sch WD6 169 D3
St Nicholas Gn CM17 118 C1
St Nicholas House Prep Sch HP3 139 B6
St Nicholas Mount HP1 123 F3
St Nicholas Sch CM17 118 F3
St Ninian's Ct 8 LU2 63 D8
St Olam's Cl LU3 45 B6
St Olives SG5 11 E6
St Pancras Ho SG8 2 D1
St Paul's CE Prim Sch WD4 152 A8
St Paul's Gdns LU1 63 E5
St Paul's Rd Hemel Hempstead HP2 124 E4
Luton LU1 63 E5
St Paul's Walden SG4 49 A1
St Paul's Walden Prim Sch SG4 66 D7
St Pauls CE Prim Sch WD4 153 C5
St Pauls Cl AL5 107 D8
St Pauls Ct 3 SG2 50 F1
St Pauls Pl AL1 128 A3
St Pauls RC Prim Sch EN7 148 B4
St Pauls Way Waltham Abbey EN9 163 D6
Watford WD24 167 C7
St Peter's Ave SG15 11 A7
St Peter's CE Prim Sch WD3 165 B1
St Peter's Cl Barnet EN5 171 B4
Bushey WD23 168 D1
Rickmansworth WD3 165 B1
St Albans AL1 127 D4
St Peter's Rd AL1 127 E4
St Peter's Sch AL1 127 E2
St Peter's St AL1 127 D4
St Peters Cl AL10 130 A6
St Peters Hill HP23 100 A4
St Peters Rd LU1 63 B7
St Peters Way WD3 164 B5
St Philip Howard RC Prim Sch AL10 130 B5
St Raphaels Ct 5 AL1 127 E4
St Ronans Cl EN4 159 D1
St Rose's RC Inf Sch HP1 124 A1
St Saviors View AL1 127 F4
St Saviours Cres LU1 63 D6
St Stephen's Ave AL3 141 B8
St Stephen's Cl AL3 141 B8
St Stephen's Hill AL1 127 C1
St Stephen's Rd EN3 162 D2
St Stephens Rd EN5 171 D4
St Teresa RC Prim Sch WD6 170 B7
St Teresa's RC Fst & Mid Sch HA3 176 C2
St Thomas Ct HA5 175 E2
St Thomas More RC Prim Sch Berkhamsted HP4 122 A4
Letchworth SG6 22 D4
St Thomas of Canterbury RC Prim Sch SG11 55 C3
St Thomas Pl AL4 108 D8
St Thomas' Dr HA5 175 E2
St Thomas's Cl LU2 46 A4
St Thomas's Rd LU2 46 A4
St Vincent de Paul RC Prim Sch SG1 51 A6
St Vincent Dr AL1 128 A1
St Vincent Gdns LU4 44 D3
St Vincent's Way EN6 159 C6
St Winifreds Ave LU3 45 C3
St Yon Ct AL4 128 E3
Sale Dr SG7 12 F1
Salisbury Ave Harpenden AL5 86 A1
St Albans AL1 128 B4
Salisbury Cl Bishop's Stortford CM23 76 F5
Potters Bar EN6 159 C7
Salisbury Cres EN8 162 D7
Salisbury Gdns AL7 110 F5
Salisbury Hall Dr AL10 129 E7
Salisbury Ho AL3 127 C2
Salisbury Rd Baldock SG7 12 F1
Barnet EN5 171 E6
Enfield EN3 162 F2
Harpenden AL5 86 D3
Hoddesdon EN11 135 C8
Luton LU1 63 D6
Stevenage SG1 37 A2
Watford WD24 154 C1
Welwyn Garden City AL7 111 A5
Salisbury Sq Hatfield AL9 130 C6
Salisbury Sq *continued*
7 Hertford SG14 113 D6
Sally Deards La AL6 68 B3
Salmon Cl AL7 90 A1
Salmons Cl SG12 93 D4
Saltdean Cl LU2 46 D4
Salter's Cl HP4 121 F6
Salters CM23 76 C4
Salters Cl WD3 165 E1
Salters Gdns WD17 167 A8
Saltfield Cres LU4 44 C4
Salusbury La SG5 33 C2
Salvatorian Coll HA3 176 E1
Salwey Cres EN10 134 F3
Samian Gate AL3 126 F1
Sampson Ave EN5 171 D4
Samuel Lucas Jun Mix Inf Sch SG5 34 D7
Samuel Sq 2 AL1 127 D2
Sancroft Rd HA3 176 F1
Sanctuary Cl UB9 173 C3
Sandalls Spring HP1 123 F5
Sandalwood Cl LU3 45 B7
Sanday Cl HP3 125 B1
Sandbrook La HP23 79 C1
Sandell Cl LU2 45 F2
Sandeman Gdns SG12 93 E2
Sander's Cnr EN2 161 B5
Sanderling Cl SG6 22 E8
Sanders Cl Hemel Hempstead HP3 138 F7
London Colney AL2 142 D4
Stansted Mountfitchet CM24 59 D6
Sanders Rd HP3 139 A7
Sandfield Rd AL1 128 A3
Sandgate Rd LU4 44 D2
Sandhurst Ct AL5 107 D6
Sandifield AL10 130 B2
Sandle Rd CM23 77 A7
Sandmere Cl HP2 125 A2
Sandon Cl HP23 99 F4
Sandon Jun Mix Inf Sch SG9 15 C1
Sandon Rd EN8 148 C1
Sandover Cl SG4 35 B6
Sandown Rd Stevenage SG1 37 C1
Watford WD24 154 C1
Sandown Road Ind Est WD24 154 C2
Sandpit Hill Cotts HP23 120 B3
Sandpit La AL1,AL4 128 C5
Sandpit Rd AL7 110 E4
Sandridge Cl HP2 105 A1
Sandridge Ct AL4 128 D7
Sandridge Gate Bsns Ctr AL1 127 F7
Sandridge Pk AL3 127 F8
Sandridge Rd AL1 127 F5
Sandridge Sch AL4 108 D1
Sandridgebury La Sandridge AL3,AL4 108 A2
St Albans AL3 127 E8
Sandringham Cres AL4 128 C8
Sandringham Gdns 6 CM23 76 E5
Sandringham Rd Potters Bar EN6 145 B1
Watford WD24 154 C2
Sandringham Sch AL4 128 B7
Sandringham Way EN8 162 D5
Sandy Cl SG14 113 B6
Sandy Gr SG4 34 F6
Sandy La Bushey WD25 168 C6
Moor Park HA6 175 A5
Sandy Lane Cvn Site WD25 168 C6
Sandy Lodge HA6 174 E8
Sandy Lodge Ct HA6 174 E5
Sandy Lodge La HA6 174 E8
Sandy Lodge Rd WD3 174 C8
Sandy Lodge Way HA6 174 E4
Sandycroft Rd HP6 150 C1
Sanfoin Rd LU4 44 A4
Sanfoine Cl SG4 35 C8
Santers La EN6 158 E6
Santingfield N LU1 63 B6
Santingfield S LU1 63 B6
Sappers Cl CM21 97 F2
Saracen Est HP2 125 B5
Saracens Head HP2 125 A4
Saracens Head Yd 1 AL1 127 D2
Sargents SG11 55 F1
Sarita Cl HA3 176 D1
Sark Ho Enfield EN3 162 D1
10 Watford WD18 166 F3
Sarratt Ave HP2 125 A8
Sarratt CE Prim Sch WD3 152 A3
Sarratt La Rickmansworth WD3 165 C6
Sarratt WD3 165 D8
Sarratt Rd WD3 165 C8
Sarum Pl HP2 124 E7
Sarum Rd LU3 44 F4
Satinwood Ct 1 HP3 124 E1
Saturn Way HP2 124 F6
Sauncey Ave AL5 86 B3
Sauncey Wood AL5 86 E4
Sauncey Wood La AL5 86 E6
Sauncey Wood Prim Sch AL5 86 D4
Saunders Cl Cheshunt EN8 148 D4
Letchworth SG6 23 C7
Savanna Ct WD18 166 F5

Savill Cl EN7 147 C6
Savoy Cl UB9 173 D1
Sawbridgeworth Rd
Hatfield Heath CM22 98 E3
Little Hallingbury CM22 98 B6
Sawbridgeworth Sta
CM21 98 A3
Sawells EN10 134 F2
Sawtry Cl LU3 45 A6
Sawtry Way WD6 157 A1
Sawyers La EN6 158 D5
Sawyers Way HP2 124 F3
Sax Ho SG6 11 E1
Saxon Ave SG5 11 F8
Saxon Cl Harpenden AL5 86 C4
Letchworth SG6 11 F1
Saxon Ct
Borehamwood WD6 169 E8
6 Hitchin SG4 34 F6
Saxon Rd Luton LU3 45 C2
Welwyn AL6 89 B3
Wheathampstead AL4 108 D7
Saxon Way Baldock SG7 13 B1
Waltham Abbey EN9 163 C6
Saxted Cl LU2 46 D1
Saxton Mews WD17 167 A7
Sayer Way SG3 68 F4
Sayers Gdns HP4 122 A6
Sayes Gdns CM21 97 F2
Sayesbury Ave CM21 97 E3
Sayesbury Rd CM21 97 E2
Sayfield Cotts SG9 26 B8
Saywell Rd LU2 46 B1
Scammell Way WD18 166 F3
Scarborough Ave SG1 50 B7
Scatterdells La WD4 138 A2
Scholar's Hill SG12 95 A4
Scholars Ct AL4 143 C8
Scholars Mews AL8 110 D8
Scholars The WD18 167 C4
Scholars Wlk 4 AL10 130 A2
School Cl Essendon AL9 131 F6
Stevenage SG2 51 B3
School Cotts SG4 47 F6
School Gdns HP4 123 B6
School Ho The 1 SG7 23 F7
School La Ardeley SG2 38 F3
Aston SG2 51 E2
Barley SG8 9 A1
Bricket Wood AL2 155 A7
Bushey WD23 168 B2
Essendon AL9 131 F6
Great Offley SG5 33 C3
Harlow CM20 117 E2
Hatfield AL10 130 C6
Luton LU4 44 D4
Preston SG4 48 E5
Tewin AL6 90 E2
Watton at S SG14 70 E3
Welwyn AL6 89 B4
Weston SG4 24 C1
School Mead WD5 153 D7
School Rd EN6 145 C1
School Row HP1 123 F2
School Wlk SG6 23 B6
Schoolfields SG6 23 C5
Schubert Rd WD6 169 D3
Scot Gr HA5 175 D3
Scotfield Ct LU2 46 D3
Scots Hill WD3 165 F3
Scots Hill Cl WD3 165 F3
Scots Mill La WD3 165 F3
Scotscraig WD7 155 F4
Scotswood EN5 171 B4
Scott Ave SG12 115 B4
Scott Cl SG8 2 D1
Scott Rd
Bishop's Stortford CM23 76 E6
Luton LU3 44 C7
Stevenage SG2 51 B6
Scott's Grotto* SG12 114 D8
Scott's Rd SG12 114 D8
Scotts Cl SG12 114 D8
Scotts View AL8 110 C5
Scottswood Cl WD23 167 E7
Scottswood Rd WD23 167 E7
Scratchwood Nature Trail*
NW7 170 D2
Scriveners Cl HP2 124 E3
Scrubbits Sq WD7 156 A4
Scrubbitts Park Rd
WD7 156 A4
Seabrook LU4 44 B3
Seabrook Rd WD4 139 D4
Seacroft Gdns WD19 175 D7
Seaford Cl LU2 46 C3
Seaforth Ct EN11 135 B4
Seaforth Dr EN8 162 D5
Seal Cl LU4 44 D3
Seaman Cl AL2 141 D6
Searches La WD5 140 C4
Seaton Rd
Hemel Hempstead HP3 124 E1
London Colney AL2 142 D5
Luton LU4 44 F3
Sebright Rd Barnet EN5 171 E6
Hemel Hempstead HP1 124 A1
Markyate AL3 83 E5
Secker Cres HA3 176 C2
Second Ave
Letchworth SG6 23 C6
Watford WD25 154 D4
Sedbury Cl LU3 45 A6
Sedge Gn EN9,CM19 135 E3
Sedgewick Ct HP2 105 B1
Sedgwick Rd LU4 44 B7
Sedley Cl EN1 162 B1
Seebohm Cl SG5 21 C1
Seeleys The CM17 118 C4
Sefton Ave HA3 176 D2
Sefton Cl AL1 127 F4
Sefton Rd SG1 37 B1
Selbourne Rd LU4 45 A2
Selby Ave AL3 127 D3
Selden Hill HP2 124 D2
Sele Mill SG14 113 B6
Sele Rd SG14 113 B6
Sele Sch The SG14 112 F6
Selina Cl LU3 44 C7
Sell Cl EN7 147 B5
Sellers Cl WD6 170 C8
Sells Rd SG12 93 F2
Sellwood Dr EN5 171 D4
Selsey Dr LU2 46 D4
Selwyn Ave AL10 129 E4
Selwyn Cres AL10 129 E5
Selwyn Dr AL10 129 E5
Sempill Rd HP3 124 E1
Senate Pl SG1 37 B3
Sentis Ct HA6 174 F4
Sequoia Cl WD23 168 D1
Sequoia Pk HA5 176 B4
Serby Ave SG8 7 D8
Sergehill La WD5 140 A5
Serpentine Cl SG1 37 C2
Service Industry Bays
CM20 117 F2
Service Rd The EN6 159 A7
Seven Acres HA6 175 A4
Seven Roe's Malting SG7 23 E8
Sevenoaks Ct HA6 174 C3
Severalls The LU2 46 B3
Severn Dr EN1 162 A1
Severn Way
Stevenage SG1 36 F3
Watford WD25 154 C5
Severnmead HP2 124 E6
Severnvale AL2 142 F4
Sewardstone Rd EN9 163 D3
Sewardstone St EN9 163 C5
Sewell Cl AL4 128 E3
Sewell Harris Cl CM20 117 F1
Sewells AL8 89 E2
Sexton Cl EN7 147 B6
Seymour Ave LU1 63 F5
Seymour Cl HA5 175 F2
Seymour Cres HP2 124 E3
Seymour Ct HP4 121 E6
Seymour Mews CM21 118 E7
Seymour Rd
Berkhamsted HP4 121 E6
Luton LU1 63 F5
St Albans AL3 127 E6
Shackledell SG2 50 F2
Shacklegate La SG4 66 E5
Shackleton Gdns CM23 76 E6
Shackleton Spring SG2 51 A3
Shackleton Way
Abbots Langley WD5 154 A7
Welwyn Garden City AL7 111 D6
Shady Bush Cl WD23 168 C2
Shady La WD17 167 B7
Shafford Cotts
Hemel Hempstead HP3 139 A5
St Albans AL3 126 F6
Shaftenhoe End Rd
Barley SG8 9 A1
Nuthampstead SG8 18 B8
Shaftesbury Ct
Croxley Green WD3 166 C4
Stevenage SG1 50 E4
Shaftesbury High Sch
HA3 176 B2
Shaftesbury Ind Ctr SG6 23 B7
Shaftesbury Quay 11
SG14 113 D6
Shaftesbury Rd Luton LU4 45 B1
Watford WD17 167 C6
Shaftesbury Way
Bedmond WD4 139 C3
Royston SG8 7 E5
Shakespeare SG8 7 D8
Shakespeare Ct EN11 115 A2
Shakespeare Ind Est
WD24 154 A1
Shakespeare Rd
Harpenden AL5 86 C1
Luton LU4 44 B2
Shakespeare St WD24 154 B1
Shalcross Dr EN8 148 F1
Shallcross Cres 6 AL10 130 A2
Shambrook Rd EN7 147 B6
Shangani Rd CM23 76 F5
Shanklin Cl
Goff's Oak EN7 147 F2
Luton LU3 45 A7
Shanklin Gdns WD19 175 C6
Shantock Hall La HP3 136 E1
Shantock La HP3 136 E1
Sharmans Cl AL6 89 F4
Sharose Ct AL3 83 E5
Sharpcroft 1 HP2 124 D5
Sharpenhoe Rd LU3 31 A5
Sharpes La HP1 123 B1
Sharples Gn LU3 45 B8
Sharps Way Hitchin SG4 22 A1
Hitchin SG4 35 A8
Shaw Cl Bushey WD23 176 E8
Cheshunt EN8 148 C3
Shaw's Cnr* AL6 88 A6
Shaws The AL7 111 C5
Shearers The CM23 76 C4
Sheares Hoppit SG12 95 D2
Shearwater Cl SG2 51 D4
Sheepcot Dr WD25 154 C5
Sheepcot La WD25 154 B6
Sheepcot Villas WD25 154 C5
Sheepcote AL7 111 A3
Sheepcote La AL4 87 F1
Sheepcote Rd HP2 124 F3
Sheepcroft Hill SG2 51 D3
Sheephouse Rd HP3 124 F1
Sheering CE Prim Sch
CM22 98 D1
Sheering Dr CM17 118 E4
Sheering Lower Rd
CM21 98 A2
Sheering Mill La CM21 97 F2
Sheering Rd
Harlow CM17 118 F4
Harlow CM17 118 F5
Sheethanger La HP3 138 A7
Shefton Rise HA6 175 A3
Sheldon Cl EN7 147 E5
Shelford Rd EN5 171 C3
Shelley Cl Hitchin SG4 35 C7
Moor Park HA6 174 F5
Royston SG8 2 D1
Shelley Ct Cheshunt EN7 148 A3
16 Harpenden AL5 86 B1
Waltham Abbey EN9 163 F6
Shelley La UB9 173 A3
Shelley Rd LU4 44 B2
Shelton Way LU2 46 A3
Shendish Edge HP3 138 F6
Shenley Ct HP2 125 B8
Shenley Hill WD7 156 B4
Shenley La AL2 142 C4
Shenley Prim Sch WD7 156 F5
Shenley Rd
Borehamwood WD6 170 B6
Hemel Hempstead HP2 105 B1
Radlett WD7 156 C4
Shenleybury WD7 156 E8
Shenleybury Cotts WD7 156 E8
Shenleybury Villas WD7 156 E8
Shenstone Hill HP4 122 E5
Shenval Ho CM20 118 A4
Shephall Gn SG2 51 B2
Shephall Green Inf Sch
SG2 51 B2
Shephall La SG2 50 F1
Shephall View SG1 51 A5
Shephall Way SG2 51 C3
Shepherd Cl
Abbots Langley WD5 153 F8
Royston SG8 7 E5
Shepherd Inf Sch WD3 165 A1
Shepherd Prim Sch
WD3 165 A1
Shepherd's La WD3 164 E2
Shepherd's Row AL3 106 B5
Shepherds Cl CM23 76 C4
Shepherds Ct SG14 92 C1
Shepherds Gn HP1 123 E2
Shepherds La SG1 50 A6
Shepherds Mead SG5 21 F2
Shepherds Rd WD18 166 F5
Shepherds Way
Brookmans Park AL9 145 D4
Harpenden AL5 85 D4
Rickmansworth WD3 165 B2
Shepherds Wlk WD23 176 D8
Shepley Mews EN3 163 A2
Sheppard Cl EN1 162 B1
Sheppards Cl AL3 127 E6
Sheppards Yd 4 HP1 124 D4
Shepperton Cl WD6 170 D8
Sheppey's La WD5 139 E3
Sheraton Cl WD6 169 F4
Sheraton Ho WD3 164 C5
Sheraton Mews WD18 166 E5
Sherborne Ave LU2 45 D6
Sherborne Cotts WD18 167 C4
Sherborne Pl HA6 174 D4
Sherborne Way WD3 166 B5
Sherbourne Cl HP2 124 E2
Sherbourne Ct AL1 127 F3
Sherd Cl LU3 44 F7
Sheredes Dr EN11 134 F4
Sheredes Prim Sch
EN11 134 F4
Sheredes Sch EN11 134 F5
Sherfield Ave WD3 173 E8
Sheridan Cl HP1 124 B2
Sheridan Rd Luton LU3 45 C2
Watford WD19 167 D2
Sheriden Wlk EN10 134 E3
Sheriff Way WD25 154 A5
Sheringham Ave SG1 36 B1
Sheringham Cl LU2 45 C7
Sherington Ave HA5 176 A3
Sherland Ct WD7 156 A4
Shernbroke Rd EN9 163 F5
Sherrards Mans AL8 89 B1
Sherrards Mews AL8 89 B1
Sherrardspark Rd AL8 110 D8
Sherrardswood Sch AL6 89 D4
Sherwood SG6 22 F8
Sherwood Ave
Potters Bar EN6 158 E7
St Albans AL4 128 B6
Sherwood Ct
20 Bishop's Stortford CM23 76 F7
Watford WD25 154 A5
Sherwood Ho WD5 153 F8
Sherwood Pl 1 HP2 124 F7
Sherwood Rd LU4 45 A2
Sherwoods Rd WD19 167 E2
Sherwoods Rise AL5 107 D8
Shetland Cl WD6 170 D3
Shetland Ho 13 WD18 166 F3
Shillington Rd SG5 20 B5
Shillitoe Ave EN6 158 E7
Shingle Cl LU3 45 A8
Ship La LU7 80 D3
Shire Cl EN10 148 F5
Shire Ct HP2 125 A4
Shire La
Chalfont St Peter,Horn Hill
WD3 172 B6
Chalfont St Peter,West Hyde
WD3 172 C4
Chorleywood WD3 164 C4
Maple Cross WD3 172 B5
Tring HP23 120 B4
Shiremeade WD6 169 F4
Shires The Luton LU2 45 D1
Royston SG8 7 E6
Watford WD25 154 C8
Shirley Cl Cheshunt EN8 148 C2
Cheshunt,Wormley EN10 148 F7
Stevenage SG2 51 C8
Shirley Rd
Abbots Langley WD5 153 F7
Luton LU1 63 C8
St Albans AL1 127 F2
Shootersway HP4 121 E4
Shootersway La HP4 121 F4
Shootersway Pk HP4 121 F3
Shoplands AL8 89 D2
Shoreham Cl SG1 50 A8
Short Hale LU7 80 D3
Short La Aston SG2 51 E4
Bricket Wood AL2 140 E2
Shortcroft CM23 77 D7
Shortlands Gn AL7 110 F5
Shortlands Pl CM23 76 F8
Shortmead Dr EN8 162 E8
Shothanger Way HP3 137 D6
Shott La SG6 23 A5
Shottfield Cl AL4 108 D2
Shrevington Gr LU3 45 C3
Shrubbery Gr SG8 7 D4
Shrubbery The HP1 123 E4
Shrubhill Rd HP1 123 F2
Shrublands AL9 145 B5
Shrublands Ave HP4 122 A4
Shrublands Rd HP4 122 A5
Shrublands The EN6 158 E6
Shrubs UB9 173 F4
Shrubs Rd UB9 173 F4
Shugars Gn HP23 100 B5
Sibley Ave AL5 107 E7
Sibley Cl LU2 46 B3
Sibthorpe Rd AL9 144 D7
Siccut Rd SG4 35 E4
Sicklefield Cl EN7 147 F5
Siddons Rd SG2 51 C6
Sidford Cl HP1 123 F3
Sidings Ct SG14 113 C7
Sidings The
Hatfield AL10 129 E4
Hemel Hempstead HP2 124 D3
Hoddesdon EN10 135 A1
Sidmouth Cl WD19 175 B8
Sidney Ct EN8 162 F5
Sidney Terr CM23 76 F6
Signal Cl SG16 10 B3
Silam Rd SG1 50 E5
Silecroft Rd LU2 64 B8
Silk Mill Ct WD19 167 B2
Silk Mill Rd
Redbourn AL3 106 B4
Watford WD19 167 B2
Silk Mill Way HP23 100 A5
Silkin Ct SG2 51 D3
Silver Birch Ct EN8 162 D8
Silver Cl HA3 176 D3
Silver Ct Ashwell SG7 4 D4
Hitchin SG5 34 F8
Silver Dell WD24 153 F4
Silver Hill WD6,WD7 157 B3
Silver Pl WD18 166 F5
Silver St Anstey SG9 29 A5
Ashwell SG7 4 D4
Goff's Oak EN7 147 D1
Guilden Morden SG8 1 F4
Luton LU1 63 E7
Stansted Mountfitchet
CM24 59 D6
Waltham Abbey EN9 163 C6
Silver Trees AL2 140 F1
Silverbirch Ave SG5 11 F8
Silverdale Ho HA6 174 F4
Silverdale Rd WD23 167 E4
Silverfield EN10 134 F1
Silverthorn Dr HP3 139 B7
Silverwood Cl HA6 174 C2
Simmonds Rise HP3 124 D1
Simon Balle Sch SG13 113 E5
Simon Dean HP3 137 A4
Simpson Cl LU4 44 D2
Simpson Dr SG7 23 F8
Simpsons Ct 3 SG7 23 F8
Sinderby Cl WD6 169 E8
Sinfield Cl SG1 51 A5
Singlets La AL3 84 C2
Sir Frederic Osborn Sch
AL7 111 B7
Sir Herbert Janes Village The
LU4 44 D4
Sir John Lawes Sch AL5 86 C3
Sir John Newsom Way
AL7 110 E3
Sir Joseph's Wlk AL5 107 A8
Sir Peter's Way HP4 81 E6
Sirus Rd HA6 175 A5
Sish Cl SG1 50 D6
Sish La SG1 50 D6
Siskin Cl
Borehamwood WD6 170 A5
Siskin Cl *continued*
Royston SG8 7 E8
Watford WD23 167 E5
Sisson Cl SG2 51 C2
Sitwell Gr HA7 176 F5
Six Acres HP3 139 A8
Six Cotts SG11 57 C6
Six Hills Way SG1,SG2 50 C4
Sixth Ave Letchworth SG6 23 C6
Watford WD25 154 D4
Skegness Rd SG1 50 A8
Skegsbury La SG4 65 F1
Skelton Cl LU3 31 B1
Skidmore Way WD3 165 E1
Skimpans Cl AL9 144 D7
Skimpot Rd LU4 44 A1
Skinners St CM23 76 C4
Skipton Cl SG2 68 F8
Skua Cl LU4 44 A5
Skye Ho 11 WD18 166 F3
Skylark Cnr SG2 51 D3
Skylark Pl SG8 7 E8
Skys Wood Rd AL4 128 B7
Skyswood Prim Sch
AL4 128 C6
Slade Ct WD7 156 A4
Sleaford Gn WD19 175 D7
Sleapcross Gdns AL4 129 C2
Sleaps Hyde SG2 51 C1
Sleapshyde La AL4 129 C2
Sleddale HP2 124 E6
Sleets End HP1 124 B5
Slimmons Dr AL4 128 A7
Slip End SG7 14 B6
Slip End Lower Sch LU1 63 B1
Slip La SG3,AL6 68 C4
Slipe La EN10 148 F7
Slipe The LU7 80 A7
Slippers Hill HP2 124 D4
Sloan Ct SG1 50 F6
Sloansway AL7 90 A1
Slowmans Cl AL2 141 C3
Slype The AL4 87 B5
Small Acre HP1 123 F3
Smallcroft AL7 111 B7
Smallford La AL4 129 B2
Smallwood Cl AL4 108 E7
Smarts Gn EN7 147 F5
Smeaton Cl EN9 163 E7
Smeaton Rd EN3 163 A2
Smith St WD18 167 C5
Smith's End La
Barley SG8 17 F8
Nuthampstead SG8 18 A8
Smithfield HP2 124 D5
Smiths Cres AL4 129 C2
Smiths La EN7 147 D5
Smiths Lane Mall 5 LU1 63 E7
Smiths Sq 6 LU1 63 E7
Smithy The
Little Hadham SG11 57 B2
Sawbridgeworth CM21 97 E3
Smug Oak Bsns Ctr AL2 141 B1
Smug Oak La AL2 141 D1
Snailswell La SG5 21 E5
Snatchup AL3 106 A5
Snells Mead SG9 40 F7
Snipe The SG4 24 B1
Snowdrop Cl CM23 76 C6
Snowford Cl 1 LU3 45 A7
Snowley Par CM23 59 B1
Soham Rd EN3 162 F2
Solar Ct WD18 166 F4
Solar Way EN3 162 F3
Solesbridge Cl WD3 164 F6
Solesbridge La WD3 165 B7
Sollershott E SG6 22 F4
Sollershott Hall SG6 22 F4
Sollershott W SG6 22 E4
Solomon's Hill WD3 165 D2
Solway HP2 124 F5
Solway Rd N LU3 45 A4
Solway Rd S LU3 45 A3
Somerby Cl EN10 135 A2
Someries Inf Sch LU2 46 C3
Someries Jun Sch LU2 46 C3
Someries Rd
Harpenden AL5 86 C4
Hemel Hempstead HP1 123 F5
Somers Rd AL9 144 C7
Somers Sq AL9 144 C8
Somers Way WD23 168 C2
Somersby Cl LU1 63 E5
Somerset Ave LU2 46 A1
Somerset Rd EN3 163 A1
Somersham AL7 111 D6
Sommer's Ct SG12 114 E8
Sonia Cl WD19 167 C2
Soothouse Spring AL3 127 F7
Soper Mews EN3 163 A1
Soper Sq CM17 118 C1
Sopers Rd EN6 146 F2
Sopwell La AL1 127 D2
Sorrel Cl Luton LU3 45 B8
Royston SG8 7 F5
Sorrel Garth SG4 35 A6
Sotheron Rd WD17 167 C6
Souberie Ave SG6 22 F5
Souldern St WD18 167 B4
South App HA6 174 D7
South Bank Rd HP4 121 F6
South Block CM21 97 F2
South Charlton Mead La
EN11 135 D5
South Cl Baldock SG7 23 F7

South Cl *continued*
Barnet EN5 .....171 F6
Chiswell Green AL2 .....141 B6
Royston SG8 .....7 B7
South Comm AL3 .....106 B5
South Cottage Dr WD3 .....164 F4
South Cottage Gdns WD3 .....164 F4
South Dene HP2 .....104 A8
South Dr Cuffley EN6 .....146 E1
St Albans AL4 .....128 E4
South Drift Way LU1 .....63 B5
South Farm Cotts AL2 .....142 C3
South Hill Cl SG4 .....35 A6
South Hill Prim Sch HP1 .....124 C2
South Hill Rd HP1 .....124 C3
South Ley AL7 .....110 E3
South Ley Ct AL7 .....110 E3
South Lodge Mews 2 SG7 .....23 F7
South Luton High Sch LU1 .....63 F5
South Ordnance Rd EN3 .....163 A2
South Park Ave WD3 .....164 F4
South Park Gdns HP4 .....122 B5
South Pl Harlow CM20 .....118 A4
Hitchin SG5 .....34 D8
Waltham Abbey EN9 .....163 C6
South Rd Baldock SG7 .....24 A7
Bishop's Stortford CM23 .....77 A5
Chorleywood WD3 .....164 C4
Harlow CM20 .....118 A4
Luton LU1 .....63 D6
Standon SG11 .....55 D2
South Riding AL2 .....141 A1
South St
Bishop's Stortford CM23 .....76 F6
Hertford SG14 .....113 D6
Stanstead Abbotts SG12 .....115 C4
South Street Commercial Ctr 1 CM23 .....76 F6
South View SG6 .....22 F5
South View Rd HA5 .....175 B4
South Way
Abbots Langley WD5, WD25 .....153 E6
Hatfield AL10 .....130 B2
Waltham Abbey EN9 .....163 C3
South Weald Dr EN9 .....163 D6
Southacre Way HA5 .....175 C2
Southall Cl SG12 .....93 D2
Southbrook CM21 .....97 E1
Southbrook Dr 2 EN8 .....148 D3
Southdown Ct AL10 .....130 A2
Southdown Ho AL5 .....107 C8
Southdown Ind Est AL5 .....107 C8
Southdown Rd
Harpenden AL5 .....107 B8
Hatfield AL10 .....130 A2
Southend Cl SG1 .....50 D7
Southern Ave SG16 .....10 C3
Southern Gn SG9 .....26 A4
Southern Rise LU2 .....85 F7
Southern Terr 2 EN11 .....115 B1
Southern Way
Letchworth SG6 .....22 E8
Studham LU6 .....82 C4
Southernwood Cl HP2 .....125 A4
Southerton Way WD7 .....156 E6
Southfield Barnet EN5 .....171 D3
Braughing SG11 .....55 F7
Welwyn Garden City AL7 .....110 D4
Southfield Ave WD24 .....154 C1
Southfield Rd
Cheshunt EN8 .....162 E7
Hoddesdon EN11 .....135 A7
Southfield Sch AL10 .....130 B1
Southfield Way AL4 .....128 D6
Southfields
Letchworth SG6 .....11 F1
Standon SG11 .....55 E2
Southgate SG1 .....50 D4
Southgate Cotts WD3 .....165 E2
Southgate Ct 5 AL5 .....86 A2
Southgate Ho 1 EN8 .....148 D1
Southgate Rd EN6 .....159 C6
Southhill HA6 .....174 E2
Southlynn Ho 2 LU2 .....63 F8
Southmead Cres EN8 .....148 F1
Southmill Ct CM23 .....77 A6
Southmill Rd CM23 .....77 A5
Southmill Trad Ctr CM23 .....77 A6
Southsea Ave WD18 .....167 A5
Southsea Rd SG1 .....50 B8
Southside SG9 .....28 A3
Southview Cl 1 EN7 .....147 E5
Southview Rd AL5 .....86 D3
Southwark Cl SG1 .....37 B2
Southwark Ho 11 WD6 .....170 A7
Southwold Cl SG1 .....50 A6
Southwold Rd WD24 .....154 C2
Soval Ct HA6 .....174 D3
Sovereign Ct WD18 .....167 A5
Sovereign Pk
Hemel Hempstead HP2 .....125 B5
Luton LU4 .....44 F1
St Albans AL4 .....128 D2
Sowerby Ave LU2 .....46 C3
Sparhawke SG6 .....12 A1
Sparrow Cl LU4 .....44 A4
Sparrow Dr SG2 .....51 D4
Sparrows Herne WD23 .....168 C2
Sparrows Way WD23 .....168 C1
Sparrowswick Ride AL3 .....127 C8
Spayne Cl LU3 .....45 B8
Spear Cl LU3 .....44 E6
Spectrum Ho EN3 .....162 E3
Speedwell Cl
Hemel Hempstead HP1 .....123 E2
Luton LU3 .....45 A8
Speke Cl SG2 .....51 D5
Spellbrook La E CM22 .....97 F8
Spellbrook La W CM23 .....97 E7
Spellbrook Prim Sch CM23 .....97 F7
Spellbrooke 5 SG5 .....34 D8
Spencer Ave EN7 .....147 E5
Spencer Cl CM24 .....59 E6
Spencer Gate AL1 .....127 E5
Spencer Ho SG5 .....11 F6
Spencer Jun Sch AL3 .....127 E6
Spencer Mews AL1 .....127 E4
Spencer Pl AL4 .....108 C2
Spencer Rd Harrow HA3 .....176 E1
Luton LU3 .....45 C2
Spencer St
Hertford SG13 .....113 E7
St Albans AL3 .....127 D3
Spencer Way HP1 .....124 A6
Spencer Wlk WD3 .....165 C4
Spenser Cl SG8 .....2 D1
Spenser Rd AL5 .....86 C1
Sperberry Hill SG4 .....35 B2
Speyhawk Pl EN6 .....145 B1
Sphere Ind Est The AL1 .....128 A2
Spicer St AL3 .....127 C3
Spicersfield EN7 .....148 A4
Spindleberry Cl AL6 .....90 A7
Spinney Cl SG4 .....35 B6
Spinney Ct CM21 .....97 E2
Spinney Jun & Inf Schs The CM20 .....118 A1
Spinney La AL6 .....68 E3
Spinney Rd LU3 .....44 D7
Spinney St SG13 .....114 A6
Spinney The Baldock SG7 .....23 E7
Berkhamsted HP4 .....121 F3
Cheshunt EN7 .....148 B1
Harpenden AL5 .....85 E3
Hertford SG13 .....113 F6
Hoddesdon EN10 .....134 F4
Potters Bar EN6 .....159 D8
Radlett WD25 .....155 D1
Stansted Mountfitchet CM24 .....59 E6
Stevenage SG2 .....51 D7
Watford WD17 .....167 A8
Welwyn Garden City AL7 .....110 E5
Spinneys Dr AL3 .....127 B1
Spires Sh Ctr The EN5 .....171 E6
Spires The
Bishop's Stortford CM23 .....76 D7
Hemel Hempstead HP2 .....124 D2
Spittlesea Rd LU2 .....64 C7
Spooners Dr AL2 .....141 C4
Spratts La LU6 .....82 F8
Spreckley Cl SG16 .....10 B5
Spring Cl Barnet EN5 .....171 D4
Borehamwood WD6 .....170 A8
Harefield UB9 .....173 D2
Latimer HP5 .....150 D3
Spring Court Rd EN2 .....161 A1
Spring Crofts WD23 .....168 A4
Spring Dr SG2 .....69 B8
Spring Field Rd HP4 .....122 A6
Spring Gdns WD25 .....154 C3
Spring Glen AL10 .....129 F4
Spring Hills CM20 .....117 B1
Spring Hills Twr CM20 .....117 A1
Spring La Cottered SG9 .....39 C5
Hemel Hempstead HP1 .....124 A4
Spring Mews CM21 .....97 E2
Spring Pl 6 LU1 .....63 D6
Spring Rd Harpenden AL5 .....85 A4
Letchworth SG6 .....22 E4
Letchworth SG6 .....22 E6
Spring Valley Ent Ctr AL3 .....127 E7
Spring View Rd SG12 .....114 C8
Spring Way HP2 .....125 C5
Spring Wlk EN10 .....134 C2
Springfield WD23 .....168 D1
Springfield Cl
Croxley Green WD3 .....166 B4
Potters Bar EN6 .....159 E8
Springfield Cres AL5 .....86 B5
Springfield Ct
Bishop's Stortford CM23 .....76 E8
Rickmansworth WD3 .....165 B1
Springfield Lodge SG13 .....113 E5
Springfield Rd
Cheshunt EN8 .....162 E7
Hemel Hempstead HP2 .....124 F4
Luton LU3 .....45 C6
St Albans AL4 .....129 B3
St Albans, The Camp AL1 .....128 A2
Watford WD25 .....154 B6
Springfields
Hoddesdon EN10 .....134 F4
Waltham Abbey EN9 .....163 E5
Welwyn Garden City AL8 .....110 B4
Springfields Ho AL8 .....110 C4
Springhall Ct CM21 .....97 E2
Springhall La CM21 .....97 E1
Springhall Rd CM21 .....97 E2
Springhead SG7 .....4 D4
Springle La SG13 .....114 F2
Springmead Jun Mix Inf Sch AL7 .....111 C7
Springs Cotts EN10 .....148 E7
Springs The
Cheshunt EN10 .....148 E6
Hertford SG13 .....113 F7
Springshott SG6 .....22 E5
Springwell Ave WD3 .....173 A8
Springwell Ct
Rickmansworth WD3 .....173 A8
Stanstead Abbotts SG12 .....115 C4
Springwell La WD3 .....173 A6
Springwood EN7 .....148 A5
Springwood Cl UB9 .....173 D2
Springwood Wlk AL4 .....128 D6
Spruce Way AL2 .....141 B4
Spur Cl WD5 .....153 D6
Spur The
3 Cheshunt EN8 .....148 D3
Stevenage SG1 .....50 E4
Spurcroft LU3 .....31 C1
Spurrs Cl SG4 .....35 B7
Square St CM17 .....118 C1
Square The
Braughing SG11 .....55 F7
Buckland SG9 .....27 D5
Hemel Hempstead HP1 .....124 C3
Hoddesdon EN10 .....148 E8
Much Hadham SG10 .....74 F3
Potten End HP4 .....123 B7
Redbourn AL3 .....105 F6
Sawbridgeworth CM21 .....97 E2
Watford WD24 .....154 B2
Squires Cl CM23 .....76 C8
Squires Ct EN11 .....135 A5
Squires Ride HP2 .....104 F1
Squirrel Chase HP1 .....123 E4
Squirrels Cl 2 CM23 .....76 F8
Squirrels The
Bushey WD23 .....168 D3
Hertford SG13 .....114 B6
Welwyn Garden City AL7 .....111 C5
Stable Block The AL6 .....90 B2
Stable Cotts SG11 .....57 E2
Stable Ct AL1 .....127 E5
Stable Mews
Northaw AL9 .....145 E3
St Albans AL1 .....127 E4
Stables The CM21 .....98 B3
Stacey Ct 9 CM23 .....76 F6
Stackfield CM20 .....118 A3
Stacklands AL8 .....110 B4
Staddles CM22 .....98 B8
Stadium Est The LU4 .....44 B1
Stadium Way CM19 .....116 F1
Staff Cotts UB9 .....173 B2
Stafford Cl EN8 .....148 B2
Stafford Ct EN10 .....135 A3
Stafford Dr EN10 .....135 A3
Stafford Ho
Bishop's Stortford CM23 .....76 F5
Hoddesdon EN10 .....135 A3
Stafford Rd HA3 .....176 C3
Staffords CM17 .....118 E4
Stag Ct WD3 .....164 C5
Stag Green Ave AL9 .....130 C7
Stag La Berkhamsted HP4 .....122 B5
Chorleywood WD3 .....164 C3
Stagg Hill EN4 .....159 E3
Stainer Rd
Borehamwood WD6 .....156 D1
Radlett WD6 .....169 D8
Stainers CM23 .....76 C5
Stains Cl EN8 .....148 F3
Stake Piece Rd SG8 .....7 C5
Stakers Ct AL5 .....86 B1
Stamford Ave SG8 .....7 D7
Stamford Cl Harrow HA3 .....176 E3
Potters Bar EN6 .....159 D7
Stamford Ct SG8 .....7 D7
Stamford Rd WD17 .....167 B7
Stamford Yd SG8 .....7 C6
Stanborough Ave WD6 .....157 B1
Stanborough Cl
Borehamwood WD6 .....157 A1
Welwyn Garden City AL8 .....110 C5
Stanborough Gn AL8 .....110 C4
Stanborough La AL8 .....110 C4
Stanborough Mews AL8 .....110 D4
Stanborough Prim Sch WD25 .....154 C4
Stanborough Rd AL8 .....110 C4
Stanborough Sch AL8 .....110 B4
Stanborough Sec Sch WD25 .....154 B4
Stanbury Ave WD17 .....153 E2
Standalone Farm* SG6 .....22 D8
Standard Rd EN3 .....162 E2
Standfield WD5 .....139 E1
Standhill Cl SG4 .....34 F6
Standhill Rd SG4 .....34 F6
Standon Bsns Pk SG11 .....55 E1
Standon Ct SG11 .....55 F1
Standon Hill SG11 .....55 D2
Standon Rd SG11 .....56 E3
Standring Rise HP3 .....138 B8
Stane Cl CM23 .....58 F1
Stane Field SG6 .....23 B3
Stane St SG7 .....13 A1
Stanelow Cres SG11 .....55 D2
Stanfields Ct CM20 .....117 E1
Stanford Rd LU2 .....46 A1
Stangate Cres WD6 .....170 E4
Stanhope Ave HA3 .....176 D2
Stanhope Rd Barnet EN5 .....171 D3
Cheshunt EN8 .....162 E6
St Albans AL1 .....127 F3
Stanier Rise HP4 .....121 F7
Stanley Ave AL2 .....141 A6
Stanley Dr AL10 .....130 B3
Stanley Gdns
Borehamwood WD6 .....169 E8
Tring HP23 .....99 F3
Stanley Livingstone Ct 2 LU1 .....63 D6
Stanley Rd Hertford SG13 .....113 E5
Northwood HA6 .....175 A2
Stevenage SG2 .....51 B7
Streatley LU3 .....31 A5
Watford WD18 .....167 C5
Stanley St LU1 .....63 D6
Stanmore Chase AL4 .....128 D2
Stanmore Cres LU3 .....44 F4
Stanmore Rd
Stevenage SG1 .....50 D7
Watford WD24 .....167 B8
Stanmount Rd AL2 .....141 A6
Stannington Path WD6 .....170 A8
Stanstead Dr EN11 .....135 B8
Stanstead Rd
Hertford SG13 .....114 A6
Hertford Heath SG13 .....114 D5
Hoddesdon EN11 .....115 B1
Stansted Hill SG10 .....75 A1
Stansted Mountfitchet Sta CM24 .....59 E6
Stansted Mountfitchet Windmill* CM24 .....59 D6
Stansted Rd
Birchanger CM23,CM24 .....59 C4
Bishop's Stortford CM23 .....59 B2
Stanton Cl AL4 .....128 D7
Stanton Rd LU4 .....44 C1
Stantons CM20 .....117 B1
Staplefield Cl HA5 .....175 E3
Stapleford AL7 .....111 D6
Stapleford Prim Sch SG14 .....92 A6
Stapleford Rd LU2 .....46 C4
Stapleton Cl EN6 .....159 D8
Stapleton Rd WD6 .....157 A2
Stapley Rd AL3 .....127 D4
Staplyton Rd EN5 .....171 E6
Star Holme Ct SG12 .....93 E1
Star St SG12 .....93 E1
Starkey Cl EN7 .....147 C6
Starlight Way AL4 .....128 C1
Starling La EN6 .....146 F3
Startpoint LU1 .....63 C7
Stately Ct LU3 .....45 D1
Statham Cl LU3 .....31 B1
Stathams Ct AL3 .....106 A3
Station App
Cheshunt EN8 .....162 E5
Chorleywood WD3 .....164 D5
Harlow CM20 .....118 C5
Harpenden AL5 .....86 B1
Hitchin SG4 .....35 A8
Kings Langley WD4 .....139 B1
Knebworth SG3 .....68 F5
Northwood HA6 .....174 E3
Radlett WD7 .....156 A4
South Oxhey WD19 .....175 D7
Station Cl
Brookmans Park AL9 .....144 E5
Potters Bar EN6 .....158 F8
Station Ct 15 SG12 .....93 D1
Station Footpath WD4 .....139 B1
Station Mews EN6 .....159 A8
Station Par SG6 .....22 F6
Station Pl SG6 .....22 F6
Station Rd Aldbury HP23 .....101 B5
Arlesey SG15 .....11 A4
Ashwell SG7 .....4 F4
Baldock SG7 .....12 F1
Berkhamsted HP4 .....122 D4
Bishop's Stortford CM23 .....77 A7
Borehamwood WD6 .....170 A5
Braughing SG11 .....55 E5
Bricket Wood AL2 .....155 A8
Brookmans Park AL9 .....144 D6
Buntingford SG9 .....40 E7
Cheddington LU7 .....79 F8
Cuffley EN6 .....146 F2
Harlow CM17 .....118 C4
Harpenden AL5 .....86 C2
Hemel Hempstead HP1 .....124 C1
Hoddesdon EN10 .....135 A3
Holdbrook EN9 .....163 A5
Kings Langley WD4 .....139 B1
Knebworth SG3 .....69 A5
Letchworth SG6 .....22 F6
Letty Green SG14 .....112 B3
Long Marston HP23 .....79 B4
Lower Stondon SG16 .....10 A4
Luton, Leagrave LU4 .....44 E5
Luton,High Town LU1 .....63 E8
Much Hadham SG10 .....74 E1
Pitstone LU7 .....80 E5
Radlett WD7 .....156 A4
Rickmansworth WD3 .....165 D2
Sawbridgeworth CM21 .....97 F3
St Albans AL4 .....129 B3
Standon SG11 .....55 E2
Stanstead Abbotts SG12 .....115 C4
Stansted Mountfitchet CM24 .....59 E6
Steeple Morden SG7,SG8 .....5 C5
Tring HP23 .....100 D4
Ware SG12 .....93 E1
Watford WD17 .....167 B7
Watton at S SG14 .....70 D3
Welwyn AL6 .....89 E3
Wheathampstead AL4 .....87 D1
Station Rdbt WD3 .....165 D2
Station Terr Hitchin SG4 .....35 A8
Park Street AL2 .....141 D5
Station Way
Letchworth SG6 .....22 E6
St Albans AL1 .....127 F3
Stationers Pl HP3 .....138 E6
Staveley Rd LU4 .....44 C1
Steeplands WD23 .....168 B2
Steeple View CM23 .....76 F8
Sten Cl EN3 .....163 A2
Stephens Cl LU2 .....46 A3
Stephens Gdns LU2 .....46 A2
Stephens Way AL3 .....105 F5
Stephenson Cl SG8 .....7 B7
Stephenson Way WD23, WD24 .....167 D7
Stephenson Wharf HP3 .....138 F6
Stephyns Chambers HP1 .....124 C2
Stepnells HP23 .....80 A1
Stepping Stones The LU3 .....44 E5
Sterling Ave EN8 .....162 D5
Sterling Rd EN2 .....161 D1
Stevenage Cres WD6 .....169 E8
Stevenage Mus* SG1 .....50 E5
Stevenage Rd Hitchin SG4 .....34 F5
Knebworth SG2,SG3 .....68 F7
Little Wymondley SG4 .....35 E3
Little Wymondley, Titmore Green SG4 .....35 E2
St Ippolyts SG4 .....35 C2
Walkern SG2 .....51 E8
Stevenage Rise HP2 .....124 F7
Stevenage Sta SG1 .....50 C5
Stevens Cl EN6 .....158 D6
Stevens Gn WD23 .....168 C1
Steward Cl EN8 .....148 E1
Stewart Cl WD5 .....154 A7
Stewart Rd AL5 .....86 B2
Stewarts The CM23 .....76 E6
Stile Plantation SG8 .....7 E6
Stilton Path WD6 .....157 A1
Stirling Bsns Pk EN8 .....162 F5
Stirling Cl Hitchin SG4 .....35 C7
Stevenage SG2 .....69 D7
Stirling Cnr EN5 .....170 D3
Stirling Ho WD6 .....170 C5
Stirling Way
Borehamwood WD6 .....170 D4
Watford WD5 .....154 A7
Welwyn Garden City AL7 .....111 E6
Stirling Way Ret Pk WD6 .....170 D3
Stoat Cl SG13 .....114 A6
Stobarts Cl SG3 .....68 F6
Stock Bank SG8 .....8 D1
Stockbreach Cl AL10 .....130 A6
Stockbreach Rd AL10 .....130 A6
Stockens Dell SG3 .....68 F4
Stockens Gn SG3 .....68 F4
Stockers Farm Rd WD3 .....173 D8
Stockfield Ave EN11 .....135 B8
Stockholm Way LU3 .....44 E8
Stocking Hill SG9 .....39 B8
Stocking La SG8 .....18 C1
Stockings La SG13 .....132 D6
Stockingstone Rd LU2 .....45 E3
Stockmen Field CM23 .....76 C5
Stockport Rd WD3 .....164 C2
Stocks Mdw HP2 .....125 A4
Stocks Rd HP23 .....101 D7
Stockwell Cl EN7 .....148 E3
Stockwell La EN7 .....148 B3
Stockwood Craft Mus & Gdns* LU1 .....63 D4
Stockwood Cres LU1 .....63 D6
Stockwood Ct 17 LU1 .....63 D6
Stockwood Pk* LU1 .....63 D3
Stone Cross CM20 .....117 D1
Stonecroft SG3 .....68 F5
Stonecroft Cl EN5 .....171 B5
Stonecross AL1 .....127 E4
Stonecross Rd AL10 .....130 B7
Stonehill Jun Mix Inf Sch SG6 .....11 E1
Stonehills AL8 .....110 D7
Stonelea Rd HP3 .....138 F8
Stoneleigh CM21 .....97 D3
Stoneleigh Ave EN1 .....162 B1
Stoneleigh Cl
Cheshunt EN8 .....162 D6
Luton LU3 .....45 B7
Stoneleigh Dr EN11 .....115 B1
Stoneley SG6 .....11 F1
Stonemason Cl AL5 .....86 A3
Stonemead AL8 .....89 D3
Stonesdale LU4 .....44 C4
Stoneways Cl LU4 .....44 C6
Stoney Brook CM24 .....59 E5
Stoney Cl HP4 .....121 F6
Stoney Comm CM24 .....59 E5
Stoney Common Rd CM24 .....59 D5
Stoney La Bovingdon HP3 .....137 C5
Chipperfield WD4 .....137 E1
Hemel Hempstead HP1 .....137 B8
Stoney Pl CM24 .....59 E5
Stoneycroft
Aldbury HP23 .....101 C5
Hemel Hempstead HP1 .....124 A3
Welwyn Garden City AL7 .....111 A7
Stoneyfield Dr CM24 .....59 E6
Stoneygate Rd LU4 .....44 D3
Stonnells Cl SG6 .....22 F8
Stony Croft SG1 .....50 E6
Stony Hills SG12 .....92 C7
Stony La
Chenies HP5,HP6 .....150 E1
Great Offley LU2,SG4 .....47 C4

Stonyshotts EN9 163 E6
Stookslade HP22 60 A3
Stopsley High Sch LU2 45 F4
Stopsley Prim Sch LU2 46 A4
Stopsley Way LU2 46 A3
Storehouse La SG4 34 F6
Storey Ct WD23 168 B4
Storey St HP3 138 D7
Stormont Rd SG5 21 F1
Stormont Sch EN6 159 D8
Stornoway HP3 125 B1
Stort Lodge CM23 76 D8
Stort Mill CM20 118 B6
Stort Rd CM23 76 F6
Stort Valley Ind Pk CM23 59 B2
Stortford Hall Ind Pk
CM23 77 B7
Stortford Hall Pk CM23 77 B8
Stortford Hall Rd [3]
CM23 77 B8
Stortford Rd
Hatfield Heath CM22 98 E4
Hoddesdon EN11 135 C7
Little Hadham SG11 57 C2
Standon SG11 55 F2
Stotfold Ho SG5 11 F6
Stotfold Rd Arlesey SG15 11 C7
Hinxworth SG7 3 C1
Hitchin SG4,SG6 22 C4
Letchworth SG6 11 D1
Stow The CM20 117 F2
Stox Mead HA3 176 D2
Strafford Cl EN6 159 A7
Strafford Ct SG3 69 A5
Strafford Gate EN6 159 A7
Strafford Rd EN5 171 E6
Straits The EN9 163 B7
Strandburgh Pl HP3 125 B1
Strangers Way LU4 44 C4
Strangeways WD17 153 E3
Stratfield Dr EN10 134 E4
Stratfield Rd WD6 170 A7
Stratford Lodge WD17 167 B8
Stratford Rd Luton LU4 45 B1
Watford WD17 167 A7
Stratford Way
Bricket Wood AL2 140 F2
Hemel Hempstead HP3 138 B8
Watford WD17 167 A7
Strathmore Ave
Hitchin SG5 21 F1
Luton LU1 63 F5
Strathmore Ct SG5 21 F1
Strathmore Inf Sch SG5 21 E2
Strathmore Rd SG4 66 E6
Strathmore Wlk LU1 63 F6
Stratton Ave EN2 161 D2
Stratton Ct [8] HA5 175 F3
Stratton Gdns LU2 45 D4
Straw Plait Way SG15 10 F4
Strawberry Field
[8] Hatfield AL10 130 A2
Luton LU3 44 E7
Strawberry Fields SG12 93 B2
Strawfields AL7 111 B7
Strawmead AL10 130 B7
Strawplaiters Cl SG3 69 A2
Straws Hadley Ct HP22 60 B2
Strayfield Rd EN2 161 B2
Stream Woods Jun & Inf Sch
AL10 130 B4
Street The Braughing SG11 55 F7
Chipperfield WD4 152 A8
Dane End SG11 53 F3
Furneux Pelham SG9 43 A4
Sheering CM22 98 E1
Wallington SG7 25 C8
Stretton Way WD6 156 E1
Stringers La SG2 51 E2
Stripling Way WD18 167 A3
Stroma Cl HP3 125 C1
Stronnell Cl LU2 46 B3
Stronsay Cl HP3 125 C1
Stroud Wood Bsns Ctr
AL2 141 E4
Stuart Ct WD6 169 D3
Stuart Dr Hitchin SG4 35 B7
Royston SG8 7 D8
Stuart Ho EN9 163 F6
Stuart Rd AL6 89 B3
Stuart St LU1 63 D7
Stuart St Pas [7] LU1 63 D7
Stuart Way EN7 162 B8
Stuarts Cl [3] HP3 124 D1
Stud Gn WD25 154 B7
Studham CE Lower Sch
LU6 82 B4
Studham La Dagnall HP4 81 D4
Whipsnade LU6 82 A7
Studio Way WD6 170 C8
Studios The WD23 168 A3
Studlands Rise SG8 7 E6
Studlands Rise Fst Sch
SG8 7 E5
Studley Rd LU3 45 D1
Stump Cross SG8 15 C6
Sturgeon's Way SG4 22 B2
Sturla Cl SG14 113 B7
Sturlas Way EN8 162 D6
Sturmer Cl AL4 128 C2
Sturrock Way SG4 35 C6
Styles Cl LU2 46 C2
Such Cl SG6 23 B7
Sudbury Ct AL1 127 E2
Sudbury Rd LU4 44 B6
Suffolk Cl
Borehamwood WD6 170 D4
London Colney AL2 142 C6
Suffolk Cl *continued*
Luton LU4 44 A3
Suffolk Rd
Potters Bar EN6 158 E7
Royston SG8 7 E6
Sugar La HP1 123 B1
Sulgrave Cres HP23 100 C5
Sullivan Cres UB9 173 D1
Sullivan Way WD6 169 C3
Summer Ct HP2 124 D5
Summer Dale AL8 89 D1
Summer Gr WD6 169 D3
Summer Hill WD6 170 A4
Summer St LU1 63 C1
Summer Wlk AL3 83 E5
Summercroft Jun & Inf Schs
CM23 77 C8
Summerfield AL10 130 A2
Summerfield Cl AL2 142 C5
Summerfield Rd
Luton LU1 62 F8
Watford WD25 154 A4
Summerhill Ct AL1 127 F4
Summerhouse La
Harefield UB9 173 A3
Radlett WD25 168 C8
Summerhouse Way
WD5 139 F1
Summerlands Rd AL4 128 C7
Summers Lodge SG6 22 D6
Summers Rd LU2 46 C1
Summers Way AL2 142 E4
Summerswood La EN6,
WD6 157 E4
Summerswood Prim Sch
WD6 170 B5
Summit Ct EN5 171 F6
Summit Rd EN6 144 E1
Sumpter Yd AL1 127 D3
Sun Hill SG8 7 C5
Sun La AL5 86 A2
Sun Sq [2] HP1 124 D4
Sun St Baldock SG7 23 E8
Hitchin SG5 34 E6
Sawbridgeworth CM21 97 F1
Waltham Abbey EN9 163 C6
Sunbury Ct
[2] Barnet EN5 171 E5
St Albans AL1 128 B2
Sunderland Ave AL1 128 A4
Sunderland Est WD4 139 B2
Sunderland Gr WD25 153 F5
Sundew Rd HP1 123 E2
Sundon Park Jun Sch
LU3 44 C8
Sundon Park Rd LU3 44 C7
Sunmead Rd HP2 124 D5
Sunningdale
Bishop's Stortford CM23 76 E6
Luton LU2 45 F3
Sunningdale Mews AL7 89 F2
Sunny Bank Prim Sch
EN6 159 A5
Sunny Hill SG9 40 F7
Sunnybank LU7 79 F7
Sunnybank Rd EN6 159 A6
Sunnydell AL2 141 B5
Sunnyfield AL9 130 D8
Sunnyhill Rd
Hemel Hempstead HP1 124 B3
Maple Cross WD3 172 D4
Sunnyside
Lower Nazeing EN9 135 F1
Stansted Mountfitchet
CM24 59 E6
Sunnyside Cotts HP5 136 A5
Sunnyside Rd SG4 35 A5
Sunridge Ave LU2 45 E2
Sunrise Cres HP3 138 F8
Sunrise Ind Est LU2 46 A2
Sunset Dr LU2 45 F3
Sunset View EN5 171 E7
Sunshine House Sch
HA6 174 D4
Surrey Pl HP23 100 A3
Surrey St LU1 63 E6
Surrey Street Prim Sch
LU1 63 F6
Sursham Ct AL3 83 E5
Sussex Cl EN11 135 A7
Sussex Pl LU2 46 D2
Sussex Rd WD24 154 A1
Sutcliffe Cl
Bushey WD23 168 C5
Stevenage SG1 51 A8
Sutherland Ave EN6 146 D3
Sutherland Cl EN5 171 E5
Sutherland Ct
Watford WD18 166 C2
Welwyn Garden City AL7 110 F7
Sutherland Pl LU1 63 D5
Sutherland Way EN6 146 E3
Sutton Acres CM22 98 D7
Sutton Cl
Hoddesdon EN10 134 E4
Tring HP23 100 B6
Sutton Cres EN5 171 D4
Sutton Ct SG12 114 E8
Sutton Gdns
Caddington LU1 62 E3
Luton LU3 44 D6
Sutton Path WD6 170 A6
Sutton Rd St Albans AL1 128 B3
Watford WD17 167 C6
Swale Cl SG1 37 A3
Swallow Cl
Bushey WD23 168 C1
Luton LU4 44 A4
Swallow Cl *continued*
Rickmansworth WD3 165 C2
Swallow Ct Enfield EN3 162 C2
Hertford SG14 113 C6
Welwyn Garden City AL7 110 F6
Swallow Dell Prim Sch
AL7 111 A5
Swallow End AL7 110 F6
Swallow Gdns AL10 130 A3
Swallow La AL1 142 B8
Swallow Oaks WD5 153 F7
Swallow Pk HP2 125 B7
Swallowdale La HP2 125 B6
Swallowfields AL7 110 F6
Swallows CM17 118 C4
Swallows The AL7 89 F2
Swan & Pike Rd EN3 163 A1
Swan Cl WD3 165 D2
Swan Ct
[2] Bishop's Stortford CM23 76 F6
Chorleywood WD3 164 C5
Swan Field Ho [3] WD3 165 D2
Swan La SG8 1 F4
Swan Mead
Hemel Hempstead HP3 138 F6
Luton LU4 44 B4
Swan Rd EN8 162 E5
Swan St SG7 4 D4
Swanfield Rd EN8 162 E6
Swangley's La SG3 69 B4
Swanhill AL7 90 A1
Swanland Rd AL9,EN6 144 B3
Swanley Bar La EN6 145 B3
Swanley Cres EN6 145 B2
Swanley Ct WD24 154 C2
Swannells Wood LU6 82 C4
Swans Cl AL4 128 E2
Swans Ct EN8 162 E5
Swanstand SG6 23 D4
Swanston Grange LU4 44 B2
Swanston Path [3]
WD19 175 C7
Swasedale Rd LU3 45 A6
Sweet Briar
Bishop's Stortford CM23 76 B6
Welwyn Garden City AL7 111 A5
Sweetbriar Cl HP1 124 A6
Sweyns Mead SG2 51 C7
Swift Cl Letchworth SG6 22 E8
Royston SG8 2 D1
Stanstead Abbotts SG12 115 C3
Swiftfields AL7 111 A7
Swifts Green Cl LU2 46 B5
Swifts Green Rd LU2 46 B5
Swinburne Ave SG5 21 C1
Swinburne Cl SG8 2 D1
Swing Gate Fst Sch
HP4 122 D3
Swing Gate La HP4 122 D2
Swingate SG1 50 D5
Swinnell Cl SG8 2 B5
Swiss Ave WD18 166 E6
Swiss Cl WD18 166 E6
Sword Cl EN10 134 D3
Sworders Yd [3] CM23 76 F7
Sycamore App WD3 166 C4
Sycamore Ave AL10 130 A4
Sycamore Cl
Hammond Street EN7 147 F4
Hitchin SG4 35 A4
Watford WD23 167 E7
Watford,Garston WD25 154 B4
Sycamore Dr
Park Street AL2 141 D4
Tring HP23 100 B4
Sycamore Ho HP2 124 E4
Sycamore Rd WD3 166 D4
Sycamore Rise HP4 122 D3
Sycamores The
Baldock SG7 23 E8
Bishop's Stortford CM23 77 B6
Hemel Hempstead HP3 137 F8
Radlett WD7 156 B5
[8] St Albans AL1 127 D2
Sydney Rd WD18 166 F4
Sylam Cl LU3 44 E7
Sylvan Cl HP3 125 A2
Sylvan Hts AL1 128 A1
Sylvan Way AL7 111 C5
Sylvandale AL7 111 C5
Sylvia Ave HA5 175 F4
Symonds Ct [13] EN8 148 D3
Symonds Green La SG1 50 A6
Symonds Green Rd SG1 50 A7
Symonds Rd SG5 34 D8

T

Tabbs Cl SG6 23 B7
Tacitus Cl [2] SG1 51 C8
Tailors CM23 76 B5
Takeley Cl EN9 163 D6
Talbot Ave WD19 167 E2
Talbot Ct HP3 124 D1
Talbot Rd Harrow HA3 176 F1
Hatfield AL10 130 A8
Luton LU2 45 F2
Rickmansworth WD3 165 E1
Talbot St Hertford SG13 113 E6
Hitchin SG5 34 C8
Talbot Way SG6 12 B1
Talisman St SG4 35 C6
Tall Trees Hitchin SG4 35 A4
Royston SG8 7 E6
Tallack Cl HA3 176 E3
Tallents Cres AL5 86 D3
Tallis Way WD6 169 E8
Tamar Cl SG1 37 A3
Tamar Gn HP2 124 F8
Tamarisk Cl AL3 127 D7
Tameton Cl LU2 46 F2
Tamworth Rd SG13 113 F7
Tancred Rd LU2 46 A4
Tanfield Cl EN7 148 A4
Tanfield Gn LU2 46 E1
Tanglewood
Harpenden AL5 85 F2
Welwyn AL6 90 A7
Tanglewood Cl HA7 176 E8
Tankerfield Pl AL3 127 C3
Tanner Ho WD19 167 B2
Tanners Cl AL3 127 C4
Tanners Cres SG13 113 C4
Tanners Hill WD5 154 A8
Tanners Way SG12 116 D8
Tanners Wood Cl WD5 153 E7
Tanners Wood Ct WD5 153 E7
Tanners Wood Jun Mix Inf
Sch WD5 153 E7
Tanners Wood La WD5 153 E7
Tannery Cl SG8 7 C6
Tannery Drift SG8 7 C6
Tannery Drift Sch SG8 7 C6
Tannery The SG9 40 E7
Tannery Yd SG4 66 F6
Tannsfield Dr [1] HP2 124 F5
Tannsmore Cl [2] HP2 124 F5
Tansycroft AL7 111 B7
Tanworth Cl HA6 174 C4
Tanworth Gdns HA5 175 C1
Tany's Dell CM20 118 A3
Tany's Dell Com Prim Sch
CM20 118 A3
Tanyard La AL6,SG4 88 B8
Tapster St EN5 171 F6
Taransay HP3 125 B1
Tarlings CM20 117 F3
Tarpan Way EN10 148 F6
Tarrant SG1 36 B1
Tarrant Dr AL5 107 D7
Tassell Hall AL3 105 F6
Tate Gdns WD23 168 E2
Tates Way SG1 36 B2
Tatlers La SG2 51 E4
Tatsfield Ave EN9 149 E8
Tatsford Villas EN9 135 C1
Tattershall Dr HP2 105 B1
Tattle Hill SG14 91 E2
Tattlers Hill HP22 60 B3
Tatton St CM17 118 C1
Tauber Cl WD6 169 F5
Taunton Ave LU2 46 B1
Taverners HP2 124 E5
Taverners Way EN11 135 A6
Tavistock Ave AL1 141 D8
Tavistock Cl
Potters Bar EN6 159 D8
St Albans AL1 141 D8
Tavistock Cres LU1 63 E5
Tavistock Rd WD24 167 D8
Tavistock St LU1 63 E6
Taylers Cotts EN6 157 F5
Taylor Cl Harefield UB9 173 C1
St Albans AL4 128 A8
Taylor St LU2 63 F8
Taylor Trad Est SG13 114 B7
Taylor's Hill SG4 34 F6
Taylor's La EN5 171 F8
Taylor's Rd SG5 11 F8
Taylors Ave EN11 135 A5
Taylors La HP23 119 C3
Taywood Cl SG2 51 B2
Teal Dr HA6 174 C3
Teal Ho WD25 154 E3
Teal Way HP3 138 F6
Teasdale Cl SG8 2 D1
Teasel Cl SG8 7 E5
Tedder Ave SG16 10 B5
Tedder Rd HP2 125 A4
Tee Side SG13 114 B7
Tees Cl SG1 36 F3
Teesdale
Hemel Hempstead HP2 124 E6
Luton LU4 44 C5
Telford Ave SG2 51 B6
Telford Cl WD25 154 D4
Telford Ct Hatfield AL10 129 F3
St Albans AL1 127 E2
Telford Rd AL2 142 C4
Telford Way LU1 63 D8
Telmere Ind Est [16] LU1 63 E6
Telscombe Way LU2 46 C3
Temperance St AL3 127 C3
Tempest Ave EN6 159 D7
Templar Ave SG7 23 F6
Templars Dr HA3 176 D4
Templars La SG4 48 D6
Temple Bank CM20 118 B5
Temple Cl Cheshunt EN7 162 A8
Luton LU2 45 E5
Preston SG5 34 B4
Watford WD17 166 F7
Temple Ct Hertford SG14 92 D1
Potters Bar EN6 158 D8
Temple Fields SG14 92 D1
Temple Gdns
Letchworth SG6 23 C8
Moor Park WD3 174 B6
Temple Ho EN7 162 A6
Temple La SG12 92 F8
Temple Mead
Hemel Hempstead HP2 124 D5
Roydon CM19 116 B1
Temple View AL3 127 C5
Templefields Ent Ctr
CM20 118 A3
Templepan La WD3 152 E2
Templewood AL8 89 D1
Templewood Prim Sch
AL8 110 D8
Tempsford AL7 111 D6
Tempsford Ave WD6 170 D5
Temsford Cl HA2 176 C1
Tenby Dr LU4 44 F3
Tenby Mews LU4 44 E3
Tene The SG7 23 F8
Tennand Cl EN7 147 F5
Tennison Ave WD6 170 B4
Tennyson Ave Hitchin SG4 35 C7
Waltham Abbey EN9 163 E5
Tennyson Cl SG8 2 E1
Tennyson Ho LU1 63 E5
Tennyson Rd
Chiswell Green AL2 141 B5
Harpenden AL5 86 A2
Luton LU1 63 E5
Tennyson Road Prim Sch
LU1 63 E5
Tenterfield Ho AL6 89 C4
Tenth Ave LU3 44 C7
Tenzing Gr LU1 63 C6
Tenzing Rd HP2 125 A3
Teresa Gdns EN8 162 D5
Terminus St CM20 117 D1
Terrace Gdns WD17 167 B7
Terrace The
Essendon AL9 131 E6
Redbourn AL3 106 A5
Tring HP23 100 A3
Westmill SG9 40 F2
Tethys Rd HP2 124 F6
Tewin Cl St Albans AL4 128 C7
Tewin AL6 90 C5
Tewin Cowper CE Prim Sch
AL6 90 E2
Tewin Ct AL7 110 F7
Tewin Hill AL6 90 F5
Tewin Rd
Hemel Hempstead HP2 125 C3
Welwyn Garden City AL7 110 F7
Thackeray Cl SG8 2 D1
Thames Ave HP2 124 F8
Thames Ct LU3 45 B3
Thamesdale AL2 142 F4
Thanet Ho [1] WD18 166 F3
Thatchers Croft HP2 124 E7
Thatchers End SG4 35 D8
Thatchers The CM23 76 C5
Thaxted Cl LU2 46 F2
Thaxted Way EN9 163 D6
Thaynesfield EN6 159 D8
Theabald's Grove Sta
EN8 162 D7
Thelby Cl LU3 44 F6
Thele Ave SG12 115 D4
Thele Est SG12 115 E4
Theleway Cl EN11 115 B1
Thellusson Way WD3 165 A2
Thelusson Ct WD7 156 A3
Theobald Bsns Ctr SG4 22 A3
Theobald Cres HA3 176 C2
Theobald Ct WD6 170 A6
Theobald St
Borehamwood WD6 169 F7
Radlett WD6,WD7 156 D2
Theobald's La
Cheshunt EN8 162 B7
Cheshunt EN8 162 D7
Theobald's Rd EN6 146 F1
Theobalds Cl EN6 146 F1
Theobalds Park Camp Site
EN7 162 A5
Theobalds Park Coll
EN7 162 A6
Theobalds Park Rd EN2 161 B3
Therfield Fst Sch SG8 15 F7
Therfield Heath Nature
Reserve* SG8 7 A5
Therfield Rd AL3 127 D6
Thetford Gdns LU2 45 E6
Thieves' La SG14 112 F7
Third Ave Letchworth SG6 23 C7
Luton LU3 44 D7
Watford WD25 154 D4
Thirlestane AL1 127 F4
Thirlestone Rd LU4 44 D1
Thirlmere SG1 37 C2
Thirlmere Dr AL1 128 B1
Thirlmere Gdns HA6 174 C4
Thirsk Rd WD6 157 A1
Thirston Path [1] WD6 170 A7
Thistle Cl HP1 123 E2
Thistle Dr AL10 129 F8
Thistle Gr AL7 111 C3
Thistle Rd LU1 63 F7
Thistlecroft HP1 124 B2
Thistles The HP1 124 B4
Thistley La SG4 34 F1
Thomas Alleyne Sch The
SG1 50 C8
Thomas Bourne Ho [9]
HP4 122 D4
Thomas Coram CE Mid Sch
The HP4 122 D2
Thomas Ct HP4 121 F5
Thomas Heskin Ct [11]
CM23 77 A7
Thomas Rochford Way
EN8 148 F4

Thomas Watson Cottage Homes The EN5 171 E4
Thomas Way SG8 2 D1
Thompson Way WD3 165 A1
Thompsons Cl
Goff's Oak EN7 147 F2
Harpenden AL5 86 A1
Thompsons Mdw SG8 1 F4
Thorley Ctr The CM23 76 D4
Thorley High CM23 76 F2
Thorley Hill CM23 76 F5
Thorley Hill Prim Sch CM23 76 F4
Thorley La CM23 76 F3
Thorley La E CM23 76 D3
Thorley La W CM23 76 B4
Thorley Park Rd CM23 76 F4
Thorn Ave WD23 168 C1
Thorn Gr CM23 77 B6
Thorn Grove Prim Sch CM23 77 B6
Thorn Tree Dr HP23 99 F4
Thornage Cl LU2 45 D7
Thornbera Cl CM23 76 F4
Thornbera Gdns CM23 76 F4
Thornbera Rd CM23 76 F4
Thornbury AL5 86 D1
Thornbury Cl
Hoddesdon EN11 115 B2
Stevenage SG2 69 A8
Thornbury Gdns WD6 170 C5
Thorncroft HP3 125 B1
Thorndyke Ct HA5 175 F3
Thorne Cl HP1 124 B1
Thorne Ho AL1 127 E4
Thorne Way HP22 99 B4
Thorneycroft Cl LU3 44 F4
Thorneycroft Dr EN3 163 A2
Thornfield Rd CM23 76 E8
Thornhill Rd Luton LU4 44 F2
Moor Park HA6 174 C6
Thornton Gr HA5 176 A4
Thornton Rd Barnet EN5 171 E6
Potters Bar EN6 145 C1
Thornton St
Hertford SG14 113 D6
St Albans AL3 127 C4
Thorntondale 5 LU4 44 C5
Thorpe Cres WD19 167 C2
Thorpe Rd AL1 127 D2
Thorpefield Cl AL4 128 D6
Thrales Cl LU3 44 E7
Three Cherry Trees La HP2 125 B7
Three Close La HP4 122 C4
Three Closes SG5 20 C4
Three Corners HP3 125 A1
Three Houses La SG4 67 D5
Three Meadows Mews HA3 176 F2
Three Rivers Mus of Local History* WD3 165 E2
Three Star Cvn Pk SG16 10 A3
Three Stiles SG2 52 E4
Three Valleys Way WD23 167 E4
Thremhall Ave CM23 77 F8
Thresher Cl CM23 76 C5
Thricknells Cl LU3 44 E7
Thrift Farm La WD6 170 C7
Thriftfield HP2 124 D5
Thrimley La CM23 58 C6
Thristers Cl SG6 23 B3
Throcking La SG9 27 C1
Throcking Rd SG9 39 D8
Thrums WD24 154 B2
Thrush Ave AL10 130 A3
Thrush Gn WD3 165 C2
Thrush La EN6 146 F3
Thumbswood AL7 111 A3
Thumpers HP2 124 E5
Thunder Hall 1 SG12 93 D2
Thundercourt SG12 93 D2
Thundridge Bsns Pk SG12 93 D7
Thundridge CE Prim Sch SG12 93 D7
Thundridge Cl AL7 111 B5
Thurgood Rd EN11 135 A8
Thurlow Cl SG1 36 D2
Thurnall Ave SG8 7 D5
Thurnall Cl SG7 23 F8
Thyme Cl LU2 45 E7
Tibbles Cl WD25 154 E4
Tibbs Hill Rd WD5 139 F1
Tiberius Rd LU3 44 F6
Tichborne WD3 172 D5
Tile Kiln Cl HP3 125 B2
Tile Kiln Cres HP3 125 B2
Tile Kiln La HP3 125 B2
Tilecroft AL8 89 D1
Tilehouse Cl WD6 169 F6
Tilehouse La UB9 172 E2
Tilehouse St SG5 34 E6
Tilekiln Cl EN7 147 F2
Tilgate LU2 46 D3
Tillers Link SG2 51 A2
Tillotson Rd HA3 176 B3
Tilsworth Wlk AL4 128 C8
Timber Orch SG14 92 A2
Timbercroft AL7 89 F1
Timberidge WD3 165 D5
Timbers Ct AL5 85 F2
Times Cl SG5 21 D2
Timplings Row HP1 124 B5
Timworth Cl LU2 46 D1
Tingeys Cl AL3 106 A5
Tinkers La HP23 121 A6
Tinsley Cl LU1 63 B5
Tintagel Cl
Hemel Hempstead HP2 124 D8
Luton LU3 45 B4
Tintern Cl Harpenden AL5 85 C4
Stevenage SG2 69 A7
Tinwell Mews WD6 170 D4
Tippendell La AL2 141 C5
Tippet Ct SG1 50 D3
Tiree Cl HP3 125 B1
Titan Ct LU4 44 F1
Titan Rd HP2 124 F6
Titchfield Rd EN3 162 E2
Tithe Barn Cl AL1 141 C8
Tithe Barn Ct WD5 139 F2
Tithe Cl SG4 67 F1
Titian Ave WD23 168 E2
Titmore Ct SG4 35 E2
Titmus Cl SG1 50 E6
Tiverton Ct AL5 107 E6
Tiverton Rd EN6 159 E8
Toddington Rd LU4 44 C6
Toland Cl LU4 44 C1
Tolcarne Dr HA5 175 A1
Tollgate Cl WD3 164 F5
Tollgate Rd
Colney Heath AL4,AL9 143 E7
Enfield EN3 162 D4
Welham Green AL9 144 A6
Tollpit End HP1 124 A6
Tollsworth Way SG11 55 D3
Tolmers Ave EN6 146 E3
Tolmers Gdns EN6 146 F2
Tolmers Mews SG13 146 E6
Tolmers Rd EN6 146 E3
Tolpits Cl WD18 166 F4
Tolpits La WD18 166 E2
Tom's Hill WD3 152 E3
Tomkins Cl WD6 169 E8
Tomlins Cl SG8 8 F1
Toms Croft HP2 124 E2
Toms Field AL10 129 E4
Toms Hill Cl HP23 101 D5
Toms Hill Rd HP23 101 D5
Toms La WD4,WD5 139 D3
Tonwell St Mary's CE Prim Sch SG12 92 E7
Tooke Cl HA5 175 E2
Toorack Rd HA3 176 D1
Tooveys Mill Cl WD4 139 A2
Topstreet Way AL5 107 C8
Tormead HA6 174 D4
Toronto Ho EN8 162 D8
Torquay Cres SG1 50 B7
Torquay Dr LU4 44 D4
Torridge Wlk 2 HP2 124 F8
Torrington Dr EN6 159 D7
Torrington Rd HP4 122 B4
Tortoiseshell Way HP4 121 F6
Torwood Cl HP4 121 F4
Torworth Rd WD6 157 A1
Tot La CM23,CM24 59 D4
Totteridge Comm N20 171 D1
Totteridge Pk N20 171 C1
Totteridge Rd EN3 162 D2
Totteridge Village N20 171 F1
Totton Mews AL3 106 B5
Totts La SG2 38 C1
Toulmin Dr AL3 127 C7
Tovey Cl
London Colney AL2 142 D5
Lower Nazeing EN9 149 F8
Tower Cl
Berkhamsted HP4 122 A3
Hertford Heath SG13 114 C2
Kneesworth SG8 2 A5
Little Wymondley SG4 35 F3
Tower Ct LU2 46 A1
Tower Ctr EN11 135 A6
Tower Hill
Chipperfield WD4 137 F1
Much Hadham SG10 74 F2
Tower Hill La AL4 108 F4
Tower Hts EN11 135 A6
Tower Prim Sch SG12 93 E3
Tower Rd Codicote SG4 67 F2
Luton LU2 64 A8
Ware SG12 93 F2
Tower St SG14 113 C8
Tower View SG4 66 D6
Tower Way LU2 64 A8
Towers Rd
Hemel Hempstead HP2 124 E4
Pinner HA5 175 E2
Stevenage SG1 50 D4
Towers The SG1 50 D4
Town Ctr AL10 130 A6
Town Farm
Cheddington LU7 80 A7
Wheathampstead AL4 108 D8
Town Farm Cl SG8 1 F4
Town Farm Cres SG11 55 F2
Town Fields AL10 130 A6
Town La SG2 52 E4
Town Mead Rd EN9 163 C5
Town Mill Mews 3 SG14 113 C6
Town Sq SG1 50 D5
Towne Rd SG8 7 D5
Townfield WD3 165 C2
Townley SG6 23 D4
Townsend HP2 124 D5
Townsend Ave AL1 127 E4
Townsend CE Sch AL3 127 C8
Townsend Cl
Barkway SG8 17 C3
Harpenden AL5 85 F1
St Ippolyts SG4 35 A3
Townsend Dr AL3 127 D5
Townsend La AL5 85 F1
Townsend Rd AL5 86 A2
Townsend Way HA6 175 A3
Townshend St SG13 113 E6
Townsley Cl LU1 63 E6
Tracey Ct 15 LU1 63 E6
Trafalgar Ave EN10 134 F2
Trafford Cl Shenley WD7 156 E7
Stevenage SG1 36 E1
Traherne Cl SG4 34 F5
Trajan Gate SG2 37 D1
Trapstyle Rd SG12 93 A2
Travellers Cl AL9 144 C8
Travellers La
Hatfield AL10 130 B2
Welham Green AL9 130 C1
Treacle La SG9 25 F3
Treacy Cl WD23 176 C8
Trebellan Dr HP2 124 F4
Treeby Ct EN3 163 A2
Treehanger Cl HP23 100 B4
Treetops AL6 89 E7
Treetops Cl HA6 174 D5
Trefoil Cl LU4 44 A4
Trefusis Wlk WD17 166 E8
Tremaine Gr HP2 124 E7
Trent Cl Shenley WD7 156 E7
Stevenage SG1 50 E8
Trent Rd LU3 45 B4
Tresco Rd HP4 121 F5
Trescott Cl LU2 46 E2
Tresilian Sq HP2 125 A8
Treslian Sq 1 HP2 124 F8
Trevalga Way HP2 124 E7
Trevellance Way WD25 154 D6
Trevelyan Pl AL1 127 C1
Trevelyan Way HP4 122 B6
Trevera Ct Cheshunt EN8 162 E6
Hoddesdon EN11 135 A7
Trevor Cl HA3 176 F3
Trevor Rd SG4 35 A8
Trevose Way WD19 175 C7
Trewenna Dr EN6 159 D7
Triangle The SG4 34 F6
Trident Ctr WD24 167 C8
Trident Ind Est EN11 135 C7
Trident Rd WD25 153 F5
Trigg Terr SG1 50 E6
Triggs Way LU2 46 E3
Trimley Cl LU4 44 B5
Trinder Rd EN5 171 C4
Tring Bsns Ctr HP23 99 E4
Tring Ford Rd HP23 100 A7
Tring Hill HP23 99 C3
Tring Ho WD18 166 E2
Tring Rd
Berkhamsted HP4 121 D7
Long Marston HP23 79 C3
Wingrave HP22 60 C1
Tring Sch HP23 100 B4
Tring Sta HP23 101 A5
Trinity Cl
Bishop's Stortford CM23 76 F6
Northwood HA6 174 E4
Trinity Ct SG14 113 C8
Trinity Gr SG14 113 C8
Trinity Hall Cl WD24 167 C6
Trinity Ho
2 Borehamwood WD6 170 A5
Cheshunt EN8 162 E7
Trinity La EN8 162 E7
Trinity Mews HP2 125 D2
Trinity Pl SG1 50 D6
Trinity Rd
Hertford Heath SG13 114 C3
Luton LU3 45 A4
Stevenage SG1 50 C6
Stotfold SG5 11 F7
Ware SG12 93 E2
Trinity St CM23 76 F6
Trinity Way CM23 76 F6
Trinity Wlk
Hemel Hempstead HP2 125 D2
Hertford Heath SG13 114 C3
Tristram Rd SG4 22 B2
Triton Way HP2 124 F5
Trojan Terr CM21 97 E3
Troon Gdns LU2 45 E7
Trooper Rd HP23 101 C5
Trotter's Gap SG12 115 E4
Trotters Bottom EN5 158 B2
Trotts Hill Prim Sch SG1 36 F1
Trout Rise WD3 165 B6
Troutstream Way WD3 165 B5
Trouvere Pk HP1 124 B5
Trowbridge Gdns LU2 45 E3
Trowley Bottom AL3 105 B8
Trowley Hts AL3 84 B2
Trowley Rise WD5 153 F8
Truemans Rd SG5 21 D2
Trumper Rd SG1 36 F1
Trumpington Dr AL1 141 D8
Truncals LU1 63 D5
Trundlers Way WD23 168 E1
Truro Gdns LU3 45 C5
Trust Cotts HP4 81 A1
Trust Rd EN8 162 E5
Tucker St WD18 167 C4
Tucker's Row 4 CM23 76 F6
Tudor Ave Cheshunt EN7 162 B8
Watford WD24 154 D2
Tudor Cl Cheshunt EN7 162 B8
Hatfield AL10 129 F2
Tudor Cl *continued*
Hunsdon SG12 116 D8
Stevenage SG1 36 C1
Tudor Cres EN2 161 C1
Tudor Ct Barnet EN5 171 F5
Borehamwood WD6 169 E7
Hitchin SG5 34 D6
Kneesworth SG8 2 B4
Rickmansworth WD3 165 A1
Sawbridgeworth CM21 97 E3
Tudor Dr WD24 154 D2
Tudor Gdns HA3 176 D1
Tudor Jun Mix & Inf Sch HP3 124 E1
Tudor Lodge 3 HA6 174 E3
Tudor Manor Gdns WD25 154 D7
Tudor Par WD3 165 A2
Tudor Rd Harrow HA3 176 D1
Luton LU3 45 B2
Pinner HA5 175 C1
St Albans AL3 127 E7
Welwyn AL6 89 B3
Wheathampstead AL4 108 E8
Tudor Rise EN10 134 E2
Tudor Sq 18 SG12 93 D1
Tudor Way
Hertford SG14 113 A7
Rickmansworth WD3 165 A2
Waltham Abbey EN9 163 D6
Tudor Wlk 17 Ware SG12 93 D1
Watford WD24 154 D2
Tuffnells Way AL5 85 D4
Tunfield Rd EN11 115 B1
Tunnel Wood Cl WD17 153 F2
Tunnel Wood Rd WD17 153 F2
Tunnmeade CM20 118 A1
Turf La SG4 36 B4
Turkey St EN1,EN3 162 C2
Turkey Street Sta EN3 162 C2
Turmore Dale AL8 110 C5
Turnberry Ct WD19 175 C7
Turnberry Dr AL2 140 E1
Turner Cl SG1 36 C2
Turner Rd WD23 168 C5
Turners Cl Bramfield SG14 91 C4
Harpenden AL5 86 C4
Turners Cres CM23 76 C4
Turners Ct EN8 162 D8
Turners Hill
Cheshunt EN8 148 D1
Hemel Hempstead HP2 124 E2
Turners Rd N LU2 46 A2
Turners Rd S LU2 46 A2
Turneys Orch WD3 164 D4
Turnford Sch EN8 148 E3
Turnford Villas EN8 148 F5
Turnpike Dr LU3 31 C1
Turnpike Gn HP2 124 F7
Turnpike La SG5 21 E3
Turnstones The WD25 154 E3
Turpin Cl EN3 163 A2
Turpin's Ride SG8 7 D5
Turpin's Rise SG2 50 F1
Turpin's Way SG7 23 F7
Turpins Chase AL6 89 F7
Turpins Cl SG14 112 F6
Turpins Ride AL6 89 F7
Tussauds Cl WD3 166 A4
Tuthill Ct SG8 15 E7
Tuxford Cl WD6 156 E1
Tweed Cl HP4 122 B5
Twelve Acres AL7 110 E4
Twelve Leys HP22 60 B3
Twickenham Gdns HA3 176 E3
Twigden Ct LU3 44 E5
Twin Foxes SG3 69 A1
Twinwoods SG1 50 F4
Twist The HP23 100 D2
Twitchell The SG7 23 F8
Two Acres AL7 110 F3
Two Beeches HP2 124 F8
Two Dells La HP5 136 A4
Two Oaks Dr AL6 90 C6
Two Waters Prim Sch HP3 138 D6
Two Waters Rd
Hemel Hempstead HP3 124 C1
Hemel Hempstead HP3 138 D8
Twyford Bsns Ctr The CM23 77 A4
Twyford Bury La CM22, CM23 77 A4
Twyford Cl CM23 77 A5
Twyford Dr LU2 46 D1
Twyford Gdns CM23 76 F4
Twyford Mews CM22 77 A3
Twyford Mill CM22 77 A3
Twyford Rd
Bishop's Stortford CM23 77 A5
St Albans AL4 128 D7
Twysdens Terr AL9 144 C7
Tye End SG2 69 B8
Tyfield Cl EN8 148 C1
Tylers AL5 86 D1
Tylers Cl Buntingford SG9 40 D7
Kings Langley WD4 138 F3
Tylers Cswy SG13 132 C1
Tylers Hill Rd HP5 150 A8
Tylers Mead LU2 45 E5
Tylers Way WD23,WD25 168 E4
Tylers Wood AL6 90 C6
Tylersfield WD5 154 A8
Tynedale AL2 142 F4
Tynemouth Dr EN1 162 A1
Typleden Cl HP2 124 D5
Tysoe Ave EN3 162 F2
Tythe Rd LU4 44 C6
Tyttenhanger Gn AL4 142 E8

U

Uckfield Rd EN3 162 D2
Ufford Cl HA3 176 B3
Ufford Rd HA3 176 B3
Ullswater Cl SG1 37 C2
Ullswater Rd HP3 125 C1
Ulverston Cl AL1 127 F3
Underacres Cl HP2 125 A4
Underhill Jun & Inf Schs EN5 171 E4
Underwood Rd SG1 36 C2
Union Chapel Ho 1 LU1 63 E6
Union Ct 19 HP4 122 D4
Union Gn HP2 124 D4
Union St Barnet EN5 171 E6
Luton LU1 63 E6
Union Terr SG9 40 E7
Unity Rd EN3 162 D2
Univ of Hertfordshire AL10 129 F3
Univ of Hertfordshire (Hertford Campus) SG13 113 E4
University Cl WD23 168 A5
Unwin Cl SG6 22 E4
Unwin Pl SG2 51 C3
Unwin Rd SG2 51 C3
Updale Cl EN6 158 E6
Upland Dr AL9 145 B6
Uplands Braughing SG11 55 F6
Croxley Green WD3 165 F3
Luton LU3 44 D8
Stevenage SG2 51 D7
Ware SG12 93 F2
Welwyn Garden City AL8 89 C2
Uplands Ave SG4 35 B6
Uplands Ct
3 Bushey WD23 168 D1
Luton LU1 63 E4
Uplands The
Bricket Wood AL2 140 E1
Harpenden AL5 107 A4
Upper Ashlyns Rd HP4 122 B3
Upper Barn HP3 138 F8
Upper Bourne End La HP1 137 B8
Upper Clabdens SG12 93 F2
Upper Culver Rd AL1 127 F5
Upper Dagnall St AL3 127 D3
Upper George St LU1 63 D7
Upper Gn AL6 90 D3
Upper Green Rd AL6 90 E3
Upper Hall Pk HP4 122 E2
Upper Heath Rd AL1 127 F5
Upper Highway WD5 153 D6
Upper Hill Rise WD3 165 B3
Upper Hitch WD19 167 E1
Upper Icknield Way
Aldbury LU7 80 E1
Aston Clinton HP22 99 A3
Tring HP23 100 D8
Upper King St SG8 7 D6
Upper Lattimore Rd AL1 127 E3
Upper Marlborough Rd AL1 127 E3
Upper Marsh La EN11 135 A5
Upper Maylins SG6 23 C3
Upper Paddock Rd WD19 167 E3
Upper Pk CM20 117 B1
Upper Sales HP1 123 F2
Upper Sean SG2 51 A3
Upper Shot AL7 111 A7
Upper Shott EN7 147 F5
Upper Station Rd WD7 156 A4
Upper Tail WD19 175 E7
Upper Tilehouse St SG5 34 E7
Upperfield Rd AL7 110 F5
Upperstone Cl SG5 11 F6
Upshire Rd EN9 163 F7
Upton Ave AL3 127 D4
Upton Cl Luton LU2 45 D6
Park Street AL2 141 D6
Upton Lodge Cl WD23 168 C2
Upton Rd WD18 167 B6
Upwell Rd LU2 46 B2
Uranus Rd HP2 124 F5
Urban Hive LU3 44 C8
Urban Rd CM23 77 B7
Uxbridge Rd WD3 173 A8
Uxbridge Rd (Harrow Weald) HA3 176 D3
Uxbridge Rd (Hatch End) HA5 175 F3
Uxbridge Rd (Pinner) HA5 175 D2
Uxbridge Rd (Stanmore) HA7 176 F4

V

Vadis Cl LU3 44 E7
Vale Ave WD6 170 B4
Vale Cl AL5 85 D4
Vale Cotts SG11 54 D5
Vale Ct AL4 108 D7
Vale Dr EN5 171 F5
Vale Ind Pk WD18 166 C1
Vale Rd WD23 167 E4
Valence Dr EN7 148 A3
Valency Cl HA6 174 F6
Valerian Way SG2 51 D8

Valerie Cl AL1 128 B3
Valerie Ct WD23 168 C2
Valeside SG14 113 A5
Vallance Pl AL5 107 C7
Vallans Cl SG12 93 D3
Vallansgate SG2 51 B1
Valley Cl Hertford SG13 113 D5
Pinner HA5 175 B1
Studham LU6 82 B4
Waltham Abbey EN9 163 C7
Ware SG12 93 B2
Whipsnade HP4 81 E7
Valley Ct CM23 76 E5
Valley Gn HP2 105 B1
Valley Gn The AL8 110 C7
Valley Ho EN8 162 D8
Valley La AL3 83 E1
Valley Rd
Berkhamsted HP4 121 F6
Codicote SG4 67 F1
Letchworth SG6 22 D7
Rickmansworth WD3 165 B3
St Albans AL3 127 F7
Studham LU6 82 B3
Welwyn Garden City AL8 110 B6
Valley Rise Lea Valley AL4 86 F2
Royston SG8 7 E6
Watford WD25 154 B6
Valley Road S SG4 88 F8
Valley Sch The SG2 50 F2
Valley The SG4 66 E7
Valley View Barnet EN5 171 E3
Goff's Oak EN7 147 C3
Valley Way SG2 51 A3
Valley Wlk WD3 166 C4
Valleyside HP1 123 F3
Valpy Cl HP23 100 D1
Vancouver Rd EN10 148 E6
Vanda Cres AL1 127 F2
Vantorts Cl CM21 97 E2
Vantorts Rd CM21 97 E2
Vardon Rd SG1 50 F8
Varna Cl LU3 45 A3
Varney Cl
Hammond Street EN7 148 A4
Hemel Hempstead HP1 123 F3
Varney Rd HP1 123 F3
Vaughan Mead AL3 106 A4
Vaughan Rd
Harpenden AL5 86 B1
Stotfold SG5 11 E7
Vauxhall Rd
Hemel Hempstead HP2 125 B3
Luton LU1,LU2 64 B5
Vauxhall Way LU2 46 B1
Vega Cres HA6 175 A5
Vega Rd WD23 168 C2
Velizy Ave CM20 117 D1
Venetia Rd LU2 46 A4
Ventnor Gdns LU3 45 A7
Ventura Pk AL2 141 F2
Venus Hill HP3 151 A8
Ver Mdw Cvn Site AL3 106 C5
Ver Rd Redbourn AL3 106 C6
St Albans AL3 127 C3
Vera Ct WD19 167 D2
Vera La AL6 90 B4
Verdure Cl WD25 154 E7
Verity Way SG1 51 B8
Veritys AL10 130 A5
Verney Cl
Berkhamsted HP4 121 F5
Tring HP23 100 C5
Vernon Ave EN3 162 E3
Vernon Ct CM23 76 E4
Vernon Dr UB9 173 C2
Vernon Rd Luton LU1 63 C8
Watford WD23 167 E4
Vernon's Cl AL1 127 E2
Veronica Ho AL7 111 B4
Verulam Cl AL7 110 F6
Verulam Gdns LU3 44 F6
Verulam Ind Est AL1 127 F1
Verulam Rd Hitchin SG5 34 F8
St Albans AL3 127 C4
Verulam Sch AL1 128 A4
Verulamium Mus* AL3 127 B3
Verulamium Roman City Walls* AL3 127 B2
Verulamium Roman Town* AL3 127 A3
Verwood Rd HA2 176 C1
Vespers Cl LU4 44 A2
Vesta Ave AL1 141 C8
Vesta Rd HP2 124 F5
Vestry Cl LU1 63 D7
Veysey Cl HP1 124 B1
Viaduct Cotts LU1 85 F8
Viaduct Rd SG12 114 E8
Viaduct Way AL7 89 F2
Vian Ave EN3 162 E4
Vicarage Cl Arlesey SG15 11 A8
18 Bishop's Stortford CM23 76 F7
Hemel Hempstead HP1 124 C2
Northaw EN6 145 F1
Shillington SG5 19 F8
St Albans AL1 141 C8
Standon SG11 55 E2
Vicarage Cswy SG13 114 B4
Vicarage Gdns
Flamstead AL3 84 B1
Marsworth HP23 80 A2
Potten End HP4 123 B7
Vicarage La
Bovingdon HP3 137 B4
Kings Langley WD4 138 F2
Pitstone LU7 80 F5
Stapleford SG14 92 B2
Vicarage Rd
Buntingford SG9 40 E8
Marsworth HP23 80 A2
Pitstone LU7 80 D3
Potten End HP4 123 A7
Ware SG12 93 E1
Watford WD18 167 A4
Wigginton HP23 100 D1
Vicarage Road Prec WD18 167 B5
Vicarage St LU1 63 F7
Vicarage Wood CM20 118 A1
Vicerons Pl CM23 76 D4
Victoria CE Fst Sch HP4 122 C4
Victoria Cl
Rickmansworth WD3 165 D2
Stevenage SG1 50 D7
Victoria Cres SG8 7 D7
Victoria Ct Harlow CM20 117 E1
Watford WD17 167 C6
Victoria Dr SG5 12 A5
Victoria La EN5 171 F5
Victoria Mews SG13 113 A1
Victoria Pl HP2 124 D3
Victoria Rd
Berkhamsted HP4 122 C4
Bushey WD23 168 B1
7 Harpenden AL5 86 B1
Waltham Abbey EN9 163 C5
Watford WD24 154 B1
Victoria Sq AL1 127 F2
Victoria St Luton LU1 63 E6
St Albans AL1 127 E3
Victoria Way SG5 34 D8
Victors Way EN5 171 F6
Victory Ct SG8 7 E5
Victory Rd HP4 122 A5
View Point SG1 50 A5
View Rd EN6 159 C7
Vigors Croft AL10 129 F4
Villa Ct 6 LU2 63 D8
Villa Rd LU2 63 D8
Village Cl EN11 135 D8
Village Ct AL4 128 D7
Village Mews HP3 137 A4
Village St SG4 49 F1
Villiers Cl LU4 44 D3
Villiers Cres AL4 128 D6
Villiers Rd WD19 167 E3
Villiers St SG13 113 E6
Villiers-Sur-Marne Ave CM23 76 D4
Vincent SG6 23 C4
Vincent Cl EN8 148 E3
Vincent Ct HA6 174 F2
Vincent Rd LU4 44 D5
Vincenzo Cl AL9 144 C8
Vine Cl AL8 110 E8
Vine Gr CM20 117 E5
Vine Tree Ct WD3 173 B8
Vines The SG5 11 E6
Vineyard The
Hertford SG14 113 D8
Ware SG12 94 A2
Welwyn Garden City AL8 110 E8
Vineyards Hill EN6 146 B2
Vineyards Rd EN6 146 A2
Vinters Ave SG1 50 F5
Violet Ave EN2 161 D1
Violet Way WD3 165 C5
Violets La SG9 43 B5
Virgil Dr EN10 148 F8
Virginia Cl LU2 45 F3
Viscount Cl LU3 45 A5
Viscount Ct 11 LU2 45 D1
Vivian Cl WD19 167 A1
Vivian Gdns WD19 167 A1
Vixen Dr SG13 114 A6
Vyse Cl EN5 171 C5

W

Wacketts EN7 148 A4
Waddesdon Cl LU2 46 D2
Waddesdon Ct EN2 161 E1
Waddington Rd 1 AL3 127 D3
Waddling La AL4 87 D1
Wade The AL7 111 A3
Wades The AL10 130 A2
Wadesmill Rd
Tonwell SG12,SG14 92 D3
Ware SG12 93 D2
Wadham Rd WD5 153 F8
Wadhurst Ave LU3 45 C4
Wadley Cl 1 HP2 124 F2
Wadnall Way SG3 68 F3
Waggon Rd EN4 159 E2
Waggoners Yd 4 SG12 93 D2
Wagon Mead CM22 98 F3
Wagon Rd EN4 159 B2
Wagon Way WD3 165 C6
Waight Cl AL10 129 E7
Wain Cl EN6 145 B2
Wainwright St CM23 76 C5
Wakefields Wlk EN8 162 E8
Walace Ct EN3 163 A2
Walcot Ave LU2 46 B1
Waldeck Rd LU3 63 C8
Waldegrave Pk AL5 86 D1
Walden End SG1 50 E4
Walden Pl AL8 110 D8
Walden Rd AL8 110 D8
Waleran Cl HA7 176 F4
Waleys Cl LU3 44 E8
Walfords Cl CM17 118 C3
Walk The Hertford SG14 113 A5
Walk The continued
Potters Bar EN6 159 B7
Walkern Prim Sch SG2 52 B8
Walkern Rd
Benington SG2 52 D5
Stevenage SG1 50 D8
Watton at S SG14 70 C6
Walkers Cl AL5 107 C7
Walkers Rd AL5 107 B7
Walkers' Ct SG7 23 F8
Wall Hall (Univ Campus) WD25 155 B3
Wallace Way SG4 22 A2
Walled Gdn The AL6 90 B2
Waller Ave LU4 44 F3
Waller Dr HA6 175 A2
Waller Street Mall 3 LU1 63 E7
Waller's Cl SG8 9 F2
Wallers Way EN11 115 B1
Wallingford Wlk AL1 141 D8
Wallington Rd SG7 13 D1
Wallis Ct EN9 163 B4
Walnut Ave SG7 24 A7
Walnut Cl
Chiswell Green AL2 141 B4
Hitchin SG4 35 A6
Luton LU2 46 B4
Much Hadham SG10 74 F2
Royston SG8 7 D6
Stotfold SG5 11 F6
Walnut Cotts CM21 97 E3
Walnut Ct
Welwyn Garden City AL7 110 E3
Wheathampstead AL4 108 D8
Walnut Dr CM23 76 D3
Walnut Gn WD23 167 F7
Walnut Gr
Hemel Hempstead HP2 124 D3
Welwyn Garden City AL7 110 E3
Walnut Ho AL7 110 F3
Walnut Tree Ave CM21 97 E4
Walnut Tree Cl Aston SG2 51 D4
Cheshunt EN8 162 D8
Hoddesdon EN11 135 A6
Walnut Tree Cres CM21 97 E3
Walnut Tree Rd SG5 20 D3
Walnut Tree Wlk SG12 114 E6
Walnut Way SG5 21 E4
Walpole Bldg WD3 165 E1
Walpole Cl HA5 176 A4
Walpole Ct SG2 69 C7
Walsh Cl SG5 34 D7
Walsham Cl SG2 69 C7
Walshford Way WD6 157 A1
Walsingham Cl
Hatfield AL10 129 F6
Luton LU2 45 D7
Walsingham Way AL2 142 C4
Walsworth Rd SG4 35 A8
Walter Rothschild Zoological Mus The* HP23 100 A3
Walters Cl EN7 147 B6
Waltham Abbey* EN9 163 C6
Waltham Cross Sta EN8 162 F5
Waltham Ct LU2 46 C3
Waltham Gate EN8 148 F5
Waltham Gdns EN3 162 C2
Waltham Holy Cross Inf Sch EN9 163 D6
Waltham Holy Cross Jun Sch EN9 163 D6
Waltham Rd
4 Hitchin SG4 34 F6
Waltham Abbey EN9 149 F5
Walton Ct EN11 135 C8
Walton Gdns EN9 163 B6
Walton Rd
Hoddesdon EN11 135 C8
Ware SG12 114 D8
Watford WD23 167 E5
Walton St AL1 127 F5
Walverns Cl WD19 167 C3
Wandon Cl LU2 46 C4
Wannions Cl HP5 136 A1
Wansbeck Cl SG1 37 A3
Wansford Pk WD6 170 E5
Warburton Cl HA3 176 D4
Ward Cl
Hammond Street EN7 148 A4
Ware SG12 93 C2
Ward Cres CM23 76 E6
Ward Hatch CM20 118 A3
Warden Ct 5 LU2 63 E8
Warden Hill Cl LU2 45 C8
Warden Hill Gdns LU2 45 C8
Warden Hill Inf Sch LU3 45 C7
Warden Hill Jun Sch LU3 45 C7
Warden Hill Rd LU2 45 C8
Wardown Cres LU2 45 E2
Wardown Ct LU3 45 D2
Wards Cotts WD6 168 F7
Ware Mus* SG12 93 D1
Ware Park Rd SG12, SG14 113 E8
Ware Rd Hertford SG13 113 E6
Hoddesdon EN11 115 A1
Tonwell SG12 92 F6
Watton at S SG14,SG12 71 C3
Widford SG12 95 D4
Ware Sta SG12 114 E8
Wareham's La SG14 113 C5
Warenford Way WD6 170 A8
Wareside HP2 105 A1
Wareside CE Prim Sch SG12 94 E3
Wareside Cl AL7 111 B5
Warham Rd HA3 176 F1
Warlow Cl EN3 163 A2
Warmark Rd HP1 123 E5
Warminster Cl LU2 46 F1
Warneford Pl WD19 167 E3
Warner Rd SG12 114 D8
Warners Ave EN11 134 F4
Warners Cl SG2 51 C3
Warners End Rd HP1 124 B4
Warren Cl Hatfield AL10 130 B8
Letchworth SG6 22 D7
Warren Cotts SG8 9 A1
Warren Ct SG8 7 D5
Warren Dale AL8 89 D1
Warren Dell Prim Sch WD19 175 C7
Warren Dr The LU1 64 C1
Warren Gn AL10 130 B8
Warren Gr WD6 170 D5
Warren La Clothall SG7 24 D7
Cottered SG9 39 B6
Stanmore HA7 176 F8
Warren Park Rd SG14 113 D7
Warren Pl 16 SG14 113 D6
Warren Rd Bushey WD23 168 D1
Luton LU1 62 F8
St Albans AL1 141 C7
Warren Terr SG14 113 D8
Warren The
Harpenden AL5 107 A6
Radlett WD7 156 B6
Royston SG8 7 D5
Warren Way AL6 89 E4
Warren Wood Ind Est SG14 91 F6
Warrenfield Cl EN7 162 A8
Warrengate La EN6 158 C8
Warrengate Rd AL9 144 C4
Warrensgreen La SG4 37 D5
Warton Gn LU2 46 E2
Warwick Ave EN6 146 D4
Warwick Cl
Bushey WD23 168 E2
Cuffley EN6 146 D4
Hertford SG13 113 C4
Warwick Ct
Chorleywood WD3 164 F6
Luton LU4 63 B8
Warwick Dr EN8 148 D3
Warwick Rd
Bishop's Stortford CM23 77 B6
Borehamwood WD6 170 D6
Enfield EN3 162 F2
Pitstone LU7 80 D3
St Albans AL1 127 F5
Stevenage SG2 51 C6
Warwick Rd E LU4 63 B8
Warwick Rd W LU4 63 B8
Warwick Way WD3 166 C5
Wash La Dancers Hill EN6 158 C3
South Mimms EN6 158 C5
Wash The
Furneux Pelham SG9 43 D5
Hertford SG14 113 D6
Washington Ave HP2 124 E8
Watchlytes AL7 111 C6
Watchlytes Jun Mix Inf Sch AL7 111 C6
Watchmead AL7 111 A6
Water End HP1 103 F2
Water End Cl WD6 169 F7
Water End Rd HP4 123 C7
Water Hall Farm & Craft Ctr* SG4 66 F7
Water La
Abbots Langley WD4 139 B2
Berkhamsted HP4 122 C4
Bishop's Stortford CM23 76 F8
Bovingdon HP3 137 B1
Hertford SG14 113 C5
Hitchin SG5 21 F1
Stansted Mountfitchet CM24 59 E6
Watford WD17 167 D5
Water Row 11 SG12 93 D1
Waterbeach AL7 111 D6
Watercress Cl SG2 51 D5
Watercress Rd EN7 147 D5
Waterdale SG13 113 C4
Waterdell La SG4 35 A2
Waterdell Pl WD3 173 B8
Waterend La
Ayot St Peter AL4,AL6 88 E1
Redbourn AL3 106 B5
Waterfield
Chorleywood WD3 164 C2
Welwyn Garden City AL7 111 B7
Waterfields Ret Pk WD17 167 D5
Waterfields Way WD17, WD23 167 D4
Waterford Comm SG14 92 B2
Waterford Gn AL7 111 B6
Watergate The WD19 175 D8
Waterhall Cotts SG13 132 D7
Waterhouse St HP1 124 C2
Waterhouse The HP1 124 C3
Waterloo La SG5 21 A6
Waterlow Mews SG4 35 E3
Waterman Cl WD19 167 B3
Watermark Way SG13 113 F6
Watermead Rd LU3 44 F6
Watermeadow AL2 141 E3
Watermill Ind Est SG9 40 E6
Watermill La
Hertford SG14 113 D8
Stansted Mountfitchet CM24 59 C6
Waters Dr WD3 165 E1
Waters End SG5 11 E6
Waterside
Berkhamsted HP4 122 D4
Kings Langley WD4 139 A2
London Colney AL2 142 E4
Radlett WD7 156 B5
Stansted Mountfitchet CM24 59 E6
Welwyn Garden City AL7 90 B1
Waterside Cotts AL9 130 E8
Waterside Ct WD4 139 B2
Waterside Ind Est EN11 135 D5
Waterside Mews UB9 173 A4
Waterside Pl CM22 98 A2
Waterslade Gn LU3 45 B6
Watersplash Ct AL2 142 F4
Waterways Bsns Ctr EN3 163 A1
Watery La
Flamstead AL3,AL5 84 E3
Hatfield AL10 129 E4
Marsworth HP23 79 F1
Watford Arches Ret Pk WD17 167 D4
Watford By-pass WD6 169 C2
Watford Coll (annex) WD23 167 D6
Watford County Ct WD18 167 C5
Watford Ent Ctr WD18 166 E3
Watford Field Rd WD18 167 C4
Watford Football Gd & Saracens RFC WD18 167 B4
Watford General Hospl (Shrodells Wing) WD18 167 B4
Watford Gram Sch for Boys WD18 166 F5
Watford Gram Sch for Girls WD18 167 B5
Watford Heath WD19 167 D2
Watford Heath Farm WD19 167 D2
Watford High Street Sta WD17 167 C5
Watford Junction Sta WD17 167 C7
Watford Mus* WD17 167 C5
Watford North Sta WD24 154 C2
Watford Rd
Abbots Langley WD4 153 C6
Chiswell Green AL2 141 A6
Croxley Green WD3 166 B3
Elstree WD6 169 C3
Kings Langley WD4 139 A1
Moor Park HA6 175 A4
Radlett WD7 155 F4
Watford Sch of Music WD17 154 A1
Watford Sta WD18 166 F6
Watkin Mews EN3 163 A2
Watkins Cl HA6 174 F2
Watkins Rise EN6 159 B7
Watling Cl 1 HP2 124 E6
Watling Ct WD6 169 D3
Watling Knoll WD7 155 F6
Watling Mans WD7 156 B3
Watling St
Park Street AL2 141 D6
St Albans AL1 141 C8
Watling View AL1 141 C8
Watling View Sch AL1 141 D7
Watlington Rd CM17 118 D4
Watson Ave AL3 127 F6
Watson's Wlk AL1 127 E2
Watton at Stone Prim Sch SG14 70 D3
Watton at Stone Sta SG14 70 D3
Watton Ho SG14 70 F3
Watton Rd Knebworth SG3 69 A5
Ware SG12 93 C2
Watton at S SG3,SG14 70 B2
Watts Cl SG11 57 C2
Waulud Prim Sch LU3 44 E7
Wauluds Bank Dr LU3 44 E7
Wavell Cl EN8 148 E4
Wavell Ho AL1 128 A2
Waveney HP2 124 F8
Waveney Rd AL5 86 C3
Waverley Cl SG2 69 A8
Waverley Gdns HA6 175 A2
Waverley Lodge AL3 127 D5
Waverley Rd AL3 127 D5
Waxhouse Gate AL1 127 D3
Waxwell Cl HA5 175 D1
Waxwell La HA5 175 D1
Wayfarers Pk HP4 121 F4
Wayletts Dr CM23 77 B7
Waynes Ct 9 LU1 63 E7
Wayre St CM17 118 C4
Wayre The CM17 118 C4
Waysbrook SG6 23 B5
Wayside
Chipperfield WD4 138 B1
Potters Bar EN6 159 D6
Shenley WD7 156 D6
Wayside Ave WD23 168 D3
Wayside Ct AL2 140 F1
Wayside The HP3 125 C2
Waysmeet SG6 23 B4
Waytemore Castle* CM23 77 A7
Waytemore Rd CM23 76 E6

Weald Fst Sch HA3 176 F3
Weald La HA3 176 D2
Weald Mid Sch HA3 176 F3
Weald Rise HA3 176 F2
Wealdwood Gdns HA5 176 B4
Weall Gn WD25 154 B7
Weardale Ct EN5 171 C4
Weatherby Rd LU4 44 D2
Weaver St CM23 76 C4
Weavers Orch SG15 11 A4
Weavers Rd HP23 99 E4
Weavers Way SG7 24 A8
Webb Cl SG6 23 C5
Webb Rise SG1 50 F7
Webber Cl WD6 169 D3
Webley Ct EN3 163 A2
Wedgewood Cl HA6 174 C4
Wedgewood Pk SG1 37 C2
Wedgewood Rd SG4 35 B7
Wedgewood Way SG1 37 B2
Wedgwood Ct SG1 37 C2
Wedgwood Gate SG1 37 B2
Wedmore Rd SG4 35 A6
Wedon Way SG7 13 C4
Weedon Cl SG16 10 C5
Weighton Rd HA3 176 D2
Welbeck Cl WD6 170 A6
Welbeck Rd 3 LU2 63 E8
Welbeck Rise AL5 107 D6
Welbury Ave LU3 45 C7
Welch Pl HA5 175 C2
Welclose St AL3 127 C3
Welcote Dr HA6 174 D4
Weldon Cl LU2 46 E1
Welham Cl
Borehamwood WD6 170 A8
Welham Green AL9 144 C7
Welham Ct AL9 144 C7
Welham Green Sta AL9 144 D8
Welham Manor AL9 144 C7
Welkin Gn HP2 125 C4
Well App EN5 171 C4
Well Croft HP1 124 B4
Well End Rd WD6 157 D1
Well Garth AL7 110 E5
Well Gn SG14 91 C4
Well La Harlow CM19 117 A1
Mentmore LU7 61 B8
Well Rd Barnet EN5 171 C4
Northaw EN6 145 E2
Well Row SG13 132 F6
Wellands AL10 130 A7
Wellbrook Mews HP23 100 B4
Wellbury Terr HP2 125 C3
Wellcroft LU7 80 F5
Wellcroft Cl AL7 111 A4
Wellcroft Rd AL7 111 A4
Wellen Rise HP3 138 E8
Wellers Gr EN7 148 A3
Wellesley Ave HA6 174 F5
Wellesley Cres EN6 158 E6
Wellfield Ave LU3 44 C8
Wellfield Cl AL10 130 A6
Wellfield Ct SG1 37 B1
Wellfield Rd AL10 130 A7
Wellgate Rd LU4 44 D2
Wellhouse Cl LU1 63 A7
Wellhouse La EN5 171 D5
Wellingham Ave SG5 21 D1
Wellington Ave HA5 175 F2
Wellington Cl WD19 175 F7
Wellington Cotts SG11 73 B7
Wellington Ct 3 LU1 63 D6
Wellington Dr AL7 111 C6
Wellington Ho 1 WD24 167 C7
Wellington Pl
Cheshunt EN10 148 C8
Kneesworth SG8 2 B5
Wellington Rd
London Colney AL2 142 D5
Pinner HA5 175 F2
St Albans AL1 128 B2
Stevenage SG2 51 C5
Watford WD17 167 B7
Wellington St
Hertford SG14 113 B7
Luton LU1 63 D7
Wells Cl
Hammond Street EN7 147 C6
Harpenden AL5 85 E4
St Albans AL3 127 C4
Wells Yd 8 Ware SG12 93 D1
Watford WD17 167 B6
Wellside Cl EN5 171 C5
Wellstones WD18 167 B5
Wellswood Cl HP2 125 B4
Welsummer Way EN8 148 D3
Weltmore Rd LU3 44 F6
Welwyn By Pass Rd AL6 89 C5
Welwyn Ct HP2 124 F7
Welwyn Garden City Sta
AL8 110 D6
Welwyn Hall Gdns AL6 89 C5
Welwyn North Sta AL6 89 F3
Welwyn Rd SG14 112 F7
Wendover Cl
Harpenden AL5 86 D1
St Albans AL4 128 C8
Wendover Ct AL6 89 C5
Wendover Dr AL6 89 C5
Wendover Ho WD18 166 E2
Wendover Way
Bushey WD23 168 C3
Luton LU2 45 F3
Wengeo La SG12 93 B2
Wenham Ct SG2 52 B8
Wenlock CE Jun Sch LU2 64 B8
Wenlock St LU2 63 E8
Wensley Cl AL5 107 D6
Wensleydale
Hemel Hempstead HP2 124 F6
Luton LU2 45 E1
Wensum Rd SG1 36 F3
Wensum Way WD3 165 D1
Wenta Bsns Ctr WD24 154 D2
Wentbridge Path WD6 157 A1
Wentworth Ave
Borehamwood WD6 169 F4
Luton LU4 44 C6
Wentworth Cl
Potters Bar EN6 159 A8
Watford WD17 153 F1
Wentworth Cotts
Dane End SG11 53 F2
Hoddesdon EN10 134 E1
Wentworth Ct EN5 171 E6
Wentworth Dr CM23 76 D6
Wentworth Rd
Barnet EN5 171 D6
Hertford SG13 113 C3
Wenwell Cl HP22 99 A3
Wesley Cl Arlesey SG15 11 A4
Goff's Oak EN7 147 C3
Wesley Ho 7 AL1 127 D3
Wesley Rd AL3 83 E5
Wessex Ct 7 EN5 171 D5
Wessex Dr HA5 175 E3
West Alley 3 SG5 34 E7
West Ave Baldock SG7 23 E8
Chiswell Green AL2 141 B6
West Burrowfield AL7 110 D4
West Chantry HA3 176 B2
West Cl Barnet EN5 171 B4
Hitchin SG4 22 B1
Hoddesdon EN11 135 A8
Stevenage SG1 50 F5
West Comm
Harpenden AL5 107 B6
Redbourn AL3 106 A4
West Common Cl AL5 107 B5
West Common Gr AL5 107 B5
West Common Way
AL5 107 A5
West Ct CM21 97 E3
West Dene HP2 104 A8
West Dr Arlesey SG15 11 B4
Stanmore HA3 176 D4
Watford WD25 154 B3
West Drive Gdns HA3 176 D4
West End SG7 4 C3
West End La Barnet EN5 171 D5
Essendon AL9 131 C5
West End Rd EN7 147 F8
West Gate CM20 117 C1
West Herts Bsns Ctr
WD6 170 B6
West Herts Coll (Dacorum
Campus) HP1 124 C4
West Herts Coll Cassio
Campus WD17 154 A1
West Herts Coll Leggatts
Campus WD24 154 A3
West Herts Coll Watford
Campus WD17 167 A6
West Hill SG5 34 D7
West Hill Rd
Hoddesdon EN11 134 F8
Luton LU1 63 E5
West Hyde La SL9 172 A4
West La Great Offley SG5 33 C2
Pirton SG5 20 D5
West Lieth HP23 99 F1
West Lodge Cotts LU2 46 D5
West Mead AL7 111 B3
West Pas HP23 100 A3
West Pl CM20 118 A3
West Rd
Berkhamsted HP4 122 A5
Bishop's Stortford CM23 76 E6
Harlow CM20 118 A4
Sawbridgeworth CM21 97 C3
Stansted Mountfitchet
CM24 59 E6
West Reach SG2 50 F2
West Riding
Bricket Wood AL2 140 F1
Tewin AL6 90 D5
West Side EN10 148 E6
West Sq CM20 117 C1
West St Hertford SG13 113 C5
Lilley LU2 32 D1
Ware SG12 93 D1
Watford WD17 167 B7
West Valley Rd HP3 138 D7
West View Hatfield AL10 130 A7
Letchworth SG6 22 E5
Standon SG11 73 A6
West View Ct WD6 169 D3
West View Gdns WD6 169 D3
West View Rd AL3 127 D4
West Way Harpenden AL5 86 C2
Luton LU2 46 C4
Rickmansworth WD3 165 B1
West Ways HA6 175 A1
Westall Cl SG13 113 C5
Westall Mews SG13 113 C5
Westbourne Mews AL1 127 D3
Westbourne Rd LU4 45 B1
Westbrook Cl SG8 5 B8
Westbrook Ct SG4 34 F5
Westbrook Hay Prep Sch
HP1 137 D7
Westbury EN8 148 D1
Westbury Cl SG5 34 D8
Westbury Farm Cl SG5 33 C3
Westbury Gdns LU2 45 E3
Westbury Pl SG6 22 E5
Westbury Prim Sch SG6 22 E5
Westbury Rd
Moor Park HA6 174 E7
Watford WD18 167 B4
Westbush Cl EN11 114 F1
Westcott AL7 111 D7
Westcroft HP23 100 A3
Westcroft Cl EN3 162 C1
Westcroft Ct EN10 135 A4
Westell Cl SG7 24 A8
Westerdale
Hemel Hempstead HP2 124 E6
Luton LU4 44 B5
Western Ave SG16 10 B3
Western Cl SG6 11 E1
Western House Hospl
SG12 93 E2
Western Rd
Lower Nazeing EN9 135 E1
Luton LU1 63 D6
Tring HP23 99 F3
Western Terr 1 EN11 115 B1
Western Way SG6 11 E1
Westfield
Welham Green AL9 144 F8
Welwyn Garden City AL7 111 A7
Westfield Ave
Harpenden AL5 86 A3
Watford WD24 154 D1
Westfield Cl
Bishop's Stortford CM23 76 E8
Cheshunt EN8 162 F8
Hitchin SG5 34 D7
Westfield Com Prim Sch
EN11 134 F7
Westfield Com Tech Coll
WD18 166 F3
Westfield Ct AL4 128 D6
Westfield Dr AL5 86 B4
Westfield Fst Sch HP4 121 F5
Westfield La SG5 34 D7
Westfield Pk HA5 175 F3
Westfield Pl AL5 86 B4
Westfield Rd
Berkhamsted HP4 121 F5
Bishop's Stortford CM23 76 E8
Harpenden AL5 86 B4
Hertford SG14 113 C8
Hoddesdon EN11 134 F7
Pitstone LU7 80 C3
Westfield Wlk EN8 162 F8
Westfields AL3 141 A8
Westgate SG1 50 D5
Westgate Ct EN3 162 D4
Westholm SG6 22 F8
Westland Cl WD25 153 F5
Westland Dr AL9 144 E4
Westland Rd
Watford WD17 167 B7
Knebworth SG3 69 A5
Westlea Ave WD25 154 E2
Westlea Cl EN10 148 F8
Westlea Rd EN10 148 F8
Westlecote Gdns LU2 45 D4
Westly Wood AL7 111 A7
Westmeade Cl EN7 148 B2
Westmill La Hitchin SG5 21 C2
Ickleford SG5 21 C3
Westmill Lawns SG5 21 D1
Westmill Rd Hitchin SG5 21 D1
Thundridge SG12 93 A3
Westminster Ct
Cheshunt EN8 162 F6
St Albans AL1 127 C1
Westminster Ho 6
WD24 167 C7
Westmorland Ave LU3 44 F5
Weston Ave SG8 7 C7
Weston Cl EN6 158 F7
Weston Prim Sch SG4 24 C1
Weston Rd SG1 36 E1
Weston Way SG7 23 E7
Westonia Ct EN3 162 E3
Westray HP3 125 C1
Westridge Cl HP1 123 F3
Westron Gdns HP23 100 B4
Westview Rise HP2 124 D4
Westwick Cl HP2 125 D2
Westwick Pl WD25 154 C5
Westwick Row HP2 125 E2
Westwood Ave SG4 35 A6
Westwood Cl EN6 145 A1
Wetherby Cl SG1 51 C8
Wetherby Rd
Borehamwood WD6 169 E8
Enfield EN2 161 C1
Wetherfield CM24 59 D7
Wetherly Cl CM17 118 F4
Wetherne Link LU4 44 C5
Wexham Cl LU3 44 E8
Weybourne Cl AL5 86 D2
Weybourne Dr LU2 45 C7
Weybrigge Cl AL3 106 A5
Weymouth St HP3 138 D7
Weyver Ct 3 AL1 127 E4
Whaley Rd EN6 159 C6
Wharf La
Berkhamsted HP4 121 C8
Rickmansworth WD3 165 E1
Wharf Pl CM23 77 A6
Wharf Rd
12 Bishop's Stortford CM23 76 F6
Hemel Hempstead HP1 124 B1
Hoddesdon EN10 148 F8
Wharf Row HP22 99 B4
Wharf Villas HP1 124 B1
Wharfdale 7 LU4 44 C5
Wharfedale HP2 124 E6
Wheat Cl AL4 128 A7
Wheat Croft CM23 76 E4
Wheat Hill SG6 22 F8
Wheatbarn AL7 111 B7
Wheatcotes SG3 69 C1
Wheatcroft EN7 148 B3
Wheatcroft Prim Sch
SG13 114 A7
Wheatfield Hatfield AL10 130 B6
Hemel Hempstead HP2 124 D5
Wheatfield Ave AL5 107 A5
Wheatfield Cres SG8 7 E6
Wheatfield Rd AL5 107 A4
Wheatfields CM17 118 D6
Wheatfields Inf Sch
AL4 128 B7
Wheatfields Jun Mix Sch
AL4 128 B7
Wheathampstead Rd
Harpenden AL5 107 E8
Wheathampstead AL5,AL4 108 A8
Wheatlands SG2 51 C7
Wheatley Cl
Sawbridgeworth CM21 97 C1
Welwyn Garden City AL7 111 A4
Wheatley Dr WD25 154 C5
Wheatley Rd AL7 111 A4
Wheatleys AL4 128 C5
Wheatlock Mead AL3 106 A5
Wheatsheaf Dr SG12 93 B3
Wheatsheaf Rd SG12 95 D1
Wheelers Cl EN9 135 F1
Wheelers La HP3 124 E1
Wheelright Cl WD23 168 B3
Wheelwrights SG4 66 C1
Wheelwrights Cl CM23 76 C4
Whempstead La SG12 71 B6
Whempstead Rd SG12 71 B7
Whetstone Cl AL6 89 E8
Whetstone Ct AL6 89 E8
Whinbush Gr SG5 34 F8
Whinbush Rd SG5 34 F8
Whippendell Hill WD4 138 C1
Whippendell Rd WD18 166 F4
Whipperley Ct LU1 63 C5
Whipperley Inf Sch LU1 63 A6
Whipperley Ring LU1 63 A6
Whipperley Way LU1 63 C5
Whipsnade Wild Animal Pk*
LU6 81 E7
Whisper Mews LU4 44 D4
Whisper Wood WD3 165 B6
Whisperwood Cl HA3 176 E3
Whit Hern Ct EN8 148 C1
Whitby Rd LU3 45 C1
Whitchurch Cl LU2 46 D2
White Beams AL2 141 C3
White Bear CM24 59 E8
White Craig Cl HA5 176 A5
White Gate Gdns HA3 176 F3
White Hart Cl SG9 40 E8
White Hart Ct HP2 125 A2
White Hart Dr HP2 124 F2
White Hart Rd HP2 125 A2
White Hedge Dr AL3 127 C5
White Hill
Ashley Green HP3,HP5 136 C7
Flamstead AL3 105 B8
Hemel Hempstead HP1 123 F2
Rickmansworth WD3 174 A4
Walkern SG2 38 C2
White Ho The 6 EN8 148 D3
White Horse La
London Colney AL2 142 E5
Welwyn AL6 90 C7
White House Cl SG14 70 E3
White House The SG6 23 B5
White La SG4 49 C7
White Lion St HP3 138 D7
White Orchards N20 171 F1
White Post Field CM21 97 D2
White Shack La WD3 152 F2
White Stubbs La EN10,
SG13 133 C2
White Way The SG2 51 C7
Whitebarns SG9 43 A5
Whitebarns La SG9 43 A6
Whitebeam Cl
4 Hammond Street EN7 147 E5
Shenley WD7 156 F6
Whitebeams AL10 130 A2
Whitebroom Rd HP1 123 E5
Whitechurch Gdns SG6 23 C3
Whitecroft AL1 142 B8
Whitecroft Rd LU2 64 A8
Whitecrofts SG5 11 F6
Whitefield Ave LU3 44 C7
Whitefield Ho AL10 130 C7
Whitefield Inf Sch LU3 44 E8
Whitefield Jun Sch LU3 44 E8
Whitefields Rd EN8 148 C3
Whitefriars Ave HA3 176 E1
Whitefriars Dr HA3 176 E1
Whitefriars Fst & Mid Sch
HA3 176 E1
Whitefriars Teaching Sch
HA3 176 D1
Whitefriars Trad Est
HA3 176 D1
Whitegale Cl SG4 35 A6
Whitegates Cl WD3 166 A5
Whitehall Cl EN9 135 E1
Whitehall Coll CM23 58 E1
Whitehall Cotts SG12 116 D8
Whitehall La CM23 58 F1
Whitehall Rd CM23 58 E1
Whitehands Cl EN11 134 F6
Whitehart Cross HP3 136 F3
Whitehaven Cl EN7 147 E3
Whitehicks SG6 12 A1
Whitehill
Berkhamsted HP4 122 D5
Welwyn AL6 89 A3
Whitehill Ave LU1 63 D5
Whitehill Cotts AL6 89 A3
Whitehill Ct HP4 122 D5
Whitehill Jun Sch SG4 35 A5
Whitehill La LU7 80 D3
Whitehill Rd SG4 35 A6
Whitehills Cl SG4 35 A6
Whitehorse St SG7 23 F8
Whitehorse Vale LU3 31 A1
Whitehouse Ave WD6 170 B5
Whitehouse Ct SG8 17 D4
Whitehouse La WD5 140 C4
Whitehurst Ave SG5 21 F1
Whitelands Ave WD3 164 C5
Whiteleaf Rd HP3 138 C8
Whiteley Cl SG12 71 E7
Whiteley La SG9 27 C8
Whitesmead Rd SG1 50 E7
Whitestone Wlk HP1 124 A6
Whitethorn AL7 111 B5
Whitethorn La SG6 23 A4
Whitethorn Way LU1 63 A6
Whitewaites CM20 117 E1
Whiteway SG6 23 C4
Whitewaybottom La LU2,
SG4 66 A3
Whitewebbs La EN2 161 F4
Whitewebbs Mus of
Transport* EN2 161 B4
Whitewebbs Pk* EN2 161 D4
Whitewebbs Rd EN2 161 C4
Whitewood Rd HP4 122 A4
Whitfield Way WD3 164 F1
Whitings Cl AL5 86 D4
Whitings Hill Prim Sch
EN5 171 C4
Whitings Rd EN5 171 C4
Whitlars Dr WD4 138 F3
Whitley Cl WD5 154 A7
Whitley Ct EN11 135 B8
Whitley Rd EN11 135 B8
Whitmores Wood HP2 125 B4
Whitney Dr SG1 36 C1
Whittingham Cl LU2 46 F1
Whittingstall Rd EN11 135 C8
Whittington La SG1 50 E4
Whittington Way CM23 76 F3
Whittle Cl
Lower Stondon SG16 10 B4
Watford WD25 153 F5
Whittlesea Cl HA3 176 C3
Whittlesea Path HA3 176 C2
Whittlesea Rd HA3 176 C2
Whitwell Cl LU3 45 B8
Whitwell Rd WD25 154 D4
Whitworth Cres EN3 163 A2
Whitworth Jones Ave
SG16 10 C5
Whitworth Rd SG1 37 B3
Whomerley Rd SG1 50 E4
Whybrow Gdns HP4 122 E5
Whydale Rd SG8 7 E5
Whytingham Rd HP23 100 C4
Wick Ave AL4 108 D8
Wick Hill LU6 82 F8
Wick Rd HP23 120 D8
Wick The Hertford SG14 92 C1
Kimpton SG4 66 D1
Wicken Fields SG12 93 C3
Wickets End WD7 156 E6
Wickets The LU2 45 E1
Wickfield SG3 69 A2
Wickfield Cl SG3 69 A2
Wickham Cl UB9 173 D2
Wickham Rd HA3 176 D1
Wickham Way SG11 55 E3
Wickhams Wharf SG12 93 E1
Wicklands Rd SG12 116 D8
Wickmere Cl LU2 45 C7
Wickstead Ave LU4 44 E4
Wickwood Ct AL1 128 B5
Widbury Gdns SG12 93 F1
Widbury Hill SG12 93 F1
Widbury Ho SG12 94 A1
Widford Rd Hunsdon SG12 95 D2
Much Hadham SG10 95 F7
Welwyn Garden City AL7 111 B6
Widford Sch SG12 95 D4
Widford Terr HP2 105 A1
Widgeon Way WD25 154 E2
Widmore Dr HP2 125 A5
Wieland Rd HA6 175 A3
Wiggenhall Rd WD18 167 C4
Wigginton Bottom
HP23 120 E8
Wiggles La HP23 99 F7
Wight Ho WD18 166 F4
Wigmore La LU2 46 D2
Wigmore Park Sh Ctr
LU2 46 E1
Wigmore Pl LU2 46 E1
Wigmore Prim Sch LU2 46 E2
Wigmores N AL8 110 D7
Wigmores S AL8 110 D6
Wigram Way SG2 51 B3
Wilbraham's Almshouses
EN5 171 F7
Wilbury Cl SG6 22 C7
Wilbury Hills Rd SG6 22 C7

Wilbury Jun Sch SG6 ....22 D6
Wilbury Lodge 2 EN5 ..171 D5
Wilbury Rd SG6 ....22 E8
Wilbury Way SG4 ....22 A3
Wilcon Way WD25 ....154 D5
Wilcot Ave WD19 ....167 E2
Wilcot Cl WD19 ....167 E2
Wilcox Cl WD6 ....170 C8
Wild Cherry Dr LU1 ....63 D5
Wild Marsh Ct EN8 ....162 E2
Wildacres HA6 ....174 F7
Wilderness The 3 HP4 ..122 C4
Wildhill rd AL9 ....131 B2
Wildman Ct SG13 ....114 A7
Wildoaks Cl HA6 ....174 F4
Wildwood HA6 ....174 D4
Wildwood Ave AL2 ....140 F1
Wildwood Ct WD3 ....164 F5
Wildwood La SG1 ....50 E3
Wilford Cl HA6 ....174 D3
Wilga Rd AL6 ....89 B5
Wilkin's Green La AL4 ..129 C4
Wilkins Gr AL8 ....110 D5
Wilkinsgreen Terr AL4 ..129 B3
Wilkinson Cl EN7 ....147 C6
Willenhall Cl LU3 ....45 A7
Willetts Mews EN11 ....135 A7
William Austin Inf Sch LU3 ....45 C4
William Austin Jun Sch LU3 ....45 C4
William Covell Cl EN2 ..160 F1
William Crook Ho HP1 ..123 F3
William Ct HP3 ....138 D7
William Pl SG2 ....51 A3
William Ransom Prim Sch SG4 ....35 B7
William St
18 Berkhamsted HP4 ....122 D4
Luton LU2 ....45 E1
Markyate AL3 ....83 E5
Watford WD23 ....167 D6
William Sutton Ct LU2 ....46 B5
Williams Way WD7 ....156 C4
Williamson St 1 LU1 ....63 E7
Williamson Way WD3 ..165 A1
Willian Church Rd SG6 ..23 A2
Willian Rd
Great Wymondley SG4 ....35 F7
Hitchin SG4,SG6 ....22 E1
Willian Way Baldock SG7 ..23 E6
Letchworth SG6 ....23 A3
Willinghall Cl EN9 ....163 D7
Williton Rd LU2 ....46 C2
Willoughby Cl EN10 ....134 E2
Willoughby Ct AL2 ....142 D5
Willoughby Rd AL5 ....86 B4
Willoughby Way SG4 ....35 A6
Willow Cl
Bishop's Stortford CM23 ....76 E8
Great Hormead SG9 ....42 A8
Hammond Street EN7 ....147 E5
Reed SG8 ....16 D5
Willow Cnr SG13 ....132 F5
Willow Cres AL1 ....128 C3
Willow Ct Harrow HA2 ..176 C1
Harrow HA3 ....176 F2
Luton LU3 ....44 E5
Willow Dene
Bushey WD23 ....168 E2
Pinner HA5 ....175 D1
Willow Dr EN5 ....171 E5
Willow Edge WD4 ....139 A2
Willow End HA6 ....175 A4
Willow Gn WD6 ....170 D4
Willow Gr AL8 ....89 D3
Willow La Hitchin SG5 ....34 D6
St Ippolyts SG4 ....35 B2
Watford WD18 ....167 A4
Willow Mead CM21 ....97 E2
Willow Path EN9 ....163 E5
Willow Tree Way SG5 ....21 F2
Willow Trees Cvn Site SG16 ....10 A4
Willow View SG12 ....114 E8
Willow Way
Chiswell Green AL2 ....141 A4
Harpenden AL5 ....86 C4
Hatfield AL10 ....129 F2
Hemel Hempstead HP1 ..124 B5
Luton LU3 ....44 E5
Potters Bar EN6 ....159 B6
Radlett WD7 ....155 E3
Willow Wlk AL6 ....89 C8
Willowdene EN8 ....148 E4
Willowfield Lower Sch LU1 ....62 F4
Willowgate Trad Est LU3 ..44 B8
Willowmead SG14 ....113 B5
Willows Cl HA5 ....175 C1
Willows La HP1 ....103 F1
Willows Link SG2 ....51 A1
Willows The
Buntingford SG9 ....40 D8
Hemel Hempstead HP2 ..125 B5
Hitchin SG4 ....35 A5
Rickmansworth WD3 ....173 A8
St Albans AL1 ....142 B7
Stevenage SG2 ....51 A1
Watford WD19 ....167 B2
Willowside AL2 ....142 E4
Willowside Way SG8 ....7 C8
Willowtree Lo HA6 ....174 F5
Willowtree Lodge 1 HA6 ....174 F5
Wilsden Ave LU1 ....63 C6
Wilshere Ave AL1 ....127 C1
Wilshere Cres SG4 ....35 C8
Wilshere Rd AL6 ....89 A5
Wilshere-Dacre Jun Sch SG5 ....34 E8
Wilsmere Dr HA3 ....176 E3
Wilson Cl
Bishop's Stortford CM23 ....76 F5
Stevenage SG1 ....36 D1
Wilsons La SG7 ....4 C4
Wilstone Dr AL4 ....128 C8
Wilton Cl CM23 ....77 B7
Wilton Cres SG13 ....113 C4
Wilton Ct WD17 ....167 C6
Wilton Rd SG5 ....21 E1
Wilton Way SG13 ....113 C4
Wiltshire Rd SG2 ....51 A4
Wimborne Cl CM21 ....97 D2
Wimborne Gr WD17 ....153 E2
Wimborne Rd LU1 ....63 C8
Wimple Rd LU4 ....44 A2
Winch Cl SG4 ....88 F8
Winch St LU2 ....45 F1
Winchdells HP3 ....139 A8
Winchester Cl
Bishop's Stortford CM23 ....76 D4
Stevenage SG1 ....37 B2
Winchester Ho AL3 ....127 C2
Winchester Rd HA6 ....174 F1
Winchester Way WD3 ..166 B4
Winchfield LU1 ....62 E4
Winchfield Way WD3 ....165 C2
Windermere Ave AL1 ....128 B1
Windermere Cl
Chorleywood WD3 ....164 D4
Hemel Hempstead HP3 ..125 C2
Stevenage SG1 ....37 D2
Windermere Cres LU3 ....44 F5
Windermere Ct 5 WD17 ....167 A7
Windermere Prim Sch AL1 ....128 B1
Windhill
Bishop's Stortford CM23 ....76 E7
Welwyn Garden City AL7 ..111 A7
Windhill Old Rd CM23 ....76 E7
Winding Hill SG10 ....75 A4
Winding Shot HP1 ....124 A4
Winding Shott SG14 ....91 C4
Windmill Ave AL4 ....128 C7
Windmill Cl Barkway SG8 ..17 C5
Pitstone LU7 ....80 F5
Stansted Mountfitchet CM24 ....59 D6
Waltham Abbey EN9 ....163 E5
Windmill Cotts SG12 ....93 D6
Windmill Dr WD3 ....165 F3
Windmill Field SG12 ....114 D8
Windmill Fields CM17 ..118 F4
Windmill Hill
Buntingford SG9 ....40 F6
Chipperfield WD4 ....151 F7
Hitchin SG4 ....34 F7
Windmill La Barnet EN5 ..170 F3
Bushey WD23 ....168 E1
Cheshunt EN8 ....148 E1
Windmill Rd
Breachwood Green SG4 ....47 D2
Hemel Hempstead HP2 ..124 F2
Luton LU1 ....63 F6
Markyate AL3,LU1 ....84 B6
Windmill St WD23 ....168 E1
Windmill Way
Much Hadham SG10 ....74 E1
Tring HP23 ....99 F4
Windmills SG12 ....71 E8
Windmore Ave EN6 ....158 C8
Windmore Hall EN6 ....158 C8
Windridge Cl AL3 ....127 A1
Windrush Cl SG1 ....37 A3
Winds End Cl HP2 ....125 A5
Windsor Cl
Borehamwood WD6 ....170 A8
Bovingdon HP3 ....137 A3
Cheshunt EN7 ....148 A1
Hemel Hempstead HP3 ..124 E2
Northwood HA6 ....175 A1
Stevenage SG2 ....69 B7
Welwyn AL6 ....89 B3
Windsor Ct
Borehamwood WD6 ....170 C7
Bushey WD23 ....168 C2
Kings Langley WD4 ....139 B2
11 Luton LU1 ....63 D6
St Albans AL1 ....128 A2
Windsor Gdns CM23 ....76 C7
Windsor Rd Barnet EN5 ..171 E3
Enfield EN3 ....162 D3
Harrow HA3 ....176 D2
Pitstone LU7 ....80 D3
Royston SG8 ....7 F6
Watford WD24 ....154 C1
Welwyn AL6 ....89 B3
Windsor St LU1 ....63 D6
Windsor Way WD3 ....165 A1
Windsor Wlk 8 LU1 ....63 D6
Windsor Wood EN9 ....163 E6
Windward Cl EN3 ....162 D4
Windy Rise SG12 ....71 F7
Winford Dr EN10 ....134 F1
Wingate Ct LU4 ....44 F2
Wingate Gdns AL6 ....89 B5
Wingate Rd LU4 ....44 F2
Wingate Way AL1 ....128 A2
Wingrave CE Comb Sch HP22 ....60 A3
Wingrave Rd Tring HP23 ..100 B6
Wilstone HP23 ....79 D1
Winifred Cl NW7 ....170 F3
Winifred Rd HP3 ....138 D7
Winkfield Cl LU4 ....44 B1
Winnington Rd EN3 ....162 C2
Winsdon Ct 1 LU1 ....63 D6
Winsdon Rd LU1 ....63 D6
Winslow Cl LU3 ....45 C4
Winslow Rd HP22 ....60 B3
Winston Churchill Way EN8 ....162 D6
Winston Cl Harrow HA3 ..176 F4
Hitchin SG5 ....34 D7
Winston Ct HA3 ....176 B3
Winston Gdns HP4 ....121 F4
Winston Way EN6 ....159 A6
Winstre Rd WD6 ....170 A8
Winters La SG2 ....38 C1
Winterscroft Rd EN11 ....134 F7
Winton App WD3 ....166 C4
Winton Cl Letchworth SG6 ..23 D8
Luton LU2 ....45 D6
Winton Cres WD3 ....166 B4
Winton Dr Cheshunt EN8 ..148 E2
Croxley Green WD3 ....166 C4
Winton Rd SG12 ....93 F1
Winton Terr AL1 ....127 E2
Wintons CM20 ....117 C2
Wisden Rd SG1 ....36 F1
Wisdom Dr SG13 ....113 E6
Wiseman Cl LU2 ....45 E7
Wisemans Gdns CM21 ....97 C1
Wistaria Dr AL2 ....142 B5
Wistlea Cres AL4 ....129 B1
Wistow Rd LU3 ....45 A6
Witchford AL7 ....111 D6
Withy Cl LU4 ....44 B4
Withy Pl AL2 ....141 C3
Witley Gn LU2 ....46 D2
Witney Cl HA5 ....175 F4
Witter Ave SG5 ....21 E4
Wiveton Cl LU2 ....45 D7
Woburn Ave CM23 ....76 C7
Woburn Cl Bushey WD23 ..168 C3
Stevenage SG2 ....69 C7
Woburn Ct LU4 ....44 D5
Wodecroft Rd LU3 ....45 B6
Wodson Park Sports & L Ctr SG12 ....93 D4
Wolfsburg Ct 4 LU4 ....44 C5
Wolsey Ave EN7 ....147 F2
Wolsey Bsns Pk WD18 ..166 D2
Wolsey Mans HA6 ....174 C7
Wolsey Rd
Hemel Hempstead HP2 ..124 D2
Moor Park HA6 ....174 D7
Wolston Cl LU1 ....63 C7
Wolverley Ho SG7 ....4 D4
Wolves Mere SG3 ....69 A2
Wolvescroft SG3 ....69 A2
Wonnacott Pl EN3 ....162 D3
Wood Cl AL10 ....130 B5
Wood Comm AL10 ....130 B8
Wood Cres HP3 ....124 E1
Wood Dr SG2 ....51 B2
Wood End AL2 ....141 C3
Wood End Cl HP2 ....125 C4
Wood End Hill AL5 ....85 D4
Wood End La AL3 ....104 E8
Wood End Rd AL5 ....85 D3
Wood End Sch AL5 ....85 D3
Wood Farm Rd HP2 ....124 E2
Wood Green Cl LU2 ....46 B5
Wood Green Rd LU2 ....46 C5
Wood Green Way EN8 ..162 E8
Wood House La EN10 ....134 A2
Wood La Birchanger CM23 ..59 E2
Hemel Hempstead HP2 ..124 D2
Meesden SG9 ....30 A6
Wood Lane End HP2 ....125 B4
Wood St Barnet EN5 ....171 D5
Luton LU1 ....63 F6
Wood Vale AL10 ....130 B5
Wood View Cuffley EN6 ..146 E4
Hemel Hempstead HP1 ..124 B5
Woodacre Dr AL6 ....90 A8
Woodbine Gr EN2 ....161 D1
Woodbridge Cl LU4 ....44 E4
Woodbrook Gdns EN9 ..163 E6
Woodbury Hill LU2 ....45 E2
Woodcock Hill
Rickmansworth WD3 ....173 E4
Sandridge AL4 ....108 E1
Woodcock Rd Luton LU1 ..63 A7
Royston SG8 ....7 E8
Stevenage SG2 ....51 D2
Woodcote Cl EN8 ....148 C1
Woodcote Ho 1 SG4 ....34 F7
Woodcroft SG5 ....34 E6
Woodcroft Ave SG12 ....115 E4
Woodfall Ave EN5 ....171 F4
Woodfield Ave HA6 ....174 E6
Woodfield Cl CM24 ....59 E6
Woodfield Dr HP3 ....125 D1
Woodfield Gdns HP3 ....125 D1
Woodfield La AL9 ....145 E8
Woodfield Rd
Radlett WD7 ....156 A3
Stevenage SG1 ....36 C1
Welwyn Garden City AL7 ..110 F6
Woodfield Rise WD23 ..168 D2
Woodfield Sch HP3 ....125 C1
Woodfield Terr
Harefield UB9 ....173 B1
Stansted Mountfitchet CM24 ....59 E6
Woodfield Way AL4 ....128 C6
Woodfields
Stansted Mountfitchet CM24 ....59 E6
2 Watford WD18 ....167 C5
Woodford Cres HA5 ....175 B1
Woodford Rd WD17 ....167 C7
Woodforde Cl SG7 ....4 E4
Woodgate WD25 ....154 B6
Woodgate Ave EN6 ....160 B7
Woodgate Cres HA6 ....175 A4
Woodgrange Ct EN11 ..135 A5
Woodhall Ave HA5 ....175 E2
Woodhall Cl SG14 ....113 C8
Woodhall Ct AL7 ....110 E5
Woodhall Dr HA5 ....175 E2
Woodhall Gate HA5 ....175 D2
Woodhall Gr CM23 ....76 D6
Woodhall Ho AL7 ....110 F4
Woodhall La
Hemel Hempstead HP2 ..124 E4
Shenley WD7 ....156 F4
South Oxhey WD19 ....175 E6
Welwyn Garden City AL7 ..110 E4
Woodhall Sch WD19 ....175 E6
Woodham Way SG12 ....115 C4
Woodhill Ho AL9 ....145 D8
Woodhouse Eaves HA6 ..175 A5
Woodhurst SG6 ....22 F8
Woodhurst Ave WD25 ..154 D4
Woodland Ave
Hemel Hempstead HP1 ..124 B2
Luton LU3 ....45 B2
Woodland Cl
Hemel Hempstead HP1 ..124 B2
Tring HP23 ....99 F2
Woodland Ct AL3 ....127 F7
Woodland Dr
St Albans AL4 ....128 C4
Watford WD17 ....166 F8
Woodland La WD3 ....164 D6
Woodland Mount SG13 ..113 F6
Woodland Pl
Chorleywood WD3 ....164 F5
Hemel Hempstead HP1 ..124 B2
Woodland Rd
Hertford Heath SG13 ....114 C3
Maple Cross WD3 ....172 D5
Woodland Rise
Studham LU6 ....82 B7
Welwyn Garden City AL8 ..110 C8
Woodland Way
Baldock SG7 ....23 F6
Bedmond WD5 ....139 F4
Goff's Oak EN7 ....147 B3
Stevenage SG2 ....51 A1
Welwyn AL6 ....90 A7
Woodlands
Bishop's Stortford CM23 ....77 C8
Brookmans Park AL9 ....145 B4
Caddington LU1 ....62 E3
Chiswell Green AL2 ....141 C4
Harpenden AL5 ....85 E3
Radlett WD7 ....156 A5
Royston SG8 ....7 E6
Woodlands Ave HP4 ....122 D3
Woodlands Cl
Borehamwood WD6 ....170 B5
Hoddesdon EN11 ....135 A5
Woodlands Dr
Bedmond WD4 ....139 C3
Harrow HA7 ....176 F4
Hoddesdon EN11 ....135 A4
Woodlands Meade SG4 ..37 B8
Woodlands Prim Sch WD6 ....170 A8
Woodlands Rd
Enfield EN2 ....161 D1
Hertford SG13 ....113 F6
Kings Langley HP3 ....139 A4
Thundridge SG12 ....93 D6
Watford WD23 ....167 E4
Woodlands Sec Sch LU3 ..44 F7
Woodlea AL2 ....141 A6
Woodlea Gr HA6 ....174 C4
Woodley Rd SG12 ....93 F2
Woodleys CM20 ....118 A1
Woodman Rd 4 HP3 ....124 E1
Woodmere LU3 ....31 A1
Woodmere Ave WD24 ....154 E1
Woodmill Mews EN11 ..135 B8
Woodpecker Cl
Bishop's Stortford CM23 ....76 C6
Bushey WD23 ....168 C1
Harrow HA3 ....176 F2
Hatfield AL10 ....129 F2
Woodridge Way HA6 ....174 E4
Woodridings Ave HA5 ....175 F2
Woodridings Cl HA5 ....175 F3
Woods Ave AL10 ....130 B4
Woods Pl HP23 ....100 A3
Woods The Radlett WD7 ..156 B5
South Oxhey HA6 ....175 A5
Woodshots Mdw WD18 ..166 D4
Woodside
Bishop's Stortford CM23 ....77 D8
Borehamwood WD6 ....169 F5
Cheshunt EN7 ....162 A8
Hertford Heath SG13 ....114 C2
Watford WD24 ....154 A3
Woodside Farm & Wildfowl Pk* LU1 ....84 A8
Woodside Gdns SG4 ....34 F7
Woodside Ho AL8 ....110 C7
Woodside Ind Pk SG6 ....23 B7
Woodside La AL9 ....131 A1
Woodside Prim Sch EN7 ....147 B2
Woodside Rd
Abbots Langley WD25 ....154 B8
Bricket Wood AL2 ....140 F2
Welwyn AL6 ....89 F3
Woodside LU1 ....63 B3
Woodstock SG3 ....68 F3
Woodstock Cl SG13 ....114 B4
Woodstock Rd
Bushey WD23 ....168 F2
Hoddesdon EN10 ....134 E4
Woodstock Rd N AL1 ....128 B4
Woodstock Rd S AL1 ....128 B3
Woodvale EN8 ....162 C4
Woodville Court Mews WD17 ....167 A7
Woodville Ct WD17 ....167 A7
Woodville Pl SG14 ....113 B8
Woodward Gdns HA7 ..176 F3
Woodwaye WD19 ....167 C2
Woodwicks WD3 ....172 D5
Woolenwick Inf Sch SG1 ..50 B6
Woolenwick Jun Sch SG1 ....50 B6
Woolgrove Ct SG4 ....22 B1
Woolgrove Rd SG4 ....22 B1
Woolgrove Sch SG6 ....23 D5
Woollam Cres AL3 ....127 C7
Woollams AL3 ....106 A4
Woollard St EN9 ....163 C5
Woolmans Cl EN10 ....134 F1
Woolmer Cl WD6 ....157 A1
Woolmer Dr HP2 ....125 C3
Woolmer's Park Mews SG14 ....112 B1
Woolmerdine Ct WD23 ..167 D6
Woolmers La SG14 ....112 B2
Woolners Way SG1 ....50 C6
Woolston Ave SG6 ....23 A4
Wootton Cl LU3 ....45 B7
Wootton Dr HP2 ....124 F8
Worboys Ct SG8 ....1 F5
Worcester Ct AL1 ....128 A2
Worcester Ho 12 WD6 ..170 A7
Worcester Rd AL10 ....129 F6
Worcesters Ave EN1 ....162 A1
Worcesters Prim Sch EN1 ....161 F1
Wordsworth Cl SG8 ....2 D1
Wordsworth Gdns WD6 ..170 A4
Wordsworth Rd
Harpenden AL5 ....86 A3
Luton LU4 ....44 A2
Works Rd SG6 ....23 C7
Worley Rd AL3 ....127 D4
Wormley Ct EN10 ....148 F7
Wormley Lodge Cl EN10 ..148 F8
Wormley Prim Sch EN10 ....148 E8
Wormleybury EN10 ....148 D8
Worsdell Way SG4 ....35 B7
Worsted La SG9 ....41 E7
Wortham Rd SG8 ....7 E4
Wortham Way SG2 ....51 B3
Wraglings The CM23 ....77 B5
Wratten Cl SG5 ....34 E6
Wratten Rd E SG5 ....34 E6
Wratten Rd W SG5 ....34 E6
Wrayfields SG5 ....12 B8
Wraysbury Cl LU4 ....44 D3
Wren Cl Kimpton SG4 ....66 B1
Luton LU2 ....46 C6
Stevenage SG2 ....51 B6
Wren Cres WD23 ....168 C1
Wren Wood AL7 ....111 B7
Wrenbrook Rd CM23 ....76 F6
Wrensfield HP1 ....124 B3
Wrestlers Cl AL10 ....130 C7
Wrexham Terr SG8 ....7 D7
Wright Cl AL4 ....108 E7
Wright's Bldgs WD17 ..167 B7
Wrights Green La CM22 ..98 D7
Wrights Mdw SG2 ....52 B8
Wrights Orch SG2 ....51 E2
Wrotham Pk* EN5 ....158 F3
Wrotham Rd EN5 ....171 E7
Wroxham Ave HP3 ....124 D1
Wroxham Gdns
Crews Hill EN2 ....161 B4
Potters Bar EN6 ....158 D8
Wroxham Sch The EN6 ..158 D8
Wroxham Way AL5 ....86 C3
Wulfrath Way SG12 ....93 C3
Wulstan Pk EN6 ....159 D7
Wulwards Cl LU1 ....63 B6
Wulwards Ct LU1 ....63 B6
Wyatt Cl Bushey WD23 ..168 E2
Ickleford SG5 ....21 D4
Wyatt's Cl WD3 ....165 A6
Wyatt's Rd WD3 ....165 A6
Wyburn Ave EN5 ....171 F6
Wych Elm CM20 ....117 C1
Wych Elm La AL6,SG3 ....68 F2
Wych Elms AL2 ....141 B3
Wychdell SG2 ....69 C8
Wychford Dr CM21 ....97 C1
Wychwood Ave LU2 ....45 E3
Wychwood Way HA6 ....174 F3
Wycklond Cl SG5 ....11 E6
Wycliffe Cl LU3 ....45 C6
Wycliffe Ct WD5 ....153 E7
Wycombe Pl AL4 ....128 B6
Wycombe Way Luton LU3 ..45 C8
St Albans AL4 ....128 B6
Wyddial Gn AL7 ....111 B6
Wyddial Rd SG9 ....40 E8
Wye The HP2 ....125 A8
Wyedale AL2 ....142 F4
Wykeham Rise N20 ....171 E1
Wyken Cl LU3 ....45 A7
Wyldwood Cl CM17 ....118 C6

Wyllyotts Cl EN6 ....158 F7
Wyllyotts La EN6 ....158 F7
Wyllyotts Pl EN6 ....158 F7
Wylo Dr EN5 ....171 A3
Wymondley Cl SG4 ....35 A7
Wymondley Jun Mix Inf Sch SG4 ....35 E4
Wymondley Rd
Hitchin SG4 ....35 B6
Letchworth SG6 ....23 A1
Wynches Farm Dr AL4 ..128 D3
Wynchgate HA3 ....176 E3
Wynchlands Cres AL4 ...128 D3
Wynd The SG6 ....22 F6
Wyndham Rd LU4 ....44 C2
Wyndhams End AL7 .....110 F2
Wynlie Gdns HA5 ....175 B1
Wynn Cl SG7 ....13 A1
Wyrley Dell SG6 ....23 A3
Wysells Ct SG6 ....22 D7
Wyton AL7 ....111 D6
Wyvern Cl LU4 ....44 E3

Y

Yardley SG6 ....23 C4
Yardley Ave LU7 ....80 D4
Yardley Ct 14 AL5 ....86 B1
Yarmouth Rd
Stevenage SG1 ....50 A7
Watford WD24 ....154 C1
Yarra Ho 3 AL1 ....127 E3
Yately Cl LU2 ....45 D7
Ye Cnr WD19 ....167 E3
Yearling Cl SG12 ....114 F7
Yeatman Ho WD24 ......154 B3
Yeats Cl SG8 ....2 D1
Yeomanry Dr SG7 ....13 A1
Yeomans Ave AL5 ....85 D3
Yeomans Cl CM23 ....76 D6
Yeomans Dr SG2 ....51 E2
Yeomans Ride HP2 .....105 A1
Yeovil Ct LU2 ....46 B2
Yeovil Rd LU2 ....46 B2
Yew Cl EN7 ....147 E4
Yew Gr AL7 ....111 C5
Yew Tree Cl HP5 ....136 A1
Yew Tree Ct
Elstree WD6 ....169 D3
Hemel Hempstead HP1 ...124 A1
Yew Tree Dr HP3 ....137 B3
Yew Tree Pl CM23 ....76 F8
Yew Wlk EN11 ....135 A5
Yewlands
Hoddesdon EN11 ....135 A5
Sawbridgeworth CM21 .....97 E1
Yewlands Dr EN11 ......135 A5
Yews Ave EN1 ....162 B3
Yewstone Ct WD18 ......167 A6
Yewtree Cl LU7 ....80 E5
Yewtree End AL2 ....141 B4
York Cl WD4 ....139 A2
York Cres WD6 ....170 D7
York Ho
13 Borehamwood WD6 ....170 A7
St Albans AL3 ....127 C2
York House Sch WD3 ...165 F7
York Rd Cheshunt EN8 ....162 E6
Hitchin SG5 ....34 E8
Northwood HA6 ....175 A1
St Albans AL1 ....127 F4
Stevenage SG1 ....36 F1
Watford WD18 ....167 C4
York St LU2 ....63 F8
York Terr EN2 ....161 C1
York Way
Hemel Hempstead HP2 ....124 E2
Royston SG8 ....7 B8
Watford WD25 ....154 E3
Welwyn AL6 ....89 C3
Yorke Gate WD17 ....167 A7
Yorke Mead Prim Sch WD3 ....166 A4
Yorke Rd WD3 ....166 A3
Yorkes Mews 16 SG12 ....93 D1
Youngfield Rd HP1 ......123 F4
Youngs Mews SG14 .....113 C6
Youngs Rise AL8 ....110 C6
Youngsbury La SG12 .....93 E8
Yule Cl AL2 ....140 F1

Z

Zambesi Rd CM23 ....76 F5